ANCIENT ROMAN VILLAS

ANCIENT ROMAN VILLAS

❊ THE ESSENTIAL SOURCEBOOK ❊

Edited and with translations by
GUY P. R. MÉTRAUX

J. PAUL GETTY MUSEUM
LOS ANGELES

© 2025 J. Paul Getty Trust

Published by the J. Paul Getty Museum, Los Angeles
Getty Publications
1200 Getty Center Drive, Suite 500
Los Angeles, California 90049-1682
getty.edu/publications

Laura diZerega, *Project Editor*
Elma Sanders, *Manuscript Editor*
Dani Grossman, *Designer*
Victoria Gallina, *Production*
Nancy Rivera, *Image and Rights Acquisition*

Distributed in the United States and Canada
by the University of Chicago Press

Distributed outside the United States and Canada
by Yale University Press, London

Printed in China

Library of Congress Control Number: 2024948263
ISBN 9781606069370 (paperback)
ISBN 9781606069387 (epub)
ISBN 9781606069394 (adobe pdf)

Front cover (top): Villa San Marco at Castellammare di Stabia, Parco Archeologico di Pompei, 62518, Courtesy of Ministero della Cultura, Parco Archeologico di Pompei; *Front cover (bottom):* Landscape *pinakes* featuring villas, Museo Archeologico Nazionale di Napoli, 9406, Courtesy of Ministero della Cultura, Museo Archeologico Nazionale di Napoli; *page 9*: detail, fig. 5; *pages 10–11*: detail, fig. 14; *pages 20–21*: detail, fig. 9; *page 28*: detail, fig. 6; *page 45*: detail, fig. 12; *pages 46–47*: detail, fig. 22; *page 48*: detail, fig. 11

Illustration Credits
Every effort has been made to contact the owners and photographers of illustrations reproduced here whose names do not appear in the captions or in the illustration credits listed at the back of this book. Anyone having further information concerning copyright holders is asked to contact Getty Publications so this information can be included in future printings.

On pp. 64–69, excerpts from *Xenophon,* Oeconomicus*: A Social and Historical Commentary* (1994) are reprinted with kind permission of Prof. Sarah B. Pomeroy.

On pp. 124–29, selections from John G. Fitch, *Palladius,* Opus Agriculturae*: The Work of Farming* (2013) are reprinted by permission of Equinox Publishing Ltd.

On pp. 132–39, selections from Ingrid D. Rowland and Thomas Noble Howe, eds., *Vitruvius: Ten Books on Architecture* (1999) are reprinted by permission of Cambridge University Press through PLSclear.

On pp. 178–80, Gregory of Nyssa's Letter 20 is used with permission of Brill, from *Gregory of Nyssa: The Letters; Introduction, Translation and Commentary* by Anna Silvas, © 2007; permission conveyed through Copyright Clearance Center, Inc.

On pp. 215–16, selections from Galen's *On Consolation from Grief* are reprinted from Clare K. Rothschild and Trevor W. Thompson, eds., *Galen's* De Indolentia*: Essays on a Newly Discovered Letter* (2014), courtesy of Mohr Siebeck.

On pp. 309–10, excerpts from Fronto's *Epistles* are reprinted from E. B Fentress, C. Goodson, M. Maiuro, with M. Andrews and A. Dufton, eds., *Villa Magna: An Imperial Estate and Its Legacies; Excavations 2006–10* (2016), courtesy of the British School at Rome.

The complete manuscript of this work was peer reviewed through a single-masked process in which the reviewers remained anonymous.

CONTENTS

List of Illustrations		8
Illustrations		12
Notes on the Presentation of This Sourcebook		49
Introduction		52

1 GREEK AND SICILIAN BACKGROUNDS OF ROMAN VILLAS

HESIOD
XENOPHON
DIODORUS SICULUS
CICERO

58

2 VILLAS IN ROMAN AGRICULTURAL TREATISES

CATO
VARRO
COLUMELLA
PALLADIUS

76

3 VILLAS IN ROMAN ARCHITECTURAL TREATISES

VITRUVIUS
FAVENTINUS

130

4 DESCRIPTIONS OF VILLAS

CICERO
PLINY THE ELDER
VARRO
HORACE
SENECA THE YOUNGER
MARTIAL
STATIUS
PLINY THE YOUNGER
APULEIUS OF MADAURUS
AULUS GELLIUS
ST. GREGORY OF NYSSA
AUSONIUS
PAULINUS OF PELLA
SIDONIUS APOLLINARIS
GERONTIUS
CASSIODORUS
CARMEN DE PROVIDENTIA DEI

141

5	VILLAS AND *OTIUM*	CICERO SENECA THE YOUNGER MARTIAL PLINY THE YOUNGER GALEN SIDONIUS APOLLINARIS	201
6	VILLA VISITS	CICERO HORACE JUVENAL MARTIAL PLINY THE YOUNGER RUTILIUS NAMATIANUS SIDONIUS APOLLINARIS	219
7	ECONOMICS AND EUERGETISM	CICERO PLINY THE ELDER PLINY THE YOUNGER JUVENAL	235
8	BUYING, BUILDING, IMPROVING, AND SELLING VILLAS	CATO CICERO PLINY THE YOUNGER MARTIAL	246
9	VILLAS AND *HORTI* IN THE LATE ROMAN REPUBLIC	PLUTARCH PLINY THE ELDER CICERO CORNELIUS NEPOS PROPERTIUS SUETONIUS LUCRETIUS SENECA THE YOUNGER HORACE *ELEGIAE IN MAECENATEM* MARCUS CORNELIUS FRONTO	262

10	EMPERORS AND VILLAS	AUGUSTUS	280
		TIBERIUS	
		GAIUS (CALIGULA)	
		CLAUDIUS	
		NERO	
		GALBA	
		VESPASIAN	
		TITUS	
		DOMITIAN	
		NERVA	
		TRAJAN	
		HADRIAN	
		ANTONINUS PIUS	
		MARCUS AURELIUS	
		LUCIUS VERUS	
		COMMODUS	
		SEVERUS ALEXANDER	
		GORDIAN III	
		TACITUS	
		DIOCLETIAN	
		ROMULUS AUGUSTULUS	

Acknowledgments	322
Abbreviations of Ancient Texts Cited	323
Abbreviations of Journals and Standard Reference Works Cited	327
Glossary	329
Notes	342
References	425
Illustration Credits	463
Index of Ancient Texts Cited	464
Index	469

LIST OF ILLUSTRATIONS

Figure 1. Plans of the ground and mezzanine floors, country house of Ischomachus................12

Figure 2. Attic Red-Figured Covered Pyxis, attributed to the Painter of the Louvre Centauromachy, Athens, ca. 430 BCE...................13

Figure 3a, b. Plan (a) and reconstruction (b) of the fishponds known as Piscina di Lucullo, Circeo, late first century BCE................14

Figure 4a, b. Drawing (a) and reconstruction (b) of an archaic hut, Palatine Hill, Rome, seventh–sixth century BCE.........................15

Figure 5. Mosaic floor (detail) from the *caldarium* of a private bath at Dar Zmèla near Thysdrus, second half of the second century–early third century CE 16

Figure 6. Wall painting, room 17 (*cubiculum*), House of the Library, Pompeii, mid-first century CE...........................17

Figure 7. Wall painting (detail), room 14 (*triclinium*), Oplontis Villa A, mid-first century CE..........18

Figure 8. *Lararium*, room 17, House of Sutoria Primigenia, Pompeii, late first century BCE–early first century CE 19

Figure 9. Peristyle, room 10, House of the Small Fountain, Pompeii, mid-first century CE...............22

Figure 10. Plan of Varro's aviary-*triclinium* at his villa at Casinum, mid-first century CE..................23

Figure 11. Orpheus mosaic, House of Orpheus, Nea Paphos, Cyprus, late second–early third century CE...........................24

Figure 12. View of atrium and south wall of *tablinum* with Third Style Painting, House of Marcus Lucretius Fronto, Pompeii, late first century BCE–early first century CE........25

Figure 13. *Pinax* of a porticoed villa, north wall of *tablinum*, House of Marcus Lucretius Fronto, Pompeii, late first century BCE–early first century CE...........................26

Figure 14. *Pinax* of waterside villas, south wall of *tablinum*, House of Marcus Lucretius Fronto, Pompeii, late first century BCE–early first century CE...........................27

Figure 15a, b. Ground plan (a) and axonometric plan (b), Via Gabina, Site 11, Phase 1c, late second–early first century BCE................30–31

Figure 16a, b. Ground plan (a) and axonometric plan (b), Via Gabina, Site 11, Phase 2a, late first century BCE–early first century CE.................32–33

Figure 17a, b. Ground plan (a) and axonometric plan (b), Via Gabina, Site 11, Phase 2b/c, early second century CE.............................34–35

Figure 18a, b. Ground plan (a) and axonometric plan (b), San Rocco villa, Period I, late second–early first century BCE........................36–37

Figure 19a, b. Ground plan (a) and axonometric plan (b), San Rocco villa, Period II and IIA, late first century BCE–early first century CE 38–39

Figure 20a, b. Ground plan (a) and axonometric plan (b), Settefinestre villa, 40s–30s BCE......40–41

Figure 21. Ground plan of Montmaurin villa, mid-fourth century CE..................42

Figure 22. Reconstruction view of the Villa Iovis (Villa of Tiberius) from the southeast, Capreae, 20s CE..................43

Figure 23. Reconstruction view of the Palace of Diocletian from the southwest, Spalato, late third–early fourth century CE.....................44

Figure 1 Plans of the ground and mezzanine floors, country house of Ischomachus (after the reconstruction by F. Pesando 1987 from Xen., *Oec.* 9.2–7)

The entrance to the ground floor (top plan) is on the right long side (A); it leads to an open courtyard with granaries and storerooms (B) and a kitchen and latrine by the stairs (C). The four contiguous rooms beyond the portico (D) were reserved for men, including a dining room (ἀνδρῶν, *andron*). The walls of *andrones* were sometimes equipped with benches to accommodate reclining diners, as indicated here on the plan. The two rooms to the right of the entrance provided nighttime accommodations for male and female enslaved workers: females in the back room, males in the front, separated by a locked door. The ground floor also had space for the cellarage of wine and olive oil (E).

The mezzanine level (bottom plan) included the bedroom (θάλαμος, *thalamos*) for Ischomachus and his wife, and a storeroom for valuable objects and cloth. One of the other rooms on the mezzanine could have been reserved for the weaving overseen by Ischomachus's wife.

Related texts: Xen., *Oec.* 9.3.

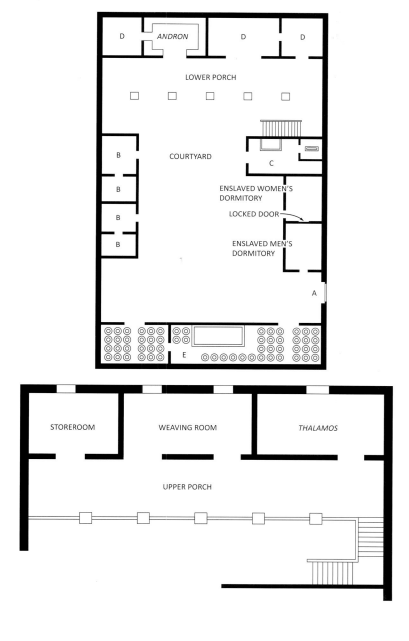

Figure 2   Attic Red-Figured Covered Pyxis, attributed to the Painter of the Louvre Centauromachy, Athens, ca. 430 BCE. Paris, Musée du Louvre, Département des Antiquités grecques, étrusques et romaines, inv. no. CA 587

A woman, most probably the wife of the dwelling's owner, is shown seated on a cloth- or skin-covered curved-back chair (*klismos*) with a footstool that denotes her high status. She holds a short distaff wound with yarn. A woman holding a hand loom approaches, her bound hair probably indicating her enslaved status.

Behind the seated woman is an open door reinforced with wood or metal crossbeams that connect with two locking devices on the right doorjamb. The room beyond is the *thalamos*, equipped with a finely carved bed covered with pillows or cloth indicating that the room is both bedroom and storeroom.

Figures 3a, b Plan (a) and reconstruction (b) of the fishponds known as Piscina di Lucullo, attached to a *villa maritima*, Circeo, late first century BCE

Writing in 37–36 BCE, Varro mentions that rich owners of seaside villas were investing in new-fangled *piscinae* to raise fish for profit and pleasure, adding that the fishponds resembled the compartmented boxes for colors invented by the Greek painter Pausias. Varro mocks pisciculture for pleasure and alleges that its commercial return did not justify the high cost of its infrastructure and maintenance. Cicero regarded rich owners of fishponds (*piscinarii*) with contempt.

Varro was wrong: even the income figures from pisciculture that he cites are impressive (Varro, *Rust.* 3.1.17.1-5 and 8). As for the pleasure of raising fish, designing fishponds may have been related to the design of pleasure gardens, an important activity for the villa-owning elite: Lucullus, Maecenas, Pliny the Younger, and many others engaged in the arts of the gardener (*topiarius*). Techniques of gardening (propagating species, irrigation, seasonal and climatic considerations) and techniques of pisciculture were not dissimilar. In fishponds, compartments separated species, while feeding, water temperatures, and the proportions of salt to fresh water were controlled via a complex system of intake and drainage by channels and sluice gates. Lucullus and his brother Marcus Lucullus succeeded with such techniques at their villas on the Bay of Naples, and their example may have prompted emulation by others. *Piscinae* at Republican maritime villas along the Tyrrhenian coast featured fanciful circular, rectilinear, and semi-circular designs, sometimes with walkways, viewing platforms, and bases for architectural structures and statues.

Related texts: Varro, *Rust.* 3.1.17.1-5 and 8 (*piscinae*); Cic., *Att.* 1.19 (*piscinarii*); Cic., *Off.* 1.39.140; Plut., *Vit. Luc.* 39.1–4 (gardens); Sen., *Ep.* 55.6–8 (*piscinae*); Plin., *Ep.* 5.6.16-20 and 32-40. (gardens); Gregory of Nyssa, Letter 20.5-6 (gardens).

Bibliography: Chiappella 1966.

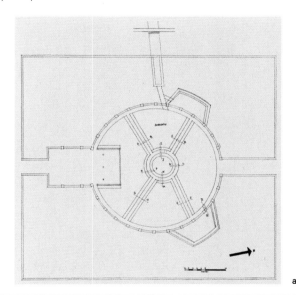

a

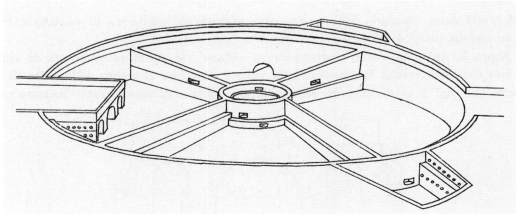

b

Figures 4a, b Drawing (a) and reconstruction (b) of an archaic hut, Palatine Hill, Rome, seventh–sixth century BCE

The Roman conception of the past included a pious admiration of the noble ancestors (*maiores*) and their habits of life (*mores*). Because the *maiores* were, by fact or legend, farmers foremost, they lived at their villas in a state of honorable ancient simplicity. However, they were also called to high civic and military duties as soldiers, generals, senators, consuls, and dictators of patrician families or the ennobled plebeian class, so the nobility of farming and its origins in the glorious past came to be exemplary for later villa owners.

Romulus, the founder of the City, was thought to have lived in similarly simple circumstances, and his supposed house or hut (the *casa* or *tugurium Romuli*) on the Palatine Hill was maintained as a patriotic monument; later, it was enshrined in a special building to protect and exhibit it. This modern reconstruction of thatched wood wattle-and-daub huts, one of several excavated on the eastern extension of the Palatine and in the Forum, illustrates how the thatched *casa Romuli* might have looked. Owners of villas in the Republican and Imperial periods no longer lived in such huts, but the example of ancestral simplicity lent ancient authenticity to contemporary villas.

Related texts: Vitr., *De arch.* 2.1.2–3 and 5–7 (see shrine of *casa Romuli* in ch. 3 and n. 21); Plut., *Vit. Cat. Mai.* 2.1–2; Rut. Namat., *De red.* 1.541–558.

Bibliography: Gjerstad 1960, vol. 3, figs. 23, 26; Yegül and Favro 2019, 244–45, fig. 5.1.

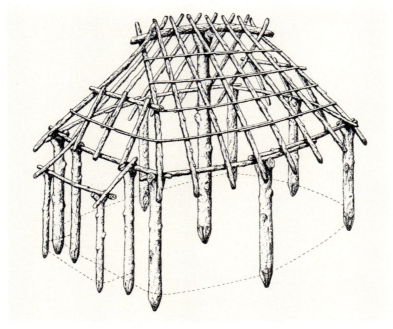

a

b

ILLUSTRATIONS 15

Figure 5   Mosaic floor (detail) from the *caldarium* of a private bath at Dar Zmèla near Thysdrus (modern El Djem), second half of the second century–early third century CE. Sousse, Musée archéologique de Sousse

Xenia were a frequent theme in Roman domestic decoration. They were painted on walls and represented on mosaic floors, becoming part of the toolbox of motifs offered by craftsmen to their clients. Images of edibles—fruit, fish, fowl, game— could be interlaced with decorative framing devices (boxes, linear or curvilinear patterns, botanical motifs) or set in fictive architecture or landscapes. In this mosaic floor from North Africa, a pattern of leafy vines emanates from large rosettes to define circular and oval shapes that frame single fish or fish braced in pairs, ducks, and various other fowl on white backgrounds (see also detail, p. 9). Good eating from hunting and fishing is a theme of *otium* at villas, but so was the promise of enjoying things fed and raised in pens and pools around the villa—the *pastiones villaticae*. This mosaic was part of a bathing facility in a private house; bathing before dining was a well-established social habit.

Related texts: *Xenia*: Vitr., *De arch*. 6.7.4; Mart., *Epig*. 7.49; Mart., *Epig*. 9.54; Mart., *Epig*. 7.31; Plin., *Ep*. 1.7.6; Plin., *Ep*. 2.1–2; Sid. Apoll., *Carm*. 21.1–4. *Pastio villatica*: Varro, *Rust*., Book 3.

Figure 6   Wall painting of room 17 (*cubiculum*), House of the Library, Pompeii (VI.17.41), mid-first century CE. Naples, Museo archeologico nazionale, MANN inv. 8594

Xenia in their simplicity could appear in painting at large scale accompanying monumental scenes. Between two red panels topped with theater masks, the central image on the end wall of a *cubiculum* depicts a grand temple-like building behind a round pavilion (*tholos*) that enshrines a statue of Venus to which female figures are making offerings of fruit (see detail, p. 28). In contrast, the two red panels on either side are hung with *xenia*: on the right, a brace of fowl, and, on the left, a brace of fish, both well over life-sized. Such images were representations of the edible abundance of fishing, hunting, or of *pastio villatica* that were suitable as gifts among friends. In Vitruvius's account of the Greek house, such *pastiones* would have been sent by the owner to his guests as a mark of hospitality.

Related texts: Vitr., *De arch*. 6.7.4.

Bibliography: Pagano and Prisciandaro 2006.

Figure 7　Wall painting (detail), Oplontis Villa A, room 14, end wall of *triclinium*, mid-first century CE. Naples, Parco archeologico di Pompei

The mark of *xenia* is their freshness and simplicity, no matter the form they took—fruit, eggs, fish, meat, live or killed game. When presented in person as gifts or sent accompanied by a letter or poem, they conveyed immediacy of feeling and the simple sincerity of friendly intent, both components of *amicitia*. Painted or mosaic *xenia*—as groups of comestibles, single images, or in decorative ensembles—may also reference the terminology of *amicitia*.

Xenia are informally presented as still lives. Here in a *triclinium* of a very grand villa, a richly colored, painted architecture with rigorous formal symmetry has a basket of ripe figs left haphazardly on an entablature. The *xenia* strikes a grace note of simplicity to both contrast with and emphasize the formality of the lavish decoration.

Figure 8　*Lararium*, House of Sutoria Primigenia, Pompeii (I.13.2), room 17, east and north walls, late first century BCE–early first century CE. Naples, Parco archeologico di Pompei

The paintings of the kitchen *lararium* of this house bring enslaved and free members of the *familia* into coordinated pious action. The niche on the north (left) wall would have contained small statues of the protective household gods (*Lares*), and the surrounding images—skewered meat and fish(?), a wineskin—offer them pictorial versions of food and drink. The snake in a garden (*agathodaimon*) served an added protective presence.

Real social action occurs on the east (right) wall. The largest figures on either side are the *Lares* themselves. On the left, a little flute player (*tibicen*) pipes an invitation to assemble at an altar. The members of the *familia* approach in two rows. In the back, two tall, veiled women lead five (or six) other figures. Four of them are men with raised right arms crossed over their chests to indicate that they are wearing togas: veils and togas denote high status. In the front row, the two male figures are smaller; their tunics, lowered arms, and bare legs indicate their enslaved status. No matter their rank, all have gathered to worship at the altar on which an officiant has lit a fire. This painting is a rare example of enslaved and free piously gathering to wish safety and prosperity for the *familia*.

Related texts: Hor., *Epod.* 2.

Bibliography: Haug and Kreuz 2021, 20–21, fig. 1.5.

Figure 9   Peristyle, House of the Small Fountain, Pompeii (VI.8.23), room 10, south wall and part of west wall, mid-first century CE. Naples, Parco archeologico di Pompei

The yard of this urban house has three surprises: the first, a pretty fountain decorated with glass mosaics (partially seen on the right); the second, sturdy Doric columns define the small open space and responding columns—albeit painted ones—give the illusion of fully-colonnaded peristyle. The third surprise was large-scale wall paintings of marine and natural landscapes made picturesque with villas, temples, and other structures in a misty, atmospheric style that contrasts with the solemn solidity of the real and fictive architecture.

In the painting on the south (left) wall (see detail, pp. 20–21), a waterside villa with a round tower set on an embankment unites two little islands. Elsewhere, an isolated temple is softened by its countrified setting. On the mainland above, a terrace supports the formal garden of a colonnaded villa with two towers. More marine scenes with waterside structures and small boats complete the painting. A bare-legged figure crosses a rustic bridge, and others stop to chat, while a fisherman nods over his rod nearby. This is not a port with wharves and enclosed harbors: it is a painting of rural delight with charming villas.

Related texts: Strabo 4.5.8; Plin., *HN* 35.116–117 (35.37); Plin., *Ep.* 2.17.1–5.

Bibliography: Fröhlich and Strocka 1996.

Figure 10 Plan of Varro's aviary-*triclinium* at his villa at Casinum, mid-first century CE (after Stierlin 1996)

Varro described the aviary-*triclinium* that he designed and had built for his villa at Casinum, southeast of Rome. This plan's reconstruction is very general but follows his description from the entrance to the hall (1) with two rectangular pools on either side (2) and cages for birds between the porticoes. At the far end, the circular perimeter and more cages enclosed the domed dining area with its pool (3), duck refuges (*navalia*), reclining couches, and the island on which the banqueters were served (4). The only elements not included in the plan are the little channels (*rivoli, canaliculi*) that brought running water to the birds and flushed their cages: Varro was not explicit about their position and construction.

Related texts: Varro, *Rust*. 3.5.8–17.

Bibliography. Stierlin 1996, 180–81.

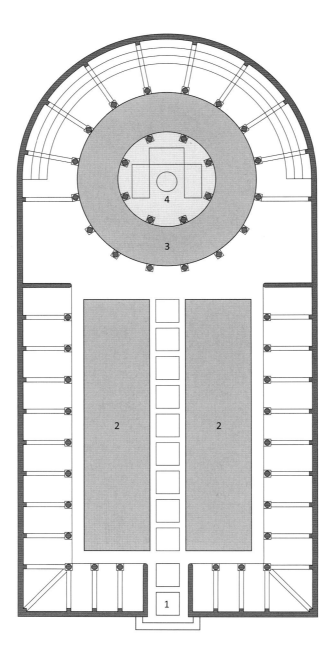

ILLUSTRATIONS   23

Figure 11   Orpheus mosaic, late second–early third century CE. 4.25 × 5.10 m; figurative panel 2.82 × 3.40 m with inscription "Titus (or Gaius) Pinnius Restitutus made this." House of Orpheus, Nea Paphos, Cyprus

In his third Book, Varro described his game park at a villa near Tusculum, where boar and deer would congregate to be fed at the sound of a trumpet. He also cites an even more impressive park owned by Q. Hortensius (Hortalus) near Laurentum in which a "Thracian Orpheus" would sing, accompanying himself on a cithara or lyre, while animals gathered to feed and be viewed by guests who dined in a specially built *triclinium*.

Such mythological and poetic allusions at villas were real-life enactments of the Thracian poet Orpheus charming the animals with his music, a scene widely represented in Roman art. In this mosaic, a ferocious but domestic animal (bull), game animals (deer, boar), and wild animals (bear, fox, tiger, leopard, and lion) gather peaceably with a snake and at least one wild bird (eagle, with two others partially damaged), one pet bird (parrot), and a partridge and a peacock that might have been raised at a villa for *pastio villatica* (see detail, p. 48).

Related texts: Varro, *Rust*. 3.13.

Bibliography: Stanley-Price 1991.

Figure 12   View of atrium and south wall of *tablinum* with Third Style painting, House of Marcus Lucretius Fronto, Pompeii (V.4.a), late first century BCE–early first century CE

In the house of M. Lucretius Fronto, the *tablinum* (reserved for the owner of the *domus*) was decorated with a theme of villas—*pastio villatica* (two *xenia* of fish) and four small views (*pinakes*) of villas (see detail, p. 45). The rest of the décor was assembled from the Third-Style painters' toolbox of motifs, but the theme may have been the owner's special request.

The principal (middle) zones of the south and north walls were defined by large red panels framing mythological scenes; the lower zone was painted with gardens and fountains, and the upper had Third Style fantasy architecture. In contrast to this elegant environment and in prominent places at the top of the large red panels on both sides, there were two vigorously painted *xenia*: freshly caught fish tumbling from a basket or in braced pairs or threes.

Figure 13 *Pinax* of a porticoed villa on the left side of central panel, north wall of *tablinum* of the House of Marcus Lucretius Fronto, Pompeii (V.4.a), late first century BCE–early first century CE

At eye level on the black panels of the middle zones, two sets of contrasting pendants are formed by four picture-postcard sized *pinakes* on spindly painted candelabras.

On the north wall (below), the left side *pinax* features an image of a porticoed villa, its formal structure fronted by an equally formal garden, all rendered in a less than atmospheric axial view that contrasts with its pendant on the right (not shown), a waterside villa with porticoes and towers shown in an oblique view, complete with picturesque figures and a rowboat.

Figure 14 *Pinax* of waterside villas on the right side of central panel, south wall of *tablinum* of the House of Marcus Lucretius Fronto, Pompeii (V.4.a), late first century BCE–early first century CE

The *pinakes* on the south wall provide similar contrasts like those on the north: on the left side, a waterside villa has a large L-shaped portico with formal herms and statues. Its pendant on the right, shown here (see also detail, pp, 10–11), conveys a picturesque, misty vision of several side-by-side villas, jostling one another in a friendly manner, one with a private quay, an embankment, and a boat promising a fine day's excursion on the water.

Related texts: Plin., *HN* 35.116–117 (35.37).

ILLUSTRATIONS 27

PLANS AND DEVELOPMENT OF VILLAS

Figures 15–21

Plans and reconstructions of excavated villas are documents of physical acts of change and aspiration in domestic architecture. The changes may have been economic: modifications in planting, new investment in agriculture, accommodations for enslaved workers, diversification of villa products. Changes to dwellings were also changes in modes of self-presentation, informed by what was socially needed (or not) in environments appropriate for the villa's inhabitants and owners at given moments of construction. In these ways, plans of villas examined over time serve as social texts in themselves, much like their manifestations in written form.

Three villas present vivid stories of architectural change at small (Via Gabina, figs. 15–17), medium-sized (San Rocco, figs. 18 and 19), and large (Settefinestre, fig. 20) structures all built in Italy during the Late Republic and modified in the Early Empire. A fourth villa (Montmaurin, fig. 21) is an example of a very large mid-fourth century CE villa in Aquitania (southern Gaul) that incorporates elements of Late Antique villa design.

Figure 15a   Ground plan, Via Gabina, Site 11, Phase 1c, late second–early first century BCE

On the Via Gabina (later Via Praenestina) about 9 km east of Rome and midway to Gabii, this villa was one of a group of dwellings in a position favorable for transporting produce to markets in either city. Built on a site inhabited since the mid-third century BCE, by the early first century BCE the villa consisted of a simple south-facing farmhouse (ca. 16 × 16 m) with a partially enclosed *hortus* on its west side. In its southeast corner, a rectangular room with robust masonry walls has been interpreted as the base of a tower, possibly used to surveil work in the fields, to dry produce, or as a decorative feature. The most important element of the villa was the U-shaped courtyard with an entrance open to the south and defined by a portico on the east (perhaps to store *instrumenta* or equipment such as wagons). From the courtyard, the villa itself (labeled *domus* on the plan) was entered through a door leading to a large transverse room with three rooms on its north long side. A series of small utilitarian spaces on the west side faced the *hortus*. This villa in its developed form lasted nearly eighty years, or about three generations.

Bibliography: Widrig 1987, 2009.

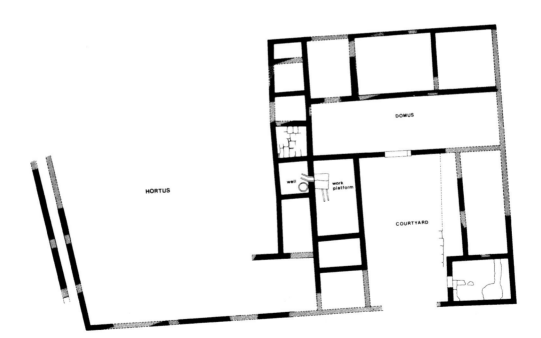

Figure 15b   Axonometric plan, Via Gabina, Site 11, Phase 1c, late second–early first century BCE

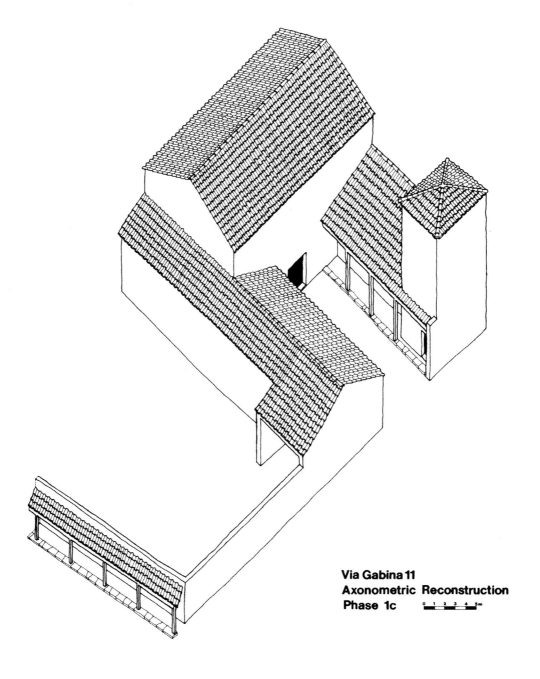

Figure 16a Ground plan, Via Gabina, Site 11, Phase 2a, late first century BCE–early first century CE

Phase 2a modifications were both thrifty and symbolic: while the structure retained its original footprint with the reuse of many interior walls, the villa became something more than a farmhouse. The most important modification was the replacement of the U-shaped courtyard with an atrium that spatially turned the villa into a formal urban *domus*. The new formality was emphasized by the addition of a *triclinium* in the northwest corner. The *hortus* on the west with its open north wall stayed the same, but additional small spaces encroached on it, including two new staircases up to a second story. A shallow portico overlooking the *hortus* extended the west side of the dwelling. Besides the new atrium, symbolic elements included adding short wall ends to define the main (south) door and a basin to the side: the wall ends gave the door a ceremonious frame, and the basin was a hospitable amenity for passersby or those seeking entrance to the villa or its *hortus* to wash up. These symbolic elements bestowed dignity and a public face upon the villa, which stayed in its Phase 2a form for about a hundred years.

Bibliography: Widrig 1987, 2009.

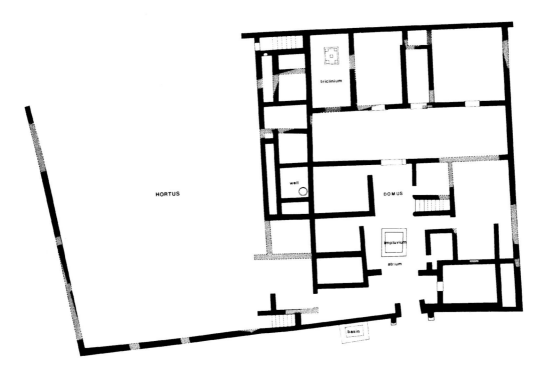

Figure 16b Axonometric plan, Via Gabina, Site 11, Phase 2a, late first century BCE–early first century CE

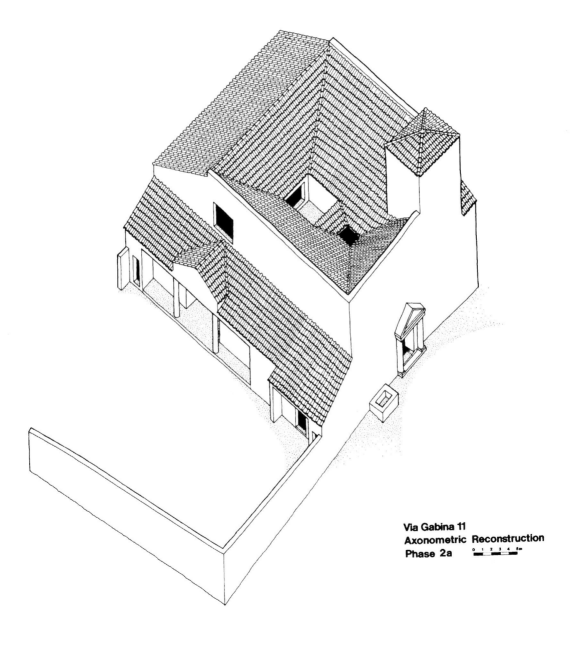

Figure 17a Ground plan, Via Gabina, Site 11, Phase 2b/c, early second century CE

Phase 2b/c thriftily maintained the villa's footprint but enhanced its productivity, comfort, and the visual relationship of the villa-*hortus*. Increased productive capacity is indicated by the installation of an impressive *cella olearia* in the northeastern part of the dwelling. New comfort came with the installation of a small but adequate bath building in the rooms facing the *hortus*. The sequence from warm-wet (*tepidarium*) to hot-dry (*caldarium*) was followed by a hot plunge; the cold-wet stage (*frigidarium*) may have been supplied by a new pool (*piscina*) built in the center of the *hortus*.

A new wall on the north side gave privacy to the *hortus*, and porticoes were added to its west and south sides. The floor and a shallow flight of stairs extended the west portico by about one meter—small, subtle changes giving the garden facade new visual height and adding picturesque distance to the view of the garden. The taste for such effects—here done in a miniaturized way—may have derived from the work of architects and landscapers at imperial villas, and been inspired by Roman landscape painting. The Phase 2b/c villa endured for about eighty years. After 180 CE, the oil press continued to function, but the dwelling and *hortus* were occupied by squatters. Agricultural activity in the area continued: a masonry *horreum* (79 × 19 m) was built near the site in the late fourth–early fifth century.

Bibliography: Widrig 1987, 2009; Yegül and Favro 2019, 269–70, fig. 5.26.

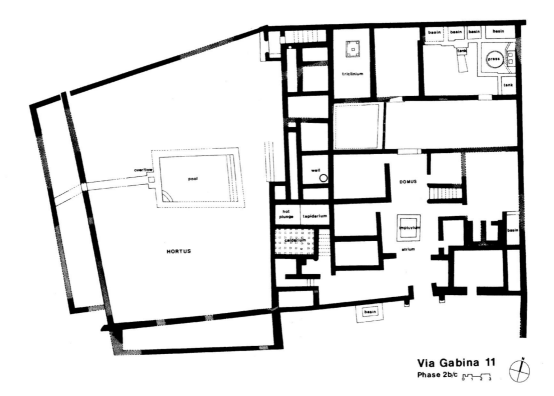

Figure 17b   Axonometric plan, Via Gabina, Site 11, Phase 2b/c, early second century CE

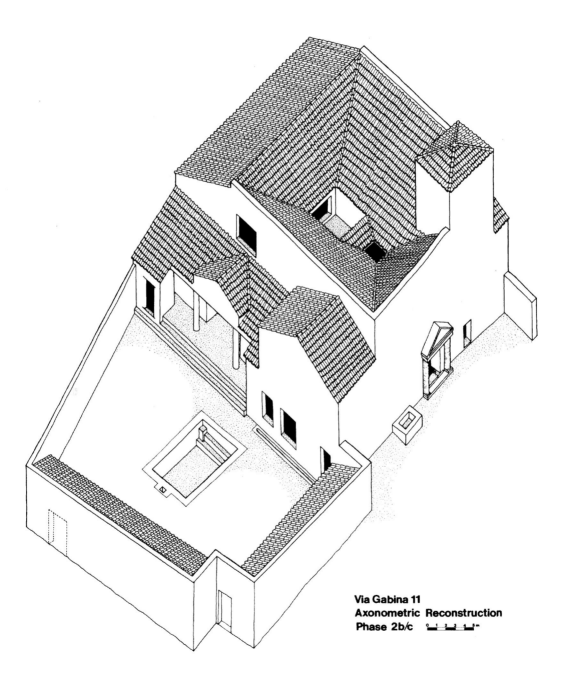

Figure 18a Ground plan, San Rocco villa, Period I, late second–early first century BCE

The modern village of Francolise is the site of the San Rocco villa in the northwest corner of the Ager Falernus, about 20 km west of the major city of Capua (modern S. Maria Capua Vetere) and close to the line of the ancient Via Appia.

The Period I San Rocco villa was a *basis villae* midway up a steep hillside terraced to separate the residential villa above a lower *pars rustica*. The upper villa had a large open courtyard (room B) and an architecturally impressive main hall (room D) with interior walls articulated with pilasters; most rooms had mosaic or *opus signinum* floors. Reservoirs and roof drains feeding a cistern assured the water supply, and a portico flanked by two staircases overlooked and gave access to the lower terrace.

The eroded remains of the lower terrace contained elements of the *pars rustica* with a well, waterproofed reservoir, cistern, and two round threshing floors indicating grain harvesting. The remains of a *dolium defossum* may indicate wine production for which the Ager Falernus was famous. Although Period I at San Rocco was comparable in date, size (a little larger), and plan (open courtyard) to Via Gabina Phase Ia, the terraced separation of residential and agricultural areas was marked. The Period I villa lasted about eighty or ninety years.

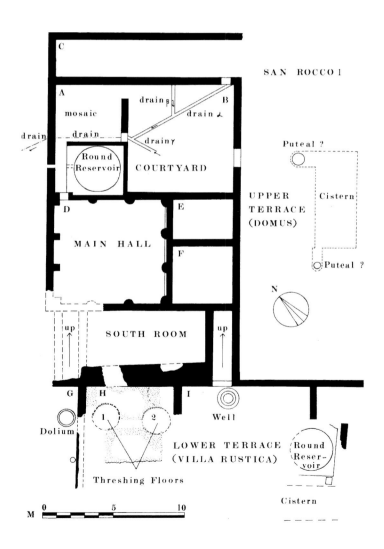

Figure 18b   Axonometric plan, San Rocco villa, Period I, late second–early first century BCE

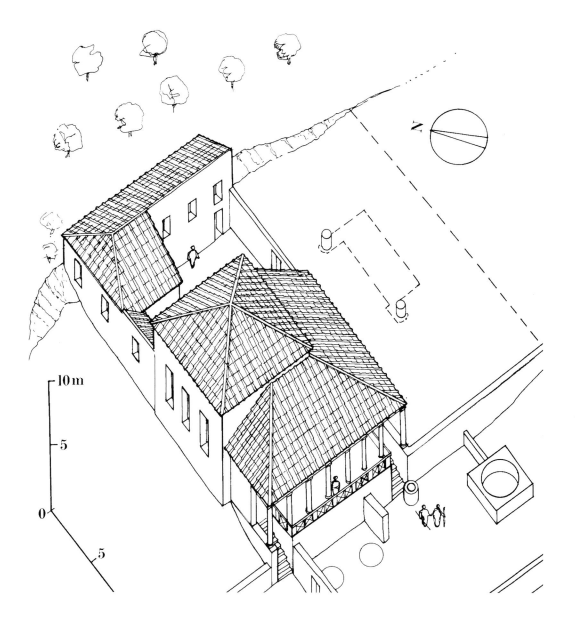

Figure 19a Ground plan, San Rocco villa, Period II and IIA, late first century BCE–early first century CE

The Period II San Rocco *basis villae* was significantly extended south and west. Two sets of cisterns (capacities of 500–565 hl) were built into the hillside. A partially paved roadway, an amenity perhaps jointly maintained with other villa owners, separated the *pars urbana* from the *pars rustica*.

The *pars urbana* (ca. 40 × 40 m, not including cisterns), on the west side of the roadway, was entered through a T-shaped passageway (A) leading to a peristyle (B) with a garden (*viridarium*) (C) and a *tablinum* on axis with adjacent *triclinium* and *exedra* (D). Other large reception rooms and *cubicula* surrounded the peristyle; all had high quality colored mosaic or decorated *opus signinum* floors. There was a second story on the west side of the peristyle, and a partially roofed kitchen (*culina*) (E) with utilitarian floors was accessed down a ramp. Some walls and floors of Period I rooms were thriftily adapted in the Period II villa. The entire *pars urbana* was extended southward with new porticoes and terraces offering spectacular views of the Ager Falernus, Mons Massicus, the Tyrrhenian sea in the distance, and, to the west, low hills and valleys.

The *pars rustica* consisted of two terraces. The larger upper terrace (ca. 35 × 35 m) included an H-shaped structure with two courtyards on either side of a long room (F) that may have accommodated enslaved workers; a room on its north side had a latrine. A large kitchen garden (*hortus*) occupied a second lower terrace (ca. 700 m^2); a room in its southwest corner could have been the lodge for the porter (*ianitor*). Courtyard 2 was open to the roadway; a three-room apartment (G) on its north side may have been for the *vilicus*. Courtyard 1 had a threshing floor and a niche with a stone pedestal on its east wall, possibly the altar of a *lararium* for the *familia*.

In the Period IIA *pars urbana* (50s–60s CE), a small hypocausted bath building (*balineum*) was built into the northwest corner of the *pars urbana*: a *frigidarium* with a cold plunge, a *sudatorium*, and a *caldarium* with a hot bathing tub. In the Period IIA *pars rustica*, a small roof-tile factory with two kilns was added to the long central room, and courtyard 1 became an impressive *cella olearia*: its well-preserved remains attest to all the processes of an *oletum*, from pitting the fruit to decanting the pressed oil from vats into amphoras. The standing amount of oil in the vats, if full, may have had a value of about 6500*HS*, and a year's harvest may have filled the vats several times. The Period II San Rocco villa with its later additions lasted about a century, becoming ruinous toward the mid-second century CE.

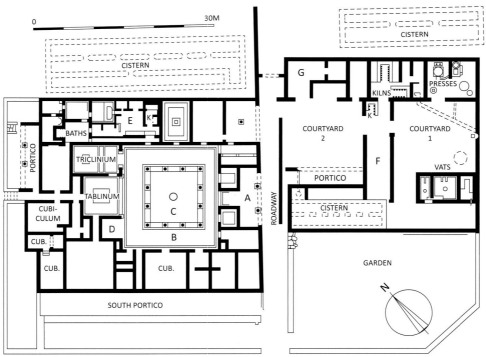

Figure 19b Axonometric plan, San Rocco villa, Period II and IIA, late first century BCE–early first century CE

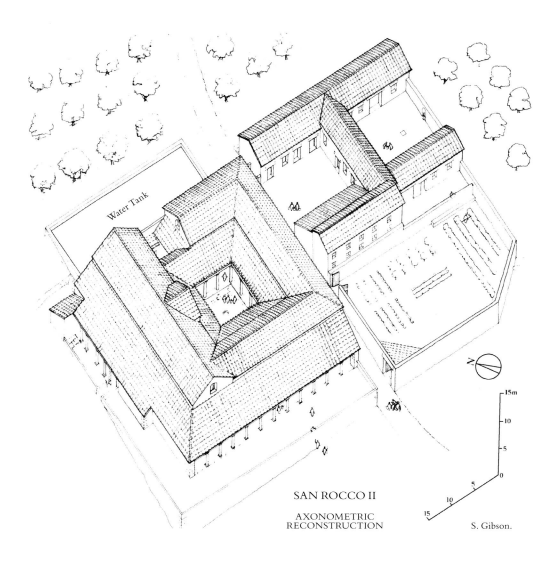

Figure 20a   Ground plan, Settefinestre villa, near Cosa (Ansedonia), 40s–30s BC

The Late Republican Settefinestre villa, near the line of the ancient Via Aurelia close to the port of Cosa, was built on raised terraces as a *basis villae* and faced northwest, overlooking the hills of the Ager Cosanus. The main residence (44.35 × 44.35 m [150 Roman feet] = 145.5 ft^2) was larger than San Rocco II. The upper terrace contained the *pars urbana*, the lower had a large *hortus*, and the lower terrace walls were amusingly decorated with miniature turrets as if fortified.

The plan of the *pars urbana* began with an entrance through a symmetrical, axial atrium-peristyle sequence that allowed for rooms to be grouped in contiguous apartments, possibly as suites of *cubicula-triclinia* for guests. The facades on the northeast and southwest were screened with porticoes, and most of the rooms were decorated with mosaic floors. At this level, corridors separated the owner's living spaces from a *pars rustica* that contained a small *cella olearia* and a *cella vinaria*. At the lower terrace level, a barrel-vaulted *cryptoporticus* with an arcade opening to the *hortus* accommodated more wine-making equipment. The villa produced wine at a large scale, some for export to Gaul; the gross value of the annual wine production of the Settefinestre villa has been estimated at about 60,000*HS*.

By the early second century CE, a large entrance court, enclosed courtyards, and a further *hortus* had been added together with a large separate barn or granary on the southeast and southwest sides, indicating diversification of agricultural production, including the addition of a large pig sty as well as accommodations for enslaved personnel.

From its beginning, the Settefinestre villa was a formal residential villa with strict separations between padronal and agricultural areas. Colonnaded porticoes with terraces allowed for pleasurable viewing of the surroundings as well as surveillance of the working areas from above. The original plan and redecoration encouraged the villa's use as a venue for hospitality. Its profitability, derived from the labor of its enslaved workers, secured the owners' social status. The villa came to the end of its function in the later third or early fourth quarter of the second century CE, about the same time as the Via Gabina Site 11 and San Rocco Period IIA villas.

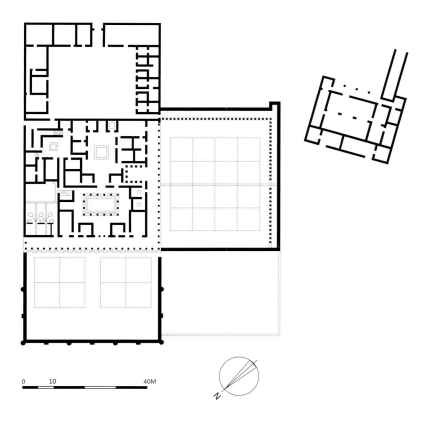

Figure 20b   Axonometric plan, Settefinestre villa, near Cosa (Ansedonia), 40s–30s BCE

Figure 21   Ground plan of Montmaurin villa, mid-fourth century CE

The villa was situated in an area of low hills near the confluence of navigable rivers (the Garonne and Save) in southwestern Gaul (about 20 km north of the modern city of Saint-Gaudens, France). A riverine trading post nearby (La Hillère) may have served as an annex to ship its produce. An earlier villa on the site survived in the form of *partes rusticae* and *fructuariae*, but in the mid-fourth century CE, the villa (with a monumental fountain and baths on the northwest side) was rebuilt, starting at the large semi-circular entrance court (an *atrium lunatum*, which included a small shrine). The residential complex rose through low terraces along symmetrically placed reception rooms, a large peristyle, courtyards, gardens, *triclinia*, *cubicula*, and small *atria* to a garden at the apex of the axis. The formal symmetry of the plan gives it a palatial character quite unlike earlier Roman villas; it was an engine of reception and representation. The decline of the villa after a fire appears to have occurred within a few years of its construction.

Bibliography: Fouet 1969.

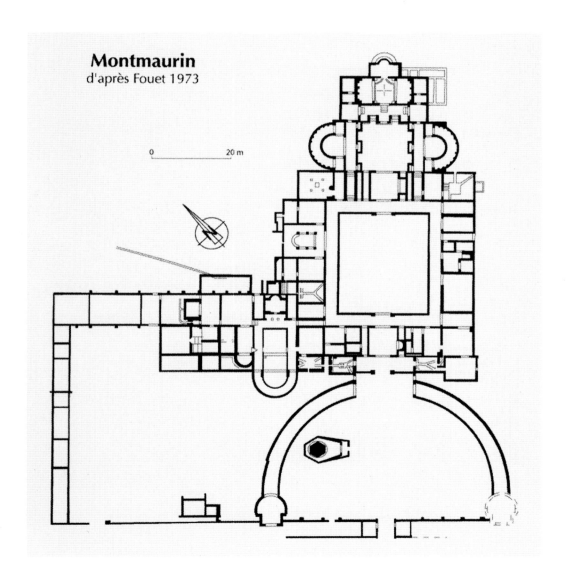

Figure 22   Capreae (modern Capri), reconstruction view of the Villa Iovis (Villa of Tiberius) from the southeast looking toward Vesuvius, 20s CE

By the reign of Tiberius (14–37 CE), securing the person of the emperor at urban residences and villas came to be a matter of architectural importance. On Capreae, Tiberius's Villa Iovis was raised on a high promontory with steep cliffs on three sides, requiring a considerable network of cisterns to make the building habitable (see detail, pp. 46–47). Later, a similar site for a villa was chosen by Domitian: the citadel-like *arx Albana* overlooking the *lacus Albanus*, but in this case the villa had been on or near a property of his father Vespasian and produced some wine. Later, at his villa at Tibur, Hadrian was secured with an architectural panoply of several rings of buildings that barred access to the emperor's presence.

Related texts: Suet., *Tib.* 38–41; Suet., *Tib.* 43; Tac., *Ann.* 4.67; Tac., *Ann.* 6.21.

Figure 23.   Spalato (modern Split), reconstruction view of the palace of Diocletian from the southwest, late third–early fourth century CE

Ultimately a secure imperial residence was achieved at Spalato, a complex planned for the emperor Diocletian near the town of Salona (modern Solin), his hometown. The emperor had evidently begun construction several years before finally retiring there after his abdication as *Augustus* in 305 CE. The strongly defended perimeter of walls with towers enclosed a cross-axial system of streets as in a military camp, but colonnaded as in a town. Barracks and military headquarters were grouped on the north side of the enclosure, while the south side included a temple of Jupiter, Diocletian's mausoleum, and the imperial residence overlooking the sea from a long colonnade on the upper level. The building—a place for retirement (*recessus*), as villas often were—thereby took on military, urban, religious, residential, and funerary aspects in a single imperial complex. No matter the site and circumstance, both Tiberius on Capreae and Diocletian at Spalato occupied themselves with the villa-like activity of growing vegetables.

Related texts: Aur. Vict., *Caes.* 39.6.

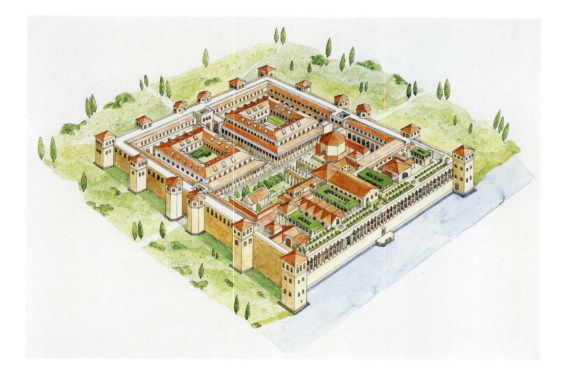

NOTES ON THE PRESENTATION OF THIS SOURCEBOOK

Villas were permanent presences in the Roman landscape and flexible in responding to the needs of the Roman economy: their estates supplied food, raw materials, some manufactured goods, and even luxuries for the changing demands of towns and cities, imperial and official projects, and military requirements. Permanence and flexibility ensured that villas could adapt to changes over time and thereby endure in recognizable form from the Republican and Imperial periods to Late Antiquity.

The culture of villas was equally both permanent and flexible. Many elements of their culture were formulated in the Late Republic and persisted in various forms, staying the same (at least in aspiration) yet modifying according to changing circumstances. In view of the versatility of villas over time, the chapters that follow are organized in two ways. Thematic chapters present the agricultural and architectural sources on villas and consider attitudes and activities such as leisure (*otium*), eating, drinking, visiting, and practical matters of purchase and construction. Villas in Republican and Imperial times are arranged chronologically, as are texts on the ancient Greek and Sicilian origins of villas.

Except in a few cases where other scholars have made superior translations, the translations (and mistakes) are mine. Poems are set into lines to convey an impression of the poets' rhythms and arrangements: the first letter of the first word in each line is capitalized, but no line numbers are given, and English metrical scansion is not attempted. For prose texts, I have tried to convey their tone and mood but, for the most part, without exclamation points and emphases in italics (such punctuation was not used in antiquity). The exception is the addition of paragraph breaks to conform to English usage and to clarify the texts.

The purpose of this sourcebook is to stimulate further studies and encourage greater interest in the topic. To supply facts and elaborate the contexts of the ancient sources, the translations are accompanied by introductions, headnotes, and endnotes intended to be explanatory rather than interpretive. This apparatus—introductions, headnotes, endnotes—lays out some of the larger architectural, economic, social, and cultural aspects of Roman villas. They are directed to students, professionals, and readers of any kind for whom the particulars of living in rural landscapes by women and men, enslaved or free, socially high or low, Roman or other, are matters of interest.

In the texts, square brackets enclose certain items for one of three purposes:

1. Ancient agriculture, villas, and domestic architecture generated terms and names for things, techniques, persons, attitudes, and concepts; some linguistic intimacy with these terms is useful. For that reason, Latin or Greek words and phrases are included within square brackets to familiarize readers of this sourcebook with the distinct vocabulary of villas, to see the variety of words associated with them, and to check the accuracy of my translations. In some cases, near English alternatives are offered. Nouns in square brackets appear in the first-person singular or plural rather than as inflected in the texts; verbs are changed to infinitives rather than in their conjugated form. At times, authors writing in Latin used Greek terms or quotations for special meaning or atmosphere, so these are placed in square brackets as well.

2. Highly inflected languages such as Latin combine references to persons or things with inflected pronouns; when they are translated, sometimes a back reference or pronoun needs to be included. These appear in square brackets, as do any further explanations needed to clarify the authors' meaning.

3. Areal sizes, weights, and amounts are given in ancient terms, followed by their approximate metric and US/UK equivalents within square brackets to convey the amounts of land, mass (metric units/avoirdupois), and dry or wet measures mentioned in the texts. Measurements of length are also given in ancient terms, followed by their approximate equivalents in metric and US/UK standards in square brackets.

Because this book was compiled and written during the COVID-19 pandemic (2020–22) when academic libraries and interlibrary systems were closed, I have used texts in reliable standard editions (e.g. Teubner, Budé, Migne *PL* and *PG*) on readily available internet sites (Internet Archive, Project Gutenberg ebooks, Perseus, Persée, HathiTrust, and The Online Books Page, https://onlinebooks.library.upenn.edu/).

For ancient sites and some bibliography, the name of sites in their ancient form is noted in Pleiades; the development of this research tool is ongoing (see pleiades.stoa.org, subscription and frequent updates are free). The main online reference works cited are *Brill's Neue Pauly* (*NP*) for its fine deployment of ancient sources and the *Oxford Classical Dictionary*, rev. ed. 4, for its firm interpretations. The endnotes take into account the long-standing bibliography on specific topics as well as parts of the vast modern scholarship on antiquity increasingly available in digital form.

The illustrations are intended to augment some of the topics readers encounter in the texts and commentaries. There are visual examples of *xenia* (presents of simple food grown, hunted, and fished for at villas): such presents were emblematic of the sincerity of friendship (*amicitia*) encountered in letters and poems. Villas themselves occur in painted (and occasionally mosaic) scenes illustrating the taste for genre images of verdant and maritime landscapes with a panoply of standard elements: views of villas on land or by water, people, animals, tombs, or statues. Picturesque genres in visual imagery had a real-life counterpart: in Nero's Domus Aurea, the emperor arranged for a view to be crafted from an imported assemblage of rural elements such as fields, vineyards, and herds of animals set in contrast with models(?) of urban buildings, marking the theme of town in country, country in town (*urbs in rure, rus in urbe*).

Plans and reconstructions of villas (figs. 15–21) are grouped to illustrate themes important in the texts without making mechanical one-to-one correlations. They are not presented in strict chronological order: their building histories overlap. Rather, they follow a small-medium-large sequence: the small Via Gabina Site 11 and San Rocco I villas, the medium-sized San Rocco II–IIA villa, and Settefinestre as an example of a large villa (in this case, a *latifundium*) built to be big all at once and added onto in impressive ways. A final example for Late Antiquity is Montmaurin—its plan is significantly different from the earlier villas. Most villas changed over time, presumably related to changes in farming and expectations of profit, investment in agriculture, and other material considerations. However, material changes are also evidence of mental changes: decisions about how to change the plan, orientation, and decoration of any domestic environment are cultural and social acts that are at once intimate and expressive of larger social norms and expectations. They constitute a history of motivation as clear as texts and can resonate with literary examples.

For ease of use, citations have been put into Arabic rather than Roman numerals in combination with Arabic. The letters of Cicero are listed first in the addressees and sequential numbering in Tyrell and Purser format, followed by the addressees, book number, and number format of other editions in parentheses: example: Cic., *Att.* 123.4-5 (6.78.4-5). Pliny the Elder's texts appear by book and paragraph number, followed in parenthesis by the book number plus the large "chunked" section numbers, for example: Plin., *NH* 15.136-137 (15.40).

Throughout, my comments and endnotes refer to enslaved persons, personnel, and individuals. "Slaves" and related terms have been retained as used in the translated texts.

—GPRM
York University

INTRODUCTION

Villa means farm in Latin. The term ranges from a rural establishment owned by a citizen farmer (*agricola*), or maintained by a grower (*cultor*), or cultivated by a tenant (*colonus*) to the property of an owner (*dominus*) of any status except enslaved, a citizen (*civis*), or a formerly enslaved person (*libertus*). Most villas were simple farms (*villae rusticae*, a modern term).[1] Others could be architecturally substantial, with separate residential, utilitarian, and storage sectors: respectively, the *pars urbana*, the *pars rustica* with quarters for free or enslaved personnel and farm gear (*instrumentum*) of all kinds, and the *pars fructuaria* for storage, according to Columella.

The texts in this sourcebook convey information about people in villas. A villa could house an owner (*paterfamilias, dominus*) who might be permanently on-site, absentee, sporadically present, or living overseas; a woman could be matriarch of the establishment as wife of the owner or owner in her own right (*materfamilias, domina*). The *familia* was a household of relatives, extended family, and free, manumitted, and enslaved personnel. The enslaved person or persons (*servus/servi, serva/servae*) were often identified by their function: the *vilicus* was an enslaved, freed, or free male who supervised the agricultural work and residential facilities as a foreman. The *vilicus* may have had a *vilica*: a helpmate, if he was enslaved, or a wife, if both he and she were freedpersons (*liberti*) or he a free man. The *vilica* could have supervisory responsibilities over the enslaved personnel. Other personnel had designated jobs and names: a *pastor* (shepherd), a *bubulcus* (ox driver), and so on. *Servi* on the villa could be bought, inherited, given and received as gifts, loaned, born enslaved to enslaved mothers on the villa property (*vernae*), and sold. Villas often provided occasional seasonal work for free laborers and tenants (*coloni*).

There were many purposes for villas. In a highly monetized but largely agrarian economy, their purpose was to grow produce (*fructus*) of all kinds for the villa's inhabitants and/or for sale at local or urban markets (*macella*) on market days every ninth day (*nundinae*) or at permanent urban markets. The return on sales of such goods was also called *fructus*. The goods could be essential to feeding the villa's inhabitants and could respond to local, regional, or export markets, for the last, especially grains, olive oil, wine.[2] A villa could specialize in other goods: wood and charcoal, fresh and salted fish, peacocks, dormice, minerals, ceramics of all kinds.[3] The term *villa* is generic, but its meaning extended across all aspects of Roman life and culture. Villas were essential in supplying food, flowers, oil, meat, and wine to towns and cities and for providing raw and finished materials (timber, clay, leather, fibers, cloth, stone, tiles) for craft industries, woven goods, and construction of buildings and boats, often from workshops in the countryside (*fabricae*). Their products contributed to civilian, official, and military needs.

However, revenue-generating *fructus* derived via harvests from horticulture, arboriculture, ranching, animal husbandry, or production of raw materials, semifinished, or finished goods was not necessary in order to call something a villa; there were plenty of villas conspicuous for their beauty, spectacular or charming sites, architecture, and decoration and furnishings (*supellex, instrumentum, apparatus*). Locations such as Tusculum and Baiae that had villas owned by socially prestigious families or individuals naturally attracted others to buy available properties or build villas in the environs.

At various times, the term *villa* designated a farm, a small villa or cottage (*villula, casa*), a shed or seasonally habitable hut (*tugurium*), an estate (*fundus, rus*), an estate of considerable extent and most often with a dwelling (*praedium*), rural villas, estates or places in the country (*ager, agri, in agro, in agris*), a substantial villa (*praetorium*), a mansion in either country or town (*aedes*), a building (*aedificium*) in a rural area, or any rural building housing an imperial person (*palatium*). These terms were used interchangeably to designate country residences, but all would be recognized as *villae*, including those generating large or small agricultural revenue, nice places in the suburbs (*suburbanum*) with kitchen gardens or decorative plantings (*hortus, horti*), substantial rural residences with some grand architectural development, and even elaborate imperial residences. In this sense, *villa* was a versatile term encompassing several material and social meanings.

Land associated with villas had various designations. Any property (urban or rural) that was bought, received as a gift, or inherited could be a *possessio*, though one that might be subject to debts and servitudes; similarly, a *portio* indicated bequeathed or inherited land, also with potential contraints. A *fundus* was a farm and might consist of earth (*terra*) and arable fields (*ager, agri*), pasturage (*pascua*), meadows (*pratus*), sparsely wooded land (*saltus*), or forested areas, either natural or in plantation (*silvae*).

Villas came to be ubiquitous, or almost so, throughout Rome's European and Mediterranean hegemony. Their presence was as recognizable as other tangible and intangible Roman phenomena: roads, laws, sewers, entertainments, temples, law court buildings (*basilicae*), suburbs, social arrangements, inscriptions, and mental attitudes. Villas were venues for pleasure, relaxation, learning, and the cultivation of friendships and the mind; they were also settings for real or alleged vice, as well as places of refuge and retirement.

This sourcebook offers selected texts in Latin and Greek to illustrate the many aspects of Roman villas, even though the texts are only loosely helpful in the interpretation of villas in the archaeological record. Instead, the selection is designed to bring villas into focus for general readers as well as scholars at any level—undergraduates, graduate students, and specialists—who are interested in a range of cultural and socioeconomic aspects in history, agricultural and landscape history, architectural development, and artistic phenomena, Roman or other. Texts by themselves do not suffice for a history of villas because they are, for the most part, narratives of the elite, or at least the owning, class. Still, villas had a multivalent relevance to many aspects of Roman life: economy, agricultural methods, social status, architecture, kinship habits and structures, military recruitment, deployment of free and enslaved workforces. For that reason, Roman villa history must combine texts with many other types of evidence.[4] Villas were close to nature and its exploitation, but they were also venues for love of nature and the exercise of taste. In many cases, they were guarantors of moral worth and affiliation, real or imagined, with the supposed habits of Roman ancestors: villas conferred an admirable collective national character (*mores maiorum*) with close contact—actual or merely supervisory—to the soil, farming, and ancestral morality. The moral ideal of the farm provided an important historical frame for villa owners, but villas were also symbols of wealth. At elite social levels, or for owners of lower status, owning at least one villa was almost obligatory, and owning more than one conferred a reputation for riches. Villas were real, but the culture of owning them could be performative.

Situating villas in the history of Roman agricultural and suburban landscapes is an interpretive act of history writing based on various kinds of archaeological and epigraphical information. Villa architecture stands at the intersections of grand or modest building traditions and the needs of domestic spaces and areas for agricultural work. Replicating, at a small level and in the countryside, the divisions inherent in Roman society seems to have been an important social function. Consequently, texts that include family and *familia* memberships, gender relationships, and treatment of enslaved men and women have been chosen to illustrate these social phenomena so that the owner's voice is tempered with others, if only indirectly. Texts that situate villas in Roman mental and cultural landscapes are included to show how villas appear in various types of writing: agricultural treatises, letters, poems, histories, biographies, and other works of literary art. These literary sources are themselves products of traditions, an imagined past, and concrete experiences. Villas were often the settings for the exercise of epistolary, poetic, and philosophical arts.

This sourcebook is intended as a tool: it attempts to coordinate its texts with other literary works and within as many of their archaeological contexts as possible. The texts themselves are chosen to give readers understanding and enjoyment—even entertainment—about villas and their importance in Roman life and, ultimately, their later manifestations in Western architectural history. The texts are supplemented by my specific comments and contextual notes; the introductions to the chapters, the commentaries that precede many of the individual texts, and the endnotes—at times extensive—may consider the relation of a text to the historical moment of its composition, offer a précis of contemporary events and actors, or draw attention to regional accounts of villas. Cross references are generously supplied throughout to guide readers to related texts within the volume.[5] Thematic chapters such as that on the special leisure (*otium*) enjoyed at villas, or on examples of buying and selling them, are included alongside chronological ones (chapter 9 on the Late Republic, chapter 10 on emperors and villas), and there are many overlaps among all of them. Readers will wish to make their own connections among the texts and to use them to illustrate other topics of research—as starting points or as the coda to a related investigation.

Two texts give an idea of the variety of sources for, and ideas about, Roman villas. Between 47 and 45 BCE, the scholar and encyclopedist Varro wrote *On the Latin Language*, a treatise in twenty-five books about Latin grammar and the origins of its words. Among the entries of the books that have survived (Books 5–10 only), Varro derives the term *villa* from verbs expressing the animated movement of goods, animals, vehicles, and people to and from the villa.[6]

VARRO   (Marcus Terentius Varro, 116–127 BCE)

***On the Latin Language (De lingua latina)*, 47–45 BCE (Varro, *Ling.*)**

Varro, *Ling.* 5.22   A *via* [road, street] is thus called an *iter* [path] because it has been worn down [*teritur*] by transportion in carts [*vehendo*].

Varro, *Ling.* 5.35   As the word highway [*actus*, a path for cattle or wagons] came from where they drove [*agebant*] cattle or wagons, so the word for street or road [*via*] came from [the surface] on which they transported [*vehebant*] their goods, and so the destinations to which they transported their produce [*fructus*] were called villas [*villae*].

The second text is by Quintilian, a famous orator and teacher of rhetoric in the late first century CE. His book *Institutes of Oratory* remains a classic in the arts of public speaking. In his text (8.3), he is discussing ornamentation in oratory (*oratio ornatus*) as well as elegance (*cultus*) of speech; these can include appropriate mixes of sublimity (*sublimitas*), richness (*magnificentia*), sober elegance (*nitor*), and authoritative demeanor (*auctoritas*) in arguing a specific legal case (*causa*; 8.3.3–4). Speech, he says, can be like swords polished to glittering effect (8.3.2) or lightning inspiring fear by its strength (*vis*) and flare (*fulgor*; 8.3.5–6). *Oratorio ornatus* must be "manly, strong, and pure (*sanctus*, holy)"; it must "not exhibit either effeminate fluency (*levitas*) or fake cosmetic color; it must shine with lifeblood (*sanguis*) and strength" (8.3.7).

To clinch his argument for his reader, Quintilian continues with a genial and nuanced simile of the agricultural activities and arrangements on a well-tended villa-estate. He evidently thought that the image of rural life would resonate with his readers.

QUINTILIAN   (Marcus Fabius Quintilianus, ca. 35–100 CE)

Institutes of Oratory (Institutio oratoria), ca. 95 CE (Quint., *Inst.*)

Quint., *Inst.* 8.3.7–11   [...] On this matter, I do not want any of our [present-day] corrupt orators to say that I am against those who speak elegantly [*culte*]: I do not deny the virtue of such elegance, but I do not concede that they have it. Should I consider that a farm [*fundus*] that freely abounds with flourishing lilies, violets, and anemones is better cultivated than one with a full harvest of grain and vines heavy with fruit? Should I settle my preference on the sterile plane tree and clipped myrtle bushes rather than on the conjugal elm[7] and the fertile olive? Wealthy men [*divites*] can have plane trees and decorative myrtle bushes, but would they be wealthy if those were the only things they had? Can ornamentation [*decor*] never be applied to [useful] fruit trees? No one would say such a thing. So I will plant my trees in a pattern [*ordo*] set at measured intervals. What could be more attractive than the quincunx, which results in straight lines from every point of view?[8] More to the point, the quincunx arrangement is directly beneficial because it draws moisture from the soil evenly. If my olive tree grows too high at the top, I will prune it with a knife, and it will spread out in a better way and soon bear fruit on more branches. A lean-flanked horse is more attractive but is also faster. The athlete with arm muscles trained with exercise may look good, but he is also better prepared for combat. Real beauty is never far from usefulness.[9]

NOTES

1 The term *villa rustica* is a modern term that does not appear in Latin texts, a fact pointed out by Lafon (2018, 456). Cato (*Agr.* 3.2) says that, by the age of thirty-six, a *pater familias* should prioritize the *rustica* parts of the villa before any other construction. *Villa urbana* appears in Cato (*Agr.* 4) and in Varro (*Rust.* 3.2.10); Varro terms a fancy villa as *perpolita* (*Rust.* 3.2.3).

2 Several new areas of research on villas have emerged recently and are in lively current development. On the coordination of farm production in relation to local and regional markets: Roselaar 2019; de Haas 2017; Kron 2017. On social relations among villa owners in the Italian countryside: Launaro 2017. On export issues in Italian villa-estates and "rationalization" of agricultural production: Heinrich 2017. On wine production in general: Brun 2004, with special attention to Italian peninsular vinting facilities at 7–59; and Dodd 2023 for recent developments in the history of Roman wine production in Italy. For an analysis of land use in Roman Etruria (intensive-extensive and ley farming, fallowing techniques): Bowes et al. 2017. For agricultural land use in the same area: Bowes 2020. A catalogue of 124 villas in central Italy that had significant production facilities (oil and wine presses, vats, *dolia defossa*, *horrea* and other storage facilities) can be found in Feige 2021.

3 Wood and charcoal: Veal 2017. Fresh and preserved fish and *garum*: extensive analysis of size and worth of maritime exploitation (with preceding bibliography) in Marzano 2010; 2013b; 2018; 2020; Marzano and Brizzi 2009. Peacocks (*pavo*, *pavones*) as commercial comestibles in *pastio villatica*: Plin., *HN* 10.45 (10.23). Edible dormice (*glis*, *glires*): Plin., *HN* 8.223–224 (8.82), *HN* 36.4 (36.2), and *HN* 16.18 (16.7). Minerals: sulphur extraction and use of the mineral in treatment for acne, medicated bandages and poultices for abscesses, respiratory conditions, finishing woolen and other fabrics, and religious fumigation/purification: Plin., *HN* 35.174–177 (35.50). On a maritime villa near Antium (modern Anzio), in a caldera with hot sulphur springs and mineral extraction: Marzano 2018, 129 and n. 30, with preceding bibliography. Ceramics of all kinds: de Haas 2017, 72–79; Peña 2017, 213–29. Rural craft production in general: Peña 2017.

4 For example, the history of social interaction among working, enslaved, and owning classes in the agricultural landscape of villas can only work by cross-coordinating archaeological, dating, and biogeological information with epigraphy, field studies, paleobotanical analysis and, very occasionally, texts. An early instance of such cross coordination (for Late Antiquity and the Early Medieval period) can be found in Duby 1973, 13–59 (Eng. trans. 1974, 5–47). Conspicuous recent work on Republican Italy in deploying such adjacencies: Launaro 2011; Roselaar 2019, 8–27, and villas in Italy at 85–93; Bowes 2020. The same issue for Late Antiquity is given case-study treatment in Bintliff 2010. For the history of specific villa landscapes leading to broad regional conclusions, recent gazetteers combined with granular statistical breakdowns are very useful: see examples in, among others, Marzano 2007 (central Italy); De Franceschini 1999 (Istria and the Veneto) and 2005 (environs of Rome); Carandini et al. 2002 (central Italy).

5 For example, the introduction to chapter 2 includes an outline of research on rural enslaved persons that will be of interest to students of the history of enslavement.

At the end of chapter 9, readers will find an appendix on Cicero's use of villas during the many periods of seriously troubled times: his exile in 85–57 BCE; his political wilderness from 60 to 53 BCE; his opposition to Caesar in 49–48 BCE; his proscription and murder in 44–43 BCE.

At the end of chapter 8, an appendix lists letters of 45 and 44 BCE in which Cicero enlisted the assistance of his friend Atticus to buy *horti* not far from Rome. To soothe his grief at her death in childbirth (February 45 BCE), Cicero attempted to find a location for a memorial to his daughter Tullia (*fanum Tulliae*) in *horti* that would affirm her domestic divinization. The *horti* might also serve as a property suitable (and affordable) for his retirement villa. The letters give readers specific instances of Cicero's attempt to enter a difficult property market around the City and—like many who pursue property with strong emotion—his ultimate failure to secure anything.

6 Book 5 of Varro's *On the Latin Language* covers the names of things derived by their analogies of sound to common language or particularly primitive, rural but still current locutions observable in the speech of simple country folk. These derivations and Varro's method gave words the authority of antique tradition and the authenticity of rural usage: the method by sound analogy may have been erroneous, but it chimed strongly with Roman self-representation—namely, that rural simplicity and ancient authority were the same. The word *villa* may have had other origins.

7 The elm tree (*ulmus*) is conjugal (*maritus*) because plantations of them are wedded, as supports, to vines: Columella, *Rust.* 5.6.1–5; 4.13.2. The method of training vines to trees is still current in Campania with poplar trees (*populi*), as also described by Columella, and is called *vite maritata*: Di Gennaro 2013, 436, 449–50; Marzano 2022, 206 and n. 30.

8 The quincunx is a figure in geometry of five equal things (trees, dots, any object) set as corners of a square with one in the middle: ∴. In a series, it sets out parallel but alternating rows of elements, an arrangement, as Quintilian says, that ensures even access of plants to moisture, air, and sun.

9 *Numquam vera species ab utilitate dividitur.*

SOURCEBOOK

1

GREEK AND SICILIAN BACKGROUNDS OF ROMAN VILLAS

HESIOD

XENOPHON

DIODORUS SICULUS

CICERO

Latin authors in any literary endeavor, and Greek authors of accounts of Roman history and culture, were well aware of the Greek historical and cultural background in many Roman fields of achievement: political structures and rhetorical techniques, literary genres of many kinds, all the philosophical and technical sciences, agriculture, and how to live. Among elite Romans, this awareness ran from outright distaste, either affected for political reasons or as a natural inclination (and its corollary in extreme cultural patriotism) to an extreme affiliation (with Greekness as the apex of civilized behavior); there were many subtle gradations between philhellenism and Hellenophobia.[1]

For the literature of villas, Hesiod, Xenophon, Diodorus Siculus, and Cicero were exponents, in different and various ways, of Roman consciousness of Greek antecedents in terms of organized, written agricultural knowledge, cultural situations, and examples of how to live in the countryside: simplicity, luxury, morality, family relations, and to how to manage resources, including the people enslaved to work on the villa-estates and provide service to its owners and free persons.

HESIOD   (mid-eighth to mid-seventh century BCE)

Works and Days (Ηργα καὶ Ἡμέραι, *Opera et Dies*) (Hes., *Op.*)

In antiquity, the *Works and Days* of Hesiod was the first agricultural treatise intended for use by farmers and estate owners: it is a manual that outlines the schedule of work appropriate to times of year, seasons, days, and even times of day.[2] Like all such treatises, it is a literary work first, useful but also elevated and inspiring. The calendar is mainly based on the movement of stars, sun, and moon, but other natural phenomena are also recorded—blossoming of fruit-bearing trees, migration of birds, appearance of snails, and so on. Hesiod includes homely advice, nostrums, what appear to be old saws and sayings, and other down-to-earth remarks that give his poem the character of an all-purpose almanac and vade mecum.

In addition, the poet presents agriculture and life in the country in personal biographical incidents: the poet and his brother, their father, the poet's anger at his brother; and as universal history: divine justice and human evil, the gods' gifts to the first woman, the passage of human generations from nobility to ignominy and from gold to iron. Proverbs, home truths, common sense, and moralizing are included, all sharpened by Hesiod's scolding of his brother Perses.

Hesiod's poems *Theogony* and *Works and Days*, both written in the majestic epic meter of dactylic hexameter, were associated in later speculations about their date (mid-eighth to mid-seventh century BCE) and authorship with those known under the name of Homer—the *Iliad* and the *Odyssey*.[3] *Works and Days* is the earliest statement of enduring themes in Western literature: growing is better than grubbing in cities, making is better than marketing, farming is better than fooling around in towns, agriculture is superior to urban culture, simple morality more acceptable to the gods than legal wrangling, purity and piety better than perversion and pollution, and so on.[4] The simple notion—that the dignity and authenticity of the work of farming and country living are superior to the degradation and depravity of life in cities—is a powerful theme in attitudes and art, with moral dimensions at many levels. Along the way, Hesiod gives good advice about marriage, proper behavior with others, including table-talk topics, protective clothing to stay dry in the rain, many moral lessons, and specifics about how to organize a house and household. The *Works and Days* is cited as a source in the agricultural treatises of Varro, Columella, and Palladius as well as very frequently in Pliny's *Natural History*. It and its author are included in Cicero's dialogue *On Old Age* excerpted below, and Cicero urged that the young son of a good friend (Quintus Lepta) study Hesiod for good character and pious inclination.[5]

The notion that the countryside and its inhabitants were superior in morality and authenticity to all cities or towns and their citizens—including the greatest *urbs* of all, the City itself, Rome—became an intellectual tradition and cultural assumption in antiquity. It persisted in various forms and still does. Hesiod may have kicked it off, but it did not need its originator to endure. Engagement with the work and activities of agriculture came to be closely associated with the Roman *mos maiorum*, in which upright behavior of ancestors and courage of all kinds were the underpinnings of the state. Many authors of the texts on villas in Greek and Latin made the noble estate-owning founder-farmers, elected officials, and the commanders and soldiers of the City into examples of the Hesiodic tradition assimilated to Roman history.[6] Morally, if not actually, Roman villa owners may have recognized and sought to emulate Hesiod's farm and his attitudes in their own villas.[7]

Hesiod's poem begins (lines 1–26, omitted here) by invoking the Pierian Muses to tell him of Zeus and his famous equalizing justice: humbling the proud, raising the humble. Then the poet goes straight to the point: "I will speak truths [ἐτήτυμα] to Perses" (Hes., *Op.* 10). This brother had cheated him of some agricultural property and had abandoned the farm they had inherited from their father to become a hanger-on of prominent men (βασιλεῖς, rulers, judges) in town. Hesiod directly addresses his brother Perses, the "you" of the poem.

Early in his poem, Hesiod sets up two manifestations of Strife (Ἔρις), defined as both a divine entity and a life principle with two opposite aspects, negative and positive.[8] The positive Strife of work and its motivations (including the spur of jealousy) follows the example of the man who ploughs and plants his fields well and organizes his house or household (οἶκός τ'εὖ τιθέναι) solidly, thereby becoming rich (πλούσιος).

Hes., *Op.* 27–41

> So that Strife with her *Schadenfreude* [κακόχαρτος] may not prompt your spirit to shirk working, Perses,
> Get this into your head [θυμός, spirit] while you listen to litigations and waste your time in the [town] assembly.[9]
> A man can have little to do with disputes and goings-on in the assembly,
> If he does not have life's necessities—Demeter's grain—that the earth brings us
> Stored up inside [his granary] in a timely way.
> After you've polished off that grain, you could start discussion and disputes about another man's property,
> But you're not going to have a second chance to behave like that:
> Instead, let's settle our dispute with just judgments, the best ones—those that come from Zeus.
> We had apportioned our farm allotment [κλῆρος, allotment of land], but you grabbed the greater part
> And went off with it to ingratiate yourself with gift-greedy rulers [βασιλεῖς]

Who want to pass judgment [on the matter of the allotment].[10]
They're simpletons: they don't know how much greater the half is than the whole,
And don't know that mallow and asphodel are a great blessing [ὄνειαρ].[11]

Hesiod's *Op.* 42–212 (omitted here) are the most famous lines of Hesiod's poem for their majesty, lofty narration, and artistic engagement. The poet lodges his discussion of farming and the superior virtues of the country in the story of Pandora, the first human, a woman, to whom all life's evil principles were given (sorrow, sickness, poverty, and so on) in a jar (*pithos*; *Op.* 60–105).[12] All were released except Ἐλπίς, usually translated as "Hope," though it can have other subtle meanings (Expectation, Anticipation, Apprehension); Hope remained under the jar's lid by the providence of Zeus. There follows an impressive account of the generations of human beings from past glory to their present existence: the generations from gold and silver, then to bronze and finally grim iron, and a description of the genesis of demigods.[13] The address to Perses then resumes:

Hes., *Op.* 213–218
O Perses, adhere to Justice [Δίκης], don't magnify hubris.[14]
For a coward, hubris is a bad thing, and hard to bear even for a brave man
Who, when he encounters obstacles, gets overwhelmed. Justice overcomes
    hubris in the end,
But a simpleton [νήπιος] comes to know this only after enduring [misfortune].

In *Op.* 219–237 (omitted here), Hesiod urges his brother to take up the virtues of good judgment and hard work, promising that men who do so become wealthy from "thick-fleeced" sheep, and fertile with "wives who give birth to children in the likeness [image] of their parents." Such men rely on harvesting the land and never go to sea. Then, in *Op.* 238–305 (omitted here), a warning of the vengeance of Zeus on cities and individuals because of hubris and cruelty is followed by a warning to rulers (βασιλεῖς) to deliver justice (Δίκη). Hesiod then addresses Perses directly and scolds him for injustice and foolishness, with a warning about famine and misery.

Hes., *Op.* 306–311
As for you [Perses], you should be glad to arrange your works [ἔργα] with care,
That way your granaries will be full of life's necessities in the right season.
It's from work that men become rich in flocks of sheep.
And if you're zealous in your work, you will be much better loved by gods and men.
Working [ἔργον] is not a dishonor, but not working is.

Hes., *Op.* 320
Valuable properties [χρήματα, goods, things needed for life] are not for the taking
    [by other humans]—properties given by god are much better.

Hesiod then remarks in *Op.* 321–334 (omitted here) on how shamelessness and impiety lead to inhospitable behavior, cruelty to those who beg for help, sins against orphans, illicit sexual relations, and disrespecting and quarreling with one's father; the vengeful anger of Zeus is at hand for such a person.

Hes., *Op.* 335–360
Now [Perses], keep your damaged spirit far away from such actions.
Instead, as far as your ability allows, sacrifice to the immortal gods
In purity and sincerity, burning splendid fleshy thigh bones,

Or at other times, offering libations and burnt offerings,
Both before going to bed and when the holy light [of dawn] comes on,
So [the god's] heart and spirit will be gracious to you,
And so you can buy other persons' farm allotments [κλῆροι], not they yours.[15]
Invite your friend to feast [with you] but ignore your enemy
And especially call [for help] from those who live in the [same] district.
If something bad should happen on your property [ἐγχώριος]
The neighbors who come [to help] are not buckled up, but kinsmen are buckled
    in [i.e., ready].
A bad neighbor is a misery in the same way that a good one is a blessing:
He who shares a good neighbor [with another person] has a stake in a good thing,
And, as long as the neighbor's not a bad person, not even one cow would go missing.
Deal fairly in a good measured way with your neighbor, and go one better [with him],
So that next time you're in need, he will come [to help].
Do not look for ill-gotten profit, for such profit is the same as ruin.
Be affectionate to your friend[s], and return visits to those who come to visit you.
Give to the man who gives, and don't give to him who doesn't.
Giving is good, grabbing is bad and is the giver of death.
In giving what he wants to give, even if it's a very big gift,
The giver takes pleasure in the gift and has a happy feeling in his spirit,
But the man who, clinging to shameless behavior, grabs [others' property?]
Freezes up his "own dear heart" [φίλος ἦτορ], if only by a little.

In *Op.* 383–396 (omitted here), Hesiod begins the agricultural calendar, marked for ploughing by the rising of the Pleiades in May and harvesting with their descent in October. He interrupts himself briefly, however, to repeat injunctions to Perses about hard work, never getting into debt, and being careful with neighbors. He then gives advice about the sequence of building, about a specific enslaved woman, and some more general advice.

Hes., *Op.* **405–413**
First a house [οἶκος], [then] a woman, and an ox for the plough:
The woman is to be bought [κτητή γυναῖκα], not to be a wife, [rather,] she's a woman
    who can help with the oxen.[16]
Get all the goods in your house in shipshape order [χρήματα ἄρμενα]
Because if you ask someone [for help] and he declines, you would be in want.

In portions not included here, Hesiod resumes (*Op.* 414–535) with the agricultural calendar of which work is to be done on certain days with the start of cold weather and the descent of Sirius. Axles for wagons and other wood implements (ploughs, yokes) are to be made at that time. Instructions and good or bad dates for ploughing and casting seed are given, and enslaved workers are told to make winter shelters for themselves at midsummer. The calendar is based on stars, changes in prevailing winds, the return of migratory birds such as cranes, the sound of cuckoos, and the appearance of snails. There is advice about waterproof clothing in January–February (the period called *Lenaion*, *Op.* 536–546), winter storms, and dry-docking a boat (*Op.* 547–640).[17] The passages into spring, summer, and fall are described with the tasks appropriate for them, and Hesiod also gives a biographical account of his father who, on account of some failure in farming or trade, had left Aeolian Cyme (Asia Minor) to settle at Ascra near Mount Helicon in Boeotia to escape poverty (*Op.* 633–640).[18]

There follows (*Op.* 641–681) a detailed account of winter, and the passage into spring and summer precedes additional instructions on how to dry-dock a boat. The biographical theme continues: Hesiod tells his listeners that the only time he took to the sea was to go to Chalcis in Euboea across the Euripus strait from Boeotia on the mainland.[19] Even though he claims to know little about seafaring and to despise it (*Op.* 663–681), his objections seem more moral than practical.

Hes., ***Op.*** **682–694**
> I myself do not praise [going to sea]: my spirit cannot find it pleasant.
> [Seagoing] is hard to master, and it's only with difficulty that you can get out
>   of a bad situation.
> But in the ignorance of their minds, men do it anyway:
> Riches [χρήματα] are a soul itself [ψυχή] for small mortal men,
> [But] it's terrible to die in the sea swell of the waves.
> I'm telling you all these things out loud and in public so you get this into your head:
> Do not load all of life's necessities into hollow boats.[20]
> Leave the greater part of it aside, load only the smaller part;
> It's a misery, too, if you freight a cart with an over-heavy load
> And break the cart's axle, and your produce [φορτία] is ruined.[21]

In *Op.* 694–705 (omitted here), Hesiod provides marriage advice: when you're around 30 years old, marry a local woman in the fifth year after her puberty, a virgin, and one of good reputation, who will take care of you when you're old. *Op.* 706–714 are advice about friendship and enmity toward others, with an urging to be forgiving of others' mistakes; be consistent in friendship.

Hes., ***Op.*** **715–726**
> Never be known [either] as entertaining [too] many guests or being stingy about hospitality,
> Do not befriend bad men and do not denigrate good ones.
> Never attempt to blame a man for [his] cursed, soul-destroying poverty,
> It's the gift of those who live forever [i.e., the gods].[22]
> Among men, a tolerant tongue is a treasure,
> And the most pleasure [χάρις] comes from measure [in speech].
> Speak evil, and right away you yourself will hear more of the same.[23]
> Don't be stormy [i.e., rude] in company when there are many guests at dinner:
> Pleasure enjoyed in common [with others] is all the greater and less expensive.
> At daybreak, never pour a libation of glistening wine to Zeus or the other immortals
>   With unwashed hands. They do not listen and reject the [evil] prayer.

Op. 727–828 (omitted here) concludes Hesiod's poem. The passage incorporates two themes: the first a series of proverbs, homely sayings, and injunctions, many against forbidden practices (e.g., washing a man in water used by women). The second consists of a list of the days, good or evil, of the month or year when certain activities (e.g., woodworking, being born, castrating goats and sheep, building fences) are religiously prescribed or proscribed.[24]

XENOPHON   (ca. 430–355/354 BCE)

Oeconomicus (Οἰκόμικος), after 394 BCE (Xen., *Oec.*).
Translation by Sarah B. Pomeroy.[25]

Xenophon's self-representation and biography as a military man, statesman, philosopher, and man of some wealth and social distinction appealed to Romans of a status and mentality that they took to be comparable to his. His conservatism, philosophical bent, and tendency to idealize both the Persian royal class and the Spartan form of government made him a natural referent to villa owners looking for cultural and social reinforcement for their own attitudes.[26] In addition, he was a farmer: at Skillous, which he says is 20 stades (about 3.75 km, or 2⅓ mi.) from Olympia on the road from Sparta, he bought an estate (τὸ χωρίον) from the proceeds of his military exploits in Asia Minor; the riverine property had meadow, forests providing good hunting (boars, stags, gazelles), and space for a miniature version of the temple of Artemis at Ephesus, which the neighboring inhabitants honored with gifts of food. He worked the land and hunted there with his sons.[27] The promise, in the *Oeconomicus*, of becoming a gentleman in society by innate personal worth, status, and shapely philosophical padding gave Xenophon's treatise a natural appeal to many of Roman elite status or those aspiring to such status, and it validates a villa owner's natural and authoritative role in society beyond considerations of profit. The Persian royal connection was another boost. It is perhaps in part for these reasons that Cicero, in a literary endeavor as a young man, translated Xenophon's treatise into Latin. He returned to it as an old man in his dialogue *On Old Age*, including the long-dead Cato the Elder as a participant in the conversations as well as referring to Cato's *De re rustica*.[28] Xenophon's Greek original, Cicero's Latin translation, and Cato's treatise projected an atmosphere of rationality and devotion to proper behavior, even though Xenophon has little on actual farming and much on behavior, and Cato much on farming techniques and only a few pointers on how to behave. Cicero was interested in both, as his *On Old Age* indicates. Passages from Xenophon's text are grouped here in several overlapping themes.

Purpose and Pleasures of Farming

Xenophon's Socrates was looking for a perfect gentleman; he found him in one Ischomachus, the main protagonist of the dialogue (*Oec.* 6.12–17). The *Oeconomicus* is a conversation in which Socrates explains the principles of good householding to Critobulus, in part his own ideas, in part by telling Critobulus what Ischomachus told him. By reputation, Ischomachus was the perfect gentleman (ἀνήρ καλός τε κἀγαθὸς), someone who is both noble and beautiful, as well as good in himself, and who embodies the abstract principles of nobility/beauty of mind and goodness (καλοκαγαθία).[29] He is presented as a wealthy citizen of the city of Athens, who owns a house in town but lives by preference at his house on his farm in the country. His wealth put him under obligation of liturgy (λειτουργία): endowing or paying for public works such as equipping ships for the Athenian navy, horses for the cavalry, sponsoring choruses and plays for festivals, providing buildings for athletic training, and other goods for the public benefit. He is married to a much younger woman (unnamed in the text) whom he both instructs and relies on for the smooth functioning of the household.[30] Socrates met Ischomachus at Athens, where he found him after a day of business, sitting in the Stoa of Zeus Eleutherius in the Agora but soon to be on his way home to his farm (*Oec.* 7.1).[31]

Xen., *Oec.* 6.4–10
SOCRATES Well, we thought that estate management [ἡ οἰκονομία] was the name of some branch of knowledge [ἡ ἐπιστήμη]. This knowledge appeared to be the science by which men can increase their estates. And an estate seemed to be identical with the total of a person's property. We said that property is what is beneficial to each person for a livelihood. And we discovered that everything which a person knows how to use is beneficial. We thought that it was impossible to learn all the branches of knowledge. And we agreed with the cities in rejecting the so-called "banausic" occupations on the grounds that we thought that they ruin men's bodies and weaken their minds.[32] We asserted that the clearest proof of this would be evident during an enemy attack against the land, if the farmers [γεωργοί] were to

be separated from the craftsmen [τεχνίται] and asked whether they preferred to defend the land or to retreat from the open country to guard the city walls. We thought that in such a situation those who are occupied with the land would vote to defend it, but the craftsmen would vote not to fight but to remain sitting down, as they have been trained to do, and to avoid exertion and danger. We decided that for a true gentleman [ἀνήρ καλός τε ἀγαθός], the best line of work and the best branch of knowledge is farming, by which human beings obtain the necessities of life. This life of work seemed to be very easy to learn and most enjoyable to practice, to make men's bodies most handsome and strong, and to provide their minds with the greatest amount of leisure to devote to their friends and their cities. We thought that farming, to some extent, stimulated those who work at it to be brave, because crops and cattle are raised outside the city walls. Therefore this way of making a living, we thought, enjoys the best reputation among cities; for they believe that it creates citizens who are both extremely brave and most loyal to the community.

Xen., Oec. 5.1–5
SOCRATES   Critobulus, I am telling you this because not even those most favored by the gods can do without farming. For concerning oneself with it seems to be simultaneously a pleasant experience, a means of increasing one's estate [οἶκος, household], and exercise for the body so that it may be capable of all those things that are suitable for a free man [ἀνήρ ἐλεύθερος]. First of all, for those who cultivate her, the earth bears the food that human beings need in order to live and provides their sources of enjoyment as well. Secondly, she supplies what they use to decorate altars and statues and to adorn themselves, and these are most pleasant to look at and to smell, too. And then there are edible delicacies: some she produces, for others she provides the means of sustenance; for the occupation of breeding livestock is closely connected with farming, so that men may propitiate the gods with sacrifices and make use of the animals for themselves.

Although the earth offers her goods most generously, she does not allow men to take them without work, but she makes them accustomed to enduring the winter's cold and summer's heat. Through exercise she gives increased strength to those who work the land with their own hands, and those who farm by supervising their laborers she makes manly by waking them up early and forcing them to move about energetically. For in the country and in the city the most urgent operations occur at a fixed time. Furthermore, if a man wishes to defend his city by serving in the cavalry, farming is best suited for providing the horse with food; if he serves in the infantry, it makes his body energetic. The earth encourages him to take rather more pleasure in the activity of hunting, providing easy access to nourishment for the hounds and nourishing the prey at the same time.[33] [...]

Xen., Oec. 5.9–11
SOCRATES   What occupation welcomes friends more generously? Where is it more comfortable to spend the winter than on a farm with a generous fire and warm baths? Where is it more pleasant to spend the summer than in the countryside with streams and breezes and shade? What occupation provides more appropriate first fruits for the gods or produces festivals with a greater abundance of offerings? What occupation is more popular with slaves, or sweeter to a wife, or more attractive to children, or more agreeable to friends? I think it would be remarkable if any free man has ever come to possess any property more pleasant than a farm, or has discovered any object of concern more pleasant or more useful for making a living.[34]

Farming as a Royal Vocation

Xen., *Oec.* 4.4–5
CRITOBULUS   Then, Socrates, which occupations do you advise us to practice?
SOCRATES   Surely we ought not to be ashamed to imitate the king of the Persians? For they say that he classifies farming [γεωργία] and the art of war among the noblest and most essential concerns, and he is seriously concerned about both of them.

Xen., *Oec.* 4.13–14
SOCRATES   And furthermore in which ever of his territories he [the king of the Persians] lives and which he visits, he is concerned that there should be gardens—the *paradeisoi*, as they are called—full of all the fine and beautiful plants that the earth naturally produces.[35] And he spends most of his time in these, except when the time of year prevents him.

CRITOBULUS   By Zeus, then Socrates, the king must be concerned that the *paradeisoi* in which he himself spends time should be furnished in the finest manner possible with trees and all the other fine things that the earth produces.

Ischomachus's Country House Itself

In these next passages of the *Oeconomicus*, Socrates is telling Critobulus what Ischomachus had said about talking with his wife regarding the plan and arrangement of their house.

Xen., *Oec.* 9.2–7
SOCRATES QUOTING ISCHOMACHUS   "Well, I thought it was best to show her the possibilities of our house first. It is not elaborately decorated, Socrates, but the rooms are constructed in such a way that they will serve as the most convenient place to contain the things that will be kept in them. So the rooms themselves invited what was suitable for each of them. Thus the bedroom [θάλαμος], because it was in the safest possible place, invited the most valuable bedding and furniture. The dry storerooms called for grain, the cool ones for wine, and the bright ones for those products [ἔργα] and utensils that need light. I continued by showing her living rooms [διαιτητήρια] for the occupants, decorated [κεκαλλωπισμένα] so as to be cool in summer and warm in winter. I pointed out to her that the entire house has its facade facing south, so it was obviously sunny in winter and shady in summer. I also showed her the women's quarters [γυναικωνῖτις], separated from the men's quarters [ἀνδρωνίτιδα] by a bolted door, so that nothing might be removed from them that should not be, and so that the slaves would not breed without our permission.[36] For, generally, honest slaves become more loyal when they have produced children, but when bad ones mate, they become more troublesome. After we had gone through these rooms," he [Ischomachus] said, "we sorted the contents by type. We first began by putting together the things that we use for sacrifices. After that we separated the fancy clothing that women wear at festivals, the men's clothing for festivals and for war, bedding for the women's quarters, bedding for the men's quarters, women's shoes, and men's shoes. Another type consisted of weapons, another of spinning implements, another of bread-making implements, another of implements used for other food, another of bathing implements, another of kneading implements, and other dining implements. And we divided all this equipment into two sets, those that are used daily and those that are used only for feasts."[37] [...]

Ischomachus has been explaining to his wife the importance of organizing objects in the household. Here, Socrates is both quoting Ischomachus directly and telling Critobulus what Ischomachus said.

Xen., *Oec.* 8.10–13

SOCRATES QUOTING ISCHOMACHUS "I believe the most beautiful and meticulous arrangement of equipment that I ever saw, Socrates, was when I boarded the great Phoenician merchant ship to see what it was like. For I saw an enormous amount of equipment arranged in separate places in the smallest receptacle.[38] For, you know," he [Ischomachus] said, "a ship needs many pieces of wooden equipment and ropes when she anchors or puts out to sea, and much rigging, as they call it, when she sails. She is armed with many devices to use against enemy ships, and she carries around with her many weapons for the crew. She also carries all the same utensils that people use at home for the various meals they eat together. In addition to all this, she is laden with all the cargo the owner takes with him to make a profit. I'm telling you from my personal experience," he said, "that all the items were stored in a space not much bigger than a dining-room large enough for eleven couches.[39] I noticed that everything was stored in such a manner that nothing got in the way of anything else, and there was no need for anyone to go and search for it. Nothing was disarranged or difficult to untie so as to cause delay when something was required for immediate use."

Xen., *Oec.* 8.18–19

SOCRATES QUOTING ISCHOMACHUS'S WORDS TO HIS WIFE "I have already told you that it is good for equipment to be arranged in order and that it is easy to find a place in the house that is suitable for each piece of it. How beautiful it looks, when shoes are arranged in rows, each kind in its own proper place, how beautiful to see all kinds of clothing properly sorted out, each kind in its own proper place, how beautiful bed linens, bronze pots, tableware! And what a facetious man would laugh at most of all, but a serious man would not: even pots appear graceful when they are arranged in a discriminating manner. It follows from this that all other things somehow appear more beautiful when they are in a regular arrangement. Each of them looks like a chorus of equipment, and the interval between them looks beautiful when each item is kept clear of it, just as a chorus of dancers moving in a circle is not only a beautiful sight in itself, but the interval between them seems pure and beautiful, too."

Ischomachus in the Country and in the City

As the *Oeconomicus* dialogue continues, Socrates later asks Ischomachus about his daily schedule between the country estate and the city.

Xen., *Oec.* 11.14–16

SOCRATES QUOTING ISCHOMACHUS "Well, Socrates," replied Ischomachus, "I usually get out of bed early enough that if there's anyone I need to see, I can find him still at home. And if I have any business to transact in town, I also use this business appointment as an opportunity to take a walk. If I haven't any urgent business in town, then my slave leads my horse to the farm, and I make the trip to the country serve as a walk, and maybe that's better, Socrates, than if I'd strolled around in the arcade [ξυστός].[40] Once I have arrived at the farm, whether I find them planting, or working the fallow, or sowing, or gathering in the crops, I always inspect how each of these jobs is being done, and put them on the right track if I know of any method superior to the one in use. Afterwards, I generally get on my horse and practice a horseman's maneuvers resembling the horseman's maneuvers that are required in war as close as I can manage them, avoiding neither hillside nor steep descent nor ditch nor stream, though, of course, I take as much care as possible not to lame the horse while performing these exercises."

Ischomachus's Wife

Ischomachus's wife has a responsibility in the house, over the household, and on the estate that is equal to but different from her husband's. While the distribution of spatial tasks is attributed to an essential difference between the sexes, neither is inherently superior or inferior to the other.[41] Household supervision results in a well-exercised body and a fine facial complexion.

Xen., *Oec.* 3.14–16
SOCRATES QUOTING ISCHOMACHUS   "I think that a wife who is a good partner in the estate [οἶκος] carries just as much weight as her husband in attaining prosperity. Property generally comes into the house through the exertions of the husband, but it is mostly dispensed through the housekeeping [δαπανητής] of the wife. If these activities are performed well, estates increase, but if they are managed incompetently, estates diminish." [...]

At one point in the dialogue, Socrates remarks that Ischomachus does not look as if he spent much time indoors. What follows is an account, later much elaborated, of Ischomachus's wife, her character, and her duties on the estate.

Xen., *Oec.* 7.3–6
SOCRATES QUOTING ISCHOMACHUS   [...] "And, Socrates, in reply to your question, I certainly do not spend time indoors, for my wife is more than capable of managing everything inside the house, even by herself."

I [Socrates] said, "I should very much like you to tell me, Ischomachus, whether you yourself trained your wife to become the sort of woman that she ought to be, or whether she already knew how to carry out her duties when you took her as your wife from her father and mother."

"What could she have known when I took her as my wife, Socrates? She was not yet fifteen when she came to me, and had spent her previous years under careful supervision so that she might see and hear and speak as little as possible. Don't you think that it was adequate if she came to me knowing only how to take wool and produce a cloak, and had seen how spinning tasks are allocated to the slaves? And besides, she had been very well trained to control her appetites, Socrates," he said, "and I think that sort of training is most important for man and woman alike."

Xen., *Oec.* 7.20–25
SOCRATES QUOTING ISCHOMACHUS   "Those who intend to obtain produce to bring into the shelter need someone to work at the outdoor jobs. For ploughing, sowing, planting, and herding is all work performed outdoors, and it is from these that our essential provisions are obtained. As soon as these are brought into the shelter, then someone else is needed to look after them and to perform the work that requires shelters. The nursing of newborn children requires shelters, and so does the preparation of bread from grain, and likewise, making clothing out of wool. Because both the indoor and the outdoor tasks require work and concern, I think the god, from the very beginning, designed the nature of woman for the indoor work and concerns and the nature of man for the outdoor work."[42]

Ischomachus's Enslaved Personnel

Socrates asks Ischomachus if he isn't keeping him from returning to the farm from town, and they converse about Ischomachus's enslaved foremen. Additional passages included here speak about other enslaved workers.[43]

Xen., *Oec.* 12.2–4

SOCRATES QUOTING FIRST ISCHOMACHUS AND THEN HIS OWN REJOINDER   "But, Socrates, I am not neglecting the matters which you mention," said Ischomachus. "I have foremen in the fields."

"When you need a foreman [ἐπίτροπος]," I said, "do you find out if there is a skilled supervisor anywhere around and try to buy him, just as when you need a carpenter, you find out, I'm sure, where you can see a man with building skills and try to get him? Or do you train your foremen yourself?"

"By Zeus, Socrates," he replied, "I try to train them myself. If someone is going to be capable of taking charge in my place when I am away, what else does he need to know other than what I do? If I am capable of supervising the various types of work, surely I can teach someone else what I myself know."[44] [...]

Xen., *Oec.* 5.14–17

SOCRATES TO CRITOBULUS   Furthermore, farming helps train people to collaborate with each other. [...] Therefore the man who is going to be a successful farmer must make his laborers eager and disposed to be obedient. [...] On many occasions, the farmer must encourage his workers no less than the general encourages his soldiers. Slaves need some good thing to look forward to no less, in fact, even more than free men so that they may be willing to stay. The man who said that farming is the mother and nurse of the other arts spoke truly. When farming is successful, all the other arts prosper, but wherever the earth is forced to lie barren, the other arts, both on earth and sea, are virtually extinguished.

Socrates reports also what Ischomachus had to say about his housekeeper, an enslaved woman.

Xen., *Oec.* 9.11–13

SOCRATES QUOTING ISCHOMACHUS   "Now when we appointed our housekeeper [ταμία], we looked for the one who seemed to have the greatest degree of self-control in eating, drinking wine, sleeping, and intercourse with men, and who, furthermore, seemed to have memory and the foresight both to avoid being punished by us for negligence and to consider how, by pleasing us in any way, she might be rewarded by us in return. We taught her to be loyal to us by giving her a share of our joy when we were happy, and if we had any trouble, we called on her to share it too. We trained her to be eager to improve the estate by taking her into our confidence and by giving her a share in our success. We instilled a sense of justice [δικαιοσύνη] in her by giving more honor to the just than the unjust, and showing her that the just live lives that are richer and better suited to a free citizen than the unjust. And so we appointed her to this post."

DIODORUS SICULUS   (fl. mid-first century BCE)

Historical Library (Βιβλιοθήκη ἱστορική, *Bibliotheca historica*) 60–30 BCE (Diod. Sic.)[45]

Few events were more terrifying to Roman authorities and citizenry than the rebellion of enslaved people.[46] Three major revolts occurred, the first in Sicily in 138/7–132 BCE and a second in 104–101 BCE; a third, between 73–71 BCE, centered on Capua in Campania, is known as the revolt of Spartacus.[47] In his account of the origins of the first rebellion, Diodorus Siculus organized his narrative along three points to provide historical warning to, and a contemporary moral lesson for, owners of estates run by enslaved workers.[48]

Diod. Sic. 34.31–32 [...] On the one hand, the praetors [οἱ στρατηγοί] tried to control the rebellious slaves, but on the other they were not bold enough to punish them because they were afraid of the power and control of their masters [οἱ κύριοι, owners] and so had to overlook the depredations to the province. That was because most of the landowners were duly appointed Roman knights, and as such they were the judges [κριταί] over provincial affairs brought up against the praetors, and so they feared their powers.

Those of the Italians who were occupied [as owners] in agriculture [γεωργία] bought a great many slaves and branded all of them but did not give them provisions and, by imposing heavy work, broke them down.

Diod. Sic. 34.33 When wielding political power, men of importance should behave kindly to those who are in inferior positions, and even in private life as well, they should be kind to their slaves in a thoughtful way. Crude arrogance leads cities [πόλεις, states] to quarrels among the free citizens, and even in households themselves, such arrogance leads to plots by slaves against masters and even to fearful rebellions against the entire state itself. [...]

Diod. Sic. 34.34–35 There was a man called Damophilus, a native of Enna, very wealthy but most of all very arrogant. Because he had a large amount of land in cultivation and had many herds of cattle, he copied the Italian landowners [κεκτημένοι] of Sicily not only in their luxury [ἡ τρυφή] but also in having many slaves and in their inhumanity and harshness [to them]. He toured his estates in four-wheeled wagons [drawn by] expensive horses and a company of slaves; he also was proud of his large band of good-looking boy slaves and a swarm of hangers-on.

Both in the town and in his villas [ἔπαυλεις], he put on a show of silver vessels in relief and expensive purple covers for dining beds, and he was furnished with lavish and kingly dinners which outdid even the Persians in luxury and expense. He also outdid them in his arrogance.[49]

CICERO   (Marcus Tullius Cicero, 106-43 BCE)

Verrine Orations (In Verrem), 70 BCE (Cic., Verr.)

In 70 BCE, Cicero was nominated to be elected aedile; he was still a youngish man in his mid-thirties. His candidacy for office was enhanced by the speeches he made in the prosecution of Gaius Verres for extortion (*repetunda*) when Verres was propraetor (governor) of Sicily in 73–71 BCE. Cicero's speeches and prosecution brought him to prominence as a rising statesman and made him famous.[50] The brilliance of his oratory and his entertaining sarcasm prompted admiration for his speeches and their later publication.[51]

There were other political events in the balance at the time, and the precarity of the situation made Cicero's selection of themes all the more vivid.[52] Verres had robbed the *domus* and villas of members of the Greek elite of Sicily, taking money, legacies, family heirlooms, works of art, personal possessions, and even entire estates, often while enjoying or having enjoyed their hospitality.[53] One of the themes Cicero emphasized was the civic virtue of the Sicilian Greek gentlemen who were Verres's victims—their endurance, moral uprightness, and thriftiness (*patientia virtus frugalitasque*)—thereby equating them with the old Roman heroes in the way of civic patriotism. He also lauded their wealth, generous hospitality, high culture, and refined tastes in their *domus* and villas as models for modern, civilized Hellenizing culture—how to live—versus modern Roman rapacity and moral depravity.[54] Cicero speaks about the produce and products of Sicily as if the whole island were a suburban villa outside of Rome.

Cic., *Verr*. 2.2.2 (5)[55]   [...] Marcus Cato *Sapiens* called Sicily the Republic's granary, the nursemaid of the Roman people. In truth, we have good experience in the hard times of the Italic

War that Sicily has not merely been a granary but rather like the well-equipped state treasury [*aerarium*] in the old days, supplying us free of charge with animal hides [*coria*, leather], tunics, and grain to clothe, feed, and arm our great armies.[56] [...]

Cic., Verr. 2.2.3 (6–7)   What shall I say? Gentlemen of the jury, what great benefits she [Sicily] gives us—we may perhaps be unaware of them. Many [Roman] citizens have become richer because they have a field of business in that fertile, faithful province close by, which they can get to easily and where they can freely oversee their business. Sicily supplies some of them with merchandise and sends them on their way with profits [*compendium*]. Others she keeps—to farm, to ranch, or to do business as merchants [*arare, pascere, negotiari*] as they prefer, and in short to build up a base and establish a home [*sedes ac domicilium*]. It's no small civic advantage for the Republic that so many of our citizens engaged in such honest, productive occupations should be so close to their [original] home [in Italy]. Indeed, our taxable lands [*vectigalia*] and our provinces are almost like estates [*praedia*] for the Roman people, and just as you [the jurors] enjoy most of all the estates you own that are close to [the City], so for the Roman people it's a pleasure to have the province [of Sicily] as a suburb.[57] In addition, gentlemen of the jury, the endurance, moral uprightness, and thriftiness [*patientia virtus frugalitasque*] of these [Sicilian] men can be seen to approach that ancestral moral discipline of ours, so different from the morality that now prevails. They are not at all like other Greeks: no laziness, no extravagance. Instead, their best work is in both public and private affairs, undertaken with great thriftiness [*parsimonia*] and zeal [*diligentia*]. In addition, they hold our people in such regard that they are the only ones who do not hate either the [Roman] tax collector [*publicanus*] or the businessman [*negotiator*, banker]. Furthermore, the Sicilians have put up with the unjust acts of our [Roman] officials in so many ways, but up to now they have not sought refuge at the altar of the law and your protection in public deliberations. [...]

Cicero took six individual Sicilians as the most important examples of Verres's extortions: Gaius Heius (Mamertinus) of Messana, Quintus Caecilius Dio of Halaesa, Heraclius of Syracuse, Epicrates of Bidis, Gnaeus Pompeius of Tyndaris, and Sthenius of Thermae.[58] There were others of lesser status, but all were examples of civic virtue and solid property, and many had taste in collecting; all had misfortunes of various kinds during Verres's maladministration.[59] Their private goods and their gifts to municipal facilities (e.g., public forums, *palaestrae*) were victims of Verres's rapacious greed for money and as a depraved connoisseur of art. In the next passages, Cicero describes the contents of their houses, giving a good idea of the model for fine living that philhellene Romans might admire and emulate.

In addition, Cicero presents a clinching argument to the jurors designed to praise the traditions of respectful hospitality shown to the Romans by the Greek gentlemen of Sicily, with Sthenius of Thermae as an example. But the example involved a further claim on the Roman jurors' emotions, namely their historical piety: in despoiling Sthenius, Verres had thereby sullied the acts of a revered person in Roman history, Scipio Africanus. Cicero made sure that the jurors became aware that Scipio's greatness involved gardens and a suburban villa.[60]

Only one of Verres's victims in Sicily is presented here, Gaius Heius of Messana. His collection of works of art—inherited and acquired—was notable and gives a sense of what may have been appealing to Roman collectors in houses and villas in the Late Republic and how they might have arranged such works.

On Gaius Heius (Mamertinus) of Messana

Cic., Verr. 2.2.5 (13)   [...] In addition, the leader of that delegation [of Messana], [Gaius Heius] the most noble citizen of the city [...] has accused Verres not only of taking his personal goods [*bona sua*] but has said that he even stole the sacred images of the family gods [*penates*] and divinities [*dei*] from his house [*aedes*, mansion], things that had been handed down from the ancestors of his house.[61]

Cic., *Verr*. 2.4.3–7 (2.4.2–3)   As all who have visited Messana will entirely agree, Gaius Heius the Mamertine [of Messana] is the most accomplished man of affairs in the city. His house is possibly the best in Messana and is for certain the best known, and the most open in the way of hospitality to us [Romans]. That house was so beautiful that it had even become the main attraction of the city until that man Verres set foot in it—that same Messana which now is mainly beautiful for its site, walls, and port ever since it has been emptied and stripped of the things that Verres finds pleasure in.

There were four statues of the very finest and most beautiful artistic worth in Heius's house, in a majestic ancient shrine room [*sacrarium*] inherited from his ancestors.[62] These were works of the highest quality [*summa nobilitas*], works that would appeal not only to a man of sensitivity and artistic appreciation [*ingeniosus et intellegens*] but that would even be able to give pleasure to any one of us—"know-nothings" [*idiotae*], as Verres calls us. One of the statues was a Cupid in marble by Praxiteles—mind you, I learned these artists' names while I was looking into matters about that man [Verres].[63] I think it's by the same sculptor who made a Cupid in the same manner at Thespiae, which is why Thespiae gets visited, since there is no other reason for people to go there except to see it.[64] Lucius Memmius, even though he took the other statues away from that city, including the Thespiades, which now are near the temple of Good Fortune, did not lay hands on the marble Cupid because it was consecrated.[65]

Let's return to that shrine room, the one in which, as I told you, there was the marble statue of Cupid. A beautifully made bronze statue of Hercules stood in another part of the room. It is said to have been made by Myron, as I believe—yes, most certainly [by that sculptor].[66] There were altars in front of both of these [images of the] gods: everyone can see [from the altars] that the shrine room had a religious character. Besides these, there were two other bronze statues, small ones but really of a special beauty, in the appearance and dress of maidens [*virginales*] lifting their hands to hold certain sacred objects on their heads. These statues were called *Canephoroe*, but who was their sculptor? Who again? You're right—they say it was Polyclitus.[67] Anyone of us Romans who visited Messana went to see them, [Heius's] doors were open daily for people to pay visits, and his house was not so much his as its owner as it was an embellishment for the city. Gaius Claudius [Pulcher], whose aedileship we know to have been of the greatest possible magnificence, included this Cupid for a short while when he arranged for the Forum to be decorated in honor of the immortal gods and the Roman people.[68] He had been the guest of the Heius family and the patron of the Mamertine population [of Messana], and he was careful to return it to those kind people who had allowed it to be included [in the public shows promoting his aedileship]. That was the way, gentlemen of the jury, that prominent men used to act some time ago. But what did I say: "Some time ago"? In fact, quite recently we have prominent men decorating the Forum and the *basilicae* not with the spoils of war of [defeated] provinces but with the [rightful] possessions of their friends, with objects loaned in the kindness of a guest's obligation [*commodi hospitum*], not by theft by bad men; however, they gave these statues and other ornaments back to each of their owners. They did not take them from the cities of allies and friends on the pretext of a pretended four-day celebration of being [elected to be] aedile, then transferring them to their own houses and villas. But, gentlemen of the jury, Verres took all the statues I've described from Heius's shrine room. I'm telling you: he left not a single one of them, except an old wooden one, the image of Good Fortune, I think. That man would not have it in his house.[69]

Cicero, *On Old Age* (*Cato Maior de senectute*), May to July 44 BCE (Cic., Sen.)[70]

In 44 BCE, twenty-six years after his brilliant start with the Verrine orations, Cicero, now in his early sixties, had been out of politics and largely absent from Rome for two years, in retirement at his villas and perhaps feeling old and ignored, and still grieving his daughter's death the year before (February 45 BCE). These feelings did not reduce the pace and intellectual penetration of his literary activity; in fact, they may have stimulated him to recall the enthusiasms of his youth and maturity, among them the poetry of Hesiod and Xenophon's philosophic dialogues.[71] Cicero, being a man of high literary education, would have known the Greek poets of great antiquity such as Hesiod, but Xenophon as a statesman, military man, philosopher, and late-age writer on practical, philosophical, and autobiographical topics would have impressed him even more. Cicero had, as a young man some forty years before, translated Xenophon's *Oeconomicus* into Latin,[72] a fact also commented on by Columella.

Cicero is not without clear-eyed humor. His version of Cato the Elder, while old, wise, and distinguished, is also grumpy and petulant: Cato bursts out that Hesiod never discussed manuring, whereas he, Cato, did.[73]

Cato is the speaker in the following excerpts:

Cic., Sen. 51 I now come to the pleasures enjoyed by farmers [*voluptates agricolarum*] that I find incredibly delightful. Having such pleasures is in no way mitigated by old age and, to me, they seem perfectly appropriate to the life of a wise man. These pleasures have an account with earth [*ratio terrae*] herself: she never rejects a pay order [*imperium*] on an account and always gives a return without a discount [*sine usura*] on the accounts she holds, sometimes at a lower rate of interest [than one would like] but most often at a higher one. Still, my enjoyment is not only in the revenue [*fructus*] but also the power and character of the earth itself [*ipsius terrae vis ac natura*]. [. . .]

Cic., Sen. 52–54 But why should I speak of the origin, planting, and growth of the vine? I cannot have enough of these things, just so you know what gives me relaxation [*requies*] and delight [*oblectamentum*] in my old age. I'm not mentioning the power of all the things that come from the earth, a power that generates stout trunks and [thick] branches from a tiny fig seed, grape pip, and the smallest seeds of other fruits and plants. Aren't mallet slips [*malleoli*], shoots [*planta*], twigs and branches [*sarmenta*], root cuttings [*viviradices*], and layerings [*propagines*] enough to give delight and induce amazement in anyone?[74] In its pendant habit, the vine falls down to the ground unless it's propped up, but with grasping hand-like tendrils, it raises itself in many twists and turns in various directions, pruned by the farmers' skill with the knife so its shoots don't get woody and take over everywhere. In the greening of spring, when the tendrils that remain bring on what's called a "jewel" [*gemma*, a bud] from which in turn, increasing with earth's sap [*sucus*, moisture] and the sun's heat, a grape appears. At first it is very sour tasting but as it matures becomes sweet; wrapped in its leaves, it does not lack for warmth in moderation and keeps off the sun's too extreme heat. What can be more pleasing in its taste or more attractive to the eye? As I've already said, to me, it's not merely the vine's usefulness that delights me but also its cultivation and its nature itself: the rows of props [*adminiculi*] joined together at the top, the method of binding [*religatio*] and layering [*propagatio*] the vines and, as I've mentioned, the way some have been pruned, others grafted. Why should I talk about the irrigation trenches [*irrigationes*], the ditching [*fossio*], the hoeing of the field that makes its earth so much more fertile? What should I say about the usefulness of manuring [*utilitas stercorandi*]?

Manuring is a topic I talked about in my book on agriculture. The learned Hesiod, even though he wrote on agriculture, said not one word about it. In contrast, Homer, who according to me lived many generations before Hesiod, had Laertes cultivating his farm and manuring it, to calm the grief he was feeling about his son.[75] The pleasures aren't only in wheat fields [*segetes*], meadows [*prati*], vineyards [*vineae*], and woodlots [*arbustae*]. They're also in the garden and the orchard, in cattle husbandry, in the swarms of bees, and in the variety of flowers. Planting is not the only delight—it's also grafting, which requires as great a skill as these others when it comes to farming.

Cic., *Sen.* 55–56   I could go on and on about the many pleasures of living in the country, but I'm aware that I've already said enough by now. Bear with me: I'm carried away by my devotion to country living [*studium rerum rusticarum*], and old age is by nature too garrulous—I say this so I won't be blamed for absolving old age of its failings. Anyway, Manius Curius [Dentatus] at the end of his life lived like this in the country after having triumphed over the Samnites, the Sabines, and Pyrrhus. When I contemplate his villa, which isn't far from mine, I cannot have enough admiration either for that man's frugality or for the disciplined restraint [*disciplina*] of his times. Curius was sitting by his hearth when the Samnite ambassadors brought him a large quantity of gold [as a bribe]; they were rebuffed. He said that it seemed to him that having the gold is not so great as ruling over those who have it. With a soul like that, don't you think that it would make old age joyful?

So I don't get off topic, I am going back to farmers. At one time senators—namely the elders [*senes*]—lived on farms [*in agris*], if it was in fact true that Lucius Quinctius Cincinnatus was driving the plough when it was announced that he had been elected dictator, and during his tenure, by his order, the master of the horse [*magister equitum*] Gaius Servilius Ahala arrested Spurius Maelius and executed him for seeking to become king. It was from the villa that [Manius] Curius [Dentatus] and others of his age [*senes*] were called to the Senate, hence the name "road-men" [*viatores*] for those who came to call them to duty. In the circumstances, was their old age so miserable, these men who found such delight in cultivating their farms [*ager*]? It's my view that, as far as I know, no life can be happier than that of cultivating one's estates [*agri*], not merely from the [honorable] duty [*officium*] it imposes, which is a benefit for all mankind, but also because of the delights I've already described, as well as the abundance [*saturitas*] and plentiful resources [*copia*] it offers for human existence [*victus hominum*] and even for the worship of the gods. Because there are some people who want such things [i.e., food and worship], I may now admit to being open to pleasure [*voluptas*] myself.[76] It's always the case that the good, persevering owner has a full wine cellar and oil store as well as a good stock of provisions, and that the villa has a prosperous aspect [*villa locuples*] and abounds in pork, goat, lamb, chickens, milk, cheese, and honey. Then there's the garden [*hortus*], which farmers call a "second serving of bacon." When there's free time, hawking and hunting give extra sauce to all this.

Cic., *Sen.* 57–58   What else do I need to say about the green of the meadows, the rows of trees, the view [*species*] of the vineyards and olive groves? I'll be brief: there's nothing more useful or more lovely than a well-cultivated farm [*ager bene cultus*], and old age, far from detracting, actually attracts and encourages such enjoyment. Where else can a man at that age find a better place to seek warmth by the hearth or to bask in the sun or, on the other hand, more easily find a cool place in shady places and with waters? Other men can keep their weapons, their horses, their spears, their bats [*clava*] and balls, their swimming and running contests. Leave the knucklebones and dice to us old men, or take those games away, if you want—old age can be happy without them.

Cic., *Sen.* 59   Xenophon's books are extremely useful on many topics, and I beg you to read them carefully, as [I know] you are doing. How abundantly does Xenophon praise agriculture in his book *Oeconomicus*, which deals with household management [*tuenda re familiari*]. So you should become aware that he [Xenophon] saw nothing less than royal status in agricultural activity: in that same book [*Oeconomicus*], Socrates in speaking with Critobulus mentions

Cyrus the Younger.⁷⁷ This Persian ruler [*rex*, satrap], outstanding in intelligence and for the fame of his rule, was visited at Sardis by Lysander the Lacedaemonian [of Sparta], a man of the highest virtue, when he brought him gifts from the [Greek] allies [of the Persians]. Along with other acts of friendliness toward his guest Lysander, Cyrus showed him a certain carefully planted enclosed garden [*consaeptus ager*]. Once Lysander had admired the majestic height of the trees arrayed in straight lines in quincunx patterns [*ordines*], the well-turned clean soil and the sweetness of the odors coming from the flowers, he said that he admired not only the care [*diligentia*] but also the skill [*sollertia*] of the man who measured [*dimensa*] and laid out [*discripta*] this garden.⁷⁸ Cyrus answered, "But it was I who measured it, its patterns are mine, it is I who laid it out. Many of those trees were planted by my own hands." Then Lysander, having looked at Cyrus's purple cloak, the elegance of his bearing, his Persian attire with a great quantity of gold and jewels, said, "Rightly and in truth, Cyrus, men call you happy because your virtue is at one with your good fortune!"

Cic., Sen. 60   Such good fortune can be enjoyed by old men, but old age does not lessen our dedication to other endeavors, first and foremost our devotion [*studium*] to agriculture, which we can maintain to the end of old age. Indeed, I understand that Marcus Valerius Corvinus, having completed life's span, continued to live on his farms and cultivate them until he was 100 years old, with forty-six years passing between his first and sixth consulates. Just as our forefathers considered that amount of time to be the beginning of old age [46 years], that was precisely his public career [*cursus honorum*], and the last part of his life was happier than its middle, because his labors were less and his authority greater [*auctoritas plus*, influence, prestige].⁷⁹

2

VILLAS IN ROMAN AGRICULTURAL TREATISES

CATO
VARRO
COLUMELLA
PALLADIUS

The Agricultural Treatises

The four agricultural treatises or manuals that survive continued, in Latin, an older tradition of Greek and Carthaginian (Punic) texts on agriculture. There had been other Latin treatises written before Cato's *De agricultura* (ca. late 160s–early 150s BCE), and an official translation into Latin of Punic texts on agriculture appeared in 146 BCE (three years before Cato's death), but the evidence for earlier Roman manuals on rural topics is sparse.[1] However, by the time of Varro's *De re rustica* written in the mid-30s BCE, writers on agriculture (agronomists) had a good stock of books, many specialized about the villa's various activities, which they could refer to, copy from, and criticize.[2] In addition, they had an audience of readers eager for practical, up-to-date enlightenment about farming and living in the country (and making an income from doing so); such information would not have been included in the ordinary course of education (which was skewed toward grammar, descriptive writing ability, and rhetorical presentation) for a Roman citizen of landed means, even though the economy was for the most part agrarian. The eagerness of readers for practical information about farming techniques began in the second century BCE and lasted into the fifth century CE—Cato to Palladius. The treatises of Varro (37–36 BCE) and Columella (60s CE) had a particular presence in their organization and range of topics. Between the times of Columella and of Palladius, other treatises were written: the Quintilius (or Quinctilius) brothers, owners of a huge villa in the suburbs of Rome and men of talent, high education, and great wealth (for which they were executed by the emperor Commodus in 182 CE and their villa confiscated) wrote an agricultural treatise in Greek (lost).[3] Manuscript versions of agricultural treatises persisted throughout the Middle Ages, with Palladius's (fifth century CE) having a particularly wide distribution.[4]

The texts from Cato, Varro, Columella, and Palladius that follow show how these writers framed their discussions and what theoretical and ethical, moral, and historical notions they used and the examples they chose. The main body of their treatises concerned farming work itself: when and what to plant (beans, flowers, vines) and to do (grafting, building granaries), how to tend to domestic animals, and other matters of great practical importance; a few of these have been included below. However, the main selections here are on the villa dwellings, their locations and spatial conceptions, and how they supported and defined the owner's *familia* of related and extended household members.[5]

Despite their factual content, however, agricultural treatises are *literary* works with atmosphere, mood, moral direction, unifying themes, and human relations, while intended to be read (or listened to) and referenced as manuals.[6] How they relate to actual agricultural practices and the archaeological record of villas anywhere is occasionally included in notes on the texts but is not the focus of these selections. No single excavated villa corresponds, as by recipe, to a written text, and the actual effect of an agricultural treatise on productive activity has not, as far as I am aware, been proved, though some techniques (methods of wine-making, how to set up an olive oil manufacture, planting and irrigation methods) are relatable to what has been found at various sites archaeologically. But as literature—as with any artistic production in antiquity—the treatises depend on giving abstract mental architecture to practical activity: their authors in varying ways are at pains to supply the *why* of what is done at the villa. For that reason, such ideas as *utilitas*—which has many nuances and meanings in these writings—and the difference, say, between *luxus* (luxury, always negative) and *voluptas* (pleasure, most often positive) are given special emphasis. Religious and historical piety—the due regard both for the gods and especially for the nature of ancient exemplars in Roman history (and its converse, feckless modern ignorance of farming)—is repeated and varied or mostly omitted altogether. These are also themes vis-à-vis villas in Latin poetry, philosophy, letters, essays, and moral philosophy. Even though he did not mention or dilate on religious observances for planting, harvesting, and villa life in his treatise, Columella thought religion in the practice of agriculture was so important that he promised his readers an entire book on the topic (Columella, *Rust.* 2.21.5–6); it is a matter of regret that he never got around to writing it.[7]

Agricultural treatises and villas are manifestations of elite mental and material culture; so, for the most part, are inscriptions (except some funerary ones), legal compendia, and other written sources. The farming content—such as growing cabbages, digging ditches—are the agronomist-authors' appropriations, even exploitations, of nonelite practices developed over time: the *agricolae*, their wives, their families and relatives tending their kitchen *hortus* giving way to the villa's landscape gardener (*topiarius*) growing roses and acanthus for an owner (*dominus*) in flower beds and training box bushes into ornamental shapes, or local hired hands digging ditches replaced with chain gangs of enslaved foreigners, abducted as spoils of war or obtained by piracy. The lives of nonelites in Roman countrysides (tenant farmers or sharecroppers, small-propertied farmers, enslaved workers) cannot be found directly in the agricultural treatises or are only indirectly reflected in them: the documentation of the rural poor and nonelite life and work can be found more directly in the archaeological record with strong and various interpretive methods.[8] Roman elites may well have flattered themselves on their authenticity and earthbound patriotism in reading and mastering—as *patres familiarum* (Cato), *ingenui genus liberali* (Columella), and *domini* (Varro, Palladius)—the methods that Cato and his fellow agronomists wrote about. They also wanted to make money from their investments and inherited properties.[9]

The Roman countryside of villas, in Italy and throughout the empire, was no less socially stratified than towns and cities. Changes in land use and the widespread introduction of enslaved workers in the second century BCE may have progressively modified the earlier landscape of small holdings and citizen farmers with access to local markets. Large estates enjoyed efficiencies of scale as well as lower costs and better productivity brought about by enslaved workers: these advantages promoted changes in the way food was supplied to towns and cities in Italy and overseas.[10] In turn, these changes may have precipitated the need for legal redress of social friction and fractures in the countryside. Agrarian legislation was the rural equivalent of the social settlements and compromises that had marked events and relationships among groups of the Roman urban citizenry throughout Republican times.[11] In addition, how the enslaved personnel, both house workers and estate workers, were housed, fed, and treated in agricultural treatises is included: villas were the assumed loci of enslavement from before Cato's day forward, and while enslavement had a changing history and regional variations within the Roman hegemony, its outlines—in historiography, interpretation, and the archaeological record—are still developing in recent studies.[12] Agricultural writers located enslaved personnel in space and seasonal occupations a little more clearly: sleeping quarters, lockups, work assignments, character, anthropology, punishments, rations, and clothing, are all topics included in the selected passages below.[13]

Enslaved workers are inseparable from any consideration of the development of Roman villas from the early second century BCE until Late Antiquity.[14] The functioning of villa-estates came to be predicated upon enslaved personnel for agricultural, domestic, and rural production, no matter the size or specialization of their *fructus*. Large villas (sometimes called *latifundia*) with substantial residences, many enslaved workers, and large land holdings (contiguous or scattered) coexisted with smaller agricultural entities, either tied to the larger estates or worked independently. No matter their size or the status of their proprietors, both exploited an enslaved workforce. In the early second century CE, for example, Pliny the Younger wanted to supply some crews of enslaved workers as part of his contribution of equipment (*instrumentum*) to the tenant farmers, free citizen farmers, or freedpersons (*coloni*) cultivating small, family-sized agricultural units on his Tuscan estate.[15] While a free peasant economy may have existed in Italy, by the time at which texts about villas appear in the mid-second century BCE, agricultural labor was, as a general rule, undertaken by enslaved persons. For that reason, this chapter begins with an outline of recent developments in studies of Roman enslavements generally, and, in specific relation to villas, will elucidate and expand on the texts presented in this and other chapters.

Enslavement and Roman Villas

Historiographies

Enslavement inevitably concerns work, most often agricultural work, construction, and mining, and as such its study involves discussion of the nature of work and the deployment of enslaved workforces as resource or capital investment in a larger frame of economic and social arrangements. Enslavement studies can also focus on the means of social force and institutional cruelty whereby it comes into being and changes historically.[16] For Greek and Roman enslavements, an essential consideration continues to be how they differ from, or relate to, more familiar later servitudes based on colonialistic and/or racial criteria, and how such servitudes inflect modern agricultural economies and domestic arrangements quite differently from any in antiquity.[17] The debate persists: DuBois and others have developed an argument that aligns ancient with modern enslavement, though the relevance of South and North American and Caribbean plantation enslavement as a model—economic and social—for Greek and Roman enslavement has been frequently challenged.[18]

In Greek and Roman antiquity, enslavement in its philosophical and social dimensions was already an important topic. The theories applied to enslaved persons conditioned Roman attitudes: the view that the enslaved were innately inferior in nature, moral level, and physique had been developed systematically by Aristotle in the fourth century BCE, with wide cultural dissemination. Roman ideas followed from that, in physical and moral traits of both enslaved populations and individuals. Enslavement as a function of nature in Aristotle is complex: his arguments are made mainly in the *Politics*, and they involve the physical and soulful aspects of the enslaved, their governance by more capable others, their lack of virtue, and other deficiencies.[19] "Natural slavery" was related to geography and climate for Aristotle: northern dwellers and those of Asia, because they live in extremes of cold and heat, cannot be compared to the ideal middle situation of the Greek race.[20] Enslaved persons had other physical characteristics, all negative, but their cultural and social status in early Latin plays—the comedies of Plautus especially, where they are numerous—gave them complex, active roles on the stage, often as successful tricksters and sly managers of their fellow enslaved, bystanders, and enslavers in the plays' plots. Actors—be they freeborn or freed—assuming an enslaved persona on the stage, and especially enslaved actors playing the part of enslavers, might well have given the audience an added frisson in watching these transgressions of social status.[21]

In the modern and contemporary historiography of ancient enslavement, the means of interpreting enslavement in its economic and social aspects and in its effects on enslaved human beings is under continual mutation. Some consideration of how enslavement has been interpreted, both factually and ideologically, must be taken into account because interpretation can skew how evidence is assembled—even archaeological evidence—in favor of ideology, or sentiment, or both. Essential questions about enslavement are many, often as usefully crude as subtle: good or bad? for whom? efficient in the short term or economically debilitating over time? should pain, abuse, and sexual exploitation predominate the discussion or should manumission and *libertus* (freedperson) status be emphasized? A historiographic contrast is often made between "schools" of interpretation, more or less between that of Joseph Vogt, who took a broadly anthropological view in attempting to square the contradiction between enslaving practices and humane intellection in antiquity, and Moses I. Finley, who factored enslavement as a normal part of the larger investment and resource systems of the ancient economy. However, the differences between Vogt and Finley are fewer than their agreements about how enslaved persons were articulated in the highly (but differently) stratified Greek, Hellenistic, and Roman societies.[22] The commodification of human beings for purposes of agricultural production, husbandry and herding, public works, manufacturing, mining, and administrative operations (as public enslaved workers) is one aspect of ancient enslavement, but enslaved persons were also convenient social and cultural commodities: they were nurses, nannies, wetnurses, secretaries, teachers, tutors, hairdressers, philosophers, actors, prostitutes, conversationalists, librarians, readers, bedmates, and occasionally friends.[23]

There was a functional distinction between the urban and rural enslaved—the former more differentiated as to the kinds of labor they were forced to perform, the latter more akin to chattel enslavement.[24] Where enslaved persons in the Roman economy came from, how they were acquired, and how many of them there were has been and continues to be a matter of investigation.[25] Enslavement was an important military and commercial enterprise in the Roman economy, and by the second century BCE, it had become integrated with many aspects of Roman political and economic assumptions about work and production, never more so than in the operation of villas supplying food and other goods to urban markets, the army, and, later, the needs of the urban annonarian systems in the Italian peninsula. Roman generals appear to have been the greatest enslavers: in their thousands, entire tribal or geographically defined populations were converted to enslaved persons under Julius Caesar in the 50s BCE. They were probably destined for rural work (men in the fields and grazing land, women in the household), for mining and quarrying, or for construction. Cicero owned enslaved agricultural and construction workers from the Gallic campaigns; his brother Quintus, as an officer with Caesar in Gaul, had privileged access to Gallic prisoners for enslavement as part of the perks of his commission (possibly before they were sold to brokers), and he offered some privately as a present to his brother for work both at Rome and on his estates. For construction, Cicero had a team of enslaved workmen with an enslaved foreman whom he called on for work as needed.[26]

Enslavement and Ethnicity at Villas

The many sources of enslaved workers in the expanding Roman hegemonies in the Mediterranean and Europe support the claim that ancient enslavement was related more to status than to race or ethnic origins. In the second quarter of the second century BCE, Cato mentions the food and clothing of the enslaved laborers as part of a villa's inventory but says nothing about their races or ethnicities: it does not occur to him to do so, even though in his day, the enslaved workforce was made up of foreigners, captured in war, or trafficked by traders battening onto Roman military successes from areas such as Gaul, Hispania, and the East.[27]

By contrast, about 120 years later, in the 40s–30s BCE when the great enslaving military campaigns had largely come to an end, Varro, who had been in active military commands in Hispania and Illyria, had specific views on enslaved persons based on their ethnicity. He preferred Gauls as herdsmen over Hispanics, and based his somewhat positive views of Illyrian workers on firsthand experience, though then introducing the prejudices of exoticism and misogyny by noting how different the Illyrian women's behavior was from Roman norms of female comportment.[28] In addition, for the sake of domestic peace at the villa and to control the enslaved workforce, Varro thought it was better to mix enslaved persons from different nations.[29]

Some eighty years after Varro, Columella, writing in the (socially) relatively peaceful mid-first century CE, mentions nothing about the ethnic origins of the persons he enslaved: what may have occurred in the intervening years is that the trade for enslaved agricultural workers, heretofore generated predominantly by overseas Roman military victories or commercial human trafficking abroad, had been supplemented by *vernae*, enslaved persons born of enslaved women on the villas or in the *domus*, members of the *familia* or saleable assets of the estates. Columella exhibits some concern and warmth toward his enslaved workers, which may imply that he had long familiarity with villa-born, villa-naturalized, and thus fully villa-homogenized enslaved persons deracinated from their foreign origins.[30] There may have been a change from foreign-born enslaved persons to internally generated enslaved persons when their importation into Italy from overseas diminished in the Early Imperial period, but it is notable that the aggregate enslaved population from all sources did not change.[31]

By the fifth century CE, Palladius speaks hardly at all about enslaved personnel in terms of their ethnicity, body types, or status; he offers his expertise to the *dominus* of the villa and its estate without much mentioning enslaved labor. The relative silence of writers in the later Roman Imperial period on enslaved individuals and enslavement in general has been taken to indicate their gradual replacement by other forms of workforce, but this has also been shown to be erroneous.[32] The use of enslaved personnel was part of the normal environment of production throughout antiquity.

Enslavement and Latifundia

Enslavement in villas, especially in Italy, has seen interpretive permutations in modern studies. Early interpretation of *latifundia*, the villas with "wide estates," were taken by many scholars to represent an early instance of capitalistic exploitation of labor—especially in large agricultural enterprises entirely dependent on an enslaved workforce—that emerged in the second century BCE. The existence of *latifundia* had been attested in written texts, and their development was known to have been a major impetus for social agitation in the mid- and late second century BCE.[33] *Latifundia* had been somewhat apparent in the archaeological record, but from the 1970s on, a combination of field survey results and excavation revealed their prominence in the agricultural landscape. *Latifundia*, most notably that of Settefinestre in the Ager Cosanus, was taken as an instance of early capitalistic practice that dislocated traditional forms of rural work, specifically that of small farms in central Italy. The narrative—both the Roman one and the modern one—was that, in the *latifundia* system, an enslaved workforce provided surplus value of labor for agricultural investment, which added to efficiencies of scale and drove out the small, citizen-worked farms. One result of the added enslaved workforce was that owners of large villas came to dominate and profit from the growing local, peninsular, and Mediterranean-wide demand for food and other products supplied from villas. Dispossession of the virtuous poor citizen families by an abundant, cheap, foreign, enslaved workforce available to the rich gave dramatic populist color to the search for how widespread enslavement came about in the Roman Republic. The narrative of the rural poor driven from their land and gravitating to Rome to swell its population and thus distort its traditional politics came to be standard. Its first expression—in protest against a sorry state of affairs in the countryside—is in the political careers of Tiberius Sempronius Gracchus and his brother Gaius.[34] Tiberius Gracchus was not protesting enslavement itself, only the way it was used to dispossess free Roman citizens. His narrative was popular on the hustings in Rome.

The use of enslaved workers in agriculture—the initial focus of modern scholarly inquiry on enslavement in ancient Rome—brought about serious differences among contemporary scholars about which interpretive strategy or strategies could best be used to assess this phenomenon. The Italian agricultural boom of the second century BCE saw an apparently vast increase, for Italian villas, in size, distribution, and profitability of wine, olive oil, grain, and certain manufactured goods (tiles, *dolia*) and the development of *latifundia*. This naturally suggested a Marxist approach to assessing the exploitation of enslaved labor: a *villa schiavistica* system. However, the pre-existing condition of such capital formation and economic integration, a real coordination of suppliers and middlemen with markets and transportation throughout an economic zone, existed only in crude forms in Roman times, and certainly not yet in the second century BCE. A notion that there was, obligatorily, an economic inevitability converting all agricultural activities into enslaved-based *ville schiavistiche* came to dominate villa scholarship in the 1980s.[35] These studies presented a monotonous landscape of widespread enslavement-based agricultural and villa landscapes in Italy in the Late Republican and Early Imperial periods. The conception of such a landscape was not entirely wrong, and it appeared to validate the picture of social dislocation in Italian agriculture drawn by Tiberius Gracchus in the 130s BCE. However, archaeological research and expansion of historical horizons soon modified the Italian landscape with a more comprehensive understanding of changes in the Mediterranean economy that occurred with Rome's overseas conquests in the second century BCE and into the Imperial period.

Taking into account how the widespread use of enslaved workers modified the Italian agricultural landscape has proved very positive for history writing and for archaeological investigation. Regional studies of the distribution of building-types (villas of varying size and social level) have become increasingly important: such studies clearly indicate that *latifundia*, and thus the enslaved workers on them, were only one part of a widely varied agricultural landscape. In such landscapes, small and large villas coexisted: *latifundia* centralizing contiguous or noncontiguous property and grand *domini* of luxury villas were simultaneously present with small holdings owned by humble freeborn citizen farmers (*agricolae*), tenants (*coloni*), and other kinds of workers.[36]

Villa owners were responsive to current economic conditions: they reacted to local or more distant demands for *fructus* (produce),[37] were eager for bigger opportunities for profit (also called *fructus*),[38] and were quite aware of how to take advantage of Mediterranean-wide holdings and trade.[39] Such sophistication implied early and continued knowledge by villa owners of commercial information as well as appropriation of existing agricultural techniques and experience developed by small farmers for a much more localized economic environment. The issue of economic integration in Italy and throughout the Roman hegemony impinges on villas with enslaved workers—large ones but also small ones—and the decisions of the villas' owners on what to grow and make.[40] An important factor in Roman economic integration is how enslavement shaped the momentum of specific economic sectors such as wine or storage-and-transport vessels (amphoras)—both produced at villas.

Rural manufactures as adjuncts to villa production must have impinged upon the lives of the enslaved and what work they did.[41]

Enslaved Persons at Villas

Two areas of scholarship on Roman enslaved people in villas are relevant to the source material presented in this book. The first considers the measures for release from enslavement, and thereby gaining freedperson status, and the motivations enslavers had in allowing such release, as much in their own self-interest as for the social advantages and legal protections extended to male *liberti* and freedwomen. The second concerns the material aspects and evidence for those objects, spaces, and environments designated for enslaved persons, which are elusive in general and particularly ghostly in villas.

Enslavement was not monolithic. In Italy and the wider empire, it had its own regional histories, variations, and differing attributes as well as varied legal definitions. And Roman enslavement was not necessarily lifelong: there were a few safety valves, and in that respect, it was unlike severe forms of enslavement in which the enslaved status was rigorously defined by law, carefully policed, and unmitigated by any social easements, intellectual insights, or legal custom. There were, in the history of Roman enslavement, some motivations and opportunities to obtain freedom and to acquire *libertus* status; there were also motivations and opportunities for owners to manumit. Freedperson status—no matter how rare it may have been—came with legal protections and social expectations. Even within the restricted sphere of agricultural treatises, there are clear differences about enslavement among their authors. In the 30s BCE, Varro exhibited care for the comfort of enslaved workers regarding their rest from work.[42] Some eighty years later, in the 50s–60s CE, Columella had assumed that vineyards would be worked by chain gangs (*servi vincti*) whose assigned members would be confined to prisons (*ergastula*) at night or when not working.[43] Around the same time, Pliny the Elder was negative on the use of any chain gangs and such prisons.[44] Some forty years later still, in the early second century CE, his nephew Pliny the Younger, whose Tiburtine property was mainly in vines, seems to assume that the enslaved personnel would live unchained and unconfined rather than in chain gangs or prisons.[45]

Release from enslavement occurs very often in Plautus's comedies in the late second century BCE: most usually, the female is released from bondage because she is recognized as the true daughter of a free citizen. Another release is that of a woman with real enslaved status bought by a free man who is in love with her; her release is affective and emotional. For male enslaved, it is different: in Plautus's *Epidicus*, the enslaved Epidicus is freed for bringing a father together with a long-lost daughter (falsely enslaved by accident) through his stratagems, intelligence, and loyalty. The theme of transition from enslavement to freedom runs through many of Plautus's plays, but these are fairy-tale happy endings intended to leave audiences feeling satisfied as they depart the theater with the pleasing thought that justice has been done. In the same plays, the alternatives for the urban enslaved deemed to be deserving of punishment were to be whipped, tortured (crucified), or sent to the mills (*in pistrinum*), which may have meant being sent to work grinding grain in the countryside (*rus*). The enslaved's reactions to the threat of such punishments was intended to amuse the audience.[46]

In practice, Roman enslavement offered motivations toward freedperson status, both for the enslaved persons and their enslavers. A real release from enslavement could be via the practice of *peculium*, whereby the enslaved person, in all cases male, could amass property sufficient to buy his freedom. The enslaved person's motivation is obvious, but the motivation of the enslaver to allow the self-purchase or grant freedom to an enslaved person without some payment or comparable advantage is another factor. *Peculium* may actually have favored the rural enslaved; at a villa, *peculium* could be a little piece of arable land to grow crops and presumably sell them, or a farm animal set aside as the *mancipium* of the enslaved, to encourage them in their work; Varro mentions both, and both accompanied the enslaved person upon sale.[47] Ultimately there were serious imperial protections for both enslaved persons and their property as well as graduation to freedom.[48] For female enslaved persons, favored individuals could be granted special treats of food; freedom could be granted after producing three or more enslaved male children who, together with any female children, would be added to the *vernae* of the villa.[49] Enslaved females could find freedom, by purchase, to be the wife of a free man or a freedman. By convention, formerly enslaved men took all or part of their enslaver's name, sometimes with the addition of their own as an identifier: the *trianomina*—*praenomen, nomen, cognomen*—were plausible tickets to status as a participant in Roman life in the way of property and law, if not as full citizens.[50] The children of *liberti* were fully free citizens.

Freedperson status conferred privileges and responsibilities: by being able to own property and present themselves before magistrates and administrative officials, freedpersons could act on behalf of, and to the profit of, their former enslavers, in compacts or contracts maintained by social tradition and law, as well as acting independently and establishing families whose children became full citizens, able to form *familiae* and businesses of their own. These empowerments gave motivation to enslavers to manumit intelligent, educated, skilled, capable enslaved persons, especially literate ones, whom they deemed advantageous to undertake wider activities on their behalf, while maintaining the preexisting power relationship framed by tradition and law.[51] Because the contract and contacts between former enslaver and former enslaved were socially strong, the freedperson would become a *cliens* in the *clientela* of the former *dominus*, now a *patronus*, and greeting him in the daily *salutatio*, to accompany him about his affairs, be it as a bullyboy, financial agent, part of the retinue, or just a talker-up at election time.

The second area of scholarship on people enslaved at villas and recorded in some of the texts is material: objects and spaces related to enslaved persons. Objects reflecting intimate, obvious enslavement are well known: they include fetters, inscribed collars or collars with tags, and other confining items with or without identification of personhood by name and ownership.[52] Branding was also used.[53] The rations (bread, olives, wine, and so on) for enslaved workers were matters of villa economy laid out in detail by Cato, as were their clothing and other gear.[54]

In the spatial record of villas and *domus,* enslaved persons are elusive, in part because spaces in Roman domestic architecture could be somewhat undetermined, often used for quite different purposes according to times of day and the schedule of domestic activities. While rooms were designated as bedrooms (*cubicula*) in the formal, patronal domestic design, enslaved persons may have slept on the floor, bedded down in common rooms, or accommodated themselves in attics (*cenacula*).[55]

Outside the villa, the locus of enslaved persons can be equally elusive.[56] The modern study of enslaved persons as represented in the visual arts (wall painting, funerary monuments), in domestic architecture, and in urban landscapes is an important addition to the social and visual armature of Roman culture.[57] Centers of research are contributing to the project, notably the resources maintained at the *Forschungen zur antiken Sklaverei* (Akademie der Wissenschaften und der Literatur, Johannes Gutenberg-Universität Mainz) on Greek and Roman enslavement,[58] and in the continuing seminars (*GIREA*) on ancient enslavement at the Université de Franche-Comté at Besançon, and at other research entities.[59]

The search for enslaved people in ancient times is not limited to the Greek and Roman eras: the search continues for the ancient Near Eastern, Egyptian, and North African cultures and economies. As far as I am aware, factoring enslavement into either the statistical history or the simulations of Roman economies has not yet been broached. The enslaved, we know, are pervasive, but often without being clearly manifested in the historical record.

CATO (Marcus Porcius Cato, 234–149 BCE)[60]

On Agriculture (De agricultura, or *De re rustica),* 150s BCE (Cato, *Agr.*)

The following excerpts show something of the homely, even crude, but very straightforward instructions on villas in Cato's *On Agriculture.* It is possible that the author purposefully wrote in this manner to address readers whom he thought were genuinely simple of understanding and reading ability. However, he also assumes that villa owners will visit their substantial, well-equipped properties only occasionally, can read and write, leave their management to enslaved managers (*vilici*), and live mostly in towns, possibly even in Rome. Cato's simplicity may be feigned: by upholding old-fashioned values going out of style, Cato was flattering his readers as being (like his own self-projection) right-thinking strong citizens and family men, good farmers and good soldiers of the old stripe (or encouraging them to be so), even though they were of the mid-to-upper, propertied, and town-dwelling classes, not simple farmer citizens. The long passage on the versatile virtues of cabbage as the staple of Roman *agricolae* may be an example of such exaggerated social conservatism, a form of showy culinary patriotism.[61]

In addition, by upholding these values as well as describing the very simple villa and estate that he recommends, Cato may have wished to contrast himself with the sophisticated, urbanized elite of the patrician and plebeian noble families of his day. Members of the Roman elite had become builders of new villas with innovative designs and interior elegance of an extravagance quite unlike the self-consciously simple farm-villa that Cato writes about.[62] His contemporaries had also developed refined tastes in food, entertainment, architecture, art, and literature, as well as other modern degenerate habits, at least according to conservatives such as Cato.[63] As a *novus homo*, a "new man," brought to prominence by service to the Roman state rather than by his place in patrician or plebeian noble society, his fetishizing of old-fashioned Roman values may be that of an outsider committing himself more strongly to the supposedly traditional values of the society that had accepted him; that society's elites had in some cases acquired more up-to-date attitudes and ways of living.

To avoid Cato's repetitive sequence of topics, his sections have been loosely rearranged into themes, with some overlap among them. The topic headings are my own, and passages are not always in the sequence in which they appear in his text.

Preface and General Advice

Cato, *Agr.* Preface   Making money in trade is desirable if it were not so risky [*periculosus*], and the same for moneylending, if it were virtuous [*honestus*]. Our ancestors thought so and put it into law: a thief [if found guilty] was required to repay [the theft] two-fold, but a moneylender was required to repay four-fold. It can be seen from this how much they considered moneylending to be worse than theft.

When our ancestors praised a good man, they did so in this way: that he was a "good farmer" [*bonus agricola*], or a "good freeholder" [*bonus colonus*]. He who was praised in such a way was considered to have been praised in the highest degree. In fairness, I reckon that a man in trade [*mercator*] is vigorous [*strenuus*] and eager to make money, but still, as I have said, trade is risky and prone to calamity. By contrast, the strongest men [*viri fortissimi*] and the most vigorous soldiers [*milites strenuissimi*] come from farmers: their work is considered most worthy [*quaestus stabilissimus*] and is not held in a bad light, and those who practice the profession are not susceptible to bad attitudes.

Now, to return to the subject that will be the beginning of that which I promised to do.

Cato, Agr. 1   When thinking of buying an estate [*praedium*], consider this: do not be too eager in acquisition and do not stint looking it over and walking around it often. As many times as you go, a good estate should look better each time. Be aware of how the neighbors' maintenance [of their estates] is undertaken; in a good district, good maintenance should be the norm. Get in there and look around so you can come out [successfully with an informed opinion].

The estate should have a good climate and not be dangerously situated, the soil must be good and worth its value. If you can, [the estate] should be located at the foot of a hill, in a healthy spot facing south, with an abundance of workers [*operarii*], a good water supply, with a well-established town [*oppidum validum*] nearby, or near the sea or a wide river that accommodates boats, or a good major roadway. It should be in a district where estates do not often change owners, or if they have been sold, the owners are sorry that they did so [afterwards]. The estate should have good buildings. Do not disdain the way others do things. Buying from a good farmer and a good builder is the best. When you arrive at the villa, look to see if there are numerous oil presses [*vasa torcula*] and wine *dolia*; if there are not many, you can tell what the product [might be] in relation to their number. See to it that the equipment is minimal in quantity and that the land is not extravagantly large. Keep in mind that an estate is like a man, no matter how productive it may be, if it is extravagant, it will not amount to much.

Were you to ask me what the best estate should be, I say this: an estate of 100 *iugera* [about 25 ha, or 62 acres] of several [different] soils in a good location. A vineyard [*vinea*] is the foremost if its produce is abundant, [after that] an irrigated garden [*hortus inriguus*]. Third, a bed of reeds [*salictum*]; fourth, an olive orchard [*oletum*]; fifth, a meadow[s] for pasturing [*pratum*]; sixth, a wheat field [*campus frumentarius*]; seventh, a plantation for timber [*silva caedua*]; eighth, a tree plantation for training vines [*arbustum*]; ninth, a grove of nut trees [*silva glandaria*].

Cato, Agr. 2   When the *pater familias* comes to the villa and, once having saluted the family Lares, on the same day if possible or [at any rate] the next day, he should go over the whole estate. When he has reckoned its condition, how the estate's cultivation is going and what has been done and still needs doing, on the following day he should call the *vilicus* before him and ask what work has been done, what remains to be done, whether what has been done was done in a timely way, if work not yet completed can be readily finished, and what the amount of wine, grain, and other produce has been.

Once he has taken stock [of these things], he should reckon the number of workmen and [their] daily output. If the work does not seem correct to him, and if the *vilicus* says he did as zealously as he could, that the slaves were no good, that there were storms, that the slaves took themselves off, that there was public [government] work [*opus publicum*] to do, and many other reasons, bring up with the *vilicus* [your] account of the work done and the workforce that did it. If there were rainstorms, what work could have been done while it rained: the *dolia* washed and sweetened, cleaning the villa, stirring the grain [in its bins], shifting manure outside, making a manure pile [or pit], cleaning seed, mending ropes [*funes*, horse tackle] and making new ones; the slaves should have mended their smocks and hoods. On holidays, old [clogged] ditches could have been cleared, the public road [*via publica*] maintained, scrub cut down, the garden worked over, the meadow cleaned up [weeded], kindling wood bundled, thorn bushes pulled out, spelt ground, and seeing to a general clean-up [*munditia*]. When the slaves were sick, they should not have been given so much food.

After [all] this has been looked into in an orderly way, [there should be] a consultation on what yet needs to be accomplished, the cash on hand, the revenue from grain, what expense has been incurred for fodder. The accounts for the wine, the oil—what has sold already, what [money] has come in, what is still due, and what is still left that could be sold. Where an obligation to pay exists, enforce the obligation to the full amount. Anything left over on account should be listed. Whatever is needed for the [next] year, order it up; whatever is left over [not needed], have it sold, and work that needs to be done by hired hands [*locari*], order it be done. Say what work you want done in-house and what you want hired out. Put your orders in writing.

Think about the livestock. Hold an auction [*auctio*]. Sell the oil if the price is good, sell what's left of your wine and grain. Sell old oxen, blemished cattle, blemished sheep, wool, hides, an old wagon, old metal hardware, an old slave [*servus senex*], a sick slave [*servus morbosus*], and anything else not needed. A *pater familias* should be a seller, not a buyer.

Cato, *Agr.* 3 A young *pater familias* should concentrate on the planting of the fields. Building should be thought about for a long time, but planting is not something to be merely considered but actually done. If you've planted your land [already], once you've reached the age of thirty-six, you should build. For building, make sure that neither the villa [takes priority] over the estate nor the estate over the villa. For the *pater familias*, it is good to have a well-built *villa rustica*, an oil cellar [*cella olearia*], a wine cellar [*cella vinaria*] with many *dolia*, so he may [store his produce in anticipation] of a rise in price. This will bring him riches [*rei*], [a reputation for] virtue, and fame [*virtus et gloria*]. He should have good press equipment so the work can be done well. The harvested olives should be pressed immediately into oil so they don't spoil. [...]

Cato, *Agr.* 4 [...] The residential villa [*villa urbana*] should be built in relation to your wealth [*copia*]. If you can live in it in comfort, you will prefer to go there and do so more often: the front of the head is better than its back.[64] Be nice to neighbors, and do not allow your [relatives or] slaves to offend them. If, in your neighborhood, you are seen to be pleasant, you will sell your produce more easily, and it will be easier to rent your workforce [to others] and easier to hire [outside] workers [*operarii*]. If you build, neighbors will help with the work, the tools, and the material, and if by "good luck" [i.e., bad luck] something happens, they will help you.[65]

Cato, *Agr.* 61 What is good cultivation? *Good ploughing.* What after that? *Ploughing.* What is the third? *Manuring.*[66] [...] When you plough a grain field, do it well and at the right time of year, and do not plough a wobbling furrow. [...]

The *vilicus* and *vilica*[67]

Cato, *Agr.* 5.1–5 The duties [*officia*] of the *vilicus* are as follows: discipline is to be maintained. Feast days [*feriae*] must be kept. He must not put his hands on other people's possessions but keep to his own. He must adjudicate disputes among the slaves: if someone does something wrong, he must punish the offender in a commensurate way. The slaves must not be badly cared for, not left cold or hungry. He should keep them closely to their work—it's easier [that way] to keep them from doing bad or strange things. If the *vilicus* does nothing wrong, the slaves will also not do so. But if the *vilicus* countenances bad behavior, the owner should not allow it. The *vilicus* should commend good work so that the others will do the same. The *vilicus* should not be a pleasure seeker [*ambulator*], he must always be sober, and must not eat outside [the villa]. He must keep the slaves to their work and make sure that what the owner has ordered is done. He must not imagine that he knows more than the owner. He must have the owner's friends as his own. He should listen to whomever he has been told to listen to. Unless it is at the Compitalia festival at a crossroads [near the villa] or at the hearth [*focus*, at home], he should not engage in religious matters [*res divina*].⁶⁸ He should not extend credit to anyone, and what the owner has loaned, he must insist on getting it back. He must give no seed grain, fodder, spelt, wine, or oil to anyone. At most, he should have only two or three other households from which he can ask for things that are needed and to which he can lend. He must often go over the accounts with the owner. He must not hire the same worker, hired hand, or skilled worker for more than one day at a time. He should not wish to buy anything without the owner's knowledge nor should he conceal anything from him. He must not have a laggard friend [*parasitus*]. He must not consult with a soothsayer [*haruspex*], an augur, a prophet [*hariolus*], or a Chaldean [astrologer]. He must not be stingy about seeding—it is unlucky [*infelix*]. He must take care to know how to do all the things that are needed [on the estate] and to actually do them, but not to the extent of fatiguing himself: in so doing, he will understand what the slaves are thinking and so they will work more happily. If he does this, he will not want to go out and about so much, will maintain better health, and sleep more enjoyably. He should be the first to rise, the last to go to bed. Before going to bed, he must see that the villa is closed for the night, that all are sleeping in their assigned places, and that the livestock have their food.

The oxen must be cared for very zealously. Treat their teamsters with some kindness so they will be disposed to be kind to the oxen. [...]

Cato, *Agr.* 142 About the duties of the *vilicus*, that is all the things that the owner [*dominus*] has ordered needed for the estate [*fundus*]—namely the things that need buying or acquiring for the estate, and how food and clothing are to be apportioned to the slaves. I am warning [him] that he do them and that he listen to the owner's instructions. In addition, he must know how to deal with the *vilica* and how to instruct her so that the owner, upon his arrival, will find that everything has been diligently anticipated and arranged.

Cato, *Agr.* 143.1–3⁶⁹ Care must be taken that the *vilica*'s duties are done. If the owner has given her to you as your wife, be constant only to her. Keep her in fear of you. She should not be extravagant. She should rarely be friends with other women in the neighborhood and receive them rarely, either in the house or in her own quarters. She must not go out for meals or walk out about. Without specific orders from the owner or the owner's wife, she must not undertake religious devotion or make someone else to do so on her behalf. She should be aware that the owner undertakes the devotions on behalf of the whole household. Let her be tidy herself; let her also keep the villa tidy; every day, she must keep the hearth and its area tidy before she goes to bed. On the kalends, ides, nones, and any other holidays, she must hang a wreath over the hearth for the gods of the house [*lares familiares*] and pray [to them] for abundance [for the house]. She must be vigilant to have cooked food on hand for you and the slaves. She must keep many hens and have eggs on hand. She must have dried pears, sorb apples, figs, raisins, sorb apples preserved in wine concentrate [*sapa*], pears, grapes, and quinces [preserved] in jars, and [fresh] quinces, grapes preserved in wine and in jars buried in the ground, recently harvested Praenestine nuts, also kept in jars buried in the ground. Scantian quinces in jars and other fruit that are habitually stored and wild fruits as well—all these she should diligently store on a yearly basis. She must know how to make good flour and finely ground spelt.

Prayers and Religious Duties of the *pater familias*

Cato, *Agr.* 131–132 When the pear trees are in bloom, make [the following] offering [*daps*] for the oxen; after that, start the spring ploughing. Start with the pebbly sandy soil, then later plough the heaviest and wettest soils.

The offering must be made in this way: Offer to Jupiter Dapalis a cup [*culigna*] of wine of any amount you want to offer. The day should be a holiday for the oxen, their teamsters, and those who make the offering. In making this offering, here is what you say:

"Jupiter Dapalis, because it is right that, in (my) house and with my household (*familia*) you should receive a cup of wine for your feast, so for that, be honored by this offering that is given to you."

Having washed your hands, take the wine [and say]:

"Jupiter Dapalis, be honored by this offering, be honored by this wine brought before you."

If you wish, you can make an offering to Vesta.[70] The offering [*daps*] to Jupiter is roasted meat and a jar of wine, presented [to him] purely and without desecration. After the offering is made, plant millet, panic grass, garlic, and lentils.

Following a discussion about cutting trees in a sacred grove (*lucus sacrus*), a *piacula* or sacrifice of a pig is to be made by the owner with a prescribed prayer to a god or goddess for benignity for himself, his household, and his *familia*. Converting a plot of soil to a new use was accompanied with ritual acts and prayers. Other acts and prayers are also part of the owner's duties.

Cato, *Agr.* **140**   If you wish [then] to work the ground [of the sacred grove], make a sacrifice [*piacula*] in the same way, saying in addition:

"For the cause of doing this work"

While the tilling is going on, the rite must be daily repeated somewhere [on the estate], and if a public or family holiday interrupts [the rite], a new sacrifice must be made.

Cato, *Agr.* **141.1–4**   Here is what is to be done to purify a field: Order the *suovetaurilia* to be led around [the land and say]:[71]

"That with the help of the gods good things may happen, I order you, 'Manius,' to ensure that my estate, my field, and my earth be purified in whatever location you think it best the *suovetaurilia* be led around or guided."[72]

With [an offering of] wine, say this prayer to Janus and Jupiter:

"Father Mars, I pray and beg you to be willing to be gracious to my house and my household [*domus familiaque*] for which I have ordered this *suovetaurilia* to be led around my field, my earth, and my estate [*agrum, terra, fundusque meus*], so that you prevent, forbid, and avert illnesses both seen and unseen, and deprivation and destruction, calamities and bad weather, and that you grant good growth and outcome to my harvests, my grain, my vineyards, and my [new] plantings, and that you keep my shepherds and my flocks in good health as well as keeping me, my house and household in good health and strength. Therefore, concerning these things, to purify my estate, my soil, my fields and making an expiation, as I have said, be satisfied with this sacrificed suckling piglet, kid, and calf [*suovetaurilia lactans*]."

Then make a pile of the cakes with a knife and have the oblation cake at the ready, then bring the victims forward. When you sacrifice the pig[let], the lamb, and the calf, say the following:

"For these things, be satisfied with this sacrificed *suovetaurilia*."[73] [...]

Inventory of an Oil-Producing Estate (*oletum*)

Much effort is made by Cato to list the equipment needed for the olive oil estate (*oletum* and *cella olearia*, *Agr.* 10 and 13.2), the vineyard (*Agr.* 11–12), and other types of properties, as well as for the olive-pressing and wine-producing areas of the villa. He even tells his readers where to buy equipment and what prices to expect for purchase, transport, and setup. His lists are long and detailed, but it is their detail that makes his treatise seem as if he is addressing an almost unenlightened readership. This could not have been the case. Local knowledge and the traditions of farming for profit among the well-to-do in the countrysides of central Italy north and south of Rome, and particularly the corridor of variegated and fertile farmlands between Rome and Naples along the Via Latina that he cites specifically, had had very well-developed villas and agricultural estates for generations.

Cato's inventories of equipment are part of Roman pride in possession and enumeration, a drive to minutely catalogue the panoply of equipment needed for any task—be it in agricultural, construction, military, or even political endeavors. For owners of villas and estates, this has been called "the romance of equipment."[74] In the following excerpt and in others, Cato begins with the enslaved personnel as equipment, followed by the animals needed for the work, then the equipment needed in the process from ploughing to storing the produce, finally to accommodation and clothing for the enslaved workers. Cato presented similar lists for wine-making equipment, and there is a good deal of overlap in the lists; some items seem to be misplaced (wine-making equipment in the list of items for making oil).

Cato, *Agr.* 10   For an olive estate [*oletum*] of 240 *iugera* [about 60 ha, or 150 acres], the following equipment is needed:

> a *vilicus*, a *vilica*, 5 slaves, 3 ox drivers, 1 muleteer, 1 swineherd, 1 shepherd, to a total of 13.
> 3 pair of oxen, 3 donkeys fit for carrying manure, 1 donkey for [to turn] the mill, 100 sheep.[75]
> 5 well-fitted oil-pressing units, 1 covered copper pot of 30 quadrantals [about 786 liters, or 203 gal.], 3 iron hooks, 3 water containers, 2 funnels, 1 five-quadrantal copper container [about 131 liters, or 34 gal.], also with a copper lid, 3 hooks, 1 small basin, 2 oil jars, 1 jar of a capacity of 50 [...corrupt passage], 3 ladles, 1 water bucket, 1 wash basin, 1 small pot, 1 water pot, 1 ladle, 1 small dish, 1 chamber pot, 1 watering can, 1 ladle, 1 lampstand, 1 container for 1 *sextarius* [about 546 ml, or 18½ fl. oz.].
> 3 big carts, 6 ploughs with ploughshares, 3 yokes with leather ties, 6 harness fittings for oxen, 1 harrow, 4 crates for manure, 3 manure baskets, 3 *semuncias* [?], 3 saddle pads for the donkeys.
> Metal tools: 8 metal tilling forks, 8 hoes, 4 spades, 5 shovels, 2 four-pronged rakes, 8 scythes, 5 pitchforks, 5 pruning knives, 3 axes, 3 wedges, 1 hand quern, 2 tongs, 1 poker, 2 grills.
> 100 *dolia*, 12 basins, 10 *dolia* for grape pips, 10 *dolia* for *amurca*, 10 [jars?] for wine, 20 for grain, 1 container for lupine beans, 10 clay jars, 1 wash tub, 1 bath tub, 2 basins for water, lids for the *dolia* and jars.
> 1 donkey mill and 1 quern, 1 Spanish quern, 3 small grinders, 1 abacus [counting board?], 2 brass disks, 2 tables, 3 large benches, 1 bench for the bedroom, 3 stools, 4 chairs [beds?], 2 seats, 1 bed for the bedroom, 4 rope beds, and 3 beds.
> 1 mortar made of wood, 1 tub for washing, 1 wide loom, 2 mortars, 1 pestle for beans, 1 pestle for spelt, 1 pestle for seeds, 1 pestle for crushing nuts, 1 container of 1 *modius* [about 8.75 liters, or 2 gal.], 1 half-*modius* container.
> 8 mattresses, 8 blankets, 16 cushions, 10 covers, 3 napkins, 6 slaves' smocks.

Shopping for Machinery and Other Hardware

Cato, Agr. 22.3-4   An olive oil press can be bought in the district of Suessa for 400 *sestertii* and 50 *librae* of oil [about 16.5 kg, or 36⅓ lb.]. Assembling the press costs 60*HS*, for transporting it with an ox train 60*HS*, plus 6 [days'] work for 6 men including the ox drivers, 72*HS*. The gear for the press bar [*cupa ornata*] is 72*HS*, plus oil [grease for wagon axles?] is 25*HS*, to a total of 629*HS*.

At Pompeii, the whole unit can be bought for 384*HS*, plus 28*HS* for transport. It is better to have the unit put together on site [at the villa] and adjust it there, work that will cost 60*HS*, to a total of 72*HS*. If you are fitting new *orbes* [half-spherical grinding stones] into an old *trapetum* [mill basin], they should be [... Cato specifies dimensions but text is corrupt]. *Orbes* can be purchased at Rufrius's building yard [in the Suessa district?] for 189*HS* and adjusted at a cost of 30*HS*. It is the same price at Pompeii.

Cato, Agr. 135.1-3   Tunics, togas, woolen cloaks, smocks, and clogs are [best] bought in Rome. At Cales and Minturnae: hoods, metal hardware, scythes, shovels, axes, [metal] fittings [*ornamenta*], and small chains. At Venafrum: shovels. At Suessa and in Lucania: wagons and sledges. At Alba and Rome: *dolia* and basins. At Venafrum: roof tiles [*tegulae*]. Roman-style ploughs are good for heavy soil; Campanian ploughs are good for dark [loamy] soil. Roman-style yokes [for oxen] are the best, and the best ploughshares are detachable ones. Olive oil presses [should be bought] at Pompeii and at Rufrius's agricultural supply yard [*maceria*] at Nola; nails and [metal?] enclosures at Rome; buckets, oil jars, water pitchers, wine jars, and other copper containers at Capua and Nola; Campanian hampers from Capua are useful. Lifting ropes and all kinds of cordage at Capua. Roman-style baskets at Suessa and Casinum. [... corrupt passage] from Rome are the best.

Lucius Tunnius at Casinum and Gaius Mennius, son of Lucius Mennius, at Venafrum, make ropes for presses.[76] [...]

Rental Contracts for Land

Cato, Agr. 136-137   Here is the formula for renting land to a sharecropper [*partiarius*]: In the environs of Casinum and Venafrum, on first-quality land, he should receive one-eighth of the grain in baskets [reaped but not threshed], on good-enough land one-seventh, on third-quality land, one-fifth. If the grain is to be divided in *modius* units [i.e., in threshed form, a *modius* is about 8.75 (dry) liters, or 2 (US dry) gal.], he should receive one-eighth. In the environs of Venafrum, on the best land, one-ninth of the grain in baskets [i.e., reaped but not threshed]. If they mill together [the owner and the sharecropper], the sharecropper will pay that part of the cost of milling in relation to his share. His share should be one-fifth of barley in *modius* units [i.e., reaped and threshed] and one-fifth of beans in *modius* units [i.e., shelled].

For a sharecropper in regard of a vineyard: He shall take good care of the estate, the orchard, and the grain field[s]. The sharecropper should have enough hay and food for the cattle that are on the estate. Everything else is shared.

Maintenance of Enslaved Workers

Cato, Agr. 56-59   Food for the slaves [*familiae*]: In winter, 4 *modii* [about 35 (dry) liters, or 8 (US dry) gal.] of wheat for the workers, and 4½ [about 39 liters, or 9 gal.] in summer. For the *vilicus*, the *vilica*, the steward [*epistates*, a Greek term], and the shepherd, 3 *modii* [about

26 liters, or 6 gal.]. The chain gang [*conpedes*, the shackled men] should have 4 *librae* of bread [about 1.3 kg, or 3 lb.] in winter, then 5 *librae* of bread [about 1.65 kg, or 3¾ lb.] when they take up work on the vines, then when they begin work on the figs, back down to 4.

Wine for the slaves: Once the grape harvest is over, for three months, they shall have pomace wine [Fr. *piquette*]. In the fourth month, a *hemina* [about 275 ml, or 9⅕ fl. oz.] per day. In the fifth, sixth, seventh, and eighth month, a *sextarius* [about 550 ml, or 18½ fl. oz.] per day or 5 *congii* [about 3.2 liters, or 3½ qt.] per month. In the ninth, tenth, eleventh, and twelfth month, 3 *heminae* per day, that is an amphora [about 26 liters, or 7 gal.]. For the Saturnalia and Compitalia festivals, an extra 3½ *congii* [11.5 liters, or 12 qt.] per man to a yearly total per man of 7 *quadrantalia* [of *amphorae quadrantal,* about 183.5 liters, or 48½ gal.], with more for the chain gang in accordance with the work they are engaged in: for them, 10 *quadrantalia* [*amphorae quadrantal*; about 260 liters, or 700 gal.] per year is not too much.

Condiment for the slaves: Store as many of the olives that have fallen [before harvest] as possible, and later the olives that will not give much oil, and [distribute them to the slaves] sparingly to make them last as long as possible. When the [stored] olives are finished, distribute fish sauce [*hallec*] and vinegar and a *sextarius* [about 550 ml, or 1½ pt.]. of oil. One *modius* of salt per year is enough.

Clothing for the slaves: One tunic 3½ *pedes* long [about 104 cm, or 3½ ft.] and a blanket every other year. When you give out the tunic and blanket, take back the old ones to use for patching. Wooden clogs are needed every other year.

Cabbage

The subject of cabbage (*brassica*) in all its varieties, versatilities, and uses—as food, as condiment, as medicine—receives the longest discussion by far in Cato, longer even than his specifications for olive and wine presses or planting advice. His virtually encyclopedic treatment of cabbage (including some old wives' remedies) indicates that his enthusiasm for the crucifer may have been impelled by moral considerations. As he says, "the cabbage is the foremost of all vegetables," and he may intend his praise to be a standing rebuke to the luxurious refined tastes and excessive eating of his upper-class contemporaries. That Cato recommends it as an antidote to overeating and hangover may be telling, but he also combines the simplicity, availability, and cheapness of cabbage with all of the parts of the body (bile, spleen, heart, liver, lungs, veins, joints) in a kind of universal catch-all of goodness for men, women, and children. Besides physical well-being, promoting health and strength is a matter of social morality and the body politic as well as the human body and mind.

Cato, *Agr.* 156.1–2   Cabbage is the foremost of all vegetables. It can be eaten cooked or raw. If you eat it raw, dip it in vinegar. It is wonderfully easy to digest and is a good laxative, and the urine [of those who eat it] is healthy in all respects. If you wish, at a feast, to drink a lot and eat with abandon, eat as much raw cabbage with vinegar as you wish before the meal and, after you have dined, eat about five leaves. This will make you feel as if you had eaten almost nothing, and you can drink as much as you want.

If you want to clear the upper intestine [bowel], take four smooth cabbage leaves and tie them into three equal bunches. Fill a pot with water, bring it to a boil, then put in one of the bunches: this will quell the boiling. After the water returns to the boil, plunge the [first] bunch [to the bottom of the pot], count to five, and remove. Do the same with the second and third bunches, combine the boiled bunches, and chop them. Then squeeze about a *hemina* [about 275 ml, or 9 fl. oz.] of the boiled cabbage juice into an earthenware cup, adding a pinch of salt about the size of a pea and enough crushed cumin so it develops a smell. Then put the cup [of cabbage juice] outside on a calm night. Before a person drinks this, he should take a hot bath, take a drink of water sweetened with honey, and go to bed without dinner. The next morning, he should drink the juice and walk for four hours, going about his business [as usual]. Then, when the feeling comes to him and he is overcome with nausea, he should lie down and purge himself. He will throw up so much bile and phlegm that he will be amazed at how much there was. After a while, when the other end begins to work, he should drink a *hemina* of the juice or a bit more. If it works more [too much], take two small measures of flour and stir them into water; after drinking [this mixture], the effect will cease.

Cato, *Agr.* 157.1–2   First of all, it is important to know the various types of cabbage and their nature. [...]

Cabbage has all the elements needed for health and adapts itself to [conditions of] heat, at once dry and moist, sweet, bitter, and acid. [...]

Dislocations can be readily treated with a daily bath of hot water and a compress of chopped cabbage; a twice-daily application will lessen the pain. [...]

For a mammary ulcer and a cancer, apply macerated cabbage to effect a cure. If the ulcer is too sensitive for this application, mix some barley flour with the macerated cabbage and apply. All ulcerations of this kind will be cured in this way, something that other medications cannot effect or clear up. For a boy or girl, barley flour should be added.

VARRO   (Marcus Terentius Varro, 116–27 BCE)

Three Books on Agriculture (*De re rustica libri III*), ca. 37–36 BCE (Varro, *Rust.*)

Varro's treatise is mainly about the work and activities of *fundi* or agricultural estates in Italy: it includes the villa in its three parts—dwelling (*pars urbana*), working areas (*pars rustica*), storage facilities (*pars fructuaria*).[77] These neat divisions are part of Varro's larger program and his direct address to readers: he intends to instruct Italian villa and estate owners in both practical and intellectual matters, on both how to manage their properties and how to understand what they are doing and why. Hence his emphasis on simple dichotomies such as usefulness (*utilitas*) versus pleasure (*voluptas*) and other ideas that would give readers a philosophical and mental structure with which to frame their villas, in addition to the common sense prescriptions and practical instructions that he also includes. He thus addressed readers who were sufficiently educated to understand abstractions but sufficiently unfamiliar with farming to need some practical advice. They were not on-the-land farmers but rather educated, town-dwelling estate owners at Rome and elsewhere, who expected to live comfortably, but not year-round, in villas from which they gained income from agricultural produce.[78]

Varro delivered his messages to readers in a form that was widely appealing in antiquity: conversations among men of different origins, wealth, and social class who all had mutual interests but differing opinions and expertises on complex topics. The three books of conversations happened on three different days, in significant religious and political circumstances, and came to satisfyingly clear conclusions. The formula was that of the Platonic dialogue, a device that would have been familiar to most educated persons in antiquity because, in simple form, its elements were used in the schoolroom. However, the whiplash speed and density of most Platonic dialogues is replaced, in Varro, with a pleasant, sometimes digressive, always informative, and loquacious exchange—agreeable to read and listen to but also easily applicable to whatever agricultural work was being discussed. The context of the dialogues need not have been actual: Varro was writing for a literate audience that would have understood that he was a writer, not a journalist or reporter, but some exciting circumstances with moral import set the stage.

Varro's topic is the ideal villa, the *villa perfecta* (*Rust.* 3.1.10). That any such entity could be conceived or even achieved is a philosophical notion in itself: practical and abstract elements are marshaled in a method not dissimilar to "scientific" Aristotelian (or Peripatetic) ways of analyzing and documenting external phenomena, in this case villas and estates. Varro's *villa perfecta*—what it might be and what it is definitely not—gives a snapshot of what upper-class Romans considered to be both normal and aspirational about villas and estates in the mid-first century BCE in central and northern Italy (he includes lands north of the Po, south of the Alps).[79]

Varro is at pains to set the books of his treatise into a narrative with speakers and events, in physical places that might be familiar to readers who lived in Rome but owned villas elsewhere. The speakers give opinions but rarely express much individual character; rather, they represent a range of differing social ranks but all with an interest in estates and agricultural methods. The framework of events—in Books 1 and 3 at Rome, on days of religious observance and political participation—gives an atmosphere of reverence and immediacy, which the selections chosen here are intended to convey.

The excerpts from the three books have been arranged by certain topics, under topic headings of my own.

Book 1

Varro, *Rust.* 1.1–7   If I had the free time [*otium*], Fundania, I would write more usefully than what I am writing now, though I am doing my best. I must hurry because, as it is said, if man is a bubble, he is even more so when he is old. My eightieth year tells me to pack my bag before leaving life.

So, because you have purchased an estate [*fundus*] and wish to profit from it by good practices [*bene colendo*], and you have asked me to give advice in this matter, I will try to do so about proper procedures [of agriculture] both while I am alive and after my death.[80]

I cannot let the [Cumaean] Sybil, who gave prophesies to humankind when she lived to people whom she did not know—even now after many years, we still refer to her books after some portent to know what we need to do in the public interest [*publice*]—without making myself useful to my family while I am alive.[81]

For that reason, I am writing three books [on agriculture] to which you can refer when you wish to know how do certain necessary things. As is said, gods help those who call out to them, so I will invoke them, but not the Muses that Ennius and Homer invoked.[82] Rather, I will invoke the twelve *Dii Consentes* [gods of good counsel], but not the twelve urban gods—six males and as many females—whose gilded statues adorn the Forum. Instead, I will invoke the twelve gods who are the patrons of farmers [*duces agricolarum*].[83]

First, Jupiter and Tellus who encompass all the products of agriculture through sky and earth and are therefore called the great parents: Jupiter is called Father, Tellus is called Mother Earth [*terra*]. Second, Sol and Luna [because] their movements are observed for planting and harvesting. Third, Ceres and Liber, because their products are essential to life—food and drink [wine] come from the farm. Fourth, Robigus, by whose care disease does not infect grain and trees, and Flora, by whom seasonal flowering occurs. Thus the public feast of the *Robigalia* has been set up for Robigus, and the *Floralia* games for Flora. I also call on Minerva and Venus: the former takes charge of olives, the latter of gardens, in whose [Venus's] name the rustic *Vinalia* has been instituted. I will not [omit] to pray to *Lympha* [sweet water] and *Bonus Eventus* [Good Outcome] because, without water, farming is dry and hard, and without success and a good outcome, farming [*agri cultura*] is just frustration, not cultivation [*frustratio est, non cultura*].

Having reverenced these gods, I will tell you about conversations about agriculture that we had lately, to which you can refer to know what you must do.[84] And if there are matters you wish to know that are not in here, I will list the [relevant] writers, both Greek ones and our own [Latin] ones.[85]

Plan of the Treatise on Agriculture

Varro, Rust. 1.1.11 I will be even more brief [sic] in three books, one on agriculture proper, the second on animal husbandry, and a third on *pastio villatica*, omitting topics that I do not consider pertinent to agriculture.[86] Having first listed these omissions, I will state the matter in its natural divisions. These come from three sources: what I have learned on my own farms, what I have read, and what I have heard from experts.[87]

The Dialogue on Agriculture Begins

Varro, Rust. 1.2.1 On the Sementivae festival, I went to the temple of Tellus [...] where I found my father-in-law, Gaius Fundanius, Gaius Agrius who is a Roman *eques* and a man of Socratic persuasion, and Publius Agrasius, a tax collector: they were looking at a painted wall map of Italy [*in pariete picta Italia*].[88] "What are you doing?" I asked, "Has the quiet of the Sementivae festival brought you here, in the same way as it brought our fathers and grandfathers?"[89] [...]

Varro, Rust. 1.2.3 When we [four] had sat down, Agrasius asked Agrius, "You, who have traveled many lands, have you seen any equal in cultivation to Italy?"

Agrius replied, "Indeed, I judge that no other land is so completely cultivated than Italy. From Eratosthenes's natural division, [we know] that the earth is divided into two parts, north and south—doubtless the northern part is the healthier [*salubriora pars*] and so more fruitful [*fructuosiora pars*], so at least Italy is better for cultivation than Asia, first because it is in Europe, in the temperate part of Europe rather than inland to the north. Inland, winter is virtually eternal, and no wonder, as it is between the northern circumference (of the earth) and the pole where there is no sunshine for six months' duration, and they say that even navigation is impossible because of ice. [...]

Varro, Rust. 1.2.6–10 On the other hand, what useful plant does not only grow in Italy but does so to perfection? What spelt can be compared to that of Campania? What wheat to that of Apulia? What wine to that of the Falernian plain? What oil to that of Venafrum?

Is not Italy so covered with trees that it seems like an orchard?[90] [...]

[Cato tells us] that, in the Gallican plain, in some places, ten *cullei* [about 5,200 liters, or 1,374 gal.] of wine are produced per *iugerum* [about .25 ha, or ⅔ acre] of vineyard. Is not the same [produced] in the plain of Faventia [in the Po valley]? Cato calls the vineyards there *trecenariae* because their yield is 300 amphoras [about 78,000 liters, or 20,605 gal.] per *iugerum*."

Agrius then turned to me [Varro] and said, "For sure, your friend Marcius Libo the chief engineer [*praefectus fabrum*] told me that such was his yield on his estate at Faventia. Italian farmers have two things in mind for cultivation: if the yield justifies the cost and labor, and whether the location is healthy or not. Absent either of these, anyone who persisted in wishing to farm has lost his mind and should be confined by family and relatives. No sane person should wish to undertake the cost and effort of farming if he sees it will not bring in produce, or if the produce is spoiled because of the location.

But I reckon that there are men here who can speak with greater authority about this, because I see that Gaius Licinius Stolo and Gnaeus Tremellius Scrofa are coming up.[91] One

[Stolo] has an ancestor who brought forward the agrarian law by which a Roman citizen could not own more than 500 *iugera* [about 125 ha, or 312 acres]. The name Stolo is confirmed by this descendant's diligence in farming: he used to dig around his trees so that no spontaneous suckers [*stolones*, sing. *stolo*] would grow from the roots. The other whom I see coming is Gnaeus Tremellius Scrofa who was your [Varro's] colleague as a member of the Commission of Twenty to apportion the [*ager publicus* or agricultural land of the] Campanian plain [into farms], a man distinguished by many virtues and considered the most expert Roman in the matter of agriculture."

"Indeed it's so," I [Varro] exclaimed, "for his estates [*fundi*] are a pleasant sight because of their cultivation, more than the majestic buildings of other owners [*regie polita aedifica aliorum*], for when people come to see his [Stolo's] villas, they do not see picture galleries [*pinacothecae*] the like of which they would see at Lucullus's villas; rather, they see larders of fruit [*oropothecae*]. [In the market] at the top of the Via Sacra," I added, "where fruit is like gold, Stolo's orchards are like that."[92] [...]

Principles and Goals of Agriculture

Varro, *Rust*. 1.2.12–14 [Agrius speaking to Scrofa] "Tell us what the goal of agriculture [*summa agri cultura*] is. Is it useful profit [*utilitas*], or pleasure [*voluptas*], or both? For they say that now you are the best in agriculture, as Stolo once was."

Scrofa replied, "First, we must distinguish among the elements of agriculture only things that are planted in the ground or else things brought into the countryside like sheep and cattle. Indeed, I notice that those who have written on agriculture in Punic, Greek, and Latin have wandered away from the proper subject."

Stolo then said, "As for me, I judge that [all] these writers should not be imitated in all things. Rather, [we should imitate] those who did better in limiting the confines of the topic by excluding things that are not relevant. [...] Grazing, which many writers discuss under the rubric of agriculture, properly belongs to the herdsman [*pastor*] rather than to the farmer [*agricola*]."[93] [...]

Varro, *Rust*. 1.3.1–4 "Now then," said Agrasius, "having parsed what sorts of things can be omitted from the discussion about agriculture, teach us about that knowledge [*scientia*] which is needed in these matters: is it a real art [*ars*, expertise] or something else, and take us along the track from the starting gates to the finish line."[94]

Fixing Stolo with a look, Scrofa said, "In age, distinction, and knowledge, you are foremost [among us], so you must speak."

Not holding back, Stolo said, "First, it's not only an art, it's a necessary and noble art. At the same time, it's a [species of] knowledge [*scientia*] that indicates what must be planted in what field and what soil reliably gives the largest harvests. Its essential elements [*principia*] are those that Ennius wrote were those of the entire world: water, earth, air [*anima*], and fire [*sol*]. You must know this before sowing your seed, the beginning of all production. Going forward, farmers should set their sights on two goals: useful profit [*utilitas*] and pleasure [*voluptas*]."

Best Sites for Villas and Farms, Types of Estates and Buildings

Varro's discussion of how to think about villas and estates is formulated on the model of Aristotelian categories and subcategories:

1. Knowledge (*cognitio*) of the farm and its soil, including the location of the site and its healthiness, its prevaling and seasonal climate, as well as the villa itself and the stables or outbuildings.

2. The *means* or equipment needed, in three important parts: devices for pressing, transportation, the enslaved workers and the help hired from outside the villa.

3. The *operations* needed for certain work, planning for them and where they are to be done.

4. The *times* of the year or season to do the work based on solar or lunar cycles.

In these categories, the texts excerpted below emphasize aspects of site and building as well as personnel for the villa and its farm as well as moral aspects of villas.

Varro, Rust. 1.7.1–2 [...] Stolo said, "As for the natural site, Cato was right that the best place for an estate is at the base of a mountain facing south."[95] [...]

Varro, Rust. 1.10.1–2 Scrofa [said], "Measuring [parcels of] land is particular to each country. In Farther Spain, it is called *iugum*, while in Campania the *versus*, and with us in the Roman and Latin district, *iugerum*. [...] Two *iugera* are a *heredium* because, in the days of [king] Romulus, that was the allotment per citizen as inheritable by heirs [*heredes*, sing. *heres*], so it is called *heredium*. Later, a hundred *heredia* were termed a *centuria*, each side 2,400 feet long [710.5 × 710.5 m, or 2,331 × 2,331 ft.]. Four *centuriae* set two-by-two on each side are called a *saltus*, for purposes of assigning land to individuals."

Varro, Rust. 1.11.1–2 [Scrofa speaking] "Many make mistakes in reckoning the size of the estate, some building a villa either smaller or larger [than what is needed], and thus not appropriate to the property and its produce. Big buildings [*maiora tecta*] are expensive and need greater maintenance; buildings that are too small [in their storage facilities] will result in spoiled produce [*fructus*]. To be sure, bigger wineries should be built on an estate with vineyards, and bigger granaries [*horrea*] on a grain-growing estate. [...]

"Above all, the villa should be built so that water is available within its walls, but if not, then very nearby; a spring is the best, but a perennial stream [brook] will do. Absent running water, covered cisterns and uncovered [artificial] ponds must be built, the former for human consumption, the other for watering the herd animals."

Varro, Rust. 1.12.1–2 [Scrofa speaking] "Care must be taken to place the villa at the base of a forested mountain [*mons*, hill] facing wide pastures, and in such a way as [to face] the area's healthiest breezes. A villa facing east [*aequinoctiales*] is the best—it will have shade in summer and sun in the winter. If you have to build by a river, take care not to have the villa facing the river as it will be very cold in winter and unhealthy in summer." [...]

Arrangements for Storerooms and Rooms for Enslaved Workers

Varro, Rust. 1.13.1–2 [Scrofa speaking] "The cow sheds are to be located in the part of the villa that is warmest in winter. Produce such as wine and oil should be stored on floored storerooms with the appropriate wine and oil containers; dry produce such as beans and hay should be stored on [raised] decks. The slaves [*familia*] should be provided for in a place where they can get their strength back comfortably when tired from work in heat or cold. The room for the *vilicus* should be close to the entrance so he can identify who comes in or goes out at night and what has been taken away, especially if there is no doorman. Care should be taken for the kitchen to be conveniently situated because much activity takes place before dawn in the way of preparing and eating food." [96] [...]

Ancient Good Sense about Villas Contrasted with Modern Folly

Varro, *Rust*. 1.13.6–7   "An estate is more profitable," Fundanius said, "if its buildings are built with the thriftiness [*diligentia*] of men of the past rather than the luxurious constructions of men of today. The former built in good relation [*ratio*] to their produce, the latter build according to their indomitable desires [*libidines indomitas*]. Thus [in the past] *villae rusticae* used to cost more than urban houses [*urbanae*], but nowadays the opposite is true in many cases. [In the past], a villa was praised if it had a good country-style kitchen [*culina rustica*], big barns, wine and oil storage facilities [*cella vinaria, cella olearia*] well suited to the size of the vineyard and olive orchard, with a sloping floor going down to a reservoir. [...] In this way, they arranged that the villa had everything it needed for agriculture.

"By contrast, men today work to make the *villa urbana* as large and elegant [*maxima ac politissima*] as the so-called villas of Metellus and Lucullus, villas built to the detriment of the public interest.[97] What men now work for and expect to have is that their summer dining rooms [*aestiva triclinaria*] should face the cool east, their winter dining rooms [*hiberna triclinia*] facing west for the sun's warmth; by contrast, men of the past attended to which sides the wine and oil storage facilities should be, because the *dolia* for wine need cooler air, while the oil jars need warmer. In the same way, if there is a hill, the house should be built there if possible, unless there is some other impediment."[98]

Villas, Roads, Rivers, Markets, Special Services, Movement

The next passages are included because they indicate the local interdependence of villas with other villas and estates and their connection to the landscape and urban markets, rather than their isolation and independence. In addition, there are remarks about outside specialists for hire and a comment about impediments to enslaved persons' movement outside the estate.

Varro, *Rust*. 1.16.1–6   [Scrofa speaking] "Another topic remains, namely what is around the estate itself, because it has important connections to cultivation. There are [four] items: whether the district is unsafe; whether it is hard to send our produce [to market] or bring necessary supplies back; third, whether roads or rivers for transport are not available or inadequate; fourth, whether adjacent estates can help or harm our own cultivations. [...]

"Profitable farms have adequate means to transport what they grow to where it can be sold and to be able to get what they need in return. Many [farms] have premises to which either grain or wine need to be imported, and not a few which need to export [their produce]. [...]

"Thus it is good to have big gardens near a city, for violets and roses, which [the city] welcomes in abundance, but such items would not be marketable on distant properties. Again, if there are nearby towns and villages or even well-maintained estates and villas owned by rich men from whom you can buy what you need for your own estate and who can take your extra produce such as props, poles, and reeds [for vineyards], the estate will be more profitable than if such items have to be brought in from afar, and even more so if you can supply them from your own property. In the same way, farmers prefer to have specialists [*artifices*] on yearly contracts nearby—doctors [*medici*], fullers [*fullones*], craftsmen [*fabri*]—rather than having them in the villa itself, because the death of one of these [specialists] can wreck the farm's profit.[99] On this score, rich men [*divites*] who are owners of large estates [*lati fundi*] habitually rely on their own personnel. If towns and villages are far away from the estate, they arrange to have other craftsmen as needed in the villa, so that the slaves do not leave their tasks on working days and loaf as if [it were] a holiday instead of making the estate [*ager*] more profitable.

"For that reason, the book by Saserna prescribes that no one shall leave the estate except the *vilicus*, the steward [*promus*], or one person whom *vilicus* designates. Should a person go out, the *vilicus* should be punished. The prescription [on this matter] should actually read: 'No one shall leave without permission from the *vilicus*, and the *vilicus* without permission from the owner [*dominus*], for any errands that prevent return on the same day, and not more often than is needed for estate business.'"[100]

"Transportation makes a farm more profitable if there are roads on which wagons can be easily driven or navigable rivers nearby." [...]

Hired Labor and Enslaved Personnel

Varro, *Rust*. 1.17.1–7 [Stolo speaking] "Now I will speak about how agriculture is to be carried out. Some have divided this topic into two parts: men themselves, and the means [*adminicula*] without which men cannot cultivate. Others have divided the topic into three parts: equipment capable-of-speech [*instrumentum genus vocale*], semi-vocal equipment [*instrumentum semivocale*], and inarticulate equipment [*instrumentum mutum*]. Equipment capable-of-speech are the slave workers [*servi*], while among the semi-vocal equipment are cattle; inarticulate equipment include [such things as] wagons [*plaustra*]. All cultivation is done by men, be they slaves [*servi*] or freeborn [*liberi*], or both. Freeborn men work for themselves, as many poor men do with their children's help, or else by hired laborers among the freeborn men [*mercenarii liberorum*] for heavy work such as the grape and grain harvests, and men in debt bondage [*obaerarii*], as it used to be called and who are still numerous in Asia, Egypt, and Illyricum. On these topics in general, I say that it is better to cultivate hard-to-work places with hired laborers than with slaves, and the same is the case even in easy-to-work land, [at the times] for storing the harvests of grapes and grain.

"Cassius [Cassius Dionysius of Utica] wrote that the [freeborn] men to be hired for this work should be capable of [heavy] work, no younger than 22 years old, and well adapted to farm labor. You can judge their aptitude by their work on other given tasks, and for new hires [debt bondsmen?], what they did for their previous master.

"Slaves should be neither timid nor spirited. Their overseers should be able to read and write and have some humane touch [*imbuti humanitate*] as well as be upright in character, older than the slaves so they [the enslaved] will pay better attention to them than they would to younger men. In addition, it is very important that the overseers be experienced in farming, not only for giving directions but also be able to do the work as well, so that the slaves can imitate them and be aware that the reason that [the overseer] is in charge of them is because of his greater knowledge [*scientia*]. They should not be encouraged to control the slaves with lashes but rather with words, to obtain the same effect. Do not have too many slaves of the same nation [*natio*] as it is very likely that domestic quarrels will ensue from that. The overseers [*praefecti*] should be made keener with rewards and by having their own property [*peculium*] and be able to have wives of their own from whom they can have children.[101] This will make them more devoted and connected to the estate—and it is for exactly this reason that slaves from Epirus are the most famous and most costly. Overseers' willingness must be won by holding them in some esteem [*honor aliquis*]. The slaves [*operarii*] whose work is better than that of others should also be asked as to how the work should be done. In this way, they will see that they are not despised and are held in some respect by their owner. Slaves will be more zealous by being treated more liberally in the way of food, or more clothing, or being let off work, or being allowed to pasture [their own] animals on the estate, in such a way that when they are ordered to do heavy work or they are punished, their willingness and good feelings to the owner can be restored." [...]

Varro, Rust. 1.19.3   [...] [Stolo speaking] "Under this head of semi-vocal equipment [*genus semivocalis*], it is to be additionally pointed out that, among other animals, only those for agriculture should be kept and those few that are the [freely held] properties [*mancipia*] of the slaves for their [own] betterment and so that they [the enslaved] will be more zealous." [...][102]

Criticisms of Cato and the Sasernas

Writers often validate their authority by criticizing earlier ones. In *Rust.* 1.18.1–8, Varro frames his principles of *imitation of past practices* and *reasoned experimentation* in terms of an extended criticism of his predecessors in agricultural treatises, Cato and the two Sasernas. His readers may have been familiar with them already, and Varro is teaching his readers how to evaluate advice. His objections may seem labored and mocking, but they appealed to readers with common sense and some practical mathematical ability. The criticisms of Cato are intended to disprove rigid formulae and nonstandard land allocations; Varro is more favorable to Saserna's estimates of man hours to amount of cultivatable land but disputes their application to new and disparate agricultural lands that Rome had acquired on the Italian peninsula and overseas. In doing so, Varro lays claim to a modern view as against old rigid prescriptions.

Varro, Rust. 1.18.1–8   [Scrofa speaking] "Cato has two prescriptions for [the number of] slaves [needed], based on the extent of the cultivation and the type of crop. First, writing about an olive oil estate of 240 *iugera* [about 60 ha, or 150 acres], he prescribes that there be 13 slaves: a *vilicus*, the wife of the *vilicus*, 5 workers, 3 herdsmen, 1 muleteer, 1 swineherd, and 1 shepherd. His [Cato's] second prescription is for a vineyard of 100 *iugera* [about 25 ha, or 62 acres] where 15 slaves are needed: a *vilicus*, a *villica*, 10 workers, a cowherd, a muleteer, and a swineherd.

"Saserna writes that one man is enough per 8 *iugera* [about 2 ha, or 5 acres] and can turn over that amount in 45 days, though 4 days are enough for him to turn over one *iugerum*, but he [Saserna] also writes that he allows 13 days [of the 45] for sickness, bad weather, idleness, and laziness.[103] These writers have not given us a satisfactorily clear template. Had Cato wanted to do so, he should have stated it such that we could add or subtract [the personnel] according to the greater or lesser size of the estate. In addition, he should not have counted the *vilicus* and *villica* as part of the slave personnel because when cultivating less than 240 *iugera* of olives, you cannot do with less than one *vilicus*, and if you cultivate an estate twice the size or more, two or three *vilici* are needed.

"It is only laborers and ploughmen that need be added for a larger estate, and that only if the land itself is homogenous. But if it is not—say, if the land is impossible to plough or is very steep—far fewer oxen and ploughmen are needed. I am omitting this: that the amount of 240 *iugera* [given by Cato for an olive oil producing estate] is neither a standard unit nor a measured lot [the standard is a *centuria* or 200 *iugera*], and deducting one-sixth from 240 or 40 *iugera*, I do not see how I will take one-sixth from 13 slaves according to [Cato's] prescription. And even if I leave out the *vilicus* and *villica*, how to take out one-sixth from the 11 remaining slaves? As for what (Cato) says about a 100 *iugera* vineyard that the work requires 15 slaves: if [the estate] is a *centuria* [200 *iugera*], half in vines and half in olives, it follows that the owner will need two *vilici* and two *villicae*, which is ridiculous. Saserna is sounder in his reasoning about how many slaves and what kind [are needed]: he says that a single *iugerum* is enough for four days' work by one workman.

"Still, if this was the case for Saserna's estáte in Gaul [*Gallia Cisalpina*], the same would not be the case for land in mountainous Liguria.[104] Thus, in terms of determining how many slaves and other equipment you will need, consider the following three things: the nature and size of the neighboring estates, how many laborers work there, and how many extra or fewer laborers you need for better or worse cultivation. Nature provides two paths to cultivation: experimentation [*experientia*] and imitation [*imitatio*]. Farmers of the past found out many things by trying them; their descendants [*liberi*][found things out] mainly by imitation. It is up to us to do both: to imitate others and to try by experimentation to do things not by hit-or-miss but in a methodical way [*ratio*][105]—for example, to do a second ploughing either more or less deep than the first, or to see what the effect [of a certain procedure] will be; and by the same reasoning [what the effect was] when a second and third weeding were done, and for delaying grafting figs from the spring season to the summer."

Lists of Equipment

Varro, Rust. 1.22.1–4. [Scrofa speaking] "On the rest of the equipment—the mute equipment—in which are included baskets, *dolia*, and other such things, this precept is to be adhered to: nothing should be purchased that grows on the estate or that can be made by its slaves, namely things made of willow and [other] materials on the estate such as baskets, things made of wicker, flails [for threshing], fans [for separating chaff from kernel], and rakes, as well as items made of hemp, flax, rushes, palm, and bulrushes such as rope, cordage, and mats. Items that the estate cannot supply and that are useful rather than showy will not detract from the profit, especially if they can be bought conveniently nearby and very cheaply. The types and number of such equipment are to be reckoned by the size of the estate, more if the estate is large."

Stolo said, "Thus Cato, on a fixed size of estate, prescribes that a person who has an olive oil producing estate of 240 *iugera* must have 5 oil presses with the following listed items: copper vessels, pots, a three-spouted pitcher, and such; of wood and iron, 3 wagons, 3 large ploughs, 6 ploughs with ploughshares, 4 manure containers, and such; then specific iron tools in the [right] number for the work—8 hoes and 8 forks, half that number of shovels, and so on. Cato's prescription for a vineyard of 100 *iugera* [about 25 ha,, or 62 acres] is that it must have 3 completely fitted-out *torcularia*, covered *dolia* for 800 *cullei* [about 419,200 liters, or 110,720 gal.], 20 grape containers, 20 grain containers, and other items like that. In fact, others recommend fewer such items, but I think that Cato prescribed that amount [800 *cullei*] so that [the producer] would not have to sell the wine that year. Old wine sells better than new wine, and that same wine can sell for more at different times [of the year]." [...]

Varro, Rust. 1.22.6. So spoke Stolo; Scrofa then took up: "A [written] inventory of the owner's equipment and estate goods must be kept both in the city and at the country estate [*in urbe et rure*], and the *vilicus* should keep all the equipment in a safe place near the villa, and whatever cannot be kept under lock and key [*sub clavi*], the *vilicus* should keep an eye on it, especially things that are not often used, such as the baskets for the grape harvest and other equipment. Things that are seen every day are less likely to be stolen."

Expense and Profit

Varro, Rust. 1.53 [Stolo speaking] "When the wheat harvest is finished and gleaning needs to be done, either in-house [by estate enslaved workers] or [hired] workers brought in, if the stalks are few and hard to gather, turn [the fields] to pasture. The highest goal to keep in view in this matter is that expense shall not be greater than profit."

Produce to Market

Varro, *Rust.* 1.69.13   [Stolo speaking] "For produce intended for sale, timing is important. Separate the [perishable] produce that cannot be kept and sell it right away, while that which can be stored should be sold when it is saleable at a high price. If you sell at the right time, stored produce will often double in price."

The Dramatic End to Book 1: An Assassination in Rome

Varro ends Book 1 of *De re rustica* with an agitated account of a fatal stabbing in the precinct of the temple of Tellus where the six gentlemen had been having their discussion on agriculture. Their host, Lucius Fundilius, the *aeditumus* or official of the cult, had been assassinated. The friends conclude that life is risky and Rome is dangerous. Cities and Rome are fearsome—better to live at a villa in the country.

Varro, *Rust.* 1.69.2–3   While he [Stolo] was speaking, a freedman of the *aeditumus* comes to us weeping and begs that we forgive him for making us wait, and asks us to come to a funeral with him the next day. We all jumped up and exclaimed together, "What? To a funeral? What happened?" Still weeping, he tells us that [his master] had been stabbed by someone and fell down. In the uproar, he couldn't tell who the perpetrator was, but he heard a voice saying that a mistake had been made. He had taken his master [*patronus*] home and sent servants to find a doctor and quickly bring him, and he begged our pardon for attending to his master rather than coming to get us. Even though he had not been able to help his master and could not ultimately prevent his [taking his] last breath, he considered that he had done rightly. Bearing him no ill will, we walked down from the temple and took leave of one another, pondering [the fact that] human fate [*casus humanus*] was greatly subject to chance, and very amazed that such an event should have happened in Rome.[106]

Book 2

Book 2 of Varro's *De re rustica* concerns choosing, breeding, caring for, and working with farm animals: cattle, sheep, goats, swine, horses, donkeys, dogs, and mules. It is dedicated to a friend, Turranius Niger, who appears to have been a cattle drover and livestock broker plying his trade from the Po River valley in the north as far as Apulia in the south of the peninsula: *Rust.* 2.2.6. Varro set the dialogue in Epirus where he was on active military duty against the Cilician pirates in 67 BCE under Pompey's command, thus some thirty years before the writing of *De re rustica*: *Rust.* 2.1.6. Turranius himself takes no part in the dialogue; there are four others who participate somewhat: Menates, Cossinius, Lucienus, and Murrius.[107] Cossinius and Murrius lay out the design of the discussion, then Varro lays out the history and Greek bibliography of farm animals from early shepherding to modern profitable herding. The principal speaker throughout is Gnaeus Tremellius Scrofa, whom we have already met in Book 1. The preface of Book 2 broaches modern folly about villas, with much sarcasm about their owners' pretensions to Greek culture and even a criticism of the Mediterranean-wide economy in foodstuffs and wine.

Preface

Varro, Rust. 2.1.1-4   It was not without good cause that our great ancestors [*maiores*] valued the Romans of the countryside [*rustici Romani*] over those of the city. In the same way that those who live in the countryside [but stay] inside their villas are lazier [*ignavior*] than those who engage themselves in the field doing whatever needs doing, they considered that those who lived in cities were more indolent [*desidiosior*] than those who worked in the countryside.

In consequence, they divided the year [*annus*, calendar] in such a way that such business as needed to be done in the city took up only the ninth day, and they worked in the countryside for the other seven days.[108] As long as they maintained this plan, they were able both to have their fields be most productive and to keep themselves in stronger health, not needing the Greeks' city-*gymnasia*. But now these days, one such *gymnasium* is considered to be barely enough, and owners do not feel that they really own a villa unless it rings with many Greek words, places called by such special names as *procoeton* [entrance], *palaestra* [exercise facility], *apodyterion* [changing room], *peristylon* [colonnade or colonnaded court], *peripteros* [colonnade], *oporotheca* [dry-fruit storage room].

Because now most *patres familiae* have furtively slid themselves behind the city walls, abandoning the sickle and the plough to occupy their hands in the theater or the circus rather than in the grain fields and vineyards, we pay some [middle]man money to bring us grain from Africa and Sardinia to fill us up, and the wine we store comes from the islands of Cos and Chios in ships.

In consequence, in this land where the shepherds who founded the City and once taught agriculture to their offspring, now their offspring in the same place have made meadows out of grain fields, out of greed and in defiance of the laws, ignorant that cultivation and pasturing are not the same. [...]

Special Profitabilities

Varro, Rust. 2.1.143   [Scrofa speaking] "The third point [about choosing livestock] is to think about the breed. On this topic the donkeys of Arcadia in Greece are distinguished, as are, in Italy, the donkeys from Reate, even to the point that I remember an ass sold for 60,000*HS* and a team of four went for 400,000*HS*!"[109]

Enslaved Workers: Physique, Ethnic Characteristics, Buying and Selling

By the second century BCE, villas and estates of any size and type relied on the labor of enslaved workers and sometimes freeborn tenants [*coloni*], even though they coexisted with farms independently cultivated by freeborn citizens. For Varro's readers in the mid- to upper social and financial classes, enslaved personnel on larger properties would have been matters of concern and planning for an estate, but little is actually said of their upkeep. However, a few passages concerning the work of enslaved personnel as herders for cattle and goats leads Varro to discuss the selection of enslaved laborers and related matters.

Varro, Rust. 2.10.1-10   [...] Then Cossinius spoke: "For herds of larger cattle, older slaves are best. For smaller animals, even boys will do, but in both it is better to have the stronger [enslaved men] for those who [must] follow the tracks than those who return daily to the estate's villa. For that reason, in open pasturing you may see young men, [sometimes] even equipped with a weapon, while on the estate, both boys and even girls may be seen tending the herds.

"The herdsmen must stay the whole day in the pastures and have the herds feed together in common, but each herdsman must be with his own herd at night. All herdsmen should be under one master herdsman [*magister pecoris*], who should be older and more experienced than the others—the others will pay attention to one who is greater in age and knowledge, but the master herdsman should not be so old that he cannot do the work because of his age. [...]

"Old men and boys do not easily stand the difficulty of the tracks and the steepness and harshness of the mountains, things that must be endured by those following the herd, especially cattle and sheep, which find their fodder among rocks and in woodlands. The body type of men to be selected [as herdsmen] should be strong and speedy, quick, nimble, and supple of limb: men who can both follow the herd and even defend it from wild animals and robbers, who can lift heavy packs onto draft animals, who can run (quickly), and who can use a javelin. Not all races are suited to be herdsmen: neither the Bastulans nor the Turdulans [are adapted to the work], but Gallic slaves are most suited [to it], especially for [work with] oxen."[110]

"In buying slaves, there are six ways to achieve legitimate ownership: (1) by right of inheritance, (2) by duly obtaining, by [the act of] *mancipium* from someone who has the legal right to do so, (3) by legal cession, by someone who has the right to do so to another who in turn has the right to receive such items, (4) by customary right of ownership, (5) by auction of the spoils of war, and finally, (6) by purchase with other goods or with confiscated items that have come to public sale. In such purchases, it is usual for the [individual slave's] *peculium* to be included unless an explicit clause is written in, and [affidavit from the seller] that he [the enslaved person] is healthy and has not been charged with robbery or damage; if [the enslaved person] has not been transmitted by *mancipium*, either double the amount or the equivalent [of the purchase price] is promised [as compensation for ill health of the slave or instances of robbery or damage], as per agreement."[111]

"The herdsmen should eat by themselves during the day with their herds, but those who are under a master herdsman should eat together. The master herdsman is in charge of all equipment needed for the sustenance of the men and the [veterinary?] needs of the herd. For that task, owners have pack animals, sometimes mares or others for the work, which can carry loads on their backs.

"On the business of breeding herdsmen: it is easy for those who always live on the estate and have [enslaved] females at the villa, because the Venus of herdsmen needs no greater room to maneuver. But those who pasture their herds in the mountains and woodlands rather than near the villa, and [need to] keep off sudden rains in their huts, many [owners] have thought it useful to add [enslaved] women to follow the herds as well as to make meals for the herdsmen and keep them up to the mark. But those slave women should be strong and not unattractive, and indeed in certain regions women are as good as men for the work: in Illyria one can see them tending the herd, carrying wood to the hearth, cooking the food, and doing what is needed in the huts. I note that for nursing [their children], they can be both child-bearers and caregivers."

At the same time, looking at me [Varro], Scrofa said, "I have heard you say that when you were in Liburnia [in Illyria], you saw slave mothers carrying logs and nursing one or two children at the same time. Our [Roman] women, when they have just given birth, lie [on beds] under canopy curtains [*conopea*] for days on end: they are worthless and contemptible."

"You are right" I [Varro] said. "And in Illyria I have even seen something more: often pregnant [slave] women, when they are about to give birth, leave their work for a moment and come back with a baby, so you would think that they had found a child rather than having given birth to one.[112] Not only that, Illyrian custom does not disallow women as old as twenty—yet still referring to them as virgins—to yield to any man they want before marriage, to walk by themselves unaccompanied, and to have children [out of wedlock]."

[Cossinius resuming]: "The master herdsman must keep a written record of the items about the health of the men and the herd that can be attended to without a doctor's care. An illiterate master herdsman is not qualified [for the job] because he cannot keep his owner's accounts of the herd correctly. The number of herdsmen is sometimes fewer, sometimes greater...."[113] [...]

Book 3

Book 3 of *De re rustica* is the apex of Varro's treatise: the *villa perfecta*. This majestic embodiment of *utilitas* and *voluptas* is conceived in the largest possible historical and social contexts and as proof of the innate civic-mindedness of owners of estates and villas. It is defined by the entire contents of all three books, and its proper relation both to Roman traditions and the new Rome of wealth and dominance is considered.

The setting and day in the political calendar are important: in the Villa Publica at Rome, on the day that the polls were open for the election of the aediles.[114] The Villa Publica was neither a dwelling nor an estate: it was a building in the Campus Martius intended for use by the censors to convene the people of the City to establish the *census* (name and property for all, list of senators, qualification for equestrian status), lists of names for military conscription, the regulation of morals, and certain financial duties (public buildings and infrastructure). Its location was ancient and even had royal associations; it was close to the Ovile or Sheep Pen, a palisaded area in which the tribal voting units could be marshaled on voting days.[115] It is to the Villa Publica that the dialogue's interlocutors go to have their discussion, to avoid the sun's heat on voting day (in July) and the bustle of the voting precinct.[116]

The gentlemen discussing *pastio villatica* of Book 3 are waiting for the results of the elections: they have gathered to support a specific candidate.[117] Certain aediles (*aediles plebis*) were in charge of the upkeep and worship of this temple (*aedes*) of Ceres and her children Liber Pater and Libera on the Aventine Hill in Rome.[118] All three divinities were important guarantors of grain and grapes, and thus bread and wine, as well as the fertility of the earth in general; Liber and Libera were also guarantors of the civil rights of plebeians. Varro's point is that sound agricultural practice, social peace, and good politics are intimately connected for the moral fabric of the *villa perfecta* and the state.

All the gentlemen in the dialogue seem to have voted, so all are Roman citizens, and all have villas, thus dividing their time between the City and their country estates. In addition, *pastio villatica* often required special costly installations, so all are wealthy: Varro wants to present a typical range of rich owners of villas who would be his readers. Some have built their villas themselves (Quintus Axius at Reate), others inherited them; another (Lucius Abbucius, not present) wanted to buy a seaside villa to raise fish for big money.[119] Varro himself built a villa near Casinum with a *musaeum* and an aviary-*triclinium*; he describes the aviary-*triclinium* in detail, comparing it favorably to the mistakes Lucullus made in his aviary-*triclinium* at his Tusculan villa. The very wealthy built game parks on their estates.[120]

Preface

Varro, Rust. 3.1.1–5 While there are two ways in which human beings traditionally live, in the countryside or in the city [*rustica et urbana*], there is no doubt, Pinnius, that they are different not only as to their location but also as to the time in which they had their origin [*origo*].[121] Living in the countryside is older by far—that is to say, at the time that men worked the land and did not have cities.

In fact, by tradition the oldest city is Thebes in Boeotia, founded by King Ogyges.[122] In the Roman area, the oldest is Rome, founded by King Romulus. On this topic, it can finally be said [no better] than what Ennius wrote: "Seven hundred years, more or less / Since illustrious Rome was founded by august augury."

Thebes, which, as is said, was founded before the flood called Ogygian, is thus about 2,100 years old. If you juxtapose this time span to the first time that fields were cultivated and men [still] lived in huts [*casae*] and cabins [*tuguria*] and knew nothing of a wall [*murus*] or a gate [*porta*], farmers [*agricolae*] preceded city dwellers [*urbani*] by very many years.

This is not astonishing: divine nature [*divina natura*] gave the countryside, [but] human artifice [*ars humana*] built cities, and because all the arts are said to have been developed in Greece within [the last] 1,000 years, there were never fields on earth that would not have been cultivated. Not only is agriculture more ancient—it is actually better [*antiquior sed etiam melior*]. Therefore it was not without [good] cause that they called the earth "Mother" and "Ceres," and considered that those who tilled it had a pious and useful life [*pia et utilis vita*] and were alone the descendants of the race of King Saturnus.[123] In view of this, the rites of Ceres are called "initiations" [*initia*] above all others.[124] [...]

Varro, *Rust*. 3.3.7–10 Because of their poverty, men mostly practiced agriculture without differentiation: those descended from shepherds grew [crops] and pastured [their flocks] on the same land. Later, as the flocks grew, they divided, some called farmers [*agricolae*], others shepherds [*pastores*].

Herding is a two-fold topic, though the difference has not been effectively made by anyone: there is *pastio villatica*, and there is herding on the [estate's] land. The latter is called *pecuaria* and is a well known and noble endeavor, and rich men have ranches [*saltus*] for this, either rented or purchased. *Pastio villatica*, by contrast, is considered of less importance and has been treated by some [authors] under the rubric of agriculture, even though it is [properly] about feeding, but no one has discussed the matter in its discrete parts, as far as I am aware.

For that reason, and because there are three sectors of rural activity that are the basis of profitable outcomes, I have written three books: the first on agriculture, the second on animal husbandry, and the third on *pastio villatica*. The first book was for my wife Fundania, on agriculture; the second, on animal husbandry, for Turranius Niger. This last book is on profits [*fructus*] from animal husbandry at the villa, and I send it to you [Pinnius] because we are neighbors and have a mutual affection, so it is written for you.

Inasmuch as you [Pinnius] had a villa with stuccoed walls [*opera tectoria*], marquetry [*opera intestina*], and notable mosaic floors [*pavimenta nobilia lithostrota*], but still it seemed to you not equal to them unless [the villa's] walls were decorated with your writings, so, in order that your villa be better decorated with produce [*fructus*, or profit or revenue], to the extent that I can, I am sending you a memoir of discussions we had on the subject of the perfect villa [*villa perfecta*]. On this topic, I will begin as follows:

The Perfect Villa

Varro directly proceeds to recount, to Pinnius, the circumstances and the details of his discussions with his fellows on the *villa perfecta*.

Varro, *Rust*. 3.2.1–11 Having cast our ballots in the elections for the aediles, Quintus Axius—a senator and fellow tribe member—and I wished to be nearby to accompany the candidate we had supported when he returned home, even though it was a warm day to be in the sun. Axius said to me, "While the ballot count is going on, wouldn't you prefer to have the shade of the Villa Publica rather than here?" [...]

I [Varro] replied, "For sure, I am not the only one who has repeated what they say: 'bad advice is the worst for the advisor,' and also that 'good advice should be taken as good for both the advisor and those whom he advises.'"

So we got up and went to the Villa Publica, where we found the augur Appius Claudius sitting on a bench so that he could be easily consulted [on matters of religious protocol] if need be. On his left sat Cornelius Merula of a consular family, and Fircellius Pavo of Reate; to his right sat Minucius Pica and Marcus Petronius Passer.

When we came near him, Axius asked Appius, "Will you receive us into your aviary where you are seated among birds?"

To which Appius replied, "You above all [are welcome], especially for the birds [of that meal] that you placed before me a few days back—I am still belching from them—at your Reatine villa on my way to Lake Velinus about the dispute [I adjudicated] between the citizens of Interamna and those of Reate."[125]

He [Appius] then asked [Axius], "Surely this villa [the Villa Publica] that our ancestors built is simpler and better than that fancy villa [*villa perpolita*] you built near Reate. Do you see any citrus wood or gold here? Or vermilion or blue paint, or *emblema* [colored mosaic?], or floors in mosaic work [*lithostrotum*]? Here, it is just the opposite. In addition, this villa is the property of the whole people, whereas yours just belongs to you. This one is for citizens and others to come to from the Campus [Martius], while yours is for mares and donkeys.[126] This villa is used for administering public business—it is where the [military] cohorts gather when they are called for conscription, for the parade of arms, and for the censors to gather the people for the census."

Axius replied, "Surely you do not mean [to claim] that [your] villa here by the side of the Campus Martius is exclusively useful [like the Villa Publica], when it is more sumptuous in luxuries than any villa owned by all the villa owners of Reate put together. Your villa [next to the Campus Martius] is crammed with paintings, not to mention statues, whereas mine [at Reate] has nothing by [the Greek sculptor] Lysippus or [the Greek painter] Antiphilus; rather, it's mostly about the [agricultural] worker and the shepherd [*sartor et pastor*]. In addition, while [my] villa is not without its large estate made tidy by tillage, yours has never had a field, an ox, or a mare on it."

[Axius continuing] "Anyway, what does your villa have in common with the villa that your grandfather and great-grandfather owned? Unlike their villas, your villa has not seen a dried hay harvest in its loft [*faenisicia arida in tabulato*], a wine harvest in its cellar [*vendemia in cella*], or a grain harvest in its warehouse [*messis in granario*]. Just because a building is outside the City does not on that account make it a villa, not any more than those just barely outside the City—those outside the Porta Flumentana or in the Aemiliana [a near suburb].'"[127]

Smiling, Appius replied, "As I do not know what a villa is, I wish you to teach me so I will not forge ahead thoughtlessly: I wish to purchase a villa in the Ostia region from Marcus Seius. If buildings are not villas unless they have that donkey you showed me that you bought for 40,000*HS*, I fear that I will buy a "Seian" villa rather than one by the sea.[128] Lucius (Cornelius) Merula, my friend, urged me to acquire this villa because, after spending several days there with him [Seius], he had never seen a villa that was more delightful, even though he had seen neither any pictures nor statues in bronze and marble, but then again, [he saw] no wine presses, oil storage jars, or olive pressing mills."

Axius turned to [L. Cornelius] Merula and said, "How can that be a villa if it has neither citified decorations [*urbana ornamenta*] nor the essential elements of the countryside [*rustica membra*]?"

Merula replied, "Is your villa at the bend of the river Velinus [near Reate], which has never seen a painter [*pictor*] or a stucco worker [*tector*], less of a villa than [your] elegant villa in the Rosia district that you and that donkey of yours own together and which is decorated with elegant stucco work [*opus tectorium*]?"

With a nod, Axius agreed that a villa that is used solely for rustic purposes is as much a villa as one that was used both for agricultural purposes and as a *villa urbana*. [...] Then he asked what conclusion he [Merula] drew in the matter. Merula answered, "Why do you ask? If your estate in the Rosia district is commendable for its pasturage and because it feeds and shelters herds, and is thereby correctly called a villa, so for the same reason [the term villa] can be applied to the large profit that can be derived from *pastiones* [*villaticae*]. If you get profit from herds, what difference is there between [a herd] of sheep or a flock of birds?" [...]

Varro, *Rust.* 3.2.13–18. [Appius speaking] "Merula did not claim that you could not have *pastiones* [*villaticae*] like Seius—it's just that I have not seen any myself. There are two kinds of pasturing, one in the fields, the other at the villa [*pastiones villaticae*]. The latter includes chickens, doves, bees, and suchlike, which are usually fed at the villa: Mago the Carthaginian and Cassius Dionysius [of Utica] and others have treated these topics in their books, but separately and in a scattered way. Seius has read these books and in consequence gets more profit from such *pastiones* than others get from an entire estate."

"You are right," Merula said, "for I have seen large flocks of geese, chickens, doves, cranes, and peafowl there, not counting also dormice, fish, boars, and other game. A freedman who served as Varro's accounts secretary and hosted me when his patron was away, told me that the villa made as much as 50,000*HS* a year!"

Axius was amazed, [so] I [Varro] said, "Surely you know my maternal aunt's estate in Sabine country—the one at the 24th milestone from Rome on the Via Salaria?"

"Of course [I know it]," said Axius, "that is where, in summertime at around noon, I usually stop on the trip from Rome to Reate, and where I camp out in winter on the way back [from Reate to Rome]."

So I [Varro] said, "I know for sure that at that villa there is an aviary, and that 5000 thrush [probably fieldfares, *Turdus pilaris*] from there sold at 3 *denarii* apiece, to the tune of 60,000*HS* from just that part of the villa, twice as much as your whole year's profit from your 200-*iugera* estate at Reate [about 50 ha, or 124 acres]!"

"What?" exclaimed Axius, "Sixty [thousand]? Sixty? You're joking!"

"Sixty," I [Varro] said. "But to make such a sum, you will need either a public banquet or a triumph like the one Metellus Scipio celebrated at that time, or else the dinners of men's clubs [*collegia*] that are making the price of food go so high.[129] In other years, if you cannot foresee a comparable income, I hope that your aviary will not fail you, but the way social customs [*mores*] are now, it will be most unusual for you to miss your mark. What year is it that you don't see a public banquet or a triumph, or a year in which members of men's clubs do not dine?"

Axius spoke, "About luxury: just now, public banquets are held daily within the gates of Rome!"

[Merula resumes] "Did not Lucius Abuccius—who, as you know, was a most learned man and wrote books in the manner of Lucilius—say that the profits of his estate [*fundus*] at Alba [near Rome] were less than the profit from his villa? His estate [*ager*] brought in less than 10,000*HS*, but his villa brought in 20,000*HS*. He also said that a seaside villa, if he had the one he wanted, would bring in more than 100,000*HS*! Look, didn't Marcus Cato, when he recently became the guardian of Lucullus, sell the fish in the fishponds for 40,000*HS*?"[130]

Axius replied, "My dear Merula, please take me as your student in matters of *pastio villatica*."

To which Merula responded, "I will do so when you promise me a small tuition payment [*minerval*]."

Axius said, "I won't refuse to pay, and I'll do so today or just after the [profit from] the *pastio* comes in."

Appius interjected, "I think you'll pay only after geese or peacocks in your flock die!"

Axius said, "What difference would it make if you ate fowl or fish that died a natural death, since you never eat them unless they are dead anyway? But, please, point me to the path of the science [*disciplina*] of *pastio villatica* and tell me about its potential [*vis*] and method [*forma*]."[131] [...]

Bees

Very good money could be made from beekeeping, the subject of detailed presentation in *Rust.* 3.16.10–38.[132] Honey, virtually the only source of sweetness in all of antiquity besides a few fruit species, was especially profitable, as a story told by Varro confirms.

Varro, *Rust*. 3.16.10–11   Merula [said], "About profit, I can say something that may satisfy you, Axius, and I can cite not only Seius, who has given out at option 5,000 *librae* of honey [about 1645 kg, or 3,625 lb.] from his apiaries, but also our friend Varro here. He told me that he had two soldiers under his command in Spain, brothers both named Veianius, from near Falerii. They were rich because, even though their father had left them a small villa and a bit of land not larger than a *iugerum* [about .25 ha, or ⅔ acre], they built an apiary all around the villa and had a garden as well. The rest of the land was planted with thyme, alfalfa, and balm. [...] The brothers usually, one way or another, never profited less than 10,000*HS* from the honey; they said that they preferred to wait for a buyer [to come to them] rather than to sell quickly to another person [whom they did not know]." [...]

Varro, *Rust*. 3.16.23   [Merula speaking] "The substance called *propolis* is what [the bees] make, mainly in summer, to make a cover over the entrance to the hive. This same substance is used [under the same name] by doctors to make [medicated] bandages, so it is even more expensive in the Via Sacra market than honey."

Fishponds

In Varro's continued recounting of the dialogue on villas, the discussion about agriculture starts breaking up because the voting is over and the candidates for the aedileship are coming out; as one of them appropriately says, the gentlemen are about to weigh anchor (*ancoras tollere, Rust.* 3.17.1). One more topic completes the account of *pastio villatica*.

Varro, *Rust*. 3.17.1–9   [...] [Axius speaking] "To finish up on this topic, it can be said that there are two kinds of fishponds [*piscinae*], freshwater and saltwater, the first available to ordinary people [*plebs*] and not without profit: in them, the Nymphs take care of the water for ordinary [domestic] fish. The other are those saltwater fishponds belonging to the nobility [*illae maritimae piscinae nobilium*] for which Neptune supplies both water and fish—these appeal to the eyes rather than to the wallet and empty their owner's purse rather than filling it. First of all, these [saltwater] fishponds are built at great expense, secondly, they are filled [with fish] at great expense, and thirdly, they are kept going at great expense. Hirrius brought in a revenue of 12,000*HS* from the buildings near his fishponds; however, all the money that came in was spent on food needed for the fish.[133] It's no wonder: at one time I recall that he loaned Caesar two thousand lampreys by weight, and also that his villa sold for 4,000,000*HS* on account of its huge number of fish.[134]

"Our pond in the countryside [*piscina mediterranea*]—which is available to the ordinary people—is rightly called 'sweet' [*dulcis*] while the other [saltwater] one is 'bitter'[*amara*]. Who among us is not satisfied with just one such [freshwater] pond? In contrast, who among those who have one saltwater fishpond does not [eventually] have many connected ones?

"Just as [the painter] Pausias and other painters of his day had large compartmented boxes to separate their painting waxes of different colors, so these owners have fishponds with compartments to separate the fish.[135] [...]

"Our friend Quintus Hortensius [Hortalus] had fishponds built at great cost of money near Bauli, but when I was at his villa, I know for a fact that he would send to Puteoli to buy fish for dinner. Having his fish fed in his fishponds was not enough for him: he had to do it himself. He took greater care that his mullets not be hungry than I worry about keeping my donkeys in victuals. With [the help of] only a young boy-slave, I keep my valuable donkeys going with a bit of barley and water from my own estate. By contrast, Hortensius kept many fishermen who also fished for little fish to feed the bigger ones. [...] Besides which, he was just as worried about a sick fish as he was about the health of a slave—he was less concerned than that a sick slave should not have imbibed overly cold water than what kind of water his fish had recently drunk. [...] He said that Marcus Lucullus was careless on the topic and that he disapproved of Lucullus's ponds because there were no special tidal basins, with the result that his fish lived in foul conditions as the water became brackish.[136] By contrast, when Lucius Lucullus cut through a mountain near Naples to let a stream of [sea-]water into his fishponds so there was a tidal flow, he yielded nothing to Neptune himself [on the expertise] of fishing. The fact is, he seemed to lead the fish himself to cool places, as if they were his own friends, just as Apulian herdsmen lead their herds along the tracks to the [higher] hills of Sabine country in hot weather. When he [Marcus Lucullus] was building near Baiae, he was so worried that he let his architect do as he wished [as if the money was his own], just so he could have an underground channel linking his fishponds to the sea with a dyke, to cool the ponds with the tide twice daily from the rising of one moon to the next."[137]

The Conclusion to Varro's *De re rustica*: Order Restored

Varro's Book 3 ends happily; Book 1 had ended in tragic violence. The arc of Varro's intentions are clear: in Book 1, attendance at a religious ceremony (the Sementivae festival) involving agricultural planting ended in a mysterious murder in broad daylight. At the conclusion of the treatise in Book 3, the gentlemen greet their candidate who has been successfully elected. He comes toward them newly clothed: before, as a candidate, he would have worn the freshly laundered toga dazzlingly whitened with chalk (*toga candida*), but now he wears the decorated toga appropriate to his new status.[138]

    The lesson is clear: what begins in civil violence and desecration ends in orderly civil process. Reasoned agricultural methods and moral balance support the emergence of social peace and civility. Varro's agricultural treatise of ca. 37–36 BCE was written in the years of political unrest and civil war that had already lasted about a century and were to continue until the Augustan settlement of 29 BCE. The author urges peace and security through a return to sound farming practices, wholesome country living in villas, and good morals.

Varro, *Rust*. 3.17.10   So there we were. Then there was a commotion to our right, and our candidate came forward into the Villa Publica wearing [a toga with] the broad [purple] stripe as aedile designate [*designatus aedilis*].[139] We meet and congratulate him and follow him to the Capitoline. From there, he went to his own home and we to ours, after having had the discussion on *pastio villatica*, dear Pinnius, of which this treatise has been an account.

COLUMELLA   (Lucius Junius Moderatus Columella, ca. 4–70 CE)

On Farming Matters (*De re rustica*) 60s CE (Columella, *Rust*.)

Columella's treatise is dedicated as a long letter to one Publius Silvinius (otherwise unknown). Columella's stance in regard to villas and estates is conservative, following the tradition of Cato and Varro and emphasizing a return to the practices of the Roman ancestors (*maiores*) by advocating a hands-on approach by owners of agricultural properties and villas.[140] While he claimed to disdain enslavement-based agriculture, by his day in the Italian peninsula there were few, if any, alternatives for owners of villas of any size and standing, so his prescriptions about enslaved workers and their treatment are detailed. Most of the treatise deals with technical matters of agriculture in ordered categories (viticulture, soils, grain, and so on) and with tips for central Italy, though his knowledge of Mediterranean-wide agriculture is also apparent. What he says about villas, their construction and orientation, and their personnel—both enslaved and free—are found in Books 1 and 12. The Preface to Book 1 outlines the author's theories, anthropological history, and social ideas about agriculture and rural life.

Columella, *Rust*. 1. Preface 1–6   I hear, repeatedly, our most distinguished men [*principes*] decrying the sterility of our fields, then again the recent bad weather as bad for growing crops. Some of them, I hear, even combine these claims, as if by well-reasoned arguments, saying that the overworking of the land in the past has depleted it, and it cannot supply human beings the food that it used to in its previous abundance.

Such reasonings, Publius Silvinius, I consider quite far from the truth: it is wrong to think that nature, whose everlasting fertility as has been destined to her by the creator of the world [*genitor mundi*], would be affected by sterility as if it were an illness. It is also incorrect for a thoughtful man [*prudens*] to believe that Earth [*Tellus*], who was allotted a divine and eternally youthful destiny, and who is called the progenitor of all things because she has always and forever brought all things into being—[it is incorrect for a thoughtful man] to think that Earth ages as we humans do.

On this topic, I reckon that disasters do not come to us from violent weather but are, instead, our own fault: agriculture, which we have given over to the worst of our slaves as if we were giving it to an executioner—agriculture, which the best of our ancestors [*maiores*] practiced in the best way.

I cannot wonder enough why those wishing to become public speakers are so choosy about the orator whom they wish to imitate; or those who study the art of measuring and calculation follow the precepts of a master of the discipline; or those who study singing and dancing are most eager to search out experts in movement and music; or those who wish to build call in [skilled] artisans and architects; or those who commit boats to the sea look for expert pilots; or those who plan to go to war call for men knowledgeable in weapons and military matters. Omitting to mention each and every discipline, the man who wishes to know about any given topic brings in the most experienced teacher. From the assembly of teachers, he then calls upon the one who can teach him [best] in the way of virtue and discernment.

But it is only agriculture that is lacking, as much in those who wish to learn as in those who can teach—agriculture [*res rustica*], which without any doubt is the closest to Wisdom [*sapientia*] itself and even is Wisdom's very own sister.

As I have said, there are now schools for rhetoricians, geometricians, and musicians, and even more astounding, centers for the most contemptible vices, which I have not just heard about but actually seen for myself—centers for the spicing of food and the selection of courses in a dinner, for masters in makeup and hairdressing. But for agricultural matters [*agriculatio*], there are neither professed teachers nor learners. Even if the State [*civitas*] lacked teachers of those arts [rhetoric, hairdressing], the Republic [*res publica*] was still able to flourish in its early days, even without professional entertainment; and even without lawyers, cities [*urbes*] went along happily enough and will do so again. But without those who cultivate the fields, it is clear that human beings can neither eat nor live.[141] [...]

Ignorance and Knowledge

Columella, having addressed his treatise to Publius Silvinius, then identifies who its reader might be: a man of good (free) birth and generous disposition (*unus genus liberale et ingenuus*). Such a man, not identified as an *agricola* (farmer, as in Cato), as *pater familias*, or only as an owner (*dominus*, as in Varro), is unique: a man who wishes to add to his household wealth through agriculture, implying that he has existing means (from other occupations or inheritance) but also promoting agriculture (rather than trade or career-advancing military or civilian appointments) as a viable alternative.

In contrast to both Cato and Varro, who assumed that the actual work of the farm and its supervision (by an enslaved *vilicus*) will be effected by enslaved personnel, Columella inveighs against the extensive use of servile labor in farming, but he adopts many of his predecessors' practices with enslaved personnel anyway. Still, there is in Columella a "back-to-the-land" attitude and even a certain pride in local good practices that dominate his treatise.

Columella, *Rust.* 1. Preface 10–15 [...] If [all] good men, as they must, avoid the bad practices that I have already mentioned, a man of good [free] birth and generous disposition [*unus genus liberale et ingenuus*] who wishes to increase his household's wealth can find it in agriculture. Even if the principles [of agriculture] were used by [ignorant] amateurs, as long as they were the owners of the properties and applied the ancient methods, agriculture would suffer less, because at least the zeal of owners [in applying the ancient methods] would greatly offset the mistakes made from [their] ignorance. Men who are governed by self-interest will not wish to be seen to be wrong-headed in business, so for that reason they will be ever more eager to learn about agriculture.

Nowadays, we disdain to cultivate our own estates ourselves. Instead, we never hesitate for a moment to call in an expert *vilicus* or, if we call in an inexperienced man, at least we call in one who is energetic and alert and can quickly make up for what he does not know. [It is bad] if a wealthy man [*locuples*] buys an estate and then chooses a man compromised by age and strength from the crowd of lackeys and litter bearers [that surrounds him]. [Agricultural] work requires not only knowledge but also a vigorous stage of life, and bodily strength to endure. [It is bad] if an owner of middling wealth [*dominus mediarum facultatum*] chooses as an overseer [*magister*] someone who has refused to pay him the rent he owes and is a liability, even as he is [also] ignorant of the work he is to be in charge of.[142]

Becoming aware of these things, and going over in my mind and thinking of the degree to which knowledge of agriculture, by evil [but universal] consent has been abandoned and disused, I am afraid that it may seem shameful [*flagitiosa*] and even dishonorable [*inhonesta*] to a well-born man [*ingenuus*]. In fact, I am reminded by the accounts of many writers that, for our ancestors, it was glorious activity [*cura gloriae*] to engage in farming: from [a life of] farming came Quinctius Cincinnatus, called from the plough to be dictator and the savior of a consul and his blockaded army, after which he laid down the *fasces* [symbols of his power] more quickly than he had taken them up when called to be *imperator* [general]. He returned to the same oxen and to his little ancestral inheritance of four *iugera* [about 1 ha, or 2½ acres].

From farming as well came C. Fabricius and Curius Dentatus—the former drove Pyrrhus from the land of Italy, the latter defeated the Sabines. Both men cultivated the seven-*iugera* [about 1.75 ha, or 4⅓ acres] portions allotted to each man from the conquered territories with an energy no less than that which they had exhibited in arms.

Not to run on about individual instances too long, when I consider that many distinguished leaders [*memorabiles duces*] of Roman stock [*Romanus genus*] prospered with the double devotion to either defending or caring for their ancestral estates [*patrii fines*] or ones they had bought, I realize that our luxury and pleasures are discordant with the habits and manly life of the past.

As Marcus [Terentius] Varro complained already in the time of our grandfathers, all of us—the *patres familiarum* [of our generation]—have put aside the sickle and the plough and slipped behind the walls [of towns], giving our hands [i.e., our attention] over to the circuses and the theaters instead of to the wheat fields and the vineyards.[143] We fix our attention on the dancing of effeminate men because, with female gestures, they falsely imitate a sex that nature denies them, and they deceive spectators' eyes. In addition, so that we can get ready for feasting, we daily sweat out our overstuffed guts in dry-heat rooms [*laconica* of baths] and develop thirst from such sweating. We seek nights of depravity and drunkenness, we spend days gambling or sleeping, and we think we are fortunate that "we see neither the sun rising nor setting."[144] [...]

Columella, *Rust*. 1. Preface 17–21   [...] The consequence of such a life is ill health: the bodies of young men are weak and feeble—death would not make much difference. By Hercules! Those true descendants of Romulus, well used to regular hunting and no less [to working in] the fields, were superior in the greatest strength of body and, when in war, were strong in the works of peaceful times. They always admired countryfolk much more than denizens of the city.

Because those who idled within the walls of their villas were considered more feckless than those who worked the soil outside, those who idly wasted time behind the walls of the city were considered lazier than those who tilled the earth or oversaw the work of field hands. Even the nine-day markets [*nundinae*] were used in this way, to be the day on which town business [*res urbana*] could be transacted, namely on the ninth day, and all the other days to attend to cultivation. As we've said before, in those days the important men of the State kept to [their] fields and, when [their] advice on public matters was needed, they were called to the Senate from [their] villas—[this is why] those called to the Senate in this way are known as "road men" [*viatores*].

As long as this custom was kept, the old Sabine *Quirites* and the Roman ancestors, despite their crops having been destroyed by the iron weapons and fire of enemies, brought to storage a much greater quantity [of produce] than we do—we, who in the present days of settled peace, should have enlarged [the scope of] agricultural activity.[145]

Even from this Latium and Saturnian district,[146] where the gods taught their offspring about the product of the fields, we bid at auction on getting grain from overseas provinces so as not to be hungry, and we bring in vintage wines [*vindemiae*] from the Cyclades and from the regions of Baetica and Gaul. No wonder, then, that farming is now seen as something that needs no set rules or principles, being that this is the common and established view: farming is a degrading occupation [*sordidum opus*].

As for me, when I look over the magnitude of the whole topic of agriculture, like the vastness of a body or the small elements of its individual parts, I fear that I will die before I can know everything about the entirety of farming practice [*universa disciplina ruris*]. [...]

Columella comes to the end of the preface to his agricultural treatise (*Rust*. 1. Preface 29–31) with a discussion of the "greater" and "lesser" arts in many fields of expertise, and he classes Roman achievements as subsequent to, but no less valid than, the monuments of Greek poetry, rhetorical culture, and art. At the same time, he says: "In trying for the top of the column (*summum columen*), it will be enough to have made it honorably to the second place (*secundum fastigium*)," meaning that if you can't make it onto the A-list, an honest spot on the B-list is just fine.[147]

Columella, *Rust*. 1. Preface 31–33   But in every branch of knowledge, the best [exponents] have received admiration and veneration, and those of lesser merit have [also] received praise.

To which can be added the person whom we wish to be a perfect farmer [*perfectus agricola*], no matter if he [as an individual] is not yet perfectly knowledgeable in the arts of farming, or if he may not have [yet] arrived at the wisdom of a Democritus or a Pythagoras in the nature of universal things, nor again in predicting, like Meton and Eudoxus, how the stars and winds move, nor again the knowledge that Chiron and Melampus had in taking care of cattle, and besides the prudent counsel of a Triptolemus and Aristaeus for cultivation of fields and soil.[148] Still, if he follows the precepts of our own Cn. Tremelius (Scrofa), the Sasernas, and our Stolones, he will equal them.[149]

As is often said, agriculture can be undertaken without much detailed knowledge, but not with a fat-headed view [*Minerva pingua*] of it.[150] Many believe—even though it is far from the case—that agriculture is an easy business and needs no special acumen. On these subjects there is no need for further discussion, because its different rubrics will be dealt with in an orderly way, with a preface [to each topic] that I consider to be pertinent to the general knowledge [of agriculture].[151]

Location of the Villa

Following the preface, Columella's Book 1 starts with some sharply delivered advice to the *dominus* before going on to the best sites, varieties of land, and orientations of the villa.

Columella, *Rust.* **1.1.18–19**   As I have said, even with these safeguards [experience and learning from mistakes], and even with the zealous work and experience of a *vilicus*, and even with money and a willingness to spend it, nothing is worth more than the presence of the owner [*praesentia domini*], for without his frequent presence, no work will get done—the same as with an army when the commander is away.[152] And it is my opinion that Mago the Carthaginian was addressing this issue specifically at the beginning of his treatise with these opinions:

> "He who buys an estate should sell his house in town, so he will prefer to worship the country *lares* over those of the *lares* of the city."[153]

If this precept could be maintained nowadays, I would not change it. Now, because ambition in political affairs [*ambitio civilis*] often calls us and, once called, even more often keeps us away [from our villas], I think that it follows that the most convenient estate will be near a city so that a daily visit is possible for the busy owner after business in the forum is concluded. Men who buy distant estates, not to mention estates overseas, are giving their patrimony to their slaves as if deeding an inheritance to them and, even worse, doing so while they themselves are still alive: for slaves are certainly corrupted with the owners' great distance, and, once corrupted, they become more interested in criminal activity than in cultivation, because they anticipate that other slaves will replace them in view of their depredations.

Columella, *Rust.* **1.2.1–5**   Therefore, my opinion is that land to be bought should be nearby [near the city] so that the owner can frequently go there and declare that his visits will be more frequent than they really will be. The *vilicus* and the slaves will be more up to the mark with this [anticipatory] fear in mind. But whenever the occasion arises, the owner should stay in the country, but not to be idle or [to relax] in the shade. The diligent *pater familias* should go over the estate minutely in all its parts, and do so frequently throughout the year, so that he may come to know intelligently the nature of the soil, be it in foliage, grass, or in crop production, that he be aware of what can best be done with it. Cato's old dictum is that an estate is most badly treated when the owner himself does not issue the instructions as to what is to be done, but instead listens to his *vilicus*. For that reason, the main worry for someone who has inherited an estate from his ancestors or one who is about to buy one is to know which district is the best, so that he can dispose of a bad one or buy a good one.

If Fortune grants [our] prayers, we will have an estate in a healthful climate, with rich soil, partly level fields, partly with hills on gentle slopes facing east or south. Some parts of the estate under cultivation, other parts wooded and left rough, not far from either the coast or a navigable river to transport produce [off the estate] and to bring in goods bought elsewhere.

The level area should be allocated to meadowland, cropland, willow plantation, and reed beds: these should be near the dwelling. Some hills for planting grain should not have trees on them, even though grain crops do better on slightly dry fields and rich flat land than on steep slopes—for that reason, even the higher grain fields should have some flat areas or a gentle slope to be like level fields. Some hills can be for olives and vines, with material for stakes to hold them [the vines]. If building is needed, some hills should have timber [*materia*] and stone [*lapis*] as well as grazing land for the herds. The hills should have streams flowing into the meadows, gardens, and willow plantations, and running water for the villa. Herds of cattle and other quadruped animals should not be lacking cultivated land and scrub pastures for grazing. However, all that we want in the way of a location is hard to find, and, because [such a location] is rare, it is only available to a few. The next best is a location that has most of these features, and the one that lacks the fewest [of these features] is tolerable.

Size of the Estate

Columella's comments on the best size for an estate, *Rust.* 1.3.8–13 and 1.4.1–4, are omitted here. He repeats the conservative views of Cato, that excessive size of villas and estates has led to modern moral depravity and an abandonment of traditional virtues, referring to early Roman history in which famous ancestors of the Roman state, holding to ancient restraint, tilled small farms. The philosophy of agriculture is the same as that for all endeavors: good limits (*modus*) and good proportion (*mensura*). He cites one of the Seven Sages of Greece, Bias of Priene, at the head of a long list of other Greek and Latin writers on agriculture; his theory of agriculture is less detailed than Varro's, but it melds Greek moral philosophy with Roman history that states, in simple terms, the idea of ancient morality, country life, and villas. He includes an apt quotation from Vergil, to discern both winds and the habits of the climate (*caeli mores*), to apply ancestral methods (*patrius cultus*), and to watch for what the locations (*habitus locorum*) can or cannot produce (Verg., *Geor.* 1.51–53).

The Buildings of the Villa

Columella, *Rust.* 1.4.5–10   [...] How the villa is to be constructed and usefully arranged is comparable to the nature of the estate and the way it should be cultivated. As memory serves [to remind us], mistakes can be made: very great men such as Lucius [Licinius] Lucullus and Quintus [Mucius] Scaevola [Pontifex] made such mistakes—the former by building too much, the latter by building not enough to accommodate the size of his estate.[154] Both [sorts of] mistakes result in working against the interests of their households. The bigger we build in the way of a complex, the more we are liable to to greater expenses; but when the buildings are smaller than the estate requires, the produce suffers. What the earth produces in the way of moist and dry crops are easily spoiled if they are stored in buildings too small and not suited to them.

In addition, the *pater familias* must live [in a house] as suited to his wealth as possible so that he may come to the countryside with pleasure and find a greater delight in being there. Of course, if the *matrona* will be in attendance with him, the spirit of her sex being more fastidious [*sexus animus delicatior*], she must be coddled with some comfort [*amoenitas*] so that she stays more willingly with her husband [at the villa]. Thus, the "farmer" [*agricola*] should build [his villa] with elegance without becoming a "builder" [*aedificator*] as such, and he should not acquire too large a property, for Cato says, "The villa may not seek its estate, nor the estate its villa."[155]

For what the site [of the villa] in general should be, I shall explain [as follows]:

As a building to be built should be located in a healthy region, so also it should be built in the healthiest part of that region. For bad air prevailing in the surroundings will be the cause of noxious bodily conditions. Certain places are not too hot in the summertime but unbearably cold in winter, such as Thebes in Boeotia; there are others that are temperate in winter but swelter in a ferocious summer heat, as Chalchis in Euboea is said to be.

A site where the air is a temperate mean between hot and cold should be looked for—this can be found halfway up a hillside where, because it is not in a low-lying place, [the villa] will not be affected by frosts in winter or baked with humid heat in summer, and, not being set up at the top of a mountain, will not be affected all the time by the passing winds or rains. The best position is therefore halfway up a hillside, but on a little rising ground so that the [villa's] foundations will not be undermined when flooded by downpours of rain coming from the hilltop.

Columella, *Rust.* 1.5.1–10 In addition, there should be a spring with a perennial flow, either inside the villa or brought in from outside; there should also be a woodlot [*lignatio*] and a pasture [*pabulum*] nearby. If running water is not available, a well should be searched for in the neighborhood, not one that is too deep for hoisting the water, and the water should not be bitter or salty. If this doesn't work and there is little hope for a source of water, capacious cisterns for people and vats for cattle must be built: rainwater is still healthy for the body and is the best, even the very best, if it is brought into a covered cistern in clay pipes. Next [in goodness] is running water coming from a source in the mountains and flowing freely over rocks, as on the Gauran mountain in Campania. The third [kind of water] is water from a well on a hillside or a valley, but not its low-lying part. The worst is water in swamps that runs sluggishly, and water that stagnates in swamps is deadly. But this water, though noxious by nature, can become drinkable with winter rains: from this process, water from the sky is understood to be most healthful because it cleans even poisonous water. Still, running streams mitigate the heat of summer and add attraction to many places. If the set-up of the site allows, I think that running streams should be piped into the villa, as long as the water is potable. However, if the stream is far from the hills and if the healthy nature of the place and the stream's higher banks allow the villa to be built above the flow, the stream should be at the back of the building rather than at its front. Also, the front of the building should be placed away from the locale's prevailing bad winds and toward its good ones. Many streams are covered with hot mists in summer, cold mists in winter, and unless they are blown away with the greater force of winds, they can be harmful to herds and people.

As I have said, the villa should face eastward or southward when the site is healthful, but it should face northward in an unhealthy location. A villa directly overlooking the sea is always in a good spot, buffeted and sprayed by the waves, but it should never be at water's edge: rather, it should be removed at some distance from the shore. It is better to set [the villa] farther back from the sea than nearer, because there is heavy vapor in between.

There should be no swamp near the villa and no nearby military road. The former generates a bad smell in hot weather and brings out dense swarms of insects with sharp stings to attack us; the swamp also sends out swimming and crawling creatures that, lacking the winter's damp, are often poisoned with mud and rotting filth from which obscure diseases can be contracted, the causes of illness that even medical doctors cannot understand. The damp damages farming tools and equipment and spoils produce both kept in the open or in storage.

In addition, being near a road is bad for the household because of the [casual] travelers [*populatio viatorum*] and those turning into the villa and insisting on its hospitality [*hospitium*].[156] For these reasons, and to avoid inconvenience, I recommend that the villa should not be next to a road but not too far from one, set on a slightly higher ground, and built so its facade is on axis of the rising sun at the equinox. In such a location, the villa occupies a middle postion between winter and summer winds, and the more to the east the site slopes, the better the villa will catch breezes in summer and the less it will be affected by winter storms, and it has the rising sun early in the morning to melt the frosts. It is almost deadly to be cut off and badly set in relation to the sun and gentle sun-warmed breezes: if the villa lacks these things, no other force can dry up or cleanse the night-born hoarfrost and whatever blight or dirt has taken over. These are noxious to men as well as to cattle, crops, and fruit.

But if one wishes to build on a slope, the work should always be started in the lower part [of the site], because when the foundations begin lower down, not only will they easily support the structures but they will also be the supports and substructure consolidating the upper part; because, if it prove convenient to enlarge the villa [later on], they will be supporting the upper part, the earlier structure acting as a strong base for the subsequent additions.

If the upper part of the villa's foundations bear the weight [of its own structure], whatever you might add below will soon have cracks and fissures. For when new building is added to old, as if unwilling to take the growing weight and yielding to the older structure pressing upon it, it falls over. Such a defect of design is to be avoided at the outset of laying down the foundations of the villa.[157]

Columella, *Rust*. 1.6.1–2. The extent [of the villa] and the number of its parts must be thought of in terms of its entire enclosure, and it should be divided into three parts: the [*pars*] *urbana*, the [*pars*] *rustica*, and the [*pars*] *fructuaria*. The *pars urbana* should be divided into winter and summer quarters; the winter bedrooms should face the [rising] sun at the winter solstice [northeast], and also the winter dining rooms [*cenationes*] face the equinoctal setting sun [west]. In turn, the summer bedrooms should face the sun at noon at the time of the equinox, but the dining rooms for the summer season should face the rising sun [east]. Bath buildings [*balnearia*] should face the direction of the summertime setting sun so that they have light from noon to dusk. The porticoes [*ambulationes*] should be open to the noonday sun at the equinox to get the greatest amount of sun in winter and the least in summer.

Tenants and Enslaved Personnel

The human interactions among the personnel of villas is a matter that Columella treats in some detail in *Rust*. 1.6 through 1.9. The following passages are selected to illustrate the villa's architectural arrangements for the enslaved personnel (including the use of bathing facilities). In addition, Columella gives recommendations about the demeanor of the *dominus* vis-à-vis the enslaved and freeborn personnel on the estate, along with some other advice.

Columella, *Rust*. 1.6.3 In the *villa rustica*, there should be a large high-roofed kitchen [*culina*] with beams to ensure against the danger of fire and to offer a useful place for the slaves to wait throughout the year. For the unfettered slaves [*servi soluti*], their rooms [*cellae*] should face the noonday sun at the equinox, but the chained slaves [*vincti*] should be in an underground prison [*ergastulum*], as healthful as possible, lit by narrow windows set so high from the floor that they cannot be reached by hand.[158] [...]

Columella, *Rust*. 1.6.7–8 [...] The dwelling for the *vilicus* should be placed near the entrance so he can monitor those who enter and exit (the villa), and the dwelling for the manager (*procurator*) over the entrance (to the villa) for the same purpose and so he can stay in contact with the *vilicus*; nearby there should be a storeroom where farm equipment can be stored, and inside it a lockup for the metal tools.

The rooms for the herdsmen and shepherds should be located near their animals so that they can take care of them if need be. All the slaves should be housed near one another so the *vilicus* in his duty does not have to walk to widely separated places, and so the slaves can observe who among them is diligent or negligent.[159]

Columella, *Rust.* 1.6.19–20 [...] The smoke-room [*fumarium*], in which recently cut timber is dried out quickly, can be built in the part of the villa near the baths for the countryfolk [*balnea rusticae*], for such baths are needed for the household slaves to bathe in, but only on holidays—frequent use of bathing facilities is detrimental to bodily vigor. [...]

Columella, *Rust.* 1.7.1–7 After all this has either been done or arranged, the urgent duty of the owner is required in other matters, but especially in the matter of the human personnel: these are either [free] tenants [*coloni*] or slaves, [the slaves being] either unchained or chained [*servi soluti aut vincti*]. He should be affable to his tenants and make himself available to them easily, and he should be more alert to their work [*opus*] than to their rents [*pensiones*], because this gives less offense [to the tenants] and also results in a more profitable outcome in general. For land that has been diligently cultivated frequently returns a profit, so the tenant does not ask for rent remission [*remissio*] unless the land has been subject to a weather disaster of unusual strength or pillaged by robbers.

The owner should not insist on every little matter to which he has bound the tenant, such as being exacting on the precise day he is to be paid or demanding firewood or other small extras. Taking care [of such demands] is a greater inconvenience than expense to the countryfolk. It is not reasonable for us to insist on all that is owed to us: it is a precept of our forefathers [*antiqui*] that extreme application of law is a torment. However, our demands are not to be entirely ignored, in that "good obligations which have not been enforced become bad debts," as Alfius the moneylender has truly said.[160] As I myself heard, Publius Volusius—an old man, a consul, and very rich—was heard to declare that the happiest estate was the one that had local tenants and maintained them as if they were born under a paternal authority from infancy and had long familiarity [with the owner]. Thus my opinion is that it is bad to often rent out an estate, and even worse if rented to a town-living tenant who prefers to have the estate worked by his slaves rather than cultivating it himself. Saserna said that a man of this kind got litigation instead of revenue, so it was better to give the work to [local] countryfolk who were zealous tenants, if it was not convenient for us to work the estate ourselves or with our own people. However, this does not [usually] happen except in districts that have bad weather and barren soil.

When even the climate is good enough and the goodness of the earth [on an estate] is adequate, no other means than one's own supervision [*sua cura*] will bring better profit than that of a tenant [*colonus*], and even than that of a *vilicus*, unless [leaving the estate to] a slave's negligence and rapacity intervenes. There is no doubt that both these offenses, either actually committed or allowed, are the fault of the owner: he has allowed the person to have charge of his business and could have removed him from the charge. However, on estates that are far away and not easy for the *pater familias* to travel to, it is reasonable for all properties to be placed in the care of free tenants [*liberi coloni*] rather than slave *vilici*, especially for a grain growing estate. On such an estate, unlike a vineyard or a tree-planted property, a tenant can do a minimum of harm, whereas slaves can do much harm: they rent out the oxen [to others] and pasture the other herd animals in a bad way, they do not work the soil properly and they claim more than the amount of seed than they have [actually] sown, and what they have sown they do not properly care to ensure its sprouting; then, when they bring the grain to the threshing floor [*area*], they diminish the threshed grain by fraud or negligent practices. They themselves steal it or do not watch out for the robbery of others, and, once [the grain is] stored, they do not account for it honestly. In this way, both the manager and the slaves have acted badly, and the estate often comes into bad repute. As I have already said, an estate of this nature should be leased [to a tenant] if the owner cannot be present himself.

The *vilicus* and *vilica*[161]

Columella, *Rust*. 1.8.1–14   Next, with regard to slaves: what duties should be assigned to which, and what kind of work to allot them. First off, I advise not to appoint a *vilicus* from the sort of slaves who are good-looking, and not from the sort who engage in citified and pleasurable occupations. The sort of lazy and half-asleep slaves, used to idleness, the Campus [i.e., Campus Martius in Rome], the circus, the theaters, to gambling with dice, to fast-food counters [*popinae*], and to brothels, never stop dreaming of such foolishness. When they transfer their dreams to cultivation, the owner [*dominus*] endures not just the loss of the slave himself as of the whole of his property. The person to be chosen is one who has been hardened by farmwork since childhood, one proven by experience. However, if such a person is not ready to hand, the one who should be given the post [of *vilicus*] should be one of those slaves who have endured hard servitude. He should be a man past his first youth but not so old as to have arrived at old age, so that his youth may not detract from the authority of his position, because older men disdain those who appear younger [than they], and one whose age has not succumbed to the hardest work. Therefore, he should be of middle age and strong of body, well versed in farming or at least conscientious enough to be quick to learn. In our [farming] business [*negotium*], it is no good to have one person give orders [for what work is to be done] and another to teach [how to do it]; nor can work be expected from someone who is being told by an unqualified person what needs doing and how to do it. Even an illiterate, as long as he has a very strong memory, can function well enough for the work. Cornelius Celsus says that such a *vilicus* often brings in more money for the owner than he would with an account book because, not knowing how to read and write, either he is less capable of falsifying the accounts [himself] or else, by falsifying them [by colluding] with others, he fears that the fraud would become known.

No matter who the *vilicus* might be, a woman must be assigned to be his mate [*contubernalis mulier adsignanda*] to keep him in control and even to help him in certain matters. The *vilicus* must be forewarned not to become a close friend with [another] domestic slave and certainly not [one who is] a stranger [to the household]. Still, on a holiday, he may summon one of the slaves to eat at his table, one who has shown continuous zeal and vigor in going about his tasks, to thereby recognize his commendable work.

Except by order of the owner, he [the *vilicus*] will offer no sacrifices. He will not admit soothsayers and sorceresses, the types of people who seduce those with stupid minds into profligacy and then into vice. He will have nothing to do with the city or the ninth-day markets [*nundinae*] unless it is to buy and sell things related to his work. As Cato says, a *vilicus* must not be a pleasure-seeker, and he should not go beyond the perimeter [of the estate] unless it is to learn something about cultivation, and only to a place nearby so he can return [promptly]. He must not allow new footpaths or shortcuts to be made, and he will receive no guest except one who is a friend or close family member of the owner.

In the same way that he must be kept away from these things, so must he be charged to take care of the equipment and metal hardware, and to keep twice as many of them in good repair and stored up as there are slaves, to avoid having to borrow them from a neighbor, because to lose [a day] of the slaves' work is more costly than the price of these items.

In the well-being [*cultus*] and clothing for the slaves, he must see to usefulness rather than looks, being especially concerned to shield them from wind, cold, and rain, all of which can be protected against by long-sleeved leather garments, garments made of patchwork, and capes with hoods [*sagi cuculli*]. Once this is done, no day is so intolerably bad that something cannot be done outside in the open.

He [the *vilicus*] should not only be an expert in agricultural work, but also have qualities of spirit, at least as far as his slavish nature [*ingenium servile*] allows, to give orders without weakness but also without cruelty, and also to encourage the better slaves, and even spare criticism of the lesser ones so they will fear his severity rather than hate his cruelty. He can effect this by preventing his subordinates from doing bad things, rather than, because of his own lack of foresight, having to punish the offenders himself. Even with the worst men, there is no better way of keeping them in line than by supervision of the work, that the tasks be correctly done, and that the *vilicus* always be there himself. In this way, the overseers [*magistri*] will be zealous in the execution of their obligations, and the others will give themselves over to rest and sleep after their tiring work rather than to pleasures.

[It would be good] if only these old rules, strong in moral force [*optimi moris*] and which these days have been set aside, could be maintained: that an overseer never employ anyone except in the affairs of his owner; that he never eat except in the sight of the household; that he never eat food different from that supplied to the others. By doing so, he will make sure that the bread is carefully made and that other food is healthfully prepared. He shall not allow anyone to go beyond the property's perimeter unless he has sent them himself or unless there is some great and immediate need. He shall not engage in self-dealing [*negotio suum*], and he will not spend the owner's money either for farm animals or other things offered for sale, because such dealings will call the *vilicus* away from his duty and not allow him to give a balance of accounts to his owner, or, when an accounting is demanded, he can show something [of value] rather than a sum of money.

In general, the most important thing that he should do is this: that he not imagine that he knows what he does not know, and that he ask to know what he is ignorant of [when he is].

While doing what needs doing skillfully is good, it is much worse to do things badly. There is one and only one principle in agriculture [*rusticatio*], which is always to do what is required, because when imprudence [*imprudentia*] and negligence [*neglegentia*] need fixing, the business itself has already suffered and cannot recoup the losses that a period [of imprudence and negligence] has brought on.

Duties of the *vilica*

Columella expanded on the duties of the woman assigned to the *vilicus* as his helpmate in Book 12 of his treatise. Its placement there is justified by a long passage in which the author enlarges on the gendered nature of work, but Columella also emphasizes the practical importance of the *vilica*'s role in the functioning of the villa. Among other things, Columella asserts that the *vilica* has taken over the household duties formerly undertaken by the *matrona* (see *Rust.* 12. Preface 1 and 4–10 in this chapter).

Columella, *Rust.* 12.1.1–3   I can say that the *villica* should be young without being exactly a girl, for the same reasons that we discussed about the age of the *vilicus*. She also should have good health and neither ugly looks nor exceptional beauty. Unlimited strength will be sufficient for long nights [of work] and other difficult tasks. Ugliness repels, but too much in the way of desirable good looks makes (the *vilicus*) overly attached. [...] But the qualities I have outlined are not the whole of what a *villica* must be: it is very important to see that she be not prone to wine, to greed, to superstition, and to sleeping, and that she be distant from men, that she understands what needs to be done and what is needed in the future, so that she may keep to the manner of behavior that we have already discussed about the *vilicus*.

Columella, *Rust*. 12.1.6   If someone in the slave household is getting sick, it is her obligation to see that the person gets the best attention. Gratitude as well as an obedient feeling are born of such attention. Those who have recovered as a result of her oversight are more eager to serve than before.

Treatment of Enslaved Persons

Columella, *Rust*. 1.8.15–20   For other slaves [than the *vilicus* and *villica*], here are the precepts [*praecepta*] that can be used, ones that I myself have used and that I do not regret having done so, namely to address country slaves [*rustici*] with more familiarity and more often than addressing slaves [*urbani*] in town, as long as they have not made trouble. And when I saw that their continual work was made lighter by the owner's geniality, I would joke with them and allow them to joke with me as well. Since then, I often call upon them to advise me on some new work project, as if they were experts, and also to find out by this means who has ability and how intelligent he might be. In addition, I notice that, if they think that their opinion and advice has been taken, they are more willing to undertake the work.

Now, on the topic of the slaves in the slave prison [*ergastulum*], it is the usual duty for all intelligent men [*circumspecti*] to look that they are properly chained, whether the place of confinement is safe and well secured, and whether the *vilicus* has unchained or chained someone without the owner's knowledge. For the *vilicus* should be very careful not to unshackle a slave whom the *pater familias* has punished in that way, unless the owner gives permission to do so, and not to free a slave whom he [the *vilicus*] has himself punished before the owner knows about the issues. The investigation by the *pater familias* should be more scrupulous on the side of the slaves, so that they would not be badly treated in the matter of clothing or in other ways, for these slaves are subject to many others—the *vilicus*, the overseers of work [*operum magistri*], the prison guards [*ergastulari*]—and so are put in greater danger of of unjust punishments. Then again, when slaves are goaded to the limit by cruelty and greed, they are to be feared even more. For that reason, a diligent owner [*diligens dominus*] asks both the chained slaves and the unchained ones which of them is the more trustworthy and whether they are getting what is correct in accordance with his [the owner's] arrangements; he looks into the quality of their food and drink by tasting it himself, he goes over their clothes, gloves, and footwear. As well, he should often give them the occasion to complain of those who cruelly or dishonestly harass them. Sometimes I give justice to those who justifiably complain and punish those who rouse slaves to revolt or who slander their overseers. But then again, I give a commendation to those who behave with strength and diligence.

I grant leisure [*otium*] to exceptionally prolific female slaves who should be honored for the number of children they bear, and even I grant her freedom [*libertas*] after they have reared many young [slaves]. To a female slave who has had three sons, remission from work [*vacatio*], and to one who has had more than that, her freedom as well.

Both such justice and care [*iustitia et cura*] by the *pater familias* confer great increase on the owner's estate. But he must keep this in mind: to worship the household gods [*dii penates*] upon returning [to the villa] from town. After that, without delay if there is time, or if not, he should go over all parts of the estate and calculate how much his absence has detracted from discipline and oversight, whether any vine, tree, or stored produce is missing. He should also make a new inventory of the herds, slaves, the estate equipment, and the household goods. If he has maintained these practices over many years, he will have achieved a civilized discipline when old age comes upon him, and he will never be despised by his slaves no matter what the years have done to him.

Selection of Work Assignments for Enslaved Workers

Columella, *Rust.* 1.9.1–9 It's necessary to speak about my views on what physique or spirit should be coordinated with what kinds of work. For shepherds, zealous and very thrifty men are to be put in charge. Both these are more important than bodily size and strength because this work needs careful attention and skill.

For a ploughman, while an innate intelligence is necessary, it is not enough if not accompanied by a booming voice and a demeanor that impresses the oxen. However, he should curb his power with kindness, because he should be more commanding than harsh, so that the oxen obey his commands and maintain their strength longer when not altogether worn out by their hard work together with the lash of the whip.

As for what the duties of the shepherds and herdsmen are, I will take up [later] in the proper place, but for now it is enough to know that, for the former, strength and height are not needed, whereas for the latter, they are extremely important. As I have said, we should appoint tall men to drive the plough, for the reason I have outlined just now, and because the work is less tiring for a taller man, because he can manipulate the plough handles almost standing upright.

The ordinary slave worker can be any height, provided he can endure the work.

For vineyards, sturdy, large-built men are needed, not tall ones, for a slave so endowed is better adapted to digging, pruning the vines, and other tasks for vineyards. For working the vineyard, [a slave's] honesty is less important than it is in other agricultural work. This is because work in vineyards must be done in a group and under close supervision. Unruly men [*improbi*] are generally more intelligent than others, and intelligence is required for this kind of work. Vineyard work requires that the slave be not only strong but also sharply intelligent [*acuminis strenuus*]. For this reason, vineyards are for the most part worked by chained slaves [*alligati*]. For all that, an honest man of intelligence will do [work] more capably than a dishonest one.

I have stated this so that no one should consider that I think that I wish my land to be worked by bad men rather than honest ones. But I think this way: the slaves' work should not be amalgamated in such a way that all the slaves carry out all the tasks [that need to be done on the estate]. [. . .] Such an arrangement brings little to the *agricola*, either because no one [of the slaves] thinks that the work [he does] is his own, or because he is working at a task that is not his own but a communal one, and for that reason works much less well. The fault lies not with one individual slave but because many have done the work. For this reason, the ploughmen must be distinct from the vineyard workers, and the vineyard workers from the ploughmen, and both of these from the ordinary slave workers.

Teams not greater than ten men should be formed: our ancestors called them *decuriae* and very much approved of them because a team of that size can be most easily supervised at work and does not divert the watchfulness of the supervisor [*monitor*] leading the men. Therefore, if the field [to be worked] is very large, the teams should be assigned to parts of it in such a way that the slaves will not be [working] singly or in pairs, because they are not easily watched if dispersed. The teams should not be greater than ten slaves, for if there is a more numerous group, each one may think that the work does not concern him. This arrangement [in teams of ten] not only fosters competition but also reveals the lazy ones: when work is spurred by rivalry, the punishment of slackers is considered just and unobjectionable.

Surely, by now we have advised the future farmer [*agricola futurus*] on those matters that must be especially planned for—namely healthfulness, a [nearby] road, the neighborhood, the water, the location of the villa, the kind of estate, the types of tenants and slaves, and the allocation of responsibilities and work. So now we have come in a timely way to the cultivation of the soil itself, which I will soon discuss extensively in the following book.[162]

Indoors and Outdoors

Columella's Book 12 is about tasks that are done indoors and mostly by women to provision the villa's *familia* with what it needs: preparation of containers, pickling, dry and cool storage, weaving, and so on. However, its preface is an extended essay on men and women, the theory of their differing but equally important abilities, outdoor and indoor tasks, the old ways of the ancestors and ancestresses, and contemporary luxury and laxity. Columella laments that *matrones familiae* of the past who were real heads of household equal to their husbands have been replaced by *matronae* who have given themselves to laziness, pleasure, and spending money. In the same way, men of old lived on their estates, whereas now men have become absentee landlords and their *vilici* have taken over their duties.

In one form or another, these ideas had become traditional and were repeated in agricultural treatises: they are endemic to the genre and its readers expected them. Ischomachus had asserted many of them to Socrates in Xenophon's *Oeconomicus* already 500 years before, and Cato had done so some 200 years before Columella's treatise in the 60s CE. A few more appear in Varro a century or so earlier.[163] For Columella, the ideal character of the enslaved *vilica* (cited above in *Rust.* 12.1.1–3) is used as reproof of modern *matronae* who, according to Columella, no longer even wished to supervise wool making and weaving, thereby losing the right to be complimented, by their husbands, for being *lanificiae*, spinners of wool. The enslaved *vilica* has become a surrogate or substitute for the *matrona*. Such social inversion upends the natural social relations of husband and wife in the villa and is a perversion of the structure of the *familia*: Columella sees social change as illegitimate, morally wrong, and deleterious to the functioning of the villa.

Columella, *Rust*. 12. Preface 1   Xenophon the Athenian in his book called *Oeconomicus* asserted that the married state was devised by nature to be the most agreeable and the most profitable social state in life: first, as Cicero says as well, so the human race might not die off over a long passage of time, and for this purpose man and woman were brought together, and second, from the same social unit [*societas*], help and security could be assured to human beings in their old age.[164] [...]

Columella, *Rust*. 12. Preface 4–10   Since the responsibilities described above required work and diligence, and because the things that need attention within the house are acquired with no small effort outside the house, it is right, as I have already said, that Nature has provided women for diligence at home, whereas men are provided for the public sphere and the out-of-doors. Thus God [*deus*] has allocated to men the will to endure cold and heat and the adventures of peace and war, meaning agricultural endeavors and military service. By contrast, and because God made them less capable for these things [endurance and adventuring], he has given women the responsibility of domestic affairs. And because he has assigned to the [female] sex responsibilities for custodial care and careful oversight in domestic affairs, for that reason he made women more timid than men because fearfulness adds greatly to the zeal of taking care of things in the home.

In turn, for those who needed to seek food out-of-doors in the open and sometime to repel assaults, for that reason he made men bolder than women. But once these qualities had been assigned, and equal amounts of memory and attention were needed for both sexes, God allocated both—memory and attention—no less to women than to men. Then nature, in her simple way, not wishing one or other [sex] to have all the good things, for that reason made both have need of the other, since what one of them lacks is often readily available in the other.

These ideas were already in and, not irrelevantly, discussed by Xenophon in his *Oeconomicus*, and by Cicero who translated that work into Latin.[165] For the Greeks and afterward among the Romans until the time in our fathers' memory, domestic work was that of the *matrona*, at a time when the *patres familiarum* would come [home] to the domestic *penates* at the end of public business and their duty [for it] accomplished. The highest reverence for harmony and oversight together was keenly espoused for emulation by [even] the most beautiful woman, to see that her husband's work be fulfilled in greater and better ways. Nothing within the house was separate, nothing that either the husband or the wife declared to be one or the other's by right: rather, they held all things in common for one another, so that the wifely work done inside the home by the *matrona* was equally valued as that done outside it [by her husband]. For that reason, there was not much for either the *vilicus* or the *villica* to do, because the owners went over and attended to their businesses themselves.

Now, however, women for the most part give themselves to luxury and idle pursuits, and do not even deign so much as to supervise wool making, and [even] have an aversion to clothes made at home; they take pleasure only in a willful desire for expensive items nearly equal to the income that the [husband's] property brings in. It is not surprising that such women are annoyed by being in the country and by farming activities: [for them] staying in the country for a few days is the dirtiest thing [*sordissimum negotium*]. In consequence, now when the ancient habits of Sabine and Roman *matrones familiarum* have not only declined but even have been extinguished, the oversight by a *villica* has crept in out of necessity, to take over [what had been] the duties of the *matrona*, in the same way that *vilici* have taken over the place of owners—owners who once by ancient custom not only cultivated their fields on their own but also lived in the country. But so that I am not perceived to have awkwardly taken on the duty of a censor about contemporary manners of behavior, I continue to the duties of the *villica*.[166]

PALLADIUS   (Rutilius Taurus Aemilianus Palladius, late fourth–early fifth century CE)[167]

***The Work of Farming* (*Opus agriculturae*), early fifth century CE (Palladius, *Op. agr.*)**
Translation by John G. Fitch[168]

The early recognition of Palladius's treatise as having a particular practical usefulness comes from Palladius's organization of his material: "chunks" of work (fieldwork, planting, grafting, pruning, harvesting, and so on) in a schedule of operations described month by month, tidy but flexible.[169] Its originality lies in its directness and relative lack of cultural or social baggage: there is a distinct "let's get on with it" attitude. From the very few references to divinities of any kind, the religious link between agriculture and rural worship is gone; absent moralizing reference to great figures in Roman history, Palladius's readers did not have to worry about their villas representing modern versions of ancient civic virtue. Some of Palladius's content, instructions, and advice is derived from Varro and Columella, but the sequence he gives considerably clarifies the material he adapted from his predecessors.

Preface

Palladius, *Op. agr.* 1.1.1–2   Common sense [*prudentia*] requires that you first assess the kind of person you intend to advise. If you want to make someone into a farmer [*agricola*], you should not emulate the skills and eloquence of a rhetorician, as most instructors have done. By speaking in a sophisticated way to countryfolk [*rustici*], they have achieved the result that their instruction cannot be understood even by the most sophisticated. But we must avoid a protracted preface, so as not to imitate those we are criticizing.

We are to speak, if heaven is kind, about every aspect of cultivation [*agricultura*], pasturing [*pascuus*], farm buildings [*aedificia*] following the authorities on construction [*magistri fabricandi*], and finding water—every detail of activity or nutrition that the farmer needs to observe for the sake of pleasure [*voluptas*] and production [*fructus*]. These topics are distributed throughout the work according to the appropriate season. One exception: on fruit trees I have decided to cover all details of their regimen under the month in which each should be planted.

The Four Fundamentals

Palladius, *Op. agr.* 1.2   First, then, the fundamentals of choosing land and cultivating it well consist of four things: air, water, earth, and application [*industria*]. Three of these things depend on nature, one on capacity and will. You should examine first the factors belonging to nature: in places you intend to cultivate, the air should be healthy and mild, the water wholesome and easily obtained (whether found on the spot or channeled in or collected from the rain), and the earth fertile and favourably situated.

Assessment of the Air

Palladius, *Op. agr.* 1.3   A wholesome air, then, is indicated by a location well away from valley bottoms and innocent of night mists, and by appraisal of the inhabitants' physique: whether their colour is healthy, their heads steady and sound, their vision unimpaired, their hearing distinct, and whether their voice comes clear and unimpeded from their throat. The benign quality of the air is determined in this way: the opposite symptoms reveal that the atmosphere of the region is harmful.[170]

Application: Maxims Essential to Farming

Palladius's *Op. agr.* 1.6.1–18 (excerpts presented here) is an interesting loosely organized collection of what J.G. Fitch astutely calls "maxims" in an "aphoristic style like old saws." Most are technical about soils, planting, and so on, so not all are included here, only the pithy ones about personnel or farming analogies which allow for easy memorization of practical wisdom. Palladius's model may have been lines 727–828 from Hesiod's *Works and Days*.[171] Many are versions of ideas found in earlier agricultural treatises.

Palladius, *Op. agr.* 1.6.1–4   After evaluating these factors [air, water, earth], which are natural and cannot be amended by human means, you need to deal with the remaining area, that of application [*industria*]. Your best means of attending to this factor will be to keep in mind particularly the following maxims, drawn from all areas of farmwork. [...]

> § The master's presence [*praesentia domini*] promotes the farm's well-being [*provectus agri*]. [...]
> § You must definitely have ironworkers [*ferrarii*], woodworkers [*lignarii*], makers of pots and barrels [*doliorum cuparumque factores*] on the farm, lest the farmhands be drawn away from their regular work by the need to visit the city.[172] [...]
> § The calculation of how many workers are required cannot be uniform, since lands are so diverse; familiarity with the soil and region will readily show what numbers should perform any given task, on woody plants or any kind of seed crop. [...]
> § In farming, young men [*iuvenes*] are best suited to carrying out tasks, older men [*seniores*] to assigning them. [...]
> § Trees like people should be transferred from bad places to better ones.

Palladius, *Op. agr.* 1.6.6–8
§ A person who rents his farm or land to an owner or tenant-farmer holding adjacent land is asking for losses and lawsuits.
§ The central areas of a farm are at risk, if the outer areas are not cultivated. [...]
§ Three troubles are equally harmful: sterility, disease, neighbors [*vicinus*]. [...]
§ Level land [*campus*] produces more abundant wine, hills nobler wine; a north wind [*Aquilo*] fecundates vines exposed to it, a south wind [*Auster*] ennobles them. So it is a matter of judgment whether to have more or better.
§ Necessity takes no holidays.[173] [...]
§ The trouble entailed in a journey [*via*] is equally detrimental to its pleasure and its usefulness.
§ One who cultivates a farm endures a creditor whose levies are demanding, and to whom he is bound without hope of discharge. [...]
§ A small plot well cultivated [*culta exiguitas*] is more productive than a large one untended.
§ A longer support [*adminiculum*] promotes the vine's growth.

Palladius, *Op. agr.* 1.6.10
[...] § A garden in a gentle climate with springwater running through it is almost free of limitations, and needs no sowing regimen.

Palladius, *Op. agr.* 1.6.12
§ Assess your abilities and observe moderation [*modum tene*] when you take on cultivation, lest you outdo your own strength, exceed your limits, and abandon in ignominy what you took on in arrogance.

Palladius, *Op. agr.* 1.6.14
§ The Greeks advise that olives, when being propagated and gathered, should be handled by pure boys and virgin girls; they are mindful, I suppose, that chastity [*castitas*] is the presiding spirit of this tree.[174] [...]
§ Well-watered land needs more dung, dry land less. [...]
§ When any rural work is recommended, it is not too early if done 15 days ahead, nor too late if done 15 days afterward.[175]

Palladius, *Op. agr.* 1.6.17
[...] § To supervise the farm you should not appoint any slave for whom you once had a tender fondness, since his reliance on that past love will lead him to expect impunity for any present fault.

Choice and Site of the Farm

Palladius goes on in Book 1 with numerous recommendations regarding the farm site and its buildings.

Palladius, *Op. agr.* 1.7.1 In choosing or buying a farm [*ager*], you will have to check whether its natural productiveness has been spoilt by the laziness of its cultivators, and whether they have wasted the soil's fertility on inferior planting. This can be corrected by grafting better stock, but it is better to have unimpaired enjoyment of these things, rather than postponed success and the hope of putting things right. [...] It will cost you much toil to correct the situation, if you purchase a farm beset by flaws like these.

Palladius, *Op. agr.* 1.7.3   The actual farmstead to be chosen should be situated as follows. In cold regions the farmstead should be exposed to the east or south: if it is cut off from these aspects by some large mountain standing in the way, it will be freezing, with the sunshine excluded by a northern aspect, or postponed till evening by a westerly one. But in hot regions one should instead choose a northerly aspect, which answers equally well to utility [*utilitas*] and pleasure [*voluptas*] and health [*salus*]. If there is a river near a planned construction site, we must check its nature, since a river's exhalations are generally harmful. If such is the case, the building will have to avoid it. But marshy ground must absolutely be avoided, especially that which faces south or west and dries out in summer, in view of the pestilence or noxious animals that it generates.

The Building

Palladius, *Op. agr.* 1.8.1–3   The planned building should be in keeping with the farm's value and the owner's wealth, since it is generally more difficult to sustain ongoing expenditure on an extravagant scale [*inmodice sumptus*] than it is to build on that scale. The size should therefore be calculated so that if some accident occurs, it can be put right with one year's income, or at most two years', from the farm in which it stands.

The site of the main building [*praetorium*] should be higher and drier than everything else, to prevent damage to the foundations and to enjoy a pleasant outlook [*laetus aspectus*].[176] [...] In addition, one must ensure that the building can be surrounded by gardens and orchards or meadows. The whole building should be oriented so that its long front faces south, receiving the early morning sun in winter on its corner, while it is somewhat turned away from the setting sun in summer. The result will be that the building is lit by the sun through the winter, and unaffected by its heat in summer.

Floors for Winter and Summer Quarters

Palladius, *Op. agr.* 1.9.1   The design should be such as to provide living quarters [*mansiones*] for both summer and winter in a small compass. Those intended for winter should be positioned in such a way that they can be gladdened by virtually the whole course of the winter sun. They will need to have suitable paved floors. [...]

Palladius, *Op. agr.* 1.9.5   But if they are summer quarters, they should face north and the sunrise at the solstice; they should be given a floor of crushed-tile mortar, as mentioned above, or of marble [*marmora*] or mosaic [*tesserae*] or lozenge-shaped stones [*scutula*], whose corners and sides should be flush so as to give a level surface.[177]

Light and Height

Palladius, *Op. agr.* 1.12   In rural construction we must ensure first and foremost that it is bright and well lit; then that we orient the seasonal quarters, as I said above, in the appropriate directions, that is, summer quarters north, winter quarters south, spring and autumn quarters east. The dimensions to be observed in dining rooms and other rooms are these: the length and breadth should be added together, and half that total should be taken as the height.

Wall Cladding

Here and elsewhere, Palladius gives detailed recipes for the mixing and application of wall treatments in villas. In all cases, the mural finishes seem to be for unpainted walls, unlike Vitruvius's detailed instructions for wall surfaces that he assumes, in most cases, will have painted decoration (*opus tectoria*: Vitr., *De arch.* 7.3.7, in ch. 3, Villas in Roman Architectural Treatises). These unpainted walls are similar to the bare walls that Sidonius Apollinaris prided himself on in his bath building at his Avitacum villa (Sid. Apoll., *Ep.* 2.2.5, in ch. 4, Descriptions of Villas). The sheen [*nitor*] achieved by buffing of these plaster walls seems to have been an important part of their appeal. Vitruvius also found well-buffed plaster very attractive.[178]

Palladius, *Op. agr.* 1.15 Here is how to make the cladding of the walls strong and shiny [*fortis et nitida*]. [...] When this crushed marble coating also begins to dry, another thinner layer should be applied. In this way it will keep both its solidity and its sheen [*soliditas et nitor*].

Cisterns

Unlike Varro and Columella, who had preferred running water for villas and farms, Palladius—perhaps responding to readers whose properties were further afield than those of well-watered central Italy—recommends the construction of cisterns.[179] He also prefers reliable cistern water from rain collected from the villa's roof runoffs to water from other sources.

Palladius, *Op. agr.* 1.16 Now one must avoid what many have done in order to have a water supply, namely burying their farms at the bottom of valleys, and placing a few days' pleasure [*voluptas*] ahead of the health of the inhabitants [*habitati*].[180] [...] If there is no spring or well, it will be advantageous to construct cisterns, in which water can be collected from the roofs of all the buildings. [...]

Palladius, *Op. agr.* 1.17.4. [...] It will be healthful to conduct water here through earthenware pipes and guide it into the covered cisterns. For rainwater is preferred to all other kinds for drinking, so that even if flowing water can be brought in, it should be reserved, if it is unwholesome, for the baths and for garden cultivation.

The Wine Room

This description of the *cella vinaria* is included because, in order to convey its shape, Palladius refers to an urban building type familiar to his readers.

Palladius, *Op. agr.* 1.18.1 We should have the wine room facing north; it should be cold and almost dark, a long way from baths, animal stalls, the furnace, dung-heaps, cisterns, water and other foul-smelling places. It should be equipped with necessities so as not to be overwhelmed at vintage time, and arranged in such a way that, basilica-like [*forma basilicae*], it has a pressing floor built at a higher level, to which one can ascend by three or four steps between two vats [*lacus*], which are sunk on each side to receive wine.[181]

The Garden

In contrast to that of other writers, the *hortus* of Palladius's villa is purely utilitarian; not even flowers or ornamentals are grown.

Palladius, *Op. agr.* **1.34.1**   The gardens and orchards will need to be close to the house [*domus*]. The garden should ideally be at the foot of the dungheap, so as to be fertilized automatically by the liquid from it; but sited well away from the threshing floor, since the dust from the chaff is injurious.

The Bath House

Palladius, *Op. agr.* **1.39.1**   It is not inappropriate, if the water supply permits, for the head of household [*pater familias*] to consider building a bath [*structura balnei*], something that contibutes greatly to pleasure and to health. We shall establish the bath, then, in an area that will be warm, on a spot raised above moisture, so there is no wet ground near the furnace to cool the place down. We shall give it light on the south side and facing west in winter, so it is cheered and brightened all day by the sunlight. [...]

Palladius, *Op. agr.* **1.39.3–5**   We shall set a water heater of lead, with a shallow copper pan beneath it, outside [of the bath building itself], between the locations of the bathing tubs [*solia*], with the furnace below it [the water heater]. A cold-water pipe should lead to this water heater, and a pipe of similar size should run from it to the bathing tub; this pipe will draw an amount of hot water into the bath equal to the cold water brought to the heater by the other pipe. The rooms should be arranged so that they are not square, but for example if they are 15 feet long, they should be 10 feet wide [4.4 m, or 14½ ft.]; for the heat will roll around more vigorously in a narrow space. The shape of the bathing tubs can be according to individual preference.

Rooms with swimming pools should be lit from the north in summer bathhouses, and from the south in winter baths. If possible, the baths should be placed so that all the gray water from them runs through the gardens. [...]

[...] If we are keen on economy [*compendium*], we can also place winter living quarters on top of the bathhouse; in this way we provide warmth from below for the living area, and make additional use of the foundations.

Veterinary Medicine

The fourteenth book of Palladius's *Opus agriculturae* is titled *De veterinaria medicina*. It is on the care of animals, but it includes, under the veterinary topics, some advice on the care of farmworkers.

Palladius, *Op. agr.* **14.1.1**   Against pestilence, it is helpful for farmworkers who are toiling in the sun's heat to take food briefly and often, so the nouishment provided can refresh them, not accumulate and weigh them down.

Palladius, *Op. agr.* **14.1.4**   Some people steep wormwood in hot water and provide this for the workers before they eat, or squill wine or vinegar, but it is better to provide the vinegar after food.[182]

3

VILLAS IN ROMAN ARCHITECTURAL TREATISES

VITRUVIUS
FAVENTINUS

Two Latin architectural treatises—that of Vitruvius and an abridgement by Faventinus—have survived, but in contrast to the agricultural treatises, there appear to have been few Latin works on architecture or even on individual buildings. Vitruvius cites some previous accounts of buildings by their architects, mainly Greek, but knowledge of agriculture in either Greek or Italian/Roman contexts predominated: both were largely agrarian economies, hence the number of agricultural treatises. The paucity of architectural works in Latin stands in contrast to the civic pride, enthusiastic patrons, and willing governments at all levels devoted to building of all kinds—ordinary, practical, grand, unusual—and these buildings were often ingenious in their design and technology.[1] Architecture and infrastructure as art and civic commodity had an important place in Roman social structure and patronage, and resourcing them may have made their reduction to written forms irrelevant or beside the point: its traditions and innovations could have been a matter of intergenerational design and craft capacities not requiring literary elucidation for a reading audience.

The exception is the treatise *On Architecture* (*De architectura*) of Marcus Vitruvius Pollio, written during the reign of Augustus and dedicated to the emperor. It is unique in its completeness and firm organization of material that had received—as the author himself plausibly claims—only scattered or partial treatment before his efforts.[2] In that respect, *On Architecture* provides, as much for its imperial dedicatee as for the general public and professional architects, something like what Varro offered for agriculture in his *De re rustica* (see ch. 2, Villas in Roman Agricultural Treatises): enough theory to frame the issues socially and politically for an intellectually engaged readership, some historical perspective along developmental lines with emphasis on Greek traditions, and plenty of good practical recipes and formulae for building and engineering solutions, including military ones.[3] Vitruvius is very readable, and he often takes pride in his clarity, downplaying any aspiration to elegant writing. Architecture as an emanation of nature is his leading principle, but the emphasis is on Roman themes and types: temples correctly designed in Greek style to convey the dignity of religious worship, public buildings arranged to frame the functions of law and ceremony, and urban amenities such as theaters, amphitheaters, sports and educational facilities (*palaestra*), infrastructure (aqueducts, sewers), and *thermae* of different sizes. The targeted readership seems mainly city-dwelling readers involved with the urban built environment, and administrators such as Frontinus, writing about 120 years after Vitruvius, who may have consulted Vitruvius's treatise as reference for both practical information and administrative talking points.[4] Villas were included in *On Architecture*, but itemizing them appears to be more for completeness in the logical structure of his treatise, which otherwise has little to do with domestic architecture.

Still, private dwellings, both *domus* and villas, are of some interest to Vitruvius, and including them was innovative. He may have been prompted to do so by Augustus himself because he claims in the dedication that the emperor had an equal concern for public and private construction.[5] However, for an architect of Vitruvius's elevated estimation in the profession, there was probably little prestige in designing and building houses or villas.

That said, no matter how relatively little text Vitruvius devoted to domestic design, the professional education and universal principles (*rationes*) of architecture outlined in his Book 1 remained paramount. The education of the architect should comprise a good understanding of all the sciences and arts and an ability to apply and coordinate them.[6] In schematic form, the principles of design in all architecture, including *domus* and villas, are *ordinatio*,[7] *dispositio*,[8] *eurythmia*,[9] *symmetria*,[10] and *decor* and *distributio*.[11] These values combine adherence to tradition, some innovation and expressiveness, and appropriateness or restraint in location, orders used, style, and decoration.[12] All buildings must embody *firmitas* (stability), *utilitas* (usefulness, purpose), and *venustas* (beauty), no matter what their status in the hierarchy of construction and design.[13] In this respect, Vitruvius did for architecture what Varro had done for agriculture about a decade before: he provided a theoretical framework for practical endeavors.

Most of Vitruvius's Book 6 is brief as to domestic design, spaces, and decoration, though the use of certain rooms is covered. Tradition—or his version of tradition—dominates his approach, with some comparison between the urban *domus* and the Greek *oikos*. The Vitruvian villa is an extension of his *domus*, but certain aspects of villas seem to relate better to Greek houses, so aspects of the latter's use and nomenclature are included here.[14]

The treatise by Cetius Faventinus, written in the late third century CE, at least 250 years after that of Vitruvius, is a shortened version of the earlier work and has an appealing air of practical efficiency and directness. The recipes for such things as floor foundations and surfaces, wall-plastering techniques, and site selection for *domus* and villas are pretty much the same with very few differences: both treatises attest the early development, success, and robust endurance of Roman methods of construction and finish. For villas, the strategies for water supply and storage in Vitruvius, Faventinus, and Palladius—ranging from the first century BCE to the fifth century CE—did not change much except in their relative importance in sustainable locations, and linings and caulkings for waterproofing persisted from much earlier practices. The continuity of construction among Roman craftsmen over several centuries maintained the building recipes that Vitruvius and Faventinus, as architects, wished to preserve and disseminate, together with the larger principles of design and traditional formulae for villas.

VITRUVIUS   (Marcus Vitruvius Pollio[?],[15] ca. 70–15 BCE)

On Architecture (***De architectura***) 27–22 BCE[16] (Vitr., *De arch*.).
Translation by Ingrid D. Rowland.[17]

Vitruvius, Book 1

In dedicating his treatise to the emperor Augustus (addressed as Caesar), Vitruvius comments on aspects of imperial policy for public and private construction.

Vitr., ***De arch***. **1. Preface 2.2**   When, however, I perceived that you were solicitous not only for the establishment of community life [*vita communi*] and of the body politic, but also for the construction of suitable public buildings, so that by your agency not only had the state [*civitas*] been rendered more august by the annexation of entire provinces, but indeed the majesty of the Empire [*maiestas imperii*] had found conspicuous proof in its public works—then I thought that I should not miss the opportunity to publish on these matters for you as soon as possible, given that I was first recognized in this field by your Father [Julius Caesar] and was a devoted admirer of his qualities. [...]

Vitr., De arch. 1. Preface 2.3 [...] For I perceived that you had already built extensively, were building now and would be doing so in the future: public as well as private constructions [*cura publicorum et privatorum aedificatorum*], all scaled to the amplitude of your own achievements so that these would be handed down to future generations. I have set down these instructions, complete with technical terms, so that by observing them you could teach yourself how to evaluate the works already brought into being and those yet to be. [...]

Vitruvius, Book 2

In Greek and Roman antiquity, it was customary to posit abstractions and human phenomena as developing from a common primitive condition modified, through time, by such things as climate, ethnicity, and particular social structure. This gave the act of building—from temples to rough dwellings to very grand houses—a historical and anthropological logic that allowed both Vitruvius and the writers on agriculture to cite the simple houses of the old ancestors of the *patria*—Romulus, Cincinnatus, even Cato—as exemplary of the *mos maiorum*.

Vitruvius has a well-developed anthropology of construction: humans first lived in caves and out-of-doors, then were united by forest fires, which prompted cooperation and language, then a search for comfort, hence construction, cooperation, and civilization.[18]

Vitr., De arch. 2.1.2–3 [...] The beginning of association [*conventus initio*] among human beings, their meeting and living together, thus came into being because of the discovery of fire.[19] When many people came into a single place, having, beyond all the other animals, this gift of nature: that they walked, not prone, but upright, they therefore could look upon the magnificence of the universe and the stars [*mundi et astrorum magnificentia*]. For the same reason, they were able to manipulate whatever object they wished, using their hands and other limbs. Some in the group began to make coverings of leaves, others to dig caves under the mountains. Many imitated the nest building of swallows and created places of mud and twigs where they might take cover.[20] Then, observing each others' homes and adding new ideas to their own, they created better types of houses [*meliora genera casarum*] as the days went by.

Because people are by nature imitative and easily taught, they daily showed one another the success of their constructions, taking pride in creation, so that by daily exercising their ingenuity in competition they achieved greater insight with the passage of time. First they erected forked uprights, and weaving twigs in between they covered the whole with mud. Others, letting clods of mud go dry, began to construct walls of them, joining them together with wood, and to avoid rains and heat they covered them over with reeds and leafy branches. Later, when these coverings proved unable to endure through the storms of winter, they made eaves with molded clay, and set in rainspouts on inclined roofs. [...]

Vitr., De arch. 2.1.5–7 [...] In Athens, on the Areopagus, there is an ancient example to this day of a house daubed with mud. Likewise, on the Capitol, the house of Romulus [*Romuli casa*] shows us and calls to mind the ancient ways, so do the wattle houses in the Citadel precinct.[21] [...] So from the making of buildings they progressed, step by step, to the other arts and disciplines, and thus they led themselves out of a rough and brutish life into gentle humanity [*mansueta humanitas*].

Then, training their own spirits and reviewing the most important ideas conceived among the various arts and crafts, they began to complete, not houses [*casae*] any longer, but real residences [*domus*], with foundations, built up with brick walls or stone, roofed with timbers and tiles.[22] Furthermore, on the basis of observations made in their studies, they progressed from haphazard and uncertain opinions [*iudici incerti*] to the stable principles of symmetry [*certas symmetriarum rationes*]. After they had noted what a profusion of resources has been begotten by Nature, and what abundant supplies for construction have been prepared by her, they nourished these with cultivation and increased them by means of skill and enhanced the elegance of their life with aesthetic delights [*voluptates*]. Therefore, I shall tell as best I can about those things which are suitable for use in construction, what their qualities are and what properties they possess.

Vitruvius, Book 6

Vitruvius discusses domestic architecture in Books 6 and 7.

Vitr., *De arch.* 6. Preface 7   [...] Therefore, because in the fifth book I wrote about the proper construction of public buildings, in this volume I shall explain the calculations for private buildings, and the dimensions of their symmetries.

Vitruvius has a complex theory of domestic architecture based in part on the location of buildings in the earth's latitudes as proved by pitch and tone in human voices and other standards of the relation of climate to sound. Bodies of people from northern climes contain more moisture, are bigger, braver, have fairer complexions and hair, and are deeper-voiced: their houses should be completely covered and face southward. Bodies of those from southern climes are drier, smaller, more timid, darker, and shriller: their houses should be more open and face north and northeast. Roman Italy is the best.[23]

Vitr., *De arch.* 6.1.10–11   [...] Thus these things have been so positioned in the cosmos by Nature, and all nations have been made different from one another by their unequal composition. Within the area of the entire earthly globe and all the regions at the center of the cosmos, the Roman People has its territories.
    The populations of Italy partake in equal measure of the qualities of both north and south, both with regard to their physiques and to the vigor of their minds, to produce the greatest strength. [...] Thus the divine intelligence established the state of the Roman People as an outstanding and balanced region—so that it could take command over the earthly orb.

In Book 6, chapter 3, Vitruvius describes the principal rooms of the *domus*, which are, with some exceptions, those of the villa, but with differences of sequence as well as some borrowings from the Greek house as Vitruvius conceived of it. For the *domus*, the "coverings" or roof-structure and support (*cavaedium*) of the atrium defined the dwelling.[24] Then the famous sequence of atrium with its *alae* or wings, then to *tablinum* to peristyle, with special discussion of *triclinia* and special *exedrae* or *oeci*, ancillary spaces off peristyle corridors or *tablina* for sitting, eating, conversation, and, in the case of the Greek house, wool working by the *matrona*.[25] The underlying principle is that of *symmetria*, which flexibly defines the width, length, and height of rooms.[26] In general, the lived use of the rooms is not specifically indicated, except in a couple of instances regarding the *alae* of the atrium and picture galleries.

Vitr., *De arch.* 6.3.6   [...] Place the *imagines* [ancestral portraits], with their ornaments, at a height corresponding to the width of the wings [*alae*]. [...]

Vitr., *De arch.* 6.3.8   [...] Picture galleries [*pinacothecae*], like *exedrae*, should be set up with generous proportions. [...]

In his Book 6, chapter 4, discussion of where various rooms in the *domus* should face for best temperature and pleasantness, Vitruvius may be thinking of villas with possibilities of multiple orientations rather than confined urban dwellings.

Vitr., *De arch.* 6.4.1 Now we shall explain where types of buildings with particular characteristics should face as befits their use and the regions of the sky. Winter dining rooms and baths [*balnearia*] should face the setting winter sun, both because they should make use of the evening light and also because the setting sun, shining full on and yielding up heat, makes this region warmer at evening time. *Cubicula* and libraries should face east, for the morning light makes them serviceable [for reading], and furthermore, the books in libraries will not rot. For in libraries that face south and west, the books are spoiled by worms and moisture, as the oncoming moist winds give rise to such things and nurture them, while as they pour forth their moist breath they corrupt the scrolls by discoloring them [with mold].

Vitr., *De arch.* 6.4.2 Spring dining rooms and autumn dining rooms should face east. Extended in this direction, with their windows facing the force of the sun, this, as it proceeds westward, moderates their temperature in the season when one is accustomed to use them. Summer dining rooms should face north because that region of the heavens does not, like the rest, become boiling hot in the heat of the solstice. Instead, because it is turned away from the course of the sun, it is always cool and when in use, a dining room so oriented affords good health and pleasure. The same orientation is appropriate for picture galleries and the workshops of brocaders, embroiderers, and painters, so that the colors in their work, thanks to the consistency of the light, will not change their quality.

In Book 6, chapter 5, Vitruvius shows he was aware how both *domus* and villa could represent the needs and habits of the elites of his day, needs that went beyond the norms of *domus* design. Atrium, *tablinum*, *triclinium*, and sometimes the peristyle were sufficient for ordinary people, but he lists the extra rooms of the very grand *domus* needed by very great owners, the kind of houses and villas that prominent members of high society in the late Republic had been building for themselves: large, with all the appurtenances of Hellenistic almost-royal state, exceptional at any scale, and richly decorated in up-to-date styles. Exceptional status required an exceptional panoply of rooms: this was the social *decor* of domestic architecture keyed to the social status of the owner.

Vitr., *De arch.* 6.5.1 Once these things have been set out with regard to the regions of the heavens, then it is time to note also by what principles the personal areas [*propria loca*] of private buildings should be constructed for the head of the family and how public areas should be constructed with outsiders in mind as well.[27] Personal areas are those into which there is no possibility of entrance except by invitation, like *cubicula*, *triclinia*, baths, and the other rooms that have such functions. Public areas are those into which even uninvited members of the public may also come by right, that is, vestibules, *cavaedia* [atria], peristyles, and any rooms that may perform this sort of function.[28] And so, for those of moderate income [*communis fortuna*], magnificent vestibules, *tablina*, and atria are unnecessary, because they perform their duties by making the rounds visiting others, rather than having others make the rounds visiting them.

Vitr., *De arch.* 6.5.2 Those who deal in farm products have stables and sheds in their entrance courts [*vestibuli*], and in their homes should have installed crypts, granaries, storerooms, and the other furnishings that have more to do with storing provisions than with maintaining an elegant correctness [*elegantiae decor*]. Likewise, for moneylenders [*feneratores*] and tax collectors [*publicani*] public rooms should be more commodious, better looking, and well secured, but for lawyers [*forenses*] and orators [*diserti*] they should be more elegant, and spacious enough to accommodate meetings. For the most prominent citizens [*nobiles*], those who should carry out their duties to the citizenry by holding honorific titles and magistracies [*honores magistratusque*], vestibules should be constructed that are lofty and lordly [*vestibula regalia alta*], the atria and peristyles at their most spacious, lush gardens [*silvae*] and broad walkways [*ambulationes*] refined as properly befits their dignity. In addition to these, there should be libraries [*bybliothecae*], picture galleries, and basilicas, outfitted in a manner not dissimilar to the magnificence of public works, for in the homes of these people, often enough, both public deliberations and private judgments and arbitrations are carried out.[29]

The difference between the design of *domus* and that of villas, according to Vitruvius, is mainly one of the sequence of spaces: villas have peristyles at the entrance to the dwelling rather than atria. Actual villas varied, however.

Vitr., *De arch.* 6.5.3   Therefore, if buildings are set out like this, by these principles and according to the individual types of persons, just as is written about correctness in Book 1, there will be nothing to reproach in them, for they will have comfortable and faultless execution in every respect. Furthermore, these principles will not only serve for buildings in the city, but also for those in the countryside, except for the fact that in the city the atria are customarily next to the entrance, whereas in the countryside and in pseudo-urban buildings [*pseudourbanae*] the peristyles come first, then afterward the atria, and these have paved porticoes around them looking into *palaestrae* and walkways. To the extent that I could record the principles for urban buildings I have set them down comprehensively. Now I shall state how the layout of rural buildings should be executed so that the buildings are convenient to use, and by what principles they should be designed.

Vitruvius's account of the villa and its buildings for processing olives and grapes, grain storage, the stabling of farm animals, and other agricultural activities is so brief that it suggests he may be relying on his readers to have access to Varro's treatise on agriculture or another like it.

Vitr., *De arch.* 6.6.1–5   First of all, as regards a healthful site, just as was written in the first book about locating city walls, the area should be inspected and the villas located accordingly. Their size should be determined according to the amount of land available and the supply of crops. The courtyards [*chortes*] and their size should be defined according to the number of cattle and however many yoke of oxen it will be necessary to keep in them. Within the courtyard, the kitchen should be laid out in the warmest possible place, the cattle stalls should adjoin them, with the mangers facing toward the hearth and the eastern region of the heavens, so that the cattle, by facing the light and fire, will not become shaggy. Likewise, farmers who are experienced in the lay of land and sky do not think that cattle should face any region of the heavens except the rising sun.

Now the widths of the cattle stalls should not be less than ten feet and not more than fifteen, and their length such that each yoke will occupy no less than seven feet apiece. The baths should also adjoin the kitchen, for by this means the facilities for heavy-duty washing will not be far off. The olive press should also be next to the kitchen, for in this way access to the olives will be convenient. It should also have a wine cellar [*vinaria cella*] connected to it whose windows face north. If it has windows in any other part, which the sun might warm, the wine in this chamber, stirred up by the heat, will be weak.

The oil room [*olearia*] should be placed so that there is light from the south and the warm regions, for the oil should not be chilled, but rather kept fluid by the warmth of heat. The size of these rooms should be made in accordance with the amount of harvest collected and the number of storage jars and if these measure one *culleus*, they should occupy a space of four feet each in diameter [1 *culleus*: about 91 liters, or 24 gal.]. The olive press itself, if it is not turned by a screw [*cocleae*], but rather compressed by handspakes [*vectes*] and a pressing lever [*prelum*], should measure no less than forty feet; in this way there will be enough room for the man at the press. Its width should be no less than sixteen feet, for in this way there will be plenty of free movement and space available to the workers when work is fully under way.[30] If the site calls for two presses, twenty-four feet should go to the width.

Sheep and goat pens should be large enough that individual sheep may have no less than four and one-half feet of space, and not more than six. Granaries should be elevated and laid out so that they face either north or northeast, and in this way the grain cannot heat quickly; instead, chilled by the breeze it is preserved indefinitely. The other regions give rise to weevils and the other little creatures whose habit it is to ruin grain. The places in the villa that are especially warm should be designated for the horse stables, so long as they do not face the hearth. For when draft animals are stabled next to fire, they become shaggy.

Likewise, mangers that are located outside the kitchen in the open air facing east are certainly useful. For when cattle are brought into them in the morning, under a clear winter sky, they become more sleek because they take their feed facing the sun. Storage barns for grain [*horrea*], haylofts [*fenilia*], and spelt [*fararia*], as well as the bread oven[s] [*pistrina*], should be constructed outside the villa, so that it will be more protected from the dangers of fire. If the villa is going to be on the more refined side, it should be designed according to the symmetries that have been recorded earlier for urban buildings, so long as this does not interfere with its serviceability as a country house.[31]

Vitruvius concludes Book 6's chapter 6 on Roman dwellings and announces his next topic, the Greek house.

Vitr., *De arch.* 6.6.7 [...] I have described the layout of the buildings of our countrymen [*nostrates*, fellow Italians, fellow citizens] as best I could, so that they would not be incomprehensible to builders [*aedificatores*].[32] Now I will also give a cursory account of how buildings are laid out according to Greek customs, so that such buildings will not be unknown to the reader.

Vitruvius's discussion of the Greek house in Book 6, chapter 7, is concerned with both the names of the rooms and their gendered uses as well as the etiquette of space for inhabitants and guests.[33] Like Varro, he is concerned with linguistic issues in the names of rooms.

The frequent appearance of *xenia* in Roman painting and mosaic is a clear reference to the kind of startlingly fresh, simple comestibles in simple bowls or baskets that were the gifts of hosts to guests.[34] These *xenia* could be isolated images or grace notes of informality in painted representations of grand buildings.[35] Gifts of villa comestibles were frequently and affectionately sent or exchanged, as the poems of Martial, Pliny the Younger, and Sidonius Apollinaris attest.[36]

Vitr., *De arch.* 6.7.1–2 The Greeks do not use atria, and so they do not build them; coming in from the front doors, they make narrow corridors [*latitudines*]. On one side of these there are horse stables and on the other the doorman's quarters [*cella ostiaria*], and then immediately after this they install interior doors. The place between the two sets of doors is called *thyroreion* in Greek. Next comes the entrance into the *peristylion*. This peristyle has porticoes on three sides; on the side facing south it has two piers standing a considerable distance apart, across which beams are carried. Whatever the distance between these piers, that expanse minus one-third goes to the depth of the portico. This place is named *prostas* by some, and *pastas* by others.[37]

Inside these places large *oeci* are put up, in which the lady[-ies] of the house [*matres familiarum*] sits[sit] with her wool workers [*lanificiae*]. To the right and left of the *prostas*, *cubicula* are located, of which one is called the *thalamos* and the other the *amphithalamos*. Around this, under the porticoes, everyday dining rooms [*triclinia cotidiana*] and *cubicula* are set out; also the servants' quarters [*cellae familiaricae*]. This part of the building is called the women's quarters, the *gynaeconitis*. [...]

Vitr., De arch. 6.7.4 [...] In these *oeci* the men's banquets [*virilia convivia*] take place. For it was never part of their custom for the ladies of their houses to join the men at dinner. Now these residential quarters with peristyles are called *andronitides*, for within them men move about without contact with women.

In addition, to the right and left small residential quarters [*domunculae*] are set up with their own entrances and convenient dining rooms and bedrooms, so that upon arrival, guests are not shown into the peristyles but into these guest quarters [*hospitalia*]. When the Greeks were more refined and more wealthy, they outfitted dining rooms and bedrooms with well-stocked pantries [*penus* or *peni cellae*] for their arriving guests, and on the first day would invite them to dinner; subsequently they would send over chickens, eggs, vegetables, fruit, and other rustic produce [*res agrestes*]. For this reason painters who in their pictures imitated the things that were sent to guests called such paintings "hospitalities," *xenia*. Thus heads of households, although guests, did not seem to be away from home, for they had in these guest quarters a generous amount of privacy [*secreta libertas*].

Vitr., De arch. 6.7.5 Furthermore, between the two peristyles and the guest quarters there are corridors, called *mesauloe*, because they are placed "in the middle between two halls"; we call these corridors *andrones*. But this is a very amazing thing, because it is not an appropriate term either in Greek or in Latin. For the Greeks apply the word *andrones* to the *oeci* where men's banquets usually take place because women do not enter there. Other terms, too, are similar in Greek and Latin, like *xystus, prothyrum, telamones*, and many other words of this kind. *Xystos* is a broad portico according to Greek terminology, where athletes train during the winter season. But we call outdoor walkways "xysta," whereas the Greeks call them *paradromides*. So, too, *prothyra* in Greek applies to the vestibules before entrance doors, and what we call "prothyra" the Greeks call *diathyra*.[38]

Vitr., De arch. 6.7.7 [...] I have explained the customs by which buildings are designed according to the Italian fashion [*more italico*] and the traditions of the Greeks [*instituta Graecorum*], and as for their proportional systems, I have recorded the proportions for individual types. Therefore, since I have written before about their beauty and correctness [*venustatis et decor*], now let us explain about sound construction, and how buildings can be designed to last until great age without flaws.[39]

Vitruvius, Book 7

Book 7 of Vitruvius's treatise concerns floor construction (*pavimentum*) and wall finishes in stucco (*albarium opus*): the recipes and methods (thickness, layering, wet and dry applications, drying times, recoating protocols) are detailed and indicate the author's experience with these crafts and his respect for their practitioners. He also gives tips on molded elements (cornices, soffits) as part of wall finishes.[40] When the subject of coloring the walls and applying paintings (*opus tectoria*) to them arises, Vitruvius has criticisms of contemporary extravagance, not unlike Varro's comments on luxurious decorated villas. Vitruvius's principle of *decor* applied to his principles of domestic decoration as well as his views on the moral relation among artistic traditions, contemporary art, and nature. A few of his comments are included here to indicate the temper of the times in the area of morality and artistic taste.[41]

Vitr., De arch. 7.3.7   [...] Walls finished with one coat of rough mortar, three coats of sanded mortar, and three coats of plaster mixed with marble dust in different grades of fineness, once polished, are ready for paint. [...]

Vitr., De arch. 7.4.4   [...] Now the walls themselves ought to have their own principles of correctness when it comes to finishing their decoration, so that they will have a dignity in keeping with their site and with the specific characteristics of the type of building. In winter dining rooms neither monumental painting nor subtle ornamentation of the ceilings with stucco and moldings will be of any value as decoration, because these will be marred by smoke from the fire and constant soot from the many lamps. Rather, for these rooms panels worked and finished in black should be arrayed above the podium, with inlaid wedges of ocher or cinnabar in between.[42] [...]

Vitr., De arch. 7.5.1–2   In the remaining rooms, that is, the spring, autumn, and summer quarters, also in atria and peristyles, the ancients [*antiqui*] have established certain secure principles for painting, based on secure phenomena [*ex certis rebus certae rationes picturarum*].[43] For a painting is an image of that which exists or can exist, like those of people, buildings, ships, and other things with definite and certain bodies, of which examples may be found and depicted in imitation [*similitudo*]. On this principle, the ancients who established the beginnings of painting plaster first imitated the varieties and placement of marble veneers, then of cornices and the various designs of ocher inlay.

Later they entered a stage in which they also imitated the shapes of buildings, and the projection into space of columns and pediments, while in open spaces like *exedrae*, because of the extensive wall space, they painted stage sets in the tragic, comic, or satiric style, and adorned their walkways, because of their extensive length, with varieties of landscape, creating images from the known characteristics of various places. For ports, promontories, seashores, rivers, springs, straits, shrines, sacred groves, mountains, herds, and shepherds are depicted; some places are portrayed in monumental painting [*megalographia*] with the likenesses of the gods or the skillfully arranged narrations of myths, such as the Trojan battles, or the wanderings of Ulysses through various landscapes, and other subjects that have been created according to nature on similar principles.[44]

FAVENTINUS   (Marcus Cetius Faventinus,[45] third century CE)

Short Book on the Art of Architecture for the Use of Private Individuals (*Artis architectonicae privatis usibus adbreviatus liber*), late third century CE (Fav., *Artis arch.*)

The date of Faventinus's *Short Book* is in doubt: it was certainly used by Palladius in the fifth century CE, and it has been tentatively given a date in the first half of the third century CE.[46] Readers in Late Antiquity and the Middle Ages were eager to acquire easily read, widely available, and even cross-referenced manuals of specialized knowledge, especially if that knowledge was based on literary texts that might have been hard to access. Palladius's *Opus agriculturae* is an example. In turn, writers like Palladius could rely on other manuals, and in his case, he turned to Faventinus's handy, well-organized abridgment of Vitruvius's treatise *On Architecture* and some other sources for what he needed in the way of architectural recipes for villas.[47]

Faventinus is unembarrassed to be writing an abridgment of Vitruvius, and he makes no apologies for omissions.[48] He apparently intended to direct his *Short Book* primarily to villa owners, telling the reader to go to the next section (chapter 14) on urban buildings (*opera urbana*) for more on the dwelling itself, thereby reversing the sequence of urban *domus* to villas that had been the case in Vitruvius's sequence of discussion.[49]

The following texts give an idea of Faventinus's methods.

Fav., *Artis arch*. 13.   HOW TO ORGANIZE THE CONSTRUCTION OF THE VILLA RUSTICA[50]
First off, the courtyards [*cortes*] and the kitchens [*culinae*] will be located in the warm parts [of the site]. The cattle stalls [*bubilia*] will be on the south side so that the cows face either the rising sun or the hearth: they acquire a sleeker [*nitidior*] look if they face toward the light. [...] The stables [*equilia*] will be set in warm parts [of the villa] but must have less light so the horses can feel safe while they eat. [...] The wine cellar [*cella vinaria*] will be located in the coldest parts with windows opening to the north so cool air maintains the wine intact: a [warm] atmosphere spoils all wines. [...].[51] If, however, you might wish to build something nicer and more elegant [*melius et nitidius*], you can take up examples from urban buildings.

Fav., *Artis arch*. 14.   SETTING URBAN BUILDINGS[52]
For pleasantness, an urban building must be full of light, especially if there are no adjacent walls to block out the light. It will be necessary to determine in advance which orientations [*caeli regiones*] are appropriate to specific rooms. For example, winter *triclinia* should face the setting sun because their use requires evening light: the setting sun not only illuminates the room but warms it with its strength. Bedrooms and libraries must face the rising sun [eastward] because their use requires early morning sun. All places that face the *Africanum* [southwest winds] are subject to deterioration due to those damp winds' corrupting moisture. Spring and autumn *triclinia* should face the rising sun [eastward] so they are more pleasant at the times they are used. Summer *triclinia* should face north because that quarter is the coolest at the summer solstice and offers, above all the others, pleasant healthiness of body. Galleries for paintings [*pinacothecae*] and embroidery studios [*officinae plumariorum*] are to be set up facing north so that the colors [colored threads] and purples [purple-dyed cloth] can be kept without harm: deterioration comes about in warm spaces.[53]

Fav., *Artis arch*. 16.5.   ON THE CONSTRUCTION OF BATHS[54]
In the *villa rustica*, the bath building and the kitchens should be placed side-by-side so that the band of agricultural slaves [*ministerium rusticum*] can go about their duties more easily.[55]

Fav., *Artis arch*. 25.   WINTER TRICLINIA MUST BE DECORATED WITH SMALLER PAINTINGS[56]
It is not a good idea to decorate winter *triclinia* with large paintings because they become sooty in the abundant lighting by candles or [oil] lamps. For that reason, it is better to have flat ceilings [*camerae planae*] so that, once the soot has been cleaned, their bright painting [*inluminatus splendor*] becomes immediately apparent.

4

DESCRIPTIONS OF VILLAS

CICERO
PLINY THE ELDER
VARRO
HORACE
SENECA THE YOUNGER
MARTIAL
STATIUS
PLINY THE YOUNGER
APULEIUS OF MADAURUS
AULUS GELLIUS
ST. GREGORY OF NYSSA
AUSONIUS
PAULINUS OF PELLA
SIDONIUS APOLLINARIS
GERONTIUS
CASSIODORUS
CARMEN DE PROVIDENTIA DEI

Villas were apt subjects for description in prose and poetry, used either as entities in themselves or as settings and prompts for letters, philosophical and moral essays, conversations in dialogue form, and thank you messages for hospitality, as invitations to visit, and little gifts (*xenia*) from the villa's garden (*hortus*) or its *pastio villatica*. In almost all cases, villas and their settings acted as tuning forks to set the tone for a wider orchestration of themes, whether incidental or the main topic. The following texts, presented chronologically (with some exceptions), give an idea of the varieties of villas owned by private citizens from the Late Republic to Late Antiquity and how they appeared in various literary genres.[1]

Cicero's Villa at Tusculum

Cicero was very proud of the villa he called his *Tusculanum* near the town of Tusculum, an ancient Latin town that had become a prestigious center of suburban villas for members of rich and prominent families in the Alban hills about 25 km southeast of the City. He appears to have bought it some years before his consulship in 63 BCE and started adding to it right away.[2] Even though he does not describe its architectural features specifically, he built at least one portico, some *oeci*, an Academy referencing Plato on a lower level or terrace, and a Lyceum referencing Aristotle above it: the Academy and Lyceum appear to have had attached *gymnasia*, and the library was in the Lyceum. He refers to the villa itself as *gymnasium*-like (γυμνασιώδη) and therefore a place of philosophical inquiry, discussion, and teaching.[3] The combination of elements indicates that Cicero thought of the Tusculanum as his teaching venue with its athletic and pedagogical aspects and as a garden for philosophical meetings.[4] Together, they supplied a Greek cultural wrapping for Cicero's writing and hospitality, underscoring his desire to bring Greek philosophy to Roman attention and to apply its principles to practical politics.

Both Cicero and Atticus in the 60s BCE were concerned with their villas: Cicero congratulates his friend on the purchase of a property in Epirus and mentions its development and consecration. The Epirote estate and its villa ultimately became Atticus's Amalthea and included inscriptions of *pensées* by Cicero sent to his friend; thus the villas, like their owners, were literary and personal alter egos of one another.[5] Atticus had another helpful function for his friend's villas: he was Cicero's agent in finding, purchasing, and arranging transport of works of art bought in Greece for the Tusculanum and other properties.

Cicero's exile from Rome between May 58 and August 57 BCE by the machinations of his political enemies on the basis of actions during his consulship in 63 BCE resulted in the confiscation of his family house in the Carinae district in Rome and the demolition of his house on the Palatine—itself expensively purchased for 3,500,000*HS* some years previously. His villas were also confiscated, and those at Tusculum and Formiae vandalized and robbed: at Tusculum, marble columns, as well as some unspecified decorations, were transferred to his enemies, the consuls of 58 BCE Aulus Gabinius and L. Calpurnius Piso Caesoninus and their relatives.⁶ Upon cancellation of his exile and his return, he received compensation from the Senate on evaluations of 2,000,000HS for the *domus* on the Palatine, 500,000HS for the Tusculanum, and only 250,000HS for the villa at Formiae.⁷ He grumbled that the assessments were too low, and he was thinking of selling the Tusculanum. If compensation for the works of art were included, he does not say.

Such descriptions of his Tusculum villa as Cicero provides occur in his treatises *On the Orator* (*De oratore*), *Tusculan Disputations* (*Tusculanae disputationes*), and *On Divination* (*De divinatione*), so they are excerpted here. He built a portico (*ambulatio* or *xystus*), and there were two athletic areas—*gymnasium* and *palaestra*—that together constituted the pedagogical and philosophical spaces recalling Greek pedagogical environments.⁸ Though not explicitly described, and therefore omitted here, Cicero's actual villa at Tusculum was also the setting of Cicero's *Brutus* (*De claris oratoribus* or *On Famous Orators*, 50 BCE) and his *Orator* (*Orator ad M. Brutum*, 46 BCE), both dedicated to M. Junius Brutus, Cicero's friend and villa neighbor at Tusculum.

CICERO   (Marcus Tullius Cicero, 107/106–43 BCE)

On the Orator (*De oratore*), 55 BCE (Cic., *De or.*)

The dialogue presented below, written in 52 BCE, obliquely describes Cicero's Tusculanum in the guise of another villa at Tusculum, that owned by one of the speakers, the famous orator L. Licinius Crassus (140–91 BCE, consul in 95 BCE), who had been Cicero's teacher and mentor in rhetoric.⁹ It is a conversation among politicians and lawyers famous for their oratory, purportedly set in 91 BCE, the year of Crassus's death; the dialogue treats the character and education of the successful orator in various philosophical and technical aspects. A short description of the setting by one of the interlocutors, Q. Lutatius Catulus, describes the villa as having a Greek architectural panoply to reinforce its educational and philosophical aspects.¹⁰ Cicero's villa at Tusculum also had such Greek architectural equipment, on the intended theme of Rome as true inheritor of Greek philosophy.

Crassus's reply to Catulus's question about the purpose of *gymnasia* may stand for the definition of the philosophic villa: that *gymnasia*, once used for teaching, were now primarily for athletic training and enjoyment, not for learning. He ends with the dictum "The real reward of *otium* is not the mind's struggle but rather the mind's release."¹¹

Cic., *De or.* 2.19 (2.5)   Then Catulus said, "However, Crassus, those Greeks who were famous great men in their own cities, in the same way as you and all of us wish to be in our own republic—those Greeks weren't at all like the Greeks of today who are now foisting themselves on our ears—but still, in their *otium*, they [those Greeks of the past] did not avoid conversations and disputations in the way we are doing now. And if those [famous great] men seem, as well they might at this time, in this place, in this day, irrelevant and lacking in good reasoning [skills], still, can this place—its portico [*ambulatio*] where we are walking, its *palaestra*, and its many seats—can these places right here not revive the memory of *gymnasia* and disputations among the Greeks?"¹²

Cicero, *On Divination* (*De divinatione*) 44 BCE (Cic., *Div.*)

Cic., *Div.* 1.8 (1.5)   [...] These topics have often been considered [by me] elsewhere [in other writings] but most recently and with greater exactitude when my brother Quintus and I were together recently at my Tusculan villa. For the purpose of having a walk, we had gone to the

Lyceum, the name by which my upper gymnasium [*superior gymnasium*] is known, when Quintus remarked....[13] [...]

Cic., *Div.* 2.8 (2.3)   After my brother Quintus had expressed his opinion about divination, and we had walked enough, we sat down in the library [*bibliotheca*], which is in the Lyceum, and I said....[...]

Cicero, *Letters to Atticus* (*Epistulae ad Atticum*) (Cic., Att.)

Cicero's condemnation to exile was rescinded by senatorial decree, and he returned to Italy and Rome in August 57 BCE.[14] His efforts to reclaim his property, which had included the destruction of his house on the Palatine and depredations at his villas, occupied him for a while but appear to have been successful despite his grumbling.[15] This letter describes the compensation amounts allocated by the Senate to Cicero for his property, mainly his house on the Palatine Hill that had been razed and maliciously replaced by a shrine to Liberty (*aedes* or *atrium Libertatis*) by Publius Clodius and his partisans.[16] Cicero initiated his requests for compensation in a speech (*De domo sua*) to the religious authorities, asking them to void the consecration of the site, as it had been made on false pretenses. His speech was successful. After that, a debate in the Senate ensued, resulting in a vote of monetary compensation for both the house and two villas.[17] The going was not straightforward. Construction on his house on the Palatine and an adjacent new construction (the portico of Catulus) was disrupted by Publius Clodius's bullyboys (*Att.* 75.3 [4.3]). The work on the villas continued, apparently without incident.

Cic., *Att.* 74 (4.2), October 57 BCE   [...] On the day after, the senatorial decree which I am sending you was enacted....[...]

The consuls, upon taking the advice of assessors, gave an estimate for the value of my house at about 2,000,000*HS*, but the other properties were stingily valued at 500,000*HS* for my villa at Tusculum and 250,000*HS* for the Formian villa. This estimate was vehemently disapproved not only by the party of conservative tendency but by the ordinary people as well. [...]

Those are my plans regarding my career as a politician, but my domestic affairs are terribly awry. My house is being built, but you know how expensive and bothersome that can be. My villa at Formia is being restored, but neither can I let it go [sell it] nor go to see it. I've offered my villa at Tusculum for sale—I can do without a suburban villa easily enough [*careo facile*].[18] [...]

Cicero, *Tusculan Disputations* (*Tusculanae disputationes*), late 45 BCE (Cic., Tusc.)

After the death of his daughter Tullia in February 45 BCE, Cicero wrote a consolatory essay or speech to himself and a major long work on the philosophy of death, grieving, mental distress, and Stoic resignation, as well as the *Tusculan Disputations* in five dialogue books, addressed to M. Junius Brutus.[19]

The architecture of the villa at Tusculum and its symbolic spaces for philosophy had been ideated and achieved, with Atticus's help with the statues and some buying in the Roman art market, in the mid-60s BCE; now, some twenty years later, they have become real settings for a dialogue set over five days at the villa, specifically in its Academy. Cicero does not describe the villa in much detail, but it recalls Crassus's villa at Tusculum which had been the setting for his *On the Orator* (*De oratore*) about a decade earlier.

The Tusculanum was not only a place for philosophical discourse: it was also luxurious. Cicero collected Corinthian bronzes at the villa, the obligatory paraphernalia of the art-loving rich Romans at the time.[20] Elsewhere in the dialogue, Cicero included a little story about the lean hospitality of Xenocrates, the third *scholarch* of Plato's Academy at Athens, to give color to his own frugality.[21]

Additional material is included here to show how Cicero set the Academy in his Tusculanum as the stage for philosophical discussions.

Cic., *Tusc.* 1.7 (1.4) […] I have always considered that speaking on questions of the greatest importance at length and in a complete way is a perfect philosophical endeavor, and I have so zealously given myself over to this endeavor that, as the Greek philosophers used to do, I have already attempted to set up a school. So, after you [Brutus] left me and, having many of my friends with me, I attempted to do something like that at my Tusculanum. […]

Cic., *Tusc.* 2.2 (2.1) […] As the knowledge of philosophy in its entirety at a universal scale may at times free us, at least in part, from our longing for things [*cupiditatis*], and from our sadness and fear: in this way, from the discussion that was had recently at my Tusculanum, a contempt for death was aroused which is not a small spur to freeing the spirit from fear. […]

Cic., *Tusc.* 2.9 (2.3) […] In my own memory, Philo, whom I often heard speak, used to contemplate the lessons of the orators at one time, then, at another time, those of the philosophers.[22] At my Tusculanum, I was prompted by my friends to adopt this [alternation of rhetoric and philosophy], so we spent our time in this way. While we spoke of this topic before midday, in the afternoon we went down to the Academy: I've told you about the conversations we had, not [merely] in a narrative summary but almost in the words as they were spoken. […]

Cic., *Tusc.* 2.32 (2.14) […] You are quite aware that if, say, something [in your collection] of Corinthian [bronze] objects went missing, the rest of them would be safe. However, if a virtue went missing—though virtue cannot really go missing—would you admit that, no longer having one [particular virtue or bronze object], would you then say that you had none at all?

Cic., *Tusc.* 3.6–7 (3.3) […] I have never ceased either discussing or writing on these [philosophical] matters.[23] These books contain what was discussed between myself and my friends at my Tusculanum. Having, in the two previous books, discussed death and sorrow, the third day of the disputations [about alleviating mental pain] will be in this volume. Then, as the day was getting on to the afternoon, we went down [*descendimus*] to my Academy, and there I asked one of those who were there to set out a topic for discussion. […]

Cic., *Tusc.* 4.7 (4.4) […] I have practiced this system [of enumerating the most probable opinions] in the other books of my *Tusculan Disputations*. Having already given you in the three foregoing books what we discussed on the three previous days, what [we discussed] on the fourth day will be related. As we did on the days before, we went down to the lower portico [*inferior ambulatio* of the Academy], and the matter was broached in this way.… […][24]

Cic., *Tusc.* 5.11 (5.4) Carneades used this method [Socratic questioning] in a sharp and copious [detailed] way, and I did the same just recently at my Tusculanum.[25] I have already sent you what we discussed on the four previous days, so on the fifth day, when we were seated in the same place [in the lower portico of the Academy], what was proposed for discussion was outlined in this way.… […]

Cicero's Villa at Tusculum: The Works of Art and Other Decorations

Collecting works of art for his villas—mainly for the Tusculanum but also for others—was a matter of grave consideration: they were environments for Cicero's intellectual work (*studium*) as well as his *otium*, and their appropriate iconography was important.[26] In the 60s BCE, both before and after his consulship in 63, Cicero was completing additions to the structure and decoration of his Tusculum villa. He wrote several letters to Atticus, at the time residing in Athens or at his villa near Buthrotum (modern Butrint) in Epirus, about statues that his friend was buying and forwarding to him; these were to decorate his villas both to amplify their philosophical and literary atmosphere and to serve as ornaments in architectural ensembles.

Three considerations motivated Cicero: that the subject matter of the works be appropriate to his self-representation as an intellectual and public figure, that they not cost too much, that they be from Greece, be in Greek materials or manufacture (marble or bronze), or depict Greek gods; these last conferred glamor and embodied the general Roman preoccupation with Greek culture.[27] Cicero was also interested in acquiring books and mentions them in the context of his villas. Most of the comments about purchases of art are contained within letters dealing with political issues, personal matters, and gossip.

Cicero, Letters to Atticus

In this next letter (*Att.* 10.5 [1.1.5]), Cicero associates his *gymnasium* with a sacred precinct in which the herm statue of Athena and Hermes was almost an object of worship. In another letter (*Fam.* 28.2–3 [7.23.2–3]), Cicero distinguished between *palaestra* and *gymnasium*: in Latinized Greek terminology, a *palaestra* was an open sports field for exercise, while a *gymnasium* with its porticoes provided spaces for pedagogy in rhetoric and philosophy. Both were venues for young men to meet their teachers and functioned as gathering places for philosophical discussion. The entire Tusculan villa evidently was a kind of *gymnasium* in Cicero's mind.

Cic., *Att.* 10.5 (1.1.5), ca. July 17, 65 BCE   [...] The Hermathena you sent me is very pleasing indeed, and it has been placed in a good spot, such that the whole *gymnasium* seems to be a sacred offering [ἀνάθημα] to it.[28] I love you dearly.

Cic., *Att.* 8.1 (1.3.1), late in the year 67 BCE   [...] The statues [*signa*] you bought for me are now on the quayside at Caieta. I haven't seen them yet as I have not been able to leave Rome, but I have sent someone to transport them. I am greatly grateful to you for the energy you expended and that you paid a small amount of money for them. [...]

Cic., *Att.* 9.3 (1.4.3), early April 66 BCE   [...] I am very pleased at what you write me about the Hermathena.[29] It is a suitable ornament to my Academy [at the Tusculanum] because Hermes is usual for all *gymnasia* and Athena is particularly appropriate here. So, in this matter do as you have written to me and send as many other items of the same kind to embellish the place. The ones you sent me before I have not yet seen—they are now at my villa at Formiae where I am now thinking of going. I will have everything transferred to my villa at Tusculum, and when that is completed, I will start decorating [*ornabo*] my villa at Caieta.

Hold onto your books and do not despair that someday they will belong to me—when that happens, I will have outstripped even a Crassus in wealth and will [be able to] disdain all their mansions and meadows.[30] [...]

The next two letters (*Att.* 1.4 [1.5.4] and *Att.* 2 [1.6.2]) were written in rapid succession in late November 68 BCE. Cicero urges Atticus to send more works of art for his villa, and quickly.

Cic., *Att.* 1.4 (1.5.4), late November 68 BCE   [...] I am happy that your purchase [of the property] in Epirus pleases you. On the things that I asked about, and, as you write, anything else that you think would be suitable at my Tusculan villa, go ahead [and buy them], as long as you can do so without inconvenience. For me, it is the only place that I can feel at ease after work and worries. [...]

Cic., *Att.* 2 (1.6.2), late November 68 BCE   [...] If by chance you are able to find any decorations for my γυμνασιώδη [*gymnasium*–like villa] that would be suitable as you are familiar with it, don't let them get away from you. I am so happy with my Tusculan villa that I am not really at ease unless I am there. [...]

Cic., *Att.* 4 (1.8.2), on or after February 13, 67 BCE   [...] As you told me to do, I have taken care to put together 20,400*HS* for the statues to pay Lucius Cincius.[31] The herms in Pentelic marble with bronze heads that you wrote to me about already please me very much.[32] Send them and anything else that would be suitable for the place and my intellectual interests [*studii*] and your tastes [*elegantiae*]. Send me as many as possible and as soon as you can, most especially if they would suit the *gymnasium* and the portico [*xystus*]. In such things, I exhibit such great zeal [*studium*] that others may sharply censure me, but I expect approval from you. If Lentulus's ships are not available, put the statues on any boat you like. [...]

Cic., *Att.* 5.2 (1.9.2), late March or early April 67 BCE   [...] I am waiting impatiently for the statues in Megarian marble and the herms that you wrote to me about. Don't hesitate to send anything else like them that you have and that you think would be appropriate for my Academy—I am sure that I have the money [*arca*].[33] Such things are my great pleasure, and I'm especially looking for things for my γυμνασιώδη. Lentulus promises [transport in] his ships, and I beg you, be quick about getting this done. [...]

Cic., *Att.* 6.1 (1.10.1) and 7.3 (1.10.3), July 67 BCE   "When I was at my villa at Tusculum" is like the remark [in your letter] "When I was at my place in the Ceramicus."[34] In any case, when I was there, a boy [*puer*] gave me a letter from you forwarded from Rome by your sister, and he told me that someone was leaving [Rome] soon and would go to see you [in Greece, and could deliver a letter from me] [...]

As you've written, send my statues and the herms [*hermeraclae*] as soon as you possibly can, and anything else that you find that would be suitable to the house [οἶκος], which you know so well, especially things that would be suitable for the *palaestra* and the *gymnasium*. I'm sitting there right now as I write to you, so the place itself suggests these items. In addition, I am giving you permission to buy some reliefs that could be set into the walls of the small atrium [*atriolus*], and two carved puteals [*putealia sigillata*].[35]

[...] Make sure not to promise your library to anyone else, even if you should find an eager buyer: I am saving up all my small fees [*vindemiolae*] for it to be a support in my old age.[36]

Cic., *Att.* 7.3 (1.11.3), July 67 BCE   [...] As soon as you can, send me what you have bought for my Academy. It's amazing how much thinking about it pleases me even when I am not actually there. Keep your books away from anyone else and keep them for me as you have promised. Literary work is my foremost preoccupation even as my disdain for other things grows. [...]

Throughout the 60s BCE, Cicero and Atticus were building the Tusculanum and the Amalthea, respectively—the former near Rome, the latter near Buthrotum in Epirus.

Cic., *Att*. 13.4 (1.13.4), January 25, 61 BCE   [...] As it happens, I don't often hear of someone setting out for Epirus [to deliver my letters to you]. I reckon that when the sacrifices [*caesus victimarum*] have been made at your Amalthea, you'll go lay siege to Sikyon right away.[37] [...]

Cicero, *Letters to Friends* (*Epistulae ad familiares*) (Cic., *Fam.*)

Atticus was not the only source for works of art for the Tusculanum; there were agents for the art market in Rome and elsewhere in Italy. Fadius was one such agent, and while Cicero seems to know him well, he rebukes him for unreliability and lack of taste.

Cic., *Fam*. 209 (7.23.2–3), to Marcus Fadius Gallus,[38] 63–61 BCE   As soon as I returned from my estates at Arpinum, your letters to me were delivered, and by the same courier I received a letter from Avianus, in which he included a very generous offer, namely to put whatever date I wanted [on the receipt] when he came to see me.[39] I ask you to think of yourself as if you were I: would it be honorable, either for you or for both of us, to quibble about the day [of sale] on which the expense was incurred or the amount of interest [on the sum]?

But of course, dear Gallus, the whole affair would have been easier, if you, as a buyer of the goods, had bought what I had wanted and within the maximum amount of money I had stipulated to spend. Anyway, all things being equal [*ista ipsa*], I will give my approval to the items you've written to me about. What's more, I will acknowledge my pleasure in them, because I clearly recognize that you had an affectionate wish to please me—you, a man whom I have always judged to be the most discriminating in matters of taste [*in omni iudicio elegantissimus*]—and that, because these things pleased you, you thought they would be worthy of me.

Still, I would prefer that Damasippus stay true to his offer [to buy the statues], because there's not one of these items that I would actually want.[40] As you did not know what my principles [*mores*] are, you have bought four or five statues for as much money as I would have estimated the cost of all statues of any type anywhere! You compare these Bacchantes to the statues of Muses in Metellus's collection, but in what way are they similar?[41] In the first place, I would never have considered that those Muses [of Metellus] would have been worth all that amount of money, and my view would have been approved by all the [nine] Muses themselves! Muses would have been appropriate for my library and appropriate to my literary activities. Where [in my villa] would there be a place for Bacchantes? They're pretty little things—I know them well and have often seen them. Still, if I had wanted them, I would have commissioned you to buy them—things that I had already seen. Indeed, I am accustomed to buying statues for my *palaestra*, to make it resemble a *gymnasium*. But, really, a statue of Mars—what would I, a promoter of peace, do with that? I'm relieved that there was no statue of Saturn [in the offering], for the two together would have put me deeply in debt. I would have preferred a statue of Mercury; that way, I think, I would have gotten a better deal from Avianus.[42]

Now about the table-support [τραπεζοφόρον] that you wanted for yourself, please take it if it pleases you, but if you've changed your mind, for sure I'll take it for myself. For the [large] sum of money [all these things have cost], it would have been better for me to have bought a *deversorium* at Tarracina [for myself] so as not to bother my host there.[43] In any case, I consider the blame to be clearly that of my freedman whom I commissioned to make these purchases, and with Junius, Avianus's friend, whom you also know.[44] In the small porticoes of my villa at Tusculum, I've installed some new *exedrae* which I have thought of decorating with pictures [*ornare tabellis*].[45] For that matter, if I enjoy anything in the way of art, it's painting that pleases me most. To conclude, if I must take possession of these items, please tell me where they are, when they can be seen, and what vehicles are needed. If Damasippus doesn't adhere to his [original] offer [to buy the statues], I will have to look around for a substitute Damasippus.[46] [...]

Cic., *Att.* 21.1 (2.1.1), June 60 BCE   [...] My "Amalthea" is waiting and longing for you.[47] The villas at Tusculum and Pompeii delight me, except that, as I am myself liable for their cost, I am overwhelmed with [the need to pay in] ordinary [bronze] coin rather than Corinthian bronzes.

Cicero, perhaps a little embarrassed at his wealth and luxury, makes self-deprecating, wordplay fun of his art collection in order to encourage his indisposed friend, G. Trebatius Testa, to be cheerful during an illness.[48]

Cic., *Fam.* 34.2 (7.11.2), to Gaius Trebatius Testa, January 53 BCE   [...] Now listen to me, what's going on with you? Has anything happened? I see some lightness of tone in your recent letters. These are better signs [*signa*] than the statues [*signa*] at my villa at Tusculum. [...]

Cicero, *Orator (Orator ad M. Brutum)* late 46 BCE[49,] (Cic., *Orat.*)

Cicero bought art (*signa*) for his villas. However, what Cicero bought was different in kind from what his noble associates and friends had bought for their villas but had also inherited.[50] The difference would have been obvious, as Cicero himself recognized: it was the difference between what we call art (for sculpture, *signa* in general, but which can also refer to portraits) and what the Romans would have called an *imago* (pl. *imagines, imagines maiorum*) when applied to ancestor images.[51] Cicero was very proud of his father and grandfather, whose memories he cherished, and he was forever grateful for the gift of fine education that their father had given to his younger brother Quintus and himself. He was also very fond of his hometown of Arpinum, its people, and its traditions. However, as a *novus homo* in Rome, he would have had few ancestral *imagines* or, more probably (as he does not mention any), none at all. He only had *signa* that he could buy.

In contrast, Brutus was descended from impeccably aristocratic patrician and plebeian noble families for more than 400 years on his father's, adoptive father's, and mother's sides, and he would have had plenty of family portraits at his Tusculan villa besides other works of art or images of historical figures he admired.[52] Cicero's deficiency in regard to *imagines maiorum* was made up, in his mind, by the glittering intellectual and rhetorical ancestry of Greek and Latin poets and orators of which he was a distinguished scion in mental power rather than in family tree. But Brutus, in his villa, had both *signa* (an *imago* of a famous Athenian orator) and *imagines maiorum*, the portraits of his ancestors.

Cic., *Orat.* 110 (30–31)   [Cicero, speaking to Brutus directly] For example, Demosthenes, whom I believe you admire, and whose bronze portrait [*imago ex aere*] I saw recently at your Tusculan villa together with images of yourself and those of your relatives [*inter imagines tuas ac tuorum*]—a Demosthenes is not inferior to Lysias in plainness, nor to Hyperides in sharpness and insight, nor to Aeschines in lightness of touch and splendor of expression.[53]

Cicero, *Letters to Atticus*

Cicero saw villas—Atticus's in Epirus and his own Tusculanum—as equivalent and related in the same way that he thought of both their lives on parallel and intersecting paths. Atticus's Amalthea was in progress of construction, and inscriptions, perhaps mentioning their friendship in verse, appear to have been part of its embellishment. Cicero wished to emulate his friend's projects.[54]

Cic., *Att.* 16 (1.16), December 61 BCE   [...] I will be pleased with the inscriptions [*epigrammata*] you have installed in the Amaltheum, most of all because Thyillus has left my company, and Archias has written nothing about me.[55] [...]

Please, if you wish, write me how your Amaltheum [Ἀμαλθεῖον] is set up, and how it is decorated and what its location [τοπθεσία] is, and tell me what you know in the way of poems and stories about Amalthea [Ἀμαλθεία] herself—it would please me to set one up at my villa at Arpinum. [...]

Cicero's Villa at His Hometown of Arpinum

Cicero, *On the Laws* (*De legibus*) 46–45 BCE (Cic., *De leg.*)

Cicero's dialogue *On the Laws* deals with the basis of civil and religious law in the natural order. It is supplemented with some circumstantial detail: a description of the setting and meaning of his villa at Arpinum. In the first book, Cicero (=Marcus), his brother Quintus, and his friend Atticus are walking and talking along walkways with occasional places to sit (*illa spatia nostra sedesque*), first by the Liris River (modern Liri River) that flows nearby (*De leg.* 1.14–15). Book 2 has the same three interlocutors, but the setting has changed to the confluence of the Fibrenus stream (modern Fibreno River) with the Liris. The theme of villas is elaborated, both for Cicero's villa at Arpinum and Atticus's Epirote villa, as well as the idea of villas in general.

Cic., *De leg.* 2.1–7 (2.1–3)
ATTICUS   "Don't you think, now that we've walked enough and you are ready to begin another topic of discussion, we should leave this place and go to the island in the Fibrenus—I think that's the name of the other river—and finally sit down to finish the rest of the conversation?"

MARCUS   "Certainly we should—that's the place that I most willingly go for thinking [when I am] by myself, or for writing something, or for reading."[56]

ATTICUS   "In truth, now that I have come to this best of all places, I cannot be more pleased, and I [have come to] disdain magnificent villas, marble floors, and coffered ceilings [*magnificae villae et pavimenta marmorea et laqueata tecta*]. Who, after seeing this place, wouldn't laugh heartily at those streams of piped water that are known as Niles and Euripi, as some call them? And so, just as a while ago you correlated all things relevant to law and justice with Nature, so too Nature is the most important element to those things relevant to the mind's calm disposition and delight. For that reason, because I had thought that there was nothing but rocks and mountains around here, and I thought so having been led to this view by your [own] speeches and poems, I used to wonder how it was that this place pleased you so much. Now, by contrast, I wonder that you can bear to be anywhere else when you are away from Rome."

MARCUS "It's true, whenever I can be away [from Rome], I seek out the beauty and healthfulness of this place, but it's not often possible. But of course, there's a reason why this place gives me another [greater] pleasure, one which you would not have in the same way."

ATTICUS "What reason might that be?"

MARCUS "I will tell you the truth. It's that this is my and my brother's own true fatherland [*germana patria*]; we were born here, descended from a very ancient family, and it is from here that our [family] rituals and our race originate; there are many traces of our ancestors here. What else is there to say? Over there you see the villa as it is now, a building made more elegant [*lautius*] by our father's effort; because he suffered from poor health, he passed most of his life in literary pursuits here. In addition, it was right here, believe me, that I was born, at the time that my grandfather was [still] living and the villa was a small affair in the ancient manner [*antiquo more parva villa*] like that of Curius in the Sabine district.[57] It's for that reason that something—I don't know how to say it—stays in my mind and consciousness and perhaps makes this place even more greatly dear to me; there was, after all, that very wise man who, it is written, rejected immortality so that he might see [his] Ithaca once more."[58]

ATTICUS "I think that you have a good reason to be eager to come here and to love the place; indeed in truth, I myself have now become fonder of the villa over there and to the whole landscape [around it], now that [I have been made aware that] this is the place that your race [*ortus*] comes from and where your birth took place. I don't know how it is, but we are moved by the common places in which there are recollections of those whom we love and admire. For me, even our own dear Athens, it is not the magnificent public buildings and the ancient, exquisite works of art that are causes of delight. Rather, it is the memory of its greatest men, where each one lived, where they sat, where it was customary for them to have discussions, and I even love to contemplate their tombs. That's the reason that I will love this place even more, because it is where you were born."

MARCUS "It makes me glad to have been able to show you what might be called my cradle."

ATTICUS "In the same way, I am glad to know the place. But still, what did you intend, when I heard you say a little while ago, that Arpinum was your [and your brother's] fatherland [*patria*]? Do you have two fatherlands? Or is the [one Roman] fatherland we share the only one? Maybe you think that wise Cato's fatherland was Tusculum [where he was born] rather than Rome?"

MARCUS "Most emphatically [*mehercule*] do I think that Cato and all citizens of [Italian] towns have two fatherlands, one by virtue of nature, the other by being citizens [of a municipality], such that Cato, even though he was born in Tusculum, was taken into the citizenship of the Roman people; in this way, he was Tusculan in origin and a Roman by citizenship, and he had one fatherland of place, another fatherland in law [*alteram loci patriam, alteram iuris*]."[59] [...]

ATTICUS [...] "But we've [now] come to the island [in the river]: really, nothing could be more pleasant. Almost like a ship's beak, it divides the Fibrenus into two equal streams, flowing fast on either bank then suddenly reuniting, so close as to leave just enough room for a small athletic field [*palaestra*]. Having done all this, and as if its only business and duty were to make some room for us to sit down for our discussion, it then throws itself headlong into the Liris, and, as if it had come into a patrician family, it forfeits its less well known name [*nomen obscurius*] and makes the Liris River much colder. I've seen many a river, but none as cold as this one—I could almost not stand to put my foot in it, as Socrates did in Plato's *Phaedrus*."[60]

MARCUS   "It's truly as you say, but as I often hear from Quintus, I imagine that the pleasant aspect of your [Amalthea by the river] Thyamis in Epirus does not yield anything [in the way of beauty] to this place."

QUINTUS   "It's just as you say: do not think that there is anything more refined than our dear Atticus's Amaltheum and its plane trees.[61] But if it seems good, let's sit down together here in the shade and return to the discussion where we left off [while we were walking]."

Cicero's Villa at Puteoli

PLINY THE ELDER   (Gaius Plinius Secundus (23/24–79 CE)

Natural History (*Naturalis historia*), mid–first century CE (Plin., *HN*)

About a century after Cicero's murder in 43 BCE, Pliny the Elder discussed the different kinds of water throughout Mediterranean lands, many having therapeutic and even curative properties: Plin., *HN* 31.6–9 (31.3). Cicero's villa at Puteoli, in the geothermic region of the Bay of Naples caldera, had hot springs (beneficial to the eyes), which had erupted on the property soon after his death. This was the villa he had received in bequest from the banker Marcus Cluvius and where he had entertained Julius Caesar and his entourage of 2,000 soldiers in December, 45 BCE. It is briefly described and, most importantly, named by Pliny who reproduces a touching poem on the spring and on Cicero as the villa's previous owner.[62]

Plin., *HN* 31.6–8 (31.3)   In the matter of the types of waters, some can heal tendons and feet, others work on sciatica, yet others on luxated joints or broken bones. Some can clear up bowel problems or heal wounds. Others work specifically on the head or the ears; however, [the waters called] Ciceronian are [good] for the eyes.

It is worth reminding ourselves that, on the track along the coast between Lake Avernus and Puteoli, there is a villa with a famous portico and a tree plantation, which M. Cicero called *Academia* after its Athenian exemplar. At this villa he wrote the books [*Academica*] after the name [he had given to the place], and there he set up memorials [*monumenta*] to himself, as if, indeed, he had not already done so all over the world.[63]

Shortly after his [Cicero's] death, when Antistius Vetus owned the villa, hot-water springs burst out, which are very effective for afflictions of the eyes.[64] These springs have been celebrated in a poem by Laureus Tullius, one of Cicero's freedmen, something that alerts us vividly [to the fact that] even those in his service drank from the authority [*maiestas*] of that man's genius. I am writing the poem out as follows, [because] it is worthy of being read everywhere, not just there [at the villa's springs]:

> You [Cicero], the champion of our great [Latin] language,
> Whose plantation of trees grows green with a better flourishing [than before]
> And its villa, made famous by the name *Academia*,
> Which [Antistius] Vetus keeps in trim with stronger measures [than you had],
> Here, waters not known before revealed themselves
> Which when applied in drops can soothe tired eyes.
> Surely the place itself gave this [memorial] to honor its [former] owner Cicero,
> When it opened up these eye-healing springs, so that,
> Because he is unceasingly read all over the world,
> There will be more [beneficial] waters to heal eyes."

VARRO (Marcus Terentius Varro, 116–27 BCE)

Three Books on Agriculture (*De re rustica libri III*), ca. 37–36 BCE (Varro, *Rust.*)

Lucullus's Aviary-*triclinium* at His Villa near Tusculum

Lucullus had an aviary at his villa at Tusculum, one of Varro's type not built purely for pleasure or profit but for both: to make money and also provide the amenities of a *villa urbana*.[65] It does not appear that Lucullus's aviary worked very well, but Varro describes it in contrast to his own much better designed aviary-*triclinium* at his Casinum villa, of which he was very proud. Varro was mocking Lucullus's famous futile luxury as well as his own ability to supply an unlimited quantity of thrush (fieldfares) for the Roman market.[66]

Varro, *Rust.* 3.4.3 [Merula[67] speaking] "Lucullus [had] an aviary at his Tusculan property, where an *ornithon* and a *triclinium* were combined: there, he could feast in luxury and see cooked birds on the dish before him and the same species of caged birds flying around the windows [of their cages]. This did not work: to see the birds flying around the windows did not offset the bad smells that filled diners' nostrils.

Varro's Villa, *musaeum*, and Aviary-*triclinium* at Casinum

Varro's villa at Casinum (modern Cassino) was one of several he appears to have owned, but it was the one where, according to Cicero, he did his writing, made scientific collections, and amassed a library.[68] The villa was equipped with buildings and imaginatively designed appurtenances to exhibit specimens of favorite animals, encyclopedic collections of art, fish, plants, books, and other miscellanies. Besides the aviary (*ornithon*), there was a *musaeum*, or retreat for study and writing, at the villa.[69] In *De re rustica*, Varro gives a brief description of the property and its buildings, then concentrates on the aviary-*triclinium*, of which he was very proud, (see fig. 10) as much for its arrangement as that he improved on Lucullus's aviary at Tusculum: science betters wealthy ignorance.[70]

Specifically, Varro's improvements appear to have been in the provisioning of water running in channels (*rivoli, canaliculi*) through the cages in both the entrance porticoes and the circular one surrounding the *triclinium* (the villa, set on a downward slope, straddled a stream). These channels provided the birds with water and could be used to flush the execreta that had discommoded the diners in Lucullus's aviary-*triclinium*. By implication, Varro is comparing his own ingenuity to Lucullus's failure, as previously described by Merula.

Varro, *Rust.* 3.5.8–17 Appius said to Axius, "If you put 5,000 birds into an aviary and there is a public banquet or a triumph [in Rome], you can then loan 60,000*HS* out right away at as high a rate of interest as you wish."[71]

Then, speaking to me [Varro], he said, "Tell us about that other type of *ornithon* that you built for pleasure near Casinum, in which you surpassed [*longe vicisse*] not only the archetype of such aviaries by their inventor, [namely] our friend M. Laenius Strabo, who was our host at Brundisium, the first to keep birds caged in an *exedra* in the peristyle, feeding them through a net, but also surpassing the large buildings of Lucullus's villa at Tusculum."[72]

I replied, "Near the town of Casinum, I own a clear, deep stream running through my villa; it has rocky banks some 57 *pedes* wide [about 15.33 m, or 55 ft., 4 in.], and bridges are needed to get from one part of the villa to the other. There is a distance of 950 *pedes* [about 281 m, or 923 ft.] from an island at the lowest part of the stream [where it conjoins with another torrent] to the upper area of the villa where the *musaeum* is located. An open walkway 10 *pedes* wide [about

3 m, or 9 ft., 9 in.] runs along the banks, and the aviary is set next to it, facing the countryside with high walls on its right and left sides. The aviary within the walls is shaped like a writing tablet with a *capitulum* [rounded headpiece]; the space between the walls is 48 *pedes* wide and 72 *pedes* long, with the rounded *capitulum* of 27 *pedes* [about 14.2 m wide × 21.3 m long × 8 m for the *capitulum*, or 46 ft., 7 in. wide × 70 ft. long × 26 ft., 2 in. for the rounded headpiece]. At the base of the writing tablet [so to speak] where there is a space, there are *plumula* [little wings] of the aviary forming an entrance to a courtyard with its cages [on either side]. Beyond [this entrance], there are porticoes with stone columns on the right and left; in front of them [in the middle] are dwarf trees in rows.

From the top of the [outside] walls to the architrave of the porticoes, there is a [horizontally spread] hemp net, and the same from the architrave to the base of the [stone] colonnade [spread vertically]. The colonnades are crowded with all kinds of birds—they are fed through the nets, and water flows along a small channel [*rivulus*]. Inside and along the colonnades, on the right and left extending from the top end of the courtyard, there are two narrow rectangular fish basins. Between them, there is an entrance to a *tholos*, a domed rotunda set on columns—you can see one in the temple of Catulus if you [can] imagine columns instead of a [solid] circular wall.[73]

Outside the columns [of the rotunda], there is an artificial grove of large trees, so light comes into the rotunda from below, and the whole enclosure has high walls on the outside. Between the circular stone colonnade of the rotunda and the inner circle of slender columns made of pinewood [fir], there is a space 5 *pedes* wide [about 1.5 m, or 5 ft.]. The colonnade is draped with nettings of gut instead of an exterior wall—this barrier does not allow birds to escape but makes for a view into the grove of trees and its features. On the inner side of the [circular] pinewood colonnade and between each column, there is netting instead of a wall.

Between the [inner pinewood] columns and the exterior [stone] columns, there is a stepped structure making a little [half-round] theater, with projecting shelves on all the columns for the birds' perches. Within the netting are all kinds of birds, mainly songsters such as nightingales and blackbirds; water comes to them through a small channel [*per canaliculum*] and they are fed under [through] the netting. Below the stylobate of the columns is a stone wall 1 *pes* 9 *unciae* in height [about 45.6 cm, or 1 ft., 6 in.] defining a platform; the platform itself is set 2 *pedes* [about 59 cm, or 2 ft.] above a pond and is about 5 *pedes* wide so guests can walk between the cushions [for lying on the platform?] and the inner [pinewood] columns. The platform defines a pond with an edge 1 *pes* wide and a little island in the middle. The platform's circumference is pierced with dry docks [*navalia*] to accommodate ducks.

On the island, there is a column holding a shaft that supports a spoked wheel instead of a tabletop; at the end of the spokes, instead of the usual braced wheel rim [felloe], there is a curved surface like a drum 2½ *pedes* and a palm high [about 74 cm, or 2 ft., 3 in. wide, and about 7.5 cm, or 3 in. high]. This can be turned by a single slave boy so that drinks and dishes of food can be distributed around to all the guests.

From the platform wall where the couch coverings [*eripetasmata*] would hang down, the ducks come out and swim in the pond. From the pond, a stream runs into the two fishponds [in the courtyard] that I've already mentioned, and small fish dart here and there. Hot and cold water from spigots is served from the revolving table at the end of the spokes, as I've mentioned, to each guest.

Inside the *tholos*, the morning [*stella lucifer*] and evening [*noctu hesperus*] stars move around the lower edge of the dome to mark the hours [of the day]. In the same hemispherical dome, in the middle, there is a wind rose of the eight winds, just like the *horologium* at Athens that the Cyrrestrian built: there is an indicator attached to a post that is moved as a wind touches it so you can tell which wind is blowing.'"[74]

Varro's Descriptions of Game Parks at Villas

Villas with plenty of space could enclose large animals for display and possibly for food; the pens were known as *leporaria* after the pens or enclosed warrens for rabbits.

Varro, *Rust*. 3.13   [Appius, speaking to Axius] "You know that boars can be kept in an enclosure without much trouble—both [wild] ones that have been captured and domesticated ones that were born there. On the estate near Tusculum that our friend Varro bought from M. Pupius Piso, you have seen how, on the trumpeting of a horn at a fixed time, wild boars and roe deer gather to eat food thrown to them from a raised deck—nuts to the boars, vetch to the deer.[75] Indeed, I have seen the same thing done in a more 'Thracian' manner on the estate of Q. Hortensius [Hortalus] near Laurentum.[76] There was a grove that, as he claimed, was a walled pen of more than 50 *iugera* [about 12.6 ha, or 31 acres], and he called it a *therotrophium* rather than a mere enclosure. In it was a high spot where we ate at a *triclinium* set up there and where he called for an 'Orpheus.' The 'Orpheus' came in with his cloak and harp and was told to sing; he blew a horn and we were surrounded by such a troop of stags, boars, and other quadrupeds that, in my view, it was no less beautiful than when the aediles stage hunts in the Circus Maximus without African animals."

HORACE   (Quintus Horatius Flaccus, 65–8 BCE)

Satires, ca. 35–33 BCE (Hor., *Sat*.)

Horace's Sabine Farm

In the late 30s BCE, Augustus's friend and political associate Maecenas gave Horace the usufruct of a small estate comprising a dwelling and five tenants in Sabine country northeast of Rome.[77] This poem is the poet's thank you note.

Hor., *Sat*. 2.6.1–19
>This was what had been in my prayers: a measure of land not too large
>With a garden and a perennial spring of water near the house
>And, above these, a small wooded area.
>The gods have given me more than this and even better: I am happy.
>O son of Maia, I ask for nothing more than this,
>Unless it is that you might make these self-same gifts to be my own.[78]
>If I had not made the gifts greater by bad means,
>Or if I had been about to make them smaller,
>Or if I didn't stupidly pray like this:
>"O, if only that nearby corner bit could be added—the one that's spoiling the squaring up of my little farm [*agellus*]!
>O, if only fortune would show me [where there is] an urn of silver coins!"
>I [the poet] would be just like that man who, having found a treasure, became the buyer of the estate that he used to plough as a hired hand [*mercennarius*],
>Becoming rich by the friendship of Hercules![79]
>Rather, if what I have makes me happy and grateful, I would pray to you in this way:
>"Make the flocks I own fat, and all the other things I own as well,
>But not my talent [*ingenium*]. As you [Maecenas] have done for so long [*soles*], keep on being my greatest guardian!"[80]

> Now that I have left the City and am up in my fortress in the hills [*in montes et in arcem ex urbe*],
> What might be the first topic for [poetic] Satires for the Muse who inspires my prose?
> Up here, evil ambition does not bother me, nor does the oppressive south wind [*Auster*],
> And neither does harsh autumn which brings in gloomy death [*Libitina*].[81] [...]

In lines 20–58 (omitted here), Horace continues with an amusing account of the inanities and distractions of the City and then continues telling us of his longing for study and simple companionship at his villa.

Hor., *Sat.* 2.6.59–76

> Lost in such nonsense, my day [in Rome] does not pass without this prayer:
> "O country home, when will I see you [again]? When will I be allowed,
> Now with the books of the ancient thinkers, now in sleep and lazy hours,
> To enjoy forgetting life's worries?
> O when will Pythagoras's beans mixed with bacon drippings be served up?[82]
> O heavenly nights and dinners! When, with my own friends, and an offering having been made
> To my own household god [*Lar*], I eat and feed my impudent house-born slaves [*vernae*].
> Then each guest drinks down from cups of different sizes according to his own taste,
> Not bound by crazy rules, neither the guest who likes a bowl with strong sharp drink,
> Nor the one who wets his whistle with more moderate cheer.
> Then a conversation begins, not [small talk] about the villas or town houses of others [*non de villis domibusve alienis*],
> Nor about whether Lepos dances badly or not.
> Rather, the talk is of what concerns us in a greater degree: we examine if ignorance is evil,
> Or whether it is wealth or virtue that make men happy and brings us to friendship,
> And what the nature of the [true] good and what its greatest manifestation is." [...]

The poem ends (lines 77–117, omitted here) with one of the guests at Horace's drinking party telling a version of the famous story of the country mouse and the city mouse. The story is referred to by the emperor Marcus Aurelius in his *Meditations* 11.22 (171–173 CE).

Horace, *Epistles* (*Epistulae*) (Hor., *Epist.*), letter–poem to Quinctius

The first part of this letter-poem describes, very briefly, Horace's Sabine farm.[83] His topographical description may have become a short template for later, more elaborate, prose descriptions of their villas by Pliny the Younger and Sidonius Apollinaris included in this chapter (Plin., *Ep.* 2.17.1–5, *Ep.* 5.6.1–46, and Sid. Apoll., *Ep.* 2.2.1–20).

Hor., *Epist.* 1.16.1–16

> Dear Quinctius—If it's necessary for you to ask about my farm,
> And whether it sustains me as its owner from its ploughed fields or makes me rich from olive crops,
> Or whether it does so with its apple crop, its meadows, or the elm trees laced with grapevines,
> I will tell you at some length about its shape and how it is set up.
> There are contiguous hills, but they are separated by a shady valley—
> A valley on which the sun shines on its right side but which, in its airborne chariot as it descends, brings a misty warmth.[84]
> You would praise the prevailing climate.
> What about [my] bushes with their cornelian-red cherries and their plums,
> That oak tree and the holly [*ilex*] that give pasturage to the cattle

And whose shade makes their owner happy?
It's possible you could say that the green growth of Tarentum was brought nearer.[85]
There's also a spring, indeed one that is more like a river,
No less cold or pure than the Hebrus river that goes through Thrace:[86]
It flows such that it is [medically] helpful to [cure] illnesses of the head and the digestion.
If you can believe me, this sweet, pleasant retreat
Keeps me healthy even in September's heat. [...]

The second part of this letter (lines 17–78, omitted here) is philosophic: a good, wise man (*vir bonus et sapiens*, line 73) who is independent in thought and action is the only one who is truly free. All those bound in other ways (city life, custom, social prejudice), Horace writes, are enslaved. The freedom of a beautiful estate and villa in the countryside is the best.

Horace's Fictitious Villa

Horace, *Epodes* (*Epodi*) (Hor., *Epod.*)

In *Epode* 2, Horace wants to make his listeners or readers laugh. The poet has made up this villa: its description seems straightforward, but every element is tinged with complex social satire that contrasts with the elevated versification in iambic meter. It presents itself as a long quotation from a speaker who is identified only at the surprise ending, giving a mock heroic, mock humble color to everything that precedes it. The poet gives hints or clues to indicate what's going on, so that his readers' knowing puzzlement or giggling along the way ends in hilarity at the final revelation.[87]

Hor., *Epod.* 2.1–70
"He's a happy man who, far away from business dealings [*negotia*]
Like men of old now dead [*prisca gens mortalium*]
Ploughs his ancestral fields [*paterna rura*] with his own oxen
Free of all usurious money lending [*solutus faenore*].[88]
He's not roused by a horrid trumpet blast like a soldier,
Nor does he fear the raging sea.[89]
He avoids the Forum and the high [proud] thresholds [*superba limina*]
Of powerful citizens.[90]
Thus he grafts [new shoots] to mature vine stocks,
Marrying them to tall poplars,
And from afar he sees, in the depths of a valley,
[His] lowing, wandering herds,
While with a sickle he cuts dead branches
To graft better shoots on them,
Or to store up honey [extruded from the combs] in well-cleaned amphorae,
Or shearing a docile sheep.
Or then, when Autumn has raised its head wreathed with ripe fruit over the fields,
He delights in picking the pears he'd grafted
And comparing [his] grapes to purple dye,
To offer them to you, O Priapus, and to you,
O Father Silvanus, guardian of [property] boundaries![91]
As he wishes, he lies down under an ancient oak tree [*ilex*, holm oak]
On thick [smooth] grass
While waters run between high banks,

Birds chirp plaintively in the woods
And fountains gurgle with free-flowing waters
That invite him to a light siesta.[92]
But then, when Winter comes, with thundering Jupiter
Bringing rain and snow,
Here and there with his pack of dogs, he flushes out
Ferocious wild boars to catch them in strong nets spread along their tracks
Or sets traps on light snare hooks
To fool the greedy thrushes,
Or puts out snares for the frightened rabbit and the stork coming in from far away—
    it's a pleasing reward![93]
But who could forget the pangs of love in all of this?
What if [there were] a modest woman who rejoiced in household affairs and sweet children [*liberi*],
A Sabine woman or a hard-working sunburned Apulian wife?[94]
She would put the well-seasoned log on the [house's] holy hearth [*sacrus focus*]
And when her man comes home,
She would enclose the fat ewes in open-roofed pens
To empty their swollen udders,
[Then] drawing the year's sweet wine from the jar,
Make meals from homegrown ingredients.[95]
Oysters from the Lucrine Lake don't please me
Nor do turbot, nor scars
Even if an easterly storm might drive some to our waters![96]
No African bird would reach my stomach,
Nor yet an Ionian partridge.
Rather, olives taken from the tree's fullest branches are more pleasant,
Meadow-loving sorrel and mallow for bodily aches,
Or the ewe sacrificed for the Terminus feast
Or the kid snatched from the jaws of the wolf.[97]
In the course of such a feast, it's a pleasure to watch the lambs scamper back to the fold
To see the tired oxen, with their lowered necks,
Dragging the plow with its upturned beam,
[And to see] the assembled home-born slaves [*vernae*], the swarming denizens of a wealthy house,

Gathered around the Lares." [98]
    So spoke the moneylender Alfius—
He, who once aspired to be a country gentleman [*rusticus*] in the future.
He got all his money out on the ides and put it back [into money lending] on the kalends![99]

Pliny the Elder's Natural History

Horace's second *Epode*, above, as well as other prose and verse descriptions of villas emphasize a strongly pictorial aspect of country life and activities. Pliny the Elder, in his chapters on Greek and Roman painting, gives instances of *tabulae* (easel paintings on cloth or wood), holding their moral and civic value and meaning for humanity in greater regard than the relatively more recent, distinctively Roman, and allegedly selfish decoration of private houses with wall paintings. Still, he had a weakness for wall paintings that showed villas and the deep landscape views with charming details that had come into being in the Late Roman Republic and continued in fashion well into Neronianic and Flavian times.[100] His remarks can also be compared to those of Vitruvius on wall painting about a century before.[101]

Plin., HN 35.116–117 (35.37) [...] Spurius Tadius, who lived in the days of the divine [emperor] Augustus, must not be omitted [from this list of famous painters].[102] He originated a very agreeable type of wall painting showing villas and porticoes, planned gardens [*topiaria opera*], groves, woods, hills, fishponds, Euripi, rivers, shorelines, and anything else one might wish for.[103] In addition, in these wall paintings there are various depictions [*species*] of people strolling around and boating; on land, people approaching villas on donkeys or in vehicles, then again some people fishing, catching birds or hunting, and even [others] harvesting grapes.

Examples of his work show grand villas entered across marshes [standing at water's edge?], men wobbling along, staggering with [the weight of their] women on their backs for a bet [*sponsio*], and many other such funny things, done in an earthy way [*argutiae facentissimi salis*]. He also originated painting [on the walls] of open terraces with scenes of seaside cities, for a lovely effect and minimal expense.

SENECA THE YOUNGER (Lucius Annaeus Seneca, ca. 4 BCE–65 CE)

Letters on Morality (Epistulae morales ad Lucilium) (Sen., Ep.)

The *Epistulae morales* from which the following excerpts are taken was one of Seneca's many writings in different genres. They were intended for publication as easily readable short essays on various moral and philosophical topics; the notional addressee was one Lucilius Junior, a younger man, who was himself ambitious to have a literary career. A few of the letters mention villas as expressions of the moral worth or turpitude of their owners. It is possible that the villa of Servilius Vatia (*Ep.* 55) as indicating an Epicurean lifestyle was intended as the opposite of that of Scipio Africanus and his villa at Liternum (*Ep.* 86), clearly Seneca's antique and Stoic ideal.

Seneca, Letter to Lucilius Junior on the villa of Servilius Vatia[104] near Cumae on the Bay of Naples, 60s CE

Sen., *Ep.* 55.1–3 I have just returned from an excursion in a litter, no less tired out by being seated as if I had walked the distance myself. Even being carried for a long time can be laborious, the more so as I am not unaware that it is against Nature—she who gave us feet to walk and eyes to see for ourselves. Our pleasures have imposed weakness on us, and what we are no longer capable of doing is [now] what we have stopped doing altogether. However, it was necessary to shake my body up, so that the bile that clogged my throat might be dislodged, or that the breath that had gotten thicker might be dispersed by some jolting that I thought would do me good. So I continued for a long time [to be carried] along that inviting beach, a narrow path curving between Cumae and the villa of Servilius Vatia, defined by the sea on one side and the lake on the other.[105] The beach was hard because of a recent storm—as you know, frequent fast-surging waves flatten the sand, but calm weather dries it out, so the water-packed sand loosens up.

In my usual way, I began to look around for something that might hold my attention and would be interesting to me. My eyes fell upon the villa once owned by Vatia. This was where that rich man of [merely] praetorian rank [*praetorius dives*], who was famous for nothing besides his [so-called] life of leisure [*otium*], spent his old age, and only because of that was he considered happy. For when men were at times plunged to ruin by their friendship with an Asinius Gallus or by their hatred of a Sejanus and then by their love for him—there was an equal danger in having offended him or loved him—they would exclaim, "O Vatia, you alone know how to live!"[106]

But Vatia only knew how to hide, not how to live. There's a great difference between living a life of leisure [*vita otiosa*] and living a life of sloth [*vita ignava*]. So whenever I passed by Vatia's villa when he was still alive, I would say, "Vatia lies here!" [107]

To come to the point, dear Lucilius, philosophy is so sacred a source of strength and so worthy of veneration that even a fakery of it pleases, as long as it resembles it in some way. Ordinary people are deceived into thinking that a man is truly at leisure [*otiosus*] when alone, happy, and living for himself, but only a wise man can actually have these things. [. . .]

Sen., *Ep.* 55.6–8   I cannot tell you much about the villa. I know only the facade and the parts visible to passersby. There are two huge manmade grottoes, which were great undertakings, both as large as a lofty hall [*atrium*], one of which does not see the sun's light, the other full of sunshine all day until sunset. A plane tree plantation borders a stream, which is fed from both the sea and the Acheronian lake and divides the plantation like a Euripus.[108] Its size supports fish even though the water flows continuously; when the sea is calm, the fishermen do not fish in the stream, they only fish in it when bad weather gives them a holiday from open-sea fishing.[109] The villa's best feature is that Baiae is nearby [*trans parietem*, over the party wall]: the villa thus avoids the disadvantages [of proximity to the resort] but enjoys Baiae's pleasures. I fully appreciate the villa's good points, and I think it is truly a year-round villa. As it happens, it faces a west wind and does so in a position that prevents that wind from blowing over Baiae. So Vatia cannot be thought stupid for choosing this place for his leisurely life [*otium*], when that leisurely life was lazy and dilapidated by age. Tranquillity of spirit is not something that a place can impart: it is the spirit [*animus*] itself that must give real ease to everything. I myself have seen men be sad in lively, lovely villas, and be lonely in the midst of the bustle of an artificial activity. [. . .]

Seneca, Letter to Lucilius on the villa of Scipio Africanus at Liternum, 60s CE
Like many of Seneca's letters intended for publication, this one is deceptively simple and circumstantial but skillfully combines three themes in its two parts: the first part (*Ep.* 86.1–15, presented here) is a description of the villa once owned by Scipio Africanus at Liternum on the flat, sandy coast of Campania north of the Bay of Naples. This provides the author with an occasion to disparage contemporary folly, praise ancient habits and virtues, and emphasize the claim that the "old Romans" were basically farmers.[110] Seneca's Letter 86 was written some 240 years after Scipio's death.[111]

The second part (*Ep.* 55.16–21, omitted here) is an account of an effective method of transplanting olive trees, vines, and elms with which Seneca was not acquainted.[112] Seneca learned the method from one Vetulenus Aegilaus, a farmer and the current owner of Scipio's villa. This allowed the author to assert himself as an "old Roman" with hands-on knowledge of farming learned from a farmer whose knowledge of arboriculture was itself traditional and handed down from remote, moral antiquity.[113]

The concatenation of themes is clear: Seneca, by visiting Scipio Africanus's villa, learns about the virtue of great men of the past, and by learning a method from Aegialus, a most diligent *paterfamilias* (*diligentissimus pater familiae*), he is learning an old method new to him that he is now transmitting to Lucilius: virtue passes from generation to generation, much like moral manliness and agricultural techniques set in villa life and work. The philosophical messages are clinched by the references to Vergil's *Georgics*, already some half a century old.

Sen., *Ep.* 86.1–15   I am staying at the villa of Scipio Africanus, and I write to you after having paid homage to his dead spirit and at an altar that I believe is that great man's tomb.[114] His soul has gone to the sky whence, indeed, it had come, not, in my view, because he led great armies—after all, Cambyses also led great armies and Cambyses was a crazy person who used his craziness to good advantage [only for himself].[115] Rather, it was because of his extreme moderation and civic feeling, which I judge to have been more commendable after the time he drew back from his native land than when he had been defending it: either Scipio must remain in Rome, or Rome should continue to be free.[116]

Scipio said, "In no way do I wish to disregard the laws or the customs: may the law be the same for all citizens. O *patria*! Use the good things I have done, but without me! I was the cause of your freedom, and I will be its pledge. I leave you, because I have become a greater man than is good for you." What can I do except admire such greatness of soul that drew him to voluntary exile and [thereby] relieve the state? The situation had developed that either liberty would work to harm Scipio, or Scipio would do the same to liberty. Both alternatives were divinely forbidden. So he followed the laws and went to [his villa at] Liternum, putting the responsibility for his exile onto the State's debt to him as much as he had been responsible for Hannibal's expulsion [from Italy].

I have seen the villa. It is built of squared stone masonry [*lapidi quadrati*].[117] Its wall encloses a forest of trees, and there are towers with bulwarks raised to defend the villa as well as cisterns below the gardens large enough for the needs of an army, as well as a measly dark bath building [*balneolum angustum*] in the old fashioned manner, because our ancestors did not think to have a hot bath unless it was in darkness. Thus I had the pleasure in contrasting Scipio's habits with our own nowadays. In this cramped bath building, the "Scourge of Carthage," to whom Rome should offer thanks that she was not overrun more than once—that [great] man bathed his body, a body worn out with work in the fields. He had the habit of working his lands himself, as had been the habit of men of the old days [*mos priscis*]. He stood beneath this lowly roof, this ordinary floor was beneath his feet.

Who these days would care to bathe in such a way? We consider ourselves poor and lowly if our walls do not glitter with large, expensive images (*orbes*); unless Alexandrian marbles are not outlined with mosaics of Numidian stone; unless they are not edged on all sides with elaborate borders resembling pictures [*picturae*]; if our rooms with vaulted ceilings [*camerae*] are not covered in glass; unless marble from Thasos—which used to be rarely seen even in temples—lines our swimming pools into which we plunge our bodies, artificially exhausted by much sweating; unless water does not pour out of silver spigots.[118]

Up to now I have spoken only of ordinary venues for bathing: What shall I say when I come to freedmen's baths [*balnea libertinorum*]? How many statues, how many columns holding up nothing except to be placed there as decoration for expensive showiness? What quantity of water pouring noisily down from level to level! Soon we will come [to demand] so many luxuries that we will [want to] tread on nothing but gems.

In Scipio's bath, there are small slits cut through the stone wall rather than windows, so that light may come in without breaching the fortifications. Of course, nowadays they call bath buildings roach-ridden [*blattaria balnea*] if they are not arranged so that the widest windows let in the sun all day, such that men can both bathe and get a tan at the same time, or cannot see both fields and the sea from their bathing tubs. In this way, baths that once garnered crowds of users and admiration when they were first dedicated are now shunned and relegated to the category of obsolete facilities as soon as Luxury has contrived something new by which to bring herself to ruin. Once long ago, bath buildings were few in number and not decorated in any special way, for why should anything that only costs a small entrance fee be decorated, something that is not intended for pleasure but rather for use?

Water was not [lavishly] poured out [in Scipio's bath building] as it is now and did not perpetually run as if from a hot spring, and people did not worry about the purity of the water in which they left their dirtiness. Good god, what a pleasure to enter Scipio's dark bath with its low roof, knowing that the great Cato when he was aedile, or Fabius Maximus, or one of the Cornelii, warmed the water with his own hands! Indeed, aediles of the highest rank once undertook this duty, having to enter these bath buildings, which were frequented by the ordinary people, making sure they were clean and brought to a temperature adequate to utility and health, unlike the temperatures currently preferred that seem like a conflagration, one in which some criminal slave must be [condemned to be] "bathed" alive. As far as I can see, there is no difference between a boiling bath and a warm one.

How many men these days condemn Scipio as a country bumpkin because he did not let the light of day into his bath's hot room [*caldarium*] through big windows, or because he did not cook himself in sunlight or loaf around to boil in the bath? [They exclaim,] "Oh ill-fated man! He did not know how to live! He bathed himself in unfiltered muddy water and even, after heavy rains, polluted water!"[119] However, bathing in that way made no difference to Scipio: he went there to wash off sweat, not perfumed oils.

And what do you think people will say about this in the future? [They will say,] "I do not envy Scipio: if he bathed himself in that way, he was truly [justly] an exile!" Rather, you should know that he did *not* wash himself every day. Indeed, those who have transmitted accounts of the ancient behavior of the City's great men [*mores prisci urbis*] tell us that they only washed their arms and legs daily—that is, the limbs that were soiled in the course of their [farm] work—and that they bathed their whole bodies only on market-days [*nundinae*]. Someone else will declare on this topic: "To me, those guys must have been very dirty! What do you think they smelled like?" [The answer is:] "They smelled of the military camp, of their farm work, and of their heroic manliness." Since then, men have become dirtier even though clean bath buildings have been invented.

Wishing to describe a bad person notoriously given to pleasures, what does Horace say? He says, "Rucillus smells of candies [*pastilli*]."[120] Show me a Rucillus now. Now a Rucillus would smell like a billy goat and would take the place of that Gargonius to whom Horace compared him in the same poem. Nowadays, because perfume loses its scent on the body, it is not enough to smell nice unless perfume is applied three times a day! Why should a man be proud of this smell as if it were his own?

If all this seems too dreary to you, [Licilius], blame it on Scipio's villa, where I have learned from the current owner, a very diligent *paterfamilias*, how to transplant a tree no matter how old it might be. We must learn this lesson in our old age: not one of us plants an olive orchard except for another [who will come after us]. I have seen such trees bear fruit after three or four years of barrenness, and you will be sheltered by the tree that is, as our dear Vergil says, "slow-growing, but gives [your] grandsons shade."[121] [...]

MARTIAL (Marcus Valerius Martialis, ca. 38/41–102/104 CE)

Epigrams (Epigrammata) (Mart., *Epig.*)

Epigram to Bassus, 87 CE

"Bassus" was Martial's notional name for a rich, unfeeling patron who owned a sterile suburban villa, which he supplied with comestibles from the city market in Rome.[122] Faustinus may have been a real person.[123] To shame Bassus, Martial describes Faustinus's ideal productive and peaceable villa in a detailed, lively description, even though it may be fictitious; the contrast is between real and fake in the way of villas.[124]

Mart., *Epig.* 3.58

The villa near Baiae that our friend Faustinus has, Bassus,
Does not take up a big area of graceless land
Arranged with useless myrtle bushes, infertile plane trees, and topiaries of box.[125]
Instead, it cheerfully enjoys its coarse countryside [*rus barbara*].
Here, grain [*Ceres*] is stuffed into every nook and cranny,
And many vessels of aged autumn wine give off a nice aroma.

Here, when winter is coming in after November,
The rugged vine dresser brings in the late-grown grapes.
Fierce bulls bellow in the long valley,
And the bull calf, his head as yet unhorned, itches for a fight.
A mixed and dirty crowd of all sorts wanders around:
The honking goose, the jeweled peacock,
The bird that gets its name from crimson feathers [i.e., flamingo],
The painted partridge, the spotted Numidian birds,
And the pheasants of the faithless Colchian peoples.[126]
The proud roosters cuddle the Rhodian hens,
And the cotes hum with the clamor of doves,
Over here a wood pigeon's chirruping, over there the iridescent [*cereus*] turtle-dove's murmur.
The eager pigs [try to] forage in the *villica*'s apron [*sinus*],
And the sweet lamb looks around for his milk-giving mother.
Slaves born and bred in the house [*vernae lactei*] gather around the quiet hearth,
And big logs blaze before the happy Lares.
There's no lazybones host [*copus*] whose skin's all white from slacking off,
Or one who oils himself up for wrestling in some sporting contest.
Instead, the host sets a net to catch hungry thrushes,
And brings up a line quivering with fish,
Or brings in a doe caught in the hunting nets.
The nicely tended garden gives an occupation to the happy town slaves [*hilari urbani*],
And the joyous children, now with their hair grown long and without their teacher to tell them what to do,
Are happy to pay [mock]attention to the *vilicus*, and even the pampered eunuch enjoys some mild work.
The local farmer, come to pay his respects [*rusticus salutator*], does not come without a gift:
He brings light [clear] honey in its waxy honeycomb and a cone-shaped milk cheese from the woodlands around Sassina.[127]
One neighbor brings in some sleepy dormice,
Another comes with a kid bleating for its shaggy nanny,
Yet another, capons never allowed to copulate.
Tall young girls, daughters of the honest tenant farmers [*coloni*],
Bring gifts from their mothers in a woven basket.
When the day's work is done, a cheerful neighbor is called [to table]:
And the table itself does not stingily keep back [some of] its meal for the next day.
Everyone eats well, and the well-fed and well-wined steward does not envy the drunken guest.
But you, [Bassus], you have a villa in the City's suburbs that's tidy and starving,
And from its tower you can overlook bare laurel trees,
Secure from worry in a house whose Priapus has no fear of being robbed.[128]
You feed your vine dresser on [bread made from] grain bought in town,
And you convey, when you have nothing else to do, vegetables, eggs, chickens, fruits, cheese, and wine to your villa.
Should it be called a rural villa [*rus*], or a town house just a bit out of town [*domus longe*]?

Martial, *Epigram*, 88 CE

The poet describes the view from the top of the Janiculum Hill, where the garden and villa of Julius Martialis were located, which does indeed give a panorama of some 180 degrees or more over the City looking northwest and southeast. The view from the villa is urban in the foreground but rural farther afield: this may be why the poet refers to the dwelling as a villa, a *rus*, and a *domus*. The "Julius Martialis" in this epigram may be a fictious person, perhaps a rich alter ego of the penurious poet himself.[129]

Mart., *Epig*. 4.64
>Some few *iugera* spread out on the summit of the Janiculum hill, and they are lovelier than the Gardens of the Hesperides.[130]
>Peaceful places [*lati recessus*] occur throughout the hillsides,
>And the smooth hilltop with its gentle undulations continuously enjoys a serene sky,
>And alone gleams with its special light while mists fill the hollow valleys below.
>The elegant towers [*culmina delicata*] of a noble villa [*celsa villa*] rise serenely to the stars.
>From this place, you can see the seven lordly hills of Rome and look over its entire area,
>You can see the hills of Albanum and those of Tusculum,
>And the cool spots that lie in the suburbs;
>You can see ancient Fidenae and little Rubra,
>And the fruit trees of Anna Perenna which enjoy virgin's blood.[131]
>A traveler can be seen on the Via Flaminia and the Via Salaria
>But his carriage is noiseless and the sound of its wheels don't disturb anyone's quiet sleep
>Which is broken neither by the call of the boatswain to the oarsmen nor by the noise of the bargemen,
>Even though the Milvian Bridge is so close by, and fast boats fly along the sacred Tiber.[132]
>This rural house [*rus*], which should really be better called a *domus*, is made agreeable by its owner:
>You could even imagine that it belongs to you, so unstintingly, liberally, and affably is its hospitality given.
>You could believe that it belongs to the household [*penates*] of an Alcinous or to that Molorchus recently made rich.[133]
>To all of you, who think that these things are nothing much, you who cultivate cool Tibur or Praeneste with a hundred spades
>And assigned the hillsides of Setia to a single tenant:[134]
>In my view, these few *iugera* of Julius Martialis are preferable by far.

STATIUS (Publius Papinius Statius, ca. 45–ca. 96 CE)

Silvae **(Stat., *Silv*.)**

Letter to Vitorius Marcellus, 94 CE or shortly after
Statius gives a geography of the towns with villas in proximity to Rome. The poet's friend Marcus Vitorius Marcellus, when elected praetor in 94 CE, was put in charge of the maintenance of the Via Latina as its official curator (*curator viae Latinae*).[135] Statius tells him not to work too hard and lists the towns along the road where villas for *otium* can be found (including the Via Latina) as well as the villa–town of Tibur. Statius instructs his letter-poem to hasten to Marcellus. The names of towns in this geography of villas are bolded.

Stat., *Silv*. 4.4.1–25
>Do not linger, my letter, hurry over the Euboean fields,[136]
>Start on the road where the famous [Via] Appia branches to the side
>And where a great embankment rests on soft sands.
>When you have reached the citadels of Romulus, look over to yellow Thybridis's right bank
>Where the Lydian river edge hems in the naval basin, and suburban gardens lie along the shallows.[137]

There you'll see Marcellus, distinguished by his good looks and spirited nature,
And you'll recognize him because he's very tall.
First off, give him a greeting in the usual way,
Then right away remember to give him this message done up in verse:
> "Now the retreat of spring releases the earth and the flying pole
> And burns the sky with Icarian barkings.[138]
> Now the high walls of crowded Rome are emptying.
> Some go to sacred **Praeneste**, others to **Diana's icy grove** [Nemi],
> To jagged **Mount Algidus** [Alba?] or to the shadiness of **Tusculum**,
> Yet others are charmed by the groves of **Tibur** or the Anio's cool waters."[139] [...]

Statius, *Silvae*, on the Villa of Manilius Vopiscus at Tibur, 90s CE(?)

Like Varro's villa at Casinum, Vopiscus's villa (termed houses [*domus*] and *praetoria*) was set astride a stream or river.[140] Statius describes the villa while recalling a visit.

Stat., *Silv.* 1.3.1–75

If he who has seen well-spoken Vopiscus's home at cool Tibur, the two dwellings
  [*gemini penates*] separated by the Anio
Or has come to know the common relationship of the friendly banks,
With the two villas competing for which would shelter their owner,
Then Sirius with its burning star has not growled at him,
And leafy Nemea's child has not glared at him, [because]
Such is the winter-like coolness of the house, and such is its merciless cold to break up the heat,
That the house does not bake in Pisa's summer heat.[141]
Pleasure herself drew you with her soft hand [...]
Then Venus anointed its gables with Idalian decoctions and stroked them with her hair,
Imparting a delightful dignity on the [two] houses, and forbidding her winged sons to ever
  leave them.[142]
A day to keep in memory for a long time! What joys come to mind,
By how many miracles [of beauty] my vision is exhausted!
How genial is the soft soil! How the beauty of the place has a shape greater than the hand of
  art [could supply]![143]
Nowhere else has Nature more generously spread herself out. Groves of tall trees bend over
  the flowing shallows,
An elusive image reflects their leaves, and their shadowy impressions rush over the long waves.
The Anio itself—imagine such a thing—with its rocks above and below quells his swollen
  anger and foaming sound,
As if he feared disturbing the Pierian days and poem-infused sleep of placid Vopiscus.[144]
The house is on both shores, and the most tranquil stream does not separate your
  [the villa's] parts.[145]
Grand buildings [*praetoria*] watch over either shore and do not challenge one another
  or complain that the stream stands in their way.
Fame should brag of the gulf at Sestos and the brave young man who swam it faster than
  the dolphins![146]
Instead, there is an eternal quiet here; here, storms have no right to be; there is no fury
  in the waters.
Seeing one another and talking across the river can be done, and even hands can almost join.
In the same way do the waves hold back Chalcis, and Bruttia isolated by the sea look toward
  Sicanian Pelorus.[147]
What will my [poem's] beginning and middle parts be, at what ending will I leave off?
Should I admire the gilded beams and many doorposts of Mauretanian wood?[148]

Or the colored veins of shining marbles?
Or the waters [*Nymphae*] piped into every bedroom?[149]
I am attracted one way by my eyes, [but] another way it's my mind that draws me on.
Should I tell of the great age of the forests? Or should I tell of you, you halls [*aula*]?[150]
One of you overlooks the stream below, the other looks back to quiet woods
Where a complete calm and an untroubled nighttime silence without any disturbance
And murmuring sounds invite you to a gentle sleep?
Or should I tell of the steaming baths [*balnea*] built up on the grassy slope and their furnace [*ignis*] set right on the cold water's edge?
Or should I tell how the river near the steaming furnaces [*fornaces*] laughs at the Nymphs panting [from the heat of the furnaces] in the waves nearby?
I saw works of art and the handiwork of ancient artists, and metals fashioned in various ways.
It's hard work to list the objects in gold or ivory and the jewels worthily begemming a finger,
Or the objects in silver, or smaller ones in bronze, or the colossal ones of huge size that the playful hand of the artist first attempted.
While wandering and looking around, making my eyes look at everything,
I was walking on riches [*opes*] without realizing they were there.
The brightness streaming down enhanced by bronze [roof?] tiles from above
Revealed the elegant floor, where the floor surface [*humus*] gladly displays its various arts
And with its unusual images outshines the *asarota*.[151]
I trembled as I walked.
Why should I wonder at the main conjoined buildings [*iungentia*] or at the separate buildings with upper stories [*tecta trichoris*]?
Why should I wonder at you, you tree, you who have been preserved in the middle of the house
You, who rise above the house's roofs and emerge into the limpid air?
You, you tree, would have suffered the [blows of a] cruel double axe under any other owner!
And now in your ignorance, you tree, you are not [even] aware that some Naiad in flight
Or some Hamadryad might owe you the years (of her life) that might otherwise have been cut short!
Why should I recount the feastings alternately held [*alternae mensae*] on both of the two high banks,
Or of the clear springs and deep pools around the whirlpool,
Or of you, Marcia, you who flow almost alongside the river itself
And [then] cross its course in valiant lead [pipes or channel-lining]?[152]
Or should the river of Elis be the only one to flow by a sweet-water passage to Aetna's harbor under Ionian waves?[153]
Here, the Anio himself, leaving his cavern and his spring in the witching hour of the night [*nocte arcana*],
Takes off his grey cloak and lies down on the soft moss around there
Or falls, huge as he is, into the ponds to swim in the glass-like waters.
Tiburnus reclines in that shade, and there the Albula wishes to dip her sulphurous hair.[154] [...]

Statius goes on (lines 76–89, omitted here) to imagine that Vopiscus's *domus* has a quasi-sanctified power, capable of drawing Diana (here called Phoebe, Diana's grandmother) from her shrine at nearby Lake Nemi, the Dryads from Mt. Taygetus in Laconia, and Pans from Arcadia. Oracular sites in Italy are also mentioned (Tibur itself, Antium), and various sites in Greece and Italy are compared unfavorably with Tibur and Vopiscus's villa. Some were coastal or inland towns made famous in Vergil's *Aeneid*. It is no coincidence that many of them—Tusculum, Baiae, Formiae, Circeii, Caieta, Antium—were also places, like Tibur, that were favored by villa owners.

Stat., *Silv.* 1.3.90–94

> Here in truth, that man [Vopiscus] contemplates weighty matters,
> Here, silence surrounds a prolific calm and a grave virtue with a serene demeanor,
> A healthy refinement and a graceful ease that has nothing of [mere] delights,
> Much like the old Gargettian had wanted when leaving his Athenian hometown
> > and his garden.[155] [...]

In lines 95–104 (omitted here), Statius asks why undergo the dangerous voyage to Athens when there is a similar delight nearby (*vicina voluptas*), namely Vopiscus's villa. He compliments his host's literary skills in composing odes in Pindaric style, epic poems, venomous satires, and beautiful letters.

Stat., *Silv.*, 1.3.105–110

> A blessing on your wealth of soul, Vopiscus—you are worthy of the riches of a Midas,
> Or that of a Croesus and of Persian treasure
> You, over whose well–watered countrysides should have flowed the golden Hermus and
> > the Tagus with its glistening silt![156]
> So may you [continue to] apply yourself to a learned *otium*, and, I pray,
> That you do so with a frank heart and live longer than even old Nestor's age![157]

Statius, *Silvae* 2.2, on the Villa of Pollius Felix at Surrentum, mid–90s CE

Statius's letter-poem on the Surrentine villa of Pollius Felix describes the villa itself (its views, some architectural elements, and some of its contents) as well as the *otium* enjoyed within and around it. The picture of the personality, property, and villa of the proprietors Pollius and Polla is an outline for this particularly important aspect of villas. The sense of detachment, cultured ease in lovely circumstances, the views of land and sea, nature in its forms both wild (the sea, the rocks) and cultivated (tree plantations, vineyards), devotion to literature, and a sense of a life well lived are the components of *otium*, the special pleasure and culture of villas. The villa had a sacred character: there were temples of Hercules and Neptune, thus land and sea, nearby.[158] There are plenty of other semi-divine denizens as well.

The site of the villa of Pollius Felix has been identified within a range of possibilities of villas on the promontories of the Sorrentine coast.[159]

Stat., *Silv.* 2.2.1–35

> A high villa [*celsa villa*] gazing out on the Dicaearchean sea stands between the walls
> Known by the Sirens' name and the rock that bears the Tyrrhenian Minerva.[160]
> The estate [*ager*] is Bromius's delight, and its grapes ripen on its high hills
> And do not envy [the fame or quality] of the Falernian wine presses.[161]
> After the five-year festival at my hometown, when a calm quiet fell on the racetrack and
> > its gray dust settled down
> And athletic shows changed over to the crowns of the Ambracian games,
> Already desiring to make my way, the lovely invitation of gentle Pollius
> And young Polla's adroit grace brings me there, by way of the well-known [Via] Appia, queen
> > of the long roads.[162]
> My stay there was a delight. A moon-shaped sea in a bay has rocks curving on either side,
> And Nature has given the place a smooth seashore with overhanging cliffs going up to the
> > land itself.
> The first welcome seen [from afar] is the steam rising from the double-domed bathhouse
> And freshwater flowing from the land to the Nymphs's [dwellings in the salty] sea.

Here, the lively followers [*chorus*] of Phorcys wish to bathe
With Cymodoce with her dripping hair and sea-green Galatea.[163]
The caerulean Ruler of the swelling waves keeps watch over the house
[Acting] as the guardian of its innocent Lar—the waves spray his altars with pleasant salty spume.[164]
Alcides oversees the happy land: the harbor enjoys a double divine presence [*numen*]—
The one protects the land, the other thwarts the angry waves.[165]
An amazing calm suffuses the sea, the exhausted waves abandon their fury,
And the wild south wind [*Auster*] blows more gently.
Here the furious winter storm dares less to provoke
And the pools lie quiet without ripples, imitating the customs of their owner.
From there [the harbor], an arched portico [*porticus arces*] rises diagonally,
A citified construction [*urbis opus*], its long ridgeline defeats the jagged rocks.[166]
Before, the sun broke through layers of dust
And the track was rough and unpleasant, but now it's a pleasure to climb.
It's just like the covered ramp [*semita*], should you approach the high crest of Bacchiadic
    Ephyre from Ino's Lechaeum.[167]

In lines 36–42 (omitted here), Statius declares (with a wealth of references) that his poetic inspiration is inadequate to describe the nature and beauty (*species cultusque*) of the villa.

Stat., *Silv.* 2.2.42–99
While I was being led from place to place, my eyes and even my feet could hardly keep up.
What a crowd of things! What to admire first? The genius of the place or that of its owner?
This section of the house faces Phoebus's rising sun; the other holds him back a little
    as the light fades,
And does not allow the tired day to diminish its light as the shadow of a dark mountain
    falls on the sea
And the villa's buildings [*praetoria*] swim on the water still as glass.
In one part, the buildings resound with the sound of the sea,
In other parts, there is no sound of the waves but the silence of the land.
In some parts, Nature predominates; in other parts, Nature has been set aside in favor
    of cultivation
And becomes sweetly tamed in ways of which she was ignorant before.
Here, where once there was a hill, now you see flat land.
Where once there were swamplands, now you see buildings,
And where now you see tall groves of trees, there wasn't even any soil.
The owner has domesticated the place, and the earth has delighted to follow as he has shaped
    and broken through the rocks.
Look at how the compliant rocks have taken up the yoke, how the buildings predominate
To make the mountain retreat.
Now may the talents of Methymne's poet, the single Theban lyre, and the glory of the
    Getic plectrum
Surrender to you [Pollius]: you move rocks as well, and high groves follow you.[168]
Why should I bring up the ancient forms in wax and bronze,
Or what the pigments of Apelles delighted to bring to life, or what the hand of Phidias carved
In such a wonderful way, even though Pisa was still empty,
Or what was brought to life by Myron's art and Polyclitus's carving,
Or the bronzes made from Isthmian ashes, more valuable than gold,
Or the faces of ancient leaders, poets [*vates*], and men of wisdom,
Those whom you take care to follow, whom you feel in your whole being,
You, who are free from worries and settled in quiet virtue, always yourself?[169]

Why would I go over describing the thousand peaks and vistas you can see [from the villa]?
Each room has its own particular pleasure, its own view of the sea,
And its own view of the landscape across the sea [*Nerea*] from its windows.
One looks out to Inarime; craggy Prochyta appears to view from another;
From yet another, Hector's companion spreads out;
From here, Nesis surrounded by the sea breathes in a foul air;
Further on is happy Euploea, [the island of] good omen for passing ships;
There's also Megalia thrown out to guard against the curving waves;
And your own Limon—grieving that you, its owner, lies on the opposite shore—
Looks toward your Surrentine buildings [*praetoria*] from so far away.[170]
There is one room, separate and set above the others,
That brings Parthenope to your view across a straight line of sea.[171]
In it are marbles chosen from deep in Greek quarries:
The vein-splashed stone of Syene in the East,
The marble of sad Synnas, white with purple striations,
Which Phrygian axes cut out in the fields where Cybele mourns;
In addition, there are the blocks cut from the mountain of Lycurgus at Amyclae
Which resemble soft grass; yellow Numidian marble gleams (in the room),
And marble from Thasos, Chios, and Carystos which delights in overlooking the waves;
They all greet the Chalcidian towers opposite [the villa].[172]
Good for you! You like all things Greek and you live in Greek land,
And may the Dicaearchean [Puteoli] city of your birth not be envious.[173]
We will both be better masters of our learning.
Why should I tell of the richness of the countryside, the new land built out over the sea,
And the cliffsides drenched in Bacchus's nectar?[174]

Lines 100–111 (omitted here) evoke the villa's land and sea environs filled with Nereids, Satyrs, and Pans, then turn to Pollius's two other villas, one probably at Tibur, the other certainly at Tarentum.[175]

Stat., *Silv.* 2.2.112–115

Here [in this villa], where Pollius practices his Pierian poetry,
Whether he is obeying his Gargettian master's teachings,
Or whether he strikes my lyre, or combines dissonant modes [of poetry],
Or whether he draws out the threat of vengeful verses.[176]

In lines 116–138 (omitted here), Pollius is said to have mastered, by his greatness of mind (*magnus pectus*), both fate (*fas*) and fortune (*fortuna*), and his verses even calm the sea's tempests. He looks down on mere mortals' ceaseless to-and-fro and doubtful joys from a sublimely elevated spot, presumably his villa. Even Pollius's Greekness—he was born at Puteoli but had been adopted by Neapolis, the nearby town that had a better claim to Hellenic tradition (see ch. 4 n. 173)—is resolved by his new mental calm. The next passage, below, takes us to the end of this letter-poem.

Stat., *Silv.* 2.2.139–146

But now the mists of affairs [*res,* business] are gone, and you see the truth: your steady boat
    has found safe harbor and a quiet place,
While others are still tossed about on the sea.
Continue as you are, and do not send that boat that has served you up to now into our storms.
And you [Polla], who in perspicacity are greater than the daughters of Latium and equal to
    any man in [strength of] mind [*mens*],

You, whose face has never avoided threatening difficulties,
You, who are always serene and happy, who has an unworried pleasant look;
For you [Pollius?], no ugly money box [*arca*] locks up your private wealth,
And no consequences from money lending [*dispendia fenoris*] tortures your spirit.
Instead, your wealth [*census*] is laid out and you enjoy it in a wise way.
No other more blessed soulful union can exist, Concordia (herself) has not taught other minds more than this.
Learn well, those of you who maintain a blended friendship [marriage] over a long time
And keep up the obligations of a chaste love.
Go onward through the ages and into the honor roll of ancient fame.[177]

PLINY THE YOUNGER   (Gaius Plinius Caecilius Secundus, 61–113 CE)

Letters (*Epistulae*) (Plin., *Ep.*)

On His Villas

Pliny the Younger's letters include many references to villas.[178] They were written at various times from the beginning of his official career in Rome in the 80s CE to his death when he was the emperor's governor (*legatus Augusti*) in Bithynia and Pontus in Asia Minor, in 113 CE. Their publication in grouped books appears to have begun in 97 CE and continued for several years after that, most addressed to friends and relatives, some in a two-way correspondence between Pliny both at Rome and while he was in office overseas and with the emperor Trajan.

Pliny the Younger's Villa at Laurentum

Letter to his friend Gallus,[179] published ca. 97–110 CE
Together with Pliny's own *Ep.* 5.6 on his Tuscan villa and a very few others, this is the most famous description of a villa in Latin literature.[180] Themes of this letter were reprised in Sidonius's description of his villa Avitacum in central Gaul some four centuries later (see Sid. Apoll., *Ep.* 2.2.1–20, in this chapter). The descriptions of the Laurentine and Tuscan (Tiburtine) villas significantly shaped the development of villas throughout Europe.[181] In this case, the villa's charm and its amenities are part of Pliny's invitation to his friend to visit him.

Plin., *Ep.* 2.17.1–5   You can marvel that my Laurentine villa [*me Laurentinum*]—or, if you prefer, my Laurentum villa [*Laurens meus*]—gives me so much pleasure, but you will stop wondering when you get to know the beauty of the villa itself, the varied aspects of its location, and the length of its seaward frontage. It's 17 miles [about 25 km, or 15 mi.] from the City, so having leisurely finished what [business] needed to be gotten through [in Rome], I can get there in a day and stay put.

There isn't just one way to reach the place: the Via Laurentina and the Via Ostiensis both take you there, but on the Via Laurentina you must leave the road at the fourteenth milestone, while on the Via Ostiensis at the tenth milestone. Either way, both roads are sandy for a while, hard and slow in a cart but quick and easy on horseback. There are views on either side: from time to time, the road passes through wooded areas, then it opens and gives prospects onto broad meadows with herds of horses as well as flocks of sheep, which have been driven down from the winter pastures in the mountains to fatten in the springtime clime.

The villa is well adapted to how it is used, but maintaining it is not excessive. The first room is the atrium, a simple room but not paltry for all that. Then there are porticoes in the shape of a letter D surrounding a small but pretty courtyard [*area*]. In bad weather, this is a good place to take shelter because it is protected by windows and even more by overhanging eaves.

On axis, there is a pleasant hall [*cavaedium*], then a *triclinium* of some beauty. The *triclinium* overhangs the shore in such a way that, when the sea is driven by the southwesterly wind [*Africus*], it is lightly sprayed by the waves breaking and backwashing in turn. It has double doors or windows the same size, such that the prospect from the sides and on axis is of three sea views; looking back, one can see the hall [*cavaedium*], the courtyard [*area*] with its two porticoes on either side, then the atrium, the woods, and the hills in the distant horizon.

On the left [of the atrium-*area*-*cavaedium*-*triclinium* sequence] and set back a little, is a large bedroom [*cubiculum*] followed by another smaller bedroom with windows that let in light at sunrise and sunset, and from it one has a view of the sea but at a safer distance. Beside both the [big] *cubiculum* and the *triclinium*, there is a passage [*angulus*] that keeps and greatly intensifies the sun's warmth, so this is the wintertime residential room and playroom for the people of my household—in it, winds do not blow unless brought in by cloudy weather, and the place can be used as before when good weather resumes.

Next to this passage there is an apsidal [D-shaped] bedroom with windows that admit the sun's light from all sides; it has one wall lined with a kind of shelving as for a library for the books that I have read and reread. Communicating with this [library-bedroom] across a corridor is a suite of bedrooms for the people of my household: the floors are raised and jacketed with pipes to admit and regulate hot air to a health-enhancing temperature. The other part of this side of the villa is allocated for the use of the slaves and freedmen, and many of the rooms are nice enough to receive guests.

On the other side [of the atrium-*area*-*cavaedium*-*triclinium* sequence], there is a large, very elegant bedroom, then another large bedroom ample enough to be used as a moderately sized dining room [*cenatio*], lit as much by the sun as by [reflections from] the sea. Behind this [large bedroom-*cenatio*] is a suite comprising a bedroom and an antechamber with a high ceiling, cool in summer, protected in winter because impervious to all winds [drafts], and there is a similar bedroom-antechamber suite across a party wall next door.[182]

After that, there is the large and lavish cold room [*frigidarium*] of the baths, which has two curved plunge pools in opposite corners; the pools have an abundant amount of water, considering that the sea is so close. Beyond is the oiling room [*unctorium*], a warm room with a hypocaust, then the hot room [*propnigeon*] of the baths. Right after are two small rooms, elegantly rather than sumptuously decorated, and attached to them is an admirable hot bath from which swimmers have a view of the sea. Not far away, there is a court for playing ball games [*sphaeristerium*], very well warmed by the sun at the end of the day.

A tall building [*turris*] standing over the bath building has two living rooms at ground level and two more above, with a dining room [*cenatio*] that gives another very wide and very long view of the shore and its pleasant villas.

There is yet another tall building: above, there is a bedroom, which receives light from the rising and setting sun, with accommodation for a storeroom and granary behind it and, at ground level, a dining room [*triclinium*] that, when the sea is agitated, almost converts its crashing into a soft and fading sound—it looks over the garden and the walkway surrounding it. The walkway is bordered by a box hedge [*buxus*] and rosemary bush[es] to fill in where the box gives out, because box grows readily where it is protected by the buildings but withers when open to the sky and subject to wind and sea spray, no matter how far away from the sea it might be.

There is a young, shade-giving vine in the middle of the walkway where the ground is soft and giving even to bare feet. The garden is densely planted with mulberry and fig trees, types of trees that this [particular] earth supports well but can be deleterious to other species. In this area, a dining room facing away from the sea enjoys a view no less pleasant than the one overlooking it. This dining room has two living rooms [*diaetae*] attached to it at the back, giving a view through windows onto the entrance [*vestibulum*] of the villa and a well-planted kitchen garden [*hortus rusticus*].

From there, an enclosed portico [*cryptoporticus*] almost as large as that of a public building extends outward.[183] It has windows on both sides, more overlooking the sea, fewer overlooking the garden because their spacing alternates [one on the garden-side to every two on the seaward side]. The windows are left open on calm days without wind, but in gusty weather they can be closed against the wind's drafts on one or the other. In front of the *cyptoporticus*, a planted walkway [*xystus*] gives off the scent of violets. With the sun's effects, the temperature in the *cryptoporticus* rises, and the building both holds the warmth and wards off the northwesterly wind [*Aquilo*], with the result that it is as warm in front as it is cool behind.[184] In the same way, it deflects the southwesterly wind [*Africus*] and breaks and confines the other winds blowing on this side or the other. The *cryptoporticus* is delightful in winter, even more so in summer. In summer, the *xystus* remains cool in the morning. In the afternoon, shade tempers the heat in the walkway area and the garden near the wall [of the *cryptoporticus*], and as daylight increases or fades, it lengthens or shortens on either side. The *cryptoporticus* is dark when the sun is at its warmest at midday and beats down on its roof. At that time, it receives and circulates westerly breezes [*Favonius*] through its open windows: its air is never stale or motionless.

At the end of the *xystus*, the *cryptoporticus*, and the garden, there are rooms in a suite [*diaeta*] that are my own true loves [*amores mei*]. I myself had them built. There is a sunroom [*heliocaminus*] facing the *xystus* on one side and the sea on the other, with sunshine everywhere. There is a bedroom with folding doors leading to the *cryptoporticus*, as well as windows giving a view of the sea. In the opposite wall, there is a small, elegantly decorated private room which can be either opened into the bedroom or closed off by opening or closing its glass doors and curtains. It accommodates a daybed and two armchairs; on one side it has the sea, with a view of villas behind and woods at a distance—the views of these places can be seen through the many windows, either singly [by closing some windows] or in unison [by opening all of them].

Next door is my own bedroom for sleeping at night: the voices of the young slaves are not heard, and neither is the susurration of the sea, nor the sound of thunder and flash of lightning, not even the light of day unless the windows are open. The reason for such great privacy and seclusion is that there is a corridor separating the bedroom from the garden so that the empty space extinguishes all noise. Next to the bedroom, there is a tiny hypocaust; a small opening circulates or maintains the heat underneath [the floor], as needed. Then there is an antechamber and another bedroom extending fully out toward the sun as soon as it rises and remaining in the sun's rays until beyond midday, though obliquely after that.

When I return to this suite of rooms alone, I feel in myself that I have left my own villa and feel great pleasure [in doing so], especially at the Saturnalia holiday when the rest of the building rings with the days' freedom for festivity and tumult: I don't impede the slaves' fun, nor they my studies.

The convenience [*utilitas*] and pleasantness [*amoenitas*] of the villa is deficient in one thing: running water. There are wells, which might better be called springs, so close to the surface is the water level. It is a remarkable natural fact all along this shoreline that wherever you dig down into the earth, drinkable water is readily found, pure water that is not even slightly brackish even though it is so near the sea. Nearby woods provide enough firewood, and the town of Ostia supplies any other necessities. In addition, a village separated [from my villa] only by a villa next door can supply one's small sundry needs. The village has three pay-for-service bathing facilities which are very useful if, either due to an unexpected visit or a shorter residence (than usual), heating up the baths at home is inadvisable.

The roofs of villas—some arranged in groups, others standing alone—grace the shore with a welcome variety; they give the impression of many cities, when seen from the sea or from the shore itself.[185] A long spell of good weather softens the sand but most often it's hardened by the constant waves. The sea hereabouts has few fish of much value, but there are good sole and prawns.[186] The villa itself provides inland necessities, especially milk: the herds of livestock converge there [at the villa] when they are looking for water and shade.

In your opinion, don't you think that I am right to choose this retreat as my preferred dwelling to live in? You are too much a man of the town not to envy it! And would that you do exactly that, indeed: envy it! That way, the many nice things of my lovely little villa will have a great addition with your presence in companionship [with me]. Farewell.

Pliny the Younger's Tuscan (Tiburtine) Villa[187]

Letter to his friend Domitius Apollinaris,[188] published ca. 97–110 CE

Plin., *Ep.* 5.6.1–46 I am moved at your worry and solicitude for me when you heard that I am spending the summer at my Tuscan villa, and that I should not do so because it is an unhealthy place, that the entire Tuscan seashore is noxious and insalubrious.[189] But where I am is well away from the sea, actually in the foothills of the healthiest of [all] mountains, the Apennines. To dispel your fears on my behalf, listen to my account of the prevailing weather of the region and the pleasant location of my villa—it will be as much of a pleasure to you in hearing about it [*quae et tibi auditu*] as the pleasure I have in writing about it.[190]

In winter, the weather is cold and frosty, so the area rejects and is hostile to myrtles, olives, and other trees that otherwise grow happily in [other] prevailing moderate climates. Laurel, however, can thrive and even flourish, and it withers not more often than it does in the environs of Rome. The summer is admirably mild, the air always being in some kind of movement, more frequently with breezes than with winds. There are many old people [in the neighborhood]: you can encounter the grandfathers and great-grandfathers of grown young men and hear old stories and talk of the forebears—if you come here, you will think that you have been reborn in another century!

The landscape of the area is very beautiful. Imagine some gigantic amphitheater, something that only nature could make. The wide-spreading plain is surrounded by mountains, mountains crowned with stands of tall old-growth trees. Up there, much hunting of various kinds is available. Downslope, there are woodlands of trees suitable for logging. Between the woodlands, there are [low] hills so rich in soil that it is hard to find a stone even if you look hard, hills [almost] as flat as level fields and just as fertile, bringing in no less of a rich harvest, though a little later in the summer.[191]

Below these, the vineyards spread out broadly, linking with one another in a uniform appearance far and wide; their lower limit is edged with stands of trees. Then come meadows and fields. In the fields, only heavy oxen and the sturdiest ploughs can be used for first breaking up the soil because its hardness is such that the first attempt makes clods that can only be finally broken down by a ninth ploughing.

The meadows are begemmed with flowers, clover, and other soft grasses that seem forever new and freshly growing. All these are watered by perennial brooks, which, though there are many of them, do not pool to form marshes because of the downslope; pooling water that is not absorbed drains into the Tiber. The river takes the water from the fields and, because it is navigable, all the [villa's] produce can be shipped downstream to Rome, but only in winter and spring—in the summer, the channel dries up, and the Tiber's reputation [*nomen*] as a great river ceases until the next autumn. You will take great pleasure if you look down upon the region from a mountaintop, because the countryside you will see appears like some landscape painting of exceptional beauty. The eyes, wherever they turn, are refreshed by its variety and what it offers.

My villa is at a low position on a hill but looks outward as if it were at the top, because the approach road rises so slightly and gently that you have no sensation [are deceived into not becoming aware] that you're climbing upward, even when you have arrived. Behind is the cordillera of the Apennines, but a long way away; from there, breezes blow even on cloudless, still days, never sharp or blustery because the distance moderates and calms them. The greater part of the villa looks southward, and its front portico welcomes the sun from midday in summer, a little earlier in winter. The portico is wide and long in extent, with many rooms [along it] and an atrium in the old style.

A planted walkway [*xystus*] stands in front of the portico—it has box hedges cut in different shapes. A low slope leads to a raised bed on which there are animals facing one another, also cut out of box, and on a level area there is a bed of acanthus so soft it could be mistaken for water.[192]

Around the *xystus* is a promenade surrounded by flowering plants cut into various shapes, and then another walkway in the [oval] shape of a circus with box cut in different shapes and small, artificially dwarfed low-clipped bushes. A masonry wall defines the whole area, hidden at its base by a box hedge cut in levels. Beyond is meadowland [*pratus*], no less lovely by nature than the other is by its artifice; then beyond that are fields and many more meadows and woodlands.

From the end of the front portico, a dining room breaks forward of the facade. Through the folding doors, it has a view of the *xystus* leading up to it, the nearby meadows, and the countryside. On the other side, windows overlook more of the *xystus* and the villa's projecting rooms, then through [a third set of] windows, there is a view of the tops of the trees next to the garden-hippodrome.[193]

Around mid-point of the front portico and a little set back from it, there is a suite of living rooms [*diaeta*] built around a little courtyard shaded by four plane trees. Between them, water flows from a marble basin and bathes the trees and their roots with a light spray. In this suite is a special bedroom [*dormitorium cubiculum*] into which neither daylight nor the sound of raised voices or [other] sounds can penetrate. Next door is an informal dining room for my friends; it looks into the little courtyard, a wing of the front portico, and what else the portico overlooks. There is another bedroom, green and shady because it is near one of the plane trees, covered from the floor up with marble as well as painting showing tree branches with birds perching on them—a picture no less attractive than the marble. There is a small fountain with a basin, giving a lovely low murmur of water from a circle of little pipes.[194]

At the angle of the front portico opposite the dining room is a large bedroom; through some of its windows, it gives a view of the *xystus*, through others the meadowland. But on axis of the windows and just below them, there is pleasure for sight and sound [*strepitu visuque iucunda*]: a lovely view of the pool as water cascading from above foams onto the marble below. This bedroom is suffused with sun and in consequence is very warm in winter; there is a hypocaust nearby that supplements the sun's heat with warm vapor on cloudy days.

Next, a large, cheerful entrance hall to the baths [*apodyterium*] leads to the cold room [*frigidarium*], in which the plunge baths are big enough but dark. If you want more room to swim and warmer water, there is a warm bath next door, and then a cold plunge bath if you're weary of warmth. The sun gives a very pleasant temperature to the rooms of the *frigidarium*, but the hot room [*caldarium*] is even warmer because it extends outward. There are three plunge baths in the *caldarium*, two in full sun, a third away from its rays but still with some light. A court for playing ball games [*sphaeristerium*] stands above the entrance hall (*apodyterium*), large enough for several groups to engage in several different kinds of exercises.

Stairs near the bath building lead to a *cryptoporticus* and then three suites of living rooms [*diaetae*]. One overlooks the little courtyard with the four plane trees, the second out to the meadows, and the third has a view to the vineyards and the entire horizon. A *cubiculum* has been walled off at the end of the *cryptoporticus*; it has a view of the garden-hippodrome, the vineyards, and the mountains. An adjoining *cubiculum*, sun-filled especially in winter, connects to a living room, which joins the garden-hippodrome to the villa. That is the aspect and structure of the villa's facade.

To one side is a summer *cryptoporticus* set at a higher level, which seems not to overlook but almost to touch the vineyards. At its midpoint is a *triclinium*, which receives wonderfully health-enhancing breezes from the valleys of the Apennines; at the back, at the entrance from the *cryptoporticus*, the vineyards can be seen through its wide windows and its folding doors. On the windowless side of this *triclinium*, there are service stairs used [by the servants] to accommodate gatherings of guests [*convivium*]. At the end, there is a *cubiculum* that looks back to the *cryptoporticus*—a view as pleasant as that over the vineyard.

Below [this summer *cryptoporticus-triclinium-cubiculum* sequence), there is a second, partially below-grade *cryptoporticus*, which retains a cool temperature throughout the summer and has enough air circulation not to need outside ventilation. Next to both [of these superimposed] *cryptoporticus*, just at the farther side of the [upper] dining room, there is a [colonnaded] portico, wintery cool before midday but summer hot by evening. This leads to two suites of rooms, one with four bedrooms, the other with three, which enjoy sunshine or shade as the sun moves.

The garden-hippodrome by far surpasses the arrangement and pleasant character of the villa's buildings. The middle part is completely open so that the whole area is immediately visible upon entering. Plane trees surround it, verdant with ivy that garbs them lower down, verdant also with their own leaves above. The ivy grows over the trunk and branches of the trees and marries one to another as it spreads [laterally]. Box hedges are planted between the trees, and outside them is a ring of laurel trees adding their own shade to that of the plane trees.

The garden-hippodrome then changes: its straight part gives way to a hemicycle at the end, and the planting is different: cypress trees surround and protect the area, with a fuller shade, denser and darker. Many circular pathways inside are in full sun; roses grow, and cool shade is varied by the welcome warmth of the sun. At the end of these various pathways [*viae*], the curve leads to a straight one, or, really, many of them, divided from one another by box hedges. Here and there between little [grassy] meadows [*pratula*] are box hedges in thousands of shapes, sometimes letters that spell out the name of the owner or that of the gardener. Miniature obelisks of box alternate with fruit trees, and then, unexpectedly within this greatly artificial [citified] planting [*in opere urbanissimo*], there appears an imitation of a rustic countryside [*ruris imitatio*]. The open space in the middle [of the garden-hippodrome] is embellished on either side with dwarfed plane trees. Behind them are the shiny waving leaves of acanthus, then more box hedges in shapes and [letters of] names.

At the far end [of the garden-hippodrome] is a curved dining facility [*stibadium*] of white marble covered by a vine; four small columns of Carystian marble hold up the vine. Water flows from little jets as if impelled by the weight of the [reclining] dinner guests; the water then pours into a stone basin and is held in a graceful marble basin regulated by a hidden mechanism so it is always full but never overflows. The dinner's appetizers and principal dishes are placed on the edge of the stone basin, while the lighter ones float on the water in vessels shaped like little boats or birds.[195] Opposite the *stibadium* is a fountain that spurts and catches its own water—a jet jumps high and then falls back upon itself into the basin, then by narrow openings jumps up again.

A *cubiculum* faces the *stibadium*; its beauty adds to the dining area as much as it is enhanced by its [important] position. It is covered with shining marble, and it overlooks and opens to greenery, with upper and lower windows framing and looking onto more greenery. A very small cubicle adjoins the *cubiculum* itself, part of it but a little separate: it has a bed and windows all around, and the light is kept low and shaded by a vigorous vine that grows upward to cover the whole building up to the roof. You can lie there as if you were in a forest, safe and sound in the woods but without rain. There is a fountain that bubbles up and then subsides. Here and there, marble chairs are positioned so strollers who are tired of walking can enjoy [a rest], much as if they were in their own bedrooms. Next to the chairs are little fountains, and everywhere in the garden-hippodrome there is the sound of streams channeled into it, the water controlled by hand to flow to one or another part of the plants, or sometimes to irrigate the whole garden at once.

For a while now, I should have tried to be less loquacious unless this letter had been intended to take you with it to every corner of the villa. For that matter, I am not worried that you might find it boring to read about what would not be boring [if you were] here, particularly if you could put this letter down and have a rest as you might wish to do [up here].

Anyway, I am indulging my loves: I love especially those places I have built myself or that I have improved from a previous state. Why should my opinion—be it good or bad—not be stated clearly to you? In the end, I consider that the first duty of a writer is to keep to his subject, to fully ask himself about the particulars he set out to elucidate, to know that he will not seem boring if he keeps it short, and will be much too long if he introduces irrelevant matters.[196] You can see how many verses there are in Homer and Vergil describing the arms of Achilles and Aeneas, but in effect they seem short because both stick to what they intended to do. You can see how Aratus does the same in following and cataloguing the smallest stars; the method works [for him, too], because it is not a digression but rather the very essence of his work.[197] It's the same with me, to go from the sublime to the small![198] I'm trying to put the whole villa before your eyes, and if I do not bring in irrelevancies, my letter describing it is not long—rather, it's my villa that's large.

To avoid being blamed for not obeying my own law if I keep going any more in this [irrelevant, off-topic] vein, I return to where I began: you now can understand why my Tuscan villa is preferable to those [or any] at Tusculum, Tibur, and Praeneste.[199] In addition, I can add this: there is better *otium* here, more calm, and lack of worry.[200] There's no need [for me] to wear a toga, and no one in the neighborhood bothers me. Tranquillity and relaxation are everywhere, and these are themselves as much a part of the healthfulness of the region as its lovely climate and pure air. Here, I have what's best for mind and body. My slaves are also healthier than anywhere else, and up to now I have not lost any one of them who came with me—pardon me for the expression. May the gods keep this villa a joy to me forever and maintain its fame. Farewell.

Pliny the Younger's Villas near Comum

Letter to his friend Voconius Romanus[201]
In giving advice to a friend about a seaside *villa maritima* under construction, Pliny describes, as exemplars, two of his villas near Comum (modern Como) by the Larian Lake (modern Lago di Como), indicating that he is adding to the existing buildings.[202]

Plin., *Ep.* 9.7.1–5 I write to you because you're building. It's a good thing because now I have you as my advisor, and my building projects can be modeled on yours. Your project is not so different from mine: you are building at the seaside, I on the Larian Lake. I have several villas there, and while two are particularly delightful, they are also a cause of some worry. One is built on rocks in such a way as to give a view of the lake, in the way that villas at Baiae do. The other is built down by the shore, also like [some other] Baiaean villas. The former I refer to as *Tragedy*, because it wears high theatrical boots, while the latter deserves the title of *Comedy* because it wears soft slippers.[203] Each one has a pleasant aspect different from the other, and each one more pleasant to their owner because of the difference between them. The former [*Tragedy*] has a wide view of the lake, whereas the latter [*Comedy*] touches the lake closely because it is built around an inlet defined by a curving terrace wall. The former is built on a high promontory crossing over two inlets, and there is a long, straight walkway extending from it high above the lake. The latter [*Comedy*] has a wide terrace gently following the curving shore. The former [*Tragedy*] is not touched by the waves, while the waves break over the latter. From *Tragedy*, you can see the fishermen, while from *Comedy* you can be a fisherman yourself, casting your hooked line from your bedroom, even from your bed, almost as if you were in a boat. These amenities are already there, and they are the reasons that I making additions to both of them. But why am I explaining myself to you? You're doing the same as I. Farewell.

APULEIUS OF MADAURUS (ca. 125–170/1 CE)

Apology (*Apologia*, or *Apologia sive Pro se de magia liber*), spoken 158–159 CE, published in written form later (Apul., *Apol.*)

The Villa of His Wife Pudentilla near Oea

In about 152 CE, Apuleius, a native of Madaurus in Numidia (Algeria), arrived in the *colonia* of Oea (modern Tripoli).[204] He was in his mid- to late twenties at the time. As a highly educated and personable man, engaging lecturer, and well-spoken literary figure, he attracted the attention of Aemilia Pudentilla, a wealthy widow some fifteen years older than he; they were soon married.[205] Pudentilla had had two sons by her first husband; the elder had recently died, but the younger, an adolescent, was alive but estranged from his mother. To impede Apuleius from receiving financial benefits from his wife at the expense of her son Pudens, a charge of magic was brought against the writer as having ensorcelled Pudentilla to marry him.[206] In the course of his defense, Apuleius describes what, from her property, he advised her to give to her sons from her possessions outright as tokens of their future inheritance. This was only part of all she owned, but even the two tokens give a picture of the villas and estates of wealthy municipal citizens in the Roman African provinces in the second century CE. She also gave Apuleius, a little farm as a modest wedding present (*dos modica*)

Apul., *Apol.* 93.4–5 [Apuleius, speaking to the judge] [I urged her to comply without delay with their demands to buy] properties at low valuations at the prices they themselves insisted on. In addition, [I urged her] to give them from her own estates the most fertile fields, a big, well-appointed house [*domus*] in town as well as a good stock of wheat, barley, wine, and olive oil and other produce, and 400 slaves, plus valuable cattle, so that they [her sons] could have certainty as to what she had assigned them [in her will] and to be fully confident that the rest of their inheritance would be coming.[207]

Apul., *Apol.* 101.4–6 [Apuleius, speaking to his accuser] So as not to omit anything before I finish, I will refute the other false allegation. You [the accuser] have said that I bought a very lovely estate (*pulcherissimum praedium*) for myself with a large sum of my wife's money. I say that it's a small property (*herediolum*) worth [only] 60,000*HS* and that it was not bought by me but bought [for me] in Pudentilla's name, and that it's registered to her and the tax of the property (*agellus*) is paid in her name. [...]

AULUS GELLIUS (ca. 123[?]–after 180 CE)

Attic Nights (*Noctes Atticae*), ca. 177–179 CE (Gell., *NA*)

The Villa of Herodes Atticus at Cephisia near Athens

In 143 CE, while he was a student in Athens, the young Aulus Gellius was often received at the villas owned by one of that city's, and Rome's, most distinguished persons. His host was none other than Lucius Vibullius Hipparchus Tiberius Claudius Herodes Atticus (ca. 101–177 CE), a man of great literary and intellectual distinction, vast wealth, high position in imperial and Athenian government, consul in 143 CE, and tutor to the emperor Antoninus Pius's designated heirs. Herodes Atticus owned other villas: an estate with a palatial villa at Marathon (his birthplace) and another at Eua Loukou in Arcadia in the Peloponnese.[208] The following brief excerpt is Gellius's memory of the Cephisia villa, in the Attic plain in the suburbs of the city.

Gell., *NA* 1.2.1–2.   Herodes Atticus, a man of great Greek eloquence who was [also] honored with the consular dignity, often received us together with [our] Athenian teachers at his villas near the city, together with the distinguished [*clarissimus*] Servilianus and some others of our countrymen who had left Rome for Greece to absorb its intellectual culture. There at the time, while we were at the villa called Cephisia in the heat of the summer and autumn's torrid sun, we warded off the unpleasant hot temperature in the shade of its extensive groves, on its long soft walkways, in the cool siting of the mansion [*aedes*] itself, in the elegant baths with their great quantity of shining water—in sum, the beauty of the villa in all its parts, humming everywhere with the sound of waters and the song of birds.[209]

ST. GREGORY OF NYSSA (ca. 335–395 CE)

Letter 20, to Adelphius the Scholasticus, ca. 376 CE.
Translation by Anna M. Silvas.[210]

Gregory, Bishop of Nyssa (372–376 and 378 CE to his death), his younger brother Basil, Bishop of Caesarea (Mazaca), and their friend Gregory of Nazianzus, Archbishop of Constantinople, were important theologians, orators, and ecclesiastics; the three are known as the Cappadocian Fathers. Besides their charitable and pastoral work, as high churchmen all three were in close communication with wealthy and influential persons in their local bishoprics, and Basil and Gregory of Nazianzus had correspondents empire-wide. In this letter, Gregory of Nyssa describes the villa of Adelphius during the course of a visit, to thank him for his hospitality.[211] The prose letter is couched in mythological and geographical references similar to the allusive imagery of the poems of Statius to his hosts.[212]

In another text (not included here), an account of the life and death of his sister Macrina, Gregory briefly described the villa-like setting of his sister's rural religious community at Anisa (Annisa: *Pleiades* s.v. "Annisa") on the river Iris in Pontus and the hospitality there.[213]

Gregory of Nyssa, Letter 20.1–21   I write you this letter from the sacred Vanota, if I do not do the place an injustice by naming it in the local dialect—do the place an injustice, I mean, because the name lacks elegance. For indeed this Galatian title does not hint at the loveliness of such a place.[214] It has need of the eye to appreciate its loveliness. For though I have till now seen many things—yes, in many places—and have also apprehended many things through the word-pictures [λόγων ὑπογραφή] in the accounts of the ancient writers, I consider that all I have seen and all I have heard [to be] a trumpery in comparison with the beauty here.

[Your] Helicon is nothing, the Isles of the Blest are a fable, the Sicyonian plain is a trifle. The accounts of the Peneius are another poetic exaggeration—that river, which they say overflows the banks on its sides and so with its rich current fertilizes for the Thessalians their far-famed plains.[215] Why, what beauty is there in any of these places mentioned that Vanota does not also unfold before us in its own beauties? Whether one seeks the natural loveliness of the place [τοῦ τόπου χάρις], it does not need any of the arts of beautification [ἐκ τῆς τέχνης καλῶν], or looks to what has been added by artifice, so much has been done and done so well that they are able even to improve the deficiencies of nature.

The gifts with which nature favors the place as it adorns the land with unstudied grace [ἀκατασκεύῳ χάριτι] are these: down below, the river Halys with its banks beautifies the place, gleaming like a golden ribbon on a deep purple robe, by reddening its current with the soil.[216] Up above, a thickly wooded mountain extends itself along a great ridge, covered on all sides with oaks, worthy of finding some Homer to sing its praises beyond that of Ithacan Neritus, which the poet calls "far-seen with quivering leaves."[217] But the native forest, in descending the hillside meets at its foot the work of husbandry. For immediately vines spread out over the slopes and flanks and hollows at the mountain's base, cladding all the lower region with color as with a green mantle. In this climate the season has also enhanced the scene, displaying the divinely sweet treasure of its grapes, which rather surprised me, because the neighboring country was displaying its fruit still unripe, whereas here it was possible to enjoy the grapes and take one's fill of their ripeness as much as one wished.

Then from afar, like some flare on a great beacon tower, the loveliness of the buildings shone out upon us. On the left as we entered was the oratory, which is being built to the martyrs [ὁ εὐκτήριος οἶκος τοῖς μάρτυσιν]. Its structure was not yet complete, for it still lacks a roof, yet it was resplendent all the same. Straight ahead of us on the road were the beauties of the house [τὰ τῆς οἰκήσεως κάλλη], one part marked off from another by some elegant contrivance, the projections of the towers and a banquet [τὸ συμπόσιον] in preparation among the wide and high-arched rows of plane trees which crowned the entrance before the gates.[218] Then lying around the buildings are the Phaeacian gardens—but let not the beauties of Vanota be insulted by comparison with those.[219] Homer never saw "the apple with shining fruit" that we have seen here, which approaches the hue of its own blossom in the high color of its skin.[220] He never saw a pear whiter than newly polished ivory. And what is one to say of the fruit of the peach tree, its variety and its many forms mingled and synthesized from different strains? For just as those who paint "goat-stags" and "centaurs" and the like commingle things of different kinds, making themselves wiser than nature, so it is with this fruit. Nature tyrannized by art [ἡ φύσις παρασοφιζόμενοι γράφουσις] makes one into an almond, another into a walnut, yet another into a cling [stone] fruit, mingled alike in name and in flavor.[221] Yet with all these, each kind noted even more for their number than their beauty.

But I do not think one can describe in words the arrangement of their planting and the artist's orderly proportions, for truly such a marvel belongs to a draughtsman [γραφεύς] rather than to a tiller of the ground, so readily has nature fallen in with the wishes of those who make these arrangements. Who could describe adequately in words the path under the overhanging vines and the sweet shade of the grapes and the new kind of wall made of lattices where the roses with their shoots and the vines with their trailers intertwine themselves together, making a wall fortified against attack from the sides, and the cistern of water at the summit of this course, and the fish being bred there?[222]

Through all this time, these who have charge of your nobility's house were eagerly guiding us around with a kind of easy affability, pointing out to us the details over which you had taken pains, as if they were showing courtesy to yourself through us. There too, one of the lads, like some conjuror, showed us a sight that one does not often come across in nature: for he plunged into the depths and brought up at will whatever fish he had a mind to. They did not slip away at the fisherman's touch but were tame and submissive under the artist's hands, like well-trained young dogs.

Then they led me to a house [οἶκος] where I was to take my rest. At least, the entrance signaled a house, but when we came inside the doors it was not a house but a portico [ἡ στοὰ] that received us. The portico was raised aloft to a great height above a deep pool. Lapped by the water, the pavement which supported the portico in a triangular shape was like a vestibule to the delights within.[223] Once inside, a house [οἶκος] occupied the projection of the triangle straight opposite us.[224] It had a lofty roof [προβολὴν τὸν ὄροφον], lit up on all sides by the sun's rays and decorated with a variety of paintings [γραφαῖς ποιχίλαις], so that this spot almost made us forget what we had previously seen.[225] The house drew us to itself, and again, the portico above the pool was a unique sight. For the superb fish would swim up from the depths to the surface, leaping up into the very air like winged things, as if meaning to mock us land creatures. They would display half their form as they tumbled through the air, and plunge again into the depth. Still others, following one another in orderly shoals, were a sight for unaccustomed eyes, while elsewhere one might see another shoal packed in a cluster round a morsel of bread, one pushing aside another, here one leaping up, there another diving down. But even this we were made to forget by the grapes that were brought us in baskets made of vine twigs, by the varied display of fruit, the preparations for lunch, the varied dainties and savory sauces and sweet cakes and the drinking of toasts and wine cups.

But now, since we are satisfied and inclined to sleep, I have stationed a scribe beside me and have drafted this babbling letter to your eloquence as if in a dream.[226] But I pray that I may be able to describe fully to you and those who love you with my own voice and tongue and not with paper and ink the beauties of your home.

AUSONIUS (Decimus Magnus Ausonius, ca. 310–393/394 CE)

The Moselle (Mosella), ca. 371 CE (Auson., *Mos.*)

For a decade, when Ausonius was appointed tutor to the imperial heir Gratian in 364 CE, he resided at Augusta Treverorum (modern Trier, Trèves). The city was, with Milan, Ravenna, and occasionally other places, an imperial residence for the western empire. Ausonius's poem describes a passage on the Moselle River, by boat and on foot, going south-southwest upstream from Bingium (modern Bingen-am-Rhein) near its confluence with the Rhenus (modern Rhine) to Augusta Treverorum. This city, as the principal civilian center and military headquarters of Belgica Prima in Diocletian's reorganization of the provinces, had been long acclimatized—like Aquitania—to the norms and habits of Roman social culture.[227] Ausonius's poem (of almost 500 hexameters) expresses a sincere love of the river's lovely landscapes as it twists through the hills; the deep views include the picturesque presence of villas and farms, and the recollection of the landscapes of his Aquitanian hometown of Burdigala (modern Bordeaux) carry the theme of affectionate remembrance through the entire account.[228] *The Moselle* was written toward the middle of Ausonius's ten-year residence at Trier, ca. 371 CE.[229]

Auson., *Mos.* 19–22

[The open views] made me see in this a picture of my lovely, well-cultivated native land of Burdigala,
The roofs of its villas [*culmina villarum*] set high above the sloping riverbanks,
Its hills green with vineyards [*Baccho*] and, below, the pleasant water of the Moselle
Flowing along with a quiet sound.

Auson., *Mos.* 169–177[230]
> The landscape scene doesn't merely please human beings:
> I can well believe that rustic Satyrs and Naiads with their gray eyes
> Come together at the river's banks, when reckless animation rouses the goat-footed Pans
> And they, leaping around and beating up the water with boisterous splashing,
> Frighten the [Naiads'] sisters trembling with fright under the water.[231]
> Often, Panope with her friends the Oreiads, when she has stolen grapes from the hills,
> Flees away from the lustful Fauns, the countryside's divine guardians [*paganica numina*].

In *Mos.* 208–210 (omitted here), Ausonius equates youths' playing to those of Cumae, and the hillside vineyards of the Moselle landscape to those of Cumae, Mount Gaurus, and "miasmic" Vesuvius; later, Cumae and Baiae will be invoked (*Mos.* 346–348). The fame of the resorts and landscapes of the Bay of Naples resonated in the later fourth century and persisted well into the sixth (see Cassiodorus, *Variae* 12.22.3–5, in this chapter).

Auson., *Mos.* 283–285
> Villas set suspended on the peak of high rocks [*pendentes saxis…culmine villaeI*] look down on scenes like these [of fishing]
> Along the blue expanses [of the river], and between them
> The river winding this way and that,
> And great mansions [*praetoria*] gracing both banks.

Auson., *Mos.* 298–304
> Who could ever accurately set out the innumerable beauties and forms [*cultusque habitusque*]
> The architectural shapes of each and every mansion [*praedia*]?
> The winged man of Gortyna would not refuse such work [*opus*, i.e., of such villas],
> He who set the plan [*conditor*] for the Euboean temple at Cumae, and who
> Trying to depict Icarus's disaster in gold, was defeated by fatherly grief.[232]
> Nor would Philo the Cecropian [Athenian], nor again the man who was praised
> By his enemy for prolonging the famous struggle [seige] of the Syracusan war.[233]

Auson., *Mos.* 318–348
> So these—or others like them—can be believed worthy of having built
> Such groupings of houses [*scaenae domorum*] in the lands of the Belgae,
> And to have raised these lofty villas as the river's adornment.
> This one is poised high on a natural outcropping of rock,
> Another built on the edge of a shore reaching out into the stream,
> This one is built farther back [but] close to itself, holding the river captive in a bay.
> Again, this one, clinging to a hill, overhangs the river
> And relishes a wide panorama over many places,
> Asserting easy eyeshot over both cultivated fields and wastelands—
> Enjoying [all] the lands as if they were the villa's own.
> Now yet another, even though it is set low on a well-watered meadows,
> Balances the nature-given dominance of a high mountain towering over the villa
> When it breaches the aether with its high roof
> And lofty tower, like the Pharos of Memphis.[234]
> Here, another villa has a way of its own to catch fish
> By capturing them in swirling pools among enclosures of sun-struck rocks.
> [Another villa] at the top of a crag has a slightly misted view of the stream gliding below.
> Why mention their entrance halls [*atria*] set into green meadows?
> Or of their elegant roofs [*nitentia tecta*] set on innumerable columns?

What [mention is needed] of the baths [*balnea*], set at the edge of the river,
Which emit smoke when Mulciber, drawn in by the fiery hidden pipe,
Belches flames and whirls them up behind the hollow plastered walls
Heaping up the imprisoned steam [smoke] with blasting heat?[235]
I personally have seen bathers, worn out by the great heat of the bath,
Disdaining the basins and the cold of the swimming pools,
Prefer the running waters; then, restored in the stream,
Splashing and swimming in the cool river.
If a traveler [*hospes*] from the shores of Cumae were to come here,
He might well have believed that this place has been given as a far-flung copy of Euboean Baiae,
Such is its beauty and elegance: its delight does not rise to [vulgar] luxury.

Ausonius, *Ephemeris* 2 (*Id est totius diei negotium*), after ca. 379–380 CE (Auson., *Eph.*)

Ausonius wrote the *Ephemeris* (diary, journal) as a series of poems in various meters sectioned by the time of day and his activities as a villa owner: his "work" or *negotium*, as he calls it.[236] The tone is wry and self-mocking, intending to make the reader smile or laugh, except for section 3, a long morning prayer. He alternates between addressing different interlocutors about the estate and quoting or speaking himself. The excerpts illustrate his daily "work" around the villa, but where the villa actually was—in Gallia Belgica or in Aquitania—is not certain. For most of the poem, he is speaking in his own voice. The commanding condescension to his enslaved attendants—as well as his complaints about their laziness, gluttony, and negligence—are part of the amusement Ausonius intends to provoke in his readers.

Auson., *Eph.* 2.1.1–9
"Bright morning is opening windows now
And now the sleepless swallow twitters from its nest,
But you, Parmeno, sleep on, as if it were still the first or middle hour of the night.[237]
Dormice sleep all winter,
But they're frugal with their food
While your reason for sleeping is because you drink a lot
And stretch out your bulk with too much food." [...]

Auson., *Eph.* 2.2.1–14
"Come here, Boy [*puer*], get yourself up!
Bring my shoes and my linen gown.
Bring me all the other things
That you've already laid out, so I can go out.
Bring me spring water so I can wash my hands, my mouth and eyes.
Open up the chapel [*sacrarium*]
But without ostentatious preparation:
Pious words, innocent prayers
Are enough for holy worship."
I don't ask for incense to be burned
Or the sacrifice of a piece of honeyed bread:
I leave hearths set on [altars of] living turf
To [worship] on the altars of vain gods.[238] [...]

Auson., *Eph.* 2.4.1–10

Enough of praying to God,
Even though it's never enough to make holy supplication.
"Boy [*puer*]! Bring me my going-out-in-public clothes [*habitus forensis*]!
It's time for a mutual Hello-Goodbye [*have valeque*] with friends."
But now that it's the fourth hour of the day,
As the sun has whipped his horses in their course
And it's coming up to miday,
It's time to talk to Sosias![239]

Auson., *Eph.* 2.5.1–8

Now's the time to call my friends to come,
So that, by me, they won't be late for lunch [*prandium*],
"Run quickly, Boy [*puer*], to the neighbors' houses [*aedes*].
You know who they are, and get back here as soon as what I say is said!"
I have invited five guests: six is the correct number for a feast—
If there are more, it's a mess!
Off he goes! Now I'm left [to talk] with Sosias.

Auson., *Eph.* 2.6.1–7

"Sosias, lunch is really, really needed. The sun has gone into the fourth hour,
And its shadow is progressing into the fifth.
Make sure the well-seasoned dishes are prepared to perfection by tasting them.
Roll the bubbling pots around in your hands and give them a stir,
Stick your fingers—but carefully!—in the pots
And lick them with your wet tongue, in and out." [...]

Auson., *Eph.* 2.7.1–21

"Come here now, Boy [*puer*]! My skillful secretary,
My quick-writing servant.
Open the two-leaved notebook
Over which so many words are spoken,
Then converted into a few signs
And finished up as one idea [*vox*, expression].[240]
I think about writing weighty books
And, fast as hail, I pour out words in a torrent,
But your ears do not fail you
And your page isn't overcrowded.
Your right hand, moving carefully,
Flies over the smooth wax.
When I hold forth, as fast as I am doing now,
Going over and around the topic,
You already have the sense of [what is in] my heart
And just as soon as my words are spoken,
You've got them on the wax."
I wish my mind had the capacity
To be as quick to understand
[How] you get ahead of me as I speak,
And [how] the speed of your right hand outruns me [my words]. [...]

Auson., *Eph.* 2.8.40–43[241]

> If sweet sleep shall calm me with its soothing breath,
> And no troubling images disturb me at night,
> I dedicate this grove for you to live in during your nightly watches—
> This elm which spreads its green leafy branches on my estate [*ager*].

Ausonius, *Ephemeris* 3 (*Domestica* 1. *De herediolo*, Domestic Poems 1. *My Little Inheritance*) (Auson., *Eph.*)

Ausonius was 73 years old when, in 383 CE, he retired to a villa near Burdigala left to him by his father, who himself had died very recently at the age of about 90. His retirement was prompted by the murder of the emperor Gratian, his former pupil and patron, who had promoted him to high office as praetorian prefect of Gaul in 375 and consul in 379 CE. After the defeat of the usurper Maximus (388 CE), the new regime of Gratian's successors, Valentinian II in the west and Theodosius I in the east, evidently had no work or favor for Ausonius, but he was happy at his villa, as his hexameter poem indicates. He gives his villa a theoretical aspect by framing its physical extent with the famous Greek aphorism—"know thyself." This gives his farm and his farming a Stoic moderation with some Epicurean appeal.

Auson., *Eph.* 3. Preface and lines 1–32
Having left the palace after many years in many very exalted appointments [*multi anni honoratissimi*], even that of consul, and as soon as he [Ausonius] returned to his native land [*patria*] and to the little villa [*villula*] that his father had bequeathed him, he wrote these amusing verses in Lucilian style:[242]

> "Greetings, my little inheritance, the kingdom of my ancestors
> Which my great-grandfather, grandfather, and father brought to perfection [*excolere*],
> And which [this last], my father, even though he was old, left to me after a much too early death.
> Alas, too I did not wish to enjoy it so soon!
> Of course, it is in [appropriate] sequence [for a son] to follow the father,
> But really, among loving kin [*pii*], a situation of shared ownership would have been more pleasing.
> Now, the work and worry are mine;
> Before, only the enjoyment was mine, the rest was my father's [work and worry].
> I admit it's pretty small, this little inheritance of mine,
> But to a man who has serenity, nothing's small, everything's harmonious.
> It's my belief that serenity about property [*res*, wealth, business] comes from the soul,
> Not his soul from his property [*res*].
> Croesus desires all things, Diogenes wants nothing.[243]
> Aristippus scatters gold among the Syrtes,
> All of golden Lydia is not enough for Midas.[244]
> He who has no limit to what he wants sets no limit to the things in his possession:
> The way to setting limit to your wealth is what you establish in your soul.
> Now it's really time for you to know the size of my estate,
> So you may get to know me and get to know yourself as well, if you can.
> However, it's hard to know oneself: γνῶθι σεαυτόν!
> We learn that [phrase] quickly, and we forget it just as readily.
> I till two hundred *iugera*; there are a hundred in vineyards;
> And half of that [50] *iugera* are in pastureland [*prata*].
> The woodlands are more than twice the extent of pastureland, vineyards, and ploughed land.[245]

The number of my farmhands is neither too great nor too few.
There's a spring nearby and a small well, and a navigable river with clear water—
Its ebb and flow bears me away from home and brings me back.
Two years' worth of the produce [of my estate] is always kept in store:
He who doesn't have an ample amount stored away will have famine very soon.
My estate is not far from the town, but not really very near it, either:
It lets me keep away from crowds and lets me enjoy its pleasures.
In this way, whenever I've had enough [*fastidium*] and want to change,
I move from one to the other, enjoying either the country or the town in turn.

Ausonius, *Epistles* (Auson., *Ep.*)

Epistle 26, to Paulinus

Ausonius wrote this letter in a rueful mood, as one villa owner to another, addressing his fellow Aquitanian and former pupil at Burdigala, Pontius Meropius Anicius Paulinus (Paulinus of Nola, ca. 354–431 CE), a substantial landowner and aristocrat. It gives a picture of a bustling and pretentious agent of Ausonius's villa and estate.

Auson., *Ep.* 26 I have many and various reasons, my son Paulinus, to be grateful to you, sometimes coming as an opportunity arises and at other times as your affable good nature affords. Now because you never refuse me anything that I might ask, you sharpen my shamelessness rather than dulling it, as you'll find out once more in the matter of Philo, my former agent [procurator]. He is in danger of being expelled in an untimely way from the use of lodging given to him by your men after he stored some goods at Hebromagus which he had bought up from various estates.[246] Unless you grant my request—that he be allowed to stay there at his convenience and that a barge [*nausus*] or other boat be made available so a good amount of the produce can be brought to the town so that [my] Lucaniacus can be freed from the danger of an imminent want of victuals—the entire *familia* of a man of literature there [at the villa] will reach the state not of [Marcus Tullius] Cicero's *Frumentaria* speeches but to the *Curculio* by Plautus.[247] So that I may obtain [what I need] more easily, or to make you fear greater fuss were you to refuse my request, I'm sending you a letter in iambic verse. It is sealed so that you will know that the messenger has not been interfered with if he arrives with the letter incorrectly unsealed. [...][248]

Auson., *Ep.* 26.1–48, to Paulinus:
　　Philo, the *vilicatus* [*vilicus*][249] of my estates,
　　Or as he's pleased to call himself, their ἐπίτροπος [overseer]—
　　Because that little Greek guy thinks that a pretentious name
　　Makes for a glamorous Dorian status—
　　Adds his own whining pleas to my requests
　　Which I myself am hesitatingly following up.[250]
　　You'll see him for himself, just as he is as he stands next to me,
　　A typical example [*imago*] of his own social status [*fortuna sua*]
　　Gray-haired, hirsute, shaggy, menacing, primitive,
　　Just like Phormio in Terence,
　　Hair unkempt, standing up like a bristly sea urchin's spines
　　Or as spiky as the lines of my verse![251]
　　This guy, when poor harvests often showed his claims to be false,
　　Took a dislike to the title of *vilicus*,
　　And having sown either too late or much too early,

Because he was ignorant of the stars,
And to get out of being blamed himself,
Lashed out at heaven and blamed the climate criminals.
He isn't any assiduous farmer, no experienced ploughman,
More a steward [*promus*] dispensing household items than a keeper [*condus*] of the storeroom.
While denouncing the earth [land] for its treachery and sterility,
He prefers to be a businessman [*negotior*]
As a dealer [*mercator*] in the buy-and-sell market [*forum venalium*]
Trading in Greek guarantees, and now,
Having become wiser than the Seven Sages of Greece,
Has taken his place as the eighth Wise Man.[252]
Now he's furnishing grain for old salt
And is newly branching out as a [big-time] merchant [*emporus*]:
He visits tenants, country places, villages, and towns,
For the trade in products of the earth and salt.
He travels the Tarnis and Garumna by dinghies [*acati*], long boats [*phaseli*], skiffs [*lintres*],
    barges [*stlattae*], and rafts [*rates*]
Claiming his profits as liabilities and fraudulently overstating his liabilities—
He gets rich and makes me poor.[253]
Now he's brought himself straight to your [villa at] Hebromagus
And made it the storage spot for his goods.
From there, he alleges, grain will be transferred by barge for my convenience.
For that reason, get him going soon with the loan of your boat
So that my Lucanianum [villa] can be freed from famine,
Like the Perusian famine before, and the Saguntum famine, too.[254]
If I can get this help [*munus*] from you,
You'll be worshiped above [the goddess] Ceres.[255]
Because this gift will be yours to me,
I'll place you well above the godhead
Of Triptolemus of ages past, the one they call Epimenides
Or Buzyges, the chief of *vilici*.[256]

PAULINUS OF PELLA (Paulinus Pellaeus, 376–ca. 461 CE)

Eucharisticus, ca. 459 CE (Paulinus, *Euch.*)

Paulinus of Pella (Paulinus Pellaeus), the only name by which he is known, and that only from his birthplace at Pella in Macedonia, was the grandson of Decimus Magnus Ausonius. Having a consul (in 379 CE) and poet as ancestor, and, for a father, a *vicarius* or lieutenant governor of Macedonia and later proconsul of Africa (378), assured Paulinus a place in the upper echelons of Aquitanian society and the imperial bureaucracy, though lower than the position achieved by his grandfather.[257] The family members' own efforts plus their marriages brought them estates, and pleasant—even luxurious—country life in villas. Certainly Paulinus's life, both as the young son of a privileged villa owner, then a villa owner himself, was agreeable: villas and estates of the provincial aristocracies in the late fourth century CE in Aquitania preserved elements of a long Roman tradition. Paulinus's autobiography includes some account of his villas.

Paulinus's pleasant life in his villas and houses changed with the occupation of Aquitania by Gothic forces beginning in 412 CE and their subsequent capture and then abandonment of Burdigala in 414 CE. Paulinus underwent several other misfortunes, but it is a tribute to his resourcefulness that he was able, by skillful management, to get back to some semblance of a comfortable life. In the end, he achieved his two goals: to praise God and to write poetry. Along the way, his account of villa life in the fifth century CE is of interest: he does not describe his villas, but he does describe his life in and with them.

The *Eucharisticus*[258] is autobiographical: a prose preface sets out Paulinus's devotion to God's grace, pity, and benign providence (*gratia, misericordia, providentia*), disclaiming any desire for fame (*gloria*). In lines 1–41 (omitted here), Paulinus proclaims his faith, tells us of his birth in Macedonia, his stay as a child at Carthage, and, on return to Burdigala (modern Bordeaux), a detour through Rome.

Paulinus, *Euch*. 42–47

>Finally, coming to the end of some long journeys,
>I came to my ancestors' land and to my grandfather's house at Burdigala
>Where the lovely Garumna draws back the Ocean's waves into a shipping entrance
>Which still provides a large harbor inside the spacious city's walls.
>That is when I first got to know my grandfather [Ausonius],
>Who was consul that year, in my first three years of life.[259]

Eucharisticus 48–175 (omitted here) gives an account of his education. From age 6 while living in the country (where his father hunted), Paulinus received a fine education in both Greek and Latin classics: his mother tongue was Greek, which facilitated his philosophical studies and appreciation of poetry. Latin was more difficult (*Euch*. 72–84). At the age of 15, he became ill with a quartan fever (*quartena acerba*); his parents allowed him to stop his studies at the point of learning oratorical skills, and doctors urged a relaxed, amusing life (*laetitia, omnia grata*). Paulinus took full advantage of their advice: perfumed gewgaws, a fast horse, a tall groom, a gilded ball brought from Rome. His health returned, and God's providence kept him from serious accidents. Paulinus was careful to avoid adultery with women against their will or with women of his own class, but with an enslaved woman of his household, he had at least one child, a son who died (*Euch*. 153–175, omitted here).

Paulinus, *Euch*. 176–219

>That was my life, and it continued in that way
>From about my eighteenth year [*ter senis circiter*] until I was almost twenty [*duo decennia*].[260]
>Then my parents' kind concern compelled me—and I admit, I was reluctant—
>To give up this pleasant way of life which I had led by force of habit,
>And made me turn to something new:
>To be married to a wife whose properties [*domus*]
>Were more magnificent for their name than for their current ability to give much pleasure.[261]
>The properties had by then become run down
>Because they had been neglected by the indifference of an owner in decline.
>His little granddaughter, inheriting after her father's death,
>Later surrendered to my marriage torches [*taeda meae*].[262]
>But once I decided to take up the work that was assigned to me,
>And with the energy of youth boosting my eagerness of spirit,
>Very soon and within a few days, I was happy to enjoy the pleasures of the house,
>Quickly compelling both myself and my people
>To change from their seductive do-nothing behaviors [*malesuada otia*] to take up unfamiliar tasks,
>Encouraging those I could by the example of my own work,
>And coercing, with an owner's severity [*rigor domini*], those unwilling to work.
>In this way, energetically persevering in the activities of the status that I had taken up,

> I looked after the cultivation of the newly restored fields right away,
> And quickly attended to the care of the worn-out vineyards in need of renewal
> In the method I had ascertained [to be the best] myself.
> What's more—and this may seem especially terrible to many men—
> By being the first to pay my tax bills [*fiscalia debita*] willingly and at the specified deadline,
> I was consequently soon able to get some solid leisure time [*fida otia*] to spend on my own personal enjoyment [*quies*].
> This personal enjoyment was always much too dearly loved by me,
> Though at first it was aligned with my natural inclination [*ingenius*]
> Which at the time was wishing for a moderate way of life.
> Later, from the luxuries close at hand and by drawing away from high ideals [*ambitio*],
> [This enjoyment] became [differently] disposed:
> That my house should have spacious rooms [*aedes*],
> And that it be set up to adapt to the different seasons of the year,
> That my table be elegant and sumptuous, that there be many young servants,
> That the furniture be plentiful and pleasingly versatile for various uses,
> That the silver be more costly in money than in its [mere] weight,
> And that there be craftsmen trained in different trades to fulfill my orders quickly,
> And next, that my stables be full of strong carriage horses
> For driving out comfortably in fine carriages.
> Still, I was less preoccupied at increasing these things
> As I was more involved with [merely] maintaining them,
> And I desired neither to add to my wealth nor to be a candidate for office [*ambitor honorum*].
> Instead, I was—I admit—a hunter of luxuries,
> But only if they could be had at minimal cost and expenditure
> And on the condition that they wouldn't go beyond a decent limit,
> And that the report of [my] being preoccupied with luxury would not taint my reputation for virtue.

Paulinus's agreeable life in his villa was coming to an end (*Euch.* 220–270, omitted here). The twelve years between the entry of the Visigoths into the empire in 406, their Sack of Rome in 410, and their settlement in Aquitania in 418 were accompanied by Paulinus's personal misfortunes: his father Thalassius died and his elder brother contested the will, and his and his mother's properties were destroyed.[263] The next passage, below, indicates that the Mediterranean-wide ownership of villas among the elites continued into Late Antiquity. Paulinus received an imperial court commission.

Paulinus, *Euch.* 271–298
> At this time, these difficulties fell especially on me, even though I had deserved them long ago,
> I, who had a second homeland in the East where I was born
> And where I was, of course, seen to be a pretty big owner [*possessor non ultimus*].[264]
> First, I was prevented on going on a long trip by the passive laziness of the people around me
> Then by the conflicted feelings of my loved ones,
> Most often by their minds made up in opposition to what I wanted.
> By chance and just as often, a recurring fear of an uncertain outcome
> Would put off the plans even when everything had already been gotten ready.
> But then, against my spirit [to leave] there was my accustomed quiet life,
> My long-held habits of *otium*, the many lovely special attractions of my *domus*,

>   Crammed with—alas!—all the great agreeable luxuries in that troubled time
>   And which, alone [at least] then, didn't yet have a Gothic guest [*hospes Gothicus*].[265]
>   What happened soon after was a disaster:
>   Because there was no one in charge who had special [legal] authority,
>   My house was given up to be plundered by the escaping people,
>   Even though I know that, out of their great sense of humanity, certain Goths
>   Zealously tried to help their hosts by protecting them.[266]
>   For me, another new misfortune was added to those circumstances already enumerated
>   By reason of a duty assigned to me in my absence: the tyrant Attalus,
>   Fumbling around for futile support, loaded me up with an empty honor,
>   That of the name of Count of the Private Largesses [*Comes privatae largitionis*].[267]
>   [Attalus] knew that the honor provided no income,
>   And he already had stopped believing in his own royal status
>   Because he was dependant exclusively on the Goths. [...]

In lines 299–405 (omitted here), Paulinus leaves the area of Burdigala to go to Vasatis (Civitas Vasatis, modern Bazas), about 60 km southeast of Burdigala.[268] He may have gone there to defend family estates against a military siege, but they were also threatened by some civil disturbances.[269]

Paulinus, Euch. 406–425

>   That's enough of what I've already said about what happened to me
>   During the long time that I frequented barbarian peoples.
>   Though I still dawdled [in Aquitania], the many misfortunes that I experienced from them
>   Convinced me to leave my native seat as soon as possible—
>   Something that would have been more advantageous to have done earlier—
>   And to travel on a straight line to that shore [land]
>   Where the great part of my mother's wealth still remained safe and sound,
>   Dispersed through many Argive [Greek] cities and those of Old and New Epirus.[270]
>   There were well set up estates [*farta praedia*], scattered but not far apart,
>   With not a few number of farmworkers [*coloni*],
>   Even a very wasteful and negligent owner could have made some good profit.
>   But now as well, there was no outcome for what I wanted,
>   Which was to be able either to emigrate to that longed-for land,
>   Or to retrieve for myself what was left of my grandfather's properties,
>   Some confiscated under the laws of war by barbarians,
>   Others by the criminality [*nefas*] of Romans acting just as they wanted against all laws
>   Thereby increasing my property losses at different times.[271]

In lines 426–519 (omitted here), Paulinus tells us that his plan to assert ownership of his mother's properties in Greece and his grandfather's estates in Gallia Belgica were thwarted by his wife, who refused to let him go. Around this time, he underwent some religious conversion.[272] Then deaths in his family multiplied: his mother-in-law died, then his mother, then his wife.[273] He had two sons, one a priest, the other a courtier in a barbarian royal entourage.[274] He was left with one resource.

Paulinus, *Euch.* 520–545

>   Finally I decided to go to Massiliae for a time,
>   A city in which there were many holy souls dear to me,
>   But only a small remaining part of my family estate.[275]
>   There was no great hope for deriving any profits:

There was no developed estate with its own workers,
No vineyards on which the city mainly depends for its own needs to import necessities from elsewhere.
There was only an urban house [*domus urbana*] with a garden [*hortus*] nearby, and a little field [*agellus*]
With a few vines and even some fruit trees, but no land worth cultivation:
This was [to be] the refuge for my exile [*perfugium secreti*].[276]
But my desire for some work made me put effort into the vacant part of the land—it was just four *iugera* [about 1 ha, or 2½ acres].
And to build a house on the top of the rocks so as not to reduce the amount of [cultivatable] land.
In addition, for the outlays to secure what's needed for living,
I put my hope in renting some fields [*agri conducti*]
As long as my household's means [*domus*] continued to have plenty of slaves
And my remaining good years supplied me continuing strength.[277]
Afterwards, as both [my slave-force and health] got worse
In a time that the prevailing condition of the times was generally changing,
After a while I admit that I was worn out with worries and age.
All alone, no money, no family: I easily changed to new plans and while vacillating among different intentions,
I thought it would be good to take myself back to Burdigala.[278]
My determination to do so was not followed up with success. [...]

Now back in Burdigala, Paulinus is humiliated and living on the charity of others (*Euch.* 546–563, omitted here). But his luck (a fluke in real estate) and God's grace mitigated his misfortune.

Paulinus, *Euch.* 564–581

However, in this same moment of my life you did not allow me to sleep in indecision,
But without my asking, God, you quickly saw fit to comfort me,
And you have always been prompt with pleasant treatments
To soothe my old age, weakened at various times with different illnesses,
In such a way that you have been able to restore it to youthfulness.
When you had shown me in a final way that there was no hope for any profit
From my grandfather's properties, and when all that I was still able to hold onto
In the way of property at Massiliae was under a contractual obligation [*adstrictus sub condicione*]
Because my [outright] ownership of it had been let go [*proprietas amissa*],
You brought me a buyer, a Goth unknown to me, who wanted to buy the small farm
That used to belong legally to me.[279]
He sent me the money voluntarily, not really the right amount [for the property's value],
But truly a gift that I had long wished for, I have to admit.[280]
Of course, with it I could prop up the long-standing ruins of my fallen wealth
And hold off any new loss to my self-esteem [*damna pudoris*].

The poem ends with a heartfelt paean to Christ for His many blessings (*Euch.* 582–616, omitted here).

SIDONIUS APOLLINARIS
(Gaius Sollius Modestus Apollinaris Sidonius, ca. 430–481/490 CE)

Letters (Epistulae) (Sid. Apoll., *Ep.*)

Letter to his friend Domitius on the Villa Avitacum of Sidonius Apollinaris and its baths, 470s CE

Sidonius's Avitacum, the villa named after his father-in-law the emperor Avitus, was near Augustonemetum (modern Clermont-Ferrand) in the Auvergne region.

Sid. Apoll., *Ep.* 2.2.1–20   You complain about my being in the country [*rus*], but I have a better reason to ask what keeps you in town [*urbs*]! Now spring is giving way to summer and the sun is traveling to its highest point in the sky to shine light on the Scythian northern lands, so why mention the climate of my district?[281] A divine plan has so set up its environment that we are mainly dominated by heat from the west. What else to say? The earth heats up, the Alpine ice has melted, the earth [soil] is scarred with jagged cracks from the heat, gravel clogs the fords, the banks are silted up, there is dust in the fields, and even streams that flow perennially will have slowed to a quiet state; their waters not only simmer but actually boil.

At this time, while one fellow perspires in linen and another sweats in silk, you, wrapped in a heavy cloak and bundled up inside it, squeezed into a deep chair of Amerian willow-work, are yawning while expounding to your students whose pallor is no less due to the heat than to their fear of you: "A Samian was my mother."[282] Come now, why not consider, if you have any thought at all for your bodily health, quickly leaving the airless narrow confines of the town and eagerly come to be a member of our fellowship in a very cool retreat, to cheat the dog days' heat?

If it pleases you, take note of the country place to which you are invited. We are at the estate [*praedium*] called Avitacum which is dearer to me than the one that came to me from my father, because it came from my wife. Such is the harmony under God's direction that I live with the members of my household, unless you fear the evil eye. On the west, there is a mountain, somewhat earthy but steep, from which small hills spill out as from a double branch [*geminus fomes*].[283] Four of these hills form a space about 4 *iugera* broad [about 1 ha, or 2½ acres]. Before opening up to make a flat area suitable for the entrance to the house, the sides of the sloping hills define the valley between them in rectilinear patterns going up to the perimeter of the villa: its facades face northwest [*Boreas*] and south [*Auster*].[284]

On the southwest side of the villa, the baths are set at the foot of a forested cliff, and when firewood is cut from the trees along the cliff's edge, they fall almost by themselves in sliding clumps into the mouth of the furnace. The hot room [*cella coctilium*] is adjacent to, and the same size as, the room used for oiling the bathers, but it has a semi-circular end with a large tub that has hot water singing sobbingly through lead pipes that pierce the wall. Within the hot room, there is a fire-like daylight and such an abundance of illumination that persons of great modesty are forced to think that they are more than just naked.

Next, the cold room [*frigidarium*] opens out: without exaggeration, [it can be said] that its size emulates public bath buildings. First of all, the builder [*conditor*] has made the roof ridge of the *frigidarium* conical and pointed. The four intersecting walls of the *frigidarium* are covered at their adjoining corners with overlapping tiles. The *frigidarium*'s dimensions have been calculated to take the exact number of seats as the [number of] bathers that the sigma-shaped swimming pools can accommodate, yet without disturbing the service by the bath attendants.[285] The builder has opened two windows at the top of the room where the vaults intersect [with the walls], thereby adding a view [of the outdoors] for the bathers looking up at a skillfully made coffered ceiling. The interior surface of the walls is adequately finished with polished white plaster.

The walls bear no foul story illustrated with beautiful painted nudes: a story that glorifies art disgraces the artist. There are no actors with outlandish faces and costumes imitating Philistion's clothes in many different colors of paint.[286] There are no wrestlers slipping and twisting in contest with hits and holds—even in actual combat, if the wrestlers start rolling around in a suggestive way, the chaste wand of the referee [*gymnasiarchus*] separates them right away.

What's more, there won't be anything written up on these "pages" [the walls] that cannot be taken to be anything but holy. Instead, here are some short verses that will make the passerby linger to read: they are minimally difficult as to content, because they do not prompt rereading and can be readily perused without tedium.

Now if you ask about marbles: in truth, Paros, Carystos, Proconnesus, Phrygia, Numidia, or Sparta from those many-colored hillsides have not contributed slabs to my bath building, nor have I any stones quarried from Ethiopian cliffs with their purple rock faces giving the illusion of being speckled with bran.[287] Still, though I am not endowed with the [cold] formality of stone brought from abroad, my buildings—or should I say my little shacks or cottages [*tuguria seu mapalia*]?—are cool enough.

However, listen to what we do have instead of what we don't have. A pool [*piscina*]—or a *baptisterium*, if you prefer the Greek word—is attached to the *frigidarium* of the bath on the east side: it holds about 20,000 modii of water [about 274,600 liters, or 72,542 gal.]. Bathers emerging from the heat of the bath go through an entrance formed of three arched openings in the middle of the wall. The middle opening is not flanked by pillars but rather by columns that the better class of architects call "purples." Into the *piscina*, a stream channeled down from the brow of the mountain is brought through pipes around the curved outer sides of the swimming pool [*natatorium*] itself.[288] The water pours through six protruding jets in the form of lions' heads; those who come in without paying attention are tricked into seeing real sets of teeth, real fierceness in their eyes, real manes ringing their necks.

In the *piscina*, if there is a crowd either of household members or of the owner's guests, it is very hard for people to hear one another, because of the loud sound of the falling water, so people must converse directly into one another's ears: an otherwise ordinary conversation becomes a ludicrously secret exchange due to the noise.

Leaving the area of the *piscina*, the facade of the women's *triclinium* presents itself; contiguous to it is the household storage pantry [*cella penaria*], separated by a wooden half wall and then a weaving-room [*textrinum*] beyond that.

A portico overlooking the lake is supported on piers rather than pompous monolithic columns. From the side of the vestibule, a long roofed passage leads inward: it has no view to the outside but is not partitioned with cross-walls, so it isn't exactly an underground corridor [*hypodromus*] but by rights can be called a *cryptoporticus*. At the very end of this passage, a space has been sectioned off to make a very cool chamber, where [we find] a very talkative group of female *clientes* and nursemaids; but the group calls for silence when I and my family make our way through to the bedrooms.

Off the *cryptoporticus*, there is a winter dining room which [the smoke from] the fire often lit in the arched fireplace has darkened with soot. But why do I mention this to you, when the last thing I am doing is inviting you to [sit around] a fireplace? Rather, let me speak of what's relevant to you and the season.[289]

From the winter *triclinium*, there is a passage into a living room or a small dining room [*cenatiunculum*], which is open to the lake and gives a view of all of it. In this room, there is a *stibadium* and an elegant sideboard [*nitens abacus*], and stairs—neither short nor narrow—gently ascend to the level or platform from the lower portico. Reclining there, if you are not busy eating, you can enjoy the pleasures of the view.

If a cold drink is offered to you from the most famous of springs, you will see pieces and powderings of snow-like mists that rises in the brimming cups when they are suddenly filled, and their glossy shine is dulled to a slippery-looking surface by the sudden cold. After that, there are liquids suited to the cups, ice cold and by the ladleful for a thirsty guest—such drinks might be feared [for their ability to make the drinker drunk], but I say nothing about this to you because you are so temperate.

From this *triclinium*, you will see how the fisherman propels his alder-wood boat out onto the open lake, how he lays out his stationary nets upheld with cork floats, and how he deploys ropes with hooks attached to them, setting them out at measured distances so that the hungry trout in their nighttime forays through the lake may be caught by their like: for what might I say that would be more appropriate than to say "fish are caught by fish?"

Dinner done, the living room [*deversorium*] will receive you. It is a real room for summer but not too hot, because it opens only to the north [*Aquilo*], so it has light but no direct sun. There is a very narrow room with benches, a place where the dozing bedroom attendants lie about in lazy sleepiness rather than real sleep.

Here [at the villa], how pleasant it is to have the chirping of cicadas at midday, the croaking of frogs at twilight, and while lying asleep at night, the honking of swans and geese, and in the songs of crowing cocks in early morning in one's ears; and [in the morning] to hear the ominous triple crowing of the rooks saluting Dawn's rosy rising torch, the nightingales [*Philomela*] singing in the berry bushes at early light, and the chirping of swallows [*Procne*] in the rafters![290] If you like, add the Camena's pastoral sound of the seven-tone shepherd's pipe which, often at night, our sleepless shepherds [*Tyrti*] play, in a nighttime song with the bells around the necks of sheep in flocks, bleating as they graze in the fields.[291] All those various sounds and melodies will entice you to sleep and seduce you to a deeper one.

Leaving the [shade of the villa's] porticoes and going out into ordinary daylight, if you want to go out to the jetty on the shore [of the lake], there is an open green area with, however, a grove of trees not far away, where there are two giant linden trees with interwoven branches, making a single shade from a double root. In that darkness, where my own Ecdidius shines his light on me, we abandon the game, but only up to the time when the trees' shadow, growing shorter, recedes and is limited to the area of the branches; the trees' shadow [at midday] makes a [cool] dice-throwing area for the tired players after the ball game is over.[292]

Now that I have told you about the building, there still remains something for you to know, so now I must tell you about the lake. The lake comes down from the east [*Eurus*], and its foaming surge driven by the wind drenches the foundations [of the villa], which are set in the lake's sandy silt. At its edge, it has marshland and pits, inaccessible to those on foot because of its sticky adhesive mud crossed by cold currents and weeds on the banks. However, the moving sheet of water is buffeted this way and that by small boats when the breeze is still, but when a south wind [*Auster*] blows in with bad weather, terrible waves are formed: the breakers rain their spray from above, even on the topmost leaves of the trees standing along the banks.

The lake, according to nautical calculations, is 17 *stadia* long [about 3.15 km, or 2 mi.]. A stream enters it, [its flow] breaking over rough rocky barriers and so froths with foaming splash, and then, passing over the steep rocks, it settles into the lake. Whether or not the stream makes the lake or merely runs into it, what is certain is that it flows beyond it; it is forced through underground strainers, which diminish its fish but not its water. The fish are forced back into a weir pool that is calmer than the lake, and there they bulk up their white bellies with reddish flesh. They can neither go back to healthy places [in the lake] nor get out [of the pool]; because they are so fat, the weir pool is an endlessly circulating prison for them.

The lake itself has an irregular, curving, and wooded shoreline on the right, and a straight, grassy and flat shoreline on the left. To the southwest [*Africus*], the water is green along the shore because the [trees'] foliage shades the water, in the same way that the water covers the [lake bed] gravel, so the shade covers the water. On the eastern shore, a circle of trees gives the water the same color. On the north [*Arctus*] side, the water looks as it does normally. The western [*Zephyrus*] side has a tangle of common weeds, often bent over by the weight of the small sailboats gliding over them, and a slippery fringe of bulrushes surrounds it; thick pieces of sedge float in the water, and the bitter sap of the grey willows is nourished by the sweet waters.

In the middle of the deep part of the lake, there is a small island on which a turning marker [*meta*] is set on a natural pile of rocks: the turning marker is dented by the impact of oars of ships circling it, and it is the place where amusing wrecks occur during the games. At this place, by tradition of our ancestors, the Contest of Drepanum in the hallowed Trojan story was reenacted.[293]

Going somewhat beyond what I need to describe, the land around here has plenty of woodland, florid meadowland, full of sheep in the pastures and wealthy shepherds.

But I will keep you no longer, for, if I let my pen go on any more, autumn will find that you are still reading! Grant me, then, a quick arrival, and you will give yourself a long visit for your own pleasure. Allow me at least to excuse this overly detailed letter. It has gone well beyond the brevity it should have had. The whole country place has been described, though there are still some parts [I have] left out so as to avoid tedium. For that reason, a good judge and an artful reader will declare that the large size is not the page of the letter, but the villa itself, whose spaciousness needs such a long description. Farewell.

Sidonius Apollinaris, *Carmina*, 460s CE (Sid. Apoll., *Carm.*)

Sidonius's bath at his villa prompts him to compare and clothe it with references to Baiae and the Bay of Naples.

Sid. Apoll., *Carm.* 18.1–12

    Dear guest, were you to condescend to visit my villa Avitacum,
    It would not displease you. [I hope that] what you have pleases you.
    It has a cone-shaped peaked roof like the one at Baiae,
    And like Baiae's bath, the top of its roof shines in the same way.
    The stream flowing from a neighboring hill makes more sound
    Than the noisy waters flowing from Mount Gauranus.
    Wealthy Campania would disdain the Lucrine pond
    If she saw the waters of our lake.
    That other shore is garlanded with red sea urchins,
    But here, dear guest, you see another kind of fish.
    No matter who you are, if you're willing and can share my happiness with a heart at peace,
    You can make a Baiae here in your imagination.

Sid. Apoll., *Carm.* 19.1–4

    After the torrid heat of the bath, give yourself to the frigid water
    So that it may strengthen your hot skin with its coldness.
    If you bathe your limbs in this wine-like water,
    My pond makes your eyes swim.[294]

Sidonius Apollinaris on the *burgus* of Pontius Leontius, between 462 and 466 CE

Sidonius's *Carmina* 22 is an ambitious work that includes a prose letter introducing a poem of 235 hexameter lines and a short prose appendix to accompany the poem. Hexameters in a combination of dactyls and spondees were, in both Greek and Latin poetry, the most formal and solemn of metrical devices, often called "heroic." I have separated the text into lines to show how Sidonius developed the narrative, but I have not attempted to mimic the meter.

The poem is addressed to Pontius Leontius, a nobleman of senatorial rank and a native of Burdigala (modern Bordeaux) in Aquitania.[295] Sidonius seems to have known Pontius Leontius well, and his visit to the family's *burgus* was the occasion of this poem which may be a bread-and-butter thank you.[296]

The description of the villa itself is impressive, but it is preceded by 100 introductory verses (omitted here) that lead the reader from origins in early Greek poetry (the *Odyssey*) through the mythic birth and triumphal return of Bacchus (Dionysus, also called Silenus and Bromius) from the Ganges Valley in India to Greece, to a prophesy about the villa by Apollo (also called Phoebus), god of light, wisdom, and art. This vast scale of scene is replete with mythological and historical references, and Sidonius calls upon Erato, Muse of lyric poetry and daughter of Jupiter, for inspiration.

The 100 introductory verses describe Apollo standing in a chariot and majestically descending from the sky with a stately escort of the nine Muses and other attendants, as he advances on Thebes in Boeotia in Greece. There, he chances to meet his half brother Bacchus, who is returning from the East at the head of an enormous procession of Satyrs, Maenads, elephants, the Phoenix, and various enslaved Indians carrying treasure. The half brothers embrace, and for the rest of the poem, Apollo speaks in prophetic mode about the villa where he and his brother will live in the future. Bacchus is silent because he is drunk; by poem's end, he has sobered up a little. The passage below quotes Apollo's prophesy about the villa and his description of it.

Sid. Apoll., *Carm.* 22.101–235

"[…] There is a place where the Garunna spins down from a wet rocky height,
And likewise, O slippery Duranius, you hurry down and emerge in a curving flood,
Then you [both] commingle your slowly subsiding flows.
Here, the sea [tide] runs against their flow with a repeated contrary current,
And rolling back and forth, both spurs and seduces the waves that the rivers roll down.
The Garunna, swollen by the waxing of the moon,
Then takes up a tidal flow on its surface and suddenly swells with a fast-moving surge
That seems to be returning downwards to its source rather than back to it.
The Duranius, even though, as the lesser river, receives less water from its flooding brother
Then also is swollen by the Ocean's tide, and its banks become seashores.[297]
Between the rivers, but somewhat closer to one of them than the other,
There is a mountain towering into the upper air [*aethera*], notable for its great height,
But it will have owners greater still, and the place where senators will be born.[298]
When [in the future] the land will be under Latin rights,[299] Paulinus Pontius, the first
    founder of the family
Will build walls around the mountain, and towers called Stateliness [*pompa*] and
    Support [*auxilium*]
Will pierce the high aether, and [both] their tops will shine with equal brilliance.
No machine, no battering ram, no tall [movable] tower or mound built close by,
No catapult hurling screeching stones,
No movable tortoise machine [*testudo*], no mantlet shed [*vinea*], no wheeled machine
Rushing up with ladders set in place—none will ever be strong enough to shake these walls.[300]
O Castle [*burgus*], for by that name I will call you, I see the future that shall be yours!
The house stands above the river's flood, and glittering bath buildings are set inside
    the ramparts.
When the tide is disturbed by the dark north wind [*Aquilo*], the rough pumice rock
Rumbles from the battered bank, and then a torrent pouring from a cranny in the rocks
Flies upward, raining down showers even on the rooftops,
Carrying sailors upward and often teasing them with threat of shipwreck,

DESCRIPTIONS OF VILLAS

And sometimes, when the torrent retreats, it strands fleets of boats in the bath
   building itself!
Of what kind and size are the columns that uphold the baths?
The pride of expensive Synnada in its purple quarry must give way to it,
And the Numidian hill that produces stone like ivory, and the [Proconnesian] marble
   that has grassy veins.
From now on, I disdain marble from Paros, marble from Carystos,
And the purple marble that holds a reddish blush seems much less to me.[301]
And if posterity should doubt who the founder of the building was,
A stone mounted at the entrance has the names of its [family's] progenitors.
There's water nearby: it washes away the marks of footsteps and clears up the mud
   with its stream.
The wall [at the front of the house] is covered with slabs of cut marble that rise to
   the ceiling,
Which itself is covered with yellow metal:
The prosperous house, not wishing to reveal itself in any secretive way,
Exhibits its wealth when it hides its ceiling in this way [with gilding].
A double portico proceeds from here, rising above a double floor [area],
And does not know the double Wain.[302]
The portico moves gently back, and these curved wings, turning inward with their horns,
Look back upon themselves.[303]
The curving portico on the right sees the rising sun while the center faces it,
And the left curve sees the setting sun. The crescent-moon shaped atrium [atrium lunatum]
Never loses any of these three cardinal quadrants of light: it is always full of sunshine.[304]
The father of Pharnaces can be seen here, hurling a quadriga of horses into the sea,
As sacrifices to the trident-bearing Jove [Neptune].[305]
You would think that the horses' bodies had really been slashed
And that real wounds were reddening with bloody spurts. The horror of the wounds
   seems true,
And the painting is alive with [the scene of] the quadriga team of slaughtered horses.[306]
On another wall, the king of Pontus [Mithridates] is besieging Cyzicus with a huge army,
And in yet another place [wall?], we see Lucullus bringing up aid,
While the soldiers of Mithridates, compelled to suffer the most terrible hazards of hunger,
Envy the besieged enemy. Here the heroism of a Roman soldier [is shown],
Drenched through and swimming in the sea, carrying his message (but keeping it)
   perfectly dry.[307]
Beyond, the warehouses stretch out under their high roofs
And the buildings burst with the quantity of their [stored] produce.
This is the place where a harvest will come like that which is grown in Africa's warm fields,
Or like the harvest coming from Calabria's lands or those of fierce Apulia,
As abundant a harvest as that which is stocked from Leontini,
Or as [Mount] Gargarus sends out from its Mygdonian furrow,
Or as [once] Eleusis in Attica, the city that once worshiped Ceres with occult dances,
Gave [as great a harvest] to the citizen Triptolemus, at the time when humans,
Renouncing the acorn, took up the golden gift of grain when the Golden Age was dying away.[308]
Next comes the summer portico open to the cold constellation of the Bears [triones];
In one part of it, a harmless heat issues from the winter baths to warm the portico
   when needed,
So this location [in the portico] is better in a cold season, because the part that flees
   the Lion's mouth
Cannot well endure the Lycaonian Bear.[309]

A stream flows into the baths from a high promontory; on the mountainside, it is enclosed and falls into narrow channels,
And moves through diverging hidden pipes.
To the west of the covered warehouses stands the owners' winter dwelling.
Here a nice fire eagerly consumes the logs set nearby,
And in a billowing cloud, its heat rising from the oven and then breaking,
Dissipates and spreads a temperate warmth throughout the upper parts of the house.
Next door are the weaving rooms [*textrina*]; the ambitious founder built them to compete with the temples of Pallas.[310]
In the future, the heavens will declare that the most respected wife of Leontius,
Whom no other wife of the Pontian house ever enjoyed the distinction of her husband's status as much [as she does],
Untangled the Syrian distaff, twisting the fine wool through thin reeds and adding a supple metal,
Making the distaff swell with a thread of gold.[311]
Next to the weaving rooms, a space with connecting walls shows the early history of the circumcised Jews.[312]
The picture will sparkle forever: time does not diminish the colors to lessen its images.
You turn to the left, and a wide curving portico with straight corridors greets you,
With, at its upper end, a dense forest of stone columns. A high-ceilinged dining room [*cenatio*] is here, equipped with folding doors.
Nearby is a metal channel [*Euripus*], and a stream falls from above,
Into a basin set above the double entrance, and fishes swimming along the conduit,
Come to their end in a watery upper dining room [*cenaculum*].
Nearby there is the first of the towers, or actually the outermost of them:
Here the owners have the custom of setting their dining beds [*sigma*] in the wintertime.
From this high and visible place, I frequently sit and overlook the mountain beloved by my Muses and by the goats.
I will stroll in the laurel thickets, and I will imagine that the fear-struck Daphne believes in me.[313]
If by chance your steps lead you to the twins of Arcturus [Ursa Major and Ursa Minor],[314]
You would come to the temple of the greatest god of all, and there you find a storeroom
And a [wine] cellar redolent of mixed delights.[315]
This place will see a lot of you, dear Brother.
Now let the places of our residence [at the *burgus*] be divided [between us] as follows:
You will grant me the spring flowing from the mountain; it is covered in its circuit by a vault of porous stone.
This area needs no improvement because Nature has given it a natural beauty.
It is pleasing that there is no artificial embellishment, no artificial stateliness,
No hammer with its echoing strokes will carve the stones, no marble will take the place of the good old tufa.
For me, this spring's flowing water will take the place of the Castalia.[316]
The rest you can have as your fine place to live: the hills may quail before your power.
Set free your captives, and may their broken chains become the happy vineyards throughout the lands of the *burgus*."
Silenus, by now more or less sober, confirmed [Apollo's] dictum, and the chorus of dancers sang in agreement:
"Nysa, Bromius says goodbye to you, and to twin-peaked Parnassus, Phoebus says goodbye as well.
Naxos shall not seek to find the one [Bacchus], nor Cirrha the other [Apollo].[317]
Instead, the *burgus* shall be our place for perpetual delight!"

Christian Donations of Villas and Properties, Fourth to Sixth Centuries CE

In the late fourth and on into the sixth century, some Christian owners of villas sold their properties for cash distributions to the poor, gave their income from lands to charity, changed the designated use of their estates and dwellings, or otherwise disbursed their wealth in the name of their faith.[318] Their motivations were various: to free themselves from material encumbrances, to sell or transfer their wealth in favor of the Church, to fund charitable donations and to set up community centers of worship, to embellish saints' *memoria* (e.g., tombs or sites of martyrdom), and to establish or fund monastic foundations for both men and women. The devices of devolution were also various: diversion of current income to charity without alienation of property, outright cash sale, and change of use from family or personal enjoyment to Christian communitarian arrangements. The older form of Roman charity, the *alimenta*, does not seem to have been an option, possibly because *alimenta* were local and municipally administered, in contrast to the new Christian horizon, which was at once more universal and more personal.

Donations in the name of elite donors are recorded in Italy, Gaul, Britain, and Africa; they included Paula of Rome (347–404 CE),[319] Paulinus of Nola (ca. 354–431 CE) and his wife Therasia,[320] Claudius Postumus Dardanus (and his wife and brother, early fifth century CE) of Segustero (Gallia Narbonensis),[321] Sulpicius Severus (ca. 363–420 CE) of Primuliacum (Aquitania),[322] and Flavius Magnus Aurelius Cassiodorus (ca. 490–585) of Vivarium (southern Italy).[323] The texts regarding their donations do not include much detail about the villas and their estates, perhaps to avoid virtue signaling.[324]

The impulse was not universal among Christian owners. Many villa owners were happy to retain their villas as they were: Sidonius Apollinaris at his own Avitacum near Augustonemetum (modern Clermont-Ferrand, Aquitania), Pontius Leontius and his wife in their *Burgus* (Aquitania), and the men of Ausonius's reading circle of religious books in his friends' libraries (probably Gallia Narbonensis).[325] Private villas could thus take on some Christian color with no sacrifice of traditional secular ownership or much change in habits of hospitality.

However, that was not enough for other owners. Melania the Younger (383–439 CE) and her husband aggressively disposed of properties on a grand scale as well as large numbers of enslaved persons for charitable purposes; her donations were so conspicuous that they elicited documentation as part of her *acta sancta*.

GERONTIUS   (ca. 395–ca. 485 CE)

Life of Melania the Younger (*Vita Melaniae Junioris*, Greek and Latin redactions), after 439 CE (Gerontius, *Vit. Mel.*)

Gerontius, who may have known Melania the Younger (ca. 383–439 CE) personally in Rome and Jerusalem, documented the life and works of his subject in detail, including her benefactions based on the sale of her property and people. He presented her as the greatest heiress of her day: she was the granddaughter of Melania the Elder, a Spanish noblewoman whose marriage into the patrician Valerii Publicolae had brought her the lustre of ancient Roman nobility. In turn, the younger Melania's marriage to Valerius Pinianus (ca. 396 CE) united several branches and properties of that noble family.[326]

Beginning around 403 CE and continuing to her death in 439 CE, Melania sold or gave away possessions in Rome and its suburbs, and others in Sicily, Hispania, Britain, and Africa. Around 407 CE, she and Pinianus resided a short time in Africa, visited Egypt, then settled permanently in Jerusalem. They were genuinely inspired to charity, and their schemes for the poor and monastic foundations were warmly encouraged at the imperial level by Serena, niece of the emperor Theodosius I, wife of Stilicho, and mother of the empress Maria, the emperor Honorius's wife. However, the sales threatened property holders of the senatorial class in Rome and the city's local economy, including Pinianus's brother Severus, so Serena had to appeal to her imperial son-in-law for his permission to void certain legal impediments to the couple's extravagant generosity.

The *Life of Melania the Younger* exists in Greek and Latin redactions that differ slightly; in some instances here, both have been used for their variations.[327]

Gerontius, *Vit. Mel.* **Latin 7.1–2**   At this time, Melania's father [Publicola] died.[328] Thanks to the [financial] security that his death brought them, they renounced the world in more definitive ways [than before] and undertook to attend the needs of pilgrims and the poor. They offered the same to holy bishops, presbyters [priests], and all pilgrims who presented themselves, and they lived in their villa in the suburbs of Rome [*in suburbano urbis Romae*], showing a goodness [to all] of no small worth. Since by now they could no longer abide to enter the City after having renounced [the world], [...] they therefore remained in their suburban villa, accomplishing what is written [i.e., Luke 21.37, Jesus on the Mount of Olives].... [...]

Gerontius, *Vit. Mel.* **Greek and Latin 9.1.2–10.1 and 10.4–6**   So they began to put their goods up for sale [*venundare possessiones*], mindful of what was said by our Lord: "...sell all..." [Matt. 16:24 and 19:21]. [...]

At the beginning of the sales, the Evil One [*inimicus*, ὁ διάβολος, Satan], who always hates good folk, used the means of the saintly Pinianus's brother [Severus] to persuade, or rather incite, the slaves (*servi*, δοῦλοι) who lived on their properties to refuse to be dispersed in the sales: if their masters in their power wished to sell their property, it should only be to his brother Severus.[329] [...] Here is the advice that that most holy woman [Melania] gave to her "brother" Pinianus:[330] "If those [slaves] who live in our suburban villa and are in the power of our [actual] presence here have had the temerity to rebel against us, what will those who live in the various provinces do—that is, those in the Hispanic provinces, in Italy, in Apulia, Campania, Sicily, and Africa [*Africa Vetus*], or [those in] Numidia or Britannia, or even [those in] the other regions?[331] It seems to me that we had better see the most pious Augusta [Serena]."[332]

Gerontius, *Vit. Mel.* **Latin 18.1–4**   The most holy one [*beatissima*, Melania] had, for a second time, to undergo the assaults of the devil, because he had been able to fill her with doubt. Indeed, she owned an outstanding property which had a bath building [*balneum*] equipped with a swimming pool [*natatorium*], such that on one side there was [a view of] the sea and on the other the glade of a forest that sheltered different animals and wild beasts [*venationes*]. There, while bathing in the swimming pool, she could see ships passing and animals in the forest [at the same time]. But the devil put various thoughts in her mind, evoking the precious marbles and the special embellishments [of the bath], or even her great income and her huge wealth. In fact, the property encompassed sixty villa-estates [*sexgintae villae*], each one having 400 slave workers.[333] The saint drove these [temptations] from her mind with pious thoughts.... [...]

Gerontius, *Vit. Mel.* **Latin 21.1 and 21.4**   There was a small town called Tagaste [modern Thagaste], in which the saintly Alypius held the office of bishop. The holy couple chose to live there because it was small and poor but mostly to be in companionship with the holy Bishop Alypius,[334] a man not only full of virtues but also with saintliness.... [...]

In addition, she gave [to the church of Tagaste] a large estate [*possessio*] that brought a large income.[335] In fact, the estate was larger than the town itself and encompassed a bath building, many different craftsmen—goldsmiths, silversmiths, brass workers—and two bishops, one of our faith, the other of the heretics [i.e., Donatists].

CASSIODORUS (Flavius Magnus Aurelius Cassiodorus, ca. 490–585 CE)[336]

Variae, Letter of September 537 CE, (Cassiod., Var.)

Cassiodorus, despite writing letters on official business for the Gothic administration at Ravenna, retained a sense of learned *otium* to share his knowledge and appreciation of villas and famous resorts with lower bureaucrats—in this case, the similarity of the Istrian peninsula and its *praetoria* with those of Baiae. The memory of past pleasures and allusion to past places is a theme in the history of villas in Late Antiquity.[337]

Cassiod., Var. 12.22.3–5   [...] It is not irrelevant to say that it [Istria] is to the King's city [Ravenna] as Campania is to Rome, the larder [*cella penaria*] of the royal capital. It is not off-topic to say it is pleasant and delicious, enjoying a temperate climate despite being so far north. Without digression, I would even say that [Istria] even has its own Baiae with its lagoons in equal play with the rolling hills. Lake Avernus [near Baiae] is not the only one: this place [Istria] is [also] famous for harboring many *garum* factories [*garismatia*] and being rich in fish. *Piscinae* for raising saltwater fish are numerous, and facilities for raising oysters are everywhere. [...]

The gleaming *praetoria* [villas] strung like pearls [along the shore] show clearly how much, in the opinion of our ancestors, that province was prized. The archipelago of the most beautiful islands, set as much for pleasant aspect as for usefully protecting ships at sea and bringing wealth to its farmers [*cultores*]. [...]

[PROSPER OF AQUITAINE?]

On God's Providence (Carmen de providentia Dei), 406–415 CE

The poem *On God's Providence* of 972 verses has been ascribed to Prosper of Aquitaine (ca. 388–455 CE) on the basis that it was written in response to the Vandal and Gothic invasion of Gaul in the early fifth century CE.[338] The theological topic is God's providence, but the homiletic message is to stand firm and humble in the face of what appears to be disaster. Toward the end of the poem, villas are invoked.

On God's Providence, 913–916
>You, who now grieve over your ruined fields,
>Your deserted *atria*, and the facades [*proscenia*] of your empty villa,
>Wouldn't it be better to lament your real woes,
>If you looked into the miserable depths of your heart. [...][339]

5

VILLAS AND *OTIUM*

CICERO
SENECA THE YOUNGER
MARTIAL
PLINY THE YOUNGER
GALEN
SIDONIUS APOLLINARIS

Villas were a venue for *otium*, a state of being and animated leisure that is always recognizable but can be hard to define. While *otium* may have had other venues besides villas, as well as nuances of meaning for individuals and elaboration over time, it endured as an instantly familiar term in written and verbal communication through Roman times and well into the Renaissance. Its nearest Greek equivalent, σχολή (*scholē*), gives it a tincture of literate and learned leisure, but its most obvious antonym, with negative prefix, *negotium*, meaning engagement in public affairs and professional duties, attending to business or to work in general, is too crudely "opposite" to define its special character.[1] For those in a position to enjoy it, most often owners of country properties, villas facilitated, often framed, the theory and practices associated with *otium*, if not exclusively then almost so.[2]

The first appearance of the term in the early second century BCE coincided with the construction of large, luxurious villas in the environs of Rome. *Otium* happens to have been first defined in military context, denoting the intervals between mobilization on a war footing, ordinary camp duties, or movement to new camps and headquarters, but "downtime" or "furlough" does not adequately signify its later meanings.[3] Cato, in his moralizing account of Roman history titled *Origines*, promotes *otium* as the necessary equal of *negotium* in the occupations and preoccupations of statesmen, and in a speech of 54 BCE, Cicero quotes Cato approvingly to promote his own *otium* as a highly active, productive, essentially intellectual time.[4] Eight years later, in his *On Duties* (*De officiis*) of ca. 46 BCE, when he was in enforced *otium* due to the political situation, Cicero defines his *otium* as *otium negotii inopia*, "leisure because of the shortage of public business (for himself)." The term was thus multivalent and could change in different circumstances; it also found further definitions, explicitly in essays such as Seneca's *On Leisure* (*De otio*) and his *On Tranquillity of Mind* (*De tranquillitate animi*), both 60s CE. Its positive meaning was more usual in Latin literature; laziness was its pejorative, but rare, meaning. However, from time to time the term slips: some authors indicate a shading of *otium* into doing nothing or even merely vacationing at a villa, which, if anything, would reinforce the connection of *otium* and villas.[5] It needs no pointing out that *otium* was an abstract concept that only concerned, for the most part, elite members of Roman society.[6]

Because *otium* is both a state of being and an activity, its manifestation can be personal, with varying meanings from one individual to another, but it can also be general, applicable to many different and varied activities. *Otium* is the necessary condition of not-working that promotes intellectual insight and writing (especially philosophy, sometimes history), creative endeavor in the arts (usually writing poetry, always the highest artistic form), healthy relaxation (such as hunting, ball games, exercise, and walking and talking), the cultivation of friendships (*amicitia*) in various ways (visits to villas, letter writing, exchange of gifts), pleasurable experiences of nature, art, and architecture, and self-knowledge, this last in its Greek form (γνῶθι σεαυτόν), the best-known philosophical and psychological dictum of antiquity since early Greek times.[7] All of these activities, while not restricted to villas, were certainly appropriate to them. Villas and the activities they fostered and framed, while in some cases entirely personal, were ultimately intended to have a positive benefit to all human beings: that was the goal of *otium*.[8]

CICERO   (Marcus Tullius Cicero, 107/106–43 BCE)

For Gnaeus Plancius (Pro Cnaeo Plancio), 54 BCE (Cic., *Planc.*)

Cicero's speech in defense of Gnaeus Plancius, who had helped him when Cicero was in exile in Greece in 58 BCE, turns on some technicalities in election procedures for candidates to public office but actually extends to a passionate plea for fair dealing and justice. In this passage, Cicero addresses one Cassius, an assistant to the prosecuting lawyer Marcus Iuventius Laterensis; Cassius had expressed admiration for Cicero's speeches.[9] Cicero begins with a rueful account of how he was humiliated when he returned to Rome from an absence on official business in Sicily and found that everyone had forgotten who he was.

Cic., *Planc.* **66 (27)**   Gentlemen of the jury, on this matter I think that it was by no means worse for me than if all had offered me congratulations. Because after that [experience], I stopped thinking about what people would hear about me, because I understood that the Roman populace's ears are rather stupid, but their eyes are quick and sharp. So I made it my business to be seen in person, I pushed myself forward in the Forum, and neither sleep nor the porter at my front door prevented anyone from gaining access to me. Need I say how my time was spent? Even when I was at leisure [*otiosus*], would my *otium* have been anything at all? Those of my speeches, Cassius, that you bring up—the ones you say you are in the habit of reading when you are at leisure—well, those speeches [are the ones] I wrote on days when there were public games or on holidays, so I never really had any real time for *otium* myself. I've always considered the guiding principle, as enunciated by Marcus Cato in his [book] *Origines*, to be majestic and noble, namely that "the attention [*ratio*] of outstanding, great men should be directed as much to their hours of *otium* as to their duties [*negotium*]."

Letters to Atticus (Epistulae ad Atticum) (Cic., *Att.*), April 59 BCE, from Antium

Cic., *Att.* **26.1 (2.6.1)**   On the work that I promised you in earlier letters and that would be finished while on this excursion, I cannot confirm just now that I have done any great amount on it. I have embraced *otium* to such an extent that I am not able to tear myself away from it. So either I enjoy my books, of which I have an ample supply at [my villa at] Antium, or else I count the waves—the weather is not good enough to catch [even] mackerel—and my spirit draws me utterly away from writing anything. [...]

Letters to Friends (Epistulae ad familiares) (Cic., *Fam.*), to Marcus Marius,[10] 55 BCE

Marcus Marius, a friend of long standing from Arpinum, was a rich invalid who owned a villa and estate near Cicero's villa at Pompeii, on the north coast of the Bay of Naples, where he so enjoyed the vista to the south and west of the cliffs and buildings of Stabiae on the south coast that he cut an opening in his bedroom wall to view it.[11] Cicero wrote to Marcus to keep him abreast of events in Rome, in this case the magnificent spectacles presented by Pompey upon the dedication of the Theater of Pompey in August 55 BCE.[12] The letter begins with Cicero's commiserating on Marius's poor health but complimenting him on his strong-minded avoidance of the events.

Cic., *Fam.* 24.1 (7.1.1)   [...] In this way, you had the pleasure of an *otium*, enjoying the pleasure [*amoenitas*] of being left all alone to savor your lovely place. However, I don't doubt, since you made that opening [in the wall], you have spent your mornings looking out from your bedroom at the little spectacles [*spectiunculi*] of the view toward Stabiae.[13] Meanwhile, the ones here who left you all alone there have been dozing while watching vulgar displays of mimes. For the remainder of the day's hours, you enjoy the pleasures that you, in your good judgment, have arranged for yourself—while we, if we can stand it, enjoy such things as Spurius Maecius has allowed us to endure.[14] [...]

Cic., *Fam.* 24.3 (7.1.3)   [...] I also think that you would not have enjoyed the Greek plays or the farces in the Oscan style [that were performed at the spectacles at Rome], mainly because you can enjoy Oscan plays in [the meetings of] your local municipal council, and you like Greek plays so little that you do not even take "the Greek road" to get to your villa.[15]

Cic., *Fam.* 24.5 (7.1.5)   [...] So, continue in the way you are doing and be careful of your poor health, so you'll be able to go around to my villas and [we] can travel together in the same litter.

***Letters to Atticus*, April 22, 55 BCE**

Cicero, mostly shut out of political affairs in Rome after the formation of the so-called First Triumvirate of Caesar, Pompey, and Crassus in 60 BCE, is turning to literary pursuits at his villa at Cumae.[16] "Those men" refers to the three triumvirs.

Cic., *Att.* 84.1 (4.10.1)   [...] Here I am grazing in Faustus's library, though perhaps you thought that I was here for the pleasures of the Puteolan and Lucrine districts.[17] It is true that they are here, but by heaven [*mehercule*], the more I am away from other enjoyments and pleasures due to [current] political life, the better am I encouraged by, and find interest in, literary pursuits. I would prefer to sit on your little stool, the one you have under the *imago* [portrait bust] of Aristotle than in those men's curule chairs;[18] I would prefer to walk with you at your place rather than having to walk with those with whom, as I can see, I will be obliged to walk. But fate will guide my walking, if there is a god who looks after such things. [...]

***Letters to Atticus*, October 54 BCE**

Still shut out of public life, Cicero is at his villas writing about oratory rather than engaging in politics and the profession of law.

Cic., *Att.* 92.2 (4.18.2)   [...] The delight of oratory consoles me for the obligation of making speeches at law. My house in town and my villas please me, and I do not dwell on the position from which I fell but on the place from which I have risen. If I have my brother [Quintus] and you with me, the rest take their own paths: I can philosophize [ἐμφιλοσοφῆσαι] with you.

***On the Ends of Good and Evil (De finibus bonorum et malorum)*, 45 BCE (Cic., *Fin.*)**

This treatise in three dialogues, only partially preserved, concerns ethical behavior in terms of its philosophical underpinnings (Epicurean, Stoic, and generally Platonic in its late Academic iterations). Cicero himself is the main protagonist, with Atticus and other interlocutors. The treatise was dedicated to Marcus Junius Brutus (*Att.* 336 [13.44]) and was written at Cicero's maritime villa at Astura in the summer of 45 BCE, when he was grieving the death, in February of that year, of his daughter Tullia. Parts were set in various locations and anachronistically some five or six years before (51–50 BCE, Books 1, 2, and 3) or much earlier, in 79 BCE, at Athens (Book 4).

Villas, or villa gardens, or other gardens were the settings for the dialogues and give flavor and immediacy to the conversations. A meeting at Cicero's villa at Cumae (Books 1 and 2) provides the circumstances for two younger interlocutors visiting a great man in retirement, while the library of Lucullus's villa at Tusculum (Books 3 and 4) shows an older and a younger man doing careful research into intellectual matters. The last dialogue (*Fin.* 5.1–3, not included here) is set in the environs of the Platonic Academy at Athens, but Atticus, an Epicurean, tells us that he spends time in the Gardens of Epicurus nearby, to tease Cicero about his Stoic preferences.

Cic., ***Fin.*** **1.5.14**   [...] Lucius Torquatus, a man of the greatest learning in all [philosophical] doctrines, had once made a sharply argued defense of Epicurus's notions on pleasure.[19] With the help of Gaius Triarius, a young man of sincerely serious disposition and great learning who was part of the discussion, I responded to him.[20] They both came to visit me at my villa at Cumae, and we first spoke of literary matters because both were eager students of them. Then Torquatus. [...]

The third dialogue of *On the Ends of Good and Evil* begins with a finely visualized vignette of a chance encounter in a villa library at Tusculum. It has many aspects beyond the charming spontaneity of the circumstances; it embodies the mutual support that villa owners and households gave one another beyond practical support for farming activities. Here, their mutuality of literary pursuits is illustrated.

The three protagonists of the scene all owned villas at Tusculum. They were unequal in age and distinction, but villas in proximity to one another brought them together. The interlocutors are Cicero himself, Marcus Porcius Cato (son of Cato the Younger "of Utica"), and Lucius Licinius Lucullus; individually, they are representatives of three quite different social backgrounds.[21] The *gens* Licinia was among the oldest of the plebeian aristocracy from the foundation of the republic with many consulships and other honors, so some 400 years. The *gens* Porcii Catones, by contrast, were much newer: their first ancestor of any prominence in Rome was Marcus Porcius Cato (the Elder, ca. 234–149 BCE), consul in 195 BCE, governor, triumphator, and censor (184 BCE), so only some 150 years. Cato's family, the Porcii Catones, came from Tusculum, and the current scion who appears in the dialogue may have owned or inherited a family villa there. Cicero himself, though by far the eldest of the three, was decidedly a *novus homo*, provincial and non-noble in origin, whose status was conferred by his personal, political, and even his short military career, as well as his prestige as an advocate and statesman. Yet he, as well as the other men of famous descent, owned a luxurious villa at Tusculum. Villas grouped in proximity provided a venue for social relations among the elite, of which Cicero was a very recent member in comparison to the other two. To the extent that a certain social democracy existed at all in Roman times, villas were one of its venues among the elite.

Cic., ***Fin.*** **3.1.7–9**   [...] I was at my villa at Tusculum and wanted to consult some books in the young Lucullus's library, so I went to his villa to search them out, as usual.[22] As I came in, I found Marcus Cato, who I had not known was there, sitting in the library totally surrounded by books on Stoicism. As you know, he had a famous appetite for reading [*aviditas legendi*], to the extent that, ignoring the disapproval of ordinary people, he often read even in the Curia itself while waiting for the Senate to convene, though he in no way ignored matters of state.[23] He appeared to be engaged so thoroughly in a great *otium* and with such a quantity of books—

a kind of gluttony, if such a word can be used to describe so distinguished an activity [*res clarus*]. Both of us were surprised at encountering one another so unexpectedly; he stood up right away, and immediately started on those greetings that are habitual upon meeting.[24] "Why are you here?" he asked, and he continued, "I think you must be at your villa, and had I known you were there, I would have come to visit you!" I replied, "The Games began yesterday so I came down from the City and arrived in the evening.[25] The reason I came here is to consult some books, and really, Cato, it's high time to make all this abundance [of books] known to our dear Lucullus.[26] It's my great concern—even though the actual duty is yours—that he should enjoy these books even better than the many other pleasures of his villa, and that he become as learned as his father and our dear Caepio, and as learned as you are as well, you to whom he is so closely related.[27]

***Letters to Friends*, to Marcus Caelius Rufus,[28] May 49 BCE, from his villa at Cumae**

At the time of writing, Cicero had sequestered himself at his maritime villa at Cumae, waiting to learn the outcome of the conflict between Pompey and Caesar.

Cic., *Fam.* 154.2 (2.16.2)   [...] But you know my little properties well: I have to live on them so as not to intrude on [the hospitality of] my friends. And while it is most agreeable to stay at my maritime place, I cannot do so without raising the suspicion that I will take ship [to escape]: maybe I would do exactly that, if *otium* could be found in doing so.[29] But if only war is to be found there, what's the use? [...]

***Letters to Friends*, to Marcus Terentius Varro, June 46 BCE**
Caesar, returning to Italy from Africa after defeating the Pompeian forces of Cato the Younger, was looking to settle accounts with Pompeian partisans remaining in Italy.[30] Cicero admires Varro's determination to pursue his studies at his villa rather than engage in politics.[31]

Cic., *Fam.* 181.4 (9.6.4)   We live in a troubled republic—who can deny it? [...]
   I have always placed you among the great men, one who has almost alone reached a port in these storms; you, who are reaping the invaluable harvest of knowledge, as you consider and investigate those things that are of highest importance. Such a familiarity [with erudition] is a delight and must be placed before all other occupations and pleasures that others enjoy. For my part, I consider that your days at your villa at Tusculum are the model of a life [*opes vitae*], and I would freely give up all my wealth and other activities to live in your manner, free from all violence.

***Letters to Friends*, to Lucius Papirius Paetus,[32] September 46 BCE**
Cicero is by himself, enjoying as best he can the enforced *otium* at his villa at Tusculum: the political situation was such that he was confined to his villas and not allowed to live in the City.

Cic., *Fam.* 191.1 (9.18.1)   I received your very agreeable letter when I was enjoying *otium* at my villa at Tusculum, having sent my "pupils" off to meet their "great friend" so that they might make themselves, as well as me, agreeable to him insofar as that is possible.[33] [...]

***Academica Posteriora* 45 BCE (Cic., *Acad. post.*)**

Villas were places where philosophy was discussed, but lovely settings could both interrupt and extend a train of thought. Contemporary taste in painted landscape views may have reinforced such moments, and they often showed villas (see, for example, fig. 9). In the earlier version of the *Academica* (often termed *Academica 2 Posteriora*), during discussions in the villa of the orator Q. Hortensius Hortalus at Bauli, notionally set ca. 63–62 BCE, Cicero sets out to analyze the variability and contingency of vision (as he had laid out in the design of the treatise, *Acad. pr.* 1.40 [1.11]). In this passage, he is under full philosophical sail about the many deficient aspects of sight but suddenly breaks off to delight in the view.[34]

Cic., *Acad. post.* 2.80–81 (2.25)   [...] "If, as you assert, a god were to ask you what more you wanted besides complete and healthy senses, what would you say? If only he would ask! He'd hear how badly he treats us! Granting that we see accurately, still, how widely do we actually see? From here and in a direct view [*ex regione*] from the environs, I can see Catulus's villa at Cumae. I can't see [Catulus's] villa at Pompeii, even though there's nothing between here and there to obstruct: it's my sense of sight that doesn't take me any further. What an amazing view! I can see Puteoli, and I can't see my friend Gaius Avianius who is probably walking in the Portico of Neptune [there].[35] [...] Thus, as fish are enveloped in murky water, we are enveloped in cloudy air.

***On Duties (De Officiis)* ca. 46 BCE (Cic., *Off.*)**

Cic., *Off.* 3.1   Marcus, my son: Cato—that Cato, who was about the same age as that Scipio who first was given the name *Africanus*, has written down [a phrase] usually attributed to Scipio, that he was never less at leisure [*otiosus*] than when he was at leisure, and never less alone than when he was actually by himself.[36] Really, this is a great statement, worthy of a great, wise man; it signifies that even when he was at leisure [*in otio*] he thought of public affairs, and that when he was alone by himself, he communed with himself—in this way, he never ceased activity and at the time never needed any other company [besides his own]. The two factors that bring about laziness in [most] others, namely *otium* and solitude, made him sharper. Would that it were possible for me to truly say the same of myself! But if by imitating him [i.e., Scipio] I cannot even in a small way rise to the greatness of that man of genius, at least I can try to do so by an act of will. But [now], because by impious [treasonous] armed force I am forbidden to engage in public activities and to practice law, I follow a life of *otium*; for that reason, I have left the City and, as I wander around and around [my] villas [*rura*], I am often alone.[37]

Cic., *Off.* 3.2   But my *otium* is not comparable to that of Scipio Africanus, and my solitude is not his. He—seeking some repose from his very great services to the republic—would seek *otium* from time to time and would absent himself from meeting and frequenting other human beings, retreating into his own solitude as if into a safe harbor. But my *otium* is because of the shortage of public business, not induced by some zeal for peace and quiet. Since the Senate was abolished and the courts have been shut, what, in view of my sense of self-worth (*dignitas nobis*), can I do either in the Curia or the Forum?

Cic., *Off.* 3.3   So I—I who once lived in the most conspicuous way and in eyeshot of the entire citizenry—am now fleeing the gaze of evil men who are everywhere, and I am withdrawing as much as possible: I am often alone. But I have learned from learned men not only that we must choose the least evil of the evils [on offer to us], but even to extract from the evils themselves whatever good might be in them. For that reason, I am making the most of my *otium*, even though it is not the kind of *otium* appropriate to a man [like myself] who [once] brought a state of peace [*otium*] to the State, and I am not allowing my solitude, coerced rather than voluntary, to make me listless. [...]

Cic., *Off.* **3.4** [...] But I am not as strong [as Scipio Africanus], I am not as able to take myself out of my solitude by silent [mental] contemplation. So I have turned all my diligence [*studium*] and attention [*cura*] to this work of writing, and as a result I have written more in a short time than during the many years in which the republic [still] stood.

SENECA THE YOUNGER   (Lucius Annaeus Seneca, ca. 4 BCE–65 CE)

On Leisure (De otio), after 49 CE (Sen., *Otio*)

Seneca's essay on *otium* associates the concept with *contemplatio* or the contemplative life, highly coordinated with the life of action for humanity but strongly and negatively contrasted with the life of pleasure. A safe place—perhaps a villa—with *otium* fosters both contemplation and thus good action.[38]

Sen., *Otio* **5** [...] In consequence, it is also possible for a man—one for whom everything [in his life] is as yet free of trouble and before he experiences any misfortunes—to take himself to a safe place [*in tuto subsistere*], to give himself over to serious studies [*bonae artes*], and to demand complete *otium* to become an exponent of the virtues [*virtutium cultor*], something that even the most retiring of men are able to do. Of course, it is required of [such a] man that he bring good things to all men: if he can, to many, but if not, to a few, and if not to a few, then to those nearest him, and if not to these, then to himself. When a man is useful to others, he works toward the public good [*commune negotium*].

MARTIAL   (Marcus Valerius Martialis, ca. 38/41–102/104 CE)

Epigrams (Mart., *Epig.*), to Castricius, late 80s–early 90s CE

Martial had a villa near Nomentum (modern Mentana) 30 km northeast of the city; Cicero's friend Atticus also had a villa there.

Mart., *Epig.* **6.43**
    While happy Baiae gives you pleasure, Castricius,
    And you swim in water silvered with sulphurous springs,
    The *otia* of my estate at Nomentum and its house
    Sitting lightly on its land [*casa iugeribus non onerosa suis*]
    Are my sunny days at Baiae and my soft [waters of the] Lucrine lake.
    Here are my riches like the riches you're enjoying there, Castricius.
    Once it was fine for me to rush off to voguish seaside watering holes
    Without fearing the long trips to get there.
    Now I like places near the City, easy hideaways [*faciles recessus*],
    Where it's nice enough if I am left [alone] to be myself.[39]

PLINY THE YOUNGER   (Gaius Plinius Caecilius Secundus, 61–113 CE)

Letters (Epistulae) (Plin., *Ep.*), to his friend Minicius Fundanus[40]

Plin., *Ep.* **1.9.1–8**   It's amazing how much, in a single day, can happen in Rome and be remembered, but over many days, nothing [that actually happened] can be recalled. If you ask someone: "What did you do today?" he will answer, "I went to a coming-of-age ceremony for a young man [*officio togae virilis*],[41] then I showed up for a betrothal or a wedding, then went to witness somebody's testamentary disposition, then went to a court hearing, then to a counsel-advisory meeting." When you do all these things on a specific day, they seem obligatory, but when you think back, they all seem absurd, especially when you leave town. On remembering, one suddenly says to oneself, "How many days I have wasted in pointless activities." This always happens to me in my Laurentine villa, when I am reading or writing and free also to do the exercise that strengthens my mind. I hear or say nothing that I would regret having heard or spoken later on, and no one bothers me with ill-meant remarks, and I have no one to blame except myself if I write with some difficulty. Neither hopes nor fears come to me, and no gossip comes to me; I engage with myself and my books. What a true and good life! O what sweet, honorable *otium* I have, better than almost any work [*negotium*] can ever be. The sea, the shore are my real and true private place of the Muses [μουσεῖον], a place for much inspiration. You should yourself take the first opportunity to flee the noise, the pointless chatter, and the many silly activities [of the City]; give yourself instead to your studies or to *otium*. Our friend Atilius has wisely and wittily said that it is better to be free from work than to work at nothing.[42] Farewell.

Letter to his friend Caninius Rufus[43]

Caninius Rufus, probably a school friend of Pliny's, was a man of wealth in their hometown of Comum (modern Como). Unlike his friend, Pliny had left Cisalpine Gaul for a greater career in Rome than any small provincial town like Comum could have offered, but his affection for the friends he left behind and the town itself were undiminished. The beginning of the letter evokes Rufus's *villa suburbana*, the second part urges him to turn from *negotium* to *otium*, the leisurely study and writing that is appropriate to a villa owner's life.

Plin., *Ep.* 1.3.1–5 How goes it at Comum, the town of our mutual delight? How goes your pleasant suburban villa, its portico where it is always springtime, the deeply shaded plane-tree plantation, the sparkling green Euripus cascading to the lake below, and the easy but firm roadway?

How goes your bath building into which the circling sun shines all day, how go your dining rooms [*triclinia*]—the one for many guests, the [other] one for just a few—the bedrooms [*cubicula*] for a daytime nap or the night's rest? Do they have you in their possession and by turns have a share in your attention? Or, as is your usual habit, are you often called to frequent distractions needed for the discharge of duties incumbent on you in the management of your household? If your villa and its portico, its plantation, the Euripus, its sunny bath building, the *triclinia*, and its bedrooms have you in their possession, you a happy, blessed man. But if not, you are just one man of many.

Shouldn't you assign those ordinary and lowly duties to another person and put yourself in a calm and comfortable place of retirement for your scholarly endeavors? This [retirement] should be both your business [*negotium*] and your leisure [*otium*], your work and your relaxation, it should take over your wakefulness and your sleep. Create something and work it over so that it will be yours forever. After your death, everything you own will be divided among this person or that, but what you have done will be your very own once it has been effected. I encourage your spirit and your genius: you yourself must strive to do your own best, and others will come to appreciate it if you do so yourself. Farewell.

Letter to his friend Cornelius Tacitus the historian[44]

For *otium*, writing was a favorite occupation of villa owners who had a literary or philosophical bent, but so was hunting.

Plin., *Ep.* 1.6.1–3   You will laugh, and you're allowed to do so. I, whom you know so well, have caught three boars, very fine ones, too.[45] "'You?' you ask." Myself indeed, and not even by changing my usual laziness in the slightest way. I was sitting near the nets, but next to me were neither a hunting spear nor a lance but rather a stylus and notebooks: thinking about something and making notes of my thoughts so that, if I came back empty-handed, I would at least have my writing-tablets [*cerae*] full.[46] Don't disdain such an occasion for intellectual work—it is amazing how the spirit is stirred up by bodily activity and movement. Great promptings for thought can come from being deep in the woods and keeping the silence that is needed in hunting.

So next time you go hunting, it's my right to be your guide [*auctor*]: take your picnic hamper and a little flask together with your notebooks: you will see that Diana does not wander in the hills any more than Minerva.[47] Farewell.

Letter to his friend Valerius Paulinus[48]
Pliny makes a distinction between *studium* and *otium* in the context of his *desidia* (idleness, slothfulness) at his villa.

Plin., *Ep.* 2.2.2   [...] For myself, I am at my villa enjoying some time off, partly engaged in study [*studium*], partly in *otium*. Farewell.

Letter to his friend Caninius Rufus
Pliny is stuck in Rome, working, while his friend is enjoying the pleasures of his villa at Comum.

Plin., *Ep.* 2.8.1–3   Are you reading, or fishing, or hunting, or all three? On our beloved Larian lake, you can do all three at once—the lake has fish, the surrounding woods have game, and your retreat [*secessus*, villa] gives you abundant occasion for study. I can't say that I am jealous of all or any one of your activities—I'm only cross that I can't enjoy them myself, and I long for them as a sick man longs for wine, a bathhouse, and a spring of water. Could I break free from these artfully made fetters if were I allowed to do so? I think not. New business mounts up before the old is completed: more links are added to the lengthening chain, and the amount of my work grows daily. Farewell.

Letter to his friend Caninius Rufus, soon after 103 CE
This letter is an account of the life and death of Silius Italicus (Tiberius Catius Asconius Silius Italicus, ca. 26–101 CE), a literary man with philosophical interests, a courtier in the entourage of the emperor Nero (54–68 CE), consul in 68 CE, and governor of Asia in 77–78 CE.[49] Silius, who greatly admired Cicero, showed his admiration by buying one of the statesman's villas on the Bay of Naples; he also admired Vergil to the extent of buying the poet's tomb near Naples.[50]

Plin., *Ep.* 3.7.6–10   [...] Most recently in his declining years, he [Silius] left the City to live in Campania and stayed there even with the excitement of the advent of the new emperor [Trajan], and it is a tribute to the magnanimity of the emperor that he allowed him to do so. He was a great lover of art [φιλόκαλος] and incurred censure for buying so much. He owned many villas in the region, neglecting the old ones in favor of the new ones. [In the villas] he had many books, statues, and portrait busts [*libri, statuae, imagines*]—or, rather, he did not own them so much as worship them, Vergil above all, whose birthday he observed even more than his own. When he was at Naples, he would visit Vergil's tomb as if visiting a temple. In this tranquil situation, he reached his seventy-fifth year, longer in comforts of the body than in the time [he] spent in illness. [...]

Letter to his friend Pomponius Bassus, ca. 104 or 105 CE
Plin., *Ep.* 4.23.1–4   It made me very happy to hear from our mutual friends that, in your wisdom, your present honorable state is to live pleasantly, in full possession of your *otium*, to exercise sometimes on land and then again in the sea, to have conversations, to be read to or to read, so that while you know most things, you can advance in knowledge every day.[51] This is the reward for a man who has been the highest in the rank of magistrates, has been an army commander, and who has given himself entirely in the public service for as long as it was possible. In youth and maturity, we give the State our all, but as the laws tell us, [in] our old age [we] can return to *otium*. When will it be allowed to me, when in an honorable old age will I be able to do the same as you, to retire to a joyful peace? When will my retirement be understood not as willfulness [selfishness] but as a desire for tranquillity? Farewell.

Letter to his friend Calpurnius Macer,[52] after 98 CE
Plin., *Ep.* 5.18.1–2   As you are well, I am well. Your wife and son are with you, and you're enjoying the sea, the brooks, the gardens, the estate, and your very pleasant villa. There is no doubt in my mind that it is very pleasant: it belonged to a man who was [already] happier than most, before he became the happiest man indeed.[53] I'm at my Tuscan villa, hunting and reading, sometimes in sequence, sometimes both at once. Between the two, I can't decide which is harder: to catch something or to write something. Farewell.

Letter to Pontius Allifanus[54]
Writing poetry was part of *otium* at villas. Pliny was proud of having published several volumes of Latin verse, and even prouder that they were being recited by professional Greek singers. This letter describes what he did at his Laurentine villa in the way of poetry.

Plin., *Ep.* 7.4–5   When returning from military service and delayed by contrary winds on the island of Icaria, I made some poems in Latin elegiac verse about the sea and that island.[55] I have attempted some poems in heroic meter, but here is the occasion for my first attempt at hendecasyllables.[56] At my Laurentine villa, I was having Asinius Gallus's account of his father in a comparison with Cicero read to me, in which there was [a quotation of] an epigram by Cicero about [his secretary] Tiro.[57] Then, as it was summertime and I had retired for a sleepless siesta, I started to go over the idea that the greatest orators had made versifying an amusement and that they considered doing so a good thing. Though I had been out of the practice [of poetry] for a long time, I put my mind to it; in a short while it came to me what I had wished to write, namely these verses....[58] [...]

Letters to his friend Caninius Rufus
Plin., *Ep.* 7.25.1–6   How many scholars are hidden and robbed of fame, either through their own modesty or a natural desire for a quiet life? We, when we are about to speak in public or do a public reading, are afraid of those who make a show of their scholarly knowledge, while those who are silent show how much better it is to honor great effort with silence. I know what I'm talking about. Terentius Junior,[59] after having completed his service with an impeccable record in a military appointment for men of the equestrian rank and having been a procurator in Gallia Narbonensis as well, then retired to his estates, giving himself over to a very tranquil *otium* rather than to the [further] official duties that were available to him.[60] When he invited me to be his guest, I reckoned him to be a good *paterfamilias* and a diligent farmer [*agricola*]; so thinking, I planned to converse with him about such [farming] matters with which I thought he would be familiar.

I started along those lines, but he brought me back to literary topics. Such elegance of speech, such fine Latin, such fine Greek! He is so well versed in both languages that he seems to excel best in the one he is speaking. What a number of books he reads, what an amount of knowledge he retains! You would think that he lives at Athens rather than in his villa. What else? He has expanded my thinking about my own opinions and has made me respect, just as much as I respect very great scholars whom I personally know, those very learned people who live in seclusion, almost as if they were country folk. I suggest you do the same: in military camps as in our realm of learning, there are many men of quite ordinary demeanor who, on closer look, you'll find are well prepared and well armed and full of ardor and intelligence. Farewell.

Letter to his friend Terentius Junior
The surprise of meeting a learned man rather than a farmer or *paterfamilias* living at a villa in the country prompted Pliny to become a friend of Terentius Junior (see *Ep.* 7.25 to Caninius Rufus, above). This letter is written as one learned villa owner to another; the tone is jocular.

Plin., *Ep.* **8.15** I am honoring you by sending you so many books, but I did so as soon as you asked for them, and anyway, since you write that the grape harvest is so meager where you are, then I know that you'll be at leisure, as they say, to read a book. I've received news that my farms have had the same poor harvest, so I'll be able to write something for you to read, as long I can buy myself some paper—but maybe I'll have to erase what I've written, be it good or bad, and write on it again. Farewell.

Letter to his friend Cornelius Tacitus the historian
Plin., *Ep.* **9.10.1–3** I want to observe your strictures, but I find it impossible to obey your commands to honor Minerva at the same time as Diana, in view of the measly number of boars.[61] So only Minerva can be worshiped, and even so, she is worshiped in a relaxed summertime manner. On my trip here, I made up some vacuous phrases that should have been discarded—phrases much like the conversations that are had while traveling in a conveyance [*in vehiculo*]. I expanded them somewhat when I arrived at the villa, as nothing else called for my attention. So now my poems are silent, those poems that you imagine are so easy to finish in woods and groves.[62] I have corrected one or so little speeches, but this is an unpleasant type of work, and even more so in that it is like having to work in the country rather than enjoying its pleasures. Farewell.

Letter to his friend Cornelius Titianus[63]
Plin., *Ep.* **9.32** What are you doing, what will you do next? I myself am living a most pleasant life, that is to say, in utter idleness [*otiosissimus*]. As a result, and even though I would like to read some letters in my idleness, I don't write longer letters to anyone, idle as I am. No man is lazier than one who is [as] pampered [as I am], but no lazy man is more curious [than I am] in his idleness. Farewell.

Letter to his friend Fuscus Salinator[64]
In this evocative letter, Pliny tells his friend what *otium* consists of at his Tuscan villa: from morning to evening, writing, reading, walking, napping, bathing, riding, hunting—always in moderation, and always in pursuit of learning and literary production.

Plin., *Ep.* **9.36.1–6** You ask me how I spend my days in the summer at my Tuscan villa. I wake when it pleases me, usually at first light, sometimes before, rarely much later. The windows remain shuttered because, in the silence and darkness, I feel free and unconstrained by distractions. I follow my mind's eyes instead of my eyes determining my mind's thoughts; I see my mind's thoughts more clearly because my eyes don't see anything. I think on what I am working on just now, thinking on how to write it and how to correct its wording. For greater or lesser results, what I am able to do depends on how easy or difficult it is to harmonize and coordinate my thoughts. I call my secretary, the light of day is let into the bedroom, and I dictate what I have formulated. The secretary leaves, I call him back, and then he's again dismissed. Four or five hours after I've gotten up—I don't actually adhere to a rigorous schedule—and as weather permits, I take myself to either the open terrace [*xyxtus*] or the *cryptoporticus*, to think about the rest of my project and dictate it. [Sometimes] I get into my carriage where I do the same as when I was walking or lying down: my intellectual resolve stays strong and is actually strengthened [by changing my routine]. I have a short nap, then I take another walk, after which I read a Greek or Latin speech out loud and with attention to its meaning, not only for vocal exercise but also for bodily stamina—both are made stronger by this method. Then I take another walk, am rubbed down with oil, do exercises, and bathe. If I am dining alone, or with my wife or some friends, a book is read [during the meal]; after eating, there is a comedy or some music. Then I walk with people in my household—many of them are well educated.[65] In this way, and with various conversations, the evenings are extended, and even when daylight lasts long, the day comes to a pleasant end.

Not infrequently, I change this routine: if I've lain on my bed for a long time or have taken a walk, after a nap and a time for reading, I ride on horseback instead of taking my carriage—it's shorter and quicker that way. For part of the day, friends come to visit me from neighboring towns, and from time to time they provide some welcome distraction when I am tired. Occasionally I hunt, but never without my notebooks, so that, if I don't catch anything, I can at least return home with something. I give some time to the tenants, who consider that [the time I give them] it is not enough. Their mundane whining on rustic matters heightens the value of our literary work and citified occupations. Farewell.

Letter to his friend Fuscus Salinator
This letter can be read with *Ep.* 9.36, above.

Plin., *Ep.* **9.40.1–3** You write that you are highly grateful for my letter to you which let you know how I spend my summertime *otium* at my Tuscan villa, and you ask how I change my routine at my Laurentine villa in winter. I make no changes, except to eliminate my midday nap and make use of much of the night by using the times either before dawn or after sundown. If there is a legal case coming up, as frequently happens in the winter, there is no comedy or music after dinner. I repeatedly work over what I have dictated and by doing so commit it to memory by frequent revision. There you have my routine, and you can add to it what I do in spring and autumn which separate winter from summer: in those seasons, nothing of the day is wasted, so only a little is subtracted from the night. Farewell.

Letter to his friend Calvisius Rufus[66]
While Pliny's visit to his retired friend Spurinna is not explicitly to Spurinna's villa, the presence of friends at leisure and the indications of walking and long drives imply space and circumstances that would not have been available in urban venues.[67] Spurinna's life in retirement is the epitome of the kind of gracious *otium* that villas framed.

Plin., *Ep.* **3.1.1–12** I cannot recall having passed time more pleasantly than when I was at Spurinna's recently, and, if becoming old is granted me, there is no one whom I would wish to emulate more in my old age than he: no other manner of living is more clearly defined than his. Indeed, the orderly life of a man pleases me the same way that the fixed movement of the stars pleases me, especially that of an old man. It's not bad for young people to have a bit of disorder and disturbance in their lives, but for the elderly, a quiet and orderly time is the best of all—for them, the work of life [*industria*] is over, and protracted ambition is unattractive. Spurinna minutely observes this rule, and he does so with orderliness and repeated sequence even in the smallest things—they would be "small" if they were not regularly repeated daily.

Every morning, he stays in bed until the second hour of the day, then calls for his shoes and takes a three-mile walk [about 4.3 km, or 2⅓ mi.], as much for his mind [*animus*] as for his body.[68] If there are friends with him, serious conversation is undertaken, but if not, a book is read [to him], and this is sometimes done even when friends are present, as long as they aren't bothered by the reading. After the walk, he sits down, and the reading continues, or preferably in conversation rather than the book. Soon after, he gets into his carriage for a drive with his wife—an exemplary woman—or one of his friends, and recently one of them was me. How pleasant this is, how sweet to be taken into confidence, what accounts of ancient events, what deeds, what men to impart such inspiring lessons! Even so, his temperament is one of such modesty that he never seems to be lecturing.

After a drive of seven miles [about 10.6 km, or 6¼ mi.], he walks another mile, then he sits again or takes himself to his bedroom and his pen, for he writes very accomplished lyric verses in both languages [Greek and Latin], verses remarkable for their sweetness, elegance, and wit, and the virtuous devotion of the writer [to his vocation] adds to their grace.

When the hour of the bath is announced—at the ninth hour in winter, in summer at the eighth—he walks naked in the sunshine if there is no wind.[69] Then he works out by vigorously throwing a ball for a long time: these are the other kinds of exercises by which he fights off old age. After bathing, he postpones dining for a while and listens to something light and pleasant being read to him. This is a time when his friends are free to join him or to do something else, as they wish.

The simple dinner is elegantly served in ancient solid silver [dishes], and there are Corinthian bronzes [i.e., dishes, utensils, plates] in common use, which he enjoys without showing them off. The dinner is often interrupted by comic performances, so its enjoyment is flavored with literary spices. Dinner goes well into the night, even in summertime, and no one finds that it lasts too long, such is the delightfulness of the company.

In this way and after seventy-seven years, the vigor of his hearing and sight are intact; his body is agile and animated, and [he has] the wisdom that comes only from old age. His is the life that I wish for myself and hope for in my thoughts, and I would eagerly enter into it whenever the realization [*ratio*] of my [advanced] age allows me to plainly declare my retirement [from business and affairs].

Meanwhile, I am hemmed in by a thousand duties, about which Spurinna himself is a help and an exemplar [to me] on such matters: because he was an honorable man, he undertook public offices, served as a magistrate, ruled provinces, and deserves the *otium* that his hard work has conferred. His race [*cursus*] is my race, and I stand ready to reach the same goal, and right now I commit myself, with you as witness, that if ever you see me going on too long, you can by rights use this letter of mine to call me out and order me to retire, as long as I can avoid the charge of laziness. Farewell.

GALEN (Aelius Galenus, ca. 129–210 CE)[70]

On Consolation from Grief (Περὶ Ἀλυπίας, *De indolentia*), **193 CE** (Gal., *De indol.*)
Translation by Clare K. Rothschild and Trevor Thompson.[71]

Cicero and Pliny the Younger give us a general picture of how *otium* was pursued in villas, but the physician and philosopher Galen gives us his plan for *otium* at his Campanian villa in the summer of 193 CE. Some friends at his hometown of Pergamum in Asia (modern Bergama) had requested a clean edition of his works, probably to present as a gift to the city library. Galen's pleasant, learned task was to fulfill his friends' request in the quiet of his villa, with help from scribes he was intending to take with him.

In anticipation of this agreeable assignment in the country, he had prudently—or so he thought—stored all the items in his urban *domus* in Rome in a rented section of a warehouse on the Sacred Way, between the Temple of Peace (Templum Pacis) and the Flavian Amphitheater (Colosseum). The stored possessions included a quantity of silverware, household goods, professional "contracts" (deeds, loan-agreements?), household goods and all his books (medicine, philosophy, philological works), his collection of medicines, medical equipment, and the beeswax models for his medical inventions. Books by him which he planned to use, correct, and have copied were to have been forwarded separately from the warehouse in Rome to his Campanian villa.[72]

He lost everything. A fire—the first of two—broke out during the winter of 192–193 CE, destroying the warehouse he (and others) had rented and all their possessions. A second fire destroyed the two great public libraries on the Palatine hill, the Library of the Palatine Apollo founded by Augustus and another housed in the Domus Tiberiana, as well as others in the precinct of the Temple of Peace.[73] In a letter-essay called *On Consolation from Grief*, Galen describes, some 250 years after Cicero and 100 years after Pliny the Younger, what his *otium* in Campania was to have been.[74]

Gal., *De indol*. 1–4 I received your letter in which you urged me to reveal to you what training, arguments, or doctrines prepared me never to be distressed. You said that, when you were here, you witnessed how I lost the slaves I kept on hand in Rome during a severe bout of long-lasting plague.[75] You also heard that such a thing had already happened to me before. I encountered severe losses to my belongings three or four times. You said that you saw I was not even a little disturbed. However, the very recent event that happened to me—when all of my possessions deposited in the storehouses on the Sacred Way were destroyed in the great fire—surpassed everything prior. You said you knew how important these objects were but learned from a messenger that I am still not in the slightest bit troubled, remaining cheerful and carrying out my customary activities as before. Of items deposited in the storehouses destroyed in the fire, what surprised you was not that I appeared to endure without distress silver, gold, silver-plates, and many contracts, but a considerable number of my writings, a wide assortment of medicines both simple and compound, and various instruments.

In *De indol*. 5–7 (omitted here), Galen lists his loss of the medical equipment (some standard, some unique of his own invention), the quantity of remedies (theriacs) and other medicines, and the books, both holographs and corrected manuscripts.

Gal., *De indol*. 8–10 Being confident that the storehouses along the Sacred Way would certainly not succumb to fire, people used to deposit their most valuable possessions in them. They trusted them because they were not made of wood apart from the doors, were not in the vicinity of a private house, and were guarded by a military garrison since the district archives of four procurators of Caesar were stored there.[76] For this very reason, those of us who leased the units paid more rent, confidently storing very valuable possessions there.

Yet, in addition to this shared misfortune, something else—a private misfortune—befell me. When I went to Campania, I placed everything at home in the storehouse—instruments, medicines, books, and not a few silver vessels—for safekeeping while I was abroad. For that reason, the entire inventory—plus the [above-mentioned] valuables—were destroyed. You said that you learned these things happened in this way, but wanted to hear about it from me for greater certainty. [...]

Galen then specifies (*De indol*. 12a–20, omitted here) certain books that were burned, especially his glossary and item-frequency of Attic words from Old Comedy and prose authors. He implies that the loss of the libraries on the Palatine could not be made up from the books in the imperial library at Antium (modern Anzio) because of theft and bad maintenance. Had the fire occurred two months later, his books would by then have been safe in his Campanian villa.

Gal., *De indol*. 21–23   All my works intended for circulation were already transcribed in duplicate, not counting those [only] intended to remain in Rome. Friends at Pergamum requested I forward all my works in order to place them in public libraries as other friends had done in other cities. I also intended to keep copies of everything in Campania. [...] For this reason, there were duplicate copies of all my works, excluding those meant to be housed [only] in Rome [i.e., not for circulation], as I said.

The fire, then, broke out at the end of winter. I planned, at the beginning of summer, to transport books to Campania, both those copies to be kept there and those to be sent to Asia when the Etesian winds blow.[77] Fortune, then, ambushed me, depriving me of many of my other books, not least the glossary of nouns. [...]

SIDONIUS APOLLINARIS
(Gaius Sollius Modestus Apollinaris Sidonius, ca. 430–before 490 CE)

Letters (Epistulae), 460s CE (Sid. Apoll., *Ep.*)

Letter to his friend Eutropius, ca. 467 CE
This letter was written when Sidonius was on this way to Rome from his Avitacum villa. He and Eutropius, a wealthy fellow nobleman but apparently a homebody, had been colleagues in the imperial service in Gaul or Rome sometime before (Sid. Apoll., *Ep.* 3.6).[78] Eutropius had just been offered a second imperial administrative post requiring his presence in Rome. Sidonius urges him to take up the honor and describes Eutropius's Aquitanian villa in doing so. Evidently he was successful: Eutropius was appointed praetorian prefect some years later (*Ep.* 3.6.1) and Sidonius tells him how happy he is that he has "achieved the *fasces*." The letter reverses the usual Roman culture of villas, perhaps temporarily in view of the circumstances, loudly encouraging *negotium* in affairs of state and denigrating the *otium* of country living.

Sid. Apoll., *Ep.* 1.6.1–5   For a while now I have been wishing to write to you and am especially wanting to do so now because I am on the road to the City, in the name of Christ's sacrifice. My only reason, but the most urgent one, for writing is to rouse you from the depths of your calm domestic environment to assume the responsibilities of the Palatine imperial appointments.[79] In addition to this, it can be said that you are, with God's help, in the prime of life and have full vigor of body and mind to match it. You also have horses, weapons, clothing, money, and a household. Unless I am mistaken, the only thing you fear is to begin, and while you are energetic at home, a sluggish-making fear makes you afraid to undertake travel abroad. But can you, a man of senatorial descent who daily associates with the images of your ancestors dressed in robes of state [*trabea*], really say that it is travel abroad when you have [already] seen, as a youth, the home of laws, the schoolroom of literary achievements, the court of high officials, the apex of the cosmos, the homeland of liberty, the one city in the entire world where only barbarians and slaves are considered foreigners?

Staying behind with boorish cowherds and grunting swineherds—what a shame that would be! Indeed, if you can still hold the wobbling plough-handle in the field, or if, bending down, you can cut the flowers of a meadow in wide arcs with a sickle, or if, stooping like a ditch-digger with a hoe, you can turn over a vineyard choked with young shoots—those achievements are now your greatest aspirations! Wake up! Do something better! Let your spirit, now withered and weak from a flabby-making *otium*, rise to something greater! A man of your birth must cultivate his public image [*persona*] as carefully as he cultivates his villa.

Finally, what you call the training of youth [*exercitium iuventutis*] is the *otium* of army veterans, whose rusty swords are exchanged for the hoe of old age in work-worn hands.[80] It's certainly the case that the grape-must from your many vineyards will foam in your cellarage, and that your barns will be stocked to bursting with grain, that your shepherd, himself well-fed, will drive a dense flock of ewes with full udders through the foul-smelling gates of the sheepfold to the milking-pails.

But what is the point of adding to your inheritance in such a filthy way and not only to hide yourself away in a filthy way but, what's worse, to hide yourself away for it? Wouldn't it be a bad thing for you, as an inglorious countrified old nobody, to be placed behind younger men who are seated in the assembly discussing matters of importance. You, an old man, standing aside and lying low, giving reverential heed to the [arrogant] lofty opinions of some impecunious man newly arrived at some honorable position. Grieving, will you not see that some men have now gone ahead of you—men for whom, in previous times, it would have been shocking to even follow behind [you and me] in our footsteps?

What else is there to say? If you let yourself be guided by this advice, I will be your friend, supporter, helper, leader, and partner in your endeavors. But if you prefer to get caught up in the seductive snares of luxurious pleasures and, as is said, give yourself to the ideas of Epicurus—the one who throws virtue aside and claims that the only highest good [in life] is its pleasure—I invoke the witness of our forebears and descendants that I will not be party to such bad behavior. Farewell.

Letter to his friend Consentius

Sid. Apoll., *Ep.* 8.4.1–2   Will your Octavianus estate [*ager*] ever see us together, my great lord, with God's help? It isn't so much that your estate is your home as it is the home of your friends! It's close to the town, the river, and the sea: it feeds your guests and feeds you with guests, and its placement is attractive to a viewer's gaze. First of all, the walls of the home are set high up in such a way as to appeal to a definite sense of architectural coordination [*concinentia architectura*]. Then again, the home's chapel [*sacrarium*], porticoes, and baths vividly catch the eye from afar, and the view of its fields, brooks, vineyards, and olive groves as well as its vestibule, its surroundings, and its hilltop setting [*collis*] is very pleasant [*amoenissiumus*]. Besides all this, there is a fully stocked pantry [*super penus*] and much furniture [equipment], and the house contains a treasury of books. There, you apply yourself as much to your pen as to the ploughshare: it's difficult to know which has been better cultivated—the owner's estate or his intelligence [*ingenium*].

On your estate, as I recall, you worked late into the night over facile iambic verses, sharply felt elegies, and compositions in well-shaped hendecasyllables—poems that will greatly increase your approval among your contemporaries [*aequaevi*] and your fame in future generations. At present, these poems, as well as your other poems scented with the flowers and thyme of the Muses, are sung in the towns of Narbo and Baeterrae.[81] [...]

Letter to his friend Syagrius

The tone of this letter is funny-sarcastic and mock-scolding to a younger, unmarried friend. There is some scoffing that passes for friendly joking.

Sid. Apoll., *Ep.* 8.8.1–3   Tell me, flower of Gallic youth, how long are you going to be so occupied [*negotiosus*] with the business of rural work that you scorn that of the town? For how long, and against all human and divine law, will the tools of planting take charge of your hands for their own uses—hands callused by casting dice? When will your Taionnacus villa wear you out—you, a [so-called] farmer of patrician rank [*patriciae stirpis agricola*]?[82] How long will you, in wintertime, sow seeds from the previous tillage, pretending to be a ploughman rather than being a gentleman [*eques*]? How long will you drive the weight of a blunt hoe to dig up planting rows? Why do you guide the plough's handle, imitating such men as a Serranus and a Camillus, while pretending to not be going for a palm-embroidered robe yourself?[83] Please spare the disgrace to the nobility [of the region] by making yourself into a countryman [*rusticarus*]. If you cultivate a farm in moderation, you own it: if not, it owns you.

Come back to your forebears, your country, and even to your faithful friends, whom in justice can be categorized as your supporters! However, if the life of a Cincinnatus pleases you so much, first marry a Racilia, she who yoked up the oxen in her husband's place.[84] It's not for me to say that a thoughtful man should not pay attention to his household business. However, on consideration, he should think about not only what he should have but what he should be!

Now, if you repudiate all the responsibilities of the nobility, and you are motivated only by the desire to increase the value of your own property, you will be able to recall your name distinguished by consular robes [*trabea*], many ivory curule chairs [*eborata curules*], gilded sedan chairs, and deep-dyed purple robes, all put into the official record.[85] [However], if all that happens, it must be said of you that you are an industrious person, but one not so much honored by the censor as by the tax-man [*censetor*].[86] Farewell.

6

VILLA VISITS

CICERO
HORACE
JUVENAL
MARTIAL
PLINY THE YOUNGER
RUTILIUS NAMATIANUS
SIDONIUS APOLLINARIS

CICERO (Marcus Tullius Cicero, 107/106–43 BCE)

Letters to Atticus (Epistulae ad Atticum) (Cic., Att.)

Traveling from villa to villa—either one's own or one's friends'—at the time of the suspension of the political calendar in the City was normal. From his Antium villa, Cicero tells Atticus what his travel plans are so that they can get together; the same kind of travel plans are listed in other letters (*Att.* 29 [2.9] and 32 [2.11]). This letter and the three following are Cicero's attempt to inveigle his friend Atticus to come for a nice visit, either at his coastal villas (Antium, Formiae), the Tusculum villa, or at the family villa at his hometown of Arpinum.

Cic., ***Att.*** **28.2 (2.8.2), April 59 BCE, from Antium**   [...] Here is my itinerary so you can fix on where we can see one another: I want to be at my villa at Formiae on the festival of Pales.[1] After that, since you think that I should avoid the *crater delicatus* at this time, I will leave Formiae on the kalends of May and will reach Antium on the fifth day before the nones of May [May 3].[2] There will be games at Antium from the fourth to the day before the nones of May [May 6], which Tullia [Cicero's daughter] wants to see. From there, I am thinking of going to my villa at Tusculum, then to Arpinum, returning to Rome on the kalends of June [June 1]. Make sure that we can see one another either at Formiae or at Antium or else at my Tusculan villa. [...]

With this letter written from his villa at Formiae, Cicero is ruefully trying to make his friend laugh. Villa life required accepting visits from neighbors and enduring the tedium of their conversation: courteous forbearance was needed.

Cic., ***Att.*** **34 (2.14), April 59 BCE, from Formiae**   [...] As for what I should be writing—something you are always nagging me about—I can do nothing. I live in a basilica, not a villa, and one too small for the denizens of Formiae even [if it were as large as] the basilica of the Aemilian clan.[3] I'm not counting the ordinary folk [*vulgus*] of Formiae, for they are only bothersome until the fourth hour.[4] However, Gaius Arrius is my direct neighbor, or rather, he is my roommate [*contubernalis*] and has told me that he didn't go to Rome on purpose, so he could spout philosophy with me all day long right here.[5] On the other side [of my villa] is one Sebosus, [who calls himself] Catulus's "buddy" [*familiaris*].[6] Which way can I turn? By Hercules, I would go to Arpinum right now if my villa at Formiae were not the best place for me to wait for your visit.[7] However, only before the nones of May [May 6]—you can see what kind of men my ears must listen to. Now's the best time of all for someone to buy my Formian villa while these guys are with me![8] [...]

Cic., ***Att.*** **35.2 (2.15.2), April 59 BCE**   [...] I had just finished writing this to you when there's that Sebosus again! I had just barely stopped groaning when Arrius pops in saying "Greetings!" That's what leaving Rome gets you! I left Rome to escape people, and here I meet these guys?

Really, I will be off "to my native hillsides and to my birthplace" soon. Anyway, if I cannot be alone, it would be better to be with real countrymen [*rustici*] rather than these [boring] city slickers [*perurbani*]. However, since you haven't written me with a date [for your visit], I will wait at my villa at Formiae until the day before the nones of May [May 5]. [...]

Still grieving his daughter's death in February of that year, Cicero lost nothing of his satirical view of intrusive neighbors while enjoying being alone at his seaside villa at Astura. The beauty of his surroundings may be alleviating his sadness.

Cic., *Att.* 246 (12.9), July 17, 45 BCE   I would be happy here and even getting happier day by day if it weren't for the reason that I have written about in a previous letter. Nothing is more pleasant than this solitude, unless it's to be interrupted by the son of Amyntas from time to time.[9] His long-drawn-out drivel is painful to me. You can't imagine how pleasant the rest of the place is: the villa, the shore, the view of the sea, the hills, everything. But these matters are not worth a longer letter than what I've written, and sleep calls me.

Cic., *Att.* 36.4 (2.16.4), May 5(?), 59 BCE   [...] I will see you at my place at Arpinum and offer you some country hospitality [*hospitium agrestum*] because you have disdained visiting my seaside villa [at Formiae].

Cicero, *Letters to His Brother Quintus* (*Epistulae ad Quintum fratrem*) (Cic. QFr.)

Cicero, writing to his brother from his villa at Tusculum and inviting him for a visit, laughingly describes an incident—a prank in poor taste—that had occurred a year or so before, when he had invited his good friend Marcus Marius to his villa (still under construction) at Baiae (for other letters to Marcus Marius, see Cic., *Fam.* 24.1 [7.1.1], in ch. 5, Villas and *Otium*). Marius, a fellow Arpinate, was a literary man who had a villa at Pompeii; he suffered from chronic poor health.[10] Cicero had once invited him to share a large closed litter escorted by soldiers rather than take more modest transport. His comment on Marius at the end of the excerpt contrasts his own strong character with his friend's weak, but attractive, nature.

Cic., *QFr.* 12.2–4 (2.9.2–4), June 56 BCE   [...] I swear to god [*mehercule*], I should have accommodated [Marcus] Marius in my own litter, not the one that King Ptolemy gave Asicius.[11] Anyway, I remember the time when I was giving Marius a lift from Naples to Baiae in Asicius's litter with its eight porters and a hundred armed bodyguards surrounding us, when he, not knowing of the escort, suddenly opened the [curtains of the] litter and almost died from fright, and I from laughing.

As I say, I should really have taken him [in my own litter] to get to know [more of] his subtle old-style manners and his supremely cultivated conversation. But I would not invite a man in such fragile health to my open-roofed villa—as it still is even now [under construction].

It will, in truth, be a distinct pleasure for me to have him here [at Baiae]: I know that to have Marius as a near neighbor [in Pompeii] is [to have] a luminous presence, so I will see if he can stay at Anicius's place.[12] For me, I have such a scholarly temperament [*philologus*] that I can live comfortably even with workmen in the house. My philosophical bent comes not from Hymettus but from our own craggy peak [Arpinum].[13] Marius is rather weak in health and character.

On the matter of interruptions, I will take from your friends just the amount of time that you allow for your writing. Hopefully you won't allow any, so it will be on your head rather than on my laziness if I don't do anything. [...]

[...] I will love you if you come quickly [to my villa]: I will console you and dispel your sorrow. As you love me, bring Marius as well, but both of you must come now. The kitchen garden [*hortus*] is [growing] well.

Cicero, *Letters to Friends (Epistulae ad familiares)* (Cic., *Fam.*)

Cic., *Fam.* 37.3 (7.18.3), to Gaius Trebatius Testa,[14] April 8, 53 BCE, from a villa in the Ager Pomptinus
I'm writing this letter from the villa of Marcus Aemilius Philemon in the Pomptine marsh, where I have already heard the croaking of my clients, or at least those whom you gave me to advise. For at Ulubrae, there's been a big strong commotion of little frogs who have banded together to honor me![15] [...]

Letters to Atticus

Cic., *Att.* 95.1 (5.2.1), May 10, 51 BCE   On the ides of May [May 10], the same day as I wrote this letter, I left my villa at Pompeii to stay for a day with Pontius at his villa at Trebula.[16] [...]
   While I was at my villa at Cumae, our friend Hortensius came to visit me, which pleased me greatly.[17] [...]
   When I was there, my villa at Cumae was a mini-Rome [*pusilla Roma*]; there was such a crowd there.... [...]

Cic., *Att.* 128.3 (7.5.3), January 13, 50 BCE   [...] I am amazed that your sister has not arrived at Arcanum.[18] [...] I will certainly not go to my villa at Tusculum just now: it is not a good place for meetings [τοῖς ἀπαντῶσιν] and is generally inconvenient [δύσχρησται]. But from Formiae I will go to Tarracina on the day before the kalends of January (December 31). After that, to the upper Pomptine marsh, and then to Pompey's villa at Albanum, from there to Rome on my birthday, the third of January.[19] [...]

Letters to Friends

This cold letter of instruction to Terentia about arrangements at the villa at Tusculum was written just prior to the couple's divorce. Its brusque tone contrasts with his previous letters to her over many years.

Cic., *Fam.* 173 (14.20), To his wife Terentia, October 1, 47 BCE   I think I will arrive at the villa at Tusculum either on the nones [October 7] of this month or the next day. Let everything be ready there. It is possible that I will have several others with me, and I reckon we will be in residence for a long stay. If there is no basin [*labrum*] in the bath building, have one installed, and do the same for other things needed for daily life and health. Farewell. From the district of Venusia, on the kalends of October.

Letters to Atticus

Cicero received Caesar on December 19, the third day (by Roman counting) of the Saturnalia festival (December 17–23) at his villa at Puteoli. The Cluviana villa, also called the Puteolana, had been a partial bequest to him in the will of Marcus Cluvius, a banker and business associate.[20] The reception of the dictator was a grand act of hospitality for the highest officer of the Republic; its expense and trouble would have been offset by the considerable prestige it conferred. The villa must have been large enough to accommodate the dictator's guard of some 2,000 soldiers, who bivouacked nearby.

Cic., *Att.* 353.1–2 (13.52.1–2), December 21, 45 BCE   Oh, my important guest leaves no regrets [ἀμεταμέλητος] behind him [about his visit]! It was more than delightful! However, when on the second day of the Saturnalia [December 18] he arrived at Philippus's place, my villa was so full of soldiers that the *triclinium* lacked enough room for even Caesar himself to eat dinner.[21] In fact, there were two thousand men! I was really very worried about what might happen the next day, until Cassius Barba helped out by loaning me some sentries.[22] A camp was set up in the fields and my villa came under guard. On the third day of the Saturnalia [December 19], he [Caesar] remained at Philippus's place until the seventh hour [1:00 pm] and received no one; I think he was going over plans [*rationes*] with Balbus.[23] After that, he strolled on the shore, after which he had a bath after the eighth hour [2:00 pm]. When he heard about Mamurra, he did so without flinching.[24]

Then he was oiled and lay down to eat. As he was having an emetic treatment [ἐμετικός], he ate and drank as he wished [ἀδεῶς] and pleasurably: it was a really splendid dinner, and not only that, it was also: "nicely cooked and herbed with good conversation—if you ask, it was very pleasant."[25]

Those who accompanied him [οἱ περὶ αὐτὸν] dined very copiously in three *triclinia*, and nothing was lacking for the freedmen of lower status and the slaves. Those of higher status were properly served. What more can I say? I am considered to be equal among men.[26] However, he is not the kind of guest to whom you might say, "I'd love for you to come back and visit me when you return." Once is enough. The conversation did not include serious matters [σπουδαῖος οὐδὲν]; rather, [the talk turned to] more philosophical [literary] matters [φιλόλογα]. What else do you want to know? He said he had enjoyed himself and was pleased. He said that he would spend a day at Puteoli, another near Baiae.[27]

There you have it—my hospitality or perhaps the forced quartering [ἐπισταθ μείαν] of troops upon me was a disturbance but not, as I have said, a disagreeable one. For a while I will be here [at Puteoli], then at my Tusculan villa. When he [Caesar] passed by Dolabella's villa, the entire body of armed men divided up to his left and right, nowhere else—Nicias [a neighbor] told me so.[28]

Letters to Friends

Cic., *Fam.* 262.1 (6.19.1), To Quintus lepta,[29] July or August 45 BCE, from Astura   I'm happy that Macula has completed his duty.[30] It has always seemed to me that his place in the Ager Falernus is precisely the place for a stopover [*deversorium*], as long as its size is large enough to take my entourage. Its location does not displease me, but I will not avoid your villa in the Petrine district for that reason—both your villa and its pleasant location make it a real place to stay in [*commemoratio*] rather than a mere stopover.[31] [...]

Cic., *Fam.* 198 (9.23), To Lucius Papirius Paetus,[32] November 17, 46 BCE   I arrived at my villa at Cumae yesterday, and maybe I'll come see you tomorrow. When I know for certain, I will let you know a little before, even though when I met Marcus Caeparius in the Gallinarian woods and asked him how you were doing, he said that you were in bed because you were suffering from pain in your feet.[33] As was right for me to do, I felt sorry for your suffering, but I am still intending to come to see you and have a proper visit and even have dinner—I don't think that your cook has arthritis [as you do]. Therefore, expect a guest who doesn't eat very much and dislikes elaborate dinners.

Besides villas, Cicero and others owned simple habitations known as *deversoria* as stopovers on the trip between villas or from villas elsewhere in the peninsula. Cicero owned one at Anagnia for the Rome to Arpinum trip, and another at Sinuessa for the journey between

Rome, Tusculum, or Astura to his Bay of Naples villas. They could be made available to friends. Otherwise, travel could be uncomfortable.[34]

Cic., *Fam.* 339.1 (12.20.1), To Quintus Cornificius,[35] spring of 46 BCE   Your letter was very pleasing to me, but not when you wrote how much you disliked my little *deversorium* at Sinuessa! My little villa will be wounded in spirit at your contempt unless you come to visit me to make up for all [the mean things] you said about it. [...]

HORACE   (Quintus Horatius Flaccus, 65–8 BCE)

Odes, ca. 23 BCE (Hor., *Odes*)

Horace is proud of the *vin de table* produced at his villa rather than the *grands crus* of the Falernian region. The poet is asking his patron Maecenas to come for a visit.

Hor., *Odes* 1.20
   Come and drink my Sabine wine out of ordinary vessels!
   It's a wine that I myself stored in a Greek container.
   It was on the same day, Maecenas *Eques*, that you were so [loudly] applauded in the theater
   And that its happy sound echoed to the banks of your hometown river from the Vatican hill.[36]
   At that time, you drank Caecuban wine and wine made from grapes crushed under presses from Cales.
   My vessels are not adulterated with either Falernian vintages or those of the Formian hills.[37]

JUVENAL   (Decimus Junius Juvenalis, late first–early second century CE)

Satires, 117–early 120s CE (Juv., *Satires*)

Juvenal describes the food from his Tiburtine farm that he will present to a friend called Persicus at a dinner, comparing it to the present-day taste for fast food cooked in takeout shops that even enslaved persons have taken up. He also inveighs against the luxurious food with which rich or pseudorich people indulge themselves. The simplicity and freshness of Juvenal's dinner are the equivalents of what the great ancestral heroes of Rome would have eaten. Even more than other writers, Juvenal disdains his social contemporaries, both those lower than and above his own station. Instead, he both aligns himself with the simplicity of the great Romans of the past and claims their high virtues for himself.[38]

Juv., *Satire* 11, 64–109
   [...] Listen to this menu: it has not been elaborated by any market-bought edibles.
   A fat kid, the most tender of the flock, will come from my Tiburtine property,
   A kid more full of milk than blood, one who has never eaten grass or dared to nibble [the shoots of] low-lying willow branches.
   There will be mountain asparagus cut by my *vilica* once she's laid aside her spindle.
   What's more, there will be large eggs, still warm in twisted beds of straw,
   And the mother hens themselves.
   And bunches of grapes, as fresh as they were on the vine though they've been kept for half a year,
   Pears from Signia or Syria, and, in the same baskets, fresh-smelling apples like those of Picenum.[39]

You don't have to worry about the apples—the cool temperatures after autumn's heat have
    dried them, so there's no danger of an acid taste.
Long ago, such a simple dinner would have been a most luxurious feast, even for [members of]
    our Senate.
On his homely hearth, [Mucius] Curius [Dentatus] cooked the little vegetables he had gathered
    from his own garden.[40]
Nowadays, even a dirty ditchdigger in a [slave] chain gang would haughtily disdain such food,
Because he remembers the pig's udders he tasted in a stuffy cookshop [*calida popina*].
Once, long ago, the custom was to have a dried chine of pork hanging from a grill [hook?] for
    festival days
Or some bacon to give their relatives on birthdays, and even fresh meat if by chance a
    [religious] sacrifice supplied it.[41]
One of their relatives, one who had held the title of consul three times
And had commanded armies and had held the office of dictator,
In his retirement [from these honors] would hasten home to a feast [like mine] earlier
    than usual,
Shouldering his shovel from the hillside he had worked over [to plant].
Once, when people trembled at the Fabii, at a harsh Cato,
At the Scauri and a Fabricius, and when the austere censor's stern morals [*mores rigidi*]
Intimidated even his colleague [in their censorial duties]
No one had in mind so a serious matter as what kind of tortoise swimming in Ocean's flow
Would make a famous and noble headrest for the "Trojan-born."[42] [...]
At that time, a soldier was a rough man who knew nothing of Greek art [*graias artes*],
And if he shared, from the plunder from a defeated city, some drinking cups made by
    famous craftsmen,
He crushed them, so his horse could enjoy ornamented tack and his helmet be decorated
With images to show, at the moment of his enemy's death, the image of Romulus's wild beast
    becoming gentle by reason of an imperial destiny [*iussae imperii*],
Or the Quirinus twins in their rocky cavern, or the image of the god himself, without shield
    or spear descending from above.
Thus the men of old poured their porridge-gruel into Etruscan bowls.[43]
Any silver they might have had, they kept to make their armor shine. [...]

MARTIAL   (Marcus Valerius Martialis, ca. 38/41–102/104 CE)

Epigrams (Epigrammata) (Mart., *Epig.*)

Estates with villas were, by tradition, productive farms. Many were, but some were unproductive and had to be supplied from urban markets. This epigram mocks a certain Bassus, a fictional figure, a vain and unsympathetic rich patron, who loaded up in the Roman market before setting out to his villa in his cart. He leaves Rome by the Porta Capena, so his villa was on the Via Appia southeast of the City. Martial's *Epigram* 3.58 recounts a similar situation.

Mart., *Epig.* 3.47
[...] ...Bassus was off in a carriage full of all the lovely produce [*omnis copia*] of a lovely
    country place [*beatum rus*].
In it you could see cabbages on noble stalks, onions and leeks [*utrum porrum*], baby lettuces,
And beets good for stomach ailments.
You could see a snare ring laden with thrushes in the carriage,
And a hare wounded by the tooth of a Gallic hunting dog,

Not to mention a suckling pig that had never yet eaten so much as a bean.
The slave running alongside was not on holiday—he carried the eggs wrapped in hay.
Was Bassus coming into the City? Oh no! He was going out to his country place!

Epigram to Severus
Xenia were small presents of fresh produce—fruits and vegetables—or meat (including poultry) and fish (including shellfish)—that would have been produced at villas. Flowers were also *xenia*. These products were part of *pastiones villaticae* and were emblematic of hospitality and friendship: their simplicity were guarantors of the sincerity of the sender's sentiment, and their freshness a promise of eternal amity.[44]

Mart., *Epig.* 7.49   I'm sending you tiny presents from the garden of my suburban villa [*suburbana*]: Eggs for your throat ailment, and some fruits to whet your appetite, Severus.[45]

Epigram to Carus (possibly a relative)
Mart., *Epig.* 9.54
   If at my country place the thrushes had gone off-color from [so many] Picenian olives,
   Or if my Sabine woods were set with nets,
   Or if a long fishing rod had brought in a wealth of fat fish,
   Or if limed twigs caught birds,
   As a sincere present, you, dear relative [*cara cognatio*], would have such a gift,
   Which would not be offered to [even] either my brother or my grandfather before you.[46]
   Around here just now, my country property [*ager*] only resounds with the sound of measly
      grackles, the complaints of finches,
   And it greens up only in spring with the shrilling sparrow.
   Still, there the ploughman answers the magpie's greetings
   And the ferocious kite flies upward to the stars.
   Because of all that, I am sending you some little presents from my farmyard [*chors*]
   If you accept them, you and I will always be close.

Epigram to Regulus
Sending presents of comestibles (*xenia*) to friends was obligatory, even if they did not come fresh from the villa's garden or estate. The tone is mock heroic.

Mart., *Epig.* 7.31
   The noisy brood of birds and eggs of the mother hen,
   The figs ripened [yellowed] by a temperate heat,
   The young kid from a bleating nanny goat,
   The olives not yet up to bearing cold temperatures,
   And the vegetables silvered with cold frosts,
   Do you imagine that they are sent to you from my country place [*rus*]?
   How utterly mistaken you are, Regulus!
   My little fields [*agelli*] produce nothing but what I need for myself.
   Whatever the *vilicus* at your Umbrian estate,
   Or the tenant [*colonus*] at your country place at the Third Milestone outside the City,
   Or what your people send you from your Tuscan place or the one at Tusculum,
   All that is produced for me in the Subura.[47]

Epigram to Caesius Sabinus
Villas at places such as Paestum, Tibur, Tusculum, and Praeneste, and those in Campania often grew flowers in their gardens, but Martial's garden at Nomentum did not. Martial is addressing the roses (perhaps in a wreath) that he bought for his friend from a florist in Rome.

Mart., *Epig.* 9.60
> If you were grown on the flatlands at Paestum or Tibur.
> Or if the land of Tusculum blushed with your flowering,
> If a *vilica* gathered you in a Praenestine garden,
> Or if by chance you were the glory of a Campanian villa [*rus*],
> In order for you to seem more beautiful to my friend Sabinus,
> Let him believe that you come from my Nomentanum property.

Epigram to Faustinus
Martial is inviting his friend to visit him at his villa near Nomentum, in the Sabine hills, about 30 km northeast of Rome.[48]

Mart., *Epig.* 5.71
> Here, well-watered Trebula goes down into cool valleys
> And the land [*ager*] is fresh and green even in the months of Cancer's sign,
> There is a country place [*rus*] never languishing under the Cleonaean Lion,
> And a dwelling [*domus*] always the friend of the Aeolian Notus wind.[49]
> They are calling to you, Faustinus. Spend the long harvest days in these hills;
> Tibur will be your place for the winter soon enough.

PLINY THE YOUNGER (Gaius Plinius Caecilius Secundus, 61–113 CE)

Letters (*Epistulae*) (Plin., *Ep.*)

Letter to Pompeia Celerina,[50] ca. 100 CE
Pliny's mother-in-law Pompeia Celerina outlived her daughter, Pliny's second wife; her death in 97 CE is indicated in his *Ep.* 9.13.4. Pliny appears to have remained on friendly terms with his former mother-in-law even after her remarriage (Plin., *Ep.* 9.13.13) and his own; he visited her often and even borrowed money from her (Plin., *Ep.* 3.19.8). She appears to have been the owner of at least five villas, one at Alsium on the Tyrrhenian coast in Etruria (modern Palo; see Plin., *Ep.* 6.10, below) and four others inland, all in central Italy north of Rome, in the environs of Ocriculum (modern Otricoli), Narnia (modern Narni), Perusia (modern Perugia), and Carsulae. Pliny is writing to Pompeia while staying in her villa at Narnia, thanking her for her hospitality even though she was not in residence.

Plin., *Ep.* 1.4.1–4 Such a quantity of riches you have at Ocriculum, Narnia, Carsulae, and Perusia, and even a bath building at Narnia! Don't worry about [replying to] my letters—the short one you sent a while ago is enough. By Hercules! What is yours seems more mine than yours, but still with this difference: I am better looked after, and more assiduously, by your slaves than by mine. The same may happen to you when you come to stay with us—and I wish you would do just that, first so that you could enjoy our goods as if they were your own, and second that my slaves might finally rouse themselves—it's certainly the case that they wait upon me in a negligent way![51] Fear of the kinder sort of masters disappears after the slaves have a long habit of [knowing] him, but they become freshly alert by [encountering] new faces and try to prove themselves to the master by working to give more to others [his guests] than they give to him. Farewell.

Letter to his friend Lucceius Albinus,[52] ca. 106 or 107 CE
The villa at Alsium owned by Pliny's former mother-in-law, Pompeia Celerina, had been the property of Lucius Verginius Rufus: Plin., *Ep.* 1.4 and *Ep.* 3.19.[53] Verginius (14–97 CE) was a distinguished man of equestrian stock, a senator and three times consul, and a successful general, defeating Gaius Julius Vindex, the rebel governor of Gallia Lugdunensis, in 68 CE. He survived the reign of Nero, the year of the Four Emperors (69 CE), and the later years of Domitian's reign.[54] When Pliny's father, Lucius Caecilius, died early, Verginius Rufus became the boy's guardian and mentor; Pliny was devoted to him (Plin., *Ep.* 2.1). Verginius retired to, and died at, the villa; his tomb was located there. This letter was written nine years later, in 106 or 107 CE.[55] The inscription is cited by Pliny in *Ep.* 9.19.1, in another, more philosophical context, but not in the context of its location at the Alsium villa.

Plin., *Ep.* 6.10.1-6 I have been staying at my mother-in-law's villa at Alsium, which belonged for a while to Verginius Rufus. Not without pain, the place itself brought back my longing for that greatest, noblest of men. He came to live here in retirement and used to call it the little nest of his old age [*senectutis suae nidulus*]. Wherever I went [at the villa], I felt how much I needed to see him. I wished to see his tomb but was struck with pain when I saw it. It is as yet unfinished, not due to any difficulties with its design—it is quite modest, even small—but because of the indifference of the man who has been put in charge of it. Indignation and pity overcame me considering that in the tenth year after his death, his ashes still lie neglected with neither an inscription nor his name, he whose memory pervades the whole earth. He even had arranged and stipulated verses to be inscribed about his divinely inspired deed:

> "Here lies Rufus, he who defeated Vindex
> And upheld the imperial power, not for himself but for his country."

Loyalty to one's friends is so rare, and the dead are so readily forgotten, that we ourselves must build our own tombs and undertake in advance all the responsibilities of our heirs. Who should not fear the same, when we can see what has happened to Verginius? The injury he has sustained is all the more undeserved because his greatness is so widely recognized. Farewell.

Letter to his friend Octavius Rufus[56] regarding an exchange of presents
Plin., *Ep.* 1.7.6 [...] I almost forgot the most important: please accept my greatest thanks for the wonderful dates—now my [present of] figs and mushrooms will have to compete with them. Farewell.

Letter to Calpurnius Fabatus[57]
Pliny here writes to his wife's grandfather, on visiting him at Comum. As an important landlord in the district of Tifernum Tiberinum, where his Tuscan villa was located, Pliny had obligations to the township.[58] This letter was written from Rome while preparing a visit to Comum with a detour to the town in Tuscany.

Plin., *Ep.* 4.1 You have wanted to see your granddaughter and me for a long time, and we are both moved by your desire to see us and feel the same just as strongly. We are both eager in wanting to be with you at your place, a visit that we are by no means postponing, and in fact we are buckling up our bags so as to get on our way as fast as the road will allow.

There will be one delay: we must break our journey at my villa in Tuscany, not to lay eyes on my land and household business [*agri resque familiaris*] there—that can wait—but to do what

I consider a necessary official act. The town of Tifernum Tiberinum is close to my estates [*praedia*]; it chose me as its patron [*patronus*] when I was scarcely more than a boy, its enthusiasm for me being greater than its soundness of judgment. The town celebrates my arrival, laments my departures, and expresses joy at my honors. To return the town's graciousness in turn—to be outdone by [others'] graciousness is disgraceful [to oneself]—I had a temple built at my own expense. Now that it is finished, it is ready to be dedicated, so delaying the ceremony any longer would be lacking in piety [*inreligiosus*]. We will therefore have to be there on the day of dedication, and I have arranged a public feast to celebrate. It may be that we will stay over the next day, but we will hurry to get on our way more quickly.

Hopefully we will find you and your daughter [Calpurnia's mother] well, and it will be pleasant (for all of us) when we arrive safely. Farewell.

Letter to his friend Junius Mauricus[59]
Plin., *Ep.* **6.14.1–2** You have asked me to visit [you] at your villa at Formia. I will come on one condition: that you do nothing to trouble yourself, and I will observe that arrangement myself. I will come not for the sea and the shore but to seek *otium* and freedom [*libertas*] with you; otherwise, I would just stay in the City. Everyone needs to decide between seeking the favor of others or one's own good opinion of oneself. I am certainly of this disposition: the whole is better than merely a part.[60] Farewell.

Letter to his friend Calpurnius Flaccus[61]
Pliny, in describing his Laurentine villa, complained of the lack of good fish obtainable on its coast (see *Ep.* 2.17.1–5, in ch. 4, Descriptions of Villas). He could not respond in kind to the *xenia* he received from friends with similarly fresh presents. This letter is his affectionate but self-deprecating substitute.

Plin., *Ep.* **2.1–2** I have received your very fine thrushes but cannot reciprocate in the same way, either from the urban markets or from the sea at my Laurentine villa because of bad weather. Receive, therefore, this rather pitiful letter and my very simple thanks, which exhibit nothing like the intelligence Diomedes showed in gift exchange.[62] However, your graciousness is such that you are quicker to forgive than when forgiveness itself is not really justified. Farewell.

Letter to Cornelius Tacitus the historian[63]
These excerpts are included to illustrate the etiquette of visits to villas. They are from Pliny's most famous letter, the account of the eruption of Vesuvius in 79 CE and his uncle Pliny the Elder's efforts to help its refugees and to observe the natural phenomenon scientifically and up close. As the commander of the imperial fleet at Misenum across the Bay of Naples, the Elder Pliny was in a good position to bring assistance. The drama of the events, both natural and human, is underscored by the Elder Pliny's arrival, by boat from Misenum across the bay, at the villa of his friend Pomponianus at Stabiae on the Surrentine coast. Arrival at a villa was normally followed by a bath and a rest before a meal.[64] To reassure his friend and the villa's household in this moment of crisis, Pliny requested this normal ceremony of arrival be maintained to give the example of calm in the midst of catastrophe and to allay the fears of his host and the household. Then they dined.

Plin., *Ep.* **6.16.11–12** [...] My uncle then considered turning back, but as soon as the helmsman warned him to do so, he told him, "Fortune steadies brave men—let's make for Pomponianus's place."[65]

He was frustrated from getting there by the width of the bay, whose shores bend gradually in a circle enclosing the sea. It was clear that he was not yet in immediate danger but soon would be, because the volcanic cloud was growing. Pomponianus had put bags [of his household goods] onto boats, for the safety of flight if the contrary [landward] wind should change. Because the wind was favorable [for his approach to the villa], my uncle was able to land, hugged his terrified host and urged him to be calm. To soothe his friend's fear with [the example of] his own composure, he ordered that he be taken to the bath. After bathing, he reclined to dine, and continued to be cheerful or to seem so, which was also a great thing to do. [...]

Letter to his friend Pontius Allifanus,[66] from a villa in Campania
Plin., *Ep.* 6.28.1–3   I know what has been the cause of your not being here in time for my arrival, but even though you are absent you might as well be here anyway, such have been the quantities of treats—both citified and countrified [*copiae urbanae rusticae*]—that have been offered to me on your behalf. Rascal that I am, I have accepted them all. The people in your household insisted that I do so, and I worried that you would be angry with me and with them if I did not. In the future, if you don't apply a limit, I will do so myself. I have told your people that if they bring me so much next time, they will have to take it back. You tell me to use all your goods as if they were mine. So be it, but I'm allowed to use your goods as mine—that is, sparingly. Farewell.

RUTILIUS NAMATIANUS
(Rutilius Claudius Namatianus, late fourth–mid-fifth century CE)

On My Return (*De reditu suo*), September–November 416 CE (Rut. Namat., *De red.*)

Rutilius Namatianus, from a Gallic aristocratic family of high imperial officials based at Tolosa (modern Toulouse) in Aquitania, wrote a long, detailed poem in elegiac couplets on his trip from Rome to Gaul and back. His trip was prompted by a need to look after his Aquitanian estates and as a holiday after a year-long appointment as *Praefectus Urbi Romae* (prefect of the City) in 413 CE, a high position in the imperial bureaucracy in the reign of Honorius (395–423 CE).[67] Like Horace's account of his trip to Brundisium, this was a road-trip account or, as we have it, a sea-trip story. Rutilius meets friends along the way, stays with them, and enjoys himself at their villas.

His journey, possibly lasting as much as a year, started on September 22, 416 CE. However, the transmission of the poem's text is truncated: the text breaks off after November 21, a month or so later that same year, just as Rutilius is about to leave the Ligurian coast for Massiliae (modern Marseille) and thus arrive in Gaul.[68]

Rut. Namat., *De red.* 1.463–468
   A northwesterly Corus, the kind of wind that even breaks [innermost parts of] dense forests,
   Made me stop right there [at Volaterrana Vada].[69]
   We were just barely safe under shelter [*domus*] to endure the wild rains,
   My friend Albinus's nearby villa was opened to me.
   Rome linked my friend with me: it was he by whom my togate power continued.[70] [...]

Rut. Namat., *De red.* 1.507–508
   [...] He [Albinus] was recently appointed *Comes Illustris* in the sacred court
   But he disdained the highest rankings in favor of his love of the country life [in Etruria].[71] [...]

Rut. Namat., *De red.* 1.541–558
   A keen southeast wind brought about the time to set to sea,
   But I wanted to see my friend Protadius,
   He whom, were anyone to wish to know him through external indications,
   Would, in a heart-felt way, be able to see him as an exemplar of virtue—

No painting would be able to give a likeness of him in colors
Than the composite image [*figura*] that comes from the assemblages of his fine qualities. [...]
Even at a distance, the steadiness of his demeanor stands out clearly
As does the essence of his sense of justice.
My praise would be less if it were only Gaul praising a Gallic citizen,
But Rome herself can attest [to the worth of] her former Prefect.[72]
Umbria replaced his ancestors' homeland with a poor place to dwell,
[but] His virtue made the one equal to the other.[73]
For this man, his unconfined [free, unconquered] mind takes small things to be great ones,
To his soul, great things themselves once had been small.[74]
A narrow bit of land was inhabited by those who had vanquished kings,
And a few *iugera* gave [us many a] Cincinnatus.[75]
This brings us nothing less than what was brought to us
By the plough of Serranus and Fabricius's homely hearth.

Rut. Namat., *De red.* 1.527–530

[...] From there we find our way to Triturrita,[76] which is the name of the villa
That lies on an island in a wave-driven channel,
It overhangs the sea on artificial mounds of stones
Because he who built the house had only to set it so. [...]

Rut. Namat., *De red.* 1.615–628[77]

[...] Now as I returned to Triturrita villa from the city of Pisa,
While I was raising the hanging sail to a steady south wind [Notus],
The arch of the air became black with clouds
And the scudding clouds threw out lightning here and there.
So we halted: who would dare to go to sea under a storm
Threatening such insane anger?
We spend the restful interruption [*otia*] from our sailing in nearby forests
And enjoy moving our limbs in pursuit of game.
The *vilicus*, our host, equips us with what is needed for the chase
And with hounds taught to catch the scent of a den.[78]
A boar, terrible in his flashing tusks, is caught by tricks and clever stratagems,
A boar that even a strong-armed Meleager might be afraid to encounter,
One which would make even Amphitryon's son quiver in his joints.[79]

SIDONIUS APOLLINARIS
(Gaius Sollius Modestus Apollinaris Sidonius, ca. 430–before 490 CE)

Letters (Epistulae) (Sid. Apoll., *Ep.*)

Letter to his friend Donidius,[80] ca. 460–470s CE

This letter is an apology for being tardy in arriving for a stay at (or return to) Nemausus (modern Nîmes) with Donidius: on his way, Sidonius had been waylaid (literally) by two friends and made to enjoy being a guest at their villas. He describes the activities they arranged for him; their competitive welcome gives a good insight into the traditions of hospitality that seem to have persisted from the Late Republic through Pliny the Younger's time to the fifth century CE. There were other guests besides Sidonius at the two villas.

Sid. Apoll., *Ep.* 2.9.1–10   You ask why, since starting for Nemausus a long time ago, I might be thwarting your anticipation of my arrival. I will give you my reasons for my tardiness, and I will not delay telling about my delay in returning [to Nemausus], for what is pleasant to me is pleasant to you as well. I have had the most wonderful time at the very pleasant villas [*agri amoenissimi*] of two most amiable hosts, Ferreolus and Apollinaris.[81] The legal boundaries of their estates [*praedia*] adjoin one another, and their homes [*domicilia*] are close by, with a track connecting them that is a tiring distance on foot but hardly anything at all on horseback. The vine dresser and the olive grower cultivate the hills above the buildings [*aedes*]— you might well think the hills to be Aracynthus and Nysa, the mountains celebrated in poetic songs.[82] One house [*domus*] overlooks a flat landscape, the other has a view over woodlands, but the difference between them is less important than that they are both equally delightful.

But why talk any more about the positions of their estates when what really remains to be described is the manner of their hospitality [*ordo hospitalitatis*]? In the first place, very expert scouts were sent out from both houses to monitor the route of my return journey, not just on the lines of the public roads but even on the winding footpaths with shortcuts and shepherds' tracks, so that I could not in any way escape the traps set up by their hospitable intentions. I was trapped, I admit, but trapped with minimum reluctance on my part, and I was immediately compelled into swearing an oath that I would not contemplate continuing on my journey before seven days were up.

There was a pleasant daily competition between the two hosts as to which of their kitchens [*culinae*] would be the first to open to prepare my meals. It wasn't even possible to maintain a fair division to balance between the two by taking turns between them, seeing that one host is related to me, the other has a tie of close relationship to my family. Ferreolus is a man of prefectorian rank: in consequence, his age and status, when considered with the duty owed to him [by family tie], gave him the first prerogative for inviting me.

Thus I was taken from one delight to yet another delight. Whichever vestibule [*vestibulum*] I entered, right away in one direction there was the circular whirling of the rival ball players at the game of *catastrophae*, then, looking another way, it was equalled elsewhere with the sounds of the competing gamblers' voices and the rattle of the dice boxes and dice.[83] In yet another place, there were books readily available, [in such a quantity] that you might think you are looking at the shelves of a scholar, at the book stacks of an Athenaeum, or at booksellers' cluttered cupboards. The books containing pious literature [*stilus religiosus*] were arranged near where the chairs for the matrons were placed, whereas the seats for the *patres familiarum* had books containing the noblest of lofty Latin eloquence [*eloquium Latiaris*].[84] However, these books [of Latin eloquence] also included certain volumes by authors who maintained a means of expression similar to others who had argued along different lines of thought, because both read the writings of men of similar knowledge [*similis scientia*]: here Augustine, there Varro, Horace here, there Prudentius.[85]

Among the books was the translation, by Turranius Rufinus, of the *Adamantius* by Origen, which was zealously examined by readers of our faith. We would discuss as equals, giving our different opinions as our hearts prompted. We discussed why certain of our theologians [*protomystari*] held Origen to be wrong, even perverse, and to be shunned, even though his work had been translated [by Turranius] with such care as to its content and spirit that Apuleius himself could not have better rendered Plato's *Phaedo*, or Cicero the *Ctesiphon* by Demosthenes into the usage and [grammatical] rules of Roman [Latin] speech.[86]

While each one of us undertook different activities as freely as he wanted, a message came from the head chef [*archimagirus*], indicating that it was now time to take care of our bodies, and as the time registered on the water clock was passing the fifth hour, he was proved to be very observant.[87] We ate in a short amount of time but lavishly, in the manner of senators whose nature and practices is to have a lot of food served on only a few platters, though the dinner combines some roasted meat with stews. For levity and learning [*laetitia peritiaque*], there were some little stories [*narrantiuculae*] while we were drinking [after dinner]: they were presented in two ways, some for laughter, others for worldly wisdom. We ate with respect, elegance, and abundance [*sancte pulchre abundanter*].

Rising [from our dinner], if we were at Vorocingus, as this estate was called, we made our way to our luggage and sleep-over rooms.[88] However, if we were at Prusianus, as the other estate is called, we made Tonantius [a young friend] and his brothers, the first and most excellent of their noble generation, get out of their beds, because it was not easy to carry our sleeping equipment around from one place to another. The drowsiness of the midday nap having been shaken off, we went for a short ride to revive our appetites that had been dulled with too much food.

Both my hosts had bath buildings [still] under construction, so neither was usable. But when the little drinking fellowship [*turba compotrix*] of my hangers-on and members of my household stopped drinking for a while—their heads had been drowned in and overpowered by the hospitable drinking bowl—a ditch would be quickly dug near a spring or stream, into which a pile of recently heated stones would be placed, and a structure in the shape of a hemispherical cave of flexible hazelwood was built while the ditch was heating up. Over this structure, a cover made of *cilicium*, which covered the spaces between the twigs and shut out the light, keeping in the steam rising from the boiling water sprayed on the hot stones.[89]

We spent many hours there, not without some humorous and pleasant conversations [*semones salsi ioculares que*], and while doing so we were surrounded by and breathed in the hissing mist that brought out a healthy perspiration. When we had sweated enough to our pleasure, we plunged ourselves into the warm waters; their soothing effect was to loosen us up and purge our indigestion. Steeling ourselves, we then gave ourselves to the cold waters of the spring or the well, or right into the river. The river is the Vardo: it flows between the two houses.[90] Except when swollen by snow and becoming cloudy, the river is reddish from the yellow gravel, and it passes along its channel clear, quiet, and rocky, but for all that no less abounding in fine fish.

I might well tell you about our very lovely dinners [*cenae unctissimae*], but if I did, there would be no end to my prolixity, which even my sense of proportion might not curtail. Even though a retelling of these dinners would make a pleasant story, I might well have blushed for blotting the back of this letter with a leaky pen.

But now I am coming to you, and under Christ's guidance we shall soon see one another, and it will be more convenient to tell you about the dinners with my friends when you and I dine together. I am hoping, first of all, that the seven days' time will soon restore the much-desired feeling of hunger, for nothing fixes a stomach upset by gluttonous consumption better than abstemious eating. Farewell.

Letter to his friend Maurusius[91]
This letter may be compared with that of Pliny, *Ep.* 2.1 above.

Sid. Apoll., *Ep.* 2.14.1–2 I hear that the vintage has responded to your own industriousness and the prayers of your community with a better result than what the otherwise unproductive year was threatening, so I suspect that you will remain for a long while in *pagus Vialoscensis*, the village once called *pagus Martialis* because the Julian legions had winter quarters there.[92] In that village you have a fruitful vineyard and also a farm as great as the greatness of its owner, and the farm detains you and your household by its copious stores of grain [*plurifaria frugum*] and its many places of accommodation [*mansiones*].

If, now that your barns, storerooms, and pantries [*horrea, apothecae, penus*] have been filled up, you plan to stay there in sooty *otium* [*otium fuliginosum*] and in the convenience of having to wear only a tunic throughout the cold months of January [*Janua*] and February [*Numa*], before the arrival of the swallow and the stork [in spring], I will, in consequence and like you, immediately cease my stay in town for good reasons so that, while you enjoy your country life, I may enjoy being with you.[93] As you know, an estate bringing in good returns is no greater pleasure or closer to my heart than a neighbor of my own age and pleasant disposition. Farewell.

Sidonius Apollinaris, *Carmina*, ca. 470s CE (Sid. Apoll., *Carm*.)

Sidonius's *Carmen* 21 accompanied a *xenia* of fish.

Sid. Apoll., *Carm.* 21.1–4
> Tonight and for the first time, four fishes were caught on my hooks.
> Of these, I am keeping two, so take two yourself.
> I'm sending you the bigger ones, and the way they have been apportioned is most correct,
> Because you are the larger part of my heart.

In *Carmen* 24, Sidonius is writing a farewell [προπεμπτικόν] to a little book of poems [*libellus*] he has written. He imagines it traveling from place to place in his friends' homes in Gaul, though it is not certain if a single copy was sent to one friend with a request to send it on to others in round robin style, or if individual copies were sent to each one. Along its way, the book will find its way to the villa called Vorocingus owned by his friend Apollinaris.[94]

Sid. Apoll., *Carm.* 24.51–74
> No matter how quickly you are undertaking your journey,
> Vorocingus will give you rest. There you will find my friend Apollinaris.
> Either he will be outfitting his home with cool marble against the heat of the angry Lion,
> Or else he will be strolling in his hidden gardens
> Like those of the honey-producing Hybla
> Or the gardens of the old man of Corycus, darkened [watered] by the black Galaesus River.[95]
> Or [Apollinaris] may be there with his violets, his garden thyme, his hedges of privet bush,
> His wild thyme, his cassia [cinnamon], his saffron crocus, his narcissus, and his
>   hyacinth flowers,
> And therefore he may spurn the lump of frankincense
> That a Sabaean salesman [*petitor*] offers him at a great price.[96]
> Or maybe he is resting in his artificial grotto [*fictus specus*] on the hillside,
> Where surrounding trees work hard to make a natural portico,
> But thereby make a cavern rather than a grove.[97]
> Who now would compare this place to the ancient orchard of the Indian king,
> And the golden vines with their shoots of greenish electrum
> That Porus made, with royal treasure tinkling on the yellow-gold metal vine shoots
> And the waving clusters of jewels?[98]

7

ECONOMICS AND EUERGETISM

CICERO

PLINY THE ELDER

PLINY THE YOUNGER

JUVENAL

Making money from agriculture was an important part of villas as businesses, as the agricultural writers indicated.[1] However, in letters and poems, and even in the agricultural writers and in Pliny the Elder's *Natural History*, reference is rarely made to actual profit or revenue amounts from villas and estates, possibly because, not unlike today, talking about money was thought to be vulgar or a matter of banal personal concern, or possibly because complaining about the high cost of maintaining houses in the country was a boastful custom among Roman elites. While some business aspects of villas can be gleaned from literary texts, much more practical information can be had from economic history based on archaeological sources or inscriptions. The workforce—enslaved workers, free farmers, or tenants—were also investment commodities that were functional parts of costs and profits.

Another aspect of business was keeping a friendly eye on villas, estates, clients, and personnel for one's friends or relatives. Cicero did this often, his friend Atticus supervised Cicero's property affairs in his absence, and Cicero looked after his brother's villas at Arpinum when Quintus was away. Pliny the Younger also helped his friends and relatives by supervising their properties, and in turn his friends who still lived at Comum kept an eye on his houses and villas there.

Purchases of villas and estates were certainly investments, but they were also part of social aspirations that might also be realized from non-land-based activities such as commerce, banking and lawyering. Horace's Alfius in his *Epode* 2 is the most obvious example: he is a satirized stereotype in the poem, but he cannot have been alone in advertising—with villa, estate, enslaved personnel—what Trimalchio in the *Satyricon* of Petronius also aspired to: social prominence conferred by land ownership in addition to other sources of wealth.[2] A villa in some sense mitigated their low social origins.

Revenue was one aspect of villas, but another was responsibility in the form of euergetism.[3] The term encompasses all aspects of donation: architecture and infrastructure, cultural goods such as libraries, religious works such as temples, public buildings (forums, basilicas, *balnea* or *thermae*), market buildings (*macella*), *horti* open to the public, gifts of statues and paintings. Such benefactions were often associated with high-status groups, individuals, or emperors, and they were characterized by such abstract concepts as *largitio* (distribution, largesse) or *liberalitas* (acts of generosity) given by persons of high status (*honestiores*) to those of lesser standing (*humiliores*).

Villas and estates in rural districts and near towns, no matter if the owner or owners were in residence, brought expectations of civic presence and participation, often at considerable outlay.[4] Pliny, for example, was treated as a kind of magistrate and celebrity in the market town near his Tuscan villa (Tifernum Tiberinum, modern Città di Castello in Umbria). He repaid the citizens of the town with thoughtful, generous gifts and wrote about them to friends and to the emperor Trajan. He was also personally generous by helping Corellia, the daughter of a friend, with the cancellation of a debt on her inheritance. At his hometown of Comum, Pliny set up an endowment for poor children: this was a private *alimenta*, meaning provisions, in this case a permanent source of income for an entity of social benefit. An inscription set up by the town recorded his generosity and included his private *alimenta*.[5]

In peninsular Italy south of the Alps, there was an important official *alimenta*, set up in the reign of Nerva and expanded in that of Trajan, in the form of obligatory, unamortizable farm loans on *fundi* and villa owners to provide local town governments with funds for the care and education of poor children, boys and some girls.[6] The *alimenta* system was celebrated in one of the panels of over-life-size reliefs on the Arch of Trajan at Beneventum: Trajan greeting children and their fathers with bread on tables for distribution, witnessed by female personifications with city-wall crowns representing the good fortune (Tyche) of the towns and townsfolk.[7]

The duty to make an estate profitable as a business and to "give back" to the local communities were parallel activities for many villa owners; the texts that follow here illustrate aspects of both. The first two excerpts from Cicero demonstrate some of the diverse ways villas might be used for profit, and Pliny the Younger's letters convey various economic and civic considerations of villa ownership related to his estates in Tuscany and at Comum. Owning a villa went beyond mere possession: it involved participation in the affairs and well-being of the local township.

CICERO   (Marcus Tullius Cicero, 107/106–43 BCE)

Letters to Atticus (Epistulae ad Atticum) (Cic., *Att.*), March 15, 60 BCE

Cic., *Att.* 1.19   [...] ...and I saw how easily my friends the tax gatherers could be separated from the Senate even though they might not separate themselves from me, while the rich [*homines beati*]—I mean those friends of yours, owners of fishponds [*piscinarii*]—did not hide their envy of me.[8] [...]

PLINY THE ELDER   (Gaius Plinius Secundus, (23/24–79 CE)

Natural History (Naturalis historia), mid–first century CE (Plin., *HN*)

Improving villa properties for vineyards could be very profitable. Pliny the Elder cites two sons of freedmen of his day who were successful: Acilius Sthenelus and Vetulenus Aegialus. They worked for patrons, but their success must have been conspicuous to have caught Pliny's attention. Seneca had met Vetulenus Aegialus at Liternum when he visited the villa that had belonged to Scipio Africanus (Sen., *Ep.* 86, in ch. 4, Descriptions of Villas). Pliny the Elder admired the improving entrepreneurs of the freedman class but had very mixed feelings about their patrons, Remmius Palaemon and Seneca. Pliny's citation of these business successes is part of his discussion of types of table grapes and wine grapes, specifically on their planting and care.

Plin., *HN* 16.47–52 (16.5)   In my [our] time, there are few examples of any great skill in this matter [i.e., planting and care of vines], so for that reason it is better not to omit [mentioning] them so that the rewards of success may be known—it's successes in any and all endeavors that stand out. So Acilius Sthenelus, the son of a freedman [*e plebe libertina*], achieved the greatest reputation [*summa gloria*] in the improvement of a vineyard near Nomentum, a vineyard not greater in size than 60 *iugera* (about 15 ha, or about 37 acres): he sold it for 400,000*HS*. In addition, Vetulenus Aegialus, also of freedman extraction, became famous at Liternum in

Campania, and he came to be even more prominent in reputation because he cultivated the estate to which [Scipio] Africanus had retired in exile.

But the greatest fame goes to the work of the aforementioned Sthenelus on behalf of Remmius Palaemon, a man famous for his writing on the art of grammar.[9] In the past twenty years, he [Remmius] bought an estate [*rus*] for 600,000*HS* in the same area around Nomentum, just where there is a side road at the tenth milestone from the City. The low price [*vilitas mercis*] of real estate in all the City's suburbs is well known, especially around there. Palaemon had bought estates [*praedia*] that had been neglected by poor management, ones that were by no means better in the way of soil than even the worst ones in the area.[10] He started to cultivate not out of virtuous intention [*virtutis animi*] but first and foremost out of vanity [*vanitas*], a trait for which he was famous. So, playing at being a farmer [*agricolam imitatur*], [but really] with Sthenelus's work on thoroughly turning over [the soil of the] the vineyards [*vinea pastinata*], he soon was rewarded in a wonderful way: in the space of [only] eight years, and with the grapes still hanging on the vines, his harvest was sold to a buyer for 400,000*HS*. Everyone ran to see the piles of the grapes in his vineyards, justifying themselves against a charge of living in a lazy district by [referring to] Remmius's very deep studies [*altiores litterae*]. Recently, Annaeus Seneca—a man as prominent in the way of erudition as he was in power, a power so excessive that it ruined him in the end—became enslaved to such a degree with desire for Remmius's estate that, even though he was, to be sure, no devotee of worthless things, he was not ashamed to cede victory to that other man [Remmius Palaemon], even though Palaemon was hateful to him and would certainly broadcast the concession. Seneca bought those vineyards for four times the price Palaemon had [originally] paid for them, within not more than ten years from the time that Palaemon had first come to manage them.

These methods [*opera*, i.e., that of Sthenelus] might well have been appropriate to employ on Caecuban and Setian farms in view of the fact that, after they were applied, one *iugera* of vineyard often produced seven sacks [*cullei*] of grapes, equal to 140 *amphorae* of must.[11] So that no one might imagine that production in times past was less than it is now, Cato has recorded that one *iugera* used to produce ten sacks of grapes. These examples demonstrate definitively that a merchant can bring in no more income by setting out rashly on the sea, seeking commodities [*merces*] on the coast of the Red Sea or India, than to find profit from a well-farmed estate at home [in Italy].[12]

PLINY THE YOUNGER (Gaius Plinius Caecilius Secundus, 61–113 CE)

Letters (Epistulae) (Plin., *Ep.*)

The web of obligations that bound villa owners to acts of personal generosity as well as to the more formal and visible acts of euergetism are illustrated in the two letters that follow, the first to the daughter of a deceased poor relation, the other arranging for a statue to be set up in a temple in Comum, his hometown.

Other instances of such very private and very public acts of generosity are also illustrated in Pliny's gift of the usufruct of a small villa to the nurse of his childhood (*Ep.* 6.3.1–2, in ch. 8, Buying, Building, Improving, and Selling Villas) and the very grand gift of imperial portraits to a temple in the market town near his Tuscan villa (*Ep.* 10.8.1–8, below).

Letter to Calvina, daughter of a relative[13]
Plin., *Ep.* **2.4.3–4** If your father were to have died in debt to several other creditors in addition to what he owed me, you might not have accepted an inheritance that would have been onerous even for a man [to undertake]. However, I was prompted by the duty owed to a relative

to settle up such debts as were immediate [*molestiores*], if not the ones needing more attention [*diligentiores*], so that I would become the only creditor [to whom debt was owed by the inheritor of the estate, namely Calvina]. While your father was living, to supplement the amount he gave you, I had given 100,000*HS* for your dowry money when you married. His amount [actually] came from me, because it had to be withdrawn from what he had [on deposit] with me.[14] This is a firm expression [*pignus*] of my good wishes [*facilitates*] so you may have the confidence [*fiducia*] to acknowledge your deceased father's reputation and innocence [*fama* and *pudor*, respectively]. As encouragement to you not merely by [my] words but, more importantly, by [my] actions, I will order that whatever sum your father [still] owed me to be listed as paid [on my accounts]. You need not worry that this gift will be a burden for me. It's the case that my resources are limited [*modicae facultates*] and the expense of my offices are great [*dignitas sumputosa*]. Income [*reditus*] from my estates in the contracts for the farms [*agelli*] is small [*minor*] and less than steady [*incertior*], but what's lacking in the way of income can be made up by frugal living.

All this—by both my words and especially by my actions—should validate what your father meant to me and encourage you to validate my view [of him]. You should not worry that this cancellation of debt is a financial burden to me. My wealth is somewhat modest and the expenses of my official appointment are very great, and the income from my properties, in the condition they are in, is both small and unpredictable, but frugal living can make up the difference.[15] It's from this frugality that the spring of [my] generosity flows. I must restrain my generosity somewhat, for fear that prodigality might diminish it, but I can keep my frugality for others—for you, it's really easy for me to clear the accounts even if doing so goes beyond the norm. Farewell.

Letter to Annius Severus[16]
Plin., *Ep.* 3.6 From an inheritance that has come to me, I have recently bought a statue made of Corinthian bronze [*Corinthium signum*]—it's small, but lively and nicely modeled as far as my taste goes, though it is quite possible that I am wrong as I know little about such things. Still, even I can see it is a [fine] statue. It is a nude figure, so it does not hide any faults it may have [in the modeling]; this also shows its good elements. It depicts an old man in a standing position; the bones, muscles, sinews, and the veins and even the wrinkles are represented as if the figure were breathing. The brow is broad with a balding, thin head of hair, the face is hollow and the shoulders slack, the breast has lost tone and the stomach is shrunken. Even from the back, as far as any [view from the] back can indicate, the same look of [old] age is apparent. From its color, the bronze itself has the look of real antique material. It's things like these—things that attract the eye of the artist as well as delighting the eye of the amateur—that prompted me to buy it despite being a mere beginner [in appreciating art].

However, I bought it not to keep it in my house—actually, I have had no such Corinthian bronzes in my house up to now.[17] Rather, in all sincerity I wish to place it in a public place in our hometown [Comum], most especially in the temple of Jupiter, because it is clearly something well suited to be an offering in a temple and to a god. Will you take care of this task—you, who usually join with me in all my projects—and immediately order a base for it to be made? Choose something you like in the way of marble, and my name and honors should be inscribed on it if you think they should be there as well.

I will send you the statue once I'm able to find someone for whom the errand won't be a nuisance, or else I'll bring it to you along with myself—you'll like that better. Indeed, I wish to go up there myself if my work schedule will allow. You'll be happy at my promising to come visit but will knit your brow when I add that it will be only for a few days: the duties that keep me here even now will not allow me to absent myself any longer. Farewell.

Calvisius Rufus was a childhood friend who had stayed at Comum after Pliny had left for Rome (see Plin., *Ep.* 1.3, in ch. 5, Villas and *Otium*). Pliny relied on Calvisius's financial advice, and in this letter he enumerates the pros and cons of buying a villa and its estate adjacent to his Tuscan villa.

Letter to his friend Calvisius Rufus[18]
Plin., *Ep.* 3.19.1–9   As is my habit, I am asking you for some advice on a personal matter. An estate next to mine has been put up for sale.[19] Many things attract me to [buying] it, but not a few discourage me from doing so. Combining the two estates is the first attraction, and no less than that is the convenience of visiting both properties together on a single visit, and having one manager [*procurator*] and the same supervisors [*actores*] for both, and only one villa to maintain and embellish, leaving the other as is.[20] My reckoning in this matter includes expenses for the furniture [*supellectiles*], the household staff [*atriensis*], the gardeners [*topiarii*], the workmen [*fabri*], and the equipment for the gamekeepers [*venatorii instrumenti*] as well: it's more economical if you keep all these things in one place than to have them in several.[21]

The counter argument is that it would be imprudent to subject so large an estate to the same prevailing bad weather and negative events [as my existing property]: against uncertain outcomes, it is better to try having estates in different places.[22] In addition, having estates in different climates is pleasant, and so is traveling among one's various properties.[23]

But the main argument in my deliberation on the matter is as follows: the soil is fertile and well watered, and the estate consists of fields, vineyards, and woodlands from which enough steady, if modest, income is produced. However, this good farming property has been ruined by incompetent cultivation. The previous owner often sold [his tenants'] farming equipment, thereby reducing the amount of rent [or produce] that they owed him over time but depleting their productivity for the future, and so their indebtedness to him became ever greater.[24] Therefore, they will have to be supplied with some good slaves, because I don't have any chained slaves [*vincti*] there and no one has any [in the neighborhood].[25]

Besides, you should know the asking price: 3,000,000*HS*, down from 5,000,000*HS*, but the reduced number of tenants as well as the current bad [economic] situation has reduced farming income, driving down the asking price.[26] You may well ask if it will be easy for me to raise 3,000,000. While it is a fact that most of my wealth is in [landed] properties, I can call in some loans and it won't be hard to borrow. I can always get money from my mother-in-law [*socrus*]—I use her fortune as if it were mine.[27] So don't worry about my ability to raise the money when you weigh the alternatives and give them your most diligent consideration. In all business affairs and the disposition of large amounts of money, your experience and foresight are the best. Farewell.

Letter to his friend Julius Naso
Plin., *Ep.* 4.6.1–3   I am told that my Tuscan estate has suffered a hailstorm, and in the Transpadine region [of my Comum properties], there has been a bumper crop resulting in falling prices; only my Laurentine villa brings me any income. There, I own only the building and the garden and the shore in front, but it's still my only source of revenue.[28] I attend to the greater part of my writing there, and so, in relation to land that I don't have, I concentrate on my literary work. In this way, I can show you full bookcases [*scrinia* (*plena*)] in the place of full barns [*horrea plena*] elsewhere.

So, I suggest that if you want a similarly predictable and abundant return on investment, buy an estate on this coast. Farewell.

Letter to Plinius Paternus, a relative
Plin., *Ep.* 1.21   I grant that you have the greatest possible capacities of judgment and eye, not so much because they are so discerning (much as you might like me to say so) but because

they are as discerning as mine. Joking aside, I think the slaves you think I should buy look decent enough. It must still be determined if they are honest, because in the matter of buying slaves, it is better to judge them by what is heard about them than by what the evidence of one's eyes might be.[29] Farewell.

Letter to his friend Julius Valerianus

Nundinae were of great importance to villas: every nine days, produce could be taken for sale (retail or wholesale) in the markets and supplies purchased for the estate.[30] They were also very valuable to town governments, which sponsored, supervised, and taxed them and welcomed the added business activity and influx of countryfolk. Holding a *nundina* on a private estate evaded municipal regulations, putting villa owners and local authorities at legal loggerheads.

Plin., *Ep.* 5.4.1–2   [...] The matter is small but could be the beginning of something not at all trivial. Sollers, a man of praetorian rank and a senator, has petitioned the Senate to be allowed to hold a market [*nundina*] on his estates [*in agris suis*]. The Vicetine representatives, with Tuscilius Nominatus as advocate, objected to this, but the matter was adjourned temporarily.[31] [...]

Letter to Calpurnius Fabatus of Comum,[32] his wife's grandfather, after 93 CE

Plin., *Ep.* 7.11.1–8   You are surprised that my freedman Hermes, as I ordered him to do, has sold my five-twelfth portion of a hereditary estate that I had offered for sale. He did so without waiting for [and in advance of] the [public] auction [*auctio*], valuing my portion at 700,000*HS*. You observe that its real price might have been 900,000*HS*, and furthermore you ask whether I confirm his action.[33] Indeed, I do: hear me out on my reasons. I am very eager to have your approval and to be pardoned by my co-inheritors if I differ from them in order to obey a higher call to duty.

I have the greatest reverence for Corellia and hold her dear, first as the sister of Corellius Rufus whose memory is sacred to me, and then again because she was my mother's dearest friend. I have a long-standing friendship with her husband Minicius Justus, a very fine man, as well as with her son who organized the games I gave during my praetorship.[34] The last time I was at your place, she let me know that she wished to buy something on the shores of our Lacus Larius. I offered her whichever of my estates [*praedia*] she might like and whatever price she wanted to pay, except those of my mother and father—those I could not sell, even to Corellia.

For that reason, when my inheritance of [part of] this estate came my way [by bequest in a will], I wrote to her indicating that it was for sale. My freedman Hermes delivered the letter, and when she requested that my portion be assigned to her account, he did so. As you can see, I must confirm the action that my freedman took in accordance with my orders. It remains to be determined if my co-inheritors countenance with an equitable attitude the fact that I sold separately what needn't have been sold at all. They do not need to follow my example, as they do not have the ties of affection with Corellia that I do. They can do what is best for themselves: what I did was for friendship. Farewell.

Letter to Caninius Rufus[35]

Plin, *Ep.* 7.18.1–5   You have asked me for advice as to how the amount of money for an [annual] banquet [*epulum*] you want to transfer to our township can be securely set up after your death.[36] It is an honor to give advice, but quick advice is not good advice. You could give the whole amount to the town's public treasury [*res publica*], but its dissipation is greatly to be feared. Or you could give agricultural properties to the public treasury, but for sure they will be neglected by the municipal bureaucrats [*publici*].

No scheme can be better than the one I came upon myself and instituted. I had promised a sum of 500,000*HS* for an *alimenta* for freeborn boys and girls. To do so, I conveyed [the title of] a part of my estates worth much more [than 500,000*HS*] to the municipal registrar [*actor publicus*].³⁷ I then received the deed back after the imposition of an official property tax [*vectigal*] of 30,000*HS*, payable annually. In this way, the monetary value of the property remains entirely in the hands of the township, the interest [*sors*] will always be reliably paid, and because the property's value is much greater than the tax charged against it, a lease holder [*dominus*] can always be found [willing] to work it.

I am not unaware that I seem to have expended more money than I would have [otherwise] given outright, because the value of so fine a property [*pulcherimus ager*] has been diminished by the tax imposed on it. However, it is necessary that private advantage [*privatus utilitas*] be set aside for public interests, and [merely] lifetime considerations for permanent objectives. It is better by far to think of public contributions than of one's own expediencies.³⁸ Farewell.

Letter to his friend Calvisius Rufus
Pliny appears to be having trouble getting the wine produced on his Tuscan villa off his hands, no matter whether because it was a good or bad year in relation to market value or in terms of the quality of his vintage.³⁹ While some Italian wines improved with age, Pliny's Tuscan vintage does not appear to have been one of them: he needed to get his wine stock out of his cellarage fast, maybe also because he was running out of storage space.⁴⁰ In any case, he shows significant concern about the situation.

Despite Pliny's claim that he was giving discounts for the sake of fairness, the necessity of having to do so indicates the extent of his dilemma. He was the social superior of the *negotiatores*, but they had the upper hand in this commercial transaction: Pliny gave the biggest rebates to the biggest buyers of his stock, plus another discount for those who paid cash. His insecurity in the matter may be revealed by his two quotations from epic poetry—Vergil and Homer—which gave a literate gloss to his somewhat desperate measures.

Plin., *Ep.* 8.2.1–8   While others visit their estates to return richer than they had been, I return poorer than I was. I sold my grape harvest to the middlemen [*negotiatores*] who were competing among themselves to buy [at the discounts]. The price was good, and at the time the market for the harvest was considered viable. Their hopes were dashed. The easy solution would have been to give all of them the same discount, but that would have been unfair. It seems to me that, in both business and personal affairs, and in great and small matters, it's best to deal as justly with others as [one would do] with oneself. If all disgraceful acts are the same, so all good deeds can be equally perceived [without qualification between or among them].

For this reason, and "so no one should leave without getting something," I returned every middleman an eighth of what he had bought.⁴¹ For those who had bought a lot more, I made a separate provision, because their loss was all the greater for having been a greater help to me [in buying my wine]. In consequence, to those who had paid more than 10,000*HS*, a tenth of what had been paid above that amount [10,000*HS*], as a bonus discount above the eighth that had been granted to all the middlemen as a group.

I'm afraid that I have not expressed myself with sufficient clarity: I must re-explain my calculation. Let's say that someone bought my wine for 15,000*HS*. He would receive one eighth of 15,000*HS*, and a tenth of 5,000*HS*. In addition, thinking about those who had paid money up front as opposed to those who had paid a small amount [an installment] in advance, and then those who had paid nothing as yet, I considered that it was not a fair deal to treat them all with the same generous discounts. I therefore went back and allowed another tenth of the money paid in advance to those who had done so. By this neat solution, I expressed my appreciation to each of them according to his past merits, and so that they would continue to buy from me in the future, as well as to encourage them to pay up [promptly].⁴²

The method—or perhaps my affability in the matter—has been expensive, but it has been worth the money. The entire region has been congratulating me on the novelty of the discounts and how they were effected. And the middlemen themselves, whom I did not measure with the same measuring rod but rewarded in a graded ranking as to which of them was the more deserving and honest, left with the feeling that I am not a person "who holds the worthy and the unworthy in the same regard."[43] Farewell.

Letter to his friend Valerius Paulinus,[44] 107 CE

Plin, *Ep.* 9.37.1–5 It is not your habit to demand ceremonious attention from your friends if it might be an inconvenience to them, and I hold you in such faithful regard that I do not fear that you might misunderstand in some way what I really want to say, namely that I will not see you actually become consul on the kalends [first of the month]: specifically, what keeps me here is the necessity of arranging the multiyear leases of my farms, and a new plan will have to be put in place. Despite the large reductions in rents that I have granted in the last lustral period [five years], the arrears have increased, and many tenants no longer want to reduce what they owe me because they despair of paying it off. They even steal and eat what they grow [seed grain] because they think there won't be anything left over for themselves.

So it is very important that this increasingly bad situation be remedied. One remedy would be to rent farms for portions of the produce rather than for cash, and then for me to appoint some of them as supervising overseers [*exactores custodes*] to watch over the produce.[45]

There is no more truly deserved harvest than that which comes from the earth, the weather, and the year's seasons. However, great honesty, sharp eyes, and many handy workmen are needed for this project. Still, I must try the experiment and see what changes might help to remedy this longstanding bad situation.

As you can see, it is not selfish fussiness that prevents me from being with you on the first day of your consulship. As if being there with you, I will celebrate it here with prayers, rejoicing, and congratulations. Farewell.

Letter to his friend Mustius

This letter provides an example of the voluntary contribution of villa and estate owners to the religious and civic well-being of a district or town. It is also an example of a religious cult open to the public, which happened to be set in private property (Pliny's, in this case); maintaining and improving the premises would have fallen on the landowner.

Plin, *Ep.* 9.39.1–6 The warnings of the soothsayers tell me that the temple of Ceres on my property must be renovated: it must be made better and bigger because it is old and much too small, especially when it is crowded on the annual celebration of its inauguration. On the ides of September [September 13], the entire population of the region comes together, there are religious ceremonies, and many vows are pledged and redeemed. There is no shelter from either rain or sun. So I consider that, as acts of munificence and piety, it would be good for me to construct a temple as beautiful as I can make it, as well as porticoes, these last as much for the goddess as for the worshipers.[46]

For this project, I wish you to buy four marble columns of whatever type seems suitable. Also, buy marble, some to apply to the floor and some to the walls. An image of the goddess also needs to be made: parts of the old wooden one have fallen off due to the statue's age. As for the porticoes, nothing comes to mind at the moment, unless you can write up a reasoned plan for their location. The porticoes cannot surround the temple, because the area adjacent to the temple has very steep slopes, and there is a river on one side and a public road on the other. On the other side of the road, there is a large meadow in which porticoes could be placed facing the temple. Unless you can come up with a better solution, you alone can solve the problems of the terrain with your expertise. Farewell.

Letter to the emperor Trajan, after ca. 103 CE
As a major local villa owner, Pliny was expected to engage in euergetism: he had sponsored the building of the temple in question (*Ep.* 3.4 and 4.1). Here, he is adding a statue of Trajan with other imperial effigies to be housed in that temple (not the temple of Ceres on his estate described in *Ep.* 9.39, just above). Having already asked the emperor Nerva for permission to add an image of him to the other statues, Pliny now seeks permission from the current emperor, Trajan, for the same. As the emperors' images had important religious or sanctified character, asking for such permission would have been obligatory.

Plin, *Ep.* 10.8.1–8 In his very fine speeches and by his noble example, My Lord [*dominus*], your divine father [Trajan's adoptive father and predecessor, the emperor Nerva] urged all citizens to engage in public munificence [*munificentia*].[47] I asked him for permission to send statues of the emperors to the municipality [Tifernum Tiberinum] some [short] distance from my estates. These statues came to me by several different bequests, and I had also asked the emperor if I might add a portrait statue of himself. He gave his approval with every mark of graciousness. I then immediately wrote to the town's *decuriones* [councillors] to set aside a location for a temple I would build at my own expense; they honored me by allowing me to choose the site.

But ill health—first my own, then your father's—and then the duties of the post conferred on me by both have prolonged the accomplishment of these projects, so it seems most advisable to see to them in person. My term in office ends on the kalends of September [last day of August], and September has many official holidays.

Before all else, I ask that you give me permission to add your statue to the collection that has been amassed to adorn the temple. After that, I ask you for the grant of a leave of absence so that I can have the work finished as soon as possible.[48] In all sincerity, I would not presume on your kindness in hiding the fact that a leave will incidentally be very useful to my personal business. I own farms in the region that rent for more than 400,000*HS* annually: I cannot delay renting them, and the new tenants [*coloni*] must be there to see what needs to be done to prune the vines. In addition, continual bad years have brought me to contemplating a reduction in rents, and I cannot arrange for that unless I am on the spot.

Therefore, My Lord, I will be indebted to you if, in your generosity, you grant me a leave for these thirty days, both to expedite the quick completion of the expression of my loyal regard for you as well as the settling of my own personal business. I cannot accomplish these tasks in less time, because the town and my estates are more than 150 miles [about 222 km, or 138 mi.] away.

Letter from the emperor Trajan to Pliny, after ca. 103 CE
The emperor replied to Pliny's requests by granting the leave of absence and the permission.

Plin., *Ep.* 10.9 You have given me many [personal and public] reasons to be granted a leave, though a mere expression of your wish would have sufficed for me [to grant it]. I do not doubt that you will return to your difficult duties as soon as you can. I permit you to place the statue of me where you wish in the temple. Even though I usually resist granting [requests for] these kinds of honors, I do not wish to appear to be putting a damper on your expression of loyalty to me.

JUVENAL (Decimus Junius Juvenalis, late first–early second century CE)

Satires, 117–early 120s CE (Juv., Satires)

This poem decries the wealth from nonlanded sources that can buy luxurious villas and estates.

Juv., Satire 7.178–190
>[...] The owner [of the villa] spends 600,000*HS* on a bath building and even more
>   for a portico
>To drive around in whenever it's raining.
>Is he supposed to get mud on his horses while waiting for good weather?
>It's much better for the animals' hooves to be spic and span.
>In another spot, a dining room [*cenatio*] rises, held up on columns of Numidian marble
>Deliberately placed to receive a bit of winter's sunshine.
>No matter how much the dwelling costs, there will be a man well trained in setting up
>   nice menus
>And [yet another] who specializes in making relishes.
>These 2,000 sesterces are enough and more than enough for "Quintilian"—nothing
>   less than what a father would spend for his son.[49]
>So how come the "Quintilian" has so many estates [*saltus*]?
>Don't dwell [too much] on [such] examples of special good luck. [...]

8

BUYING, BUILDING, IMPROVING, AND SELLING VILLAS

CATO

CICERO

PLINY THE YOUNGER

MARTIAL

The principle of *dominium* guided Roman property law, including ownership of villas and estates: some of its aspects are addressed in the texts below. In the context of rural property, and barring exceptional political or other circumstances, *dominium* was absolute ownership of land of any kind (taxed or untaxed), its boundary markers, fences, and buildings, the equipment attached to it including enslaved workers, any features of running or still water on the property, woods and coppices, tame and wild animals, and produce either extant or potential. Following the *Institutes* of Gaius (160s CE), which were based on earlier legal manuals, the enumeration of items was very often related to the management of villas and estates.[1] Jurists classed such things as ownable, tangible things (*res mancipi*) which could be bought, enjoyed, profited from, given away, sold, inherited, and bequeathed: some of the texts excerpted in this chapter are examples of these forms of ownership and conveyance.[2] *Res mancipi* could be sold: there were forms of direct sale (*mancipatio* and others), and villas could be acquired by other means (*traditio* or gifting, *usucapio* or presumption of possession over time, inheritance) leading to right of possession (*possessio*).[3] Villas and estates could also be given or leased in limited use (*usus*) or profit- or income-making usufruct (*usufructus*) without cession of ownership: their use, or their enjoyment and profit (especially produce) combined, could be allocated by their *domini* to others for monetary advantage (leasing), kindness, or other reasons, for a specified period or for a lifetime.[4] Unsurprisingly, disputes over usufruct of villas, estates, and enslaved persons were numerous and take up large amounts of space in Roman legal compendia, opinions, and hypothetical case studies.[5]

Ownership of villas and estates and their disposition (*res mancipi*) were subject to three types of limitations:

1. The right of general enjoyment by humans and animals of running or still water, air, and ocean, (called *res communes*). There were two public rights: those of public entities over roads, *ager publicus*, rural, riparian, maritime infrastructure, and the like (called *res publicae*) and, in towns and cities, those owned by the municipalities, such as streets, basilicas, and fire stations, (called *res universitatis*, and not much of an issue for villas). Another important limitation was the rights of things that no one owned: the seashore itself was an independent entity, and all things that were devoted to public religion were protected by gods, or were consecrated to private devotion, such as temples, tombs, boundary markers, and city walls (called *res nullius*).[6]

2. The second limitation on *res mancipi* were obligations generally defined as intangible (*res nec mancipi*) attached to the property itself: debts and liens, mortgages, tax obligations if relevant, private or public *alimenta* as previously set up, *usus* or usufruct arrangements under dispute, arrangements for inheritance or bequest, and current lawsuits about property.[7]

3. Land could be subject to servitudes (*servitus, servitudines*), which were arrangements agreed upon among owners or between owners and local authorities, or ordered by authorities, for rights to pasture animals, deviation and use of water, right-of-way across another's property, the seasonal right to cross others' properties for transhumance of pasturing herds, roads privately and/or jointly maintained, and other easements and restrictions.[8]

Buying and building were two separate operations in the two treatises that addressed the issues in practical ways: Cato's in the 150s BCE and Vitruvius's in ca. 27–22 BCE. Their approaches were quite different. Cato starts with the land itself, estimating its potential and its near neighbors and the equipment needed, including enslaved workers; he advises that the villa be built after the estate has proved itself profitable—the young owner should initially be a planter, not a builder.[9] What he says about actually building the residence from the ground up is short: it seems to be a memorandum to consider while negotiating with a contractor, giving minimal standards of construction and pricing to avoid getting cheated. In contrast, Vitruvius has a fair amount to say about urban *domus* but little to say about villas, and while construction methods and techniques are his real topic, he eschews much discussion about prices, land, or practical advice to villa owners.[10] Evidently he thought of villas as existing entities in the landscape not needing his professional attention or advice, only explanations of what was usual or needed or appropriate according to his principles of *decor*.

Varro, in the third book of his *De re rustica* (37–36 BCE), mentions that one of the protagonists in the discussion, Quintus Axius, had built a villa near Reate for himself (*Rust.* 3.2.3). In the group of villa owners, he is the only builder of a new villa: the other gentlemen assembled in the *Villa Publica* had either inherited their villas or bought them, making improvements either with decorative amenities (floors, wall painting), collections of works of art, or profit-making additions such as *piscinae* for fish farming.[11] Varro says nothing at all about actual construction, assuming, in the late first century BCE, that a landscape densely equipped with existing villas or villas for sale was the norm. He was right: in central Italy, the accretion of villas for elite habitation and other kinds of rural establishments was conspicuous in the close to 120 years between Cato and Varro.[12] Ninety to 100 years after Varro, Columella makes the same assumption: villas had become ubiquitous and the norm in the Italian countryside. At the elite level, owning more than one villa—profitable or not—came to be a norm as well.

Once built, villas had to be maintained, and at the elite level recorded in written texts, both absentee ownership and personnel were important issues. Cicero kept his eye on his brother Quintus's projects, and Pliny the Younger kept his eye on his father-in-law's property in Campania, while his father-in-law kept his eye on his son-in-law's properties at Comum: such friendly mutual monitoring was normal. Trustworthy, well-trained personnel was also needed, and in this chapter and elsewhere, texts about *vilici*, the *vilica*, other specialized enslaved workers or hired hands, tenants (*coloni*), and freedmen give an idea of how such maintenance was effected.[13]

Villas could be bequeathed, given, and sold: the texts in this book, especially in this chapter and in chapters 4 and 9 give some idea of these transactions, but with the exception of villas received in bequest or inheritance, little about sales is known.[14]

CATO (Marcus Porcius Cato, 234–149 BCE)

On Agriculture (*De agricultura*), 140s BCE (Cato, *Agr.*)

Cato's formula for building a new villa combines great detail (some seemingly irrelevant) with vague and cursory listing of what needs to be done. His method of projecting costs according to the size of the roofing tiles, presumably to give an approximate areal measurement of the building, is not helpful.

Cato, Agr. 14.1-5   If you plan a new villa to be built from scratch [*ab solo*], the builder [*faber*] should be required to do the following: All walls are to be built as [you have] ordered, of rubble [*caementum*] and mortar, masonry uprights of solid cut stone [*pilae ex lapide angulari*], [supply] all that's needed in the way of the lumber [*tigna*], thresholds [*limina*], posts [*postes*, door posts], crossbeams [*iugumenta*, lintels], beams [*asseres*], props [*fulmenta*], winter stalls and summer fodder feeders for cattle, a horse stall, rooms for slaves, 3 spaces for meat, a round [table?], 2 copper [cauldrons?], 10 coops, 1 hearth.

One major entrance-door [*ianua maxima*] and another as the owner wishes; for windows: 10 window grates for the bigger windows two *pedes* high [about 60 cm, or 2 ft.], 6 shutters.

3 benches, 5 stools, 2 wide looms, 1 small wheat mill, 1 tub for washing, doorframes, two presses.

That [the above list] are the building-materials in wood that the owner [*dominus*] will supply for the work and will send to the building site, as well as 1 saw and 1 plumb line. The builder [*conductor*] himself is to cut, work, true up, and smooth the timber. [The owner will supply] stone, lime, sand, water, straw, and clay earth [*terra unde lutum*, mortar dust].

If the villa is touched by lightning from the sky, a prayer about that event must be made.

For a good owner who supplies the materials that the work requires and pays in good faith, one *sestertius* per tile. The roof [*tectum*] is estimated as follows: each whole tile, [and] one of which is cut down by one quarter less than a whole [?], shall be reckoned as a whole counted as two, the cover tiles are reckoned as two, and the single tiles [*imbrices*, pantiles] as four.

For a villa of stone and mortar walls: the walls from their foundations should rise above ground by a *pes* [about 30 cm, or 1 ft.], with the rest in brick [mud brick?], and the lintels and door frames to be added according to the project. The rest of the villa [to be finished] in stone and mortar as specified. The cost per tile will be 1*HS*. The prices quoted are for an honest owner in a healthy location: the cost of labor will be reckoned on a [final] accounting. In an unhealthy location, where working in summertime cannot [easily] be done, the honest owner will add a 25% tip to the final bill.

The walls [of the enclosure are to be] of *caementum*, mortar, and gravel as supplied by the owner. It should be 5 *pedes* high [about 1.5 m, or 4 ft., 10 in.] with a 1 *pes* top, 1½ *pedes* [about 45 cm, or 18 in.] thick, 14 *pedes* [about 4.5 m, or 14 ft., 9 in.] long; the plaster coating should be subcontracted. If he subcontracts the walls of the villa [for plastering] by units of 100 *pedes*, that is 10 *pedes* on both sides, [he should] reckon 5 *libellae* [1/2*HS*] per *pedes* and 10 *victoriati* [1 1/4*HS*] per a perch rod measuring 1 *pes* by 10. The owner will build the foundation wall 1½ *pes* thick [about 45 cm, or 1 ft., 6 in.] and supply one *modius* [about 8.7 liters, or 2 gal.] of lime and two *modii* [about 17.5 liters, or 4 gal.] of sand per foot.

Cato, Agr. 128   To plaster [the walls] of the dwelling: Very chalky or clayey earth, pour in *amurca*, add chopped straw. Let it steep for four days, then, when well steeped, remix with a spade. When it is smooth, plaster [*deluta*]. In this way, damp will not affect [the walls], mice will not tunnel into them, weeds will not grow, and cracks will not appear in the plaster.

CICERO   (Marcus Tullius Cicero, 107/106–43 BCE)

Letters to Atticus (Epistulae ad Atticum) (Cic., Att.)

Atticus, having returned from a long residence at Athens and at his villa Amalthea near Buthrotum in Epirus, is looking to buy a villa at Antium where his friend had a villa.

Cic., *Att.* 79.1–2 (4.8.1–2), May 56 BCE   [...] I find nothing in the way of a house in the countryside [*in agris*] for you. There's something quite close to me, but it's in town, and it's doubtful that it's for sale. This I know: Antium is the Roman Buthrotum, and exactly what Corcyra is to your Buthrotum.[15] There is nowhere more tranquil, nowhere more agreeable: here is my own dear home. [...]

Since Tyrannion has put my books in order, an understanding mind [*mens*] seems to have appeared in my house, and your [slaves] Dionysius and Menophilus were helpful in their wonderful tasks.[16] Nothing is nicer than the bookcases after the books have been classified with their titles [*syllabi*]. [...]

Letters to His Brother Quintus (Epistulae ad Quintum fratrem) (Cic. QFr.)

While his brother was on official business in Sardinia, Cicero was left in charge of the construction of his and his brother's domus in Rome as well as Quintus's villas near Arpinum.

Cic., *QFr.* 8.2–3 (2.4.2–3), March 56 BCE   [...] Your son Quintus [Minor], a very good boy, is being taught in an excellent way, and I have an even better perception [of his instruction] because Tyrannion is giving the lessons at my house. The houses that are being built for us are going well, and I've made sure that your contractor [*redemptor*] has been paid half his fee. I hope that we will be living side-by-side [*contubernales*] before the winter.[17]

Cicero writes to his brother, still in Sardinia, about family and political matters, but mentions their Roman houses, houses in their hometown of Arpinum, and some villas under construction. Cicero's consulship (63 BCE), return from exile (May 58–August 57 BCE), and an attempt to restore his political prominence obliged him to live in an expansive way. Evidently his brother commented on this, which Cicero explains as a new duty, without specifying which of his villas he is referring to, but one of them may have been his villa at Cumae.

Cic., *QFr.* 9.3 (2.5.3), April 11, 56 BCE   [...] Now about what you tend to call [my] hand-over-fist extravagance [ἀμφιλαφία],[18] I like it a lot but in a good way, in the way that I patiently await [while hunting] an incoming but still-hidden prey, without arousing it. That said, I am building in three places and renovating the others [*tribus locis aedifico reliqua reconcinno*]: I am living somewhat more amply than has been my habit, but it's been my duty to do so. Were we together, I would give the builders a little more leeway. But I hope that soon we'll be able to share some opinions on this matter. [...]

Cic., *QFr.* 10.3 (2.6.3), April 9, 56 BCE   [...] After I left your son [Quintus Minor], I went to see your construction site [*area*]. The work is going ahead with many workmen [*structores*], and I told Longilius, the contractor [*redemptor*], to get a move on, and he promised me that he would give us something that would please [you]. It will be a great house [*domus egregia*], and we can now see more clearly what it will be than when we looked over the first plan [*forma*]. My house is going up quickly as well.[19] [...]

[...] I am writing this letter before dawn on the second day before the ides of April [April 11] and will soon be on my way: I'll stay at Titus Titius's place at Anagnia, but the day after I plan to be at Laterium, then spend five days at Arpinum, then go to my villa at Pompeii, then go to see my villa at Cumae on my way back to Rome, to be there on the nones of May.[20] [...]

Cicero's brother Quintus, now on military service with Julius Caesar in Gaul and Britain, had left his brother in charge of five villas near their hometown at Arpinum and a *domus* in Rome. In this letter, Cicero interrupts his news of political and legal events in Rome to inform about projects at three of his brother's villas and estates and his house in the City. The five villas were on an estate called Arcanum, another called Manilian, an estate bought by Cicero on behalf of his brother (the Fufidian estate), a Bobilius(?) estate, and an estate and villa called Laterium; the projects included construction and finishing, water supply, installation of sculpture, and landscaping.[21] The Bobilius estate had legal problems with its water supply but could be sold or kept for pleasure.

Elsewhere in the letter, Cicero mentions buying a villa in the suburbs of Rome for his brother as well as rebuilding of his own house on the Palatine that had been dismantled when he was in exile.

Cic. *QFr.* 21.1–6 (3.1), September 54 BCE   After the hot weather—in fact, I do not recall any hotter—I have been restoring myself at Arpinum with the pleasant aspect of the river during the days of the Games, having put the members of our tribe in the care of Philotimus.[22]

I was at Arcanum on the fourth day before the ides of September [September 10], and Mescidius and Philoxenus were working on the water supply [*aqua*], which they are channeling to a spot not far from the villa. Despite the current great dry spell, I saw that the water was flowing really well, and they told me that they were about to arrange for an even more abundant flow. All is well at Herius's place.[23]

At the Manilian estate, I bumped into Diphilus wasting more time than even Diphilus himself is [usually] capable of![24] Still, there is nothing left for him to do except the bath buildings [*balnearia*], a walkway [*ambulatio*], and the aviary [*aviarium*]. The villa is really very pleasing: the paved portico [*porticus*] has a great presence [*dignitas*], something that was noticeable to me only just now since the whole portico is presently set out and the [surfaces of the] columns have been polished [*columnae politae*].[25] The main thing is for the plastering [*tectorium*] be done properly—I'll watch to see how it's going. The floors were being correctly laid. There were some vaulted ceilings [*camerae*] that I did not like, so I ordered them to be modified.

Now about the location in the portico for a small entrance hall [*atriolum*, small atrium]—the location that, they say, you wrote out in some instructions—I think it [the portico] is better as is. That's because there isn't enough space for even such a small entrance hall, and besides, such entrance halls are not customarily built except in buildings that have a large atrium. Also, the small entrance hall could not have bedrooms or similar rooms attached to it. As the portico is now, its dignified covering [*honesta testudo*] will make it usable as a good room in the summer, but if you think otherwise, write me on the matter as soon as you can.

In the bath buildings [*balnearia*], I had the [hot-water] stove [*assus*] moved to the other corner of the *apodyterium* because it was positioned in such a way that its steam pipe, from which flames can erupt, was right under the bedrooms. I very much like that fairly large bedroom and the other one with a high ceiling for use in the winter: both were large and placed to the side of the walkway [*ambulatio*] where the bath buildings are. Diphilus placed the columns so they are neither straight nor aligned, so clearly he will have to dismantle them. Someday he will learn to use a plumb line and a measuring rod. Anyway, I hope that Diphilus's work will be finished in a few months—Caesius, who was with me, is watching his work very carefully.[26]

From there [the Manilian estate], I went straight along the Via Vitularia to your Fufidian estate, the one that I bought for you from Fufidius on the last market days [*nundinae*] at Arpinum for 101,000*HS*.[27] I've never seen a shadier spot in the summertime anywhere else, with water flowing freely from many places and plenty of it. What else would you want? Caesius considered there would be no trouble for you to irrigate 50 *iugera* [about 12.5 ha, or 33 acres] of meadow. On this property, I can truly say—and it's something I know more about than many [other people]—that you will have a lovely villa to live in, if a fishpond and a water channel can be added, as well as a *palaestra* and a nicely staked vineyard.

I now hear that you want to keep the Bobilius [?] estate, but you'll have to decide what exactly is to be done about it.[28] Caesius has asserted that, with the [estate's] water supply blocked, were a perpetual contract [*servitus* for water-rights] on that [neighboring] estate established, we could still get its purchase price back if we wanted to sell it. I had Mescidius with me, and he said that he made a deal with you for 3 sesterces per foot [*pes*, for a channel or aqueduct] and claimed he had paced it out at 3,000 *passus*.²⁹ It looked more than that to me, but I'll tell you truly: you couldn't invest your money better on anything else. [To do the work] I had called Cillo to come from Venafrum, but four of his fellow slaves and apprentices had been injured [working] in a tunnel.

On the ides of September [September 13], I arrived at Laterium. I looked over the road, which pleased me so much that I thought it was a public works project [*opus publicum*] except for some 150 paces [about 222 m = 728 ft.] of it: I paced off the distance myself, from the little bridge near the shrine of Furrina, walking toward Satricum.³⁰ Just there, there was dusty earth rather than tamped gravel [*glarea iniecta*], so it will have to be changed. That stretch of the road is very steep, but I understand it couldn't be graded to another slope, especially because you did not want to route it either through Lucusta's or Varro's property.³¹ In front of his own estate and alongside it, Varro has seen to the roadbed, but Lucusta has not, so I will take him up on the matter in Rome and, I think, will prompt him [to do something]. At the same time, I will speak to Marcus Taurus, who is now in Rome, and ask him about the promise he made to you—as far I have been led to believe—on the subject of channeling water [to your property] through his estate.

I much approve of Niecephorus, your *villicus*. I asked him if you had sent anything to him about the little building [*aedificatiuncula*] at Laterium—the one [you] mentioned to me. He then answered that he himself would be the contractor for the building at a cost of 16,000*HS* but that you had made many additions to the project without adding any payment for them, so he stopped working on it. Truly [*mehercule*], it makes me happy that you want to have these additions as you had planned, but as it stands, the villa has a rather "philosophical" look [*tamquam philosopha*], one that scolds the crazy extravagance of other villas [*ceterarum villarum insania*]. With what you want to add, it will be lovely. I praised your gardener: he has dressed ivy over everything, not only the foundations of the villa but also the spaces between the columns in the walkway—it seemed as if the *pallium* wearers [statues] were the gardeners and were meaning to sell their ivy!³² Just now, the *apodyterium* is the coolest room, and it's covered with moss.

That's it for what's going on in the country. Philotimus and Cincius are getting on with the embellishment of your town house [*urbanae expolitio*], but I go and see them quite often—it's easy for me to do, and I wish you to be free from worry on these matters.³³ [...]

Cicero is reporting on family affairs and construction for the brothers' houses in Rome; Quintus's villas at Arpinum are finished except for water and road-access problems already noted in a previous letter (Cic., *QFr.* 21.4).

Cic., *QFr.* 23.1 (3.3.1), October 21, 54 BCE   [...] Our affairs [*negotia nostra*] are in this state, with the domestic ones as we want them to be. The boys are well, learning attentively and being taught in a meticulous way. The final embellishments [*expolitiones*] of both our houses are in hand, but the work on your villas at Arcanum and Laterium is already finished. I wrote to you a while back in a letter about the water and the road [at Laterium] in some detail and leaving nothing out.... [...]

Quintus, still in Gaul, is urged by his brother to buy a suburban villa, perhaps as much as a backdrop to a political career as for relaxation in the country, but close to the City.³⁴

Cic., *QFr.* 24.5 (3.4.5), October 24, 54 BCE   [...] On [buying] a suburban villa, I admire you for not being in a hurry to do so, but I do urge you to buy one. [...]

Cic., QFr. 27.4 (3.7.4), December 54 BCE   The campaigns of Caesar in Gaul and Britain resulted in drafts of newly enslaved persons for sale or gift; Quintus, as an army commander, was in a good position to acquire them and offer some to his brother, who thanks him. In these portions of his letter to his brother, Cicero returns to the construction of Quintus's Manilian estate, then again to the Arcanum estate.

Cic., QFr. 27.4 (3.7.4)   On the slaves [*mancipia*] that you've promised me, I thank you: as you say, I lack slaves both in Rome and on my estates [*praedia*]. But please, dear brother, don't even think of doing something for my benefit unless it is at your complete convenience and entirely easy for you to do.

Cic., QFr. 27.7 (3.7.7)   Take the building down? Every day it pleases me more: the lower portico and its adjacent rooms [*conclavia*] are being built in a fine way. As for the Arcanum [villa], we really very much [*mehercule*] need Caesar's sense of these things [*Caesaris opus est*] or that of others in things even more elegant [(*res*) *elegantiores*].[35] Your busts [*imagines istae*], the *palaestra*, the fish pool, and the *Nile* would have been better off with many of those that Philotimus [would have supplied] rather than any at all [supplied] by that Diphilus![36]

Letters to Friends (Epistulae ad familiares) (Cic., *Fam.*), to Publius Cornelius Lentulus Spinther[37] (in Cilicia), from Rome, December 54 BCE

The Mediterranean-wide commerce in property and multiple ownership of villas and estates is illustrated here. In a letter having to do with important matters of state and high politics, Cicero asks his friend Lentulus, at the time governor of Cilicia, for help in securing a property at Arpinum adjacent to his brother Quintus's estate; the property was owned by an owner living in Cilicia.

Cic., Fam. 20.24 (1.9.24)   [...] Concerning my brother Quintus's business, you write that, having fallen ill last summer, you could not go into Cilicia to complete the deal but that now you will soon see to its completion. I know that, in this matter, my brother considers that, if the property can be added to his [existing estate], it is by your intervention that his inheritance has been consolidated.

Letters to Atticus, July 51 BCE

Cicero, on his way to taking up the proconsular governorship of Cilicia in Asia Minor, has left Atticus in charge of his affairs. He writes about some construction at one of his villas, probably that at Tusculum.

Cic., Att. 105.3 (5.12.3)   [...] Since you are staying in Rome, look after my affairs carefully, please. Also, on a matter that I forgot to mention when I wrote: on the bricks [*strues laterum*] and the aqueduct [*aqua*], please do what can be done, as you usually do with your good nature. [...]

Letters to Friends, to Quintus Minucius Thermus,[38] governor of Asia, winter 51 BCE

Cicero wrote many letters of recommendation and introduction for friends, young acquaintances, and business associates. This letter was written by Cicero as governor (propraetor) of Cilicia to his colleague Minucius, governor of the neighboring province of Asia, to recommend

Marcus Cluvius, a banker at Puteoli.[39] The rest of the letter lists several cities in the province of Asia that owed money to Cluvius as well as individuals who held his mortgage bonds, and Cicero requests Minucius's help in closing the accounts. When Cluvius died in 45 BCE, Cicero was one of his heirs, a bequest that included a villa and property at Puteoli (which Cicero calls his *Cluviana* or *Puteolana*, and even his *Academia*), in gratitude to the well-connected statesman for his help on this and other matters.[40]

Cic., *Fam.* 131.1 (13.56.1)   Cluvius of Puteoli greatly respects me and is a great friend of mine. He has convinced himself that the businesses [*negotia*] he has in your province must be counted as lost and in desperate straits unless, while you are in charge of your province, he will have been able to get a recommendation from me.

Letters to Atticus

Gifts of land, villas with estates, gardens, and other property were often offered as inducements to individuals for political support. Another ploy was favorable bidding on confiscated property during the proscriptions or in consequence of legal judgments. Here, Cicero notes that Pompey had attempted to secure the loyalty of Lucius Cornelius Balbus, a rich, politically adroit man of Hispanic origins and equestrian rank by a gift of land.[41] Cicero is forwarding Atticus a copy of a letter from Balbus. To me, sarcasm seems intended.

Cic., *Att.* 180.8 (9.13.8), March 24, 49 BCE   [...] ... but I have received a letter from Balbus of which I have sent you a copy. I beg you to read it and especially the good Balbus's remark at the end—[is this the same] Balbus to whom our friend Pompey gave a place to build for his estate [*horti*] and whom he most often favored over us?

Cicero, having taken refuge in his villa at Formiae to avoid extreme danger as Caesar was advancing on Rome, has information about villas for sale and is still interested. Here, he speculates on a property at Lanuvium (near Tusculum) and compares it to what its value was seven years before, noting that recent financial problems and the precarity of the political situation had depressed prices.[42]

Cic., *Att.* 176.4 (9.9.4), March 17, 49 BCE   [...] Now about the Lanuvium property, as soon as I heard of Phamea's death, I very much wished for one of my friends to buy it, [at least] as long as there is a future for this Republic, but I didn't think of you, my greatest friend.[43] I know that it is your principle to ask "in what year?" and "how much on its own [revenue]?" would [a property] return its purchase price—I've seen your account books both for Rome and Delos. Anyway, it's true that, no matter how nice the property is, I value it [now] lower than what I had estimated its value during the consulship of Marcellinus.[44] At that time, because of owning my villa at Antium, I thought that the little gardens at the [Lanuvium] property would please me more and cost less than what I was spending on fixing up my Tusculanum villa. I priced the place at half a million sesterces. I offered that amount for the property when it was for sale, but he refused my offer. Now, I imagine that all such properties have fallen in price because of the [general] lack of ready money [*caritas nummorum*]. It would be very convenient to me—or, rather, to us—if you were to buy it. Beware of being disdainful of the previous owner's crazy ways: the property is really lovely. However, all such encumbered places seem doomed to ruin, in my view. [...]

Cic., *Att.* 180.6 (9.13.6), March 24, 49 BCE [...] I made a mistake about Phamea's estate at Lanuvium—I was dreaming about a Trojan estate.[45] I had wanted it for half a million sesterces, but the asking price is more than that. Even so, I would have wished you to buy the other one on my behalf, if I could see that there was any hope of my enjoying it. [...]

One way of acquiring property, including desirable villas, was to be the beneficiary of political confiscations during proscriptions, either as direct gifts or by being permitted to bid at forced auctions for below-market prices. Cicero reminds Atticus that the Pompeians and Caesarians were alike in anticipating the spoils of political partisanship for property.

Cic., *Att.* 217.6 (11.6.6), November 27, 48 BCE [...] It's a fact that Lucius Lentulus at one time assigned Hortensius's house [in Rome] to himself [as a reward] as well as Caesar's gardens [on the right bank of the Tiber or those on the Esquiline] and a villa at Baiae.[46]

Letters to Friends, **to Lucius Papirius Paetus,**[47] **October 46 BCE**

Cicero, who already owned villas on the bay at Cumae, at Puteoli, and at Pompeii (besides the ones at Arpinum, Tusculum, Formiae, Antium, Caieta, and Astura) is thinking of purchasing something in the Neapolitan region.

Cic., *Fam.* 196.3 (9.15.3) [...] As to what you write in your other letter to justify that you had not advised me not to buy a place [villa or house] in the Neapolitan region but that you were only urging caution in the matter, that was clear, and I took it in no other way. [...]

Letters to Friends, **to Lucius Papirius Paetus, September 46 BCE**
Many real estate opportunities came Cicero's way.

Cic., *Fam.* 190.10 (9.16.10) [...] On Selicius's villa, you have undertaken the matter very carefully and written wittily about it. I think that I will pass on the property. I have enough salt [*salis*]—it's the salt cellars [*salina*] that I lack.[48] [...]

Letters to Atticus, **July 30, 45 BCE**

Cic., *Att.* 352.1 (13.47a.2) Yesterday, in the evening, Lepidus sent me a letter from Antium, which is where he is now as he has a house there that I sold him. [...]

Letters to Friends, **to Tiro,**[49] **December 45 BCE**

Tiro, Cicero's highly educated freedman who worked as his secretary and ultimately his literary executor, suffered from poor health, which required that he spend some time at the villa at Tusculum; Cicero lists some health-improving villa occupations in a very jocular way as well as some improvements in the garden and water supply, ongoing issues raised also in Cic., *Att.* 310.1 (13.6.1).

Cic., *Fam.* 219.1–3 (16.18.1–3) [...] I am happy that your sweatings [διαφόρησεις] have worked well, and if the villa at Tusculum has also worked well [for you], by god how much more pleasant it will be to me! But, as you love me—and on this matter, either you do so or you do such a good job seeming to do so, and you do a good job in the task [of seeming to do so]. Anyway, take care of your health, because up to now, in the business of serving me, you haven't ministered to it enough. What it requires, you are not ignorant of: digestion, rest, walking in moderation, bodily enjoyment, and easy defecations.[50] Come back in a good state. It would make me love you more—not just you, but my villa at Tusculum as well.

Wake that Parhedrus up so he decides on the lease on the garden for himself—in doing so, you'll stir up the [present] gardener. That good-for-nothing Helico paid 1,000*HS* when there was no sunny part in the garden [*apricus hortus*], no water channel [*emissarium*], no walled enclosure [*maceria*], no lock-up shed [*casa*].[51] Is the [current] gardener to make fun of me at my expense after such outlay? Put some fire under that man [Parhedrus], as I do with Motho so I get a good quantity of flowers [flower wreaths?] from him.[52]

On the Crabra aqueduct, even though just now the [amount of] water is enough, I would still like to know [more] about what is being done.[53] I will send you a sundial and some books if the weather stays dry. And you—don't you have some little books [*libelli*] to read? Or are you composing something Sophoclean?[54] We'll see what work you've produced. [...]

Letters to Friends, from Cicero's son (Marcus Tullius Cicero Minor),[55] to Tiro, September, 44 BCE
Cicero's son, while attending lectures in rhetoric and philosophy at Athens at the age of 19 to 20, missed Tiro, his father's secretary-freedman, who had had a part in his earlier education. His letter, replying to one from Tiro, details his studies and sends his affectionate regards. As Tiro had recently bought a property (perhaps in some co-ownership deal with the family) complete with a *vilicus* and the rest of a villa owner's panoply, Tullius congratulates him condescendingly on his new status, as would have been appropriate for a *patronus*, no matter how young, to a client who had been his father's formerly enslaved secretary.

Cic., *Fam.* 337.7 (16.21.7)   [...] Your concern for me and your advice are very welcome and are well-received by me, and I am aware that your time is limited as I also know how busy you usually are.

I'm happy that you've bought an estate, and I hope that your purchase will be a happy one. Don't be surprised that I congratulate you [on your purchase] in this place [at the end of my letter]—you did the same in the letter you wrote letting me know.

You've finally got it [*habes*]! Now your citified manners [*urbanitates*] must be shed: you've become a true Roman countryman [*rusticus*]! Even now a very pleasant picture of you comes to my eyes! I seem to see you buying farm tools, conferring with your *villicus*, and secretly putting grape pips [*semina*] in a fold of your garment [*in lacinia*] after dessert [*mensa secunda*].[56] On the business part of the matter, I am as sorry as you are that I was neglectful when it happened. However, never doubt, my dear Tiro, that I am always here to support you, if my own luck holds. I am aware that the estate was purchased jointly [*fundus communis*] with us. [...]

Letters to Atticus

Cicero learned, a little late, from a messenger (one Pollex, not from his agent Vestorius) about a bequest from his banker friend, Marcus Cluvius, whom he had helped in 51 BCE by writing to the governor of Asia on financial matters: see above, Cic., *Fam.* 131.1 (13.56.1). Cluvius died in the summer of 45 BCE. His bequest was a sum of money to Cicero, another sum to Terentia (Cicero's former wife), some other commercial or residential buildings, and a maritime villa near Puteoli, which Cicero called his *Cluviana* or *Puteolana*. Cicero was one of several co-heirs with Julius Caesar and others, and ultimately he bought out his co-beneficiaries in installments so he could keep the villa for himself, which he is said to have called *Academia*. It was at the *Cluviana* or *Puteolana* that he received Caesar on December 21 later that year.

Cicero also was the beneficiary of commercial (*tabernae*, shops) and rental properties at Puteoli. They were in bad condition—even falling down—but brought income between 80,000*HS* and 100,000*HS*. They are mentioned in several letters not included here: Cic., *Att.* 363.1 (14.9.1, April 17, 44 BCE); *Att.* 364.3 (14.10.3, April 19, 44 BCE); *Att.* 365 (14.11.2, April 21, 44 BCE); *Att.* 365 (14.11.2, April 21, 44 BCE); later, in still more dangerous circumstances, he is still thinking about Cluvius's bequest: *Att.* 409.5 (16.1.5), July 8, 44 BCE.

Cicero appears to have been a bad landlord: in one, he thanks "Socrates and Socratics" for giving him the correct philosophical indifference to "such matters," namely the suffering of his tenants when some buildings collapsed (*Att.* 363 [14.9]).

Cic., *Att.* 338.3 (13.46.3), August 12, 45 BCE   [...] That Vestorius is so negligent![57] I learned tardily [and not from him but] from Pollex what the terms were to accept Cluvius's bequest [*cretio*], namely voluntary acceptance before witnesses within sixty days.[58] I was afraid that I would have to have him [Vestorius?] brought to me, but now I [only] have to send someone with instructions from me, namely Pollex. In addition, I discussed Cluvius's estate with Balbus.[59] He could not have been more gracious and said he would write to Caesar right away; also, [he told me] that Cluvius left Terentia 50,000*HS* and provision for his own tomb and other things, to be taken from the bequest made to Titus Hordeonius, nothing from my share.[60] Please scold Vestorius, but do so mildly. [...]

Quintus, Cicero's brother, had recently divorced his wife Pomponia (Atticus's sister) intending to marry a wealthy woman named Aquilia; there must have been a rumor that Quintus wanted to install her in a nice villa in a fashionable location. Quintus's son (of the same name) was hostile to his father's possible new union.

Cic., *Att.* 367.1 and 367.5 (14.13.1 and 14.13.5), April 26, 44 BCE   It took seven days for your letter of the thirteen days before the kalends of May [April 19] to be delivered to me. You ask me in your letter—as if you think that I would not know myself—which I find more delightful: a view of mountains or a walk on the shore? By Hercules [*mehercule*], both are equally so pleasant that I doubt which to prefer over the other.[61] [...]

Now back to your letter. You write that there are rumors that the villa by the lake which I own is to be sold and that my little villa [*minuscula villa*] will be transferred to Quintus for some unheard-of price so that, as the young Quintus claims, Aquilia the heiress may be accommodated there.[62]

Really, I have had no thought on selling the villa unless I come upon something that pleases me better. Quintus himself is not thinking of purchasing just now...[and] says that nothing more than a one-person bed could be better for him. [...]

Villas could be venues for hospitality and places to stay over when traveling, but they could also be made available to friends, or leased to customers or clients, for longer residence. In this case, Cicero has made his Baiae villa near the Lucrine lake available to Pilia, Atticus's wife; he is transferring his household and himself to Puteoli or Pompeii. Several letters mention this transfer. The full series of letters was written over a seven-day period; those omitted here are Cic., *Att.* 369.3 (14.15.3, May 1, 44 BCE); *Att.* 371.1 (14.17.1, May 4, 44 BCE); *Att.* 372.6 (14.19.6, May 7, 44 BCE); *Att.* 372.6 (14.19.6, May 8, 44 BCE).

It is possible that by early May 44 BCE, when these arrangements were made, Cicero was thinking of the inevitable troubles that would follow—were already following—Caesar's assassination in March six weeks earlier. He may even have already been contemplating leaving Italy but, in case of trouble, was securing his properties by loaning them to close friends, in this case his best friend's wife Pilia.

Cic., *Att.* 370.1 (14.16.1), May 3, 44 BCE   On the fifth day before the nones [May 3], I am sending this letter as I leave in an oar-equipped skiff from the gardens of my Cluviana villa, after I transferred my villa near the Lucrine lake to our dear Pilia together with its slave overseers [*vilici*] and managers [*procuratores*].⁶³ For myself, I am threatening our friend Paetus with his cheese-and-salt-fish hospitality for the same day, then in a few days will sail back to my estates [*regna*] in Puteoli and Cumae. What pleasant places to spend time in, if one did not have to flee them because of the crowd of petitioners!⁶⁴ [...]

Cicero, on the eve of an aborted departure from southern Italy to join the forces of Caesar's assassins, Brutus and Cassius, in Greece, regrets leaving his friend and his "little villas" but is sufficiently confident of success and return to ask Atticus to attend to affairs of his Cluviana properties and the villa at Puteoli as well as paying off his obligation to repay his ex-wife Terentia's dowry.

Cic., *Att.* 414.2 (16.6.2), July 25, 44 BCE   [...] Why am I not with you? Why can I not see my little villas [*villulae meae*], my darlings of Italy [*ocelli Italiae*]? [...]

Cic., *Att.* 414.3 (16.6.3)   [...] "For god's sake, pay my debts and put them in order. There is a good amount remaining [in my account]. Be especially careful that the debt to my co-heirs for the Cluviana properties be paid on the first of August.⁶⁵ [...]

PLINY THE YOUNGER   (Gaius Plinius Caecilius Secundus, 61–113 CE)

Letters (Epistulae) (Plin., *Ep.*)

Letter to his friend Baebius Hispanus⁶⁶
Gaius Suetonius Tranquillus, the historian who wrote *The Lives of the Twelve Caesars* and much else, was Pliny's friend to whom he addressed three letters and mentioned several times; they shared a devotion to literary pursuits.⁶⁷ Pliny is writing to a friend to see if a villa and estate can be found for Suetonius. Its tone is sincere but exhibits some condescension toward Suetonius.

Plin., *Ep.* 1.24.1–4   My friend Tranquillus [Suetonius] wants to buy an estate, one which a friend of yours wishes to sell. I ask you to ensure that it is sold for a fair price so that he can take pleasure in his purchase. A bad bargain is never welcome, especially as it seems to reproach the buyer for his gullibility. In addition, if the price is right, there are many features to this property that stimulate my friend Tranquillus's interest: it is near Rome and on a good road, the villa is unpretentious, and there is land enough to divert him without distracting him [from his work]. Scholars like Tranquillus who then become owners of estates do not need more land than is necessary to clear their minds, refocus, and tread their property's single pathway to get to know each vine and every little bush.

  I am telling you this so you may know the extent to which he will be grateful to me, and me to you, if he is able to buy this little property with all its fine features at a good price without buyer's remorse. Farewell.

Letter to his friend Julius Valerianus⁶⁸
Plin., *Ep.* 2.15.1–2   How is it going at your old Marsian estate?⁶⁹ And what about your new acquisition? Are you happy with the new estate [*agri*] after you've made it yours? It is a rare feeling: once acquired, nothing is as pleasing as it used to be when it was not yet purchased. My mother's estate [*praedia materna*] is somewhat abusing me, but I still love it for having been my

mother's. Anyway, my long-standing patience has made me tough. Continual whining [*adsiduae querellae*] ends from the shame of whining itself. Farewell.

Letter to his agent Verus
Romans of Pliny's social class were expected to pay dutiful respect and support to enslaved domestic servants whom they had known in their youth and who had attended to their family: a nurse or *nutrix* might figure importantly in the *familia* throughout her life and for several generations of her owners. Pliny appears to have assigned the income or usufruct of a small estate (not the estate itself) to his old nurse, and he is writing to its estate manager on this matter.

Plin., *Ep.* **6.3.1–2** I am grateful that you have taken up the management of the small estate that I gave my nurse [*nutrix*]. When I gave it, it was worth 100,000*HS* but subsequently its revenue fell and its value has gone down, but with you in charge it will come back. In these matters, remember that I have committed not merely the trees and the land to your care: I've committed my little gift as well, that it be no less profitable for she who is the object of my gift, as [it has been] to me who gives it. Farewell.

Letter to Calpurnius Fabatus of Comum, his wife's grandfather[70]
Calpurnius Fabatus was the grandfather of Calpurnia, Pliny's third wife. As he lived at Comum, he looked after Pliny's villas and estates there. Pliny reciprocates with a report on a villa in Campania owned by Calpurnius. Pliny gives some report on its poor condition and who might be delegated to take care of it.

Plin., *Ep.* **6.30.1–5** By Hercules, I must celebrate your birthday as if it were my own because my contentment depends on you: by your diligence and care, I can be happy and secure here and do not worry about what happens there.

The villa Camilliana that you own in Campania is decidedly run down due to age, but the more important parts are either still intact or have suffered very little damage, so I am looking after it and will have it repaired as best as can be.

I have thought about my many friends, but I find no one who is the person you are looking for or who could do the work: my friends are all wearers of the toga and city slicker types [*togati et urbani*]. The management of country properties requires a strong man of the soil [*durus aliquis et agrestis*] for whom the work will not be too hard or who would not be unhappy at being isolated. It is very good that you are considering Rufus—he was your son's friend. However, I am not sure of what he might do for us [at your villa], but I think he wants to do as best he can.

MARTIAL (Marcus Valerius Martialis, ca. 38/41–102/104 CE)

Epigrams (*Epigrammata*) (Mart., *Epig.*),

Epigram to Domitian
The emperor Domitian gave Martial the usufruct of a villa and a small house in Rome. The villa came with an irrigating device for the poet's gardens in the country, but he asks for a connection to the Aqua Marcia for his *domus* in the City.[71]

Mart., *Epig.* 9.18
I have—and I pray to continue to enjoy, with your favor, Caesar—
A very small country place [*rus minimum*], as well as a little home in the City [*in urbe parvi lares*].
But [for the villa in the country], with much work, a curved screw pump [*curva antlia*] brings
water to my thirsty gardens from a small valley.[72]

My house in town is bone dry [*sicca domus*] and complains that it has had no water,
Even though the nearby Marcia gurgles within my earshot.[73]
Were you to grant water to my home [*penates*], Augustus,
It will be like the Castalian spring for me, or like showers [providentially] sent by Jupiter.[74]

Epigram to Stella
The poet needs something to wear, perhaps a new toga, not just building material for his villa. The poem is addressed to his patron Lucius Arruntius Stella.[75]

Mart., *Epig*. 7.36
When my villa could not withstand Jupiter's sodden sky and rains,
And was overwhelmed by winter floods,
You sent me a present of enough roof tiles [*tegulae*] to hold off any sudden showers.
Listen how dreadful December resounds with the screaming north wind [*Boreas*]!
But Stella: you covered my villa, but you didn't cover the farmer [send me something to wear]!

Pliny the Younger, *Panegyric on the Emperor Trajan* (*Panegyricus Plinii Secundi dictus Traiano Imp.*), delivered in the Senate, 100 CE (Plin., *Pan.*)

Pliny's speech honoring the new emperor Trajan (r. 98–117 CE) was motivated as much by his bad experience in the reign of Domitian (r. 81–96 CE) as his delight in the new regime. Domitian's confiscations of the property of political foes had included houses and villas; by contrast, Trajan is liberal in making such properties newly available and putting suburban villas or gardens in imperial ownership near Rome up for sale to private buyers.

Plin., *Pan*. 50.5–6 [...] At that time [under Domitian], it was fatal for any of his entourage to have a large house or a nice villa [*laxior domus . . . amoenior villa*]. Now, our prince [Trajan] seeks out for owners for such places and makes them known [to them] himself. We can even make offers on, buy, and live in the suburban gardens of a famous general [*magni imperatoris horti*] that had always belonged to the Caesars. [...]

Afterword: Cicero's Efforts to Purchase *Horti*

Between mid-March and July 27 of 45 BCE, Cicero wrote many letters to Atticus about his plan to found a garden as a monument to honor his deceased daughter Tullia. He was also considering possibilities of a villa for his old-age retirement and his own tomb. The extensive correspondence is summarized here.

Having finished his treatise on rhetoric, *De oratore*, in January 45 BCE, Cicero remained at Rome to await the birth of a grandchild: Cic., *Fam*. 218.5 (6.18.5). The death of his daughter Tullia (78–45 BCE) in childbirth in February, some months after her divorce from Publius Cornelius Dolabella late in the preceding year, was an important event in Cicero's emotional life.[76] The child was saved but died some months later.

Cicero retired, alone, to Atticus's villa at Nomentum, then to his own at Astura on the coast: Cic., *Fam*. 249.2–3 (4.6.2–3); he praises the loveliness of the location while lamenting his loneliness. For more than a year, in the troubled times before and after Caesar's assassination in March 44 BCE, Cicero began to plan a monument (*fanum*) to Tullia and even a villa for his retirement and old age, possibly also his own tomb. From mid-March to July 27 of 45 BCE, Cicero's letters to Atticus from the Astura villa about buying gardens on the right bank of the Tiber average one every third or fourth day, and daily letters are not uncommon.[77]

At first, he thought the *fanum Tulliae* could be at his Astura estate, but then decided that the place was too isolated. He wanted the *fanum* to be consecrated (*consecratus*), easily accessed (*celeber*), have *horti* around it, and be finished by the summer of that year: Cic., *Att.* 233.1 (12.19.1). The island at Arpinum was possible for a real consecration (ἀποθέωσις) but was too far away (ἐκτοπισμός), which would result in loss of honor (τιμή): *Att.* 258.2 (12.20.2); *Att.* 259.1 (12.12.1).[78] By March 17, he had decided on *horti* just outside the City, across the Tiber River in the *Transtiberim* or on the Janiculum Hill: *Att.* 260.2 (12.21.2). Money was short, but he had the *horti* of several individuals in mind: *Att.* 261.3 (12.22.3) and *Att.* 262.3 (12.23.3). A friend offered him a site in Ostia. For a Janiculum Hill location, he was prepared to pay 1,200,000*HS* from a loan due to him and from cash at home: *Att.* 264 (12.25), where he mentions growing old (ἐγγήραμα). This gives him an idea: buy *horti* for the *fanum* with a little villa (*villula*) that would be accessible to the public in a good public position (*sequor celebritatem*) and also be a place where he could grow old and even set up his own tomb (ἐντάφιος): *Att.* 266.1 (12.27.1). He also asked Atticus to solicit Gaius Oppius and Lucius Cornelius Balbus, Caesar's notorious henchmen, to fix the deal as guarantors (*auctores*): *Att.* 268.2 (12.29.2). Another villa is old but has a nice tree plantation: *Att.* 272 (12.31). Raising money continued to be an issue: if the *fanum Tulliae* was set up on private property (the *horti* or at the Tusculanum), an equal sum had to be given to the public treasury. This was going to be expensive, so perhaps the *fanum* could be built in open land (*in agro*) despite possibly losing its sacred character if the land (or the *Tusculanum*) changed hands: *Att.* 274 (12.35); *Att.* 275.1 (12.36.1); *Att.* 276.2 (12.37.2). Cicero is prepared to build a villa if can find the right *horti*, and is prepared to take over an existing but ugly villa with a large *balneum* and a smaller one that could be used as a winter residence; taking advice from an architect, he could build a portico the same size as the one at his Tusculum villa at half the cost. Other properties were possible: Cic., *Att.* 300.1–2 (13.29.1–2) and *Att.* 302.4 (13.31.4).

All these deals fell apart. It is possible that the amount of money Cicero was prepared to spend for *horti* became known and sellers raised their prices or became coy. At one point, he thought of buying some commercial subdivisions on the river banks in the City below the Vatican Hill that were going to be offered for sale and some others to be auctioned (*Att.* 269.1 [12.33.1]), but he was warned against that because on July 9, 45 BCE, a friend told him that Caesar was planning to straighten the course of the Tiber, starting from the Milvian Bridge along the whole length of the river's passage through the City, and that the Campus Martius and Vatican river banks would be built over: *Att.* 330.1 (13.33a.1): "Caesar wants it so."

At this point, Cicero abandoned the project for the *fanum Tulliae*, the *horti*, his old-age villa, and his tomb; Caesar's assassination in March of the following year put an end to both men's projects. Still, it was on his mind about a year later (June 13, 44 BCE), almost on the eve of his abortive departure to join Caesar's assassins in Greece (*Att.* 15.15.3). The decision to abandon the project was outlined in a dialogue with himself (the *Consolatio*, now lost) and other philosophical writing, notably the *Tusculanae disputationes*: Englert 2017.

9

VILLAS AND *HORTI* IN THE LATE ROMAN REPUBLIC

PLUTARCH
PLINY THE ELDER
CICERO
CORNELIUS NEPOS
PROPERTIUS
SUETONIUS
LUCRETIUS
SENECA THE YOUNGER
HORACE
ELEGIAE IN MAECENATEM
MARCUS CORNELIUS FRONTO

Roman villas and gardens of the Late Republic stood at the intersection of several agricultural, cultural, and infrastructure developments as well as some attitude-shaping political and social events specific to the second (particularly in its second half) and first centuries BCE.[1] Land confiscated from the towns of defeated enemies in Italy was professionally parceled throughout the inland and coastal peninsula into smaller and larger parcels of *iugera* to establish social divisions familiar to Roman colonists and often respecting existing local arrangements or modifying them.[2] By the mid-second century CE, Italy presented an agricultural landscape that was somewhat socially complete, well equipped with both free and enslaved personnel, productive for local and export markets, providing a big catchment area for drafts of Italian military recruits and capable of supporting Roman military expansion into Hispania, Africa, Sicily, Greece, Asia Minor, and ultimately Gaul.

These events resulted in a demand for agricultural knowledge, which took the form of the early agricultural treatises (Cato and Varro) and their later manifestations (Columella and Palladius). Important ideas—notably *otium*—were also developed, and so were certain social values—villas as the sites of philosophy and learning, the cultivation of friendships, the loci of both family and *familia*, and the appreciation of nature, besides the display of wealth and status from business, profession, political conflict, corruption, and war. These overlapping themes interconnect seemingly disparate literary sources and are the bases for the texts selected in this chapter and throughout this sourcebook.

Chronologically, the long century and a half between the end of the Third Punic War (146 BCE) and the death of Augustus (14 CE) had plenty of events affecting villas that conditioned their later development in literary sources of all kinds and in the archaeological record. Some themes can be discerned:

1. Wealth and ideas. Wealth derived from spoils of war abroad included the influx of taxes and treasure, enslaved workforces, unfettered commercial opportunities, ownership of land and businesses overseas, occasions for corrupt enrichment, as well as the importation of cultured and artistic persons, free and enslaved, from Greece, Egypt, and the East, and a taste for works of art, whether acquired as war booty, bought, or copied.

2. Social friction. The sources presented in this chapter begin with the question of *latifundia* ("wide" estates)—that is, the implantation of villas with large estates run by enslaved labor and the consequent dispossession of poor citizen farmers and their families. In political terminology, the picture was of a populace devoted to soil, work, gods, community, traditional values, and so on being driven off the land by uncaring rich owners; this gave opportunities for political advancement to politicians (like the Gracchi and others later), defining themselves in opposition to the oppressive social status quo; violent reaction and temporary reconciliations were inevitable.[3]

3. Social representation in villas: morality and luxury. The image of the citizen farmer is the Roman reinforcement of a long social and cultural tendency in antiquity: that rural

living is better than city dwelling, that simplicity is preferable to modern comfort, that sober noble honor is more admirable than anything else.[4] Almost all writers, in one form or another, repeat again and again the glorious examples of great men of the past, very often in their villas as settings, to the point of fetishization. Of course, fetishization of frugal simplicity implies the existence of simplicity's opposite: luxury and sophistication in all its civilized and sometimes vicious forms. Villa owners could have it both ways: they had the assurance of moral worth without enduring any material discomfort or intellectual penury. Such ambidextrous advantages grew as their wealth grew. The prestige of luxury (either extravagant or in lesser emulations) became almost obligatory among the elites of the Late Republic, but so did the pretense of simplicity.[5]

4. Villas endured but were vulnerable. While the massacre, in Rome, of Marius's and Cinna's enemies in 85 BCE had been limited to the lives of their opponents, settling of political scores soon took the form of proscription (*proscriptio*, pl. *proscriptiones*), which originally meant the public posting of lists of properties of named individuals, with a new implication that the owner and often his relatives and associates could be killed as well; valuable bounties to their murderers were offered. The proscriptions of Sulla in 82 BCE extended to conspicuous villa properties throughout Italy; the more desirable they were, the more quickly they were put on the list. The proscriptions of the Second Triumvirate in 43 BCE (in which Cicero and his brother lost their lives) were reportedly the worst, with some 2,000 listed for death and the seizure and forced sale, commandeering, or auction of their property. There appears to have been a lot of swapping out of villa and *domus* ownership in consequence.

5. Development of gardens around Rome. *Hortus*, in the singular, is a generic entity, referring as much to a kitchen garden as to something more grand. However, in the plural and with the addition of a name of an owner, *horti* denoted assemblages often combining a villa-like dwelling or dwellings, terracing, raised beds, trees, shrubs, flowers and other plants (native, exotic, or newly introduced), irrigation, fountains, collections of works of sculpture and paintings, and many other amenities.[6] The great "named" villas and *horti* of the Late Republic are best known from inscriptions, topographical studies, and archaeological investigation; some of the very few written notices are included here.[7]

From the mid-second to the late first century BCE in the archaeological record, there was a significant expansion of Late Republican villas in many forms. These included farming estates producing primary foodstuffs for urban markets, secondary products (tiles, cloth, leather), and *pastiones villaticae* centered on an upscale dwelling; newly large estates depending on enslaved labor and with villas raised on platforms (*basis villae*), or hillside, cliffside, lakeside, and maritime villas; villas set on terraces and in gardens along Eastern or Hellenistic lines; and even the pictorial representation of villas as ideals of living, in wall paintings of urban *domus*.[8] The shores of the Bay of Naples provided the backdrop for many such villas, but there were others nearer Rome.[9] Some were described or mentioned in texts, in part because they were new or, in some cases, notorious for other reasons. With the need for new formulae as the conditions of imperial security and prerogative developed even before Augustus's coming to power, Late Republican prototypes were adopted for emperors' gardens and villas.

PLUTARCH   (ca. 46–after 119 CE)

Parallel Lives (*Vitae parallelae*, Βίοι παράλληλοι), late first–early second century CE.
Life of Tiberius Sempronius Gracchus (Plut., *Vit. Ti. Gracch.*)

Tiberius Sempronius Gracchus (ca. 163–133 BCE) together with his younger brother Gaius Sempronius Gracchus (ca. 154–121 BCE) merged the greatest plebeian and patrician nobilities on their paternal and maternal sides, respectively; their mother, Cornelia Africana, was the daughter of Publius Cornelius Scipio Africanus who in 202 BCE had defeated Hannibal in the Second Punic War. They were therefore in a good social position to identify, address, and shape, politically, what had become a major problem in the mid-second century BCE, namely the amalgamation of agricultural property to form large estates based on enslaved labor and to build residential villas that went well beyond simple farm dwellings. It was alleged that these measures had dispossessed the free population of citizen farmers (*coloni, agricolae*) from their land and livelihood and were continuing to do so, forcing such citizens into towns and some into the City itself, with various grave social consequences.[10] Tiberius and Gaius Gracchus were not the first to champion the rights and inflame the resentments of ordinary citizens, but their populist advocacy strongly inflected Late Republican political divisions, resulting in their assassinations (Tiberius in 133 BCE, Gaius in 121 BCE) and the murder of their adherents by conservative, reactionary senatorial partisans.[11] Plutarch's account of what had prompted Tiberius Gracchus's agitation against enslaved-based agricultural estates, together with Pliny the Elder's comments on *latifundia*, constitute the seminal texts of what would become a major social issue and source of political friction in the second half of the second and throughout most of the first centuries BCE and, in political opinion, even beyond. Villa construction was also involved. Whether the issue of agricultural enslavement and dispossession of free-citizen families was as stark as claimed is doubtful on archaeological grounds,[12] but the allocation of *ager publicus*, whether in Italy or abroad, and whether allocated to demobilized legionary veterans or to poor, but free, Roman citizens, was a continuing issue in the history of the period.

Plut., *Vit. Ti. Gracch.* 8.7   [...] When Tiberius [Sempronius Gracchus] came back from the war [... he proposed] a measure that would rouse great expectation for those involved. [...] in a certain letter, his brother Gaius [Sempronius Gracchus] has written that when he [Tiberius] was traveling through Tyrrhenia [Etruria] to Numantia, he saw the depopulation in the countryside [ἐρημία τῆς χώρας] and that those who farmed it and tended its flocks were barbarian slaves brought in from elsewhere.[13] That was when the idea of the [agrarian] law first came to him, the measure that was to be the cause of a thousand evils for both of them. However, it was the people themselves who fired up Tiberius's passion and ambition by writing graffiti on porticoes, walls, and memorial buildings calling on him to recover public land [δημοσία χώρα, *ager publicus*] for the poor citizens [πένητες].

PLINY THE ELDER   (Gaius Plinius Secundus, 23/24–79 CE)

Natural History (*Naturalis historia*), mid–first century CE (Plin., *HN*)

Pliny the Elder, writing some two centuries after the Gracchi and some fifty years before Plutarch, was opposed to the concentration of farms into streamlined agricultural estates (*latifundia*) worked by enslaved laborers, impelled by a profit motive, and capable of maintaining luxurious villas. In his Book 18, which deals with agricultural soils, he makes a series of remarks on these topics that express his devotion to ancient frugalities and contempt for modern prodigalities, moral and material.[14] Pliny especially detested owners of houses and villas equipped with big fishponds and kitchens. He sarcastically calls the courtiers of Nero's reign "slaves."

Plin., *HN* 18.7 (18.2)   Two *iugera* were considered sufficient for a citizen of the Roman people, and in those days no more was allocated.[15] But who—those who were recently slaves [courtiers] of the emperor Nero—would have been satisfied with a *viridarium* of such a [small] size [these days]? They want fishponds [*piscinae*] bigger than that, and it's a mercy that they don't want the same for the size of their kitchens.

Pliny then complains about the increase of prices for agricultural goods. But he goes on from there: he regards the profits of agriculture from enslaved labor as less than what could be gained from the old methods of the "generals," namely the citizen farmers of history.

Plin., *HN* 18.18–21 (18.4) This [increase of prices] was not due to *latifundia* owned by individual proprietors who drove their neighbors off their land, considering that the law of Licinius Stolo prescribed that the maximum amount of land was 500 *iugera* [about 125 ha, or 311½ acres], and he himself was adjudged for an infraction of his own law for owning more than that amount by the subterfuge of [designating] his son as owner.[16] That was the degree [of ownership over the stipulated amount] at a time when the Republic had already become luxurious.[17] [...]

But at the present time, this [agricultural] work is done by slaves in chain gangs and by the hands [workforce] of criminals with branded faces. The Earth [*tellus*]—she who is called our progenitor and whose cultivation is akin to religious worship—is not so stupid. When agricultural work is done by such men, we can well believe that it is not done according to her wish; in fact, it is done to her indignation. And then we are astonished that we can't get the same profit from the inmates of slave prisons [*ergastula*] that we used to get when the work was done by generals!

Plin., *HN* 18.35 (18.7) In the old days, it was thought, in principle, that moderation was better in what was needed in the way of a farm, because it was more satisfactory to sow less and plough better, and I note that Vergil said the same. To state the truth, *latifundia* have ruined Italy and in truth are doing the same in the provinces: [only] six landowners owned half of Africa at the time that the emperor Nero executed them.[18] Gnaeus Pompeius [Magnus] should not be denied one more indication of his greatness: he was never in the market for the land of an adjacent estate. Mago introduces his treatise with the instruction that someone who has bought an estate must sell his house in town, but this is too hard and actually contrary to the public good, but it does emphasize the need for the owner's attentive supervision [*assiduitas desiderata*].[19]

CICERO   (Marcus Tullius Cicero, 107/106–43 BCE)

***On Duties (De officiis)*, ca. 45 BCE (Cic., *Off.*)**

Cicero urges moderation in the domestic arrangements and building plans (*descriptio aedificandi*) of a highly placed person (*honoratus, homo clarus*) in a high social position (*principio*) for serviceability (*finis est usus*). He modernizes the trope of ancient frugality by citing examples of immoderate building (Gnaeus Octavius, Marcus Aemilius Scaurus) and adds good advice for his own fellow villa owners, but he seems to be doubtful that it ever has or ever will be followed.[20]

Cic., *Off.* 1.39.140 It is important to avoid going beyond the limits of expense and showy display [*magnificentia*], especially if you are building for yourself: in such matters, bad things can happen, if only by giving a bad example. Along those lines, there are many who are [overly] scrupulous in imitating the behavior of great men [*principes*]. Who [actually] imitates the virtues of Lucius Lucullus, that great man?[21] But how many men have imitated the showy display of his villas [*villarum magnificentia*]! It is certainly the case that a limit should be applied to this, and a modest mean [*mediocritas*] should once again become the standard way [of going about building], and that this modest mean can be the normal way for life and civilized behavior [*cultus*]. But that's enough of that.

Plutarch, *Parallel Lives. Life of Marcus Porcius Cato Maior* (Plut., Vit. Cat. Mai.)

Plutarch presents Cato the Elder's villa and domestic economy as examples of the opposite of what some villas belonging to prominent men had come to be, and came to be, in the Late Republic.

Plut., Vit. Cat. Mai. 2.1–2 [...] The villa [ἔπαυλις] that had belonged to Manius Curius [Dentatus], thrice *triumphator*, was near his properties. He [Cato] would visit it often. Walking around and seeing the small amount of land and the tiny villa put him in mind of their owner, that frugal man who, even though he had become the greatest of the Romans, the one who had utterly defeated the warlike greatest peoples and had expelled Pyrrus from Italy, still tended his small estate by his own efforts and lived in its villa, even after three triumphs.[22] It was when he was sitting in his villa at its hearth cooking turnips that the Samnite ambassadors came to offer him a large quantity of gold, but he dismissed them, saying that someone for whom such a dinner was sufficient did not need gold, and that, to his mind, it was a much better thing to be victorious over those who possessed gold than to own it. Then Cato would go away turning these things over in his mind, and when later he saw his own house and lands and servants [θεράποντες] and how he lived [δίαιτα], he would add to the work he did himself and decrease his luxuries.

Plut., Vit. Cat. Mai. 4.4 [...] Once, he [Cato] received an embroidered Babylonian tapestry as an inheritance, but he sold it immediately; not one of his villas had plastering; he never bought a slave for more than 1,500 drachmas....[23] [...]

Plut., Vit. Cat. Mai. 25.1–2 [In his old age] he [Cato] wrote speeches and then turned to writing on many [different] topics as well as histories; as for farming, he gave it his attention when he was a young man, and he did so out of poverty. In fact, he said that there were only two ways to make a livelihood: farming and thriftiness. But as he grew old, engagement with the land as a theoretical activity became a way of passing time. He also put together a book on agriculture in which he wrote out recipes for flatbreads and preserved fruits—in all things, his ambition was to be outstanding and special. The dinners he gave at his country place were very ample, and he always invited pleasant neighbors from the farms nearby, and he entertained them genially. He was considered a pleasant and desirable acquaintance not just by his contemporaries but also by young[er] men, because he had varied experience in many things and had read and witnessed things that were worthy of note. He considered the dinner table to be the best means to friendship; [at his table] much was said in praise of good and true citizens, and unworthy and bad men were completely ignored, because Cato did not allow anything, good or bad, to be said about them.

Pliny the Elder, *Natural History*

Plin., HN 18.7 (32–33) The tried and true way is for the farm not to be insufficient in relation to the villa and the villa not to be insufficient to the farm.[24] This happened—in divergent ways even though at the same period—in the case of the neighboring estates of Lucius Lucullus and Quintus Scaevola: Scaevola's villa could not warehouse his farm's produce, and Lucullus's farm could not support his villa, for which there was a censorial reprimand [for Lucullus's villa] that there was less [land] to plough than [floors] to sweep.[25] Getting this [balance] right cannot be done without a certain skill. Very recently, Gaius Marius, seven times elected consul, built a villa in the area of Misenum, using the experience he had with military camps, and even Sulla Felix remarked that others [who built villas there] had been blind [in comparison to Marius's skill in planning his villa].[26] It is the case that a villa should not be placed near a marsh or with a river near it—be the river in front or behind [the villa]. Homer was of the soundest opinion in having declared that unhealthy vapors always come from a river before dawn. The villa should be oriented northward in warm districts but eastward in temperate locations.

Plutarch, Parallel Lives. Life of Gaius Marius (Plut., Vit. Mar.)

Plutarch's method in writing his biographies includes pointing out the incongruities of a person's character and life and how conflicting tendencies are revealed in action and biography, in this case Gaius Marius and his villa at Misenum.[27]

Plut., Vit. Mar. 2.2 [...] [As a youth] it was only after a certain time that he saw a city or learned about citified ways of life, and meanwhile [before that time] he lived in a village called Cereatae in the region of Arpinum. His life was pretty rough when compared with the smooth life in a town, but it was a well-balanced life, much like the upbringing that the ancient Roman ancestors provided for their children.[28] [...]

Plut., Vit. Mar. 34.1–2 The people vacillated, some in favor of Marius, others supporting Sulla and telling Marius to go to the bathing establishments at Baiae for the health of his body, which was weakened with age and infirmities, as he himself admitted.[29] Near Misenum, there was a grand, costly villa owned by Marius equipped with such luxuries and effeminate furnishings as to seem out of place for a man who had been himself at the center of so many wars and strategic undertakings. We are told that this was the house that Cornelia [Sulla] bought for 75,000 drachmas and that shortly afterward Lucius Lucullus paid 2,500,000 for it: [this shows] how quickly great expenses grew and how much the addiction to luxurious living [ἡ ἐπίδοσις πρὸς τρυφὴν] had taken hold.[30]

Plutarch, Parallel Lives. Life of Lucius Cornelius Sulla (Plut., Vit. Sull.)

Villas were vulnerable. In 85 BCE, Sulla's political opponents had burned his villas,[31] but three years later as dictator, he took up an equally cruel settling of political scores in the form of proscription (*proscriptio*, pl. *proscriptiones*) of both lives and properties.[32] There were frightening stories of cruelty and courage, among them the bravery of an enslaved attendant attempting to save the life of his enslaver.[33]

Plut., Vit. Sull. 31.5–6 Those poor wretches who were killed through the hatred of others were nothing compared to those who were killed for their properties, and even those who executed them used to say that his great house killed this man, another man's garden killed him, and yet another's hot baths killed him. Quintus Aurelius, a retiring, quiet man, who thought that his only role during the bad state of affairs was to sympathize with others affected by misfortunes, [when] he came into the Forum and read the list of those who had been proscribed and saw his own name on it, he exclaimed "Oh woe is me! My Alban villa [*Albanum*] is accusing me [informing against me]!" And he didn't get far before he was killed by someone who was after him.

Pliny the Elder, *Natural History*

Pliny the Elder praises the old Roman tradition of honoring great men and their achievements with a simple crown of grass (*corona graminea*) instead of crowns of gold, gems, or other metals and materials.[34] In doing so, he tells us about a wall painting in Sulla's villa at Tusculum, the villa later bought by Cicero.[35]

Plin., *HN* 22.4 (12–13)   Sulla the Dictator also wrote that he himself was given this crown by the army at Nola when he was [military] legate during the Marsian War, and the event was later painted in his villa at Tusculum.

Plutarch, *Parallel Lives. Life of Lucius Licinius Lucullus* (Plut., *Vit. Luc.*)

Plutarch sets out Lucullus's character and education as the basis for his later life of *otium* in his villas.

Plut., *Vit. Luc.* 1.3–5   Lucullus was educated to speak both languages [Latin and Greek] with equal fluency, such that Sulla dedicated his own memoirs to him as being someone who would summarize and set out the history of [his] times better than he could. [Lucullus's] manner of speaking was efficient and prompt to the matter, the equal of any other man's in the Forum. [...]

Even as a very young boy, he [Lucullus] chose a pleasant and liberal education stressing the καλός [the ideal Good, the ultimate beauty].[36] And when he became older, and after many struggles, he directed his mind to be at leisure [σχολάζειν, to enjoy *otium*] and to be quiet, seeking the thoughtful aspect of himself, and after his quarrel with Pompey, to curtail his lust for glory at an appropriate time.[37] [...]

In 66 BCE, Lucullus, having been replaced as commander in the East by Pompey, found himself cheated of a triumph by the machinations of Gaius Memmius.[38] Plutarch describes some of the circumstances that prompted Lucullus's turn toward building villas at Baiae and Tusculum but only mentions in passing the most famous of the general's creations, the Horti Lucullani with its villa on the Pincian Hill northeast of the Forum, overlooking the Campus Martius.[39]

Plut., *Vit. Luc.* 38.4   [...] Crassus and Pompey made fun of Lucullus for turning to retirement and costly luxury, as if a life at ease was not just as bad for an old man as engaging in political and military affairs.[40] [...]

Plut., *Vit. Luc.* 39.1–4   It is certainly the case that Lucullus's life, like an ancient comedy,[41] can be seen, in its first part, as dealing with political affairs and military matters, then later on with drinking, banquets, and torch-lit processions at night and all kinds of childish things. For I consider that his expensive buildings [τά οἰκοδομές πολυτελεῖς], his [open] porticoes [τὰς κατασκευὰς περιπάτων], and his baths, and even more so his paintings and his statues [τὰι γραφαί καὶ ἀνδριάνται], as well as his great enthusiasm for these arts, as childish; he amassed these things at great expense, pouring out for them from the huge and splendid amounts of money he had garnered from his military commands, such that, even as luxury has increased to the point it is at now, the Gardens of Lucullus are [still] considered to be the most expensive of the emperors' gardens by far.[42] About his works on the seashore and around Neapolis, where he raised whole hillsides over huge tunnels and surrounded his houses with the sea and with water channels to breed fish, and had dwellings built out into the sea—well, when Tubero the Stoic philosopher saw these things, he called him Xerxes in a toga.[43] He also had houses in the country [ἐγχώριοι δίαιται] near Tusculum with belvederes [κατασκοπαὶ] and open dining halls [οἱ ἀνδρῶνες] and porticoes [οἱ περίπατοι], and when Pompey saw them, he said to Lucullus that he had built his villa [ἔπαυλις] very well for the summer [weather], but it would be impossible to live in during winter. Lucullus laughed straight out and said, "Do you think, then, that I am not as smart as cranes and storks and that I don't move among my houses season to season?" [...]

Plut., Vit. Luc. 39.5 [...] Flaccus [i.e., Horace] the poet mentioned this story when he [Lucullus] said that he did not consider a dwelling to be [really] rich if the things that were overlooked [by visitors] and not in evidence [to them] were not greater [in quantity or quality] than those that were [actually] visible.[44]

Plut., Vit. Luc. 40.1 The ordinary [daily] banquets [νεόπλουτα δεῖπνα τὰ καθ'ἡμέραν] that Lucullus gave were those of a nouveau riche [νεόπλουτος], and that not only because of the colored covers of his dining beds and the gem-incrusted drinking goblets as well as the choruses and recitations [during dinner] but also for the variety of meat dishes and nice confections: he made himself into an object of envy by people of base character.[45] [...]

Plut., Vit. Luc. 42.1-4 [However,] what he did in the way of setting up a collection of books is worthy of enthusiastic praise. He collected many clearly [copied and] written items, [even if] the way he made use of them was more honorable than the way he had acquired them:[46] his libraries were free for all to use as well as the adjacent porticoes, and the study centers for scholars [σχολαστηρίοι] were open without restrictions to the Greeks who visited them as if they were the dwellings of the Muses, and they spent the day with one another, happy to be relieved of their other work.[47] He himself [Lucullus] often joined them when he wasn't busy, walking in the porticoes among the philosophers, and he would help their leaders in what needed doing, and thus his house was a home-hearth and *prytaneum* for those Greeks resident in Rome.[48] He liked all types of philosophy and was kindly minded and welcoming to all of them, but he had a special strong preference for the Academy, but not the one that is called the New [Academy], even though in Philo's teaching it had a strong advocate for the philosophy of Carneades.[49] Rather, he preferred the Old Academy, which was represented at that time by an eloquent and powerful man, Antiochus of Ascalon. Lucullus eagerly made Antiochus into a friend and associate and set him against the followers of Philo—one of whom was Cicero. Cicero, in fact, wrote a very fine treatise on this philosophical school: he has put the argument about "how to know" [κατάληψις] as being that of Lucullus, while taking the opposite argument himself. The book is called *Lucullus*.[50]

CORNELIUS NEPOS (ca. 110–20s BCE)

On Famous Historians (or *Lives of the Famous Historians*; *De viris illustribus*) 25: Atticus (Nep., Att.)[51]

Cornelius Nepos was a literary figure in Rome whose personal friendships with artists such as the poet Catullus and consulars such as Cicero gave him an entrée into the highest intellectual and social circles of Late Republican Rome. He exercised his talents in writing biographies of the great men of the past and those of his own day, among them the *eques* Titus Pomponius Atticus, Cicero's great friend. Nepos's account of Atticus and his manner of life, including his villas, combines admiration with affection: no good quality was absent in his character and mode of life. Nepos's dictum—"a man's own character [*mores*] makes his destiny [*fortuna*]"[52]—is embodied in Atticus, and so was the domestic economy of his houses, villas, hospitality, and even his learned enslaved servants.

Nep., Att. 13.1–7   In his bearing [*habitus*], this man was as good a *pater familias* as he was a citizen [*civis*]; for even though he was very rich, no one was less of a spendthrift [*emax*] or less eager to build [extravagantly, *aedificator*]. Still, he lived quite as well as the best of them and was accustomed to the finest things. He lived in Tamphilius's house [*domus Tamphilianum*] on the Quirinal Hill. The house had come to him from the inheritance of his uncle; its pleasant character [*amoenitas*] was not so much in the structure itself as in the wooded park [*silva*] surrounding it.[53] Indeed, the building had been built long ago and was more elegant than extravagant, but he made no changes to it except what its age made necessary.[54] [...]

Nep., Att. 14.1   [...] He owned no *horti*, no extravagant *villa suburbana* or *villa maritima*, no country estates in Italy except those near Arretium and Nomentum; all the revenue of his wealth came from his possessions in Epirus and the City.[55] From this can be deduced that he customarily managed his affairs by reason [*ratio*] rather than by the amount of his wealth.[56]

Plutarch, *Parallel Lives. Life of Marcus Licinius Crassus* (Plut., Vit. Crass.)

There were other ways of acquiring villas than by buying them or proscribing their owners. Marcus Licinius Crassus was famous for his wealth acquired from urban real estate, often in doubtful transactions during and following the dictatorship of Sulla.[57] This is an example of how he got his hands on one.

Plut., Vit. Crass. 1.2   One of his brothers having died, he married the widowed wife and [they] had children, in this way conducting himself in as orderly a way as Romans are able. However, later on, when he was older, he was accused of having illicit relations with Licinia, one [of the College] of the Virgins of the goddess Vesta, and a certain Plotius brought a charge against her in court.[58] Now Licinia owned a nice suburban villa [τὸ προάστειος καλός], which Crassus wanted to buy for small money, so he was always hanging around the lady and being pleasant to her until he came to be suspected of evil intent. In this way, it was his greed [ἡ φιλοπλουτία] that excused him [from the accusation of interfering with a Vestal], and he was acquitted by the judges. Still, he did not cease relations with Licinia until he had acquired her property.

Plutarch, *Parallel Lives. Life of Gnaeus Pompeius, called Magnus* (Plut., Vit. Pomp.)

After his third triumph (61 BCE), Pompey built a grand permanent theater in the Campus Martius surrounded by a porticoed precinct and gardens. He added a house for himself, emulating the villas in *horti* that had been part of the adjacent Quirinal Hill since Lucullus's gardens.

Plut., Vit. Pomp. 40.5   However, afterwards, when Pompey was building the beautiful and famous theater that is named after him, he also built a house like a small boat in tow to it, more distinguished than the one he lived in before.[59] But for all that, an owner [who possessed it] after Pompey was astonished [by its simplicity], and asked where the "Great Pompey" used to dine. At least that's what they say.

PROPERTIUS (Sextus Propertius, ca. 50 BCE–15 CE)

Elegies, ca. 20 BCE (Prop., *Elegies*)

The portico of Pompey became a favorite place for amorous rendezvous in Rome, but villas around towns of the *suburbium* were also love venues. The poet Propertius, in love with an older woman he calls Cynthia, scolds her for spending time at resorts with villas (sometimes on religious pretexts) when she might just as well spend time with him walking in the villa-like garden of the Porticus of Pompey in Rome, which he describes.

Prop., *Elegies* 2.32.7–16
Cynthia! If only you would spend time here when you're at leisure,
But the ordinary crowd forbids me to believe
When they see you, carrying torches and lights, hastening to the goddess Trivia.[60]
He who sees you is a sinner, so he who sees you not
Will not desire you: the eyes, in looking, give witness to the crime [of desire].
At Praeneste, O Cynthia, why do you seek ambiguous oracles
Within the walls of Aeaean Telegonus?[61]
Why does your carriage take you to Herculean Tibur,
Or the Via Appia so often to Lanuvium?[62] [...]
None of these holds any charms for you![63]

Plutarch, *Life of Gnaeus Pompeius*

Villas were a place where great generals and leaders like Lucullus and Pompey, harassed by political opposition, could find some rest. In 59 BCE, an alliance between Pompey and Julius Caesar was forged by Pompey, then in his mid-forties, marrying Caesar's daughter Julia, then in mid-adolescence.

Plut., *Vit. Pomp.* 48.4-6 [...] Meanwhile, Cato [the Younger] spoke in an inspired way in the Senate as if knowing what the future would bring to the City and to Pompey; and Lucullus at the same time gave himself to peace and quiet [ἡσυχία] saying he was not up to politics—Pompey declared that easy living [τρυφή] was more inappropriate to an old man than political engagement. However, he [Pompey] himself pretty soon gave way to his love for his young wife [Julia], spending most of his time with her at country villas and gardens [ἐν ἀγροῖς καὶ κήποις] and ignoring events in the Forum.[64] [...]

Suetonius on Julius Caesar

Gaius Julius Caesar (100–44 BCE, dictator 48/47–44) was of the family Iulii Caesares, who were of patrician descent but had not had notable political presence or significant wealth for some generations. As one of the principal politicians of the Late Republic, Julius Caesar made up for these deficiencies quickly, in part by building villas—a sure sign of serene possession of wealth and cultured *otium*—at Nemi and Lavicum (Labicum) near Rome and another at Misenum on the Bay of Naples.[65] In Rome, he owned *horti* on the Esquiline Hill near the Porta Collatina and in the Transtiberim.[66] He also emulated his predecessors' collections of art and *objets de vertu* and composed memoirs of the Gallic, Alexandrian, African, and Hispanic wars, as well as an account of the Civil War of 49–45 BCE. He may have gone beyond his predecessors who wrote political essays and poems, having tried his hand also at verse, plays, and rhetorical discourses while still a youth. He also appears to have had property large enough to breed and raise horses.[67] Building villas—in this case farmhouses for citizens assigned allotments under the Julian Laws of 59 BCE—even revealed a sign (one of many) foretelling his murder.[68] The passages assembled here indicate how, in his behavior with country properties including villas, he followed the behavior of other politicians of the Late Republic.

SUETONIUS   (Gaius Suetonius Tranquillus, 69–after 122 CE)

Lives of the Twelve Caesars (*De vita Caesarum*), early second century CE. *The Divine Julius* (*Divus Iulius*) (Suet., *Iul.*)

Suetonius wrote his biography of Julius Caesar in the early second century CE, some 150 years after Caesar's assassination.

Suet., *Iul.* 46   First [i.e., at the beginning of his career], he lived in a modest house in the Subura, but after entering the post of *pontifex maximus*, he lived in the *domus publica* in the *Sacra Via*.[69] Many have reported that he had a strong proclivity for elegant things and luxuries, and that, after starting a villa at Nemi from the foundation up and finishing it at great expense, because it did not correspond to what he had in mind [*ad animum ei*], he tore the whole thing down, even though he was poor and in debt at that time.[70] On his campaigns, he carried mosaic and *opus sectile* floors about with him.[71]

Suet., *Iul.* 47   [...] ... and that he was a greatly enthusiastic collector of gems [*gemmae*], carvings [*toreumata*], statues [*signa*], and paintings [*tabulae*] by ancient artists, and also slaves of fine bearing and great accomplishment for such large prices that he himself was ashamed and forbade the amount to be entered into his ledgers. [...]

Suet., *Iul.* 50   But above all others, he loved Servilia, the mother of Marcus [Junius] Brutus, for whom in his first consulship he bought a pearl worth 6,000,000*HS*. During the Civil Wars, he added to this present, besides other gifts, some very fine country properties [*praedia*] at auction for small money, and when people said they were astonished at the flagrantly low prices, Cicero jokingly said, "It's better than you think: there was a third [*tertia*/Tertia] taken off [the bidding price]!" In fact, it was thought that Servilia was acting as Caesar's procuress for her own daughter Tertia.

Suetonius indicates that Caesar made his will on the ides of September (September 13) 45 BCE at his villa Lavicanum.

Suet., *Iul.* 83.1–2   Following the request of Lucius [Cornelius] Piso, the will which he had made on the ides of the preceding September at his villa near Lavicum [*Lavicana*] was opened and read in [Mark] Antony's house and consigned to the chief of the [College of] Vestals. [...] He left his *horti* near the Tiber to the People for use by all [*publice*] and 300*HS* to each man [*viritim*, male householder].

Two Moralizing Conclusions on Republican Villas: Lucretius and Seneca the Younger

Poets and authors of the Late Republic sought to define the moral character of villas in their social and physical aspects. For such villas, Lucretius (ca. 99–55 BCE), as a contemporary observer of their builders in the second quarter of the first century BCE, chose to identify their structures and maintenance as distractions from human endeavor and destiny. Seneca the Younger, writing much later, in the 60s CE, uses the villas near Baiae quite differently, as noble retreats from mundane pleasures and vice; in doing so, he criticizes Baiae, the premier venue for villas and vice.

LUCRETIUS (Titus Lucretius Carus, ca. 99–55 BCE)

On the Nature of Things (De rerum natura) (Lucr.)

Lucretius's Latin poem of nearly 7,500 lines in dactylic hexameter proclaims and extends the ideas of the Greek philosopher Epicurus (late fourth–early third century BCE). The poet brings to bear the most sublime invocations of the gods and many moments of mythology in arguing his case for philosophy against traditional belief (*religio*, or superstition). Divinities and famous humans are treated as examples or personifications of abstract, universal ideas and realities, but human beings' place in these constructs are also important. In consequence, the third book of the poem concerns the nature of the human soul, *res natura animi ... animae atque ...* (3.35–36). *Animus* is identified as the thinking mind with reactive emotions; *anima* is the soul itself with its faculties of sensation. The union of *animus* and *anima* is explained as a harmony (3.136–176, with further elaboration at 3.94–829).

Lucretius (like Epicurus) is concerned with individual human happiness, and his famous homely example of what troubles humankind is about *domus* or *aedes*, the public places of towns, and villas—a man seeking, in vain, some happiness in *urbs*, in public places, and in *rus*, the country. None of these mitigate the underlying agitation; only *studium* and *cognitio* are any help. In Lucretius's day and that of his slightly older contemporaries Cicero, Atticus, and others, villas were often venues of study and knowledge, so perhaps the poet thought of villas as the place to start finding contentment.

Lucr., 3.1053–1075
> In the same way that men can feel
> A heavy mass on their mind [*animus*],
> With its great weight bearing down [on them],
> If only such men could understand its origins [reasons, *causae*]
> And what that weight of evils on their breast [*pectus*][72] might consist of,
> They would no longer live the life that we see most of them living:
> Not knowing what he might want,
> Always trying to change his location, as if he could put the impediment aside.
> Tired of being at home, he leaves his house [*aedes*], then goes back to it right away,
> Because he feels no better when he's out in public places [*in foris*, in town].
> Driving his horses [*manni*, small horses] at breakneck speed, he hastens to his villa
> As if determined to bring help to a burning building.
> [But] then, as soon as he crosses the villa's threshold, he yawns,
> And either falls into a deep sleep or seeks forgetfulness,
> Or, moving fast, goes back to see the city again.
> In this way, each man seeks to escape from himself,
> But of course, to get away like that can never be,
> He holds on [to himself] against his will, hating doing so,
> Because, being sick, he does not know the cause of his illness.
> If he could see his situation clearly, he would put his affairs [*res*, business, businesses] aside
> And begin, at last, the task of mastering the nature of things,[73]

Because the state of wandering is not merely for one hour, but for an eternity of time,
All that time that remains after death for every human being.

SENECA THE YOUNGER (Lucius Annaeus Seneca, ca. 4 BCE–65)

Letters on Morality (Epistulae morales ad Lucilium) (Sen., *Ep.*)

Letter 51, ca. 62–64/65 CE, to Lucilius in Sicily

The debilitating effect on morals that a luxurious environment incubates is the topic of Seneca's Letter 51. The resort of Baiae on the Bay of Naples is a particular case: by the early first century BCE, it had become the supreme example of a seaside resort with hot-water bathing establishments, spas, shops, drinking holes, brothels, and other entertainments, all surrounded by villas.[74] Baiae had been the site of villas of the Late Republican generals and politicians; Seneca interprets the villas as examples of drawing away from the resort while dominating it from above, especially from the promontory of Misenum. It is also possible that, besides its thermal baths, the resort developed in consequence of the prestigious villas bringing fame to the area. Lucilius, who was practicing his writing with Seneca's help, was traveling in Sicily when Seneca wrote this letter. Seneca's doleful Stoic lessons occasioned by Baiaean villas are in abundant evidence. Seneca's only real approval is for Scipio's retirement to a villa at Liternum, some distance from Baiae.[75]

Sen., *Ep.* **51.1-6** I do what I can and have to be content with being at Baiae, which I left the day after I arrived: Baiae must be avoided because, despite some natural positive features, Luxury has taken over the place for herself as something to be celebrated. You could say, "What then? Should any place be indicted as a hateful place?" "By no means," I would reply.

As certain clothes are more appropriate to wise and honest men than other clothes, setting aside any personal dislike of a specific color but because he thinks that a certain color is incompatible with the frugal life he has chosen, so the wise man disposed to wisdom will avoid places that are hostile to good morality. For that reason, he will never decide to go to Canopus if he is seeking isolation [from the world], even though a Canopus does not in itself disallow a frugal life, and neither does Baiae—both places have become rooming houses of vice.[76] The former [Canopus] has given itself completely to luxury, while the latter [Baiae] has done so even more so, as if the place itself had a permission to [cultivate, flaunt its] vice by right.

We must choose a place [to live] that is as good for our bodily health as for our moral health. I do not choose to live in a torture room, nor do I live in a cook shop. Is it really necessary to see drunkards staggering along the shore, to see the revelers on boats, and hear the lakes echoing with songsters' singing and the other ways by which Luxury, when unrestrained by any law, not only commits sins but loudly advertises them? We must act in such a way as to flee as far away from stimulations to vice as possible. Hardening our souls is needed to remove them from the seductions of pleasure. One winter's dose of pleasure in Campania ruined Hannibal's strength, he who had weathered the Alpine snows.[77] He conquered by force of arms, but he was conquered by vice. [...]

[...] Once a man has realized how great the work he is undertaking, he will see that nothing should be done fussily or weakly. What are they to me, all those hot baths? Or those hot rooms [*sudatoria*] with dry heat to sweat out the body? Sweating should only be a consequence of work.

Sen., *Ep.* **51.10-13** [...] A man thinking about such things must choose (to live in) a sober and holy place. Pleasant circumstances [*amoenitas*] weaken spirits, and there is no doubt that an excessively pleasant dwelling can undermine one's vigor. Cattle can put up with any road if their hooves have been hardened on rough terrain, but when cattle are fattened on soft marshy pastures their hooves soon wear out. Stronger soldiers come from rough regions; the weak one is a city dweller or a homebody. When a pair of hands moves [naturally, easily] from the plough grip to the weapon, no work [of any kind] is ever objected to, but a sleek, well-lotioned man is weakened by dust. Discipline undertaken in harsher locales strengthens [a man's] native ability and gets it ready for great enterprises.

For Scipio, it was more honorable to retire to Liternum than to Baiae: his disgrace did not need a soft venue. Men like Gaius Marius, Gnaeus Pompey, and [Julius] Caesar—men to whom, first of all, fortune transferred the wealth of the people of Rome—also had villas in the environs of Baiae, but they built them on the pinnacles of hills. To look down from a great height on views far and wide seemed more soldierly. Look at the positions they chose, at the buildings they built and their type: you will see that these are not villas at all, but military camps.[78] Do you think that Cato would ever have lived in such a place [as seaside Baiae] even for a moment?—so he could count the adulterous women as they sailed by, the different kinds of multicolored skiffs, the roses strewn over the [Lucrine] lake, or so he could listen to the noisy nocturnal sounds of singers? Wouldn't he have preferred to lie down in a trench dug out by his own hands, for a night's rest? Wouldn't any man who is a [real] man prefer to be woken from his sleep by a [military] trumpet blast rather than by songsters?

But that's enough condemning Baiae, and while I could never cease condemning vice, I beg you, Lucilius, it is from vice that I wish you to flee, always and never endingly. [...]

The *Horti* of Rome in the Late Republic

The *horti* of Rome were gardens in which a villa-like *domus* was an element together with terraces, planting, water effects, and the full panoply of *luxus* in the way of statues, paintings, and display of dining spaces and equipment. While they appear to have been private pleasure gardens for the personal use of their owners, family, and friends not much different from a *villa suburbana*, they may also have signaled affiliation with innovative Hellenistic cultural tastes in defiance of their cultural opposites—devotion to native Roman frugalities.[79] Their proximity to the capital gave them a natural political presence; between 66 and 63 BCE, Lucullus may have used his Horti Lucullani on the Pincian Hill to entertain, possibly in support of the voting of his triumph. In 61 BCE, Pompey used his *horti* in the Campus Martius to pay money to the tribes to support his candidacy for consul.[80] In 54 BCE, Cicero invited Crassus to dinner, just before that general's departure for the Syrian campaign. Cicero used his son-in-law's *horti* on the Via Appia (Horti Cassipedis), perhaps because Crassus had already been voted the *imperium* and so had to stay outside the city, or possibly because Cicero's own house on the Palatine was still undergoing restoration.[81]

Later, the *horti* could be used as dwellings—by Tiberius before becoming emperor, by Vespasian to emphasize his availability to all comers—or as venues—by Nero to view the great fire of 64 CE from the Horti Maecenatis—but most notices tell us little about them.

Despite their fame, Roman *horti* are much better known from modern topographical studies of the City, analysis of inscriptions, and archaeological investigation and analysis of their sculptural panoply than from contemporary or even later texts.[82] The *horti* have been the findspots of many notable works of architecture and sculpture as well as promptings to study their origins in Hellenistic landscape architecture and the visual concepts of how nature and cityscape interact: *rus in urbe*.

Two poems of Horace, another by an anonymous poet, and a reference by Marcus Cornelius Fronto give some information about the Horti Maecenatis.

HORACE (Quintus Horatius Flaccus, 65–8 BCE)

Epodes (Epodi) (Hor., *Epod.*)

Epode 9, shortly after September 2, 31 BCE

This poem marked a banquet, apparently in the Horti Maecenatis in celebration of the victory of Octavian over Mark Antony and Cleopatra at Actium, as well as the defeat, some years earlier, of Sextus Pompeius Magnus Pius, a son of Pompey and an opponent of Octavian, Antony, and Lepidus (Second Triumvirate). The *alta domus* has been interpreted as the tower in the Horti Maecenatis from which Nero viewed the great fire of Rome in July 64 CE (Suet., *Nero* 38), but the existence of such a tower has been questioned.[83]

Hor., *Epod.* 9.1–5

Joyful [as I am] at Caesar's victory, when will I drink Caecuban wine stored up
    for a banquet in celebration
With you, happy Maecenas, in [your] high house [*alta domus*], by god's grace,
With the lyre's sound mixing with [the piping of] flutes,
That one Dorian, the others foreign [to it].[84]

Horace, *Odes*, ca. 23 BCE (Hor., *Odes*)

Horace wants his patron Maecenas to come to dinner at his house or at his Sabine villa.

Hor., *Odes* 3.29.1–16

There is sweet wine at my house not yet poured for you, Maecenas, scion of
    Tyrrhenian royalty,
With rose blooms and balsam to be mingled in your hair. Take yourself off right away,
Stop looking down on Tiber's stream, the slanting Aefulian fields,
And the ridge of Telegonus the parricide.[85]
Leave your pointless affluence behind
And your fortress house [*moles*] that almost touches the high-flying clouds.
Stop admiring the smoke, the wealth, and the noise of blessed Rome.
Most often it's a pleasant change for rich men:
In a poor man's house [*sub lare pauperum*] without canopies of purple cloth,
A welcome, plain dinner smooths a furrowed brow.

Elegiae in Maecenatem

A group of poems called *Elegiae in Maecenatem*, by a poet whose name has not been recorded, praise Maecenas for his modesty, his *horti*, and his love of nature.[86]

1.31–36

It was more noble to have been able [to be great] but not to wish for triumphs,
It was greater to have held back from great actions.
He preferred the shade-giving oak tree, cascading waters,
Some settled fruit-bearing *iugera*,
Cultivating the [Pierian] Muses and Phoebus [Apollo] in gentle *horti*,
Talking, while sitting among the chattering birds.

FRONTO (Marcus Cornelius Fronto, ca. 100–170 CE)

Epistles (Epistulae) (Fronto, Ep.)

The *horti*, unless or until they had entered the *res privata* or personal possession of the emperors, could be bought or assigned. Marcus Cornelius Fronto owned the Horti Maecenatis in the early 140s CE, more than 175 years after they were laid out, though whether by purchase or imperial assignment of usufruct is not known.[87] In this letter of late 143 CE, Fronto confirms the gardens' fame in literature by associating his ownership with Maecenas as patron of Horace, who knew the *horti* and their owner well.[88]

Fronto, *Ep.* 2.1.5 (37)[89]   In the matter of Polemon the rhetorician, whom you [recently] claimed, in your letter, to be "Ciceronian," I am referring [you to] a philosopher of whom I spoke in an oration that I gave in the Senate—a philosopher of truly ages past, unless I am mistaken. What would you say, Marcus, how does [this] Polemon's story the way I've presented it seem to you? For sure, the famous Horatius Flaccus [Horace], the poet who is not unfamiliar to me through Maecenas and my gardens of Maecenas [*Maecenatiani horti mei*], gave me many funny instances in the matter. For this Horatius, as I recall in his second book [of *Satires*], told this story about [another] Polemon. [...]

Afterword: Cicero and Villas as Places of Refuge and Safety

Cicero's estate at Arpinum, inherited from his father, confirmed his and his brother Quintus's patrimonial locus and their locally notable family; the villa with its extensions, and Quintus's new villas in the region, gave a solid—architectural and even decorative—basis for their claim to full participation as citizens in Roman political, military, and social affairs.[90] However, Arpinum was a bit out of the way and perhaps more rustic than Cicero's eventual status required; he tried to get his friend Atticus to come to his villas at either Formiae or Antium rather than receiving him at Arpinum.[91] By contrast, his villa at Tusculum was much closer to Rome and gave him access to neighbors who were socially and politically important. The Tusculanum became Cicero's main matter of pride and source of enjoyment; it was also a locale for *otium*, writing, reflection, and hospitality often designed to welcome philosophical or political conversations. These qualities extended to his coastal villas from Antium to Astura, Circeii, and Caieta, and to his villas on the Bay of Naples (Pompeii, Puteoli, Baiae, and Cumae). These were also located on the favored routes, and in the resorts of Roman high society, as they traveled to the bay area and back to the City. In receiving the dictator Caesar at his Puteolana on December 19, 45 BCE, Cicero had achieved the apex of social distinction.[92]

Villas were also places of safety. Their remoteness and isolation could provide some refuge from the dangers to which prominent politicians and their families were often exposed in Late Republican times. In 58 BCE, when he was exiled and his house and villas confiscated, Cicero made his way to Greece to observe the senatorial order that he reside at least 400 or more miles (about 608 km, or 378 mi.) from the capital. Right away, his friend Atticus invited him to stay at his Amalthea in Epirus; but Cicero demurred, fearing the presence of enemies in the district.[93] He would do so again nine years later on his way to join Pompey in Greece: Atticus again invited him to stay at the Amalthea for safety's sake, but Cicero again refused the invitation.[94]

Upon his return from exile in early 57 BCE, the villa at Tusculum became Cicero's refuge from the frozen political situation at Rome during the dominance of Pompey, Caesar, and Crassus between 60 and 53 BCE (the so-called First Triumvirate). At Tusculum, he engaged in philosophical writing and poetry as well as in pedagogical instruction of young men of good family and high status, thereby gaining some of the influence he had lost.[95] Plutarch's account of this period indicates that Cicero rarely went into Rome itself, and only did so to pay his respects to Caesar.

The fifteen months between January 49 and March 48 BCE saw the fracture between Caesar and Pompey following the defeat of Crassus in Syria in 53 BCE. Caesar's march southward upon crossing into Italy at the Rubicon in January 49 BCE threatened Rome itself and Cicero's family with it.[96] As an important Pompeian adherent, Cicero undertook a position of authority in Campania requiring his absence from Rome; he himself was in danger and feared the confiscation of his properties. He kept his son and namesake with him. His main concern was for his family and *familia*; on two successive days in January 49 BCE, he wrote to his wife Terentia and his daughter Tullia, asking them to be guided by other women of rank (*dignitas*) whether to leave the city or stay, and to consider going to one of his estates (*praedia*), even though Publius Cornelius Dolabella, an adherent of Caesar and Tullia's husband, could protect them if they stayed in Rome.[97] He feared both famine (*fames*) and rise in prices; living at one of his villas would be cheaper for the whole *familia*. In March, Cicero went to Arpinum to celebrate his son's coming of age, an important family ceremony witnessed by the local citizenry; the young man's bordered toga of youth would have been exchanged for the entirely white *toga pura* of the full citizen.[98] By June 7, on the eve of leaving Italy for Greece and Pompey's camp, he wrote again, urging his wife and daughter to go to Arpinum with the entire staff of their Roman *domus* and join the rural *familia* at the villa.[99]

The months after Caesar's assassination in March 44 BCE brought Cicero to new prominence in political affairs and new personal dangers. He wrote to Atticus on May 19 that he wished to return to his dear home (οἶκος φίλος) at Tusculum from a villa on negligible little banks (*ripulae*) at a beautiful place (*loca venusta*, i.e., Arpinum or Astura). Tusculum was evidently too dangerously close to the unsettled conditions at Rome, so he moved to his villa at Antium. That was the venue for the momentous deliberations, on June 8, 44 BCE, among Brutus, Brutus's mother Servilia, his half sister Tertulla, and his new second wife Porcia, and Cicero himself (with Cassius joining the meeting later). To Cicero's disgust ("No plan [*consilium*], no logic [*ratio*], no strategy [*ordo*]"), no good resolution was reached (Cic., *Att.* 389 [15.11]).

Villas are part of the many accounts of the deaths of Cicero and his brother Quintus and their futile attempts to seek refuge from assassination. The events between the ides of March 44 BCE and the murder of the Cicero brothers on December 7, 43 BCE, are well known. Antony, Octavian, and Lepidus agreed to proscribe them, among many others,[100] at a meeting at Bononia (modern Bologna) in November 43 BCE. Assassinating Cicero in particular came to be a desirable honor to win the triumvirs' approval. More than a century later, no less than thirty-eight versions of the death of Cicero—mainly as didactic examples of courage, fate, or cruelty, or else narrative accounts—were known to Seneca the Elder (ca. 54 BCE–39 CE).[101] The most famous is Plutarch's account: the Cicero brothers were at the villa at Tusculum, then left, borne on litters, for the coast; but Quintus, after a sad farewell, returned to Tusculum for money or important papers.[102] Quintus hid from his trackers, and his whereabouts were concealed by his son even after torture. But both—father and son—were killed.[103]

Meanwhile, Cicero had reached his villa at Astura. His next move was by boat, to the promontory of Circeii (modern San Felice Circeo), where he had a villa. He attempted to walk on the Via Appia back to Rome, but then returned to Astura for the night. His next move was by boat to Caieta (modern Gaeta), where he owned a seaside villa in a wooded area. He was killed there. His assassins had little trouble guessing where he was; they merely had to track him southward from Astura, from one of his villas to the next.

10

EMPERORS AND VILLAS

※

AUGUSTUS
TIBERIUS
GAIUS (CALIGULA)
CLAUDIUS
NERO
GALBA
VESPASIAN
TITUS
DOMITIAN
NERVA
TRAJAN
HADRIAN
ANTONINUS PIUS
MARCUS AURELIUS
LUCIUS VERUS
COMMODUS
SEVERUS ALEXANDER
GORDIAN III
TACITUS
DIOCLETIAN
ROMULUS AUGUSTULUS

The villas of emperors shared and even continued the culture of Republican-period villas but ultimately became different; perhaps new security measures, social hierarchies, etiquette, and the nature of emperorship itself changed. While the notion of *otium* remained as an underlying conception, the *imperium* with which emperors were invested and the cults, or condemnations, of their personalities modified accounts of their villas. In consequence, the sources describing or characterizing them are seen in the light and color in which their imperial owners or builders were viewed—either at the time or later—and are thus subject to political and moral interpretation that the Greek and Latin historians of Rome chose to emphasize. The result is that the sources for emperors' villas are relatively sparse vis-à-vis the literary sources for private villas in the imperial centuries (included in chapter 4), and they are often biased and vituperative. Setting aside the special villa-like Domus Aurea of Nero in Rome, the two great imperial villas *in rure*, namely the Albanum of Domitian and Hadrian's Villa at Tibur, were objects of ridicule and hatred for the former, and the latter garnered a mere two or three sentences. Texts about imperial villas appear well after the fact; only a few are first-hand accounts. That's about it: the archaeological and architectural records of emperors' villas in general outstrip their written sources, and except for Hadrian's Villa, even these records are somewhat sparse in number despite their importance. The selection of these texts for inclusion or exclusion in this collection is based on the following:

1. Mentions of villas that are merely incidental or circumstantial but provide no special information, for example, a villa in which an emperor happened to die or be buried, some event that happened in such and such a villa. These are listed in the endnotes for completeness but are rarely included among the texts.

2. Appearance of imperial villas in written notices of any kind, including villas in historical accounts as well as in poems, speeches, and other descriptive sources. Because historians mine earlier historians' accounts, any significant differences from original to version are cited in endnotes. Differences among texts can indicate variations of interpretation and report of current or past prejudices about the emperors themselves; how villas were part of later biases and prejudices, but not their actuality, is part of the history of both villas and emperors.

3. First-hand or near first-hand accounts. These are the most valuable for the lived experience of emperors' villas. The accounts of Pliny the Younger (for Trajan), Marcus Cornelius Fronto (for Antonius Pius and Marcus Aurelius), and the young Marcus Aurelius (for Antonius Pius) give some detailed impressions of imperial life *in rure*.

Villas and houses on any level are—and have always been—expressive of their owners and commissioners, whether they obey or break with architectural or other conventions. The meaning of a villa associated with an emperor can be outlined with reference to the obligatory or voluntary glorification of the emperor or to some denigration of him. There are subtleties within both glorification and denigration: for most writers of any kind, Augustus, Vespasian, and Trajan were viewed as benign, whereas Tiberius, Gaius, Nero, and Domitian were generally malign, with Hadrian somewhere in the middle. Writings about their villas follow suit: authors are careful to associate the rulers' characters with their dwellings, and villas were one way of magnifying their benignity or maligning their malignity.

At a level higher than villas, the arbitrary nature of these categorical divisions in modern writing of Roman history eventually became apparent and has prompted corrective reinterpretations and critical evaluations of the biases of the sources themselves.[1] This has led, justly and inevitably, to modern rehabilitations of the "bad" emperors and qualification of praise for the "good" ones. Tiberius, Nero, and recently Domitian are conspicuous examples of rehabilitation: the constancy of Tiberius in continuing the Augustan policies, or the intelligence of Nero's foreign relations are examples, and three edited volumes for Domitian follow along these lines.[2] The sources for imperial reigns are, with very few exceptions, "senatorial," which is to say that emperors who were polite to the senatorial elite were written up positively, whereas those who punished senators with exile, confiscation of property, or execution—whether just or unjust—were negatively viewed.[3]

The same "senatorial" prejudice is present in almost all the writers who discuss emperors' villas, no matter what their date: Tacitus, Suetonius, Pliny the Younger, Plutarch, Cassius Dio, Herodian, and the writer or writers of the *Historia Augusta*. The grounds for their disapproval are tediously predictable: sometimes (as with other building projects) they were deemed excessively costly, and very often there were repetitious accusations that villas were venues for sexual misconduct and violent cruelty. Many of these accounts seem to be court gossip, and it was justly said, of a "good" emperor: "There is no emperor who is not smeared with evil rumor."[4] Except for Pliny's laudatory description of Trajan's maritime villa at Centum Cellae (modern Civitavecchia), the villas of "good" emperors are usually described innocuously, as dwellings on family estates, which they loved and to which they returned. Seneca's dour views of emperors' villas, despite what was said of his own luxurious way of living, prevailed; innovations such as the villa-like urban palace of Nero's Domus Aurea, or Domitian's Albanum as the venue for major hunting, gladiatorial, and cultural festivals—no matter how brilliant architecturally or culturally—were seen as negative. "Lists" of good and bad emperors were made.[5] Poets, who were not of senatorial rank, were an exception; they often aspired to emperors' patronage for cultural cachet and social advancement, so they could be kinder about their villas.

While there was great variety in villas over the long imperial centuries from Julius Caesar and Augustus to the Late Antique period, certain themes reoccur. Tiberius grew cucumbers in specially invented frames on mobile beds fitted with windows of a transparent mineral to let in the sun. Diocletian, having abdicated in 305 CE after twenty years as *Augustus* and gone to his specially built palace-fortress at Spalatum (modern Split, Croatia) near his hometown of Salona on the Dalmatian coast, occupied his retirement by growing green vegetables (*olera*), praising his crop with the praise that Cato had conferred on cabbages some 450 years before. The adolescent Romulus Augustus, nicknamed Augustulus, notionally the last Roman emperor, was deposed by the barbarian king Odovacar in 476 CE and sent into exile to the Castellum Lucullanum (modern Castel dell'Ovo) on the island of Megalia (modern Megaride, now connected to the Pizzo Falcone neighborhood of Naples by a causeway). Lucullus had built a villa there after his return to Italy from the East in the 60s BCE. With the exiled young emperor Romulus's pious help, the Castellum Lucullanum soon became a monastery dedicated to St. Severinus.[6]

Augustus (Caesar Augustus, born Gaius Octavius, also known as Octavian, 63 BCE–14 CE, reigned 27 BCE–14 CE)

The only site for a villa or villas known to have been acquired by Augustus himself is the entire island of Capreae (modern Capri), which he exchanged for that of Aenaria (modern Ischia) in an arrangement with the city of Neapolis (modern Naples); he may have done so for security reasons, since the larger island was inhabited and had harbors whereas Capreae was small, naturally defended by steep cliffs, and approached with difficulty.[7] Otherwise, Suetonius judges that his villas were simple affairs, even though his granddaughter Julia built a very luxurious one, which he disapproved of; the frugal Augustus seems to have contented himself with borrowed villas where he was a guest, or villas in the environs of Rome (Lanuvium, Praeneste, Tibur) that had already been developed in the Late Republic and were the normal venues for villas.[8] However, his personal modesty about luxurious villas was different from the divine honors that accrued to him even during his lifetime, such that places associated with him came to have a numinous power, as did the house on the Palatine Hill in Rome in which he was born, the villa where he grew up, and the family villa where he died.[9]

SUETONIUS   (Gaius Suetonius Tranquillus, 69–after 122 CE)

Lives of the Twelve Caesars (De vita Caesarum), early second century CE

The Divine Augustus (Divus Augustus) (Suet., Aug.)

Suet., Aug. 5   Augustus was born in the consulates of Marcus Tullius Cicero and Gaius Antonius a little before sunrise on the ninth day before the kalends of October [September 28, 63 BCE] at "The Ox-Heads" in the area of the Palatine Hill; there is a shrine there that was built a little after he died.[10] [...]

Suet., Aug. 6   Even now, there is a modest room much like a storeroom [*nutrimentorum locus*] that is shown as his nursery in his grandfather's suburban villa near Velitrae, and opinion in the neighborhood has it that he was born there.[11] Unless out of necessity and having sought religious purification, no one dares to enter the room because of an ancient opinion that those who do so are seized with dread and terror, and this has recently been verified. For when a new owner of the villa went to bed in the room—either by chance or to investigate the matter—what happened is that after a very few hours of the night he was found thrown outside by a sudden unknown force and found half alive, laid low in front of the entrance to the room.

In his houses and villas, Augustus was very observant of strange occurrences and omens.

Suet., Aug. 92.1–2   [...] But he was especially moved by prodigies. When a palm tree sprouted in the cracks of the flagstones in front of his house, he transplanted it to the open area [*compluvium*, in his atrium] next to the Penates of the gods [the *lararium* of the house] and made sure, with great effort, that it grew. He was so happy at the revival of the branches of an old oak that had already drooped to the ground when he landed on the island of Capreae that he traded it [the whole island] for Aenaria [modern Ischia] with the city of Neapolis. [...]

After describing the modesty of Augustus's urban houses in Rome (near the Forum and on the Palatine) and their simple decoration, Suetonius gives his readers some idea of his villas and his habits.[12]

Suet., *Aug.* 72 [...] In the other aspects of his life, it has been observed that he was entirely self-controlled and never gave rise to even the suspicion of having any vices. [...] If he planned to work quietly alone and without interruption, there was a room at the top of his house that he called "Syracuse" and "workroom" [*technyphion*]. He would take himself there or else to the suburban villa of one of his freedmen, and when he felt unwell, he would sleep at Maecenas's house.[13] For holidays he most often visited the seashore and islands of Campania or went to towns near the City: Lanuvium, Praeneste, Tibur, and at Tibur he often held [judicial] court in the colonnades of the Temple of Hercules. He disliked large, elaborate country mansions [*ampla et perose praetoria*]. He ordered that a big, complicated country mansion built by his granddaughter Julia to be razed to the ground, and his own villas were not so much decorated with statues and paintings as with terraced walkways, groves, and things remarkable for their age and rarity, among them, at Capreae, parts of giant whales [*beluae*] and wild animals called "bones of giants" and weapons that had belonged to heroes [of the past].[14]

Augustus and Capreae

CASSIUS DIO   (Lucius Cassius Dio, ca. 165–ca. 235 CE)

Roman History, early third century CE (Cass. Dio)

Cass. Dio 52.43.2   In exchange for other lands, he [Augustus] obtained Capreae from the Neapolitans, who had originally owned it; it lies not far off the mainland around Surrentum and is completely worthless, but its fame in the present day is because Tiberius had a dwelling there.[15]

Augustus and the Villa of Vedius Pollio at Pausilypon

In 15 BCE, a friend of Augustus, Publius Vedius Pollio, died, leaving his house in Rome and his villa at Pausilypon (modern Posilippo) between Neapolis and Baiae on the Bay of Naples as bequests to the emperor.[16] Augustus ordered that Vedius's house on the Oppian Hill be torn down and its site be converted to public and religious uses, namely the Porticus Liviae honoring his wife Livia. The transition from private luxury to public amenity had become an Augustan policy.

Vedius's villa at Pausilypon was not torn down. Its subsequent fame came from a scene plausibly, if not definitively, set there: it was a *villa maritima* with sea-level space for the *piscinae* that made its owner's cruelty infamous and served to advertise Augustus's justice, humane empathy, and magnanimity.[17] When the emperor was its owner's guest at a dinner, the villa—or rather the villa's reputation—served as the mise-en-scène for Vedius's cruel ferocity tempered and redeemed by the emperor's benign authority. It remained an imperial property: some renovations to its water system were made in the reign of Hadrian.[18]

Cass. Dio 54.23.1–6   In this year [15 BCE], Vedius Pollio died. He was a man who, being descended from freedman stock and was a knight, had done nothing that might be memorable; still, he had become well known for this great wealth and his cruelty beyond all others, so for that he deserves a mention in history. Other things about him would be pointless to tell. However, I may report that he kept large moray eels [or lampreys] that were trained to devour men, and he was pleased to throw them the slaves he wanted to punish. At one time when he was Augustus's host, his wine bearer broke a crystal [or rock crystal] wine cup, and he [Pollio] ordered the slave to be thrown to the lampreys, without reckoning with [the presence of] his guest. At this [order], the young slave [παιδὸς] fell on his knees and implored him; first, Augustus attempted to persuade Pollio not to take such a measure, but when Pollio ignored him, the emperor said, "Bring me all the other wine cups and others like them, any that you own that are valuable." When they were brought, he ordered them to be smashed. When he [Pollio] saw this, he was angry. But he could not be angry about [merely] one cup when so many more had been broken, and he could not punish the servant for what Augustus himself had also done, so he kept quiet unwillingly. That's the kind of man this Pollio was. In death, he left much [many bequests] to many people, and to Augustus a large part of his property including the Pausilypon, a place between Neapolis and Puteoli, with an order that a very beautiful public work [δήμῳ περικαλλὲς ἔργον] be built on the site. Augustus had the [urban] house [οἰκία] razed to ground level, pretending to be laying down the foundation of the [previous] project but then building the portico, inscribing it with Livia's name, not Pollio's.[19] But in fact this was done so he [Pollio] would not be memorialized in the City [in any way].

The Villa of Livia at Primaporta

PLINY THE ELDER   (Gaius Plinius Secundus (23/24–79 CE)

Natural History (Naturalis historia), mid-first century CE (Plin., *HN*)

Livia owned a villa at Primaporta on the Via Flaminia, about 11 km north of Rome, built out on a long terrace facing southwest; its structure was similar to *basis villae* at Tibur and elsewhere.[20] It may have been part of her dowry portion when she married Tiberius Claudius Nero in 44 or 43, which reverted to her when she divorced him to marry Octavian in January 38 BCE.[21] Its story became part of the imperial legend. In this text, Pliny is actually writing about trees with medicinal and herbal properties. An embroidered variant of the legend about the Primaporta villa, with some significant differences, can be found in Suetonius's life of Galba: Suet., *Galb*. 1–3; Suetonius's account is followed by Cass. Dio, *Epit. Bk.* 68.29.3.

Plin., *HN* 15.136–137 (15.40)   There are other aspects of the laurel that are worthy of reminding ourselves: they concern the Divine Augustus. When Livia Drusilla—who took the name Augusta when she married[22]—was engaged to Caesar [Augustus], an eagle dropped a hen of dazzling whiteness, completely unharmed, from the sky into her lap as she was seated. She looked on the strange happening [*miraculum*] with wonderment but without alarm. But that was not all: the hen held a sprig of laurel laden with its berries in its beak! The priests [*haruspices*] ordered that the bird and its chicks were to be preserved and that the branch itself was to be planted and taken care of with ritual devotion.[23] This happened in the villa of the Caesars on the Tiber River at the ninth milestone on the Via Flaminia, for which it is called Ad Gallinas, and the grove has grown up in a wonderful way. Afterwards, Caesar [Augustus], when in triumph, held a branch of this laurel in his hand and a crown of it on his head. From that time, the succeeding Caesars as emperors have done the same, and the practice [*mos*] of planting the branches they held [in the triumphal procession] became a tradition. The groves [or trees] survived, each one with his own name, so it was perhaps from this that there was a change in the triumphal accessories.[24]

Death of Augustus at His Ancestral Villa

Suetonius, *Lives of the Twelve Caesars. The Divine Augustus*

Suetonius's account of the death of Augustus follows him from one villa to another in the Capreae–Bay of Naples region.

Suet., *Aug.* 97.1–2 In addition, I will give an account of his death and his deification after death—things that were foretold by very clear signs. [...]

[...] At the point of sending Tiberius to Illyricum and intending to travel with him as far as Beneventum, people interrupted him as he was hearing law cases and detained him with one case after another, he exclaimed that he could not remain in Rome after this—something that soon was taken to be an omen [of his death]. Then he went only as far as Astura: from there, against his custom [but] on the chance of a favorable wind, he embarked by night, contracting an illness with effusion of the bowels.

Suet., *Aug.* 98.1–6 Then, sailing along the Campanian shoreline and around the nearby islands, he spent four whole days at the Capreae villa [*Caprearum*] giving himself entirely to *otium* and friendly encounters [*comitas*]. Along the gulf of Puteoli, it so happened that a ship from Alexandria had just landed, and the passengers and crew, dressed in white clothes and crowned with wreaths, burning incense for good luck [*tura fausta*], in unison heaped him with praises, [saying] that they lived by him alone, that by him they [had] sailed [safely], and that they enjoyed liberty and good fortune from him.[25] [...]

[...] He constantly watched the [training] exercises of the ephebes, of which there were still a number on Capreae as there had been in the past. He also offered them a feast with himself being present, both allowing and even requesting freedom in joking and rushing for tickets for fruit, food, and other things he scattered about. He did not abstain from any kind of fun.

He called an island near Capreae *Apragopolis* in accordance with the slothfulness of some of those of his entourage who had withdrawn there [with him].[26]

In his last illness, Augustus returned to the villa and estate of his Octavius ancestors at Nola near Naples.[27]

Suet., *Aug.* 100 He died in the same room in which his father had died, on the fourteenth day before the kalends of September [August 19, 14 CE]... thirty-five days before his seventy-sixth birthday. [...]

Tiberius (Tiberius Julius Caesar Augustus, 42 BCE–37 CE, reigned 14–37 CE)

Tiberius, the elder of the two sons of Augustus's third wife Livia, was named by the emperor as his political heir after complex struggles among the descendants of the Julian and Claudian founders of the imperial regime, after the death of Julius Caesar and of several other, more favored successors. Tiberius's generalship in Germany and official civil appointments brought him distinction, but the precarity of his position prompted his removal from active political life to Rhodes for a year in 6 CE, where he lived as a private citizen. Suetonius's account emphasizes the modesty of both his house in town and a villa in the country as well as his affability to the Rhodians.[28] Upon returning to Rome, Tiberius left the Domus Pompeiana in the Carinae, where he had lived before, and dwelled modestly in the Gardens of Maecenas.[29]

As emperor, following the death of his son Drusus in 23 CE and other difficulties, Tiberius removed himself permanently from the City to Capreae in 26 CE, leaving Lucius Aelius Sejanus, prefect of the Praetorian Guard and ultimately consul in 31, in authority in the imperial administration. With Tiberius's construction of the Villa Iovis on the island, villas assumed a palatial aspect as well as an entirely personal one, emphasizing retirement and *otium* and, in Tiberius's case, vice—at least in the prejudiced views of his biographers.[30]

Suetonius, *Lives of the Twelve Caesars. Tiberius* (Suet., *Tib.*)

Writing on Tiberius and his villa at Capreae, Suetonius depicts villas as places of both retirement and debauchery.

Suet., *Tib.* 38–41   For two entire years after becoming emperor, he did not set foot beyond the gates [of the City], and after that he went nowhere except to towns nearby or, at most, to Antium, and holding himself back even going there very rarely and for only a few days. Even so, he often announced that he would visit the provinces and the armies, and almost every year [made a show of] preparing for departure by renting wagons and getting supplies arranged in the municipalities and colonies. [...]

After both of his sons had died—Germanicus died in Syria, Drusus at Rome—he sought retirement in Campania, and almost everyone held the firm view, and said so out loud, that he would never return and would soon die. Both predictions almost came true: he never returned to Rome, and a few days after, while he was dining at a grand villa called The Cave [*praetorium Speluncae*] near Tarracina, it so happened that many huge stones fell down, crushing several guests and servants, but he was fortuitously spared.[31] [...]

Traveling in Campania, he dedicated the Capitolium at Capua and a temple to Augustus at Nola, which he feigned to be the reason for his tour, and then he went to Capreae, especially attracted to the island because it could be approached only at one shoreline, everywhere else having huge high jagged stone cliffs and deep water. Right away he was called back [to the mainland] by the continual requests of the people, because at Fidenae more than 20,000 people had been killed in the collapse of an amphitheater during a gladiatorial exhibition.[32] [...]

Returning to the island, he completely abandoned any attention to duty, and from that time forward never brought the decuries [jury duty groups] of the knights up to strength, did not change the [appointments of] military tribunes or the governors of any of the [imperial] provinces, and left Spain and Syria without consular [senatorial] governors. He allowed Armenia to be occupied by Parthia.[33] [...]

Suet., *Tib.* 43   In his Capreae retirement he invented, as a place for his secret lust, *sellaria* in which selected bands of girls and male prostitutes called Spintrians who engaged in especially monstrous sexual couplings, three at a time, so at the sight of them he revived his fading sexual capacities.[34] For the many bedrooms, there was a supply of paintings and figurines showing the most lascivious images and configurations as well as the books of Elephantis to give lessons in case someone needed a model for a specific position.[35] In the woods and groves [throughout the island] as well in its caves and rocky retreats he set up places for both sexes dressed as Pans and Nymphs to have sex.[36] Playing on the name of the island, wits tagged the place *Caprineum* [the goat's place].[37]

CORNELIUS TACITUS
(Publius Cornelius Tacitus, best known as Tacitus, ca. 56–ca. 120 CE)

***Annals* (*Annales*), early second century CE (Tac., *Ann.*)**

According to Tacitus and Suetonius, the evil Sejanus gained the trust of Tiberius by saving him in an accident at a villa on the coast near Tarracina (modern Terracina) near the modern town of Sperlonga.[38]

Tac., *Ann.* 4.59   At that time a dangerous accident happened to the Caesar [Tiberius] which stimulated these pointless rumors and confirmed him in the matter of Sejanus's friendship and loyalty to an even greater degree. They were eating in a villa called the Cave [*Spelunca*] between Amyclae and the mountains at Fundi.[39] Some of the servants were crushed by a sudden slide of rocks, causing those present to flee in panic. Sejanus warded off the falling stones by arching himself over the Caesar with knee, face, and hands, and he was found in that position by the soldiers who came to the rescue. Though his counsel would prove deadly, this [event] made him greater [in the emperor's opinion], as a person not concerned for himself, so his advice could be taken with confidence. [...]

Tac., *Ann.* 4.67   The Caesar [Tiberius] at this time was dedicating temples in Campania, and even though he had warned, by edict, that no one was to interrupt his privacy [*quies*], and the crowds of the towns were fended off by a military guard detailed for that purpose, he took such a dislike for the municipalities, colonies, and other things on the mainland that he took himself to the island of Capreae, separated from the tip of the promontory of Surrentum by a strait 3 miles wide [about 4.5 km, or 2¾ mi]. I might well believe that the island's isolation [*solitudo*] was its most pleasing aspect, because it is surrounded by a sea without good ports [*importuosus*] and approaches that are barely adequate for small boats, and no one can land there without being seen by a guard. In winter, the barrier of mountains that defends it from the harsh winds gives the island a gentle climate. In summer, it faces the Favonius [western wind from the sea] and is made very agreeable by the open sea all around. It gave a view of the most beautiful bay, at least until the fiery mountain, Vesuvius, changed the topography of the area. Its history is that it was held by Greeks, with Capreae being settled by Teleboans.[40] Now, however, Tiberius occupied it with the buildings of twelve villas with names, he who once was so very preoccupied with the cares of public business was now as much fixed on hidden excess and evil *otium*.[41]

Tacitus writes of Tiberius's residence on Capreae, the Villa Iovis,[42] and how its cliff-top position was used as a device for summary execution, potential or actual. The fortune teller referred to is the "Chaldean" fortune teller Thrasyllus, to whom Tiberius was devoted. They had met at Rhodes in 6 CE; the emperor brought him to Rome and then installed him on Capreae.[43]

Tac., *Ann.* 6.21   He used the highest part of the villa for any such deliberations [about foretelling the future] with the complicity of a freedman. The villa is set above a cliff, and this illiterate, strongly built fellow led him [Thrasyllus] along the trackless steep heights because Tiberius had decided to test his [the fortune teller's] ability so that, on the way back, if there was any suspicion of empty prediction [*vanitas*] or fakery [*fraus*], he should be thrown into the sea below, just in case he should be an informer who would reveal the secrets [of the emperor's fate].[44]

Cassius Dio, *Roman History*

In cataloguing the emperor Tiberius's vices, Cassius Dio tells a curious story of the emperor's friend, involving a villa and a two-day act of hospitality.

Cass. Dio 58. 22. 2–3   There was one Sextus Marius, a friend of his [i.e., of Tiberius]. He had acquired [from his friendship with the emperor] great wealth and power. When he [Sextus Marius] was angry at a neighbor, he invited him to to dine [and kept him as his guest] for two days. On the first day, he had his neighbor's villa completely razed to [below] ground level then, on the second day, had it rebuilt much better and greatly enhanced [from what it had been]. When the neighbor, saying that he did not know who had done these things, Marius acknowledged that he had done both, saying clearly, "This shows that, in my revenge and my reciprocation, I have both the knowledge and strength to defend myself against anything and can do so."

Gaius (Gaius Caesar Augustus Germanicus, known as Caligula, 12–41 CE, reigned 37–41 CE)

The execration of Gaius, also known as Caligula, and his short reign were such that, while Suetonius records some of the public works completed from previous imperial projects and a few initiated by the young emperor, the memory of his works was generally passed over. His pontoon bridge from Baiae to the harbor mole of Puteoli across the bay, partially made of commandeered commercial vessels tied together and heaped with earth and a stone roadbed for parades, is the most famous from his early reign.[45] The second great project was also on water: the two huge boats set afloat on Lake Nemi near Ariccia about 30 km southeast of Rome. Nemi was a center for villas, among them that of Julius Caesar,[46] and was close to other villa-resorts—Tusculum, Lanuvium, Velitrae (modern Velletri), and Alba. The boats, which were seaworthy and equipped to move and be maneuvered as well as anchored in place, comprised a rich decoration as well as heated baths, running water, marble and mosaic floors, gardens, moving bases for statues, and what may have been shrines.[47] These floating villas did not find a record in literary accounts, but Suetonius includes a muddled account of other ships of another type, also richly equipped, which may represent poorly transcribed notes about the boats at Nemi, so it is included here.

Pliny the Elder, *Natural History*

On the subject of outstanding plane trees, Pliny discusses the famous tree in the Academy of Athens and others, including one associated with the emperor Gaius (Caligula).[48]

Plin., *HN* 12.5 (10–11)   Another example was at a villa at Velitrae belonging to the emperor Gaius [Caligula] who was astonished at the floor space provided by a single plane tree with dining benches laid out in the open on its branches as if they were beams; he [Gaius] had dinner there in a *triclinum* capable of holding fifteen guests and their servants, with himself contributing to some of the shadiness [of the venue].[49] He called this dining room his nest.

Suetonius, *Lives of the Twelve Caesars. Gaius Caligula* (Suet., *Calig.*)

Suet., *Calig.* 37.2-3   [...] He also built *liburnae* with ten banks of oars and sterns decorated with gems, awnings of many colors, huge baths and colonnades, big *triclinia* and even vines and various kinds of fruit-bearing trees so that, reclining [at table] during the day, he could sail along the shore of Campania accompanied by dancing singers and musicians.[50] In the construction of grand houses in the country [*praetoria*] and villas, he cared little for any plan except for wanting things that could not be done. So moles were built out into the turbulent deep sea, rocks of hardest flint were gouged out, plains were raised to mountain heights, and mountain ridges razed to the level of flat lands. All this was done with incredible speed, because the consequence of delay was death. So as to not get [too far] into details, in the space of less than a year, he spent huge amounts of wealth, including the entire amount of 2,700,000,000*HS* that Tiberius Caesar [had left].

PHILO OF ALEXANDRIA (ca. 20 BCE–50 CE)

Embassy to Gaius (Legatio ad Gaium), after 41 CE (Philo, *Leg.*)

Philo of Alexandria was a major intellectual who sought to interrelate Greek Stoic philosophy and Jewish traditions. He was also a leading citizen of that city. In 39 or 40 CE, following a complex series of events—and partially in consequence of the emperor Gaius Caligula having declared himself a god to be worshiped in statue form in all shrines of the empire including the Temple of Jerusalem—there were civil disturbances against the Jewish community in its greatest center in the Mediterranean, Alexandria in Egypt. Philo and four other representatives were sent to the court of the emperor at Rome to plead for exemption from the imperial command on behalf of both the Alexandrian and Judaean Jews.[51] Gaius received them at two places, one at an imperial villa at Puteoli on the Bay of Naples, the other at the two villas in the Horti Maecenatis and the Horti Lamiani on the Esquiline Hill in Rome. As an eyewitness, Philo describes the reception at one of the villas in the Esquiline *horti* in interesting detail.[52]

The emperor gave the Jewish ambassadors a tour of the villa, but he was accompanied by a delegation arguing against—in fact, mocking—the ambassadors, who were hard put to speak, in view of the emperor's hostility and increasing agitation. I have omitted from Philo's account most of the terrifying three-way interchange among the emperor, the parties opposing the Jewish claims and requests, and the Alexandrian ambassadors, but Philo emphasizes the themes of a sinister theatrical situation and that of a prejudiced courtroom and judge, as the tour of the villa progresses.[53]

Philo, Leg. 29 (185)   We had set out from Rome to the Bay [κόλπος] around Dichearchea [i.e., Puteoli], following Gaius, who had come down to the sea and was idling there, going from one to another of his many villas.[54]

Philo, Leg. 44 (350–352)   The events of the meeting revealed a pitiless tyrant with a harsh expression on his brow. [...] He called the officials of the Gardens of Maecenas and Lamia, which were adjacent to one another and close to the City, and where he had been enjoying himself for three or four days. [...] He ordered the officials to leave the villas open so he could inspect them. [...]

Philo, Leg. 45 (358–359)   While saying these things, he continued his tour of the villas, viewing all the rooms—the men's chambers [ἀνδρῶνας], the women's quarters, the rooms on the ground floor and the ones above—criticizing some for their deficiencies of construction, and, for others, proposing ideas of his own to make them more sumptuous.[55] In this way we were driven along, following him up and down, while being ridiculed by our enemies, like actors in theatrical mimes; indeed, the whole thing was a mime. [...]

Philo, Leg. 45 (361)   After having issued orders about the buildings, he asked us this important and solemn question, "Why do you refuse to eat pork?" There was laughter from some of our enemies at this because they were amused. [...]

The emperor told the ambassadors to address the issue of Jewish citizenship.

Philo, Leg. 45 (364–366)   We began speaking to make the argument for him, but when he had savored our reasoning and saw that it could not be easily ignored in any way, he set aside our initial arguments before we could give stronger ones, and he rushed at full speed into the main room; walking around in it, he ordered the windows everywhere to be replaced with transparent stones which, like clear glass, do not block light from coming in but keep out the wind and the heat of the sun. Then he turned and asked, in a less agitated manner, "What are you saying?" When we started on the next set of arguments, he once more ran into another room and ordered original paintings to be installed there. Our claims having been torn to shreds and cut to pieces, ... we gave up. We had no more strength. [...]

Claudius (Tiberius Claudius Caesar Augustus Germanicus, 10 BCE–54 CE, reigned 41–54 CE)

No villas are recorded from Claudius's reign except for what is known of the Gardens of Lucullus, but there is an inscription that records a villa at Baiae, probably connected to the structure at Punta dell'Epitaffio.[56]

Tacitus, *Annals*

The Gardens of Lucullus had by now changed owners, but their beauty and renovations excited others to covet them, in this case the emperor Claudius's wife Valeria Messalina.[57]

Tac., *Ann*. 9.1 [...] She [Valeria Messalina] believed that Valerius Asiaticus, who had been twice consul, had been her [Poppaea Sabina's] adulterous lover, and because she was also eager to acquire the Gardens laid out by Lucullus, which he [Asiaticus] was building back up in a notably magnificent way, she charged Suillius to bring indictments against both of them.[58] [...]

Asiaticus was condemned by Claudius and given permission to choose how he would die.

Tac., *Ann*. 9.3 Urged by certain people to a slow death by starvation, Asiaticus said that he would refuse that kind offer. Then he did the exercises that he customarily did, bathed, and dined pleasantly, saying that it would have been more honorable to have died by the cunning of a Tiberius or the violence of a Gaius Caesar [Gaius Caligula] than to have been destroyed by a woman's deceit and Vitellius's shameless mouthings.[59] He opened his veins, but before [doing so] he went to see his funeral pyre [in the Gardens of Lucullus] and ordered it to be moved to another place, for fear that the shade trees might be damaged by the smoke of the fire. So free from worry was he at the end [of his life]![60]

Nero (Nero Claudius Caesar Augustus Germanicus, 37–68 CE, reigned 54–68 CE)

Nero had maritime villas at Antium and Bauli near Baiae, but there are only passing references to them. There is no direct literary reference for a villa built in his reign, and probably for him, at Sublaqueum (modern Subiaco).[61] Nero's most famous construction, the villa-like Domus Aurea, is included here, as well as a discussion about villas and property between the emperor and his former tutor, Seneca the Younger.

Tacitus, *Annals*

After Nero's accession in 54 CE, his relations with his mother, Agrippina the Younger, by whose machinations he had come to be emperor, became increasingly antagonistic, so he urged her to seek *otium* at her villas. Nero wished to avoid murdering his mother by sword, knife, or poison, so in March 59 CE, while in residence at the imperial villa at Bauli, he invited her to dinner. Afterwards, when she was returning to her own villa on the Lucrine lake at night, he offered her a special boat, in fact a device to have her drowned. The habit of villa owners of maritime villas to travel between residences by boat gave a plausible occasion for her murder. Such pleasant boating would have normally been for hospitable purposes, not murderous ones. The passage below indicates the etiquette of hospitality at villas among members of the imperial family.

Tac., *Ann.* 14.3–4 For these reasons, Nero avoided face-to-face meetings with her, and encouraged her to seek *otium* when she went to her gardens [*horti*] and country places [*agri*] at Tusculum and Antium. [...]

[...] The scheme was pleasing and so was the timing because he [Nero] usually celebrated the Quinquatria holidays at Baiae.[62] He enticed his mother to come there, remarking repeatedly that a parent's resentment had to be borne with a quiet spirit, and thereby give an impression of reconciliation [between them] and getting Agrippina to accept [his invitation] with the easy credulity that women have for pleasant situations. As she came there—she was arriving from Antium—he met her down at the shore, grasped her hand, kissed her, and led her to Bauli.[63] That was the name of the villa at the edge of the water by the promontory of Misenum and the lake of Baiae.[64] [...]

Tacitus wrote of Seneca the Younger[65] and his precarious situation with the emperor Nero. Imperial largesse—and the properties that could be acquired from it—had been showered on the philosopher, and in 49 CE, he had been appointed by Agrippina to be tutor to her son Nero, and when Nero became emperor in 54 CE, Seneca became an imperial confidant and advisor along with Sextus Afranius Burrus, prefect of the Praetorian Guard. A series of accusations brought by Publius Suillius Rufus beginning in 58 CE, and the death of Burrus in 62 CE, made Seneca's position vulnerable.[66] Speeches against him about his wealth, malfeasances, and villas were recorded by Tacitus and Cassius Dio.[67] Tacitus reproduces (or paraphrases) Seneca's fine Stoic speech to Nero in his defense against the accusations of his detractors as well as Nero's reply: Seneca is actually asking to resign and leave the imperial entourage. Both philosopher and emperor mention gardens and villas.

Tac., *Ann.* 14.52–53 The death of Burrus diminished Seneca's power because the exercise of good intentions was weakened when one of the two [good counsellors] was removed, and also because Nero was tending to [listen to] worse ones. These [bad counsellors] charged Seneca with various crimes, namely that he was even at present adding to the wealth that went beyond that of a private fortune [*privatum modum opes*], that he solicited the attention of citizens for himself, and was outstripping even the emperor in the pleasantness of his gardens and villas [*hortorum . . . amoenitas . . . villarum*]. They even objected that he [Seneca], by writing poems more frequently now that Nero had come to love verses [as well], was appropriating all praise of eloquence to himself alone.

Seneca was by no means unaware of the charges against him—they were conveyed to him by those who [still] had some honorable concerns, and Caesar [Nero] was declining any close familiarity with him. He asked for an appointment to talk, his request was accepted, and he began in this way: "It has been fourteen years, Caesar, since I was assigned to you in your expectation [of being emperor] and eight since you obtained the *imperium*. In that time, you have loaded me with honors and wealth, such that the only thing that prevents me from being happy is moderation [in having these gifts].[68] [...] And in relation to your generosity, what else besides my zealous concerns have I been able to demonstrate? Zealous concerns [*studia*] undertaken, I might say, in quiet places away from shadowy [public?] venues? From those concerns has come my fame, because I am considered to have been there for you in your early youthful moments. The prize [of fame] for such things is great indeed! But you have endowed me with such gratitude, with such immense wealth, that I often ask myself, "Is it really I who is numbered among the great men of the State—I, who come from the equestrian rank and a provincial place? Has my [brash] new fame come to shine among these noblemen loaded with ancient honors? Where is that spirit [I used to have] that was pleased enough with a moderate existence [*mediocritas*]? A man like that—one who builds up gardens and strolls about in suburban villas [*suburbana*], enjoying big estates and important investments [*latus faenus*]? There's only one defense [for such a man as I]—that I should not [dare to] decline your generous gifts.'"[69]

Tac., *Ann.* 55   To which Nero replied in this way, more or less [*ferme*], [...] "If I am able to respond right away to your thoughtful speech, it is because I first received it [that capacity] among the gifts you taught me, which is [to speak] not solely with careful preparation but also spontaneously. [...] As long as life continues, the strength of your gifts to me will be eternal. What you have in the way of gifts from me—gardens, investments, and villas [*horti et faenus et villa*]—are fleeting [*obnoxius*]. They may seem great, but many men by no means your equal in talent have had more."[70] [...]

JUVENAL   (Decimus Junius Juvenalis, ca. 55–ca. 127 CE)

Satires, 117–early 120s CE (Juv., *Satires*)

Juvenal records the events of the conspiracy against Nero by Gaius Calpurnius Piso in 65 CE that included Seneca's *horti* being confiscated, as was the villa (*aedes*) on the Caelian Hill that belonged to Plautius Lateranus, consul-designate of that year. The theme of *Satire* 4 is the iniquity of desire for money, high office, and fame.[71]

Juv., *Satires* 4.10.12–18
> Even more people are strangled by money garnered with excessive worrying
> And by wealth that overwhelms all other inheritances,
> Like a British whale overwhelms [little] dolphins.
> That's the reason why, in those terrible times and under the orders of Nero,
> [It took] a whole cohort [of soldiers] to surround Longinus
> And the huge *horti* of that immensely wealthy Seneca and lay siege to the remarkable
>   house [*egregia aedes*] of the Laterani.[72]
> A soldier rarely [is called upon] to invade a [mere] attic room [*cenaculum*].

The Domus Aurea of Nero (64–69 CE)

The dates of the written sources for the Domus Aurea are indicative of how their authors came to view Nero's project in moralizing and political light: Pliny the Elder (mid-first century CE) could have witnessed its construction but devoted little space to it. Thirty years or so later, Tacitus and Suetonius (elder and younger contemporaries writing in the early second century CE) would never have seen the palace, its outbuildings, and its villa-like setting, even though some of it survived to the reign of Titus (79–81 CE). Martial, writing in the later 80s and 90s CE, refers to its components only as the hated predecessors of the constructions that replaced it, primarily the Flavian Amphitheater (colloquially known as the Colosseum).[73] Cassius Dio (late second–early third century CE) does not actually mention Nero's Domus Aurea, only opinions about it the year after Nero was killed.[74] The written sources included here are examples of how the Domus Aurea came to be vulnerable politically in succeeding reigns.[75]

Fires that began on July 19, 64 CE, nearly destroyed ten of Rome's fourteen urban administrative districts and neighborhoods (*regiones* subdivided into *vici*), which had been established by Augustus in 7 BCE.[76] Catastrophe gives rise to opportunity and changes space and time: space, by providing new areas for building and spurring architectural imagination; time, by hastening the acts of construction through necessity.[77] As many of the monuments and houses of the Palatine Hill were burned, the area to its northeast and southeast sides offered a bowl of land defined by the lower reaches of the Oppian Hill on the north and the rise of the Caelian Hill on the south.[78] This became the site of the *horti* and villa-like complex called the Domus Aurea. While not complete at Nero's death in 69 CE, its buildings and landscaping may well have provided much-needed temporary work for the urban craftsmen, builders, shopkeepers and the like who had been forced out of their usual occupations.[79] The palace and park appear to have been planned in tandem with their connection to the Via Sacra and the Forum, with a *rus in urbs, urbs in rus* intention.[80]

Descriptions of his buildings, and especially the landscaping of the Domus Aurea, give a snapshot of how villas—in this case, on a gigantic scale within an urban area—had come to be viewed in the second half of the first century CE. In addition, the Domus Aurea, with its complex relationship of country to City, City to countryside, *rus in urbs, urbs in rus*, at the elite level, elicited a popular jibe about the ancient town of Veii as an emblem of the rustic towns of the hinterland, as recorded by Suetonius: "Rome is becoming a *domus*! Get yourselves to Veii, *Quirites*, unless that *domus* occupies Veii as well!"[81]

The date of completion of the Domus Aurea is uncertain and its later fate mixed. In the year 69 CE, when there were several contenders for the imperial dignity, in January of that year, Marcus Salvius Otho, in one of the first acts as emperor, restored the statues of Nero that had been vandalized after Nero's suicide in June 68 CE and authorized a sum of 50,000*HS* for the completion of the Domus Aurea.[82] His successor, Aulus Vitellius, arrived in Rome in April 69 CE; he and his wife Galeria Fundana found the Domus Aurea to be substandard as far as imperial residences were concerned.[83] By the time of Martial's *On the Spectacles, Epigram* 2 in the late 80s CE, some twenty-five years after it was begun, the memory of its topography persisted.

Pliny the Elder, *Natural History*

Pliny sets the palace of Gaius (Caligula) on the Palatine Hill, which may have been an extension of the Domus Tiberiana of the previous reign, and the Domus Aurea of Nero among the expensive and wasteful instances of the *domus* construction of the Late Republic. Pliny is being unusually sarcastic in these passages.[84]

Plin., *HN* 36.111–112 (36.23)   But two *domus* surpassed all of these. We have seen the City completely ringed by the *domus* of the emperors Gaius and Nero, and the latter's *domus*, not to be outdone, is called the Domus Aurea. No doubt about it: those who contributed so much to the empire lived in such houses, men who left plough and hearth to defeat other peoples and return to triumphs, men whose farm properties took up smaller space than those emperors' latrines [*sellaria*]. Really, it's something to think about: how small in size the land allotments which used to be granted to invincible generals by the State to build their houses. The highest of these honors, as in the case of Publius Valerius Publicola…was that, by special decree, such houses were allowed to have doors opening outward so as to stand open to the public thoroughfare.[85]

Suetonius, *Lives of the Twelve Caesars*. Nero (Suet., *Nero*)

Suet., *Nero* 31.1–2   There was nothing more disastrous than his building: he had a house [*domus*] built from the Palatine Hill to the Esquiline, which he called at first the Domus

Transitoria, but soon after it was finished and destroyed in a fire, he called it the Domus Aurea once it was rebuilt.[86] Its size and embellishment will be amply described as follows: its entrance court [*vestibulum*] was large enough to accommodate a statue of him [Nero] 120 feet high and of such a size as to contain a triple portico a mile long. There was also a lake [*stagnum*] the size of a sea surrounded by buildings in the likeness of cities [*ad urbium speciem*] and with assorted rural landscapes as well: ploughed fields, vineyards, pastures, and woods, and large numbers of animals, domesticated and wild. Other parts were all covered in gold and studded with gems together with mother-of-pearl... [...]. When the house was finished to this standard and he dedicated it, he approved it just so far, saying that he was beginning, at last, to live like a man.[87]

Tacitus, *Annals*

After describing some examples of Nero's vices and violence, Tacitus takes up the events of 64 CE.

Tac., *Ann.* 15.38   A disaster followed, and whether it was accidentally or by the emperor's criminality is not certain: there are writers who support either one. But to all writers, it was the most serious and tragic conflagration that has happened to the City. It first broke out in that part of the Circus that is near the Palatine and Caelian Hills. [...]

Tac., *Ann.* 15.42   Despite all this, Nero found some advantage in the ruination of his fatherland by building a *domus* distinguished not by its gems and gold, things customary in previous buildings and made vulgarly common by displays of luxury, but rather in its fields, lakes, and an atmosphere of solitude [*modus solitudinis*], with wooded places here, there some open areas and views.[88] The designers and engineers [*magistri et machinatores*] were Severus and Celer; such was their intelligence and daring [*ingenium et audacia*] that they sought to do by their art [*ars*] what nature refused to do and to [thereby] squander the emperor's assets [*vires*].[89]

MARTIAL   (Marcus Valerius Martialis, ca. 38/41–102/104 CE)

On the Spectacles (*Spectacula*), Epigram 2, late 80s–90s CE (Mart., *Spect.*)

This poem celebrates the Flavian constructions that replaced Nero's Domus Aurea.[90] The poet's praise for the new buildings and the conversion of Nero's private buildings to public amenities (the Colosseum, the Baths of Titus, urban streets) and the spectacles that went with them alludes to some aspects of Nero's villa-like palace, by Martial's day largely forgotten except as an example of the emperor's arrogance.[91]

Mart., *Spect.*, *Epig.* 2
   Right here, where the star-studded Colossus sees the heavens close up
   And where tall pageant floats [*pegmata celsa*] are now built in the street,
   The hated halls of a king once glittered.[92]
   And a single house took up the whole City.
   Here, where the sacred and spectacular Amphitheater raises its walls
   There once were Nero's ponds [*stagna*].[93]
   Here, where we now wonder at the Baths, a gift [*munera*, i.e., to the public] so quickly built,[94]
   There was once a pretentious planting field [*superbus ager*], which had displaced the homes
      of poor people.
   Where the Porticus of Claudius now extends its deep shade,

There was once the last remaining ruin of an abandoned hall.[95]
Under your rule, Caesar [i.e., Domitian], Rome has returned to being herself,
And what were once the luxuries of a tyrant are now the delights of the people.

Galba (Servius Sulpicius Galba, 3 BCE–69 CE, reigned 68–69 CE)

Galba's ancestors had been distinguished in the late third century BCE, but their importance waned as partisans of one or another side in the civil wars of the first century BCE. Galba himself, consul in 33 CE and governor of Africa and Hispania under the emperors Gaius (Caligula), Claudius, and Nero, ultimately became emperor for a short time in 68–69 CE after Nero's death. The villa at Tusculum may have been a family possession, as the story of Galba's statue there takes place when he was in his mid-teens. The numinous nature of Galba's villa is not unlike the omen-laden Villa of Livia at Primaporta, and the fall and assassination of the emperor were predicted by his statue, as the end of the Julio-Claudian imperial line was predicted by the hens and the laurel trees.[96]

Suetonius, *Lives of the Twelve Caesars. Galba* (Suet., *Galb.*)

Suet., *Galb.* 4.1   The emperor Servius Galba was born in the consulships of Marcus Valerius Messala and Gnaeus Lentulus on the eighth [ninth] day before the kalends of January [3 BCE], in a villa set on a hill near Tarracina, on the left side of the track going toward Fundi.

Suet., *Galb.* 4.3   When he had taken the *toga virilis*, he had a dream in which [the goddess] Fortuna told to him that she was tired of standing at his front door [*fores*] and that unless she was quickly allowed in, she would soon be picked up by the first passerby.[97] Upon awakening, he found a bronze statue of the goddess more than a cubit high [about 44.5 cm, or 17½ in.] close to the entrance of the open atrium. He carried it bodily himself to Tusculum, where he usually spent the summer, consecrated it in a section of the house [*aedes*], and ever since worshiped it with monthly prayers and a vigil once a year.

Suet., *Galb.* 18.2–3   [...] As he entered the City and after that the palace, there was an earthquake and a sound like cattle lowing. Even clearer [ominous] indications soon followed these events.[98] From all the rich objects [of the palace], he had reserved a necklace of pearls and gems to apply as ornament for his Fortuna at Tusculum. Then he changed his mind and dedicated it to the Capitoline Venus as [an object] being worthy of a more prominent place. The very next night he had a dream of Fortuna complaining of having been cheated of the gift he had intended to give her, and warning him that she could take back what she herself had given. When, at first light, he hurried in terror to Tusculum to avert the dream's warning, sending men in advance to make the ritual arrangements, he found nothing but warm ashes on the altar and an old man robed in black holding the incense in a glass bowl and the wine in a clay cup.[99]

Vespasian (Titus Flavius Vespasianus, 9–79 CE, reigned 69–79 CE)

The Flavian dynasty enjoyed, in the accounts by Tacitus and Suetonius, a good beginning presaging an evil end: Vespasian and Titus were generally good, whereas Domitian was bad. Such "senatorial" opinions are clinched by the kind of villa anecdotes that Suetonius had included for Augustus. Vespasian's villas appear to have been few in number and more in the nature of dwellings on family properties, in contrast to the many villas of his second son, Domitian.[100]

Suetonius, *Lives of the Twelve Caesars*. The Divine Vespasian (*Divus Vespasianus*) (Suet., *Vesp.*)

Suetonius's account of Vespasian's homely childhood at his grandmother's villa near Cosa is in line with the historian's estimate of the future emperor's character.

Suet., *Vesp.* 1.2   Vespasian was born in the Sabine district, in a small village called Falacrina just beyond Reate [modern Rieti] in the evening of the fifteenth day before the kalends of December in the consulates of Quintus Sulpicius Camerinus and Gaius Poppaeus Sabinus [November 17, 9 CE], five years before Augustus died. He was raised by his paternal grandmother Tertulla on her estates near Cosa. For that reason, even as emperor, he regularly visited the place of his childhood, and the villa was kept as it had been [when he was a child] so that nothing that he used to see ever would ever perish, and he was so attached to the memory of his grandmother that, on days of a religious character and on holidays, he maintained a tradition of drinking from a little silver cup that had been hers.

Portents of future greatness often occurred at villas for those beyond the bloodline of the descendants of Augustus. The second shoot from the oak tree symbolized Vespasian's elder brother, Titus Flavius Sabinus.[101]

Suet., *Vesp.* 1.5.2   There was an ancient oak tree, sacred to Mars, on the suburban property of the Flavii [near Reate]. On each of the three times that Vespasia [Polla, Vespasian's mother] gave birth, the tree suddenly grew branches from its trunk, indicating with no uncertainty what the fate [of the child] would be. The first was thin and soon dried up, just like the female child who, though born, did not last a year. The second [that of the elder brother, Titus Flavius Sabinus] was very healthy and of considerable length, promising great success. The third [that of Vespasian] was [so large that it was itself] the living image of a tree. From this, they say that Sabinus, his father, further emboldened by the inspection of the entrails of sacrificial animals, announced to his mother that the grandson born to her would be a Caesar, but she laughed out loud at this, amazed that she was still of sound mind while her son was already out of his.

Suet., *Vesp.* 1.5.4   Once, while he was breakfasting [or lunching], a stray dog brought a human hand [*manus*], picked up at the crossroads, and dropped it under the table.[102] Again, once while he was reclining at dinner, an ox that had been at the plough threw off its yoke, burst into the *triclinium*, scattering the servants, and then, as if suddenly tired, fell at Vespasian's feet, lowering its neck [to him].[103] Yet again, a cypress tree on his grandfather's country place was torn up by its roots and toppled without the violence of a storm, but the next day it revived greener and stronger [than before].[104]

Cassius Dio, *Roman History*, Epitome of Book 65 (*Epit. Bk.*)

Avoiding places associated with Nero—the Domus Tiberiana on the Palatine and especially the Domus Aurea buildings—was important to the new regime and to Vespasian himself. His lack of formality was more typical of life in the country than in Rome: hence he chose to live at the *domus* in the Gardens of Sallust in villa-like lack of ceremony.

Cass. Dio, *Epit. Bk.* 65 (66).10.4   The way he organized his life can be described this way: he resided very little on the Palatine Hill [παλάτιον] but lived mainly in the Gardens of Sallust, where he received anyone who wanted to speak to him, not only the Senators but others who were admitted, and with his friends he would chat even before dawn while still lying down, and others would approach to salute him in the streets.

Titus (Titus Flavius Vespasianus, 39–81 CE, reigned 79–81 CE)

Suetonius, *Lives of the Twelve Caesars, The Divine Titus* (*Divus Titus*) (Suet., *Tit.*)

No villas are recorded for Titus's short reign, but his civic and religious responses to a fire at Rome, the disasters in the towns of the Bay of Naples in 79 CE with the eruption of Vesuvius, and a plague are recorded: they are similar to those of Nero in the fire in Rome fifteen years before.

Suet., *Tit.* 2.3.3 [...] Of the City's disaster by fire, he said nothing officially except [to say] that he himself was bereft, distributing the decorations of his villas [or equipment, *praetoriorum suorum ornamenta*] to public buildings and temples and, so the work could be done as quickly as possible, commissioned several members of the equestrian order to undertake the work.

Suet., *Tit.* 2.11.1 [...] He died in the same villa as his father, two years, two months, and twenty days after succeeding his father, on the ides of September, in his forty-second year.[105] [...]

Domitian (Titus Flavius Domitianus, 51–96 CE, reigned 81–96 CE)

Domitian was the foremost builder of public buildings and temples in Rome. In contrast, he appears to have been content to use his predecessors' villas on the Tyrrhenian coast and on the Bay of Naples, though he greatly enlarged his father Vespasian's villa at Alba.[106]

Suetonius, *Lives of the Twelve Caesars. Domitian* (Suet., *Dom.*)

Suetonius relates a story about Domitian, as a young man, diverting himself at a villa at Alba where Pompey and Tiberius had had villas and where Vespasian had one, too; but this was well before he built the Albanum, the great palatial complex where as emperor he would conduct official business. A villa at Alba was a place where Domitian could stay, out of the way of his father and brother, when Vespasian returned to Italy from Egypt in the summer of 70 CE. Domitian's idleness and fatuity in villa retirement, at the age of 19, are emphasized. The writers of senatorial disposition (Suetonius, Tacitus, Cassius Dio) present a different picture of Domitian than the poets (Martial, Juvenal, and Statius) who experienced the Albanum later on.

Suet., *Dom.* 3.3.1 At the beginning of his reign, he was accustomed every day to retire by himself for hours and do nothing more than to catch flies and spear them with a sharp stylus, and when someone asked who was in there with the Caesar [Domitian], Vibius Crispus joked wittily that there wasn't even a fly in there.[107]

Cassius Dio, *Epitome of Book 65*

Cass. Dio, *Epit. Bk.* 65.3.4 Now Domitian began to fear his father, because of all the things that he had done already and no less strongly than for what he planned doing—his plans were not small ones. For that reason, he spent a great deal of time at the Alban villa and gave himself over to his love for Domitia, the daughter of Corbulo.[108] [...]

Martial, *Epigrams* (*Epigrammata*), late 80s–90s CE (Mart., *Epig.*)

Martial gives a geography of Domitian's villas; the only one missing is the emperor's villa at Baiae.[109]

Mart., *Epig.* 5.1

I am sending this to you, Caesar [Domitian], whether you are enjoying Alba's hills
Or are viewing Trivia on one side, and Thetis on the other.[110]
Or whether the truthful sisters learn your [oracular] words [*responsa*]
Where the still sea sleeps near the town.[111]
Or whether Aeneas's nurse or the Sun's daughter pleases you,
Or bright Anxur with its health-fortifying waters.[112]
You, the happy guardian of all things—your safety allows us [me] to believe that Jupiter
    gives his thanks [to you].[113]
Please accept this gift: I will assume you have read it and be honored to enjoy a
    Gallic credulity.

Domitian's famous lechery was allegedly exercised at his villas, at least according to Martial. Here, the poet makes fun of Paula (a wife, otherwise unknown) who, in the subsequent reign of the virtuous Nerva (96–98 CE), can no longer give her foolish husband the excuse that Domitian had ordered her to present herself at the Albanum or the villa at Circeii, when her real absence was for adulterous purposes with another lover rather than the emperor.

Mart., *Epig.* 11.7.1–6

Now for sure, Paula, you will not be able to say to that stupid husband of yours,
"Caesar has ordered me to come to the Albanum tomorrow morning,
Caesar has ordered me to Circeii."
When you want to meet an adulterous lover somewhere else [*longius*].
The time for such tricks is over now.
Under the emperor Nerva you can please yourself being a Penelope,
But your itch, your old natural inclination, won't allow it.[114]

Martial indicates that Domitian had a villa at Baiae with a *piscina* to raise fish (they licked his hand); he characterizes the emperor as emulating the prodigal *piscinarii* who made pets of their fish.[115]

Mart., *Epig.* 4.30.1–7

I am warning you, fisherman, flee far from the lake at Baiae,
Unless you want to be found guilty when you leave it.[116]
These waters are aswim with sacred fish
Who recognize their master and lick his hand,
That hand that no other hand in the world is greater.
What's more, those fish have names and come to their master's call right away.[117]

Domitian's Villa at Alba: The Albanum

Tiberius, and later Vespasian, may have had a villa or villas at Alba which Domitian inhabited before his father died, and for that reason, Domitian may have chosen to build his Albanum, the great villa built over the crest of the crater of the Lacus Albanus (modern Lago di Albano), overlooking the line of the Via Appia and the coast around Ostia on the west and the Alban lake on the east.[118]

Suetonius, *Lives of the Twelve Caesars. Domitian*

As of his accession in 81 CE, Domitian's principal residence was his Albanum.[119] The palace of the Palatine Hill (the Domus Flavia plus the Domus Augustana) would have been under construction.

Suet., *Dom*. 3.4.4   Every year at his Albanum he celebrated the Quinquatria of Minerva, for whom he instituted a *collegium* of priests chosen by lot to be its supervisors and to produce remarkable hunting shows and theatrical presentations, as well as contests [*certamina*] among orators and poets.[120]

Cassius Dio, *Epitome of Book 67*

Cass. Dio, *Epit. Bk.* 67.1.2   Of the gods, the one he especially revered was Athena [Minerva], and on her account the Panathenaea was celebrated magnificently; he held competitions of poets, orators, and gladiators nearly yearly at his Albanum.[121] He had set up this estate [χωρίον] at the base of the Alban hill from which it was named as if it were an acropolis.

Martial, *Epigrams*

Martial's thirteenth volume of poetry is a versified catalogue of foodstuffs from eggs to capons, all sorts of fish and flesh, and the best vegetables. The little two-line entries (107 to 125) give a helpful list of the finest wines available from the great *terroirs* (Falernian, Massican) to the obscure (Nomentan); all are Italian vintings except four: one from Hispania, two from Gaul, one from Crete. The two lines on Alban wine, from the vineyards around the Albanum, are presented here; they indicate that the villa had some agricultural part and was not merely a palatial country residence.[122]

Mart., *Epig.* 13.109
> Albanum. This mild vintage comes out of [one of Domitian] Caesar's wine cellars
> Which takes pride in being from the Julian mountain.[123]

PLINY THE YOUNGER   (Gaius Plinius Caecilius Secundus, 61–113 CE)

Panegyric of the Emperor Trajan (Panegyricus), 100 CE (Plin., *Pan.*)

Hunting and boating were typical pastimes at villas, private and imperial. Pliny gives an account of the leisure activities at the Albanum in Domitian's time when he is praising the hunting and boating abilities of Trajan. Elsewhere in the *Panegyric*, Pliny lists the athletic and other virtues required of a hunter, in this case those of Trajan and thus imperial ones, to embody the *exemplum virtutis* or acme of virtues (see below under Trajan: Plin., *Pan.* 81.1–4).[124]

Plin., *Pan.* 81.3–4   [...] Those emperors [Domitian et al.] also falsely claimed the glory [of the hunt] when they were not actually able to do so; they even claimed it on the basis of a deceitful skill, with wild animals that had been kept in pens and broken [in spirit] and then sent out to be killed for fun—what else? [...]

Plin., *Pan.* 82.1–2   How unlike he [Trajan] is to that man [Domitian], who could not bear the calm of the Alban lake and the still quiet water of Baiae [the Lucrine lake], and could not bear the rhythmic sound and splash of oars without cringing in craven fright at each stroke! [...]

Letters (*Epistulae*) (Plin., *Ep.*)

Letter to his friend Cornelius Minicianus, after ca. 98 CE

Domitian used the Albanum as the venue for a legal proceeding of the highest religious and state importance. Besides many other issues, using the Albanum as a judicial venue was shocking to Pliny. The letter conveys some gossip about Valerius Licinianus and his fall from being a senator, orator, and lawyer at Rome to being a teacher of rhetoric somewhere in Sicily, a descent into obscurity that Pliny terms sad and much to be pitied (*tristia et miseranda*). Licinianus had been dragged into the affair of the Vestal Virgin Cornelia who was judged and condemned by Domitian and executed in the ancient penalty of live burial.[125] This was a major event in the emperor's reign.

Plin., *Ep.* 4.11   Domitian was then roaring and seething with tremendous anger, having been thwarted in his spite. For he had decided to bury Cornelia, the chief Vestal, alive, to make the time of his reign [*saeculum*] famous by such an example [of severity]. He called the other priests to meet at his Alban villa rather than at the Regia [in Rome], by his authority as Pontifex Maximus but really more for his savagery as a tyrant and his lawlessness as a ruler. He found her guilty of incest, in absentia and without hearing her defense,[126] a crime no less in itself than the one he was pretending to punish, because he had committed incest with his own brother's daughter.[127] [...]

Juvenal, *Satires*

Juvenal came to hate Domitian, whom he called a "bald Nero" (*calvus Nero*: *Satires* 4.38), but the special target for his hatred was an Egyptian called Crispinus, mentioned as the example of a rich foreigner of low extraction, now a jumped-up highly placed courtier (Juv., *Satires* 1.26–30), lecherous, overdressed, and owning land and colonnades in the country (i.e., villas). Crispinus's ownership of land shades into an allegation that he seduced a Vestal Virgin, a reference to Domitian's judgment at the Albanum of the Vestal Virgin Cornelia.[128]

Juv., *Satires* 4.5–10   What's the point, then, of telling how he tires out his carriage animals [*iumenta*] in big colonnades, what the number is of his shady groves through which he is driven along, how many *iugera* near the Forum he owns, how many mansions he has bought? No bad man can be fortunate [*felix*], certainly not a rapist [*corruptor*] and polluter [*incestus*], one who recently bedded a priestess wearing the ritual bands [*vittata*] who will be buried alive, with pulsing blood.

Suetonius, *Lives of the Twelve Caesars. Domitian*

Suetonius recounts omens about Domitian's death.[129]

Suet., *Dom.* 3.15.2   There was thunder from the sky that struck the Capitoline temple [of Jupiter] and the temple of the Flavian family, and even the inscription on the base of a statue of him as Triumphator was broken off and landed on a tomb nearby. The [cypress] tree that, when Vespasian had still been a private citizen had been toppled and then had revived, now fell down again.

Nerva (Marcus Cocceius Nerva, 30–98 CE, reigned 96–98 CE)

No texts regarding Nerva and villas are presented here. Even though Nerva had been a prominent courtier under Nero and all three Flavian dynasts, he is recorded to have chosen to reside in the villa of the Gardens of Sallust rather than in Domitian's palace on the Palatine. In doing so, he may have signaled an implicit turn away from the extravagances of Domitian and a return to the unpretentious values of Vespasian, who also chose to live there instead of in one of Nero's residences. Living in villas in the *horti* and adopting new, good political values went together.[130]

Trajan (Marcus Ulpius Traianus, 53–117 CE, reigned 98–117 CE)

Trajan's accession to the imperial dignity in 98 CE began a period of stable imperial rule that lasted almost a century; his reign saw the expansion of Roman territory to the northeast with the addition of Dacia and the trans-Danubian areas (101–102 CE) and the conquest of parts of the Parthian Empire (113–117 CE), partially fulfilling, for the Romans, a dream of eastern conquest that had preoccupied rulers since Alexander the Great. Trajan reorganized the military and instituted administrative reforms throughout the empire. In Italy, he continued and expanded the *alimenta*, a system of municipal poor relief supporting the children of citizen families, both those who farmed agricultural lands as *coloni* and those who lived in towns. The *alimenta* funds were generated from the interest on obligatory loans assigned to owners of villas and estates on the peninsula.[131]

The only villa that Trajan built and used known from literary accounts is that at Centum Cellae (modern Civitavecchia). Its description by Pliny the Younger is brief but explicit: the villa was suitable to the imperial pleasure and hospitality (its beauty and convenience), to be a working environment (Trajan acted as magistrate for lawsuits brought to the emperor's attention), and it was built so its harbor could supplement, with a good roadstead and sheltered port, the long stretch of coast between Ostia and the port of Pisae (modern Pisa), Triturrita (modern Porto Pisano), that had not had a modern shipping facility before.[132] Another attraction may have been the hot springs at Thermae Taurianae, 5 km from the villa, mentioned by Rutilius Namatianus.[133]

Pliny the Younger's account of the still-under-construction villa and harbor works at Centum Cellae ("one hundred rooms") may date to about 104–107 CE, namely in the hiatus between the Dacian and Parthian campaigns, when Trajan, who liked to go to war in person, had time and attention to plan and use its facilities.[134] Pliny's account gives a good picture of how a senior civil servant and lawyer would have experienced the villa as an honored guest and how it functioned. The Centum Cellae villa, possibly because of its well-located harbor, lasted a long time.[135] One of the reasons for its obscurity as an imperial residence (but not its port) after Trajan's reign may have been due to its greater distance—some 60 km from the City—than Tibur (about 19 km, built and used by Hadrian), or Alsium and Lorium (respectively about 36 and 19 km, both favored by Antoninus Pius and Marcus Aurelius).

Trajan is known, from the archaeological record only, to have built an inland villa at Arcinazzo Romano some 50 km east of Rome, in the foothills of the Appenines in the valley of the Anio (modern Aniene).[136] The site was—and still is—set in steeply mountainous and heavily forested terrain. While not explicitly mentioned in literary sources, the villa was in good hunting country, and hunting was Trajan's favorite pastime, so Pliny the Younger's landscape description could very well be of the area of this villa.

Pliny the Younger, *Epistulae,* **letter to his friend Cornelianus, between 104 and 107 CE**

The emperor Trajan built a new maritime villa at Centum Cellae on a site not previously known as an imperial residence, on a stretch of flat coast between the great port of Ostia-Portus at the mouth of the Tiber and that of Portus Herculis (modern Porto Ercole near Cosa) or Pisae farther north. Pliny, as an experienced lawyer and a member of the *centumviral* court dealing with private legal matters, was called to the villa to give advice on cases brought before the emperor acting as chief magistrate. The main part of this letter is about the emperor's judgments in cases of libel, adultery, and forgery (this last adjourned for further inquiry). Pliny was the emperor's guest for three days at the villa and describes the imperial hospitality as well as the setting of the residence and some of its harbor installations under construction.

Plin. *Ep.* **6.31.1–2** It was a great pleasure to be called by our emperor to be his [legal] advisor to Centum Cellae, as the place is called. What could have been more pleasant than to witness the emperor's justice in a countryside retreat where, in a relaxed atmosphere, it can be fully appreciated? His thinking and the value of his judicial virtues were tested in various cases. The first was the case of.... [...]

Plin. *Ep.* **6.31.13–17** As you can see, the days were honorably spent because they were on serious matters, but there were very pleasant relaxations afterward. We ended every day with a dinner: the dinner was modest considering who the host was. At times we heard recitations, sometimes the night was filled with very pleasant conversations. On the last day, we all received gifts, so eager is the emperor in his kindness. The importance of the cases, the honor of being an advisor, the agreeable simplicity of the company, and the villa itself were more than delightful.

The villa is surrounded by bright green fields and is very beautiful. It faces the beach, and a bay is quickly being made into a harbor. The left arm of the harbor, very impressively built, is almost finished, and the other is under construction. An island is rising at the mouth of the port to break up wind-driven waves so ships can enter the harbor from both sides. The method by which it is being constructed is worth seeing: giant boulders are brought up on ships, then thrown one on top of another to stabilize their position by their own weight and to form, gradually, something like a defensive hill. This is now rising [above the water] and makes a stony ridge that breaks the waves and throws them back—the noise is tremendous and the sea foams around them. In time, projecting supports will be built on the ridge and finally an island will appear, looking as if it was always there. The port, already named for its builder [the emperor], will be a very good thing for safety [for boats at sea] by providing this long expanse of shoreline with a haven that it lacks. Farewell.

RUTILIUS NAMATIANUS
(Rutilius Claudius Namatianus, late fourth–mid-fifth century CE)

On My Return **(***De reditu suo***), September to November 416 CE (Rut. Namat.,** *De red.***)**

After several years in high administrative posts in Rome, Rutilius Namatianus decided to visit his family estates in Aquitania. Rutilius's description of Trajan's maritime villa and harbor at Centum Cellae on the Etrurian coast was written more than three centuries after its construction. Having embarked at Ostia on September 22, 416 CE, his boat passed Alsium, mentioned by Pliny the Younger and the site of a villa built by Antoninus Pius and used by Marcus Aurelius. The ruins of famous old cities such as Caere (modern Cerveteri) and Castrum Novum are mentioned, and Rutilius notes that big villas have replaced little towns. The harbor of Pyrgi is passed, then a night's mooring is found at Centum Cellae.[137]

Rut. Namat., *De red.* 1.223–228

> The land of Alsium is sailed past, [the port of] Pyrgi fades [from view].
> Now there are large villas [where] once there were small towns.[138]
> Then the sailor points to the area where Caere's boundaries once were—
> Old Agylla lost its name over time.
> Next we [pass] Castrum [Novum], ruined by both the sea's waves and time
> An old gateway is a token of the half ruined spot.[139]

Rut. Namat., *De red.* 1.237–248

> At Centum Cellae we veered into a strong south Wind [*Auster*]
> The ships moor in the quiet harbor.
> An amphitheater of water is surrounded by jetties
> And a man-made island protects the narrow roadsteads.
> On it, two towers rise to accommodate approaches on both sides.
> [Because] it was not enough to build berths with wide docks
> [And] so the restless breeze will not disturb the boats at anchor,
> A curving basin has been made among the buildings [of the villa]—
> Its calm waters are not touched by the shifting air,
> Like the water filling the Euboean [Cumaean] swimming pools
> Which buoys a swimmer's alternating strokes.

Pliny the Younger, *Panegyric of the Emperor Trajan*

In his speech of 100 CE celebrating Trajan's first two years in power, Pliny uses the new emperor's prowess in plying the oars and hunting in the rough to contrast with Domitian's unmanly weakness on the water and killing penned prey. Hunting is seen as an imperial duty to protect the farmers' work in the fields, so venery in general is a vocation appropriate to villas.[140] In this case, Trajan's personal virtues are the same as those he exhibits in sportsmanlike hunting and those required of an emperor, so both Trajan and hunting are *exempla virtutis*. Pliny also commends Trajan's strength of body (*duritas corporis*) and his seriousness (*gravitas*), moral worthiness (*sanctitas*), and moderation or self-control (*temperentia*) (Plin., *Pan.* 82.8).

Pliny describes Domitian's deficiencies in tandem with Trajan's virtues in the matter of villa activities—sailing and hunting. Domitian's cowardice on water and shooting penned animals (Plin., *Pan.* 81.3–4 and 82.1–2, earlier in this chapter) stands in contrast to Trajan's skills and demeanor.

Plin., *Pan.* 81.1–4 But once you have mastered the ever-incoming number of tasks [that you must attend to], the kind of relaxation [*refectio*] you like is really just a change of work![141] Your only enjoyment [*remissio*] is to hike through forests [*lustrare saltus*], to drive wild beasts [*excutere feras*] from their dens, to climb [*superare*] huge mountain ranges and to place your foot [*gradum inferre*] on rough cliffs, with no one offering a helping hand or showing the track and, in all this, to go into sacred groves with a pious mind [*pia mente*] and approach the gods [*occursare numinibus*] there.[142] Long ago, such was both the training [*experientia*] and pleasure [*voluptas*] of youth, and future leaders [*duces futuri*] were formed with such disciplines [*artes*], to compete [*certare*] in swiftness with the animals' speed, with steadiness [*robor*] against their courage, and with skill [*cum astu*] against their cunning. In quiet, peaceful times, there was honor [*decus*] enough in clearing the fields of an invasion of wild animals and raising their siege of the citizen farmer's hard work [*obsidione agrestium labor*]. But this Caesar [Trajan] works up as much sweat in tracking the quarry as in capturing it [*capiendi quaerendique sudor*] and takes the greatest pleasure in the hardest task [*gratissimus labor*]: spying out where the quarry is.

What's more, if he should want to show his bodily strength on the water, it's not in his nature to follow the billowing sails merely with his eyes' gaze or his hands' gestures. Instead, now he takes the helm, at other times he competes with the strongest of his companions to cut through the waves, taming the winds in his face [*venti reluctantes*] and, by plying the oars himself, breaks against the upstream current.

Hadrian (Caesar Traianus Hadrianus Augustus, born Publius Aelius Hadrianus, 76–138 CE, reigned 117–138 CE)

Hadrian's family was of Spanish origin, and his father had risen to senatorial rank, but Hadrian himself was raised in Rome in the household of Trajan and was soon admitted to high positions in the military and political *cursus honorum*. His early proficiency in Greek studies and his proclivity for them earned him the nickname of *Graeculus*—"little Greek"—and all his biographers emphasize his many cultural interests and achievements, including writing poetry, a tendency of taste in literary matters toward antiquarianism (e.g., a preference for Ennius rather than Vergil), and accomplishments in the way of arithmetic, geometry, painting, flute playing, and singing, forming friendships with and honoring philosophers, actors, rhetoricians and grammarians, and astrologers.[143] The way Hadrian behaved with regard to hospitality and visits to the villas [ἀγροί] of others is briefly recorded by Cassius Dio.[144]

Hadrian was preoccupied with architectural design and with construction itself.[145] Of the many buildings associated with his reign in Rome and throughout the empire, six villas are known: three inland, two on the Bay of Naples and one at Antium on the Tyrrhenian coast. Inland, Hadrian's villa at Tibur is the most famous, but there were two others: one just south of Praeneste (modern Palestrina, about 35 km east of Rome), and another called the Villa Magna. The villa near Praeneste is not known in any literary sources, but it was a substantial construction with a cistern system, gardens, and a large residence; its location near Praeneste represents a continued frequentation of the town, and especially of the Temple of Fortuna Primigenia, since Republican times.[146] The Villa Magna is not known from any literary source of Hadrian's own time, but its main fabric is Hadrianic, even though it may have been started in the late years of Trajan's reign.[147] It continued in use in the reign of his successor Antoninus Pius and was described in lively detail by the future emperor Marcus Aurelius on holiday there, so sources for it are set out in the section on Antoninus Pius below. Its location, like Trajan's villa at Arcinazzo Romano, was located in fine hunting country, which both Hadrian and Marcus Aurelius liked very much.[148]

At Antium, the maritime villa built by Nero continued in use; its library was still functioning in the 190s CE, though not in good condition. A comment on Hadrian's villa or palace [τὰ βασίλεια] at Antium occurs in Philostratus's *Life of Apollonius of Tyana*, with the claim that the emperor was the fondest of the Antium residence among all of his villa-palaces in Italy.[149]

On the Bay of Naples, Hadrian died at a villa at Baiae. Another villa nearby at Pausilypon, the villa that had belonged to Vedius Pollio in the reign of Augustus, underwent a renovation in the name of Hadrian; it was the personal property of emperors.[150]

Hadrian's Villa at Tibur

The Villa Hadriana at Tibur (modern Tivoli) is Hadrian's most famous architectural achievement, one in which he appears to have had a hand in the inception, design, development, and decoration. However, it must tell its own story: only four literary sources mention it, and three are so cursory that they do not merit separate inclusion here.[151]

Fortunately, Hadrian's villa has had many modern exponents.[152] Its location at Tibur, roughly 30 km east-northeast of Rome, is in no way unusual; Tibur had been part of the geography of villas since the mid-second century BCE. However, many of the villas there were conspicuously older than those at other popular sites: the big, very prominent ones at Tibur are datable for the most part to the mid- to late second century BCE unlike the first-century ones at Tusculum, Alba, and the Tyrrhenian coast.[153] It is possible that Hadrian chose Tibur precisely for the density—and the historical authenticity and associations—of its Republican villas.[154] In maturity as emperor, he also may have remembered enjoying the place when he was a child: Tibur appears to have been the resort of choice for new members of Roman high society of senatorial rank whose families, though originally from Italian towns and regions, had been naturalized in the provinces of Roman Hispania and had more recently found new distinction in the imperial capital.[155] Hadrian and his sister Paulina were born of just such parents, Publius Aelius Hadrianus Afer of Italica (modern Santiponce) and Domitia Paulina of Gades (modern Cádiz), and they may well have found congenial summer society in the villas of "Spanish" Tibur with their children.

In the *Historia Augusta*, certain of the names (*nomina*) were assigned, possibly by Hadrian himself, to the Villa at Tibur; some are allusions to places that Hadrian would have seen on his many travels in the empire, others perhaps drawn from literary sources or even from other villas.[156]

***Historia Augusta** (Scriptores Historiae Augustae)*, **fourth century CE.** *Hadrian (HA, Hadr.)*

HA, Hadr. 26.5   He built his villa at Tibur in a wonderful way [*mire*], in a manner that, in it, he might assign the names of provinces and the most famous places [*provinciarum et locorum celeberrima nomina*]; for example, the Lyceum, the Academy,[157] the Prytaneum,[158] the Canopus,[159] the [Stoa] Poikile,[160] the [Vale of] Tempe.[161] So as not to omit anything, he even constructed an Underworld [*inferi*].[162]

Antoninus Pius (Titus Aelius Hadrianus Antoninus Pius, 86–161 CE, reigned 138–161 CE)

Like Trajan, Antoninus Pius was devoted to the villa where he was brought up, or at least to its location at Lorium where he built a residence as emperor and where he died.[163] Even at the beginning of his official career, as *quaestor*, he preferred to live in the country. In other respects, he was substantially different from Hadrian, in part because his residence in Italy was more continuous, and rather than build anew, he chose to maintain and visit his predecessor's—notably the great villa at Tibur and the Villa Magna near Anagnia (modern Anagni)—rather than new country establishments. He also had a villa at Lanuvium where he was born.[164] While many wars were fought during his reign, he delegated the campaigns to his generals and preferred to live in the capital. The imperial family, after his death in 161 CE, are known to have used Domitian's Albanum, a villa at Formiae (Formianum), and another at Capua; these residences may have continued in use from Antoninus Pius's reign but are only briefly mentioned as imperial dwellings after his death, in letters between Marcus Aurelius and his wife Faustina.[165]

Antoninus Pius's presence at Hadrian's villa at Tibur is attested by a bust portraying him in the villa. Literary texts regarding the villas he used are found in the correspondence of his adoptive sons' tutor, Marcus Cornelius Fronto.[166] Fronto's career as an eminence at the Antonine court is documented in letters to the emperor himself, but especially in letters to and from his imperial pupils after 138 CE, when Fronto became tutor to the *Caesares* who would later jointly rule as Marcus Aurelius and Lucius Verus. The villas most often mentioned in connection with Antoninus Pius are in locations significantly different locations from those around or in the towns to the east and southeast of Rome (Tusculum, Praeneste, Alba) or those on the Tyrrhenian coast but southwest of Rome (Antium, Circeii) or on the Bay of Naples (Baiae, Bauli). Instead, he and his adoptive son Marcus Aurelius used two villas northwest of the City, a maritime villa at Alsium where Julius Caesar had had a villa, another inland at Lorium on the Via Aurelia running north-northwest from Rome and Alsium.[167]

Historia Augusta, Antoninus Pius (HA, Ant. Pius.)

HA, Ant. Pius. 3.1.8–9   Antoninus [Pius] himself was born on the thirteenth day before the kalends of October [September 19] in the twelfth Consulate of Flavius Domitian and that of Cornelius Dolabella [86 CE], at a villa at Lanuvium. He was brought up at Lorium on the Via Aurelia, where he later built a palace [*palatium*] of which there are ruins still standing.[168] [...]

HA, Ant. Pius. 3.2.10–11   He was a generous *quaestor* and an excellent praetor and consul with Catilius Severus.[169] In private life, he spent the greatest part of his time on his estates [*in agris*], though he was well known everywhere. He was chosen by Hadrian to be in charge of that section of Italy in which the major part of his estates were located. Hadrian was aware of the honorable nature of such a man and of his firm hand.[170]

HA, Ant. Pius. 3.7.11–12   He sold excess imperial apparatus [*species imperatoriae*] and its properties [*praedia*] and lived on his own estates according to [the changing of] the season, and he did not make any journey except to visit his estates [*agri sui*] in Campania, saying that no matter how frugal he might be, it was a bad thing for provincials to be burdened with [the needs of or visits from an emperor].

HA, Ant. Pius. 3.11.2–3   He enjoyed the arts of the theater as well as fishing and hunting, and he loved walking accompanied by his friends and having conversations with them. He took part in the grape harvest with friends as if he were an ordinary person.

MARCUS AURELIUS   (Marcus Aurelius Antoninus, 121–180 CE)

Meditations (Τὰ εἰς ἑαυτόν, *Thoughts to Oneself*), 171–173 CE (M. Aur., Med.)

As emperor on the front in the battle against the German tribes in the early 170s, Marcus Aurelius wrote a philosophic and moral text in twelve books. Book 1 gives an account of his adoptive father, Antoninus Pius, his character, morals, and habits of life, including a mention of his villas.

M. Aur., Med. 16.8   He did not bathe off-schedule [ἀωρί], and he did not have a mania for building [φιλοικοδόμος], he was indifferent to matters of eating or to the look and color of his garments, or his attendants' physiques.[171] His cloak [στολὴ, robe] came from his inland villa [κάτω ἔπαυλις] at Lorium, and for other things, there was enough at Lanuvium. [...]

The Villa Magna in the Reign of Antoninus Pius

Besides the villa at Lanuvium, the *palatium* at Lorium and a possible presence at the Villa Hadriana at Tibur, the third villa known to have been lived in by Antoninus Pius was the Villa Magna. The archaeological record indicates that its main structures were built in the reign of his predecessor Hadrian, but no literary record of its initial construction or how Hadrian came to choose its location has survived. It was in the area of Anagnia where Cicero had had a *deversorium* at which to break his journey from Rome to his hometown of Arpinum and his (and his brother's) villas there.[172]

The Villa Magna was reached by a side road running south-southwest from the religious site known as Compitum Anagninum near the junction of the Via Latina and the Via Labicana, some 75 km (about 47 mi.) east-southeast of Rome: the town of Anagnia itself was a short distance from the Via Latina on another side road running north-northeast. Its location had made the area a good stopping place for the trip between the capital and the Bay of Naples, an alternative to the more westerly Via Appia. It also connected Rome with the rich agricultural region of the valley of Latium to Casinum (modern Cassino) and its Ager Casinus, and the northern part of the Ager Falernus to Teanum Sidicinum (modern Teano), Capua (modern Santa Maria Capua Vetere), and Casilinum where it joined the Via Appia. This was the corridor of agricultural estates and villas making up the Roman *Latium vetus* which was the trajectory and geographical center of Cato's *De agricultura*.[173]

In the reign of Antoninus Pius, the sources for the Villa Magna and how it was used are found in three letters from his successor Marcus Aurelius to his tutor Fronto. Hadrian's original building does not seem to have changed much since its construction some twenty years before, so his intentions for its use and arrangements may well be present in the young man's letters.

FRONTO   (Marcus Cornelius Fronto 100–170 CE)

Epistles (*Epistulae*) (Fronto, *Ep.*).
Translation by Margaret A. Andrews.[174]

Three letters from Marcus Aurelius, early 140s CE(?)

In an arrangement brought about by Hadrian in January 138 CE, the emperor adopted Antoninus Pius as his son and heir; Antoninus in turn adopted Marcus Aurelius together with Lucius Verus, Marcus's very distant younger relative. Marcus and Lucius were named *Caesares* to identify them as imperial heirs-apparent. The letters from Marcus Aurelius to Fronto, the *Caesares*'s tutor, were part of the collection of the tutor's letters as preserved in the second century CE; most deal with matters of philosophy and oratory, but these three below describe life at the Villa Magna with the emperor in residence. Their date in the early 140s indicates that Marcus was a very young man, just barely in his early twenties.[175]

The three letters bear the marks of schoolroom *progymnasmata*, or training in descriptive writing, in this case about the terms of *otium* in villas at the court of Antoninus Pius in the early years of the reign: Marcus's trip getting to the villa, his occupations from dawn (awaking) to dusk (going to bed), reading, hunting, bathing, feasting, conversations, listening to others. In both reading and listening to others, an interest in linguistic antiquities (Novius), arcane expressions (on the Anagnia gate), and rustic speech (that of the enslaved personnel in the winery) have a Varronian character in keeping with the antiquarian tastes of his teacher Fronto.[176] They are also elements of learned *otium* at villas on holidays. A familial and pupil–master competitiveness as to who loves the more or the best is also part of the emotional atmosphere.

Fronto, *Ep.* 4.4 (59)

After I climbed up into the carriage and said goodbye to you, we had a not so uncomfortable journey, but were sprinkled by rain for a little bit. Before we got to the villa, though, we turned off toward Anagnia almost a mile from the road, and then we saw that ancient town. It is quite insignificant indeed, but it contains many ancient things—temples, shrines, and rituals beyond measure. There was no corner where there was not a temple or a sanctuary or a shrine. Above all, there were many records written on linen [*libri lintei*] pertaining to sacrifices. Then, on the gate, when we left, there was written the following on both sides: *flamen sume samentum*. I asked one of the townsfolk what this word was, and he said that it meant in the Hernician language the skin from the sacrificial victim that the priest puts over his pointed cap when he enters the city.[177] We also learned many other things that we wanted to know. Indeed, the only things that we did not want was that you were away from us: this is the greatest anxiety for us.[178]

Now you then left afterward—was it along the Via Aurelia or into Campania that you went? Make sure you write me whenever you begin the grape harvest and whenever you bring a heap of books to the villa and also this: whenever you miss me; but I ask this foolishly since you certainly do. Now if you miss me and love me, send me your letters frequently, as they will be solace and consolation for me. For I would ten times rather collect your letters than all the Massican or Gauranian vines: these vines of Signia have bunches too rancid and grapes too acidic—to the point that I would rather drink wine than must![179] Besides, you can chew these grapes more comfortably dried than when ripe, for surely I would prefer to tread on the latter with feet than eat them with my teeth. But they would still be favorable and peaceful, and they deliver good indulgence for this laughter.

Farewell, my most dear friend, most charming, most pleasant teacher. Whenever you see must swirling in the *dolium*, let it remind you that my longing for you springs forth and overflows and foams in my chest.[180] Farewell as always.

Fronto, *Ep.* 4.5 (60)

Hail, my dearest master!

We are doing well. Today I studied from the ninth hour of the night to the second hour of the day, being well disposed from food; from the second hour to the third, I walked around most cheerfully in front of my bedroom in my sandals [*soleatus*]. Then I put on proper shoes [*calceatus*], as well as my cloak (for we had been instructed to appear like this), and went out to greet my lord.[181] We set out for a hunt and carried out rather great feats. We heard some talk that boars had been captured, but there was no chance to see anything. Still, we climbed a pretty steep hill, then after midday, we went back home, and I set myself to my books. So, with my shoes off and my clothes set aside on the bed, I stayed on my couch for two hours and read Cato's oration *On the Property of Pluchra* and another one in which he impeached a tribune. "Hey," you say to your slave, "go as fast as you can and bring me these speeches from the library of Apollo!" But you send him in vain, for these books came with me! You must get around that librarian of Tiberius's palace: you should take [i.e., give him] a bribe [*res insumenda*], which he and I will share when I get back to town.[182]

When I finished browsing these speeches, I wrote for a little while, though poorly—only something I could dedicate to the nymphs or to Vulcan.[183] Today I have truly been unfortunate in writing, clearly the musing of a hunter or a vintager, like those who make noise through my window with their wild cries as tedious and repulsive as those of the lawyers.[184] But what have I said?! Indeed, my master is an orator!

I seem to have caught a cold, whether because I walked around in my sandals in the morning or because I wrote poorly, I do not know. In any case, I am certainly full of phlegm, and today I seem to be much more sniveling. So I will pour oil onto my head and begin to sleep; I do not think I put a drop into the lamp today since the riding and sneezing wore me out.

Farewell, most dear and sweet teacher, whom I dare say I miss more than Rome herself.

Fronto, *Ep.* 4.6 (61)

Hail, most charming teacher!

We are well. I overslept a bit on account of a slight cold, but this seems to have subsided. From the eleventh hour of the night until the third hour of the day I read from Cato's *De agricultura* a bit and wrote a bit (less badly than yesterday, thank god).[185] Then, after greeting my father [Antoninus Pius], I relieved my throat by swallowing honey water all the way down and then spitting it back out (better I say this than *gargling*, though this word is found in Novius and others, I think).[186] So with my throat tended to, I set out for my father and stood by him at the sacrifice.[187] Then I went to lunch. What do you think I ate? Just a small bit of bread, but I saw others eating beans, onions, and small fish with roe inside. Then we set ourselves to the task of picking the grapes; we seated, and rejoiced, and, as another author says, "we left some high-hanging grapes surviving the harvest."[188] At the sixth hour we returned home.

I studied for a little while, and ineptly at that. Then I spoke a lot with my mother, who was sitting on the couch.[189] My conversation was this: "What do you think my Fronto is doing just now?" Then she said, "What, on the other hand, do you think my Gratia is doing?" Then I said, "What about our little sparrow, small Gratia?"[190] While we were chatting and conversing about these things (which one of us loved the one or the other of you more) the gong rang—that is, it was announced that my father was going over to the bath.[191]

Washed, we therefore dined in the pressing room [*torcularium*] (we did not bathe in the pressing room, but, having washed, we ate there) and we happily heard the peasants bantering.[192] Then I came back, but before turning over on my side and beginning to snore, I set out my homework and gave my kindest master an account of the day. I would gladly endure the annoyance of missing him a bit more, if I could.

Farewell, my Fronto, wherever you are, most sweet, my love, my delight. How do I fare with you? I love you, though you are not here.

Marcus Aurelius (Marcus Aurelius Antoninus, 121–180 CE, reigned 161–180 CE)

Marcus Aurelius, like his adoptive father Antoninus Pius, was conservative in his use of villas: he stuck to Lorium for the countryside and Alsium for the shore, and would readily return to Rome from Campanian villas for important duties in the Senate. He was also devoted to the villa in the gardens of his mother (Horti Domitiae Lucillae) on the Caelian Hill where he was born and brought up: he called its site "my Caelian Hill."[193] Later, he lived in the Domus Tiberiana while in the City instead of in Domitian's Palace on the Palatine.[194] Still, Marcus could not have been unfamiliar with the life of luxury villas in famous resorts, as a letter to his tutor Fronto indicates.

Marcus Aurelius may have continued to use the Villa Magna after his stay there in the early years of Antoninus Pius's reign, but that villa disappears from the literary sources until the late second century in the reign of the Severi, and then only in an inscription and a portrait.[195]

Fronto, *Epistles*, 140s CE

While this letter of the young Marcus Aurelius to his tutor Fronto does not mention villas specifically, it is a geography (and weather map) of regions and resort towns in which villas were abundant. Evidently a topic of conversation for owners of villas in these or any other venues was, as now, the weather.

Fronto, *Ep.* 2.6.3 (44)   The Neapolitan climate is very agreeable but violently changeable—from one moment to the next, it can get colder, a bit warmer, or more wild. At first, it is warm at midnight, as in the Laurentine area, but then quite cold at the cock's crow at dawn, as in the Lanuvium, and also cold in the drear of night and [continuing cold to] just before dawn and until sunrise, as icy as [Mount] Algidus. Then, sunny in the morning, as in the Tusculanum region. After that, a ferocious heat at noon, as in the Puteolana. But when the sun dips into the ocean, the climate (temperature) becomes quite mild, as around Tibur, and continues this way through the evening and into the early night until "the dead of night tumbles down," as Marcus Porcius [Cato] says.[196] [...]

This is a letter of 143 CE from Marcus Aurelius to his tutor Fronto about a speech by Polemon of Laodicea the young *Caesar* had recently heard.[197] It is a model-letter based on analogy; in this case, analogy that criticizes Polemon's rhetorical style by reference to a villa-estate, its revenue-generating monocultures, and its lack of loveliness.

Fronto, *Ep.* 2.5 (35)   So that we can have a gossip about men,[198] I heard Polemo give a speech three days ago. If you ask me my opinion of him, read this. To me he seems like a diligent farmer [*agricola*], equipped with a high degree of expertise, who has taken possession of a large estate [*latus fundus*] entirely planted with grain crops and vines, from which, indeed, the harvest is the most abundant and its return the greatest [*fructus pulcherrimus et reditus uberrimus*]. But nowhere on that estate is there a Pompeian fig tree or a vegetable from the valley of Aricia [cabbage] or a Tarentine rose; nowhere is there a pleasant grove of trees or a dense plantation or a shade-giving plane tree.[199] It's all set up more for usefulness [*usus*] than for pleasure [*voluptas*], something that must prompt praise [*laudare oporteat*] rather than inviting love [*amare non libeat*]. [...]

Fronto, *Epistle 3, On the Holidays at Alsium* (*De feriis Alsiensibus*), early 160s CE (Fronto, *Ep.*)

According to Fronto, Marcus Aurelius, after he became emperor in 161 CE, worked too hard when on holiday at his villas, in this case the maritime villa at Alsium. Too much time was spent on administrative and judicial work. The dour Stoic in the emperor was, his old tutor thought, excessive, going well beyond the balance that a philosophic life needed. To redress the balance, Fronto supplied Marcus Aurelius with a complex argument and genealogy of healthy *otium* at villas, with historical and literary parallels.[200] He urges the emperor to get more sleep.[201]

Fronto, *Ep.* 3.1   What? Do [you think that] I didn't know that you went to Alsium with the thought in mind to get some change of habit and give yourself some amusement, fun, and rest [*ludus, iocus, otium*] for four days? I don't doubt that you have taken the opportunity to enjoy the holidays in your seaside retreat in this way: after the usual lie-down nap at noon, you might call Niger [an enslaved secretary-assistant] that he bring you some books. Then, as soon as you were disposed to the activity of reading, you would refine your knowledge of Plautus or complete your knowledge of Accius or soothe yourself with Lucretius or fire yourself up with Ennius.[202] [...] If he [Niger] had brought you [some of] Cicero's discourses, you would have listened to them. Then you would have gone right off as far as possible and sought out the seashore and walked around in the [frog-infested] noisy marsh. Then, if it seemed to be a good idea, you got on board some boat and, with nice weather all around, set off to sea, taking pleasure in the sight and sound of the oarsmen and the coxswain's pace. From there, you'd get yourself over to the baths, make your body thoroughly sweat itself out, then get yourself involved with a royal dinner [*regium convivium*] of various seafoods... and dainty [birds?] fattened up for a long while, apples, dainty snacks, pastries, lovely wines, and translucent wine cups unmarked by an informer's sign [*delatoria nota*].[203]

Fronto continues with a long passage on curiosities of old Latin words in plays by Plautus.

Fronto, *Ep.* **3.2–6**   [...] Now tell me, Marcus, I beg of you: have you gone to Alsium to starve yourself while in full sight of the sea? What? Couldn't you just as well have exhausted yourself with hunger and thirst and engaging in [official] work at Lorium? [...] They say that [even] the sea itself goes on holiday at the kingfisher's time [*alcedonia*, halcyon days], so is the kingfisher [*alcedo*] with her chicks more worthy of tranquil *otium* than you with your children?[204]

But you claim that the situation [*res*] clearly requires—what [does it require]? study [*studium*]? work [*labor*]? sleeplessness [*vigilia*]? official duties [*munera*]? What bow is always stretched taut? What mooring lines [*fides*] are always drawn tight? Eyes see [best] by blinking, but they stop [seeing] when staring continuously. A garden [*hortus*], if it's over-planted, will die without manure and will produce weeds and only undersized vegetables, whereas for real grain crops and substantial harvests, a fallowed field is the best choice—the soil's productivity is restored by *otium*.

What about your ancestors—the ones who so greatly added to the Roman state and its empire with huge expansions? Your great-grandfather,[205] a great warrior, sometimes took pleasure in [being with] actors and drank quite a lot as well. Still, the Roman people, in consequence of his triumphs, often had honeyed wine to drink. Then again, we know that your grandfather,[206] a learned emperor who was not only conscientious in ruling the whole world but eager to travel around it, was nonetheless given to music making [*modulus*] and pipers [*tibicen*] and, besides that, was a hearty eater at rich feasts. Then there's your father,[207] that man of a divine nature, whose vigilance, continence, thriftiness, blamelessness, piety, and upright behavior were greater than the virtues of all emperors—still, he exercised in the *palaestra*, went fishing, and laughed at clowns.

I'm not even mentioning Gaius [Julius] Caesar, Cleopatra's bitterest enemy, or Augustus, Livia's husband. Romulus himself, the City's founder, having killed the enemy leader in hand-to-hand combat and dedicated the great spoils [*opima spolia*] to Jupiter Feretrius—do you think that he made do with a measly meal [after that]? [...] Do you fast on feast days? And I'll say nothing about that Chrysippus of yours who, it's said, used to get drunk every day.[208] [...]

Since you have launched a war on play [*ludus*], on *otium*, on an agreeable way of life [*satietas*], and on pleasure [*voluptas*], it's good, at least, for you to [enjoy some] sleep as if you were a free man [*homo liberus*].[209] Having worked intensely to the end [of daylight] do you persist doing so [at night] until first light? Since no one has yet snatched fire [the light of the sun] from heaven, doesn't the sun [daylight] give you enough time to go about your duties as a judge?

Marcus Aurelius, *Meditations*, **170s CE**

Throughout the book of his thoughts conventionally called *Meditations*, written at the front in the German wars of the early 170s, Marcus Aurelius laments the transience of human greatness and lives, material goods, and even the study of language that had long been part of *otium*. Even the distinguished dead—once revered as exemplars of morality, patriotism, and modesty—are lost to memory. He illustrates his thoughts from the country estates, gardens, and villas of the great men of the past, in no special order and without much reference.

M. Aur., *Med.* **4.33.1**   Phrases that were formerly in common use are now outdated [πάλαι γλωσσήματα], with the result that the names of the highly praised are now also somewhat obsolete: Camillus, Caeso, Volesus, Dentatus, then a bit later Scipio and Cato, then again Augustus, then also Hadrian and Antoninus.[210] All things are quickly forgotten and become mythic; just as quickly, a complete oblivion covers them. I'm speaking of men who shone marvelously. For those [of us] who remain, once breath goes out, the dead indeed are dead [ἄιστοι, ἄπυστοι].[211]

M. Aur., *Med.* 12.27.2 [...] Think about this: "Where is all that now?" Smoke and ash and a myth that's not even a myth. Come to this kind of knowledge: Fabius Catullinus in the countryside, Lusius Lupus in his gardens, Stertinius at Baiae, Tiberius at Capreae, and Velius Rufus—all things that are [now] utterly swaggering oddities.[212]

Lucius Verus (Lucius Aelius Aurelius Verus, 130–169 CE, reigned 161–169 CE)

Lucius Verus was adopted as joint successor to Antoninus Pius with the 17-year old Marcus Aurelius, his senior by nine years, in a scheme of dynastic arrangements devised by Hadrian in the year of that emperor's death, 138 CE. The death of Antoninus Pius in 161 brought Marcus Aurelius to the imperial power as conferred by the Senate, but Lucius Verus was, by his adoptive brother's wish, also raised to the dignity of *Augustus* as co-emperor. From 162 to 166 CE, he spent most of the joint rule campaigning in the east, headquartered at Antioch and celebrating a triumph in 166 CE. In 169, he died of illness at Altinum in northern Italy on the return journey to Rome, after having joined Marcus Aurelius on the Danubian front the year before.

No written records of Lucius Verus's construction or ownership of villas are known, but the large villa at the modern site of Acquatraversa, about 7 km north of Rome on the Via Cassia appears to have been his, given his portraits and a quantity of high-quality statues found there. The accounts of his profligacy might have accorded well with villa ownership, but his short residence in Rome and Italy may have abbreviated the opportunity.[213]

Commodus (Caesar Marcus Aurelius Commodus Antoninus, born Lucius Aelius Aurelius Commodus, 161–192 CE, reigned 180–192 CE)

Even accounting for the biases of the writers of the *Historia Augusta* and those of Cassius Dio and Herodian, the reign of Commodus, though enduring nearly twelve years, was troubled. He was born at Lanuvium, where there must have been a villa of the Aurelii Fulvi; it may have become an imperial property after Antoninus Pius was adopted by Hadrian in 138 CE, though there is no indication that Marcus Aurelius went there. It was used by Commodus. Trajan's villa at Centum Cellae apparently continued to be visited, if the atrocity story (with a happy ending) of 173 CE when Commodus was 12 years old (related below) is true. For medicinal reasons, an outbreak of plague in Rome prompted Commodus's move to Laurentum on the coast, where Pliny the Younger had had a villa. In Rome, while the imperial residences on the Palatine Hill are mentioned, Commodus apparently lived on the Caelian Hill, in the Vectilian *domus*, where he was murdered in 192 CE.[214] By 190 CE, he was living in a very grand suburban villa confiscated from the Quintilii.[215] He returned to the City and the Vectilian *domus* to preside over chariot races as well as to supervise measures of assistance in the emergency of the fire in the winter of 192 CE.[216]

EMPERORS AND VILLAS

Historia Augusta, Commodus (HA, Comm.)

The writer provides an account of the pedagogical personnel and education of the imperial son in his youth.

HA, Comm. 1.2   [Commodus] himself was born on the day before the kalends of September, together with a twin brother, Antoninus, at Lanuvium where his maternal grandfather is said to have been born.

HA, Comm. 1.7–9   In any case, his teachers in all these studies were of no benefit to him. So much for either the force of a natural disposition or else for the [kind of] teachers that are housed in a palace. From his first youth, he was shameful and dishonorable, cruel and lustful, used dirty language, and was debauched. Even at the time, he was proficient in such things as are beneath the dignity of an emperor: he made goblets, danced, sang, and whistled, and he showed perfect talent in being a clown and a gladiator.[217] An early indication of his cruelty occurred at Centum Cellae when he was 12 years old. When it so happened that his bath had been prepared too cool, he ordered the bath attendant to be thrown into the furnace. At this, his attendant slave [*paedagogus*] to whom the order had been given, instead burned the skin of a wether in the furnace, to give him proof certain from the foul stench that the punishment had been carried out.

HA, Comm. 8.5   He was also called the Roman Hercules because he had killed wild animals in the amphitheater at Lanuvium, and as a matter of habit he killed beasts on his own [Lanuvium?] estate [*domus*].

HERODIAN

History since [the Death of] the Emperor Marcus [Aurelius] (τῆς μετὰ Μάρκον βασιλείας ἱστορία), early third century CE (Hdn.)

Hdn. 1.12.1–2   At this time a severe plague occurred in Italy and its virulence was greatest in the city of Rome, a city usually very crowded anyway and still having people coming in from elsewhere; the result was terrible sickness as much for men as for beasts of burden. Commodus, as advised by certain of his doctors, moved to Laurentum, a pleasantly cooler spot, shaded with the laurel plantations that give the place its name. It was considered safer because it was said to be unaffected by the airborne plague due to the pleasant scent of the laurels and the agreeable shade of the trees.

Historia Augusta, Pescennius Niger (HA, Pesc. Nig.)

Commodus had *horti*, probably in Rome, which may have included a villa having a curved portico with its back wall(?) decorated partially or entirely in mosaic; in the mural, Pescennius Niger was depicted as a friend of Commodus undertaking the rites of the Egyptian goddess Isis.[218] Pescennius Niger's self-restraint was apparently famous, suitable to one acting as a priest of Isis.

HA, Pesc. Nig. 6.8–9   He [Pescennius] undertook certain sacred rituals in Gaul which are always given, by general consent, to the most chaste for celebration. We can see him on the curved portico in the *horti* of Commodus: he is shown in mosaic among Commodus's closest friends, initiating the rites of Isis.

Emperors and Villas after Commodus

Written sources regarding emperors' villas become sparse for Roman emperors after the murder of Commodus and the often shaky or nonexistent familial connection among those who followed him (despite Septimius Severus's and his sons' claim to be somehow descended from the Nerva-Antonine adoptive and natural dynasty of which Commodus was the last). This does not mean that villas available for imperial residence ceased to exist or ceased to be built, or that life and construction of villas stopped for those in private ownership. It means that the writers who might otherwise have documented emperors' villas almost stopped doing so, possibly because the necessities of imperial lives changed, along with the themes of history writing in Greek and Latin taking on different emphases and subjects, in changed circumstances.

The main writers of the period from after 192 CE to the early fourth century—the authors of the *Historia Augusta* as well as Cassius Dio, Herodian, Aurelius Victor, and a few others—vary in date, intention, authenticity, and ability, but they share a similar lack of interest in the circumstances of emperors' lives and therefore of much of anything about their villas. Sometimes they repeat tropes that were to be found in Suetonius's biographies: the numinous or prophetic value of what happened at villas (especially in childhood), what kind of *otium* certain emperors enjoyed there, and so on. The writers of the *Historia Augusta*, on Suetonius's model, tended to concentrate on the education, family background, and military and political career of their subjects, but many emperors were not well educated, only a few came from socially and regionally established families, and most had had careers on the continually-upward-moving escalators of military achievement. These circumstance may have allowed little occasion for traditional *otium* and its villa venues, so villas they owned or used may have seemed unimportant to their biographers. Even Cassius Dio, who was a senator, consul, and eyewitness to the reigns of Commodus, Pertinax, Didius Julianus, Septimius Severus, Caracalla, Elagabalus, and Severus Alexander, hardly mentions villas of emperors of his own day, even though—prompted by and faithful to his sources—he had included them in his accounts of earlier emperors. The lack of *otium* in emperors' lives of this period may have stemmed from considerations of security as well: the militarization of the imperial entourages, even in Rome itself, may have made villas undesirable.[219] The emperors succeeding Domitian had in some cases avoided living in the palace on the Palatine Hill, preferring the Domus Tiberiana (Marcus Aurelius, Commodus), villas in the *horti* (Nerva, Trajan), or on the Caelian Hill (Nerva, Marcus Aurelius) for convenience and perhaps to advertise, like Vespasian and Trajan, their easy approachability and perhaps their self-distancing from Domitian: Nerva had actually renamed the palace—the Domus Flavia and Domus Augustana complex—the *aedes publicarum* to accord with this distancing.[220] However, after Commodus left it for the Vectilian *aedes*-villa on the Caelian and, later, the suburban Villa of the Quintilii, within a year the palace came—because of ease of entry by soldiers to murder Pertinax there in March 193 CE—to be fortified with grates [κιγκλίδες] and reinforced doors [θύραι ἰσχυραί]. To no avail and to much popular amusement, as despite these precautions, Didius Julianus was murdered there later that year.[221] Villas in the countryside may have been considered even less secure.

It is also possible that, in the imperial milieux, the nature of *otium* had changed: the emulation of elite behavior among Late Republican villa owners on the model of Cicero and Lucullus may have seemed dated, and the enjoyment of a Domitian or Hadrian in very grand villas compared to the less grand, almost rustic hunting-lodge villa of Trajan (Arcinazzo Romano) or faux-rustic villa such as Villa Magna may have seemed too small and remote for housing the imperial bureaucracy and the military escorts. Enjoying villas and the pleasures of *otium* did not cease for *privati*, but they may have diminished for emperors.

The historians also note the shortness of the reigns of emperors (except for those of Septimius Severus at eighteen years' duration and Severus Alexander's at thirteen) and the fact that many did not have family roots in Italy.[222] The places where they were born or raised is a theme in the villa sites of Hadrian (his villa at "Hispanic" Tibur where he may have spent youthful holidays) and Antoninus Pius (Alsium and Lorium); following Suetonius's model, some writers included the portents of greatness at the villas where emperors were born, or the omens at the villas presaging their deaths, but even these begin to dwindle in imperial biographies after the end of Commodus's reign in 192 CE. Pliny indicates that utility—building a much-needed port on the Tyrrhenian coast—had prompted Trajan to make his villa at Centum Cellae. However, in the case of most of their successors, lack of time spent and hometown affiliations in Italy, as well as the hurly-burly of securing and maintaining power, may have curtailed much villa construction at the imperial level. Many of the emperors were, for the most part, absent from Rome and Italy altogether, campaigning in Gaul, Germany, and the East. Such emperors who resided in Rome (Caracalla, Elagabalus) used villas very sporadically, or else existing villas belonging to Roman families came to be associated with their members who happened to become emperors (the Gordians). Maxentius (r. 306–313 CE) is recorded as being proclaimed *imperator* "at his villa six miles from the City itself, on the road to Lavicum," but that is the sum of texts about this villa.[223] His huge villa at the third milestone on the Via Appia, where he appears to have lived and where he dedicated a precinct tomb and a grandiose circus for horse racing to his son Romulus, is known only from an inscription.[224]

For a number of emperors of the later second and the third centuries, some desultory mentions by writers of their villas or rural properties are here referenced in the endnotes. These include Pertinax (reigned a few months in 193 CE),[225] Clodius Albinus (reigned a few months late 196–early 197 CE),[226] Septimius Severus (r. 193–211 CE),[227] Caracalla (r. 211–217 CE),[228] Elagabalus (r. 218–222 CE),[229] Maximinus Thrax (r. 235–238 CE),[230] Valerian (r. 253–260 CE),[231] his son Gallienus (r. 260–268 CE),[232] and Tetricus the Younger (r. 273–274).[233]

For only a few emperors and their villas in the later second, throughout the third, and into the early fourth centuries are there sources substantial enough to merit inclusion to complete this chapter: Severus Alexander (r. 222–235 CE), Gordian III (r. 238—244 CE), and Tacitus (r. 275–276 CE). Besides them, two texts bring the account of emperors and villas to a close: one a comment of the emperor Diocletian about his gardening activities in retirement from his *palatium* (modern Spalato, Split, Croatia) near Salona in 308 CE, the other concerning the exile of Romulus Augustus to the Lucullanum in 476 CE.

Severus Alexander (Marcus Aurelius Severus Alexander, born Alexianos, or Bassianus, 208–235 CE, reigned 222–235 CE)

Historia Augusta, Severus Alexander (HA, Sev. Alex.).

HA, Sev. Alex. 18.13.5-6–18.14.1   It is said that on the day after he was born, a star of the first brightness was to be seen for the whole day at Arca Caesarea and that the sun was circled with a shining ring near his father's house.[234] The soothsayers, when they had subjected the day of his birth [to scrutiny], declared that one day he would hold the highest power, on the basis that sacrificial victims had been brought from a villa belonging to the emperor [Septimius] Severus, which the farmers [of the estate] had gotten ready in his [the future Severus Alexander's] honor. In his house, a laurel tree grew next to a peach tree [*persicum arbor*], and within a year the laurel tree had grown taller than the peach; from this, the interpreters foretold that the Persians [*Persi*] would be defeated by him.

Severus Alexander restored many buildings and temples in Rome as well as constructing new works on the Bay of Naples.

HA, Sev. Alex. 18.26.9–11   He was remarkably devoted to his mother Mamaea,[235] to such a degree that, in Rome, he built special rooms [*diaetae*] for her in the palace called *Mamaeae*, which to this day ignorant low-class people call *Ad Mammam*. Besides these, he built near Baiae [*in Baiano*] a palace [*palatium*] with a pool, still designated with the name of Mamaea even today. Elsewhere around Baiae he built magnificent public buildings [*opera*] in honor of his relatives as well as huge pools made by letting in the sea.

The following famous passages are included because their author indicates clearly that many of the young emperor's pursuits were undertaken outside of Rome, in places—most probably villas—where he could ride, fish, walk, and hunt. Riding and walking could certainly be done in any one of the *horti* close to or even within Rome, but fishing and hunting are better done well outside the City, at villas. It also appears that his two *lararia* with portraits were portable and were taken wherever he went. The books he liked reading were those of traditional literary *otium*.

HA, Sev. Alex. 18.29.1–3   Before discussing his wars, campaigns, and victories, I will speak a little of his daily life and domestic arrangements. His customary way of life was as follows: first, if it were feasible—that is, if he had not had sexual relations with his wife [*non cum uxore cubisset*]—at the break of day he would pray in his *lararium* in which there were statues [*effigies*, likely busts] of the deified [*divi*] emperors, chosen only from among the best ones, and holier souls [*animae sanctiorae*], among them Apollonius and, according to a writer of his day, Christ, Abraham, and Orpheus as well as certain others who shared their character, and [images of] his ancestors.[236] If this [praying] could not be done, depending on the nature of the place he would ride, fish, walk, or hunt. Next, if time allowed, he would give himself to all kinds of work, both civilian and military. [...]

HA, Sev. Alex. 18.30.1–4   After conducting public business of a civilian or military nature, he would give himself even more eagerly to reading in Greek, perusing the books of Plato's *Republic*. When he turned to reading in Latin, there was nothing that he read more frequently than Cicero's *On Duties* (*De officiis*) and his *Republic* (*De re publica*), unless it was speeches and works by poets, among them those of Serenus Sammonicus, whom he had known personally and had enjoyed, and Horace.[237] He also read the life of Alexander the Great, whose example he often imitated, even though he abhorred Alexander's drunkenness and cruelty to his friends, and despite the assertion by reliable writers that these [Alexander's] faults were not true, he [Severus Alexander] often believed their assertions. After a time of reading, he would give himself to activity in the *palaestra* or to a ball game or to mild wrestling, then, having anointed himself with oil, he would bathe, but never in hot water—or at least rarely; rather, he used the swimming pool, staying in it for almost an hour and, without having eaten, would drink a *sextarius* of cold water from the Aqua Claudia.[238] Emerging from the bath.... [...]

HA, Sev. Alex. 18.31.1–5   He devoted his afternoons to signing and reading letters. [...]
   He called Vergil the Plato of poets, and he had his portrait [*simulacrum*] with that of Cicero in his lesser [*secundum*] *lararium* where there were portraits of Achilles and [other] great heroes. Alexander the Great was consecrated in his greater *lararium*, with the greatest men and the deified emperors.

Gordian III (Marcus Antonius Gordianus, 225–244 CE, reigned 238–244 CE)

In the *Historia Augusta*, the "senatorial" bias of the writer of the Gordian dynasty—father and son, then a nephew who reigned briefly between 238 and 244 CE—is very evident: their allegedly noble affiliations, high education, strong morality, and personal attractions are emphasized together with the splendor of their suburban villa and their works for public enjoyment in the Campus Martius.[239] The suburban villa of the Gordiani on the Via Praenestina is one of the few mentioned or described in the *Historia Augusta*; its construction is attributed to Gordian III, nephew of Gordian I and cousin of Gordian II.[240] However, the description appears to indicate that it was a long-established villa suitable to a distinguished family. The impressive remains of a Late Antique villa on the Via Praenestina (Villa di Tor de' Schiavi, "dei Gordiani") has been identified as this villa; its archaeological record indicates construction before the 230s and continuing into the fourth century.[241] The family's (or only Gordian III's) patronage of public works on the left bank of the Tiber in the Campus Martius is included, even though the description of the project may have been made up to praise their public-spirited efforts. Either way, the projects of the Gordiani within the urban area of Rome—to create *horti* for the public in the Campus Martius—reverted to private ownership quite soon.

Historia Augusta, The Three Gordians (Gordiani Tres) (HA, Gord.)

HA, Gord. 32.1–8 The *domus* of the Gordians, which was beautifully adorned by this Gordian [III], still exists today. There is a villa of theirs [*villa eorum*] on the Via Praenestina, which has two hundred columns in the peristyle [*tetrasylum*], fifty of Carystian marble, fifty of Claudian, fifty of Synnada, and fifty of Numidian, all of equal size.[242] In this villa there were three basilicas 100 feet [about 29.6 m, or 97 ft., 1 in.) in length and other things appropriate to the building, and *thermae* of such a nature as nowhere else in the world besides the City itself as it was then [*praeter urbs ut tunc*].[243] The Senate passed a motion that the descendants of the family of Gordian [III] should in perpetuity never be obliged to act as guardians [*tutores*], envoys [*legati*], or in [other] public capacities unless they wished to do so.[244] None of the Gordians' buildings in Rome survive except for fountains and *balnea*, and the *balnea* were for ordinary people [*homines privati*] and so he furnished them to an ordinary standard [*usus privatus*].[245] In the Campus Martius under the hill, he had once undertaken [to build] a portico 1,000 feet long planned to face another [in parallel], also 1,000 feet long, with a space 500 feet wide between them; in this space there would have been gardens [*viridaria*] planted with laurel, myrtle, and box hedges on either side of a central mosaic floor [*lithostrotum*] with small columns and miniature statues [*columnae et sigilla*] on both sides making a promenade [*deambulatorium*] with a basilica 500 feet long at the end.[246] In addition, with Misitheus he had once planned for summer *thermae* to be built behind the basilica and dedicated in his name, with corresponding winter *thermae* at the entrance to the porticoes, so that neither the gardens nor the porticoes would be without practical benefit [*usus*].[247] But all this area is now covered by the properties, gardens, and houses [*aedes*] of private individuals [*possessores privati*].

Tacitus (Marcus Claudius Tacitus Augustus, ca. 200–276 CE, reigned for six months, 275–276 CE)

When called to imperial dignity by the Senate in 275 CE, Tacitus had had a long and distinguished career as senator and as consul in 273, but he was already in his seventies, so he may have been in retirement at his villa after an interregnum following the murder of Aurelian earlier that year.[248]

Historia Augusta, Tacitus (HA, Tac.)

HA, Tac. 27.7.5–7 It cannot be omitted, at this point, that many in their writings report that Tacitus was away and living in Campania when he was called to the principate—this is a fact and I cannot prevaricate on the matter. When the rumor emerged that he was to be made emperor, he retired and stayed [at his house] near Baiae for two months. Having been brought back from there, he participated [voted] in senatorial decision [*senatus consultum*] as if he were merely a private person and could refuse the imperial power at will [*quasi vere privatus et vere recusaret imperium*].

Tacitus and his brother Florian were memorialized with statues on their rural property at the family hometown of Interamna (modern Terni) in central Italy. Tacitus was depicted in a wall painting or mosaic(?) in the "Quintilian [house]," which probably refers to the Villa of the Quintilii that had been confiscated by Commodus in the early 180s; it was evidently still in imperial hands ninety years later.

HA, Tac. 27.15.1 The [two brothers'] statues, of marble and 30 *pedes* in height, were put up at Interamna on their own land [*in solo proprio*]. [...]

HA, Tac. 27.16.1–3 [...] His portrait was placed in the villa of the Quintilii in a five-part panel: in one, he was wearing a toga [*togatus*], in another, a short *chlamys* [*chlamydatus*]; in yet another, wearing armor [*armatus*]; then again in a [Greek] *pallium* [*palliatus*]; and once in hunting dress [*venatorius habitus*].[249]

When he was inaugurated as *Augustus* in late September 275 CE, and thereafter confirmed by military representatives, Tacitus had been the first for nearly two centuries to become emperor by nomination in the Senate. The writers of the *Historia Augusta* made much of this momentous event, and in doing so reproved senators' retirement to villas and *otium* in favor of active political engagement in the new circumstances. Tacitus's biographer includes documents in the form of letters; they are of doubtful authenticity and authorship but energetic and enthusiastic in tone to illustrate the senators' new attitudes. Their elation, however, was short-lived. The emphatic italics are mine.

HA, Tac. 27.19.3–5 "Claudius Sapilianus to his uncle Cereius Maecianus, greeting. We have achieved, reverend relative [*pater sancte*], what we have always wished for: the Senate has returned to its ancient position. We make emperors [*principes*], the ruling powers [*potestates*] are in our Order. Thanks to the Roman army, [now] truly Roman [once again]: it has given back to us the power that we had always had. *Away with retirements at Baian and Puteolan villas!* Bring yourself to the City, bring yourself to the Senate House [*Curia*]! Rome prospers, the whole State prospers! *We* designate the emperors, *we* empower the princes; we who have *made* them can *depose* them! A word to the wise is enough."

Diocletian (Gaius Aurelius Valerius Diocletianus, born Gaius Valerius Diocles; ca. 242 or 245 to 311 or 312, reigned 284 to abdication 305 CE)

Diocletian's rise in the military led to his proclamation as emperor with the death of the emperors Carus and his son Numerian and the defeat of Carus's younger son Carinus. He set up a system of coequal *Augusti*, one for the east with its main capital at Nicomedia (modern İzmit, Turkey) which he took for himself, the other for the west with its capital at Mediolanum (modern Milan) to which Maximian was appointed. In 293 CE, two *Caesares* (Galerius and Constantius) were commissioned as aides, Galerius with Diocletian, Constantius (Chlorus) with Maximian, in a system called the tetrarchy. By mutual agreement, the *Augusti* both retired in May 305, Diocletian going to a specially built *palatium* (modern Spalato, Split, Croatia) on the Adriatic sea near Salona (modern Solin) in Dalmatia where he had been born; Maximian to a villa in southern Italy. By 308 CE, the events of a civil war prompted a request to Diocletian from his former colleagues Maximian (Herculius) and Galerius to return to power. His answer—that of a villa owner in retirement—was recorded in Aurelius Victor's *Epitome de Caesaribus*:

AURELIUS VICTOR   (Sextus Aurelius Victor, ca. 320–ca. 390 CE)

Epitome de Caesaribus, late fourth century CE (Aur. Vict., Caes.)

Aur. Vict. Caes. 39.6:   It was he [Diocletian] who when asked to resume the *imperium* by Herculius [Maximian] and Galerian, answered as if to ward off some plague: "If you could see the green vegetables [*olera*, cabbages] that have been planted by our own hands, you would never even think that [a return to *imperium*] could be anything of a temptation for me."

Romulus Augustus (Augustulus, 461 or 465 to 511 CE or after, reigned 475 to deposition 476 CE)

Romulus was appointed *Augustus* by his father the *patricius* Orestes in 475 CE; when his father was defeated by Odoacer at the head of a mixed barbarian army including Goths,[250] Romulus was deposed and sent to the villa on an island (Megalia, Megaride) in the Bay of Naples called the Castellum Lucullanum (modern Castel dell' Ovo, probably the site of a villa built by Lucullus upon his return from the east in the 60s BCE). The memory of the villa had endured in its name for some five centuries.[251]

JORDANES

History of the Goths (*De origine actibusque Getarum*, known as *Getica*), 550s CE (Jord., Get.)

Jordanes wrote a history of the origins and presence of the Goths in Italy in the mid-sixth century CE based on an account, now lost, by Cassiodorus of about twenty-five years earlier. This account is repeated almost verbatim in two other texts: in the *Chronicon* of Marcellinus *comes* 14 for the year 476 CE, and in the *Excerpta Valesiana* (*Anonymus Valesianus*).[252]

Jord., Get. 242-243 Soon after Augustulus had been named *imperator* by his own father, Orestes, at Ravenna, Odoacer, king of the Torcilingi accompanied by the Sciri and the Heruli, occupied Italy, killing Orestes, deposing his son Augustulus from power, and condemning him to exile at the Castellum Lucullanum in Campania. In this way, the Roman empire of the west, which the first of the *Augusti*, Octavian Augustus, had begun to rule in the 709th year from the founding of the City, came to an end with this Augustulus 522 years since the beginning of his predecessors' reigns. Since then, Rome and Italy have been held by Gothic kings.

ACKNOWLEDGMENTS

Kenneth Lapatin, curator of antiquities at the J. Paul Getty Museum, and John R. Clarke, professor of art history at the University of Texas at Austin, suggested that Getty Publications entrust this project to me. I hope that their confidence has been fulfilled with this book: it is intended to convey my thanks. Karen Levine, formerly editor in chief at Getty Publications, now with University of Chicago Press, gave me the double gift of time and space—extra time to complete the work, extra space to bring about its ambition.

My greatest thanks go to my project editor at Getty Publications, Laura diZerega. Her guidance and commitment to this book have been invaluable to me. I am grateful to her for suggestions on how to organize the many topics into thematic or chronological chapters as compactly as possible as well as her insistence that the apparatus to the texts induce a sense of intellectual participation in all readers. Laura also encouraged, even advocated for, the expansion of the project to include the contexts of older and current scholarship on villas. She also ensured that the development of the project had some limits, on the wise principle "it's not how much you write, it's how much you cross out."[1] Elma Sanders's skillful manuscript editing combined rigorous logic with elegant solutions, sparing readers many obscurities and awkward phrasing. The mistakes that remain are entirely mine. I also wish to thank Victoria Gallina, senior production coordinator, Dani Grossman, designer, and Nancy Rivera, associate rights specialist, the team at Getty Publications whose expertise and hard work transformed my many manuscript pages into an exquisite bound book.

Suggestions from anonymous evaluators solicited by Getty Publications were a great help in shaping the manuscript. The staff of York University Libraries, Professor Joy Kirchner, dean of libraries, and the Ontario Omni borrowing system must all be thanked, with particular thanks extended to Dr. Scott McLaren, associate librarian for humanities.

This book is a present for my friend Professor Annalisa Marzano, Università di Bologna, in thanks for her support and friendship and to express my admiration for her scholarship.

The dedication of this book is to my wife, Michèle Métraux, to mark my gratitude for her patient help over many years and for her support in more ways than I can say.

—GPRM
Toronto, Canada
October 2024

---

[1] Adapted from Kenneth Clark, *Another Part of the Wood: A Self-Portrait* (New York: Harper and Row, 1974), 85.

ABBREVIATIONS OF ANCIENT TEXTS CITED

Abbreviations are based primarily on Simon Hornblower, Antony Spawforth, and Esther Eidinow, eds., *The Oxford Classical Dictionary*, 4th ed. (Oxford: Oxford University Press, 2012).

App., *B. Civ.*	Appian, *Bella civilia*
App., *Hisp.*	Appian, Ἰβηρική
App., *Mith.*	Appian, Μιθριδάτειος
Apul., *Apol.*	Apuleius of Madaurus, *Apologia*
Arist., *Oec.*	Aristotle, *Oeconomica*
Arist., *Pol.*	Aristotle, *Politica*
Asc., *Mil.*	Asconius Pedianus, Commentary on Cicero, *Pro Milone*
Aur. Vict., *Caes.*	Aurelius Victor, *Caesares*
Aur. Vict., *De vir. ill.*	Aurelius Victor, *De viris illustribus*
Auson., *Ep.*	Ausonius, *Epistles*
Auson., *Eph.*	Ausonius, *Ephemeris*
Auson., *Mos.*	Ausonius, *Mosella*
Cassiod., *Var.*	Cassiodorus, *Variae epistulae*
Cassiod., *Inst.*	Cassiodorus, *Institutiones divinarum et saecularium litterarum*
Cass. Dio	Cassius Dio, *Roman History*
Cass. Dio, *Epit. Bk.*	Cassius Dio, *Epitome* of the *Roman History*
Cato, *Agr.*	Cato, *De agricultura*, or *De re rustica*
Cic., *Acad. post.*	Cicero, *Academica Posteriora*
Cic., *Acad. pr.*	Cicero, *Academica Priora*
Cic., *Ad Brut.*	Cicero, *Epistulae ad Brutum*
Cic., *Att.*	Cicero, *Epistulae ad Atticum*
Cic., *Brut.*	Cicero, *Brutus*, or *De claris oratoribus*
Cic., *Cael.*	Cicero, *Pro Caelio*
Cic., *Cat.*	Cicero, *In Catilinam*
Cic., *De leg.*	Cicero, *De legibus*
Cic., *De or.*	Cicero, *De oratore*
Cic., *Div.*	Cicero, *De divinatione*
Cic., *Dom.*	Cicero, *De domo sua*
Cic., *Fam.*	Cicero, *Epistulae ad familiares*
Cic., *Fin.*	Cicero, *De finibus bonorum et malorum*
Cic., *Leg. Agr.*	Cicero, *De lege agraria*
Cic., *Nat. D.*	Cicero, *De natura deorum*
Cic., *Off.*	Cicero, *De officiis*
Cic., *Orat.*	Cicero, *Orator ad M. Brutum*
Cic., *Phil.*	Cicero, *Orationes Philippicae*
Cic., *Planc.*	Cicero, *Pro Cnaeo Plancio*
Cic., *QFr.*	Cicero, *Epistulae ad Quintum fratrem*
Cic., *Sen.*	Cicero, *Cato Maior de senectute*
Cic., *Top.*	Cicero, *Topica*
Cic., *Tusc.*	Cicero, *Tusculanae disputationes*
Cic., *Verr.*	Cicero, *In Verrem*
Columella, *Rust.*	Columella, *De re rustica*
Diod. Sic.	Diodorus Siculus, *Bibliotheca historica*
Diog. Laert.	Diogenes Laertius, *Lives and Opinions of Eminent Philosophers*

Dion. Hal., *Ant. Rom.*	Dionysius of Halicarnassus, *Antiquitates Romanae*
Fav., *Artis arch.*	Faventinus, *Artis architectonicae*
Frontinus, *Aq.*	Frontinus, *De aquae ductu urbis Romae*
Fronto, *Ep.*	Fronto, *Epistulae*
Fronto, *Ep. gr.*	Fronto, *Epistulae graecae*
Gal., *De indol.*	Galen, *De indolentia*
Gell., *NA*	Aulus Gellius, *Noctes Atticae*
Gerontius, *Vit. Mel.* Greek	Gerontius, *Vita Melaniae Junioris*, Greek redaction
Gerontius, *Vit. Mel.* Latin	Gerontius, *Vita Melaniae Junioris*, Latin redaction
HA, Ant. Pius	Historia Augusta (Scriptores Historiae Augustae), Antoninus Pius
HA, Aurel.	Historia Augusta (Scriptores Historiae Augustae), Aurelian
HA, Avid. Cass.	Historia Augusta (Scriptores Historiae Augustae), Avidius Cassius
HA, Clod.	Historia Augusta (Scriptores Historiae Augustae), Clodius Albinus
HA, Comm.	Historia Augusta (Scriptores Historiae Augustae), Commodus
HA, Gall.	Historia Augusta (Scriptores Historiae Augustae), Gallieni duo
HA, Gord.	Historia Augusta (Scriptores Historiae Augustae), Gordiani tres
HA, Hadr.	Historia Augusta (Scriptores Historiae Augustae), Hadrian
HA, M. Ant.	Historia Augusta (Scriptores Historiae Augustae), Marcus Aurelius Antoninus (Caracalla)
HA, M. Aur.	Historia Augusta (Scriptores Historiae Augustae), Marcus Aurelius
HA, Pert.	Historia Augusta (Scriptores Historiae Augustae), Pertinax
HA, Pesc. Nig.	Historia Augusta (Scriptores Historiae Augustae), Pescennius Niger
HA, Sev.	Historia Augusta (Scriptores Historiae Augustae), Septimius Severus
HA, Sev. Alex.	Historia Augusta (Scriptores Historiae Augustae), Severus Alexander
HA, Tac.	Historia Augusta (Scriptores Historiae Augustae), Tacitus
HA, Tyr. Trig.	Historia Augusta (Scriptores Historiae Augustae), Tyranni Triginta
HA, Verus	Historia Augusta (Scriptores Historiae Augustae), Lucius Verus
Hdn.	Herodian
Hdt.	Herodotus
Hes., *Op.*	Hesiod, *Opera et dies*
Hes., *Theog.*	Hesiod, *Theogony*
Hom., *Il.*	Homer, *Iliad*
Hom., *Od.*	Homer, *Odyssey*
Hor., *Ars P.*	Horace, *Ars poetica*
Hor., *Epist.*	Horace, *Epistulae*

Hor., *Epod.*	Horace, *Epodi*
Hor., *Odes*	Horace, *Odes* or *Carmina*
Hor., *Sat.*	Horace, *Satirae*
Jerome, *Ep.*	Jerome, *Epistulae*
Jord., *Get.*	Jordanes, *Getica*
Joseph., *AJ*	Josephus, *Antiquitates Judaicae*
Juv., *Satires*	Juvenal, *Satires*
Lactant., *Div. inst.*	Lactantius, *Divinae institutiones*
Livy	Livy, *Ab urbe condita*
Livy, *Per.*	Livy, *Periochae*
Lucr.	Lucretius, *De rerum natura*
Macrob., *Sat.*	Macrobius, *Saturnalia*
M. Aur., *Med.*	Marcus Aurelius, *Meditations*
Mart., *Epig.*	Martial, *Epigrams*
Mart., *Spect.*	Martial, *Spectacula*
Nep., *Att.*	Cornelius Nepos, *Atticus*
Ovid, *Ars am.*	Ovid, *Ars amatoria*
Ovid, *Fasti*	Ovid, *Fasti*
Ovid., *Her.*	Ovid, *Heroides*
Ovid, *Met.*	Ovid, *Metamorphoses*
Palladius, *Op. Agr.*	Palladius, *Opus agriculturae*
Paulinus of Nola, *Ep.*	Paulinus of Nola, *Epistulae*
Paulinus of Nola, *Carm.*	Paulinus of Nola, *Carmina*
Paulinus, *Euch.*	Paulinus Pellaeus, *Eucharisticus*
Paus.	Pausanius, *Description of Greece*, Ἑλλάδος Περιήγησις
Petron., *Sat.*	Petronius, *Satyricon*
Philo, *Leg.*	Philo of Alexandria, *Legatio ad Gaium*
Pindar, *Ol.*	Pindar, *Olympian Odes*
Plaut., *Cas.*	Plautus, *Casina*
Plaut., *Pseud.*	Plautus, *Pseudolus*
Plin., *Ep.*	Pliny (the Younger), *Epistulae*
Plin., *Pan.*	Pliny (the Younger), *Panegyricus*
Plin., *HN*	Pliny (the Elder), *Naturalis historia*
Plat., *Cra.*	Plato, *Cratylu*
Plat., *Phdr.*	Plato, *Phaedrus*
Plut., *Cons. ad Apoll.*	Plutarch, *Consolatio ad Apollonium*
Plut., *Lyc.*	Plutarch, *Lycurgus*
Plut., *Vit. Artax.*	Plutarch, *Vitae parallelae, Artaxerxes*
Plut., *Vit. Caes.*	Plutarch, *Vitae parallelae, Caesar*
Plut., *Vit. Cam.*	Plutarch, *Vitae parallelae, Camillus*
Plut., *Vit. Cat. Mai.*	Plutarch, *Vitae parallelae, Cato Maior*
Plut., *Vit. Cat. Min.*	Plutarch, *Vitae parallelae, Cato Minor*
Plut., *Vit. Cic.*	Plutarch, *Vitae parallelae, Cicero*
Plut., *Vit. Crass.*	Plutarch, *Vitae parallelae, Crassus*
Plut., *Vit. Luc.*	Plutarch, *Vitae parallelae, Lucullus*
Plut., *Vit. Lys.*	Plutarch, *Vitae parallelae, Lysander*
Plut., *Vit. Mar.*	Plutarch, *Vitae parallelae, Marius*
Plut., *Vit. Pomp.*	Plutarch, *Vitae parallelae, Pompeius*
Plut., *Vit. Rom.*	Plutarch, *Vitae parallelae, Romulus*
Plut., *Vit. Sull.*	Plutarch, *Vitae parallelae, Sulla*
Plut., *Vit. Ti. Gracch.*	Plutarch, *Vitae parallelae, Tiberius Gracchus*

Polyb.	Polybius, *The Histories*
Prop.	Propertius, *Elegies*
Quint., *Inst.*	Quintilian, *Institutio oratoria*
Rut. Namat., *De red.*	Rutilius Namatianus, *De reditu suo*
Sen., *Clem.*	Seneca (the Younger). *De clementia*
Sen., *Ep.*	Seneca (the Younger), *Epistulae morales ad Lucilium*
Sen., *Otio*	Seneca (the Younger), *De otio*
Sid. Apoll., *Ep.*	Sidonius Apllonaris, *Epistulae*
Sid. Apoll., *Carm.*	Sidonius Apllonaris, *Carmina*
Stat., *Silv.*	Statius, *Silvae*
Strabo	Strabo, *Geographica*
Suet., *Aug.*	Suetonius, *Divus Augustus*
Suet., *Calig.*	Suetonius, *Gaius Caligula*
Suet., *Claud.*	Suetonius, *Divus Claudius*
Suet., *Dom.*	Suetonius, *Domitianus*
Suet., *Galb.*	Suetonius, *Galba*
Suet., *Iul.*	Suetonius, *Divus Iulius*
Suet., *Nero*	Suetonius, *Nero*
Suet., *Tib.*	Suetonius, *Tiberius*
Suet., *Tit.*	Suetonius, *Divus Titus*
Suet., *Vesp.*	Suetonius, *Vespasian*
Symm., *Ep.*	Symmachus, *Epistulae*
Tac., *Ann.*	Tacitus, *Annales*
Tac., *Hist.*	Tacitus, *Historiae*
Ter., *Phorm.*	Terence, *Phormio*
Val. Max.	Valerius Maximus
Varro, *Ling.*	Varro, *De lingua latina*
Varro, *Rust.*	Varro, *De re rustica libri III*
Vell. Pat.	Velleius Paterculus
Verg., *Aen.*	Vergil, *Aeneid*
Verg., *Geor.*	Vergil, *Georgics*
Vitr., *De arch.*	Vitruvius, *De architectura*
Xen., *An.*	Xenophon, *Anabasis*
Xen., *Cyr.*	Xenophon, *Cyropaedia*
Xen., *Oec.*	Xenophon, *Oeconomicus*

ABBREVIATIONS OF JOURNALS AND STANDARD REFERENCE WORKS CITED

AA	Archäologischer Anzeiger
AJP	American Journal of Philology
ANRW	Aufstieg und Niedergang der römischen Welt, ed. H. Temporini, 31 vols. (Berlin 1972–)
AntCl	L'Antiquité Classique
ArchCl	Archeologia Classica
AtlasAncRome	The Atlas of Ancient Rome: Biography and Portraits of the City, ed. Andrea Carandini and Paolo Carafa, 2 vols. (Princeton 2017)
ATTA	Atlante Tematico di Topografia Antica
BICS	Bulletin of the Institute of Classical Studies of the University of London
BullCom	Bullettino della Commissione archeologica Comunale di Roma
CAH	Cambridge Ancient History, 31 vols. (Cambridge 1924–1939 and 1970–2005)
CÉFR	Collection de l'École française de Rome
CIG	Corpus inscriptionum graecarum, ed. August Böckh et al. (Berlin 1825–)
CIL	Corpus inscriptionum latinarum, ed. Theodor Mommsen et al. (1853–)
CJ	Classical Journal
CPhil	Classical Philology
EAA	Enciclopedia dell'arte antica, classica ed orientale, 8 vols. plus supplements (Rome 1958–1966)
ILS	Inscriptiones latinae selectae, ed. Hermann Dessau, 3 vols. (Berlin 1892–1916)
JECS	Journal of Early Christian Studies
JRA	Journal of Roman Archaeology
JRS	Journal of Roman Studies
LIMC	Lexicon iconographicum mythologiae classicae, John Boardman, 8 vols. (Zurich 1981–2009)
LTUR	Lexicon topographicum urbis romae, ed. Eva Margareta Steinby, 6 vols. (Rome 1993–2001)
LTUR Suburbium	Lexicon topographicum urbis Romae: Suburbium, ed. Adriano La Regina, 5 vols. (Rome 2001–2008)
MAAR	Memoirs of the American Academy in Rome
MÉFRA	Mélanges de l'École française de Rome, Antiquité
MGH-AA	Monumenta Germaniae Historica, Auctores Antiquissimi, 15 vols. (Berlin 1827–1919)
NP	Brill's New Pauly: Encyclopaedia of the Ancient World. Antiquity, ed. Hubert Cancik and Helmuch Schneider, 16 vols. (Boston 2002–2010)
OCD4	Oxford Classical Dictionary, 4th ed., ed. Simon Hornblower, Antony Spawforth, and Esther Eidinow (Oxford 2012)

ODCC4	*Oxford Dictionary of the Christian Church*, 4th ed., ed. Andrew Louth (Oxford 2022)
ODCW	*Oxford Dictionary of the Classical World*, ed. John W. Roberts (Oxford 2005)
ODLA	*Oxford Dictionary of Late Antiquity*, ed. Oliver Nicholson, 2 vols. (Oxford 2018)
PBSR	*Papers of the British School at Rome*
PECS	*Princeton Encyclopedia of Classical Sites*, ed. R. Stillwell et al. (Princeton 1976)
PG	*Patrologia Graeca*, ed. Jacques-Paul Migne, 161 vols. (Paris 1857–1866)
PIR²	*Prosopographia Imperii Romani, Saeculi I, II, III*, 2nd ed., 9 vols. (Berlin 1933–2014)
PL	*Patrologia Latina*, ed. Jacques-Paul Migne, 217 vols. (Paris 1841–1855)
Pleiades	*Pleiades*, https://pleiades.stoa.org/. Online gazeteer. Institute for the Study of the Ancient World and Ancient World Mapping Center
PLRE	*The Prosopography of the Later Roman Empire*, J.R. Martindale et al., 3 vols. (Cambridge 1971–1980)
RA	*Revue Archéologique*
RM	*Römische Mitteilungen*
TAPA	*Transactions of the American Philological Association*
ZPE	*Zeitschrift für Papyrologie und Epigraphik*

GLOSSARY

Note: Latin and Greek nouns are given in the nominative singular form, then the nominative plural form; some Latin nouns do not change from singular to plural. The English equivalents are in the singular.

actus, actus. A cattle path, a road. Also used as a unit of linear measure: 120 *pedes* (about 35.5 m, or 116½ ft.); as a unit of areal measure, a square of 120 *pedes* (one-twelfth ha, or 3 acres).

aedes, aedes. A temple or any impressive or memorable building, including a *domus* or a villa.

agellum, agella. A meadow or a field, hence sometimes an estate, property, or farm.

ager, agri. Land, field, territory, region, countryside. *In agro, in agris*, with the preposition *in*, means a villa and its estate. The adjective *agrestis* (*agreste*), *agrestes* (*agrestia*) indicates that something is rural but also wild, uncivilized, boorish.

Ager Falernus. The agricultural area in northern Campania between the Mons Massicus on the north and the Vulturnus River (modern Volturno River), crossed from northwest to southeast by the Via Appia from Sinuessa to Capua and Neapolis (modern Naples) as of 312 BCE, and along its coast by the Via Domitiana as of ca. 95 CE. It was famous for its wine, with several regions enjoying a particularly high regard by connoisseurs.

Ager Gallicana. The fertile farming plain of the Padanus River (modern Po River).

ager publicus. Land in the *possessio* of the Roman people that was taken from conquered communities by treaty or annexation. Its disposition was in the hands of censors, who could lease, centuriate, and assign it to *coloni*.

agricola, agricolae. A farmer, usually one holding Roman citizenship.

aheneus. Copper, but also brass.

ala, alae. Literally, wings; in a Roman *domus*, the atrium could have cross-axial extensions of its space at its further end, providing space for *imagines* (see below) and as architectural backdrops for members of the family to receive guests.

alimentum, alimenta. An official financial scheme in local towns and cities in Italy for the support of disadvantaged boys and girls, initiated in the reign of Nerva (r. 96–98 CE) and greatly expanded under his successors, notably Trajan. The *alimenta* were funded by nonamortizable loans assigned to owners on their self-declared valuation of their land at low rates of interest, paid annually to the local administration, which would distribute the funds. Private *alimenta* in the form of endowments could be set up on a similar basis, either in the lifetime of the donor or as a bequest in a will for the permanent support of public goods such as annual banquets for citizens or for special groups, processions, entertainments (theatrical, acrobatic, athletic), lectures, libraries, payments to poor families, or faithful freedmen.

ambulatio, ambulationes. A promenade, a walkway, paths in gardens, also a portico.

amoenitas. Pleasure, pleasant circumstances, delightful or luxurious surroundings.

amphora, amphoras. Ceramic or terracotta containers with narrow necks for sealing, and larger bodies for holding liquids (*garum*, wine, olive oil) and occasionally dry goods or preserved or live comestibles. Greek versions could be decorated, but Roman ones were typically plain or stamped by the maker and sometimes labeled as to contents, owner, destination. Some had pointed bases for pouring or rounded ones for transport by cart or boat.

andron. A dining room.

annona. Beginning in 123 BCE, an official measure ensuring the subsidized sale of wheat in the amount of 5 *modii* (about 33.5 kg) per month to adult male citizens; as of 58 BCE, the allocation became gratis, with some reform of eligible recipients in 2 BCE; an official bureaucracy for the *cura annona* under an equestrian *praefectus* was established. In the third century CE, oil, wine, and pork were added to the annonarian distributions.

apodyterium, apodyteria. In a bath building, the vestibule or room in which the users removed and stored their clothes before entering the facility; from Greek ἀποδύω, to remove, to strip.

apotheca, apothecae. A storeroom or warehouse.

apparatus, apparati. As a participle, anything gotten ready or prepared. As a noun (*apparatus, apparatus*), movable equipment, furnishings, appurtenances; can also mean magnificence in decoration, embellishments; see also *supellex*, below).

arbustum, arbusti. An orchard or plantation; in villas, a vineyard with vines wedded to trees.

area, areae. Any open, flat area, a precinct; in the *pars rustica*, a threshing floor.

atrium, atria, also *cavaedium, cavaedia*. The formal room of a house of Roman-Italic type, centralized to other surrounding rooms such as bedrooms (*cubicula*) and corridors but leading, on axis, to the room specially allocated to the *paterfamilias*, the *tablinum*. Its position in a *domus* could be directly after the entrance area from the street (*vestibulum, fauces*) or, in villas, preceded by a peristyle, according to Vitruvius (*De arch.* 6.5.3).

auditorium, auditoria. A square or rectangular room, often with a square or round apse, for hearing legal cases, lectures, poetry readings, and entertainments. *Auditoria* were part of the architectural panoply of *domus* and villas of socially elevated persons, especially in Late Antiquity.

augur, augures. A priestly soothsayer, one who foretold divine intention and good or bad futures by observing events (such as lightning, actions of birds) occurring in a defined viewing quadrant (*templum*) that had a sacrosanct character.

balneum, balnea, balinarium, balinaria, also *balnarium, balnaria*. A bath building, in context smaller than the large public facilities (*thermae*) but available in various sizes as public facilities and usual in *domus* and villas for private use. Sequence, size, and number of rooms varied, but *balnea* could be equipped with an *apodyterium* for disrobing, then a cold-room (*frigidarium*) with a plunge bath or swimming pool (*natatio*), a warm room (*tepidarium*), a hot-and-wet room (*caldarium*) with plunge bath or basin (*labrum*), and a hot-and-dry room (*laconicum*, or *sudatorium*) for sweating. The sequence of use was cold to hot-dry, then in reverse. Radiant heat could be supplied from a hollow floor (*hypocaustum*) raised on supports (*pilae*) and from thermal jacketing of the walls through tubes (*tubuli*) fed with hot air from a furnace (*praefurnium*), and hot water made available from metal boilers.

basilica, basilicas. The Roman form of law court was a rectangular room with an apse (semi-circular or square) at a short end to frame the magistrate's seat (curule chair) and those of his advisors and assistants, sometimes set on a tribunal or dais. Some public basilicas had colonnades along the long ends; others had mezzanines where businessmen (*negotiatores*) exchanged commercial information and transacted business. Vitruvius lists *basilicae* as part of the panoply of rooms appropriate to important persons such as senators, but they are rare in Early Imperial-period private dwellings. In Late Antiquity, as the elite owners of *domus* and villas began to assume quasi-magisterial authority, they became more numerous.

basis villae. The term for the terraced platform and the villa built on it, sometimes with sublevel or adjacent cisterns to supply water; the structure gave views, light, and cross ventilation to the dwelling and its gardens.

bibliotheca, bibliothecae, also *bybliotheca, bybliothecae.* A library or collection of books, public or private.

caementum. See *opus caementicium.*

Caesar. Name and title of emperors. Gaius Octavius took the name Gaius Julius Caesar Octavianus upon adoption by Julius Caesar in 44 BCE. The Senate added the title *Augustus* to Octavian's name in 28 BCE. *Caesar* and Augustus became the name and title for emperors in the direct succession of Augustus, and both were appropriated by later emperors. In the second century CE and later, *Caesar* became the title of an heir-designate or junior colleague to senior Augusti.

Campania. The area south of the Mons Massicus including the Ager Falernus, running from the west coast of the Italian peninsula inland to the Apennine range, with its southern extent on the south side of the Surrentine cordillera. Its major cities in Roman times were Capua (modern Sta. Maria Capua Vetere), Nola, Neapolis (modern Naples), Puteoli (modern Pozzuoli), and the towns and resorts around the Bay of Naples, including Herculaneum, Pompeii, and Surrentum.

casa, casae. small villa or dwelling, sometimes a hut. In association with a man of famous ancestral status such as Romulus, the humble Casa Romuli came to embody the modesty and frugality of men of the noble past.

cavaedium, cavaedia. See **atrium.**

cella, cellae. Any special room. In religious architecture, the principal space for worship. In villas, the room or rooms with special functions.

cella olearia, also *oletum, oleta.* The facility in which separation of olive pits from flesh in a mill (*trapetum, mola*) prepared the fruit for crushing in a bin (*galeagra*) set on a platform (*ara*). The press (*torcularium*) could be either a screw press, or a winched machine with a lever (*prelum*) connected to a cylindrical rope drum (*sucula*) set in counterweights and tightened with handspakes; the machine was stabilized by cross-braced uprights (*arbores*). The first pressings were channeled into vats for filtering before transport in amphoras or other containers. Successive pressings determined the quality of the oil; final treatments with boiling water produced a residue (*amurca*) that was used as a lubricant and preservative (similar to modern Cosmoline). Both the facility and the villa producing it would be termed an *oletum.*

cella vinaria, vinetum. The room or rooms in which grapes were crushed and their must channeled into containers for fermentation into wine. The containers, *dolia*, were sometimes partially buried below ground (*dolia defossa*) to stabilize temperature. Ultimately, the wine was decanted into transport vessels such as amphoras or barrels. A villa whose product was wine was a *vinetum*.

cenaculum, cenacula. A room on an upper floor of a *domus* or villa, an attic, sometimes a *triclinium*.

cenatio, cenationes. A dining room, equivalent to *cenaculum*, or *coenatio*; another word for a *triclinium*.

Chaldean astrologer. In Roman context, a soothsayer or astrologer from the East.

city, City. See *urbs*.

civis, cives. A free citizen.

cliens, clientes. The term designates a person in dependency or subordinate association to a patron (*patronus*); the social institution had various degrees of definition, from a one-to-one relationship to a patron having entire cities or even entire provinces as clients. The *clientela* (*clientelae*) designated the patron's dependent group.

collegium, collegia. Any organized group devoted to professional, commercial, or social/charitable activities, often receiving official recognition and legal status with permission to own property and retain funds.

Collis Hortulorum. The hill known later as the Mons Pincius (modern Pincio, Pincian Hill) running from the ravine on the west side of the Quirinal Hill (where the Horti Sallustiani were located) to the modern area of the Porta Flaminia; site of many *horti*, including the Horti Lucullani. Its name is indicated in Suet., *Nero* 50.

colonus, coloni. A tenant farmer, a sharecropper, sometimes an assignee of *ager publicus*.

Compitalia. An ancient winter festival celebrated in *domus* and villas in honor of the Lares Compitales, or household deities; the entire *familia*, notably including the enslaved members, participated in the celebration.

corona, coronae. A crown made of metal, or, very commonly, wreaths of flowers or leaves (laurel, oak, wild celery).

cryptoporticus, cryptoporticus. A covered passageway, gallery, or portico that is walled on both sides; could be entirely or partially underground, free-standing, or supporting structures above, *Cryptoporticus* provided cool environments for relief from heat and for moderate-temperature storage.

cubiculum, cubicula. Bedroom.

culina, culinae. Kitchen.

cultor, cultores. A cultivator, a farmer.

cursus honorum. The course of honors included the initiation to elected office and the ascent to higher position, by election (Republican period) or election and appointment (Imperial period).

custodia, custodiae. Guardianship, duty to protect.

Cyzicene dining room. A type of *triclinium* fronted by the north-facing colonnade of a peristyle: Vitr., *De arch.* 6.7.3.

descriptio, descriptiones. A plan, image, representation, drawing.

diaeta, diaetae. A living room or rooms, places for domestic relaxation and conversation.

dignitas, dignitates. The measure of respect in which a person is held, the worth of a person, the social or political status of a person.

diligentia, diligentiae. Careful oversight, attention, diligence in tasks.

dolium, dolia. Heavy, thick-walled, round-bodied and bottomed terracotta containers used mainly to ferment grape must into wine, often set half-buried below ground for temperature control (*dolia defossa*); see also *cella vinaria*, above.

domina, dominae. A female property owner in her own right, but usually designating the wife of the *dominus* or *paterfamilias*.

dominus, domini. The property owner (male).

domus, domus. An urban house; sometimes designating a villa.

the East. The geographical areas to the east of the Italian Peninsula with which the Romans had connections, including Greece, Asia Minor as far as Armenia, Syria-Palestine as far as the Euphrates and the border with Persia, and Egypt.

epulum, epula. A banquet, public banquet, feast, meal.

euergetism. A modern term describing the beneficent action of individuals or groups in promoting or funding goods or events in the public interest. From Greek εὐεργέτης (doer of good things); can refer to any public good, often expensive and beyond the ordinary means of governments (naval vessels, banquets for citizens, processions and festivals, athletic and cultural contests).

Euripus, Euripi. Geographically, Euripus is the (partially tidal) strait separating the island of Euboea from mainland Boeotia in central Greece; by extension, in architecture and gardens a euripus is any canal or channel of water, often with a flow and sometimes connected to a fountain.

exedra, exedrae. An architectural extension of a main space, curvilinear or angular, usually open to the main space.

fabrica, fabricae. A workshop.

familia, familiae. The human household, including a *paterfamilias*, his wife (*uxor, domina, materfamilias*), their children, their relatives living with them, clients, formerly enslaved persons (*liberti, libertae*), and enslaved persons (*servi, servae*).

flumen, flumines. River.

fructus, fructus. Anything enjoyable, or profit or income resulting from professional or commercial activity; in an agricultural context, harvest of any kind as well as the profit or income derived from such produce.

frumentum, frumenta. Any grain, but most often wheat.

frux, fruges. Crops, produce.

fullo, fullones. A fuller.

fundus, fundi. A villa, agricultural estate.

Gallia Cisalpina, also **Gallia Citerior, Gallia Togata.** That section of the Italian peninsula defined on the north by the Alps as far as the Lacus Lemanus (modern Lake Geneva), and on the south by the Rubico (modern Rubicon) and Arno Rivers, which marked its border with Italia. The area ran from the Ligurian sea on the west to the Adriatic on the east, divided into Gallia Transpadana and Gallia Cispadana on either side of the Padanus River (modern Po River).

Gallia Transalpina. Ultimately, that section of western Europe beyond the Alps comprising all of Gaul, with Aquitania, the Moselle area, and the Rhineland, to the North Sea. At first, with the foundation of Narbo (Colonia Narbo Martius, modern Narbonne), it was limited to little more than modern Provence (Gallia Narbonensis), but with the westward extension to Tolosa (modern Toulouse) and Burdigala (modern Bordeaux), Aquitania and Septimania were added; the other parts to the northwest and northeast—Gallia Celtica, Gallia Belgica—were administered from Lugdunum (modern Lyon), hence Gallia Lugdunensis, but administrative changes resulted in different nomenclatures and administrative capitals in the Imperial period.

garum. A fermented fish sauce used as a common condiment in cooking. Equivalents are *hallec* (Greek) and *liquamen* (Latin).

hallec, or *allec*. Another term for *garum*.

harena, harenae, also *arena, arenae*. Sand, hence a sandy place or beach, or the sand-strewn spectacle floor of an amphitheater.

haruspex, haruspices. A priestly official who determined divine will by interpretation of the organs of sacrificial animals.

hemina. A unit of liquid measure equaling about 273 ml, or 9¼ fl. oz.

horologium, horologia. Any timepiece; in Varro, a wind indicator (not a true *horologium*).

horreum, horrea. A warehouse.

hortus, horti. A garden. In the plural, often denotes an extensive landscaped garden, sometimes terraced, with special planting (shrubs, trees), decorations (statues, paintings), water features (fountains, cascades, euripi), seating, and views.

HS. Abbreviation for sesterces. The *sestertius* (*sestertii*), was the most common Roman small silver coin in the Republican period, later bronze in the Imperial period; commonly used for stating and estimating prices in both periods.

ianitor. A porter.

imago, imagines. Images of ancestors kept in various forms by Romans of elite and ordinary status; the most frequent were portrait images on funerary reliefs (very common for couples of freedmen and women, sometimes shown with a son of citizen status). Others were portable portrait masks used in funerary processions and, according to Vitruvius, kept in the *alae* of the *tablinum* in the family *domus* as ancestral memorials.

imbrex, imbrices. A curved terracotta roof tile covering the flanged seam between the *tegulae*.

imperium. The power of command conferred, by vote or appointment, on an individual for a specific time of tenure (in many elective civilian offices, one year) or activity (a military campaign, a term of proconsul of a province). *Imperium* was held by aediles, praetors, consuls, *magister equitum* (master of the horse, the adjunct to a dictator), and dictator. Emperors held *imperium* permanently.

ingenium, ingenia. Innate character, ability, intelligence.

instrumentum, instrumenta. Farm gear of any kind, mobile equipment (baskets, wagons), also fixed agricultural facilities or infrastructure (drains, mills); *instrumentum vocalis* (Varro's term, "equipment capable-of-speech") were the enslaved personnel of a villa and were considered part of its inventory.

iugerum, iugera. In Latin texts, the most frequently used term to denote areal measurement of land: a unit of 28,800 sq. Roman ft., about .25 ha, or ⅔ acre. Its multiples were also standard descriptors: ½ iugera = 1 *actus*; 2 *iugera* = 1 *heredium*; 200 *iugera* = 1 *centuria*; 800 *iugera* = 1 *saltus*.

Jupiter Daps, or **Jupiter Dapalis**. In Cato, the manifestation of Jupiter in specific reference to the offering of food from the villa's *fructus*.

labor, labores. Activity, work, task.

Lacus Velinus. A lake in Sabine territory between Interamna (modern Terni) and Reate (modern Rieti), partially drained by Manius Curius Dentatus in 272 BCE.

Lar, Lares. The divine household spirit associated with Vesta as guardian of the hearth and the Di Penates who protected the entire *familia* (see above); see also Vesta.

lararium, lararia. The altar in a *domus* or villa, sometimes in the *atrium* or nearby, or in the *culina* so the free and enslaved members of the *familia* could participate equally in worship.

lectus triclinaris, lecti/ae/a triclinaris. The couch or daybed, cushioned and draped, sometimes simple, often painted, gilded, and with applied decorations in metal; used for reclining to eat in *triclinia*.

liber, libri. A book, referring equally to a *rotulus* (roll) and a codex.

liberta, libertae. A freedwoman (rare usage).

libertus, liberti. A freedman.

liberus, liberi. A child, by extension the child of free persons or those of freed status.

macellum, macella. A market or market building, most usually in a town or city.

maior, maiores. An ancestor, either personal to an individual or, in the plural, a collective ancestry. Individual *maiores* frequently cited in Latin literature are Camillus, Cincinnatus, Curius Dentatus, Fabricius, and Serranus; these men exhibited the virtues of the *mos maiorum* (see below).

mancipium. The subjugation of a person or thing to its owner, or any right of *possessio* (see below) or acquisition by purchase. Also, any owned thing (pl. *mancipia*) including enslaved persons (*mancipii*).

marbles. (Listed here are marbles and other decorative stones mentioned in the texts, including porphyries and granites.)

Carystian marble. From Carystus (Karystos), a town on Euboea, which exported the marble quarried at nearby Marmarium: Strabo 9.5.16 and 10.1.6. It is yellow-cream in color with prominent green, gray, and/or purple veins; sometimes called *cipollino, cipollino verde,* or *cipollino ondato* in Italian. Plin., *HN* 4.51 (4.6) and 4.64 (4.12, on geography) and 36.49 (36.7, on luxury); van Dam 1984, 250–51; Newlands 2011, 144–45. Corsi Collection: nos. 89, 90.

Chian marble. A richly colored and veined marble from Chios in the Aegean; the modern Italian name is *portasanta*. Plin., *HN* 36.46 (36.5); van Dam 1984, 250; Newlands 2011, 144. Corsi Collection: nos. 77–88.

Laconian "marble." "Marble from the mountain of Lycurgus at Amyclae" (Stat, *Silv.* 2.2.90, in ch. 4, Descriptions of Villas) is the gray-green porphyry (not technically a marble) from Amyclae near Sparta in southern Greece; its modern Italian name is *serpentino antico* or *porfido serpentino*. The mountain of Lycurgus is Mt. Taygetus: Strabo 4.8.52–53; Mart., *Epig.* 4.42.11. It is not clear why Lycurgus, the lawgiver of Sparta, had a mountain or quarry named after him, unless the mountain had become proverbial: Plut., *Lyc.* 29 and 31. There were other memorials to him; Paus., 3.2.3–4, 3.14.8., 3.16.6., 3.16.10, and 3.18.2. For the Laconian "marble": van Dam 1984, 249–50; Newlands 2011, 144. Corsi Collection: nos. 797–802.

Megarian marble. A soft white marble from near Megara in the Megarid between Attica and Corinth; mentioned in Cic., *Att.* 5.2 (1.9.2). Its modern Italian name is *lumacella bianca antica*. Corsi Collection no. 215.

Numidian marble. Quarried at Simithus (or Simithuum, Simithu, modern Chemtou) on the border of the Roman provinces of Africa Vetus and Numidia. It was widely used for its fine yellow and red, heavily veined surface that took a high shine. Called *giallo antico* in Italian. Plin., *HN* 35.3 (35.1) and 36.49 (36.7, on foolish luxury); *HN* 5.22 (5.2) and 5.29 (5.4, on geographical location); Suet., *Aug.* 85; Sid. Apoll., *Carm.* 5.37; van Dam 1984, 250; Newlands 2011, 144. Corsi Collection: nos. 22–34, 40.

Pentelic marble. From Mt. Pentelicus in Attica, northeast of Athens, a golden white marble of medium hardness suitable for use in both architectural elements and sculpture. Strabo 9.1.23; Vitr., *De arch.* 2.8.49. Corsi Collection: no. 3.

Syene marble. A red granite from Egypt. *Ethiopia lapis Syenitiis*: Plin., *HN* 36.63 (36.13); this is the "granite of the obelisks" as known in Rome, Alexandria, and Egypt: Plin., *HN* 36.63–74 (36.14–15). See Charlesworth 1926/2016, 247, and note on 21–22; van Dam 1984, 248–49; Newlands 2011, 143. Corsi Collection: nos. 831–33, 837, 839-840, 992.

Synnas marble. From Phrygia, a white marble with purple spots. The modern Italian name is *pavonazzetto*. Plin., *HN* 37.115 (37.37); van Dam 1984, 248; Newlands 2011, 143. Corsi Collection: nos. 123–24, 420, 431, 917–18.

Thasian marble. A white or white-gray veined marble from the island of Thasos off the eastern coast of Macedonia. Plin., *HN* 36.44–46 (36.5, first import of colored, veined marble to Rome); Sen., *Ep.* 5.37 (on luxury); van Dam 1984, 250; Newlands 2011, 144. Corsi Collection: nos. 5–7.

Other marbles in widespread use in Roman times were Parian marble, from the islands of Paros (Plin., *HN* 36.14 [36.4]; Corsi Collection no. 2) and Proconnesian, from the island of Proconnesus (modern Marmara, Marmara Adası; Plin., *HN* 5.151 [36.43]; Corsi Collection no. 4).

mater familias, matres familias, also *materfamilias, matresfamilias, matres familiarum.* The female head of household, most usually the wife of the *dominus* or *paterfamilias*.

matrona, matronae. The wife of a *paterfamilias*; more specific than *materfamilias*.

meus, mei, meorum. My people, people of my household, my enslaved personnel, my household.

modius, modii. A unit of dry measure, about 8.75 liters, or 1.9 gal.

Mons Gauraunus, or **Mons Gaurus** (modern Monte Barbaro). A mountain inland from Puteoli (modern Pozzuoli), overlooking the area between Cuma and the cape of Misenum.

mons, montes. Hill, mountain.

mos, mores. Manners, habits, demeanor, behavior.

mos maiorum, mores maiorum. The traditional habits, behavior, and character of the collective ancestry, with a stress on their personal virtues, civic devotion, military courage, modesty, and frugality.

nundina, nundinae. The market day in both rural and urban calendars, marking the ninth day in an eight-day workweek. It was the occasion for rural folk to visit local towns to sell the *fructus* of their agricultural activities or craftsmanship, to visit, stay informed, and be entertained. The *nundinae* were important occasions of social activity and revenue from commerce for towns and villages in Roman agricultural landscapes.

oil. In the context under consideration, always signifies olive oil.

oletum, oleta. A facility in a villa for processing olives into oil, or a villa specifically geared to producing olive oil; see *cella olearia*, above.

opus, opera. Work, method; here, especially in construction and certain types of decoration.

opus *in construction:*

opus caementicium. Structural work made of stone (quarry stone, field stone, marble pieces or fragments) that is mortared with *caementum* (Roman concrete: a mixture of aggregates such as gravel or sand, pozzolanic dust, ash of various types, and lime clasts). The surface finish varied both regionally and chronologically and could include:

opus incertum. Stonework using field stones cut on the exposed side, set randomly, though often in large zigzag vertical fields for strength.

opus latericium. Opus caementicium with a surface of brick for waterproofing.

opus mixtum. Combination of *opus reticulatum* and *latericium*, sometimes with brick leveling courses.

opus quadratum. Stonework using cut ashlar blocks.

opus reticulatum. Stonework of tufa elements cut square for the surface but pyramidally behind, set in a regular pattern suggesting a net (Latin *rete*).

In decorative or utilitarian floors:

opus musivum, or ***opus tessellatum.*** Any surface treatment (floor, wall, ceiling, vault) made of tesserae (sometimes just black and white, sometimes colored); most commonly used for floors.

opus sectile. A floor treatment made of pieces of cut marble and colored stones set in geometric patterns or figural motifs, as a whole floor or in combination with *opus musivum*; sometimes applied to walls.

opus signinum. A floor treatment of *caementum* mixed with tile dust and pottery fragments, especially good for waterproofing; might be left plain or decorated with tesserae in patterns (Italian, *cocciopesto*; English, *terrazzo*).

opus spicatum. Surface work laid in herringbone pattern, using bricks or tiles (sometimes marble tiles).

opus vermiculatum. Surface treatment composed of especially small colored tesserae; often used for small separate items in floors, on tables, or on other surfaces.

ordo, ordines. A grouping of persons of equivalent high social status, such as senators and equestrians.

palatium, palatia. An imperial palace, derived from the imperial residences of the Palatine Hill in Rome; later, the dwelling or locale wherever the emperor and his entourage were located.

parasitus. A person considered to be a sponger, a hanger-on.

pars fructuaria, partes fructuariae. The area of a villa devoted to storage of produce (Columella).

pars rustica, partes rusticae. The area of a villa allocated to agricultural activities, husbandry, some *pastiones villaticae*, housing oil and wine presses, milling, kilns, stables, service courtyards; the dwelling of the *vilicus* and quarters for enslaved personnel might be in this area.

pars urbana, partes urbanae. The area of a villa comprising the dwelling of the owner, more refined than the *pars fructuaria* and *pars rustica* (Columella).

pascuus, pascua. Pertaining to pasturage, pastureland, a field for grazing. As *pascua* (neuter plural): pasturage, pasturelands.

pastio, pastiones. The pasturing, feeding, and taking care of the nourishment of animals.

pastio villatica, pastiones villaticae. Literally, "villa feeding." This was the raising of poultry, fish, and other items (honey, dormice), partially for home consumption but usually primarily destined for sale in local *macella*. It could be a substantial source of income for a villa. Flowers were also grown for profit.

pastor, pastores. A shepherd.

pater familias, patres familias, also ***paterfamilias, patresfamilias, patres familiarum.*** The male head of the *familia* or household.

patrician, patriciate. The term signified members of ancient families associated with the foundation and regal periods of Rome and the early years of the Republic. Their noble, aristocratic social status was unassailable and was usually confirmed by election to high office over several generations.

patronus, patroni. From father (*pater*), designating a person with authority over another as master, and by extension, a patron of another person, of a client, or especially of a formerly enslaved individual, who was bound to the *patronus* by strong ties of social tradition. See *cliens*, above.

peculium, peculia. The money savings, land, or other goods (e.g., grazing animals) that an enslaved person (usually male) could acquire, which could be used for better food or to purchase the status (and duties) of a freedman from his owner.

peristyle. A four-sided architectural space consisting of an open area surrounded by porticoes of columns or pillars.

pictor, pictores. A painter.

piscina, piscinae. In *balnea*, a swimming pool, plunge bath, or pool of any size; in other architecture, a pool or artificially constructed body of water; in villas, freshwater or saltwater fishponds.

piscinarius, piscinarii. Literally, "owner of fish-basins," designating a rich person who owned or commissioned expensive basins for the breeding of fish for pleasure or profit, often in luxurious maritime villas; a term of contempt for dilettante wealthy persons.

plebs, plebes. The people, the common people. Plebeian could refer to the character of ordinary folk, but families originally plebeian could rise to noble, aristocratic status by election to higher offices, such as that of consul; hence there existed a plebeian aristocracy.

plumula. Literally, "little wings," used of small architectural extensions.

portio. In a bequest or inheritance of property, the allocated portion of a subdived property.

possessio. Ownership, possession, right of possession.

praedium, praedia. An estate, most often with a dwelling and most often of considerable size.

praefectus, praefecti. In villas, the overseer, steward.

praetorium, praetoria. Regarding villas, an estate with a dwelling of considerable size; derived from the military term for a military commander's headquarters.

pratus, pratus. A meadow, open grassland.

publicus. The State itself, or the public interest in general.

puer, pueri. A boy, but also an enslaved male child or adult.

quirites, quirites Sabini. See **Sabine region**.

res publica. The State itself.

rus, rura. The countryside in general; in the context under consideration, a villa with a *fundus*, an estate, cultivated lands.

Sabine region, Sabines. The region north and east of Rome, bordering Latium on the south, east of Umbria, west of Picenum but east of Etruria; Umbria lay to the north. The Sabine peoples were associated as both associates and enemies of the Romans since the foundation of the City. By the 290s BCE, the Sabine region had been largely absorbed into the Roman state. Its main towns in Roman times were Crustumerium and Nomentum. *Quirites* was a term for citizens in early Roman periods; *quirites Sabini* indicated an acceptance of the Sabines as citizens of Rome.

saltus, saltus. Open land with trees and bushes, sometimes meaning ranchland; also a unit of areal measure of 800 *iugera* (see above).

Saturnalia. The festival in honor of Saturn in his double character of Italic deity and protector of agriculture; celebrated in late December with feasting, drinking, exchange of gifts, and reversal of social roles (e.g., enslavers-enslaved).

serva, servae. Enslaved females (rare usage).

servus, servi. Enslaved males; collective group of enslaved personnel.

sesterces. See *HS*.

sextarius, sextarii. In liquid measure, about half a liter, or 17 fl. oz.

silva, silvae. Woods and forest, either natural or planted.

species, species. Outward appearance, spectacle; hence showiness.

stibadium, stibadia. An arrangement for dining forming a half-sigma (ς) shape, an alternative to the angular positioning of couches (*lectus triclinaris*) in *triclinia*. The semicircular reclining surface, cushioned and draped, provided for more numerous diners and often had an architectural backdrop to display them in a theatrical, public way. *Stibadia* could be made of movable segments in wood or of fixed masonry.

studium, studia. Literary work of any kind, study, acquisition of knowledge.

suburbanum, suburbana. An adjective in the neuter signifying a villa or estate in the suburbs of a town or city, especially Rome.

sumptus, sumptus. As a noun and in context of domestic economy: costs, maintenance expenses of a household.

suovetaurilia. The sacrifice of a pig (*sus*), sheep (*vetus*), and bull (*taurus*); the most solemn ritual act of any kind, domestic or public.

supellex, supellectiles. Movable equipment of any kind, including kitchen utensils, fine furniture, anything of use in any dwelling; see also *apparatus*, above.

tablinum, tablina. See **atrium**.

tegula, tegulae. The terracotta pantiles of roofs, flat with flanges on either side; see also *imbrex*, above.

terra. Earth, soil, particularly cultivated earth, also the earth as an abstract entity

tessera, tesserae. Any small six-sided object. In mosaic floors, the cubic elements of *opus musivum* or *tessellatum* (see above); also used for a ticket or token of this shape.

thalamos. A bedroom.

thermae. Hot springs, but by extension, bath buildings equipped with warm and hot water; in the plural and with the addition of the name of the donor (emperor, magistrate), refers to large urban bathing facilities open to the public (e.g., Thermae Diocletiani). *Thermae* were equipped with latrines; they could have a *palaestra* or a *gymnasium* for exercise, and spaces for lectures, readings, and other cultural events.

tholos, tholoi. Any building of circular plan, with a curving wall and with or without an exterior colonnade; domed or truss-roofed.

torcularium, torcularia. See ***cella olearia***.

trapetum, trapeta. See ***cella olearia***.

triclinium, triclinia. A dining room, so called from an original arrangement of couches (Latin *lecti triclinari*) or dining beds (Greek κλίναι) in a squared U shape; the name persisted even when the number of couches increased or other arrangements such as *stibadia* (see above) came into use.

triumphator. The general who overcame an enemy army in a defeat which met certain conditions was awarded the privilege of entering Rome in a chariot accompanied by his army and a procession including defeated commanders and soldiers and spoils of war (money, weapons, exotic objects).

tugurium, tuguria. A shed or hut, sometimes inhabitable.

turris, turres. A tower; but in domestic architecture, can designate an upper floor.

urbanum, urbana. An adjective in the neuter used to describe a *domus* in a town or city.

urbanus, urbana, urbanum. An adjective meaning urban, citified.

urbs, urbes. Any city or town, but in context signifies Rome: *Urbs*, "the City" (as "the city," for many Americans, signifies New York City).

uxor, uxores. Wife.

ventus, venti. Wind, breeze.

verna, vernae. Enslaved persons born to the enslaved members of a *familia* within a villa or *domus*.

Vesta. An ancient goddess with particular valence as the protector of the *familia*, the *domus* or villa itself, and its hearth (*focus*). The larger family of the Roman people also worshiped Vesta, in her own temple, served by priestesses from patrician families vowed to virginity called Vestales. Their dwelling in the Roman Forum contained the Trojan or City hearth (*Iliacus focus, Urbis focus*), recalling the Trojan origins of the Roman people.

vilica, vilicae, also **villica, villicae.** Most often the female helpmate assigned to the *vilicus* who had responsibilities for the *familia* in the villa. She was subject to the free members of the household but had some authority over the enslaved personnel. With her position as assigned to the *vilicus*, she was an enslaved person herself.

vilicus, vilici, also **villicus, villici.** The foreman or manager of a villa, often an enslaved person.

villula, villulae. A small villa.

vinetum, vineta. A vineyard, or a villa specifically geared to producing wine.

viridarium. A garden.

xenia. From the Greek ξενία; hospitality both actual and as an abstract principle of behavior. Vitruvius (*De arch.* 6.4) uses the term both to signify the gifts of country produce (*res agrestes*; namely poultry, eggs, vegetables, and fruit) sent by hosts to guests after an initial feast in their honor. *Xenia* could also be fish and game. The term also extends to the representation of such edible items in paintings.

NOTES

NOTES TO CHAPTER 1

1 A recent analysis of Cato the Elder's famous Hellenophobia shows it to be as much performative for reasons of social advancement as political persona: Bur 2021.

2 Some 1,300 years later, Palladius's agricultural treatise *Opus Agriculturae* followed the same general model in seasonal calendar form.

3 These four (and a few others) are the foundational poems and artistic inspiration of later Greek and Latin literature and beyond.

4 For an evaluation of Hesiod: *NP* s.v. "Hesiodus" (G. Arrighetti); most recently, West 2008, incorporating commentary from his earlier studies and translations of the poems. For dates: West 2011, 15–19. On themes of Hesiod's poems and later reception: articles in Montanari et al. 2009.

5 Cic., *Fam.* 219.1.5 (16.18.5). On Hesiod in Latin literature of all kinds: Rosati 2009.

6 A person such as Cato the Elder, despite his lifelong involvement in urban politics, may have modeled himself on the Roman version of the noble *maiores* and their villas. Among members of the educated elite who owned villas, it came to be assumed that life in the country was more natural than any other, no matter what their actual behavior might be: what began with Hesiod was reinforced by Vergil and found resonance in poetry, letters, and philosophical essays from the late republic well into Late Antiquity and even to this day.

7 Roman villa owners may also have found the poet's farm physically recognizable; despite his brother having taken more than half of their father's estate, Hesiod's farm as described was a substantial holding. He frequently mentions enslaved workers in the household and on the estate, farm animals for ploughing and transport, and boats. Of human personnel, enslaved men and women (δμώς, δμωάς, for δοῦλος, δοῦλοι) are mentioned: a bought woman (*Op.* 405), enslaved males for ploughing (*Op.* 458–461), who need to build their huts in anticipation of winter (*Op.* 502–503), who are scything in summer (*Op.* 572–573), winnowing (*Op.* 597–599), tending to oxen (*Op.* 607–608), receiving rations (*Op.* 765–766). It is not clear if the mature ploughman and younger seed sower are enslaved males (*Op.* 441–447) but they probably are. A male hireling is to be let go for the winter and replaced with a childless (enslaved?) woman as servant (ἔριθος), possibly for wool working in the house (*Op.* 600–603 and 779). The farmer is also able to contract with a neighbor and the neighbor's brother for their help (*Op.* 370–371). Equipment and animals mentioned: elements of the plough and two young oxen (*Op.* 435–437), oxen and mules (*Op.* 45–46, 606–607, 790–791, 815–816). Horses, pigs, and dogs are also part of the farm's complement, as well as carts.

8 In the *Works and Days*, positive and negative Strife (Ἔρις) are counterparts and competitors in human relations and actions. Greater success in farming and neighborliness are positive, but envy of others' successes is negative, as are anger, envy, war, cruelty, and much else. By contrast, in Hesiod's *Theogony*, there was only one, the negative, Ἔρις; she had a different genealogy, gave birth to some evil children, and had no positive competitor: Hes., *Theog.* 225–226. For that reason, in translating *Works and Days*, I have preferred to use the English word Strife for Ἔρις because that is its closest meaning in this poem; it can also be translated as Discord. The Latin equivalent is *lis*, which is used in similar context by Ovid (*Met.* 1.21).

9 While *Schadenfreude* is a relatively recent introduction in English usage, it is an expressive equivalent and widely current term for the Greek term κακόχαρτος meaning "rejoicing in the misfortunes of others."

10 Βασιλεῖς can denote kings, rulers, and judges, men of prominence in the town market, assembly, and law courts.

11 By "how much greater the half is than the whole," Hesiod indicates the superiority of rural simplicity over urban sophistication.

Edible mallow (*Malva* in various forms of *Malvaceae*), a humble and easily cultivated plant, appears to have had a poetic presence as a vegetable of choice for those claiming simplicity, even poverty: Horace, *Odes* 31.15; Dioscurides 2.144.

Asphodel (*Asphodelaceae* in the *Asparagales* order) and its flowers are associated in mythology with death, Persephone, and Hades, but here its presence is for its roots as an edible in wild and cultivatable forms and as simple food for the poor. Their association with asparagus also associates it with rural simplicity of diet in both Greek and Roman times: Juvenal, *Satires* 11.69; Dioscurides 2.199 (asphodel), and 2.152 (asparagus); for its many mentions (flower and root) in Greek and Latin authors: Verpoorten 1962, 111–18; Biraud 1993, 37–42.

12 The story and Pandora's name in the *Works and Days* appear to be a reprise of her appearance in the *Theogony* (560–612), though her name is omitted there.

13 The theme of the ages of humankind was taken up (before 8 CE) by Ovid (*Met.* 1.89–150).

14 I have retained the transliteration "hubris" for the Greek ὕβρις because its many meanings have made it into a useful, multivalent, almost portmanteau, English term in numerous humanistic and artistic disciplines to signify violence, pride, arrogance, outrageous behavior, threatening acts, and even tempting fate or the gods: *OCD4* s.v. "hubris" (N.R.E. Fisher); *ODCW* s.v. "hubris"; Fisher 1992, with extensive preceding bibliography.

15 Greek and Roman sacrifices included burning the fatty parts and femurs or other leg bones with some flesh adhering to them in honor of the gods as well as other tokens of wine and other gifts, often immolated on altars. For Hesiod, piety generously backed up with sacrifices will guarantee wealth and increase in property.

16 Earlier, Hesiod had indicated that Perses has a wife (or plans to have one) and children (*Op.* 399). What work this enslaved woman would do with the ploughing is not clear (the verb, ἕπομαι, can mean "to attend," "to escort," "to follow"), so it may be that she is for household work or as a companion for the enslaved ploughmen.

17 For the *Lenaion*: *NP* s.v. "Months, names of the" II. Greece (C. Trümpy); the *Lenaion* is comparable to the Attic month of *Gamelion*: *NP* s.v. "Dionysia" (F. Graf). For calendars and regional calendars with *Lenaion*: Hannah 2008, 20–26, 32, 72–73, 75–76.

18 For bibliography and analysis regarding these biographical and geographic details: *NP* s.v. "Hesiodos" (G. Arrighetti).

19 There he won the competition in poetry at the Amphidamas contests and dedicated his trophy, a tripod, to the Heliconian Muses in gratitude for having guided him in his vocation to poetry.

20 Elsewhere, however, Hesiod gives instructions for the right time of year to make things of wood and build boats (*Op.* 805–809) and to launch them (*Op.* 817–818); however, these may be boats to ship agricultural produce off the estate rather than commercial vessels.

21 I have interpreted the terms ὁ φόρτος and τά φορτία as "agricultural" produce rather than generic "goods," "load," or "cargo" because, in the next section, Hesiod appears to be making a distinction between things that Perses has harvested and prepared for loading onto a big boat for transport, and things on-boarded for commercial exchange (ἐμπορία) of nonagricultural enterprise, not for sale as food.

22 Hesiod means that a man's poverty is part of his divine fate sent by the gods and is not to be judged by mere human beings.

23 In an English equivalent: "Evil be to him who evil thinks," the motto of the British Order of the Garter: *Honi soit qui mal y pense*.

24 It is possible that Cato later structured his somewhat disjointed treatise on the listing of a mixed bag of items about agriculture and ethics that had characterized Hesiod's lines at *Op.* 727–828. On lucky and unlucky days for activities, in ancient Greek sources: Hannah 2008, 20–25.

25 Sarah B. Pomeroy, Hunter College and Graduate School, City University of New York. Her commentary is invaluable for its range and detail in interpreting the text; Pomeroy 1994. I am grateful to her for granting permission to reproduce sections of the translation. The passages translated here have been reordered thematically rather than in the order of Xenophon's text. The only other changes to Pomeroy's translations are the addition of some of my own notes, and some Greek terms added in square brackets and minor punctuation changes to align with the presentation of other texts in this sourcebook.

I have not seen the translation and commentary by Verity and Baragwanath 2022.

26 The study of Xenophon has greatly increased in the past five decades, prompted in part by the study of the *Oeconomicus* in its political and philosophical dimensions by Leo Strauss (1970), which has given intellectual impetus to other scholars of the text and continues to do so. Strauss broached the difficult question of the relation of Xenophon's Socrates and Plato's Socrates and how sincere either philosopher was—or any philosopher can be: Is philosophy necessarily an esoteric, secret activity? Or one with application to the world? For an outline of the issues: Kronenberg 2009, 7–11, 39–74.

The question can be extended: is household management a good model for statesmanship? Xenophon affirmed that it is: Pesando 1987, 71–81 and fig. at 80. Most recently, Helmer (2021, 87–114) has posed the question differently: what is the difference between the master's knowledge, the enslaved person's knowledge, and the overseer's knoweldge?

Pomeroy's 1994 commentary on her translation has also impelled other studies, and she had earlier extended her views on women and enslavement in the *Oeconomicus*: Pomeroy (1989) 2010, 31–40. The question of Xenophon's separation of household management from statesmanship has recently been outlined in Jeirani 2020 (esp. 37–41, nn. 4, 5, and 7) and Nadon 2021, and more extensively in Dorion 2001 (2010), Johnson 2021, and esp. Helmer 2021, 23–65. On specific themes: essays in Gray 2010 and Burns 2015. For a close evaluation of the text: Danzig 2003–2004.

Another question was: if, as Xenophon believes, the household is the basis of human exchange and government, is the *Oeconomicus* really about economics? The question was answered negatively by Finley 1999, 18–21, who viewed it as a treatise on ethics, and by Mossé 1975, 175–76, who considered whether economics is a valid category with regard to antiquity.

27 At the time, Xenophon was in exile from Athens: Xen., *An.* 5.3.7–13. For Skillous: *Pleiades* s.v. "Skillous."

28 Cicero's translation is attested by Quintilian: *Inst.* 10.1.33.

29 In linguistic shorthand, such men are known as καλοὶ κἀγαθοί and as having the quality of καλοκαγαθία. Ischomachus may have been Xenophon's fictitious alter ego, but his name is that of other known Athenians: Pomeroy 1994, 259–64; Kronenberg 2009, 37–38 and n. 110.

30 *NP* s.v. "Liturgy" I. Political, A. Definition, B. Athens (P.J. Rhodes); *ODCW* s.v. "Liturgy, euergetism."

31 On the stoa of Zeus Eleutherius: Travlos 1971, 527–33.

32 Banausic occupations are those associated with a craftsman or craftsmen (βάναυσος, pl. βάναυσοι) in general, specifically those associated with manual crafts requiring working with metal and clay (ignoble substances) and with fire in forges or kilns. Their indoor work in proximity to heat wrecks their bodies and make them womanish. The result is that they become ugly, unsociable, even quarrelsome; in some states, craftsmen are not even allowed to be citizens (*Oec.* 4.2–3). Only military and agricultural activities are worthwhile: Pomeroy 1994, 235–37. Also *NP* s.v. "Education/Culture" B. History 4. Banausia (J. Christes).

33   The list that follows enumerates the many advantages conferred on the gentleman farmer: convenience for owning and exercising horses, early rising, acuity developed by supervision, preparing to defend the land if invaded by enemies, and training for athletic competitions such as running, throwing, and the long jump.

34   Farming the earth also gives the benefit of military preparedness: the command of enslaved personnel on the estate is good preparation for commanding soldiers in battle (*Oec.* 5.12–13).

35   On *Paradeisoi* in Achaemenid, Greek-Hellenistic, and Roman gardens: *NP* s.v. "Paradeisos" (L. Käppel and H.D. Galter) and s.v. "Paradise" I. Concept (B. Ego.); Nielsen 2001a; 2013; Bremmer 2008, 35–55; Zarmakoupi 2010; 2023. On "Persian" farming: Kronenberg 2009, 42–44.

36   Ischomachus, or actually Xenophon, is using the terms γυναικωνῖτις and ἀνδρωνίτιδα for the enslaved persons' gendered sleeping-quarters in the house, but these terms also had general meanings of "women's quarters" and "men's quarters," respectively, for the free inhabitants of an οἶκος.

37   The large bibliography on Greek houses, both urban and rural, is summarized in Jones 1975; Pesando 1987; 1989; Nevett 1999; 2010; Ault and Nevett 2005, 83–98.

38   Adolf Loos (1870–1933) and Le Corbusier (Charles-Édouard Jeanneret, 1887–1965) both modeled the perfect house on ships and the efficiency of maritime space and storage. Loos in particular cited the design of ships as the basis of his *Raumplan* or three-dimensional concept of domestic space: Loos as quoted in Loos 2011, 43. Le Corbusier 1923, *passim* and cover image.

39   Pomeroy concludes that a dining room of this size with 10 or 11 couches (6.30 × 6.30 m, about 20 ft., 8 in. square) would have been large by any standard for the later fifth century BCE: Pomeroy 1994, 288–89. See also Dunbabin 1998.

40   It is possible that ξυστός denoted a deep portico like that of the Stoa of Zeus Eleutherius in Athens. The term became *xystus* in Latin architectural vocabulary and is often used by Pliny the Younger to denote terraced walkways; see Cic., *Att.* 4 (1.8.2), and Plin., *Ep.* 2.17.1–5 in ch. 4, Descriptions of Villas.

41   The only exception is that the husband has a pedagogical duty to the wife to teach her what needs to be done. For example, Ischomachus tells her that directing the enslaved women in spinning and weaving, showing the baker how to knead dough, and taking charge of the folding, airing, and storing of household goods will result in both a well-exercised body and a fine facial complexion not needing cosmetics (*Oec.* 10.9–11).

42   In subsequent passages, Ischomachus defines his wife as guardian and defender of his property, acting as the queen bee of the farm and its personnel (including nursing the enslaved when sick) and teaching spinning and weaving to the female enslaved; the wife is his equal but she is differently endowed, and she has a greater affection for newborn babies (*Oec.* 7.7–19).

43   For attitudes about enslavement and enslaved persons, see ch. 2, Villas in Roman Agricultural Treatises.

44   The conversation continues, and the qualities for the foreman are the male versions of those for the housekeeper: loyalty (εὔνοια) to the owner and his family, not drinking too much (οἴνου ἀκρατής), not sleeping too much, not being in love with money (κερδαίνω ἐρωτικῶς), not succumbing to amorousness for boys (δύσερως), and careful concern to work or attentiveness to it (ἐπιμελής).

45   The texts of Books 33–40 of Diodorus Siculus's *Bibliotheca historica* (like some other ancient histories) exist only in fragments quoted, with some overlapping versions and differences, in the *Excerpta constantiniana* compiled in the reign of Constantine VII Porphyrogenitus (913–959 CE). There are several accounts of the same events, in part because the Byzantine editors combined an account by Posidonius with others attributed to Diodorus. The standard modern edition is Boissevain et al. 1903–10, now quite rare. Instead, I have used an edition available online: Fischer 1969, based on the 1866–68 edition by Ludwig Dindorf: https://archive.org/details/bibliothecahisto0006diod/page/n3/mode/2up. Diodorus's Book 34 is in vol. 6, 96–97, of that edition. For analysis of Diodorus's text: Dumont 1987, 200–20.

46   Dumont 1987, 291–98.

47   The term "Servile Wars" is modern. See a good account of the rebellions in Dumont 1987, 161–308.

48   Diodorus gives three reasons or causes for the first rebellion (138/7–132 BCE). The first was a conflict of authority between the Greek landowners of Sicily (οἱ κύριοι), who were also Roman knights, in overawing the Roman authorities (οἱ στρατηγοί, praetors) of the province in effective quelling of the rebellions (Diod. Sic. 34.31–32; praetors were officials sent from Rome to govern certain provinces; Gaius Verres was propraetor or governor in Sicily, appointed in 74 BCE and serving there from 73–70 BCE). Diodorus's point is that weak government leads to divided authority and then violence. The conflict, as Diodorus presents it, is anachronistic: he alleges that the praetors were afraid of the Sicilian landowners who had become Roman knights and so could sit as jurors (κριταί) in cases brought against Roman provincial administrators for maladministration. However, as of 149 BCE and the *lex Calpurnia de repetundis*, only senators served on such juries; knights became jurors only later, in 123 BCE and confirmed in the *lex Servilia Caepio* of 106 BCE: Lintott 1992, 25.

The second cause was the cruelty to enslaved people by owners of agricultural estates. Diodorus blames the landowners for their cruelty but also condemns the violence of the enslaved workers.

Diodorus uses a case study to illustrate the third cause: Damophilus, a native of Enna in the center of the island and evidently a Greek in culture, took up the luxury and cruelty of the new Italian, namely Roman, landowners who had bought estates and enslaved people in the province. In this way, power, morality, and assimilation of ethnic origins combined to cause the rebellion.

49 The rest of the account of Damophilus is predictable: his evil nature and a sinister fate led to his destruction and that of his equally cruel wife. On Damophilus: *NP* s.v. "Damophilus" 2, with preceding bibliography (K. Meister); *NP* s.v. "Slave revolts" (H. Schneider); Lintott 1992, 25–27. For the history of the slave rebellions: Bradley 1989.

On Greek villas in the Late Republic on Sicily: Wilson 2018a, 196–98; see also Fentress et al. 1986; Fentress 1998. On Greek rural establishments in southern Italy: Lippolis 1997 and 2006.

50 Cicero had undertaken a three-month pretrial tour of the province to collect evidence and verify the claims that the Sicilian towns, cities, and individuals had produced against Verres. As Cicero had been quaestor in Sicily five years before, he was in a good position to get information.

For the circumstances of the trial: *NP* s.v. "Verres" (J. Bartels); Michel 2000.

51 The published versions of the orations did not correspond exactly with the events of the proceedings: Verres skipped town and went off to Massalia (modern Marseille) before the decision of the judges was voted.

52 In part, a decision was pending concerning the composition of the court responsible for probing and punishing extortion by officials (the *quaestio de pecuniis repetundis*). Originally, only senators could serve (confirmed by the *lex Calpurnia de repetundis* of 149 BCE), but later, members of the equestrian order were assigned to it (in 123 BCE and by the *lex Servilia Caepio* of 106 BCE); then the court changed back to exclusive senatorial control in 80 BCE in the Sullan reforms. In 70 BCE, at the time of Cicero's prosecution of Verres, mixed membership of senators, knights, and financial officials had been instituted (by the *lex Aurelia iudicaria*), bringing to an end, for a while, the political competition between the two higher orders.

53 On the moral and customary obligations of hospitality: Wallace-Hadrill 2018, 72–73.

54 This gave scope to the long-standing philhellenism of some of the Roman elite who would have been jury members, opposing the counter-current of anti-Greek attitudes that Gaius Marius and Cato had espoused. In fact, despite its Greek origins and elite culture mixed with some lingering native presence, much of Sicily had been a Roman province since 241 BCE, the end of the First Punic War, with settled arrangements with Rome for more than 170 years and providing an essential source of the food supply of the City in Late Republican times.

55 The number in parentheses is a designation that some modern texts use for portions of the *Verrine Orations*.

56 *Sapiens* was the nickname given to Marcus Porcius Cato the Elder for his great wisdom.

On the *elogium* or praise of Sicily, Cicero's views were taken up by Strabo, who listed grain, honey, proximity to Italy, supplying Rome, cattle, hides, and wool as assets of the island: Strabo 6.276 (6.7).

57 *Suburbanitas* is the quality of living in a *suburbana*, a villa in the *suburbium* or near environs of Rome.

58 Sthenius of Thermae (modern Termini Imerese, north coast) was frequently mentioned because he was the most important of Cicero's witnesses and sat beside him at the trial in Rome: Cic., *Verr.* 2.2.82–91 (2.2.34–37).

59 Besides Sthenius of Thermae, the most important victims of Verres's depredations were:

Quintus Caecilius Dio of Halaesa (near Cefalù, north coast): Cic., *Verr.* 2.1.27–29 (2.1.10–11). Dio was robbed of valuable mares from his stud farm as well as silver and cloth, and his property was escheated to the temple of Venus of Eryx, which in practice meant that it went to Verres.

Heraclius of Syracuse: Cic., *Verr.* 2.2.35–47 (2.2.14–19). Heraclius, supposedly the richest man in Syracuse, had inherited by bequest a large sum of money and a house with much silver feasting equipment with relief figures (*caelati argenti*), rich cloth, and numerous enslaved personnel. The condition of the inheritance was that certain statues were to be made and set up in the public *palaestra*. A series of bogus legal *démarches* resulted in the confiscation, by Verres, of Heraclius's entire property.

Epicrates of Bidis: Cic. *Verr.* 2.2.53–57 (2.2.22–23). The leading citizen of a small town near Syracuse, he was cheated of his property in the same way as Quintus Caecilius Dio of Halaesa had been: a false charge that he had not fulfilled the terms of a bequest to have statues made for the town's *palaestra*.

Gnaeus Pompeius (once called Philo) of Tyndaris: Cic., *Verr.* 2.4.47–49 (2.4.22). When he was a guest at Philo's villa near Tyndaris (modern Tyndari, north coast), Verres tore the embossed decorations off his host's silver plate, and he did the same to silver cups when he was a guest of Eupolemus of Calacte (Kale Akte, modern Marina di Caronia, north coast).

60 Verres had been a guest in Sthenius's house at Thermae and had absconded with his host's private collection of works of art: these included elegant objects in Delian and Corinthian bronze, paintings, and expertly made silver. Cicero tells the jury that Sthenius's purpose in acquiring these objects in Asia (when he was there as a young man) was not for his own pleasure but to give pleasure to those Romans who might, in the way of being friends and guests, come to visit him. Sthenius's misfortunes at the hands of Verres became more complicated, but a charge that Cicero brought against the governor—one calculated to shock the jury for its offense against famous events of Roman history—was about public and historical works at Thermae. Scipio Africanus, after his victory over Carthage in the Second Punic War (218–201 BCE), had established a postwar settlement of Sicilian affairs some 130 years before.

Cicero's account was as follows: the town of Himera had been occupied and despoiled by the Carthaginians (406 BCE), its population transferred to the site of Thermae nearby, and its many statues (*ornamenta*) taken away. At the end of the war, Scipio made sure to return such objects to the Sicilian towns, and the Himeritans-Thermaeitans nearby were glad to have the statues of their old town back. Among the works in bronze (*signa ex aere*) was a beautiful statue of Himera herself (both the river and the town), a statue of the lyric poet Stesichorus (sixth century BCE) who had resided at Himera, and a pretty statue of a nanny goat (*capella*). Cicero supplies Scipio's noble motivation: he returned the statues to the Himeritans-Thermaeitans not because he had no gardens [*horti*] or a villa in the suburbs of Rome [*suburbanum*] or some other place of his own to put them, but because he knew that, once he had taken them away to his home, they would be known as belonging to Scipio only for a short time, then after his death they would be known in the name of whoever came after him, instead of as "Scipio's statues." Verres had wanted the statues for himself and leaned on Sthenius to get them for him, but Sthenius refused. Cicero's account against Verres masterfully appealed to Roman sense of the past, reminded them of Scipio's modesty and magnanimity, and the jury's empathy with other citizens' pride in civic *ornamenta*; for further interpretation: Wallace-Hadrill 2018, 72–73 (hospitality); Wilson 2018a, 196–98 (Sicilian villas of the Late Republic).

61 Heius had a somewhat equivocal position: the Mamertine population of Messana actually supported Verres even though he, as the leader of their court delegation in Rome, had personally suffered under the governor: *NP* s.v. "Heius" (K.-L. Elvers). On his family images: Roloff 1938, 51 and n. 2.

62 For detailed analysis of Heius's *sacrarium*: Zimmer 1989.

63 On the Cupid (Eros) of Praxiteles: Pollitt 1965, 131–33; Stewart 1990, 1:280. The statue owned by Gaius Heius must have been a copy: Strabo, writing in the second decade of the first century CE, about ninety years after Cicero, indicates that the original statue was no longer at Thespieae. More than a century after Strabo, Pausanias (ca. 150 CE) confirms that the original statue was no longer there; he tells us that Praxiteles's original had been taken from Thespiae to Rome by the emperor Gaius during his reign (37–41 CE), then it was returned to the town by Claudius (41–54 CE), then taken back to Rome by Nero (54–68 CE): Paus. 9.27.3–5. He also attributes the statue he saw at Thespiae during his visit there as a copy by Menodorus of Athens. Pliny, writing in the 60s CE, indicates two statues of Eros by Praxiteles: one in Rome, exhibited in the Porticus of Octavia (perhaps the one Nero retrieved from Thespiae), and another, nude, kept at Parium in the Propontis, a town at the entrance to the straits between Europe and Asia: Plin., *HN* 36.22–23 (36.4). Cicero, and other Roman writers, neither claim nor might have cared if the work was an original or a copy: the prestige of both was sufficient to command respect. On originals and copies in Roman art and their historiography in Roman art history: Gazda 2002, with preceding bibliography; Weisberg 2002, 25–41.

64 On Thespiae (Thespiai) and the statue of Cupid: Strabo 9.410 (9.25); *Pleiades* s.v. "Thespiai." Strabo shares, or repeats, Cicero's view that there is nothing to see there, perhaps because it had become depopulated like other habitation centers in Boeotia, or because all three were drawing on some earlier negative judgment about the town.

65 The Thespiades, or statues of the Muses (Thespiae is at the foot of Mount Helicon where the Muses lived), had been taken by Lucius Memmius upon his defeat of the Achaean League in 146 BCE. A general rounding up and confiscation of works of art from temples and cities as spoils of war took place, mainly and most famously at Corinth, but in other cities and towns as well; they were often exhibited in temples. At around the same time, a temple surrounded by a portico (*aedes Felicitatis*, Happiness personified) was consecrated at Rome by Lucius Licinius Lucullus (grandfather of the later general) for his victories in Hispania in 151–150 BCE. The Thespiades were placed near or in its portico. For *aedes Felicitatis*: App., *Hisp.* 52 (vowing of temple); portico of the *aedes*: *LIMC* 8.1.1, s.v. "Aedes Felicitatis" (P. Müller); the temple: *LTUR* 2 244–45 (C. Palombi); Richardson 1992, s.v. "Felicitas, Aedes"; the area: *LTUR* 5 102–8 (F. Guidobaldi and C. Angelelli); *AtlasAncRome* 1 165–66, 168; 2 pls. 14, 15, 26, 30.

The original statue of Cupid (Eros) by Praxiteles, when it came into the possession of his mistress (named either Phryne or Glykera), had been dedicated [ἀνέθηκε from ἀνατίθημι] by her to the Thespians; the verb can indicate it was dedicated in some religious form, or merely presented or given: Strabo 9.410. If it was set up as a votive offering in the fourth century BCE when the statue was made, and then its copy in Gaius Heius's *sacrarium* set up with an altar in front, the religious nature of both original and copy may have prompted Lucius Memmius to avoid sacrilege and not take it, whereas Verres had no such scruples.

66 The Herakles (Hercules) by Myron of Eleutherai (fl. 480–440 BCE); its original location is not indicated. The copy in the *sacrarium* of Gaius Heius preceded the statue later claimed by Pliny the Elder to be in an *aedes Pompei Magni* in the Circus Maximus in Rome. This is possibly the *aedes Herculis Invicti ad Circum Maximum* (Richardson 1992, s.v. "Hercules Invicti, aedes"; *AtlasAncRome* 1 431, 437) or the *aedes Herculis Pompeiani* (Richardson 1992, s.v. "Hercules Pompeianus, aedes"; *AtlasAncRome* 1 438 n. 1, pl. 171), but there were other temples of Hercules in the City. On the statue: Plin., *HN* 34.57 (34.19); Pollitt 1965, 61–62 and n. 24; Stewart 1990, 1:255–56.

Here and elsewhere in the *Verrine Orations*, Cicero interjects little phrases like this one: "as I believe—yes, most certainly" (*ut opinor et certe*) as if he were not in command of facts and names of art and artists. However, this is a pose to differentiate himself from Verres who knew all about art and was a connoisseur; in fact, Cicero also had a well-developed taste in Greek art, as his collecting for his Tusculanum and other villas indicates. His pose of ignorance about art can be interpreted as an affected upper-class disdain for material (banausic) objects, but his letters do not bear this out. Rather, these little phrases may have been introduced to give circumstantial authenticity to the published versions of the speeches, as if he were consulting his notes or getting whispered information from a secretary.

67   On the Canephoroe: Pollitt 1965, 91; Stewart 1990, 1:264.

Later, Cicero tells us that Verres's claim to have bought the works he stole from Gaius Heius were fraudulently receipted in Verres's account books with their prices: the marble Cupid of Praxiteles, the bronze Hercules of Myron, and the two bronze Canephoroe of Polyclitus together sold for the small sum of 1600*HS*. Cicero then launches into a storm of sarcasm, comparing great works by great Greek artists of incomparable value to little bronzes on the art market that could sell for relatively high prices (400*HS*): Cic., *Verr.* 2.4.6 (12–14).

68   Gaius Claudius Pulcher was quaestor in 105 BCE and aedile in 99 BCE, attaining the consulship in 92: Broughton 1951–1960, 3:57–58; *NP* s.v. "Claudius" I 28 (K.-L. Elvers). Cicero would not have known his aedileship: he was only 4 or 5 years old at the time.

69   Verres may have thought that, being of wood, it was of ignoble material, not like the noble materials of bronze and marble.

70   *On Old Age* was written between May and July of 44 BCE. Its form is a dialogue among three interlocutors, with the principal speaker being Cato the Elder (Cato Maior) represented by Cicero as being in his eighty-fifth year, so the notional date of the dialogue is 150 BCE, more than forty years before Cicero's birth. Among the many advantages to old age, the love of earth, agriculture, prosperous villas, and moral living according to ancestral virtue were prominent. Cicero's lyrical effusions predate but anticipate Vergil's *Georgics* and pastoral themes in the work of other poets.

The second interlocutor is Publius Cornelius Scipio Africanus Aemilianus, sometimes called Scipio Aemilianus or Scipio Africanus the Younger (ca. 185–129 BCE), the son of Lucius Aemilius Paulus Macedonicus, but who changed his name upon adoption by Publius Cornelius Scipio and thus was the adoptive grandson of Publius Scipio Africanus the Elder. He had a distinguished military career at Numantia (Hispania) and against Carthage in the Third Punic War, celebrating two triumphs; consul in 148 and censor in 142 BCE; a political opponent of his relatives by marriage, the Tiberius and Gaius Sempronius Gracchus: *NP* s.v. "Cornelius" I 70 (K.-L. Elvers). At the notional time of the dialogue, Scipio Aemilianus would have been about 35 years old.

The third interlocutor is Gaius Laelius (ca. 186–129 BCE), called *Sapiens* (wise), a student of philosophy and a patron of the playwright Terrence; a distinguished soldier and statesman, senator and consul in 140 BCE. His friendship with his near contemporary Scipio Aemilianus (above) was memorialized, in the same years that *On Old Age* was written, in Cicero's *On Friendship* (*De amicitia*): *NP* s.v. "Laelius" I 2 (K.-L. Elvers). At the notional time of the dialogue, Laelius would have been about 36 years old.

71   *On Old Age* was written in the same years (45–44 BCE) as the lost *Consolation* (*Consolatio*) to himself about his daughter's death, the *Tusculan Disputations* (*Tusculanae disputationes*), *The Nature of the Gods* (*De natura deorum*), *On Divination* (*De divinatione*), *On Fate* (*De fato*), *On Friendship* (*De amicitia*), a work on technique in argumentation (*Topica*, where at 1.1 he mentions sitting with its dedicatee in the library of his Tusculan villa unrolling scrolls), and *On Duties* (*De officiis*). For detailed commentary on *On Old Age*: Powell 1998.

72   Cicero mentions his translation, which no longer exists, in *On Duties* (Cic., *Off*. 2.87 [2.24]), saying there to his son, Cicero minor, that he had written it when he was about the same age as the boy. His son was born in 65 or 64 BCE and was a student in Athens in 44 BCE, so about 20 years old, thus giving a date of ca. 85 BCE for Cicero's translation of the *Oeconomicus*. Columella was familiar with it: Columella, *Rust.* 1. Preface 6 (list of Greek authorities), 11.5 (duties of the *vilicus* from the *Oeconomicus*), 12. Preface 1–7 (on marriage and the owner's wife), 12.7 (a virtual paraphrase of Cicero's translation on the orderliness of the Phoenician commercial ship). Columella also includes Hesiod as one of the many Greek agronomists he consulted: *Rust*. 1. Preface 6–7. Hesiod was well known among Greek scholars in the Roman period and was extensively commented on by Plutarch (who wrote a biography of the poet, now lost): Hunter 2014, 167–74.

Cicero also knew Xenophon's account of the life of Cyrus the Great: Cic., *Sen*. 30 (on vigor in old age), and *Sen*. 79–81 (21–22) (on body, soul, and memory), from Xen., *Cyr*. 8, where the character of Cyrus is treated in detail.

73   Cicero may be somewhat irreverently remarking that Cato's dictum on three essentials of farming was quaint and lacking in contemporary elegance: "ploughing…ploughing…manuring" (Cato, *Agr*. 61). It certainly was.

The appearance of Cato as a figure in Cicero's dialogue is similar to other Latin dialogues in which the historical personalities fit with the philosophical or moral stance they embody. On the genre: articles in Müller 2021, esp. Föllinger 2021; Lucciano 2021 (Socrates in Latin dialogues); and Sedlmeyr 2021 (Cicero's late dialogues including *On Old Age*); see also Föllinger and Müller 2013.

74   For grafting in Roman agricultural practice in general and especially for shrubs and trees, the most complete account is in Pliny, *HN* 17.96–140 (17.21–31); see also Marzano 2022, 130–76. For vines, Palladius included a poem *On Grafting* (*De insitione*) as the fourteenth book of his *Opus agriculturae*, but its content is more literary than practical. The terms used by Cicero here had been defined in Greek and Latin agricultural treatises earlier than the date of *On Old Age* and they continued in use in later manuals:

Malleoli (sing. *malleolus*) are mallet slips or shoots from a vine, in two parts, the base (called an arrow, *sagitta*) and the shoot itself: Varro, *Rust*. 2.40–41 (with many variations of technique for different plants, both growing and trenching); Columella, *Rust*. 3.6.1–4 (cuttings and grafting in general), 3.10 and 3.17–19 (mallet slips), 11.2 (schedule of operations including vine propagation); Plin., *HN* 17.156

(definition); Palladius, *Op. agr.* 14.47–50.

Planta (pl. *plantae*) is a shoot or sapling: Columella, *Rust.* 5.9, 10.150–154.

Sarmenta (sing. *sarmentum*) are twigs or branches, either young or old: Cato, *Agr.* 36; Varro, *Rust.* 31 (method of pruning vines); Columella, *Rust.* 4.13–14 (branch cutting in general), 11.2 (schedule for cutting).

Viviradices (sing. *viviradix*) are root cuttings: Cato, *Agr.* 41–42; Varro, *Rust.* 40; Columella, *Rust.* 4 (Book 4 is entirely devoted to vine cultivation); Plin., *HN* 17.173 (17.35) (method for vines).

Propagines (sing. *propago*; the method is called *propagatio*) are parts of the mother plant tied together, bent, and either weighted or buried for propagation by layering: Cato, *Agr.* 32 and 41 (method for vines); Varro, *Rust.* 17.204–205 (methods); Columella, *Rust.* 4.17 (vines) and 5.4; Plin., *HN* 17.96–99 (17.21).

75 Laertes, king of the Cephallenians, was the father of Odysseus: *NP* s.v. "Laertes" (R. Nünlist). In the long absence of his son at Troy, and a widower after the death of his wife Anticleia from grief, he retired to his farm. At first he was said to have neglected it (Hom., *Od.* 16.137–145) but then he is said to be working it when Odysseus finds him (Hom., *Od.* 24.239–301). Laertes is turning over the soil, but there is no mention in the description of any manuring as asserted by Cato in Cicero's words.

76 Cicero seems to be playing on Cato's reputation for severity by having him say that he is open to pleasure in the case of agriculture.

77 Xen., *Oec.* 4.17–25. Cicero would have been familiar with the story from Xenophon's *Anabasis* as well as the *Oeconomicus*, but later accounts (by Plutarch and others) repeat substantially the same story.

Cyrus the Younger was satrap of Lydia and Ionia for his father Darius II and his brother Artaxerxes II, the Achaemenian king: Xen., *An.* 1.1.9; Plut., *Vit. Artax.* 1.1–3 and *Vit. Lys.* 3–4 (434), 6 (436), 9 (437); *NP* s.v. "Cyrus" 3 (J. Wiesehöfer).

78 The quincunx is a geometric and decorative device: five equal things (trees, dots, any object) set as corners of a square with one in the middle: ⸫. See also the introduction to this volume, n. 8.

79 Cato, in Cicero's fictitious account, then turns to the next theme, that of *auctoritas*, or influential presence, as another asset of old age.

NOTES TO CHAPTER 2

1 Some aspects of the Greek tradition are represented by Hesiod's *Works and Days* (late eighth–early seventh century BCE) and Xenophon's *Oeconomicus* (after 394 BCE). On Decimus Junius Silanus's translation commissioned by the Senate in 146 BCE: Plin., *HN* 18.22–23; *NP* s.v. "Iunius. D. Silanus" I 28 (K.-L. Elvers). Varro lists the Greek and Carthaginean agricultural writers that Cato had omitted: see ch. 2 n. 83 below.

2 For consideration of these lost works, especially that of the Sasernas, father and son: Martin 1971, 81–85; White 1973; 1975, 20–21; *NP* s.v. "Sasernae" (K. Ruffing).

3 Sextus Quinctilius Condianus, consul in 151 CE: *NP*. s.v. "Quinctilius" II 1 (W. Eck); *PIR*² Q 21; and his brother and fellow consul, Sextus Quinctilius Valerius Maximus: *NP* s.v. "Quinctilius" II 6 (W. Eck); *PIR*² Q 27.

4 Rogers 1975a; Fitch 2013, 21–28.

5 The term *familia* encompasses the entire blood-related and dependent or nondependent people associated with a genetic family headed by a *pater familias*; it could even include friends, and it certainly included freedmen of the owner and his wife and children, enslaved personnel, sharecroppers on estates, and so on. At other times, the term *familia* can denote only the enslaved persons within the villa or *domus*, but in all cases it defines an identifiable group within which there may have been individuals who enjoyed different, but well-defined, status. The bibliography is vast: *NP* s.v. "Family" B. Rome 1–2, 4–7 (M.-L. Diesmann-Merten); articles in Rawson 1986, esp. 243–57 for preceding bibliography; Rawson and Weaver 1997; articles in Bradley 1991; Dixon 1992.

6 For a profound analysis of the literary and specifically "philosophic" nature of Xenophon's *Oeconomicus* and Varro's *De re rustica libri III* in the genre of Menippean satire: Kronenberg 2009; she extends her argument to include Vergil.

7 Columella notes that, while anything done for the good of vegetables (*causa holorum*) is legitimate, some of the purifications, rituals, prayers, and restrictions on work (animal and human) on holidays (*feriae*) have been maintained, but that others have fallen into abeyance. He states his wish to write a book on them and other religious observances that are good for the harvests (*quae pro frugibus*): Columella, Rust. 2.21.1-6.

8 See most recently Bowes 2020; Dyson 2021. See also Greene 1986; Scheidel 2004; 2005; Lewit 2004; articles in Bowman and Wilson 2013a; for northern areas, articles in Roymans and Derks 2011.

9 Stringer 2020.

10 These changes have been termed "innovative intensifications" in agricultural practice: Horden and Purcell 2000, 201–24.

11 Agrarian legislation: Weber 1891, English trans. 2008 remains the best overview; *NP* s.v. "Agrarian laws" (M.H. Crawford).

12 The historiography of enslaved populations and the systems for which enslaved persons were purposed in Roman times has recently been studied in Vlassopoulos 2021. For an overview of enslavement in antiquity: Herrmann-Otto 2009; in Italy: Augenti 2008; Scheidel 2005. It was an important topic in antiquity and has been in modern historiography, and it continues to be so in Western historical and political consciousness.

13 Specifically on the duties of the *vilicus* and *vilica* in Cato's treatise: detailed analysis in Hallet 2021.

14 This brief overview and its endnotes are offered with the hope that they can serve readers as tools for further research into villas and their enslaved personnel.

15   See Plin., *Ep*. 3.19.1–9, in ch. 7, Economics and Euergetism.

16   As early as the 1520s and in his writings in the 1540s and 1550s, Bartholomé de las Casas (1484–1566) protested the enslaving-systems for agricultural and mining workforce of the native populations in the new Spanish hegemonies after 1500; his writings brought the abuses vividly to light, and his arguments are among the first in modern Western consciousness. Las Casas had proposed that enslaved Black Africans be substituted as the workforce, but then repented of this view: Comas 1971. On Bartolomé de las Casas's life and work: Friede and Keen 1971.
   Slavery is not merely a historical issue of a distant past: the multi-volume *Cambridge World History of Slavery* (2011–2021) brings the material forward from antiquity to the last decade; the Oxford Reader *Slavery* (2001) includes issues of modern slavery.

17   On these topics: Dumont esp. 1988, but also 1987; Finley 1998; useful summaries in Momigliano 2006, esp. 3–7 on Marxist interpretations; Carandini 1989a; critical analyses in Carlsen 1984 and 2010.

18   DuBois 2010; for a thorough review of the historiographic issues of the parallel of North and South American with Caribbean chattel enslavement and ancient enslavement: Alston 2011; succinct account in de Wet 2022.

19   Physical and soulful aspects of enslaved persons (ἡ φύσις τοῦ δούλου): Arist., *Pol*. 1254b 11–38 (1.2.11–12); their need for governance by others (δεσποτεῖ): *Pol*. 1255b 13–40 (1.2.21–23), their lack of virtue and other moral qualities, among them balanced wisdom (σωφροσύνη): *Pol*. 1259b 24–1260a 15 (5.3–7); their deficiency in virtue: *Pol*. 1259b 24–26 (5.3); Heath 2008.
   On Greek theories of enslavement in literary texts earlier than Aristotle: Schlaifer 1936, 167–73, 184–89; and in Plato, 167–73, 184–89, and 190–99.

20   Greeks are therefore spirited and intelligent (Ἑλλήνων γένος . . . ἔνθυμον καὶ διανοητικός): *Pol*. 1327b 19–38 (7.6.1-2); this is an anthropological version of the *laudes Italiae* for agriculture, on which see Varro, *Rust*. 1.2.3 ch. 2 n. 88.

21   These negative physical and soulful characteristics of enslaved persons are analyzed, both in visual representations and from texts, in Weiler 2002, esp. 16–18; George 2002; DuBois 2010; 2021. On Greek issues of enslaved bodies: McKeown 2002.
   On the special character and place of the enslaved in the plays of Plautus: Segal 1987, 99–169. The visibility of enslaved persons in Latin literature is outlined in Joshel 2011; her conclusion (239) defines the enslaved as "the projection or vessel of masters' imagination."

22   Vogt 1972 (Eng. trans. 1974); discussion in Deissler 2010. Finley 1968 and esp. 1998; discussion in Andreau 1982. For comparisons between conflicting views and methods: McKeown 2007; 2010. In general on Greek enslavement: Vlassopoulos 2023; in general on Roman enslavement: Lenski 2023; Roman Republican-period enslavement: Bradley 2011; East Greek enslavement: Lewis 2018; enslavement in Late Antiquity and Early Christian–period developments: de Wet 2017. Recent developments are reviewed in McKeown 2007 and 2010; Vlassopoulos 2021. Historiographic developments for Late Antiquity: de Wet 2017; Gebara da Silva 2022 (Gaul).

23   The variety of functions for which enslaved persons served can be found in Bodel 2011; Finley had emphasized this variety in Finley 1998; see also Saller 2006, esp. n. 2; Edmonson 2011, with extensive preceding bibliography at 360–61. An interesting aspect of enslavement is the multiplication of the numbers of the enslaved and "ornamental" designations for showy luxury: Clemente 1981; Mouritsen 2011, 194–96.
   Enslaved persons could also be assigned to municipal authorities: Weiss 2004; Luciani 2020; 2022, with epigraphic evidence. Enslaved personnel in the entourage of the imperial family often found freedom, and in this new status they formed associations (*collegiae*) to construct and maintain impressive collective tombs in the cemeteries of Rome: Borg 2018; Bodel 2008, 195–97, 210–19.

24   For urban and rural issues concerning enslaved workers: Carandini 1988; Augenti 2008 (urban workers); Temin 2020, with preceding bibliography.

25   Scheidel 2011, 293–97, with table 14.2 at 295; Bradley 2006, 53–81, with a clear tabulation as to dates and number of enslaved persons brought to market (mainly as captives from war) in table 1 at 57; Bradley 2011, 245–53.

26   For Cicero's thank you to Quintus (Cic., *QFr*. 27.4 [3.7.4]), and on a construction team being called from another project: Cic., *QFr*. 21.5–6 [3.1.5–6] in ch. 8, Buying, Building, Improving, and Selling Villas.

27   Bradley 1994; 2006; Mouritsen 2011.

28   See Varro, *Rust*. 2.10.4 (herdsmen) and *Rust*. 2.10.9–10 (Illyrians), in this chapter. On status designation versus racialized enslavement: Dumont 1988; DuBois 2021.

29   Varro, *Rust*. 1.17.4, in this chapter; see also Varro, *Ling*. 8.9; Wiedemann 1981, 30–31.

30   Columella, *Rust*. 1.8.15–19, in this chapter; Scheidel 2011, 305–8; Giardina 1997b; Bradley 2006; 2011.

31   Scheidel has shown that the sources of enslaved labor (military, purchase, reproductive) contributed to maintaining a numerically constant pool of enslaved workers from the Late Republic on: Bradley 2006; Scheidel 2011, 293–97. See also Eltis et al. 2017b, 9–13; Higman 2017, 33–34, 41–42 and n. 25, 45–46.

32   Whittaker 2006, with preceding bibliography; Lewit 2004.
   The situation in Roman Italy after some attrition in the supply of foreign enslavable people may have been comparable to the changes that occurred with the nominal cessation of the trafficking of human beings as provided in the Slave Trade Act 1807 in the British Parliament and the Prohibiting Importation of Slaves Act, also of 1807, prompted by Article 1, Section 9 of the United States Constitution. The trade of human beings captured in Africa and sent to the American South and the Caribbean continued until 1820 in a diminished way and theoretically

(if not practically) ceased thereafter (except to Brazil), with consequences on enslaved demography and rates of reproduction among enslaved persons, as noted in Whittaker 2006.

33 Plin., *HN* 18.18–21 (18.4); White 1967, esp. 64–72 for texts and inscriptions.

34 The text relative to the Gracchi postdates their careers by 230 years: see Plut., *Vit. Ti. Gracch.* 8.1–7, in ch. 9, Villas and *Horti* in the Late Roman Republic.

35 The clearest systematic application of such analysis can be found in articles gathered in Giardina and Schiavone 1981. These quickly generated further studies along the same socioeconomic lines: Carandini 1981; Manacorda 1981; Carandini 1988 (suggesting that agricultural work became more repetitive and more alienating, but more efficient and thus more productive); Giardina 1997b; Augenti 2008 (on different forms of work carried out by enslaved persons). The crown jewel supporting these studies was the great Settefinestre villa near Cosa north of Rome, its exemplary archaeological publication, and the elaborate interpretive frame about it: Carandini and Ricci 1985. Enslaved laborers as means of production in *latifundia* were at the foreground, and this conviction prompted an interest in the study of villa sites in different parts of the Italian peninsula: volume two of Giardina and Schiavone 1981 included excellent coverage of villa sites in Sicily and in southern and central Italy as they were known at the time.

36 Rathbone 1981; 1983; Kron 2017; Marzano and Métraux 2018b, 16–17 and nn. 91–93. For an early consideration of the variety of villas of different sizes and uses and the nuances of the term *latifundium*: Martin 1967, 64–72; 1995 on literary sources. On the term itself: White 1967. On regional variety of villas and other settlements: Bowes 2020; Bowes et al. 2017; Bradley 2011, 248–50; Rathbone 1981; 1983; Corbier 1981; Fentress and Perkins 2016, ch. 19, table 19.1, map figs. 19.4, 19.5. Regional studies of types of villas and settlements in the Tiber valley: Patterson and Millett 1998;

A.I. Wilson 2008. Interpretation of the "slave-villa system" (*villa schiavistica*) and certain features of the Settefinestre villa in relation to the villa of the Volusii Saturnini at Lucus Feroniae: Marzano 2007, 125–53; Marzano and Métraux 2018b, 16–18 and nn. 90–99, with analysis in Joshel 2013, 104–6. For population characteristics, employment, and numbers of enslaved persons at villas: Scheidel 2004; 2005.

37 For an example of modification of agricultural methods to respond to demand in wheat production in the Tiber valley: Goodchild 2013. This may have been due to "agricultural intensification" in the Late Republic in Italy in general: Dermody, Chiu-Smit, and van Beek 2022, 214–15.

38 Varro's villa owners have an extended conversation about profits in fish farming: Varro, *Rust.* 3.17.1–8, in this chapter.

39 The larger Mediterranean trade exchanges can be found in articles gathered in D'Arms and Kopff 1980. For the macroeconomic aspects of the Mediterranean, with surprising results (e.g., that Hispania was a bigger supplier of wheat to Rome than North Africa and Egypt, traditionally held to be her main suppliers): Dermody, Chiu-Smit, and van Beek 2022, 213–14.

An example of such (thrifty and knowledgeable) integration is the owner, in the 150s–160s CE, of the villa known as Gara delle Nereide at Tagiura near Tripoli (Libya). He built his grand North African villa with imported bricks stamped with the names of Italian manufacturers, quite possibly villa owners themselves, as he sent boats loaded with his villa's *fructus* (probably olive oil) to Italian markets, and his boats returned with heavy building materials (as ship ballast) for the construction site of his villa: Di Vita 1966a, 133; 1966b, 16–20; Marzano and Métraux 2018, 3 and n. 8; R.J.A. Wilson 2018b, 286–87, with preceding bibliography.

40 On villas and economic integration: de Haas 2017; Launaro 2017; Feige 2021; Roselaar 2019 with particular attention to villas.

41 Crafts in general: Peña 2017. Wine, production at villas: Brun 2004; review of recent research on Roman wine in Italy: Dodd 2023; ceramic production: Manacorda 1981; Tchernia 1986 (amphoras); *dolia* production and especially their value as indicated by their careful repair: Cheung 2021.

42 Good accommodation: Varro, *Rust.* 1.13.1. Varro was particularly careful about the things owned by enslaved workers: see Varro, *Rust.* 1.19.3 (*mancipia*), and *Rust.* 1.17.4 (*peculium*), in this chapter.

43 Columella, *Rust.* 1.9.4–5, in this chapter.

44 See Plin., *HN* 18.18–21 (18.4), in ch. 9, Villas and *Horti* in the Later Roman Republic.

45 See Plin., *Ep.* 3.19.1–9, in ch. 4, Descriptions of Villas.

46 Being sent to the villa was a fearful punishment for an urban enslaved person: in Plautus's *Casina*, Olympio the *vilicus* of an estate, tries to get his master to send his rival Chalinus (a personal attendant to the master's son) out to the countryside as punishment, and the *rus* and villa are much talked about: Plaut., *Cas.*, 420–488. In same playwright's *Pseudolus*, Simo the enslaver and Pseudolus the enslaved have a witty exchange in which Simo's ability to send Pseudolus to the mills (*in pistrinum*) is presented as part of the fun: Plaut., *Pseud.* 491–536; the phrase is frequent in Plautus. *In pistrinum* came to be an idiom denoting hard, meaningless work of any kind: Cicero uses the phrase to lament the sad fate of an educated orator condemned to petty law work instead of bigger things: Cic., *De or.* 11.46.

47 See Varro, *Rust.* 1.19.3 and 2.10.5, in this chapter. Mouritsen 2011, 159–80. Special considerations for the female enslaved population: Mouritsen 2011, 190–94. Analysis of the legal and practical aspects of *peculium*: Gamauf 2023.

48 Certain laws and especially imperial decrees in the second century CE protected some aspects of the enslaved persons' well-being and transfer to other owners; there were also legal protocols for owners' sales to others or inheritance of the enslaved: *Institutes of Gaius* 1.53; *Digesta* 1.6.2 and 48.8.2–4; analysis of legal issues most recently in Schermaier 2023b. Enslavement in Roman agriculture and villa estates was a matter of considerable legal concern in the way of ownership, inheritance, and disputes among owners; all categories are covered in detail in Roman legal commentaries and imperial decrees: Bodel 2011, 326–30, and 336 for preceding bibliography on enslavement in legal sources; in general, Watson 1987; Wiedemann 1981 cites many of the legal sources for enslavement, helpfully listed in chronological order (*Institutes* and *Digesta* mentioned above) rather than by listings as presented in the compilations.

49   Columella, *Rust.* 1.8.19, in this chapter.

50   Alfius, in Horace's *Epode* 2, was most probably a freedman; he had a career as a banker, then became a villa owner and an enslaver himself; he may have bought his wife out of enslavement; on Alfius and his villa, see Hor., *Epod.* 2, in ch. 4, Descriptions of Villas.

51   The study of freedmen and their status, obligations, and powers is extensive: Fabre 1981; Eck and Heinrichs 1993, 212–16; Mouritsen 2011, 36–51 (status within the *familia*), 51–65 (legal and cultural principles of obligation), 202–5 (motivation of enslavers). Augustus set up the confraternity of the Augustales of freedmen (and others of similarly lower status) as an important corporate and quasi-religious cult for his, then his successors', *genius*): *NP* s.v. "Augustales" (J. Scheid).

52   Joshel 2013; Joshel and Petersen 2016.

53   See Plin., *HN* 18.18–20, in ch. 9, Villas and *Horti* in the Late Roman Republic.

54   Cato, *Agr.* 56–59, in this chapter.

55   At the San Rocco II villa at Francolise, the *villa rustica* had a large, long room (marked F on fig. 19a) that could have served to accommodate enslaved agricultural workers; the room had an oven at one end, so it was not uncomfortable in winter. In the padronal area, a staircase (southwest of B and D on fig. 19a) led to an attic, which might have served as living or dormitory quarters for the enslaved persons of the household.

56   Overviews in Cameron 2023; Dyson 2021; Hunt 2018. For a remarkable study of possible places of sale and confinement of enslaved persons: Fentress 2005. For discussion of the so-called enslavement courtyard at Settefinestre, as advanced in the original publication (Carandini et al. 1982, vol. 1, and vol. 3:505–9) and challenged later: Marzano and Métraux 2018, 17–18 and nn. 94–99, with preceding bibliography.

57   The determined work of scholars on both the representation of enslaved persons and their physical presence in domestic and urban contexts is an ongoing project: articles in George 2013; Joshel and Petersen 2016, with preceding bibliography; Joshel 2010; 2013; George 2010.

58   For the bibliography and image bank of the *Forschungen zur antiken Sklaverei*: Binsfeld 2010 (image bank); Vogt and Bellen 1983 (bibliography); Herrmann-Otto 2010 (mission statement, with preceding bibliography).

Also, the *Institute for the Study of Slavery* at the University of Nottingham (UK) has study days and its members publish on ancient enslavement, but the institute's main focus is on later manifestations of systems of enslavement: https://www.nottingham.ac.uk/isos.

59   The *Groupe International de Recherche sur l'Esclavage dans l'Antiquité* (*GIREA*), Université de Franche-Comté at Besançon (France), has study days and colloquia. Its proceedings can be found at https://www.persee.fr/collection/girea.

60   For Cato's life and career, Astin's 1978 account remains authoritative; see also *NP* s.v. "Agrarian writers" B 1 (E. Christmann); *NP* s.v. "Cato" 1 and B.b (W. Kierdorf); White 1970, 19–20.

61   Cato's cabbage recipes were later lampooned by Varro: *Rust.* 1.2.22–28.

62   For the many luxurious and ingeniously terraced villas (*basis villae*) at Tibur built in Cato's lifetime: Tombrägel 2012.

63   For Cato and villas in his day: Terrenato 2012; for social status: Bur 2021.

64   The phrase "the front of the head is better than its back" (*frons occipitio prior est*, literally "the forehead is better than the occipital side") has a proverbial force and means "eyes are in the front of the head, not the back," or "it's better for the master to see things on the spot than to be absent," or "seeing directly is better than listening to a report." The phrase is cited by Pliny, *HN* 18.6 (26).

65   Cato says "good luck" (*bona salute*) in sarcastic-ironic reverse to avoid writing "bad luck."

66   Cicero, in *On Old Age* (*Cato Maior de senectute*), imagines Cato crossly criticising Hesiod because, in the *Works and Days*, nothing was said about manure, whereas he (Cato) discusses it at length: see Cic., *Sen.* 54, in ch. 1, Greek and Sicilian Backgrounds of Roman Villas.

67   Texts of Cato use the spelling *vilicus* and *vilica*. In Varro and Columella, however, these appear as *vilicus* and *villica*. I have maintained the difference.

68   As an enslaved worker, the *vilicus* could validly undertake the religious duties of this festival, which was held on the estate and in eyeshot of the villa: Cic., *Att.* 7.7.3. The Compitalia festival was a homely holiday celebrated after the Saturnalia, usually in January; it was oriented toward the *familia* or extended household and directed toward the enslaved personnel as well as the free members of the community: Varro, *Ling.* 6.25 and 6.29; Dion. Hall., *Ant. Rom.* 4.14.3–4; *NP* s.v. "Compitalia" (U.W. Scholz).

69   The following is addressed as speech to the *vilicus* in the case of an enslaved female given to him as a wife and female manager of the villa and estate. After a few sentences, the imperative third person singular picks up: "she must . . ." Such changes in conjugation are typical of Cato's text: he often switches back and forth between the third person singular imperative ("it must . . .") to the second person singular present or future imperative ("you must/you shall . . .") to address the reader or listener.

70   Vesta or Hestia was the guardian of the hearth and thus of the entire household.

71   In the *suovetaurilia* rite, three animals are sacrificed to purify agricultural land. This form of *suovetaurilia* is that of the *suovetaurilia minora* or *lactans* (young animals); another form with a boar, ram, and bull was known as the *suovetaurilia maiora*. While Cato says to pray to Janus and Jupiter, the form of the prayer is to Mars, apparently the deity originally invoked. *NP* s.v. "Suovetaurilia" (A.V. Sibert).

72   "Manius" is a fill-in-the-blank name, in this case referring to a local divinity; it can also mean "anybody."

73   Cato continues with instructions to add further sacrifices and addresses to Mars if the sacrifice proves unacceptable.

74   Purcell 1995. Purcell's insights are invaluable in understanding why these lists were important to Cato's readers.

75   The inclusion of routing and grazing animals (pigs and sheep) and personnel (a shepherd) indicates that animals were pastured in the olive orchard; the muleteer and donkey were there to run the mill, and the orchard could also be used for planting crops between the trees.

76   Cato continues to describe how to make leather ropes for the lever bars or winches (*sucula*) for the presses and other uses.

77   *NP* s.v. "Agrarian writers" B.2 (E. Christmann); *NP* s.v. "Varro" 2 and section IV.e (K. Sallmann); White 1970, 22–24; analysis in Kronenberg 2009.

78   For extended analysis of Varro, his literary methods and his readership: Kronenberg 2009, 11–13, 76–130.

79   A translation into Italian of parts of Varro's *De re rustica* coordinated minutely with the remains of the villa at Settefinestre in the Ager Cosanus can be found in Carandini et al. 1985, 1:107–85.

80   Varro frames all three of his books on farming for his wife "Fundania" (and, further on, his father-in-law, Gaius Fundanius), but there are different dedicatees for Books 2 and 3. Whether Fundania ("she who owns a farm [*fundus*]" or merely "from the town of Fundi") and her father Gaius Fundanius were real persons and not aptly named fictions seems an open question. Fundania may have been a second wife, much younger than Varro, the daughter of a Gaius Fundanius who would have been a member of the obscure but old *gens* Fundania attested at Rome by the mid-third century BCE when one of its members, Gaius Fundanius, attained the consulship in 243 BCE after being plebeian aedile in 246 BCE: Broughton, *MMR* 2 216–17. The same is the case with Lucius Fundilius, the host of the dialogue. Gaius Agrius and Gaius Agrasius may be wholly fictional: their names are based on *ager*, a cultivated field, estate, or a farming district, and *ager* can also be used interchangeably for *villa*.

81   By mentioning his great age and death, he identifies himself as an oracle, a prophet of sorts, like the Cumaean Sibyl, whose wisdom and sayings were for the ages and a matter of state importance.

82   "Gods help those who call out to them": *dei facientes adiuvant*.

83   Evoking the homely rustic gods and their festivals, the benign ones that guide agriculture (earth and sky, water, "good outcomes," and so on), is significant because farming and piety go together, but in ways different in Varro than they had in Cato more than a century before. Rustic reverence embodied simple values unlike the formal worship of the great urban gods who had statues in the Forum. The theme is thus the opposition of town and country and the superior morality and religious difference of the rustic life: the theme had been a commonplace in Hesiod's *Works and Days* and continued in Cato, in later manuals, and in the culture of life in villas throughout the Roman period.

84   The dialogue form would have appealed to even moderately educated readers because it is modeled on the familiar form of the Platonic dialogue and, in a rudimentary form, on interaction in schoolrooms. In addition, besides circulating in written formats, books were "published" in public readings for which the dialogue form was very appropriate.

85   Varro then lists forty-seven Greek authors (including the philosophers Aristotle and Theophrastus) who wrote on agriculture in prose, two in verse (notably Hesiod), and the Carthaginian "Mago" who wrote in Punic (Varro, *Rust.* 1.1.8–11). This work by "Mago" was translated into Greek by Cassius Dionysius of Utica and dedicated to the praetor Sextilius (P. Sextilius Rufus?); it was later abridged and extended by one Diophanes of Nicaea who dedicated his six-volume book to King Deiotarus of Galatia in the mid-first century BCE. These are the agricultural treatises that constitute Varro's bibliography of sources. See discussion in Hentz 1979; White 1970, 15–18.

Strangely, Varro omits listing the translation from the Punic into Latin of the "Mago" treatise by Decimus Junius Silanus, commissioned by the Roman Senate after the defeat and destruction of Carthage in 146 BCE: Plin., *HN* 18.22–23. Mago is the generic name given by Romans to any persons of prominence or consequence at Carthage. For considerations of the Magonian tradition: Martin 1971, 37–52.

Significantly, Varro's list also omits earlier Latin agricultural manuals, notably those of Gnaeus Tremellius Scrofa (who appears later on in Book I), the Elder and Younger Sasernas, and M. Porcius Cato, even though Cato is often cited in Varro's text itself. Varro's reverence for Cato may have been culturally obligatory but did not cloud his judgment about his questionable advice.

86   *Pastio villatica* (pl. *pastiones villaticae*): specialized items for household consumption or for urban markets that could be raised on the estate, often in proximity to the villa dwellings: birds, dormice, rabbits, fish, honeybees, flowers, and other niche items for the urban market for fresh, often perishable, produce.

87 The triple authentication of his work—his own experience, his reading, and his consultation with experts—combines practical, scholarly, and immediate expertise in a an Aristotelian/Peripatetic divisioning. Farming is thus set in majestic religious and intellectual contexts, though Varro is also appealing to old-fashioned simplicity and practicality. It is significant that, even though he is dedicating his book to an owner of an estate (his wife), he emphasizes that he invokes the gods of farmers (*agricolae*) to include a larger, more generic category of readers.

88 The temple of Tellus (*aedes Telluris*), built in the third century BCE, was in the Carinae district on the Esquiline Hill; it was the focus of agricultural rituals in the City: *LTUR* 5 24–25, Tellus, aedes (F. Coarelli); *AtlasAncRome* 1 287, 291, 302 n. 164, 303 n. 255, figs. 79 and 83, ill. 15; 2: tabs. 104, 105; Haselberger et al. 2002, 241 (E.A. Dumser), map 351; Richardson 1992, s.v. "Tellus, Aedes." By starting in Rome on the day of an ancient but distinctly rural sowing festival, the *Sementivae feriae*, Varro continues the contrast between city and country; the festival was movable, but was held in April and in villages (*pagi*, sing. *pagus*) in honor of Tellus and Ceres: Ovid, *Fasti* 1.657–704, with details of rituals and sacrifices; *NP* s.v. "Sementivae feriae" (C.R. Phillips III).

The gentlemen are waiting for a friend, an official of the temple or the cult of Tellus, called an *aditumus*, and Varro introduces the speakers in the dialogue after some antiquarian digression (omitted here). A map of Italy prompts praise of the centrality and favorable temperate climate of the peninsula (including Gallia Cisalpina or the Gallican plain, namely the area of the Po River valley south of the Alps) and its astonishing fertility—these are declarations of providentially endowed, patriotic attributes called *laudes* (sing. *laus*). The glories of Italy (or another locale) are customary in agricultural treatises, geographical descriptions, and poetry: Strabo praises all Italy for its fauna, flora, and fruits (5.3.1) and often points out certain regions for their particular fertility (such as that of Campania: 5.4.3). Strabo even praises cities for their productive industry (such as that of Patavium, modern Padua: 5.1.7 and 5.1.12). The most famous are the praises of Italy (*laudes Italiae*) in Vergil's *Georgics* 2.136–175.

Painted maps, or maps in other materials, were known in Rome, but this is specified as a map of Italy. Later, around 20–15 BCE, a world map will be painted in the Porticus Vipsania built by Agrippa and completed by Augustus after his death: Plin., *HN* 3.17 and 6.139; Dilke 1987, 205 (map of Italy in *aedes Telluris*), and 205–9 (other maps and Agrippa's map in the Porticus Vipsania); Talbert 2012b, 167–70; Boatwright 2015, 255–59.

89 The seven interlocutors in Book 1 are a mix of social status: (1) Varro is of senatorial rank and a former praetor (in 68 BCE) but not consular. (2) His father-in-law Gaius Fundanius is an apparently wealthy and knowledgeable farmer from Reate, which was Varro's hometown. (3) Gaius Agrius is a philosophically minded *eques* (knight) and thus a member of the social rank just below the senatorial elite. (4) Gaius Agrasius is a *publicanus* or state-contracted tax collector, most probably also an *eques*. (5) Their host, one Lucius Fundilius, is an official (*aeditumus*) of the Tellus cult and so of at least equestrian rank but more probably senatorial; he does not appear in the dialogue (his assassination is described at the end of Book 1).

Later, two others come in: (6) Gaius Licinius Stolo, claimed to be of an old family of the plebeian nobility that had achieved senatorial and consular distinction. The Licinii Stolones had become extinct by the mid-Republic, so this Licinius is Varro's creation: *NP* s.v. "Licinius" I 43 (C. Müller) and I 44 (T. Frigo). (7) Gnaeus Tremellius Scrofa, a renowned expert on farming whose books may have been already familiar to Varro's potential readers: *NP* s.v. "Tremellius" 3 (J. Fündling); *NP* s.v. "Agrarian writers" B.2 (E. Christmann); White 1970, 21. Stolo represents an early moment in agrarian legislation some 330 years in the past, whereas Scrofa participated in a near-contemporary instance of land distribution.

The variety of rank and occupation in men who own villas and estates provides a template for the readership to which Varro's agricultural treatise was addressed: upper middle to upper class, but not at the pinnacle of society. For agrarian legislation and villas, a fundamental study remains that of Max Weber 1891 (Eng. trans. 2008); comprehensive discussion in Kehoe 2007; *NP* s.v. "Agrarian laws" (M.H. Crawford). For the arrangements made for Pompey's veterans in Julius Caesar's settlement in the Ager Campanus: Cic., *Leg. Agr.* 2.54; Cic., *Att.* 1.18.6.; Cass. Dio 38.5.2 and 42.54–56; Suet., *Iul.* 20.1–3 and 38.1; App., *B. Civ.* 2.10 and 2.94; *NP* s.v. "Veterans" I. Republic (H. Schneider). Texts in Crawford 1989; Crawford and Cloud 1996, 2:763–67.

90 "Is not Italy . . . an orchard?": *Non arboribus consita Italia, ut tota pomarium videatur*?

91 The appearance of Stolo and Scrofa is designed to give the reader a large historical context for the discussion as well as a more recent iteration directly involving Varro himself. Gaius Licinius Stolo reminds the reader of the old laws (in this case, one of the *leges Liciniae Sextiae* of 367 BCE) that had limited the amount of land any Roman citizen could legally own (500 *iugera*, maximum, about 125 ha, or 312 acres) in an attempt to reduce agrarian inequality and poverty due to debt in the apportionment of public land (*ager publicus*). By the time of Varro's treatise, the laws were some 330 years old, and their texts or intentions had become unclear, but the principle of measured distribution of farmland is Varro's point. Gnaeus Tremellius Scrofa comes in as a Commissioner, with Varro, for the recent distribution of public land in Campania to bring the principle of limiting landholdings up to date. Scrofa and Varro himself had been commissioners for the surveying and allotment of land in Campania (Ager Campanus) mandated by Julius Caesar in 59 BCE (*lex Julia Agraria*), in a measure intended for distribution to Pompey's veterans and to other Roman citizens, especially the poor of Rome itself: Vell. Pat. 2.44.4; Suet., *Iul.* 20; Plut., *Vit. Cato Minor* 33; Crawford and Cloud 1996, 2:763–67; *NP* s.v. "Agrarian legislation" (M.H. Crawford). For an interpretation of Scrofa: Kronenberg 2009, 77–80.

92 The upper (south) end of Rome's Via Sacra had a market in Republican times. On the various areas in the City where commercial specializations were concentrated: Papi 2002; Rieger and Scricciolo 2019, 31–33, fig. 1.

93 The conversation continues with a discussion, omitted here, of the names of the personnel and the differences among their occupations and duties: *magister pecoris* (the master shepherd or master of grazing livestock) and *vilicus*, then a derivation of the term *villa*. On the term *villa*: Varro's analysis (*Ling.* 5.22 and 35) is given in the introduction to this sourcebook.

94 The phrase is from the racetrack: *a carceribus ad metas*, the "prisons" or *carceres* being the gated holding pens into which the horses and chariots were driven before the start, and the *metae* can mean the turning mark of the oblong track but here indicates the finish line.

95 See Cato, *Agr.* 1.3, in this chapter.

96 Scrofa continues (*Rust.* 1.13.2–5) with detailed consideration of roofed and unroofed sheds for farm vehicles and equipment (to prevent damage from weather or stealing by thieves), inner and outer courtyards (*cohortes*), the inner one with a reservoir for watering and washing cattle (oxen) and watering geese and pigs, and the outer courtyard with a pond elsewhere to steep dried beans and other comestibles needing softening. Two dung pits (*sterclina*, sing. *sterclinum*), one for fresh, the other for well-rotted wet manure, are needed near the villa, and the enslaved workers' privies can be placed on one of them. The *nubilarium* or covered shed needs to be well ventilated with windows and big enough to store all the estate's produce; it should be next to the threshing floors so the wheat separated from the chaff can be quickly stored. These practical and common sense prescriptions are followed with the impassioned denunciation of contemporary luxury villas by Varro's father-in-law, Fundanius (*Rust.* 13.6–7).

97 "…villas built to the detriment of the public interest": *villis pessimo publico aedificatis certant*.

98 The issue of recent and contemporary luxury villas is important in Varro's and others' treatises and occurs frequently. Two themes emerge: first, that modern luxury villas are a detriment to the *publicus*, which can mean "the State" or, more generally, the public interest. Second, that luxury (*luxuria*) is the opposite of sensible old-fashioned thrift (*diligentia*), which has historical and patriotic justification.

The last sentence of this passage, about building on a hill, may refer obliquely to the sites of villas on landscape promontories to free up space for planting, but it may also refer to the placement of grand villas on high terrace walls (*basis villae*) to catch the breezes, give an impressive aspect, and provide views. Later, Varro mentions the stone walls (*maceriae*) of villas at the town of Tusculum (*Rust.* 1.14.4); these may also be the terrace walls of villas. On grand terraced villas of Late Republican date at Tibur: Tombrägel 2012.

99 This reliance on local professional expertise readily available in proximity to the villa is significantly different from the comment offered by Palladius some 400 years later: see *Op. Agr.* 1.6.2, in this chapter.

100 This rule about enslaved persons is eerily resonant with a similar sign announcing a much more severe punishment posted on the door of the *triclinium* in the house of Trimalchio, in the section of the *Satyricon* of Petronius (dated to the reign of Nero, 54–68 CE) called the *Cena Trimalchionis* (Trimalchio's dinner). Having had a fine, if somewhat drunken, bath, the guests are then escorted to the dining room; on its doorpost is a sign reading: "Any slave who leaves the house without the permission of his owner will receive a hundred lashes": Petron., *Sat.* 28.6–8. One hundred lashes could be a death sentence.

101 This indicates that the overseers (*praefecti*) are themselves enslaved workers, who were allowed to collect *peculium*, or small amounts of money, possessions, and animals, even small properties: *NP* s.v. "Peculium" (J. Heinrichs). Enslaved persons could use their *peculium* to buy their freedom from their owner. Although *peculium* was not limited to enslaved persons (it could be a son's present of things or money from his father or other relatives), in this case it is linked to the owner's permission or order to an enslaved couple to form an informal union and to procreate (enslaved persons had no rights to socially recognized marriage): Mouritsen 2011, 159–80.

102 The *mancipia* here means the *peculium* whereby an enslaved person might buy graduation to freedperson status; see the introduction to this chapter.

103 This means that in a period of 45 days, the working man-hours are calculated to be 28–29% below 100% productivity.

104 With *Gallia Cisalpina*, Varro is describing the flat plain or low hills of the valley of the Padanus River (modern Po River) to the Adriatic coast on the east, circumscribed on the north by the Alps and the coastal mountains of Liguria on the west.

105 "… not by hit-or-miss": *sequentes non aleam* (not by the throw of the dice).

106 This gives topographical authenticity to the account: the temple was on the Esquiline Hill, so the gentlemen walk down (*descendimus*) on their way home: see ch. 2 n. 88.

107 Cossinius may have been the Lucius Cossinius mentioned by Cicero as a mutual friend with Atticus in letters of the 60s BCE—that is, some thirty years before Varro's writing of *De re rustica* but in the years that Book 2 is set: Cic., *Att.* 20.6 (1.2.60) and *Att.* 21.1 (2.1)

108 The "seven days" included the eighth day in the series of counted days. Roman counting always included both the day and the day hence in the calculation, as in French, where "next Thursday" is phrased *jeudi en huit*: an English-speaker might take that to mean Friday, but it means "a week Thursday." In English, "in a fortnight" is two weeks or fourteen days hence, expressed in French as *dans quinze jours*.

109 Reate was Varro's hometown in Sabine country, and its mules and donkeys were highly praised by Strabo (5.3.1).

110 Bastulia or Bastetania: the location of a pre-Roman people of southern Hispania: Strabo 3.1.7, 3.2.1, 3.4.2, and 3.3.7 (picturesque details); see also *Tesauros del Patrimonio Cultural de España* s.v. "Bastetania-Bustulia": http://tesauros.mecd.es/tesauros/toponimiahistorica/1211480.html. By Varro's day, the Turduli (or Turduli Veteres) had settled in the west-central part of Lusitania in Hispania from an original location in the south: Strabo 3.1.6.

111 Varro's outline (through Cossinius) of how enslaved persons could be acquired is a digression on his recommendations about enslaved persons (men, boys, even girls) working with livestock. *Mancipium* was a special way of acquiring enslaved persons or other property: in a ceremony (*mancipatio*) before six adult male citizens as witnesses (one holding a weighing scale) and in the presence of the owner, the buyer would place his hand on the object or enslaved individual and claim ownership of it/him/her, then strike the scale with a bronze coin and give it to the former owner. The action was symbolic (the enslaved individual would presumably cost more than a single bronze coin) but the witness to the property transfer was important in law and for further legal demarches if needed: *NP* s.v. "Mancipio" and "Manicipatio" (both D. Schanbacher).

112 This account, implausible on its face, is invented by Varro to impute strangeness to the Illyrian women's physique and their culture as well as to contrast them with contemporary Roman women.

113 Book 2 builds to an end that coordinates sheepshearing with the importation, "400 years after the foundation of the City of Rome," of barbers (*tonsores*) to cut men's beards: the juxtaposition of the mundane with the almost mythical seems intended to prompt a smile in the reader. This concern with hairdressing is perhaps an instance of modern luxury or vanity: Varro's proof (*per* Cossinius) is that some statues of the men of old (*antiquorum statuae*) showed them with long hair and big beards: *Rust.*

2.11.10. In Jane Austen's *Emma* (1815), getting a haircut is a mark of vain affectation in a young man (Frank Churchill).

114 The aediles were a body of legal officials in charge of registering acts of the Senate and other legislative bodies as well as the care and upkeep of temples and the sponsorship and management of festivals: Livy 3.55, 6.42, and 31.50–56 (different rankings); *NP* s.v. "Aediles" (C. Gizewski).

115 *LTUR* 5 202–5 (S. Agache); The Villa Publica of Varro's Book 3 was that of 194 BCE: Livy 34.44.5; for the Villa Publica and the Ovile: *AtlasAncRome* 1 155, 161 and n. 422, 496–98, fig. 187 (shows a two-story structure); 2: tabs. 207, 208, 214, 222, 223; Haselberger et al. 2002, 273 (A.B. Gallia); Richardson 1992, s.v. "Villa Publica"; Claridge 2010, 177–79; Coarelli 2014, 273; Yegül and Favro 2019, 187, 194; *NP* s.v. "Saepta" (C. Höcker); Masciale 2019, 62 and n. 67; excavations in Filippi 2015b. Later, in Augustus's reign, the functions of the Villa Publica and the Ovile would be replaced by the Saepta Julia precinct (begun by Julius Caesar in 54 BCE but completed only in 26 BCE, after Varro's treatise). The Saepta Julia was a precinct for corralling the tribal voting delegations en masse: a capacious building for counting the votes, called the Diribitorium, was built next to it: Plin., *HN* 16.201 and 36.102; Cass. Dio 55.8. *AtlasAncRome* 1 162; 2: tabs. 222, 223, and 227; Yegül and Favro 2019, 212 and fig. 4.30

116 Seven interlocutors are present in Book 3 (*Rust.* 3.2.1–3): (1) Varro himself (senatorial but not consular): *NP* s.v. "Varro" 2 (K. Sallmann). (2) Quintus Axius, a senator from Varro's hometown of Reate, who was an acquaintance and host of Cicero in 54 BCE: *NP* s.v. "Axius" II 1 (K.-L. Elvers). Q. Axius (Varro, *Rust.* 2.1.8) and Cicero (Cic., *Att.* 90 [4.15]) had villas there. The drainage of Lacus Velinus caused quarrels between Reate and Interamna: Cic., *Att.* 90 [4.15.5]; Cic., *Pro Scauro* 12.27; Tac., *Ann.* 1,79; *NP* s.v. "Lacus Velinus" (G. Uggeri). (3) Appius Claudius, described as a priest and augur representing the state religion (therefore a patrician) as well as a member of one of the most illustrious noble and notorious families of the Republic, but which of this family is not specified. (4) Lucius Cornelius Merula, supposedly a member of a consular family (Cornelii) but probably fictitious (his cognomen means "Blackbird"). (5) Fircellius Pavo, a provincial farmer from Varro's hometown of Reate, but probably fictitious (his name means "Peacock"). (6) Minucius Pica and (7) Marcus Petronius Passer, two men of undefined status and probably fictitious (their names mean "Magpie" and "Sparrow," respectively).

The stage is set for discussion of birds, one of many topics in Book 3 (including Varro's aviary at Casinum), though how the character of the birds relates to the gentlemen's characters is not certain: *Rust.* 3.2.4. The tone is jocular at times: there is some good-natured teasing but also some competitive repartee.

In the Roman order of social status, these interlocutors run from Appius Claudius as priest and patrician of an ancient family with consular nobility at the very top, to the consular L. Cornelius Merula, then to the senatorials Varro and Quintus Axius, then to those of undefined status.

117 In the *cursus honorum*, the aedileship was a (nonobligatory but usual) step between the first lap (the quaestorship) in the *cursus honorum*, before becoming praetor (just below consular candidacy). In Varro's day, it was for men in their mid-30s, so the gentlemen are looking to support a candidate in the following one or two younger generations of candidates.

118 They also were in charge of the other temples in the City and had other civic duties.

119 Lucius Abbucius: Bannon 2009, 226.

120 Varro, *Rust.* 3.4.3 (Lucullus's aviary), *Rust.* 3.8–17 (Varro's aviary), and *Rust.* 3.13.1 (game parks): for Varro's villa and *triclinium*-aviary at Casinum, see Varro, *Rust.* 3.5.8–17, in ch. 4, Descriptions of Villas.

121 The dedicatee, Pinnius, was Varro's friend, evidently quite rich and a villa owner: *Rust.* 3.1.10.

122 Ogyges was king of the area that would later become Boeotia and the area around Thebes: Paus. 9.5.1. Used as an adjective here, Ogygian, it gives the sense of something mythically old.

123 Varro, *Ling.* 5.64; Cic., *Nat. D.* 2.67; on Vergil's *Georgics*, Servius 1.7. King Saturnus or Saturn was the mythical patron of farming, Italy itself, sowing, and fertility in general: Varro, *Ling.* 5.54; *NP* s.v. "Saturnus" A–C (A. Mastrocinque).

124 Varro's sequence of an ancient Saturnian racial descent (*soli reliqui...ex stirpe Saturni regis*) for those who engage in agriculture, then followed by an initiation of later farmers into the rites of Ceres, emphasizes agriculture as a sacred vocation. Cato had included prayers for events in farming activities (Cato, *Agr.* 131–132, 140, and 141.1–4 in this chapter), but his prescriptions were formulaic. In contrast, Columella regarded religion and agriculture as so intimately entwined that he wanted to write an entire book on the subject (p. 78 and n. 7 in this chapter).

125 See p. 105 and n. 116 in this chapter for Reate and three of the interlocutors (Appius Claudius, Quintus Axius, and Fircellius Pavo) of *Rust.* 3.

126 See further on regarding the potentially great revenues from donkey breeding.

127 The Porta Flumentana opened through the old (Servian) walls of Rome at the southern extremity of the open Campus Martius; in Republican times, there were villas to its south. The Aemiliana district was nearby, also outside the Servian walls: Tac., *Ann.* 15.40; *CIL* 15 7150; Cic., *De republica* 1.9.; *LTUR* 3 327–28 (F. Coarelli); *AtlasAncRome* 1 535 nn. 390 and 396; 2: tab. IB at N; Haselberger et al. 2002, 195 (with discussion, D. Borbonus and L. Haselberger); Richardson 1992, s.v. "Porta Flumentana"; Coarelli 2014, 309.

128 The reference to Marcus Seius is unclear, but the use of the derived adjective Seian (as in *villa Seiana*) in a pejorative sense may indicate that Marcus Seius is a mistake for a story about a scribe, one Gnaeus (not Marcus) Seius. In the 50s BCE, Gnaeus Seius owned a fine big horse that belonged to four persons in succession (Seius himself, Cornelius Dolabella, Cassius the Tyrranicide, and Mark Antony). The horse brought bad luck to all of them. This may indicate that Seius refers to an anybody, a nobody, a person down-on-his luck or bringing bad luck to others. Seius's villa near Ostia had no farm equipment or luxurious works of art, so it seems to have been nothing at all. However, the source of the Gnaeus Seius story is much later, in the 170s CE, so its relevance may be doubful: Gell., *NA* 3.9.

129 For Metellus Scipio (Quintus Caecilius Metellus Pius Scipio Nasica), see n. 41 in ch. 4, Descriptions of Villas.

The *collegia* were associations of any kind (craftsmen, firefighters, shippers, tradesmen), and in this case social clubs for men of similar status, interests, and wealth.

130 Marcus Porcius Cato the Younger became the guardian of Lucius Licinius Lucullus's son (of the same name) upon the general's death in 56 BCE. The indication that this was a recent event gives a notional date of about 56 BCE to the dialogue of Varro's third book, even though it was written some thirty years later: Cic., *Att.* 310.2 (13.6.2); Varro, *Rust.* 3.2.17; Treggiari 2019, 96 and n. 53.

131 Merula continues the discussion under three headings: aviaries (*ornithones*), rabbit hutches (*leporaria*), and fishponds (*piscinae*). Among the aviaries is that of Lucullus at his Tusculan villa. There were also game parks at villas: see Varro, *Rust.* 3.13, in ch. 4, Descriptions of Villas.

132 Varro tells us that apiaries were sometimes set in the portico of the villa (*porticus villae*) itself for good protection from the elements: *Rust.* 3.17.15.

133 Gaius Hirrius (Postumius?), of a family that rose to the praetorship in 88 BCE, is identified as the son-in-law of Cossinius: *Rust.* 2.1.2. See also Varro, *Rust.* 2.5, and Plin., *HN* 9.55.

134 Loan to Caesar for the triumphs of 46 and 45 BCE: Plin., *HN* 9.171; Marzano 2013b, 299–300; Beard 2009, 102–4, 179.

135 Pausias of Sicyon: Plin., *HN* 35.123; Paus. 2.27.3.

136 Marcus Licinius Lucullus was the brother of the general and triumphator Lucius Licinius Lucullus and the equal of his sibling in luxury and building.

137 *Contra* Varro, on the actual profitability of *piscinae* and pisciculture for saltwater fish, Marzano and Brizzi 2009; Marzano 2010; 2013b, 199–233, 281–300; 2020. On Cicero's contempt for owners of fishponds (*piscinarii*): see Cic., *Att.* 1.19, and n. 8 in ch. 7, Economics and Euergetism.

138 On the *toga candida*: Goette 1990, 166; *NP* s.v. "Toga" (R. Hurschmann); Edmonson 2008, 26–27 and nn. 24, 25.

139 Their candidate has now entered into the dignity of a designated elected magistracy and has the right to wear the purple-striped *toga praetexta* and sit in a *sella curulis* reserved for magistrates. It may also indicate that he has been elected from the ranks of the patrician families for whom certain aedileships were reserved.

140 *NP* s.v. "Agrarian writers" B.3 (E. Christmann); *NP* s.v. "Columella" (E. Christmann); White 1970, 26–28.

141 In a section omitted here, *Rust.* 1. Preface 6–10, Columella describes in detail the squalour, humiliation, and hypocrisies of men living in towns and having to cater in servile ways to the rich and powerful. The sophism of lawyers and the business of banking (*faeneratio*) come in for a great deal of his condemnation.

142 The implication appears to be that, in order to work off a debt, a free man of whatever status is then indentured to be supervisor of the debt holder's property.

143 Columella's notions of the historical development from countrymen-citizens to city dwellers are similar to those of Varro: see above, Varro, *Rust.* 2.1.1.

144 Cato, quoted by Seneca in *Ep.* 122.2.

145   *Quirites* (sing. *Quiris*) was the term designating a person as a Roman citizen: *NP* s.v. "Quirites" (H. Galsterer).

146   "Latium and Saturnian district": Columella is referring to the locations, in Latium near Rome, of his own properties as well as to the area of Etruria around Saturnia.

147   Columella, *Rust.* 1. Preface 29: *Summum enim columen adfectantes satis honeste vel in secundo fastigio conspiciemur*. Columella expresses himself in architectural terms: top of the column (*summus columnae*), lower (*secundum*) *fastigium* (roof, triangular pediment).
Columella notes that Vergil has been honored in temples along with lesser poets; poets after Homer did not give up poetry because of the brilliance of their master; Cicero's speeches did not discourage lesser and younger orators from rhetorical endeavors of their own; Columella may be modeling this idea on Cicero's assertion that he was not cowed in his orations and philosophy by Demosthenes and Plato: Cic., *Orat.* 1–2. Columella continues with other examples: the great Greek artists—Protogenes, Apelles, and Parrhasius the painters as well the sculptor Phidias—did not discourage painters and sculptors who followed them (for example, Bryaxis, Lysippus, Praxiteles, and Polyclitus) from their own efforts. The list is impressive.

148   These are references to the most exalted intellectual and mythological persons of Greek antiquity. Democritus: Deocritus of Abdera (ca. 460–370 BCE), Greek philosopher and mathematician. Pythagoras: Pythagoras of Samos (ca. 570–495 BCE), Greek philsopher and mathematician. Meton: Meton of Athens (second half of the fifth century BCE), a geometer and astronomer, inventor of the nineteen-year lunisolar calendar. Eudoxus: Eudoxus of Cnidus (ca. 390–330 BCE), a student of Archytas and Plato, an astronomer and mathematician. Chiron: a Centaur, wise in all the arts of athletics and healing (including veterinary science), teacher of Achilles, and adept at pharmacology for humans and animals. Melampus: a mythical seer of Argos who could understand the language of animals; his many adventures involved cattle. Triptolemus: either a demigod or a prince of Eleusis near Athens, associated with Demeter, goddess of agriculture, after the kidnapping of the goddess's daughter Persephone (Kore); he learned the arts of agriculture from the goddesses and was sent on a mission to teach them everywhere. Aristaeus: a demigod, patron of many agricultural arts including beekeeping, wine and beer making, leather tanning and working, and other useful occupations.

149   For Scrofa and the Stolones: Varro, *Rust.* 1.2.9–10, in this chapter; for the Sasernas: Varro, *Rust.* 1.1.7, and 1.18.1–4, in this chapter. Varro mentions the Sasernae (father and son) in *Rust.* 1.16.5 and 1.2.22, which are not included here.

150   *Minerva pingua*: as goddess of wisdom, Minerva's name denotes wisdom; fat (*pingua*) wisdom is foolishness.

151   Before moving on to his main topics, Columella gives a long account of previous writers on agriculture, Greek, Carthaginean, and Roman, which he has consulted (*Rust.* 1.1.7–14). He starts with Hesiod's *Works and Days*, Xenophon's *Oeconomicus*, Cato, the Sasernas, Stolo, and Varro, his principal source.

152   Cato, *Agr.* 4; Plin., *HN* 18.31; Palladius, *Op. Agr.* 1.6.1.

153   For Mago's agricultural treatise, see ch. 2 n. 85.

154   Quintus Mucius Scaevola Pontifex: *NP* s.v. "Mucius" I 9 (K.-L. Elvers and T. Giaro).

155   Cato, *Agr.* 3.1. The idea of moderate proportionality in villas is taken up by Varro (*Rust.* 1.11.1) and Pliny (*HN* 18.32).

156   The sequence is intentional: bugs and unannounced guests are both pests.

157   Vitruvius had included some instructions for defensive walls for towns and other walls, but nothing as specific as Columella's that seem to indicate walls for *basis villae*. Vitruvius on walls: *De arch.* 1.6.3–8, 2.8.1–9, and 2.8.17–19.

158   On *ergastula*: Étienne 1974. Columella continues his recommendations for the *pars rustica* with specifications for the stabling of cattle and oxen (*Rust.* 1.6.4). He will briefly take up the accomodation (in the *pars rustica*) for the *vilicus* and the manager (*procurator*) of the estate at *Rust.* 1.6.7–8, in this chapter.

159   In *Rust.* 1.6.9–24, Columella deals with the arrangements of the *pars fructuaria* at some length: storage rooms for oil, presses, wine, secondary treatment of pressed olives and grapes, haylofts, granaries. Convenience of access, ventilation, and control of humidity and temperature are treated in some detail, as are vaulting, plastering, and vermin and insect control. The type of hard flooring of crushed tile and mortar known as *opus signinum* (modern terrazzo) is recommended, as is the finishing of surfaces with the lees of pressed olives (*amurca*).

160   This may be the freedman Alfius the banker in Horace's *Epode* 2.2: see ch. 4, Descriptions of Villas. As Alfius appears to have been a fictional character, Columella has made up this quotation.

161   See ch. 2 n. 67.

162   Columella's Book 2, not excerpted here, treats types of soil as well as draining, ditching, ploughing methods, and sowing of legumes. It ends with consideration of religious practices in agriculture and rural life and a promise to write a book about them.

163   For these themes in Xenophon's *Oeconomicus*: Xen., *Oec.* 3.14–16, 7.20–25, and *Oec.* 8.10–13 in ch. 1, Greek and Sicilian Backgrounds of Roman Villas. Cato in his introduction inveighs against trade and the abandonment of farming: Cato, *Agr.* Preface, in this chapter. Varro also repeats some of these themes: Varro, *Rust.* 2.1.1–4 and 2.10.1–10, also in this chapter.

164   See discussions of Hesiod and Xenophon in ch. 1, Greek and Sicilian Backgrounds of Roman Villas.

165   For Cicero's translation of Xenophon, see n. 28 in ch. 1, Greek and Sicilian Backgrounds of Roman

Villas, and Columella, *Rust.* 12. Preface 4–10, in this chapter.

166 For the *vilica*'s duties and character, see Columella, *Rust.* 12.1.1–3, in this chapter.

167 Also: Palladius Rutilius Taurus Aemilianus. *NP* s.v. "Palladius" II 1 (K. Ruffing); White 1970, 30–31.

168 Prof. Fitch, of the University of Victoria, Canada, has graciously given me permission to use his translation (Fitch 2013); I am grateful to him and to the publisher, Prospect Books (Totnes, UK), and to Catheryn Kilgarriff for endorsing his permission. While keeping Fitch's structure and titles, I have adapted his topic headings, added notes and comments, and included some Latin terms in square brackets to align with the presentation of other texts in this book; some punctuation has been brought in line with the current publication.

169 On the manuscripts and early use of the treatise: Rogers 1975a; Fitch 2013, 21–28; Martin 1976, i–xxxviii; Guirard and Martin 2010, 1–12. Palladius's method is similar to part of the agricultural content of Hesiod's *Works and Days* from the late eighth–early seventh century BCE, some 1,200 years earlier: see Fitch 2013, 11–20, for a shrewd assessment. In Hesiod's poem, as of line 383, planting, harvesting, and ploughing are timed in relation to the April–May and October–November rise of the constellation of the Pleiades, forestry projects in relation to seasonal and celestial movements of Sirius in the autumn, and so on. Palladius goes month by month in a more methodical way but with an ingenious check: he refines the days of work within the month by noting—and advising his readers on—the changing length of a man's shadow; Fitch 2013, 85 n. 32 for explanation.

170 Palladius continues with sections (*Op. Agr.* 1.5–6, omitted here) on water and soil issues, as he promised.

171 See my comment on Hes., *Op.* 727–828, in ch. 1, Greek and Sicilian Backgrounds of Roman Villas.

172 This list of specialized workers seems to be an aspirational list rather than an instruction about indispensible personnel. Many of these craftsmen would exercise their expertise in towns or as itinerants in the countryside. Palladius appears at times to be thinking of an isolated villa and estate, and he does not assume or even advise about water or road transport for people and produce. However, a manorial set-up or even partially self-sufficient circumstances for a villa do not seem to be in his mind.

173 "Necessity takes no holidays": *necessitas feriis caret.*

174 Athena/Minerva, the goddess of wisdom, weaving, and war, was also a virgin and patron of the olive tree, its fruit, and its products.

175 Farther on, after the first two books, Palladius's treatise is set up in monthly units from January to December, with the farmwork listed by days or weeks; this statement indicates that some latitude can be exercised.

176 Palladius's emphasis on the high position of the *praetorium* and the pleasant outlook from it may indicate that he is thinking of the terraced villas (*basis villae*) such as those of Tibur: Fehr 1969; Tombrägel 2012.
 Palladius uses the word *praetorium* for the main residential dwelling of the villa, presumably the *pars urbana*. This is unusual: *villa* is his normal collective word, sometimes *ager* for villa and estate in general, often *aedificium*, and even *domus*. Giving military names such as *praetorium* to villas has been claimed to be part of a general militarization of language and society in Late Antiquity: MacMullen 1963, 23–48; Ripoll and Arce 2000, 64–65; discussion in Métraux 2018, 404 and n. 25.
 However, already in the mid-first century CE, Seneca had used military terms for the villas of Marius and Julius Caesar at Misenum, calling them *castra*, or military camps, in which the general's headquarters and dwelling would have been the *praetorium*: Sen., *Ep.* 51.11, and my discussion in ch. 9, Villas and *Horti* in the Late Roman Republic. Seneca had emphasized the military aspects of Scipio Africanus's villa at Liternum: *Ep.* 86.1–15, discussed in ch. 4, Descriptions of Villas. A little later (end of the first century CE), Statius called the two parts of the villa of Manilius Vopiscus at Tibur *praetoria*, and he used the word for the complex of villa buildings of Pollius Felix at Surrentum and his villas or buildings on the island of Limon: see Stat., *Silv.* 1.3.1–75 and 2.2.1–35, also in ch. 4. It is true that later, by the fifth and sixth centuries CE, *praetorium* had been naturalized as a term for villas in Ausonius and Cassiodorus, but the term had had earlier manifestations: see Auson., *Mos.* 283–285, and Cassiod., *Var.* 12.22, also in ch. 4.

177 Palladius's recipes for floors, both for residential rooms and utilitarian spaces, are based partially on the utilitarian floors described in Faventinus's treatise, which in turn were derived from Vitruvius's recipes in Book 7 of his *De architectura*. Here, Palladius exceptionally mentions marble and mosaic floors without dilating on their techniques; such floors were probably works commissioned by villa owners from speciality craftsmen. The floors made of *scutula* (sing. *scutulum*, diminutive of *scutum*, shield) had been widely used in Italy in the Late Republic and Early Empire, then fell out of favor. Such floors are called *scutulata pavimenta*, their appeal being the random distribution, usually on a field of white mosaic tesserae, of irregularly shaped many-colored veined marbles and colored limestones of different sizes. They would not have been a current formula for floor decoration in Palladius's day: Morricone 1980, but see Guidobaldi and Salvatori 1988 for revision of Morricone's dating.
 On the persistence of nonmosaic floor and wall treatments (mortars, plasters): most recently Lancaster 2021, with considerable bibliography; also Gros 2003.

178 Vitruvius: *De arch.* 7.3.7, in ch. 3, Villas in Roman Architectural Treatises; Sidonius Apollinaris: *Ep.* 2.2.1–20, in ch. 4, Descriptions of Villas.

179 Much more than those of his predecessors in writing of agriculture, Palladius's strategies for finding water at a villa site are elaborately and minutely outlined in his Book 9.8–10 (for the month of August).

180 This distinction (pleasure versus the health of the inhabitants) indicates that Palladius is distinguishing between the owners' pleasure at visiting the villa for a few days and the workers who have to live there all the time. Evidently the old habit of absenteeism by owners, already countenanced disfavorably by Cato at least five centuries before, was still a norm in Palladius's day. A theory of Late Antique villas—that the "boom" in construction of numerous very grand and grandly decorated villas was due to the abandonment, by the provincial notables, of civic participation in towns and cities (in Italy, southeast Gaul, and Hispania, especially)—has been largely discarded in favor of more complex analyses of changing economic, agricultural, and ecclesiastical conditions in the fourth and fifth centuries: Ripoll 2018, 426–28 and nn. 4–7, with preceding bibliography; Fixot 2000, 44–48; Ripoll and Arce 2000, 66–70.

181 The long, narrow shape of the legal basilica in Roman towns and cities, sometimes with interior galleries, defined a space with a raised dais or tribunal on the axis of its length or crosswise on its width. The dais raised the chair (*sella*) of the presiding magistrate (and more chairs for his advisers, if any) into a prominent position over the floor of the basilica; there was often an architectural backdrop of some kind. The type is known throughout the empire and would have been instantly recognizable to readers: Vitr., *De arch.* 5.4–7.

182 Wine to which slices of the bulb of squill (*Scilla/Urginea maritima*) were added was used as an expectorant and for other conditions: Dioscurides 2.202; 5.25 (vinegar); 5.526 (wine).

NOTES TO CHAPTER 3

1 Vitruvius lists mainly Greek sources in several prefaces to the books of his *De architectura*, some on architecture but others on topics relevant to his idea of the universal knowledge required to be a professional architect. As examples, Archimedes of Syracuse (third century BCE) is cited on problems in water channels (*De arch.* 1.1.7); Pythius of Priene's *Commentaries* appear in relation to his temple of Athena at Priene (*De arch.* 1.12.1); Hermogenes's work is cited on Ionic temples and his temple at Teos (*De arch.* 3.8–9); Epicurus, Plato, and many other philosophers are listed as the predecessors (*maiores*) who have transmitted both wisdom and knowledge necessary to the practice and theory of architecture (*De arch.* 7 Preface 2).

2 For the date of *On Architecture* and comments on the author's name: Nichols 2017, 1–2, nn. 7, 9 and 10, with preceding bibliography.

3 Vitruvius was familiar with Varro's work on machinery (*De arch.* 7. Preface 14) and linguistics (*De arch.* 9. Preface 17).

4 Frontinus, *Aq.* 1.25; Pliny the Elder mentions Vitruvius as a source: Pliny, *HN.* 16.35–36. On other aspects of Vitruvius's readership: Gros 1994b; Nichols 2017, 3–6, 10–13, 15–18.

5 Vitr., *De arch.* 1.3. He states that the public and private buildings will be a testament to the greatness of what the Romans have achieved and will transmit their memory to future generations.

6 *De arch.* 1.1.2–17. Vitruvius is disarmingly grateful to his parents for giving him the education he needed to succeed as a professional in the field: *De arch.* 6. Preface 4.

7 It is best to read Vitruvius's explanation of these terms, but their extension and use in later times and other terminologies is also important. I have used Rowland's (in Rowland and Howe 1999) here for the best definitions, but there are many others. Vitruvius himself supplied the Greek equivalents.
For *ordinatio* (ordering [Rowland], Gk. τάξις, meaning internal logic of the minute and overall modular parts): *De arch.* 1.2.1–2.

8 *Dispositio* (design [Rowland] translated as design or arrangement, Gk. διάθεσις, the internal congruence of elements in plan, elevation, and perspective): *De arch.* 1.2.2.

9 *Eurythmia* (shapeliness [Rowland], often called proportion or proportionality of parts in size and spatial relationships): *De arch.* 1.2.3.

10 *Symmetria* (harmonious correspondence of parts): *De arch.* 1.3.4.

11 *Decor* (correctness [Rowland], appropriateness or propriety, and good ordering, Gk. οἰκονομία). *Distributio* (efficient management of resources and work on the site [Rowland]: *De arch* 1.3.5.

12 The deployment of these values can be complex but logical and precise: only certain places in the city are appropriate to temples of certain gods, and certain gods can only be housed in temples built in certain architectural orders: Doric for Minerva and Mars; Corinthian for Venus, Ionic for Diana and Liber Pater, and so on: *De arch.* 1.2.5.

13 *De arch.* 1.3.2.

14 Vitruvius's treatment of houses can be contrasted with the expansion of private construction of *domus* and villas during his professional career: the City was greatly expanding, as were Italian towns, and new villas were being built, and existing ones were being expanded in size, distribution, and local density. His near-contemporary Dionysius of Halicarnassus noticed these expansions, as did Strabo in the next generation, and Suetonius records Augustus's measures: Dion. Hal., *Ant. Rom.* 4.13.4 (for Rome); Strabo 5.4.8 (on the density of villas surrounding the Bay of Naples); Suet., *Aug.* 30. On villas around Rome: Guidobaldi 2000; De Franceschini 2005, 297, fig. 1. On Italy in general during Vitruvius's lifetime: Patterson 2006. On the particular nature of the urban-rural relation: Jolivet 2018. Both Jolivet and Wallace-Hadrill argue that for Vitruvius the villa as a separate architectural type did not really exist: Wallace-Hadrill 2018, 63–64.

15 The name Pollio (or Polio) has been questioned as belonging to him; its application to him may have been a mistake in transmission: Nichols 2017, 1 and nn. 7 and 10, with previous bibliography.

16 For possible dates of his treatise: Gros 1994b, 75–76; Nichols 2017, 1 and n. 9.

17 Ingrid D. Rowland, Department of History, Notre Dame University, Rome Center; Rowland and Howe 1999. I have added headnotes and prefatory comments for this volume, and some punctuation has been brought in line with the current publication. While keeping Rowland's structure and numbering of the Latin text, I have added my own notes and put some Latin terms in square brackets to align with the presentation of other texts in this book. My additions are not meant to substitute for Rowland's very complete commentary, and they follow the meticulous, expert illustrations and explanations by Thomas Noble Howe (Southwestern University, Georgetown, Texas) which accompany Rowland's translation; Rowland and Howe 1999.

18 Discussion in Romano 1987.

19 In the previous section (*De arch.* 2.1.1), the taming of fire was discussed in detail.

20 The study of the "original" primitive house in the historical imagination is the topic of Rykwert 1972.

21 The House of Romulus, *tugurium Romuli* or *casa Romuli*, was situated on the southwestern scarp of the Palatine Hill, but another was later exhibited on the Capitoline: Plut., *Vit. Rom.* 20.4; Dion. Hal., *Ant. Rom.* 1.79.11; Cass. Dio 48.43.4 and 53.16.4, citing a house of Romulus on the Palatine. *NP* s.v. "Rome" III B (topography and archaeology of the city of Rome, Bronze and Iron Ages) (M. Heinzelmann); Capitoline House of Romulus, *Casa Romuli*: *AtlasAncRome* 1 156, 217; 2: tabs. 7 and 20, fig. 269; Gjerstad 1953–73: 1960, vol. 3, 48–55; 1966, vol. 4, 45–49 (Palatine Settlement); Pensabene and Falzone 2001, 81–92; most recently on the Palatine House of Romulus: Carafa and Bruno 2013, 731–38, fig. 8, plan at fig. 10b and section at fig. 11. Vitruvius locates it on the Capitoline hill (*De arch.* 2.5).

22 Houses with foundations: *domus fundata*; walls built of brick or stone: *latericii parietes aut e lapide*; timber and tiled roofs: *materiaque et tegula tecta*.

23 *De arch.* 6.1.1–9. See also the *laudes Italiae* in Varro, *Rust.* 1.2.3–7, in ch. 2, Villas in Roman Agricultural Treatises.

24 He describes atria with a central square opening or *compluvium*: Tuscan, Corinthian, tetrastyle, and displuviate; atria with no *compluvium* and consequently and covered (*testudinate*, "turtle-shelled"): *De arch.* 6.3.1–4.
    Vitruvius's authority in the Renaissance was such that the names he gave to the rooms of both the Italian and Greek houses have become conventions in modern scholarship. There were Latin alternatives to the Vitruvian nomenclature, and there were certainly differences of use and domestic practice in actual houses than Vitruvius's typology of spaces would lead us to believe: Leach 1997; Nevett 2010, 89–118; for a specific example, the *vestibulum*: Speksnijder 2022.

25 At his villa at Tusculum, Cicero had *exedrae* in the small porticoes, which he decorated with easel paintings (*tabellae*); see Cic., *Fam.* 209 (7.23.2–3), in ch. 4, Descriptions of Villas.

26 On *tablina, triclinia*, and *exedrae* or *oeci*, and for advice on lighting and placement of windows: *De arch.* 6.3.5–11.

27 ".... Principles the personal areas... for the head of the family": *privatis aedificiis propria loca patribus familiarum*; "public areas ... with outsiders": *communia cum extraneis*. This discussion comes after chapter 4 on the orientation of the different rooms of the house.
    For private versus public in general: *NP* s.v. "Private Sphere and Public Sphere" III. Rome (C. Höcker); most recently, Bartz 2019b, with preceding bibliography; also Wallace-Hadrill 1988; and Grahame 1997, 137–64, a study applying a special method of urban structural analysis (based on Hillier and Hanson 1984) to a house; but see my review: Métraux 2003.

28 In this instance, Vitruvius uses *cavaedium* to designate the atrium itself rather than its covering.

29 "...Public deliberations and private judgments and arbitrations": *publica consilia et privata iudicia arbitriaque*.

30 In the *pars rustica* of the San Rocco villa at Francolise, the room housing the press for the olives was 3.75 m wide × 5.70 m deep, but the pressing was done in a wood container (*galleagra*) with its lever (*prelum*) tightened with handspakes (*vectes*). The room was not deep enough to accommodate the full length of the lever, but rather the lever protruded from the wide entrance into the room itself, giving the workers space to operate it. When not in use, out of the processing season, the wood components could be dismantled and stored: Cotton and Métraux 1985, 69–76.

31 ".... The more refined side": *quid delicatius in villis faciundum*; "serviceablity as a country house": *rusticae utilitatis*.

32 Rowland's perceptive translation separates *nostrates* from *aedificatores* to emphasize, correctly, that Vitruvius is speaking to a reader "like us" who is going to hire a builder and give him clear instructions, not, as in other translations, "our" builders.

33 On Vitruvius and Greek houses: Krause 1977; Raeder 1988; Reber 1988. On Greek houses, classical to Hellenistic: Nevett 2010, 89–118; also Hoepfner and Schwandner 1994; Pesando 1987; 1989; Walter-Karydi 1996.

34 Regarding *xenia* in verse and ekphrasis: Martial's *Epigram* 13 is entirely devoted to short descriptions of these gifts, including wine; other more elaborate ones appear in *Epig.* 7.49 and 9.54, and he describes market-bought *xenia* (i.e., not from his villa) in *Epig.* 7.31 and 9.60 to entertain his readers with his sly subterfuge. There are other descriptions—sincere ones— in Pliny, *Ep.* 21.1–2, in Sidonius Apollinaris, *Carm.* 21.1–4, and elsewhere; see also Plin., *Ep.* 1.7.6, in ch. 6, Villa Visits. Grand displays of food are described in Philostr., *Imag.* 1.31 and 2.26. On *xenia* in mosaics: Balmelle et al. 1990; Darmon 1990, 107–12. On *xenia* in Campanian painting: Croisille 1965; 1982.

35 They could also be found on walls of bars and fast-food counters (*popinae, cauponae*), but there as advertising and menu listings for the prepared dishes and drink on offer.

36 See discussions in headnote to Vitr., *De arch.* 6.7.4, in this chapter and ch. 3 n. 34; and in headnote to Mart., *Epig.* 7.49, in ch. 6, Villa Visits, and ch. 6 n. 44.

37 For the correct use of these terms: *NP* s.v. "House" II B 1 (*pastas* house), II B 2 (*prostas* house), and II B 4 (peristyle house) with plans and drawings (C. Höcker); *NP* s.v. "Pastas" (C. Höcker); *NP* s.v. "Private Sphere and Public Sphere" II. Greece (C. Höcker); Hoepfner and Schwandner 1994, s.v. "*pastas, prostas*," 354–60; Müller-Wiener 1988, 176–81; Nevett 2010, 89–118.

38 See analysis in Speksnijder 2022.

39 The final part of Book 6 (*De arch.* 6.8.1–7) is devoted to the foundations for private dwellings, very briefly with respect to ground-level houses and those with basements or those with vaulted ceilings or underground or partially below grade *cryptoporticus*. Relieving arches within walls are also discussed. The longest discussion (*De arch.* 6.8.5–7) concerns terrace walls, either with wall buttresses or smooth, and sometimes with complex compartments behind them to hold the fill of the terrace and reduce its pressure on the retaining wall. These devices are the terracing foundations of the *basis villae*: Fehr 1969, 1–65; Tombrägel 2012.

40 *De arch.* 7.3.4.

41 On *luxuria* and Vitruvius in the context of morality: Nichols 2017, 83–98, 169–78; extensive and expansive discussion in Romano 1994.

42 The rest of this section gives instructions on how to make a floor for a winter *triclinium*: an excavation should be made, then filled with packed substrate topped with crushed charcoal, in turn covered with a layer of gravel, ashes, and lime flattened and polished. The result is a smooth, dark floor that readily dries in case wine is spilled on it, and retains heat so that the barefooted enslaved servers of food and drink do not catch cold.

43 "…. Certain secure principles for painting": *certae rationes picturarum*; "secure phenomena": *res certae*.

44 The section that follows (omitted here) is famous as a denunciation of fanciful wall-painting styles exhibiting what Vitruvius calls depraved "modern" taste (*iniqui mores, novi mores*): *De arch.* 7.5.3–4. He appears to be targeting the Third Style of Pompeian painting on the general basis that art must follow nature, but his calculated vehemence may have resonated with readers for whom old-fashioned decorative sobriety had been a norm for a generation. For consideration of this important topic: in general, Ling 1991, 18–51. But the bibliography is vast; it originated with Mau's categorization of the four styles: Mau 1882; discussion in Bragantini 2014 and 2015.

45 *NP* s.v. "Cetius Faventinus, M." (K. Sallmann).

46 Cam 2001, xiii–xvii. The book is sometimes called *De diversis fabricis architectonicae* (*On Various Building Matters of Architecture*). The most recent and definitive edition of the text, with French translation and very extensive commentary, is Cam 2001; earlier in Plommer 1973.

47 On Palladius's use of Faventinus around 400 CE or later: Martin 1976, xxxiii–xxxviii. Faventinus himself says that his little book (*libellus*, 29.5) is written in a middling style (*sermo mediocriter*, Prologue) to appeal to readers of ordinary or lesser competence (*humiliores ingenii*). The effectiveness and popularity of both Faventinus's and Palladius's treatises is attested by the large number of medieval copies and their wide distribution: Cam 2001, lxxi–lxxii.

48 The omissions are listed in Cam 2001, 50–166. The gap between Faventinus and actual villa construction in the second and third centuries CE in the western Roman provinces is striking at a time when, in Aquitania and Hispania, villas were reaching an apex of complexity and variety for architectural inventiveness and decorative exuberance; see Balmelle 2001 and articles in Eristov and Monier 2014 (Aquitanian villas); Teichner 2018 and Ripoll 2018 (Hispanic villas). The elements that Faventinus omits may indicate that his intended readers were at a moderate level of status and wealth: he does mention *bybliothecae* and *pinacothecae* in passing as well as the technology and construction of bath buildings (*Artis Arch.* 16, 17, parts of 18 and 24 for the floors), but he says nothing at all about their decoration or sequence of use. The only mention of wall paintings is about maintaining them. Marble floors and revetments and mosaic on floors or other surfaces are not included (marble and mosaic had been largely absent from Vitruvius's earlier *On Architecture*, even for *opera urbana*), even though marble and mosaic are mentioned in Palladius later on: *Op. Agr.* 1.9.5. For villas specifically, Faventinus's chapter 13 mentions the orientations and arrangements for kitchens, *cella olearia, cella vinaria*, cattle stalls, stables, and enclosures for sheep, pigs, and goats, derived in large part from Vitruvius's *De arch.* 6.6.1–5. At this time, villa owners were also greatly expanding their production and storage facilities, but he is silent on those topics: Métraux 1998, 3–12.

49 As in Vitr., *De arch.* 6.3 and 6.4 (urban *domus*) with 6.6 (villa) afterward.

50 *De fabrica villae rusticae dispondenda*. The rubrics are Faventinus's. Here in the notes, I give the Latin rubrics as transcribed in Cam 2001, and give my translations in the text.

51 The text continues rapid-fire with instructions on the proper placement of the oil production area (*cella olearis*, on the south), the granaries (on the north), and warehouses (*horrea*), haylofts (*fenilia*), and ovens (*pistrina*) outside the villa in case of fire.

52 *De dispositione operis urbani*.

53 This list omits many of the other rooms that Vitruvius had listed as appropriate to the *domus* of highly placed persons: Vitr., *De arch.* 6.5.1–3.

54 *De fabrica balnearum*.

55 This may indicate that the bath was accessed from both the villa and from the outside so that agricultural workers could also use it but without coming into the villa itself; Columella has a similar solution or something like it: see Columella, *Rust.* 1.6.19–20, in ch. 2, Villas in Roman Agricultural Treatises. Such an arrangement was the case at the villa at Sidi Ghrib in Africa Vetus (modern Tunisia), where the large bath building was connected to the residential villa on the west and to the agricultural fields on the east: Ennabli 1986a and 1986b; Ennabli and Neuru 1994; Wilson 2018b, 281–85, fig. 16.13.

56 *Triclinia hiberna minoribus picturis esse ornanda.*

NOTES TO CHAPTER 4

1 The texts in this chapter range from the first century BCE to the sixth century CE. The later history of villas, including the architectural changes to rural dwellings—new and reused—in Italy and elsewhere in the early Medieval period, have been the subject of two collections of articles: Cavalieri and Sacchi 2020, and Cavalieri and Sfameni 2022. The topics include documentation and analysis of continuities from, and changes to, earlier villas and their structural determinants: land use, ownership (private, imperial, ecclesiastical), personnel (free and enslaved), legal issues, plantings and husbandry practices, transport, and trading venues.

2 Cicero's Tusculanum had been owned by the dictator Lucius Cornelius Sulla Felix (138–78 BCE) and subsequently by Quintus Lutatius Catulus (the younger, son of a namesake, ca. 121–60 BCE), consul in 102 BCE and triumphator the following year as well as a poet, orator, and man of wealth; Cicero bought the property from Lucius Vettius (Cic., *Att.* 80 [4.5.2]). The environs of the town comprised villas belonging to political and aristocratic members of Cicero's day as well as earlier and later prominent persons, notably Lucullus, M. Aemilius Scaurus (praetor in 56 BCE), Metellus, Lentulus (P. Cornelius Lentulus Spinther, ca. 63–48 BCE), Pompey, M. Junius Brutus, G. Asinius Polio (ca. 76 BCE–5 CE), and Varro the encyclopedist.

3 For the portico, see also Cic., *Att.* 300.1 (13.29.1).

4 Cic., *Tusc.* 2.3.

5 The name Amalthea may have been conferred by the nearby Amaltheion dedicated to the nanny goat wet nurse of the infant Zeus. Atticus's villa was much admired by Cicero (Cic., *De Leg.* 2.7 [2.3.7] and Cic., *Att.* 16.15 and 18 [1.16]); he supplied some quotations to animate its walls. Its site may be that of the ruins of a villa at Malathrea southeast of Buthrotum: Papaioannou 2018, 329 and n. 18.

6 The urban *domus* was consecrated as a shrine to Liberty (*aedes Libertatis* or *monumentum Libertatis*) and part of its site annexed by his enemy and neighbor Publius Clodius Pulcher; Cicero was able later, with a speech to the priests of the shrine and to the College of Pontiffs, to secure reassignment of the land from religious to secular designation and some compensation: Cic., *De domo sua* 24; see, most recently, Manuwald 2021, though this does not include *De domo sua*; Tamm 1963, 25–28; Picard 1964.

Recent investigations on the Palatine hill have identified a possible location of the *domus Tullii Ciceronis*: Carafa and Bruno 2013, 742–48; for Cicero's house and that of his brother Quintus: *AtlasAncRome* 1 232; 2: tab. 64 at X 91; older discussion in Cerutti 1997; Allen 1939.

7 The consuls arrived at these figures following the estimate by the opinion of professional advisors (*de consili sentenia*; Cic., *Att.* 74.5 [4.2.5]). For the *domus* on the Palatine, the difference between the 3,500,000HS Cicero paid and the 2,000,000HS in compensation is striking: he may have overpaid for it, or the house had decreased in value, or the troubled times had depressed real estate in general, or the damage was not as great as first thought, or the Senate's advisors were stingy—perhaps some combination of these factors.

8 The two—*gymnasium* and *palaestra*—seem to have been different, but their difference seems obscure even in Cicero's distinction between them: see Cic., *Fam.* 209 (7.23.2–3), in this chapter.

9 Lucius Licinius Crassus, consul in 95 BCE, thereafter proconsul in Gaul: *NP* s.v. "Licinius" I 10 (C. Walde).

10 Quintus Lutatius Catulus, consul in 78 BCE, an adherent of the dictator Sulla: *NP* s.v. "Lutatius" (K.-L. Elvers).

11 *Verum oti fructus est non contentio animi, sed relaxatio.*

12 The point being made by Catulus (and Cicero) is that the present-day Greek successors of the great Greek philosophers are inferior in every respect, and that the Romans are their true successors. That was one of Cicero's agendums in his philosophical writings.

13 Cicero specifies here that the Lyceum is the upper gymnasium of the Tusculanum. In *Tusculan Disputations* (see *Tusc.* 3.6–7, in this chapter), he uses the verb *descendo* (to go down) to indicate movement into the Academy, thereby establishing an upper and lower position for these spaces in the villa. It is possible that there were two *gymnasia*: one associated with the Academy, on a terrace or lower level, and this one higher up adjacent to the Lyceum and its library.

14 His anxiety to redress his financial affairs and reestablish his presence and influence are shown in many letters to Atticus and others: e.g., Cic., *Att.* 73 (4.1) of September 57 BCE.

15 The difference of compensation amounts between his urban house and his villas is notable, indicating that the villas suffered less damage or were valued at lesser amounts, or both, and that the Tusculanum near Rome was considered more valuable than the villa at Formiae on the coast.

16 Carafa and Bruno 2013, 742–48; Picard 1964.

17 The *post reditum* or "after my return" speeches Cicero made on these matters are analyzed with translations in Manuwald 2021.

18 A variant reading in the negative (*careo non facile*) changes this to "I can't easily do without a suburban villa," but the previous claim that he has put it up for sale seems to contradict this; Cicero does not indicate that he wants to sell in order to buy another suburban villa, so the variant reading (addition of *non*) would be illogical.

19   The *Consolatio* is lost but is referenced in Cic., *Tusc.* 1.27, 1.31, and 3.28. His preoccupation for many months in 45 and into 44 BCE was to find a suitable location for a memorial for his daughter, a *fanum Tulliae*: for discussion, see Afterword in ch. 8, Buying, Building, Improving, and Selling Villas.

20   Also alluded to in *Tusc.* 4.14 (32). For Corinthian bronzes: *NP* s.v. "Corinthian alloy" (R. Neudecker); *EAA* 2 s.v. "Corinthiarius" (I. Calabi Limentani); Jacobson and Weitzman 1992; Mattusch 2003.

21   Cicero's story about Xenocrates of Chalcedon (396–314 BCE) is as follows: Xenocrates, the director (*scholarch*) of the Platonic Academy from 339/8 BCE to his death, was once offered 50 talents of silver (a huge sum) for some political advice and influence in Athens by ambassadors of Alexander the Great. He invited them to dinner. When the ambassadors asked to whom they should forward the sum, he said "Did you not understand from yesterday's sparse little dinner [*cenula*] that I don't need money?" But when he saw the ambassadors' dismay, he relented and accepted a gift of 30 *minae*: Cic., *Tusc.* 5.91 (5.32). (An Attic talent of silver [*talanto*] equals in weight about 1 amphora of water, or about 26 kg, or about 56 lbs., 60 *minae* equals 1 talent, so 30 *minae* is about half a talent, a relatively small sum.) The anecdote thus associates a Greek philosopher with the frugality of the Roman ancestors.

22   Philo of Larissa (ca. 159–84 BCE) was the head of the Platonic Academy at Athens from 110/109 BCE; Cicero heard him speak in 88 BCE when Philo had left Athens for Rome during the First Mithridatic War. Cicero mentioned him often: Cic., *Fam.* 63.2 (13.1); *Acad. post.* 1.14 (1.4); *Acad. post.* 2.11–112 (2.4).

23   Cicero, in a book on technical issues of argumentation called *Topica*, mentions sitting in the library of his Tusculanum with his friend and dedicatee of the work, G. Trebatius Testa; they sat and unrolled scrolls of Aristotle while chatting: Cic., *Top.* 1.1.

24   See ch. 4 n. 13.

25   Carneades of Cyrene (ca. 214–129 BCE), associated with the Academy at Athens, had lectured in Rome in 155 BCE: Plut., *Cato Maior* 22; Lactant., *Div. inst.* 5.14–15; *NP* s.v. "Carneades" 1 (K.-H. Stanzel).

26   On the particular nature of Cicero's villa environment, *studium/otium*, and self-representation: Hutchinson 2016; on his use of villas: Dalfen 2000.

27   For Roman collecting in overview: Rutledge 2012, 59–64 on Cicero; Leen 1991. More than a century later, Pliny the Elder often mentioned who purchased works of art and where they were exhibited. In both matters of expense and ostentatious display, Pliny inherited something of Cicero's concern for appropriate (or inappropriate) subject matter and frugality while idolizing Greek art. Among other instances, he notes that Cicero's older contemporary, orator, and fellow lawyer Quintus Hortensius Hortalus paid 144,000*HS* for a painting of the Argonauts by Cydias and installed it in a shrine (*aedes*) at his villa at Tusculum: Plin., *HN* 35.130 (35.40), 60s CE; *NP* s.v. "Cydias" 3 (N. Hoesch); Pollitt 1965, 180 (Kydias).

28   Hermathena: a double bust of Hermes (Mercury) and Athena (Minerva), half siblings of their father Zeus (Jupiter), probably in the form of a herm or square pillar with the two faces on opposite sides. Hermes represented eloquence in general, Athena wisdom. On the type: *EAA* 3 s.v. "Erma" (P. Mingazzini); *NP* s.v. "Herms" (R. Neudecker); and esp. Wrede 1986.

29   If the Hermathena mentioned here is the same statue that was mentioned a year before (Cic., *Att.* 10.5 [1.1.5] above), it had been repositioned from the *gymnasium* to the Academy. However, this one may have been a new acquisition.

30   Cicero had long wished to buy Atticus's library for himself. By "a Crassus," Cicero means any proverbially rich person, a reference deriving from M. Licinius Crassus (ca. 115–53 BCE), a politician and general, consul in 70 and 55 BCE, and the third member of the so-called First Triumvirate (with Pompey and Caesar).

31   L. Cincius, an employee of Atticus, is often mentioned in Cicero's letters: Shackleton-Bailey 1996, 33.

32   Herms with marble or stone shafts and bronze heads were a common formula in Hellenistic and Roman art: Wrede 1986.

33   An *arca* is a chest or box; metal or metal-strapped versions in wood were used as safes to stow cash and valuables, so by extension meaning money: *NP* s.v. "Arca" (R. Hurschmann).

34   The Ceramicus (Kerameikos) was a suburb of Athens where Atticus apparently had a villa that Cicero equates with his villa at Tusculum.

35   *Puteal*: a round wellhead in any material giving access to the water in a cistern or dug well; ones in marble were often carved in relief.

36   As lawyers did not charge for professional services, "small fees" (*vindemiolae*, sing. *vindemiola*, literally, small harvest of grapes) could be generated from perquisites or gifts received for ordinary legal consultation, not the great presents of money or inheritances received for major defenses or prosecutions in court.

37   Atticus may have inaugurated his Amalthea or celebrated its completion with a ritual involving sacrifices.

Sikyon, a town in the northern Peloponnese, refers to Atticus's purchases of art for his friend's villa. It was the birthplace and hometown of famous artists such as the painter Pausias and the sculptor Lysippus, therefore an "art town."

38   M. Fadius Gallus, an art jobber: Shackleton Bailey 1992, 50.

39   The sculptor and dealer C. Avianus Evander had evidently paid for the goods "on spec" and did not ask for down payment or charge interest on his outlay: Cicero apparently was prestigious enough as a customer to be an advertisement, so Avianus could forgo any profit or interest. Avianus Evander had an interesting later career with Mark Antony in Egypt, and later back in Rome: *NP* s.v. "Evander" 4 (R. Neudecker); Shackleton Bailey 1995, 22.

40 The dealer L. Licinius Crassus Damasippus was well known to the art-buying elite and was satirized later by Horace (*Sat.* 2.3.64–68); he was perhaps the descendant or freedman of Lucius Junius Brutus Damasippus, a partisan in the Marian-Sullan conflicts of the 80s BCE: Cic., *Att.* 268 (12.29); *NP* s.v. "Licinius" I 17 (W. Will); *NP* s.v. "Art, interest in," B. Rome (H.G. Döhl); Shackleton Bailey 1995, 45.

41 Bacchantes were female followers of Bacchus, god of wine, and expressed their devotion to him by wild dancing and drunkenness. They were the opposite of Muses, the inspirers of art and devotees of Apollo. Metellus was known to have a villa at Tusculum, so Cicero may well have seen them there.

The Metellus referred to is Quintus Caecilius Metellus Pius Scipio Nasica (100/98 BCE–46 BCE), a famous conservative politician, art collector, and luxury-loving aristocrat. *NP* s.v. "Caecilius" I 32 (W. Will); Broughton 1951–1960, 2:234–35.

42 Mars, as god of war, and Saturn, ambivalently god of procreation and death, were figures of misfortune. Mercury was a god of good luck and effective rhetoric, so his image promised good fortune and the gift of fine speaking, appropriate to Cicero himself.

43 Cicero notes his exasperation at the cost of these objects and indicates that he would have been better off buying a *deversorium* at Tarracina. *Deversoria* were simple buildings used as places to stay while traveling. In the case of Tarracina, its location on the Via Appia at the road's run along the coast to turn inland to cross Campania was a good place to break the trip from Rome to his villas on the Bay of Naples. He evidently had a "loaner" he could use at Tarracina: he mentions a host in or near the town.

Cicero owned a *deversorium* at Anagnia on the Via Latina to break his journey between Rome and his ancestral villa at Arpinum: Cic., *Att.* 248.1 (12.1.1). He could also use the Via Latina to travel to and from the Bay of Naples: it joined the Via Appia at Capua (modern Sta. Maria Capua Vetere). The *deversorium* at Anagnia may have been the place where he had left his baggage (*impedimenta*) when he was in dangerous circumstances being courted politically by both Octavian and Caesar's assassins Brutus and Cassius and was uncertain whether to stay put at his villa at Puteoli or go to Rome or Arpinum: *Att.* 418.1 (16.8.1).

44 Junius is otherwise unknown: Shackleton Bailey 1995, 58.

45 An *exedra* was any square, rectangular, or apsidal extension of a space, portico, or room that afforded architectural dignity with some privacy. Domestic *exedrae* could also be used for readings, lectures, conversations, and other quiet pursuits.

46 As a dealer in art, Damasippus had a long-enduring bad reputation. In his *Satire* 2.3.64–68 (published ca. 30 BCE), Horace does not hesitate to underscore it, saying that anyone who invests as *creditor* in his art business is going to be cheated, with the implied lesson to not throw good money after bad. The rest of this letter has to do with a real estate transaction.

47 To entice him to visit, Cicero is wittily calling his own villas by the same name, Amalthea, as Atticus's villa in Epirus.

48 G. Trebatius Testa was a well-known jurist and bon vivant: *NP* s.v. "Trebatius" 2 (T. Giaro); Shackleton Bailey 1995, 98. Trebatius was sufficiently prominent to be used, much later, as an advisor to Horace on bad libellous satire versus good epic poetry: Hor., *Sat.* 2.1 (published ca. 30 BCE).

49 Cicero's *Orator* (*Orator ad M. Brutum*) brought to a close arguments developed in two related treatises, also written in 46 BCE, *On the Orator* (*De or.*) and *Brutus* (*Brut.*). The topics concern the comity of philosophy and oratory. All three are in dialogue form: the speakers included Brutus, Atticus (whose recent historical account *Liber Annalis* formed the basis of the treatises), and himself. In *Orator*, Cicero criticizes the new fashionable style—very stripped down and unemotional—that Brutus and others had adopted in their speeches, contrasting it with his own varied and often vehement manner of presentation. By mentioning Brutus's villa at Tusculum and his portrait of Demosthenes, the most eclectic and varied of Athenian orators, Cicero is comparing his own style with that of Brutus.

50 On works of art and collections in villas: Neudecker 1988. Cicero mentioned Metellus's collection of Muses—these would have been *signa*: Cic., *Fam.* 209.3 (7.23.3), in this chapter.

51 An *imago* (pl. *imagines*) can mean a portrait of any kind, but *imagines maiorum* refers specifically to inherited ancestral portraits. The difference among the categories *signa*, *imagines*, sculpture, craft, painting, *objets de vertu* is a long-standing and profound issue in the history of Roman art, as much in antiquity (where Greek vase painting was never discussed and Roman mosaics almost never) as in modern scholarship. For portrait sculpture in funerary and nonfunerary contexts, sources in both Greek and Latin are at issue: Polybius, seeking to explain to his Roman and Greek readers how the rise of Rome in the second century BCE was coming about, devoted most of his Book 6 to analyses of Roman constitutional and military arrangements. However, at the end of this long decipherment of Roman greatness and personal bravery, Polybius included a short section in the language of ethnographic reportage of kinship culture: Romans are great and brave because they honor their ancestors with laudatory rhetoric at their funerals, making an image or likeness [τό πρόσωπον] of them, mounting them in shrines in their homes, and using them in funeral processions with the togas and other implements (*fasces*) appropriate to their achievements (Polyb. 6.53.1–10). The making of the masks in colored wax or wood, ancestral portraits in other media like bronze or marble, and details of their use were later taken up by Pliny the Elder (*HN* 35.6 [35.2]) and by Seneca the Younger (*De beneficiis* 3.28.2). The tradition both endured and spread outside of Italy: much later, Sidonius Apollinaris mentioned his friend Eutropius's images of his ancestors (*imagines maiorum*) in his villa in Aquitania: see Sid. Apoll., *Ep.* 1.6.2, in ch. 5, Villas and *Otium*.

The mention of masks has greatly stimulated the imagination of modern scholars: it appears to solve the paradox of the simultaneity of a certain bold realism and a smooth classicism in Roman art. The arguments are complex and subtle: portraits of elite individuals in the Late Republic have a vigorous realism (sometimes termed "veristic") claimed to be native to Roman artistic disposition, even though adapted from earlier Hellenistic and local peninsular (Etruscan) exemplars: Dillon 2006, 86–98, emphasizing types and methods of Hellenistic character representations; Gazda 1973, Etruscan connections; Zanker 1976b, Hellenistic connections in Italy; Smith 1981, Hellenistic-Roman connections and preceding bibliography; Kleiner 1992, 31–40; most authoritatively on all the issues: Flower 1996. With the expansion of portrait representation in the Late Republic and Early Imperial period, this elite mode of realism was taken up by freedmen at the same time that classicizing modes were adopted by the elite in the late first century BCE and later: Kleiner 1977; Lahusen 1985; Kleiner 1992, 40–42. Further considerations of Roman portraiture: *NP* s.v. "Imagines maiorum" (W. Kierdorf); *NP* s.v. "Portraits" II. Italic and Roman Portraits (R. Neudecker); *EAA* 2 s.v. "Busto" (V. Scrinari); Bažunt 1995, historiography of Roman portraits.

52 On *imagines*: Plin., *HN* 35.4–8 (35.2), famous men in homes and public places; *HN* 35.9–11 (35.2), in libraries and as book illustrations in Varro; *HN* 12–14 (35.2–3), on *clipei* [shields] and other formats or materials; Roloff 1938, 24 and n. 6. For an analysis of Cicero's discussion, here and elsewhere, of the ancestors of the Bruti and other significant families (Scipiones, Servilii): Roloff 1938, 144–45 and n. 9..

53 Earlier in *Orator* (*Orat.* 109), Cicero aligned himself with Quintus Ennius of Rudiae in Calabria (ca. 239–169 BCE), a prolific poet and adapter of Greek plays into Latin and a protégé of such diverse patrons as Cato the Elder, Scipio Africanus, and Marcus Fulvius Nobilior. The poet's multilingual origins (Greek, Latin, Oscan) contributed to his versatility in various literary domains: Aul. Gell., *NA* 17.17.1; *NP* s.v. "Ennius" (W. Sauerbaum).

On the Athenian orators: Lysias (late fifth–early fourth century): *NP* s.v. "Lysias" 1 (M. Weissenberger). Hypereides (ca. 390–322 BCE): *NP* s.v. "Hypereides" (M. Weissenberger). Aeschines (ca. 399–322 BCE): *NP* s.v. "Aeschines" 2 (J. Engels).

54 In another passage in this letter, Cicero mentions that Publius Clodius accused him of spending time at luxurious, morally suspect Baiae, even though Cicero owned a villa nearby and would not have hesitated to make himself visible there in the course of ordinary social obligations. Cicero retorted that Clodius's patron, Gaius Scribonius Curio, had himself bought the villa of Marius (for small money) at Baiae in the forced sales during the Sullan proscriptions of 81 BCE. These are accusations intended to smear rivals in court: Badian 1973, 121, 124–25, 130–31; Haywood 1958.

55 In this letter, "Amaltheum" appears in both Latin and Greek and so designates some entity or character other than, or somewhere in, the villa itself. The villa was called Amalthea from the nearby Amaltheion, the shrine to the nanny goat that suckled Zeus in infancy. By Amaltheum, Cicero may mean a shrine to the nanny goat that Atticus was dedicating in the Amalthea or on its estate.

It is also possible that Cicero is being mildly sarcastic: by giving the entire villa a grand name that would otherwise designate a religious shrine, he is teasing his friend for the grandiose attention he is giving to his dwelling.

Some fifteen years later, in the *De legibus* of 46–45 BCE, Atticus's Amalthea has become an Amaltheum with plane trees, giving it a philosophical character: Cic., *De leg.* 2.1–7 below.

Thyillus was a poet of unknown career in the Late Republic; his epigrams appear in the *Greek Anthology*: Shackleton Bailey 1995, 97. Aulus Licinius Archias (ca. 120–61 BCE), a Greek poet, had been defended in the previous year, 62 BCE, by Cicero in the matter of his Roman citizenship, in the speech *Pro Archia poeta*; Archias had been planning a poetic account of Cicero's consulship, which remained unfinished: Shackleton Bailey 1995, 61; *NP* s.v. "Archias" 7 (C. Selzer).

56 Marcus is Cicero; Atticus is his friend, Titus Pomponius Atticus; Quintus is Cicero's brother, Quintus Tullius Cicero, who also owned villas near Arpinum.

57 Manius Curius Dentatus, consul in 290 and 275 BCE, was one of the farmer-statesmen of ancient Rome whose villa and life were a model of ancient domestic frugality.

58 Odysseus, who rejected the nymph Calypso's offer of eternal life to return to his home at Ithaca: Hom., *Od.* 1.55–60 and 5.135–136.

59 Cicero explains the two citizenships on the analogy of Theseus's foundation of the city of Athens: he orders the people to leave the fields or villages (*ex agris*) and live in the new city (*astu*). He then asks which of the two *patriae* commands the greater devotion; the answer is the adopted *patria* of law rather than that of birth: *De leg.* 2.4 (2.2). By bringing in Cato and Theseus, Cicero aligns himself with both the ancestral heroes and with the grandeur of the Athenian past.

60 Socrates tested the temperature of the water of the Illisus River near Athens when he and Phaedrus found a place to sit down under a plane tree after walking and talking: Plat., *Phdr.* 229a, 230b. The reference to the *Phaedrus* may also evoke the habitation of the Attic countryside—and thus the environs of Cicero's Arpinum villa—by nymphs and other natural divinities such as Achelous, a river god, and Boreas, the north wind, all near the Illisus.

61 Quintus uses the term "Amaltheum" (instead of Amalthea) to give a certain sanctified character to Atticus's villa in Epirus. Its plane trees, like the plane tree in Plato's *Phaedrus*, marked it as a venue for philosophy and wisdom, as did the plane tree in the Platonic Academy near Athens. In the previous dialogue (*On the Laws* 1.1–2), the loci and meanings of different species of trees was discussed: an oak tree (related to Jupiter) at

Arpinum in the grounds of Cicero's villa is related to Gaius Marius, also a native of Arpinum, in Cicero's lost poem *Marius* (a fragment quoted in Cicero's *On Divination* 1.106–119). The olive tree (related to Athena) on the Acropolis of Athens and the palm on the island of Delos (related to the birth of Apollo and Artemis) are also discussed.

62   On the villa Cluviana or Puteolana, see Cic., *Att*. 116 (6.2), 363 (14.9), and 338.3 (13.46.3), in ch. 8, Buying, Building, Improving, and Selling Villas; Cic., *Att*. 353.1–2 (13.52.1–2), in ch. 6, Villa Visits; and Plin., *HN* 31.6–9 (31.3), in this chapter.

63   Pliny means that Cicero's real *monumenta* are his famous writings.

The fame of Cicero's Academia at Puteoli continued: one account (fourth century CE) of the emperor Hadrian's death at Baiae in the summer of 138 CE claims he was buried there: HA, *Hadr*. 1.25.8. In contrast, Cassius Dio reports only that he was buried in his own mausoleum near the Pons Aelius (Ponte Sant'Angelo) in Rome: Cass. Dio 69.23.1.

64   Gaius Antistius Vetus, suffect consul in 30 BCE, had begun as an adherent of Brutus and Cassius but changed sides to Octavian and Antony: *NP* s.v. "Antistius" II 6 (W. Eck).

65   Raising birds in aviaries or other animals for profit or pleasure is part of Varro's discussion on the topic of *pastio villatica*: see Varro, *Rust*. 1.1.11, 3.2.13–18, 3.3.7–10, 3.16.10, 3.17.1–5, and 3.17.10, all in ch. 2, Villas in Roman Agricultural Treatises.

66   On the fine profit that Varro's maternal aunt made on supplying thrush for festivities in Rome, see *Rust*. 3.2.14 in ch. 2, Villas in Roman Agricultural Treatises.

67   Lucius Cornelius Merula, possibly a fictitious person, was a participant in the discussion throughout Varro's Book 3; Varro, *Rust*. 3.2.1–11 and elsewhere, and n. 116, in ch. 2, Villas in Roman Agricultural Treatises.

68   Casinum: *Pleiades* s.v. "Casinum"; *NP* s.v. "Casinum" (G. Uggeri). Besides his property or properties at Reate and that at Casinum, Varro owned villas at Tusculum, Cumae, and in the Vesuvian region; (see Cic., *Fam*. 181 [9.6.4] and Cic., *Att*. 309 [13.33] (Tusculum); Cic., *Acad. pr*. 1.1 (Cumae); Varro, *Rust*. 1.15 (Vesuvian region); D'Arms (1970) 2003, cat. I, 41, 197–98.

69   For later attempts to locate the *musaeum*: Cellauro 2015.

70   Varro's Casinum villa was a topic of invective by Cicero against Mark Antony and the two others of the Second Triumvirate, in the second of his famous fourteen speeches called *Philippics* (September 2, 44 BCE to April 21, 43 BCE). Their name is in emulation of Demosthenes's speeches against Philip II of Macedon in 351–341 BCE: Cic., *Ad Brut*. 2.4 (2.3.4). *Philippics* 2 is a pamphlet purportedly reproducing a speech to the Senate session of September 19, 44 BCE.

In April or May 44 BCE, Mark Antony and an entourage went to Capua and Casilinum to assign land and (illegally) found colonies to demobilized veterans of Caesar's army: Cic., *Phil*. 2.40–41 (102–105). On their way back to Rome along the Via Latina, the men and their leader stopped at Varro's villa at Casinum and lived riotously and lasciviously in it for a while (Mark Antony appears to have proscribed Varro and confiscated his properties, possibly because of Varro's laudatory biography of Pompey [*De Pompeio libri III*] who had recently been defeated at Pharsalus and assassinated in Egypt in 48 BCE). The villa's character as a retreat for *studium*, scholarly *otium*, and virtuous pursuits is Cicero's theme: Varro's scholarly virtue versus Antony's vice.

Varro himself, in his account of his villa in *De re rustica* written some eight or nine years later, does not mention the invasion of his villa, possibly because by then Mark Anthony's position had become unassailable.

71   Appius Claudius and Quintus Axius were participants in Varro's Book 3; see ch. 2, Villas in Roman Agricultural Treatises.

Varro distinguishes two types of aviaries: those for profit (*ornithones fructus causa*) and those for pleasure (*ornithones delectationis causa*): Varro, *Rust*. 3.4.2.

72   M. Laenius Strabo, a Roman knight of Brundisium, is mentioned as the inventor of aviaries by Plin., *HN* 10.141 (10.72).

73   A *tholos* is a circular building, often with a domed roof. The temple of Catulus was dedicated to the Fortune of This Day (*aedes Fortuna Huisce Diei*) and built by Quintus Lutatius Catulus (149–87 BCE) in 101 BCE to commemorate his joint triumph, with Gaius Marius, over the Cimbri. The temple, one of several at the site in modern Rome called the Area Sacra di Largo Argentina, was circular, with exterior columns and a dome set on a solid circular wall defining the *cella*; it was not far away from the Villa Publica in the Campus Martius. It would have been very familiar to Varro's interlocutors: *AtlasAncRome* 1 503–04; 2: tabs. 222 I and 223 (for the building in Varro's day); Haselberger et al. 2002, 54–56, 128 (E.J. Kondratieff).

74   The *horologium*, as Varro calls it, is the so-called Tower of the Winds in the Roman agora at Athens, built and dedicated by Andronicus of Cyrrhus around 50 BCE; it was an octagonal structure of Pentelic marble with reliefs showing personifications of the eight prevailing winds and a vane, sundials, and a *clepsydra* (waterclock): Travlos 1971, 281, figs. 362–78. Varro's morning and evening stars as hour markers seem an improvement on the Athenian model.

75   M. Pupius Piso: a descendant of Marcus Pupius Piso Frugi Calpurnianus, a politician of the early first century BCE: *NP* s.v. "Pupius" I 3 (J. Bartels).

76   Quintus Hortensius Hortalus had been a friend of Cicero's and a famous orator. Varro may be signaling his disapproval of such foolish outlay at a villa. He may also be signaling his disdain for the word *therotrophium* ("monument for wild animals") as the kind of affectation among Romans of giving Greek names to parts of villas.

The reference to "Thracian" is to the primitive ferocity of the people and land of Thrace and to its famous musician, Orpheus, whose lyre playing tamed wild beasts.

77   Horace probably was not given outright ownership of the estate but rather its usufruct, namely enjoyment of its villa, its produce, and the income from the tenants' rent: Nisbet 2007, 14–15. This allowed him to live in quiet, modest dignity and concentrate on his artistic work without the burden of ownership (*Odes* 3.1). The location of the villa is known, but the present state of its remains is later by about eighty years than what Horace may have enjoyed in the 30s BCE: Marzano 2007, 393, with preceding bibliography. Such gifts of usufruct were appropriate to gifted associates or old freedmen or other dependents: Pliny the Younger gave his aged nurse the gift of a small villa and estate in usufruct rather than freehold, possibly on the same conditions (*Ep.* 6.3.1–2 in ch. 8, Buying, Building, Improving, and Selling Villas); Weeda 2019, vii and 296.

78 Maia's son was Mercury, god of good fortune and profit in land and business.

79 Hercules was the patron of those who come upon unexpected good fortune.

80 The bad man is praying to find unexpected treasure in a field to give him the means to buy the land he had previously worked as a laborer. This is contrasted with Horace's prayer to his benefactor to maintain him in the gift and patronage of his little farm. Material wealth and the poet's talent (*ingenium*) are contrasted: the poet owns his talent, but enjoys the farm without the trouble of owning it. He wishes the things he owns (his farm animals) to fatten, but hopes that his talent remains lean and sharp.

81 Libitina: a minor deity, in charge of death and funerals; Schilling 1954, 202–6; *LTUR* 3 189–90 (F. Coarelli); *NP* s.v. "Libitina" (F. Prescendi).

82 The Greek philosopher and mystic Pythagoras forbade his disciples from eating beans, but Horace is looking forward to a plate of them from his farm. In Horace's day and a little later, the vegetarianist rules and the forbidding of eating beans attributed to Pythagoras and his followers were current, so the combination of beans and bacon drippings seems like a quiet joke on the poet's part. Cicero was familiar with both Pythagorean habits (*Div.* 1.62 and 2.119) as was Ovid (*Met.* 15.75–142), who follows up by presenting part of an apochryphal speech by Pythagoras himself, as remembered by an old citizen of Croton (*Met.* 15.143–478). On Cicero, Pythagoras, and Pythagoreanism in Rome: Flinterman 2014, 348–51.

83 On *otium* in Horace's *Epistulae*: Eickhoff 2016b.

84 The god Apollo drives the chariot of the sun.

85 Quinctius, the addressee of the poem, seems to live in a praiseworthy way at a villa near Tarentum (modern Taranto) in admirable isolation; Tarentum, on the south coast of the peninsula, more than 500 km distant from Rome, was a venue where other villa owners, such as Pollius Felix, had residences: see n. 175 in this chapter.

86 The Hebrus is a river in northeastern Greece, famous in Greek and Latin poetry for its beauty (modern Évros, Maritsa, Meriç).

87 The analysis of this complex poem will be elucidated in terms of its versification, literary structure, and importance by Prof. Duncan MacRae in a forthcoming publication. Its language is busy, charged with linguistic and philological intensities and references, which MacRae's study will elucidate. While analysis (and imitation) of Horace's work has been abundant since the eighteenth century, the *Epodes* are the least studied of his poems: Watson 2007.

Horace had contempt for people who, with money, transgressed social barriers. In *Epode* 4, he decried a rich former slave for working a thousand *iugera* worth of farms (*fundi*) in the Ager Falernus, making ruts in the Via Appia with his carriages, wearing an overly large toga, sitting in seats reserved for knights at the theater, and so on, on the principle that wealth does not alter low birth (... *fortuna non mutat genus*).

88 The hints at the beginning ("far away from business dealings and free of money lending") alerted the Roman reader to who the speaker is: no country gentleman (*rusticus*) and villa owner. In fact, he is a *faenerator* or moneylender who has merely aspired to a higher social land-owning level as a country gentleman by buying a villa. As such, he was probably an intelligent, enterprising freedman (*libertus*), given his freedom to engage in business such as money lending, in partnership with his former master (*patronus*) and for himself. By identifying him solely by his occupation rather than his social status (e.g., a knight, or *eques*), Horace places him at a social level unworthy of consideration except as a straw man of satire, despite the fact that the poet's own father had been a freedman and, quite possibly, a banker-auctioneer (*coactor*) and businessman at a low level: Hor., *Sat.* 1.6.71–92.

"Ploughs his ancestral fields with his own oxen": this would have been particularly ludicrous. A freedman would have no such thing as *ancestral* fields: individuals formerly enslaved have no landed ancestors.

89 In Horace's day, freedmen could not aspire to military careers or official civic positions in the *cursus honorum*, so not being in the army made no difference to the speaker's choice of occupation, a fact well known to Horace's readers and amplifying their amusement.

90 Freedmen could be—and typically were—the clients of their former masters and by custom were closely tied to them, hanging around their town houses and villas.

91 Priapus: the divine protector of vineyards and gardens, a guarantor of fertility. Silvanus: a minor deity, protector of both wild and plantation trees, the god of forests (*silvestris deus*). Terminus: a minor deity, protector of property boundaries, honored with sacrifices in February.

92 Plowing with his own oxen, grafting his own vines and trees, and putting up his honey in spring, preserving fruit—these are very doubtful occupations for a villa owner of any wealth in the third quarter of the first century BCE. Rather, they are the imagined occupations of the old Roman ancestors (*maiores*) which, by Horace's day on estates and at villas, would have been assigned to enslaved workers, tenants, or hirelings. For owners, napping and hunting are more likely activities.

93 Hunting was a favorite pastime for villa owners; see Pliny the Younger's letters to Cornelius Tacitus: Plin., *Ep.* 1.6.1–3 and 9.10.1–3, in ch. 5, Villas and *Otium*.

94 By identifying the children of the speaker and the "modest woman" imported from the countryside as *liberi* (sing. *liberus*), Horace identifies the speaker as a freedman (*libertus*) whose children could be fully free (*liberi*). While *liberi* can refer to children in general, and not necessarily freeborn children, Horace himself was the freeborn son of a *libertus*. Characterizing the woman as "sunburned" (*perusta*) with the addition of *solibus*, meaning sunburned from days working in the sun, indicates that the woman had been an agricultural enslaved worker, but now, her freedom bought by the freedman Alfius, she had become the speaker's wife. On children in Roman antiquity: Wiedemann 1989, 5–48; articles in Laes and Vuolanto 2017; specific studies: Vuolanto 2016; McGinn 2013.

95 Having homegrown produce from the estate was better than buying comestibles at urban markets, which was considered common.

96 The Lucrine Lake (*Lucrinus lacus*), a small lake near Baiae separated by a narrow causeway from the Bay of Naples on the north side, was famous for its oysters, first commercially produced by Gaius Sergius Orata and widely considered a luxurious delicacy: Marzano 2013b, 174–79. Scars (parrotfish) are a Mediterranean delicacy.

97 Eating meals cooked from the estate's produce is better than luxury comestibles. The speaker disdains shellfish from the famous oyster beds of the Lucrine Lake, fancy fish, or exotic birds, and so on. Despite his disdain, he seems to know quite a lot about food much richer than the sorrel, olives, mallow, lamb, or goat that supposedly constitute his simple villa feast.

98 Feasting while watching the herd and work animals returning to the villa and the homebred enslaved (*verna*) congregating around the *lararium* at the end of their workday conveyed at least four messages or images to Horace's readers: (1) A deep landscape scene with people and animals seen from afar together with images of rustic work would have corresponded to early instances of such *pastorales* in contemporary Early Imperial wall and easel painting. The bibliography for Roman landscape painting is vast; most recently Zarmakoupi 2023. (2) Specifying the enslaved persons as homebred (*vernae*) indicates that the villa and its estate had been in the ownership of the speaker Alfius for a generation or more, which will be proved false at the surprise ending. (3) The enslaved personnel, oxen, ploughs, sheepfolds, villa, and the estate constituted a package or legal entity in matters of purchase and disposition: in Roman law, the property, dwelling, goods and chattels, equipment, and any rights and easements went together and could not be separated: Kehoe 2016 and 1997. (4) The gathering at the altar of the Lares or *lararium* indicates that the villa and the estate had, in the past, been owned by another person and purchased by the speaker. *Lararia* were domestic altars to which both the owner and his *familia* (relatives, associates, friends, enslaved individuals) came to worship for the safety and continuity of the social unit (see fig. 8). These altars stayed with the dwelling (urban house or villa), but the surprise ending shows it was some previous owner's family altar, not Alfius's.

Horace is doing double duty in this poem: he is mocking the social aspirations of the freedman moneylender Alfius and his pretense to gentlemanly status. He is also lampooning the pretense of ostentatious simplicity that members of the rich, often noble, Roman elite frequently affected (grafting vines, ploughing, when in fact enslaved persons are doing the work, eating plain, healthy, homegrown food, and so on). Alfius may have bought the estate lock, stock, and barrel from a social superior eager to sell for some reason (bankruptcy, impending confiscation, legal difficulties), and in doing so bought the "package."

99 Alfius the city-dwelling moneylender evidently found that owning a villa and estate was boring and not worth the prestige. He didn't last more than half a month (ides to kalends) at the villa, selling up fast and putting his money back into usury in town, to the amusement of Horace's Roman readers. Moral: living at a villa and taking care of an estate is boring, so stay in your lane.

100 Pliny goes on to say that easel painting (*tabulae*) was the medium by which Greek artists such as Protogenes and Apelles became famous, not wall painting in private houses, even their own. Their fame was due to their *tabulae*, their skill (*ars*) to the advantage and credit of their cities, and a shared possession (*res communis*) of the world: Plin., *HN* 35.118 (35.37).

101 Vitr., *De arch.* 7.5.1–2, in ch. 3, Villas in Roman Architectural Treatises.

102 The painter's first name is often given as Spurius but another praenomen-nomen with Studius and Ludius in combination has been suggested; discussion in Robertson 1975, 610; for Studius: Ling 1977, 1–16; 1991, 142–49; *Union List of Artist Names* (*ULAN*) 500057631 https://www.getty.edu/research/tools/vocabularies/ulan/.

On landscape painting: Bergmann 1991; 1992; Kuttner 1999a.

103 A variant for *porticus* in some copies of the text is *portus*, harbors, which can mean large maritime installations or smaller ones adjoining villas.

104 Servilius Vatia: *NP* s.v. "Servilius" II 6 (W. Eck).

105 Members of the Servilius Vatia family had achieved some distinction in the Late Republic, but which of their descendants in the reign of Tiberius this one might have been is not known. His name had satirical value for Seneca: Henderson 2004, 69–79. He was rich, but stopped at the elected rank of praetor in the *cursus honorum*, a mark of laziness and lack of ambition. Seneca's letter on this villa, which he saw only from the outside, is an example of the long literary tradition by which houses and villas represent the character—in this case the moral turpitude—of its owner. Detailed analysis in Henderson 2004, 62–92, with very lively translation, 64–66.

106 Asinius Gallus (G. Asinius Gallus Saloninus, d. 33 CE) and Sejanus (L. Aelius Seianus, d. 31 CE), courtiers of the reign of Tiberius, were executed on the emperor's orders: they and their followers were conspicuously fawning to the emperor and demanded the same from their subordinates.

107 Servilius Vatia seems to have died recently; Seneca says that he had passed by the villa when its owner was in residence.

108 The villa had a stream running through it (*Euripus*) bringing water from "Acheron" or the Acheronian Lake (*Acherusia lacus*), which is probably the lake known as *Acherusia palus* (modern Lago Fusaro) or the *lacus Avernus* (modern Lago d'Averno), both west of the beach Seneca describes: Strabo 5.4.5. Seneca's name "Acheron" for the *lacus Avernus* is an allusion to Vergil (*Aen.* 6.107) which misapplies the name *palus Achernus* to the *palus Acherusia* on the analogy of its being an entrance to Hades similar to the Acheron River in Epirus in northwestern Greece. The mistake is intentional, intended to underscore the deathly aspect of a body of water near the villa.

109 The description of the stream with plentiful fish indicates that the on-site supply of fish was maintained for ornamental purposes but not for daily use as food: off-site sea fishing supplied the villa's needs, and the on-site stream was fished only when the weather prevented the launch of fishing boats. The passage is obscurely phrased, but Seneca may not have understood that channeling fresh water into salt water fish-farming basins would have prevented brackish buildup and acclimatize the water for the health and spawning of the fish: Marzano and Brizzi 2009; Marzano 2010; 2018; and 2020.

110 Detailed analysis in Henderson 2004, 53–61, 93–118; lively translation, 57–61.

111 The villa, as Seneca describes it, was within sight of the seashore: it was fortified with towers, gates, and cisterns large enough to withstand a siege. Such arrangements were needed because the piracy that had dominated the eastern Mediterranean in the third and second centuries BCE had arrived on the Italian coasts by the late third century BCE, and villas—as well as inland villages and towns—were easy targets for pirate bands. Until the effective campaigns of Pompey in 66 BCE, villas by the shore and other dwellings needed fortifications to defend against pirates: efforts against seagoing robbers throughout the third century and for much of the Late Republican period had largely failed: Plut., *Pomp.* 24–26; Cass. Dio 36.20–24 and 36a–37. In 102 and 74 BCE, the Senate had given commands to the namesakes—both grandfather and father, respectively—of Mark Antony for the extirpation of the pirates based in Cilicia in Asia Minor and on Crete, but their success was mediocre: *NP* s.v. "Antonius" I 7 and I 8 (K.-L. Elvers). The breakthrough of action against the pirates occurred in the important campaigns of Pompey, who was invested with *imperium* to extirpate them in 67–66 BCE (*lex Gabinia*): Plut., *Pomp.* 25.2–26; Cass. Dio 36.23.4; Broughton 1951–1960, 2:144 (*lex Gabinia*), 146 (Pompey's *imperium*); piracy in general, sources in Omerod (1924) 1978. Pompey's success in the task, and his defeats of Mithridates in the East, effectively gave Roman fleets hegemony of the coasts from Hispania to Syria, allowing maritime villas and others close to the coasts to enjoy security, and the villas proliferated greatly. By the Early Imperial period, the coasts were largely pacified and secure, as Strabo indicates: Strabo, 8.7.5; 11.1.6; 12.6.2; 14.5.8.

However, such had not been the case in the early years of the second century BCE, when Scipio Africanus retired to Liternum. An extremely charming story about the great general, his entourage, and a band of pirate captains is recorded by Valerius Maximus (late first century BCE–early first century CE) about forty years before Seneca's letter (Val. Max. 2.10.2). It goes as follows: the pirate captains were eager to see and honor Scipio at his fortified villa (called a *praesidium*, military headquarters). Scipio, when warned of their approach but given shouted assurances that they were friendly, ordered the gates to be opened. The pirate captains approached the gates as if entering a temple, shook hands with him, covered him with kisses, then left happy, leaving gifts in the vestibule worthy of a divinity. Conclusion: the moral virtue of a great man has something of the divine. See also Henderson 2004, 94–95.

112 Henderson 2004, 158–70.

113 Vetulenus Aegialus's success in farming is also described in Pliny, *HN* 14.47–52 (16.5). More than 230 years after the death of Scipio Africanus, he had become the owner of the great general's villa at Liternum. Seneca, who described meeting him there, learned a technique of tree transplanting that he had not known. For detailed analysis with Seneca's equation of Scipio Africanus and Aegialus in relation to tree planting: Sen., *Ep.* 86, in this chapter; Henderson 2004, 160–65.

114 In 185 BCE, despite his victory over Carthage in the Second Punic War (218–201 BCE) and great popularity at Rome, Scipio was accused of financial irregularities by Cato the Elder and others, whereupon he retired to his villa. He died some two or three years after and may have been buried at the Liternum villa or elsewhere, but not in the Tomb of the Scipios just outside the Porta Capena near the junction of the Via Appia and the Via Latina. Strabo also indicates (5.4) that Liternum was the site of Scipio Africanus's tomb.

115 Cambyses II (d. 522 BCE), ruler of the Achaemenid Empire; his hubris, cruelty, and madness became proverbial among Greek and Latin writers.

116 To be officially exiled to one's villa or another place was the mark of being a pariah, a person with no direct political presence in the capital. Self-exiling oneself to one's villa or elsewhere was a mark of nonparticipation that often signaled disdain for political life and withdrawal from factions.

117 By Seneca's day, it was rare to build a villa out of cut stone in any method, and certainly not in *opus quadratum*; brick was preferred, or local variations of rubble masonry.

118   By Alexandrian marbles, Seneca may be referring to the granite of the *mons Claudianus* in the eastern desert of Egypt, exported through Alexandria. Numidian stone is the yellow-pink marble from Simitis (modern Chemtou) on the border of Numidia and Africa Vetus in modern Tunisia; its modern Italian name is *giallo antico*. Marble from Thasos is sparkling white. On the marbles, see Glossary.

119   Seneca is sarcastically quoting the current criticism of such a lowly bathing facility.

120   Hor., *Sat.* 2.27. Some texts have "Bucillus" for this unknown person's name: a dandy, a delicate person.

121   Vergil, *Georgics* 2.58.

122   See Martial's lampooning of Bassus in *Epig.* 9.100; for Bassus supplying his villa from the City market, see *Epig.* 3.47 in ch. 6, Villa Visits.

123   See Martial, *Epig.* 5.71 in ch. 6, Villa Visits. Martial mentions Faustinus in a friendly way in *Epig.* 3.2, 3.25, 3.47, and others.

124   In *Epig.* 3.4, Martial says that he had exiled himself to a town in Cisalpine Gaul (Forum Cornelii, modern Imola) because he could not bear to have to dress in a toga (*vana toga*) to maintain himself as the client of a patron in Rome. See Pliny's remark on his Tibertine villa: *Ep.* 5.6.45, in this chapter.

125   I have preferred the reading of *ingratia lati spatia campi* as "big area of graceless land," but the very subtle interpretation by Ann Kuttner is also possible if *Epig.* 3.58 is taken as a comment on the Porticus Pompeiana in Rome, with *campus* referring to the Campus Martius: Kuttner 1999, 369. Similarly, the plane trees without vines trained to them are "infertile" in my reading, but Kuttner's extended interpretation is different and could be correct: Kuttner 1999b, 366–67.

126   Breeding peacocks for the table was profitable: Pliny says that in the 60s BCE, Marcus Aufidius Lurco was the first to do so and made 60,000*HS*: Plin., *HN* 10.45 (10.23); Varro, *Rust.* 3.6.1; *NP* s.v. "Aufidius" I 6 (K.-L. Elvers).

The inhabitants of Colchis were "faithless" because they practiced witchcraft, notably the witch princess Medea.

127   Sassina or Sarsina: A town in the northeast of central Italy, evidently famous for its cheese: Plin., *HN* 3.241 (3.97); *NP* s.v. "Sarsina" (M.M. Morciano); *Pleiades* s.v. "Sarsina."

128   Priapus was a minor god, both the patron and the emblem of fruits, vegetables, livestock, and male fertility. That nothing could be stolen from him means that he wasn't there—the garden and cupboard contained nothing worth stealing.

129   *NP* s.v. "Iulius" II 91 (W. Eck).

130   The Hesperides, daughters of the west wind Hesperus, lived in gardens on islands of the Atlantic, west of the Pillars of Hercules (Gibraltar): *LIMC* 5.1 394–406 (I. McPhee); *NP* s.v. "Hesperides" (A. Ambühl).

131   Fidenae was a town 8 km north-northeast of Rome on the Via Salaria. Rubra, also known as Saxa Rubra, was a village 14 km north of Rome, on the Via Flaminia.
    Anna Perenna and virgin's blood: the worship of Anna Perenna is attested at Rome and in Latin literature (Ovid, *Fasti* 3.523–540) and Vergil (*Aen.* 4.6–53, 630–640); she is sometimes identified as the sister of Dido, queen of Carthage and lover of Aeneas. No known instance of sacrifice, human or otherwise, to her is known, but a grove sanctuary at Rome is known: *NP* s.v. "Anna Perenna" (F.Graf); *LTUR Suburbium* 1 59–63 (M. Piranomonte; *AtlasAncRome* 1 480, 496; 2: tab. Ib at 8; Piranomonte et al. 2002; Capanna 2006; Piranomonte 2010, with preceding bibliography.

132   Milvian or Mulvian Bridge (Pons Mulvius): a bridge rebuilt in stone (from a wood predecessor) during the censorship of M. Aemilius Scaurus in 109 BCE; it crossed from the *Transtiberim* on the right bank of the river (where the Janiculum Hill is located much farther downstream) to the northern part of the Campus Martius: Aur. Vict., *De vir. ill.* 72; *LTUR Suburbium* 4 (G. Messineo).

133   Alcinous was the king of the Phaeacians on the island of Scheria who gave a generous welcome to Odysseus and his companions (Hom., *Od.* 6–13).
    Molorchus was a poor man who hosted Hercules before the Labor of the Lion of Nemea: *NP* s.v. "Molorchus" (A. Ambühl). Domitian had recently established a shrine in Rome to commemorate this instance of hospitality, so Molorchus is now rich: Dufallo 2013: 219–24.

134   Setia: a district and town 70 km south of Rome; its environs had many Roman villas: *NP* s.v. "Setia" (G. Uggeri); *PECS* s.v. "Setia" (B. Conticello); *Pleiades* s.v. "Setia."

135   Vitorius (ca. 60–130s CE) was a patron of both Martial and Statius: *NP* s.v. "Vitorius" 2 (W. Eck).

136   The Euboean fields is a term for Campania in general because Cumae on the Bay of Naples had been founded as a colony of Chalcis on Euboea.

137   The citadels of Romulus may refer to the Servian walls of Rome or to the Palatine Hill. Thybris or Thybridis is a name for the river Tiber: Vergil, *Aen.* 2.782 and 3.500. The right bank of the Tiber on its Etruscan side is Lydian because the Etruscans originated in Lydia. The left bank was its Latin side. The naval basin is the *stagnum navale* or *naumachia Augusti*, an artificial lake surrounded by a park and gardens on the right bank of the Tiber, in the gardens of the Transtiberim. It had been dedicated by Augustus in 2 CE along with his forum and Temple of Mars Ultor: *LTUR* 2 289–94, esp. 291–92 for Mars Ultor temple (V. Kockel); *AtlasAncRome* 1 555; 2: tab. 247; Mars Ultor temple: *LTUR* 3 337 (A.M. Liberati); *AtlasAncRome* 1 555; 2: tab. 247; Haselberger et al. 2002, 179 (Ö. Harmanşah); Richardson 1992, s.v. "Forum Augusti" and "Naumachia Augusti."

138   The flying pole may refer to the constellation Cygnus (Swan), the Northern Cross in the northern sky; it moves east to west in the northern hemisphere's sky from spring to fall.
    Icarian barkings refer to the dog Maera, owned by Icarius, a king of Sparta; the dog became a star after its death and was equated with the

star Procyon in the constellation of Canis Minor and thus with the dog days of summer.

139 Diana's icy grove refers to Alba and Ariccia where Diana, goddess of the hunt, was worshiped; both were sites of villas.

140 Manilius was Statius's patron, a poet, and a courtier of the emperor Domitian: Statius, *Silv.* 1 preface 25–28 (the poet claims his poem on the villa at Tibur was done in only one day); *NP* s.v. "Manilius" II 4 (W. Eck). On Varro's villa at Casinum: Varro, *Rust.* 3.5.8–17, in this chapter.

141 The following clues indicate that Statius's visit was in July: Sirius with its burning star denotes the rising of Sirius in the constellation Canis Major at the beginning of summer's dog days. Nemea's child is the Olympic games, because the games at Nemea in the Peloponnese, normally held the year before and the year after the four-year Olympic cycle, are thus the "parent" of the next games. Olympia was near Pisa on the west coast of the Peloponnese; the games there began at the first full moon after the summer solstice, so in July.

142 Idalian decoctions are herbal perfumes from Mount Ida on Crete. Venus's winged sons are *erotes*, small versions of Eros, sprites of love.

143 *Forma beatis ante manus artemque locis*: this notion that the place is naturally more beautiful than artifice recurs often in villa literature: see Gregory of Nyssa's similar locution about the Vanota villa of Adelphius: Gregory of Nyssa, Letter 20.1–21, in this chapter.

144 Pierian days are days spent in writing poetry, from the Pierian spring near Mt. Olympus which was sacred to the Muses.

145 Varro's villa at Casinum was also on both sides of a river: Varro, *Rust.* 3.5.8–17, in this chapter.

146 The brave young man at Sestos is Leander, a youth who lived at Abydos on the Asian side of the Hellespont. He was in love with Hero, a priestess of Venus who lived at Sestos on the European side; she guided Leander to her with the light of a lamp. Leander swam each night to visit Hero, but one night a storm at sea extinguished the lamp, and he was drowned in the waves: Ovid, *Her.* 18 and 19; for the dolphin image, *Her.* 18.131; *NP* s.v. "Hero" 2 (K. Waldner). Statius's point is that the amicable relations of the two riverbanks at the Tibur villa are unlike the opposing, dangerous shores at Sestos.

147 Chalcis, on the southwest coast of Euboea (modern Evia), was on the strait called *Euripus* separating the island from Boeotia on the mainland. Similarly, the region of Bruttium (part of modern Calabria) is separated at the "toe" of Italy by the Strait of Messina from Pelorus (modern Capo del Faro) on Sicily.

148 Mauretanian wood is citrus wood or thyine wood, a fragrant wood grown in North Africa. These woods were both rare and subject to use by special workmen: Verboven 2007, 21 and n. 129.

149 Nymphs, semi-divine inhabitants of water, stand for water.

150 The text reads "hall" (*aula*) but I have put "halls" because what follows indicates that there are two halls: one each for the two parts of the villa.

151 *Asarota* (Lat. from Gk. *asaroton*, pl. *asarota*): these refer to a famous mosaic floor of a room called the ἄσαρτος οἶκος or "Unswept Room" by Sosus of Pergamum (second century BCE) which showed the remains of shellfish, fish, meat bones, fruit, and vegetables discarded by diners during a banquet: Plin., *HN* 36.184. It was often copied in various versions by mosaicists in Italy and elsewhere in the Roman Empire: Dunbabin 1999, 26 and n. 27, fig. 26.

152 Statius may be describing a feat of hydrological engineering. *Marcia* is the Aqua Marcia, one of the principal aqueducts of Republican Rome (built 144–140 BCE) and the third after the Aqua Appia (late fourth century BCE) and the Aqua Anio Vetus (third century BCE). Its source was northeast of Tibur, ran through the town alongside the Anio River and crossed it, then took a southward loop to enter the City on its east side at the Porta Tiburtina; it was extensively renovated in Augustan times and later. The structures that allowed the water of the Anio channeled by the Aqua Marcia to cross the river itself at or above Tibur may have been partially equipped with lead pipes or channels waterproofed in lead, or so Statius thought: hence, "valiant" lead. It is also possible that Statius is describing a water supply system special to the villa itself: a source of water on one bank was piped to the villa on the other. On the Aqua Marcia at Tibur and its construction: Frontinus, *Aq.* 6–7; on its superior water, Frontinus, *Aq.* 92, and Vitruvius, *De arch.* 8.3.1.

153 Elis stands for Olympia. In various mythological accounts, the Alpheus River at Olympia in Elis ran under the Ionian Sea south of the Italian peninsula to surface on Ortygia, the island that is part of the city of Syracuse in Sicily, supplying the water for the fountain called Arethusa. Aetna (modern Etna) is the famous volcano on Sicily and so stands for the island itself; Aetna's harbor is Syracuse. The fact that the river Alpheus crossed *below* the sea from Greece to Sicily is the poetic equivalent of the Aqua Marcia crossing *above* the Anio River at Tibur. For the myth: Ovid, *Met.* 5.573–641; for the geography: Strabo 6.2.4; Polybius 12.4d5–8; Pliny, *HN* 2.225 (2.106); *NP* s.v. "Arethusa" 7 (F. Graf).

154 Tiburnus or Tiburtus was the founder of Tibur. Albula refers to the sulphurous water of the Aquae Albulae, ponds and springs west of Tibur that drained into the Anio: Vergil, *Aen.* 2.782 and 3.500; Vitruvius, *De arch.* 8.3.2; Pliny, *HN* 31.6; *NP* s.v. "Aquae" A. Albulae (G. Uggeri); *NP* s.v. "Tiber," sometimes known as Albula (S. Quilici Gigli); *NP* s.v. "Albula" 2 (S. Quilici Gigli).

155 The old Gargettian is Epicurus who, though born in the Attic deme of Gargettus, lived in Athens, where he had his philosophical teaching garden. Vopiscus, like Pollius, was an Epicurean.

156 Midas and Croesus: these kings in Asia Minor and Mesopotamia were famous for their wealth. Persian treasure: a reference to the royal Persian vocation of villa owners, see Cic., *Sen.* 59 and n. 77, in ch. 1, Greek and Sicilian Backgrounds of Roman Villas. The Hermus River (modern Gediz) is in Asia Minor and may represent the easternmost point of Statius's geography, while the Tagus River in Lusitania may represent Rome's westernmost extent, in a majestic geospatial analogy.

157 King Nestor of Pylos, one of the Greeks before Troy, was old and wise.

158 Van Dam 1984, 187–95; Bergmann 1991, 50–52.

159 D'Arms 2003, 123, 125, Cat. II, 209–10; Filser et al. 2021, with preceding bibliography; Mingazzini and Pfister 1946, 54–70; Bergmann 1991; Russo 2004 and 2006.

160 "Walls with Sirens' names" is the Bay of Naples in general: the Surrentum coast on the south arm may have derived from the "Sirens' archipelago" (Σειρενούσσαι) of islands: Strabo 5.4.9. The north coast derived from the Siren Parthenope, who was buried, after her suicide, at the later city of Neapolis (modern Naples). Minerva is "Tyrrhenian" because Tyrrhenus led a Lydian population from Asia Minor to Italy, later known as the Etruscan people (Hdt. 6.137; Thuc. 4.109; Strabo 1.94.) Strabo locates a temple of Athena (Minerva) there and calls it *Athenaeum* (Strabo 5.3).

161 Bromius is an epithet of Dionysus/Bacchus, god of wine. Falernian wine made from grapes of the Ager Falernus north of Naples was famous and highly prized by connoisseurs.

162 These elements indicate that Statius's visit to Pollius's villa happened in late summer. The quinquennial festival called the Actia Ludi, was held in mid-August every fifth year at Neapolis in honor of Augustus and was attended by Augustus a few days before his death on August 19, 14 CE: Strabo 7.325 (Actia for Apollo taken over by Augustus); Suet., *Aug.* 18.298; Cass. Dio 51.3; *NP* s.v. "Actia" (W. Decker). The crowns of the Ambracian games refers to the prizes given at the Actia Ludi at Actium in Epirus and in many other Roman cities including Neapolis in early September commemorating the Battle of Actium (September 2, 31 BCE), which took place at the narrow entrance of the Gulf of Ambracia near the city of that name. These perishable crowns were customarily made of twigs or leaves (celery, laurel) or pine branches.

163 Because he was the son of Earth (Gaia) and Sea (Pontos), Phorcys, a sea god, combined earth's freshwater with the salty sea. Cymodoce is one of the fifty Nereids, divinities of the sea and protectors of sailors, and Galatea is one of them.

164 The ruler of caerulean (blue) is Neptune, god of the sea.

165 Alcides is another name for Hercules (Pseudo-Apollodorus, *Bibliotheke* 2.4.12); *NP* s.v. "Alcides" (F. Graf). He guards Pollio's estate while Neptune guards the villa itself, and Phorcys protects the harbor.

166 "An arched portico rises diagonally" or "a portico on an arched foundation": Pollius's villa began at a level higher than the harbor and beach, so a diagonal or zigzag colonnaded ramp or steps were needed to lessen the ascending grade. Such switchback ramps from the sea and private jetties are known in cliffside villas at nearby Stabiae (modern Castellamare di Stabia): Howe 2018, 105–7.

167 Bacchiadic Ephyre: this refers to Corinth, as the ancient ruling nobility of Corinth, the Bacchiads, descended from King Bacchis. Ephyre refers to Acrocorinth, the mountain and citadel of Corinth. Lechaeum: Lechaeum or Lechaion is the port of Corinth. After many events, Ino, the queen of Thebes, while attempting to escape the anger of Hera, fell into the sea at Lechaeum on the Isthmus of Corinth with her son Melicertes. As guardians of sailors, Ino (worshiped as Leucothera) and Melicertes (worshiped as Palaemon [Lat. Portumnus]) were the patrons of the Isthmian Games, held in years alternate to the Olympic and Pythian (Delphic) Games. Besides sporting or agonistic events, competitions among poets were included. On painted images in the villa "of Augustus" at Somma Vesuviana: Aoyagi, De Simone, and De Simone 2018: 148–49, fig. 9.8, and pl. VI.

168 Methymne's poet is Arion, a famous lyre player (*kitharode*) and inventor of the dithyramb, a mode of hymns for singing and dancing in praise of Dionysus. Theban lyre: Amphion and Zethus built the walls of the citadel (Cadmea) of Thebes. Amphion made the stones of the walls of Thebes fall magically into place by playing on the lyre given to him by his lover Hermes; his brother Zethus had no such instrument and had to do the building work by great effort: Paus. 6.20.18. Getic plectrum: Orpheus was the son of King Oeagrus of Thrace and Calliope, the Muse of Music: Pindar *Threnoi* 3 5–12; Thrace, being the home of the barbarian people called Getae, thus claimed Orpheus as a Getic poet: Strabo 7.3.13–14; Plin., *HN* 4.43 (4.11).

169 "Pisa was still empty" refers to the Temple of Zeus at Olympia near the Greek town of Pisa; the temple had no image of the god before the chryselephantine (gold and ivory) statue by Phidias was installed in the 430s. Isthmian ashes: Corinth, on the Isthmus linking central Greece to the Peloponnese and separating the Saronic Gulf from inlets of the Aegean, is often called Isthmian, and the "ashes" refers to the metal foundries in which luxurious Corinthian bronzes were produced.

More important than works of art and luxury items was the portrait collection of ancient great men, poets, and philosophers with whom Pollius empathizes and whose virtue he emulates. Such collections were not uncommon in villas and houses: see Cic., *Orat.* 110 (30–31) in ch. 4, Descriptions of Villas. For portraits in villas, a notable example is the series of small-scale portraits of philosophers and others in the Villa dei Papyri at Herculaneum: Hallett 2019, 74–75, fig. 11.5a–d and nn. 30–35 with preceding bibliography. For sculpture, including portraits of authors and philosophers in villas: Neudecker 1988. For portraits of intellectuals in general: Zanker 1995.

170 Inarime (modern Ischia, usually known as Aenaria by the Romans) and Prochyta (modern Procida) are islands off the north coast of the Bay of Naples. By "Hector's companion (*armiger*

Hectoris) spreads out" is meant the promontory of Misenum: it bears the name of Misenus, at first Hector's armor- and spear-bearer at Troy, then Aenaeas's companion and trumpeter for the Trojan prince in his travels to Italy. Misenus was drowned there because he was in divine disfavor for having challenged the gods to a trumpet contest and so punished by Triton, the master of the conch trumpet: Verg., *Aen.* 6.162–174. Misenus was buried on the promontory, and elaborate funeral games were held all along the north coast of the Bay of Naples.

Nesis (modern Nisida), Euploea, Megalia (Megaride, modern Castel dell'Ovo), Limon: these are the names of small islands ringing the entrance to the port of Neapolis (modern Naples) at the promontory of Bagnoli and Cape Posillipo. Statius implies that Limon was owned by Pollius himself (*tuus Limon*: Stat., *Silv.* 2.2.82). For these islands: Strabo 5.4.9.

171   Parthenope: another name for Neapolis because the Siren Parthenope was buried at the site of the later city.

172   For these marbles, see Glossary. All are Greek except the Syene granite.

Cumae on the north shore of the Bay opposite Pollius's villa, had been founded from Chalcis, a Greek town on Euboea. The term "Chalcidian" became a general name for the entire coastline from Cumae to Neapolis.

173   While both were Graecophiles, Statius, having been born in Neapolis, a city that had maintained its Greek character and culture, seems to claim a superior Greekness, in contrast to Pollius who was born at Puteoli, a city which had a lesser claim to Greekness. Both men had competed in Greek-style competitions in Italy and in towns around the Bay of Naples (as had Statius's father).

174   Bacchus's nectar: wine.

175   The poet hopes that Pollius and Polla won't go to them but will stay put in Surrentum.

One villa is "Tirynthian," indicating probably a villa at Tibur: Tiryns, an Achaean (Mycenaean) fortress-palace, was the Peloponnesian locale from which Hercules set off for his Labors and so refers to the Temple of Hercules at Tibur, a site for villas. The other is called "Therapnean-Galaeasan." Pollius and Polla owned a villa near Tarentum (modern Taranto) in southern Italy, the Galaesus River (modern Galeso) refers to that town, called "Therapnean" because Tarentum was originally founded by Greek colonists from Sparta. Therapne was a village near Sparta; Therapnean was used as the equivalent of Spartan or Laconian: Livy 25.11; Horace, *Odes* 2.6.10; Vergil, *Geor.* 4.126; Propertius 2.34 and 3.32; Martial, *Epig.* 12.63.3; Van Dam 1984.

176   The Gargettian master is Epicurus: see ch. 4 no. 155. Pollius was an Epicurean in his intellectual affiliations. "Vengeful verses" refers to the type of sarcastic, cruelly satirical poetry in iambic meter (*iambus*) of which Juvenal and Martial were the masters; Statius's poem is in hexameters, a verse form better suited to nobler topics.

177   A long marriage and villa ownership obviated the shame of moneylending and, perhaps, low parentage. A little more than 140 years before, in Horace's *Epode* 2, villa ownership had not worked in the same way for the *foenerator* Alfius: Hor., *Epod.* 2.1–70 and nn. 97–98, in this chapter.

178   For a review of Pliny's letters in relation to *otium*: Neger 2016.

179   Birley 2000, 60 (Gallus 2).

180   Clusinius Gallus, to whom the letter is written, was a friend of Pliny's and perhaps a fellow Transpadane; they both may have had Comum (modern Como) as their hometown. Gallus wrote to Pliny asking him to defend Corellia Hispulla, a daughter of Corellius Rufus, also a Transpadane, whose sister had property at Comum (*Ep.* 7.11 and 7.14). Gallus may have been a school friend, like Caninius Rufus (*Ep.* 1.3.1–5), because the letter, as an example of descriptive prose, recalls schoolboy training in ekphrasis that they might have shared: Métraux 2014, 27 and n. 2, also 36–37; Kennedy 2003; Webb 1999 and 2001.

181   Parts of the corpus of Pliny's letters had been discovered and printed in 1471, but the editio princeps was that of the Aldine Press in 1508. For the influence of his letters on later European villa and country house architecture: du Prey 1994 and 2018, 467–70.

182   Details of the description indicate that the villa at Laurentum was used as a winter residence. On possible remains of the coastal villa itself at Castel Fusano: Marzano 2007, cat. no. L59, 309, with preceding bibliography.

183   On *cryptoporticus*: Étienne (1972) 2019.

184   This phrase may also mean that the *cryptoporticus* is warm in the early part of the year and cool later in summer, or warm in cool weather and cool in hot.

185   The aspect of contiguous villas forming a continuous wall like that of a city was noticed for the Bay of Naples in Augustus's day, a century earlier: Strabo 4.5.8.

186   Another source confirms the poor quality of fish at Laurentum. Martial, visiting a friend called Maternus at a villa there, makes fun of its ugly frogs, thin fish, and underweight mullet. Instead, for a real fish dinner at his seaside villa, his host had to rely on the urban market (*macellum urbanum*): Mart., *Epig.* 10.37.5–8.

187   On the site of Pliny's Tuscan villa near Città del Castello (Umbria): Marzano 2007, cat. no. U223, 736, fig. U23b, with preceding bibliography.

188   Birley 2000, 56.

189   For analysis of this opening to *Ep.* 5.6.1–46 and other parts of the letter in terms of *otium* as a picturesque, sublimely beautiful rustic idyll (*die Landidyll*): Harter 2016, 36. On *otium* in general, see chapter 2.

190   Letters were often read aloud to the addressee, hence Pliny's emphasis on the oral-auditory aspect of his message.

191   Some four centuries later, Sidonius Apollinaris describes the setting of his Avitacum in much the same way: see Sid. Apoll., *Ep.* 2.2.3, in this chapter.

192 The botanical name for the Mediterranean genus of *acanthaceae* is *acanthus mollis* (soft).

193 I have hyphenated garden-hippodrome to designate the villa's garden: Pliny means that the garden is in the shape of a racetrack, with one short end at ninety degrees to the long walls and the opposite end rounded for the turn of the track.

194 This suite of rooms: bedrooms (two, in this case), a small dining room, and a courtyard with a fountain constitute a cozy ensemble known as a *hospitalium* (pl. *hospitalia*, Gk. *xenodochium*) in a villa. Such facilities could be allocated to guests as private quarters during a visit in the manner described by Vitruvius for the Greek house: *De arch.* 7.4. The Villa of the Mysteries at Pompeii, the Settefinsestre villa, and others had no less than four such suites: Wallace-Hadrill 2018; Förtsch 1993.

195 Yegül and Favro 2019, 285.

196 This passage and what follows seems to be a prompted by the memory of school-day lessons in correct composition, the introductory exercises in ekphrasis that were parts of the *progymnasmata* or early instruction in writing and ultimately rhetoric that were part of the Roman curriculum: on *progymnasmata*; see discussion at headnote to Fronto, *Ep.* 4.4 (59), in ch. 10, Emperors and Villas.

197 Aratus was a late fourth–early third century poet and physician. Part of his poem *Phenomena* (Gk. Φαινόμενα) treats of constellations, in hexameters: Kidd 1997; J. Martin 1998.

198 Paraphrasing Vergil, *Geor.* 4.176.

199 Pliny is not implying that he owned villas at these places; rather, that his Tuscan villa, in its simplicity and great beauty, was better than any of the villas near those resort towns.

200 For analysis of the specific type of *otium* as freedom (*die Freiheit*) in this letter: Harter 2016, 34–35.

201 Birley 2000, 101.

202 On lakeside and maritime villas: Lafon 2001.

203 "…*quasi cothurnis*…*quasi socculis*": actors in tragedies wore high boots (*cothurnus*, pl. *cothurni*, Eng. buskin, Fr. *cothurne*) to increase their height on stage, whereas actors in comedies wore slippers or socks (*socculus*, pl. *socculi*, light slippers or socks, from *soccus*) suitable for dancing and miming. On *cothurnus*: Ovid's dialogue between *Tragoedia* (Tragedy embodied) and *Elegia* (the Elegy) characterizes the buskin worn by actors in tragedies as Lydian and hard: *cothurnus Lydius* and *cothurnus durus*: Ovid, *Amores* 3.1.14 and 45; *NP* s.v. "Cothurnus" (R. Huschmann). The *soccus* versus the *cothurnus* was identified by Horace as equally adopted by Archilochus of Paros (seventh century BCE) for his iambic trimeter: Hor., *Ars P.* 79–82; Pliny, as an amateur poet himself, may have known this work.

204 Oea was one of the three towns (with Sabratha and Leptis Magna) that constituted the Tripolitan *regio* of Africa Nova between Africa Vetus and Cyrenaica.

205 Her fortune was estimated by her relatives as worth 4,000,000*HS*: Apul., *Apol.* 71.6. Apuleius says she is a *mulier locupletissima*: *Apol.* 91.7–8.

206 While the events before the trial were complicated, the younger son's financial interests vis-à-vis his mother's property and will in court were supervised by an uncle, Sicinius Aemilianus, and a professional court lawyer. The case was heard in the assizes of the proconsul (Claudius Maximus) of Africa Nova at Sabratha, sometime in 158 or 159 CE.

One part of the court proceedings was that the marriage of Pudentilla and Apuleius took place quietly, not in her urban dwelling but in her *villa suburbana* and was thereby invalid in some way. Apuleius counters that it was held out at the villa to avoid the trouble and expense of having crowds of townsfolk gathering for dinners (*cena*) and treats (*sportulae*) at the wedding (Pudentilla had recently spent 50,000*HS* for her elder son's ceremony of coming-of-age [*toga virilis*] and his marriage celebrations). He also justifies using a villa for a wedding by invoking the fertility of nature and women and the Roman ancestors (*maiores*) as receiving the honors of the consulate and dictatorial powers at their villas: *Apol.* 87.11–88.7.

207 The size of the properties and produce and the number of enslaved workers is impressive, especially considering that these were donations by Pudentilla to her son from her own propertied estate. The size and population of imperial estates in the second century CE was comparable: Plin., *HN* 18.35 (comment on African estate owners); Kehoe 1988.

208 Herodes Atticus: *NP* s.v. "Herodes" 16 (E. Bowie). On the almost unimaginable artistic, epigraphic and architectural panoply of the Marathon and Eua Loukou villas: G. Spyropoulos 2018; Papaioannou 2018, 339–51; T. and G. Spyropoulos 2003; see also G. Spyropoulos 2001 (sculpture); 2006; 2015; and 2018; Neudecker 2014 (sculpture); on the Marathon inscription: Keeling 2012; Bowie 2013, 251–53.

209 The villa must have been in the Attic plain, near the Cephissus river north-northeast of Athens.

210 Anna M. Silvas, University of New England, Armidale, New South Wales, Australia, has graciously given me permission to present her translation; I am grateful to her as well as to the publisher, Brill; Silvas 2007, 181–87. Headnotes and prefatory comments have been added for this volume. Most of the notes presented here are condensations of Dr. Silvas's more extensive ones, and some phrases have been added in parentheses to align with other texts in this book; some notes are mine, to follow the way other texts have been presented.

211 Adelphius as "Scholasticus" was an imperial official who rose to consular status for the Galatian region in 392 CE: *PLRE* 1 13 (Adelphius 2 is probably Adelphius 3).

212 Stat., *Silv.* 1.3.1–75 and 2.2, in this chapter.

213 Gregory of Nyssa, *Life of Macrina* 21.1–7: Migne, *PG* 46 960–1000; Maraval 1971. I am grateful to Dr. Silvas for pointing this passage out to me.

214   For the location of the site: Silvas 2007, 182–83, nn. 316, 324, with previous bibliography; the site of Vanota or Venasa is discussed in Coindoz and Jouvenot 1997, 28–29.

215   Mount Helicon in Boeotia was the source of springs associated with the Muses: Hes., *Theog.* 1–35; Paus. 9.25.5–9. Islands of the Blest: islands beyond the Pillars of Hercules (Gibraltar) in the far west, where reincarnated souls rested in a landscape of beauty and abundance: Pindar, *Ol.* 2.69–74. Sicyonian plain: Sikyon, a town northwest of Corinth, was known not for its beauty but as the hometown of beauty because it was the birthplace of many painters and sculptors; Cicero indicates the same: see *Att.* 13.4 (1.13.4), in this chapter. The Peneius River in Thessaly (northeast Greece) ran through the Vale of Tempe, also associated with the Muses and famous for its beauty, the site of Apollo's pursuit of Daphne (Ovid, *Met.* 1.260–269). The Thessalian plains are the delta of the Peneius at its mouth at Eurymenae (modern Stomio) at the base of Mount Ossa: Strabo 9.5.22; Hansen and Neilsen 2004, 718.

216   The image of a golden ribbon may refer to the Pactolus stream at Sardis, which brought pannable gold to the Lydian capital: Herodotus 1.93; Propertius, *Elegy* 1.6; Ovid, *Met.* 11.136–144.

217   Hom., *Od.* 9.19–24. Neritus or Neriton is the mountain of Odysseus's home island of Ithaca, which he describes when identifying himself to King Alcinous and the Phaeacian royal family and nobility.

218   The locus of the banquet appears to have been outside the villa proper, but not necessarily al fresco. It is possible that a large forecourt is intended as analyzed for other villas and *domus*: Speksnijder 2022. It could have been in a separate external *triclinium* or *stibadium*; such arrangements are known in villas of the Roman period in Greece: Papaioannou 2018, 333 and nn. 61, 62. Rossiter's plan of the villa at Yakto near Antioch shows two apsidal structures to the southwest and southeast of a three-sided portico outside the perimeter of the dwelling: Rossiter 1989, 107–8, fig. 4. The apsidal structures could well have served as architectural backdrops for *stibadia*: see Marzano and Métraux 2018b, 23 and n. 129, with previous bibliography; Dunbabin 1991; Ellis 1991.

219   Phaeacia was the kingdom of Alcinous who gave hospitality to Odysseus on his return from Troy; his gardens were famous for their beauty and abundance: Hom., *Od.* 7.112–132. In alluding to the Phaeacian gardens and the banquet in preparation, Gregory of Nyssa seems to align his host Adelphius with King Alcinous and his famous Homeric hospitality, and thereby himself with Odysseus; the banquet in preparation at the Vanota villa may be the equivalent of the Phaeacian noblemen getting ready for a feast in the palace gardens.

220   Hom., *Od.* 7.114–116.

221   As far as I am aware, Gregory of Nyssa's equation of hybrid or composite animals and combined animal-human figures in paintings (e.g., centaurs, critons) with the practice of grafting in horticulture is unique and highly imaginative: it wonderfully extends his theme of art and nature. Grafting and grafting stock of different species (pears, plums, peaches, apples, and so on) was a well-known and widespread practice in antiquity and described by all the agronomists. Palladius is especially complete: his poem *On Grafting* (*De insitione*) 95–98 described peach grafting and was part of his prose manual *Opus agriculturae*. Palladius on grafting different species: *Op. Agr.* 3.8 (peaches), 5.4 (peaches grafted in April), 7.2 (June grafting), 12.6 (winter grafting of peach onto plum, almond, and older peach trees). On grafting in Roman horticulture: Marzano 2022, 130–76.

222   The image of roses and grapes mingling on a lattice or trellis has a surprising resonance in the sonnet *El Desdichado* from *Les Chimères* (1853) by Gérard de Nerval: "Rends-moi le Pausilippe et la mer d'Italie, [...]/ Et la treille où la pampre à la rose s'allie."

223   Gregory of Nyssa's description of the portico as "triangular" [στοάων τριχώνῳ τῷ σχήματι] is given careful consideration by Rossiter, who suggests a square or rectangular courtyard with three colonnades standing before the uncolonnaded facade of the house itself, a preferable solution in my view: Rossiter 1989, 106–8, figs. 2–4. For villas in the western empire described with towers in Latin literature: Métraux 2018, 412.

224   Οἶκος can refer to the whole house, but in this the word designates the main living quarters, which had their facade at one end of the porticoes and overlooking the pool.

225   The description is not clear: where the paintings were, whether on the inside walls or on the facade outside is not indicated. If the paintings were inside, they were apparently high up and visible by illumination under the "lofty roof": it is possible that Gregory of Nyssa is describing windows in the upper wall of a grand high-roofed room [ὑψώροφος] similar to that described (but imagined) by Lucian in his *On the Hall* (Περὶ τοῦ οἴκου; Lat. *De domo*) 9. There are similar examples of walls with paintings high up, "illuminated" by fictive windows, in the royal box in the theater at Herodium: Netzer et al. 2010, which illustrates other examples at Pompeii; Métraux 2015, 144–45 and n. 28.

226   "Your eloquence" [λογιότητι χαρθάπερ ἐνύπιον] is a form of address to his host to compliment him on his learning and fine speech.

227   For Trier: Wightman 1971, 25–70; 1985, 12–67; general account of Gallia Belgica: King 1990. Ausonius in Trier: Métraux 2018, 416–18 (herms from Welschbillig villa).

228   A section (lines 75–149) describes in entertaining detail the fish of the river, where they live, that they are prey to "boyish angling" (*praeda puerilibus hamis*, line 126), spearing, and seining, and even how to cook them (frying, grilling, boiling); Ausonius was justly complimented on the liveliness of these passages by his friend Quintus Aurelius Symmachus (ca. 345–402 CE) in a letter appended to the poem.

229   On his stay at Augusta Treverorum: Auson., *Mos.* 399–437 (on the town and its river), and 448–453 (on his appointments).

230   This excerpt is included because of the prevalence of Pans, Fauns, nymphs and other demigods in landscapes viewed from villas: the model may have been Statius's vision of Pollius Felix's villa at Surrentum or Tiberius's alleged sexual depravities at his villa on Capreae.

231   Nymphs of the water are sisters of the the land Naiads.

232   There follows a long list of famous architects. The "winged man of Gortyna" is Daedalus, the Cretan (or Athenian) architect of the Labyrinth to enclose the Minotaur, the monstrous bull-headed, man-bodied son of King Minos of Crete and his wife Pasiphaë. Gortyna stands in for Crete in general, and Daedalus is the ultimate architect, sculptor, craftsman, and crafty trickster. To escape Crete, Daedalus constructed wings of wax and feathers for himself and his son Icarus: Icarus flew too high, his wings melted in the sun's heat, and he fell into the sea and drowned. Daedalus tried to make a gold memorial to his son but was too sad to finish it.

233   Philon of Athens was an architect of the late fourth century BCE; he worked at Eleusis and designed the naval Arsenal at Piraeus: Vitr., *De arch.* 7.12 and 7.17; Plin., *HN* 7.125 (7.37). Athenians can be called Cecropius from Cecrops, a mythical patron of the city. The "man who was praised" is Archimedes, a philosopher, mathematician, and polymathic inventor whose engines repelled the Roman ships and soldiery during the seige of Syracuse in 213–212 BCE.
   Ausonius then follows with a list of famous Hellenistic architects and others mentioned in Varro's *Imagines*.

234   Memphis stands in for all of Egypt, and the Pharos is the Pharos (lighthouse) of Alexandria built in the third century BCE; its height guided shipping into the roadsteads of the city and was used to deny passage to hostile marine forces.

235   Mulciber is another name for Vulcan, god of fire, thus fire itself. The rest of the description indicates the method by which walls were radiantly heated with hollow jacket tiles, usually rectangular, applied to the walls and covered with plaster; they drew heat from the furnace (*praefurnium, propigneum*), which fed hot air into a suspended floor (*hypocaustum*) and then up into the jacket tiles.

236   The text is fragmentary but, as we have it, proceeds from awakening, activities of the day, going to bed, and dreaming. We find out the setting in a villa only at the end. The subtitle *Id est totius diei negotium* means "This is a whole day's work." The sequence within Ausonius's *Opuscula* has been established in Peiper 1886.

237   Parmeno appears to be enslaved (*puer*, boy), also addressed in Section 2, but not as secretary.

238   Ausonius appears to revere Christ and God the Father in this poem and disdain the pagan divinities, but in other writings he is less firmly Christian. For altars of turf: Juv., *Sat.* 12.2–3 (*caespes*) and 12.85 (*mollis gleba*).

239   The fourth hour is about 10:00 AM. Sosias is the villa's cook.

240   The enslaved secretary would have used a hinged double *tabula* covered with smooth wax (*tabula cerata*) to take dictation.

241   These lines, which end the poem, indicate that what has taken place during the day is *in agro*—at a villa on an estate. The immediately preceding part (omitted here) is about dreams.

242   Gaius Lucilius (ca. 148[?]–103 BCE), a widely admired and very influential poet, the originator of the Latin *satura*, or satirical commentary: Gruen 1992, 272–317.

243   Croesus, king of Lydia in the mid-sixth century BCE, was famous for his wealth: in Greek and Roman antiquity, he is the proverbial rich man. Diogenes of Sinope was a famous Cynic philosopher of the fourth century BCE: he mocked Alexander the Great, promoted poverty, and made an example by living in a *dolium*, a large jar, outside Athens.

244   Aristippus of Cyrene (c.435–356 BCE), though Socrates's pupil of some sort, took an opposite view of his philosophic mission, emphasizing luxurious living, hedonistic attitudes, and sensual delight. The Syrtes are the people of the wide gulf of Syrte (modern Sidra) where Cyrene is located.
   Midas, king of Phrygia, was famous in antiquity for the curse of the golden touch; in two versions of the story, to end the affliction Midas is told to bathe in the river Pactolus in Lydia: Hyg., *Fab.* 191; Ovid, *Met.* 11.127–145.

245   Ploughed land: 200 *iugera* equals 1 *centurium*, or about 50.5 ha, or 125 acres. Vineyards: 100 *iugera* equals about 25 ha, or 62 acres. Pasture: 50 *iugera* equals about 15 ha, or 37 acres. The combined total is 350 *iugera*, or 90.5 ha, or 224 acres. To this must be added at least 700 *iugera* (2 × 350) of woodland to a minimum total of 1,050 *iugera* for the estate, or 263 ha, or 554 acres.

246   The archaeological museum at Eburomagus (modern Bram), which may be Hebromagus, has a collection of metal farm implements and amphoras of Roman date: Bram city website, https://www.villedebram.fr/culture-tourisme/eburomagus-archeologique/#1565251945452-f2a1b083-ffd8.

247   *Lucaniacus* may be the name of Ausonius's villa. By Cicero's *Frumentaria* is meant the third section of the Second Verrine oration of 70 BCE, which was in great part on Gaius Verres's mismanagement of the Sicilian grain supply (*frumenta*) for Rome: Cic., *Verr.* 29–32. Plautus's *Curculio* (weevil) involves a deceitful go-between of that name who seeks to thwart lovers' meetings and unions with trickery (third century BCE).

248   The letter continues in iambic verse.

249   By adding the pejorative *-atus* to *vilicus*, Ausonius is expressing his disdain for Philo: cf. *-accio* in Italian.

250   Dorian usages were regarded as the earliest Greek

language, ethnicity, and habits, so anything "Dorian" gives the authority of antique custom.

251 Phormio is the title and title character of a play by Terence (Publius Terentius Afer, ca. 195/185–159? BCE) produced in the 160s BCE. His character is that of a trickster and defrauder, bluff but cunning.

252 "Greek guarantees" in commercial language means trading with hard cash on the barrel rather than promises to pay or buy later: Auson., *Ep.* 6.42.

253 Philo's boats appear to be coastal and riverine craft for commercial uses: Casson 1971, 159–60 (*akatos*), 167–68 (*phaselos*), 333 (*linter* and *stlatta*), and 217 (*ratis*). The Tarnis (modern Tarn) River is a tributary of the Garumna (modern Garonne), so Philo's field of commercial operation was pretty extensive, from well into Gallia Narbonensis, almost to the Rhone River valley to the Atlantic Ocean at the estuary of the Garonne River.

254 Mark Antony's brother Lucius Antonius was besieged at Perusia by Octavian in 41 BCE. The town of Saguntum in Hispania was an ally of Rome; in 218 BCE, at the start of the Second Punic War. Hannibal invested the town, causing a famine that last nearly nine months.

255 Ceres: goddess of agriculture and grain.

256 Triptolemus was a prince of Eleusis to whom Ceres (Demeter) taught the arts of agriculture in exchange for his kind hospitality. Epimenides and Buzyges are alternative names for him.

257 *NP* s.v. "Paulinus" 4 (M. Roberts); *PLRE* 1 677–78, 1135 (stemma 8); Dümler 1999; Moussy 1974; McLynn 1995, including McLynn's critique of Moussy and the date of the text. On the wider context: Colombi 1996; Ausonius family: Sivan 1993, x (stemma) and 49–73.

Paulinus's grandfather Ausonius (Decimius Magnus Ausonius) had large property holdings in Gaul, probably as a result of his tenure as imperial tutor. In a letter to Paulinus of Nola (Meropius Pontius Anicius Paulinus), he makes fun of Philo, his former (enslaved) *vilicatus* (*vilicus*) who had, presumably on being manumitted, become a trader and quite boastful: Auson., *Ep.* 26.1–34; analysis in Gebara da Silva 2022, 174–77.

258 *Eucharisticon* (*Eucharisticus* in Latin) or Εὐχαριστικόν, is Paulinus's name for his poem: the subtitle in translation is *A Εὐχαριστικός to God in the Guise of an Account of (My) Life*. He tells us that he was in his eighty-third year of life (the "twelfth hebdomad") when he composed it, so around 459 CE: *Euch.* 8–16. For redating of the year of his birth (to 377 CE) and time of composition (to 470 CE): Coşkun 2002, 331–32, nn. 2 and 4, and 333–34.

259 Paulinus had been born in Macedonia in 376 or 377, then lived at Carthage when his father was proconsul of Africa, then had a short stay in Rome but reached Burdigala in 379 during his grandfather Ausonius's consulship. Because his father was very fond of hunting, Paulinus's parents then seem to have transferred to the family's estates near Civitas Vasatica, also called Cossio (modern Bazas), about 60 km southeast of Burdigala: *NP* s.v. "Vasates" (M. Polfer). Paulinus grew up and was educated there.

260 This implies a date of 396 or 397 CE; not directly discussed in Coşkun 2002.

261 On these properties in the dowery of Paulinus's wife: Gebara da Silva 2022, 184.

262 Roman marriages were celebrated with singing and carrying torches of hawthorn wood (*spinae albae*) along the bride's way to her new husband's house.

263 What Paulinus calls the Gothic presence in Aquitania, and what historians specify as Visigothic to differentiate them from other groups, began in 412 and was confirmed by the western emperor Honorius in a general settlement in 418: Coşkun 2002: 338–39, nn.14, 15. In the interim, Burdigala was attacked by a Vandal force, then by a Visigothic force in 414. Without being specific, Paulinus is describing events in these years, from the Visigothic occupation in 412 to 414 CE. A year or two after, his father Thalassius died and his brother's suit contesting their father's will was brought (possibly a half brother from his mother's first marriage or from a previous marriage by his father: Coşkun 2005, 118–20).

The Visigothic king Atlauf abandoned Burdigala in 414, at which time Paulinus's and his mother's houses in the town or its suburbs were ransacked by Visigothic soldiers and burned; he went to live at Civitas Vasatica, where the family owned property. His grandfather Ausonius had called Vasates his homeland (*patria*), though Burdigala was his home (*lares*): Ausonius, *Carmina* 4.1–4 (speaking in the name of his father, Paulinus's great-grandfather); Ausonius, *Opuscula* 1.5–8.

The history of this period is difficult to reconstruct, not least because the sources are later than the events and are contradictory: the primary historical documents can be found in Blockley 1981; Dunn 2015; review of materials: Thompson 1956; history of the period: Heather 1991; Nixon 1992; on the Visigothic presence in Gaul and Hispania: Heather 1992; Kulikowsky 2001; analysis in Coşkun 2002; on villas: Percival 1992.

264 Paulinus's father had married his widowed mother (a second marriage for her) when he was *vicarius* of Macedonia: Sivan 1993, x (stemma). There were properties in northern Greece which had belonged to her and which Paulinus ultimately inherited.

265 In referring to a Gothic guest, Paulinus may be sarcastically indicating that Gothic soldiers who ransacked and burned his house were his "guests." Another explanation is that their presence as part of the arrangement of 418 CE with the emperor Honorius by which the Goths were admitted to Roman territory as *hospes* (guests). Later in the century, this was the case with Sidonius Apollonaris: in his *Carmina* 12, lines 1–19, he complains that his house is full of Germans/Burgundians (Goths) seven feet tall pomaded with rancid butter, so he is not able to compose six-foot lines of poetry (*senipedes stilus*) or endure their garlic breath after their giant breakfasts (*decem apparatus*). Elsewhere, Sidonius complains that the imperial arrangement with the barbarian *hospes* have deprived him of two-thirds of the property he received from his mother-in-law, the wife of the emperor Avitus: the rest went to one or another of the barbarian occupiers, of which there were a number: *Ep.* 8.9.21–44; Wolfram 1979.

266 These were events of 414 CE, when the Visigothic forces under King Atlauf evacuated Burdigala; his mother also suffered damage to her property.

267 *Notitia Dignitatum Occ.* 12.4 (Seeck 1876, 154). The *Comes privatae largitionis* was a court appointment directly subordinate to the *Comes rerum privatarum* who supervised the personal finances or privy purse and the properties of the emperor: *PLRE* 1 677–78, Paulinus of Pella 10. Priscus Attalus was a puppet supported by the Visigothic King Alaric I as emperor against Honorius, emperor of the Roman west; he had two tenures, once in 409 CE for a year, another during the reign of Alaric and Alaric's successor Atlauf in 414–415. After that, he was captured by Honorius and exiled. Paulinus was lucky that Priscus Attalus's reign was short, but Paulinus's imperial appointment identified him as an imperial official, which led to his being treated as an enemy by the Visigoths. At this time, both Paulinus's properties and his mother's were confiscated, though their lives were spared. These events are described in lines 299–326. On Paulinus's court appointment: Coşkun 2005, 122–24, and esp. n. 23.

268 The Ausonius family had long held property in Civitas Vasatis; Ausonius had mentioned it frequently in his exchange of letters with his friend Paulinus of Nola.

269 Paulinus gives a unique and exciting account of complicated events: the seige of Civitas Vasatica, which led to a rupture between the Visigoths and their fellow barbarians, the Alans (lines 337–405). Paulinus had a hand in these events that lifted the seige of the town. The military dangers were, in his view as a property owner, dangerous enough, but there was another: before the siege, enslaved farmworkers had been fomented to rebellion by young, freeborn hotheads determined to murder the local nobility (*caedes nobilitatis*).

At around the same time that Paulinus is describing the disturbances of mobs bent on killing noblemen in Aquitania—namely the first quarter of the fifth century CE—there were destructions of villas and murders of landowners and their families by similar mobs in Africa, as attested by St. Augustine, who attributes the depredations of the *circumcelliones* (tramps) to fervor induced by heretical beliefs (the Donatist movement) leading to social anger: Augustine of Hippo, *Ep.* 76.2; *Ep.* 93.3, 11, 24–25; and Augustine's *Correction of the Donatists* 2.6–5.20; Park 2013, 109–10. Villas were especially vulnerable.

270 On his mother's estates in Greece, see ch. 4 n. 264.

By Argive, Paulinus references the area in the Peloponnese around the city of Argos, but this stands for Greece in general. In the reign of Diocletian (late third–early fourth century CE), Epirus was reorganized with a southern part opposite Corcyra (modern Corfu) being called Epirus Vetus (Old Epirus) and a northern part (largely modern Albania) called Epirus Nova (New Epirus). When the empire was organized again into dioceses in the 360s CE, the two were affiliated with the diocese of Moesia, then with those of Macedonia and Dacia.

271 Besides traveling to Epirus to regain his mother's properties, he also wanted to travel elsewhere—Gallia Belgica, perhaps, certainly elsewhere in Gaul—to claim his grandfather Ausonius's properties, which might have been acquired when he was resident in Trier as tutor to the imperial heir Gratian. Paulinus's relatives seem to have had a hand in the legal depredations of these properties.

272 He considered becoming a monk but then changed his mind (lines 468–478): Coşkun 2005, 135–36, dates this to 427 CE.

273 Paulinus never listed what and how much of his own or inherited property or that of his sons from their grandmother and other family sources might have been. It may have been considerable, despite confiscations or other losses.

274 Paulinus had been married ca. 396–397 CE. He had three children, two sons and a daughter (the daughter was married and had left home before the time of the family's troubles). If the children were born in quick succession, the sons' early maturity when they left their father must have been in the 420s. It is very unclear when and if the first brother's apparently natural death was followed by the second brother's execution due to the king's anger (*ira regis*). After 414–415 CE, Burdigala was no longer a Visigothic stronghold: it had been replaced by Toulouse, and after 415 by transfer of the Visigoths to Spain (King Atlauf was murdered there in Barcina, modern Barcelona). So Paulinus must have suffered the death of his sons when he was in his mid- to late forties, but a date after 427 is also possible, when he was in his late fifties: Coşkun 2005, 135–39.

275 The date of Paulinus's move to Massiliae (also spelled Massaliae, modern Marseilles) is not indicated in the poem.

276 On the state of Massiliae and other Roman cities—Arelate (modern Arles), Narbo Martius (modern Narbonne), Mediolanum Santonum (modern Saintes), Burdigala (modern Bordeaux)—especially with the truncation of the city center by the construction of walls and the consequent reversion of some urban spaces to rural: Garmy and Maurin 1996; Gros 1998b; Goodman 2007; Sivan 1992; Métraux 2018, 407–8, with preceding bibliography nn. 45, 46.

277 Paulinus, by now cash-poor and property-bereft, was apparently still rich in enslaved workers, so he decided to rent land to farm besides the four *iugera* inherited from his grandfather Ausonius, which he owned outright. He does not tell us the size of the land he rented. On Paulinus's enslaved personnel and his Massilian property: Gebara da Silva 2022, 183–84.

278 It is not clear how long Paulinus spent farming in Massiliae: see ch. 4 n. 280.

279 To the small urban house with its garden and four *iugera*,

Paulinus has told us that he had added some more rented land to make a viable farm. This may have entailed a mortgage agreement or loan secured against the land (in addition to the house he built). The combination was sufficiently attractive to the Gothic buyer to amortize whatever mortgage may have existed (or to pay back a loan) and unite the two properties, thereby releasing the encumbrance.

280 Paulinus does not tell when he left Massiliae, when he returned to Burdigala, or when the Goth's offer of purchase occurred. If he was in his late forties, or even mid-fifties when he went to Massiliae, he may have spent ten or fifteen years farming before returning to Burdigala. At that point he was in his mid-sixties and lived in the "semblance" of a house for a while, in humiliating dependency. If the Goth's offer was soon after that, and he wrote his poem at age 83 or 84, no matter how unsatisfactory the amount of money he got for his Massiliae property, he maintained himself in decent comfort for about twenty years as a *rentier*. Despite his self-pity, his efforts with villas and farming were actually quite successful.

281 Sidonius considers Scythia the northernmost outpost of the world.

282 Ameria (modern Amelia) in Umbria produced willow goods for baskets and furniture.
  "A Samian was my mother" is a quotation from a play by Terence, *Eunuchus*, and means something like "I cannot tell a lie."

283 Some aspects of Sidonius's Avitacum resemble Pliny's descriptions of his own Tuscan villa: Plin., *Ep.* 5.6.1–46, in this chapter.

284 Sidonius defines the cardinal points according to the winds coming from approximately that direction: Boreas means north even though the wind itself comes from the northeast, and so on.

285 "Sigma-shaped" means that the pools are semi-circular as in the upper part of the lowercase Greek letter sigma at the end of a word (ς).

286 Philistion was a famous writer and impresario of mimes in the reign of Augustus, five centuries before: *NP* s.v. "Philistion" 3 (W.D. Furley). The disgust for theatrical or pantomimic spectacles became a trope in the later fourth century CE: St. Ambrose inveighs against the spectacle of actors in costume and imitating the gestures of women: Ambrose, *Ep.* 58.5.

287 For these marbles and granites, see Glossary.

288 The phrase "brow of the mountain" is adapted from Vergil, *Geor.* 1.108.

289 Sidonius is inviting his friend to come for a summertime visit.

290 Nightingales and swallows are referenced by their Greek, specifically Attic mythological counterparts Philomela and Procne, respectively. These were two sisters who prayed to be changed into birds to avoid vengeance and death.

291 Tityrus is a shepherd in Vergil's *Eclogue* 1. The Camena is a group of four Latin female deities with various responsibilities (helping women in childbirth, monitoring certain types of prophesy); they have a distinctly pastoral character.

292 Ecdidius was the brother of Sidonius's wife Papianilla and son of his father-in-law, the emperor Eparchius Avitus. Ecdidius was admired by Sidonius for his valor during one of the many Visigothic sieges of the Arvernian capital Augustonemetum between 471 and 475 CE: Sidonius Apollinaris, *Ep.* 3.3. A little before, perhaps in 470 CE, Sidonius became bishop of the town.

293 The Contest of Drepanum refers to the sailing race and other contests that were part of the commemoration of the death of Anchises, father of Aeneas, on the coast of Sicily (Vergil, *Aen.* 5).

294 Sidonius means that the fine water supplied to his swimming pool is like wine: "swimming eyes" is an indication of inebriation as Bacchus's eyes are said to be sweetly swimming (*dulce natant oculi*): Sid. Apoll., *Carm.* 22.33.

295 *PLRE* 2 674–75, Pontius Leontius 30. He was a descendant of Pontius Paulinus, identified in the poem as the founder of the *Burgus*: *PLRE* 1 681 or 676, Pontius Paulinus 19 or 5.

296 The *burgus* or "castle," was a luxurious semi-fortified villa in far western Gaul. The site of the villa has been tentatively identified: Balmelle 2001, 144–45.

297 The *burgus* overlooked the confluence of the Garunna (modern Garonne) and Durdanius (modern Dordogne) Rivers, which were close to the estuary of the Gironde (Lat.: *Magnus Garumna*) in far western Gaul, hence the detailed account of the effects of the estuary's tidal effects.

298 Pontius Leontius, his father Paulinus Pontius, his son Pontius Paulinus, and the villa itself are mentioned elsewhere by Sidonius: *Ep.* 9.125.

299 The theme of Latin rights (*ius Latii*) is important to this poem and to Sidonius's self-image and self-fashioning. He claims, through Apollo's prophesy, Latin rights of citizenship for the Gallic people, including the Pontius family, as if they had always been natural-born Italians. This was not the case: the emperor Caracalla had granted Latin rights of citizenship to all free citizens of the empire by the *Constitutio Antoniana* of 212 CE: Eberle 2021. However, in 455 CE, when Sidonius's father-in-law Eparchius Avitus (an Arvernian and fellow nobleman of Gaul) became emperor, Sidonius claimed in his long poem, the *Panegyric of Avitus* (*Carm.* 7.139–141), that the Gallic peoples had Latin rights by blood descent. The poet has Jupiter speaking: "There is a land that proudly holds its head as born of Latin blood," and continues with other compliments to Gaul, its land, and its citizens. This establishes the Romanitas and the early, divinely sanctioned claim of the Aquitanians to citizenship. At the time Sidonius delivered his *Panegyric of Avitus*, the Aquitanians were under severe, if sporadic, pressure of invasion and occupation by the Goths, so they were perhaps eager to emphasize their Roman and Latin, rather than their local, identity.

On Eparchius Avitus: *PLRE* 2 196–98.

300 These are Roman seige devices for attacking, weakening, or undermining fortifications; some are described in Vitruvius's *De arch.*, Book 10. A *testudo* can mean an infantry movement in which the soldiers cover themselves with their shields and move in unison; it can also be a movable defensive roof on wheels. A mantlet shed is similar.

301 For all these marbles, see Glossary. The purple marble with a reddish blush may be Chian marble (*portasanta*). Sidonius appears to say that such marbles were not part of the architectural elements of the bath building but that marble slabs were an *incrustatio* or covering of the front wall of the villa. Numidian marble (*antico giallo*) is from Simitis (modern Chemtou) in North Africa; it does not look at all like ivory.

302 The description of the portico at the entrance to the villa is difficult. I interpret "…double portico…rising above a double floor (*area*)" as two parts or sides of a portico raised on some steps or platform above grade rather than a two-story portico. The "double Wain" (wagon) is Ursa Major and Ursa Minor (Big Dipper and Little Dipper), the constellation or asterism that points to celestial north; by "does not know the double Wain," the poet means that the portico faces in any direction except north, as he will specify later on. For poetic flourish, the play on thrice-repeated *duplex* (double portico, double floor, and double Wain) was irresistible to Sidonius.

303 This indicates that the two sides of the raised portico are semi-circular or partially curved, with the two arcs of the portico ("horns") being visible to each other (…"Looking back upon themselves") across their curve. A large semi-circular colonnade facing southeast and curving toward the entrance is known at the Late Roman villa at Montmaurin in Aquitania (fig. 21 and Métraux 2018, 409–10, fig. 21.2), and there are smaller ones at other grand villas in Gaul and Sicily: Balmelle 2001, 379–85.

304 In other words, the entrance portico faces south. Sidonius could not resist the paradoxical play of the crescent-moon shaped atrium (*atrium lunatum*) full of sun (*sol*) all day.

305 The section beginning "…father of Pharnaces…" introduces a description of the wall paintings that appear to be on the walls of the *atrium lunatum*; the scenes shown in these paintings are of the Third Mithridatic War (73–63 BCE), the last of the wars of Rome against Mithridates VI, king of Pontus (First Mithridatic War, 88–84 BCE; Second, 83–81 BCE). Mithridates was the father of Pharnaces II of Pontus, king of Cimmerian Bosporpus (lands north of the Black Sea) after the death of his father.

306 The sacrifice of a chariot (*quadriga*) and horses to Neptune refers to an incident in the spring of 74 BCE during the first year of the Third Mithridatic War: Mithridates sacrificed four white horses to Neptune, god of the sea, to ask for the god's help for his newly built navy: Appian, *Mith.* 70.

307 The wall painting depicts more incidents of 73 BCE in the Third Mithridatic War. Cyzicus, a city strategically located on a peninsula in the Sea of Marmara on the north coast of Asia Minor, had allied itself with the Roman invasion army; Mithridates laid a siege to the city. In turn, the Roman general L. Licinius Lucullus counter-besieged Mithridates's besiegers, forcing them to near starvation. To give courage to the besieged Cyzicans, Lucullus sent them a message telling them that help was on the way, by way of a soldier equipped with a flotation device made of skins: the soldier got wet but kept the message dry and delivered it successfully: Florus, *Epitome* 40.15–16.

308 These are references to agricultural fertility. The agricultural lands of the Greek colony of Leontinoi or Lentini on the north coast of Sicily were famously fertile, as were those of Mygdonia, the region at the northern head of the Gulf of Therma (modern Thessaloniki) in Thrace. Gargarus is a peak of the mountainous massif of Mount Ida in northwestern Asia Minor (modern Kaz Daği) associated with Rhea, a Titaness, daughter of Gaia (Earth) and Ouranos (Sky); she was generally associated with harvests and the earth, sometimes known as Ops or plenty, abundance.

Attic Eleusis is a town northwest of Athens at which the mystery cult of Demeter (Ceres), goddess of agriculture, and her daughter Persephone, queen of Hades or the Underworld, was centered. Demeter/Ceres's daughter Persephone was kidnapped by Hades, god of the Underworld. Prince Triptolemus of Eleusis welcomed the goddess when she was mourning the loss of her daughter; to reward his hospitality, mother and daughter (after her return) taught the prince the arts of sowing, reading, harvesting, saving seed grain, and storing and milling wheat grain, and they sent him out to teach other humans these agricultural arts.

In Greek and Roman mythology, the change from a hunting-gathering society (hence acorns) to agriculture marked the transition from a natural, primitive, peaceful, and thus ideal Golden Age to one of civilization, cities, wars, and social strife. (Hesiod, *Works and Days* 109–126; Plato, *Cra.* 397e; Ovid, *Met.* 1.89–150, with "land of milk and honey at 111–112).

309 To be cool in summer, the summer portico faces north. The astrological sign of Leo (the Lion's mouth) denotes the period in late summer (July to mid-September) when the sun transits that constellation. The Bear of Lycaon refers to Callisto, a devotee of Minerva (Artemis). Callisto, a daughter of King Lycaon of Arcadia, was raped and impregnated by Jupiter (Zeus); she was saved from the vengeance of Jupiter's wife Juno (Hera) by being changed into the constellation Ursa Major, therefore the asterism pointing to the North Star. Sidonius means that the heat coming out of the bath building's furnace is dispersed by the northward orientation of the portico.

310 Pallas is another name for Athena, goddess of wisdom and weaving; as patron of the latter, weaving rooms are her temples.

311 Pontius Leontius's wife uses her distaff, a pointed stick used to gather wool into skeins. In her case, it is used to wind wool that has been dyed with precious Syrian purple dye made from the bodies of murex snails, a speciality of the Phoenician coast of modern Syria-Palestine. The *matrona* of the house, having made a skein of purple-dyed wool, then processes it through a sieve of reeds and adds gold thread before sending the wool to the loom. She is weaving cloth of purple and gold, a fabric of high royal—even divine—connotations.

312   The wall paintings of Jewish history indicates that Pontius Leontius's household as well as his wife and he were Christians; Jewish, and of course Roman, history were suitable themes for a noble Christian and Aquitanian family at the time (cf. Paulinus of Nola, *Carm.* 27.508–595 on wall paintings on Old Testament themes). Sidonius, in a letter to a friend (*Ep.* 8.12.5), remarks that "Apollo is . . . not a god for you": the pagan gods were welcome as presences in poetic art rather than an expression of a family's faith.

313   Daphne, a Naiad or spirit of springs and other sources of water and the daughter of a river god, was pursued by Apollo; Daphne called on her father to save her from rape and was turned into a laurel tree, which then became Apollo's symbol. Crowns of laurel were awarded to poets, singers, and artists of all kinds, as well as victorious generals and emperors. The phrase "fear-struck Daphne believes in me" (*mihi credere*) may also mean that, in the poet's imagination, Daphne relies on the *poet* to save her. Story of Daphne: Ovid, *Met.* 1.452–567.

314   Arcturus is the star near the constellations or asterisms of Ursa Major and Ursa Minor (Big and Little Dippers) and denotes celestial north, hence arctic.

315   Apollo is being sarcastic and teasing his brother Bacchus: the phrase "the temple of the greatest god of all" is a back-handed compliment to where he will take up residence (not a reference to a Christian chapel in the villa). Bacchus, Apollo says, will live in the storeroom (*apotheca*) and cellar (*penus*) of the *burgus*, facilities for the estate's produce; as Apollo is speaking to Bacchus, god of wine, *penus* may refer to a wine cellar—that is where Bacchus would normally live and so have his temple.

316   Castalia is the spring at the entrance to the sanctuary at Delphi, sacred to Apollo and the Muses.

317   Silenus is another name for Bacchus, Apollo's half brother, and Nysa is the place where the Nyseids or nymphs raised him from babyhood, saving him from the vengeance of Juno (Hera). Bromius ("roaring") is an epithet for Bacchus.

Phoebus ("shining") is an epithet for Apollo, and Parnassus is the mountain where his oracular sanctuary at Delphi was located. Cirrha is the region around Delphi.

Naxos is the Cycladic island where Bacchus, on his return from India, found Ariadne, princess of Crete, who had been abandoned there by Theseus after killing the Minotaur. Bacchus fell in love with Ariadne and made her his spouse.

318   For general considerations including gifts to local churches, communities, and bishoprics: Ripoll and Arce 2000.

319   Paula of Rome: *PLRE* 1 674–75; *NP* s.v. "Paula" (S. Letsch-Brunner). The main outlines of Paula's life and renunciation of her status as a woman of senatorial status in Rome are known from Jerome's letter to her daughter Eustochium: Jerome, *Ep.* 108, dated to shortly after her death in Jerusalem in 404 CE. She was the daughter of two families said to have been descended from ancient noble Roman *gentes* of the second century CE (Cornelii Scipiones, Valerii Publicolae, and Sempronii Gracchi) on her mother's side, and from Agamemnon on her father's side, thus uniting ancient Roman and legendary Greek lines of descent, at least according to the standards of family claims and reputations in the early fourth century CE: Mommaerts and Kelley 1992, 120–21; Matthews 1998, 23 (Gracchi), 352 and 356 (Valerii). Descent from the royal Atreus and the ill-fated Atreides, of which Agamemnon was a member, seems a strange claim. Her marriage had resulted in daughters and a son, but the prospect of an uneventful life of easeful luxury did not suit her faith. She remained in possession of her wealth but used its income for poor relief.

320   Paulinus of Nola (Meropius Pontius Paulinus) and Therasia: on Paulinus, *PLRE* 1 681–83; *NP* s.v. "Paulinus" 5 (M. Günther); on Therasia, *PLRE* 1 909. The couple appear to have sold their properties in Gaul, Hispania, and Italy outright, including an estate at Fundi near Nola (*Ep.* 32.17). After a distinguished official career in Rome (suffect consul in 378) and as proconsular in Campania where he had come to admire the worship of a local saint, Felix of Nola (martyred ca. 253–255 CE), Paulinus returned to his native Aquitania and his hometown Burdigala (394 CE), then went to Barcina (modern Barcelona). There he married Therasia, an heiress from Hispania Tarraconiensis (many of his letters are sent in both their names). He was ordained in 395 CE and became bishop of Nola some years later.

The couple sold their properties around the same time: directly stated in his *Ep.* 1.37, obliquely stated in *Ep.* 4.4, and Paulinus renounced both literary pursuits and his properties in *Ep.* 5.6 (396 CE), even though most of his letters and poems date from after that. The theme of renunciation of property is developed in *Ep.* 24.1, 3, and 7, and at length in *Carm.* 21.428–473 (also in *Carm.* 15, 16, 18, 23, 24, 26, and 27–29). He compliments others on doing the same: *Ep.* 13.13 to Vammachus (funding a banquet for the poor in St. Peter's basilica). He defined his renunciations saying: "Others can enjoy the annual income (*pensitatio*) of the profit on inherited estates (*reditus de patrimoniis*)," but he will enjoy income from the love of Christ: *Ep.* 39.1. He called his properties *facultates*, which means both land and other income (loans, investments, rents, resources in general); Therasia's properties are said to be *praedia*, landed estates. The couple then went to live at Nola in Campania, where they embellished and developed a pilgrimage shrine to Felix: Ambrose, *Ep.* 58.1–3. The architectural works at Nola are described in Paulinus's poems (*Carm.* 21.365–394 and 428–473), and in a detailed letter to his friend Sulpicius Severus (*Ep.* 32.10–12) which also mentions a basilica at Fundi (*Ep.* 32.17), both datable to ca. 403–404 CE; modern account for these and later buildings at Nola in Lehmann 2004, with preceding bibliography; Trout 1996. Paulinus even describes paintings of the history of the Jews on the portico walls of the forecourt of the basilicas that he had painted, intending to amuse the simple pilgrims and thereby prevent them from drinking too much on holidays: *Carm.* 27.508–595, and cf. Sidonius Apollinaris, *Carm.* 22.200–201 (paintings in a secular setting of the same subject). His idea of organizing pilgrims is a variation on earlier forms of hospitality at villas: Mratschek 2001.

Some themes of Paulinus's letters are replete with the social habits of villa owners and the knowledge of agriculture that the *dominus* of an estate would have known, even though some are also allusions to the earth- and agriculture-bound aspects of the Old Testament and the Parables of the New Testament: in *Ep.* 5.16, he mentions that he is leaving the (little) kitchen garden (*hortulus*) of secular pursuits to join Christ in the larger vineyard of faith, and he sends some Campanian bread (*panis Campanus*) in a wooden box to his addressee as a *xenia*, in the manner of many earlier owners of villas. In *Ep.* 11.14, he says that he is exchanging a little garden (*hortulus*) for the larger *hortus* of Heaven, and in *Ep.* 10.2–3, spiritual wealth and manuring fields are equated. Christ's cross is a plough (*Ep.* 31.2), perhaps in response to the gift of a sliver of the Holy Cross given to him by Melania the Elder when she visited Nola in 400 CE (*Ep.* 29.5–13). Like Cicero for Atticus's villa at Buthrotum in Epirus, he sent his friend Sulpicius Severus some little verses to be written on the walls of his *basilicae* at Primuliacum, much like the verses that Sidonius Apollinaris had in his bath at the Avitacum villa: *Ep.* 32.5 and 9–10; analysis in Baratte 2017. Paulinus, touchingly, says that Felix, the local saint whom he revered, gave up his property to become a mere *plantator* who cultivated just three *iugera* (less than a hectare, less than two acres) rented from a neighboring tenant farmer (*colonus*); he did so with his own hands and without any extra help in the form of a servant or enslaved person (*famulus, Carm.* 16.284–289 and *Carm.* 21.84–104). This gave Felix the character of the *maiores*, the heroic Roman ancestors who cultivated their small plots with their own hands yet served the Roman state as consuls, dictators, and so on.

321 Claudius Postumus Dardanus (late fourth–early fifth century CE), a *patricius* and twice praetorian prefect of Gaul, together with his wife and brother, founded a Christian community on his own property. On Claudius Postumus Dardanus: *PLRE* 2 346–47; *NP* s.v. "Dardanus" 5 (H. Leppin); on Naevia Galla (his wife), *PLRE* 2 491; on Claudius Lepidus (his brother): *PLRE* 2 675. Jerome corresponded with Dardanus in 414 CE on a matter of biblical interpretation after Dardanus's second praetorian prefectural appointment: Jerome, *Ep.* 129.

Dardanus founded the community on his own estate (*in agro proprio*) at Segustero (modern Sisteron), near the provincial capital of Gallia Narbonensis Secunda (Narbo Martius, modern Narbonne), sometime late in the first decade of the fifth century CE. The property was renamed *Theopolis*, "God's city." It was complete with walls and gates (*muri, portae*); the new place-name implied a new religious character for the property; the source of this information is an inscription: *ILS* 1279. On the Theopolis: Salway 1981, 452–53; Matthews 1998, 323–35; Ripoll and Arce 2000, 97; Métraux 2018, 412 and n. 81.

322 Sulpicius Severus became famous for his *On the Life of St. Martin* (*De vita Beati Martini*), bishop of Civitas Turonum (modern Tours) from 371 to his death in 397 CE. This was an edifying and miracle-filled biography, which found a wide readership; Sulpicius also wrote letters, a world history (*Chronicorum*), and some theological works in dialogue. Instead of selling his family property, Primuliacum, in Aquitania, around 394 CE he appears to have converted it to Christian and communitarian and hospitable uses as its *donor* and a dweller in the new community (but retaining his workers, still enslaved, as personnel for the new hostel): Paulinus of Nola, *Ep.* 24.1, 24.3, and 24.7; *Ep.* 30.2–3 and 6; *Ep.* 32.1–9 (*PL* 61, cols. 322–23 and 330–32;) Alciati 2011, with preceding bibliography; Métraux 2018, 414 and n. 99. For his property, which used to be indicated as Prémillac in the Périgord but no longer with certainty, *Pleiades* s.v. "Primuliacum." On Sulpicius: *NP* s.v. "Sulpicius" II 14 (U. Eigler); *PLRE* 2 1006; detailed biography in Ghizzoni 1983.

Sulpicius built two *basilicae* with a baptistry between them; the churches contained important saints' relics and a fragment of the True Cross sent to him by Paulinus (which had been a gift from Melania the Elder); Paulinus sent him verses to be written on the walls of the complex. Like Paulinus, Sulpicius retained some of the habits of villa owners: in the baptistry, around the immersion font, he wished to set up two portraits: one of St. Martin, the subject of his biography and by then venerated as a saint, the other of his friend Paulinus of Nola, whom he regarded as a living saint. The idea was for the catechumens to enter the baptismal water with the *imago* of the deceased saint as ancestor and to emerge, reborn, with the example of the living one: the *exempli* of the past and present in the new Christian family through portraits, as in earlier *domus* and villas. When Paulinus received a request for his portrait from his friend Sulpicius, he demurred on religious grounds, but added that if the artist botched the work, it might not be a good likeness (Paulinus of Nola, *Ep.* 30.6). A letter attributed to Sulpicius also expresses his anger at the mistreatment of some poor farmers (*miseri aratores, coloni*) on pleasant villa estates (*amoena diversoria*); he goes on to say that a *iugerum* (in other redactions, twenty *iugera*) needs more than one *cultor*. This letter reflects his past: Sulpicius had been a lawyer, but as a villa owner, he is scolding an interloper (a certain Salvius) for usurpation and cruel bad management of an estate (Sulpicius Severus, *Ep.* 5, in *PL* 20, cols. 243–44).

In whatever way Paulinus of Nola and Sulpicius Severus maintained their property, their personnel remained enslaved. The position of enslaved persons and the persistence of enslavement in Gaul and in Christian literature of the fourth and fifth centuries is discussed in detail by Gebara da Silva 2022, 170–87, esp. 186; also in Gebara da Silva 2022, on Paulinus of Pella and his enslaved assistant, 183–85; for a fifth-century play called *Querolus*, 177–79; and on Salvian of Marseilles (ca. 400–480 CE) and his essay *On the Government of God* (*De gubernatione Dei*), 179–83.

323 Flavius Magnus Aurelius Cassiodorus, sometimes with the addition of "Senator" to his name, had one of the most distinguished possible careers at the court of the Gothic and Visigothic king Theodoric and his son Athalaric at Ravenna, beginning as the manager of the palace (*quaestor sacri palatii*, 507–511 CE) and rising to praetorian prefect for Italy (533–537 CE). At this time, he compiled a collection of letters on various administrative topics (*Variae epistulae*) as a record of official acts, which also contains disquisitions on various topics: purple dye (Cassiod., *Var.* 1.2), public works at Rome (*Var.* 1.21), an astonishing description of the delights of sea and land at Baiae (*Var.* 9.6), and many others. On Cassiodorus: *PLRE* 2 265–67, Cassiodorus 4; on his ancestors: *PLRE* 1 263–65.

After time spent at Constantinople around 550 CE, Cassiodorus returned to ancestral estates near Squillace on the south coast of Bruttium (in modern Calabria), which he had inherited from three generations of Cassiodori, also high civil servants since the mid-fifth century. There he founded a monastic community of cenobitic monks called *Vivarium*, with an adjacent "desert" for anchorites/eremitics (hermit monks) called *Castellum* (Cassiod., *Inst.* 29.1). To get the Vivarium on a sound basis of physical tasks and literary work, he wrote the *Institutions* (*Institutiones divinarum et saecularium litterarum*, ca. 555 CE). The *Institutions* equipped the monastic community with instructions for work (land management, Latin bibliography on farming and fishing including Columella: *Inst.* 28.5–6) and literary tasks (copying and correcting classical and Old and New Testament texts, correct spelling, and so on): they were intended to give space and occupation to monks of lesser or greater levels of education and intelligence.

Cassiodorus, like Paulinus of Nola and Sulpicius Severus, had a villa owner's eye for what was needed in the way of making the Vivarium agriculturally viable.

324 Jerome's letter to Paula of Rome's daughter Eustochium indicates that the saint never sought her wealth or charitable works to be discussed or recorded: *Ep.* 108.3. Melania the Younger avoided meeting the Augusta Serena (the emperor's mother-in-law) to avoid her compliments: Gerontius, *Vit. Mel.*, Latin redaction 11.2. This detail is not included in the Greek redaction.

325 See the description of the villas in Sid. Apoll., *Ep.* 2.9.1–10, in ch. 6, Villa Visits.

326 Melania the Elder (ca. 340–410): *PLRE* 1 592–93, Melania 1; she was widowed early (ca. 362), leaving a son in Italy: *PLRE* 1 753 and 754, Publicola 1 and Publicola 2. She spent time in Alexandria, with the Desert Fathers in the Nitrian district, and in Jerusalem, returning in 400 CE, when she visited Paulinus of Nola and gave him a sliver of the Holy Cross, then returned to Palestine. It is possible that her stay in Italy was to sell her Sicilian properties: Palladius, *Lausiac History* 54.

Melania the Younger: *PLRE* 1 593, Melania 2; Valerius Pinianus: *PLRE* 1 702; on the Valerii and Valerii Publicolae: *NP* s.v. "Valerius" (K.-L. Elvers). Melania and Pinianus had two children who had died young; after that, they began the great donations and eventually settled in Palestine, at which point Valerius and Pinianus are described and lauded by Paulinus of Nola: *Carm.* 21.294–305. She corresponded with, and was mentioned by, Augustine and Jerome. She estimated her annual income in the range of 120,000 gold pieces, not including the value of her properties (*mobiles*, rentals, leases) and her husband's income and properties: *Vit. Mel.* Latin 15.1.

327 Citation for the Greek redaction, *Vit. Mel.* Greek; for the Latin redaction, *Vit. Mel.* Latin. For texts, see Gorce 1962 (Greek); Laurence 2002 (Latin). For a lively recent translation of the Latin text and complete learned account of Melania the Younger's life, see Clark 2021. For analysis of the differences between the Greek and Latin redactions, see Laurence 2002, 109–41.

328 The Greek and Latin redactions differ in their accounts of Publicola's death (ca. 403 or 404 CE?) but confirm that the young couple—now 20 and 23 respectively—began to live an even more rigorous life than before. To do so, they left Rome and went to live at their suburban villa.

329 The Greek redaction is more pointed by quoting the enslaved workers' words directly.

330 Melania and Pinianus had decided, after several years of connubial relations and the death of two children, to suspend physical relations for what would be the rest of their lives, hence she calls him *frater* (brother). The locution is not in the Greek redaction.

331 Later on, the couple listed more properties in Mauretania besides those in Numidia and Africa (Africa Vetus): *Vit. Mel.* 20.

332 In both the Latin and Greek redactions, the stately coming of the couple into the presence of the *Augusta* Serena, the protocol or nonprotocol of Melania's head covering, the gifts (embroidered silk cloth and clothes, silver, and rock crystal goblets) that Melania offered Serena and her entourage, and the *Augusta*'s graciousness and condescension, indicate the elaborate rituals of the imperial court. The *Augusta* even greeted the couple at the entrance portico of the palace, hugging Melania and kissing her eyes, seating her on her own golden throne: *Vit. Mel.* 12.1. The *Augusta* asked the emperor Honorius to arrange for the sale of the couple's properties empire-wide. There are chronological difficulties with this account: Clark 1984, 101; Laurence 2002, 177 n. 3. (It is at this point that Gerontius indicates his presence in Melania's entourage, in the Latin redaction). The gifts accepted, the *Augusta* sent the couple home with compliments and an escort. They tried to sell their palatial *domus* in Rome, but it did not sell and was later burned in the Visigothic sack of Rome (410 CE): *Vit. Mel.* 15.2. In the Greek redaction, they offered to sell it to the *Augusta*, but she demurred, saying that even she "could not buy it at its real worth," but she accepted Melania and Pinianus's offer of some precious marbles (οἱ μάρμαροι πολυτίμο): *Vit. Mel.* Greek 14.2. The sales completed, they distributed the funds in relation to the needs of the recipients: *Vit. Mel.* 15.1–6.

333 Where this villa was is uncertain; possible locations in Italy, Sicily, and Numidia have been proposed. For the number of workers, the Latin redaction has a total of 24,000 enslaved workers, but one manuscript has only forty workers in each of the sixty villa-estates, so 2,400: Laurence 2002, 190–91, n. 6. Either way, the number of villas and enslaved personnel was substantial.

334 Alypius was a friend and traveling companion of Augustine: *PLRE* 1 47–48, Alypius 8.\

335 By this point, Melania and Pinianus had been advised that selling and giving to the poor or to churches and monasteries or other communities needed to be amended: the bishops Augustine of Hippo, Alypius of Thagaste, and Aurelius of Carthage advised them to give capital funds, instead of cash, to ensure reliable income to the institutions they funded: *Vit. Mel.* Greek 20.

336 See ch. 4 n. 322.

337 The letter informs the local bureaucrats of Istria that the Gothic administration was converting money taxes (*solidi*) to contribution in kind because of the peninsula's estates having produced a bumper crop of wine, oil, and grain in the tax period (indiction) of 557–558 CE. The villas of Istria are numerous and some magnificent from the second century CE into Late Antiquity: De Franceschini 1999; Bowden 2018.

338 *PL* 51, cols. 617–38, authorship noted as *incertus*. Latin texts and English translations, with discussion: Marcovich 1989; McHugh 1964; 1968; 1970; C. White 2000, 113. The theme of disastrous contemporary events in Gaul in the early fifth century is taken up in another poem, *Carmen ad uxorem*, an *epithalamium* or marriage poem, in this case urging a chaste marriage "among the tableaux of contemporary ruin": Chiappiniello 2007, 115–38, esp. 125–27.

339 *Proscenia* can mean theater stages on several levels, thus possibly describing a *basis villa* on terraces, but I prefer "facades" as more direct.

NOTES TO CHAPTER 5

1 On *scholē*, *otium*, and *negotium* in Greek and Latin: compact analyses in Fechner and Scholz 2002; Eickhoff, Kofler, and Zimmermann 2016, 8–9; papers in Sigot 2000, esp. Panagl 2000.

2 In German, *die Muße* is perhaps closer to *otium* than the French *loisirs*, most often in the plural and suggesting extroverted hobbies and diversions more than inward-looking states of mind. The terms have found scholarly elaboration in edited volumes: André, Dangel, and Demont 1996, which comprehensively includes *les loisirs* in Greek and Roman sport, philosophy, religious festivals, theater, and so on—their themes through the early twentieth century in European literature. A thorough review of the term *otium* in its semantic variations with contexts and applied adjectives can be found in Harter 2016, elucidating such variations (and paradoxes) as *otium negotiosum* (24–27), *otium liberale*, with a tripartite breakdown of the term in a kind of Venn diagram (23, fig. 1); see also Eickhoff, Kofler, and Zimmermann 2016, esp. 8–9, for *otium* and concepts such as freedom, idyllic contemplation, pleasure (*Freiheit, Idyll, Glück*). For analysis of the spatial/psychological conditions of *Muße* and thus *otium*: Figal 2016.

3 Neither does the German *der Urlaub* nor the French *le congé*, or *la permission* in military terms, adequately express *otium*.

4 Also used by Ennius in the early second century BCE; see André 1962, and 1966, which remain the definitive studies of the term; more recently, Dosi 2006. Cato's *Origines* is lost, but its influence was assured by quotations from it a century later by Cicero, who cites it directly in his speech of 54 BCE, *For Gnaeus Plancius* (*Pro Cnaeo Plancio*), excerpted below.

5 The general equivalent in Italian is *ozio*, but since at least the eighteenth century, the word *villegiatura* in Italian has meant a vacation time spent at a country villa; *villégiature* was adopted a little later in French. In 1761, Carlo Goldoni wrote three comedies, collectively known as *La Villegiatura*, for a theater in Venice: *Le smanie della villeggiatura* (*Crazy Manias for Holidays at a Villa*), *Le avventure della villeggiatura* (*Adventures of Villeggiatura*), *Il ritorno dalla villeggiatura* (*Return from Villa Holidays*).

6 On its development in the Late Republican and Early Imperial periods in elite self-representation: Wiegandt 2016; on leisure in Augustan times: Keith 2016; and on *scholē* in Libanius (late fourth century CE): Fiorucci 2016.

7 In a slightly different form, the *gnōthi seauton*, together with two other proverbial phrases, was inscribed on the pronaos of the temple of Apollo at Delphi: Paus. 10.24.1; the phrase or injunction had wide radiance in Plato (*Protagoras*, *Laws*, and elsewhere) and Xenophon (*Memorabilia of Socrates* 4.2.24) but also had a much more popular life in inscriptions on mosaic floors in Roman domestic settings. A *caupona*, or tavern, in Ostia (the port of Rome) shows images of Greek philosophers, seated, in elevated classical style, with mocking comments by the barflies written below. Among them are Thales of Miletus (or Phemonoë or Chilon of Sparta) to whom the phrase is attributed by Diogenes Laertius (Diog. Laert. 1.36, 1.40). Both Thales and Chilon are shown in the *caupona*: Clarke 2006, 51, figs. 4 and 5, with preceding bibliography.

8 The use of contemplation and the exemplary exercise of virtue—the primary components of productive *otium*—are the main themes of Seneca the Younger's essay *On Leisure* (*De otio*), written in the early 60s CE.

9 Marcus Iuventius Laterensis: Shackleton Bailey 1992, 60.

10 *NP* s.v. "Marius" I 6 (J. Fündling); Shackleton Bailey 1995, 68, 149.

11 On Marcus Marius and his villa at Pompeii: D'Arms (1970) 2003, 182–83, cat. I 29; Shackleton Bailey 1995, 68, 149. On Cicero's other encounters with Marcus Marius, see Cic., *QFr.* 12.2–4 (2.9.2–4) in ch. 6, Villa Visits.

12 Cicero found games and festivals at Rome to be boring and noisy, even ones dictated by the religious calendar; he avoided them as much as possible, often going to one of his villas rather than stay in the City. On the Horti Pompeiani surrounding the Theater of Pompey: Cicero, *Phil.* 2.109; Asconius Pedianus, *Mil.* 33; Plutarch, *Vit. Pomp.* 44; Velleius Paterculus 1.603; Appian, *B. Civ.* 3.14; Kuttner 1999b. On the Theater of Pompey itself: Monterroso Checa 2010.

13 Marius's framing up of a long view over water of distant landscapes with picturesque buildings (by cutting an opening in his bedroom wall) corresponds to a new taste for such views in Roman painting at this time (see figs. 12, 13, and 14). The buildings at Stabiae would not have been the magnificent showy villas of the reign of Tiberius and later. Rather, the view would have been of a rustic village with a few villas standing above dramatic cliffs, with the cordillera of the Surrentine peninsula behind, the whole illuminated by the morning sun from the vantage point of Pompeii.

14 Spurius Maecius Tarpa was Pompey's impresario for the spectacles inaugurating his theater: Horace, *Sat.* 1.10.38, and *Ars P.* 386–387; *NP* s.v. "Maecius" I 2 (J. Fündling).

15 Greek plays and Oscan farces: Greek plays, both tragedies and comedies of many different dates, were customarily revived on the Roman stage. Oscan farces, also called Atellan plays (*ludi*), were an ancient form of comedy from the town of Atella in Oscan territory, originally in Oscan, later in Latin: *NP* s.v. "Atellana fabula" (J. Blänsdorf). Cicero is mocking the provincial wrangling of local councils as being like such amusing plays.
"The Greek road": a wordplay on some local highway, otherwise unknown.

16 In a letter written the following year, once again from his Cumaean villa (*QFr.* 25.1 [3.5.1], October 54 BCE), Cicero tells his brother Quintus of a reading, in the presence of the historian Sallust (Gaius Sallustius Crispus, ca. 86–35 BCE) of his *On the Republic* (*De republica*), which he was writing. Sallust commented that Cicero put himself in the dialogue because he was "not just some Heraclides Ponticus but a man with actual experience as a consul, well versed in great political affairs." Heraclides Ponticus, a student of Plato, was most famous for his astronomical speculations, but he also wrote on political affairs without practical knowledge of them: *NP* s.v. "Heraclides" 16 A–C (F. Zaminer and K.-H. Stanzel).

17 Faustus Cornelius Sulla (ca. 86–46 BCE), senator and quaestor in 54 BCE, son of the dictator Lucius Cornelius Sulla: *NP* s.v. "Cornelius" I 87 (K.-L. Elvers); on the villa at Bauli and its library: D'Arms (1970) 2003, 170–71, cat. I 11.

18 The *sella curulis* was a portable (foldable) chair that accompanied a high magistrate; it would be opened for him to sit on for hearings, judgments, or audiences to signify the presence of *imperium* or magisterial or military power: *NP* s.v. "Sella curulis" (L. de Libero). Election to a curule magistracy conferred noble status (*nobilitas*) on the person and his descendants.

19 Lucius Manlius Torquatus was of a noble family. Praetor in 49 BCE and an adherent of Pompey, he was killed after the battle of Thapsus in 45 BCE: *NP* s.v. "Manlius" I 17 (J. Fündling). On *otium* and Epicureanism: Erler 2016.

20 Gaius Triarius: Gaius Valerius Triarius, also an adherent of Pompey and killed at Pharsalus in 45 BCE, was Cicero's friend and named him guardian of his children in the event of his death: *NP* s.v. "Valerius" I 53 (J. Bartels).

21 In an amusing comment in his speech *For Gnaeus Plancius* (*Pro Cnaeo Plancio*), Cicero gives a description of the main street of the little town of Tusculum, completely surrounded by grand villas, including his own: consuls and other grand folk walked about in close proximity, rubbing shoulders: Cic., *Planc.* 19–21 (8).

22 Lucius Licinius Lucullus, son of the general of the same name, had inherited his famous father's villa at Tusculum with its buildings, works of art, gardens, and especially its philosophical library: *NP* s.v. "Licinius" I 28 (T. Frigo). For the foundation of the library, see Plut., *Vit. Luc.* 42, in ch. 9, Villas and *Horti* in the Late Roman Republic.

23 Marcus Porcius Cato (73–42 BCE), son of Marcus Porcius Cato the Younger ("of Utica," 95–46 BCE), supported his father's anti-Caesarean political stance and, like him, was a strongly moralistic Stoic; he was killed at Philippi in 42 BCE; *NP* s.v. "Porcius" I 8 (T. Frigo). At the notional time of the dialogue (51–50 BCE), Marcus Cato would have been in his early 20s, but the picture of him reading in the Curia while waiting for the Senate to convene would have been a glimpse of him much later, when he had become a senator.

24 Cicero never hesitates to point out the deference that others pay him. Marcus Cato stands up in his presence, as would have been normal for a younger man in relation to an elder, but also as a young man would do to a former consul, governor of a province, member of the College of Augurs, and a famous orator and literary figure. His simple act of rising confirms Cicero's prestige to the reader.

25 Which of the many multiday festival and holiday games held at Rome Cicero was avoiding that day is not known from the dialogue itself.

26 Ever the pedagogue, Cicero tells Marcus Cato that they have to work together on educating the young Lucullus.

27 Caepio: probably Quintus Servilius Caepio, half brother of Cato the Younger and thus half uncle of Marcus Porcius Cato (see above); guardian of Marcus Junius Brutus; died 59 BCE: *NP* s.v. "Livia" 1 (H. Stegmann).

28 Marcus Caelius Rufus: Shackleton Bailey 1995, 28.

29 In this case, *otium* designates the peace that contributes to the nonpolitical pursuits of literary and philosophical studies.

30 At the beginning of the letter, Cicero mentions that Julius Caesar owned a villa at Alsium.

31 A year later, Cicero wrote again to Varro, to announce the imminent publication of his dialogues *Academica* which, he says, were based on conversations at his Cumaean villa, and to tell him that Varro would be the dedicatee and would appear as Antiochus of Ascalon in the conversation, while Cicero would be Philo of Larissa, both upholding the Stoic view of philosophy. Antiochus of Ascalon had been head of the Platonic Academy in Athens when Cicero was a student there in 79 BCE; Philo of Larissa was Antiochus's predecessor at the Academy and had lectured in Rome in 88 BCE with the young Cicero in his audience: Cic., *Fam.* 29 (9.8.1) to M. Terentius Varro, July 45 BCE. A decade later, Varro adopted the dialogue format with several speakers in his *Three Books on Agriculture* (*De re rustica libri III*); see ch. 2, Villas in Roman Agricultural Treatises.

32 Lucius Papirius Paetus: Shackleton Bailey 1995, 75.

33 His "pupils," whom he was instructing in oratory, were Aulus Hirtius, a friend and military legate of Julius Caesar, consul in 43 BCE (*NP* s.v. "Hirtius, Aulus" [W. Will]) and Publius Cornelius Dolabella, also a friend of Caesar and a military man, consul in 44 BCE, and Cicero's son-in-law between 50 and 46 BCE (*NP* s.v. "Cornelius" I 29 [K.-L. Elvers]). The "great friend" is Caesar.

34 Though written in 45 BCE, the *Academica 2* or *Academica Priora* is notionally set in 63–62 BCE, first at Cicero's villa at Cumae, then at Bauli. On Hortensius: *NP* s.v." Hortensius" 7 (G. Calboli). The models were Plato's and Xenophon's dialogues, which were always site-specific, were set in specific circumstances, and had named interlocutors; Varro also set his dialogues on agriculture in distinct political locations and times with appropriate interlocutors.

35 Cicero continues his thought with the way birds can see, and that certain human beings are endowed with supernatural powers of sight; then he continues to the difference between how humans and fish see.

Gaius Avianius Evander or Evandrios, a sculptor and art dealer; Cicero bought sculptures from him: Cic., *Fam.* 209 (7.23), 314 (13.2), and 78 (8.2). See *NP* s.v. "Evander" 4 (R. Neudecker); Plin., *HN* 36.3 (work as a restorer).

36 This passage is analyzed by Keith 2016, 270–73.

Publius Cornelius *Scipio Africanus* (ca. 236/235–183 CE); the cognomen *Africanus* was given to him after his defeat of Hannibal in the Second Punic War as a *cognomen ex virtute*, for "services rendered," or in the Prussian and German military and civil honors, "*Pour le Mérite*."

37 I have translated *rura* as "villas" or "country dwellings" because the term is often used in that way, and going from one of his villas to another was what Cicero was doing in 46–44 BCE.

38 For negative connotations of *otium*, see Seneca's *Ep.* 55 on the villa of Servilius Vatia: Sen., *Ep.* 55.1–3, in ch. 4, Descriptions of Villas.

39 The poem ends with the epigram: *satis est pigro si licet esse mihi*, "it is nice enough if I am left (alone) to be myself."

40 Minicius Fundanus: Birley 2000, 72–73. On this and other letters by Pliny: Wagner 2010.

41 The passage to adulthood for males was marked in their mid teens by a ceremony. Its main event was robing the young man with a white *toga virilis*: Cicero conferred the toga on his son at the family villa at Arpinum in 43 BCE: Cic., *Att.* 189 (9.19.1); Dolansky 2008 with preceding bibliography; *NP* s.v. "Age(s): D. Rome and Italy (G. Binder and M. Saiko).

42 Atilius Crescens: Birley 2000, 39–40. For Pliny's correspondents, Syme (1968) 1979; (1985) 1988.

43 Caninius Rufus: Birley 2000, 47; *OCD4* s.v. "Caninius Rufus" (J. B. Campbell). On this letter: Harter 2016, 36–37.

44 Publius (or Gaius) Cornelius Tacitus (ca. 56–120 CE) had a distinguished military and civilian career, ending as suffect consul in 97 CE. He was the author of numerous historical works dealing with the early decades of the empire (*Annales, Historiae*), a biography of his father-in-law (*Agricola*), a description of the land and peoples east of the Rhine (the *Germania*), and works on rhetoric. He gave the funeral oration for Pliny's mentor Lucius Verginius Rufus in 97 CE and was the addressee of several of Pliny's letters: *NP* s.v. "Tacitus" (E. Flaig); Oliver 1977; Birley 2000, 53.

45 On boar hunting, see Plin., *Ep.* 9.10.1–3, also addressed to Cornelius Tacitus.

46 Boar was hunted with the help of beaters to drive the animals into nets.

47 Minerva is the goddess of wisdom; Diana the goddess of the hunt.

48 Valerius Paulinus: Birley 2000, 97.

49 Silius Italicus: Birley 2000, 89.

50 Silius had retired to Campania sometime after his governorship of Asia in 78 CE but was still prominent enough to be expected to attend, but excused from, the celebrations for the first year of Trajan's reign in 98 CE. His main literary work, the *Punica* (an account of the Second Punic War), was written in his retirement: *NP* s.v. "Silius" II 5 (C. Reitz). For Martial's admiration of him: Mart., *Epig.* 7.63; for his ownership of Cicero's properties and Vergil's tomb: Mart., *Epig.* 11.48 and 50 (49). Silius committed suicide by starvation in 101 CE to avoid suffering and death from an incurable tumor.

The domed mausoleum in the Mergellina district of modern Naples has often been identified on doubtful grounds as that of Vergil, but its image and atmospheric aspect has been recorded in poetic and visual form from the fourteenth to the nineteenth century: Garrison 2018; Hendrix 2018, 288–91.

51 This letter is addressed to Titus Pomponius Bassus, a senator and suffect consul in 94 CE, Governor of Asia and Cappadocia-Galatia, then a high official in the early years of the reign of Trajan with special duties regarding the *alimenta*, retiring shortly there-

52   Calpurnius Macer: Birley 2000, 46.

53   Calpurnius was the current owner of a villa that previously had been owned by a man "already happy" or a "lucky man" who had subsequently made out even better than before and had become the happiest (*felicissimus*) of all. The reference could be to a property once owned by the emperor Trajan or to another political or military leader who had been elevated to rank higher than his previous one. On Calpurnius: *NP* s.v. "Calpurnius" II 11 (W. Eck).

54   Pontius Allifanus: Birley 2000, 82.

55   Pliny had been on military service with a legion stationed in Syria in 81 CE: Gibson 2020, 89. Icaria is an island to the west of Samos, on the sea lanes between the Roman Levant and Italy: *Pleiades* s.v. "Ikaros (island)."

56   Elegiac verse is composed in couplets: the first in dactylic hexameter, the second in dactylic pentameter. Hendecasyllables are poems written with eleven syllables per line, in varying sequences of stress or accenting.

57   Gaius Asinius Gallus Saloninus (ca. 38 BCE–33 CE) was a senator and politician during the reign of Tiberius: *NP* s.v. "Asinius" II 5 (W. Eck). He evidently wrote a biography of his much more famous father, Gaius Asinius Pollio (75 BCE–4 CE), who had a distinguished military career, was consul in 40 BCE, a partisan of Julius Caesar, and became a revered figure in the early years of Augustus's reign: *NP* s.v. "Asinius" I 4 (P. L. Schmidt); Birley 2000, 39. The son earned fame as a literary man and historian of his own times as well as the founder of a Greek and Latin library in the Hall of Liberty (Atrium Libertatis) in Rome (Plin., *HN* 35.10 [35.2]); he was a patron of Vergil and Horace.

Tiro was a talented enslaved person whom Cicero had manumitted and made his secretary and man of affairs; he ultimately became Cicero's literary executor. For a letter to him from Cicero's son, see Cic., *Fam.* 337.7 (16.21.7), in ch. 8, Buying, Building, Improving, and Selling Villas.

58   What follows is a curious poem, somewhat sexually suggestive and not in the eleven-syllable form, about Cicero and Tiro.

59   Also the addressee of *Ep.* 8.15, below.

60   It is not certain who, among the members of the *gens* Terentia, this Terentius Junior might be, though an inscription (*ILS* 2.1 6120) found near Perusia (modern Perugia) on a bronze tablet mentions a property of his and identifies his praenomen as Gaius. After meeting, they became friends (see Plin., *Ep.* 8.15, in this chapter); Birley 2000, 91.

61   The letter was written from Pliny's Tuscan villa. As in *Ep.* 1.6 to Cornelius Tacitus (in this chapter), Minerva represents learning and Diana embodies hunting.

62   Later, Pliny retired to a villa at Tusculum, probably one belonging to a friend, to write some "little thing" (*opusculum*) or some poetry: *Ep.* 4.13.1–2 (to Cornelius Tacitus).

63   Cornelius Titianus: Birley 2000, 53–54.

64   Pedanius Fuscus Salinator the younger: Birley 2000, 77–78.

65   Among these might have been Encolpius, who accompanied Pliny to the Tuscan villa; he read to his master but had a throat irritation, much improved in the healthy surroundings of the villa (Plin., *Ep.* 8.1). Pliny's favorite was the multitalented freedman Zosimus of whom he was very fond (Plin., *Ep.* 5.19). Pliny sent him to Egypt to cure his cough, and even asked a friend, Valerius Paulinus, to write to the personnel of his villa at Forum Julii (modern Fréjus) in southern Gaul about a health-restoring vacation for his freedman.

66   Calvisius Rufus: Birley 2000, 46–47.

67   Titus Vestricius Spurinna (ca. 24–105 CE) had a military career and was consul in 72 CE, governor of Germania Inferior in 97 CE, and consul again in 98 CE, retiring after that: *NP* s.v. "Vestricius" (W. Eck); Birley 2000, 100–01.

68   The second hour is one hour after sunrise.

69   The ninth hour in winter is around 2:00 pm, the eighth in summer around 1:30 pm.

70   *NP* s.v. "Galen" (V. Nutton), with extensive bibliography.

71   Clare K. Rothschild, Lewis University, Romeoville, Illinois, and Stellenbosch University, South Africa, and Trevor W. Thompson, Abilene Christian University, Abilene, Texas; Rothschild and Thompson 2014a. Professors Rothschild and Thompson have graciously given me permission to use their translation and have my thanks, and I am grateful to Fr. Elizabeth Wener of Mohr Siebeck (Tübingen) for confirming their generosity. Headnotes and prefatory comments have been added for this volume, and some punctuation has been brought in line with the current publication.

72   It is not known where his Campanian villa might have been, whether inland or on the Bay of Naples, but Cicero had used the library of Faustus Sulla, which may have ultimately been bought or amalgamated for use by others: Nicholls 2014, 69–70, nn. 11–13. See Cic., *Att.* 84.1 (4.10.1), in this chapter.

73   Galen notes that the loss of these libraries was greater by far than his personal losses and misfortune; the catalogues and shelflists were also destroyed. The library in the Domus Tiberiana was the facility from which Marcus Aurelius had "borrowed" some copies of speeches by Cato to read on his autumn holidays at the Villa Magna fifty years before; see Fronto, *Ep.* 4.5 (60), in ch. 10, Emperors and Villas.

74   The letter-essay to an unknown correspondent was known by title in Galen's list of his own works but was considered lost until the stunning discovery of a copy in the Vlatadon monastery in Salonika in 2005; for a full review of the text, its bibliography, and its interpretation: Rothschild and Thompson 2014b.

75 This was the Antonine Plague, a pandemic beginning in 165–166 that killed many throughout the Mediterranean empire, including Galen's enslaved personnel and possibly the emperor Lucius Verus; *NP* s.v. "Epidemic diseases" III. Rome (V. Nutton); *NP* s.v. "Diseases" D. Pathocenosis and epidemiology (A. Touwiade).

76 The warehouse was of rubble or masonry, and its premises were guarded because official archives of trials or documents of prospective trials were housed there: Houston 2003.

77 According to Vitruvius (*De arch.* 1.9), the Etesian winds blow from the northeast, but variably from the northwest. They are seasonal in the eastern Mediterranean from late spring to early autumn. Galen may mention them because they would have assured safe landfall at Aeolian ports for ships carrying his books to his friends at Pergamum.

78 Eutropius was appointed praetorian prefect of Gaul some years later: *PLRE* 2 444–45 Eutropius 3.

79 Palatine: an appointment in the direct proximity to the *palatium* or palace of the emperor.

80 Sidonius appears to be unconsciously reprising the much older notion of *otium*, that it was related to military leave or furlough: see discussion of the term at the beginning of this chapter and n. 3.

81 Narbo Martialis (modern Narbonne) and Baeterrae (modern Béziers).

82 Taionnacus villa: This refers to a place-name not securely identified.

83 Serranus: either Gaius Atilius Regulus Serranus, consul in 257 and 250 BCE, of a distinguished family and triumphator in the First Punic War, or an earlier, more famous relative, Marcus Atilius Regulus, consul in 267 and 256 BCE. The latter was captured by the Carthaginians, released, then voluntarily returned to his captivity, becoming a symbol of heroic self-sacrifice: C. Atilius Regulus Serranus: Polyb. 1.41–48; Diod. Sic. 24.1.1–4 (for his military exploits); *NP* s.v. "Atilius" I 17 (K.-L. Elvers): M. Atilius Regulus: Cic., *Off.* 3.99–108; *NP* s.v. "Prisoners of War" III. Rome (Y. Le Bohec).

Camillus: Marcus Furius Camillus (ca. 446–365 BCE), was a famous general against the Etruscan city of Veii, against the invading Gauls in 390 BCE, and in other military exploits, triumphator four times, named dictator five times, and famous for his inflexible high morals and bravery: Plut., *Vit. Cam.*; Beard 2009, 234–35; *NP* s.v. "Furius" I 13 (W. Eder).

Palm-embroidered tunic: together with other objects and garments, the *tunica palmata*, worn under the purple and gold-edged *toga picta*, was the unique perquisite of the Roman triumphator: *ODLA* s.v. "toga picta" (M. Parani); Beard 2009, 81.

84 As a result of political and military emergencies, Lucius Quinctius Cincinnatus (ca. 519–430 BCE) was called by the consuls of 458 BCE to save the state; they found him ploughing a field on his own farm on what is now the Vatican side of the Tiber River. Calling his wife Racilia to fetch his toga, he organized an army, defeated the hostile Aequi, then returned to his farm. In a later call to be dictator in 439, Cincinnatus bravely upheld the rights of the patrician order against lawlessness. Sidonius would have known of Cincinnatus from Livy, 3.26.6–12, and Cic., *Sen.* 16.56.

85 *Trabea*: the toga, dyed purple or with purple edging, worn by consuls or those with consular status: *NP* s.v. "Trabea" (R. Hurschmann). On curule chairs, *sella curulis*, see supra n. 18.

86 "…censor as by the tax-man (*censetor*)." Sidonius means that the censor, who determined the social rank of citizens according to their career, family, and wealth, would not (or could not) raise Syagrius to any higher status than he already enjoyed, but the censor's taxation officer would be alerted to Syagrius's wealth and come after him for payment of taxes.

NOTES TO CHAPTER 6

1 The festival of Pales, a deity of shepherds and cowherds, was celebrated on April 21, in a festival called the *Parilia* or *Palilia*: Varro, *Ling.* 6.15; *NP* s.v. "Parilia" (G. Baudy) and "Pales" (F. Prescendi). On the temple of Pales in Rome, *LTUR* 4 50–51 (J. Aronen); Richardson 1992, s.v. "Pales, Templum"; *AtlasAncRome* 1 218–19, 224.

2 *Crater delicatus*: "the lovely crater (bowl)," Cicero's name for the Bay of Naples. Atticus may have advised Cicero to avoid the bay because it was full of members of high society (which would be distracting) and political persons (who might be Cicero's enemies) on holiday from the City.

3 Cicero, as an important person, found that he had more company at his villa than he liked: he might as well be on professional business in the law court—the basilica of the Aemilian clan. This building, the Basilica Aemilia, was a major public legal venue, commercial facility, and capacious gathering place in the Roman Forum, built or restored in 179 BCE by Marcus Aemilius Lepidus and frequently embellished by members of the noble *gens* Aemilia: on the building in use in Cicero's day (the Basilica Aemilia or Fulvia-Aemilia itself): *LTUR* 1 167–68 (E.M. Steinby); *LTUR* 173–75; *LTUR* 1 183–87 (H. Bauer); *AtlasAncRome* 1 161, 289–90; 2: tab. 92a; Haselberger et al. 2002, 66 (C.F. Noreña); Richardson 1992, s.v. "Basilica Paulli"; Claridge 2010, 67; Coarelli 2014, 48–49; Yegül and Favro 2019, 21 and fig. 1.11. In 55–54 BCE, after this letter was written, the basilica was rebuilt and dedicated in the name of Lucius Aemilius Paullus, becoming the Basilica Paulli; it was rebuilt and restored twice after that.

4 Fourth hour: 10:00 am between the spring equinox and summer solstice. Cicero would have had some citizens of Formiae as *clientes*, and they would have been the first to salute him in the morning *salutatio*.

5 Gaius Arrius, otherwise unknown, was a member of the *gens* Arria of non-Roman origins, also mentioned in Cic., *Att.* 380 (15.3). His only claim to fame was to have been Cicero's neighbor at Formiae, but Cicero lukewarmly admired his ancestor Quintus Arrius: Cic., *Brut.* 242–243; *NP* s.v. "Arrius" I 2 (K.-L Elvers); Shackleton Bailey 1995, 18.

6   Sebosus is claiming (on doubtful grounds) to be a close friend of Quintus Lutatius Catulus (ca. 120–60 BCE), an important politician and aristocrat, consul in 78 BCE. The Statius Sebosus known to be a geographer is probably not Cicero's neighbor; Plin., *HN* 6.184, 6.202, 9.46, and Pliny frequently mentions him as an authority.

7   For some reason, Cicero feels that he cannot adequately receive Atticus at Arpinum, perhaps because it was too small: in Cic., *Att.* 317 (13.9), he calls it a *praediola*.

8   Cicero is joking: his villa at Formia was not for sale, but with Arrius and Sebosus as neighbors, he wants out.

9   Amyntas's son was Philip II, king of Macedon. This is a wordplay on the name of Lucius Marcius Philippus, consul in 56 BCE: *NP* s.v. "Marcius" I 14 (J. Fündling); D'Arms (1970) 2003, 181, cat. I 28, for his villa at Puteoli. Cicero may have considered him a trimmer in the politics of the day and a bore as a neighbor. L. Marcius Philippus was also Julius Caesar's host at Puteoli when Cicero served the dictator dinner in December of that year: see Cic., *Att.* 353.1–2 (13.52.1–2), in this chapter.

10   Marcus Marius: *NP* s.v. "Marius" I 6 (J. Fündling); Shackleton Bailey 1995, 68.

11   King Ptolemy's litter was a royal gift or loan from the Egyptian king Ptolemy XII Auletes to Publius Asicius, a minor agent in Pompey's attempt to restore the king to his Egyptian throne. The king had been expelled from Egypt and had sought asylum at Rome in 58 BCE before returning to Alexandria in 55: *NP* s.v. "Ptolemaeus" 18. Pompey's agent Publius Asicius had been accused of a murder in the affair, prosecuted by Gaius Licinius Calvus, but was successfully acquitted with Cicero's defense in a trial (56 BCE) a year before this letter was written: Cic., *Cael.* 23. The royal litter was accompanied by a hundred soldiers; Marius was frightened by them.

12   Gaius Anicius: D'Arms (1970) 2003, 59, 165, cat I, 1; Broughton 1951–1960, 2:487.

13   Mount Hymettus overlooks Athens; Cicero uses it to refer to Athens and its famous schools of philosophy in general. Some versions supply Psyrie (Ψυρία) for *ab arce nostra* ("our craggy peak"). Psyrie is a Greek island north of Chios, mentioned in Homer's *Odyssey* (3.171), that Cicero may have equated with his hometown of Arpinum, perhaps because of its isolation and rustic character: Cic., *Att.* 424 (16.13a.2).

14   Trebatius, a young lawyer whom Cicero befriended as a mentor, was on a military tour of duty in Britain; *NP* s.v. "Trebatius" 2 (T. Giaro); Shackleton Bailey 1995, 98. Trebatius was a property owner in the Ulubrae district; he had asked Cicero to keep an eye on his properties, clients, and petitioners.

15   Marcus Aemilius Philemon was a rich freedman of Marcus Aemilius Lepidus and a witness to the murder of Cicero's enemy Publius Clodius Pulcher in 52 BCE: Asc., *Mil.* 37. Ulubrae was a village southwest of Rome on the Via Appia, near the Palus Pomptinus (modern Agro Pontino), a swampy region southeast of Rome on the coast just north of Tarracina, hence the frogs: *Pleiades* s.v. "Ulubrae"; *NP* s.v. "Ulubrae" (G. Uggeri) and "Ager Pomptinus" (H. Sonnabend). The tone of the letter is jocular.

16   Several towns in Italy had the name Trebula; that closest to Pompeii was in central Campania. Its location seems far for Cicero to travel there on the tenth of May, then leave on the eleventh to get back to Cumae that same day: Cic., *Att.* 96 (5.3) and 97 (5.4).

17   Quintus Hortensius Hortalus (ca. 114–50 BCE), a famous lawyer and rhetorician, whose pleading made him wealthy and a bon vivant; he owned villas and fish tanks on the Bay of Naples, for which Cicero called him a *piscinarius*; Varro, *Rust.* 3.17.3–10; Plin., *HN* 9.172 and 10.23; Cicero in Macrob., *Sat.* 3.15.6.

18   Atticus's sister, Pomponia, was the wife of Cicero's brother Quintus.

19   Cicero had two friends who had villas in the Pomptine marsh, near a village called Ulubrae: Gaius Trebatius Testa and Marcus Aemilius Philemon: Cic., *Fam.* 37 (7.18.3). Arcanum was Quintus's villa and estate at Arpinum.

20   See *Att.* 116 (6.2) and 338 (13.46.2), in ch. 8, Buying, Building, Improving, and Selling Villas.

21   Lucius Marcius Philippus, consul in 56 BCE, was Cicero's neighbor on the Bay of Naples and owner of the villa where Caesar spent the night. He was distantly related by marriage to Caesar and was the stepfather of Gaius Octavius (later, Caesar's heir and son by adoption, the future emperor Augustus) and his sister Octavia, later wife of Mark Antony: *NP* s.v. "Marcius" I 14 (J. Fündling); Shackleton Baily 1995, 67.

22   A friend of Caesar: Shackleton Baily 1995, 31.

23   Lucius Cornelius Balbus, consul in 40 BCE, was a close associate of Caesar's: *NP* s.v. "Cornelius" I 6 (K.-L. Elvers).

24   Mamurra: a soldier, engineer (*praefectus fabrum*), and close associate of Caesar's: *NP* s.v. "Mamurra" (J. Fündling). What had happened to him that was reported to Caesar is not indicated in the letter. On the post of *praefectus fabrum*: Welch 1995; Cafaro 2021.

25   "…nicely cooked and herbed": Cicero is quoting himself from his *On the Ends of Good and Evil* (*De finibus bonorum et malorum*), or, rather, citing Laelius on a passage of Lucilius (Cic., *Fin.* 2.8.25); the quotation is part of a refutation of Epicureanism and is placed here to emphasize the decent sobriety and frugality of the meal that he served Caesar and the philosophical conversation it prompted: food for thought as much as food to eat.

26   This phrase—*homines visi sumus*—is hard to translate. Cicero means that he is fully a man, that he has the great capacities of a superior human being, that he knows how to behave and act in society. It is the Ciceronian equivalent of

Nero's exclamation on moving into the Domus Aurea: *ut se diceret quasi hominem tandem habitare coepisse* (The only thing he said when he moved in was that he was "at last able to live like a man [*homo*]"): see Suet., *Nero* 31.2, in ch. 10, Emperors and Villas, with discussion and bibliography at n. 87.

27 "…a day at Puteoli, another near Baiae": the prepositional construction is *ad Puteolis, ad Baias*, which could refer to villas, even villas possibly owned by Caesar: D'Arms (1970) 2003, Cat I 19, 176.

28 Dolabella is Publius Cornelius Dolabella, the former husband of Cicero's daughter Tullia and a vigorous partisan of Julius Caesar: *NP* s.v. "Cornelius" I 29 (K.-L. Elvers). He had a villa at Baiae: D'Arms (1970) 2003, 176–77, Cat. I 9.

Caesar's guard dividing in two may mean that, having been in easy- or ruck-march formation or line array (*agmen quadratum*?), the men changed temporarily to brisk showy quick-march formation (*agmen pilatum*?) out of compliment to Dolabella, though these marching formations are mainly for hostile conditions, as described by Varro; they are not parade formations: Taylor 2014, 308–9; for Varro: Serv., *Aen.* 12.121 in Thilo and Hagen, vol. 2, 590.

29 Quintus Lepta was an engineer in Cicero's service: Shackleton Bailey 1995, 61. On a villa site possibly related to Cicero: Marzano 2007, cat. no. L24, 283.

30 Publius Pompeius Macula, a friend or acquaintance who owned a villa in the Ager Falernus north of Naples: Cic., *Fam.* 262 (6.19); Shackleton Bailey 1995, 65.

31 Petrine district: Petrina was a village in the northwestern corner of the Ager Falernus in Campania, just south of Sinuessa and the Mons Massicus.

32 Lucius Papirius Paetus, a friend, was addressed in a letter discussing the *gens* Papiria by Cicero, *Fam.* 188 (9.21) and other letters; *NP* s.v. "Papirius" I 22 (J. Fündling); Shackleton Bailey 1995, 75; D'Arms (1970) 2003, 59, 183, cat. I 30.

33 This Marcus Caeparius is not the person of the same name who had been a henchman of Catiline in 63 BCE (Cic., *Cat.* 3.6); Shackleton Baily 1995, 28. The Gallinarian woods: a pine grove near Cumae: Juv., *Satires* 3.307.

34 Villas were expected to be venues of hospitality (*hospitium*), either by invitation to friends or upon request by passing travelers, for shorter or longer stays. To avoid casual travelers' demands for lodging, Columella recommended that villas be not too near main roads (Columella, *Rust.* 1.5.7). While some very wealthy owners like Cicero owned their own simple layover places (*deversoria*) on the routes of their travels, others relied on the *hospitium* of villa owners to put them up. For Cicero's *deversorium* at Anagnia, which he used on his way to and from Rome and Tusculum to Arpinum: Cic., *Att.* 248 (12.1). In 38 BCE, Horace, in a party with some poet friends (including Vergil), accompanied Maecenas and his entourage (on diplomatic mission to Greece) as far as Brundisium (modern Brindisi). In his poem known as *iter Brundisium*, Horace amusingly describes their wretched lodging in an inn (*caupona*) and a crude official guesthouse (*villula*), finally finding comfortable lodging at a fellow traveler's villa at Causium near Beneventum: Hor., *Sat.* 1.5.49–50.

35 Quintus Cornificius was the son of Cicero's friend of the same name. He held important governorships during Caesar's dictatorship, and besides owning villas on the Bay of Naples, he and Cicero were colleagues in the College of Augural Priests: *NP* s.v. "Cornificius 3" (C. Kugelmeier); Shackleton Baily 1995, 42; D'Arms (1970) 2003, 50.

36 Maecenas's family (the *gens* Cilnia) was based at Arretium (modern Arezzo) in Etruria above the Arnus River (modern Arno), which flowed nearby. It was Etruscan in origin, and Horace elsewhere compliments his patron as having royal descent (Hor., *Odes* 1.1: *Maecenas atavis edite regibus*). In this poem, Horace emphasizes Maecenas's retaining equestrian rank as a mark of his modesty and authenticity.

No theater is recorded on the Vatican hill, so the reference to the applause being heard "to the banks of your hometown river from the Vatican hill" may be to the right bank of the Tiber (including the Vatican area) as being the Etruscan side nearest Rome, whereas Rome's side was in Latin areas.

37 Caecuban wine, grapes from Cales, Falernian, and Formian vintages: these were prestigious wines from districts in the Ager Falernus north of Naples, near the summit and on the slopes of the Mons Massicus or Mons Falernus (modern Monte Massico) around Formiae and in the *ager* itself around Cales; they were the most sought-after wines of Roman Italy and are classed as the *grands crus* in Plin., *HN* 14.61–66 (14.8); see also Hor., *Odes* 1.37.5 (Caecuban wine was kept in one's grandfather's cellarage until a suitably festive occasion, in this case to celebrate the death of Cleopatra, Rome's great enemy); Hor., *Odes* 2.3.1–8 ("lie down on smooth grass and drink Falernian from your cellar"); Strabo 5.3.6; there are many other tributes to these wines later than Horace, notably; Juv., *Satires* 13.310–316 (aging effects of fine wine); Mart., *Epig.* 2.40.5–6; 8.55.13–14; 8.77.6; 11.49.7, and many other places—it was apparently Martial's favorite. On Falernian wine in comparison to others: Plin., *HN* 14.61–63; Tchernia 2013a; list of *appellations d'origine* in Salviat and Tchernia 2013 (2014), 217–25; *NP* s.v. "Wine" D. Wine varieties and qualities (A. Gutsfeld).

For lying down on the grass at villas, see Hor., *Epode* 2, in ch. 4, Descriptions of Villas.

38 Juvenal continues with a description of the simplicity of his *triclinium*'s dining beds, the uncorrupted youth of his prepubescent cupbearer, the absence of an erotic floor show, the quiet of the countryside, not having to wear a toga (*effugiat . . . toga*), and so on. Throughout *Satire* 11, the poet's simple hospitality is compared to the luxuries of contemporary villas and in recollection of the simple lives of the *maiores*, thereby signalling Juvenal's own virtues.

39 Juvenal is being sweetly sarcastic and whimsically playing on consonance and assonance. Signia (modern Segni) was a town about 70 km southeast of Rome, an ordinary center of agricultural production; *Pleiades* s.v. "Signia." Far away and exotically glamorous Syria was its opposite, not a likely source of pears for an Italian table.

40 Mucius Curius Dentatus was famous for his frugal meal of roasted turnips: see Plutarch's account in Plut., *Vit. Cat. Mai.* 2.1–2, in ch. 9, Villas and *Horti* in Late Republican Rome.

41 Sacrificed animals were butchered after the ceremony, with the fat and bones burned as a symbolic offering to the gods and the meat distributed among the priests and congregants.

42 Fabii: the *gens* Fabia was among the high patrician families in several branches, the Fabii Maximi producing generation on generation of high officials; such as Quintus Fabius Maximus Gurges (consul in 292 BCE), his son or grandson Quintus Fabius Maximus Verrucosus Cunctator (ca. 280–203 BCE; consul five times, dictator, censor, commander against Hannibal in the Second Punic War) and others. The "austere censor" is Cato the Elder.

Scauri: members of the Aemilii Scauri patrician family included Marcus Aemilius Scaurus, consul in 115 BCE, a successful general and censor in 109 BCE greatly admired by Cicero, and others who attained high office. Fabricius: Gaius Fabricius Luscinus, a famous general, consul in 282 and 278, censor in 275 BCE, a paradigm of austerity and incorrupt morals.

"Trojan-born" is a sarcastic epithet for the luxurious, corrupt generations of contemporary Romans flaunting their supposed descent from Aeneas and the Trojan founders of the Latin race.

43 "Romulus's wild beast…imperial destiny" and the "Quirinus twin boys" are images of Romulus and Remus suckled by the she-wolf in the cave called the Lupercal; the "god…descending" is Mars, god of war but here in disguise without weapons, on his mission to father the twins of Rhea Silvia.

"Etruscan (or Tuscan) bowls" denote ceramic bowls, in contrast to the fine metal goblets made by Greek craftsmen and broken up by the old Romans above.

44 For the origins of *xenia* and discussion, see Vitr., *De arch.* 6.7.4, in ch. 3, Villas in Roman Agricultural Treatises.

45 Galen and Pliny the Elder recommended eggs for ailments of the throat and pharynx: Galen, *On the Properties of Foodstuffs* (*De alimentorum facultatibus*; Περὶ τῶν ἐν νεφροῖς παθῶν διαγνώσεως καὶ θεραπείας) 706; see Powell 2003, sec. 21, 134. Plin., *HN* 29.42–51 (29.11), and for throat inflammation, egg yolk, at 29.42, and for cough at 29.47.

46 The letter must have been sent in the depths of winter (mid- to late February) because of the address to "*Cara cognatio*." There was an annual festival honoring the memory of parents (the Parentalia) in mid-February: Ovid, *Fasti* 2.533–546; *NP* s.v. "Parentalia" (G. Baudy). It was followed about nine days later by the Cara Cognatio or Caristia during which living relations were celebrated by the exchange of small gifts like those alluded to in Martial's poem: Ovid, *Fasti* 2.617–638. That is why *living* brother and *dead* grandfather are mentioned.

47 A district of residential slums, tenements (*insulae*), and markets in the ravine running east-northeast between the Viminal and Esquiline Hills, east of the Roman Forum. Renkert 2019, map at fig. 1, and with preceding bibliography; *LTUR* 4 379–83 (K. Welch); *AtlasAncRome* 1 170–74 and 283–87; 2: tabs. 89m 180, and 190 (the Subura in Martial's day); Haselberger et al. 2002, s.v. "Subura" (E.A. Dunser); Richardson 1992, s.v. "Subura" 2.

48 Nomentum: *Pleiades* s.v. "Nomentum;" *NP* s.v. "Nomentum" (G. Uggeri).

49 Trebula was one of two places in the Sabine hill country northeast of Rome: Trebula Mutusca (modern Monteleone Sabino); see *Pleiades* s.v. "Trebula"; or Trebula Suffenas: *Pleiades* s.v. "Trebula Suffenas."

Cancer's sign appears in late June to late July. The Cleonaean Lion: the sun is in the constellation Leo in late August to late September; Cleonaea is a district in northern Peloponessus, near the lair of the Lion of Nemea, which was made into a constellation after Hercules destroyed it in his First Labor. The Aeolian Notus is the south wind.

50 Pompeia Celerina: *NP* s.v. "Pompeia" 4 (W. Eck); Birley 2000, 80; Sherwin-White 1966, 92–93, 754; Gibson 2020, 106, 139–41.

51 Complaining of the slovenliness and other deficiencies of servants and enslaved personnel was as endemic among Roman enslavers as it was in later times.

52 Gnaeus Lucceius Albinus, an orator: *NP* s.v. "Lucceius" II 2 (W. Eck); Birley 2000, 69.

53 Alsium: *Pleiades* s.v. "Alsium"; *NP* s.v. "Alsium" (S. Bianchetti). Verginius Rufus: *NP* s.v. "Verginius" II 1 (W. Eck).

54 *NP* s.v. "Verginius" II 1 (W. Eck); Sherwin-White 1966, 142–46, 761.

55 Bodel 1997, 21–22.

56 Gaius Marius Marcellus Octavius Publius Cluvius Rufus: Sherwin-White 1966, 754; Birley 2000, 76.

57 Calpurnius, to whom Pliny was devoted in friendship and respect, was grandfather to Calpurnia, Pliny's third wife: Sherwin-White 1966, 71, 264–65, 742; *NP* s.v. "Calpurnius" II 7 (W. Eck); Birley 2000, 46–47. He had a military career that ended during Nero's reign (Tac., *Hist.* 16.8.3) and was recorded in his funerary inscription from Comum (*CIL* 5 5267 = *ILS* 2721). Calpurnia's mother (not named) was apparently also the addressee of this letter. In retirement, Calpurnius lived at Comum but owned property elsewhere, and Pliny wrote to him on villa matters several times: see Plin., *Ep.* 7.11.1–8, in ch. 7, Economics and Euergetism.

58 For other instances of his obligations and euergetism, both at Tifernum and Comum, see Plin., *Ep.* 3.6, *Ep.* 7.18.1–5, *Ep.* 9.39.1–6, and *Ep.* 10.8.1–8, in ch. 7, Economics and Euergetism.

59 Iunius Mauricus, a senator and friend, who like Pliny had suffered under Domitian: *NP* s.v. "Iunius" II 20 (W. Eck); Birley 2000, 67.

60 The whole: *ut nihil nisi totum et merum velit*, Pliny meaning that,

61   Calpurnius Flaccus: Sherwin-White 2003 (1966), 742; his son, Gaius Calpurnius Flaccus, had a military and administrative career in the reign of Hadrian: *NP* s.v. "Calpurnius" II 8 (W. Eck); Eck 1983, 152–58; Birley 2000, 45–46.

62   Diomedes, the king of Argos and an Achaean warrior at Troy, was famous for the advantageous exchange he made with Glaucus, a strong Trojan opponent. In a fight to the draw, the two exchanged armor as a sign of mutual respect, but Diomedes's armor was of bronze, whereas Glaucus's was made of pure gold: Hom., *Il.* 6.119–236.

63   For Tacitus, see discussion at Plin., *Ep.* 1.6.1–3 and n. 44 in ch. 5, Villas and *Otium*.

64   For the promise of a bath upon arrival at a villa, Stat., *Silv.* 2.2.1–35, in ch. 4, Descriptions of Villas.

65   *Fortes Fortuna iuvat*: a version of *fortis Fortuna adiuvat*—Fortune favors the brave (Ter., *Phorm.* 203) and *audentis Fortuna iuvat* (Verg., *Aen.* 10.284) or *audentes/audaces Fortuna iuvat* in other formulations of the same idea.

66   Lucius Pontius Allifanus: Sherwin-White 1966, 755; *NP* s.v. "Pontius" II 1 (W. Eck); Birley 2000, 82.

67   Rutilius Claudius Namatianus: *PLRE* 2 770, Namatianus 2.

68   Matthews 1998, 325–28.

69   Volaterrana Vada, the port of the ancient Etruscan, and later the Roman, city of Volaterra: *NP* s.v. "Volaterrae" (M.M. Morciano); *Pleiades* s.v. "Vada Volaterrana."

70   Albinus (Caecina Decius Acinatius Albinus) was *Praefectus Urbi Romae* in 414 CE, the year following Rutilius's tenure of the post: *PLRE* 2 50–51, Albinus 7; but see also 2 50, Albinus 2; and 2 53, Albinus 10. The post was "togate" because it was reserved for Roman citizens who were wearers of the toga; men in magisterial positions such as prefect of the City would have worn specially decorated togas.

71   *Comes Illustris* designated a person who was appointed member of several honorific ranks in the courtier groups of the imperial court.

72   Protadius had been *Praefectus Urbi Romae* in 400 or 401 CE: *PLRE* 1 751, Protadius 1.

73   His friend was originally from Augusta Treverorum (modern Trèves/Trier) on the Mosella River (modern Moselle/Mosel) in Gallia Belgica but had moved to the south of Gaul (indicated in a letter to Protadius from Symmachus [Symm., *Ep.* 4.30]): Rutilius and he were thus fellow Gauls.

74   "Enjoy the little things in life because one day you'll look back and realize they were the big things"; attributed to Kurt Vonnegut (1922–2007), American writer.

75   Cincinnatus had a farm of four *iugera* (about .25 ha, or ⅔ acre) on the Vatican side of the Tiber River. The small size of his holding contrasts with his civic and military distinction (Livy, 3.26).

76   Rutilius's boat had by now passed Corsica and was coming to Triturrita (location unknown), which appears to have been a port near Pisae: *Pleiades* s.v. "Triturrita" and "Pisae."

77   In lines 531–614, omitted here, Rutilius describes going to the market in Pisae, then gets held up by a storm.

78   Rutilius says that the *vilicus hospes* equipped him and his company with hunting equipment. *Vilicus hospes* is sometimes translated as "innkeeper" or "peasant," but both seem wrong to me. The poet is enjoying the hospitality of a villa, and its *vilicus* is acting as host to a distinguished visitor in the absence of the owner.

79   Meleager is the Greek hero who led the hunt against the mythical Boar of Calydonia. Amphitryon's son is Hercules: Amphitryon, king of Tiryns, after marrying Alcmene, accepted Zeus's son Hercules by her as his own, so he was the hero's stepfather.

80   Donidius: a friend and recipient of many of Sidonius's letters: *PLRE* 2 376–77, Donidius.

81   Ferreolus was a relative of Sidonius's wife Papianilla; Apollinaris was Sidonius's friend (no relation).

82   Aracynthus: a mountain range in Aetolia (northern Greece). Nysa: which of many mountains of that name in Greece and Asia Minor is not certain, but the Nyseion was where the Nymphs raised the baby Dionysus, so vines, grapes, and wine are associated with it.

83   Ball games and dicing parties appear to be taking place in the *vestibula* of these villas, indicating they were rather large; the large size of vestibules is discussed in Speksnijder 2022 but this example is not cited. It is possible that what Sidonius has in mind is the courtyard-like size of the semicircular entrance court of the villa at Montmaurin or what he describes as the *atrium lunatum* (semi-circular courtyard) in the *Burgus Pontii Leontii*: see Sid. Apoll., *Carm.* 22.101–235, in ch. 4, Descriptions of Villas and fig. 21.

84   *Eloquium Latiaris* literally means "eloquence of Latium," giving the region around Rome and its people to stand for their language.

85   Sidonius is setting out parallels of similarity in Latin for Christian and pagan authors: prose writers such as Varro "go with" the oeuvre of the prolific St. Augustine, bishop of Hippo (Aurelius Augustinus Hipponensis, 354–430 CE), while the pagan Horace is paired with Prudentius (Aurelius Prudentius Clemens, 348–405/413 CE), a native of Hispania Tarraconensis (northern Spain) and author of a cycle of martyrs' biographies called *On the Crowns* [of the Martyrs] (*Liber Peristephanon*), among other works.

The easy alignment of Greek and Latin writers—poets and philosophers or theologians—was a norm in the later fifth century CE among learned *littérateurs* like Sidonius. In his *City of God* and other writings, Augustine had discussed Varro's lost work *Antiquities of Human and Divine Things* in 41 books (*Antiquitates rerum humanarum et divinarum libri XLI*) in detail, especially the section on Greek and Roman divinities; Augustine's many books would have been in circulation and available to Sidonius: Hadas 2017.

Sidonius couples Horace, for him the preeminent Latin poet, with the Christian poet Prudentius, whose works would also have been well known and in circulation in Aquitania and southern Gaul in Sidonius's day.

86 Sidonius indicates that he and his friends were puzzled by the reception of Origen's *Adamantius*: they were not wrong to be so. These gentlemen, in a kind of book club for conversation in a villa, are considering the text of an anonymous early fourth-century theological dialogue called *On the True Faith in God* (Περὶ τῆς εἰς θεὸν ὀρθῆς πίστεως) in its Latin translation *De recta in Deum fide* by Turranius Rufinus (also called Tyrannius of Aquileia, ca. 345–410 CE). Turranius's translation had appeared nearly 175 years after the dialogue was written, supposedly by Origen of Alexandria (ca. 184–253 CE) sometime in the second quarter of the third century. Turranius was a prolific historian and translator of the works of Origen. The dialogue, colloquially known at the time as *Adamantius*, was erroneously attributed by Rufinus and others to Origen, who in consequence was sometimes called Origen Adamantius. The mistaken identity was current in the fifth century and shared by Sidonius, his friends, his hosts, and many others. The dialogue is in the form of three speakers supporting one or another Gnostic theologies in disputation with an interlocutor called Adamantius, who upholds an orthodox view and is declared victor on the basis of his logic by Eutropius, a pagan judge: *ODCC*4 s.v. "Adamantius" (M. Edwards); Ramelli 2018; 2020.

Origen's writings on the development of Christian theology, apologetics, biblical exegesis, ethics, and formulae for sermons (homiletics) strongly influenced many Christian authors, among them St. Jerome and St. Augustine (late fourth–early fifth century). There had been some warning signs: while Origen's writings had been defended by many Church fathers (including Jerome), they were listed as heretical in the *Panarion* (*Adversus haereses, Against Heresies*) of ca. 375 CE by St. Epiphanius of Salamis; the Council of Alexandria in 400 CE had condemned Origenism, but the controversy—and Origen's prestige and interest as a theological writer—continued throughout the fourth and well into the fifth century.

That changed in 397 CE when the translation by Turranius Rufinus appeared: this is the one which was read by Sidonius and his friends at the villa. Soon after, Jerome raised an immediate and furious objection to it and made a new, corrected translation; some seventy years later, Sidonius's implied defense of Turranius's version as being done "with such care as to its content and spirit" (*ad verbum sententiamque translatus*) seems out of touch. However, Sidonius lived at the time when the controversies about the orthodoxy of Origen and Origenism were cresting, so his and his friends' perplexity is understandable. They were not theologians but men of fine literary taste.

Ultimately, some of Origen's writings were unofficially condemned in the Synod of Constantinople in 543 and in letters issued at the Second Council of Constantinople ten years after that. See Roth 2015b, with preceding bibliography.

87 The fifth hour was about 10:30 am.

88 For the villa Vorocingus, see also Sid. Apoll., *Carm.* 24.

89 *Cilicium*, originally made from the wool of goats from Cilicia in Asia Minor, was a woven sackcloth used for bags, tarpaulins, and other rough fabrics.

90 The modern Gard River.

91 A friend and fellow villa owner near Augustonemetum where Sidonius's Avitacum was located: *PLRE* 2 738, Maurusius.

92 The village known as Pagus Martialis refers to Mars, god of war: Julius Caesar had levied several legions in the district, but which ones bivouacked in this village is not certain.

93 Wearing only a tunic meant that Maurusius did not have to put on a toga to engage in any official duty or socially important activity. Pliny also liked his Tuscan villa because there was no need for him to wear his toga: see Plin., *Ep.* 5.6.1–46, in ch. 4, Descriptions of Villas.

94 A distant relative and friend; his villa was near Nemausus: *PLRE* 2 113–14, Apollinaris 2.

He was the addressee of Sidonius Apollinarius's *Ep.* 2.9, above.

95 The angry Lion: the July through September period of the hot sun in zodiacal Leo.

Hybla: the name of several sites in Sicily; the Greek colony of Megara Hyblaea was the most famous, but the Hyblaean mountains in southeastern Sicily are probably intended. Corycus and Galaesus: respectively, a region and a river near Tarentum celebrated by Vergil in his *Georgics* 4.125–148: a simple farmer takes a piece of infertile ground and turns it into a thriving garden with roses, apples, bees and honey, flowers of all sorts, and other produce. Galaesus River: *Pleiades* s.v. "Galaesus."

96 Sabaean refers to a person from Arabia, the source of frankincense. Apollinaris is refusing to buy exotic foreign frankincense because he has enough natural perfumes in his flower and herb gardens.

97 The meaning of the grotto and cavern with the trees as a portico is obscure. On artificial grottos: Miller 1982.

98 Porus: the fabulously rich Indian king who was defeated by Alexander the Great at the battle of the Hydaspes River in 326 BCE. The gold and jewels of the artificial garden of the Indian king are unfavorably compared to the natural loveliness of Apollonius's villa garden.

NOTES TO CHAPTER 7

1 Most recently, the topic of revenues and investment in business, including villas and estates as businesses, has been the subject of articles brought together in Erdkamp, Verboven, and Zuiderhoek 2020. Several address and review the historiography of major developments in Roman economic history, others are specific studies of water machines, fishponds, and other types of investment. On capital deployment in agriculture: Broekaert and Zuiderhoek 2020; Heinrich 2017; Launaro 2017. On the nomenclature of agricultural revenue pertaining to villas and estates: Stringer 2020.

2 For Alfius, see Hor., *Epod.* 2, in ch. 4, Descriptions of Villas. The description of Trimalchio's urban *domus* and the rhythm of his hospitality (entrance to the house and its decorated walls, bathing before the *cena*, drinking, the menu) are satirical takes on contemporary life in Neronian times (mid-50s–60s CE) by Gaius Petronius (*Satyricon* 26–78) . I have not included them in this sourcebook because the author's exaggeration for laughs caricatures rather than characterizes how villa interiors and hospitality are recorded in other sources, and the urban setting designates the house as a *domus* rather than a villa; see analysis in Bodel 1999. There are many fine translations of the *Satyricon* in numerous languages. For English: esp. Gaselee 1910 (also 1927 and 1944), notable also for its illustrations by Norman Lindsay.

3 "Euergetism" is a modern term for a historical phenomenon derived from the Greek nouns εὐεργεσία (benefaction) and εὐεργέτης (the benefactor); the verb εὐεργετέω (to act for the benefit of others) corresponded to Greek institutional and social practices: detailed account in Domingo 2016.

At the basic (but large-scale) level, food and entertainment were daily euergetistic realities: from the second century BCE in Republican times through Late Antiquity, the doles (*annona*) assured a free supply of grain to the poorer citizens of the City. The *annona* and *ludi* together were lampooned by Juvenal as "bread and circuses" (*panis et circenses*: Satire 10.76–81): he was expressing his satirical contempt for the decadent citizens who were recipients of such largesse and entertainment—not its givers, imperial ones in this case.

At another level, the givers' motivations could come from family pride, from individuals wishing to leave a mark on society, and from traditional or political considerations, but the result was an impressive panoply of investment in humane endeavors and cultural goods. While the capital and major cities of the empire were the main venues for showy euergetism, towns in imitation of them everywhere also enjoyed generous gifts from groups or individuals. Such benefactions brought sustenance, joy, pride, and civic identity to townsfolk. Generous displays of fellow feeling for one-time events could also be part of family ceremonies and funerals, promotions, accession to public office, and the like; inscriptions from Italian sites attest their effectiveness: Forbis 1993; 1996.

At these local levels, such ideas as *beneficium* (kindly favor) and *gratia* (gracious generosity) operated. Sponsorship of poetry competitions, putting on theatrical plays of all kinds (tragedy, comedy, pantomime, dancing), contests of oratory, and lectures, and often useful and impressive buildings as their venues could fulfill the euergetistic drive coming from emperors, local town councillors, and regional grandees, including women of the citizen class and grateful freedpersons: Eck 1997. On Greek and Roman euergetism in general: *OCD4* s.v. "Euergetism" (A.J.S. Spawforth); *NP* s.v. "Euergetism" (H.J. Gehrke); *NP* s.v. "Endowments" (G. Weiler); *EAA* s.v. "Munificentia" (W. Köhler); on female benefactors: Hemelrijk 2015. On private *alimenta* in Italy: Forbis 1996. On the terminology of *philanthropia*: McGuckin 2010, 50–57 (classical Greek) and 57–71 (Byzantine). On Late Antique euergetism, sometimes in obligatory funding by local aristocracies for towns: J.-U. Krause 1987.

On the abstract principles and terminology of euergetism: Forbis 1993; Wallace-Hadrill 1981. On "bread and circuses," Veyne 1976, in French, is still definitive; Veyne 1990 is the abridged English translation. On Late Antique and Byzantine *philanthropia* and public charities: Patlagean 1977; review of secondary sources in McGuckin 2010.

The *annona* was the system of grain distribution begun for the city of Rome already in Republican times: *NP* s.v. "Annona" (W. Jongman); *OCD4* s.v. "Food Supply: Roman" (D.W. Rathbone); Pavis d'Escurac 1976 (personnel); Rickman 1980a; 1980b; Sirks 2001; Erdkamp 2005; Kessler and Temin 2007; Jongman 2002 (sociopsychological effects); Marzano and Métraux 2018b, 4–5, n. 15; possible physical effects on villas: Métraux 1998, 14–15.

4 Private euergetism by villa owners was all the more necessary in Italy because the land tax (*tributum soli*), which was applicable to town-held land, had not been imposed on private property owned by Roman citizens since 167 BCE. The exemption was for property throughout the peninsula, including Gallia Cisalpina (where Comum was located) and the Transpadane areas south of the Alps (but not Sicily): Eberle 2021, 83–87. In the more than 250 years between 167 BCE and Pliny's day, the number and size of towns in Italy had grown, as had the number of villas and estates: Launaro 2017, 86–91; de Haas 2017, 58–65. The result was to squeeze the finances of local authorities in Italy in providing social benefits and, indeed, many of the institutional and physical elements that made a Roman town.

5 After Pliny's death in 113 CE, his fellow citizens listed his many gifts—lifetime and posthumous—to the town. The inscription was perhaps in the baths at Comum, which he had given to the town (*CIL* 5 5262 = *ILS* 2927). It lists his name, father's name, and tribe, then his positions starting with the greatest (consul) and religious positions, governorships overseas (Pontus and Bithynia), down to youthful military appointments. His lifetime and posthumous gifts to Comum are listed in this order: baths (THERM[*as*]) plus 300,000*HS* to maintain them (ORNATUM); an *alimenta* of 1,866,666 2/3*HS* to the city (TUTELA) for 100 of his freedmen (LIBERTOR SUORUM HOMIN C), then funds for an annual dinner for the citizenry ([*pl*]EB URBAN); in his lifetime, the *alimenta* of 500,000*HS* for the boys and girls of the citizenry (PUEROR ET PUELLAR PLEB URBAN), which Pliny describes in his letter to Caninius Rufus (*Ep.* 7.18.1–5); finally, 100,000*HS* to the city for the library (IN TUTELAM BYBLIOTHECAE). The benefactions appear to be listed from the greatest amount (the baths themselves plus their maintenance endowment) to the least, the library endowment.

6   The official *alimenta* was a system whereby local villa owners had their properties permanently encumbered with annual payments of 3–5% on the self-declared value of their estates for expenses related to the support of children of poor parents. It appears to have been instituted around 98 CE; it may have been replaced in 272 CE by a reformed and extended *cura annonae* under Aurelian, which reorganized comestible subsidies for Rome and possibly other centers: *HA, Aurel.* 35 and 48; Aur. Vict., *Caes.* 12.4 (attrib. to Nerva); Southern 2015, 181–82, nn. 396–402; Rickman 1980a; 1980b, 187–209.

The *alimenta* are known from inscriptions written on bronze tablets, one found at Ligures Baebiani near Beneventum in Campania, the other from Veleia in Liguria (*Pleiades* s.v. "Ligures Baebiani" and "Veleia"). These accounts list the names of owners, the names of their villas and properties as recorded, and the amount of the loans, together with a statement of the amount of interest revenue to the town and how many children were included in the alimentary scheme. For the *alimenta* accounts at Ligures Baebiani: *ILS* 6509; Veyne 1957; 1958; Champlin 1981. For the *alimenta* accounts at Veleia: *ILS* 6675; De Pachtère 1920; Criniti 1991; for both towns: Cao 2010. General considerations: Duncan-Jones 1964; 1982, 288–342, 382–385; Garnsey 1968; Lo Cascio 2000b; Jongman 2002.

7   Kleiner 1992, 224–29, fig. 190.

8   This remark by Cicero is included because it relates to income from villas. Cicero, as well as Varro, regarded *piscinarii* (sing. *piscinarius*), meaning "owners of fishponds," as contemptible rich persons of luxurious habit and pointless hobbies. Fishponds were thought to be expensive and ostentatious, an opinion Cicero repeats elsewhere (Cic., *Att.* 20 [1.20]). Both were wrong: in fact, building fishponds large enough to supply urban markets was a high-investment commercial proposition available only to the very rich who owned maritime villas, and investment in them was very profitable, not a frivolous luxury. However, the prejudice persisted. *Contra* Cicero and Varro: Marzano and Brizzi 2009; Marzano 2013; 2018; 2020; in general: Higgenbotham 1997.

9   On Quintus Remmius Palaemon: *NP* s.v. "Remmius" 2 (P.L. Schmidt).

10   While Sthenelus's efforts may have been decisive, Palaemon's own cleverness cannot be discounted no matter what Pliny says. Palaemon may have seen that buying up scattered properties that were not profitable because they were too small in order to create a single large productive estate with efficiencies of scale and management costs may well have been Palaemon's intention. His vanity or the prestige of owning *praedia* may have been only one motivation.

11   These were prestige wines of Latium: Plin., *HN* 14.61; Columella, *Rust.* 3.8.5; and see Tchernia 2013c.

12   Pliny's assertion that Italian agriculture was as profitable as the trade between the Roman empire and India through the Red Sea is a mere moral preference; the Roman-Indian commerce was very profitable and a source of considerable customs revenue: Tomber 2008; McLaughlin 2014; Cobb 2018, 116–26.

13   On Calvina: Birley 2000, 46.

14   Pliny may have acted as Calvinus's banker, taking sums on deposit.

15   Though the date of this letter is not known, Pliny's appointments were numerous: he was a high official of the state treasury (*praefectus aerarii Saturni*) as of 98 CE after a stint in the same post for the military treasury. He became a senator in 100 CE and was appointed suffect consul that same year; later, he was charged with overseeing the banks of the Tiber (*curator alvei Tiberis*). He was elected an augur in the state religious system as of 103 CE.

16   Annius Severus appears to have been Pliny's agent in Comum, evidently a friend as well; Birley 2000, 37.

17   By saying that "up to now' (*adhuc*) he had no such works of art in his house, Pliny is either disingenuously pleading poverty or else his law practice before becoming a senator and being appointed to a high treasury post had not yet brought him the wealth that would have allowed him to collect them.

18   On Calvisius Rufus: Birley 2000, 46–47

19   There was evidently a lively market in Roman central Italy for buying and selling agricultural estates with villas, even though in this case the asking sale price had gone down by 40% from its notional value of 5,000,000HS through bad management.

20   The logic of concentrating wealth by amalgamating two estates to achieve economy of scale is clear. What is also clear is that only one residential villa will survive functionally—the other will be abandoned. This gives a picture that does not support, as has been claimed, an economic downturn in Italian agricultural properties in Pliny's day. If anything, it indicates a streamlining of the agricultural economy for purposes of greater profit by concentration of estates: Gibson 2020, 149–51; Marzano and Métraux 2018b, 21–22; Métraux 1998, 2–3.

21   Pliny clearly had learned the lessons of frugality in villa management advocated by the writers of agricultural treatises insofar as the *pars rustica* aspects of property were concerned. The owner's side of the estate, the residential *pars urbana*, was another matter, as Pliny's description of his villas and their gardens tell us.

22   Pliny is explaining the logic, practiced among Roman villa owners, of owning several properties, not just in the Italian peninsula but ultimately throughout the Mediterranean provinces: spreading out risk to agricultural income due to weather, blight, or other localized misfortunes.

23   The pleasure of traveling from one estate to another is amply attested by Cicero's and many others' peregrinations to countryside and coastal villas.

24   Tenants (*coloni*) were an important part of an estate's

value, and abusing them had consequences on the viability of ownership and ultimately the value of the property: general account in De Neeve 1984. In this case, Pliny is planning to supply tenants with some enslaved workers as a normal part of their tenancy: the enslaved workers were part of their equipment. For more on Pliny's tenants, see Plin. *Ep.* 10.8.1–8, in this chapter.

25 It is unclear whether Pliny himself did not use enslaved persons in chain gangs (*servi vincti*), or if using them was not customary in the neighborhood. Certainly Columella (*Rust.* 1.9) had assumed that vineyards should be worked by *servi vincti*, and Pliny's Tuscan property was mainly dedicated to viticulture. In this case, Pliny assumes that they will live unchained and but still confined in slave prisons (*ergastula*) rather than in chain gangs. His uncle Pliny the Elder was negative on the use of chain gangs or slave prisons: Plin., *HN* 18.21 (18.5); Étienne 1974.

26 For evidence of problems in the price of agricultural goods, namely wine, see Pliny's letter about discounts to middlemen (*Ep.* 8.2, in this chapter).

27 For the friendly relations between Pliny and Pompeia Celerina, the mother of his deceased second wife, see *Ep.* 1.4.1–4, in ch. 6, Villa Visits; they visited one another in their villas. In addition, the ability of Pliny and those of his social circle to avail themselves easily of family-based fortunes was normal, giving both financial flexibility and financial clout to the upper social classes in Rome and elsewhere.

28 However, in *Ep.* 2.17.1–5 (see ch. 4, Descriptions of Villas), Pliny mentions cattle on the estate as well as pasturage, trees, and sources of water, so some revenue may have come from them as meat or dairy products.

29 Enslaved persons were an important workforce commodity for villas; care was required when acquiring them.

30 Overview in Frayn 1993. A good review of *nundinae* in North Africa and Italy is in MacMullen 1970 (339–41, figs. 2 and 3), which analyzes a fascinating inscription on marble from Suessula in Campania with a schedule of the *nundinae* in towns between Rome and the Bay of Naples. The schedule made sure that its tradesman-owner got to the right town's market on the right day. On other aspects of *nundinae* in Campania and Latium: Storchi Marino 2000; Andreau 2000.

31 The rest of this letter concerns technicalities concerning legal fees in the Roman courts; the Vicetines had made an initial deposit for services of 6,000*HS* plus another 4,000*HS* to Nominatus—fairly large sums. Whether this was ethical or was setting a questionable precedent is Pliny's concern. Because of the economic importance of *nundinae*, requests to hold private ones could be heard adversarially as high as the level of the Senate: Cracco Ruggini 2000. Some seventy-five years before this dispute between Sollers and the town government of Vicetia in Gallia Cisalpina (modern Vicenza), the future emperor Claudius had petitioned the consuls to hold a market on his private estate: Suetonius, *Claud.* 12.2.

32 On Lucius Calpurnius Fabatus: Birley 2000, 45.

33 This letter gives the approximate price of land in a good lakeside location suitable for the construction of a villa on the Lacus Larius (modern Lake Como). It also indicates that the price of properties might well vary according to the relationship between seller and buyer, in this case a matter of affection and long-standing affiliation. As the bequest to Pliny was less than half of the whole property, its valuation upon the death of its owner must have been over 1,000,000*HS*.

34 Pliny was elected praetor in 93 CE. On Hermes: Birley 2000, 62; on Minicius Justus: Birley 2000, 75; on Corellia Hispulla and Quintus Corellius Rufus: Birley 2000, 51.

35 On Caninius Rufus: Birley 2000, 47.

36 Pliny speaks of his euergetism in *Ep.* 3.4, on his donation of a statue to Comum; and in *Ep.* 4.1, on the enlargement of a temple at Tifernum Tiberinum, mentioned early in this chapter.

37 Pliny does not state the actual value of the properties he conveyed, but at a tax of 30,000*HS* representing the 3–5% interest charged on the public (imperial) *alimenta* loans, a real value of 1,000,000*HS* or more is not an unreasonable estimate. The agreement between the municipal official and Pliny offset the lowering of the property's value and made the *alimenta* for boys and girls permanent.

38 Pliny was generous to his friends' relatives (in the case of Calvina), but his public donations to the town of Comum and to Tifernum Tibertinum were much greater. For the inscription (*CIL* 5 5262 = *ILS* 2927) recording them, see n. 5 in ch. 7. That inscription does not mention the statue he gave to the temple of Jupiter (see *Ep.* 3.6 in this chapter). Other inscriptions mention Pliny and include his priesthood: *CIL* 5.5263l; *CIL* 5.5667 (Vercellae).

In *Ep.* 1.8, Pliny mentions that he has written a speech to his fellow citizens (*apud municipes meos*) on the occasion of the dedication of the library at Comum; it is possible that he also funded and built the library, not just endowing its upkeep (*tutela*) in his bequests. Later in the same letter (*Ep.* 1.8.10), he states that he is emphatically not paying for games and gladiators but has preferred to undertake the annual expenses of an *alimenta* for children (*ludi et gladiatores sed annuos sumptus in alimenta ingenuorum*). The letter is about modesty versus pride in good works, and how difficult it is to avoid virtue signaling.

To the town of Tifernum Tibertinum, he gave a temple (*Ep.* 4.1), had a temple of Ceres on his property rebuilt, the image of the goddess replaced, and porticoes built adjacent to it (*Ep.* 9.39.1–6). He donated statues to another temple, which he appears to have built for the express purpose of housing them (*Ep.* 10.8.1–8, in this chapter).

39 On the region's wine: Gibson 2020, 149. On Pliny's finances in general, including wine: Sirago 1957; Duncan-Jones 1965; R. Martin 1967. On the history of Italian wine economics: Carandini 1989.

40 For wines improving with age, Tchernia 2013a; 2013b; 2013c.

41 "…so no one should leave without getting something" is quoted from Vergil, *Aen.* 5.305.

42 Analysis in Sherwin-White 1966, 449–50. The problem with the price of wine is not certain. A good year may have resulted in a glut of wine on the general market causing decline in prices, or possibly a price war among large vintners or from overseas wine producers competing against Italian producers. We have seen that Pliny (*Ep.* 3.19.1–9, in this chapter), and doubtless others, had recognized that having different estates in different prevailing climates and places minimized losses on their agricultural income due to weather or other causes.

43 "…a person who holds the worthy and the unworthy in the same regard" is quoted from Hom., *Il.* 9.319.

44 Valerius Paulinus (M. Lollius Paulinus Decimus Valerius Asiaticus Saturninus, ca. 69–134 CE) was a high courtier and imperial official during the Flavian dynasty and through the reign of Hadrian: *NP* s.v. "Lollius" II 3 (W. Eck). In 94 CE, and again in 107, he was inducted as suffect consul for four months. It appears to be the latter occasion that Pliny is apologizing for having to remain at his Tuscan villa on farm business instead of attending the ceremony.

45 This letter has been cited as an example, in Roman Italy, of the *mezzadria* method of farm tenancy that was common in central Italy in the later Middle Ages through modern times: Cato, *Agr.* 136–137. The difference is that the norms of *mezzadria* included the estate owners' obligation to provide or subsidize agricultural hardware and equipment for their tenants: Pliny does not mention that obligation here. However, in another letter (*Ep.* 3.19.1–9, in this chapter), he notes that he may have to supply prospective tenants with enslaved workers—*instrumentum vocale*, as Varro put it (*Rust.* 1.17.1)—so a modified *mezzadria* system may have existed. The rough equivalent of *mezzadria* in French is *métayage*; in English, sharecropping.

46 On euergetism, see nn. 3 and 4 in ch. 7.

47 Pliny addresses the emperor as *dominus*, which in this context means "lord." Suetonius tells us that Domitian (r. 81–96 CE) was the first emperor to insist on this title with the addition of *et deus* (and god); it was considered very shocking (Suet., *Dom.* 13). However, by Trajan's day, *dominus* had become normalized in court etiquette as a title of address to the emperor.

48 Besides other duties, Pliny is asking for a leave of absence from the post of *praefectus aerarii Saturni* or keeper of the state treasury. These duties often rotated among a team of officials, but presence in the City was considered part of the job.

49 The "Quintilian" referred to is not the famous writer on jurisprudence (Marcus Fabius Quintilianus, ca. 35–100 BCE) but merely a name by which Juvenal denotes any typically rich lawyer, a class that Juvenal particularly hated—and he hated their rich offspring even more. In his view, buying villas with wealth generated by non-land-based professions was contemptible.

NOTES TO CHAPTER 8

1 The *Institutes* of Gaius are chosen for primary citation here because their date (early 160s CE) makes their prescriptions and definitions closer to legal issues concerning villas from Republican times and into the empire than the more elaborated jurisprudence of Justinian's legal reforms some four centuries later (530s CE). Justinian's *Institutes* and *Digesta* are cited secondarily because they include the views of earlier jurists (including Gaius), sometimes verbatim, sometimes as indirect quotations, that also deal with questions of villas, estates, personnel, and equipment.

For the definition of *dominium*, ownership, in both divine/religious and human aspects of *patrimonium potestatis*, the power of ownership: Gaius, *Institutes* 2.1–114 (Gneist 1880, 61–63; English translation: Gordon and Robinson 1988, 124–77) [= Justinian, *Institutes* 2.1, English translation: Birks and McLoed 1987, 55–61]; analysis in Johnston 1999, 56–58. Distinctions are made between a thing or things owned by someone capable to be conveyed or sold to another (*res mancipi*) and a thing or things in a religious designation or in a natural category belonging to no one (*res nullius*) and not available for conveyance or sale (*mancipatio*).

Confiscation of property and change in its legal category could be a penalty for crime or for falling afoul of authority in political circumstances. When Cicero's house on the Palatine Hill in Rome was dismantled by senatorial decree in May 58 BCE and its land allocated to religious purposes (the *aedes Libertatis*), it is possible that there was a conversion of its plot from *res mancipi* to *res nullius*. To resume ownership of the house plot, Cicero convinced the priests to change its designation the following year (Cic., *Dom.*). His villas at Tusculum and Formiae were also damaged and despoiled, though probably without change of legal designation: see Cic., *Att.* 74 (4.2), in ch. 4, Descriptions of Villas.

2 *Res mancipi* with exemptions and limitations: Gaius, *Institutes* 1.119–122 (Gneist 1880, 35–36; English translation: Gordon and Robinson 1988, 79–83); *res non mancipi*: Gaius, *Institutes* 2.14–22 (Gneist 1880, 67–68; English translation: Gordon and Robinson 1988, 127–33).

The categories of conveyable property also included bequests and inheritances. Pliny the Younger gives an example of inheritance by a widow from a husband: Plin., *Ep.* 8.18.7–9. He comments that "she inherits very pleasant villas and a large amount of money" from an old, sick husband in a second marriage that was beneath her as to rank and reputation: analysis in Sherwin-White 1966, 469.

3 On *mancipatio* (for sale of land and enslaved persons, ceremony of witnessing sales): Gaius, *Institutes* 1.119–122 (Gneist 1880, 36; English translation: Gordon and Robinson 1988, 85–87).

On *possessio* in general: Johnston 1999, 67–68; Baldus 2016.

4 *Usus* and *usufructus*: Gaius, *Institutes* 2.28–39 (Gneist 1880, 69–70; English translation: Gordon and Robinson 1988, 79–83) [=

Justinian, *Institutes* 2.5.1–6; English translation: Birks and McLoed 1987, 63–65]; further elaboration in the *Digesta* of Justinian 7.1.1–9 (Watson 2009, 1:216–18); analysis in Johnston 1999, 67–68. For an example of *usus*: Cicero's arrangements to cede his villa at Baiae to Pilia, wife of his friend Atticus: Cic., *Att.* 369 (14.15), 370 (14.16), 371 (14.17), and 371A (14.17A), May 1 to May 8, 44 BCE.

On *usufructus*: Pliny gave the usufruct of a villa to his nurse (Plin., *Ep.* 6.3.1–2, in this chapter); Maecenas gave the usufruct of a villa, its estate, and the rental income from five tenants to Horace (Hor., *Sat.* 2; see ch. 4, Descriptions of Villas); Martial had the usufruct of a villa given to him by the emperor Domitian (Mart., *Epig.* 9.18, in this chapter).

5   Gaius, *Institutes* 2.30–33 (Gneist 1880, 69; English translation: Gordon and Robinson 1988, 135–37); for elaborations on usufruct: *Digesta* of Justinian 7.1.1–74 (Watson 2009, 1:216–31).

6   Gaius, *Institutes* 2.1–14 for religious limitations (Gneist 1880, 61–63; English translation: Gordon and Robinson 1988, 124–29).

7   Gaius, *Institutes* 2.35–38 (Gneist 1880, 69–70; English translation: Gordon and Robinson 1988, 139–41). Ultimately the distinction in property designation between tangible and intangible things was dissolved in the *Novellae* of Justinian, so encumbrances such as mortgages or disputes about usufruct came to be included as assets or liabilities in the sale of properties.

8   Gaius has little to say about servitudes on rural estates: Gaius, *Institutes* 2.17 (Gneist 1880, 67; English translation: Gordon and Robinson 1988, 92–94). However, rural servitudes were an occasion for serious disputes and took up much in legal intelligence and ink by lawyers and jurists. Except for a brief section (8.2) on urban problems, the entire eighth book of the *Digesta* of Justinian is devoted to the jurisprudence on disputes about servitudes on rural estates.

Cicero describes the servitudes or similar arrangements for Quintus's villa at Laterium: Quintus wished to avoid a servitude on Lucusta's and Varro's properties by grading a road in an awkward spot, but Cicero was planning for a water servitude arrangement with Marcus Taurus, whose property was adjacent (see Cic., *QFr.* 21, in this chapter).

9   This may be a manifestation of a sparse stock of existing villas in the first half of the second century BCE relative to their greater geographical density in the second half, but it may also be Cato's desire to give expression to a pioneering spirit to his readers: e.g., Cato, *Agr.* 3, in ch. 2, Villas in Roman Agricultural Treatises.

10   See Vitr., *De arch.* 6.5.3, 6.6.1–5, and 6.6.7, in ch. 3, Villas in Roman Architectural Treatises.

11   See Varro, *Agr.* 3.2.3, in ch. 2, Villas in Roman Agricultural Treatises.

12   The archaeological evidence for villas comes as much from observation on the ground as from below-grade archaeological excavation. Spreads of datable pottery of all kinds, datable masonry methods, presence of implements (querns, millstones, vats, spindle whorls) can be analyzed in conjunction with survey and photographic methods to determine wall lines and other features. The result is a fairly reliable picture of villa spread in a landscape in chronological sequence. For an overview of methods for the South Etruria survey (1950s–1970s) and the ongoing Tiber Valley project: Patterson and Millet 1998, esp. 7–9; Launaro 2017; de Haas 2017; most recently, Bowes et al. 2020.

The increase in newly built villas in central Italy in the first century BCE is shown in the appendices of Marzano 2007. Even allowing for the skewing of the data due to the varying intensity and geographic spread of modern investigation of the countryside, the results in Marzano's study can be summarized as follows: for all known or recorded villas in Latium around Rome, Tuscany, and Umbria (appx. A, 759–69), the majority of sites showed early construction phases firmly in the first century BCE, very few earlier. The histograms of the incidence of datable villas and their start of occupation in Latium, including the city of Rome (appx. B, 771 and 773, respectively) clearly show a sudden increase of villas in the first century BCE over the number in both the previous century and the first century CE, and with an occupation lasting from the first century BCE well into the second century CE and sometimes beyond. The same is the case for Tuscany and Umbria, though over fewer villa sites: between Cato writing in the 160s BCE and Varro in 37–36 BCE, villas had indeed become the norm in the Italian landscape. Most recently on villas south of Rome: Ippoliti 2020.

Elsewhere, Campania, and especially the area of the Bay of Naples, was well provisioned with existing villas by the end of the first century BCE: in the 60s to the 40s BCE, Cicero (wealthy enough, but by no means the richest, villa owner) was buying (at Pompeii and Baiae) and receiving by bequest (at Puteoli) and adding to the stock of villas (at Cumae), besides inheriting his ancestral villa (at Arpinum). His brother was both buying and building at their hometown. For villas in inland Campania: Frederiksen 1981; 1984; Arthur 1991a;1991b; for coastal villas but not on the Bay of Naples: *EAA* s.v. "Liternum" (A. De Franciscis); Gargiulo 2000; 2002; 2007. Farther south, in the *regiones* II and III of Italy (Apulia, Lucania, Bruttium), villas of central Italian type appeared equally suddenly in the first century BCE: Gualtieri 2018, 160, nn. 18–19; Lippolis 2006, 43–84; Olshausen 2010. For overviews of the growth of agricultural exploitation in Italy in the Late Republic: Pleket 1993, 317–42; Lo Cascio 1999; articles in Coarelli and Patterson 2008; articles in Carlsen and Lo Cascio 2010; Bowman and Wilson 2013a, 5–6.

13   For an overview of the various types of personnel: Carlsen 2001.

14   On Cicero's real estate finances: Rauh 1986; 1989.

15   Atticus's villa at Buthrotum (modern Butrint) was across a strait from the town of Corcyra, a large, busy place on the island of the same name (modern Corfu). Buthrotum: *Pleiades* s.v. "Buthrotum"; Corcyra: *Pleiades* s.v. "Corcyra."

16   Tyrannion is the nickname of Theophrastus of Amisus: in 72 BCE, Lucullus had brought him as a war captive to Rome where he worked as librarian and teacher for Cicero

and others: *NP* s.v. "Tyrannion" 1 (M. Baumbach); Shackleton Bailey 1995, 104. Dionysius and Menophilus were enslaved household members or freedmen of Atticus engaged in literary and librarian activities: Shackleton Bailey 1995, 46 (Dionysius) and 69 (Menophilus).

17 These *domus* are probably the adjacent houses on the Palatine, now in the course of being rebuilt after Cicero's return from exile. Cicero's villas may also be under restoration. On their houses in Rome, see n. 6 in ch. 4, Descriptions of Villas.

18 ἀμφιλαφία: this term means "on two hands" or "extravagant," which I have translated as "hand-over-fist" expenses.

19 This is the house on the Palatine that had been dismantled by his enemies (along with the villa at Tusculum being vandalized) while Cicero was in exile: it was being rebuilt at the expense of the Senate: Cic., *Att.* 74 (4.2), in ch. 4, Descriptions of Villas.

20 Laterium was a property and villa owned by his brother near Arpinum; Cicero appears to have owned their father's and grandfather's villa at Arpinum, their hometown; he had made some additions. The phrase "to see [*adspicere*] my villa at Cumae" indicates that it was under construction and not yet habitable.

21 In the same year, Quintus's Laterium estate had unspecified problems, possibly with the approach road to the villa or with requests for water servitudes on the estate. Cicero mentioned these problems to Atticus because they were causing a local scandal: Cic., *Att.* 79 (4.8).

22 The Roman Games (*ludi Romani*) were held annually in the City in early September and consisted of processions, chariot racing, and dramatic representations. Cicero, as the leading Arpinate in Rome, has left one Philotimus to entertain and find accommodation for his relatives, fellow members of the Arpinate tribes, and townspeople who had come to Rome for the events.

The river is the Fibrenus (modern Fibreno).

23 Mescidius and Philoxenus: enslaved workers or freedmen of the brothers. Herius was perhaps a neighbor.

24 Manilian estate: either a property near the Arcanum villa, or a villa on another property called "Manilian" because it had been previously owned by one Manilius. Diphilus: an architect or builder, but the contemptuous condescension suggests he was an enslaved person or freedman: Shackleton Bailey 1995, 46.

25 ". . . columns have been polished": this indicates that the columns were of brick or rough masonry with stuccoed surfaces rather than monolithic in stone or marble; the next sentence deals with plastering.

26 Caesius: an agent in charge of Quintus's properties: Shackleton Bailey 1995, 28.

27 The Via Vitularia ("the cattle road") was the informal name of a road linking Arpinum with the Tyrrhenian coast: Leoni 2008, 181, fig. 61.

28 Some emendations have this estate as near Bovillae in Latium, but that town was not near Arpinum and not on the Via Vitularia: De Rossi 1979, 298–323; *NP* s.v. "Bovillae" (G. Uggeri). At the time, it was in some legal limbo as to water rights with a neighbor: Cic., *Att.*77.3 (4.7.3).

29 Mescidius: a local real estate estimator, or a water engineer? In Mescidius's computation, and not allowing for Cicero's observation that the distance was greater, the cost for the water supply of the Bobilius estate would have been 45,000*HS* (15,000 *pedes* × 3*HS* per *pes* = 45,000*HS*). The distance was considerable: 1 Roman *pes* = 29.44 cm or 11.65 in. In this calculation, 3,000 *passus* at 5 Roman feet to a *passus* = 15,000 *pedes*, about 4,440 m (4.4 km), or 14,562 ft. (2¾ mi.).

30 Furrina: a local goddess. Satricum: a town west of Arpinum and the Laterium villa: Heldring 1998; Attema, de Haas, and Tol 2011; *NP* s.v. "Satricum" (M.M. Morciano).

31 Locusta and Varro: neighboring property owners near Quintus's villa at Laterium. It is not certain if the Varro in question was Cicero's learned correspondent, Marcus Terentius Varro, who also owned a villa farther away, at Casinum, but he may have owned others nearer Arpinum.

32 "*Pallium* wearers": Cicero is joking. The statues standing between the columns or in the garden in Quintus's art collection were supposedly Greek, and Greek dress was the *pallium*, so Greek statues were "those who wear the *pallium*."

33 Philotimus and Cincius: enslaved workers or freedmen skilled as builders or decorators at work on Quintus's urban *domus*. Philotimus was also in charge of hosting the Arpinates attending the Roman Games in Cicero's absence: Shackleton Bailey 1995, 78.

34 The rest of the letter has to do with political and legal news as well as the purchase and sale of Greek and Latin books in Quintus's library.

Quintus and his villas and *domus* had come up seven years earlier: in Cic., *Att.* 14.7 (1.14.7) of February 61 BCE, Cicero reported that his brother has bought "three-fourths" of his house on the Argiletum for 725,000*HS* (perhaps paying off a mortgage or loan) to buy another urban house, perhaps better value for a political career. The sum can be compared to what Cicero had paid for his house on the Palatine (3,500,000*HS*), a much more desirable district compared to the Argiletum.

The Argiletum was the main road entering the Forum from the Subura from the northeast, extant in Cicero's time but later covered by the construction of the imperial forums: *AtlasAncRome* 1 148 (topography), 161 (formation in the third century BCE), 166 (development by Cicero's day); and 2: pls. 89 and 92a (plans of Argiletum from Forum to Carinae, first century BCE); Haselberger et al. 2002, s.v. "Argiletum" (E.A. Dumser); *LTUR* 1 125–26 (E. Tortorici); Richardson 1992, 39.

35 Apparently, Julius Caesar had fine taste, or else Cicero is giving his brother Quintus a topic to chat about with his commanding general.

36 The *imagines istae* in this case are not portraits or busts of Quintus's (and Cicero's) ancestors: they are works of art independent of ancestral *imagines*. In context, Cicero is saying that, had Philotimus been in charge, the decorations and accessories of the villa would have been better than if Diphilus had been in charge—that was why Julius Caesar's opinion was needed. Diphilus was, in Cicero's view, an incompetent slacker. Philotimus was much better at supervising construction for Quintus's *domus* in Rome and was given other important tasks, but neither Philotimus nor Diphilus was perfect in their work: see Cic., *QFr.* 21 (3.1): D'Arms (1970) 2003, cat. I 19, 175–76. On ancestral *imagines*, see discussion of Cic., *Orat.* 110 (30–31) and n. 51 in ch. 4, Descriptions of Villas.

37 Publius Cornelius Lentulus Spinther ("Spinther" was a nickname) was consul in 57 BCE and subsequently governor of Cilicia; though he had been an early associate of Julius Caesar, he became a prominent partisan of Pompey. Cicero and he had a long friendship, and as consul he effected Cicero's recall from exile: *NP* s.v. "Cornelius" I 54; Shackleton Bailey 1995, 41.

38 The brother of a prominent politician and military man, Marcus Minucius Thermus, consul in 81 BCE; Shackleton Bailey 1995, 67.

39 On Cluvius and other business friends: Rauh 1986. On Marcus Cluvius: Shackleton Bailey 1995, 37.

40 For Cluvius: Cic., *Att.* 116 (6.2) and 363 (14.9). See also Cic., *Att.* 338.3 (13.46.3) in this chapter and Plin., *HN* 31.6–9 (31.3), in ch. 4, Descriptions of Villas.

41 Lucius Cornelius Balbus of Gades (d. after 32 CE), suffect consul in 40 BCE, was a close associate of Caesar and had been defended on a charge of illicitly claiming Roman citizenship in Cicero's speech *Pro Balbo*: *NP* s.v. "Cornelius" I 6 (K.-L. Elvers).

42 In general on buying and selling: analysis in Rauh 1989.

43 On Phamea: Shackleton Bailey 1995, 77.

44 Gnaeus Cornelius Lentulus Marcellinus (ca. 90–48 BCE) was consul in 56 BCE, seven years before: *NP* s.v. "Cornelius" I 52 (K.-L. Elvers); Shackleton Bailey 1995, 40.

45 By "Trojan," Cicero designates the area between Lanuvium and the coastal area around Lavinium south of Ostia where the Trojan prince Aeneas had landed and founded cities: Torelli 1984; Appian *apud* Photius 52–53.

46 Lucius Cornelius Lentulus Crus (ca. 97–48 BCE), consul in 49 BCE; during the First Triumvirate, he had thought that his reward for political partisanship might be the properties belonging to opposing partisans: *NP* s.v. "Cornelius" I 50 (K.-L. Elvers); Shackleton Bailey 1995, 40.

47 A friend of Cicero who lived permanently in Naples and often received letters from him: *NP* s.v. "Paetus" I 22 (J. Fündling); Shackleton Bailey 1995, 75.

48 By *salis*, Cicero may mean salty wit, so he praises his friend for the facetious way he had described the villa in question. He may also mean money, in the same way that "bread" in English is slang for money, so he himself is both witty and rich. However, in the absence of salt cellars (*salinum*, pl. *salina*), namely sources of readily available cash rather than money in loans, businesses, and mortgages, he can't buy the villa.
    For *salinum*, Pliny inveighs against valuable silver ones, which have replaced ones in humbler materials: Plin., *HN* 33.153 (54).

49 Marcus Tullius Tiro: as a former enslaved household member manumitted by his owner Cicero, Tiro took the *praenomen* and *nomen* of his former master as a compliment to him: *NP* s.v. "Tiro" 1 (M. Zelzer); Shackleton Bailey 1995, 103.

50 The list in Greek: πέψις (*pēpsis*, digestion), ἀκοπίας (*akopias*, rest), περίπατος σύμμετρος (*perĭpatos sŭmmetrios*, moderate walking), τρίψις (or τρυφή, *trĭphe*, bodily enjoyment), εὐλυσία κοιλίας (*eulosĭa koilĭas*, easy defecations). On Tiro's illnesses (possibly malaria) and on the relationship between Cicero and Tiro: Spurny 2021, 253 and nn. 7 and 8; also 254–56 for a list of letters about Tiro's illnesses and other matters.

51 Parhedrus and Helico: neighbors(?) of Cicero's at Tusculum who had rented (*conducere*) the villa's garden in the past. Helico had been a former lessee, but, having made improvements since Helico's lease expired, Cicero wants to get a better rent and is suggesting that Tiro ask one Parhedrus to take up the lease. Shackleton Bailey 1995, 75 (Parhedrus); 54 (Helico).

52 Motho: perhaps a gardener in Rome whom Cicero was able to cajole into giving him good quantities of flowers or flower wreaths: Shackleton Bailey 1995, 70.

53 The Aqua Crabra was an aqueduct supplying the Tusculan district; for a fee, Cicero was able to siphon water from it for his villa garden: Cic., *Leg. Agr.* 3.9.7; Frontinus, *Aq.* 9.4.1; Bannon 2009, 80–85; Marzano 2007, 167–69; 2022, 125 and nn. 186, 187 on Cicero's Tusculanum garden, and 117–25 on irrigation of *horti* in the *suburbium* of Rome in general.

54 "…little books": Cicero means books for light reading. The contrast with Sophocles is meant to contrast the slight with the sublime.

55 On Cicero Minor: *NP* s.v. "Tullius" I 10 (J. Fündling); in his father's correspondence: Shackleton Baily 1995, 101. On Tiro, see ch. 8 n. 49.

56 "…in a fold of your garment": the young Cicero imagines Tiro thriftily collecting grape pips or other fruit seeds spat out during dinner, for planting later on his new estate.

57 Vestorius, a businessman: Shackleton Bailey 1995, 106; on Marcus Cluvius, see nn. 39 and 40, this chapter.

58 Heirs could refuse bequests if the estate or building was encumbered with inheritable debt or other servitudes, or was in bad condition; accepting an inheritance was thus a matter of legal affirmation. That was the case with Corellia's inheritance, as described in Pliny's letter to her: Plin., *Ep.* 7.11.1–8, in ch. 7, Economics and Euergetism.

59 Lucius Cornelius Balbus, consul in 40 BCE, was Caesar's henchman and financier. As Cicero wished to buy Caesar out of his part of the bequest, it was normal to approach Balbus.

60 Terentia was Cicero's soon-to-be ex-wife.

61 On Cicero's and others' appreciation of nature: Morvillez 2017.

62 The lake is the Lucrine Lake (*lacus Lucrinus*) near Baiae, where Cicero owned a small villa.

63 Such arrangements, with or without a lease, and even with no rent or security payment, involved the entire functional and personnel parts of the villa given to the *usus* (but not *possessio*) of the designated person: the storerooms (*cellae*), enslaved overseers (*vilici*), and managers (*procuratores*) were all to be under Pilia's authority. No mention is made of usufruct: she may have been able to reside, but not profit from, whatever *fructus* or profit from produce the villa generated.

64 By the time of writing, Cicero himself had, in his opposition to Mark Antony and the Casesarean supporters and his defense of Caesar's assassins, become prominent once again in affairs of state. In consequence, his villas appear to have had crowds of clients and petitioners, something he complains about.

65 Cicero is asking Atticus to finish buying the co-heirs out of their portion of the inheritance so as to acquire exclusive possession of Cluvius's properties and the villa at Puteoli.

66 Commentary in Sherwin-White 1966, 140–41, and on Baebius Hispanus: 741; also Syme (1968) 1979, 146.

67 The letter appears to have been written in the first years of Trajan's reign (r. 98–117 CE) but before Pliny's appointment as imperial governor of Bithynia and Pontus in 110 CE. At the time of writing, probably between 98 and 110 CE, Suetonius was a lawyer and mid-level functionary in the imperial archives, not yet having achieved the important posts of secretary for archival and diplomatic letters for Hadrian, the succeeding emperor (r. 117–138 CE). On Suetonius's career and acquaintances: Wallace-Hadrill 1984.

68 Sherwin-White 1966, 750.

69 This designates a property in the Marsian district east of Rome near the Fucine lake.

70 Commentary in Sherwin-White 1966, 390, and on Calpurnius Fabatus, 742; also on Fabatus, Plin., *Ep.* 6.30.1–5, in this chapter.

71 The contrast between purer country water and city water delivered through lead pipes is one of the topics in Horace, *Epist.* 1.10.20–21; on pipes for city water sent to fountains and private houses: Strabo 5.8.

72 The *curva antlia* is a form of the Archimedean screw pump: a simple one made of wood hooped with iron and waterproofed with pitch is described by Vitruvius (*De arch.* 10.6): this could be operated by one man and was probably what Martial needed; Vitruvius describes a more complicated one in bronze invented by the Alexandrian Greek engineer Ctesibius (third century BCE) at *De arch.* 10.7; Oleson 2000; K. D. White 1970, 157, pl. 18.

73 The *fons Marcia* appears to denote the Aqua Marcia bringing water from the Anio River (modern Aniene) to Rome from the east-southeast, entering the City at the Porta Tiburtina and dividing to bring water to both the northeast and south-southwest urban areas: for the Marcia in Martial's day: Frontinus, *Aq.* 1.4 (list of aqueducts), *Aq.* 1.7–8 (construction of the Aqua Marcia and others), *Aq.* 1.12–14 and 19 (lines and distribution in the City), *Aq.* 2.125 (Augustan remodeling); Strabo 5.13 (sources); *AtlasAncRome* 1 164 (construction), 174 and n. 779 (terminus in Forum); 330 and n. 159 (Augustan remodeling); Coarelli 2014, 447 and fig. 130; Claridge 2010, 58.

74 The Castalian spring was the spring at the entrance to the Sanctuary of Apollo at Delphi.

75 Lucius Arruntius Stella, a Senator and suffect consul in 101 CE, is mentioned as a friend and patron by Martial and Statius and was a poet himself: *NP* s.v. "Arruntius" II 12 (J.A. Richmond).

76 Treggiari 2007, 136–38, 141; Späth 2010.

77 Analysis of these letters in Hilbold 2021, 118–21.

78 Cicero wished to endow the *fanum Tulliae* with an unusual solemnity, hence his frequent use of Greek terms in letters describing his plans. He uses the Greek *entáphios* for *sepulchrum* or another term for his own burial; *ektopismós* (too far away) instead of the Latin *procul*; *apothéōsis* for the Latin *consecratio*; and *timē* to convey the honor in which the *fanum* was to be held. These Greek terms gave special meaning to the project, taking it out of a merely local or personal context and giving it an abstract, universal character.

NOTES TO CHAPTER 9

1 Any summary regarding Roman villas and gardens must begin as early as 752 BCE with the establishment of colonies of citizens (*coloniae civium*, *coloniae maritimae*) to defend the City: see Livy 1.9–11; on the colonies: *Pleiades* s.v. "Antemnae, Crustumerium"; on Antemnae: Quilici and Quilici-Gigli 1978b; on Crustumerium and ongoing excavations there by Groningen Institute of Archaeology: Attema et al. 2017. Later, wars with other Italic peoples resulted in Latin colonies (*ius Latii*) set up throughout Italy, resulting in an occupation, sociopolitical stabilization, and agricultural exploitation throughout the peninsula: the foundation of colonies is covered in Cornell 2008 and most recently in Terrenato 2020. For map and table of the *coloniae civium* and Latin colonies: Cornell 2008, 390 (map), 391 and fig. 48 (list of colonies). For settlement patterns and statistics, Launaro 2011, 149–89. Mass enslavement of Italic people began early and increased in the second century; for numbers of enslaved persons from Italian locales: Cornell 2008, table 8 at 389.

2 The allocation of land in parcels and its designation of category of use (wooded, hilly, flat, riverside, marginal, and so on) were determined by teams of surveyors (*agrimensores*) whose various written instruction books survive, compiled as the *Corpus Agrimensorum Romanorum*: Campbell 2000; Dilke 1971; 1987; 1995 (French trans.). For the *Liber Coloniarium*: Libertini 2018; Libertini and Lorenz 2019 (English trans.); *NP* s.v. "Limitation" (H.-P. Kuhnen); for discussion of texts: *NP* s.v. "Land Surveying (M. Folkerts). The work of the surveyors established the *census* of wealth and political participation of local citizens.

3 The conflict, if it actually existed, between citizen farmers and owners of *latifundia* based on enslaved workers was paralleled by successive campaigns of land division (*centuratio*) and award of agricultural properties in Italy, Greece, Gaul, Hispania, and Africa Vetus (approximately northern modern Tunisia) to drafts of citizens enrolled to become colonists and to demobilized soldiers recompensed, by political actions on their behalf by their former military leaders, with farms. For the history of this period: Lintott 2008, 1–15; on the *latifundia* question: White 1967; Roselaar 2010; for the coexistence of small and large agricultural enterprises: Kron 2017.

4 The ancient authority of the idea in Greek poetry and prose (notably Hesiod's *Works and Days* and Xenophon's *Oeconomicus*), and a new self-consciousness of their own past and national destiny among Romans themselves, resulted in a continual trope, through succeeding centuries, of writing about villas as the ultimate in how to live morally. For analysis: Edwards 1993, esp. 143–206. The superiority of country living over urban existences is even a theme in a late second-century CE novel by Largus, *Daphnis and Chloe*, written in Greek: Bowie 2006.

5 In both cases, owning a villa was a multivalent way of defining oneself and of gaining or confirming high social status, be it by Horace's Alfius the banker or, in the case of Cicero and others, by creating villas as environments of intellection, art, and friendship.

6 Pliny the Elder comments that in his day (60s CE), people could have the pleasure (*delicia*) of having *horti*, farms (*agri*), and even villas inside the City (*in ipsa urbe*), despite the fact that *horti* were originally a resource for the poor (*pauperes*): Plin., *HN* 19.50–51 (19.19); Häuber 1998b, 64. *Horti* were generally very close to, usually within eyeshot of, Rome itself but outside the official and sacred limit (the *pomerium*). They were not exactly villas, but neither were they villas far enough away to be *villae suburbanae* nor so within the urban space to be *domus*. Some were very grand; but others, such as those which in 45 BCE Cicero attempted to buy for the memorial to his daughter, appear to have been simple garden retreats on the Janiculum or riverine subdivisions in the plain of the Vatican. A century or more later, impressive ones had appeared such as that of Julius Martialis on the Janiculum (see Mart., *Epig.* 4.64, in ch. 4, Descriptions of Villas). They are part of the Roman appropriation of Hellenistic architectural types and ideas into central Italian Roman architecture: general documentation on Hellenistic architecture in central Italy: Delbrück 1907–1912; on terraced architecture: Demma 2010–2011; on *horti* and gardens: Wallace-Hadrill 1998, 1–2 and n. 1; Zarmakoupi 2010; Nielsen 2013.

7 A partial list includes those of Lucullus (Horti Lucullani, on the Quirinal Hill), Pompey (Horti Pompeiani, around his theater complex in the Campus Martius), Maecenas (Horti Maecenatis), Sallust (Horti Sallustiani), of the Licinius family (Horti Liciniani), and those of Caesar and others, these last on the Equiline Hill Capanna 2012. There were others of the Imperial period, such as the Horti Lolliani.

8 For wall paintings located in urban houses showing villas: Zanker (1979) 1990; Wallace-Hadrill 1998, 12–13.

9 For the Bay of Naples area, the account and Catalogues I (Republican) and II (Imperial) in D'Arms (1970) 2003 are indispensable; on *villae suburbanae* near Rome: De Franceschini 2005; Marzano 2007, 770–78; on Tibur: Tombrägel 2012.

10 Plutarch attributes the social and agrarian problems to the Roman conquest and colonization of Italy, selling some of the enemies' land and designating other parts as public land [δημοσία, Lat. *ager publicus*] to be allocated in amounts of thirty *iugera* to poor citizens for a small tax. Ultimately, richer citizens bought out the poor or bullied them off their small holdings, resulting in a law that limited ownership to no more than 500 *plethra* (about 500 *iugera*, 125 ha, or 311½ acres). Plutarch was also of the opinion that the dispossessed poor no longer wished to serve in the army or have children. He attributes Tiberius's motivations to his jealousy of another politician and to his mother Cornelia "because she often criticized [both] her sons for the fact that, while the Romans called her the mother-in-law of Scipio [Aemilianus], she was not yet called the mother of the Gracchi" (Cornelia Africana was Scipio Africanus's daughter; her daughter Sempronia married Scipio Aemilianus, the victor of the Third Punic War): Plut., *Vit. Ti. Gracch.* 8.1.

Appian, writing a generation after Plutarch, gives a very detailed history of land divisioning in the new Italian colonies, the abuses that ensued in the conflict among rich and poor landowners, and the political consequences in Rome that ended with the murder of Tiberius Sempronius Gracchus, who had tried to redress the wrongs to the poor with agrarian legislation: App., *B. Civ.* 1.26–72 (7–17).

The history of Roman agrarian legislation is a long one; its modern outline begins with that of Max Weber 1891 (2008 English trans.). See Cornell 1995, 327–40, but also analysis of texts and dates of agrarian legislations in Forsén 1991; Oakley 1997–2005, 1:645–61; analysis of texts in Martin 1971; succinct presentation and analysis of the landscape history—human and agricultural—in central Italy: Dyson 2003; Marzano and Métraux 2018, 15–16, nn. 81–89.

11 The designation of populist partisans as *Populares* and conservatives as *Optimates* is irrelevant here—too crude to cover the continual switching of politicians from one side to another; this is a major theme in Syme's study of the period: Syme (1958) 2002.

12 See discussion of enslavement in ch. 2, Villas in Roman Agricultural Treatises.

13 In 137 BCE, on his way from Rome to take up his military appointment as quaestor to the general in charge of the seige of Numantia in Hispania, Tiberius would have taken the Via Aurelia. At many spots to the left and right of the inland line of the road, he could easily have seen many villas and large estates—and the conditions of their workers—along the way. In addition, it would not have been unusual, as a well-connected young man on the rise in his career, to have been offered hospitality in villas by their owners and so observe the estate condtions closely. Around Cosa some 150 km northwest of Rome, there was a particular proliferation of such establishments of the mid-second century BCE, and this area of Etruria was conspicuously rich in large, well-appointed residential villas with agricultural quarters, equipment, and production capacities indicating use of enslaved labor. For what he could have seen: Quilici and Quilici-Gigli 1978a (*basis villae* with little fortress-like towers); Carandini 1980; Rathbone 1981 and 1983; Carlsen 1984; Celuzza 2002 (centuriation); Carandini, A. et al. 2002; Fentress and Perkins 2016; de Haas 2017, 67–72; Marzano and Métraux 2018, 13, nn. 68–69.

14 It is possible that, by the mid-first century CE, Pliny is expressing conventional but out-of-date opinions: issues of land allocation and resolution of social problems (including food supply and distribution) had become matters of imperial administration, *latifundia* had proliferated in tandem with small farms, and the imperial system had assured a measure of social peace in Italian cities.

15 Pliny is referring to the days of Romulus, founder-king of Rome, some 800 years before.

16 Gaius Licinius Calvus Stolo was tribune with Lucius Sextius Lateranus; they passed two of three proposed laws (*Lex Licinia Sextia*) in 368 BCE, one of which (*Lex de modo agrorum*) limited the amount of land that could be held by private citizens and addressed grazing rights on public land: Livy 6.35, 36.1–6, 37.12; Cornell 2008, 384–96. The size of land ownership and the allocation of public land were still issues 300 years later: Varro presented a later descendant of Licinius Stolo in his books on agriculture: Varro, *Rust.* 1.2.9, in ch. 2, Villas in Roman Agricultural Treatises.

17 Pliny goes on in this passage to mention Manius Curius Dentatus and Cincinnatus on his four-*iugera* farm on the Vatican as examples of small but productive holdings.

18 Pliny mentions *latifundia* in Gaul: Plin., *HN* 18.262 (18.67) and 18.296 (18.72). On African estates: in the time of Nero, Kehoe 1988, 20–26; on later developments in imperial holdings in Africa and the leasing of large estates and villas continuing well into the second century CE: Kehoe 2007, 56–72; 2016, 652–53; Hoffmann-Salz 2011; de Vos 2013.

19 See Cato, *Agr.* 4, in ch. 2, Villas in Roman Agricultural Treatises.

20 Cic., *Off.* 1.39.138–139.

21 Lucius Licinius Lucullus (ca. 118–57 or 56 BCE), of the ancient noble plebeian *gens* Licinia, rose through a military career to be named governor of Africa (77–75 BCE), was elected consul in 74 BCE and, in the following year, given the *imperium* against Mithridates VI of Pontus. That king's energetic conquests accompanied by diplomatic and dynastic strategies in Asia Minor beginning in the early 80s BCE had challenged Roman interests in the East. Lucullus's military successes against him in the Third Mithridatic War (73–63 BCE) brought Roman power into permanent prominence in the East. His replacement by Pompey in 66 BCE prompted his return to Rome; during the three years he waited for permission to celebrate a triumph, he used the enormous fortune garnered from his eastern campaigns to build the Horti Lucullani on the Pincian Hill (*collis hortulanorum*), a grand villa with a library at Tusculum, and villas on the Bay of Naples (near Naples itself, on the promontory of Misenum, and on the island of Nisida). Plut., *Vit. Luc.*; *NP* s.v. "Licinius" I 26 (W. Will); Keaveney 1992.

Cicero, who knew Lucullus well, is using Lucullus in the triple capacity of a great moral exemplar almost the equal of the *maiores*, a highly cultured person, and the embodiment of extravagant luxury in his life and villas.

22 Manius Curius Dentatus was consul in 290, 275, and 274 BCE, censor in 272; his triumphs and an ovation were celebrated in the 280s: *NP* s.v. "Curius" 4 (K.L. Elvers). Cato was a young farmer in the 210s–190s BCE, so he was writing sixty or seventy years after Curius.

23 On Cato and his treatment of his enslaved workers, Plutarch has much to say disapprovingly: Plut., *Vit. Cat. Mai.* 5. The statement that none of Cato's villas had plastered walls is modified by Cato's own recipe for wall plaster that he gives in his *Agr.* 128.

24 Much of this passage is culled directly from Cato's *De agricultura* or from Pliny's notes about Late Republican villas that had existed more than a century in the past. The result is a jumble, but one with interesting facts. Pliny's citation of Cato is an appeal to ancient authority that had become conventional by frequent repetition.

25 Quintus Mucius Scaevola (ca. 140–82 BCE) was an important jurist, consul in 95 BCE, governor of Asia, and *pontifex maximus*: *NP* s.v. "Mucius" I 8 (K.L. Elvers).

26 "Felix" (the fortunate one) was a contemporary nickname for Sulla.

27 Gaius Marius (ca. 157–86 CE), famous for his two defeats of Germanic invaders of Italy and his military expeditions in Spain, Numidia, Asia Minor, and the East, seven times consul, and one of the upholders of the rights of the ordinary citizens (*Populares*) of Rome against the oppressions of the elite classes (*Optimates*). In part of this passage, Plutarch claims to have seen a marble portrait [εἰκόνα] of him at Ravenna (Cisalpine Gaul) that showed his harsh character [ἦθος]. Plutarch also opines that a better education and some Greek culture would have softened Marius in his ferocious old age; [...] "he never spoke Greek for anything of consequence, because he said it was laughable to learn literature from teachers who were the slaves of others": Plut., *Vit. Mar.* 2.1–2. On the very complex history of Hellenic culture in the Roman Republic: Gruen 1992, 58–83, 223–71. On Marius's character, Plutarch and Pliny the Elder's views on the topic differ widely, and Plutarch's account colored that of Cassius Dio a century later: Cass. Dio 26.89.2–3 and 7, and 27.94.1–2.

28   According to Cicero, Arpinum claimed Marius and himself as distinguished native sons.

29   These are events at the end of the Social War of 91–89 BCE when Marius's command was questioned for lack of success.

30   Cornelia Sulla was the eldest daughter of the dictator Sulla. She was in a good position to have bought Marius's villa at Misenum at a cut-rate price when it was offered for sale or brought to forced auction in her father's proscriptions of Marius and his partisans in 82 BCE. Lucullus may have bought it in 66 BCE when he returned from Asia and command of the war against Mithridates; if so, Plutarch's indication that he bought it "shortly after" is wrong: D'Arms (1970) 2003, 28, n. 31; cf. Badian 1973.

31   Plut., *Vit. Sull.* 22.1.

32   Proscription originally meant the public posting of lists of properties of named individuals, with a further implication that the owner and often his relatives and associates could be killed as well; valuable bounties to their murderers were offered. While the massacre, in Rome, of Marius's and Cinna's enemies in 85 BCE had been limited to the lives of their opponents, the proscriptions of Sulla in 82 BCE extended to conspicuous villa properties throughout Italy; the more desirable they were, the more quickly they were put on the list. On the legal means and procedures of proscription: Hinard 1985, 17–50; on the Sullan proscription of 82 BCE, Hinard 1985, 104–43.

Thirty-nine years later, the proscriptions of the Second Triumvirate in 43 BCE (in which Cicero and his brother lost their lives) were reportedly worse, with some 2,000 listed for death and the seizure and forced sale, commandeering, or auction of their property. There appears to have been a lot of swapping out of villa ownership in consequence: Hinard 1985, 228–64, and for number of victims, 264–69. For a remarkable and perceptive analysis of the proscriptions in the Marian and Sullan regimes: Cass. Dio 31.12 and 33.108–109, esp. 109.11–21.

33   In an account by Appian, Antony's wife Fulvia wished to acquire an apartment building [συνοικία περικαλλή] adjacent to a property she owned. Its owner, Publius Caesetius Rufus, a member of a plebeian family of minor office-holders, had refused to sell it, then offered to give it to her gratis to save his life, but he was proscribed and executed anyway. Fulvia had Rufus's head nailed to the apartment building.

In contrast to this atrocity, Appian continues with an account of an enslaved servant attempting to save his enslaver who owned a lovely, shady villa for which he was proscribed. The servant tried to impersonate his owner but was betrayed by another enslaved attendant and so was not successful. Later on, he was rewarded with his freedom on account of his bravery: App., *B. Civ.* 29.124: also Val. Max. 9.5.4 (on P. Caesetius Rufus, identified as a senator).

34   Plin., *HN* 22.4–8 (6–17). He laments the novelty of the new Roman crowns and tells us that the Germans honorably retain the custom of the *corona graminea*. He goes on to express his disgust that Sulla got any crown at all, in hindsight of his later cruelty.

35   The events described were those of the Social War (91–89 BCE) and Sulla's defeat of the Samnite people and their allies led by Lucius Cluentius at Nola. The next year, Sulla became consul. It is not known when he acquired the villa at Tusculum later bought by Cicero in the mid-60s BCE.

36   Τὸ κάλος or τὸ κάλλος, the Good/Beautiful/Noble—something that expressed an inextricable unity of goodness, beauty, and nobility—were abstract references to Platonic forms; this was the reputation of Ischomachus in Xenophon's *Oeconomicus*: see ch. 1, Greek and Sicilian Backgrounds of Roman Villas.

37   By σχολάζειν is meant to engage in leisurely literate activities or *otium*.

38   Gaius Memmius (ca. 98–44/46 BCE), of a noble plebeian family, was married to Sulla's elder daughter Fausta Cornelia; he was tribune in 66 BCE at the time of these events: *NP* s.v. "Memmius" I 3 (T. Frigo). Marcus Terentius Varro Lucullus (ca. 116–56/57 BCE) was Lucullus's younger brother, who had been adopted by a member of the Terentii Varrones (no relation to the encyclopedist) but reverted to the name Marcus Lucullus and is identified as such. Consul in 73 BCE and governor of Macedonia, he was charged, by Gaius Memmius, with various crimes while a partisan of Sulla in 82–80 BCE but was acquitted: *NP* s.v. "Licinius" I 27 (T. Frigo).

39   Horti Luculani or Lucullani: Plut., *Vit. Luc.* 39; Vell. Pat. 2.33.4; later ownership by Messalina in Cass. Dio 66.30.5; *AtlasAncRome* 1 478, 481–82, 485; 2: tab. III at 1. *LTUR* 5 67–70, Horti Lucullani (H. Broise and V. Jolivet); Haselberger et al. 2002, 144 (A.B. Gallia); Richardson 1992, s.v. "Horti Lucullani."

40   Plutarch then tells the reader (in a section omitted here) that Marius and Cicero should have chosen the same path as Lucullus after their great victories, to avoid the later catastrophes to which fate and character subjected them.

41   By "ancient comedy," Plutarch is invoking the plots of Attic Old Comedy of the fifth century BCE, specifically to those of Aristophanes (ca. 446–386 BCE), which included references to contemporary political events with much satire and unbridled gaiety.

42   Frass 2006, 298–99.

43   Quintus Aelius Tubero was a well-connected philosopher and legal scholar of the late second century BCE; his dates make it unlikely that he would have made this remark in the 60s BCE: *NP* s.v. "Aelius" I 17 (W. Kierdorf).

The epithet "Xerxes in a toga" is repeated in Pliny (*HN* 9.171 [9.80]). For Plutarch, and Greek and Latin writers in general, the reference to Xerxes the Achaemenid monarch (ca. 518–464 BCE, r. 486–464) is to a king whose power, grand accomplishments and projects at the Persian capital at Persepolis, and ultimate failure to conquer Greece in 480–479 BCE were examples of the catastrophes brought on by fate and character, as Crassus and Pompey had remarked about Lucullus. Plutarch may be using Tubero anachronistically to refer to Lucullus in ironic reversal: after having failed to defeat Mithridates completely, Lucullus then turned to building and other grand projects.

44 Horace references a story about Lucullus having an almost infinite supply of colored garments to loan: Hor., *Epist.* 1.6.45–48.

45 Plutarch continues in this vein of disapproval with some anecdotes of Lucullus's dazzling hospitality and its almost-royal organization involving Cicero and Pompey, as well as how much pride and pleasure it gave him to live in that way, ending with this remark: "In this manner, he used his wealth in a wanton way, indeed, as if it were a captive barbarian": Plut., *Vit. Luc.* 41.1–5.

There may have been another reason for Lucullus to build his *horti* and its villa-like dwelling for prodigal hospitality. Lucullus had returned to Rome in 66 BCE with expectation of a triumph for his victories in the East against Mithridates and his allies. In this, he was disappointed by political maneuvering: Plut., *Vit. Luc.* 37.1. A general invested with *imperium* (authority) who had been hailed as *imperator* by his troops was, at the conclusion of a war, eligible to be an official *triumphator* as declared by a commission called the *comitia curiata*; by this time the *comitia curiata* was diluted in its membership and authority but still had the power to grant the initial *imperium* to a commander for a war and to award a triumph at its conclusion: in general, Beard 2009. However, Lucullus did not lay down his *imperium* until his triumph had been voted, and so was forbidden from crossing the *pomerium* defining the City until his triumph had been promulgated. In order to curry popular favor, hospitality in a spectacular setting to win popular votes may have prompted him to build. He was awarded a triumph in 63 CE. Later *horti*—the gardens in the porticoes of Pompey's theater and the gardens of Julius Caesar—had a distinct political purpose: Frass 2006, 188–92; Marzano 2022, 17–18, 228–46.

46 Plutarch implies that he seized them as war booty in his eastern campaigns.

47 Although Plutarch specifies libraries and does not specify where they were, it is likely, from Cicero's evidence of a major library in what had been Lucullus's villa at Tusculum, that the books were collected and kept there rather than in his Roman *horti* on the Quirinal; but see Russell 2015, 150–51. In addition, the spaciousness of the buildings and their porticoes as described makes the Tusculan villa the better candidate for the library. It is there that Cicero met the young son of Lucullus: see Cic., *Fin.* 1.5.14, in ch. 5, Villas and *Otium*, and Marzano and Métraux 2018, 23 and n. 126. For the Horti Lucullani, see ch. 9 n. 39. Russell (2015) seems to imply that the library he opened to all was in the Roman *horti* on the *collis hortulorum* rather than at his villa at Tusculum.

48 The *prytaneum* (Gk. Πρυτανεῖον) in Greek towns and cities was a meeting place for town councillors, often sheltering the communal hearth dedicated to the goddess Hestia.

49 Philo of Larissa (ca. 159–84 BCE), the head of the Old Academy; Cicero attended his lectures when he was in Rome as of 88 BCE: Brittain 2001.

50 Cicero's works called the *Academica* were written and published in stages in 45 BCE but set earlier, in 62 BCE. The first appearance of the treatise (called the *Academica priora* or *First Academic*) was in two parts: *Catulus* (named for Quintus Lutatius Catulus Capitolinus, consul in 78 BCE, *pontifex maximus*, censor, deceased in 59 BCE) and *Lucullus*. The *Lucullus* section is placed at the villa of Quintus Hortensius Hortalus at Baiae. The second, later treatise (*Academica posteriora*) was dedicated to Varro.

51 Cornelius Nepos's *On Famous Historians* appears to have been divided into Greek and Latin authors. It is a fragmentary text of which only two Latin authors' biographies survive: Cato the Elder and Atticus. The biography of Atticus is item 25 in the text, but it is normally cited only by its title *Atticus* (*Att.*). An initial biography was written while Atticus was alive, then reedited after his death ca. 35 BCE.

52 *Sui cuique mores fingunt fortunam hominibus*: Nep., *Att.* 25.11.6.

53 The *domus Tamphilianum* must have been a villa in a park similar to the luxurious villa that Lucullus built farther to the northeast, well outside of the main habitation area of the City. The plebeian aristocrat Marcus Baebius Tamphilus was a senator, consul in 181 BCE, awarded a triumph for campaigns in Italy, a legislator with Cato, and governor in the East; Tamphilus may have initiated such building on the Quirinal. The contrast between Atticus's old house and his frugal ways in food and drink with Lucullus's new villa on the *collis hortulorum* and his extravagant banquets is striking, especially given that the two may have been acquaintances: Nep., *Att.* 25.5.1; and see Plut., *Vit. Luc.* 39.1–4, 39.5, and 40.1, all in this chapter.

54 *Plus salis quam sumptus*: this nicely turned phrase is capable of many translations, e.g. "more earthy than sumptuous," "basic, not grand," with *salis* (salt) here having metaphorical value as in "salt of the earth." Atticus inherited the Tamphilian house along with 10,000,000*HS* from his maternal uncle Quintus Caecilius Metellus Pius (ca. 128–63 BCE), a devoted adherent of Sulla, senator, consul in 80 BCE, and military commander in Hispania during the Sertorius rebellion: Nep., *Att.* 25.5.2–3. Metellus's great wealth, patrician lineage, and literary patronage earned him a reputation as one of the brilliant men of his day.

55 Cicero's correspondence with Atticus does mention a villa at Nomentum (modern Mentana) but not one at Arretium (modern Arezzo); his main residential villa was the Amalthea near Buthrotum in Epirus where he welcomed and sheltered political refugees, including Cicero: (Nep., *Att.* 3.4, 4.5, and 11.1–3. Arretium: *Pleiades* s.v. "Arretium"; Nomentum, *Pleiades* s.v. "Nomentum."

56 Atticus's frugal elegance can be contrasted with the prodigality of his near contemporary, Marcus Aemilius Scaurus (ca. early first century–after 53 BCE). Elected aedile in 58 BCE, Scaurus treated the City's population to plays in a monumental but temporary theater, the Theatrum Marci Scauri. After the celebrations, the props and costumes (worth 30,000,000*HS*) were sent for safekeeping in Scaurus's villa at Tusculum, but of the theater's 360 marble columns, four of them (38 Roman feet high, about 11.75 m, or 37 ft.) were transferred to the atrium of his house on the Palatine. Later, Augustus incorporated these four columns into the *scaenae frons* of the Theater of Marcellus to show his disapproval of such merely private extravagance. On Scaurus, marbles, and morality: Plin., *HN* 36.4–8 (36.2–3); 36.50 (36.8); and 36.113–115 (36.23); Coarelli 1987; Phillips 2001.

57 Marcus Licinius Crassus (ca. 115–53 BCE) was consul twice and a member, with Pompey and Caesar, of the so-called First Triumvirate: *NP* s.v. "Licinius" I 11 (W. Will). He was defeated and killed at the Battle of Carrhae in Syria against the Parthian forces.

58 The charge of interfering with a Vestal Virgin (*Vestalis*) was extremely serious, and for a Vestal to abrogate her vow of chastity was a capital offense punishable by live burial. The College of Vestals was of great antiquity; two (later four or six) young girls from noble patrician (later also noble plebeian) families were inducted for a thirty-year tenure and supported by the state to maintain certain rituals, including a communal hearth fire in buildings in the Roman Forum. They wore special clothes and were restricted from many activities but enjoyed numerous privileges including owning property in their own right.

59 This was the villa-like house of Pompey in his gardens: Russell 2016, 185; *AtlasAncRome* 1 505; earlier, he had lived in the Carinae: *AtlasAncRome* 1 291; 2: tabs. 89–90.

60 Trivia was one of the names of the goddess Diana Nemorensis, worshiped at a famous shrine at Aricia (modern Ariccia) near Lake Nemi and Tusculum, about 30 km south of Rome. The area was famous as a resort; Julius Caesar had a villa there: see ch. 10, Emperors and Villas.

61 The spectacular Late Republican temple to Fortuna at Praeneste was a famous pilgrimage venue for those seeking responses from the goddess by drawing lots (*sortes*). The town was legendarily founded by Telegonus, son of Circe, the witch-queen of the island of Aeaea, and Odysseus when returning from Troy; Telegonus also founded nearby Tusculum.

62 Tibur (modern Tivoli) was especially rich in villas; a major temple to Hercules was there. Lanuvium (modern Lanuvio), on the Via Appia about 30 km southeast of Rome, also had many villas. Propertius gives an amusing picture of his Cynthia on her way to Lanuvium by the Via Appia: Prop., *Elegies* 4.8.15–22.

63 The shade of the Porticus Pompeia is also mentioned in Propertius, *Elegies* 4.8.75: Cynthia is mock angrily ordered by her lover Propertius to be more modest in public: "Don't get yourself dolled up and walk around in the Pompeian shade!" The Porticus Pompeia, with a double or two-part plantation of trees (*nemus duplex*) within it, is mentioned by Martial (*Epig.* 2.14.10); the shadiness of the colonnades is also mentioned (Mart., *Epig.* 11.47.3), as are the gold-embroidered awnings of its colonnades (Propertius's "Attalid tapestries"; Mart., *Epig.* 11.47.3) more than a century after their installation. The shadiness of its promenades is cited in Ovid (*Ars am.* 1.67). For a catalogue of poets in the porticus: Russell 2015, 179–82; Gleason 1994; analysis in Kuttner 1999. The Porticus Pompeia is mentioned by Vitruvius (*De arch.* 5.9.1) in relation to the Theater of Pompey.

64 Pompey had a villa at Alba, his Albanum, where his wife buried his body or ashes after his murder in Egypt: Plut., *Vit. Pomp.* 80.6.

On Cato the Younger, Plutarch mentions that, for all his stern sobriety, he had a comfortable villa in Lucania where he went often with friends to enjoy literary *otium*: Plut., *Vit. Cat. Min.* 20.1.

65 Labicum or Lavicum was in the Alban hills, about 21 km (13 mi.) southeast of Rome. On the villa at Misenum near Baiae on the Bay of Naples, see Seneca, *Ep.* 51, in this chapter.

66 For Caesar's gardens northeast of the City called *Ad portam Collinam*, with others adjacent: *AtlasAncRome* 1 456–57; 2: tab. III at 2–3; Richardson 1992, s.v. "Horti Caesaris (1); Frass 2006, 288.
Caesar's *horti* and villa on the right bank of the Tiber in the Transtiberim, with others adjacent: *AtlasAncRome* 1 554–55; 2: tab. III at 23; Richardson 1992, s.v. "Horti Caesaris (2)"; Frass 2006, 286–88..

67 Literary activities: Suet., *Iul.* 56.1 and 56.7, and horse: 61.1.

68 The story (Suet., *Iul.* 81.1) was verified by Caesar's friend Cornelius Bibulus: months before Caesar's assassination, the colonists building villas near Capua on the allotments assigned to them by the *lex Iulia agraria* and other measures in the Ager Campanus by Caesar (in his first consulate of 59 BCE) near Capua disturbed the tomb and grave goods of Capys, the founder of the nearby city. A Greek inscription foretold a murder of a Roman by his relatives and its avenging.

69 Caesar was elected *pontifex maximus* in 63 BCE. The *domus publica* or Regia was a building reserved for the residence of the *pontifex maximus* as head of the Roman religion; it was located adjacent to the Via Sacra, which ran south-southeast to north-northwest from the east side of the Palatine Hill to the base of the Capitoline Hill; on recent excavations indicating changes in the previous dating and plan: Brocato and Terrenato 2017.

70 In a letter from Laodicea in Cilicia written in 51 BCE, Cicero mentions Caesar's building of his villa near Nemi (*in Nemore*): Cic., *Att.* 115 (6.1.25).

71 *tessellata et sectilia pavimenta*: Suetonius juxtaposes Caesar's villa at Nemi with the mosaic and *opus sectile* floors he transported in travel baggage when on active duty in the field to send the message of Caesar's love of luxury. Such floors had become the norm in Late Republican villas and houses.

72 The bodily location of *animus* (mind with sensation) is in the central part of the chest (*situs media regione in pectoris*, Lucr. 3.140): for that reason, the burden on the mind is also a weight on the body, both unrelieved by going back and forth from the villa-owning Roman gentleman's three loci—home, forum, villa.

73 *naturam primum studeat cognoscere rerum*: the emphasis is on *studium* (study) and *cognitio* (knowledge), both components of *otium*.

74 Haywood 1958; Rakob 1961; Secchi Tarugi 2002. There was even a commercial facility where copies of Greek bronze sculpture could be made or chosen from plaster cast models: Landwehr 1985; Métraux 2006, 136–37.

75 See Sen., *Ep.* 86, in ch. 4, Descriptions of Villas.

76 Canopus (Canobus) was one of the westernmost branches of the Nile River at the Delta, east of Alexandria. Its banks were famous for their beauty and their facilities for eating, drinking, and debauchery. Juvenal uses its name to signify luxury and moral corruption: Juv., *Satires* 1.26, 6.82–84, and 15.44–46.

77 In the Second Punic War (218–201 BCE), the Carthaginian general Hannibal led an army from Hispania across the Alps into Italy in the winter of 218. He occupied most of the southern peninsula including Campania with its main city of Capua (modern Santa Maria Capua Vetere) as of 216 BCE. Polybius describes the beauty and luxury of the city in some detail, as well as the famous Falernian wine of the area: Polyb. 3.91.2–10 and 7.1.1 (frag.). Seneca is borrowing Livy's claim that when Hannibal quartered his army there in the fall and winter of 216 BCE, he and his men lost their fighting spirit in Capua's luxurious amenities.

78 Seneca's remark about Marius's villa at Misenum is directly contradicted by the judgment of Plutarch in *Vit. Mar.* 34.1–2, in this chapter.

79 In general on the Roman cultural welcome of Greek culture in this period: Gruen 1992, 131–82.
A Horti Scipionis outside the *pomerium* of the City is mentioned by Cicero, though which Scipio (Gaius Scipio Africanus or his son Gaius Scipio Aemilianus Africanus) is not indicated: Cic., *Nat. D.* 2.4.11. In either case, it would mean *horti* in existence already by the first half of the second century BCE, as Cicero is analyzing a technical issue of religious observance in 163 BCE during the second consulship of Tiberius Sempronius Gracchus: *NP* s.v. "Sempronius" I 16 (K. Bringmann); Marzano 2022, 46. These *horti* may have belonged by inheritance to Cornelia Africana, the elder Scipio's daughter and the consul's wife.

80 Plut., *Pomp.* 44.3. On the political uses of *horti*, see ch.9 n. 44.

81 Cic., *Fam.* 20.21 (1.9); as befitted Crassus's higher position, he invited himself to dinner, even though Cicero was his host. Cicero's son-in-law at the time was Furius Crassipes, husband to his daughter Tullia from 56 to about 53 BCE: *NP* s.v. "Furius" I 16 (K.-L. Elvers) and s.v. "Tullia" 2 (M. Strothmann). Analysis in Hildbold 2021, 121–25 and n. 34, with preceding bibliography.

82 For *horti*: notices in *AtlasAncRome* with map at vol. 2, tab. III. For excellent bibliography, ancient literary references, and analysis: Frass 2006, and 203–366 for a catalogue of *horti* and their owners from the Late Republic to Late Antiquity. In general: articles in Cima and Talamo 2008; Hellenistic origins: Wallace-Hadrill 1998; Demma 2010–2011; review of several gardens: Andreae 1996, 51–56, 67–95; socioeconomic aspects, ancient sources, modern bibliography: Frass 2006; Esquiline Hill: Cima 2008; Häuber 2014 (Esquiline-Oppian Hill); Häuber 1998a and 1998b (early gardens there); articles on specific topics in Cima and La Rocca 1998; water supply to the *horti* of Lucullus: Broise and Jolivet 1994; 1999; Horti Maecenatis: *LTUR* 3 70–74, Horti Maecenatis (C. Häuber); Horti Lamiani: Cima and La Rocca 1986; Horti of Sallust Talamo 1998; Hartswick 2004; *horti* in imperial times: Moretti Cursi 2019.

83 Wiseman 2016, 141–44. Elsewhere, it has been claimed that Horace is referring to the Horti Maecenatis as covering an old cemetery beyond the *agger* (the earth mound above the fosse) of the original walls of Rome at the brow of the Esquiline Hill, but this has also been questioned: Wiseman 1998.

84 The Dorian mode was for the lyre and had a formal character associated with poetic recitation and thus with Apollo, whereas the Phrygian pipes (Lat. *tibia*, Gk. αὐλός) were associated with choral singing and dancing and thus with Dionysus. The poet's joy was a mixture of Dorian elevation and Phrygian enthusiasm.

85 The *domus* in Maecenas's *horti* looked down on Rome, therefore the Tiber. Maecenas's other villas are obliquely mentioned: the Aefulian fields is Maecenas's villa near Tibur: *NP* s.v. "Aefulae" (S. Quilici Gigli); *Pleiades* s.v. "Aefulae." The ridge of Telegonus refers to Tusculum where Maecenas had a villa; Telegonus, who killed his father Odysseus by accident, was the town's founder: *NP* s.v. "Telegonus" (S. Zimmermann) and "Tusculum" (M.M Morciano); *Pleiades* s.v. "Tusculum."

86 For the poem: Baehrens 1879, 1:122–34. His love of nature is discussed in Morvillez 2017.

87 On the sale, purchase, and assignment of *horti*: Frass 2006, 45–84.

88 This letter is a reply to Marcus Aurelius, who had written to Fronto about a popular rhetorician whom he had heard recently, Marcus Antonius Polemon of Laodicea: see ch. 10, Emperors and Villas. Fronto is referencing an anecdote, from Horace's *Satirae* (2.3.247–559; 33 BCE), about another Polemon and the power of philosophical discourse: the carefree dandy Polemon, drunk, intruded by chance into a lecture by Xenocrates in the Academy at Athens, became sober and wise, and ultimately succeeded as *scholarch* of the Academy. The connection is: Fronto-Horace-*horti*-philosopher-emperor, a strained connection but an associative one.

Elsewhere, Fronto needed a new bath building, either at the villa in Fronto's Horti Maecenatis or in another he owned. His friend Aulus Gellius, in his *Attic Nights*, tells us that Fronto was prepared to spend 350,000HS on it, more or less [*praeterpropter*, the word that is the topic of the essay], with an interesting vignette about a patron choosing from among different plans: Gell., *NA* 19.10.1–8.

89 The numbering of the *Epistles* of Fronto is based on the standard modern edition in Naber 1867.

90 Described by Cicero in *De leg.* 2.1–7 (2.1–3); see ch. 4, Descriptions of Villas.

91 Cic., *Att.* 28.2 (2.8.2) and *Att.* 36.4 (2.16.4), respectively of April and May 59 BCE. Cicero says that he can only offer countrified hospitality (*hospitium agrestum*) at Arpinum.

92 See Cic., *Att.* 353.1–2 (13.52.1–2), in ch. 6, Villa Visits.

93 Cic., *Att.* 52 (3.7) and 53 (3.8), respectively from Brundisium on April 29, and Thessalonica on May 26, 58 BCE.

94 Cic., *Att.* 179 (9.12.1) and 198 (10.7.1), respectively March and April 49 BCE.

95 The account is much later; Plutarch was writing about 140 years after the events, so it may be apocryphal: Plut., *Vit. Caes.* 40.

96 Caesar's march on Rome, and the strange insanity (*mirus furor*) of the city's population fearful of his arrival, is vividly described: Cic., *Fam.* 146.1–4 (16.12.1–4).

97 Cic., *Fam.* 144.1–2 (14.18.1–2) and 145 (14.14), respectively January 22 and January 23, 49 BCE. Writing to Atticus, he begs his friend to convince Terentia and Tullia, as well as Atticus's sister Pomponia, to leave Rome: Cic., *Att.* 138 (7.14.3) of February 49 BCE. He noted that in the same month, many adherents of Pompey had even left their villas and *horti* near Rome for safer places farther away: Cic., *Att.* 152 (8.2.3), February 17, 49 BCE. From February to May 49 BCE, he himself is going from villa to villa or staying at his little villas (*villulae*, probably *deversoria* for overnight visits): Arpinum, Formiae, Cumae, Pompeii, Quintus's villas at Laterium and Arcanum, and elsewhere: Cic., *Att.* 167 (9.1.3), 170 (8.9.3), 340 (10.1.1), 341 (10.2.1), 375 (10.10) through 395 (10.18).

98 Cicero had wanted to have the ceremony in Rome, but it was too dangerous: Cic., *Att.* 189 (9.19.1) of March 31, 49 BCE. Marcus Tullius Cicero Minor was about 16 years old at the time. In 43 BCE, Cicero sent his son to Greece before the proscriptions (App., *B. Civ.* 51.1). The son was later pardoned and rose to be consul in 30 BCE, then governor in Syria and Asia.

99 Cic. *Fam.* 155 (14.7). Cicero's concept of family, *familia*, and *domus* is analyzed in Harders 2021, 205–08 (Tullia and Terentia); 208–12 and 217–18 (*familia*, idea of *domus*, and "his people").

100 Appian (late first–early second century CE) gives a lengthy account of these proscriptions and mentions that ownership of nice villas and city dwellings could be the cause of their owners being added to the proscription lists: "On this account, they were proscribed for their lovely villas and their houses" [ἤδη δέ τις καὶ διὰ κάλλος ἐπαύλεως καὶ οἰκίας προεγράφη]: App., *B. Civ.* 4.6, 4.17, 4.19–20. On the proscription of 43 BCE: Hinard 1985, 227–326, 413–522.

101 Seneca the Elder, *Suasoriae* 6–7, incorporates these various accounts or comments on Cicero's death.

102 Plut., *Vit. Cic.* 47–49.

103 In the late second–early third century CE, Dio Cassius gives examples of heroic concealment of the proscribed, including Quintus's son, by friends, relatives, and even his enslaved personnel as well as the atrocity story of Antony's wife Fulvia and the public exhibition of Cicero's head and hands: Dio Cass. 47.10–11.

NOTES TO CHAPTER 10

1 Arnaldo Momigliano and Sir Ronald Syme were early exponents of the modern critical examination of the ancient texts, especially the *Historia Augusta*: Momigliano 1954, esp. 22–25 and notes, with preceding bibliography; Syme 1968; 1971.

2 For a thorough review of the historians treating Tiberius to Domitian: Rutledge 2009; for analysis of the historiographical principles in writing the lives of emperors used by Suetonius and Tacitus: Duchêne 2020; on Nero and Domitian in Tacitus's *Agricola*: Schulz 2022, 343–47 on Suetonius's methods of biography.

Tiberius: while Tiberius had a fawning contemporary admirer in Velleius Paterculus writing during his reign, the emperor's reputation quickly waned for reasons stemming as much from political and dynastic actions of his successors as from his supposedly innate bad character: Vell. Pat. 2.94–131; for a positive assessment of Tiberius in general: Levick 1999a, 176–80 for his late and posthumous reputation among ancient historians.

Nero: most recently, Schulz 2022, 330–31 (Nero and Domitian in Tacitus's *Agricola*); Drinkwater 2019; Barrett 2020, 7–31, 416–21; Moormann 2003 with comments on the enlightened aspects of Nero's urban plans for Rome; *Nero: The Man Behind the Myth*, exhibition at the British Museum 2021.

Domitian: Marks and Mogetta 2021; articles in Cominesi et al. 2021; *God on Earth: Emperor Domitian*, exhibition at the Rijksmuseum van Oudheden, Leiden, 2021–22; Lengrand 1994; Corbier 1994; Syme (1983) 1988.

3 Rutledge 2009, 33–41. The clearest statement of the "senatorial" point of view can be found in the author of the biography of Marcus Aurelius in the *Historia Augusta*: "He gave the Senate cognizance over many decisions, even those that involved his own right of judgment. […] None of the emperors respected the Senate more than he. To honor the Senate, he assigned decisions involving disputes to many of those of praetorian and consular ranks who had resumed private life, to increase their authority in matters of law":

HA, M. Aur. 10.2–3). Another writer in the *Historia Augusta* claims that Hadrian, after executing four ranking members of that body, attempted to repair the breech with the Senate: "Finally, he censured [the memory of] those emperors who had accorded less honor [than he] to the senators": *HA, Hadr.* 1.8.10.

4 *HA, M. Aur.* 15.5.

5 Examples in the *Historia Augusta* include *Pescennius Niger* 12.1–3; and *Antoninus Elagabalus* 1.1–2.

6 Eugippus, *Vita Severini* 46. On conversions of estates into Christian communities, see headnote and text of Gerontius, *Vit. Mel.*, in ch. 4, Descriptions of Villas.

7 Cass. Dio 52.43.2. The islands of the Bay of Naples are enumerated in Statius's later description of the Pollius Felix villa at Surrentum: Stat., *Silv.* 2.2.42–99, in ch. 4, Descriptions of Villas.

8 For geographies of inland and coastal towns with villas, see Statius, *Silv.* 4.4.1–25, in ch. 4, Descriptions of Villas, and Mart., *Epig.* 5.1, in this chapter.

9 Numinous events at villas are a frequent theme in imperial biographies of later emperors: the writers of the *Historia Augusta* were following Suetonius in this theme.

10 In Suetonius's day or a little earlier, owning Augustus's birth house in Rome was used as a ploy to persuade judges to leniency in a lawsuit brought against a later owner (*possessor*) of the house; this owner (one Gaius Laetorius) called himself its *aedituus* (custodian of a *templum* or consecrated place) and so requested judicial indulgence. The judges apparently ordained that part of the house (*pars domus*) be consecrated as holy property: Suet., *Aug.* 5.

11 Velitrae (modern Velletri), about 40 km southeast of Rome in the Alban hills, was the hometown of the plebeian Octavius family, which had achieved equestrian rank by the end of the third century CE but had not attained a consulship until Octavian was elected in 43 BCE.

12 An analysis and revision of the remains of a so-called House of Augustus on the Palatine, and a new interpretation in light of Claridge's investigations (2014) can be found in Wiseman 2019, 19–29, 90–95, figs. 38, 40, 42, and 46 (location of Augustus's house); on the iconography of the house, 104–21.

13 For discussion of this house in the Horti Maecenatis, see Hor., *Epod.* 9.1–5, Hor., *Odes* 3.29.1–16, and the *Elegiae in Maecenatem* 1.31–36, all in ch. 9, Villas and *Horti* in the Late Roman Republic.

14 In a preceding section, Suetonius included a calumny by Mark Antony about Augustus's collection of Corinthian bronzes, but in following sections, Suetonius described Augustus's moderation in the way of dress (a toga neither too full or too skimpy, woven at home by his daughter and granddaughters), frugality in the way of furniture and decoration, and his extremely formal hospitality and social discrimination about invitations to his dinners: Suet. *Aug.* 70.1–2 and 2.73–74, respectively.

No date is attached to Augustus's destruction of a villa built for or by his granddaughter Julia. If it was before her exile in 8 CE, it would have been an example of his modest frugality; after her exile, an example of his vengeful resentment at her treachery.

15 Tacitus claimed that Augustus built twelve villas on Capreae: Tac., *Ann.* 4.67. On Roman Capreae in general: Federico and Miranda 1998. On Augustus and Capreae and the structure called Palazzo a Mare: Di Franco 2015, 21–92.

16 On Vedius's Roman *domus* and the Porticus Liviae: Ovid, *Fasti* 6.637–648 (Vedius's huge house—*tecta immensae domus*); *LTUR* 4 127–29 (C. Panella); Richardson 1992, s.v. "Porticus Liviae"; Haselberger et al. 2002, s.v. "Porticus Liviae" (A.G. Thein); Zanker 1987. Vedius's house probably had *horti*; Pliny records the report of a productive vine still growing in the Porticus Liviae, possibly left over from a previous garden: Plin., *HN* 14.11 (14.3). On Vedius himself; *NP* s.v. "Vedius" II 4 (W. Eck); Cicero may have met him many years before: Cic., *Att.* 115 (6.1.25); Sen., *On Anger* (*De ira*) 3.40.1–5; Tac., *Ann.* 1.9 and 4.67; Cass. Dio 54.23.2–5; Syme (1961) 1979.

17 Seneca discusses Vedius Pollio's cruelty in the context of the merciful treatment of enslaved servants (*Clem.*, 1.18.2) and Augustus's greatness of soul and self-control (*De ira* 3.40.1–5). Citing Seneca, Pliny mentions Pollio's cruelty, his ponds of eels, the Pausilypon villa, and the great age of the eels: Plin., *HN* 9.76 (39) and 9.167 (78). Pollio's evil reputation and atrocities became proverbial and lasted well into the late second century CE: Tac., *Ann.* 1.10 and 12.60; Tert., *De Pallio* 5.6.1–2.

18 The most recent and complete study of the Pausilypon villa is Busen 2023, which supersedes Gunther 1913. It was a grand maritime villa on several terraced levels and built in masonry compatible with a Late Republican date but with later additions in the first and second centuries CE. It remained an imperial property; a stamped lead water pipe indicates that its water system underwent renovations in the reign of Hadrian: Gunther 1913, 129, fig. 78; Rockwell 1971, 110; Scott 1939; Pappalardo 2009, 29–30; Varriale 2016.

19 It seems Pollio had requested that a public work be built on the site of his Pausilypon villa. Evidently Augustus ignored this request and built the Porticus of Livia on the site of Pollio's *domus* in Rome, though by becoming imperial property, the Pausilypon villa may have become the public work specified in Pollio's will: by Hadrian's time (120s–130s CE), it had been considerably changed and enlarged; see the preceding note.

20 *NP* s.v. "Prima Porta" (M.M. Morciano); *Pleiades* s.v. "Ad Gallinas Albas"; De Franceschini 2005, 27–45, no. 7; Carrara 2005; Marzano 2007, 519; Clark Reeder 2001; Calci and Messineo 1984; Messineo and Calvelli 2001; Flory 1989; Klynne and Liljenstolpe 2000 (statue of Augustus).

21 The omen and its sequel described here are part of Pliny's discussion of the laurel and the olive; the laurel was associated with Apollo, Augustus's personal divine referent, and with other numinous qualities appropriate to the celebration of victories and triumphs. However, Pliny also points out that the Roman use of the laurel as a triumphal symbol may come more from Augustus's use of a branch rather than any more ancient tradition: other branches, especially olive, had been used before. As a natural history writer, Pliny is never above putting in an interesting, perhaps current, anecdote (in this case about laurel trees) that will stick in the minds of his readers, thereby conveying knowledge by flattering them with knowledgeability.

22 This is anachronistic: Octavian became Augustus only in 27 BCE, and Livia was recognized as *Augusta* only posthumously, in 42 CE. In addition, while Pliny the Elder's version says that it was before her wedding to Octavian, Suetonius says it was after: Suet., *Galb.* 2.

23 Suetonius omits the haruspices' advice and says that Livia herself undertook to raise the chickens and plant the laurel trees, perhaps to endow her with priestly insight: Suet., *Galb.* 2.

24 To the account of the *triumphatores* planting sprigs, Suetonius adds the omen that when they were about to die, the tree so planted would wither and die, and when Nero, as the last blood relative in the Julio-Claudian family died, the entire grove died, as did all the chickens. Suetonius also includes other omens foretelling the death of Nero: Suet. *Nero* 45–46.

25 Suetonius's account continues: the emperor, mightily pleased, gave forty gold coins to members of his entourage on condition that they spend it on goods brought to port on the Alexandrian ship. Later, he gave (Roman) togas and *pallia* (cloaks in the Greek style), asking that the Romans and Greeks exchange both clothes and language.

26 *Apragopolis* is a Latinization of ἄπραγος + *polis* (city), from ἀ + πράγματα, without business or effort, or an "easytown."
A difficulty is that Apragopolis is said to be an island near Capreae (*vincina insula*), but the island is actually alone along this part of the Surrentine coast, unlike the many islands on the opposite north coast. The difficulty was tentatively resolved in a speculation by Della Corte that what was meant was a public building—the *insula civica*—of the Greek population of Capreae itself, of which the youths in exercise were treated to the banquet: Della Corte 1934, 146–49. The situation of both textual and topographical issues about Capreae is brilliantly (and hilariously) discussed in Senatore 2015.

27 Suetonius merely describes where Augustus died, without comment, but Tacitus calls the vulgar chatter (*pleris sermo*) about such meaningless coincidences to be stupid (*vana*): Tac., *Ann.* 1.9. On his death at Nola: Vell. Pat. 2.123.1; Cass. Dio 56.29.2; the room where he died became a shrine (τεμένος), according to Cassius Dio (56.46.3). See also Della Corte 1934; Aoyagi, De Simone, and De Simone 2018, 143 and n. 10.

28 Suet., *Tib.* 11. A different context to Tiberius's retirement without the circumstances of his life there besides his philosophical studies (παιδεία) is given in Cass. Dio 55.9.5–8; analysis in Levick 1972.

29 Suet., *Tib.* 15; Tac., *Ann.* 1.5.

30 Tac., *Ann.* 1.43; Cass. Dio 57.12.6, 58.1.1, and 58.5.1; Levick 1999a; Yegül and Favro 2019, 285, fig. 5.43; Ciardello 2019; Krause 2003.
Tiberius had other villas inland: in 34 CE, when thinking of returning to Rome after the fall of Sejanus, he made use of villas at Alba and Tusculum: Cass. Dio 58.24.1. Tiberius, by then quite ill, left Capreae in March 37 to return to Rome but died (or was murdered) in the villa once owned by Lucullus on the promontory of Misenum: Tac., *Ann.* 6.50.

31 Drusus died in 23 CE, but Tiberius's definitive transfer to Capreae happened only in 26 CE; the events at the cave near Sperlonga described by Tacitus must have happened in that three-year period, after Sejanus became prominent in affairs of state as the emperor's *socius laborum* (associate in my labors): Tac., *Ann.* 4.59. Another reason was his quarrel with his mother Livia: Cass. Dio 57.12.6.

32 Fidenae was a town 9 km north of Rome on the Via Salaria. The collapse of the amphitheater is recorded by Tacitus with a larger number of casualties: Tac., *Ann.* 4.62.

33 In the next section, Suetonius tells of Tiberius's early drinking history as a young soldier and the nicknames his mates gave him, going on to accuse him of assigning important public duties to drinking companions: Suet., *Tib.* 42. One of these was Pomponius Flaccus (consul in 17 CE) as governor of Syria whose death in office was documented with satisfaction by Philo of Alexandria (*In Flaccum*).

34 A *sellarium* can mean a toilet or latrine, as a communal place where there are seats for urination and defecation. Here, *sellaria* perhaps gains meaning from *sella*, a chair or seat, thus a place to put one's buttocks, hence a place for anal intercourse. For Spintrians, Tac., *Ann.* 6.1. *Spintriae* were small brass tokens, sometimes with erotic scenes, used as payment in brothels: Campana 2009; *NP* s.v. "Spintria" (G. Stumpf). For a thorough review of these terms and variations on them, as well as an assessment and reinterpretation of Tiberius's habits on Capreae: Champlin 2011; see also Coleman 2006, 212–17 (on Martial, *Epig.* 30 [26]).

35 The books of Elephantis refer to a manual or manuals on sex written in Greek by one or more female poets (first century BCE) mentioned here and in Mart., *Epig.* 43.1–4; and in *Priapeia carmina* 3.

36 For images of Nymphs or other salt- and sweet-water denizens on seashores or riverine banks, Stat., *Silv.* 2.2.12–26, and Auson., *Mos.* 169–177, both in ch. 4, Descriptions of Villas; for make-believe Nymphs and Pans, Suet., *Tib.* 43, in this chapter. The use of mythological characters and stories of all kinds marshaled for evocative or pornographic purposes has an equivalent in paintings and statues in domestic and garden decoration as well as in the spectacles arranged for the execution of criminals: Clarke 1998 (domestic erotica); Coleman 1990; 2006, lxxii–lxxv, 62, 63, 82–96, 97–100, and 174–81 (executions in mythological guise).

37 Suetonius continues to describe Tiberius's sexual behavior as well as atrocity stories on Capreae, but these relate to his character rather than the uses of the Villa Iovis itself: Suet., *Tib.* 44–45 and 60.

38 See Suet., *Tib.* 39, in this chapter. The villa (modern name: Villa Prato) was originally built on a promontory above a cliff with a good view of the sea but with an extensive inland property; its masonry indicates a date in the first century BCE: Broise and Lafon 2001. The grotto at sea level was modified into a *triclinium* with a famous group of statues (Blinding of Polyphemus, Transfer of the Palladium), probably for Tiberius himself; it was here that Sejanus saved the emperor's life, possibly sometime between 23 and 26 CE. On the statues in the Spelunca: Andreae 1964; 1974; 1994; 1995; Conticello and Andreae 1974; Andreae and Conticello 1987; articles in de Grummond and Ridgway 2000; Ridgway 2000; Champlin 2013; Neudecker 1988, 41–43, 220–23, n. 62 (with older literature on statues); Himmelmann 1995 (origins of statue groups); Sauron 1997 (analysis of interpretations); good plan in Yegül and Favro 2019, 285, figs. 5.44, 5.45; Zarmakoupi 2023, 41, fig. 23.

39 Amyclae was the name given to the area of Tarracina from a foundation legend ascribing it to Spartan colonists from Laconia: Vergil, *Aen.* 10.564; Martial, *Epig.* 13.115).

40 From Acarnania in western Greece.

41 The reference to twelve named villas recalls a feast given by Augustus at which the guests appeared as the twelve Olympian gods, and Augustus himself as Apollo; it is possible that such a program of villas on Capreae was before Tiberius, but with Tiberius fixing on the Villa of Jove—Villa Iovis—as his special dwelling. The feast of the twelve gods was a calumny of Augustus by Mark Antony: Suet., *Aug.* 70.

42 Ciardello 2019; Krause 1998; 2003; Yegül and Favro 2019, 285, fig. 5.43; Savino 2002; R. Edwards 2011; Di Franco 2015.

43 Casaburi 2002. For another atrocity in the same vein with no happy outcome: Suet., *Tib.* 60; discussed in Champlin 2008, esp. 408.

44 After hearing some general predictions, Tiberius asked Thrasyllus what his own birth horoscope might be; Thrasyllus mapped his planetary and starry fate, became fearful, and told the emperor that the greatest crisis of his life was about to happen. Tiberius admitted his intention and took the fortune teller back into his confidence.

45 Suetonius's grandfather told him stories of the emperor's bridge-road construction and why he built it: Suet., *Calig.* 19.1–3; Wardle 2007.

46 On Julius Caesar's villa at Nemi: Suet., *Iul.* 1.46, in ch. 9, Villas and *Horti* in the Late Roman Republic.

47 The shrine on the smaller boat may have been for the worship of Isis, but Lake Nemi was especially numinous because it was the site of the shrine to Diana Nemorensis and its priest. On what is known of the ships: "Navi di Nemi 1895–1947," *Museo Nazionale Scienza e Tecnologia Leonardo da Vinci*, https://archivi-online.museoscienza.org/detail/IT-MUST-ST003-0000001/navi-nemi; also Ucelli 1950; Carlson 2002; Kroos 2011.

48 On plane trees associated with royal Persian gardens: Herodotus 7.27 and 7.31; also Pliny, *HN* 12.4–12 (12.2–5).

49 The emperor was very tall: Suet., *Calig.* 50.1.

50 Suetonius seems mistaken in identifying the boats that would have been used: *liburnae* were shallow-draft military biremes (originally pirate boats) with double banks of fewer oars than the heavy triremes (three-banked galleys) and were relatively much lighter and more agile: Casson 1971, 141–43; Zaninović 1988.
By "during the day" (*de die*), Suetonius indicates that Gaius's dinner cruises began just after midday rather than in the late afternoon or evening. This would have extended the time for feasting, merging *prandium* (a small afternoon meal) with the evening's *cena*: Lindsay 1913, s.v. "*cena, prandium.*"

51 The *Embassy to Gaius* was the introductory chapter to an essay by Philo on virtue; it concluded with a section, now lost, on the emperor's murder. For the historical circumstances, Tac., *Hist.* 5.9; Joseph., *AJ* 18.8.1 (257–259), 18.9 (305); and 19.5.1–2 (278–291) on the happy outcome and reversal of Gaius's order by Claudius.

52 Which Late Republican villa in what garden—that of Maecenas or the Lamian family—is not clear in the text. The *domus* in the Horti Maecenatis had been undergoing some redecoration in the previous reign (Tiberius, r. 14–37 CE), so perhaps it was the Lamian villa that needed the renovations. On the villas and the *horti*: Cima and La Rocca 1986; Barbera et al. 2010, with preceding bibliography; Häuber 2014; Frass 2006, 289–90.

53 The situation was resolved by the murder of the emperor, so the installation of statues in the temple was rescinded. Philo's account sometimes has the hindsight of an easy resolution, so he uses sarcastic litotes to characterize the emperor's remarks and his disgust for them.

54 This meeting at the imperial villa at Puteoli was inconclusive. Philo and the Alexandrian ambassadors next met the emperor at Rome.

55 While ἀνδρῶνας means "men's quarters," here it probably refers to dining rooms.

56 *CIL* 5 5050. On the Punta Epitaffio at Baiae, there are remains of the structures and statues of a now submerged complex, perhaps relating to a villa: Pappalardo 2009, 31–32, fig. 7; Belli 2009; Zevi and Andreae 1982 (site excavation); Tocco Sciarelli 1983b; Andreae 1983a (sculpture); 1983b (Emperor Claudius imagery); good plan and reconstruction in Yegül and Favro 2019, 285, figs. 5.44, 5.45.

57 Between Lucullus and Valerius Asiaticus, the owner of the gardens was identified by an inscription as being Marcus Valerius Messalla Corvinus, a friend of Augustus. The inscription indicates that the garden wall (*maceria*) was the private property of Messalla: *CIL* 6 29789 = *ILS* 5990, which reads: locus in quo | maceria est et | maceria privata | M. Mes [sallai] | Corvini.

58   Valeria Messalina was Claudius's third wife; Poppaea Sabina was a highly placed woman of the court; her daughter of the same name was Nero's second wife. Decimus Valerius Asiaticus, suffect consul in 35 CE and consul in 46, was a Gallic senator who had acquired great wealth from Mediterranean-wide real estate holdings. His and Poppaea Sabina's deaths by suicide in consequence of the accusations of Publius Suillius Rufus and the machinations of Lucius Vitellius, themselves lawyers and friends of the emperors Tiberius and Gaius, resulted in the Gardens of Lucullus becoming imperial property, which is what Messalina had wanted.

59   By "the exercises he customarily did," Tacitus is referencing Asiaticus's fame as a body builder.

60   Messalina subsequently met her end by execution in the Gardens of Lucullus on the order of Claudius: Tac., *Ann.* 9.37–38.

61   On Nero's villa and harbor at Antium: Suet., *Nero*. 1 (his birthplace), 9.1 (established a *colonia*), and 25.1; Tac., *Ann.* 15.23. On the Sublaqueum villa: Di Matteo 2005; Quilici 1997.

62   The Quinquatria was a celebration of Minerva, March 19–23: Varro, *Ling*. 6.14.

63   The villa at Bauli had been owned by Quintus Hortensius Hortalus (ca. 114–50 BCE), consul in 69 BCE, a famous orator and famously rich; Cicero named his dialogue *On Philosophy* (*De philosophia*, also called *Hortensius*) of 45 BCE after him. The dialogue, anachronistically presented among the dead—Hortensius in 50, Lucullus in 57/56, Quintus Lutatius Catulus Capitolinus in 59 BCE, and the still-living Cicero himself—is lost. All four had villas in the area of Baiae. Hortensius's villa is mentioned by Cicero in *Academia priora* 2.9; Cic. *Att*. 185 (5.2.1); and by Varro, *Rust*. 3.17.5; detailed discussion in D'Arms (1970) 2003, 181, n. 17. It was inherited by his son Quintus Hortensius: Cic., *Att*. 402 (10.16.5); D'Arms (1970) 2003, 182, n. 18. On the view toward Pompeii from Hortensius' villa: Cic., *Acad. post*. 2.80–81 (2.25) in ch. 5, Villas and *Otium*.

64   What follows is Tacitus's exciting account of the deadly barge Nero insisted his mother use to return to her villa on the Lucrine lake. The boat was designed to collapse and both crush the *Augusta* from a weighted canopy and throw her down into the sea. Her companions were either crushed or killed by the crew, but the empress-mother, a woman in her mid-forties, though wounded, saved herself. Then she returned to her own villa on the Lucrine Lake: Tac., *Ann.* 14.5–9 and 14.9–11, with her subsequent death by execution and her burial. Tacitus indicates where her tomb was located: "Later on, with the faithful care of her household servants, an unassuming tomb was built for her beside the road to Misenum and to the villa of the dictator Caesar, which dominates the bay from its great height."

Tacitus's account is detailed, but the story, with very different motivations and circumstances for the execution of Agrippina and varied events, appears in Suet., *Nero* 34.1–5, and Cass. Dio, *Epit. Bk.* 62.1–14. These events were recalled by Martial some fifty years later in a poem for a certain Caerellia, who was drowned in the passage from Bauli to Baiae: Mart., *Epig*. 4.63.

65   *NP* s.v. "Seneca" 2 (J. Dingel).

66   Sextus Afranius Burrus: *NP* s.v. "Afranius" 3 (W. Eck); Publius Suillius Rufus: *NP* s.v. "Suillius" 3 (W. Eck).

67   Tac., *Ann.* 13.42 (Suillius against Seneca); Cass. Dio, *Epit. Bk.* 61.10 (adulteries) and *Epit. Bk.* 62.2 (his crooked deals); Braund 2015, esp. 15–21.

68   Seneca continues to compare the greatness of Nero's ancestry to the lowliness of his own provincial and merely equestrian forebears. He also cites "the grandfather of your grandfather" (*abavus tuus Augustus*) having awarded influence, riches, and honorable retirement to Marcus Agrippa and Gaius Maecenas, and then continues to his own situation.

69   Accepting any given circumstance, be it great misfortune or great wealth and suburban villas, is the prime virtue of the Senecan Stoic. Tacitus may be engaging in some sarcasm in relaying—or making up—Seneca's speech to the emperor.

70   The emperor (or Tacitus) may be countering Seneca's acceptance of his wealthy circumstances by reminding him that wealth, villas, and the like are impermanent: a Stoic trope. Seneca's request to resign was not fully accepted; three years later (65 CE) he was invited to commit suicide, which he did at his villa at the fourth milestone south of Rome after dining with his wife Pompeia Paulina and two friends: Tac., *Ann.* 15.60; Cass. Dio, *Epit. Bk.* 62.24–25.

71   The most famous sentence is at line 356: [to pray for] a sound mind in a sound body (*mens sana in corpore sano*).

72   Gaius Cassius Longinus, suffect consul in 30 CE, a member of Nero's court, was part of the conspiracy against the emperor. Plautius Lateranus, the owner of the *egregia aedes* on the Caelian Hill, was also involved; he was a nephew of Aulus Plautius Silvanus, Claudius's general in the conquest of Britain, and on that basis had been forgiven by Claudius for adultery with his wife Messalina. Epictetus cites the death of Lateranus: Arrian, *Discourses of Epictetus* 1.1.18–19.

The villa, apparently on several levels, was covered by the construction of the Cathedral of St. John Lateran: Krautheimer, Corbett, and Frazer 1977, 27–29. Most recently, a difference of interpretation of the *egregia aedes* and its remains is in Liverani 2020 and Spinola 2020.

73   Pliny the Elder mentions the Palatine *domus* of Gaius (Caligula), which may refer to an extension of the Domus Tiberiana of Tiberius; Pliny was a late adolescent in that emperor's reign, in his early forties when Nero's Domus Aurea was begun, and in his mid-forties when Nero was deposed and murdered.

74   Cassius Dio describes the fire of 64 CE in some detail, including the destruction of the buildings of the Palatine Hill, but he does not mention the Domus Aurea: Cass. Dio, *Epit. Bk.* 62.16–18; Palatine destroyed: 62.18.2–3. By his day in the early third century, all traces of the Neronianic constructions would have disappeared under other buildings.

75 Nero was the last emperor in blood descent from Augustus, so Vespasian appears to have encouraged propaganda designed to stain Nero's memory figuratively and actually dismantled his architectural achievements.

The Domus Aurea was also vulnerable physically: the areas of Regio I (Porta Capena), II (Caelimontium), and III (Isis et Serapis) became areas of urban expansion beyond the City's old southeast perimeters: Ippoliti 2020.

76 The initial fire burned for some six days, then reignited for another three or four. Tacitus says that the fire broke out "in that part of the Circus that is near the Palatine and Caelian Hills"; he names some of the many ancient buildings and temples that were burned but remarks that the private houses, tenements, and places of work were too numerous to list. While repeating the calumny that Nero had some hand in the fire, Tacitus is explicit that the emperor did all he could to help: opening his own *horti* and the official buildings of the Campus Martius for refuge, ordering temporary housing for the displaced citizens, commandeering food from Ostia, and lowering the price of grain. Tacitus's description of the human reaction to the fire and the paths of its destructive power is well worth reading for its humane empathy: Tac., *Ann.* 15.38–39; Moormann 2003; 2020; Barrett 2020, 233–63.

77 The fire of 64 CE marked an important inflection point in the history of Roman architectural innovation and imagination in urbanism and design: widespread use of new materials (fireproof brick); municipal codes (firefighting measures, party walls, traffic), new forms of housing (*insulae*), as well as major spatial concepts, natural and artificial lighting effects, served and servant spaces, and many other ideas and measures: Yegül and Favro 2019, 240–45. The Domus Aurea itself embodied some of these new ideas. Nero's new Rome was indeed new, but there were inevitable complaints: some grumbled that the old narrow streets sheltered the City from the sun, whereas the new open streets were hot: Tac., *Ann.* 15.43.

The literature on Neronian Rome and the Domus Aurea in the history of Roman architecture and urbanism is too vast to summarize adequately, but there are notable accounts and analyses: Moormann 1998; 2003; 2020; *LTUR* 2 51–63 (L. Fabbrini); Boethius 1960, 94–128; Ball 2003; Gros 2001; 2002a, 242–51; Yegül and Favro 2019, 227–40.

78 The area was connected to the Forum by the Via Sacra running on a north-northwest line below the Palatine and stood within the line of the *pomerium* and the traditional defensive boundary of the Servian Wall: these two defined, numinously and physically respectively, the ancient boundaries of the City proper.

79 Before the fire, Nero had been attempting to unite the imperial habitations on the northern areas of the Palatine with the *collis hortulorum*, namely the Republican *horti* and their *domus* to the east and southeast (Horti Maecenatis, Horti Lamiani, and Horti Lolliani, all by then imperial property like the Horti Lucullani). His awkward device was to project, from the Domus Tiberiana and the buildings of Gaius (Caligula), a building called the Domus Transitoria: Suet., *Calig.* 22.2; Frass 2006, 272–75. How far along this building was in 64 CE is not known, but it burned with many of the Palatine buildings: *LTUR* 2 199–202 (M. de Vos); Gros 2002a, 244–46; Tomei 1998; *AtlasAncRome* 1 293; 2: tabs. 111, 112.

80 On this theme: Purcell 1987.

81 Suet., *Nero* 39.1–3. Suetonius claims this to have been one of many circulated to express popular opinion (*hominum vulgata*), but the jibes and graffiti he gives us, with their historical and mythological references, sound more like elite senatorial quips than popular raillery. *Quirites* is the very old term for Latin and Sabine citizens of Rome as established in the laws of civilian status after the founding of the City. Veii, a rich, powerful Etruscan town north of Rome, had been destroyed in 396 BCE and was now a country village: Livy 1.14–15.

82 Suet., *Otho* 7.

83 Gluttony and high living are Cassio Dio's theme for Vitellius who, he claims, found the Domus Aurea lacking in comfort and amenity. His wife, Galeria Fundana, considered the paucity of decoration laughable: Cass. Dio, *Epit. Bk.* 64.4.

84 Pliny parenthetically mentions the Domus Aurea in two other places: Plin., *HN* 33.54 (33.16) and *HN* 36.111 (36.24).

Pliny does have some positive view of Nero's painter and decorator of the Domus Aurea, Famulus (Fabullus or Famullus in some texts), whom he praises as a rare Roman exception of a painter whose work was "closer to the work of ancient (Greek) painters (*antiquis similior*)." The style of Famulus was stately (*gravis*) and severe (*severus*) but also florid (*floridus*) and rich (*tumidus*); he worked few hours in any day, dressed formally in a toga; his works are rare because the (destroyed) Domus Aurea was their prison (*carcer*): Plin., *HN* 35.120 (35.34); Pollitt 1965, 146.

85 Doors opening beyond the facades of private houses saved private space for houses but were a nuisance to the public right-of-way, so there was honor in such an arrangement; Vitruvius specifies that doors in the Attic style open outward, but he is describing temple doors: Vitr., *De arch.* 4.6. Hippias, the tyrant of Athens, charged (or taxed) the city's citizens for permission to have outward-opening doors, implying that they had been forbidden before: Arist., *Oec.* 1347a4–7.

86 This is incorrect: the two were quite different buildings.

87 Nero's "live like a man" (*quasi hominem habitare*): Champlin 1998; Moormann 1998; Blaison 1998. The phrase is similar to that used by Cicero (*homines visi sumus*; Cic., *Att.* 13.52.2, in ch. 6, Villa Visits). The term *homo* in Latin has a connotation of fullness and authenticity with a plenitude not reproduced in the English "man." In the plural (*homines*), it can take on a diffuse meaning, as in the people in general.

88   The villa and landscape of the Domus Aurea, at least as Tacitus describes them, differ widely from the taste for windows of gems and paintings that the emperor Gaius had been proposing for renovations in the Horti Lamiani or Maecenatis villas some twenty years before.

89   Before this, Severus and Celer had been commissioned to design and build an inland waterway from the Bay of Naples to the mouth of the Tiber at Ostia. This would have connected the port of Puteoli to Rome, supplementing or even bypassing the approach to the roadsteads of Ostia and Portus, which were hard to navigate; see also Suet., *Nero* 31.

90   Detailed analysis in Coleman 2006, 14–36.

91   The conversion of the Domus Aurea into other buildings and spaces had begun in the reigns of Vespasian and Titus, but here Martial is addressing the emperor Domitian.

92   Colossus: this was a statue of Nero, according to Suetonius 120 Roman feet high (about 30.3 m, or 99 ft.): Suet., *Nero* 31.1; according to Pliny, 106.5 Roman feet high: Plin., *HN* 34.45–46 [34.18]). It was constructed between 64 and 68 CE by Zenodorus for the vestibules of the Domus Aurea. Vespasian had the head changed to the image of Sol with a radiate crown, and Hadrian had it moved to a position to the north of the Flavian amphitheater, to which it may have given its name: Suet., *Vesp.* 18; *HA, Hadr.* 19. Commodus changed it yet again into a portrait of himself: Cass. Dio, *Epit. Bk.* 73.22.3.

Translating *crescunt media pegmata celsa via* as "pageant floats built in the street" is justified because Martial is emphasizing the newly public character of the Flavian constructions. To delight the audiences, the spectacles of the Colosseum and of triumphal processions would have needed space to construct the stage properties and sets for the shows. Watching the machines of spectacles being built can be part of the fun of seeing them in operation: in 1989, the architect Carlos Ott provided for the Opéra Bastille in Paris a broad window from the street into the atelier in which stage decor and props are constructed: Charlet 1989.

By designating the entrance to the Domus Aurea as royal (*atria regia*), Martial is equating Nero to a king, a term of political suspicion and contempt ever since the founding of the republic in the sixth century BCE. The contrast is between the benign, distinctly nonroyal (but no less imperial) rule of the Flavians and that of Nero.

93   The Domus Aurea park had ponds or expanses of water between the main block of rooms on the east side below the Esquiline Hill that could be viewed from its porticoes, with the Palatine and Caelian Hills as their background.

94   The Baths of Titus (Thermae Titi) and the Flavian Amphitheater were both dedicated in 81 CE during the brief reign of Titus; the baths were hastily put up (*therm*[*ae*]...*celeriter extruct*[*ae*]) and partially covered the northern constructions of the Domus Aurea.

95   The Porticus of Claudius refers to the Temple of the Divine Claudius, or the Claudianum or Claudium, begun in 54 CE by the emperor's widow, Agrippina. It was situated on a massive platform on the south side of the area where Nero built his Domus Aurea, which partially destroyed its structures, but the platform and temple were restored by Vespasian when Nero's works were converted to public uses: Suet. *Vesp.* 9; *LTUR* 1 277–8 (C. Buzzetti); Richardson 1992, s.v. "Claudius, Divus, Templum"; *AtlasAncRome* 1 347–50, fig. 125 and ill. 18; 2: tabs. 135–37.

96   On Livia's villa Ad Gallinas Albas: Plin., *HN* 15.136–137 (15.40) in this chapter. There are other accounts in Suet., *Galb.* 1–3, which is followed Cass. Dio, *Epit. Bk.* 68.29.3.

97   A shorter version of this story is in Cass. Dio, *Epit. Bk.* 63 (64).1. Galba would have been around 15 or 16 at this time; the white *toga virilis* (the toga of manhood, the *toga alba* or *toga pura*) was part of the rite of passage to full citizenship: Dolansky 2008, 48–50.

98   The events in question occurred between January 1 and 15, 69 CE, when Galba's blunders while emperor ended in his murder by the praetorian guard. His former friend Marcus Salvius Otho then became emperor for a few months, followed by Aulus Vitellius; Titus Flavius Vespasianus (Vespasian) brought the wrangling for the imperial dignity to an end when proclaimed emperor by the Senate in late 69 CE.

99   i.e., instead of a properly robed attendant with incense smoke to perfume the premises and vessels of silver or other metals.

Horti could be used for burials. Galba was murdered in January 69 CE by assassins sent by Otho. His beheaded body was retrieved by his steward (*dispensator*), who paid some money for the head, which had been previously sold, then buried both in Galba's private gardens on the Via Aurelia: Suet., *Galb.* 20.

100   On "senatorial" opinion, see ch. 10 n. 3. For analysis of the successes of Nero's reign and his modern rehabilitation: Levick 1999a.

101   Suffect consul of 47 CE and a general. He was murdered at Rome in 69 CE during the events that brought his brother to the imperial dignity: *NP* s.v. "Flavius" II 40 (W. Eck).

102   Suetonius and Cassius Dio (*Epit. Bk.* 65.2–3) specify that it was a human hand (*munus humana*, χεῖρα ἀνθρωπίνην) rather than a simian paw or the appendage of another beast. The meaning of "hand" is multiplied through various languages: "laying on of hands," "the hand of God," "the hand of fate," *main d'oeuvre* (workforce in French), handshake (*dextrarum junctio*), certain forms of marriage (*cum manu*, *sine manu*), and so on: Brilliant 1963, 18–48.

103   Both Suetonius and Cassius Dio tell this anecdote about the kneeling ox. The recognition by animals of future or actual greatness (in contrast to human beings who are blind to its presence) has a long history: e.g., Isaiah 3.

This kneeling by animals was also a circus trick: Trajan, during the Parthian campaign of 113–117 CE, received a horse that did the same, as a gift from satraps and princes: Cass. Dio, *Epit. Bk.* 68.18.2.

104 This portentous anecdote is repeated in Cass. Dio, *Epit. Bk.* 65 (66).1.2. In his life of Domitian, Suetonius returned to the fateful cypress tree: "The tree [at the Reate villa] that had been toppled but had revived, at the time that Vespasian was a private citizen, now suddenly fell down once more": Suet., *Dom.* 3.15.2.

Suetonius also says that before dying, Vespasian had returned to his family estates near Reate, seeking a cure at a nearby spa: Suet., *Vesp.* 1.24.1.

105 *Epitome de Caesaribus, Titus,* http://www.forumromanum.org/literature/victor_ep.html#9; Jerome, *Interpretation of Eusebius, Chronicon* 2 for the year 82: *PL* 27, col. 462.

106 Moorman 2003; 2020; B.W. Jones 2002, 79–88 (buildings in Rome), 88–93 (restorations), 93–94 (completions), 95–97 (Palatine).

107 There seems some misdating by Suetonius here: Domitian was nominated *Caesar* by his father Vespasian in 69 CE but became *Augustus* only in 81 CE, so "beginning of his reign" as emperor is premature: spearing the flies in the villa at Alba happened between 69 and 81 CE, not after. Cassius Dio repeats the story about spearing flies but is more correct in his chronology: Cass. Dio, *Epit. Bk.* 65.3.4. Cassius Dio says that Domitian was living in retirement at Alba: the verb used for "living in retirement" is ἰδιάζω which means "living by oneself" from ἴδιος or ἰδιώτης (roots of Eng. "idiot"), which here has a distinctly prejorative connotation of evil, selfish living, a negative form of productive *otium*: Cass. Dio, *Epit. Bk.* 65.9.4.

108 Domitia Lepida, a descendant of Augustus in the female line, became Domitian's wife and was named Augusta; she outlived him by many years: Raepset-Charlier 1987, 1:287–88, no. 327; vol. 2 stemmata XII–XIV; Levick 2002; Foubert 2021; Jones 2002, 35–38; Métraux 2015, 143–44, n. 23. Her father, Gnaeus Domitius Corbulo (ca. 7–67 CE), suffect consul in 39 CE, was a famous general for Claudius in Germania and for Nero in the East; he was ordered to commit suicide in 67 CE.

109 On Domitian's villas as well as his dwellings on the Palatine: Cominesi and Stocks 2021.

110 Martial's picture of Domitian's "viewing" is figurative: not all the places of his villas could be seen from the villa at Alba. Alba itself took the place of Alba Longa, founded by Ascanius, Aeneas's son. "Trivia" refers to the sanctuary of Diana Nemorensis on Lake Nemi near Ariccia; the reference to Thetis, a sea goddess and mother of Achilles, contrasts the fresh water of the lake with the salt water of the coastal villas that follow.

111 The "truthful sisters" refers to an oracle determined by lots at Antium, where there had long been imperial villas.

112 All these are sites of maritime villas: Aeneas's nurse was buried at Caieta (Vergil, *Aen.* 7.1–9) on his way to the area around Alba; Circe, for whom Circeii was named, was a daughter of Helios/Apollo, god of the Sun; Anxur, near Tarracina, was the cliff-top site of Jupiter the Thunderer. On a villa with architecture attributed to Domitian: Marzano 2007, cat. no L78, 339.

113 Domitian had completed the rebuilding of the Temple of Jupiter Capitolinus in Rome in 82 CE after it had burned in the events of 69 CE; Vespasian had started the reconstruction: Cass. Dio, *Epit. Bk.* 65.10.2. That temple was destroyed again in a fire of 80 CE, then was rebuilt by Domitian: Plutarch, *Publicola* 15.3–4 (105).

114 Penelope, queen of Ithaca and Odysseus's wife, waited virtuously at home during her husband's ten-year absence at Troy.

115 Varro, *Rust.* 3.17; Cic., *Att.* 1.19.6 and 1.20.3.

116 This may refer to a horror story about Tiberius on Capreae: a fisherman who scaled the cliffs with a mullet and a lobster or crab (*locusta*) as a gift to the emperor was, for breaching security, punished by having his gifts rubbed in his face: Suet., *Tib.* 50.

117 The rest of the poem describes a "Libyan" poacher who was punished by blinding and beggary for his transgression.

118 For Tiberius at Alba: Tac., *Ann.* 15.23; Cass. Dio 58.24.1.

119 On Domitian's Albanum: Valeri 2021, with preceding bibliography.

120 Martial celebrated the devotion of Domitian to Minerva (the "Tritonian goddess") on the emperor's birthday, in a poem that mentions the emperor's gift of "Alban gold," making the Albanum into a Villa Aurea, and the emperor into a god: Mart., *Epig.* 4.1.

Both Martial and Statius competed in the Ludi Capitolini (Capitolia) in Rome and in the Quinquatria for Minerva at the Albanum. Martial missed the prize of a gold olive-leaf crown at the Albanum but tells us that Carus, who won it, gave his crown to Domitian or to a statue or bust of the emperor: Mart., *Epig.* 9.23. Carus became golden; the verb used is *flavescere*, in compliment to Domitian's family, Flavius. In another poem, Carus is rewarded with a crown from Minerva herself: Mart., *Epig.* 9.24.

Statius commemorates his winning the golden crown at the Albanum but missing it at the Capitolia; he thanks his wife for giving him a hug when he won and empathizing when he lost: Stat., *Silv.* 3.5.28–31. Domitian invited Statius to dinner in the new palace on the Palatine Hill in Rome; Statius responded with a bread-and-butter thank you for the sacred dinner (*sacra cena*) at the lordly table (*domina mensa*): Stat., *Silv.* 4.2.63–67. In the same poem, the new palace is described in architectural and mythological detail, with a list of its marbles (4.2.18–35).

Hunting and prowess in its skills was also practiced at Domitian's Alban retreat (*in Albano sucessu*). Domitian was lazy and disliked walking, but was a famous archer: "He shot with such dexterity at a slave [*puer*] standing and stretching out the palm of his right hand as a target that the arrows passed harmlessly between the fingers": Suet., *Dom.* 3.19.1. In 91 CE, the consul Manius Acilius Glabrio was ordered by the emperor to kill a large lion at the Juvenalia festival at the villa, which he did successfully but was later exiled for it: Cass. Dio, *Epit. Bk.* 67.14.3.

The Albanum could be mocked while also being a sinister fortress. It is called the Alban citadel (*arx Albana*) in a mock-heroic account of a solemn council about what to do with a huge fish worth 6,000*HS* that had been presented to Domitian by Crispinus: Juv., *Satires* 4.144–149.

121   By the Panathenaea, Cassius Dio means the festival at the Albanum called the Quinquatria: also Tac., *Ann.* 14.4; Suet., *Dom.* 4.4.

122   Pliny the Elder classes Alban wine as a third-level wine, along with that of Surrentum; it was sweet but dry, but both had commercial value: Plin., *HN* 23.33 (20.1). Juvenal comments that it and the most famous *grand cru*, Falernian, were expensive and affectedly disdained by so-called connoisseurs who didn't know anything about wine: Juv., *Satires* 13.210–216.

123   The Julian mountain is the area of Alba where Ascanius Iulus had founded Alba Longa; Iulus was the ancestor of the *gens* Julia and thus of the Julio-Claudian dynasts.

124   The *Panegyric* offers a description of what hunting meant to Romans in Pliny's day: it was clearly an *exemplum virtutis* or mark of virtue, as well as a training ground for strength, cunning, skill, talent, benign activity to rid fields of predators and thereby promote farmers' work (*agrestium labor*), and as preparation for war. Pliny's letters to Cornelius Tacitus about writing or reading while hunting may have something of this *exemplum virtutis*.

125   This letter contains some gossip about Valerius Licinianus, whose descent into obscurity Pliny terms sad and much to be pitied (*tristia et miseranda*). It invokes several events that ocurred in 91 CE during the reign of Domitian centering on the emperor's trial of the Vestal Cornelia and his condemning her to death. Pliny considered that the trial venue at the imperial villa, the Albanum, was illegitimate. He goes on to describe other details and legal conundrums, but none are more important than his opinion that the Vestal Cornelia seemed innocent of having sexual relations with Licinianus, that Licinianus may have been innocent of the crime (even though, by a legal stratagem, he was forced to admit to it), and that Domitian was a cruel tyrant.

Licinianus appears to have been smeared with the charge of adultery with Cornelia when his only crime was to have hidden one of the priestess's freedwomen (a possible witness?) in his house. To deny that he had done so would have resulted in being charged in a cover-up and flogged to death: by admitting to the crime (either spuriously or truthfully), he received the emperor's clemency and was merely exiled to Sicily. At the same time, a knight called Celer was accused of complicity in the affair but denied any guilt while being flogged.

Besides his tyrannical cruelty, Domitian may have had an antiquarian reason from ancient Roman history for his determination to try the Vestal Cornelia at the villa at Alba instead of the Regia in the Roman Forum: before their foundation at Rome by King Numa, the first Vestals were priestesses at Alba Longa, near which the Albanum was built. This town was the community whose people had descended from the Trojan prince Aeneas and from which Rome had been founded. Both Livy and Dionysius of Halicarnassus tell the story of the first Vestal, named either Ilia or Rhea Silvia (both in Dionysius, Rhea Silvia in Livy) who was from Alba Longa: Livy 1.3–4. According to Dionysius, she was the first to suffer the punishment; her twin sons Romulus and Remus were saved and Romulus became the founder of Rome: Dion. Hal., *Ant. Rom.* 1.76–78. Livy dryly associates the condemnation and execution of Vestals with times of social strife and external danger: Livy 2.42.11 (Oppia); Livy, *Per.* 2 (Opillia).

126   A Vestal Virgin who broke her vows of chastity was technically guilty of incest as a female daughter of society as a whole, not an independent member of a specific family: Parker 2004; Kroppenberg 2010.

127   The rumor had been that he had an incestuous relationship with his neice Flavia Julia (Julia Titi), his brother Titus's daughter.

128   See Pliny the Younger, *Ep.* 4.11, in this chapter.

129   Domitian was murdered in September 96 CE; his body was taken by his nurse Phyllis to her villa on the Via Latina and cremated there, then the ashes put into the Flavian mausoleum: Suet., *Dom.* 17.3.

130   For Nerva's residence in the Gardens of Sallust: Jerome, *Interpretation of Eusebius, Chronicon* 2, for the year 98: in *PL* 27, col. 462.

131   See discussion of the *alimenta* in ch. 7, Economics and Euergetism..

132   Correnti 1990; Marconi 1998a; 1998b; Reggiani 2018.

133   Rutilius Namatianus, *De reditu suo* 249–276.

134   The date of Pliny's letter, between 104 and 107 CE, is in good accord with the dates of both the Centum Cellae villa, then still under construction, and the villa at Arcinazzo Romano. Their construction beginning in 102 but before 116 is known from lead water pipes (*fistulae plumbeae*) marked with the name of Hebrus, described as a freedman and agent (*procurator*) of the emperor. The stamps on the pipes give the emperor's cognomen as Germanicus, already awarded to him by Nerva in 97 or 98 CE, and Dacicus, conferred by the Senate for the Dacian campaign and Triumph in 102 and renewed in 106. The cognomen Parthicus for the Parthian campaign appears on coins only in 116, so 102–116 CE is the span of construction years for these villas, both probably begun in 102. Hebrus was the agent for both: *CIL* 15(1) 7770 and 7771 (Centum Cellae); *CIL* 15(1) 7894 and 7895a, b, and c (Arcinazzo Romano).

Trajan also had a villa at Talamone on the Tuscan coast, and Hebrus was also involved with its construction (a pipe is stamped with his name): Marzano 2007, cat. no. T47, 705.

135   The villa and harbor evidently endured some three centuries: it was still functional in 416 CE. See Rut. Namat., *De red.* 1.237–248, in this chapter.

136 Arcinazzo Romano was near Sublaqueum (modern Subiaco), where Nero had had a villa. Fiore Cavaliere and Mari 1999; Mari 2004; 2014; Cinti and Lo Castro 2011, with preceding bibliography.

137 For accounts of the hospitality he received at his friends' villas north of Centum Cellae, see Rutil. Namat., *De red.*, l.463–468, 1.507–508, and 1.541–558, in ch. 6, Villa Visits.

138 The Latin is particularly strongly worded: *nunc villae grandes, oppida parva prius*. Later in the poem (413–414), Rutilius says, of ruins near Populonia, "We should not feel anguish when men's bodies break down, [because] we can see from such examples [of their ruins] that towns [themselves] can die": Fentress 2021.

139 Though an Etruscan city, Caere was known as Agylla in Greek accounts of the Tyrrhenian coast: Strabo 5.2.3. Its harbors were Pyrgi and, in Roman times, Castrum Novum, as the city itself was some 6 km from the coast.

140 Trajan, by choosing the wooded area around Arcinazzo Romano, would have found good hunting and may have started an imperial trend: both his successor Hadrian everywhere he went, and the young Marcus Aurelius at the Villa Magna, loved hunting, especially boars. Trajan's contemporaries, Pliny the Younger and the historian Cornelius Tacitus, went boar hunting as well: see Pliny's letters to Tacitus: Plin., *Ep.* 1.6.1–3 and 9.10.1–3, in ch. 5, Villas and *Otium*.

141 Some sixty years later, Fronto (see *Ep.* 3[170].2–6 in this chapter) underlined the need for relaxation after *negotium* to Marcus Aurelius, citing Trajan's habits.

142 I have followed the suggestion of the excavators and curators of the Arcinazzo Romano villa and museum that good hunting would have been available in the area, then as now: Cinti and Lo Castro 2011, 20.

143 *HA, Hadr.* 14.8–9, 16.1, and 8–10; Fronto, *Ep.* 1.9 (on Hadrian's antiquarian speech, fragment); Cass. Dio, *Epit. Bk.* 69.4.6 (preferring Antimachus of Colophon, writer of epic poems, fourth century BCE, to Homer); Plutarch also records Hadrian's antiquarian literary tastes: Plut., *Cons. ad Apoll.* 9.2.

144 Cass. Dio, *Epit. Bk.* 69.7.3.

145 Two accounts present Hadrian's engagement with architecture. The first is that of Cassius Dio concerning Hadrian's relationship to Trajan's architect, Apollodorus of Damascus; the architect insulted the future emperor's sketches for buildings by telling him to go away and "draw your gourds," often cited as the young Hadrian's innovative plans and domical designs. Cassius Dio continues with a story about Hadrian's design for the Temple of Venus and Rome and its statues: Apollodorus said the site should have been excavated so the temple would appear more prominent and have room in the basement to prepare scenery for the Flavian Amphitheater (on the floats and scenery for the spectacles, see Mart., *Spect., Epig.* 2, in this chapter). This account ends by alleging that Hadrian had Apollodorus executed shortly after his accession in 117 CE, but internal inconsistencies of sequence and dates indicate that Cassius Dio is recopying court gossip of no value in order to impugn the emperor's character: Cass. Dio, *Epit. Bk.* 69.4.1–6.

The second account is in the *Historia Augusta*. The writer lists the Pantheon, the Saepta Julia, the Basilica of Neptune, various temples, the Forum of Augustus, and the Baths of Agrippa as buildings that Hadrian restored or even rebuilt, and the new constructions of the Pons Aelius, his own mausoleum, and a temple to the Bona Dea. He then continues about the engineering feat of moving the Colossus of Nero to stand adjacent to the Flavian Amphitheater and recast as Sol, with another Colossus, Luna, proposed by Apollodorus of Damascus: *HA, Hadr.* 19.12–13.

146 Gatti 2005; Fentress and Gatti 2015, 150–56.

147 Fentress et al. 2016, 78; Fentress and Gatti 2015, 161–62. The late Trajanic possibility is on the basis of brick stamps, but building material was often reused, and the balance of the masonry evidence points to Hadrianic date.

148 As a young man, Hadrian was criticized for excessive devotion to the hunt, but he continued to hunt wherever he traveled: *HA, Hadr.* 2.1–2, 20.13 (bear), and 26.3–4 (lion); Cass. Dio, *Epit. Bk.* 69.7.3. For Marcus Aurelius at the Villa Magna, see Fronto, *Ep.* 4.4 (59) and 4.5 (60), in this chapter.

149 Philostratus (ca. 170–250 CE) wrote his biography of Apollonius of Tyana (ca. 3–97 CE?), a philosopher, miracle worker, eccentric *anima sanctiora*, and philosopher of Cappadocian orgin as part of a larger project of philosophic documentation for the instruction of the Augusta Julia Domna and her intellectual court at Rome, about a 120 years after the death of Apollonius and some eighty years after the death of Hadrian. Here is the story: leaving Olympia, Apollonius went to Lebadea (modern Livadeia) in Boeotia, to the cave oracle of Trophonius carrying a book of the teachings of Pythagoras. He entered the cave and emerged seven days later, the book having been endorsed as good by the oracle. The book was later owned by Hadrian, who revered it because of its origin [αιτία], and he preserved it and some letters by Apollonius at the Antium residence: Philostratus, *VA* 19–20.

150 On his death at the Baiae villa and temporary burial at the Puteolana of Cicero: *HA, Hadr.* 25.5–8; *HA, Ant. Pius* 5.1. For the Vedius villa at Pausilypon, see Cass. Dio 54.23.1–6, in this chapter.

151 Two writers of the *Historia Augusta* mention the Villa Hadriana. The first indicates that Hadrian conducted official business there, including arrangements for his succession: *HA, Hadr.* 23.7–8.

The second identifies either the Villa Hadriana (called a *palatium*) or some place nearby called *Concha* as the place of exile for Queen Zenobia of Palmyra. Zenobia fought against and was defeated by the emperor Aurelian in 272 CE and may have been exhibited as a trophy in his triumphal parade, afterward living as a Roman matron with her children at Tibur for the rest of her life. Other accounts of her fate differ. For the place called

Concha, I cannot find a contemporaneous indication of Concha near Tibur, but an early nineteenth-century visitor claims it was known in 1828: Fosbroke 1828, s.v. "Tibur," 303–6, esp. 303.

In the late fourth century, Sextus Aurelius Victor, in a compendium of imperial biographies, indicates that it was to the Villa Hadriana that Hadrian, like other rich people, went to enjoy feasting and collecting statues and paintings: Aur. Vict., *Caes.* 14.5–7.

152   The bibliography on Hadrian's Villa is vast: see esp. Yegül and Favro 2019, 373–99, bibliography 405–8; MacDonald and Pinto 1995; Salza Prina Ricotti 2001; articles in Giuliani and Verduchi 1975; Gros 2002b; Lugli 1927 (the villa in Late Antiquity).

153   Tombrägel 2012.

154   The Villa Hadriana at Tibur was built near, and partially over, earlier Republican-period villas, which used a form of masonry surfacing over rubble cores called *opus reticulatum* (Vitruvius, *De arch.* 2.8.1–4). By Hadrian's day, this form had gone out of use in any major buildings (including those of Hadrian himself) in favor of brick, with the exception of the Tibur villa. I have argued that this antiquarian form of construction was intended, by Hadrian, to associate himself with Marcus Agrippa and Augustus: Métraux 2015.

155   Syme (1982) 1988; Métraux 2015, 140–41 and n. 10.

156   On the *nomina*: MacDonald and Pinto 1995, 6–7. On Hadrian's travels: Syme (1988) 1991.

157   Specifically, the Lyceum and the Academy may refer to the venues of philosophic study at Athens (Aristotelian and Platonic, respectively), but they refer equally well to Cicero's Lyceum and Academy at his villa at Tusculum and to the name (Academia) of Cicero's villa at Puteoli. Such were the many-angled aspects of Roman iconography that Hadrian might well have wished to project.

158   The Prytaneum at Hadrian's villa might reference the Prytaneion of Athens or any other such municipal building in Greek cities, but in a Roman context it may also refer to Plutarch's calling Lucullus's villa and its libraries at Tusculum a Prytaneum in which Greek scholars, philosophers, and literary artists resident in Rome could meet: see Plut., *Vit. Luc.* 42.1–4, in ch. 9, Villas and *Horti* in the Late Roman Republic.

159   Many of these *nomina* had multiple meanings—exotic, but also close to Roman themes and to Hadrian himself. *Canopus* as a term standing for Egypt as a whole may well allude to Augustus's assimilation of Egypt to Roman rule after his defeat of Cleopatra. In 130 CE, Hadrian visited Egypt; Antinous died there (*HA*, *Hadr.* 14.5–7).

160   The Poikile (ποικίλη στοά, Painted Stoa) fronting the north side of the Athenian Agora was as famous for being the building that exhibited large paintings of mythological scenes and military depictions of Athenian victories as it was for being the site from which Zeno taught the form of philosophy called Stoicism. Hadrian collected paintings and was an amateur painter, and the *Liber de Caesaribus* of Sextus Aurelius Victor specifically mentions the collection of paintings at the Tiburtine Villa: see ch. 10 n. 151.

161   Hadrian had visited Athens and Attica in 124 CE and was inducted into the mysteries of Demeter and Kore at Eleusis; the following year he toured the Peloponnese but made his way north, visiting Tempe: *CIL* 3 7362 and 14206. He was at Athens again in 128 CE. The Vale of Tempe was the haunt of Apollo and the Muses and the site of a temple of Apollo, which may also have had Augustan echo: Augustus's wide-ranging Apollonian imagery included his taking on the guise of Apollo at his famous banquet of the gods: see ch. 10 n. 41. The reference may well allude to the view of steep hills from the villa at Tibur to the cliffs on either side of the passage of the Peneius River from the plain of Larissa to the sea in Greece recalling the Vale of Tempe. On the Greek site: Plin., *HN* 4.31 (4.8), and description in Paus. 10.5.7.

As a literary connoisseur, Hadrian would have been well aware that Horace had praised Tibur as being more beautiful than Tempe: the poet had specifically praised Tibur, its spring (Albunea), and its Anio River, comparing it favorably to sites of lesser beauty such as Ephesus, Athens, Larisa, and especially Delphi and "Thessalian Tempe," the latter two famous for Apollo and, by implication, Augustus: Hor., *Odes* 1.7. Elsewhere, Horace mentions Augustus in relation to the Pax Romana: Hor., *Odes* 1.21.9–12; Augustus and Apollo: Hor., *Odes* 1.2.30–52; Tempe as a beautiful spot: Ovid, *Met.* 1.568–576.

Though not in the *Historia Augusta* writer's list, another famous venue can be added to the Villa Hadriana: the round Temple of Aphrodite at Knidos. Hadrian is not known to have visited Knidos, but as a connoisseur of Greek art, he would have known of Praxiteles's famous statue, the Knidian Aphrodite; on the statue: Plin., *HN* 34.69–70 (34.19) and 36.20 (36.4); see other references in Pollitt 1965, 128–31. On the round Doric temple at the Villa Hadriana: De Franceschini 1991, 446–50 ("Ninfeo Fede"); Ortolani 1998, esp. 165–202 on Hadrian and Greek culture; MacDonald and Pinto 1995, 59, fig. 50.

162   The author or authors of the *Historia Augusta* often exhibit a puckish sense of humor. After the list of impressive allusions, I take the phrase "he even constructed an Underworld" as sarcastic and mocking.

163   On his death at Lorium in 161 CE: *HA*, *Ant. Pius* 12; Aur. Vict., *Caes.* 15.7.

164   *Pleiades* s.v. "Lanuvium"; Neudecker 1988, 164–66, cat. no. 22.

165   The references to villas are found in the compilation of letters and copied correspondance of Marcus Cornelius Fronto: *Ep.* 9.7 (Albanum); 9.11 (Formianum and Capua); 10.1 (Formianum). The letters date from mid-175 to 176 CE and concern mainly family matters, though one mentions the rebellion of Gaius Avidius Cassius. These letters were included in a biography of Marcus Aurelius by Marius Maximus and are quoted in Avidius Cassius's biography in *HA*, *Avid. Cass.* 6.5–7 and 9.5.12.

Antoninus Pius was also conservative with respect to where he lived in Rome: instead of living in Domitian's Domus Augustana and using the facilities of the Domus Flavia, he lived in the old Domus Tiberiana that Nero had abandoned for his Domus Aurea. Antoninus Pius's successors also maintained it as their residence in the capital: *HA, Ant. Pius* 10.4; *HA, M. Aur.* 6.3; for Marcus Aurelius, also Cass. Dio, *Epit. Bk.* 72.35.4; Lucius Verus grew up there: *HA, Verus* 2.5.

166 Fronto (ca. 110–160s CE) was suffect consul in 142 CE, declining the governorship of Asia the next year on grounds of poor health.

167 Alsium had been a place for villas: Caesar had one there (*in Alsiense*): Cic., *Fam.* 181 (9.6.1) as had Pliny's mentor Verginius Rufus, then his mother-in-law Celerina (Plin., *Ep.* 6.10); Fentress 1984.

168 The author of Antoninus Pius's biography in the *Historia Augusta* wrote at least 150 years after the death of his subject, so the *palatium* at Lorium may well have become ruinous. Aurelius Victor says that his villa was 12,000 *passus* (about 18 km, or 11⅙ mi.) from the City: Aur. Vict., *Caes.* 15.7.

169 He was consul in 120 CE.

170 The division of Italy into four big areas assigned to exconsuls appears to have been a measure that Hadrian undertook in the 130s CE. For Antoninus Pius, who was consul in 120 but appointed governor of Asia by Hadrian only in 134 or 135, there was a hiatus during which he returned to private life, presumably on his estates on the "Etruscan" or right bank of the Tiber, at Lorium, so he was put in charge of Etruria: *HA, Hadr.* 22.13.

171 The term ὑφάς, ὑφάσματα for garments means "things woven" and may imply that the Lorium villa functioned as a place where woolen garments were made by women domestically, whether or not the Augusta Faustina did this herself. The reference may be to the younger women of Augustus's family weaving his clothes under Livia's supervision: Suet., *Aug.* 64.2.

172 On Cicero's *deversorium* at Anagnia, see n. 43 in ch. 4, Descriptions of Villas.

173 The area has the medieval and modern name Ciociaria, with its main town at Frosinone, part of the larger Campagna Romana.

174 Margaret A. Andrews, Harvard University, with thanks for her gracious permission and that of the editor of the Villa Magna excavation account, Elizabeth B. Fentress; Fentress et al. 2016, 29–31. I have added my own notes and additions in brackets to specify details in the young *Caesar*'s description of his life at the Villa Magna. Headnotes and prefatory comments have been added for this volume, and some punctuation has been brought in line with the current publication.

175 The numbering of Fronto's letters, both those of Andrews and the others in my translation, are from the modern text of van den Hout 1988. Marcus Aurelius's age (late teens, early twenties) can be deduced from Fronto's letter to him of 143 CE indicating that he no longer considers his imperial pupil (born 121 CE) to be twenty-two years old in view of his intellectual maturity: Fronto, *Ep.* 2.1.4 (37). For dates in Fronto's correspondence: Champlin 1974, 144 and 158.

176 See the Introduction for Varro on the etymology of the word "villa."

177 The excursion to look at antiquities and to comment on them is a good instance of antiquarian *otium* appropriate to villa life. Anagnia was the ancient capital of the Hernici and had been an important agricultural center in Latium since 306 BCE. On the *libri lintei*, an inscribed strip of linen (used to wrap an Egyptian mummy) is preserved in Zagreb, Croatia: Belfiore 2010.

178 For the first part of the first letter (4.4), the translation correctly renders Marcus Aurelius's conjugation in the third person plural, "we," which is correct for highly placed individuals. Elsewhere, I have translated the locution as the first person singular, "I"—as with Cicero and Sidonius Apollinaris—because it better conveys the authors' intentions, especially in letters.

179 The young writer seems to be comparing the toothsomeness of the various grapes rather than the wines themselves, and by preferring the wine to the must of local Signian grapes is also signaling his usual abstemiousness and his fine palate. For the wines: Massican or Falernian (ancient and well known) in Mart., *Epig.* 13.111; Plin., *HN* 14.62–63, 65 (14.8); wine of Mons Gaurus (modern Monte Barbaro) near Baiae, Plin., *HN* 14.39 (14.4); wine of Signia (modern Segni) near Anagnia and the Villa Magna (deemed constipative by Mart., *Epig.* 13.115; dry by Plin., *HN* 14.65 [14.8], both negative attributes).

180 Must foaming in *dolia* is an image also used by Sidonius Apollinaris: Sid. Apoll., *Ep.* 1–5 in ch. 5, Villas and *Otium*.

181 After the autumnal equinox (grape harvesting season), the ninth hour of the night to the second hour of the day would be about 3:00 AM to around 8:00 AM; the second to third of the day, about 8:00 to 9:00 AM. By switching from sandals (*soleae*) to covered shoes (*calcei*) and a short cloak of military style (*sagulum*), the young Caesar was dressing himself to greet his lord (*dominum*) in the morning *salutatio*, the muster of family, friends, and clients to greet the *Augustus*.

182 Domus Tiberiana: *LTUR* 2 189–97 (C. Krause) and 297-99 (H. Hurst); Tomei and Filetici 2011, 59-85; *AtlasAncRome* 1 237–40, 246–50, figs. 63, 64; 2: tabs. 76–81; Wiseman 2019, 122–39, figs. 65, 66.

There were two libraries on the Palatine: the Bibliotheca Apollinis Palatini (Library of the Palatine Apollo) was founded in 28 CE by Augustus, with Gaius Julius Hyginus as its first librarian: Suet., *Aug.* 29.1 and 31.1; Cass. Dio 53.1.3.

The second was the library of the Domus Tiberiana: Aul. Gell., *NA* 13.20.1; and in the *Historia Augusta, Ant. Pius* 3.10.4 and *Probus* 28.2.1; in this last text, dated to 276–282 CE, the library of the Domus Tiberiana is claimed to be still active, even after the fire of 192 that destroyed it. The importance of this library and others in Rome has come to light in a letter-essay known to have been written by Galen in 193 CE. Galen's letter-essay was thought lost until the discovery of a copy in 2005 in a monstery in Thessaloniki,

On Consolation from Grief (Περὶ Ἀλυπίας, *De indolentia*): Rothschild and Thompson 2014a, with preceding bibliography and ongoing discussions. Galen's essay and its circumstances are discussed in relation to Gal., *De indo*. 1–4 and 8–10, in ch. 5, Villas and *Otium*, describes the two fires in 192 CE that destroyed the holdings and even the catalogues of the two Palatine libraries, and the Greek and Latin libraries of the Forum Pacis, as well as the destruction of the House of the Vestals: Cass. Dio, *Epit. Bk.* 73.24; Hdn. 1.14.2–4.

Galen's account indicates that books did not circulate from the two Palatine libraries, but both the young Marcus Aurelius as *Caesar* and Fronto as his tutor may have had informal borrowing privileges, reinforced by bribes (*rei insumendi*) and their high status. Galen indicates that "robbery" had compromised the collections even before their destruction in 192 CE (*De indo*. 18).

For the circumstances of Galen's loss and the two Palatine libraries and that at Antium: Rothschild and Thompson 2011; 2012; 2014b; Tucci 2008; 2009; 2013; Nicholls 2011; 2014.

183 Marcus is joking, with a mythological twist: what he wrote was so short and so bad (*paululum misere scripsi*) that it should be thrown into a pond, lake, or river to join the nymphs who inhabit bodies of water, or burned in the fires of Vulcan's forge, god of volcanic heat and metalsmithing.

184 Pliny the Younger was also bothered by the chatting of enslaved individuals outside his window: Plin., *Ep*. 2.17.1–5, in ch. 4, Descriptions of Villas.

185 Marcus was an eager, early riser: the eleventh hour of the night was about 5:00 AM; the third hour of the day was 9:00 AM.

186 Referencing Novius indicates an interest in linguistic and cultural antiquities in specifically rural environments: Quintus Novius and Lucius Pomponius, Late Republican playwrights, composed modernized versions of the traditional and much older rustic Atellan farces (*Atellanae*), perhaps also imitating the quaint old-fashioned words of the old plays. Aulus Gellius also studied Novius for his words and definitions: Aul. Gell., *NA* 17.2. There may have been a revival of both the traditional farces and those of Novius because Hadrian, the builder of the Villa Magna, had *Atellanae* presented at dinners: *HA*, *Hadr.* 26; Antoninus Pius also liked the theater; *NP* s.v. "Atellana fabula" (J. Blänsdorf). Interest in linguistic and cultural antiquities was shown in Marcus's previous two letters: Fronto, *Ep*. 4.4 (59) and Fronto, *Ep*. 4.5 (60), in this chapter.

187 Marcus Aurelius had become *Caesar* with the accession of Antoninus Pius in 138 CE and so was inducted by the Senate into the various priesthoods of the state religion: *HA*, *M. Aur.* 6.3.

188 I am not aware of the source of Marcus's quotation.

189 Marcus uses the term *matercula*, little mother. To whom he is referring is not clear: Faustina Augusta Major, the emperor Antoninus Pius's wife, had died a year or two before the letters were written. He may be referring to his natural mother, Domitia Lucilla, who died only in the late 150s CE; Fronto wrote to her as well: Fronto, *Ep*. 2.1.7 (37); *Ep. gr*. 1 (30); *Ep. gr*. 2 (47).

190 Gratia was Fronto's daughter.

191 The residence was at some distance from the bath. The bath itself, small but luxuriously finished, was connected to the *torcularium* and its *dolia defossa* and the other wine-making spaces and machines. The structure of the entrance and exit to the bath building and thence to the *triclinium* indicates that members of the imperial family and their entourage were transported in a litter (*lectica*, pl. *lecticae*); ramps with widely spaced risers and broad treads ensured that the porters (*lecticarii*) would not jolt the person being carried: Dufton 2016, fig. 5.2, pls. 5.5, 5.8, 5.9, 5.12, 5.14, 5.19, and 5.21.

192 The *triclinium* with its *stibadium* of the Villa Magna was in a semi-circular room facing into the wine-pressing room (*torcularium*), which could be seen through an arched architectural screen with pilasters. Eating while observing enslaved individuals at work treading the grapes in a vat, with the must directed into *dolia defossa*, may have served as rustic entertainment, like the *Atellanae* that Hadrian had presented at feasts. The "happily heard the peasants bantering" (*rustici cavillanti*) with their crude but quaint conversations is an example, I think, of the authenticity and antiquarian value of old and rustic language as had been researched and popularized by Cato and Varro some centuries before. Later, Aulus Gellius continued this fascination with parsing ancient phrases and accents in the Catonian-Varronian manner: *NA* 11.2.

193 *mons Caelius meus*: Fronto, *Ep*. 2.6 (Marcus Aurelius to Fronto). These gardens and their villa must have been inherited, among other villas and properties, by his mother Domitia Lucilla from his grandmother of the same name, the Domitia Lucilla, widow of Gnaeus Domitus Tullus, who had been mentioned, with some sarcasm, by Pliny the Younger: *Ep*. 8.18.4.

194 Fronto's correspondence with Marcus Aurelius is often from Alsium or Lorium or mentions both locations. For his residence in the Domus Tiberiana, *HA*, *M. Aur.* 6.3; Cass. Dio, *Epit. Bk.* 72.35.4.

195 Severan inscription: Fentress et al. 2016, 30, fig. 3.1; portrait: 87–89, figs. 5.24, 5.25.

196 This quotation may be from a lost essay by Cato, *Carmen de moribus* (*On Morals*).

197 Marcus Antonius Polemon (ca. 85–144 CE) of Laodicea in Phrygia, a teacher of rhetoric at Smyrna in Asia and at Rome. The date of this letter from Marcus Aurelius to Fronto in 143 CE is inferred from the address to Fronto as consul; he was suffect consul for two summer months in that year. See Fronto, *Ep*. 2.1.5 (37) and n. 88, in ch. 9, Villas and *Horti* in the Late Roman Republic.

198 Marcus Aurelius expresses himself in Greek (ἵνα τι καὶ περὶ ἀνθρώπων λαλήσωμεν) and means that he wants to talk about people for a change, not ideas.

199 Pompeian fig ("of Pompey"): Plin., *HN* 15.71 (15.19); Arician cabbage from the valley of the Fortore river: Plin., *HN* 19.141 (19.41); Tarentine rose: a subspecies of myrtle bush (*myrtus* *communis subspecies tarantina*) producing abundant rose-shaped flowers: Plin., *HN* 15.119–126 (15.36–38), esp. 122 (15.37). The absent plane tree means that philosophy is also absent from Polemon's speech, because plane trees were always part of philosophical milieux: Cic., *De leg.* 2.1–7 (2.1–3) and nn. 60 and 61, in ch. 4, Descriptions of Villas.

200 The group of five letters in which this appears is called *De feriis Alsiensibus*: Champlin 1974, 155 and 159. Fronto's letters are sequenced in relation to the manuscripts in which they were found, in this case those in the Ambrosiana Library in Milan: Champlin 1974, 136. Marcus Aurelius began interrupting his villa stays with work even before his accession: in 147 CE, he wrote from Lorium (απο λωριου) as *Caesar* to priests of a temple at Smyrna, thanking them for congratulations on the birth of his son: *CIG* 2² 3176 (Böckh 1843).

201 Pliny had cited Trajan's ability to relax at the Centum Cellae villa as a distinct aspect of his wisdom and balance: see Plin. *Ep.* 6.31.1–2 and 13–17, in this chapter.

202 Fronto is listing early Latin writers. Plautus: Titus Maccius Plautus, ca. 254–184 BCE, a writer of comedies, often popularly revived and often cited in learned discourse. Accius: Lucius Accius (ca. 170–86 BCE), a poet and dramatist, wrote adaptations of Greek classical plays and others on events in Roman history as well as treatises on grammar and pronunciation. Lucretius: Titus Lucretius Carus (ca. 99–55 BCE), an Epicurean philosopher and poet whose long poem *De rerum natura* (*On the Nature of the Universe*) was widely admired and influential in antiquity, as much for its content as for its poetic form. Ennius: Quintus Ennius (ca. 239–169 BCE), Latin poet and playwright, a protégé of both Cato the Elder and Scipio Africanus; his *Annales*, an epic poem on Roman history, was much admired, and Marcus Aurelius's adoptive grandfather Hadrian had preferred him to Vergil (*HA*, *Hadr.* 1.16.5–7); on the reception of Ennius: Badian 1972.

203 The "wine cups unmarked by an informer's sign" is a compliment to Marcus Aurelius himself—and to Antoninus Pius as well—who both promised that they would not reinstitute the system of *delatores* and *quadruplatores* (informers, spies) to terrorize opponents of their regimes. *HA, Ant. Pius.* 7.3, and *HA, M. Aur.* 11.1.

204 On kingfishers and calm seas, Plin., *HN* 10.90 (10.47) and 18.231 (18.62); Plutarch, *Moralia, On the Intelligence of Animals, Whether Land or Sea Animals Are More Intelligent* (*De sollertia animalium*) 35 (982E to F-983E); Arnott 2007 s.v. "Alkyôn, -yonis," 20–21.

205 The emperor Trajan, by adoption.

206 The emperor Hadrian, by adoption.

207 The emperor Antoninus Pius, by adoption.

208 Chrysippus of Soli, mid-third century BCE, a Stoic philosopher widely influential in the Late Republic and the Imperial period. His death while drunk is reported by Diogenes Laërtius, *Lives of the Eminent Philosophers* (Βιοι και γνωμαι των εν φιλοσοφια ευδοκιμησαντων; *Vitae philosophorum Chrysippus*) 7.184 (by drinking wine unmixed with water) and 7.185 (by laughing at a donkey that had eaten his figs, and so he asked for wine): http://www.perseus.tufts.edu/hopper/text?doc=Perseus:tet:1999.01.0258:book=7:chapter=7.

209 Fronto means that the emperor's reward for all the work he does should result in the relaxation (or at least sleep) to which any ordinary person—any freeman—has a right.

210 Marcus Furius Camillus (ca. 446–365 BCE), a senator, consular tribune, dictator, and famous military commander; Caeso is probably Lucius Caeso Quinctius, a fifth-century BCE patrician and opponent of plebeian claims (Dion. Hal., *Ant. Rom.* 10.8; Livy 3.14); Volesus, a Sabine aristocrat and ancestor of the Roman patrician *gens* Valeria at the founding of Rome, which produced many famous members, notably Publius Valerius Poplicola, consul in 509 CE; Manius Curius Dentatus, of plebeian origins but consul in 290, 284, 275, and 274 BCE, *triumphator* in 290 and 275.

211 Or, "those unseen are no longer heard of," or "out of sight, out of mind."

212 Marcus lists a congery of distinguished dead men who retired to their estates, to Baiae, or to their villas: Quintus Fabius Catullinus, a senator, governor of Africa, consul in 130 CE; *NP* s.v. "Fabius" II 5 (W. Eck). Lucius Cornelius Lentulus Lupus, a senator, consul in 156 BCE (Lucilius, a fragment or title of *Satire* 1.2; *NP* s.v." "Cornelius" I 51 (Elvers, K.-L). Lucius Stertinius Avitus, a senator, suffect consul in 92 CE; Tiberius, emperor 14–37 CE; Gaius Velius Rufus (ca. 40–100 CE?), a military commander and procurator of Domitian in Panonnia, Dalmatia, and Rhetia, took part in the war against Decebalus (Mart., *Epig.* 9.31), active in the East.

213 *NP* s.v. "Verus" (W.Eck); Birley 2000, 132–94. For the villa at Acquatraversa: *LTUR Suburbium* 5 242–49, Veri Villa (V. Mastrodonato); *Pleiades* s.v. "Acquatraversa"; Mastrodonato 1999–2000; Caserta 2010–2011; 2015. Sculpture: Neudecker 1988, 200, cat. no. 45.

214 On this building: *LTUR* 211 (D. Palombi); *AtlasAncRome* 1 343, 349; 2: tab. 135. Record of death: Chron. of 354 and Chron. of Prosper Tiro, in Mommsen 1894b, I:147, 432.

By Commodus's day, the imperial villa on Capreae had been turned into places of exile for his wife Crispina, in 180 CE, and later for his sister Lucilla: *HA, Comm.* 4.5–6 and 5.11; Cass. Dio, *Epit. Bk.* 73.4.5–6.

215 The Quintilii (or Quinctilii)— the brothers Sextus Quintilius Valerius Maximus and Sextus Quintilius Condianus—were famous for their learning, their love for one another, their wealth, and their capacities in many domains, including writing a treatise on agriculture: Cass. Dio, *Epit. Bk.* 72.5.34.; *NP* s.v. "Quinctilius" II 1 (Sextus Quinctilius Condianus; W. Eck); and II 6 (Sextus Quinctilius Valerius Maximus;W. Eck). In 151 CE, they were consuls jointly in the reign of Antoninus Pius. They were also jurists: Ulpian records a judgment by them on a technicality on inheritance by freedmen's children: "This was an opinion by the Quintilius brothers": *Digesta of Justinian* 38.2.16.4. They were executed in consequence of the Quadratus and Lucilla plot of 180 CE and their property confiscated: Cass. Dio, *Epit. Bk.* 72.5.34. and 72.10.1; Hdn. 1.8.3–8; *HA*, *Comm.* 5.9.

Their villa is a complex of buildings near the fifth milestone on the Via Appia, set in an estate of some 25 ha (roughly 62 acres); its proximity to the City characterized it as προάστεια, a suburb. The various sectors included an early *basis villae*, with additions of a large *villa urbana*, gardens, bath buildings, fountains, and porticoes. Initial construction began in the reign of Trajan and continued in that of Hadrian, but further additions were made by the brothers during the reign of Marcus Aurelius: *LTUR Suburbium* 3 31–39; Frontoni, Galli, and Paris 2010; Ricci 1998, 607–15. Its decorations in the way of large scale sculpture, found in the excavations of Gavin Hamilton in 1776, are notable for their quality: Cassidy 2012.

216   Cass. Dio, *Epit. Bk.* 73.16.1 and 73.24.1–2. On this fire, see discussion in Gal., *De indol.* 1–4 and 8–10, in ch. 5, Villas and *Otium*.

217   By "making goblets" he means, I think, that he engaged in making vessels out of clay—that is, mud, an ignoble substance.

218   Pescennius Niger (ca. 135–194 CE), claimed imperial dignity and reigned for thirteen months in 193–194 CE, after the death of Commodus. Egyptian cults had long been popular in Rome, especially in the period of Cassius Dio's career in the late second to early third century CE: Cordier 2005. In general, Versluys 2005.

219   Cassius Dio notes that the senatorial elite disapproved of Septimius Severus's reliance on his military entourages and advice as well as innovations in the imperial guards: Cass. Dio, *Epit. Bk.* 25.2.2–6.

220   On the renaming of Domitian's palatial complex on the Palatine to *aedes publicarum*: Plin., *Pan.* 47.4.

221   Cass. Dio, *Epit. Bk.* 74.16.4; at 77.4.2, Cassius Dio indicates the gates were still up in the reign of Septimius Severus in 202 CE.

222   Trajan was from Hispania though of an Italian family, as was Hadrian's family; Antoninus Pius was born at Lanuvium; Marcus Aurelius was born and reared in Rome, and his son Commodus was born at Lanuvium. By contrast, Pertinax was born in Liguria, Didius Julianus in Mediolanum (modern Milan) in Cisalpine Gaul, Septimius Severus at Leptis Magna in Africa, Maximinus in Thrace, and so on.

223   Villa on the road to Lavicum: Aur. Vict., *Caes.* 40.2.

224   Villa of Maxentius on the Via Appia: De Franceschini 2005, 192–96, cat. no. 69, figs. 69.1–69.6.

225   Pertinax (Publius Helvius Pertinax, ca. 126–193 CE, reigned early January 193–late March 193 CE): *HA*, *Pert.* 3.2–4, 9.4–7., and 13.4–5; Cass. Dio, *Epit. Bk.* 73.1; some details in Aur. Vict., *Caes.* 18.1–6. Pertinax was born at Alba Pompeia in Liguria, the son of a freedman whose business had made him wealthy enough to afford some education for his very capable [*pertinax*] son. The future emperor grew up at a villa in the Apennines, and as a young man exchanged the profession of grammar teacher (*grammaticen*) for a military appointment and rose through the ranks; by 175 CE, he had become senator, suffect consul, and held a full consulship in 192 CE with Commodus as his colleague. Around 185 CE, court politics forced him to retire to his father's villa and estates at Vada Sabatia in Liguria. There, he took over his father's felt-cloth business (*coactilila taberna*), which made him rich, and he bought more land and villas, supplementing his wealth with bribes during his short reign in 193 CE. *Coacta* and *coacta lana* was felt, used in footwear, clothing, and as protective padding under armour, helmets and other military gear; the wealth of the business may have been generated from military purchases.

226   Clodius Albinus (Decimus Clodius Albinus, ca. 150–197, declared *imperator* and *Augustus* in 193 and 196, reigned late 196 to February 197 CE): *HA*, *Clod.* 12.5.1, 12.11.7–8 and 12.11.12; Cass. Dio, *Epit. Bk.* 76.6.2. Although no villas of Clodius Albinus or his noble family of Hadrumetum in Africa (modern Sousse, Tunisia) are known, in later life and despite his busy career as a military officer, consul in 194 CE, and pretender to imperial status, he appears to have taken up the traditional villa activities of *otium*: a little lovemaking, writing on agriculture, composing poems on pastoral themes (in the manner of Vergil), and devising erotica in the form of Milesian tales (Μιλησιακά, picaresque and erotic versions of the stories by Aristides of Miletus [second century BCE], also imitated by Petronius and Apuleius: *NP* s.v. "Milesian Tales" [M. Fusillo and L. Galli]). His efforts were much mocked by the *Historia Augusta* writer and even by his successor Septimius Severus: Hdn. 3.6.7.

227   Septimius Severus (Lucius Septimius Severus, 145–211 CE, r. 193–211 CE): *HA*, *Sev.* 10.4.4–7. Septimius Severus is not recorded as having owned villas before the start of his career; he only had a small estate in Venetia and a modest house in Rome. However, in 190 CE, at the crest of his civilian career and the beginning of his military commands, he acquired *horti* and agricultural properties appropriate to his social position; *horti* often included villas or villa-like residences. In his *horti*, there was a curious little exchange between Septimius Severus and his young son Lucius Septimius Bassianus, the future emperor Caracalla about an incident during a picnic that seemed to prophesize the boy's great destiny: *HA*, *Sev.* 4.6–7.

228   Caracalla (Lucius Septimius Bassianus, 188–217 CE; reigned with his father 198–211 CE; with his brother Geta 211 CE): Cass. Dio, *Epit. Bk.* 78.9.5. The historian Cassius Dio tells his readers with some bitterness how his fellow senators were forced to provide and pay for "all kinds of temporary houses" (οἴκιαι παντοδαπάι) for the emperor when he was on travels outside of Rome; these must have been the equivalent of *deversoria*. He makes no other mention of villas.

229 Elagabalus, or Heliogabalus (Varius Avitus Bassianus, Marcus Aurelius Antoninus, ca. 204–222 CE, r. 218–222 CE): *HA, Antoninus Elagabalus* 17.14.4–6 (lived in the villa of the Horti Spei Veteris on the Esquiline); 17.28.1 (childish harnessing of dogs and deer on his estates); 17.30.7–8 (building and immediately destroying *praetoria* [official headquarters] and pleasure pavillions [*diaetae*]). Elagabalus had owned family estates at Emesa and elsewhere in Syria. His reign was characterized by his contempt for the traditional orders and the Roman vocations of farming and landowning; he called senators "slaves in togas" and the Roman people a tiller of only a single farm (*unius fundi cultor*): *HA, Antoninus Elagabalus* 17.20.1.

230 *HA, The Two Maximini* (*Maximini Duo*) 19.4.4 and 19.5.1–2. These references are to the emperor Maximinus Thrax (Gaius Julius Verus Maximinus, called Thrax, ca.173–238 CE, r. 235–238 CE). The prejudices of the writers of the *Historia Augusta* about low birth, virtually barbarian antecedents, no inherited property, and no connections to the Antonine-Severan dynasty are on full display in this biography. After Caracalla's murder, at the instance of Marcus Ophellius Macrinus (reigned thirteen months, 217–218 CE), Maximinus left his military commands and bought properties (*possessiones*) near the village in Thrace where he had been born; from there, he engaged in commerce with the Gothic population across the Danube. He rose to be civilian tribune in the reign of Elagabalus but spent three years "busying himself with his properties [*agri*], at other times with *otium*, then again with pretended bouts of illness." The fact that Maximinus bought his properties is contrasted with the more noble inheritance of villas; Censorinus, one of the usurpers (the Thirty Tyrants) but a man of distinguished family and career, had inherited his property: *HA, Tyr. Trig., Censorinus* 33.2.

231 Valerian (Publius Licinius Valerianus, ca. 199–260/264 CE, r. 253–260 CE). The emperor Valerian, a member of an Italian senatorial family and consul himself in 238 CE, then again as emperor in 254, 255, and 257, owned a villa; its location is unknown. However, his villa must have been large because it received, from the future emperor Aurelian (at the time a military official in service on the Dacian frontier and in high favor with Valerian), a present of living booty: 500 enslaved persons, 2,000 cows, 1,000 horses, 10,000 sheep, and 15,000 goats: *HA, Aurel.* 26.10.2–3.

232 Gallienus (Publius Licinius Gallienus Augustus, ca. 218?–268 CE, coemperor 253–260 with his father Valerian, sole emperor 260–268). Gallienus, often praised by the writers of the *Historia Augusta* for his cultural accomplishments, appears to have used or established *horti* near Rome in his own name: see n. 246 in this chapter.

233 Tetricus Iunior (Gaius Pius Esuvius Tetricus Caesar, associated with the reign of his father Tetricus I, 271–274 CE): *HA, Tyr. Trig., Tetricus the Younger* 25.1–4. Tetricus the Younger was one of the listed thirty-two usurpers (or tyrants, or pretenders) in the section of the *Historia Augusta* called *The Thirty Tyrants* (*Tyranni Triginta*). His father had opposed the emperor Aurelian (r. 270–275 CE) but was defeated and led in Aurelian's triumphal procession along with his son and namesake. After that, they were pardoned and returned to their senatorial status. The Tetrici had a house in the garden district of the Caelian Hill, which contained villas and villa-like settings. The *Historia Augusta* writer gives an appreciation of the *domus* of the Tetrici "on the Caelian Hill between two groves of trees" and describes a mosaic (wall or floor) showing Aurelian giving the *toga praetexta* and senatorial rank to father and son.

234 Also called *Caesarea ad Libanum*, Arca in Phoenicia (modern Tell 'Arqa, Lebanon): *EAA* (Treccani) s.v. "Tell 'Arqa" (S.M. Cecchini).

235 Julia Avita Mamaea: *NP* s.v. "Iulia" 9 (H. Stegmann).

236 Apollonius of Tyana (ca. 3 BCE–97 CE) was a wandering philosopher and magician, the subject of a long biography by Philostratus that made Apollonius very popular in imperial circles due to the interest in him taken by Septimius Severus's wife Julia Domna. Apollonius of Tyana struck the imagination of later Romans to such an extent that a ghost or vision of him appeared to the emperor Aurelian in 272 CE, at the seige of Tyana itself: *HA, Aurel.* 26.14.1–9.

Orpheus is the mythological musician and poet of Arcadia who by Severus Alexander's time had become a figure in the asceticism of the mystic Orphic cult: *NP* s.v. "Occultism" D. Orpheus and Orphism (K. von Stuckrad).

237 While Plato's *Republic* on the ideal state was set in the hurly-burly of the port city of Piraeus and Cicero's *On Duties* is formulated as a letter to his son, the *De re publica* was set at a time long before both Cicero's day and Severus Alexander's, in 129 BCE, and *in hortos*, the gardens being those of Scipio Africanus Aemilianus (ca. 185–129 BCE), the final victor over Carthage. The young emperor would have been inspired by both the dialogue's garden setting and its evocation of other great names of the Republic who participate in the dialogue. Serenus Sammonicus was an antiquarian writer and courtier in the entourage of Septimius Severus and tutor to Caracalla and Geta; executed 212 under Caracalla: *HA, M. Ant.* (Caracalla) 13.4.4. *NP* s.v. "Serenus" 2 (P.L. Schmidt).

238 *Sextarius*: about 550 ml, or 1 pint. The waters of the Aqua Claudia rose in the valley of the Anio River (modern Aniene) east of Rome and entered the City with other aqueducts at the Porta Maggiore; it supplied the Palatine Hill and was extended by Nero to the Caelian: Frontinus, *Aq.* 13–14.

239 On "senatorial" bias, see ch. 10 n. 3.

Gordian I (Marcus Antonius Gordianus Sempronianus Romanus Africanus, ca. 159–238 CE), Senator, suffect consul in the reign of Elagabalus, and governor of Africa Proconsularis, was highly educated and widely read (Plato, Aristotle, Cicero, Vergil), connected to the highest nobility, and had owned the *domus* of Pompey the Great (the *domus rostrata*) on the Carinae (Esquiline Hill) in Rome as an ancestral home. This house had passed into the hands of Mark Antony and, later, the emperor

Tiberius; it contained a painting of the more than 1,000 exotic animals that were in the *munera*, the games, that Gordian I gave when *quaestor*: *HA, Gord.* 20.3.5–8, 20.6.5–7, and 20.7.1.

Gordian II (Marcus Antonius Gordianus Sempronianus Romanus Africanus, ca. 192–238 CE) was equally lauded by the writer of the *Historia Augusta*: *HA, Gord.* 20.17–22.

240   Marcus Antonius Gordianus III (225–244, r. 238–244 CE): *HA, Gord.* 20.22. *NP* s.v. "Gordianus" 2 (T. Franke).

241   De Franceschini 2005, 144–56, figs. 53.1–53.33, cat. no. 53; Sfameni 2006, 98, 137; *LTUR Suburbium* 3 31–39.

242   For more on these marbles, see Glossary.

243   The phrasing "as it was then" indicates that the writer identifies the villa and its baths as being old, not contemporary, an historic family property rather than a new building.

244   To be a *tutor* and undertake a *tutela* was a legal designation for financial matters or guardianships over minors, widows, and wills in probate. Serving as a *legatus* or envoy was to undertake ambassorial duties in a *legatio*, honorable but expensive.

245   The writer distinguishes between the near-public or imperial *thermae* in the villa of the Gordians to the simple, smaller *balnea* that Gordian III or his family had supplied in the City; supplementing the grand public *thermae* under imperial patronage and regulation might have been very welcome in neighborhoods.

246   The description is labored, but the configuration of Gordian III's two porticoes facing each other in parallel is clear. These porticoes must have been well north of the monumental area of the Campus Martius (around the Pantheon) and north of the Horologium of Augustus. How they related to the Mausoleum of Augustus is not clear. To be "under the hill" means to be along the western scarp of the *collis hortulorum*, or Pincian Hill, with its villas overlooking the Campus,

therefore in the flat area on either side of the Via Flaminia extension of the Via Lata bounded by the Tiber on the west and the (modern) Porta Flaminia on the north. These buildings would have been planned and possibly completed in Gordian III's reign, 238–244 CE.

About twenty years later, in the reign of Gallienus (260–268 CE), *horti* were planned in the form of a portico, perhaps an extension and emulation of that of Gordian III, running north of the area of the Porta Flaminia. The portico, four or five rows of columns deep, with the first row supporting statues, is described as running some 5 km along the Via Flaminia northward from the (modern) Porta Flaminia through the Aurelian Wall to the Mulvian Bridge: *HA, Gall.* 23.18.5. Gallienus's portico, if it was built, would have served as a grand entrance for travelers to the City from the north and a fine farewell to those on their way to Etruria and northern Italy.

247   Misitheus is Gaius Furius Sabinius Aquila Timesitheus (ca. 190–243 CE), a high military and civilian official since the reign of Septimius Severus and father-in-law to Gordian II: *HA, Gord.* 20.24.1–2; 20.27.9–10, and 20.28.1–6; Zosimus, *Historia Nova* (Ἱστορία Νέα) 1.17.2.

248   Tacitus was much admired by the writer of his biography for his generosity, frugality, and sharp eye for display of any kind: *HA, Tac.* 10.5–6 and 11.4–6. He was said to have advised Aurelian to ban the use of gold on garments, ceilings [*camerae*], and leather goods: *HA, Aurel.* 46.1. However, gilded ceilings were still made well into the fifth century, as in the *burgus* of Pontius Leontius: Sid. Apoll., *Carm.* 22.101–235 ("a ceiling covered . . . with yellow metal"), in ch. 4, Descriptions of Villas; for an earlier gilded ceiling in the villa of Pollius Felix: Stat., *Silv.* 1.3.1–75, also in ch. 4.

249   By the third century CE, the *chlamys* had become a short cloak pinned at the right shoulder; it had military connotations. *Pallium* (originally a distinctively Greek garment) had come to signify the large garment, unpinned, worn by Greek philosophers; a cloak, pinned on the left shoulder, was

hunting garb. The writer of the *Historia Augusta* reports that much fun was made of this five-persona image in varied clothing, but such costumed biographies were known in the mid-third century CE; a sarcophagus in Naples, for example, shows the same man four times: togate as a bridegroom and inducted consul, palliate as a Greek philosopher with a scroll, and senatorially togate again: Métraux 2008, 283–85, fig. 14.8; see also a multicostumed figure in Koortbojian 2008, 76–85, figs. 3.3–3.5.

250   Procopius, *The Gothic War (De bello Gothico)* 5.1.2–6; Latin: Haury 1905–1913, vol. 2 (1905), 4; English: Dewing 1916. On Romulus Augustus: *PLRE* 2 949–50; on Orestes, *PLRE* 2 811–12.

251   In ironic coincidence, Saint Severinus of Noricum, a missionary and monk in Pannonia and southern Germania, had prophesized that Odoacer, who later defeated and killed Romulus Augustus's father, Orestes, was to reign in Italy for between thirteen and fourteen years: Jord., *Get.* 32–33. After Severinus's death, his body was brought to the Castellum Lucullanum sometime in the 480s, where Romulus Augustus was living in exile: Jord., *Get.* 46. A mausoleum for the saint was built at the expense of a noble woman (*inlustris femina*) Barbaria and her husband: *PLRE* 2 210.

252   Jord., *Get.*: Latin: Mommsen 1882, 120; English: Mierow 1915, under XLVI. Marcellinus *comes, Chronicon*: Latin: Mommsen 1882, 91; *PL* 51, col. 932. *Excerpta Valesiana*: Latin: cited in Moreau and Velkov 1968 (*non vidi*); *PL* 51, col. 932; English: Rolfe 1939, 533.

REFERENCES

30 ans au service. 1986. *30 ans au service du patrimoine: De la Carthage des Phéniciens à la Carthage du Bourguiba*. Tunis: Ministère des Affaires Culturelles.

Actes du colloque 1972. 1974. *Actes du colloque 1972 sur l'esclavage, Besançon 2–3 mai 1972*. Actes des colloques du Groupe de recherche sur l'esclavage dans l'antiquité 3. Besançon: Presses Universitaires de Franche-Comté.

Agnoletti, M., ed. 2013. *Italian Historical Rural Landscapes: Cultural Values for the Environment and Rural Development*. Environmental History 1. Amsterdam: Springer.

Albertson, F. C. 2001. "Zenodorus's 'Colossus of Nero.'" *MAAR* 46, 95–118.

Alciati, R. 2011. "And the Villa Became a Monastery: Sulpicius Severus' Community of Primulacium." In Dey and Fentress 2011, 85–98.

Allen, W. Jr. 1939. "The Location of Cicero's House on the Palatine Hill." *CJ* 35:3, 134–43.

Alston, R. 2011. "Rereading Ancient Slavery." In Alston, Hall, and Proffitt 2011, 1–33.

Alston, R., E. Hall, and L. Proffitt, eds. 2011. *Reading Ancient Slavery*. London: Bristol Classical.

André, J.-M. 1962. "Recherches sur l'*Otium* romain: Les origines de l'*Otium*; Conjectures étymologiques et réalités sémantiques." *Annales littéraires de l'Université de Besançon* 52:5–25.

André, J.-M. 1966. *L'otium dans la vie morale et intellectuelle romaine, des origines à l'époque augustéenne*. Faculté des Lettres de Paris, Recherches 30. Paris: Presses universitaires de France.

André, J.-M., J. Dangel, and P. Demont, eds. 1996. *Les loisirs et l'héritage de la culture classique: Actes du XIIIe congrès de l'Association Guillaume Budé (Dijon, 27–31 août 1993)*. Collection Latomus 230. Brussels: Peeters.

Andreae, B. 1964. "Beobachtungen im Museum von Sperlonga." *RM* 71, 238–244.

Andreae, B. 1974. "Die römischen Repliken der mythologischen Skulpturengruppen von Sperlonga," (with contributions by P. C. Bol) In *Die Skulpturen von Sperlonga* (Antike Plastik 14), 61–105.

Andreae, B. 1983a. "Le sculture." In Tocco Sciarelli 1983a, 49–66.

Andreae, B. 1983b. "L'imperatore Claudio a Baia." In Tocco Sciarelli 1983a, 67–72.

Andreae, B. 1994. *Praetorium speluncae: Tiberius und Ovid in Sperlonga*. Akademie der Wissenschaften und der Literatur Mainz. Abhandlungen der Geistes- und Sozialwissenschaftlichen Klasse 12. Wiesbaden: Franz Steiner.

Andreae, B. 1995. *Praetorium Speluncae: L'antro di Tiberio a Sperlonga ed Ovidio*. Antiqua et nova, Sezione Archeologia 4. Italian edition of Andreae 1994.

Andreae, B. 1996. *"Am Birnbaum": Gärten und Parks im antiken Rom, in den Vesuvstädten und in Ostia*. Mainz: Philipp von Zabern.

Andreae, B., and B. Conticello. 1987. *Skylla und Charybdis: Zur Skyllagruppe von Sperlonga*. Akademie der Wissenschaften und der Literatur. Abhandlungen der Geistes- und Sozialwissenschaftlichen Klasse 14. Weisbaden: Franz Steiner.

Andreau, J. 2000. "Les marchés hebdomadaires du Latium et de Campanie au Ier siècle ap. J.-C." In Lo Cascio 2000b, 69–91.

Andreau, J., ed. 1982. *Problemi della schiavitù: Un incontro con M. I. Finley su Ancient Slavery and Modern Ideology*. Special issue *Opus* 1(1).

Aoyagi, M., C. Angelelli, and S. Matsuyama. 2021. "Somma Vesuviana, cd. Villa di Augusto: Il post 79 nell'area a nord del Somma." In Coralini 2021, 270–93.

Aoyagi, M., A. De Simone, and G. F. De Simone. 2018. In Marzano and Métraux 2018, 141–56.

Arthur, P. 1991a. *Romans in Northern Campania: Settlement and Land-Use around the Massico and Garigliano Basin*. Archaeological Monographs of the British School at Rome 1. London: British School at Rome.

Arthur, P. 1991b. "Territories, Wine and Wealth: Suessa Aurunca, Sinuessa, Minturnae and the ager Falernus." In Barker and Lloyd 1991, 153–59.

Astin A. E. 1978. *Cato the Censor*. Oxford: Clarendon Press University Press.

Attema, P. A. J., T. C. A. de Haas, J. F. Seubers, and G. W. Tol. 2017. "In Search of the Archaic Countryside: Different Scenarios for the Ruralisation of Satricum and Crustumerium." In Lulof and Smith 2017, 195–203.

Attema, P., T. de Haas, and G. Tol. 2011. *Between Satricum and Antium: Settlement Dynamics in a Coastal Landscape in Latium Vetus*. Amsterdam: Peeters.

Augenti, E. D. 2008. *Il lavoro schiavile a Roma*. Arti e mestieri nel mondo romano 3. Rome: Quasar.

Ault, B. A., and L. C. Nevett, eds. 2005. *Ancient Greek Houses and Households: Chronological, Regional, and Social Diversity*. Philadelphia: University of Pennsylvania Press.

Badian, E. 1972. "Ennius and His Friends." In Skutsch 1972, 149–99.

Badian, E. 1973. "Marius' Villas: The Testimony of the Slave and the Knave." *JRS* 63, 121–32.

Baehrens, E. 1879–1886. *Poetae Latini Minores*. 6 vols. Leipzig: Teubner. https://catalog.hathitrust.org/api/volumes/oclc/50846027.html.

Baird, J. A., and A. Pudsey, eds. 2022. *Housing in the Ancient Mediterranean World: Material and Textual Approaches*, 322–53. Cambridge: Cambridge University Press.

Baldus, C. 2016. "Possession in Roman Law." In du Plessis, Ando, and Tuori 2016, 537–52.

Ball, L. F. 2003. *The Domus Aurea and the Roman Architectural Revolution*. Cambridge: Cambridge University Press.

Balmelle, C. 2001. *Les demeures aristocratiques d'Aquitaine: Socièté et culture de l'antiquité tardive dans le sud-ouest de la Gaule. Aquitania* Suppl. 10. Bordeaux: Ausonius.

Balmelle, C., A. Ben Abed-Ben Khader, W. Ben Osman, J.-P. Darmon, M. Ennaïfer, S. Gozlan, R. Hanoune, with note by A.-M. Guimier-Sorbets. 1990. *Recherches Franco-Tunisiennes sur la mosaïque de l'Afrique antique I, Xenia. CÉFR* 125. Recherches d'Archéologie africaine publiées par l'Institut National d'Archéologie et d'Art de Tunis. Rome: École française de Rome.

Bannon, C. J. 2009. *Gardens and Neighbors: Private Water Rights in Roman Italy*. Ann Arbor: University of Michigan Press.

Baratte, F. 2017. "Les inscriptions dans le décor des églises paléochrétiennes: L'exemple de Paulin de Nole à Cimitile." In Corbier and Sauron 2017, 27–33.

Barbera, M., S. Barrano, G. de Cola, S. Festuccia, L. Giovanetti, O. Menghi, and M. Pales. 2010. "La villa di Caligola: Un nuovo settore degli Horti Lamiani scoperto sotto la sede dell'ENPAM a Roma." *FastiOnline* 194, 1–59. https://www.fastionline.org/docs/FOLDER-it-2010-194.pdf.

Barker, G., and J. Lloyd, eds. 1991. *Roman Landscapes: Archaeological Survey in the Mediterranean Region*. Archaeological Monographs of the British School at Rome. London: British School at Rome.

Barrett, A. A. 2020. *Rome Is Burning: Nero and the Fire That Ended a Dynasty*. Princeton: Princeton University Press.

Barton, I. M., ed. 1996. *Roman Domestic Buildings*. Exeter: University of Exeter Press.

Bartsch, S., and A. Schiesaro, eds. 2015. *The Cambridge Companion to Seneca*. Cambridge: Cambridge University Press.

Bartz, J., ed. 2019a. *public / private: An Exhibition of the Q-Kolleg at the Winckelmann-Institut Humboldt-Universität zu Berlin in Cooperation with the Dipartimento Scienza dell' Antichitá of the Sapienza-Università di Roma, 19/06/2019-31/12/2019*. https://doi.org/10.18452/20022.

Bartz, J. 2019b. "Public and Private Spaces in Antiquity: A Problem of Alternative Definitions?" In Bartz 2019a, 13–29.

Bayet, J. 1964. *Cicéron, Correspondance: Texte établi et traduit*. Paris: Les Belles Lettres.

Bažant, J. 1995. *Roman Portraiture: A History of Its History*. Prague: Konisch Latin Press.

Beard, M. 2009. *The Roman Triumph*. Cambridge, MA: Harvard University Press.

Becker, J. A., and N. Terrenato, eds. 2012. *Roman Republican Villas: Architecture, Context, and Ideology*. Ann Arbor: University of Michigan Press.

Belfiore, V. 2010. *Il liber linteus di Zagabria: Testualità e contenuto*. Biblioteca di Studi Etruschi 50. Pisa and Rome: Fabrizio Serra.

Belli, R. 2009. "Il ninfeo di Punta Epitaffio: *Antrum cyclopis* e l'ideologia di un imperatore." In De Simone and Macfarlane 2009, 49–52.

Bergmann, B. 1991. "Painted Perspectives of a Villa Visit: Landscape as Status and Metaphor." In Gazda and Haeckl 1991, 49–70.

Bergmann, B. 1992. "Exploring the Grove: Pastoral Space on Roman Walls." In Hunt 1992, 20–46.

Bingen, J., G. Cambier, and G. Nachtergael, eds. 1975. *Le monde grec: Pensée, littérature, histoire, documents; Hommages à Claire Préaux*. Brussels: Éditions de l'Université de Bruxelles.

Binsfeld, A. 2010. "Archäologie und Sklaverei: Möglichkeiten und Perspektiven einer Bilddatenbank zur antiken Sklaverei." In Heinen 2010, 161–77.

Bintliff, J. L. 2010. "Prosperity, Sustainability, and Poverty in the Late Antique World: Mediterranean Case Studies." In Jacobs 2010, 319–83.

Biraud, M. 1993. "Usages de l'asphodèle et étymologies d' ἀσφόδελος." In Manessy-Guitton 1993, 35–46.

Birks, P., and G. McLeod, eds. and trans. 1987. *Justinian's Institutes*. Texts in Roman Law. London: Duckworth.

Birley, A. R. 2000. *Onomasticon to the Younger Pliny: Letters and Panegyric*. Munich: K. G. Saur.

Blaison, M. 1998. "Suétone et l'ekphrasis de La 'Domus Aurea' (Suét., Ner. 31)." *Latomus* 57(3):617–24.

Blockley, R. C. 1981. *The Fragmentary Classicising Historians of the Later Roman Empire: Eunapius, Olympiodorus, Priscus and Malchus*. ARCA Classical and Medieval Texts, Papers and Monographs 6. Cambridge: Francis Cairns.

Boatwright, M. T. 2015. "Visualizing Empire in Imperial Rome." In Brice and Slootjes 2015, 235–59.

Bodel, J. 1997. "Monumental Villas and Villa Monuments." *JRA* 10:5–35.

Bodel, J. 1999. "The Cena Trimalchionis." In Hofmann 1999, 32–43.

Bodel, J. 2008. "From Columbaria to Catacombs: Collective Burial in Pagan and Christian Rome." In Brink and Green 2008, 177–242.

Bodel, J. 2011. "Slave Labour and Roman Society." In Bradley and Cartledge 2011, 311–36.

Boethius, A. 1960. *The Golden House of Nero: Some Aspects of Roman Architecture*. Jerome Lectures 5. Ann Arbor: University of Michigan Press.

Boissevain, U., C. de Boor, T. Büttner-Wobs, and A. Roos, eds. 1903–1910. *Excerpta Historica iussu imperatoris Constantini Porphyrogeniti Confecta*. 4 vols. Berlin: Weidmann.

Boissier, G. 1865, 13th ed. 1905. *Cicéron et ses amis: Étude sur la societè romaine au temps de César*. Paris: Hachette. https://www.atramenta.net/telecharger-ebook-gratuit/oeuvre18946.html.

Boissier, G. (1897) 1970. *Cicero and His Friends: A Study of Roman Society in the Time of Caesar*. New York: Cooper Square Publishers. Reprint of the English translation by A. D. Jones, London.

Bon-Harper, S., and Jones, R., eds. 1997. *Sequence and Space in Pompeii*. Oxford: Oxbow.

Borg, B. 2018. "Roman Cemeteries and Tombs." In Holleran and Claridge 2018, 403–24.

Bosman, L., I. Haynes, P. Liverani, eds. 2020. *The Basilica of Saint John Lateran to 1600*. British School at Rome Studies. Cambridge: Cambridge University Press.

Bowden, W. 2018. "Villas of the Eastern Adriatic and Ionian Coastlands." In Marzano and Métraux 2018, 377–97.

Bowes, K., ed. 2020. *The Roman Peasant Project 2009–2014: Excavating the Roman Rural Poor*. 2 vols. University Museum Monograph 154. Philadelphia: University of Pennsylvania Museum of Archaeology and Anthropology.

Bowes, K., A.-M. Mercuri, E. Rattigheri, R. Rinaldi, A. Arnoldus-Huyzenfeld, M. Ghisleni, C. Grey, M. MacKinnon, and E. Vaccaro. 2017. "Peasant Agricultural Strategies in Southern Tuscany: Convertible Agriculture and the Importance of Pasture." In de Haas and Tol 2017, 170–99.

Bowie, E. 2006. "Vertus de la campagne, vices de la cité dans *Daphnis et Chloé* de Longus." In *Passions, vertus et vices* 2009, 13–22.

Bowie, E. 2013. "Marathon in the Greek Culture of the Second Century AD." In Carey and Edwards 2019, 241–53.

Bowman, A. K., and A. I. Wilson, eds. 2013a. *The Roman Agricultural Economy: Organisation, Investment, and Production*. Oxford Studies on the Roman Economy. Oxford: Oxford University Press.

Bowman, A. K., and A. I. Wilson. 2013b. "Introduction: Quantifying Roman Agriculture." In Bowman and Wilson 2013a, 1–35.

Bradley, K. R. 1989. *Slavery and Rebellion in the Roman World, 140 B.C.–70 B.C.* Bloomington: University of Indiana Press.

Bradley, K. R. 1991. *Discovering the Roman Family: Studies in Roman Social History*. Oxford: Oxford University Press.

Bradley, K. R. 1994. *Slavery and Society at Rome*. Cambridge: Cambridge University Press.

Bradley, K. R. 2006. "On the Roman Slave Supply and Slavebreeding." In Finley 2006, 53–81.

Bradley, K. R. 2011. "Slavery in the Roman Republic." In Bradley and Cartledge 2011, 241–64.

Bradley, K. R. and P. Cartledge, eds. 2011. *The Cambridge World History of Slavery*. Vol. 1, *The Ancient Mediterranean World*. Cambridge: Cambridge University Press.

Bragantini, I. 2014. "La pittura a Pompei nell'opera di August Mau, Geschichte der dekorativen Wandmalerei in Pompeji (Berlin 1982): Note di lettura." In Eristov and Monier 2014, 9–18.

Bragantini, I. 2015. "Roman Painting in the Republic and Early Empire." In Pollitt 2015, 302–69.

Braund, S. 2015. *"Seneca Multiplex:* The Phases (and Phrases) of Seneca's Life and Works." In Bartsch and Schiesaro 2015, 15–28.

Bremmer, J. N. 2008. *Greek Religion and Culture, the Bible, and the Ancient Near East*. Leiden: Brill.

Bricault, L., M. J. Versluys, and P. G. P. Meyboom, eds. 2005. *Nile into Tiber: Egypt in the Roman World. Proceedings of the 3rd International Conference of Isis Studies, Leiden, May 11–14 2005*. Religions in the Graeco-Roman World 159. Leiden: Brill.

Brice, L. L., and D. Slootjes, eds. 2015. *Aspects of Ancient Institutions and Geography: Studies in Honor of Richard J. A. Talbert*. Impact of Empire 19. Leiden: Brill.

Brilliant, R. 1963. *Gesture and Rank in Roman Art: The Use of Gestures to Denote Status in Roman Sculpture and Coinage*. Memoirs of the Connecticut Academy of Arts and Sciences 14. New Haven: Connecticut Academy.

Brink, L., and D. Green, eds. 2008. *Commemorating the Dead: Texts and Artifacts in Context. Studies of Roman, Jewish, and Christian Burials.* Berlin: De Gruyter.

Brittain, C. 2001. *Philo of Larissa.* Oxford: Oxford University Press.

Brocato, P., and N. Terrenato 2017. *Nuovi studi sulla Regia di Roma.* Paesaggi antichi 2. Cosenza: Pellegrini.

Broekaert, W., and A. Zuiderhoek. 2020. "Capital Goods in the Roman Economy." In Erdkamp, Verboven, and Zuiderhoek 2020, 99–145.

Brogiolo, G. P., and A. Chavarría Arnau. 2018. "Villas in Northern Italy." In Marzano and Métraux 2018a, 178–94.

Brogiolo, G. P., N. Gauthier, and N. Christie, eds. 2000. *Towns and Their Territories between Late Antiquity and the Early Middle Ages.* Leiden: Brill.

Broise, H., and V. Jolivet. 1994. "Des jardins de Lucullus au Palais des Pincii: Recherches de l'École française de Rome sur le versant occidental du Pincio." *RA* n.s. 1:188–99.

Broise, H., and V. Jolivet. 1998. "Il giardino e l'acqua." In Cima and La Rocca 1998, 189–201.

Broise, H., and X. Lafon. 2001. *La villa Prato de Sperlonga.* CÉFR 285. Rome: École française de Rome.

Broughton, T. R. S. 1951–1960. *The Magistrates of the Roman Republic.* 3 vols. New York: American Philological Association.

Brughmans, T., and A. I. Wilson, eds. 2022. *Simulating Roman Economies: Theories, Methods, and Computational Models.* Oxford Studies on the Roman Economy. Oxford: Oxford University Press.

Brun, J.-P. 2004. *Archéologie du vin et de l'huile dans l'Empire romain.* Paris: Errance.

Bur, C. 2021. "L'antihellénisme de Caton l'Ancien: Une image publique construite par un homo novus?" In Bur and Humm 2021, 43–76.

Bur, C. and M. Humm, eds. 2021. *Caton l'Ancien et l'hellénisme: Images, tradition et réception.* Collections de l'Université de Strasbourg. Études d'archéologie et d'histoire ancienne. Paris: De Boccard.

Burns, T. W. 2015. *Brill's Companion to Leo Strauss' Writings on Classical Political Thought.* Brill's Companions to Classical Reception 4. Leiden: Brill.

Busen, T. 2023. *Die römische Kaiservilla Pausilypon: Gesamtanlage und Bauten des oberen Plateaus.* Denkmäler antiker Architektur 21. Weisbaden: Deutsches Archäologisches Institut.

Cafaro, A. 2021. *Governare l'impero: La "praefectura fabrum" fra legami personali e azione politica (II sec. a.C.-III sec. d.C.).* Stuttgart: Franz Steiner.

Calandra, E., and B. Adembri, eds. 2014. *Adriano e la Grecia: Villa Adriana tra classicità ed ellenismo.* Studi e ricerche. Milan: Electa.

Calci, C., and G. Messineo. 1984. *La Villa di Livia a Prima Porta.* Rome: Soprintendenza archeologica di Roma.

Cam, M-T, ed. and trans. 2001. *Cetius Faventinus: Abrégé d'architecture privée.* Collection des universités de France. Auteurs latins, textes latins et traductions françaises 363. Paris: Les Belles Lettres.

Cameron, C. M. 2023. "Injection: An Archaeological Approach to Slavery." In Pargas and Schiel 2023, 109–19.

Campana, A. 2009. "Le spintriae: Tessere Romane con raffigurazione erotiche." In *La Donna Romana* 2009, 43–96.

Campbell, J. B. 2000. *The Writings of the Roman Land Surveyors: Introduction, Text, Translation and Commentary.* Journal of Roman Studies Monographs 9. London: Society for the Promotion of Roman Studies.

Cao, I. 2010. *Alimenta: Il racconto delle fonti.* Padua: Il Poligrafo.

Capanna, M. C. 2006. "Il culto di Anna Perenna al I miglio." In Carandini, D'Alessio, and Di Giuseppe 2006, 65–70.

Capanna, M. C. 2012. "Gli horti." In Carandini 2012, 74–78.

Capozzi, R., G. Fusco, and F. Visconti, eds. 2019. *Villa Jovis: Architettura e paesaggi dell'archeologia.* Naples: Aión.

Carafa, P., and D. Bruno. 2013. "Il Palatino messo a punto." *ArchCl* 64 (n.s. 2,3, Sapienza Università di Roma), 719–86. Rome: "L'Erma" di Bretschneider.

Carandini, A. 1980. "Il vigneto e la villa del fondo di Settefinestre nel Cosano: Un caso di produzione agricola per il mercato transmarino." *MAAR* 36:1–10.

Carandini, A. 1981. "Sviluppo e crisi delle manifatture rurali e urbane." In Giardina and Schiavone 1981, 2:249–60.

Carandini, A. 1988. *Schiavi in Italia: Gli strumenti pensanti dei Romani fra tarda repubblica e medio impero*. Studi NIS archeologia vm. Rome: La Nuova Italia Scientifica.

Carandini, A. 1989a. "La villa romana e la plantagione schiavistica in Italia (II secolo a.C.–II d.C.)." In Momigliano and Schiavone 1988–1992, 4:101–92. Turin: Einaudi.

Carandini, A. 1989b. "Economia italica fra tarda repubblica e medio impero considerata dal punto di vista di una merce: Il vino." In Lenoir, Manacorda, and Panella 1989, 505–21.

Carandini, A, ed. 2012. *Atlante di Roma Antica: Biografia e ritratti della città*. Milan: Mondadori Electa.

Carandini, A., F. Cambi, M. G. Celluzza, and E. B. Fentress, eds. 2002. *Paesaggi d'Etruria: Valle dell'Albegna, Valle d'Oro, Valle del Chiarone, Valle del Tafone*. Rome: Edizioni di Storia e Letteratura.

Carandini, A., and P. Carafa. 2017. *The Atlas of Ancient Rome: Biography and Portraits of the City*. Translated by A.C. Halavais. 2 vols. Princeton: Princeton University Press. (Original edition: A. Carandini, ed. 2012. *Atlante di Roma antica*. Milan: Mondadori Electa.)

Carandini, A., M. T. D'Alessio, and H. Di Giuseppe, eds. 2006. *La fattoria e la villa dell'Auditorium nel quartiere Flaminio di Roma*. BullComm. Suppl. 14. Rome: "L'Erma" di Bretschneider.

Carandini, A., and A. Ricci, eds. 1985. *Settefinestre: Una villa schiavistica nell'Etruria romana*. 3 vols. Modena: Panini.

Carey, C., and M. Edwards, eds. 2019. *Marathon—2,500 Years: Proceedings of The Marathon Conference 2010*. BICS Suppl. 124. Oxford: Oxford University Press.

Carlsen, J. 1984. "Considerations on Cosa and Ager Cosanus." *Analecta Romana Instituti Danici* 13:49–58.

Carlsen, J. 2001. "Landowners, Tenants and Estate Managers in Roman Italy." In Herz and Waldherr 2001, 41–55.

Carlsen, J. 2010. "Land, Labour and Legislation in Late Republican Italy." In Carlsen and Lo Cascio 2010, 303–15.

Carlsen, J., and E. Lo Cascio, eds. 2010. *Agricoltura e scambi nell'Italia tardo-repubblicana*. Bari: Edipuglia.

Carlson, D. N. 2002. "Caligula's Floating Palaces." *Archaeology* 55:26–31.

Carrara, M. 2005. "La Villa di Livia a Prima Porta da praedium suburbanum a villa Caesarum." In Frizell and Klynne 2005.

Casaburi, M. C. 2002. "Chaldaei e mathematici a Capri: Sopravvivenze di Mesopotamia nell'Occidente greco-romano." In Casaburi and Lacerenza 2002, 25–40.

Casaburi, M. C., and G. Lacerenza, eds. 2002. *Lo Specchio d'Oriente: eredità afroasiatiche in Capri antica; Atti del convegno, Capri, 3 novembre 2001*. Naples: Isituto universitario orientale, Dipartimento di studi asiatici.

Caserta, E. 2010. "Roma (Via Cassia): La Villa di Lucio Vero alla luce delle recenti indagini archeologiche." *Notizie degli scavi di antichità* 21–22, 2010–2011, 53–191.

Caserta, E. 2015. "La Villa di Lucio Vero sulla Via Cassia a Roma in località Acquatraversa." *JRA* 28:179–91.

Cassidy, B., ed. 2012. *The Life and Letters of Gavin Hamilton (1723–1798): Artist and Art Dealer in Eighteenth-Century Rome*. 2 vols. London: Harvey Miller.

Casson, L. 1971. *Ships and Seamanship in the Ancient World*. Princeton: Princeton University Press.

Cavalieri, M., and F. Sacchi, eds. 2020. *La villa dopo la villa* 1: *Trasformazione di un sistema insediativo ed economico in Italia centro-settentrionale tra tarda Antichità e Medioevo*. Louvain: Presses universitaires de Louvain.

Cavalieri, M., and C. Sfameni (eds.) 2022. *La villa dopo la villa 2: Trasformazione di un sistema insediativo ed economico nell'Italia centrale tra tarda Antichità e Medioevo*. Louvain: Presses universitaires de Louvain.

Cellauro, L. 2015. "In Search of a Setting for Learning in Roman Antiquity: Renaissance Surveys of Varro's Garden *musaeum* at Casinum." *Renaissance Studies* 29:2, 204–26.

Celuzza, M. G. 2002. "Cosa, la centuriazione." In Carandini et al. 2002, 121–23.

Centlivres Challet, C.-E., ed. 2021. *Married Life in Greco-Roman Antiquity*. London, Routledge.

Cerutti, S. M. 1997. "The Location of the Houses of Cicero and Claudius and the Porticus Catuli on the Palatine Hill." *AJP* 118(3):417–26.

Champlin, E. 1974. "The Chronology of Fronto." *JRS* 64:136–59.

Champlin, E. 1981. "Owners and Neighbours at Ligures Baebiani." *Chiron* 11:239–64.

Champlin, E. 1998. "God and Man in the Golden House." In Cima and La Rocca 1998, 333–44.

Champlin, E. 2008. "Tiberius the Wise." *Historia* 57:408–25.

Champlin, E. 2011. "Sex on Capri." *TAPA* 141:315–32.

Champlin, E. 2013. "The Odyssey of Tiberius Caesar." *Classica et Mediaevalia* 64:199–46.

Charlesworth, M. P. (1926) 2016. *Trade-Routes and Commerce of the Roman Empire*. Reprint. Cambridge: Cambridge University Press.

Charlet, G. 1989. *L'Opéra de la Bastille: Génèse et réalisation*. Bilingual French-English edition. Paris: Éditions du Moniteur.

Cheung, C. 2021. "Precious Pots: Making and Repairing Dolia." In Hochscheid and Russell 2021, 171–88.

Chiappella, V. G. 1966. "Esplorazione della cosiddetta 'Piscina di Lucullo' sul lago di Paola." *Supplemento Notizie degli Scavi d'Antichità* 19. Rome: Accademia nazionale dei Lincei.

Chiappiniello, R. 2007. "The Carmen ad uxorem and the Genre of the Epithalamium." In Otten and Pollmann 2007, 115–38.

Christol, M., and O. Masson, eds. 1997. *Actes Xe Congrès International d'Épigraphie grecque et latine*, Nîmes, 4–9 octobre 1992. Paris: Éditions de la Sorbonne.

Ciardello, R. 2019. "Architettura e paesaggio a Villa Jovis: Alcune osservazioni." In Capozzi, Fusco, and Visconti 2019, 74–79.

Cima, M. 2008. "Gli horti dell'Esquilino." In Cima and Talamo 2008, 63–105.

Cima, M., and E. La Rocca 1986. *Le tranquille dimore degli dei: La residenza imperiale degli horti Lamiani*. Venice: Marsilio.

Cima, M., and E. La Rocca, eds. 1998. *Horti Romani: Atti del Convegno Internazionale, Roma, 4–6 maggio 1995*. *BullComm* Suppl. 6. Rome: "L'Erma" di Bretschneider.

Cima, M., and E. Talamo, eds. 2008. *Gli Horti di Roma Antica*. Milan: Mondadori Electa.

Cinti, T., and M. Lo Castro, eds. 2019. *Il Museo e il Parco Archeologico della Villa di Traiano ad Arcinazzo Romano*. Rome: Soprintendenza per i Beni Archeologici del Lazio.

Cinti, T. and M. Lo Castro. 2011. *Arcinazzo Romano*. Guida ai musei 20. Rome: Soprintendenza per i Beni Archeologici del Lazio.

Ciotta, G., ed. 2001. *Vitruvio nella cultura architettonica antica, medievale e moderna: Atti del convegno internazionale di Genova, 5–8 novembre 2001*. 2 vols. Genoa: De Ferrari.

Claridge, A. 2010. *Rome: An Oxford Archaeological Guide*. 2nd ed.. Oxford: Oxford University Press.

Claridge, A. 2014. "Reconstructing the Temple of Apollo on the Palatine Hill in Rome." In Häuber, Schütz, and Winder 2014, 128–52.

Clark, E. A., ed. and trans. 1984. *The Life of Melania the Younger*, by Gerontius. Studies in Women and Religion 14. Oxford: Oxford University Press.

Clark, E. A. 2021. *Melania the Younger: From Rome to Jerusalem*. Oxford: Oxford University Press.

Clark, K. 1974. *Another Part of the Wood: A Self Portrait*. New York: Harper and Row.

Clark Reeder, J. 2001. *The Villa of Livia ad Gallinas Albas: A Study in the Augustan Villa and Garden*. Archaeologia transatlantica 20. Providence: Center for Old World Archaeology and Art, Brown University.

Clarke, J. R. 1998. *Looking at Lovemaking: Constructions of Sexuality in Roman Art, 100 B.C.–A.D. 250*. Berkeley: University of California Press.

Clarke, J. R. 2006. "High and Low: Mocking Philosophers in the Tavern of the Seven Sages, Ostia." In D'Ambra and Métraux 2006, 47–57.

Clemente, G. 1981. "Le leggi sul lusso e la società romana tra III e II secolo a.C." In Giardina and Schiavone 1981, 3:1–14.

Coarelli, F. 1989. "La casa dell'aristocrazia romana secondo Vitruvio." In Geertman and de Jong 1989, 178–87, figs. 1 and 2.

Coarelli, F. 2014. *Rome and Environs: An Archaeological Guide*. Translated by J. J. Clauss and D. P. Harmon, illustrations adapted by J. A. Clauss and P. A. Mackay. Updated edition. Berkeley: University of California Press.

Coarelli, F. and H. Patterson, eds. 2008. Mercator Placidissimus: *The Tiber Valley in Antiquity; New Research in the Upper and Middle River Valley, Rome, 27–28 February 2004*. Rome: Quasar.

Cobb, M. A. 2018. *Rome and the Indian Ocean Trade from Augustus to the Early Third Century CE*. Mnemosyne Suppl. 418. London: Brill.

Coindoz, M., and C. Jouvenot. 1997. "Avanos vu par Grégoire de Nysse au IVème siècle." *Dossiers d'Archéologie* 121:26–29.

Coleman, K. 1990. "Fatal Charades: Roman Executions Staged as Mythological Enactments." *JRS* 80:44–73.

Coleman, K., ed. and trans. 2006. *Martial:* Liber Spectaculorum. Oxford: Oxford University Press.

Coletti, C. M. 2007. "La villa delle terme: L'impianto termale," in Volpe 2007, 201–15.

Colombi, E. 1996. "*Rusticitas* e vita in villa nella Gallia tardoantica: Tra realtà e letteratura." *Athenaeum* 84:405–32.

Comas, J. 1971. "Historical Reality and the Detractors of Father Las Casas." In Friede and Keen 1971, 487–537.

Cominesi, A. R., N. de Haan, E. M. Moormann, and C. Stocks, eds. 2021. *God on Earth: Emperor Domitian. The Re-invention of Rome at the End of the 1st Century AD*. Papers on Archaeology of the Leiden Museum of Antiquities 24. Leiden: Sidestone Press.

Cominesi, A. R., and C. Stocks. 2021. "Living Like the Emperor: A Portrayal of Domitian in His Villas and on the Palatine." In Cominesi et al. 2021, 105–9.

Constantelos, D. J. 1991. *Byzantine Philanthropy and Social Welfare*. New Rochelle, NY: A.D. Caratzas.

Conticello, B., and B. Andreae. 1974. *Die Skulptoren von Sperlonga*. Antike Plastik 14. 2 vols.. Berlin: Gebr. Mann.

Cooley, A. E., ed. 2016. *A Companion to Roman Italy*. Blackwell Companions to the Ancient World. New York: Wiley.

Cooley, A. E. 2018. "The Last Days of Augustus." In Goodman 2018, 32–43.

Coralini, A., ed. 2021. Extra Moenia: *Abitare il territorio della regione vesuviana*. Rome: Scienze e lettere.

Corbier, M. 1981. "Proprietà et gestione della terra: Grande proprietà fondiaria ed economia contadina." In Giardina and Schiavone 1981, 1:427–44.

Corbier, M. 1994. "Conclusion." In Pailler and Sablayrolles 1994, 421–23.

Corbier, M., and G. Sauron, eds. 2017. *Langages et communication: Écrits, images, sons.* Paris: Comité national des sociétés historiques et scientifiques. OpenEdition Books.

Cordier, P. 2005. "Dion Cassius et les phénomènes religieux 'égyptiens': Quelques suggestions pour un mode d'emploi." In Bricault, Versluys, and Meyboom 2005, 89–110.

Cornell, T., and K. Lomas, eds. 1995. *Urban Society in Roman Italy.* London: St. Martin's Press.

Cornell, T. J. 1995. *The Beginnings of Rome: Italy and Rome from the Bronze Age to the Punic Wars (c. 1000–264 BC).* Routledge History of the Ancient World. London and New York: Routledge.

Cornell, T. J. 2008. "The Conquest of Italy." *CAH* 7, pt. 2, 351–419.

Cornell, T. J., and K. Lomas, eds. 1995. *Urban Society in Roman Italy.* London: Routledge.

Correnti, F. 1990. "Centumcellae: La villa, il porto e la città." In Maffei and Nastasi 1990, 204–14.

Corsi Collection. *Corsi Collection of Decorative Stones.* Database. Oxford: Oxford University Museum of Natural History. http://www.oum.ox.ac.uk/corsi/catalogue/home.

Coşkun, A. 2002a. "Chronology in the *Eucharisticos* of Paulinus Pellaeus: A Reassessment," *Mnemosyne* 55:329–44.

Coşkun, A. 2002b. *Die gens Ausonia an der Macht: Untersuchungen zu Decimius Magnus Ausonius und seiner Familie.* Prosopographia et Genealogica 8. Oxford: Oxford Unit for Prosopographical Research.

Coşkun, A. 2005. "Notes on the *Eucharisticos* of Paulinus Pellaeus: Towards a New Edition of the Autobiography." *Exemplaria classica* 9:113–53.

Cotton, M. A., and G. P. R. Métraux. 1985. *The San Rocco Villa at Francolise.* Rome and New York: British School at Rome and Institute of Fine Arts, New York University.

Cracco Ruggini, L. 2000. "Plinio il Giovane a proposito di *nundinae* private inter-cittadine: Dispositivi giuridici e collusioni di fatto tra centro e periferia." In Lo Cascio 2000b, 161–75.

Crawford, M. H. 1989. "The Lex Iulia Agraria." *Athenaeum* 67:179–90.

Crawford, M. H., and J. D. Cloud, eds. 1996. *Roman Statutes.* 2 vols. *BICS* Suppl. 64. Oxford: Oxford University Press.

Criniti, N. 1991. *La tabula alimentaria di Veleia.* Parma: Presso la Deputazione di storia patria per le province parmensi.

Croisille, J.-M. 1965. *Les natures mortes campaniennes: Répertoire descriptif des peintures de nature morte du Musée National de Naples, de Pompéi, Herculanum et Stabies.* Collection Latomus 76. Brussels: Latomus.

Croisille, J.-M. 1982. *Poésie et art figuré de Néron aux Flaviens: Recherches sur l'iconographie et la correspondance des arts à l'époque impériale.* Collection Latomus 179. Brussels: Latomus.

Dalfen, J. 2000. "Ciceros 'cum dignitate otium': Einiges zur (nicht unproblematischen) Freizeitkultur großer Römer." In Sigot 2000, 169–87.

D'Ambra, E., and G. P. R. Métraux, eds. 2006. *The Art of Citizens, Soldiers and Freedmen in the Roman World.* BAR International Series 1526. Oxford: Archaeopress.

Danzig, G. 2003–2004. "Why Socrates Was Not a Farmer: Xenophon's *Oeconomicus* as a Philosophical Dialogue." *Greece and Rome* 50(1):57–76.

Darmon, J.-P. 1990. "En guise de conclusion: Propositions pour une sémantique des *xenia*." In Balmelle et al. 1990, 107–12.

D'Arms, J. H. (1970) 2003. *Romans on the Bay of Naples and Other Essays on Roman Campania*, ed. Fausto Zevi. Bari: Edipuglia. Reprint of *Romans on the Bay of Naples*, Cambridge, MA: Harvard University Press.

D'Arms, J. H., and E. C. Kopff, eds. 1980. *The Seaborne Commerce of*

Ancient Rome: Studies in Archaeology and History. MAAR 36. Rome: American Academy in Rome.

Dasen, V., and T. Späth, eds. 2010. *Children, Memory, and Family Identity in Roman Culture.* Oxford: Oxford University Press.

De Blois, L., P. Erdkamp, O. Hekster, and G. De Kleijn, eds. 2003. *The Representation and Perception of Roman Imperial Power: Proceedings of the Third Workshop of the International Network Impact of Empire (Roman Empire, c. 200 B.C.–A.D. 476), Rome, March 20–23, 2002.* Leiden: Brill.

De Franceschini, M. 1991. *Villa Adriana: Mosaici, pavimenti, edifici.* Rome: "L'Erma" di Bretschneider.

De Franceschini, M. 1999. *Le ville romane della X Regio (Venetia et Histria): Catalogo e carta archeologica dell'insediamento romano nel territorio, dall'età repubblicana al tardo impero.* Rome: "L'Erma" di Bretschneider.

De Franceschini, M. 2005. *Ville dell'Agro Romano.* Rome: "L'Erma" di Bretschneider.

De Grummond, N. T., and B. S. Ridgway, eds. 2000. *From Pergamon to Sperlonga: Sculpture and Context.* Berkeley: University of California Press.

de Haas, T. 2017. "The Geography of Roman Italy and Its Implications for the Development of Rural Economies." In de Haas and Tol 2017, 51–82.

de Haas, T. C. A., and G. Tol, eds. 2017. *The Economic Integration of Roman Italy.* Leiden: Brill.

Deissler, J. 2010. "Cold Case? Die Finley-Vogt-Kontroverse aus deutscher Sicht." In Heinen 2010, 77–93.

Delbrück, R. 1907–1912. *Hellenistiche Bauten in Latium.* 2 vols. Strassburg: K. J. Trübner.

Della Corte, M. 1934. Unpublished; transcribed and translated as "Augustus in His Last Visit to Campania: Capri and Apragopolis; Octavianum and Summa Villa" in De Simone and Macfarlane 2009, 144–56.

Demma, F. 2010–2011. "*Leucado Cepit*: Praeneste, Roma e la conquista dell'Oriente." *Rendiconti della pontificia accademia romana di archeologia* 83:3–57.

De Neeve, P. W. 1984. *Colonus: Private Farm-Tenancy in Roman Italy during the Republic and Early Principate.* Amsterdam: J.C. Gieben.

De Pachtère, F. G. 1920. *La table hypothécaire de Veleia: Étude sur la propriété foncière dans l'Apennin de Plaisance.* Bibliothèque de l'École des hautes études, sciences historiques et philologiques 228. Paris: Champion.

Dermody, B., A. Chiu-Smit, and R (L. P. H.) van Beek 2022. "A Model of Grain Production and Trade for the Roman World." In Brughmans and Wilson 2022, 196–225.

De Rossi, G. M. 1979. "Bovillae." In *Forma Italiae Regio I.* Ser. 2, vol. 26, 298–323. Florence: Olschki.

De Simone, G. F., and R. T. Macfarlane, eds. 2009. *Apolline Project.* Vol. 1, *Studies on Vesuvius' North Slope and the Bay of Naples.* Quaderni della Ricerca Scientifica dell'Università "Suor Orsola Benincasa" 14. Naples: Suor Orsola Benincasa nell'Università.

de Vos, M. 2013. "The Rural Landscape of Thugga: Farms, Presses, Mills, and Transport." In Bowman and Wilson 2013a, 143–218.

De Wet, C. L. 2017. *The Unbound God: Slavery and the Formation of Early Christian Thought.* London: Routledge.

De Wet, C. L. 2022. "Introduction: Late Antique Studies and the New Polyphony for Slave Studies." In De Wet, Kahlos, and Vuolanto 2022, 1–12.

De Wet, C. L., M. Kahlos, and V. Vuolanto, eds. 2022. *Slavery in the Late Antique World, 150–700 CE.* Cambridge: Cambridge University Press.

Dewing, H. B., ed. and trans. 1916. *Procopius: History of the Wars.* Vol. 3, *Books 5–6.15.* Loeb Classical Library. Cambridge, MA: Harvard University Press.

Dey, H., and E. B. Fentress, eds. 2011. *Western Monasticism* ante litteram: *The Spaces of Monastic Observance in Late Antiquity and the Early Middle Ages*. Turnhout: Brepols.

Di Franco, L. 2015. *Capreensia disiecta membra:. Augusto a Capri e la villa di Palazzo a Mare*. Quaderni di Oebalus 6. Rome: Scienze et Lettere.

Di Gennaro, A. 2013. "Campania." In Agnoletti 2013, 435–52.

Dilke, O. A. W. 1971. *The Roman Land Surveyors: Introduction to the* Agrimensores. London: David and Charles (rev. ed. in French translation by J. Gaudey, *Les arpenteurs de la Rome antique*. 1995. Sophia Antipolis: Éditions APDCA).

Dilke, O. A. W. 1987. "Maps in the Service of the State: Roman Cartography to the End of the Augustan Era." In Harley and Woodhouse 1987, 1:201–11.

Dillon, S. 2006. *Ancient Greek Portrait Sculpture: Contexts, Subjects, and Styles*. Cambridge: Cambridge University Press.

Di Matteo, F. 2005. *Villa di Nerone a Subiaco: Il complesso del Simbruina Stagna*. Studia Archaeologica 1131. Rome: "L'Erma" di Bretschneider.

Dindorf, L. A. 1866–68. *Diodori Bibliotheca Historica*. 5 vols. Leipzig: B. G. Teubner.

Diogenes Laërtius, *Lives of the Eminent Philosophers* (Βίοι καὶ γνῶμαι τῶν ἐν φιλοσοφίᾳ εὐδοκιμησάντων; *Vitae Philosophorum*) http://data.perseus.org/citations/urn:cts:greekLit:tlg0004.tlg001.perseus-eng1:7.7.

Di Vita, A. 1966a. "Archaeological News 1963–1964. Tripolitania – Tagiura." *Libya Antiqua* 2, suppl. 3:132–33.

Di Vita, A. 1966b. *La villa della "Gara delle Nereidi" presso Tagiura: Un contributo alla storia del mosaico romano, ed altri scavi e scoperte in Tripolitania*, 13–64. *Libya Antiqua* suppl. 2. Tripoli: Directorate-General of Antiquities, Museums and Archives.

Dixon, S. D. 1992. *The Roman Family*. Baltimore: Johns Hopkins University Press.

Dodd, E. 2023. "The Archaeology of Wine Production in Roman and Pre-Roman Italy." *AJA* 126:443–80.

Dolansky, F. 2008. "*Togam virilem sumere*: Coming of Age in the Roman World." In Edmonson and Keith 2008, 47–70.

Domingo, G. M. 2016. *Benefaction and Rewards in the Ancient Greek City: The Origins of Euergetism*. Cambridge: Cambridge University Press.

Dominik, W. J., J. Garthwaite, and P. A. Roche, eds. 2009. *Writing Politics in Imperial Rome*. Leiden: Brill.

Döpp, S., and W. Geerlings, eds. 1998. *Lexikon der antiken christlichen Autoren*. 2nd ed. Freiburg: Herder.

Dorion, L.-A. (2001) 2010. "L'exégèse strausienne de Xénophon: Le cas paradigmatique de *Mémorables* IV 4." *Philosophie Antique* 1:87–118, translated and reprinted as "The Straussian Exegesis of Xenophon: The Paradigmatic Case of *Memorabilia* IV 4" in Gray 2010, 283–323.

Dosi, A. 2006. Otium: *Il tempo libero dei romani*. Rome: Quasar.

Drinkwater, J. F. 2019. *Nero: Emperor and Court*. Cambridge: Cambridge University Press.

Drinkwater, J. F., and H. Elton, eds. 1992. *Fifth-Century Gaul: A Crisis of Identity?* Cambridge: Cambridge University Press.

DuBois, P. 2010. *Slavery: Antiquity and Its Legacy*. Oxford: Oxford University Press.

DuBois, P. 2021. "How to Tell a Slave." In Hodkinson, Kleijwegt, and Vlassopoulos 2016–.

Duby, G. 1973. *Guerriers et paysans VII–XIIe siècle : Premier essor de l'économie européenne*. Paris: Gallimard.

Duby, G. 1974. *The Early Growth of the European Economy: Warriors and Peasants from the Seventh to the Twelfth Century*. English translation by H.B Clarke. Ithaca, NY: Cornell University Press.

Duchêne, P. 2020. *Comment écrire sur les empereurs?: Les procédés historiographiques de Tacite et Suétone*. Scripta antiqua 137. Bordeaux: Ausonius.

Dufallo, B. 2013. *The Captor's Image: Greek Culture in Roman Ecphrasis*. Oxford: Oxford University Press.

Dufton, J. Andrew 2916. "The Plan of the Villa." In Fentress et al. 2016, 64–69.

Du latifundium au latifondo. 1995. *Du latifundium au latifondo: Un héritage de Rome, une création médiévale ou moderne? Actes de la Table ronde internationale du CNRS, organisée à l'Université Michel de Montaigne, Bordeaux III, les 17–19 décembre 1992*. Publications du Centre Pierre Paris 25. Paris: De Boccard.

Dümler, B. 1999. "Paulinus von Pella." In Döpp and Geerlings 1999, 482–86.

Dumont, J.-C. 1987. *Servus: Rome et l'esclavage sous la République. CÉFR* 103. Rome: École française de Rome.

Dumont, J.-C. 1988. "Esclavage blanc, esclavage noir." *Bulletin de l'Association Guillaume Budé* 2:173–94.

Dunbabin, K. M. D. 1991. "*Triclinium* and *Stibadium*." In Slater 1991, 121–48.

Dunbabin, K. M. D. 1998. "Ut Graeco more biberetur: Greeks and Romans on the Dining Couch." In Nielsen and Nielsen 1998, 81–101.

Dunbabin, K. M. D. 1999. *Mosaics of the Greek and Roman World*. Cambridge: Cambridge University Press.

Duncan-Jones, R. 1964. "The Purpose and Organization of the *Alimenta*." *PBSR* 32:123–46.

Duncan-Jones, R. 1965. "The Finances of the Younger Pliny." *PBSR* 33:177–88

Duncan-Jones, R. 1982. *The Economy of the Roman Empire: Quantitative Studies*. 2nd ed. Cambridge: Cambridge University Press.

Duncan-Jones, R. 1990. *Structure and Scale in the Roman Economy*. Cambridge: Cambridge University Press.

Dunn, G. D. 2015. "Flavius Constantius, Galla Placidia, and the Aquitanian Settlement of the Goths." *Phoenix* 69(3/4):376–93, 451–52.

du Plessis, P. J., C. Ando, and K. Tuori, eds. 2016. *The Oxford Handbook of Roman Law and Society*. Oxford: Oxford University Press.

du Prey, P. de la Ruffinière. 1994. *The Villas of Pliny from Antiquity to Posterity*. Chicago: University of Chicago Press.

du Prey, P. de la Ruffinière. 2018. "Conviviality *versus* Seclusion in Pliny's Villas." In Marzano and Métraux 2018, 467–75.

Dyson, S. L. 2003. *The Roman Countryside*. Duckworth Debates in Archaeology. London: Duckworth.

Dyson, S. L. 2021. "Material Evidence: Looking for Slaves? The Archaeological Record: Rome." In Hodkinson, Kleijwegt, and Vlassopoulos 2016–.

Eberle, L. P. 2021. "Fiscal Semantics in the Long Second Century: Citizenship, Taxation, and the *Constitutio Anonianiana*." In Lavan and Ando 2021, 69–99.

Eck, W. 1997. "Der Euergetismus im Funktionszusammenhang der kaiserzeitlichen Städte." In Christol and Masson 1997, 306–31.

Eck, W., and J. Heinrichs. 1993. *Sklaven und Freigelassene in der Gesellschaft der römischen Kaiserzeit*. Darmstadt: Wissenschaftliche Buchgesellschaft.

Edmonson, J. 2008. "Public Dress and Social Control in Late Republican and Early Imperial Rome." In Edmonson and Keith 2008, 21–46.

Edmonson, J. 2011. "Slavery and the Roman Family." In Bradley and Cartledge 2011, 337–61.

Edmonson, J., and A. Keith, eds. 2008. *Roman Dress and the Fabrics of Roman Culture*. Phoenix: Journal of the Classical Association of Canada. Suppl. 46. Toronto: University of Toronto Press.

Edwards, C. 1993. *The Politics of Immorality in Ancient Rome*. Cambridge: Cambridge University Press.

Edwards, R. 2011. "Tacitus, Tiberius and Capri." *Latomus* 70(4):1047–57.

Eickhoff, F. C. 2016a. "Inszenierungen von Muße durch die Gattung Brief in den *Epistulae* des Horaz." In Eickhoff 2016b, 75–94.

Eickhoff, F. C., ed. 2016b. *Muße und Rekursivität in der antiken Briefliteratur: Otium*. Studien zur Theorie und Kulturgeschichte der Muße 1. Tübingen: Mohr Siebeck.

Eickhoff, F. C., W. Kofler, and B. Zimmermann. 2016. "Muße, Rekursivität und antike Briefe: Eine Einleitung." In Eickhoff 2016b, 1–11.

Ellis, S. P. 1991. "Power, Architecture and Decor: How the Late Roman Aristocrat Appeared to His Guests." In Gazda and Haeckl 1991, 117–34.

Eltis, D., S. L. Engerman, S. Drescher, and D. Richardson, eds. 2017a. *The Cambridge World History of Slavery*. Vol. 4, *AD 1804–AD 2016*. Cambridge: Cambridge University Press.

Eltis, D., S. L. Engerman, S. Drescher, and D. Richardson. 2017b. "Introduction." In Eltis et al. 2017a, 3–19.

Engerman, S., S. Drescher, and R. Paquette, eds. 2001. *Slavery*. Oxford Readers. Oxford: Oxford University Press.

Englert, W. 2017. "Fanum and Philosophy: Cicero and the Death of Tullia." *Ciceroniana On Line* 1(1):41–66. https://ojs.unito.it/index.php/COL/article/view/2202/1940.

Ennabli, A. 1986a. "Les thermes du thiase marin de Sidi Ghrib (Tunisie)." *Monuments et mémoires de la Fondation Eugène Piot* 68:1–59.

Ennabli, A. 1986b. "Mosaïque des thermes privés de Sidi Ghrib." In *30 ans au service* 1986, 183–85.

Ennabli, A., and L. Neuru. 1994. "Excavation of the Roman Villa at Sidi Ghrib, Tunisia, 1985–1992." *Échos du Monde Classique / Classical Views* 38, n.s. 13:207–20.

Erdkamp. P., ed. 2005. *The Grain Market in the Roman Empire: A Social, Political and Economic Study*. Cambridge: Cambridge University Press.

Erdkamp, P., K. Verboven, and A. Zuiderhoek, eds. 2020. *Capital, Investment, and Innovation in the Roman World*. Oxford Studies on the Roman Economy. Oxford: Oxford University Press.

Erdmann, E., and H. Kloft, eds. 2002. *Mensch, Natur, Technik: Perspektiven aus der Antike für das dritte Jahrtausend*. Münster: Aschendorff.

Eristov, H., and F. Monier, eds. 2014. *L'héritage germanique dans l'approche du décor antique: Actes de la table ronde organisée à l'École Normale Supérieure le 23 novembre 2012*. Collection de l'Association française pour la peinture murale antique; Pictor 2. Bordeaux: Ausonius.

Erler, M. 2016. "*Otium* als *negotium*—Epikureische Briefe, Themen und Funktionen." In Eickhoff 2016b, 61–73.

Étienne, R. 1974. "Recherches sur l'ergastule." In *Actes du Colloque 1972 sur l'esclavage*. Annales littéraires de l'Université de Besançon 163, 249–66. Paris: Les Belles Lettres.

Étienne, R. (1972) 2019. "Vitruve et les cryptoportiques." *Revue d'Études Ligures* 38:62–65. Reprinted in *Itineraria Hispanica: Recueil d'articles de Robert Étienne; Textes réunis par Françoise Mayet*, 335–38. Scripta Antiqua 15. Pessac: Ausonius.

Evans Grubbs, J., T. Parkin, and R. Bell, eds. 2013. *The Oxford Handbook of Childhood and Education in the Classical World*. Oxford: Oxford University Press.

Fabre, G. 1981. *Libertus: Recherches sur les rapports patron-affranchi à la fin de la République romaine*. CÉFR 50. Rome: École française de Rome, Palais Farnèse.

Favro, D., F. K. Yegül, J. Pinto, and G. Métraux, eds. 2015. *Paradigm and Progeny: Roman Imperial Architecture and Its Legacy; Proceedings of a Conference Held at the American Academy in Rome on 6–7 December 2011 in Honor of William L. MacDonald*. JRA Suppl. 101. Portsmouth, RI: Journal of Roman Archaeology.

Fechner, D., and P. Scholz. 2002. "*Schole* und *otium* in der griechischen und römischen Antike: Eine Einführung in die Thematik und ein historischer Überblick anhand ausgewählter Texte." In Erdmann and Kloft 2002, 83–148.

Federico, E. 1999. "Masgaba: Uno scomodo libico alla corte di Augusto." *Quaderni di storia* 50:163–71.

Federico, E., and E. Miranda, eds. 1998. *Capri antica: Dalla preistoria alla fine dell'età romana*, 225–40. Capri: La Conchiglia.

Fehr, B. 1969. "Plattform und Blickbasis (für Friedrich Matz anlässlich seines 80. Geburtstags)." *Marburger Winckelmann-Programm* 1969:1–67.

Feige, M. 2021. *Landwirtschaftliche Produktionsanlagen römischer Villen im republikanischen und kaiserzeitlichen Italien*. Berlin: De Gruyter.

Fentress, E. B. 1984. "Via Aurelia, Via Aemilia." *PBSR* 52:72–76.

Fentress, E. B. 1998. "The House of the Sicilian Greeks." In Frazer 1998, 29–41.

Fentress, E. B. 2005. "On the Block: *Catastae*, *Chalcidica* and *Cryptae* in Early Imperial Italy." *JRA* 18:220–34.

Fentress, E. B. 2021. "Nunc Villae Grandes, Oppida Parva Prius: *Private Agency and Public Utility in the Tuscan Maremma*." In Sebastiani and Megale 2021, 39–47.

Fentress, E. B., and S. Gatti. 2015. "Hadrian's Other Villas." In Favro et al. 2015, 150–65.

Fentress, E. B., C. Goodson, and M. Maiuro, with M. Andrews and A. Dufton, eds. 2016. *Villa Magna: An Imperial Estate and Its Legacies; Excavations 2006–10*. Archaeological Monographs of the British School at Rome 23. London: British School at Rome.

Fentress, E. B., D. Kennet, and I. Valenti. 1986. "A Sicilian Villa and Its Landscape (contrada Mirable, Mazara del Vallo)." *Opus* 5:75–90.

Fentress, E. B., and P. Perkins. 2016. "Cosa and the Ager Cosanus." In Cooley 2016, 476.

Figal, G. 2016. "Räumlichkeit der Muße." In Eickhoff 2016b, 15–20.

Filippi, F., ed. 2015a. *Campo Marzio: Nuove ricerche; Atti del Seminario di studi sul Campo Marzio, MNR Palazzo Altemps, 18–19 marzo 2013*. Rome: Quasar.

Filippi, F. 2015b. "L'area di palazzo Venezia: Nuovi dati archeologici e considerazioni topografiche." In Filippi 2015a, 77–102.

Filser, W., B. Fritsch, W. Kennedy, C. Klose, R. Perrella, and M. Reinfeld. 2021. "La villa maritima del Capo di Sorrento: Ricerche dell'Istituto Winckelmann, Humboldt-Universität zu Berlin." In Coralini 2021, 131–43.

Finley, M. I. 1968. *Slavery in Classical Antiquity: Views and Controversies*. Cambridge: Heffer.

Finley, M. I. 1998. *Ancient Slavery and Modern Ideology*, 2nd ed., edited by B. D. Shaw. Princeton: Markus Wiener.

Finley, M. I. 1999. *The Ancient Economy*. Updated edition with new foreword by I. Morris. Sather Lectures 43. Ann Arbor: University of Michigan Press.

Finley, M. I., ed. 2006. *Classical Slavery*. New York: Routledge.

Fiore Cavaliere, M. G., and Z. Mari. 1999. *La Villa di Traiano ad Arcinazzo Romano: Guida alla lettura del territorio*. Rome: Tipigraf.

Fiorucci, G. 2016. "Ozio e lavoro in Libanio." In Eickhoff 2016b, 232–49.

Fischer, C. T., ed. 1964–67. *Diodorus, Bibliotheca Historica* (ex recensione Ludovici Dindorfii). 6 vols. Stuttgart: B. G. Teubner.

Fisher, N. R. E. 1992. *Hybris: A Study in the Values of Honour and Shame in Ancient Greece*. Warminster, UK: Aris & Phillips.

Fitch, J. G., ed. and trans. 2013. *Palladius: The Work of Farming (*Opus Agriculturae*) and Poem on Grafting*. Totnes, UK: Prospect Books.

Fixot, M. 2000. "La cité et son térritoire: L'exemple du Sud-Est de la Gaule." In Brogiolo, Gauthier, and Christie 2000, 37–62.

Flinterman, J.-J. 2014. "Pythagoreans in Rome and Asia Minor around the Turn of the Common Era." In Huffman 2014, 341–59.

Flory, M. B. 1989. "Octavian and the Omen of the 'Gallina Alba.'" *CJ* 84, 343–56.

Flower, H. I. 1996. *Ancestor Masks and Aristocratic Power in Roman Culture*. Oxford: Clarendon Press.

Föllinger, S. 2021. "Ethopoiie und Fiktionalität des Dialogs." In Müller 2021, 55–68.

Föllinger, S., and G. M. Müller, eds. 2013. *Der Dialog in der Antike: Formen und Funktionen einer literarischen Gattung zwischen Philosophie, Wissensvermittlung und dramatischer Inszenierung*. Berlin: De Gruyter.

Forbis, E. 1993. "Liberalitas et Largitio, Terms from Private Municifence in Italian Honorary Inscriptions." *Athenaeum* 81:483–98.

Forbis, E. 1996. *Municipal Virtues in the Roman Empire: The Evidence of Italian Inscriptions*. Beiträge zur Altertumskunde 79. Stuttgart: Teubner.

Forsén, B. 1991. *Lex Licinia Sextia de modo agrorum: Fiction or Reality?* Commentationes Humanarum Litterarum 96. Helsinki: Societas Scientiarum Fennica.

Förtsch, R. 1993. *Archäologischer Kommentar zu den Villenbriefen des jüngeren Plinius*. Mainz: Philipp von Zabern.

Fosbroke, Rev. T. D. 1828. *Foreign Topography; Or, An Encyclopedick Account, Alphabetically Arranged, of the Ancient Remains In Africa, Asia, and Europe; Forming a Sequel to the Encyclopedia of Antiquities*. London: J. B. Nichols and Son.

Foubert, L. 2021. "Imperial Women and the Dynamics of Power. Managing the Soft Power of Domitia Longina and Julia Titi." In Cominesi et al. 2021, 97–101.

Fouet, G. 1969. *La Villa gallo-romaine de Montmaurin (Haute-Garonne)*. Supplément à Gallia 20. Paris: Éditions du C.N.R.S.

Franciosi, G., ed. 2002. Ager Campanus: *La storia dell'Ager Campanus, i problemi della limitatio e sua lettura attuale: Atti del convegno internazionale: Real sito di S. Leucio 8–9 giugno* 2001. Naples: Jovene.

Frass, M. 2006. *Antike römische Gärten: Soziale und wirtschaftliche Funktionen der* Horti Romani. *Grazer Beiträge* Suppl. 10. Horn, Austria: Verlag F. Berger & Söhne.

Frayn, J. M. 1993. *Markets and Fairs in Roman Italy: Their Social and Econonomic Importance from the Second Century BC to the Third Century AD*. Oxford: Oxford University Press.

Frazer, A., ed. 1998. *The Roman Villa: Villa Urbana; First Williams Symposium on Classical Architecture held at the University of Pennsylvania, Philadelphia, April 21–22, 1990*. Philadelphia: University Museum, University of Pennsylvania.

Frederiksen, M. 1981. "I cambiamenti dell strutture agrarie nella tarda repubblica: La Campania." In Giardina and Schiavone 1981, vol 1, 265–88.

Frederiksen, M. 1984. *Campania*. Edited, with additions, by N. Purcell. London: British School at Rome.

Friede, J., and B. Keen, eds. 1971. *Bartolomé de Las Casas in History: Toward an Understanding of the Man and His Work*. DeKalb: Northern Illinois University Press.

Frizell, B., and A. Klynne, eds. 2005. *Roman Villas around the Urbs: Interaction with Landscape and Environment; Proceedings of a Conference at the Swedish Institute in Rome*. Rome: Swedish Institute. https://isvroma.org/en/2021/11/10/2-roman-villas-around-the-urbs-interaction-with-landscape-and-environment-proceedings-of-a-conference-at-the-swedish-institute-in-rome-september-17-18-2004-eds-b-santillo-frizell-a-klynne-2/.

Fröhlich, T. and V. M. Strocka. 1996. *Casa della Fontana Piccola*. Hauser in Pompeji, Bd. 8. Munich: Hirmer Verlag.

Frontoni, R., G. Galli, and R. Paris. 2010. *Villa dei Quintili*. Milan: Electa.

Gamauf, R. 2023. "*Peculium*: Paradoxes of Slaves With Property." In Schermaier 2023a, 87–124.

Gargiulo, P. 2000. "Liternum: Nuovi dati." In Gialanella 2000, 115–17.

Gargiulo, P. 2002. "Il territorio di Liternum." In Franciosi 2002, 203–8.

Gargiulo, P. 2007. "La via Domitiana antica nel territorio di Liternum." In Sirano 2007, 299–317.

Garmy, P., and L. Maurin. 1996. *Enceintes romaines d'Aquitaine: Bordeaux, Dax, Périgueux, Bazas.* Documents d'archéologie française 53. Paris: Éditions de la Maison des Sciences de l'Homme.

Garnsey, P. 1968. "Trajan's *Alimenta*: Some Problems." *Historia* 17:367–81.

Garrison, I. P. 2018. "The Tomb of Virgil between Text, Memory, and Site." In Goldschmidt and Graziosi 2018, 265–80.

Gaselee, S., ed. 1910. *Petronius: A Revised Latin Text of the Satyricon with the Earliest English Translation (1694).* London: privately published. (Republished 1927 and 1944 as *The Complete Works of Gaius Petronius Done into English by Jack Lindsay*. New York: Wiley Book Co.)

Gatti, S. 2005. "La villa imperiale di Palestrina." In Quilici and Quilici-Gigli 2005, 67–89.

Gazda, E. K. 1973. "Etruscan Influence in the Funerary Reliefs of Late Republican Rome: A Study of Roman Vernacular Portraiture." *ANRW* 1.4 855–70.

Gazda, E. K., ed. 2002a. *Ancient Art of Emulation: Studies in Artistic Originality and Tradition from the Present to Classical Antiquity. MAAR* Suppl. 1. Ann Arbor: University of Michigan Press.

Gazda, E. K. 2002b. "Introduction." In Gazda 2002a, 1–23.

Gazda, E. K., and A. E. Haeckl, eds. 1991. *Roman Art in the Private Sphere: New Perspectives on the Architecture and Decor of the Domus, Villa, and Insula.* Ann Arbor: University of Michigan Press.

Gebara da Silva, U. 2022. "Rural Slavery in Late Roman Gaul: Literary Genres, Theoretical Frames, and Narratives." In De Wet, Kahlos, and Vuolanto, eds. 2022, 170–87.

Geertman, H., and J. J. de Jong, eds. 1989. *Munus Non Ingratum: Proceedings of the International Symposium on Vitruvius' De Architectura and the Hellenistic and Republican Architecture, Leiden 20–23 January 1987. BABesch* Suppl. 2., 178–87.

George, M. 2002. "Slave Disguise in Ancient Rome." In Wiedemann and Gardner 2002, 41–54.

George, M. 2010. "Archaeology and Roman Slavery: Problems and Potential." In Heinen 2010, 141–60.

George, M., ed. 2013. *Roman Slavery and Roman Material Culture.* Toronto: University of Toronto Press.

Ghizzoni, F. 1983. *Sulpicio Severo.* Università degli Studi di Parma. Istituto de lingua e letteratura latina 8. Rome: Bulzoni.

Gialanella, C., ed. 2000. *Nova antiqua Phlegraea: Nuovi tesori archeologici dai campi flegrei; Guida alla mostra*, 115–17. Milan: Electa Napoli.

Gianfrotta, P. A. 1983. "L'indagine archeologica e lo scavo." In Tocco Sciarelli 1983a, 25–48.

Giardina, A. 1997a. "L'Italia, il modo di produzione schiavistico e i tempi di una crisi." In Giardina 1997b, 233–64.

Giardina, A., ed. 1997b. *L'Italia Romana: Storie di una identità incompiuta.* Rome: Laterza.

Giardina, A., ed. 2000. *Roma Antica.* Bari: Laterza.

Giardina, A., and A. Schiavone, eds. 1981. *Società romana e produzione schiavistica.* 3 vols. Vol. 1, *L'Italia: Insediamenti e forme economiche*; Vol. 2, *Merci, mercati e scambi nel Mediterraneo*; Vol. 3, *Modelli etici, diritto e trasformazioni sociali.* Rome: Laterza.

Gibson, R. K. 2020. *Man of High Empire: The Life of Pliny the Younger.* Oxford: Oxford University Press.

Giraud, C. ed., and R. Martin, trans. 2010. *Palladius: Traité d'architecture.* Vol. 2, *Livres III à V.* Collection des Universités de France. Paris: Les Belles Lettres.

Giuliani, F. C., and P. Verduchi, eds. 1975. *Ricerche sull'architettura di Villa Adriana*. Rome: De Luca.

Gjerstad, E. 1953–1973. *Early Rome: Acta Instituti Romani Regni Sueciae*. 6 vols in 7. Skrifter utgivna av Svenska institutet i Rom 17. Lund: C.W.K. Gleerup.

Gleason, K. L. 1994. "Porticus Pompeiana: A New Perspective on the First Public Park of Ancient Rome." *Journal of Garden History* 14(1):13–27.

Gleason, K., ed. 2013. *A Cultural History of Gardens in Antiquity*. Vol. 1 of *A Cultural History of Gardens*, edited by M. Leslie and J. D. Hunt. London: Bloomsbury Academic.

Gliozzo, E., and A. Pizzo, eds. 2021. "Mortars, Plasters and Pigments: Research Questions and Answers." *Archaeological and Anthropological Sciences* 13:192.

Gneist, R., ed. 1880. *Institutionum et regularum iuris romani syntagma*. Leipzig: B. G. Teubner. HeinOnline.

Goette, H. R. 1990. *Studien zu römischen Togadarstellungen*. Deutsches Archäologisches Institut, Beiträge zur Erschliessung hellenistischer und kaiserzeitlicher Skulptur und Architektur 10. Mainz: Philipp von Zabern.

Goldschmidt, N., and B. Graziosi, eds. 2018. *Tombs of the Ancient Poets: Between Literary Reception and Material Culture*. Oxford: Oxford University Press.

González Fernández, J., ed. 2000. *Trajano Emperador de Roma*. Rome: "L'Erma" di Bretschneider.

Goodchild, H. 2013. "GIS models of Roman Agricultural Production." In Bowman and Wilson 2013, 55–86.

Goodman, P. J. 2007. *The Roman City and Its Periphery from Rome to Gaul*. Abingdon, UK: Routledge.

Goodman, P. J., ed. 2018. *Afterlives of Augustus, AD 14–2014*. Cambridge: Cambridge University Press.

Gorce, D., ed. and trans. 1962. *Vie de Sainte Mélanie*, by Gerontius. Sources Chrétiennes 90. Paris: Les Éditions du Cerf.

Gordon, R. L., and F. Marco Simón, eds. 2010. *Magical Practice in the Latin West: Papers from the International Conference Held at the University of Zaragoza, 30 Sept.–1st Oct. 2005*. Religions in the Graeco-Roman World 168. Brill: Leiden.

Gordon, W. M., and O. F. Robinson, eds. and trans. 1988. *The Institutes of Gaius*. London: Duckworth.

Grahame, M. 1997. "Public and Private in the Roman House: The Spatial Order of the Casa del Fauno." In Laurence and Wallace-Hadrill 1997, 137–64.

Gray, V., ed. 2010. *Xenophon: Oxford Readings in Classical Studies*. Oxford: Oxford University Press.

Greene, K. 1986. *The Archaeology of the Roman Economy*. London: B. T. Batsford.

Gros, P., ed. 1994a. *Le projet de Vitruve: Objet, destinataires et réception du* De architectura. *CÉFR* 192. Rome: École française de Rome.

Gros, P. 1994b. "*Munus non ingratum*: Le traité vitruvien et la notion de service." In Gros 1994a, 75–90.

Gros, P., ed. 1998a. *Villes et campagnes en Gaule romaine*. Paris: Comité national des sociétés historiques et scientifiques.

Gros, P. 1998b. "Ville et 'non-villes': Les ambiguïtés dans la hiérarchie juridique et de l'aménagement urban." In Gros 1998a, 11–25.

Gros, P. 2001. *L'architecture romaine du début du IIIe siècle av. J.-C. à la fin du Haut-Empire*. Vol. 2, *Maisons, palais, villas et tombeaux*. Paris: Picard.

Gros, P. 2002a. *L'architecture romaine du début du IIIe siècle av. J.-C. à la fin du Haut-Empire*. Vol. 1, *Les monuments publics*, 2nd rev. ed. Paris: Picard.

Gros, P. 2002b. "Hadrien architecte: Bilan des recherches récentes." In Mosser and Lavagne 2002, 33–53.

Gros, P. 2003. "L'*opus signinum* selon Vitruve et dans la terminologie archéologique contemporaine." In Ciotta 2003, 1:142–52.

Gruen, E. S. 1992. *Culture and National Identity in Republican Rome*. Ithaca, NY: Cornell University Press.

Gualtieri, M. 2018. "Roman Villas in Southern Italy." In Marzano and Métraux 2018a, 159–76.

Guidobaldi, F. 2000. "Le abitazioni private e l'urbanistica." In Giardina 2000, 133–62.

Guidobaldi, F., and A. Salvatori. 1988. "The Introduction of Polychrome Marbles in Late Republican Rome: The Evidence from Mosaic Pavements with Marble Insertions." In Herz and Waelkens 1988, 171–75.

Gunther, R. T. 1913. *Pausilypon, the Imperial Villa near Naples, with a Description of the Submerged Foreshore and with Observations on the Tomb of Virgil and on Other Roman Antiquities on Posilipo*. Oxford: Oxford University Press. https://archive.org/details/pausily ponimper00gunt/page/4/mode/2up.

Hadas, D. 2017. "St. Augustine and the Disappearance of Varro." *BICS* 60:2, 76–91.

Hallet, C. H. 2019. "Sculpture: Statues, Busts, and Other Villa Furnishings of Bronze and of Marble." In Lapatin 2019, 71–97.

Hallett, J. P. 2021. "*Vilicus* and *Vilica* in the *De Agri Cultura*: The Elder Cato's Script for a Farming Couple." In Centlivres Challet 2021, 59–75.

Hannah, R. 2008. *Time in Antiquity*. London: Routledge.

Hansen, M. H., and T. Nielsen, eds. 2004. "Thessaly and Adjacent Regions." *An Inventory of Archaic and Classical poleis*. Danish National Research Foundation.; Københavns universitet. Polis centret 718. Oxford: Oxford University Press.

Harley, J. B., and D. Woodhouse, eds. 1987. *History of Cartography*. 3 vols. Chicago: University of Chicago Press.

Harrison, S., ed. 2007. *The Cambridge Companion to Horace*. Cambridge: Cambridge University Press.

Harter, B. 2016. "*De otio*—oder: die vielen Töchter der Muße. Ein semantischer Streifzug als literarische Spurensuche durch die römische Briefliteratur." In Eickhoff 2016b, 21–42.

Hartswick, K. J. 2004. *The Gardens of Sallust: A Changing Landscape*. Austin: University of Texas Press.

Haselberger, L., D. G. Romano, and E. A. Dumser, et al. 2002. *Mapping Augustan Rome*. *JRA*. Suppl. 50. Portsmouth, RI: Journal of Roman Archaeology.

Häuber, C. 1998. "The Esquiline Horti: New Research." In Frazer 1998, 55–64.

Häuber, C. 2014. *The Eastern Part of the Mons Oppius in Rome: The Sanctuary of Isis et Serpis in Regio III, the Temples of Minerva Medica, Fortuna Virgo and Dea Syria, and the Horti of Maecenas*. BullComm Suppl. 22. Rome: "L'Erma" di Bretschneider.

Häuber, C., F. X. Schütz, and G. M. Winder, eds. 2014. *Reconstruction and the Historic City: Rome and Abroad*. Beiträge zur Wirtschaftsgeographie München 6. Munich: Ludwig-Maximilians-Universität.

Haug, A. and P.-A. Kreuz. 2021. "The Diversity of Pompeii's Domestic Cult Activity." *Open Arts Journal* (January 2021).

Haury, J., ed. 1905–1913. *Procopii Caesariensis opera omnia*. 3 vols. in 4. Leipzig: B. G. Teubner.

Haywood, R. M. 1958. "Let's Run Down To Baiae." *Archaeology* 11(3):200–205.

Heath, M. 2008. "Aristotle on Natural Slavery." *Phronesis* 53(3):243–70.

Heather, P. 1991. *Goths and Romans*. Oxford: Oxford University Press.

Heather, P. 1992. "The Emergence of the Visigothic Kingdom." In Drinkwater and Elton 1992, 84–94.

Heerink, M., and E. Meijer, eds. 2022. *Flavian Responses to Nero's Rome*. Amsterdam: Amsterdam University Press.

Heinen, H., ed. 2010. *Antike Sklaverei: Rückblick und Ausblick. Neue Beiträge zur Forschungsgeschichte und zur Erschliessung der archäologischen Zeugnisse*. Stuttgart: Steiner.

Heinrich, F. 2017. "Modelling Crop-Selection in Roman Italy: The Economics of Agricultural Decision Making in a Globalizing Economy." In de Haas and Tol 2017, 141–69.

Heldring, B. 1998. *Satricum: A Town in Latium*. Satricana 1. Amsterdam: Dutch Center for Latium Studies.

Helmer, É. 2021. Oikonomia: *Philosophie grecque de l'économie*. Paris: Classiques Garnier.

Hemelrijk, H. 2015. *Hidden Lives, Public Personae: Women and Civic Life in the Roman West*. Oxford: Oxford University Press.

Henderson, J. 2004. *Morals and Villas in Seneca's Letters: Places to Dwell*. Cambridge: Cambridge University Press.

Hendrix, H. 2018. "Virgil's Tomb in Scholarly and Popular Culture." In Goldschmidt and Graziosi 2018, 281–98.

Hentz, G. 1979. "Les sources grecques dans les écrits des agronomes latins." *Ktema* 4:151–60.

Herrmann-Otto, E. 2009. *Sklaveri und Freilassung in der griechisch-römischen Welt*. Studienbücher antike 15. Hildesheim: George Olms.

Herrmann-Otto, E. 2010. "Das Projekt 'Forschungen zur antiken Sklaverei' an der Akademie der Wissenschaften und der Literatur, Mainz." In Heinen 2010, 61–76.

Herz, N., and M. Waelkens, eds. 1988. *Classical Marble: Geochemistry, Technology, Trade*. NATO ASI Series E: Applied Sciences 153. Dordrecht: Kluwer Academic.

Herz, P., and G. Waldherr, eds. 2001. *Landwirtschaft im Imperium Romanum*. Gutenberg: Scripta Mercaturae.

Higgenbotham, J. A. 1997. Piscinae: *Artificial Fishponds in Roman Italy*. Chapel Hill: University of North Carolina Press.

Higman, B. W. 2017. "Demographic Trends." In Eltis et al. 2017, 20–48.

Hilbold, I.. 2021. "Les *horti* de Rome, 'une maison comme les autres'? Pratiques résidentielles aristocratiques dans la *Correspondance* de Cicéron." In Späth 2021, 115–29.

Hillier, B., and J. Hanson. 1984. *The Social Logic of Space*. Cambridge: Cambridge University Press.

Himmelmann, N. 1995. *Sperlonga: Die homerischen Gruppen und ihre Bildquellen*. Nordrhein-Westfälische Akademie der Wissenschaften und der Künste; Vorträge: Geisteswissenschaften 340. Opladen: Westdeutscher Verlag.

Hinard, F. 1985. *Les proscriptions de la Rome républicaine*. CÉFR 83. Paris: De Boccard.

Hochscheid, H., and B. Russell, eds. 2021. *The Value of Making: Theory and Practice in Ancient Craft Production*. Studies in Classical Archaeology 13. Turnhout: Brepols.

Hodkinson, S., M. Kleijwegt, and K. Vlassopoulos, eds. 2016–. *The Oxford Handbook of Greek and Roman Slaveries*. Oxford: Oxford University Press. https://academic.oup.com/edited-volume/40302.

Hoepfner, W., and G. Brands, eds. 1996. *Basileia: Die Paläste der hellenistischen Könige*. Schriften des Seminars für Klassische Archäologie der Freien Universität Berlin 12. Mainz: Philipp von Zabern.

Hoepfner, W., and E.-L. Schwandner. 1994. *Haus und Stadt im klassischen Griechenland*. Wohnen in der klassischen Polis 1. 2nd ed. Munich: Deutscher Kunstverlag.

Hoffmann-Salz, J. 2011. *Die wirtschaftlichen Auswirkungen der römischen Eroberung: Vergleichende Untersuchungen der Provinz Hispania Tarraconensis, Africa Proconsularis und Syria*. Historia Einzelschrift 218. Stuttgart: Franz Steiner.

Hofmann, H. ed. 1999. *Latin Fiction: The Latin Novel in Context*. London: Routledge. E-book.

Holleran, C., and A. Claridge, eds. 2018. *Blackwell Companion to the City of Rome*. Malden, MA: Wiley-Blackwell.

Houston, G. W. 2003. "Galen, His Books, and the Horrea Piperataria at Rome." *MAAR* 48:45–51.

Howe, T. N. 2018. "The Social Status of the Villas of Stabiae." In Marzano and Métraux 2018a, 97–119.

Huffman, C. A., ed. 2014. *A History of Pythagoreanism*. Cambridge: Cambridge University Press.

Hunt, J., ed. 1992. *The Pastoral Landscape*. Studies in the History of Art 36. London and Washington, DC: Center for Advanced Study in the Visual Arts and National Gallery of Art.

Hunt, P. 2018. *Ancient Greek and Roman Slavery*. Chichester, UK: Wiley Blackwell.

Hunter, D. G., P. J. J. van Geest, and B. J. Lietaert Peerbolte, eds. 2018. *Brill Encyclopedia of Early Christianity Online*. Leiden: Brill. https://referenceworks.brillonline.com/entries/brill-encyclopedia-of-early-christianity-online/.

Hunter, R. 2014. *Hesiodic Voices: Studies in the Ancient Reception of Hesiod's* Works and Days. Cambridge: Cambridge University Press.

Hutchinson, G. 2016. "Muße ohne Müßiggang: Strukturen, Räume und das Ich bei Cicero." In Eickhoff 2016b, 97–111.

Ippoliti, M. 2020. *Tra il Tevere e la via Appia: Caratteri e sviluppo di un paesaggio suburbano di Roma antica tra IX secolo a.C. e VI secolo d.C*. Rome: Quasar.

Jacobs, I., ed. 2010. *Production and Prosperity in the Theodosian Period*. Proceedings of the Interdisciplinary Studies in Ancient Culture and Religion 14. Leuven: Peeters.

Jacobson, M., and P. Weitzman. 1992. "What Was Corinthian Bronze?" *AJA* 96:237–47.

Jeirani, Y. 2020. "The Politics of Benefit: On the Identity of Household Management and Politics in Xenophon's *Memorabilia*." *Greek, Roman, and Byzantine Studies* 60:36–60.

Johnson, D. M. 2021. *Xenophon's Socratic Works*. Routledge Monographs in Classical Studies. Abingdon, UK: Routledge.

Johnston, D. 1999. *Roman Law in Context*. Cambridge: Cambridge University Press.

Jolivet, V. 2018. "Urbs in rure: La lezione di Vitruvio." In Sciaramenti 2018. http://www.otium.unipg.it/otium/article/view/48/48.

Jones, B. W. 2002. *The Emperor Domitian*. London: Taylor and Francis e-Library; Routledge 1992.

Jones, J. E. 1975. "Town and Country Houses of Attica in Classical Times." In Mussche, Spitaels, and Goemare-De Poerck 1975, 63–136.

Jongman, W. 2002. "Beneficial Symbols: *Alimenta* and the Infantilization of the Roman Citizen." In Jongman and Kleijwegt 2002, 47–80.

Jongman, W., and M. Kleijwegt, eds. 2002. *After the Past: Essays in Ancient History in Honour of H.W. Pleket*. Leiden: Brill.

Joshel, S. R. 2011. "Slavery and Roman Literary Culture." In Bradley and Cartledge 2011, 214–40.

Joshel, S. R. 2013. "Geographies of Slave Containment and Movement." In George 2013, 99–128.

Joshel, S. R., and L. H. Petersen. 2016. *The Material Life of Roman Slaves*. Cambridge: Cambridge University Press.

Keaveney, A. 1992. *Lucullus: A Life*. London: Routledge.

Keeling, C. M. 2012. "The Marathon Casualty List from Eua-Loukou and the Plinthedon Style in Attic Inscriptions." *ZPE* 180:139–48.

Kehoe, D. P. 1997. *Investment Profit and Tenancy: The Jurists and the Roman Agrarian Economy*. Princeton: Princeton University Press.

Kehoe, D. P. 1988. *The Economics of Agriculture on Imperial Estates in Roman North Africa*. Hypomnemata 89. Göttingen: Vandenhoeck & Ruprecht.

Kehoe, D. P. 2007. *Law and the Rural Economy in the Roman Empire*. Ann Arbor; University of Michigan Press.

Kehoe, D. P. 2016. "Tenure of Land and Agricultural Regulation." In du Plessis, Ando, and Tuori 2016, 646–58.

Keith, A. 2016. "Imperial Leisure: The Politics, Poetics, and Philosophy of Leisure in Augustan Rome." In Eickhoff 2016b, 269–94.

Kennedy, G. A. 2003. *Progymnasmata: Greek Textbooks of Prose Composition and Rhetoric*. Atlanta, GA: Society of Biblical Literature.

Kessler, D., and P. Temin. 2007. "The Organization of the Grain Trade in the Early Roman Empire." *Economic History Review*, 60(2):313–32.

Kidd, D., ed. and trans. 1997. *Aratus: Phaenomena*. Cambridge: Cambridge University Press.

King, A. 1990. *Roman Gaul and Germany*. London: British Museum Publications.

Kleiner, D. E. E. 1977. *Roman Group Portraiture: The Funerary Reliefs of the Late Republic and Early Empire*. New York: Garland.

Kleiner, D. E. E. 1992. *Roman Sculpture*. New Haven: Yale University Press.

Klynne, A., and P. Liljenstolpe. 2000. "Where to Put Augustus? A Note on the Placement of the Prima Porta Statue." *AJP* 121(1):121–28.

Knoell, P., ed. 1886. *Eugippii Opera: Vita Severini*. Corpus Scriptorum Ecclesiasticorum Latinorum 9.2:Vienna: C. Gerold Sohn. https://books.google.ca/books?id =T7_mTaZ7QnYC&printsec =frontcover&redir_esc=y#v =onepage&q&f=false

Koortbojian, M. 2008. "The Double Identity of Portrait Statues: Costumes and Their Symbolism at Rome." In Edmonson and Keith 2008, 71–93.

Krause, C. 1977. "Grundformen des Griechischen Pastashauses." *AA* 1977:164–79.

Krause, C. 1998. "L'edificio residenziale di Villa Iovis." In Federico and Miranda 1998, 225–40.

Krause, C. 2003. *Villa Jovis: Die Residenz des Tiberius auf Capri*. Mainz: Philipp von Zabern.

Krause, J.-U. 1987. "Das spätantike Städtepatronat." *Chiron* 17:1–80.

Krautheimer, R., S. Corbett, and A. K. Frazer. 1977. *Corpus Basilicarum Christianarum Romae*. Vol. 5, *The Early Christian Basilicas of Rome (IV–IX Cent.)*. Vatican City: Pontificio Istituto di Archeologia Cristiana.

Kron, G. 2017. "The Diversification and Intensification of Italian Agriculture: The Complementary Roles of the Small and Wealthy Farmer." In de Haas and Tol 2017, 112–40.

Kronenberg, L. 2009. *Allegories of Farming from Greece and Rome: Philosophical Satire in Xenophon, Varro, and Virgil*. Cambridge: Cambridge University Press.

Kroos, K. A. 2011. "Central Heating for Caligula's Pleasure Ship". *International Journal for the History of Engineering and Technology* 81:291–99.

Kroppenberg, I. 2010. "Law, Religion and Constitution of the Vestal Virgins." *Law and Literature* 22(3):418–39.

Kulikowsky, M. 2001. "The Visigothic Settlement in Aquitania: The Imperial Perspective." In Mathisen and Shanzer 2001, 26–38.

Kuttner, A. L. 1999a. "Looking Outside Inside: Ancient Roman Garden Rooms." *Studies in the History of Gardens and Designed Landscapes* 19(1):7–35.

Kuttner, A. L. 1999b. "Culture and History at Pompey's Museum." *TAPA* 129, 343–73.

Lacerenza, G. 2002. "Masgaba, dilectus Augusti." In Casaburi and Lacerenza 2002, 73–92.

La Donna Romana. 2009. *La Donna Romana: Immagini e Vita Quotidiana. Atti de Convegno, Astina, 7 Marzo 2009*. Cassino: Diana.

Laes, C., and V. Vuolanto. 2017, eds. *Children and Everyday Life in the Roman and Late Antique World*. London: Routledge.

Lafon, X. 2001. *Villa maritima: Recherches sur les villas littorales de l' Italie romaine (IIIe siècle av J.-C. /

IIIe siècle ap. J.-C.). Bibliothèque de l'École française de Rome 307. Paris and Rome: De Boccard and "L'Erma" di Bretschneider.

Lafon, X. 2018. Review of Marzano and Métraux 2018. *Topoi. Orient-Occident* 22:453–68.

Lahusen, G. 1985. "Zur Funktion und Rezeption des römischen Ahnenbildes." *RM* 92: 261–89.

Lancaster, L. C. 2021. "Mortars and Plasters—How Mortars Were Made: The Literary Sources." In Gliozzo and Pizzo 2021.

Landwehr, C. 1985. *Die antiken Gipsabgüsse aus Baiae: Griechische Bronzestatuen in abgüssen römischer Zeit*. Berlin: Gebr. Mann.

Lapatin, K., ed. 2019. *Buried by Vesuvius: The Villa dei Papiri at Herculaneum*. Los Angeles: J. Paul Getty Museum.

Launaro, A. 2011. *Peasants and Slaves: The Rural Population of Roman Italy (200 BC–AD 100)*. Cambridge: Cambridge University Press.

Launaro, A. 2017. "Something Old, Something New: Social and Economic Developments in the Countryside of Roman Italy between Republic and Empire." In de Haas and Tol, 85–111.

Laurence, P., ed. and trans. 2002. *Gérontius: La vie latine de Sainte Mélanie*. Studium Biblicum Franciscanum Collection minor 41. Jerusalem: Franciscan Printing Press.

Laurence, R., and A. Wallace-Hadrill, eds. 1997. *Domestic Space in the Roman World: Pompeii and Beyond*. JRA Suppl. 22). Portsmouth, RI: Journal of Roman Archaeology.

Lavan, M., and C. Ando, eds. 2021. *Roman and Local Citizenship in the Long Second Century CE*. Oxford Studies in Early Empires. Oxford: Oxford University Press.

Leach, E. W. 1997 "Oecus on Ibycus: Investigating the Vocabulary of the Roman House." In Bon-Harper and Jones 1997, 50–72.

Leach, E. W. 2003. "*Otium* as *Luxuria*: Economy of Status in the Younger Pliny's Letters." *Arethusa* 36:147–65.

Le Corbusier (Charles-Édouard Jeanneret) 1923. *Vers une architecture nouvelle*. Paris: Éditions G. Crès et Cie. (1st ed., many reprints and translations).

Lee Too, Y., ed. 2001. *Education in Greek and Roman Antiquity*. Boston: Brill.

Leen, A. 1991. "Cicero and the Rhetoric of Art." *AJP* 112:229–45.

Lehmann, T. 2004. *Paulinus Nolanus und die Basilica Nova in Cimitile/Nola: Studien zu einem zentralen Denkmal der spätantik-frühchristlichen Architektur*. Wiesbaden: Reichert.

Lengrand, D. 1994. "'L'essai sur le règne de Domitien' de S. Gsell et la réévaluation du règne de Domitien." In Pailler and Sablayrolles 1994, 57–67.

Lenoir, M., D. Manacorda, and C. Panella. 1989. *Amphores romaines et histoire économique: Dix ans de recherche; Actes du colloque de Sienne, 22–24 mai 1986*. Rome : École française de Rome.

Lenski, N. 2023. "Slavery in the Roman Empire." In Pargas and Schiel 2023, 87–107.

Leoni, V. 2008. "La forma antica di Arpinum." In Quilici and Quilici-Gigli 2008, 127–90.

Levick, B. 1972. "Tiberius' Retirement to Rhodes in 6 BC." *Latomus* 31:779–813.

Levick, B. 1999a. *Tiberius the Politician*. Roman Imperial Biographies. 2nd ed. London: Routledge.

Levick, B. 1999b. *Vespasian*. Roman Imperial Biographies. Oxford: Routledge.

Levick, B. 2002. "Corbulo's Daughter." *Greece & Rome* 49(2):199–211.

Lewis, D. M. 2018. *Greek Slave Systems in Their Eastern Mediterranean Context, c. 800–146 BC*. Oxford: Oxford University Press.

Lewit, T. 2004. *Villas, Farms and the Late Roman Rural Economy (Third to Fifth Centuries AD)*. Rev. ed. of T. Lewit, 1991, *Agricultural Production in the Roman Economy, A.D. 200–400*.

BAR International Series 568. Oxford: Archaeopress.

Libertini, G. 2018. *Liber Coloniarum / Libro delle Colonie*. English translation by G. Libertini and W. Lorenz: 2019, *Liber Coloniarium (The Book of the Colonies)*. Naples: Istituto di Studi Atellani.

Lindsay, J., trans. (1927) 1944. *The Complete Works of Gaius Petronius Done into English*. London: Fanfrolico Press. Reprint New York: Wiley.

Lindsay, W. M., ed. 1913. *Sexti Pompei Festi De verborum significatu quae supersunt cum Pauli epitome; Thewrewkianis copiis usus*. Leipzig: B. G. Teubner.

Ling, R. 1977. "Studius and the Beginnings of Roman Landscape Painting." *JRS* 67:1–16.

Ling, R. 1991. *Roman Painting*. Cambridge: Cambridge University Press.

Lintott, A. 1992. "The Roman Empire and Its Problems in the Late Second Century." *CAH* 9, pt. 1, 16–39.

Lintott, A. 2008. "The Crisis of the Republic: Sources and Source-Problems." *CAH* 9, pt. 1, 1–15.

Lippolis, E. 1997. *Fra Taranto e Roma: Società e cultura urbana in Puglia tra Annibale e l'età imperiale*. Taranto: Scorpione.

Lippolis, E. 2006. "Aristocrazia romana e italica nelle ville della Regio II." In Ortalli 2006, 43–84.

Liverani, P. 2020. "The Evolution of the Lateran: From the *Domus* to the Episcopal Complex." In Bosman, Haynes, and Liverani 2020, 6–24.

Lo Cascio, E. 1999. "Popolazione e risorse agricole nell'Italia del II secolo a.C." In Vera 1999, 217–45.

Lo Cascio, E. 2000a. "*Alimenta Italiae*." In González Fernández 2000, 287–312.

Lo Cascio, E., ed. 2000b. *Mercati permanenti e mercati periodici nel mondo romano: Atti degli Incontri capresi di storia dell'economia antica, Capri, 13–15 ottobre 1997*. Pragmateiai 2. Bari: Edipuglia.

Lomas, K., and T. Cornell, eds. 2003. *"Bread and Circuses": Euergetism and Municipal Patronage in Roman Italy*. London: Routledge.

Loos, C. B. 2011. *Adolf Loos: A Private Portrait*. Los Angeles: Doppelhouse Press. Translated by C. Pontasch and N. Saunders of C. B. Loos, 1936, *Adolf Loos Privat*. Vienna: Verlag der Johannes-Presse.

Lucciano, M. 2021. "Socrate comme personnage de dialogue à Rome: Quelques exemples chez Plaute, Lucilius et Cicéron." In Müller 2021, 69–87.

Luciani, F. 2020. "Public Slaves in Rome: 'Privileged' or Not?" *Classical Quarterly* 70:368–84.

Luciani, F. 2022. *Slaves of the People: A Political and Social History of Roman Public Slavery*. Stuttgart: Franz Steiner.

Lugli, G. 1927. "Studi topografici intorno alle ville suburbane: Villa Adriana; Le fasi della Villa di Adriana al tardo impero." *BullComm* 54–55, 139–204.

Lulof, P. S., and C. J. Smith, eds. 2017. *The Age of Tarquinius Superbus: A Paradigm Shift? Rome, 7–9 November 2013*. BABesch Suppl. 29. Louvain: Peeters.

L'Urbs: Espace urbain et histoire. 1987. *L'Urbs: Espace urbain et histoire (1er siècle av. J.-C.–IIIe siècle ap. J.-C.): Actes du colloque international de Rome (8–12 mai 1985)*. CÉFR 98. Rome: École française de Rome.

MacDonald, W. L. 1982. *The Architecture of the Roman Empire*. Vol. 1: *An Introductory Study*. New Haven: Yale University Press.

MacDonald, W. L. 1986. *The Architecture of the Roman Empire*. Vol. 2: *An Urban Appraisal*. New Haven: Yale University Press.

MacDonald, W. L., and J. Pinto. 1995. *Hadrian's Villa and Its Legacy*. New Haven: Yale University Press.

MacDougall, E. B., ed. 1987. *Ancient Roman Gardens*, Dumbarton Oaks Colloquium on the History of Landscape Architecture 10. Washington, DC: Dumbarton Oaks Trustees for Harvard University.

MacMullen, R. 1963. *Soldier and Civilian in the Later Roman Empire*. Cambridge, MA: Harvard University Press.

MacMullen, R. 1970. "Market Days in the Roman Empire." *Phoenix* 24:333–41.

Maffei, A., and F. Nastasi, eds. 1990. *Caere e il suo territorio: Da Agylla a Centumcellae*. Rome: Istituto Poligrafico e Zecca dello Stato.

Manacorda, D. 1981. "Produzione agricola, produzione ceramica e proprietari nell'ager Cosanus nel I secolo a.C." In Giardina and Schiavone 1981, 2:3–54.

Manessy-Guitton, J., ed. 1993. *Les phytonymes grecs et latins: Actes du Colloque international tenu à Nice les 14–16 mai 1992*. Centre de Recherches comparatives sur les Langues de la Méditerranée ancienne 12). Nice: LAMA.

Manuwald, G., ed. and trans. 2021. *Cicero,* Post reditum *Speeches*. Oxford: Oxford University Press.

Maraval, P., ed. and trans. 1971. *Grégoire de Nysse: Vie de Sainte Macrine*. Sources chrétiennes 178. Paris: Editions du Cerf.

Marcellinus comes, Chronicum. In J. P. Migne, *Patrologia Latina* 51, 917–48. https://play.google.com/books/reader?id=8UCLym0mN28C&pg=GBS.PA915&hl=en_GB.

Marconi, G. 1998a. "Le origini di Centumcellae." *Rivista di cultura classica e medioevale* 40(3/4):195–214.

Marconi, G. 1998b. "Traiano, Plinio ed il Porto di Centumcellae." *Rivista di cultura classica e medioevale* 40(1/2):33–40.

Marcovich, M., ed. and trans. 1989. *Prosper of Aquitaine:* De providentia Dei. Suppl. to Vigiliae Christianae 10. Leiden: Brill.

Mari, Z. 2004. "La villa di Traiano ad Arcinazzo Romano." *FastiOnline*. www.fastionline.org/docs/2004-1.pdf.

Mari, Z. 2014. "La Villa di Traiano ad Arcinazzo Romano: Stato delle ricerche e itinerario di visita." *Atti e Memorie della Società Tiburtina* 87, 97–124.

Marks, R., and M. Mogetta, eds. 2021. *Domitian's Rome and the Augustan Legacy*. Ann Arbor: University of Michigan Press.

Martin, J., ed. and trans. 1998. *Aratos: Phénomènes*. 2 vols. Paris: Collection Budé.

Martin, R. 1967. "Pline le Jeune et les problèmes économiques de son temps." *Revue des Études Anciennes* 69, 62–97.

Martin, R. 1971. *Recherches sur les agronomes latins et leurs conceptions économiques et sociales*. Paris: Les Belles Lettres.

Martin, R., ed. and trans. 1976. *Palladius: Traité d'agriculture, Livres I et II*. Collection des Universités de France. Paris: Les Belles Lettres. (See also Girard and Martin 2010).

Martin, R. 1995. "Les Sources littéraires de la notion de 'latifundium.'" In *Du latifundium au latifondo* 1995, 97–106.

Marzano, A. 2007. *Roman Villas in Central Italy: A Social and Economic History*. Columbia Studies in the Classical Tradition 30. Leiden: Brill.

Marzano, A. 2010. "Le ville maritime tra *amoenitas* e *fructus*." *Amoenitas: Rivista di Studi Miscellanei sulla Villa Romana* 1:21–33.

Marzano, A. 2013a. "Capital Investment and Agriculture: Multi-Press Facilities from Gaul, the Iberian Peninsula, and the Black Sea Region." In Bowman and Wilson 2013a, 107–41.

Marzano, A. 2013b. *Harvesting the Sea: The Exploitation of Marine Resources in the Roman Mediterranean*. Oxford Studies in the Roman Economy. Oxford: Oxford University Press.

Marzano, A. 2018. "Maritime Villas and the Resources of the Sea." In Marzano and Métraux 2018a, 125–40.

Marzano, A. 2020. "A Story of Land and Water: Control, Capital, and Investment in Large-Scale Fishing and Fish-Salting Operations." In Erdkamp, Verboven, and Zuiderhoek 2020, 275–305.

Marzano, A. 2022. *Plants, Politics and Empire in Ancient Rome*. Cambridge: Cambridge University Press.

Marzano, A., and G. Brizzi. 2009. "Costly Display or Economic Investment? A Quantitative Approach to the Study of Roman Marine Aquaculture." *JRA* 22:215–30.

Marzano, A., and G. P. R. Métraux, eds. 2018a. *The Roman Villa in the Mediterranean Basin: Late Republic to Late Antiquity.* Cambridge: Cambridge University Press.

Marzano, A., and G. P. R. Métraux. 2018b. "The Roman Villa: An Overview." In Marzano and Métraux 2018a, 1–41.

Masciale, L. 2019. "Atria publica populi romani: Structures Contaminated by Memory." In Bartz 2019a, 48–78.

Mastrodonato, V. 1999–2000. "Una residenza imperiale nel suburbio di Roma: La Villa di Lucio Vero in località Acquatraversa." *ArchCl* 51:157–235.

Mathisen, R. W., and D. Shanzer, eds. 2001. *Society and Culture in Late Antique Gaul: Revisiting the Sources.* London: Routledge.

Mathisen, R. W., and H. Sivan, eds. 1996. *Shifting Frontiers in Late Antiquity: Papers from the First Interdisciplinary Conferences on Late Antiquity, the University of Kansas, March, 1995.* Brookfield, VT: Variorum.

Matthews, J. 1998. *Western Aristocracies and Imperial Court A.D. 364–425.* Oxford: Oxford University Press.

Mattusch, C. C. 2003. "Corinthian Bronze: Famous, but Elusive." In *Corinth, The Centenary: 1896–1996,* 219–32.

Mau, A. 1882. *Geschichte der decorativen Wandmalerei in Pompeji.* Berlin: Reimer.

McGinn, T. A. J. 2013. "Roman Children and the Law." In Evans Grubbs, Parkin, and Bell 2013, 341–64.

McGuckin, J. A. 2010. "Embodying the New Society: The Byzantine Christian Instinct of Philanthropy." In *Philanthropy and Social Compassion in Eastern Orthodox Tradition: Papers of the Sophia Institute Academic Conference, New York, Dec. 2009,* 50–71.

McHugh, M. P. 1964. *The Carmen de Providentia Dei Attributed to Prosper of Aquitaine: A Revised Text with an Introduction, Translation, and Notes.* Catholic University of America Patristic Studies 97. Washington, DC: The Catholic University of America Press.

McHugh, M. P. 1968. "Observations on the Text of the *Carmen de Providentia Dei.*" *Manuscripta* 12(1):3–9.

McHugh, M. P. 1970. "Observations on the Text of the *Carmen de Ingratis.*" *Manuscripta* 14(3):179–85.

McKeown, N. 2002. "Seeing Things: Examining the Body of the Slave in Greek Medicine." In Wiedemann and Gardner 2002, 29–40.

McKeown, N. 2007. *The Invention of Ancient Slavery?* London: Duckworth.

McKeown, N. 2010. "Inventing Slaveries: Switching the Argument." In Heinen 2010, 39–59.

McLaughlin, R. 2014. *The Roman Empire and the Indian Ocean: The Ancient World Economy and the Kingdoms of Africa, Arabia and India.* Barnsley, UK: Pen & Sword Military.

McLynn, N. B. 1995. "Paulinus the Impenitent: A Study of the *Eucharisticos.*" *JECS* 3(4):461–86.

Messineo, G., and L. Calvelli. 2001. "Ad Gallinas Albas: Villa di Livia." *BullCom* Suppl. 8. Rome: "L'Erma" di Bretschneider.

Métraux, G. P. R. 1998. "Villa rustica alimentaria et annonaria." In Frazer 1998, 1–19.

Métraux, G. P. R. 2003. Review of Laurence and Wallace-Hadrill 1997, *Phoenix* 57(2):394–99.

Métraux, G. P. R. 2006. "Consumers' Choices: Aspects of the Arts in the Age of Late Roman 'Mechanical' Reproduction." In D'Ambra and Métraux 2006, 134–51.

Métraux, G. P. R. 2008. "Prudery and *Chic* in Late Antique Clothing." In Edmonson and Keith 2008, 271–93.

Métraux, G. P. R. 2014. "Some Other Literary Villas of Roman Antiquity Besides Pliny's." In Reeve 2014, 27–40.

Métraux, G. P. R. 2015. "Masonry and Memory in Hadrian's Architecture and

Architectural Rhetoric." In Favro et al. 2015, 139–49.

Métraux, G. P. R. 2018. "Late Antique Villa: Themes." In Marzano and Métraux 2018a, 401–25.

Metzger, E., ed. 1998. *A Companion to Justinian's "Institutes."* Ithaca, NY: Cornell University Press.

Michel, E. 2000. "La justice selon Verrès." *Revue d'histoire du droit* 78, 661–70.

Mielsch, H. 1987. *Die römische Villa: Architektur und Lebensform.* Munich: C.H. Beck.

Mierow, C. C., trans. 1915. *The Gothic History of Jordanes in English Version.* 2nd rev. ed. Merchantville and Princeton: Evolution Publishing and Princeton University Press. http://ia800303.us.archive.org/1/items/gothichistoryofj00jord/gothichistoryofj00jord.pdf.

Miller, N. 1982. *Heavenly Caves: Reflections on the Garden Grotto.* New York: Braziller.

Mingazzini, P., and F. Pfister. 1946. *Surrentum.* In *Forma Italiae: Regio I.* Vol. 2:54–70. Florence: Sansoni.

Momigliano, A. 1954. "An Unsolved Problem of Historical Forgery: The *scriptores historiae augustae*." *Journal of the Warburg and Courtauld Institutes* 17(1/2):22–46.

Momigliano, A., and A. Schiavone, eds. 1988–1992. *Storia di Roma.* 4 vols. Turin: Einaudi.

Momigliano, A. 2006. "Moses Finley on Slavery: A Personal Note." In Finley 2006, 1–8.

Mommaerts, T. S. M., and D. H. Kelley. 1992. "The Anicii of Gaul and Rome." In Drinkwater and Elton 1992, 119–29.

Mommsen, T., ed. 1882. *Iordanis, Romana et Getica: De Origine Actibusque Getarum,* 53–138. MGH-AA 5.1. Berlin: Weidmann.

Mommsen, T., ed. 1894a. *Cassiodori Senatoris Variae.* I: *Epistulae Theodericianae Variae,* 10–392. MGH-AA 12. Berlin: Weidmann. https://archive.org/details/cassiodorisenato12cass/page/n5/mode/2up?view=theater.

Mommsen, T., ed. 1894b. *Chronica Minora Saec. IV.V.VI.VII: Marcellini V.c. Comitis Chronicon,* 60–108. MGH-AA 11. Berlin: Weidmann. https://archive.org/details/sim_monumenta-germaniae-historica_1894_11.

Montanari, F., A. Rengakos, and C. Tsagalis, eds. 2009. *Brill's Companion to Hesiod.* Leiden: Brill.

Monterroso Checa. A. 2010. *Theatrum Pompei: Forma y arquitectura de la génesis del modelo teatral de Roma.* Serie Arqueológica 12. Madrid: Consejo Superior de Investigaciones Científicas.

Moormann, E. M. 1998. "Vivere come un uomo: L'uso dello spazio nella *Domus Aurea.*" In Cima and La Rocca 1998, 345–61.

Moormann, E. M. 2003. "Some Observations on Nero and the City of Rome." In De Blois et al. 2003, 376–88.

Moormann, E. M. 2020. *Nerone, Roma e la Domus Aurea: Unione Internazionale degli Istituti di Archeologia, Storia e Storia dell'Arte in Roma Conferenze 33.* Rome: Arbor Sapientiae.

Moreau, J., and V. Velkov, eds. 1968. *Excerpta Valesiana.* Leipzig: K.G. Saur.

Moretti Cursi, G. 2019. "Roman *horti*: A Topographical View in the Imperial Era." In Bartz 2019a, 124–40.

Morricone, M. L. 1980. *Scutulata pavimenta: I pavimenti con inserti di marmo o di pietra trovati a Roma e nei dintorni.* Studi e materiali del Museo della civiltà romana 9. Rome: "L'Erma" di Bretschneider.

Morvillez, É. 2017. "'Avec vue sur jardin': Vivre entre nature et paysage dans l'architecture domestique, de Cicéron à Sidoine Apollinaire." *Cahiers mondes anciens* 9. https://doi.org/10.4000/mondesanciens.1926.

Mossé, C. 1975. "Xénophon économiste." In Bingen, Cambier, and Nachtergael 1975, 169–76.

Mosser, M., and H. Lavagne, eds. 2002. *Hadrien, Empereur et architecte: La Villa d'Hadrien. Tradition et modernité d'un paysage culturel; Actes du colloque international organisé par le Centre culturel du Panthéon en collaboration avec la Mairie de Paris*. Geneva: Vögele.

Mouritsen, H. 2011. *The Freedman in the Roman World*. Cambridge: Cambridge University Press.

Moussy, C. 1974. *Paulin de Pella: Poème d'action de gràces et Prière*. Paris: Les éditions du Cerf.

Mratschek, S. 2001. "*Multis enim notissima est sanctitas loci*: Paulinus and the Gradual Rise of Nola as a Center of Christian Hospitality." *JECS* 9:511–53.

Müller, G. M., ed. 2021. *Figurengestaltung und Gesprächsinteraktion im antiken Dialog*. Palingenesia 126, 55–68. Stuttgart: Franz Steiner.

Müller-Wiener, W. 1988. *Griechisches Bauwesen in der Antike*. Munich: C.H. Beck.

Mussche, H., P. Spitaels, and F. Goemare-De Poerck, eds. 1975. *Thorikos and the Laurion in Archaic and Classical Times: Papers and Contributions of the Colloquium Held in March, 1973, at the State University of Ghent*. Miscellanea Graeca 1. Ghent: Belgian Archaeological Mission in Greece.

Naber, S. A., ed. 1867. *M. Cornelii Frontonis et M. Aurelii Imperatoris Epistulae: L. Veri et T. Antonini Pii et Appiani Epistularum Reliquiae: Post Angelum Maium cum codicibus Ambrosiano et Vaticano iterum contulit G. N. du Rieu*. Leipzig: B. G. Teubner.

Nadon, C. 2021. "Leo Strauss's First Brush with Xenophon: 'The Spirit of Sparta or the Taste of Xenophon.'" *Review of Politics* 83:69–90.

Neger, M. 2016. "*Satius est enim otiosum esse quam nihil agere*: Die Inszenierung von Mußezeit und Mußeräumen im Briefkorpus des Jüngeren Plinius." In Eickhoff 2016b, 133–60.

Netzer, E., Y. Kalman, R. Porath, and R. Cachy-Laureys. 2010. "Preliminary Report on Herod's Mausoleum and Theatre with a Royal Box at Herodium," *JRA* 23:84–108.

Neudecker, R. 1988. *Die Skulpturenausstattung römischer Villen in Italien*. Mainz: Philipp von Zabern.

Neudecker, R. 2014. "Die Villa Hadriana als Modell für Herodes Atticus." In Calandra and Adembri 2014, 135–54.

Nevett, L. C. 1999. *House and Society in the Ancient Greek World*. Cambridge: Cambridge University Press.

Nevett, L. C. 2010. *Domestic Space in Classical Antiquity*. Cambridge: Cambridge University Press.

Newlands, C. E. 2011. *Statius: Silvae Book II*. Cambridge: Cambridge University Press.

Nicholls, M. C. 2011. "Galen and Libraries in the *Peri Alupias*." *JRS* 101:123–42.

Nicholls, M. C. 2014. "A Library at Antium?" In Rothschild and Thompson 2014a, 65–78.

Nichols, M. F. 2017. *Author and Audience in Vitruvius'* De architectura. Cambridge: Cambridge University Press.

Nielsen, I. 2001a. "The Gardens of Hellenistic Palaces." In Nielsen 2001b, 165–85.

Nielsen, I., ed. 2001b. *The Royal Palace Institution in the First Millennium BC: Regional Development and Cultural Interchange between East and West*. Athens: Danish Institute at Athens.

Nielsen, I. 2013. "Types of Gardens." In Gleason 2013, 41–74.

Nielsen, I., and H. S. Nielsen, eds. 1998. *Meals in a Social Context: Aspects of the Communal Meal in the Hellenistic and Roman World*. Aarhus: Aarhus University Press.

Nisbet, R. 2007. "Horace: Life and Chronology." In Harrison 2007, 7–28.

Nixon, C. E. V. 1992. "Relations between Visigoths and Romans in Fifth-Century Gaul." In Drinkwater and Elton 1992, 64–74.

Oakley, S. P. 1997–2005. *A Commentary on Livy Books VI–X*. 4 vols. Oxford: Oxford University Press.

Oleson, J. P. 2000. "Water-Lifting." In Wikander 2000, 217–302.

Oliver, R. P. 1977. "The Praenomen of Tacitus." *AJP* 98(1):64–70.

Olshausen, E., 2010. "The Augustan Division of Rome and Italy into Regions: II Italy." In *Brill's New Pauly Supplements I*. Vol. 3, *Historical Atlas of the Ancient World*, English edition by Christine Salazar.

Omerod, H. A. (1924) 1978. *Piracy in the Ancient World: An Essay in Mediterranean History.* Liverpool: University Press of Liverpool. Reprint Totowa, NJ: Rowman and Littlefield.

Opper, T. 2021. *Nero: The Man behind the Myth, 27 May 2021–24 Oct 2021.* Exhibition catalogue. London: Trustees of the British Museum.

Ortalli, J., ed. 2006. *Vivere in villa: La qualità delle residenze agresti in età romana: Atti del Convegno, Ferrara, gennaio 2003.* Florence: Le lettere.

Ortolani, G. 1998. *Il Padiglione di Afrodite Cnidia a Villa Adriana: Progetto e Significato.* Rome: Librerie Dedalo.

Osbaldeston, T. A., and R. P. A. Wood, trans. 2000. *Dioscurides:* De Materia Medica. Johannesburg: Ibidis.

Otten, W., and K. Pollmann, eds. 2007. *Poetry and Exegesis in Premodern Latin Christianity. The Encounter between Classical and Christian Strategies of Interpretation.* Suppl. to *Vigiliae Christianae* 87.

Pagano, M. and R. Prisciandaro. 2006. *Studio sulle provenienze degli oggetti rinvenuti negli scavi borbonici del regno di Napoli: Una lettura integrata, coordinata e commentata della documentazione.* 2 vols. Naples: Nicola Longobardi.

Pailler, J.-M., and R. Sablayrolles, eds. 1994. *Les années Domitien: Colloque organisé à l'Université de Toulouse-Le Mirail, les 12, 13 et 14 octobre 1992 à l'initiative du Groupe de recherche sur l'Antiquité classique et orientale (GRACO).* Pallas 40. Toulouse: Presses universitaires du Mirail.

Panagl, O. 2000. *"Otium honestum—labor improbus*: Wortgeschichtliche Betrachtungen im Sinnbezirk von Muss, Muße und Müßiggang." In Sigot 2000, 66–81.

Papaioannou, M. 2018. "Villas in Roman Greece." In Marzano and Métraux 2018a, 328–76.

Papi, E. 2002. "La turba inpia. Artigiani e commercianti del Foro Romano e dintorni (I sec a.C.–64 d.C.)." *JRA* 15:45–62.

Pappalardo, U. 2009. "The Roman Villas on the Bay of Naples." In De Simone and Macfarlane 2009, 25–48.

Pargas, D. A., and J. Schiel, eds. 2023. *The Palgrave Handbook of Global Slavery throughout History.* Cham, Switzerland: Palgrave Macmillan.

Park, J.-E. 2013. "Lacking Love or Conveying Love? The Fundamental Roots of the Donatists and Augustine's Nuanced Treatment of them." *Reformed Theological Review* 72:103–21.

Parker, H. N. 2004. "Why Were the Vestals Virgins? Or the Chastity of Women and the Safety of the Roman State" *AJP* 125(4):563–601.

Pasco-Pranger, M. 2015. "Finding Examples at Home: Cato, Curius Dentatus, and the Origins of Roman Literary Exemplarity." *Classical Antiquity* 34:296–321.

Passions, vertus et vices. 2009. *Passions, vertus et vices dans l'ancien roman: Actes du colloque de Tours, 19–21 octobre 2006, organisé par l'université François-Rabelais de Tours et l'UMR 5189, Histoire et Sources des Mondes Antiques.* Collection de la Maison de l'Orient méditerranéen ancien. Série littéraire et philosophique 42. Lyon: Maison de l'Orient et de la Méditerranée Jean Pouilloux.

Patlagean, É. 1977. *Pauvreté économique et pauvreté sociale à Byzance, 4e–7e siècles.* Paris: Mouton.

Patterson, H., and M. Millett 1998. "The Tiber Valley Project." *PBSR* 66:1–20.

Patterson, J. R. 2006. *Landscapes and Cities: Rural Settlement and Civic Transformation in Early Imperial Italy.* Oxford: Oxford University Press.

Pavis d'Escurac, H. 1976. *La Préfecture de l'annone, service administratif impérial d'Auguste à Constantin*. BÉFAR 226. Rome: École française de Rome.

Peiper, R., ed. 1886. *Decimi Magni Ausonii Burdigalensis: Opuscula*. Leipzig: B. G. Teubner.

Peña, J. T. 2017. "Issues in the Study of Rural Craft Production in Roman Italy." In de Haas and Tol, 203–30.

Pensabene, P., and S. Falzone. 2001. *Scavi del Palatino I: L'area sud-orientale del Palatino tra l'età protostorica e il IV secolo av.C.; Scavi e materiali della struttura ipogea sotto la cella del Tempio della Vittoria*. Rome: "L'Erma" di Bretschneider.

Percival, J. 1976. *The Roman Villa: An Historical Introduction*. London and Berkeley: Batsford and University of California Press.

Percival, J. 1992. "The Fifth-Century Villa: A New Life or Death Postponed?" In Drinkwater and Elton 1992, 156–64.

Pesando, F. 1987. *Oikos e ktesis: La casa greca in età classica*. Pubblicazioni degli istituti di storia della Facoltà di lettere e filosofia. Rome: Quasar.

Pesando, F. 1989. *La casa dei greci*. Milan: Longanesi.

Phillips, D. 2001. "Tertullian on the Opening of Pompey's Theater in Rome." *Syllecta Classica* 12:208–20.

Picard, G.-Ch. 1964. "'L'aedes Libertatis' de Clodius sur le Palatin." *RA* 1964(2):198–99.

Piranomonte, M. 2010. "Religion and Magic at Rome: The Fountain of Anna Perenna." In Gordon and Simón 2010, 191–213.

Piranomonte, M., J. Polakova, and I. A. Rapinesi. 2002. *Il santuario della musica e il bosco sacro di Anna Perenna*. Milan: Ministero per I Beni e le Attività Culturali. Soprintendenza Archeologica di Roma.

Pleket, H. W. 1993. "Agriculture in the Roman Empire in Comparative Perspective." In Sancisi-Weerdenburg et al. 1993, 317–42.

Plommer, H. 1973. *Vitruvius and Later Roman Building Manuals*. Cambridge: Cambridge University Press.

Pollitt, J. J. 1965. *The Art of Greece 1400–31 B.C. Sources and Documents in the History of Art*. Englewood Cliffs, NJ: Prentice-Hall.

Pollitt, J. J. 1966. *The Art of Rome c. 753 B.C.–337 A.D. Sources and Documents in the History of Art*. Englewood Cliffs, NJ: Prentice-Hall.

Pollitt, J. J., ed. 2015. *The Cambridge History of Painting in the Classical World*. Cambridge: Cambridge University Press.

Pomeroy, S. B. 1994. *Xenophon, Oeconomicus: A Social and Historical Commentary*. Oxford: Clarendon Press.

Pomeroy, S. B. (1989) 2010. "Slavery in the Greek Domestic Economy in the Light of Xenophon's *Oeconomicus*." *Quaderni camerti di studi romanistici* 17:11–18. Reprinted in Gray 2010, 31–40.

Powell, J. G. F. 1988. *Cicero: Cato Maior De Senectute*. Cambridge: Cambridge University Press.

Powell, O., ed. and trans. 2003. *Galen: On the Properties of Foodstuffs*. Cambridge: Cambridge University Press.

Puglia, E. 2011. "La Rovina dei Libri di Anzio nel *De Indolentia* di Galeno." *Segno e Testo* 9:1–10.

Purcell, N. 1985. "Wine and Wealth in Roman Italy." *JRS* 75:1–19.

Purcell, N. 1987. "Town in Country and Country in Town." In MacDougall 1987, 187–203.

Purcell, N. 1987. "Tomb and Suburb." In Hesberg and Zanker 1987, 25–41.

Purcell, N. 1988. Review of Tchernia 1986 and Carandini and Ricci. 1985. *JRS* 78:194–98.

Purcell, N. 1995. "The Roman Villa and the Landscape of Production." In Cornell and Lomas. 1995, 157–84. London: St. Martin's Press.

Purcell, N. 1996. "The Roman Garden as a Domestic Building." In Barton 1996, 121–51.

Quilici, L. 1997. "I 'Simbruina Stagna' di Nerone nell'Alta Valle dell'Aniene." In Quilici and Quilici-Gigli 1997, 99–142.

Quilici, L., and S. Quilici-Gigli. 1978a. *Antemnae*. Rome: Consiglio nazionale delle ricerche, Centro di studio per l'archeologia etrusco-italica.

Quilici, L., and S. Quilici-Gigli. 1978b. "Ville dell'agro cosano con fronte a torrette." *Rivista dell'istituto nazionale d'archeologia e storia dell'arte* 2(1):11–64.

Quilici, L., and S. Quilici-Gigli, eds. 1997. *Uomo, acqua e paesaggio: Atti dell'Incontro di studio sul tema Irreggimentazione delle acque e trasformazione del paesaggio antico, S. Maria Capua Vetere, 22–23 novembre 1996. ATTA* Suppl. 2. Rome: "L'Erma" di Bretschneider.

Quilici, L., and S. Quilici-Gigli, eds. 2005. *La forma della città e del territorio, 2. ATTA* 14.2. Rome: "L'Erma" di Bretschneider.

Quilici, L., and S. Quilici-Gigli, eds. 2008. *Edilizia pubblica e privata nelle città romane. ATTA* 17. Rome: "L'Erma" di Breitschneider.

Raeder, J. 1988. "Vitruv, de architectura VI 7 (*aedificia Graecorum*) und die Hellenistische Wohnhaus und Palastarchitektur." *Gymnasium* 95:316–68.

Raepset-Charlier, M.-T. 1987. *Prosopographie des femmes de l'ordre sénatorial (Ier–IIe siècles)*. 2 vols. Fonds René Draguet 4. Louvain: Peeters.

Rakob, F. 1961. "Litus beatae Veneris Aureum." *RM* 68:114–49.

Ramelli, I. L. E. 2018. "De recta in Deum fide." In Hunter, van Geest, and Lietaert Peerbolte 2018.

Ramelli, I. L. E. 2020. "The Dialogue of Adamantius: Preparing the Critical Edition and a Reappraisal," *Rheinisches Museum für Philogie* 163:40–68.

Rathbone, D. W. 1981. "The Development of Agriculture in the 'Ager Cosanus' during the Roman Republic: Problems of Evidence and Interpretation." *JRS* 71:10–23.

Rathbone, D. W. 1983. "The Slave Mode of Production in Italy." *JRS* 73:160–68.

Rauh, N. K. 1986. "Cicero's Business Friendships: Economics and Politics in the Late Roman Republic," *Aevum* 60:3–30.

Rauh, N. K. 1989. "Finance and Estate Sales in Republican Rome," *Aevum* 63:45–76.

Rawson, B., ed. 1986. *The Family in Ancient Rome: New Perspectives*. Ithaca, NY: Cornell University Press.

Rawson, B., and P. Weaver, eds. 1997. *The Roman Family in Italy: Status, Sentiment, Space*. Oxford: Oxford University Press.

Reber, K. 1988. "Aedicificia Graecorum: Zu Vitruvs Beschreibung des grieschischen Hauses." *AA* 1988, 653–66.

Reeder, J. C. 1997. "The Statue of Augustus from Prima Porta, the Underground Complex, and the Omen of the Gallina Alba." *AJP* 118:89–118.

Reeve, M. M. ed. *Tributes to Pierre du Prey. Architecture and the Classical Tradition, from Pliny to Posterity*. Turnhout: Brepols.

Reggiani, A. M. 2018. "La *villa pulcherrima* di Traiano a Centumcellae: Una proposta." *Veleia* 35:129–49.

Renkert, T. 2019. "An Approach to Understand the *subura*: The "Argiletum" and Its Function between Public and Private Spaces in Rome." In Bartz 2019a, 102–23.

Ricci, A. 1986. "La Villa dei Quintili." *Bollettino Commissione Archeologica Comunale –BullComm* 91:607–15.

Ricci, A., ed. 1998. *La Villa dei Quintili*. Rome: Lithos.

Richardson, L., Jr. 1992. *A New Topographical Dictionary of Ancient Rome*. Baltimore: Johns Hopkins University Press.

Rickman, G. E. 1980a. "The Grain Trade under the Roman Empire." In D'Arms and Kopff 1980, 261–75.

Rickman, G. E. 1980b. *The Corn Supply of Ancient Rome*. Oxford: Clarendon Press.

Ridgway, B. S., 2000. "The Sperlonga Sculptures: The Current State of

Research." In De Grummond and Ridgway 2000.

Rieger, P., and E. Scricciolo. 2019. "Public and Private Spheres of the Fora in the City of Rome." In Bartz 2019a, 30–47.

Ripoll, G. 2018. "Aristocratic Residences in Late-Antique Hispania." In Marzano and Métraux 2018a, 426–52.

Ripoll, G., and J. Arce. 2000. "The Transformation and End of Roman *Villae* in the West (Fourth–Seventh Centuries): Problems and Perspectives." In Brogiolo, Gauthier, and Christie 2000, 63–114.

Roberts, M. 2002. "Barbarians in Gaul: The Response of the Poets." In Drinkwater and Elton 1992, 97–106.

Robertson, M. 1975. *A History of Greek Art.* London: Cambridge University Press.

Rockwell, K. A. 1971. "Vedius and Livia (Tac. *Ann.* 1.10)." *CPhil* 66(2):110.

Rogers, R. H. 1975a. *An Introduction to Palladius.* BICS Suppl. 35. London: Institute of Classical Studies.

Rogers, R. H. 1975b. *Palladii Rutilii Tauri Aemiliani viri inlustris opus agriculturae, de veterinaria medicina, de insitione.* Bibliotheca Scriptorum Graecorum et Romanorum Teubneriana. Leipzig: Teubner.

Rolfe, J. C., ed. and trans. 1939. *Ammianus Marcellinus: History.* Vol. 3, *Books 27–31. Excerpta Valesiana* (*Anonymus Valesianus*), 508–69. Loeb Classical Library. Cambridge, MA: Harvard University Press.

Roloff, H. 1938. "Maiores bei Cicero." PhD diss. Universität Leipzig. Göttingen: Dieterische Universität-Buchdruckerei.

Romano, E. 1987. *La capanna e il tempio: Vitruvio o dell'archittetura.* Palermo: Palumbo.

Romano, E. 1994. "Dal *De officiis* a Vitruvio, da Vitruvio a Orazio: Il dibattito sul lusso edilizio." In Gros 1994a, 63–73.

Rosati, G. 2009. "The Latin Reception of Hesiod." In Montanari, Rengakos, and Tsagalis 2009, 343–73.

Roselaar, S. T. 2009. "References to Gracchan Activity in the *Liber Coloniarum*." *Historia: Zeitschrift für Alte Geschichte* 58:198–214.

Roselaar, S. T. 2010. *Public Land in the Roman Republic: A Social and Economic History of* Ager Publicus *in Italy, 396–89 BC.* Oxford: Oxford University Press.

Roselaar, S. T. 2019. *Italy's Economic Revolution: Integration and Economy in Republican Italy.* Oxford: Oxford University Press.

Rossiter, J. J. 1978. *Roman Farm Buildings in Italy.* BAR International Series 52. Oxford: Archaeopress.

Rossiter, J. J. 1989. "Roman Villas of the Greek East and the Villa in Gregory of Nyssa *Ep.* 20." *JRA* 2:101–10.

Roth, D. T. 2015a. *The Text of Marcion's Gospel.* Leiden: Brill.

Roth, D. T. 2015b. "The Adamantius Dialogue as a Source." 347–95. In Roth 2015a, 347–95.

Rothschild, C. K., and T. W. Thompson. 2011. "Galen: 'On the Avoidance of Grief.'" *Early Christianity* 2:110–29.

Rothschild, C. K., and T. W. Thompson. 2012. "Galen's *On the Avoidance of Grief*: The Question of a Library at Antium." *CPhil* 107(2):131–45.

Rothschild, C. K., and T. W. Thompson, eds. 2014a. *Galen's* De Indolentia: *Essays on a Newly Discovered Letter.* Studies and Texts in Antiquity and Christianity 88. Tübingen: Mohr Siebeck.

Rothschild, C. K., and T. W. Thompson. 2014b. "English Translation." In Rothschild and Thompson 2014a, 21–36.

Rowland, I. D., and T. N. Howe, ed. and trans. 1999. *Vitruvius: Ten Books on Architecture.* Translated by I. D. Rowland; commentary by T. N. Howe. Cambridge: Cambridge University Press.

Roymans, N., and T. Derks, eds. 2011. *Villa Landscapes in the Roman North: Economy, Culture, and Lifestyles.* Amsterdam: Amsterdam University Press.

Russell, A. 2015. *The Politics of Public Space in Republican Rome.* Cambridge: Cambridge University Press.

Russo, M. 2004. "Alla ricerca della villa sorrentina di Pollio Felice nella baia di Puolo." In Senatore 2004, unpaginated.

Russo, M. 2006. *La villa romana del Capo di Sorrento: Con i fondi agricoli acquistati dal Commune.* Sorrento: Centro di studi e ricerche multimediali Bartolommeo Capasso.

Rutledge, S. H. 2009. "Writing Imperial Politics: The Social and Political Background." In Dominik, Garthwaite, and Roche 2009, 23–61.

Rutledge, S. H. 2012. *Ancient Rome as a Museum: Power, Identity, and the Culture of Collecting.* Oxford: Oxford University Press.

Rykwert, J. 1972. *On Adam's House in Paradise: The Idea of the Primitive Hut in Architectural History.* Museum of Modern Art Papers on Architecture 2. New York: Museum of Modern Art.

Saller, R. 2006. "Slavery and the Roman Family." In Finley 2006, 82–110.

Salviat, F., and A. Tchernia, eds. 2013. *Vins, vignerons et buveurs de l'Antiquité.* Saggi di storia antica 31. Rome: "L'Erma" di Bretschneider.

Salway, P. 1981. *Roman Britain.* Oxford: Oxford University Press.

Salza Prina Ricotti, E. 2001. *Villa Adriana: Il sogno di un imperatore.* Rome: "L'Erma" di Bretschneider.

Sánchez, C., and I. Escobar, eds. 2015. *Dioses, héroes y atletas: La imagen del cuerpo en la Grecia antigua.* Alcalá de Henares: Museo Arqueológico Regional.

Sancisi-Weerdenburg, H., R. J. Van der Spek, W. C. Teitler, and H. T. Wallinga, eds. 1993. *De agricultura: In memoriam Pieter Willem de Neeve (1945–1990).* Dutch Monographs on Ancient History and Archaeology 10. Leiden: Brill.

Sauron, G. 1997. "Un conflit qui s'éternalise: La guerre de Sperlonga." *RA* 1997:261–96.

Savino, E. 2002. "Agrippa I e la Capri di Tiberio." In Casaburi and Lacenza 2002, 41–51.

Scheidel, W. 2004. "Human Mobility in Roman Italy, I: The Free Population.'" *JRS* 94:1–26.

Scheidel, W. 2005. "Human Mobility in Roman Italy, II: The Slave Population." *JRS* 95:64–79.

Scheidel, W. 2011. "The Roman Slave Supply." In Bradley and Cartledge 2011, 287–310.

Schermaier, M., ed. 2023a. *The Position of Roman Slaves: Social Realities and Legal Differences.* Berlin: De Gruyter.

Schermaier, M. 2023b. "Without Rights? Social Theories Meet Roman Law Texts." In Schermaier 2023a, 1–24.

Schilling, R. 1954. *La religion romaine de Vénus depuis les origines jusqu'au temps d'Auguste.* BÉFAR 178. Paris: De Boccard.

Schlaifer, R. 1936. "Greek Theories of Slavery from Homer to Aristotle." *Harvard Studies in Classical Philology* 47:165–204.

Schmidt, O.-E. 1899. *Ciceros Villen.* Leipzig: Teubner.

Schulz, V. 2022. "Historiographical Responses to Flavian Responses to Nero." In Heerink and Meijer 2022, 325–50.

Sciaramenti, B., ed. 2018. *Ruri: Abitare la campagna nell'Italia antica; Atti del Convegno Internazionale (Todi 26–27 novembre 2016).* OTIVM 4(4).

Scott, K. 1939. "Notes on the Destruction of Two Roman Villas." *AJP* 60(4):459–62.

Sebastiani, A., and C. Megale, eds. 2021. *Archaeological Landscapes of Roman Etruria: Research and Field Papers.* MediTo: Archeological and Historical Landscapes of Mediterranean Central Italy 1. Turnout: Brepols.

Secchi Tarugi, E. 2002. "*Litus beatae veneris aureum:* Aspetti della presenza di Baia negli autori latini." PhD diss., Università di Siena, Bibliotheca di Area Umanistica.

Sedlmeyr, J. 2021. "Der Einfluss des Ideals akademischen Philosophierens auf die Figurengestaltung in den Spätdialogen Ciceros." In Müller 2021, 127–42.

Seeck, O., ed. 1876. *Notitia Dignitatum accedunt Notitia Urbis Constantinopolitanae et Laterculi Povinciarum.* Berlin: Apud Wiedmannos.

Segal, E. 1987. *Roman Laughter: The Comedy of Plautus.* 2nd rev. ed. Oxford: Oxford University Press.

Senatore, F., ed. 2004. *Pompei, Capri e la Penisola Sorrentina: Atti del quinto ciclo di conferenze di geologia, storia e archeologia; Pompei, Anacapri, Scafati, Castellamare di Stabia, ottobre 2002– aprile 2003*. Capri: Oebalus.

Senatore, F. 2015. "Masgaba 'il fondatore': Questioni topografiche capresi." *Oebalus: Studi sulla Campania nell'Antichità* 10:39–80.

Sfameni, C. 2006. *Ville residenziali nell'Italia tardoantica*. Bari: Edipuglia.

Shackleton Bailey, D. R. 1992. *Onomasticon to Cicero's Speeches*. 2nd ed. Stuttgart: B. G. Teubner.

Shackleton Bailey, D. R. 1995. *Onomasticon to Cicero's Letters*. Stuttgart: B. G. Teubner.

Shackleton Bailey, D. R. 1996. *Onomasticon to Cicero's Treatises*. Stuttgart: B. G. Teubner.

Shane Bjornlie, M., trans. 2019. *Cassiodorus, The* Variae: *A Complete and Annotated Translation*. Los Angeles: University of California Press.

Sherwin-White, A. N. 1966. *The Letters of Pliny: A Historical and Social Commentary*. Oxford: Oxford University Press.

Sigot, E., ed. 2000. *Otium—Negotium: Beiträge des interdisziplinären Symposions der Sodalitas zum Thema Zeit*. Vienna: Edition Praesens.

Silvas, A. M., ed. and trans. 2007. *Gregory of Nyssa: The Letters*. Vigilae Christianae Suppl. 83. Leiden: Brill.

Sirago, V. A. 1957. "La Proprietà di Plinio il Giovane." *AntCl* 26:40–58.

Sirano, F., ed. 2007. *In Itinere: Ricerche di archeologia in Campania; Atti del I e del II ciclo di conferenze di ricerca archeologica nell'Alto Casertano*. Sant'Angelo in Formis: Lavieri.

Sirks, A. J. B. 2001. "Food for Rome: The Legal Structure of the Transportation and Processing of Supplies for the Imperial Distributions in Rome and Constantinople." *Tijdschrift voor Rechtsgeschiedenis / Revue d'histoire du droit / The Legal History Review* 69(3):361–67. https://doi.org/10.1163/15718190119685431.

Sivan, H. 1992. "Town and Country in Late Antique Gaul: The Example of Bordeaux." In Drinkwater and Elton 1992, 132–43.

Sivan, H. 1993. *Ausonius of Bordeaux: Genesis of a Gallic Aristocracy*. New York: Routledge.

Skutsch, O., ed. 1972. *Ennius: Sept exposés suivis de discussions*. Entretiens sur l'Antiquité classique 17. Geneva: Fondation Hardt/Vandoeuvres.

Slater, W. J., ed. 1991. *Dining in a Classical Context*. Ann Arbor: University of Michican Press.

Smith, R. R. R. 1981. "Greeks, Foreigners and Roman Republican Portraits." *JRS* 71:24–38.

Southern, P. 2015. *The Roman Empire from Severus to Constantine*. 2nd ed. Abingdon, UK: Routledge.

Späth, T. 2010. "Gender-Specific Concerns for Family Tradition? Cicero, Tullia, and Marcus." In Dasen and Späth 2010, 147–73.

Späth, T., ed. 2021. *Gesellschaft im Brief: Ciceros Korrespondenz und die Sozialgeschichte. La Correspondance de Cicéron et l'histoire sociale*. Collegium Beatus Rhenanus 9. Stuttgart: Franz Steiner.

Speksnijder, S. 2022. "The Elusive *vestibulum*." In Baird and Pudsey 2022, 322–53.

Spier, J., and S. E. Cole, eds. 2022. *Egypt and the Classical World: Cross-Cultural Encounters in Antiquity*. Los Angeles: J. Paul Getty Museum. http://www.getty.edu/publications/egypt-classical-world/.

Spinola, G. 2020. "The First Residential Phases of the Lateran Area and a Hypothesis to Explain the So-Called Trapezoidal Building." In Bosman, Haynes, and Liverani 2020, 71–90.

Spurny, M. 2021. "*Omnia a te data mihi putabo, si te valentem videro*: Tiros Beziehung zu Cicero während seiner Krankheitsphasen aus sozial- und medizingeschichtlicher Sicht." In Späth 2021, 253–80.

Spyropoulos, G. 2001. *Drei Meisterwerke der griechischen Plastik aus der Villa des Herodes Atticus zu Eva Loukou*. Frankfurt-am-Main: Peter Lang.

Spyropoulos, G. 2006. Η Έπαυλη του Ηρώδη Αττικού στην Εύα Λουκού Κυνουρίας [*The Villa of Herodes Atticus at Eua Loukou in Kynouria*]. Athens: Olkos.

Spyropoulos, G. 2015. "La villa de Herodes Attico en Eva/Loukou, Arcadia." In Sánchez and Escobar 2015, 392–95.

Spyropoulos, G. 2022. "Appropriation and Synthesis in the Villa of Herodes Atticus at Eva (Loukou), Greece." In Spier and Cole 2022, https://www.getty.edu/publications/egypt-classical-world/06/.

Spyropoulos, T., and G. Spyropoulos. 2003. "Prächtige Villa, Refugium und Musenstätte: Die Villa des Herodes Atticus im arkadischen Eua." *Antike Welt* 34:463–70.

Stanley-Price, N., ed. 1991. *The Conservation of the Orpheus Mosaic at Paphos, Cyprus*. Los Angeles: Getty Conservation Institute. http://hdl.handle.net/10020/gci_pubs/orpheus_mosaic.

Stewart, A. 1990. *Greek Sculpture: An Exploration*. 2 vols. New Haven and London: Yale University Press.

Stierlin, H. 1996. *The Roman Empire*. Vol. 1, *From the Etruscans to the Decline of the Roman Empire*. Cologne: Taschen.

Storchi Marino, A. 2000. "Reti interregionali integrate e circuiti di mercato periodico negli *indices nundinarii* del Lazio e della Campania." In Lo Cascio 2000b, 93–130.

Strauss, L. 1970. *Xenophon's Socratic Discourse: An Interpretation of the Oeconomicus*. Ithaca, NY: Cornell University Press.

Stringer, M. 2020. "*Impensae, operae,* and the *pastio villatica:* The Evaluation of New Venture Investments in the Roman Agricultural Treatises." In Erdkamp, Verboven, and Zuiderhoek 2020, 253–73.

Syme, R. (1958) 2002. *The Roman Revolution*. 1 vol., reprint of 2 vols. Oxford: Oxford University Press.

Syme, R. (1961) 1979. "Who Was Vedius Pollio?" *JRS* 51:23–30. Reprinted in *Roman Papers 2*, edited by E. Badian, 518–29. Oxford: Clarendon Press.

Syme, R. 1968. *Ammianus and the Historia Augusta*. Oxford: Clarendon Press.

Syme, R. (1968) 1979. "People in Pliny." *JRS* 58:1–2, 135–51. Reprinted in *Roman Papers 2*, edited by E. Badian, 694–723. Oxford: Clarendon Press.

Syme, R. 1971. *Emperors and Biography: Studies in the* Historia Augusta. Oxford: Clarendon Press.

Syme, R. (1978) 1984. "Sallust's Wife." *Classical Quarterly* 28:292–95. Reprinted in *Roman Papers 3*, edited by A. R. Birley, 1085–89. Oxford: Clarendon Press.

Syme, R. (1982) 1988. "Spaniards at Tivoli." *Ancient Society* 13/14:241–63. Reprinted in *Roman Papers 4*, edited by A. R. Birley, 94–114. Oxford: Clarendon Press.

Syme, R. (1983) 1988. "Domitian: The Last Years." *Chiron* 13:121–146. Reprinted in *Roman Papers 4*, edited by A. R. Birley, 252–77. Oxford: Clarendon Press.

Syme, R. (1985) 1988. "Correspondents of Pliny." *Historia* 34(3):324–59. Reprinted in *Roman Papers 5*, edited by A. R. Birley, 440–77. Oxford: Clarendon Press.

Syme, R. (1988) 1991. "Journeys of Hadrian." *ZPE* 73:159–70. Reprinted in *Roman Papers 6*, edited by A. R. Birley, 346–57. Oxford: Clarendon Press.

Talamo, E. 1998. "Gli *horti* di Sallustio a Porta Collina." In Cima and La Rocca 1998, 113–169.

Talbert, R. J. A., ed. 2012a. *Ancient Perspectives: Maps and Their Place in Mesopotamia, Egypt, Greece and Rome*. Chicago: University of Chicago Press.

Talbert, R. J. A. 2012b. "*Urbs Roma* to *Orbis Romanus*: Roman Mapping on the Grand Scale." In Talbert 2012a, 163–91.

Tamm, B. 1963. Auditorium *and* palatium: *A Study on Assembly-Rooms in Roman Palaces during the 1st Century B.C. and the 1st Century A.D*. Acta Universitatis Stockholmiensis, Stockholm

Studies in Classical Archaeology 2. Stockholm: Almqvist and Wiksell.

Taylor, M. J. 2014. "Roman Infantry Tactics in the Mid-Republic: A Reassessment." *Historia* 63(3):301–22.

Tchernia, A. 1986. *Le vin de l'Italie romaine: Essai d'histoire économique d'après les amphores.* BÉFAR 259. Rome: École française de Rome.

Tchernia, A. 2013a. "Acre Falernum: *Juvénal, XIII, 213–216*." In Salviat and Tchernia 2013, 189–94.

Tchernia, A. 2013b. "Le cercle de L. Licinius Crassus et la naissance de la hiérarchie des vins à Rome." In Salviat and Tchernia 2013, 175–88.

Tchernia, A. 2013c. "Les appellations d'origine dans l'antiquité grecque et romaine." In Salviat and Tchernia 2013, 217–25.

Teichner, F. 2018. "Roman Villas in the Iberian Peninsula (Second Century BCE–Third Century CE)." In Marzano and Métraux 2018a, 235–54.

Temin, P. 2020. "Slaves and the Roman Economy." In Hodkinson, Kleijwegt, and Vlassopoulos 2022.

Terrenato, N. 2012. "The Enigma of 'Catonian' Villas: The *De agri cultura* in the Context of Second-Century BC Italian Architecture." In Becker and Terrenato 2012, 69–93.

Terrenato, N. 2020. *The Early Roman Expansion into Italy: Elite Negotiation and Family Agendas.* Cambridge: Cambridge University Press.

Thilo, G., and H. Hagen, eds. 1881–1902. *Servii Grammatici qui feruntur In Vergilii carmina commentarii.* 4 vols. Leipzig: B. G. Teubner.

Thomas, J. A. C., ed. and trans. 1975. *The Institutes of Justinian.* Amsterdam: North Holland.

Thompson, E. A. 1956. "The Settlement of the Barbarians in Southern Gaul." *JRS* 46:65–75.

Tierney, J. J. 1963. "The Map of Agrippa," *Proceedings of the Irish Academy* 75(Sect. C):151–66.

Tocco Sciarelli, G., ed. 1983a. *Baia: Il Ninfeo imperiale sommerso di punta Epitaffio.* Naples: Banca Sannitica.

Tocco Sciarelli, G. 1983b. "Inquadramento storico e topografico." In Tocco Sciarelli 1983a, 17–24.

Tomber, R. 2008. *Indo-Roman Trade—from Pots to Pepper.* Duckworth Debates in Archaeology Series. London: Duckworth.

Tombrägel, M. 2012. *Die republikanischen Otiumvillen von Tivoli.* Deutsches Archäologisches Institut, Palilia 25. Wiesbaden: Reichert.

Tomei, M. T. 1998. *The Palatine.* Electa Guides for the Soprintendenza archeologica di Roma. Milan: Electa.

Tomei, M. A., and M. G. Filetici, eds. 2011. *Domus Tiberiana: Scavi e restauri 1990–2011.* Ministero per i Beni e le Attività Culturali; Soprintendenza Speciale per i Beni Archeologici di Roma. Milan: Electa.

Torelli, M. 1984. *Lavinio e Roma: Riti iniziatici e matrimonio tra archeologia e storia.* Rome: Quasar.

Travlos, J. 1971. *A Pictorial Dictionary of Ancient Athens.* London: Thames and Hudson.

Treggiari, S. 2007. *Terentia, Tullia and Pubilia: The Women of Cicero's Family.* Women of the Ancient World. London: Routledge.

Treggiari, S. 2019. *Servilia and Her Family.* Oxford: Oxford University Press.

Trout, D. E. 1996. "Town, Countryside, and Christianization at Paulinus' Nola." In Mathisen and Sivan 1996, 175–86.

Trout, D. E. 1999. *Paulinus of Nola: Life, Letters, and Poems.* Berkeley: University of California Press.

Tucci, P. L. 2008. "Galen's Storeroom, Rome's Libraries, and the Fire of A.D. 192." *JRA* 21:133–49.

Tucci, P. L. 2009. "Antium, the Palatium, and the Domus Tiberiana Again." *JRA* 22:398–401.

Tucci, P. L. 2013. "Galen and the Library at Antium: The State of the Question." *CPhil* 108(3):240–51, responding to Rothschild and Thompson 2012.

Tyrrell, R. Y., and L. C. Purser. 1904–1933. *The Correspondance of Cicero*, 2nd ed. 7 vols. Dublin and London: Hodes, Figgis and Longmans, Green.

Ucelli, G. 1950. *Le navi di Nemi*, 2nd ed. Rome: Libreria dello Stato.

Valeri, C. 2021. "'*Albanum Domitiani*': Domitian's Villa in Castel Gandolfo." In Cominesi et al. 2021, 137–43.

Van Dam, H.-J. 1984. *P. Papinius Statius, Silvae, Book II: A Commentary*. Mnemosyne, Bibliotheca Classica Batava Suppl. 82. Leiden: Brill.

Van den Hout, M. P. J., ed. 1988. *M. Cornelii Frontonis Epistulae*. Bibliotheca Scriptorum Classicorum Teubneriana. Leipzig: Teubner.

Varriale, I. 2016. "*Otium* and *Negotium*—The Breakdown of a Boundary in the Imperial Villas: The Case Study of Pausilypon." In Weissenrieder 2016, 283–301.

Veal, R. 2017. "Wood and Charcoal for Rome: Towards an Understanding of Ancient Regional Fuel Economics." In de Haas and Tol 2017, 388–406.

Vera, D., ed. 1999. *Demografia, sistemi agrari, regimi alimentari nel mondo antico*: Atti del Convegno Internationale di Studi (*Parma* 17–19 ottobre 1997). Pragmateiai 3. Bari: Edipuglia.

Verboven, K. 2007. "The Associative Order: Status and Ethos among Roman Businessmen in Late Republic and Early Empire." *Athenaeum* 95:1–31.

Verity, A., and E. Baragwanath, ed. and trans. 2022. *Xenophon: Estate Management and Symposium*. Translated by A. Verity; introduction by E. Baragwanath. Oxford World's Classics. Oxford: Oxford University Press.

Verpoorten, J. M. 1962. "Les noms grecs et latins de l'asphodèle." *AntCl* 31:111–29.

Versluys, M. J. 2005. "Aegyptiaca romana: The Widening Debate." In Bricault, Versluys, and Meyboom 2005, 1–14.

Vessey, D. W. T. 1976. "Statius to His Wife: Silvae III.5." *CJ* 72(2):134–40.

Veyne, P. 1957. "La Table des Ligures Baebiani et l'institution alimentaire de Trajan." *MÉFRA* 69:81–135.

Veyne, P. 1958. "La Table des Ligures Baebiani et l'institution alimentaire de Trajan." *MÉFRA* 70:177–241.

Veyne, P. 1976. *Le pain et le cirque: Sociologie historique d'un pluralisme politique*. Paris: Le Seuil.

Veyne, P. 1990. *Bread and Circuses: Historical Sociology and Political Pluralism*. Abridged, translated by B. Pearce. London: Allen Lane, Penguin Press.

Vlassopoulos, K. 2021. *Historicising Ancient Slavery*. Edinburgh Studies in Ancient Slavery. Edinburgh: Edinburgh University Press.

Vlassopoulos, K. 2023. "Slavery in Ancient Greece." In Pargas and Schiel 2023, 67–85.

Vogt, J. 1972. *Sklaverei und Humanität: Studien zur antiken Sklaverei und ihrer Erforschung*, 2nd rev. ed. Wiesbaden: Steiner. English translation by T. Wiedmann: 1974, *Ancient Slavery and the Ideal of Man*. Oxford: Blackwell.

Vogt, J., and H. Bellen 1983. *Bibliographie zur antiken Sklaveri*. Bochum: Norbert Brockmeyer.

Volpe, R., ed. 2007. *Centocelle II: Roma S.D.O le indagini archeologiche*. Rome: Rubbettino Editore.

Von Hesburg, H., and P. Zanker, eds. 1987. *Römische Gräberstrassen. Selbstdarstellung, Status, Standard; Kolloquium in München vom 28. bis 30. Okotober 1985*. Munich: Verlag der Bayerischen Akademie der Wissenschaften.

Vuolanto, V. 2016. "Child and Parent in Roman Law." In du Plessis, Ando, and Tuori, 487–97.

Wagner, Y. 2010. "*Otium* und *negotium* in den epistulae Plinius des Jüngeren: Zwischen Tradition und Wertewandel." *Diomedes: Schriftenreihe des Fachbereiches Altertumswissenschaften, Alte Geschichte, Altertumskunde und Mykenologie der Universität Salzburg* n.f. 5:89–100.

Walbank, F. W., A. E. Astin, M. W. Frederiksen, R. M. Ogilvie, and A. Drummond, eds. 2008. *CAH* 7, pt. 2, *The Rise of Rome to 220 BC*. 2nd ed. Cambridge: Cambridge University Press.

Wallace-Hadrill, A. 1981. "The Emperor and His Virtues." *Historia* 30:298–323.

Wallace-Hadrill, A. 1984. *Suetonius: The Scholar and His Caesars*. New Haven: Yale University Press.

Wallace-Hadrill, A. 1988. "The Social Structure of the Roman House." *PBSR* 56:43–97.

Wallace-Hadrill, A., ed. 1989. *Patronage in Ancient Society*. London: Routledge.

Wallace-Hadrill, A. 1998. "*Horti* and Hellenization." In Cima and La Rocca 1998, 1–12.

Wallace-Hadrill, A. 2018. "The Villa of the Mysteries at Pompeii and the Ideals of Hellenistic Hospitality." In Marzano and Métraux 2018a, 63–74.

Walsh, P. R., ed. and trans. 1966. *Letters of St. Paulinus of Nola*. 2 vols. Westminster, MD: Newman Press.

Walter-Karydi, E. 1996. "Die Nobilitierung des griechischen Wohnhauses in der spätklassischen Zeit." In Hoepfner and Brands 1996, 56–61.

Wardle, D. 2007. "Caligula's Bridge of Boats—AD 39 or 40?" *Historia* 56: 118–120.

Watson, A. 1987. *Roman Slave Law*. Baltimore: Johns Hopkins University Press.

Watson, A., ed. and trans. 2009. *The Digest of Justinian*. 4 vols. Philadelphia: University of Pennsylvania Press.

Watson, L. 2007. "The Epodes: Horace's Archilochus?" In Harrison 2007, 93–104.

Webb, R. 1999. "*Ekphrasis* Ancient and Modern: The Invention of a Genre." *Word and Image* 15:7–18.

Webb, R. 2001. "The *Progymnasmata* as Practice." In Lee Too 2001, 289–316.

Weber, M. 1891. *Die römische Agrargeschichte in ihrer Bedeutung für das Staats- und Privatrecht*. Stuttgart: F. Enke. English translation by R. I. Frank: 2008, *Roman Agrarian History*. Claremont, CA: Regina Books.

Weeda, L. 2019. *Horace's Sermones Book 1: Credentials for Maecenas*. Berlin: De Gruyter.

Weiler, I. 2002. "Inverted *Kalokagathia*." In Wiedemann and Gardner 2002, 11–28.

Weisberg, R. 2002. "Twentieth-Century Rhetoric: Enforcing Originality and Distancing the Past." In Gazda 2002a, 25–46.

Weiss, A. 2004. *Sklaven der Stadt: Untersuchungen zur öffentlichen Sklaverei in den Städten des römischen Reiches*. Stuttgart: Franz Steiner.

Weissenrieder, A., ed. 2016. *Borders: Terminologies, Ideologies, and Performances*. Tübingen: Mohr Siebeck.

Welch, K. 1995. "The Office of *Praefectus Fabrum* in the Late Republic." *Chiron* 25:131–45.

West, M. L., ed. and trans. 2008. *Hesiod, Theogony and Works and Days*. Rev. ed. of 1966 and 1978. Oxford: Oxford University Press.

West, M. L. 2011. *The Making of the* Iliad: *Disquisition and Analytical Commentary*. Oxford: Oxford University Press.

White, C. 2000. *Early Christian Latin Poets*. London: Routledge.

White, K. D. 1967. "*Latifundia*: A Critical Review of the Evidence on Large Estates in Italy and Sicily up to the End of the First Century A.D." *BICS* 14:62–79 (texts and inscriptions, 64–72).

White, K. D. 1970. *Roman Farming*. Ithaca, NY: Cornell University Press.

White, K. D. 1973. "Roman Agricultural Writers I: Varro and His Predecessors." *ANRW* 1.4, 439–97.

White, K. D. 1975. *Farm Equipment of the Roman World*. Cambridge: Cambridge University Press.

Whittaker, C. R. 2006. "Circe's Pigs: From Slavery to Serfdom in the Later Roman World." In Finley 2006, 111–54.

Widrig, W. M. 1987. "Land Use at the Via Gabina Villas." In MacDougall 1987, 225–60.

Widrig, W. M. 2009. *The Via Gabina Villas: Sites 10, 11, and 13*. Houston: Rice University Press.

Wiedemann, T. 1981. *Greek and Roman Slavery*. Baltimore: Johns Hopkins University Press.

Wiedemann, T. 1989. *Adults and Children in the Roman Empire*. London: Routledge.

Wiedemann, T., and J. Gardner. 2002. *Representing the Body of the Slave*. London: Routledge.

Wiegandt, E. 2016. "*Otium* als Mittel der literarischen Selbstinszenierung römischer Aristokraten in Republik und Früher Kaiserzeit." In Eickhoff 2016b, 43–55.

Wightman, E. M. 1971. *Roman Trier and the Treveri*. London: Hart Davis.

Wightman, E. M. 1985. *Gallia Belgica*. Berkeley: University of California Press.

Wikander, Ö, ed. 2000. *Handbook of Ancient Water Technology*. Technology and Change in History. 2 vols. Leiden: Brill.

Williams, C. K. II, and N. Bookidis. 2003. *Corinth, The Centenary: 1896–1996*. Athens: American School of Classical Studies at Athens.

Wilson, A. I. 2008. "Villa, Horticulture and Irrigation Infrastrcuture in the Tiber Valley." In Coarelli and Patterson 2008, 731–68.

Wilson, R. J. A. 2018a. "Roman Villas in Sicily." In Marzano and Métraux 2018a, 195–219.

Wilson, R. J. A. 2018b. "Roman Villas in North Africa." In Marzano and Métraux 2018a, 266–307.

Wiseman, T. P. 1998. "A Stroll on the Rampart." In Cima and La Rocco 1998, 13–21.

Wiseman, T. P. 2016. "Maecenas and the Stage." *PBSR* 84:131–55.

Wiseman, T. P. 2019. *The House of Augustus: A Historical Detective Story*. Princeton: Princeton University Press.

Wolfram, H. 1979. "The Goths in Aquitaine." *German Studies Review* 2(2):153–68.

Wrede, H. 1986. *Die antike Herme*. Trierer Beiträge zur Altertumskunde 1. Mainz: Philipp von Zabern.

Yegül, F., and D. Favro. 2019. *Roman Architecture and Urbanism: From the Origins to Late Antiquity*. Cambridge: Cambridge University Press.

Zaninović, M. 1988. "Liburnia Militaris." *Opuscula Archeologica* 13:43–67.

Zanker, P., ed. 1976a. *Hellenismus in Mittelitalien*. 2 vols. Göttingen: Akademie der Wissenschaften in Göttingen.

Zanker, P. 1976b. "Zur Rezeption des hellenistischen Individualporträts in Rom und in den italischen Städten." In Zanker 1976a, 2:581–609.

Zanker, P. (1979) 1990. "Die Villa als Vorbild des späten pompejanischen Wohngeschmacks." *Jahrbuch des Deutschen Archäologischen Instituts* 94:460–523. Reprinted in *Die römische Villa*, edited by F. Reutti, 150–171. Weg der Forschung 182. Darmstadt: Wissenschaftliche Buchgesellschaft.

Zanker, P. 1987. "Drei Stadtbilder aus dem augusteischen Rome." In *L'Urbs: Espace urbain et histoire* 1987, 475–89.

Zanker, P. 1995. *The Mask of Socrates: The Image of the Intellectual in Antiquity*. The Sather Lectures 59. Translated by H.A. Shapiro. Berkeley: University of California Press.

Zarmakoupi, M. 2010. "The Architectural Design of Roman Luxury Villas around the Bay of Naples (circa 100 BCE–79 CE)." *Amoenitas* 1:33–41.

Zarmakoupi, M. 2021. "Tra concezione e percezione dello spazio: Le rappresentazioni di paesaggio nella pittura romana." In Coralini 2021, 115–27.

Zarmakoupi, M. 2023. *Shaping Roman Landscape: Ecocritical Approaches to Architecture and Wall Painting in Early Imperial Italy*. Los Angeles: J. Paul Getty Museum.

Zevi, F., and B. Andreae. 1982. "Gli scavi sottomarini di Baia." *La parola del passato* 37:114–56.

Zimmer, G. 1989. "Das Sacrarium des C. Heius." *Gymnasium* 96:493–520.

ILLUSTRATION CREDITS

Figs. 1, 10, 18a, 19a, 20a Redrawn by Anthony Paular

Fig. 2 © RMN-Grand Palais / Art Resource NY

Figs. 3a, 3b Courtesy of Accademia dei Lincei

Fig. 4a Courtesy Swedish Library Institute

Fig. 4b Ministero della Cultura — Parco Archeologico del Colosseo

Fig. 5 G. Dagli Orti / © NPL — DeA Picture Library / Bridgeman Images

Fig. 6 Wall painting, entrance to a sanctuary with *tholos*, Pompeii (VI 41 Insula Occidentalis) by ArchaiOptix. Licensed under CC BY-SA 4.0

Fig. 7 Photo: © Patrice Carter. All rights reserved 2024 / Bridgeman Images

Fig. 8 Image courtesy of Dr. Johannes Eber

Fig. 9 Photo: Andrew Smith / Alamy Stock Photo

Fig. 11 Getty Conservation Institute / Photo: Vassos Stylianou

Figs. 12, 13, 14 Ministero della Cultura — Parco Archeologico di Pompei

Figs. 15a, 15b, 16a, 16b, 17a, 17b Walter Widrig Papers at Woodson Research Center, Rice University, Houston, Texas, Repository

Figs. 18a, 18b, 19a, 19b Courtesy British School at Rome

Fig. 20b Maura Medri

Fig. 21 Reproduced with permission of Cambridge University Press through PLSclear

Fig. 22 © Jean-Claude Golvin

Fig. 23 © Universal Images Group (UIG) / Media Storehouse

INDEX OF ANCIENT TEXTS CITED

Page numbers appear in boldface type. Abbreviations are based primarily on S. Hornblower, A. Spawforth, and E. Eidinow, eds., *The Oxford Classical Dictionary*, 4th ed. (Oxford: Oxford University Press, 2012).

A

Ambrose, *Epistulae* 58.1–3: **381n320**; 58.5: **379n286**
App., *B. Civ.* 1.26–72 (7–17): **402n10**; 2.10: **353n89**; 2.94: **353n89**; 3.14: **385n12**; 4.6: **408n100**; 4.17: **408n100**; 4.19–20: **408n100**; 29.124: **404n33**; 51.1: **408n98**
App., *Hisp.* 52: **356n65**
App., *Mith.* 70: **380n306**
Apul., *Apol.* 71.6: **374n205**; 91.7–8: **374n205**; 87.11–88.7: **374n206**; 93.4–5: **177**; 101.4–6: **177**
Arist., *Oec.* 1347a4–7: **413n85**
Arist., *Pol.* 1254b 11–38 (1.2.11–12): **349n19**; 1255b 13–40 (1.2.21–23): **349n19**; 1259b 24–26 (5.3): **349n19**; 1259b 24–1260a 15 (5.3–7): **349n19**
Arrian, *Discourses of Epictetus* 1.1.18–19: **412n72**
Asc., *Mil.* 33: **385n12**; 37: **389n15**
Augustine of Hippo, *Epistulae* 11: **378n269**; 24–25: **378n269**; 76.2: **378n269**; 93.3: **378n269**; 185 (*On Correction of the Donatists*) 2.6–5.20: **378n269**
Aur. Vict., *Caes.* 12.4: **395n6**; 14.5–7: **417n151**; 15.7: **418n163, 419n168**; 18.1–6: **422n225**; 39.6: **44, 320**; 40.2: **422n223**
Aur. Vict., *De vir. ill.* 72: **370n132**
Auson., *Carmina* 4.1–4: **377n263**
Auson., *Ep.* 6.42: **377n252**; 26.1–34: **377n257**; 26: **185**; 26.1–48: **185–86**
Auson., *Eph.* 2.1.1–9: **182**; 2.2.1–14: **182**; 2.4.1–10: **182**; 2.5.1–8: **183**; 2.6.1–7: **183**; 2.7.1–21: **283**; 2.8.40–43: **183**; 3 Preface and lines 1–32: **184–85**
Auson., *Mos.* 19–22: **180**; 169–177: **181, 410n36**; 283–285: **181, 358n176**; 298–304: **181**; 318–348: **181**; 399–437: **376n229**; 448–453: **373n229**
Auson., *Opuscula* 1.5–8: **377n263**

C

Cassiod., *Var.* 1.2: **383n323**; 12.22.3–5: **200, 358n176**
Cassiod., *Inst.* 29.1: **383n323**
Cass. Dio 26.89.2–3: **403n27**; 26.89.7: **403n27**; 27.94.1–2: **403n27**; 31.12: **404n32**; 33.108–109: **404n32**; 36a–37: **369n111**; 36.20–24: **369n111**; 36.23.4: **369n111**; 38.5.2: **353n89**; 42.54–56: **353n89**; 48.43.4: **360n21**; 51.3: **372n162**; 52.43.2: **284**; 53.1.3: **419n182**; 54.23.2–5: **409n16**; 52.43.2: **409n7**; 53.16.4: **360n21**; 54.23.1–6: **284, 417n150**; 55.8: **355n115**; 55.9.5–8: **410n28**; 56.29.2: **410n27**; 56.46.3: **410n27**; 57.12.6: **410n30, 410n31**; 58.1.1: **410n30**; 58.22.2–3: **288**; 58.24.1: **410n30, 415n118**; 66.30.5: **404n39**; 69.23.1: **366n63**
Cass. Dio, *Epit. Bk* 25.2.2–6: **422n219**; 62.1–14: **412n64**; 61.10: **412n67**; 62.2: **412n67**; 62.16–18: **413n74**; 62.18.2–3: **413n74**; 62.24–25: **412n70**; 63 (64).1: **414n97**; 64.4: **413n83**; 65.2–3: **414n102**; 65.3.4: **298, 415n107**; 65.9.4: **415n107**; 65.10.2: **415n113**; 65 (66).10.4: **297**; 67.1.2: **300**; 67.14.3: **415n120**; 68.18.2: **414n103**; 68.29.3: **285, 414n96**; 69.4.1–6: **417n145**; 69.4.6: **417n143**; 69.7.3: **417n144, 417n148**; 72.5.34: **421n215**; 72.10.1: **421n215**; 72.35.4: **418n165, 420n194**; 73.16.1: **422n216**; 73.22.3: **414n92**; 73.24: **419n182**; 73.24.1–2: **422n216**; 74.16.4: **422n221**; 76.6.2: **422n226**; 77.4.2: **422n221**; 78.9.5: **422n228**
Cato, *Agr.* Preface: **85–86, 357n163** 1: **86**; 1.3: **354n95**; 2: **86–87**; 3: **87, 398n9**; 3.1: **357n155**; 4: **87, 357n152, 403n19**; 5.1.1–5: **87–88**; 10: **90**; 14.1.5: **249**; 22.3–4: **91**; 32: **347n74**; 36: **347n74**; 41: **347n74**; 41–42: **347n74**; 56–59: **91–92, 351n54**; 61: **87, 347n73**; 128: **249, 403n23**; 131–132: **88–89, 356n124**; 135.1–3: **91**; 136–137: **91, 397n45**; 140: **89, 356n124**; 141.1–4: **89, 356n124**; 142: **88**; 143.1–3: **88**; 156.1–2: **92–93**; 157.1–2: **93**
Cic., *Acad. post.* 1.14 (1.4): **363n22**; 2.11–112 (2.4): **363n22**; 2.80–81 (2.25): **207, 412n63**
Cic., *Acad. pr.* 1.1: **366n68**; 1.40 (1.11): **207**
Cic., *Ad Brut.* 2.4 (2.3.4): **366n70**
Cic., *Att.* 1.4 (1.5.4): **147**; 1.18.6: **353n89**; 1.19: **14, 237, 356n137**; 1.19.6: **415n115**; 1.20.3: **415n115**; 2 (1.6.2): **147**; 4 (1.8.2): **147, 344n40**; 5.2 (1.9.2): **147, 336**; 6.1 (1.10.1): **147**; 7.3 (1.10.3): **147**; 7.3 (1.11.3): **147**; 7.7.3: **351n68**; 8.1 (1.3.1): **146**; 9.3. (1.4.3): **146**; 10.5 (1.1.5): **146, 363n29**; 13.4 (1.13.4): **148, 375n215**; 13.52.2: **413n87**; 14.7 (1.14.7): **399n34**; 15.15.3: **261**; 16 (1.16): **150**; 16.15: **362n5**; 16.18 (1.16): **362n5**; 20.6 (1.2.60): **354n107**; 21.1 (2.1.1): **149, 354n107**; 26.1 (2.6.1): **203**; 28.2 (2.8.2): **220, 408n91**; 29 (2.9): **220**; 32 (2.11): **220**; 34 (2.14): **220**; 35 (2.15.2): **220**; 36.4 (2.16.4): **221, 408n91**; 52–53 (3.7–8): **408n93**; 73 (4.1): **362n14**; 74 (4.2): **144, 399n19**; 74.5 (4.2.5): **362n7**; 75.3 (4.3): **144**; 77.3 (4.7.3): **399n28**; 79.1–2 (4.8.1–2): **250, 399n21**; 80 (4.5.2): **362n2**; 84.1 (4.10.1): **204, 387n72**; 90 (4.15): **355n116**; 92.2 (4.18.2): **204**; 95.1 (5.2.1): **222**; 96 (5.3): **389n16**; 97 (5.4): **389n16**; 105.3 (5.12.3): **253**; 115 (6.1.25): **406n70, 409n16**; 116 (6.2): **366n62, 389n20, 400n40**; 128.3 (75.3): **222**; 138 (7.14.3): **408n97**; 152 (8.2.3): **408n97**; 167 (9.1.3): **408n97**; 170 (8.9.3): **408n97**; 176.4 (9.9.4): **254**; 179 (9.12.1): **408n94**; 180.6 (9.13.6): **255**; 180.8 (9.13.8): **254**; 185 (5.2.1): **412n63**; 189 (9.19.1): **386n41, 408n98**; 198 (10.7.1.): **408n94**; 217.6 (11.6.6): **255**; 233.1 (12.19.1): **261**; 246 (12.9): **221**; 248 (12.1): **364n43, 390n34**; 258.2 (12.20.2): **261**; 259.1 (12.12.1): **261**; 260.2 (12.21.2): **261**; 261.3 (12.22.3): **261**; 262.3 (12.23.3): **261**; 264 (12.25): **261**; 266.1 (12.271): **261**; 268 (12.29): **364n40**; 268.2 (12.29.2): **261**; 269.1 (12.33.1): **261**; 272 (12.31): **261**; 274 (12.35): **261**; 275.1 (12.36.1): **261**; 276.2 (12.37.2): **261**; 300.1–2 (13.29.1–2): **261, 362n3**; 302.4 (13.31.4): **261**; 309 (13.33): **366n68**; 330.1 (13.6.1): **255**; 310.2 (13.6.2): **356n130**; 317 (13.9): **389n7**; 330.1 (13.33a.1): **261**; 338.3 (13.46.3): **257, 366n62, 389n20, 400n40**; 340 (10.1.1): **408n97**; 341 (10.2.1): **408n97**; 352.1 (13.47a.2): **255**; 353.1–2 (13.52.1–2): **223, 366n62, 389n9, 408n92**; 363 (14.9): **257, 366n62, 400n40**; 364.3 (14.10.3): **257**; 365 (14.11.2): **257**; 366 (13.4.4): **204**; 367.1 (14.13.1): **257**; 367.5 (14.13.5): **257**; 369–371, 371A (14.15–17, 14.17A): **398n4**; 369.3 (14.15.3): **257**; 370.1 (14.16.1): **258**; 371.1 (14.17.1): **257**; 372.6 (14.19.6): **257**; 375 (10.10)–395 (10.18): **408n97**; 380 (15.3): **388n5**; 389 (15.11): **279**; 395 20 (1.20): **395n8**; 402 (10.16.5): **412n63**; 409.5 (16.1.5): **257**; 414.2 (16.6.2): **258**; 414.3 (16.6.3): **258**; 418.1 (16.8.1): **354n43**; 424 (16.13a.2): **389n13**

Cic., *Brut.* 242–243: **389n5**; **364n49**
Cic., *Cael.* 23: **389n11**
Cic., *Cat.* 3.6: **390n33**
Cic., *De leg.* 1.14–15: **150**; 2.1–7 (2.1–3): **150–52**, **365n55**, **420n199**, **408n90**; 2.4 (2.2): **365n59**; 2.7 (2.3.7.): **362n5**
Cic., *De or.* 2.19 (2.5): **143**; 11.46: **350n46**; **364n49**
Cic., *De republica* 1.9: **356n127**
Cic., *Div.* 1.8 (1.5): **143–44**; 1.62: **367n82**, 2.8 (2.3): **144**; 2.119: **367n82**
Cic., *Dom.* **397n1**
Cic., *Fam.* 20.21 (1.9): **407n81**; 20.24 (1.9.24): **253**; 24.1 (7.1.1): **204**, **221**; 24.3 (7.1.3): **204**; 24.5 (7.1.5): **204**; 28.2–3 (7.23.2–3): **146**; 29 (9.8.1): **386n31**; 34.2 (7.11.2): **149**; 37.3 (7.18.3): **222**, **389n19**; 63.2 (13.1): **363n22**; 78 (8.2): **386n35**; 131.1 (13.56.1): **254**, **256**, 144.1–2 (14.18.1–2): **408n97**; 145 (14.14): **408n97**; 146.1–4 (16.12.1–4): **408n96**; 154.2 (2.16.2): **206**, 155 (14.7): **408n99**; 173 (14.20): **222**; 181 (9.6.1): **419n167**; 181.4 (9.6.4): **206**, **366n68**; 190.10 (9.16.10): **255**, 191.1 (9.18.1): **206**; 196.3 (9.15.3): **255**; 198 (9.23): **223**; 209 (7.23.2–3): **148–49**, **360n25**, **362n8**, **364n50**, **386n35**; 218.5 (6.18.5): **260**; 219.1–3 (16.18.1–3): **255–56**; 219.1.5 (16.18.5): **342n5**; 249.2–3 (4.6.2–3): **260**; 262 (6.19): **390n30**; 262.1 (6.19.1): **223**; 314 (13.2): **386n35**; 337.7 (16.21.7): **256**, **387n57**; 339.1 (12.20.1): **224**
Cic., *Fin.* 1.5.14: **205**, **405n47**; 2.8.25: **389n25**; 3.1.7–9: **205–6**; 5.1–3: **205**
Cic., *Leg. Agr.* 2.54: **353n89**; 3.9.7: **400n53**
Cic., *Nat. D.* 2.4.11: **407n79**; 2.67: **356n123**
Cic., *Off.* 1.39.138–139: **403n20**; 1.39.140: **14**, **267**; 2.87 (2.24): **347n72**; 3.1: **207**; 3.2: **207**; 3.3: **207**; 3.4: **208**; 3.99–108: **388n83**
Cic., *Orat.* 1–2: **357n147**; 110 (30–31): **149**, **372n169**, **400n36**
Cic., *Phil.* 2.40–41 (102–105): **366n70**; 2.109: **385n12**
Cic., *Planc.* 19–21 (8): **385n21**; 66 (27): **203**
Cic., *Pro Scauro* 12.27: **355n116**
Cic., *QFr.* 8.2–3 (2.4.2–3): **250**; 9.3 (2.5.3): **250**; 10.3 (2.6.3): **250**; 12.2–4 (2.9.2–4): **221**, **384n11**; 21.1–6 (3.1): **251–52**, **398n36**, 21.4: **252**; 21.5–6 (3.1.5–6): **349n26**; 23.1 (3.3.1): **252**; 24.5 (3.4.5): **252**; 25.1 (3.5.2): **385n16**, 27.4 (3.7.4): **253**, **349n26**, 27.7. (3.77): **253**
Cic., *Sen.* 16.56: **388n84**; 30: **347n72**; 51: **73**; 52–54: **73**; 54: **351n66**; 55–56: **74**; 57–58: **74**; 59: **74–75**, **371–72n156**; 60: **75**; 79–81 (21–22): **347n72**
Cic., *Top.* 1.1: **363n23**
Cic., *Tusc.* 1.7 (1.4): **145**; 1.27: **363n19**; 1.31: **363n19**, 2.2 (2.1): **145**; 2.3: **362n4**;

2.9 (2.3): **145**; 2.32 (2.14): **145**; 3.6–7 (3.3): **145**; 3.28: **363n19**; 4.7 (4.4): **145**; 5.11 (5.4): **145**; 5.91 (5.32): **363n21**
Cic., *Verr.* 2.1.27–29 (2.1.10–11): **345n59**; 2.2.2 (5): **70**; 2.2.3 (6–7): **71**; 2.2.5 (13): **71**; 2.2.35–47 (2.2.14–19): **345n59**; 2.2.53–57 (2.2.22–23): **345n59**; 2.2.82–91 (2.2.34–37): **345n58**; 2.4.3–7 (2.4.2–3): **72**; 2.4.6 (12–14): **347n67**; 29–32: **376n247**
Columella, *Rust.* 1 Preface 1–6: **111**; 1 Preface 6: **347n72**; 1 Preface 10–15: **112–13**; 1 Preface 17–21: **113**; 1 Preface 29: **357n147**; 1 Preface 29–31: **113**; 1 Preface 31–33: **113–14**, 1.1.7–14: **357n151**; 1.1.18–19: **114**; 1.2.1–5: **114–15**; 1.4.5–10: **115–16**; 1.5.1–10: **116–17**; 1.5.7: **390n34**; 1.6.1–2: **117**; 1.6.3: **117**; 1.6.4: **357n158**; 1.6.9–24: **357n159**; 1.6.7–8: **117–18**, **357n158**; 1.6.19–20: **118**, **362n55**; 1.7.1–7: **118**; 1.8.1–14: **119–20**; 1.8.15–20: **121**, **349n30**, **351n49**; 1.9.1–9: **122**, **396n25**; 1.9.4–5: **350n43**; 2.1.1.: **356n143**; 2.1.2: **356n133**; 2.2.1.5–6: **78**; 2.2.1–6: **348n7**; 3.6.1–4: **347n74**; 3.8.5: **395n11**; 3.10: **347n74**; 3.17–19: **347n74**; 4.13.2: **57n7**; 4.13–14: **348n74**; 4.17: **348n74**; 5.4: **348n74**; 5.6.1–5: **56n7**; 5.9: **348n74**; 10.150–154: **348n74**; 11.2: **347n74**, **348n74**; 11.5: **347n72**; 12 Preface 1: **123**; 12 Preface 1–7: **347n72**; 12 Preface 4–10: **123–24**, **358n165**; 12.1.1–3: **120**, **358n166**; 12.1.6: **121**; 12.7: **347n72**

D
Diod. Sic. 24.1.1–4: **388n83**; 34.31–32: **70**, **344n48**; 34.33: **70**; 34.34–35: **70**
Diog. Laert. 1.36: **384n7**; 1.40: **384n7**
Dion. Hal., *Ant. Rom.* 1.76–78: **416n125**; 1.79.11: **360n21**; 4.13.4: **359n14**; 10.8: **421n210**
Dioscurides 2.144: **342n11**; 2.152: **342n11**; 2.199: **342n11**; 2.205: **359n182**; 5.25: **359n182**; 5.526: **359n182**

E
Elegiae in Maecenatem 1.31–36: **277**, **409n13**
Eugippus, *Vita Severini* 4.6: **409n6**

F
Fav., *Artis arch.* 13: **140**, **361n48**; 14: **140**; 16.5: **140**; 16–18: **361n48**; 24: **361n48**; 25: **140**; 29.5: **361n47**
Florus, *Epitome* 40.15–16: **380n307**
Frontinus, *Aq.* 1.4: **401n73**; 1.7–8: **401n73**; 1.12–14: **401n73**; 1.19: **401n73**; 1.25 **359n4**; 2.125: **401n73**; 6–7: **371n152**; 9.4.1: **400n53**; 13–14: **423n238**; 92: **371n152**
Fronto, *Ep.* 1.9: **417n143**; 2.1.4 (37): **419n175**; 2.1.5 (37): **278**, **420n197**; 2.1.7: **420n189**; 2.5 (35): **311**; 2.6: **420n193**; 2.6.3 (44): **311**; 3.1: **311–12**; 3.2–6: **313**;

4.4 (59): **309**, **374n196**, **417n148**, **420n186**; 4.5 (60): **309**, **387n73**, **417n148**, **420n186**; 4.6 (61): **310**; 9.7: **418n165**; 9.11: **418n165**; 10.1: **418n165**
Fronto, *Ep. gr.* 1 (30): **420n189**; 2 (47): **420n189**

G
Gal., *De indol.* 1–4: **215**, **419n182**, **422n216**; 5–7: **210**; 8–10: **215**, **419n182**, **422n216**; 12a–20: **215–16**; 18: **419n182**; 21–23: **216**
Gell., *NA* 1.2.1–2: **178**; 3.9: **356n128**, 13.20.1: **419n182**; 17.2: **420n186**; 17.17.1: **365n53**; 19.10.1–8: **407n88**
Gerontius, *Vit. Mel.* Greek: 9.1.2–10.1: **199**; 10.4–6: **199**; 12.1: **383n332**; 14.2: **383n332**; 15.1–6: **383n332**; 15.2: **383n332**; 20: **383n335**
Gerontius, *Vit. Mel.* Latin 7.1–2: **199**; 9.1.2–10.1: **199**; 10.4–6: **199**; 11.2: **383n324**; 12.1: **383n332**; 15.1–6: **383n332**; 15.1: **383n326**, 15.2: **383n332**; 18.1–4: **199**; 20: **383n331**; 21.1: **199–200**; 21.4: **199–200**
Gregory of Nyssa, *Letters* 20.5–6: **14**; 20.1–21: **178–79**, **371n143**
Gregory of Nyssa, *Life of Macrina* 21.1–7: **374n213**

H
HA, Antonius Elagabalus (*Heliogabalus*) 1.1–2: **409n5**; 17.14.4–6: **423n229**; 17.20.1: **423n229**; 17.28.1: **423n229**; 17.30.7–8: **423n229**
HA, Ant. Pius 3.1.8–9: **307**; 3.2.10–11: **307**; 3.7.11–12: **307**; 3.10.4: **419n182**; 3.11.2–3: **307**; 5.1: **417n150**; 7.3: **421n203**; 10.4: **418n165**; 12: **418n163**
HA, Aurel. 26.10.2–3: **423n231**; 26.14.1–9: **423n236**; 35: **395n6**; 46.1: **424n248**; 48: **395n6**
HA, Avid. Cass. 6.5–7: **418n165**; 9.5.12: **418n165**
HA, Clod. 12.5.1: **422n226**; 12.11.7–8: **422n226**; 12.11.12: **422n226**
HA, Comm. 1.2: **314**; 1.7–9: **314**; 4.5–6: **421n214**; 5.9: **421n215**; 5.11: **421n214**; 8.5: **314**
HA, Gall. 23.18.5: **424n246**
HA, Gord. 20.3.5–8: **423n239**; 20.6.5–7: **423n239**; 20.7.1: **423n229**; **423n239**; 20.17–22: **423n239**; 20.22: **424n240**; 20.24.1–2: **424n247**; 20.27.9–10: **424n247**; 20.28.1–6: **424n247**; 20.71: **423n239**; 32.1–8: **318**
HA, Hadr. 1.8.10: **408n3**; 1.16.5–7: **421n202**; 1.25.8: **366n63**; 2.1–2: **417n148**; 14.5–7: **418n159**; 14.8–9: **417n143**; 16.1: **417n143**; 16.8–10: **417n143**; 19: **414n92**; 19.12–13: **417n145**; 20.13: **417n148**; 22.13: **419n170**; 23.7–8: **417n151**; 25.5–8: **417n150**; 26: **420n186**; 26.3–4: **417n148**; 26.5: **306**

HA, M. Ant. 13.4.4: **423n237**
HA, The Two Maximini (Maximini Duo) 19.4.4: **423n230**; 19.51-2: **423n230**
HA, M. Aur. 6.3: **418n165, 420n187, 420n194**; 10.2-3: **408n3**; 11.1: **421n203**; 15.5: **409n4**
HA, Pert. 3.2-4: **422n225**; 9.4-7: **422n225**; 13.4-5: **422n225**
HA, Pesc. Nig. 6.8-9: **314**; 12.1-3: **409n5**
HA, Probus 28.2.1: **421n182**
HA, Sev. 4.6-7: **422n227**; 10.4.4-7: **422n227**
HA, Sev. Alex. 18.13.5-6-18.14.1: **316**; 18.26.9-11: **317**; 18.29.1-3: **317**; 18.30.1-4: **317**; 18.31.1-5: **317**
HA, Tac. 10.5-6: **424n248**; 11.4-6: **424n248**; 27.7.5-7: **319**; 27.15.1: **319**; 27.16.1-3: **319**; 27.19.3-5: **319**
HA, Tyr. Trig. 25.1-4: **423n233**; 33.2: **423n230**
HA, Verus 2.5: **418n165**
Hdn. 1.8.3-8: **421n215**; 1.12.1-2: **314**; 1.14.2-4: **419n182**; 3.6.7: **422n226**
Hdt. 1.93: **375n216**; 6.137: **372n160**; 7.27: **411n48**; 7.31: **411n48**
Hes., Op. 1-26: **60**; 27-41: **60-61**; 42-212: **61**; 109-126: **380n308**; 213-218: **61**; 219-237: **61**; 238-305: **61**; 306-311: **61**; 320: **61**; 321-334: **61**; 335-360: **61-62**; 383-396: **62**; 399: **343n16**; 405-413: **62**; 414-535: **62**; 536-546: **62**; 547-560: **62**; 633-640: **62**; 641-681: **62-63**; 682-694: **63**; 694-705: **63**; 706-714: **63**; 715-726: **63**; 727-828: **63, 343n24, 358n171**; 805-809: **343n20**; 817-818: **343n20**
Hes., Theog. 1-35: **375n215**; 225-226: **342n8**; 560-612: **342n12**
Hom., Il. 6.119-236: **392n62**; 9.139: **397n43**
Hom., Od. 1.55-60: **365n58**; 3.171: **389n13**; 5.135-136: **365n58**; 6-13: **370n133**; 7.112-132: **375n219**; 7.114-116: **375n220**; 9.19-24: **375n217**; 16.137-145: **348n75**; 24.239-301: **348n75**
Hor., Ars P. 79-82: **374n203**; 386-387: **385n14**
Hor., Epist. 1.6.45-48: **405n44**; 1.10.20-21: **401n71**; 1.16.1-16: **156**
Hor., Epod. 2.1-70: **157-58, 373n177**; 2: **19**; 9.1-5: **277, 409n13**
Hor., Odes 1.1: **390n36**; 1.2.30-52: **418n161**; 1.7: **418n161**; 1.20: **224**; 1.21.9-12: **418n161**; 1.37.5: **390n37**; 2.3.1-8: **390n37**; 2.6.10: **373n175**; 3.1: **366n77**; 3.29.1-16: **277, 409n13**; 31.15: **342n11**
Hor., Sat. 1.5.49-50: **390n34**; 1.10.39: **385n14**; 1.6.71-92: **367n88**; 2.1: **364n48**; 2.3.64-68: **364n40, 364n46**; 2.3.247-559: **407n88**; 2.6.1-19: **155-56**; 2.6.20-58: **156**; 2.6.59-76: **156**; 2.6.77-117: **156**; 2.27: **370n120**
Hyginus, Fabulae 191: **376n244**

J
Jerome, Ep. 108: **381n319**; 129: **382n321**
Jord., Get. 32-33: **424n251**; 46: **424n251**; 242-243: **321**
Joseph., AJ 18.8.1 (257-259): **411n51**; 18.9 (305): **411n51**; 19.5.12: **411n51**
Juv., Satires 1.26-30: **301, 407n76**; 3.307: **390n33**; 4.5-10: **301**; 4.10.12-18: **293**; 4.38: **301**; 4.144-149: **415n120**; 6.82-84: **407n76**; 7.178-190: **245**; 10.76-81: **394n3**; 11: **390n38**; 11.69-342n11**; 13.210-216: **416n122**; 13.310-316: **390n37**; 15.44-46: **407n76**

L
Lactant., Div. inst. 5.14-15: **363n25**
Livy 1.3-4: **416n125**; 1.9-11: **401n1**; 1.14-15: **413n81**; 2.42.11: **416n125**; 3.14: **421n210**; 3.26: **392n75**; 3.26.6-12: **388n84**; 3.55: **355n114**; 6.35: **403n16**; 6.42: **355n114**; 25.11: **373n175**; 31.50-56: **355n114**; 34.44.5: **355n115**; 36.1-6: **403n16**; 37.12: **403n16**
Livy, Per. 2: **416n125**
Lucr. 3.35-36: **274**; 3.94-829: **274**; 3.136-176: **274**; 3.140: **407n72**; 3.1053-1075: **274-75**

M
Macrob., Sat. 3.15.6: **389n17**
M. Aur., Med. 4.33.1: **312-13**; 11.22: **156**; 12.27.2: **313**; 16.8: **307**
Mart., Epig. 2.14.10: **406n63**; 2.40.5-6: **390n37**; 3.2: **370n123**; 3.4: **370n124**; 3.25: **370n123**; 3.47: **225-26, 370n122, 370n123**; 3.58: **162-63, 370n125**; 4.1: **415n120**; 4.3.1-4: **410n35**; 4.30.1-7: **299**; 4.42.11: **336**; 4.63: **412n64**; 4.64: **164, 402n6**; 5.1: **299, 409n8**; 5.71: **227, 370n123**; 6.43: **208**; 7.31: **16, 226, 360n34**; 7.36: **260**; 7.49: **16, 226, 360n34, 361n36**; 7.63: **386n50**; 8.55.13-14: **390n47**; 8.77.6: **390n47**; 9.18: **259-60, 398n4**; 9.23: **415n120**; 9.24: **415n120**; 9.31: **421n212**; 9.54: **16, 226, 360n34**; 9.60: **227, 360n34**; 9.100: **370n122**; 10.37.5-8: **373n186**; 11.7.1-6: **299**; 11.47.3: **406n63**; 11.48: **386n50**; 11.49.7: **390n47**; 11.50 (49): **386n50**; 12.63.3: **373n175**; 13: **360n34**; 13.109: **300**; 13.111: **419n179**; 13.115: **411n39, 419n79**
Mart., Spect. 295-96: **417n145**

N
Nep., Att. 3.4: **405n55**; 4.5: **405n55**; 11.1-5: **405n55**; 13.1-7: **271**; 14.1: **271**; 25.5.1: **405n53**; 25.11.6: **405n52**; 25.52-3: **405n54**

O
On God's Providence (Carmen de Providentia Dei) 913-916: **200**
Ovid, Amores 3.1.14: **374n203**; 3.1.45: **374n203**

Ovid, Ars am.1.67: **406n63**
Ovid, Fasti 1.657-704: **353n88**; 2.533-546: **391n46**; 2.617-638: **391n46**; 3.523-540: **370n131**; 6.637-648: **409n16**
Ovid., Her. 18: **371n146**; 18.131: **371n146**; 19: **371n146**
Ovid, Met. 1.89-150: **380n308**; 1.111-112: **380n308**; 1.260-269: **375n215**; 1.452-567: **381n313**; 1.568-576: **418n161**; 5.573-641: **371n153**; 11.127-145: **376n244**; 11.136-144: **375n216**

P
Palladius, Lausiac History 54: **383n326**
Palladius, Op. Agr. 1.1.1-2: **124-25**; 1.2: **125**; 1.3: **125**; 1.5-6: **358n170**; 1.6.1-4: **125, 357n152**; 1.6.2: **354n99**; 1.6.6-8: **126**; 1.6.10: **126**; 1.6.12: **126**; 1.6.14: **126**; 1.6.17: **126**; 1.7.1: **126**; 1.7.3: **127**; 1.8.1-3: **127**; 1.9.1: **127**; 1.9.5: **127, 361n48**; 1.12: **127**; 1.15: **128**; 1.16: **128**; 1.17.4: **128**; 1.18.1:128**; 1.34.1: **129**; 1.39.1: **129**; 1.39.3-5: **129**; 3.8: **375n221**; 5.4: **375n221**; 7.2: **375n221**; 12.6: **375n221**; 14.1.1: **129**; 14.1.4: **129**; 14.47-50: **347n74**
Paulinus of Nola, Ep. 1.37: **381n320**; 4.4: **381n320**; 5.6: **381n320**; 5.16: **382n320**; 10.2-3: **382n320**; 11.14: **382n320**; 13.13: **381n320**; 24.1: **381n320, 382n322**; 24.3: **381n320, 382n322**; 24.7: **381n320, 382n322**; 29.5-13: **382n320**; 30.2-3: **382n322**; 30.6: **382n322**; 31.2: **382n320**; 32.5: **382n320**; 32.1-9: **382n322**; 32.9-10: **382n320**; 32.10-12: **381n320**; 32.17: **381n320**; 39.1: **381n320**
Paulinus of Nola, Carm.15: **381n320**; 16: **381n320**; 16.284-289: **382n320**; 18: **381n320**; 21.84-104: **382n320**; 21.294-305: **383n326**; 21.365-394: **381n320**; 21.428-473: **381n320**; 23: **381n320**; 24: **381n320**; 26: **381n320**; 27.508-595: **380n312, 381n320**; 27-29: **381n320**
Paulinus, Euch.1-41: **187**; 8-16: **377n258**; 42-47: **187**; 72-84: **187**; 153-175: **187**; 176-219: **187-88**; 220-616: **188-90**
Paus. 2.27.3: **356n135**; 3.2.3-4: **336**; 3.14.8: **336**; 3.16.6: **336**; 3.16.10: **336**; 3.18.2: **336**; 6.20.18: **372n168**; 9.5.1: **356n122**; 9.25.5-9: **375n215**; 9.27.3-5: **346n63**; 10.5.9: **418n161**; 10.24.1: **384n7**
Petron., Sat. 28.6-8: **354n100**
Philo, Leg. 29 (185): **290**; 44 (350-352): **290**; 45 (358-359): **290**; 45 (361): **290**; 45 (364-366): **290-91**
Philostratus, Imagines 1.31: **360n34**; 2.26: **360n34**
Philostratus, Life of Apollonius of Tyana (V A) 19-20: **417n149**
Pindar, Ol. 2.69-74: **375n215**
Pindar, Threnoi 3 (fragment 128c) 5-12: **372n168**

Plaut., *Cas.* 420–488: **350n46**
Plaut., *Pseud.* 491–536: **350n46**
Plin., *Ep.* 1.3.1–5: **209, 373n180**; 1.4.1–4: **228, 396n27**; 1.6.1–3: **210, 368n93, 387n61, 392n63, 417n140**; 1.7.6: **16, 228, 360n34**; 1.8: **396n36**; 1.9.1–8: **208–9**; 1.21: **240–41**; 1.24.1–4: **258**; 2.1–2: **16, 228, 229, 360n34**; 2.2.2: **210**; 2.8.1–3: **210**; 2.15.1–2: **258–59**; 2.17.1–5: **22, 156, 170–73, 229, 344n40, 396n27, 420n184**; 2.4.3–4: **238–39**; 3.1.1–12: **213–14**; 3.4: **396n36**; 3.6: **239, 391n58, 396n38**; 3.7.6–10: **210**; 3.19.1–9: **240, 349n15, 350n45, 397n42, 397n48**; 3.19.8: **227**; 4.1: **228–29, 396n36, 396n38**; 4.6.1–3: **240**; 4.11: **301**; 4.13.1–2: **387n62**; 4.23.1–4: **211**; 5.4.1–2: **241**; 5.6.1–46: **156, 173–76, 379n283, 393n93, 370n124**; 5.6.16–20: **14**; 5.6.32–40: **14**; 5.18.1–2: **211**; 5.19: **387n65**; 6.3.1–2: **238, 259, 367n77**; 6.10.1–6: **228, 419n167**; 6.14.1–2: **229**; 6.16.11–12: **229–30**; 6.28.1–3: **230**; 6.30.1–5: **259, 401n70**; 6.31.1–2: **303, 397n4, 421n201**; 6.31.13–17: **303, 421n201**; 7.4–5: **211**; 7.11: **373n180**; 7.11.1–8: **241, 391n57, 400n58**; 7.14: **373n180**; 7.18.1–5: **241–42, 391n58, 394n5**; 7.25.1–6: **211–12**; 8.1: **387n65**; 8.2.1–8: **242–43, 396n26**; 8.15: **212, 387n60**; 8.18.4: **420n194**; 8.18.7–9: **397n2**; 9.7.1–5: **176–77**; 9.10.1–3: **212, 368n93, 386n45, 417n140**; 9.13.13: **227**; 9.19.1: **228**; 9.32: **212**; 9.36.1–6: **212–13**; 9.37.1–5: **243**; 9.39.1–6: **233–34, 391n58, 396n38**; 9.40.1–3: **213**; 10.8.1–8: **238, 244, 391n58, 395n24, 396n38**; 10.9: **244**
Plin., *Pan.* 47.4: **422n220**; 50.5–6: **260**; 81.3–4: **300**; 82.1–2: **301**; 82.8: **304–5**
Plin., *HN* 2.225 (2.106): **371n153**; 3.17: **353n88**; 3.241 (3.97): **370n127**; 4.31 (4.8): **418n161**; 4.43 (4.11): **372n168**; 4.51 (4.6): **335**; 4.64 (4.12): **335**; 5.22 (5.2): **336**; 5.29 (5.4): **336**; 5.151; (36.43): **336**; 6.139: **353n88**; 6.184: **389n6**; 6.202: **389n6**; 7.125 (7.37): **376n233**; 8.223–224 (8.82): **56n3**; 9.46: **389n6**; 9.55: **356n133**; 9.76 (39): **409n17**; 9.167 (78): **409n17**; 9.171 (9.80): **356n134, 404n43**; 9.172: **389n17**; 10.23: **389n17**; 10.45 (10.23): **56n3, 370n126**; 10.90 (10.47): **421n204**; 10.141 (10.72): **366n72**; 12.4–12 (12.2–5): **411n48**; 12.5 (10–11): **289**; 12.14 (35.2–3): **365n52**; 14.11 (14.3): **409n16**; 14.47–52 (16.5): **369n113**; 14.61–66 (14.8): **390n37, 419n179**; 14.61: **395n11**; 14.139 (14.4): **419n179**; 15.71 (15.19): **420n199**; 15.119–126 (15.36–38): **420n199**; 15.136–137 (15.40): **285, 414n96**; 16.18 (16.7): **56n3**; 16.35–36: **359n4**; 16.47–52 (16.5): **237–38**; 16.201: **355n115**; 17.96–99 (17.21): **348n74**; 17.96–140

(17.21–31): **347n74**; 17.156: **347n74**; 17.173: **348n74**; 18.6 (26): **351n64**; 18.7 (18.2): **265–66**; 18.7 (32–33): **267–68**; 18.18–21 (18.4): **266, 350n33, 350n44, 351n53**; 18.21 (18.5): **396n25**; 18.22–23: **348n2, 352n86**; 18.31: **357n152**; 18.32: **357n155**; 18.35 (18.7): **266, 374n207**; 18.231 (18.62): **421n204**; 18.262 (18.67): **403n18**; 18.296 (18.72): **403n18**; 19.50–51 (19.19): **402n6**; 19.141 (19.41): **420n199**; 22.4 (12–13): **269**; 22.4–8 (6–17): **404n34**; 23.33 (20.1): **416n122**; 29.42–51 (29.11): **391n45**; 31.6–9 (31.3): **152, 366n62, 371n154, 400n40**; 33.54 (33.16): **413n84**; 33.153 (54): **400n48**; 34.45–46 (34.18): **414n92**; 34.57 (34.19): **346n66**; 34.69–70 (34.19): **418n161**; 35.3 (35.1): **336**; 35.4–8 (35.2): **365n52**; 35.6 (35.2): **364n51**; 35.9–11 (35.2): **365n52, 387n57**; 35.116–117 (35.37): **22, 27, 159**; 35.118 (35.37): **368n100**; 35.120 (35.34): **413n84**; 35.123: **356n135**; 35.130 (35.40): **363n27**; 35.174–177 (35.30): **56n3**; 36.3: **386n35**; 36.4 (36.2): **56n3**; 36.4–8 (36.2–3): **406n56**; 36.14 (36.4): **336**; 36.20 (36.4): **418n161**; 36.22–23 (36.4): **346n63**; 36.44–46 (36.5): **336**; 36.46 (36.5): **335**; 36.49 (36.7): **335, 336**; 36.50 (36.8): **406n56**; 36.63 (36.13): **336**; 36.63–74 (36.14–15): **336**; 36.102: **355n115**; 36.111 (36.24): **413n84**; 36.111–112 (36.23): **294**; 36.113–115 (36.23): **406n56**; 36.184: **371n151**; 37.115 (37.37): **336**
Plat., *Cra.* 397e: **380n308**
Plat., *Phdr.* 229a: **365n60**; 230b: **365n60**
Plut., *Cons. ad Apoll.* 9.2: **417n143**
Plut., *Lyc.* 29: **336**; 31: **336**
Plut., *Vit. Artax.* 1.1–3: **348n77**
Plut., *Vit. Caes.* 40: **408n95**
Plut., *Vit. Cam.* **388n83**
Plut., *Vit. Cat. Mai.* 2.1–2: **15, 267, 391n40**; 4.4: **267**; 5: **403n23**; 25.1–2: **267**
Plut., *Vit. Cat. Min.* 20.1: **406n64**
Plut., *Vit. Cic.* 47–49: **408n102**
Plut., *Vit. Crass.* 1.2: **271**
Plut., *Vit. Luc.* 1.3–5: **269**; 37.1: **405n45**; 38.4: **269**; 39.1–4: **14, 269–70, 405n53**; 39.5: **270, 404n39, 405n53**; 40.1: **270, 405n53**; 41.1–5: **405n45**; 42.1–4: **270, 385n22, 418n158**
Plut., *Vit. Lys.* 3–4 (434): **348n77**; 6 (436): **348n77**; 9 (437): **348n77**
Plut., *Vit. Mar.* 2.2: **268**; 2.1–2: **403n27**; 34.1–2: **268, 407n78**
Plut., *Publicola* 15.3–4 (105): **415n113**
Plut., *Vit. Pomp.* 40.5: **271**; 44: **385n12**; 48.4–6: **272**; 80.6: **406n64**
Plut., *Vit. Rom.* 20.4: **360n21**
Plut., *Vit. Sull.* 22.1: **404n31**; 31.5–6: **268**
Plut., *Vit. Ti. Gracch.* 8.1–7: **265, 350n34, 402n10**

Polyb. 1.41–48: **388n83**; 3.91.2–10: **407n77**; 6.53.1–10: **364n51**; 12.4d5–8: **371n153**; 7.1.1: **407n77**
Priapeia carmina 3: **410n35**
Prop. 1.6: **375n216**; 1.223–228: **304**; 1.237–248: **304**; 2.32.7–16: **272**; 2.34: **373n175**; 3.32: **373n15**; 4.8.75: **406n63**; 4.18.15–22: **406n62**

Q
Quint., *Inst.* 8.3.7–11: **55**; 10.1.33: **343n28**

R
Rut. Namat., *De red.* 1.223–228: **304**; 1.237–248: **304**; 1.413–414: **417n138**; 1.463–468: **230**; 1.507–508: **230**; 1.527–530: **231**; 1.541–558: **15, 230–31**; 1.615–628: **231**

S
Sen., *Clem.* 1.18.2: **409n17**
Sen., *De ira* 3.40.1–5: **409n16; 409n17**
Sen., *Ep.* 5.37: **336**; 51.1–6: **275**; 51.10–13: **275–76**; 51.11: **358n176**; 55.1–3: **159–60**; 55.6–8: **14, 160**; 86.1–15: **160**
Sen., *Otio* 5: **208**
Sen. *De beneficiis* 3.28.2: **364n51**
Sid. Apoll., *Ep.* 1.6.1–5: **216–17**; 1.6.2: **365n51**; 2.1–20: **191–94**; 2.9.1–10: **232–33**; 2.14.1–2: **233–34**; 3.6: **216**; 8.4.1–2: **217**; 8.8.1–3: **217–18**; 8.9.21–44: **377n265**
Sid. Apoll., *Carm.* 5.37: **336**; 18.1–12: **194**; 19.1–4: **194**; 21.1–4: **16, 234**; 22.33: **379n294**; 22.101–235: **195–97**; 22.200–201: **381n320**; 24: **393n88**; 24.51–74: **234**
Stat., *Silv.* 1 Preface 25–28: **371n140**; 1.3.1–75: **358n176, 424n248**; 1.3.1–110: **165–67**; 2.2.1–35: **358n176, 392n64**; 2.2.1–146: **167–70**; 2.2.12–26: **410n36**; 2.2.42–99: **409n7**; 2.2.82: **373n170**; 2.2.90: **336**; 3.5.28–31: **415n120**; 4.1.1–25: **164–65, 409n8**; 4.2.18–35: **415n120**; 4.2.63–67: **415n120**
Strabo 1.94: **372n160**; 3.1.6: **355n110**; 3.1.7: **355n110**; 3.2.1: **355n110**; 3.3.7: **355n110**; 3.4.2: **355n110**; 4.5.8: **22**; 4.8.52–53: **336**; 5.1.7: **353n88**; 5.1.12: **353n88**; 5.2.3: **417n139**; 5.3: **372n160**; 5.3.1: **353n8, 354n109**; 5.3.6: **390n37**; 5.4: **369n114**; 5.4.3: **353n88**; 5.4.5: **369n108, 373n185**; 5.4.8: **359n14**; 5.4.9: **372n160, 373n170**; 5.9: **401n71**; 5.13: **401n73**; 6.2.4: **371n153**; 6.276 (6.7): **345n56**; 7.3.13–14: **372n168**; 7.3.25: **372n162**; 8.7.5: **369n111**; 9.1.23: **336**; 9.410 (9.25): **346n64, 346n65**; 9.5.16: **335**; 9.5.22: **375n215**; 10.1.6: **335**; 11.1.6: **369n111**; 12.6.2: **369n111**; 14.5.8: **369n111**
Suet., *Aug.* 2.73–74: **409n14**; 5: **283, 409n10**; 6: **283**; 18.298: **372n162**; 29.1: **419n182**; 30: **359n14**; 31.1: **419n182**; 64.2: **419n171**; 70: **411n41**; 70.1–2:

409n14; 72: 284; 85: 336; 92.1–2: 283; 97.1–2: 286; 98.1–6: 286; 100: 285
Suet., *Calig.* 19.1–3: 411n45; 22.2: 413n79; 37.2–3: 289; 50.1: 411n49
Suet., *Claud.* 12.2: 396n31
Suet., *Dom.* 3.3.1: 298; 3.4.4: 300; 3.15.2: 301–2, 415n104; 3.19.1: 415n120; 4.4: 416n121; 13: 397n47; 17.3: 416n129
Suet., *Galb.* 1–3: 285, 414n96; 2: 410n22, 410n23; 4.1: 296; 4.3: 296; 18.2–3: 296; 20: 414n99
Suet., *Iul.* 20: 353n91; 20.1–3: 353n89; 38.1: 353n89; 46: 273; 411n46; 47: 273; 50: 273; 56.1: 406n67; 56.7: 406n67; 61.1: 406n67; 81.1: 406n68; 83.1–2: 273
Suet., *Nero* 1: 412n61; 9.1: 412n61; 25.1: 412n61; 31.1–2: 294–95, 389n26, 414n89, 414n92; 34.1–5: 412n64; 38: 277; 39.1–3: 413n81; 45–46: 410n24; 50: 332
Suet., *Otho* 7: 413n82
Suet., *Tib.* 11: 410n28; 15: 410n29; 38–41: 44; 287, 410n38; 42: 410n33; 43: 44; 287, 410n36; 44–45: 411n37; 50: 415n116; 60: 411n37, 411n43
Suet., *Tit.* 2.3.3: 298; 2.11.1: 298
Suet., *Vesp.*1.2: 297; 1.5.1: 297; 1.5.4: 297; 1.24.1: 415n104; 9: 414n95; 18: 414n92
Symm., *Ep.* 4.30: 392n73

T
Tac., *Ann.*1.5: 410n29; 1.9: 409n16, 410n271.10: 409n17; 1.43: 410n30; 1.79: 355n116; 4.59: 288, 410n31; 4.62: 410n32; 4.67: 44; 288, 409n15, 409n16; 6.1: 410n34; 6.21: 44; 288; 6.50: 410n30; 9.1: 291; 9.3: 291; 9.37–38: 412n60; 12.60: 409n17; 13.42: 412n67; 14.3–4: 292; 14.4: 416n121; 14.5–9: 412n64; 14.9–11: 412n64; 14.52–53: 292–93; 15.23: 412n61, 415n118; 15.38: 295; 15.38–39: 413n76; 15.40: 356n127; 15.42: 295; 15.43: 413n77; 15.60: 412n70; 55: 293
Tac., *Hist.* 5.9: 411n51; 16.8.3: 391n57
Ter., *Phorm.* 203: 392n65
Tertullian, *De Pallio* 5.6.1–2: 409n17
Thucydides 4.109: 372n160

V
Val. Max. 2.10.2: 369n111; 9.5.4: 404n33
Varro, *Ling.* 5.22: 54, 354n93; 5.35: 54, 354n93; 5.54: 356n123; 5.64: 356n123; 6.25: 351n68; 6.29: 351n68; 6.14: 412n62; 6.15: 388n1; 8.9: 349n29
Varro, *Rust.* 1.1–7: 94–95; 1.1.7: 357n1491.1.8–11: 352n85; 1.1.11: 95, 366n65; 1.2.1: 95; 1.2.3: 95, 349n20; 1.2.3–7: 360n23; 1.2.6–10: 95–96; 1.2.9: 403n16; 1.2.9–10: 357n149; 1.2.12–14: 96; 1.2.22: 357n149; 1.2.22–28: 351n61; 1.3.1–4: 96; 1.7.1–2: 97; 1.10.1–2: 97; 1.11.1–2: 97, 357n155; 1.12.1–2: 97; 1.13.1–2: 97–98, 350n42; 1.13.2–5: 354n96; 1.13.6–7: 98, 354n96; 1.14.4: 354n98; 1.15: 366n68; 1.16.1–6: 98–99; 1.16.5: 357n149; 1.17.1–7: 99–100, 349n29, 350n42, 397n45; 1.17.5: 412n63; 1.18.1–4: 357n149; 1.18.1–8: 100–101, 1.19.3: 100, 350n42, 350n47; 1.22.1–4: 101; 1.22.6: 101; 1.53: 101; 1.69.13: 102; 1.69.2–3: 102; 2.1.1–4: 103, 356n143, 357n163; 2.1.2: 356n133; 2.1.6: 102; 2.1.8: 355n116; 2.1.143: 103; 2.2.6: 102; 2.5: 356n133; 2.10.1–10: 103–4, 349n28, 350n47, 357n163; 2.11.10: 355n113; 2.40–41: 347n74; 3.1.1–5: 105–6; 3.1.10: 355n120; 3.1.17.1–5: 14; 3.1.17.8: 14; 3.2.1–3: 355n116; 3.2.1–11: 106–8, 366n67; 3.2.3: 56; 3.2.4: 355n116; 3.2.10: 56; 3.2.13–18: 108, 366n65, 366n66; 3.2.17: 356n130; 3.3.7–10: 106, 366n65; 3.4.2: 366n71; 3.4.3: 153, 355n120; 3.5.8–17: 23, 153–54, 355n120, 371n140, 371n145; 3.6.1: 370n126; 3.8–17: 355n120; 3.13: 24, 155, 355n120, 356n131; 3.16.10–11: 109, 366n65; 3.16.23: 109; 3.17: 415n116; 3.17.1–9: 109–10, 350n38, 366n65; 3.17.3–10: 389n17; 3.17.10: 110, 366n65; 3.17.15: 356n132; 17.204–205: 347n74; 31: 347n74; 40: 347n74
Vell. Pat. 1.603: 385n12; 2.123.1: 410n27; 2.33.4: 404n39; 2.44.4: 353n91; 2.94–131: 408n2
Verg., *Aen.* 2.782: 370n137; 3.500: 370n137, 4.6–53: 370n131; 5: 379n293; 5.305: 397n41; 6.107: 369n108; 6.162–174: 372n171; 7.1–9: 415n112; 10.284: 392n65; 10.564: 411n39
Verg., *Geor* 1.51–53: 115; 1.108: 379n288; 2.58: 370n121; 2.136–175: 353n88; 4.125–148: 393n95; 4.126: 373n175; 4.176: 374n198
Vitr., *De arch.* 1. Preface 2.2: 132; 1. Preface 2.3: 133; 1.1.2–17: 359n6; 1.1.7: 359n1; 1.2.1–2: 359n7, 359n8; 1.2.3: 359n9; 1.2.5: 359n12; 1.3: 359n5; 1.3.2: 359n13; 1.3.4: 359n10; 1.3.5: 359n11; 1.6.3–8: 357n157; 1.9: 387n77; 1.12.1: 357n1; 2.1.1: 360n19; 2.1.2–3: 15, 133; 2.1.5–7: 15, 133–34; 2.5: 360n21; 2.8.1–4: 418n154; 2.8.1–9: 357n157; 2.8.17–19: 357n157; 2.8.49: 336; 3.8–9: 357n1; 4.6: 413n85; 5.4–7: 359n181; 5.9.1: 406n63; 6. Preface 4: 359n6; 6. Preface 7: 134; 6.1.1–9: 360n23; 6.1.10–11: 134; 6.3.1–4: 360n24; 6.3: 361n49; 6.3.5–11: 360n26; 6.3.6: 134; 6.3.8: 134; 6.4: 361n49; 6.4.1: 135; 6.4.2: 135; 6.5.1: 135; 6.5.1–3: 361n53; 6.5.2: 135–36; 6.5.3: 136; 6.6: 361n49; 6.6.1–5: 136–37, 361n48; 6.6.7: 137; 6.7.1–2: 137–38; 6.7.3: 332; 6.7.4: 16, 17, 138; 6.7.5: 138; 6.7.7: 138; 6.8.1–7: 361n39; 7. Preface 2: 359n1; 7. Preface 14: 359n3; 7.12: 376n233; 7.17: 376n233; 7.3.4: 361n40; 7.3.7: 139; 7.4: 374n194; 7.4.4: 139; 7.5.1–2: 139; 7.5.3–4: 361n44; 8.3.1: 371n152; 8.3.2: 371n154; 9. Preface 17: 359n3; 10.6: 401n72; 10.7: 401n72

X
Xen., *An.* 1.1.9: 348n77; 5.3.7–13: 343n27
Xen., *Cyr.* 8: 347n72
Xen., *Memorabilia of Socrates* 4.2.24: 385n7
Xen., *Oec.* 3.14–16: 67, 357n163; 4.4–5: 66; 4.13–14: 66; 4.17–25: 348n77; 5.1–5: 65; 5.9–11: 65; 5.14–17: 69; 6.4–10: 64–65; 7.1: 64; 7.3–6: 68; 7.20–25: 68, 357n163; 8.10–13: 67, 357n163; 8.18–19: 67; 9.2–7: 12, 66; 9.11–13: 69; 11.14–16: 67; 12.2–4: 69

Z
Zosimus, *Historia Nova* 1.17.2: 425n247

INDEX

Page numbers in *italics* refer to illustrations.

A

Achaemenid Empire, 348n77, 369n115, 405n43
Adelphius the Scholasticus, 178–80, 371n143, 374n211, 375n219
Aegialus, Vetulenus, 160, 237–38, 369n113
Aeneid (Vergil), 166; Aeneas, 176, 299, 373n170, 391n42, 396n42, 400n45, 415n110, 415n112, 416n125; Anchises, 379n293; Ascanius, 415n110, 415n123
Africa, 177, 186, 198, 377n259, 378n269, 402n3; Africa Nova, 374n204, 374n206; Africa Vetus, 199, 336, 362n55, 370n118, 374n204, 383n331, 402n3; governors of, 296, 403n21, 421n212; North Africa, 16, 84, 300n301, 350n39, 371n148, 396n30; Roman military expansion into, 206, 263, 272; slavery and slave trade, 349–50n32, 349n16
Ager Falernus, 223, 308, 329, 331, 367n87, 390nn30–31; wines from, 37, 329, 372n161, 390n37, 416n122. *See also* San Rocco villa
agriculture: abandonment of, 357n173; advantages and nobility of, 15, 64–69, 344nn33–34; Ceres, goddess of, 60, 162, 357n148, 377n255, 380n308; Elagabalus's contempt for, 423n229; ethics and, 343n24; farm animals, 84, 102, 120, 136–37, 342n7, 367n80; Palladius's maxims for, 125–26; religious worship and, 78, 124, 348n7, 352n83, 356n124, 383n323, 387n162; Saturn, mythical patron of, 356nn123–24; slave-based, 110; superiority to city life, 60–61; treatises on, 54, 77–79, 263, 353n88, 395n21. *See also De agricultura*; *On Farming Matters*; *Three Books on Agriculture*; *Work of Farming, The*; *Works and Days*
Agrippa, Marcus, 353n88, 412n68, 417n145, 418n154
Agrippina the Younger, 291–92, 412n64, 414n95
Alba, 165, 289, 306, 307, 371n139, 415n112; imperial villas at, 298, 299, 410n30; "Julian mountain," 300, 416n123; Pompey's villa at, 406n64. *See also* Albanum
Albanum (Domitian's villa at Alba), 43, 281, 298–301, 306; citadel, 43, 415n120; hunting, 415–16n120; luxury and vice, 282, 299; Quinquatria of Minerva, 300, 415n120, 416n121; retirement at, 298, 415n107; Vestal Cornelia, trial of, 301, 416n125
Alexander the Great, 302, 317, 363n21, 376n243, 393n98
Alexandria, 389n11, 401n72, 407n76; "Alexandrian marbles," 370n118; Council of Alexandria, 393n86; Jews in, 290; Melania the Elder in, 383n326; "Pharos of Memphis," 376n234; "ship from Alexandria," 410n25; Syene marble, 169, 336, 373n172; wars, 272. *See also* Origen of Alexandria; Philo of Alexandria
Alps, 333, 354n104, 407n77; Italy south of, 94, 237, 353n88, 394n4
Alsium, 227, 228, 419n167. *See also* Antoninus Pius; Caesar; Marcus Aurelius
Alypius, 199, 383n334, 384n335
Amalthea (Atticus's villa at Epirus, near Buthrotum), 142, 150, 152, 249, 382n320, 405–6n55; "Amaltheum," 152, 365n55, 365–66n61; Cicero invited to, 278, 405–6n55; Cicero's inscriptions for, 142, 150; construction of, 147–48, 150; inauguration of, 363n37; name of, 362n5, 364n47, 365n55
Anagnia, 306, 308, 419n177; Cicero's *deversorium* at, 223, 364n43, 390n34
Anio River, 302, 371nn152–54, 401n73, 418n161, 423n238
Annals (Tacitus): Augustus, 409n15, 410n27; Claudius's wife, 291; Flavian dynasty, 296; Nero and the Domus Aurea, 291–93, 295, 412n64, 412nn69–70, 413n76, 414n88; Tiberius and the Villa Iovis, 287–88, 410nn31–32
Annius Severus, 239, 395n16
Antiochus of Ascalon, 270, 386n31
Antium, 249, 255, 287, 307, 415n111; imperial library at, 216. *See also* Cicero, villa at Antium; Hadrian; Nero
Antoninus Pius (emperor), 178, 306–8, 312, 313, 418–19n165, 419n170, 421n203, 421n207, 422n215; conservatism, 310, 418n165; Hadrian's adoption of, 308, 313, 419n170; Lanuvium, born in, 306, 307, 422n222; Marcus Aurelius, adoptive son of, 307, 308, 310, 313, 420n187; theater and, 187, 307, 420n186; villas: at Alsium, 302, 304, 307, 316; at Lanuvium, 306, 308; at Lorium, 302, 306–8, 316, 419n168; at Tibur, 306–8; Villa Magna and, 306, 308, 310; wife of, 420n189
Antony, Mark, 273, 356n128, 364n39, 366n64; Augustus, calumny of, 409n14, 411n41; brother of, 377n254; Cicero and, 279, 366n70, 401n64; Fulvia, wife of, 404n33, 408n103; Octavia, wife of, 389n21; Octavian's victory over, 277; pirates, extirpation of, 369n111; Pompey's *domus* and, 423n239. *See also* Second Triumvirate
Apelles, 168, 357n147, 368n100
Apollo, 215, 309, 366n61, 381n312, 407n84, 412n112; Augustus and, 215, 411n41, 418n161, 419n182; Bacchus, brother of, 381n315, 381n317; Daphne, pursuit of, 197, 375n215, 381n313; laurel tree, 197, 381n313, 409n21; Muses, devotees of, 364n41, 418n161; Phoebus, name for, 168, 195, 197, 277, 381n317; prophesy, 195–97, 379n299; sanctuary at Delphi, 381nn316–17, 384n7, 401n74, 418n161; sun chariot, 156, 195, 367n84, 415n112; Vale of Tempe, 306, 375n215, 418n161
Apollonius of Tyana, 153, 209n149, 212n236
Appian, 402n10, 404n33, 408n100
Apuleius of Madaurus, 177, 232, 422n226; *Apology*, 177, 374nn204–7
Aquitania, 194, 198, 333–34, 361n48, 381n312, 382n322; Eutropius's villa in, 216–17, 365n51; Goths' occupation of, 186, 188, 377n263, 379n299; Paulinus of Nola and, 381n320; Paulinus of Pella and/on, 186, 189, 377n263, 378n269; Prudentius known in, 393n85; Rutilius Namatianus's estates in, 230, 303. *See also* Ausonius; Montmaurin villa
Arcadia, 103, 166, 178, 380n309, 423n236
Arcanum. *See* Cicero, Quintus
Arcinazzo Romano. *See* Trajan
Ariccia, 145, 186n139, 204n60, 208n110
Aristotle, 94, 349n19, 352n85, 363n23, 423n239; categories, 96–97, 353n87; on enslavement, 79; *imago* of, 204; Lyceum, 142, 418n157
Armenia, 287, 333
Arpinum. *See* Cicero, villa at Arpinum; Cicero, Quintus
Arretium, 271, 390n36, 405n55
Asia Minor, 62, 170, 333, 372n160, 380n307, 403n21; Cilicia, 253, 369n111, 393n89; Hermus River, 167, 372n156; kings in, 371n156; military campaigns in, 64, 263, 403n27; mountains, 380n308, 392n82

469

Asiaticus, Valerius, 291, 411n57, 412n58, 412n59
Asinius Gallus, 159, 211, 369n106
Astura. *See* Cicero, villa at Astura
Athena/Minerva, 210, 212; Athenaeum, 232, 372n160; Callisto, devotee of, 380n309; Domitian, devotee of, 300, 412n62, 415n120; Doric order, 359n12; Hermathena, 146, 363n28; olive tree, 94, 358n174, 366n61; Pallas, name for, 380n310; Quinquatria, 292, 300, 412n62, 415n120, 416n121; temple at Priene, 359n1; "Tyrrhenian," 372n160; wisdom, 357n150, 358n174, 363nn28–29, 380n310, 386n47, 387n61
Athens, 64, 343n27; Acropolis, olive tree on, 366n61; Areopagus, 133; Cecropius, mythical patron of, 181, 376n233; Ceramicus, 147, 363n34; founding of, 365n59; Hadrian in, 418n161; orators of, 14, 364n49; Poikile, 418n160; Prytaneion, 418n158; Stoa of Zeus Eleutherius, 64, 344n40; Tower of the Winds, 366n74. *See also* Platonic Academy
Atlauf, 377n263, 378nn266–67, 378n274
Attica, 196, 336, 418n161
Atticus, 203, 220–22, 237, 249–50, 274, 399n16; Cicero, buying art for, 142, 144, 146–48, 363n37; Cicero, helping with properties of, 56n5, 236, 253, 258, 261, 399n16, 401n65; Cicero invited by, 278; Cicero inviting him to visit, 278, 389n7; in Cicero's *On the Ends of Good and Evil*, 204–5, 365n56; in Cicero's *On the Laws*, 150–52; *domus Tamphilianum*, 405nn53–54; enslaved workers, 271, 399n16; frugality, 405n53, 406n56; *Liber Annalis*, 364n49; library, 363n30; Nepos on, 270–71, 405n51; sister of, 257, 408n97; villas: at Ceramicus, 363n34; at Nomentum, 260, 405n55; wife of, 257, 398n4. *See also* Amalthea
augur, 88, 105, 330, 395n15; Appius Claudius, 106, 355n116; college of, 385n24, 390n35
Augusta Treverorum (Trier), 180, 378n271, 392n73
Augustine of Hippo, 232, 378n269, 383n326, 384nn334–35, 393n85; *City of God*, 392n85; Melania the Younger and, 383n326; Origen's influence on, 393n86
Augustonemetum, 191, 198, 379n292, 393n91
Augustus (Octavian) (emperor), 159, 260, 282–87, 296, 313, 409n11, 409–10n22, 412n57; Acta Liudi, 372n162; Actium, victory at, 277; Apollo and, 215, 409n21, 411n41, 418n161, 419n182; Augustales of Freedmen, 351n51; *Augustus* added to name of, 331, 410n22; Caesar, adopted son of, 389n21; Cicero and, 279, 364n43; Cleopatra, defeat of, 277, 312, 418n159; coming to power, 264; death of, 263, 285–86, 297, 410n27; descendants of, 297, 413n75, 415n108; forum of, 417n145; friends of, 155, 411n57; frugality, 283, 406n56, 409n14; Hadrian and, 418n154; horologium of, 424n246; house on the Palatine, 409n10, 409n12; laurel, 409–10n21; library founded by, 215, 419n182; Livia, wife of, 284–85, 312, 410n22, 419n171; marble columns, 406n56; Mark Antony's calumnies of, 409n14, 411n41; omens regarding, 283; *On Architecture* dedicated to, 131, 132; Pax Romana, 418n161; Porticus Vipsania, 353n88; reputation, 282, 409n17; Tiber, park on, 370n137; *vicis*, 293–94; villa of granddaughter Julia, 283, 284, 409n14; villa of Vedius Pollio, 284–85, 305, 409n17, 409n19; villas at Capreae, 283–86, 409n15. *See also Lives of the Twelve Caesars*
Aulus Vitellius (emperor), 294, 415n98
Aurelian (emperor), 417n151, 423n231, 423n233, 423n236, 424n248; *cura annonae*, 395n6; murder of, 319
Aurelius Victor, 315, 417n151; *Epitome de Caesaribus*, 320, 418n160, 419n168
Ausonius, 180, 358n176; Burdigala, born in, and retired to, 180, 184, 377n263; consulship, 377n259; *Ephemeris*, 182–85; Gaul, property holdings in, 376n247, 377n257, 378n268, 378n271, 378n277; *The Moselle*, 180–82, 375n228, 376n233, 376n238; *Opuscula*, 376n236. *See also* Paulinus of Nola
aviaries. *See* Lucullus, villa-aviary at Tusculum; *Three Books on Agriculture*; Varro, villa at Casinum
Avitacum (Sidonius Apollinaris's villa), 170, 191, 198, 216, 379n289, 379n294, 393n91; description of, 156, 191–94, 373n191, 379n283; verses inspired by bath building, 128, 194, 379n281, 382n320
Avitus (emperor), 9, 191, 378n265, 379n292, 379n299

B
Bacchantes, 148, 364n41
Bacchus/Dionysus, 195, 197; Apollo, brother of, 381n315; Ariadne and, 381n317; Bacchantes, followers of, 364n41; Bromius, name for, 167, 195, 197, 372n161, 381n317; dithyramb, 372n168; India, return from, 195, 381n317; Phrygian pipes, 407n84; Silenus, name for, 195, 197, 381n317; wine, 169, 195, 364n41, 372n161, 373n174, 379n294, 381n315, 392n82
Baiae, 53, 160, 166, 268, 284, 289, 307, 383n323, 390n27, 412n64, 421n212; Ausonius on, 181–82; Cassiodorus on, 200, 383n323; Dolabella's villa at, 390n28; Hadrian's death at, 305, 366n63; imperial villas at or near, 291, 292, 299, 301, 317; Lucrine Lake near, 368n96, 401n62; luxury and vice, 274–76, 365n54; Martial on, 162–63, 208; Pliny the Younger on, 176; Punta Epitaffio, 411n56; Sidonius Apollinaris on, 194. *See also* Cicero, villa at Baiae; Hortalus, Quintus Hortensius; Lucullus
Balbus, Lucius Cornelius, 389n23, 400n41; Cicero and/on, 223, 254, 257, 261, 400n41, 401n59
ball games, 171, 174, 193, 202, 317, 392n83
Basil of Nazianzus, 178
basis villae, 264, 285, 331, 354n98, 357n157, 384n339; Tibur, 285, 358n176; Vitruvius on devices for, 361n39. *See also* San Rocco villa; Settefinestre villa; Villa of the Quintilii
Bauli, 307, 386n34, 413n64. *See also* Hortalus, Quintus Hortensius; Nero
Bay of Naples, 181, 194, 203, 264, 308, 331, 372n160, 388n2, 414n89; contiguous villas, 373n185; disasters in, 298; funeral games in, 373n170; Greek-style competitions in, 373n173; imperial villas in, 284, 285, 290, 298, 305, 307; islands of, 409n7; Severus Alexander's constructions in, 317. *See also* Baiae; Bauli; Cumae; Megalia; Misenum; Puteoli
Beneventum, 237, 286, 390n34, 395n6
boating, 292, 300, 304–5
Britain, 198, 250, 253, 389n14, 412n72
bronze, 61, 67, 146, 166, 391n62, 401n72, 407n74; coins, 149, 334, 355n111; herms, 363n32; noble material, 347n69; tablets, 387n60, 395n6
bronze statues and portraits, 72, 107, 147, 149, 296, 346n60, 347n67; ancestral, 364n51; Hercules, 72, 347n67. *See also* Corinthian bronzes
Brutus, 149, 366n64, 385n27; Caesar's assassination, 258, 279, 364n43; Cicero texts addressed to, 143–45, 149, 204, 364n49; Servilia, mother of, 273, 279, 364n49; villa at Tusculum, 149, 362n2, 364n49
Bryaxis, 357n147
Burdigala. *See* Ausonius; Visigoths
Buthrotum. *See* Amalthea

C
Caecilius, Lucius, 228
Caelian Hill, 294, 414n93, 423n238; fire of 64 CE and, 295, 413n76; imperial residences on, 310, 313, 315; Lateranus's villa on, 293, 315n72; Tetrici's house on, 423n233
Caere, 304, 417n139
Caesar (Julius Caesar), 132, 223, 255, 261, 272–73, 276, 312, 393n92,

400n36; art collecting, 272; assassination of, 257, 258, 260, 261, 273, 279, 286; *Caesar* as title, 331; Cicero and, 56n5, 152, 222, 256, 278, 279, 389n9, 400n35, 401n59; Quintus Cicero's military service with, 80, 250, 400n35; gardens of, 272, 405n45; Gaul campaign, 250, 253; henchmen and partisans of, 261, 386n33, 387n57, 390n28, 400n37, 401n59; *lex Julia Agraria*, 353n91; Octavian, adopted son of, 389n21; Pompey and, 206, 272, 279; *pontifex maximus*, 273, 406n69; Rome, advance on, 254; Saepta Julia, 355n115; villas, 272, 273, 282, 358n176, 390n27; at Alsium, 307, 386n30, 419n167; at Lake Nemi, 272, 273, 289, 406n60, 406n70, 407n71. *See also* First Triumvirate

Caieta, 146, 166, 255, 278, 279, 415n112

caldarium, 16, 34, 39, 162, 174, 330

Caligula. *See* Gaius (Caligula)

Camillus, Marcus Furius, 218, 313, 335, 388n83, 421n210

Campania, 215, 227, 248, 259, 331, 353n88, 353n91, 398n12; Cicero in, 279; "Euboean fields," 370n136. *See also* Alger Falernus; Capua; Neapolis; Nola; Pompeii; Puteoli; Scipio Africanus, villa at Liternum

Campus Martius, 19, 261, 269, 318, 356n127, 370n132, 413n76, 424n246; Pompey's *horti* in, 271, 402n7, 405n45. *See also* Theater of Pompey; Villa Publica

Capreae, 410n26. *See also* Augustus; Villa Iovis

Capua, 36, 91, 308, 329, 331, 366n70, 406n68, 407n77; Capitolium, 287; imperial villa at, 306; revolt of Spartacus, 69; on the Via Appia, 364n43

Caracalla (emperor), 315, 316, 422nn227–28; Latin rights, 379n299; murder of, 423n230; tutor to, 423n237

Carinus (emperor), 320

Carneades of Cyrene, 145, 270, 363n25

Carthage, 187, 370n131, 377n259, 384n335; Scipio's victory over, 345n60, 347n70, 352n85, 369n114, 423n237

Carus (emperor), 320

Casas, Bartholomé de las, 349n16

Casinum, 91, 308. *See also* Varro, villa at Casinum

Cassiodorus, 198, 200, 320, 383n323; *Variae epistulae*, 200, 358n176, 383n323

Cassius, 258, 356n128, 364n43, 366n64

Cassius Dio, 292, 313, 315, 422n218; *Roman History*, 284, 288–89, 404n27, 410n27; "senatorial" bias, 282, 298, 313. *See also Roman History*, *Epitome of*

Cassius Dionysius of Utica, 99, 108, 352n85

Castrum Novum, 304, 417n139

Cato the Elder (Cato), 133, 205, 225, 238, 276, 311, 313, 369n114, 405n51; in Cicero's *On Duties*, 207; in Cicero's *On Old Age*, 64, 73, 347n73, 348n76, 348n79, 351n66, 385n24, 385n26; in Cicero's *On the Ends of Good and Evil*, 205–6; in Cicero's *On the Laws*, 151; Ennius, protégé of, 421n202; Hellenophobia, 342n1, 345n54; legislator, 161, 205, 405n53; *maiores*, 342n6; morality, 115, 343n24, 385n23, 420n196; Nepos on, 405n51; *On Morals*, 420n196; *On the Property of Pluchra*, 309; *Origines*, 202, 203, 384n4; Plutarch on, 403n23; rustic language, 420n192; *Sapiens*, 70, 345n56; villa, 267. *See also De agricultura*

Cato the Younger, 205, 206, 272, 385n23, 385n27, 406n64

Catullus, 270

Celerina, Pompeia, 227–28, 396n27, 419n167

Centum Cellae. *See* Trajan (emperor), villa at Centum Cellae

Ceres/Demeter, 94, 105, 106, 186, 356n124; agriculture and grain, 60, 162, 357n148, 377n255, 380n308; cult in Eleusis, 196, 380n308, 418n161; festival, 353n88; Persephone, daughter of, 357n148, 380n308; Pliny's temple of, 243–44, 396n38; Triptolemos taught by, 377n256

chariot races, 313, 354n94, 399n22

Chrysippus of Soli, 312, 421n208

Cicero: consulship, 142, 146, 250, 365n55; Epicureanism and, 389n25; Greek art, connoisseur of, 142, 146, 346n66, 347n67; *Oeconomicus*, translation of, 73, 347n72, 348n77; Platonic Academy and, 142, 144–45, 205, 418n57; proscription and murder of, 56n5, 279, 404n32, 408n98; son of, 279, 386n41, 408n98, 408n103; Stoicism and, 144, 204, 205, 385n31; Terentia, wife of, 222, 256–58, 279, 401n60, 408n97; Tullia, daughter of, 220, 279, 390n28, 407n81, 408n97; grieving the death of, 144, 205; memorial to, 56n5, 260–61, 363n19, 401n78. *See also* Antony, Mark; Atticus; Augustus; Balbus, Lucius Cornelius; Brutus; Caesar; Cicero, Quintus; Crassus, Marcus Licinius; Dolabella, Publius Cornelius; Lucullus; Marius, Gaius; Pompey

Cicero, correspondence: *Letters to Atticus*, 144, 146–48, 150, 203, 204, 220–23, 237, 249–50, 253–58, 260–61, 362n14; *Letters to Friends*, 206, 253–56, 385nn12–13, 386n31. *See also* Cicero, Quintus

Cicero, exile, 56, 142–44, 203, 278; *domus* on the Palatine demolished during, 142–44, 251, 276, 362n7, 397n1, 399n17, 399n19, 399n34; rescinding of, and return from, 143, 144, 250, 399n17, 400n37

Cicero, villa at Antium, 203, 220, 249, 250, 254, 255, 278, 279

Cicero, villa at Arpinum, 148–50, 250–51, 253, 255, 261, 278–79, 365n60; Atticus invited to, 220–21, 278, 389n7, 408n91; description of, 150–52; *deversorium* for, 148, 192, 223, 224, 308, 364n43; inheritance of, 278, 398n12; son's coming of age celebrated at, 279, 386n41

Cicero, villa at Astura, 223–24, 255, 261, 279, 286; grieving daughter's death, 205, 221; *otium*, 278

Cicero, villa at Baiae, 221, 223, 257, 278, 365n54, 397–98n4, 398n12, 412n63

Cicero, villa at Caieta, 146, 255, 278, 279

Cicero, villa at Cumae, 222, 223, 250, 255, 258, 278, 389n16, 398n12, 408n97; *Academica* and/in, 207, 386n31, 386n34; Cicero sequestered at, 204, 206; construction of, 399n20; letters from, 204, 206, 385n16; in *On the Ends of Good and Evil*, 205–6

Cicero, villa at Formiae, 220, 222, 255, 388n4, 408n97; artworks, 146; Atticus invited to, 220–21, 278; damage to, 142–43, 362n15, 397n1; neighbors of, 389nn5–6, 389nn8–9; as refuge, 254

Cicero, villa at Pompeii, 149, 222, 250, 255, 257, 398n12, 408n97; neighbor of, 203, 221; *otium*, 278

Cicero, villa at Puteoli (Academia), 152, 255, 278, 364n43; bequest, received as, 152, 222, 398n12; Caesar received at, 152, 222–23, 254, 389n9; fame of, 366n63; name of, 418n157

Cicero, villa at Tusculum (Tusculaneum), 142–45, 220–24, 255, 261, 278–79; Academy and Lyceum, 142, 144–47, 362n13, 418n157; Atticus invited to, 220; Atticus's villa equated to, 150, 363n34; in Cicero texts, 143, 205, 206, 363n34; construction at, 253, 254; *deversoria* to and from, 222–23, 390n34; as *gymnasium*, 142, 146–48; high value of, 362n15; neighbors of, 400n51; *otium*, 206, 278; Quintus Cicero invited to, 221; as refuge, 278–79; Sulla's prior ownership of, 269, 362n2, 362n13, 404n31; Tiro at, 255–56; vandalized, 397n1, 399n19; works of art, 146–50, 346n66, 360n25, 363n27

Cicero, works: *Academica*, 152, 206–7, 363n22, 386n31, 386n34, 405n50; *Brutus*, 143, 364n59; *Consolation*, 347n71; *For Gnaeus Plancius*, 203, 384n4, 385n21; *Letters to Friends*, 206, 253–56, 385nn12–13, 386n31; *Marius*, 366n61; *On*

Divination, 143–44, 347n71, 366n61, 367n82; *On Duties*, 202, 207–8, 266–67, 317, 347nn71–72, 423n237; *On Old Age*, 60, 64, 73–75, 347nn70–72, 347n74, 351n66; *On Philosophy*, 412n63; *On the Laws*, 150–52, 365–66n61; *On the Orator*, 143, 144, 364n49; *On the Republic*, 317, 385n16; *Orator*, 364n49; *Philippics*, 366n70; *Pro Archia poeta*, 365n55; *Topica*, 347n71, 363n23; *Tusculan Disputations*, 143–45, 347n71, 362n13, 363n19, 363n21. See also *Verrine Orations*
Cicero, Quintus, 143–44, 149, 204, 257, 389n18, 399n26, 399n32; Cicero's letters to, 221, 250–53, 385n16, 399n34, 400nn35–36; in Cicero's *On the Laws*, 150, 152, 365n56, 365n61; *domus* in Rome, 250–51, 399n33, 400n36; enslaved workers, 80, 253, 399n33; military service, 250, 252, 253, 400n35; proscription and murder of, 279, 408n103; son of, 250, 257, 279, 408n103; villas: at Arpinum (Arcanum), 236, 248, 250–53, 278, 279, 365n56, 408n97, 488n97; Laterium, 250–52, 398n8, 399n21, 399n31, 408n97
Cincinnatus, Lucius Quinctius, 133, 218, 335, 388n84; four-*iugera* farm, 392n75, 403n17; plough, 388n84
Circeii, 166, 278, 279, 299, 307, 415n112
civil wars, 110, 272, 296, 320
Claudius (emperor), 291, 346n63, 396n31, 411n51; generals for, 412n72, 415n108; "Porticus of Claudius," 295, 414n95; Valeria Messalina, wife of, 291, 412n58, 412n60, 412n72
Cleopatra, 277, 312, 390n37, 418n159
Clodius Albinus (emperor), 316, 422n226
Cluvius, Marcus, 152, 222, 254, 256–57, 401n65
Columella. See *On Farming Matters*
Commodus (emperor), 313–16, 421n214, 422n222, 422n225; Colossus altered by, 414n92; murder of, 315, 422n218; Quintilii and, 77, 319
Comum. See Pliny the Younger, villas near Comum
Constantinople, 178, 383n323, 393n86
Constantius, 320
Corinth, 336, 372n167, 372n169, 375n215; confiscation of works of art, 346n65
Corinthian bronzes, 214, 239, 372n169; collections of, 145, 149, 345n60, 409n14
Corinthian order, 359n12, 360n24
Cosa, 40, 297, 303, 350n35, 403n13
Crassus, Lucius Licinius, 143, 144, 362n9
Crassus, Marcus Licinius, 269, 271, 363n30, 405n43, 406n57; Cicero's dinner with, 276, 407n81; defeat and death of, 279, 406n57; wealth of, 146, 271, 363n30. See also First Triumvirate
Crete, 300, 369n111, 371n142, 376n232, 381n317
Crispinus, 301, 416n120
Croesus, 167, 184, 371n156, 376n243
Cumae, 159, 181, 207, 304, 370n136; Cumaean Sibyl, 352n81; founding of, 373n172; Gallinarian woods, 390n33; Varro's villa at, 366n68. See also Cicero, villa at Cumae
cypress tree, 175, 298, 302, 415n104
Cyrus the Younger, 75, 347n72, 348n77

D
Dacia, 302, 378n270, 416n134, 423n231
Damasippus, L. Licinius Crassus, 148–49, 364n40, 364n46
Danube, 302, 313, 423n230
Dardanus, Claudius Postumus, 198, 382n321
De agricultura (Cato the Elder), 77, 78, 85–93, 111, 123, 263, 308, 398n12, 403n22; absenteeism, 359n180; building a villa, 248–49; cabbage, 85, 92–93, 282, 351n61; Columella and, 110–12, 114–15, 119; enslaved labor/*vilicus* and *vilica*, 80–81, 84, 87–88, 119, 248; gods and festivals, 352n71, 352n73, 352n83; Jupiter Dapalis, 88–89, 335; morality, 115, 343n24, 385n23; *oletum*, 90; *pater familias*, 56n1, 78, 88–89; in Pliny, 403n24; Varro and, 95, 97, 100–101, 108, 351n61, 352n85, 357n155; *villa urbana*, 56n1; wall plaster, 403n23
Delphi, 372n167, 381n317, 408n161; Sanctuary of Apollo, 381n316, 384n7, 401n74
Demosthenes, 149, 232, 357n147, 364n49, 366n70
Dentatus, Manius Curius, 74, 313, 335, 403n17, 403n22; consulship, 403n22, 421n210; frugality, 225, 365n57, 391n40; Sabines, defeat of, 74, 112; *triumphator*, 267, 421n210
Diana, 166, 210, 212, 371n139; hunt, 371n139, 386n47, 387n61; Ionic order, 359n12; shrine at Lake Nemi, 165, 166, 406n60, 411n47, 415n110
Didius Julianus (emperor), 315, 422n222
Diocletian (emperor), 180, 282, 320, 340, 378n270; palace-fortress at Spalato, 44, 44, 282, 316, 320
Diodorus Siculus, 59; *Historical Library*, 69–70, 344n45, 344–45n48, 345n49
Diogenes of Sinope, 184, 376n243
Diomedes, 229, 392n62
Dionysius of Halicarnassus, 359n14, 416n125
Dolabella, Publius Cornelius, 307, 356n128; Caesar and, 223, 279, 386n33, 390n28; Cicero's son-in-law, 260, 279, 386n33, 390n28
Domitian (emperor), 228, 296, 301, 370n133, 371n140, 421n212; archery, 415n120; architecture and construction under, 298, 415n113; cruelty, 260, 282, 296, 415n107, 416n125; *dominus et deus*, 397n47; later emperors' distancing from, 302, 310, 315; laziness, 298, 415n107, 415n120; lechery, 299; Martial and, 259–60, 296, 398n4, 414n91; Minerva and, 300, 412n62, 415n120; murder of, 416n129; omen regarding, 301–2, 415n104; palace on the Palatine Hill, 300, 302, 310, 315, 415n120, 418n165; Pliny the Younger and, 260, 391n59; Trajan compared with, 304–5; Vespasian, father of, 296, 298; villa at Baiae, 299, 301; wife of, 415n108. See also Albanum
Domus Augustana, 300, 316, 419n165
Domus Aurea, 282, 291, 293–97, 301, 390n26, 413n74, 414n88, 414n95, 419n165; Colossus of Nero, 295, 414n92, 417n145; entrance to, 414n92; Flavian emperors' distancing from, 413n74, 414n91, 414n94; literature on, 413n77; Martial on, 293–96; park, 414n93; Pliny the Elder on, 293, 294, 412n73, 413n84; *rus in urbs, urbs in rus*, 51, 281, 294; Suetonius on, 293–95; vulnerability of, 413n75
Domus Flavia, 300, 316, 419n165
Domus Pompeiana, 286, 423–24n239
Domus Tiberiana, 315, 418n165; extension of, 294, 412n73; library in, 215, 387n73, 419n182; Marcus Aurelius and, 310, 315; Nero and, 297, 413n79, 418n165
Doric order, 22, 359n12
Drusus, 286, 287, 410n31

E
easel painting, 158, 273, 360n25, 368n98, 368n100
Egypt, 84, 99, 198, 263, 333, 350n39, 387n65; Canopus, 407n76, 418n159; cults in Rome, 422n218; Isis, 411n47; king of, 389n11; Mark Antony in, 364n39; Memphis, 376n234; mummies, 419n177; Pompey's murder in, 366n70, 406n64; Vespasian's return from, 298. See also Alexandria
Elagabalus (emperor), 315, 316, 409n5, 423n229, 423n239
Eleusis, 357n148, 376n233, 377n256, 380n308, 418n161
emperors: "good" versus "bad," 282, 284, 414n92; imperial villas, 34, 281–82; *imperium*, 281, 292, 319, 320, 334. See also Albanum; Domus Aurea; Villa Hadriana; Villa Iovis; Villa Magna
Ennius, Quintus, 94, 96, 105, 305, 311, 365n53, 384n4, 402n1, 421n202;

472 INDEX

Annales, 421n202; Cicero and, 365n53
enslavement and enslaved personnel, 52–54, 56nn4–5, 80–81, 263–65, 383n333; accommodations for, 12, *12*, 29, 39, 41, 90, 350n42, 351n55; chain gangs, 78, 83, 266, 396n25; depictions of, 19, 351n57; donations of, 198, 382n322; ethnicity of, 80–81, 349–50n32; historiography, 79–80, 348n12; *instrumentum vocalis*, 334, 397n45; *latifundia* and, 81–82, 263, 265–66, 350n35, 402n3; laws and decrees protecting, 350–51n48; rations for, 78, 84, 342n7; rebellions of, 69–70, 344–45n48; rustic speech, 308; terminology, 333–36, 338–41, 348n5, 354n102, 355n111; theories applied to, 79; urban, 80, 83, 350n46; *vernae*, 52, 81, 84, 340, 368n98; *vilica*, 52, 120, 123, 248, 340–41; *vilicus*, 39, 52, 87–88, 112, 119–20, 256, 338, 340–41; at villas, 79–85. *See also* Africa; *De agricultura*; *Oeconomicus*; *On Farming Matters*; *Three Books on Agriculture*
Ephesus, 64, 418n161
Epicrates of Bidis, 71, 345n59
Epicureanism, 204–5, 371n155, 421n202; Cicero and, 389n25; Pollius Felix and, 373n176; Stoicism versus, 159, 184
Epicurus, 205, 217, 274, 359n1, 371n155, 373n176
Epigrams (Martial), 162–64, 225–27, 259–60, 370n124, 386n50; "Bassus," 162–63, 225–26; books of Elephantis, 410n35; Domitian and his villas, 259–60, 298, 299, 398n4, 414n91, 415n110, 415n120; Faustinus, 162–63, 227; foodstuffs, 300, 373n186, 390n37; Julius Martialis, 163–64, 402n6; Porticus Pompeia, 406n63; *xenia*, 137, 226, 360n34, 391n36
Epirus, 99, 102, 189, 271, 378nn270–71; Acheron River, 369n108; Actia Ludi, 372n162. *See also* Amalthea
Epodes (Horace), 157–58, 367n87, 401n71; Alfius, 158, 236, 351n50, 357n60, 373n177, 402n5; Horti Maecenatis, poem on, 277
Esquiline Hill, 290, 354n106, 391n47, 407n83, 422n229; Caesar's gardens on, 255, 272; Pompey's *domus* on, 423–24n239; temple of Tellus, 353n88. *See also* Domus Aurea
Etruria, 339, 357n146, 390n36, 403n13, 419n170, 424n246. *See also* Caere; Centum Cellae; Tyrrhenian sea and coast; Veii
Eudoxus of Cnidus, 113, 357n148
euergetism, 236–37, 333, 394nn3–4; Pliny the Younger and, 238–40, 244, 396n36, 397n2

F
Faventinus. *See Short Book on the Art of Architecture*
feasting, 308, 345n59, 368n98, 411n50, 417n151
festivals, 64, 282, 333, 352n83, 355n114, 384n2, 385n12; Actia Ludi, 372n162; Compitalia, 87, 92, 332, 351n68; Juvenalia, 416n120; Pales, 220, 388n1; Parentalia, 391n46; Quinquatria, 292, 300, 412n62, 415n120, 416n121; Saturnalia, 92, 172, 222–23, 339, 351n68; Sementivae, 95, 110, 353n88
Fidenae, 164, 287, 370n131, 410n32
fires: of 64 CE, 276–77, 295, 413n74, 413nn76–77, 413n79; of 192 CE, 215–16, 313, 420n182
First Mithridatic War, 363n22, 380n305
First Punic War, 345n54, 388n83
First Triumvirate, 204, 278, 363n30, 401n46, 407n57
fishponds, 338, 393n1; Cicero on, 14, 237, 251, 395n8; Piscina di Lucullo, 14, *14*, 108, 110; *piscinarii*, 14, 237, 299, 338, 395n8; Pliny the Elder on, 266; profitability of, 14, 108, 109, 395n8; Varro on, 14, 108–10, 154, 356n131, 395n8
Flavian dynasty, 158, 295, 296, 302, 397n44, 414n92. *See also* Domitian; Titus; Vespasian
Formiae, 166, 224, 229, 306, 390n37. *See also* Cicero, villa at Formiae
Forum, 15, 269, 283, 391n47, 399n34, 413n78; Basilica Aemilia, 388n3; Domus Aurea's connection to, 294; gods' dwellings and statues in, 340, 352n83, 406n58; Regia, 301, 406n69, 416n125
Frontinus, 131
Fronto, Marcus Cornelius, 281, 307, 420nn189–90; Horti Maecenatis, 276, 278, 408n88; imperial tutor, 307, 308, 310, 420n182; letters from Marcus Aurelius, 308–11, 420n186, 420nn193–94, 420n197, 421n200; letters to Marcus Aurelius, 307, 311–12, 407–8n88, 417n141, 419n175, 421n202, 421n209; Palatine libraries, borrowing privileges at, 420n182; suffect consul, 419n166, 420n197
Fundana, Galeria, 294, 413n83
Fundanus, Minicius, 208–9

G
Gabinius, Aulus, 142–43
Gaius (Caligula) (emperor), 282, 289–91, 296, 411n50, 413n79, 414n88; *domus* on the Palatine Hill, 294, 412n73
Gaius Heius. *See Verrine Orations*
Galba (emperor), 285, 296, 414nn97–99
Galen: *On Consolation from Grief*, 214–16, 387nn72–74, 388nn75–77, 419–20n182; *On the Properties of Foodstuffs*, 391n45
Galerius (emperor), 320
Gallia Belgica, 182, 189, 334, 378n271, 392n73
Gallia Cisalpina, 101, 333, 353n88, 354n104, 394n4, 396n21
Gallienus (emperor), 316, 423n232, 424n246
Gardens of Lucullus. *See* Horti Lucullani
Gardens of Maecenas. *See* Horti Maecenatis
Gardens of Sallust. *See* Horti Sallustiani
Garonne River (Garunna, Garumna), 42, 186, 187, 195, 377n253, 379n297
Gaul, 40, 184, 216, 333, 384n338, 388n83; Cisalpine, 209, 370n124, 403n27, 422n222; donations of villas, 198, 381n320; grand villas, 359n180, 380n303; *latifunda* and enslaved labor in, 81, 253, 382n322, 402n3, 403n18; Roman military expansion into, 80, 81, 250–53, 263, 316; southern, 387n65, 393n85; Vandal and Gothic invasion of, 200; wines from, 300. *See also* Aquitania; Ausonius; Avitacum; Rutilius Namatianus
Gellius, Aulus: *Attic Nights*, 178, 408n88, 420n186, 420n192
Germanicus, 287
Germany, 286, 316, 387n67, 415n108, 424n251; invaders from, 403n27
Gerontius: *Life of Melania the Younger*, 198–200, 383nn326–32
Geta (emperor), 422n228, 423n237
Gnaeus Pompeius, 71, 266, 271, 345n59
Gordian I, 318, 423–24n239
Gordian II, 318, 424n239, 424n247
Gordian III (emperor), 316, 318, 424nn245–46
Goths, 320–21, 383n323, 423n230; administration in Italy, 200, 384n337. *See also* Aquitania
Gracchus, Gaius, 82, 265, 347n70
Gracchus, Tiberius, 82, 264–65, 347n70, 402n10, 403n13, 407n79
Gratian (emperor), 180, 184, 378n271
Greece: Hellenophobia, 59, 342n1, 345n54, 404n27; philhellenism, 59, 71, 345n54; Seven Sages of Greece, 115, 185
Greek art, 107, 225, 357n147; painting, 14, 107, 158, 364n51, 368n100, 413n84; Pliny the Elder on, 158, 363n27, 368n100. *See also* Cicero; Hadrian
Greekness, 59, 169, 373n173
Greek philosophy and philosophers: depictions of, 384n7, 424n249; *pallium* worn by, 424n249; Rome as inheritor of, 142, 143, 145, 362n12, 363n21. *See also* Epicureanism; Epicurus; Pythagoras

Greek plays, 204, 365n53, 385n15
Gregory of Nazianzus, 178
Gregory of Nyssa, 178–80, 371n243, 375n219, 375n221, 375n223, 375n225

H

Hades, 342n11, 369n108, 380n308
Hadrian (emperor), 282, 305–8, 313, 315, 392n61, 397n44, 419n170, 421n202, 421n206; antiquarianism, 305, 417n143, 417n149, 418n154; architecture and construction, 284, 305, 414n92, 417n145, 417n147, 422n215; art collector, 417n151, 418n160; Colossus and, 414n92; death of, 305, 313, 366n63, 417n149; Greek culture and, 305, 417n145, 417n149, 418n158, 418n161; hunting, 417n140, 417n148; Senate and, 409n3; Spanish origins of, 305, 306, 422n222; Suetonius and, 401n67; Vedius Pollio's villa during reign of, 282, 409nn18–19; villa at Antium, 305, 306, 418n149. *See also* Villa Hadriana; Villa Magna
Hannibal, 161, 265, 275, 377n254, 386n36, 391n42, 407n77
Hellenistic culture, 135, 264, 276, 363n32; architecture, 376n233, 402n6; portraiture, 365n51
Hera/Juno, 372n167, 380n309, 381n317
Hercules, 113, 220, 227, 257, 259, 392n79; Alcides, name for, 168, 372n165; good fortune, 155, 367n79; Labors, 370n133, 373n175, 391n49; Myron's statue of, 72, 168, 346n66, 347n67; Pillars of Hercules, 370n130, 375n215; temples of, 167, 284, 346n66, 373n175, 406n62
Hermes/Mercury, 372n68; eloquence, 148, 363n28, 364n42; good fortune, 148, 364n42, 367n78; Hermathena, 146, 363nn28–29
herms, 27, 146, 147, 363n28, 363n32
Herodes Atticus, 178
Herodian, 282, 313, 315; *History since [the Death of] the Emperor Marcus [Aurelius]*, 314
Hesiod, 59; *Theogony*, 59, 342n8, 342n12. See also *Works and Days*
Hispania, 198, 296, 355n110, 381n120, 402n3; grand villas, 359n180, 361n48; Hadrian and Trajan from, 422n222; Roman military expansion into, 81, 263, 272, 306, 346n65, 369n111, 403n13, 405n54, 407n77; Saguntum, 377n254; wheat, 350n39; wines from, 300
Historia Augusta, 282, 313, 315, 318, 408n1, 409n9, 418n162, 423n230, 424n249; Antoninus Pius, 307, 418n165, 419n168, 421n203; Clodius Albinus, 422n226; Commodus, 314, 421nn214–15, 422n217; Elagabalus, 409n5, 423n229; Gallienus, 423n232,
424n246; Gordians, 318, 423–24n239, 424n243, 424nn244–46; Hadrian, 306, 366n63, 409n3, 417n148, 417–18n151, 418n159, 418n161, 419n170, 420n186, 421n202; Marcus Aurelius, 408–9n3; Maximinus Thrax, 423n230; Pescennius Niger, 314, 409n5, 422n218; Severus Alexander, 316–17; Tacitus, 319, 424n248; Tetrici, 423n233
Homer, 59, 73, 94, 179, 242, 268, 357n147. *See also Iliad; Odyssey*
Honorius (emperor), 198, 230, 377n263, 377n265, 378n267, 383n332
Horace, 162, 232, 270, 317, 364n48, 393n85, 405n44, 418n161; Brindisium, trip to, 230, 390n34; Damasippus satirized by, 364n40, 364n46; Fronto's reference to, 278, 407n83, 407–8n88. *See also Epodes*
Horace, Sabine farm, 155–57, 278, 366–67n77, 398n4; description of, 156–57; Maecenas, thank-you poem for, 155–56; Maecenas invited to, 277; wine produced at, 224
Hortalus, Quintus Hortensius, 366n76, 389n17; villas: at Baiae, 255, 405n50, 412n63; at Bauli, 109–10, 207, 412n63; near Laurentum, 24, 155
horti, 53, 264, 294, 317, 332, 334, 402nn6–7, 408n97, 409n16; for burials, 414n99; Caesar's, 405n45, 406n66; Cicero's efforts to purchase, 56n5, 260–61; Commodus and, 314; Gallienus and, 423n232, 424n246; Horti Scipionis, 407n79; Horti Spei Veteris, 422n229; Late Republican, 276–78; Nero's, 413n76; Pliny the Elder on, 402n6; political purpose of, 405n45; Pompey's, 271, 402n7, 405n45; for the public, 236, 318; Seneca's, 293; Septimius Severus's, 422n227; villas in, 302, 315
Horti Lamiani, 290, 413n79, 414n88
Horti Lucullani, 269, 291, 332, 402n7, 405n45, 405n47, 411–12n57; hospitality, 405n45; imperial property, 412n58, 413n79; money to build, 403n21; Valeria Messalina executed in, 412n60
Horti Maecenatis, 276–78, 286, 290, 402n7, 411n52, 413n79; *Elegiae in Maecenatem*, 277; Fronto's ownership of, 277, 408n88; Horace's poem on, 277, 407n83
Horti Pompeiani, 276, 402n7
Horti Sallustiani, 297, 302, 332, 402n7
hospitality, 41, 198, 222, 231–33, 257, 278, 288–89, 341, 381n320, 390n34, 392n78, 394n2, 403n13; Alcinous's, 370n133, 375n219; Atticus's, 271; Augustus's, 409n14; Hadrian's, 305; at imperial villas, 292, 302; Lucullus's, 405n45; simple or rustic, 390n38, 408n91; thank-yous for, 142, 178–80,
227; Trajan's, 302–3; Triptolemus's, 377n256, 380n308; *xenia* as, 17, 226; Xenocrates's, 145
hubris, 342n14, 369n115
hunting, 64, 300, 317, 367–68n92, 368n93, 377n259, 392n78; Domitian and, 415n120; *exemplum virtutis*, 300, 304, 416n124; festivals, 282; garb, 424n249; -gathering society, 380n308; Hadrian and, 417n140, 417n148; as *otium*, 16, 202, 209–13, 309; Trajan and, 300, 303–5, 315, 416n124, 417n140, 417n142; *xenia* and, 17, 51. *See also* Diana

I

Iliad (Homer), 59, 391n62, 397n43; Achilles, 176, 317, 357n148, 415n110
Illyria, 81, 104, 355n112
Illyricum, 99, 286
imago, 149, 334, 364–65n51, 382n322; *imagines istae*, 400n36; *imagines maiorum*, 149, 364–65n51; *signa*, 146, 273, 346n60, 364nn50–51
imperium, 276, 334, 385n18; emperors and, 281, 292, 319, 320, 334; generals invested with, 369n111, 403n21, 405n45
India, 195, 238, 381n317, 395n12
Ionia, 158, 166, 348n77
Ionian Sea, 371n153
Ionic order, 359n1, 359n12
Ischomachus. See under *Oeconomicus*
Istria, 200, 384n337
Italica, 306

J

Jerome, 324n324, 381n319, 382n321, 383n326, 393n86
Jerusalem, 100, 146, 191n319, 192n326
Jews, 197, 290, 381n312, 382n320
Jordanes: *History of the Goths*, 320–21
Julian Laws, 273
Julio-Claudian dynasty, 286, 296, 410n24, 416n123. *See also* Augustus; Claudius; Gaius (Caligula); Nero; Tiberius
Justinian (emperor), 397n1; *Digesta*, 397n1, 398n8, 421n215; *Institutes*, 397n1; *Novellae*, 398n7
Juvenal. *See Satires*

L

Lanuvium, 272, 289, 311, 400n45, 406n62; Cicero's interest in property at, 254–55; Commodus born in, 313, 314. *See also* Antoninus Pius; Augustus
Lateranus, Plautius, 293, 412n72
Laterium. *See under* Cicero, Quintus
latifundia, 79, 81–83, 263, 350n35, 402n3; Pliny the Elder's opposition to, 265–66, 403n14, 403n18; Settefinestre villa, 51
Latium, 169, 308, 339, 357n146, 398n12,

399n28, 419n177; *eloquium Latiaris*, 232, 392n84; wines from, 395n11
laurel tree, 163, 173, 175, 314, 318; Apollo and, 197, 381n313, 409n21; Augustus and, 409–10n21; crowns, 285, 332, 372n162, 381n313; as omen, 29, 285, 316–17, 409n21, 410nn23–24
Laurentum, 313, 314. *See also* Hortalus, Quintus Hortensius; Pliny the Younger
Laureus Tullius, 152
Lentulus, 147, 253, 255, 362n2, 400n47
Lepidus, 255, 277, 279
Letters on Morality (Seneca the Younger), 159–62, 274–76, 368n105, 369nn107–9, 407nn77–78; emperors' villas, 282; military aspects of villas, 358n176; Scipio Africanus's villa, 160–62, 237, 358n176, 369n111, 369n113, 369–70n117, 370nn118–20; Servilius Vatia's villa, 159–60, 368n105, 369nn107–9; villas at Baiae, 274–76
Licinianus, Valerius, 301, 416n125
Liguria, 101, 230, 354n104, 395n6, 422n222, 422n225
Liternum. *See* Scipio Africanus, villa at Liternum
Lives of the Twelve Caesars (Suetonius), 258, 315, 414nn102–3; Augustus, 283–86, 359n14, 409n10, 409n14, 410nn22–23, 410n25, 410n27; Caesar, 273, 407n71; Domitian, 300–302, 397n47, 415n104, 415n107; Gaius (Caligula), 289, 411n45, 411n50, 413n81; Galba, 285, 296; *Historia Augusta* modeled on, 315, 316, 409n9; Nero's Domus Aurea, 293–95, 410nn24–25, 413n81, 414n92; omens and numinous events, 301–2, 315, 316, 409n9, 410n24, 415n104; Tiberius, 286, 287, 410n25, 410n33, 411n37; Titus, 296, 298; Vespasian, 296–97, 415n104
Livia, 286, 312, 410n22, 410n31, 419n171; portico of, 284, 285, 409n16, 409n19; villa of, 285, 296, 410nn23–24
Livy, 388n84, 407n77, 416n125
Longinus, Gaius Cassius, 293, 412n72
Lorium. *See* Antoninus Pius; Marcus Aurelius
Lucius Verus (emperor), 307, 308, 313, 388n75, 418n165
Lucretius, 273–74, 311, 421n202; *On the Nature of Things*, 274–75, 407nn72–73, 421n202
Lucullus, 14, 196, 356n130, 385n26, 398n16, 405n43, 412n57; brother of, 14, 110, 356n136, 404n38; in Cicero texts, 266–67, 403n21, 405n50, 412n63; Hispania victories, 346n65; Plutarch on, 269–70, 404n40, 405n43, 418n158; Pompey's replacement of, 269; son of, 385n22,

385n26, 405n47; Third Mithridatic War, 380n307, 403n21, 405n43, 405n45; villas, 96, 98, 115, 266–70, 272, 315; at Baiae, 110, 269, 412n63; at Castellum Lucullanum, 14, 282, 320; at Misenum, 404n30, 410n30. *See also* Horti Lucullani
Lucullus, villa-aviary at Tusculum, 105, 153, 356n131, 362n2, 385n22, 418n158; library, 205–6, 405n47
Lydia, 184, 370n137, 372n160, 374n203; Croesus, king of, 372n203; Cyrus the Younger, satrap of, 348n77; gold brought to, 375n216; Pactolus river, 376n44
Lysippus, 107, 357n147, 363n37

M
Macula, Publius Pompeius, 223, 390n30
Maecenas, 14, 284, 407n85, 412n68; *Elegiae in Maecenatem*, 277; Horace, patron of, 155–56, 224, 277, 278, 390n34, 390n36, 398n4; villas, 407n85, 414n88. *See also* Horti Maecenatis
maiores, 15, 103, 335, 359n1, 367n92, 374n206, 382n320; Cato the Elder modeled on, 342n6; Lucullus as, 403n21; return to, 110–11; simple lives of, 390n38
marble, 335–36; Carystian, 169, 175, 195, 318, 335; Chian, 169, 192, 335, 380n301; columns, 142; floors, 150, 289, 358n177, 361n48; herms, 147; Laconian, 336, 373n175; Megarian, 147, 336; noble material, 347n69; Numidian, 161, 169, 245, 318, 336, 370n118, 380n301; Parian, 36, 192, 195, Pentelic, 147, 336, 366n74; Proconnesian, 192, 195, 336; sculptures, 72, 107, 146; Synnas, 169, 336; Synnadic, 169, 336; Thasian, 161, 169, 336
Marcus Aurelius (emperor), 306–7, 313, 315, 387n73, 408–9n3, 422n222; Antoninus Pius, adoptive father of, 307, 310; *Caesar*, 420n182, 420n187, 421n200; Hadrian, adoptive grandfather of, 421n202; hunting, 417n140; joint rule, 307, 313; *Meditations*, 156, 307, 312–13; Villa Magna and, 305, 308, 310; villas: at Alsium, 303, 307, 310–13, 421n194; at Lorium, 302, 310. *See also* Fronto
maritime villas, 14, 264, 338, 369n111, 395n8, 415n112; fishponds, 14, 395n8; Marcus Aurelius's, 307, 311; Nero's, 291–92, 305. *See also* Cicero, villa at Astura; Cicero, villa at Cumae; Cicero, villa at Puteoli; Trajan (emperor), villa at Centum Cellae; Vedius Pollio
Marius, Gaius, 366n73, 403–4n27, 404n29, 404n32; anti-Greek attitudes, 345n54, 403n27; Cicero on, 366n61, 404n28; Plutarch on,

268, 403–4n27, 404n40; villas: at Baiae, 276, 365n54; at Misenum, 268, 358n176, 404n30, 407n78
Mars, 89, 148, 359n12, 364n42; temple of, 370n137; war, 364n42, 391n43, 393n92
Martial, 370n135, 373n176, 401n72, 401n75; *On the Spectacles*, Epigram 2, 293–96, 414n92; villa near Nomentum, 208, 227, 370n123. *See also Epigrams*
Maxentius (emperor), 316
Maximian, 320
Maximinus Thrax (emperor), 317, 423n230
Maximus, 184
Mediterranean: Antonine Plague, 388n75; economy, 82, 102; piracy in, 369n111; trade, 82, 350n39; villas, ownership of, 188, 253, 395n22
Megalia, 169, 373n170; Castellum Lucullanum, 282, 320–21, 424n251
Melania the Elder, 198, 382n320, 382n322, 383n326
Melania the Younger, 198–200, 383n324, 383n326, 383nn330–31, 383–84n332, 384n335
Meleager, 231, 392n79
Memmius, Gaius, 269, 404n38
Memmius, Lucius, 72, 346n65
Messalina, Valeria, 291, 412n58, 412n60, 412n72
Metellus, 108, 364n41, 405n54; villa at Tusculum, 98, 362n2; collection of Muses, 364n41, 364n50
Midas, 371n156, 376n244
Middle Ages, 77, 139, 397n45
Milan, 180, 320, 420n200, 422n222
Minicianus, Cornelius, 301
Misenum, 229, 275, 336, 373n170, 412n64. *See also* Caesar; Lucullus; Marius, Gaius
Mithridatic Wars. *See* First Mithridatic War; Third Mithridatic War
Mons Massicus, 38, 329, 331, 390n31, 390n37
Montmaurin villa, 29, 42, *42*, 51, 380n303, 392n83
mosaic, 22, 127, 161, 314, 319, 364n51, 423n233; Orpheus, 24, *24*; villas depicted in, 51; *xenia* depicted in, 16, *16*, 18, 137
mosaic floors, 16, *16*, 36, 38, 40, 106, 107, 289, 318, 340; *asarota*, 371n151; inscriptions on, 384n7; Palladius on, 358n177; transported by Caesar, 406n71
Moselle River, 180–82, 333, 392n73
mos maiorum, 53, 60, 133, 335, 336
Muses, 94, 156, 195, 197, 209, 217, 270, 381n318; Bacchantes, opposite of, 364n41; Calliope, 372n168; Erato, 195; Mount Helicon, 343n19, 346n65, 375n215; Pierian spring, 60, 277, 371n144; Thespiades, 346n65; Vale

INDEX 475

of Tempe, 375n215, 418n161. *See also* Apollo; Metellus
Myron: Herakles, 72, 168, 346n66, 347n67

N

Natural History (Pliny the Elder), 236, 267–68, 293, 346n66, 389n6; Alban wine, 416n122; ancestral portraits, 364n51; art purchases, 363n27; Cicero's villa at Puteoli, 152; eggs for ailments, 391n45; Gaius's (Caligula's) *domus* on the Palatine, 294, 412n73; *horti*, 402n6; *latifundia* and enslaved labor, 83, 265–66, 396n25; laurel, 409–10n21; olive, 409–10n21; painting, 158–59, 269; plane trees, 289; Villa of Livia, 285, 410n22; vineyards, 237–38; Vitruvius as source, 359n4; "Xerxes in a toga," 405n43
Neapolis, 169, 269, 283–85, 329, 331, 373n1n72–73; Actia Ludi, 372n162; Parthenope, name for, 372n160, 373n171; port of, 373n170; Vergil's tomb near, 210
Nemi, Lake: Diana's shrine at, 165, 166, 406n60, 411n47, 415n110; floating villas, 289. *See also* Caesar
Nepos, Cornelius, 270–71; *On Famous Historians*, 271, 405n51
Neptune/Jove, 109, 110, 207, 372nn164–65, 411n41; sacrifices to, 196, 380n306; temples of, 417n145
Nero (emperor), 228, 291–96, 346n63, 354n100, 391n57, 394n2, 415n108; ancestry of, 412n68; conspiracy against, 293, 412n72; courtiers of, 210, 265–66, 302, 412n72; fire of 64 CE and, 276, 277, 298, 413n76; "live like a man," 295, 413–14n87; mother, murder of, 291–92, 412n64; omens regarding, 410n24; reputation, 282; Vespasian's distancing from, 297, 302, 413n75, 414nn91–92; villas: at Antium, 291, 305; at Bauli, 291, 292; at Sublaqueum, 291, 417n136; wife of, 411n58; works converted to public uses, 414n95. *See also* Domus Aurea; Domus Tiberiana
Nerva (emperor), 237, 244, 299, 302, 315, 329, 416n134
Nola, 286–87, 331, 404n35, 410n27. *See also* Paulinus of Nola
Nomentum, 237, 238, 271, 339. *See also* Atticus; Martial
Novius, Quintus, 308, 310, 420n186
Numerian (emperor), 320
nundinae, 52, 162, 251, 336–37, 396n30; Columella on, 113, 119; importance of, 241, 337, 396n31; Pliny the Younger on, 241

O

oak tree, 156, 157, 179, 221, 277, 283, 332; Jupiter and, 365–66n61; Vespasian and, 297
Octavian. *See* Augustus
Odoacer (Odovacar), 282, 320, 321, 424n251
Odyssey (Homer), 59, 195, 348n75, 389n13; Alcinous, 370n133, 375n217, 375n219; Ithaca, 365n58, 375n217; Laertes, 348n75; Odysseus, 365n58; Penelope, 415n114; Telegonus, 406n61, 407n85; Troy, 348n75, 373n170, 375n219, 392n62, 406n61, 415n114
Oea (Tripoli), 177, 350n39, 374n204
Oeconomicus (Xenophon), 63–69, 74, 123, 343n26, 348n1, 402n4, 404n36; Cicero's translation of, 73, 347n72, 348n77; Columella on, 357n151; farming, advantages of, 64–66, 344nn33–34; Isomachus, Xenophon's alter ego, 343n29, 344n36; Isomachus's enslaved personnel, 68–69, 344n36; Isomachus's wife, 68, 344nn41–42
olive oil estates (*oletum, cella olearia*), 34, 39, 40, 90–91, 331, 337, 361n48, 361n51
olive tree, 55, 160, 358n174, 366n61, 410n21
Olympia, 64, 371n141, 371n153, 372n169, 411n41, 417n149
On Architecture (Vitruvius), 131–39, 248, 359nn6–7, 360n32, 388n77; Attic-style doors, 413n85; Augustus, dedicated to, 131–33; *basilicae*, 136, 331; *cavaedium*, 134, 330, 360n28; *curva antlia*, 401n72; domestic architecture, 131–32, 134, 248, 359n14, 361n53; Faventinus's abridgment of, 131, 132, 139–40, 358n177, 361n48, 418n154; floors, 138, 358n177, 361n48, 418n154; Greek house, 17, 134, 374n194; House of Romulus, 360n21; *imago/imagines*, 334; military architecture, 357n157, 380n300; Porticus Pompeia, 406n63; as reference, 331, 359n4, 360n24; sources, 391n1; Varro and, 131, 359n3; wall painting, 138, 158, 361n44; wall surfaces, 128, 138–39; *xenia*, 341
On Farming Matters (Columella), 56n7, 73, 77, 78, 110–24, 248, 263, 356n141, 356n143, 390n34; bath building, 362n55; defensive walls, 357n157; enslaved personnel/*vilicus* and *vilica*, 81, 83, 117–24, 396n25; location of the villa, 114, 390n34; *pars fructuaria*, 52, 117, 337, 357n159; *pars rustica*, 52, 117, 357n158; *pars urbana*, 52, 117, 338; Publius Silvinius, dedicated to, 110, 111; religion and agriculture, 78, 348n7, 356n124, 383n323, 387n162; sources, 60, 347n72, 357n151; "top of the column," 113, 357n147; water supply, 115, 116, 128
Oplontis, Villa A, 18, *18*
Oppius, Gaius, 261
oracles and oracular sites, 166, 272, 352n81, 381n317, 415n111, 417n149
Orestes, 320, 321, 424n251
Origen of Alexandria, 393n86; *Adamantius*, 232, 393n86
Orpheus, 24, 155, 317, 366n76, 372n168; cult of, 423n236; mosaic of, 24, *24*
Ostia, 261, 356n128, 413n76; *caupona* in, 384n7; coastal area of, 299, 302–4, 400n45, 414n89
Otho (Marcus Salvius Otho) (emperor), 294, 414nn98–99
otium, 16, 50, 54, 164, 202–18, 263, 272, 281, 291, 315, 407n73; antiquarian, 419n177; art collecting as, 146; Cicero and, 143, 146, 202, 206, 278, 366n70; hunting as, 16, 202, 209–13, 309; learned and literary, 200, 317, 366n70, 385n29, 404n37, 407n73; Lucullus and, 269; in Marcus Aurelius–Fronto correspondence, 308, 311–12, 417n141; military context of, 202, 384n3, 388n80; negative views of, 415n107, 423n230; *negotium* and, 202, 209, 216; Pliny the Younger and/on, 176, 209–15; Pollius Felix's villa and, 167; Seneca on, 202, 208, 384n8; *studium* versus, 210; as a term, 202, 384nn2–3, 384n5; Villa Iovis and, 286; writing as, 94

P

Padanus River, 329, 333, 354n104
Painter of the Louvre Centauromachy, 7, *7*
Palaemon, Remmius, 237–38, 395n10
Palatine Hill, 313, 337, 370n137, 406n56, 406n69, 413nn78–79, 414n93; archaic hut, 15, *15*; fire of 64 CE and, 294, 295, 413n74, 413n76, 413n79; House of Romulus, 15, 360n21; libraries on, 215–16, 420n182; water supplied to, 423n238. *See also* Augustus; Cicero; Domitian; Domus Tiberiana; Gaius (Caligula)
Palladius. *See Work of Farming, The*
Parallel Lives (Plutarch), 265; Caesar, 408n95; Cato the Elder, 267, 403n23; Cato the Younger, 406n64; Cicero, 279; Crassus, 271; Gaius Marius, 268, 403–4n27, 407n78; Gnaeus Pompeius, 271; Lucullus, 269–70, 404n30, 404nn40–41, 405n43, 405nn45–47, 418n58; Sulla, 268, 404n30; Tiberius Gracchus, 264–65, 402n10
Parthian Empire, 287, 302, 406n57, 415n103, 416n134
pastio villatica, 17, 264, 338, 352n86; peacocks, raising of, 24, 56n3; Varro on, 95, 105–10; *xenia* and, 16, 17, 25, 142, 226

476 INDEX

Paula of Rome, 198, 381n319, 383n324
Paulinus of Nola, 381–82n320, 383n323, 383n326; Ausonius's correspondence with, 184–85, 377n257, 378n268, 382n320; donations made by, 197, 381–82n320, 382n322
Paulinus of Pella, 186; Ausonius, grandson of, 186, 187, 377n257, 377n263, 378n277; *Eucharisticus*, 186–90, 377nn358–64, 377–78n265, 378nn266–78, 378–79n279
Pausias, 14, 109, 363n37
Pausilypon. *See under* Vedius Pollio
Peloponnese, 178, 371n141, 372n169, 373n175, 378n270; games at Nemea, 371n141; Hadrian's tour of, 418n161; Sikyon, 363n37
Penelope, 299, 415n114
Pergamum, 214, 216, 371n151, 388n77
Persephone/Kore, 342n11, 357n148, 380n308, 418n161
Persia, 63–66, 70, 74–75, 317, 333, 371–72n156; Persepolis, capital of, 405n43
Pertinax (emperor), 315, 316, 422n222, 422n225
Pescennius Niger (emperor), 314, 409n5, 422n218
Petronius, Gaius, 422n226; *Satyricon*, 236, 354n100, 394n2
Phidias, 168, 357n147, 372n169
Philemon, Marcus Aemilius, 222, 389n15, 389n19
Philo of Alexandria, 290, 410n33; *Embassy to Gaius*, 290–91
Philo of Larissa, 363n22, 386n31, 405n49
Philostratus, 360n34; *Life of Apollonius of Tyana*, 305, 417n149, 423n236
pinax, 25–27, *25*, *26*, *27*
Pinianus, Valerius, 198–99, 383n326, 383n330, 383n332, 384n335
Pisae, 302, 303, 392nn76–77
Piso, Gaius Calpurnius, 293
Plancius, Gnaeus, 203, 384n4, 385n21
Plato, 204, 357nn147–48, 359n1, 384n7, 385n16, 423n239; *Phaedo*, 232; *Phaedrus*, 151, 365nn60–61; Platonic dialogue, 93, 352n84, 386n34; Platonic forms, 404n36; *Republic*, 317, 423n237; Socrates and, 343n26
Platonic Academy, 363n25, 408n88; Cicero dialogue set in, 144–45, 205; Cicero villas' references to, 142, 418n57; directors of, 145, 363nn21–22, 386n31, 407n88; famous tree, 289, 365n61
Plautus, Titus Maccius, 79, 83, 311, 312, 421n202; *Casina*, 350n46; *Curculio*, 185, 376n247; *Epidicus*, 83; *Pseudolus*, 350n46
pleasure gardens, 14, 276
Pliny the Elder, 229, 404n27. *See also Natural History*

Pliny the Younger: Domitian and, 260, 391n59; enslaved labor and, 79, 83, 396n24, 420n184; *horti*, 14; mentor of, 419n167; *otium*, 209–15; "senatorial" bias, 282; villa at Laurentum, 170–73, 313, 373n182; *xenia*, 137. *See also* Trajan; usufructs
Pliny the Younger, correspondence: euergetism, 238–44, 394–95n5; *otium*, 208–15; Pompeia Celerina's (mother-in-law) villa, 227–28, 396n27, 419n167; villa for Suetonius, 258; villa visits, 227–30
Pliny the Younger, Tuscan (Tiburtine) villa, 228, 240, 374n199, 379n283, 387n65, 393n93, 397n44; description of, 170, 173–76, 379n283; enslaved personnel, 83; *otium*, 176, 212–13; public donations and acts of generosity, 236–38, 396n38; wine produced at, 242–43
Pliny the Younger, villas near Commum, 176–77, 210, 236–37, 240, 248; hometown, 209, 236, 238–39, 373n180; public donations, 394–95n5, 396n36, 396n38
Plutarch, 282, 347n72, 348n77. *See also Parallel Lives*
Polemon, Marcus Antonius, 278, 311, 407–8n88, 420n197, 421n199
Pollius Felix: villa at Surrentum, 167–70, 358nn158–77, 367n85, 376n230
Polybius, 364n51, 407n77
Polyclitus, 168, 357n147; Canephoroe, 72, 347n67
Pompeii, 91, 331, 375n225, 385n13, 389n16; House of Marcus Lucretius Fronto, 25–27, *25*, *26*, *27*; House of Sutoria Primigenia, 19, *19*; House of the Library, 17, *17*; House of the Small Fountain, 20–21, 22, *22*; Third Style, 25, *25*, 361n44; Villa of the Mysteries, 374n194. *See also* Cicero, villa at Pompeii
Pompey, 102, 277, 353n91, 369n111, 389n11, 405n43; adherents of, 385nn19–20, 400n37, 408n97; Caesar and, 206, 272, 279; Cicero and, 254, 278, 279, 405n45; *domus* in Rome, 423–24n239; Lucullus replaced by, 269–70, 403n21; murder of, 366n70, 406n64; portico of, 272; Varro's biography of, 366n70; villas, 222, 272, 276, 298, 362n2, 406n64. *See also* First Triumvirate; Horti Pompeiana; Theater of Pompey
pontifex maximus, 273, 301, 403n25, 405n50, 406n69
Pontius Leontius. *See* Sidonius of Apollinaris
Praeneste, 164, 165, 176, 227, 272, 307; Augustus in, 283, 284; Hadrian's villa near, 305; Temple of Fortuna Primigenia, 305, 406n61
Praetorian Guard, 286, 292, 414n98

praetorium, 53, 181, 200, 284, 287, 289, 339; Manilius Vopiscus's villa, 165; Palladius on, 127, 358n176; Pollius Felix's villa, 168, 169; as a term, 358n176
Praxiteles, 357n147; Cupid, 72, 346n63, 346n65, 347n67; Knidian Aphrodite, 418n161
Priapus, 157, 163, 367n91, 370n128
Primaporta, 285, 296
Propertius: *Elegies*, 272, 406nn60–63
Prosper of Aquitaine(?): *On God's Providence*, 200, 384nn338–39
Protogenes, 357n147, 368n100
Prudentius, 232, 393n85
Ptolemy III, 221, 389n11
Publicolae, Valerii, 198, 199, 381n319
Publius Valerius Publicola, 294, 421n210
Pudentilla, Aemilia, 177, 374nn206–7
Pulcher, Gaius Claudius, 72, 347n68
Pulcher, Publius Clodius, 144, 362n6, 365n54, 389n15
Punic Wars. *See* First Punic War; Second Punic War; Third Punic War
Puteoli, 109–10, 169, 207, 285, 286, 290, 331, 336, 390n27; harbor mole of, 289; imperial villa at, 290, 411n54; Pollius Felix born in, 373n173; port of, 414n89. *See also* Cicero, villa at Puteoli
Pyrgi, 304, 417n139
Pythagoras, 113, 156, 357n148, 367n82, 417149

Q
Quintilian, 245, 397n49; *Institutes of Oratory*, 55, 56n8
Quintilii, 77, 348n3, 421–22n215; villa of, 77, 313, 315, 319, 422n215
Quintus Caecilius Dio of Halaesa, 71, 345n59
Quintus Lutatius Catulus, 362n2, 362n10, 366n73, 389n6, 405n50, 412n63
Quintus Mucius Scaevola, 115, 403n25

R
Ravenna, 180, 200, 321, 383n323, 403n27
Red Sea, 238, 395n12
Rhodes, 163, 286, 288
Roman History, Epitome of (Cassius Dio), 413n83, 414n102, 414–15n103, 422n221; Caracalla, 422n228; Domitian, 298, 300, 415n107, 416n121; Hadrian, 305, 366n63, 417n145; Nero and the fire of 64 CE, 293, 297, 413n74; Septimius Severus, 422n219, 422n221
Rome: Antonine Plague, 215, 388n75; Aqua Marcia, 259, 371nn152–53, 401n73; Area Sacra di Largo Argentina, 366n73; Aurelian Wall, 424n246; Aventine Hill, 105; Baths of Agrippa, 417n145; Baths of Titus, 295, 414n94;

INDEX   477

Capitoline Hill, 110, 301, 360n21, 406n69; Carinae, 142, 286, 353n88, 399n34, 406n59, 423n239; Circus Maximus, 155, 346n66; Colosseum (Flavian Amphitheater), 215, 293, 295, 414n92, 414n94, 417n145; Curia, 205, 207, 319, 385n23; Milvian Bridge, 164, 261, 370n132; Oppian Hill, 284, 294; Pantheon, 418n145, 425n246; Pincian Hill, 269, 276, 332, 403n21, 424n246; Porta Flaminia, 332, 424n246; Porta Flumentana, 107, 356n127; Porta Maggiore, 423n238; Porticus of Livia, 409n19; Quirinal Hill, 271, 332, 402n7, 405n47, 405n53; Roman Games, 206, 251, 399n22, 399n33; Saepta Julia, 355n115, 417n145; Servian walls, 356n127, 370n137; Temple of Peace, 215; Temple of the Divine Claudius, 414n95; Vatican Hill, 224, 261, 388n84, 390n36, 392n75, 402n6, 403n17. *See also* Caelian Hill; Campus Martius; Domus Tiberiana; Esquiline Hill; Forum; Palatine Hill

Romulus, 97, 113, 164, 225, 370n137, 391n43, 403n15; founding of Rome, 15, 105, 312, 403n15, 416n125; house of, 15, 133, 331, 360n21; *mos maiorum*, 133

Romulus Augustus (emperor), 282, 316, 320, 424n251

Rubra, 164, 370n131

Rufinus, Turranius, 232, 393n86

Rufus, Corellius, 241, 373n180

Rutilius Namatianus, 230, 303–4; *On My Return*, 230–31, 302–4, 392nn69–79, 416n138, 417n139

S

Sabina, Poppaea, 291, 412n58

Sabine region, Sabines, 108, 110, 124, 151, 158, 339, 354n109, 421n210; Dentatus's defeat of, 74, 112; Lacus Velinus, 335, 355n116; Martial's villa in, 226, 227; *quirites*, 113, 294, 339, 357n145, 413n81; Trebula, 222, 227, 389n16, 391n49; Vespasian born in, 297. *See also* Horace, Sabine farm

Sack of Rome, 188, 383n332

sacrificial animals, 65, 89, 158, 297, 334, 352n71, 380n306; burning the bones and fat of, 61, 342–43n15, 391n41; *haruspex*, 334, 410n23; *suovetaurilia*, 339, 352n71

Salona, 44, 282, 316, 320

San Rocco villa, 29, 360n30; phase I, 36, *36*, 37, *37*, 51; phase II and IIa, 38–41, *38*, *39*, 51, 351n55

Sardinia, 103, 250

Satires (Juvenal), 373n176, 391n39, 407n76, 416n122; "bread and circuses," 394n3; hatred for Crispinus, 301, 416n120; hatred for Domitian, 298, 301; Nero, conspiracy against, 293; nonlanded wealth, 244–45, 397n49; Tiburtine farm, 245, 390n38, 390–91n39, 391nn40–43

Saturn, 106, 364n42; agriculture, 356nn123–24. *See also* festivals

Scaurus, Marcus Aemilius, 266, 362n2, 370n132, 391n42, 406n56

Scipio Africanus, 71, 207–8, 313, 347n60, 402n10; *Africanus* added to name of, 207, 386n36; Ennius, protégé of, 365n53, 421n202; gardens of, 407n79, 423n237. *See also* Second Punic War

Scipio Africanus, villa at Liternum, 159, 160–62, 237, 358n176, 369n111, 369n113; retirement to, 238, 275–76, 369n111, 369n114

Second Punic War, 377n254, 391n42, 407n77; *Punica*, 386n50; Scipio Africanus's victory in, 265, 345–46n60, 369n114, 386n36

Second Triumvirate, 264, 277, 366n70, 404n32

Sejanus, Lucius Aelius, 159, 286–88, 369n106, 410n30; Tiberius's life saved by, 287–88, 410n32, 411n38

"senatorial" bias, 282, 296, 298, 318, 408n3, 413n81

Seneca the Elder, 279, 408n101

Seneca the Younger, 237–38, 282, 291, 292, 409n17, 412n68; ancestral portraits, 364n51; *horti*, confiscation of, 293; Nero and, 291, 412nn68–70; *On Leisure*, 202, 208, 384n8; *On Tranquillity of Mind*, 202; Stoicism, 159, 275, 292, 412nn69–70; Tacitus on, 292, 412nn69–70; vineyards, 237–38. *See also* Letters on Morality

Septimius Severus (emperor), 315, 316, 422n221, 422nn226–27, 423n237, 424n247; birthplace of, 422n222; military entourage, 422n219; wife of, 423n236

Settefinestre villa, 29, 40, *40*, 41, *41*, 51; enslaved labor at, 41, 81, 350nn35–36; wine production, 40

Severinus, St., 282, 424n251

Severus Alexander (emperor), 315–17, 423nn236–37

Short Book on the Art of Architecture (Faventinus), 131–32, 139–40, 361n46, 361nn48–51, 361n53, 361–62n55; Palladius's use of, 139, 358n177; popularity and readership of, 139, 361nn47–48

Sicily, 198, 199, 345n54, 384n333; Aetna, 166, 371n153; Cicero in, 203, 345n50, 345n56; Hybla, 393n95; rebellion of enslaved people, 69, 344n48; Roman military expansion into, 263; Verres's victims in, 70–71

Sidonius Apollinaris, 216–18, 231–34, 360n34, 419n180; on Eutropius's villa, 216–17, 365n51, 388n78; on Pontius Leontius's *burgus*, 194–98, 379n298, 381nn311–12, 424n248; villa visits, 231–34; *xenia*, 137. *See also* Avitacum

Sikyon, 148, 363n37, 375n215

Silius Italicus, 210

Silvae (Statius), 164–70, 178; Domitian and the Albanum, 298, 415n120; Manilius Vopiscus's villa, 165–67, 358n176, 371nn140–55, 371–72n156, 372n157; Pollius Felix's villa, 167–70, 358n176, 372n162, 373n170, 373n173, 373n176, 376n230, 409n7

Socrates, 95, 343n26, 365n60, 376n244, 384n7; Cicero and, 145, 257; in Plato's *Phaedrus*, 151; in Xenophon's *Oeconomicus*, 64–69, 74, 123

soothsayers, 88, 119, 243, 316–17, 330, 332

Sophocles, 256, 401n54

Spalato. *See under* Diocletian

Sparta, 64, 75, 370n138, 384n7; colonists from, 373n175, 411n39; marble, 192, 336

Sperlonga, 287, 410n31

Stabiae, 203, 204, 229, 372n166, 385n13

Statius, 370n135, 401n75. *See also Silvae*

Sthenelus, Acilius, 237–38, 395n10

Stoicism, 144, 184, 269, 311, 418n160, 421n208; Cato and, 385n23; Cicero and, 144, 204, 205, 386n31; Philo of Alexandria and, 290; Seneca and, 159, 275, 292, 412nn69–70

studium, 274, 312, 339, 407n73; Cicero and, 146, 147, 208, 274, 366n70; Pliny on, 210

Sublaqueum, 291, 417n136

Suetonius, 258, 401n67; "senatorial" bias, 282, 296, 298. *See also Lives of the Twelve Caesars*

Suillius Rufus, Publius, 292, 412n58

Sulla, Lucius Cornelius, 268, 271, 345n52, 364n40, 404n35; adherents of, 362n10, 404n38, 405n54; daughter of, 268, 404n30, 404n38; "Felix," nickname for, 268, 403n26; proscriptions, 264, 268, 365n54, 404n32, 404n34; son of, 204, 385n17, 387n72; villa at Tusculum, 268, 362n2, 404n35

Sulpicius Severus, 198, 381–82n320, 382n322, 383n323; *Chronicorum*, 382n322; *On the Life of St. Martin*, 382n322

Surrentum, 229, 284, 288, 331, 385n13, 410n26; name of, 372n160; wine from, 416n122. *See also* Pollius Felix

Syria, 224, 287, 369n111, 380n311, 387n55, 391n39, 408n98, 410n33; Crassus's campaign and defeat in, 276, 279, 406n57; Elagabalus's properties in, 423n229; Syria-Palestine, 333, 381n311

T

Tacitus (emperor), 316, 319
Tacitus (historian), 386n44, 417n140; Pliny's letters to, 209–10, 212, 229–30, 387n61, 416n124; "senatorial" prejudice, 282, 298. See also *Annals*
Tarracina, 222, 287, 296, 389n15, 411n39, 415n112; Amyclae, 411n39; Cicero on *deversorium* at, 148, 364n43
Telegonus, 272, 277, 406n61, 407n85
Tempe, 418n161; Vale of Tempe, 306, 375n215, 418n161
Terence: *Eunuchus*, 379n282; *Phormio*, 185, 377n251
Terentius Junior, 211–12, 387n60
Tetricus I (emperor), 423n233
Tetricus the Younger (emperor), 316, 423n233
Theater of Pompey, 203, 271, 385n14, 402n7, 405n45, 406n63
Theodoric, 383n323
Theodosius I (emperor), 184, 198
thermae, 131, 236, 318, 330, 340, 424n245
Theseus, 365n59, 381n317
Thetis, 299, 415n110
Third Mithridatic War, 380nn305–7, 403n21, 405n43, 405n45
Third Punic War, 263, 347n70, 402n10
Thrace, 155, 157, 366n76, 380n308; Maximinus born in, 422n222, 423n230; Orpheus born in, 24, 366n76, 372n168
Three Books on Agriculture (Varro), 60, 77, 93–110, 123, 248, 263, 352n63, 356n130, 366n76, 403n16; apiaries, 109, 356n132; aviaries, 153, 355n116, 366n65, 366n71; on Cato, 100–101, 348n1, 351n61; Columella versus, 110, 112, 115, 356n143; *domini*, 78, 112; enslaved labor, 81, 83–84, 97–100, 103–4, 112, 334, 350n42, 351n67, 355n111; fishponds, 14, 109–10, 350n38, 356n131, 395n8; "Fundania" (wife), dedicated to, 352n80; game parks at villas, 24, 155, 356n131; *horologium*, 154, 334, 366n74; *instrumentum vocalis*, 334, 397n45; interlocutors, 93, 353n89, 355n116, 366n73, 366n78, 386n31, 386n34; luxury villas, 354n98; Palladius versus, 124, 128; Pinnius, dedicated to, 105, 106, 110, 355n21; readership, 353n89; as reference, 357n151; religion, 352n83, 356n124; rustic language, 308; sources, 352n85, 353n87; *villa perfecta*, 94, 105–8; Vitruvius and, 37, 131, 132, 136, 139, 359n3
Tiberius (emperor), 276, 282, 286, 309, 368n105, 387n57, 402n10, 403n13, 411n37; *domus* of Pompey, 423n239; Domus Tiberiana, 412n73; executions ordered by, 369n106; friends of, 288–89, 412n58; military career, 410n33; reputation, 282, 408n2; Sejanus and, 287–88, 410n30, 411n38; Thrasyllus and, 288, 411n44; villa at Alba, 298, 299, 410n30; villas from reign of, 286, 385n13. See also Villa Iovis
Tiberius Claudius Nero, 285
Tiber River, 164, 173, 261, 273, 285, 360n37, 407n85, 424n246; left bank, 318; mouth of, 303, 414n89; Pliny the Younger, overseer of, 395n15; right bank, 255, 260, 370n137, 390n36, 406n6, 419n170; Thybris (Thybridis), name for, 370n137; Vatican side, 388n84, 392n75
Tibur, 164–65, 227, 272, 311, 406n62; Aqua Marcia at, 371nn152–53; Augustus at villas in, 283, 284; *basis villae*, 285, 351n62, 358n176; founder of, 371n154; Maecenas's villa at, 407n85; Pollius Felix's villa at, 167; Temple of Hercules, 284, 373n175. See also Antoninus Pius; Juvenal; Pliny the Younger's Tuscan (Tiburtine) villa; Villa Hadriana; Vopiscus, Manilius
Titianus, Cornelius, 212
Titus (emperor), 293, 295, 296, 298, 414n91, 414n94
Titus Flavius Sabinus, 297
Torquatus, Lucius Manlius, 205, 385n19
Trajan (emperor), 302–5, 386n50, 387n53, 397n47, 417n141, 417n147, 421n205, 422n215; *alimenta*, 237, 302, 329, 386n51, 395n6; architect of, 417n145; Arch of Trajan, 237; Hadrian raised by, 305; Hispanian heritage, 422n222; kneeling horse, 415n103; Pliny the Younger's correspondence with, 170, 236, 244; Pliny the Younger's speech honoring, 260, 300–301, 304–5; reputation, 282; villa at Talamone, 416n134
Trajan (emperor), villa at Arcinazzo Romano, 302–3, 416nn134–35, 417n136; hunting at, 303, 305, 315, 417n140, 417n142
Trajan (emperor), villa at Centum Cellae, 302, 313, 316, 416n134; Commodus's cruelty at, 314; Pliny the Younger on, 282, 302, 303, 421n201; Rutilius Namatianus on, 303–4
Triptolemus, 113, 186, 196, 357n148, 377n256, 380n308
Triturrita, 231, 302, 392n76
Tubero, Quintus Aelius, 269, 404–5n43
Tuscany, 398n12, 416n134. See also Pliny the Younger's Tuscan (Tiburtine) villa
Tusculum, 53, 166, 176, 227, 289, 292, 306, 307, 311, 406nn60–61, 408n85; imperial villas at, 296, 410n30; in Martial, 164–65, 227; Pliny's retirement to villa at, 387n62; Scaurus's villa at, 406n56. See also Brutus; Cicero, villa at Tusculum; Lucullus, villa-aviary at Tusculum; Metellus; Sulla, Lucius Cornelius
Tyrrhenian sea and coast, 38, 277, 298, 307, 372n160, 399n27, 417n139; port on, 316; villas on, 14, 227, 305, 306

U

usufructs, 247, 259, 278, 367n77, 398n7, 401n63; Domitian to Martial, 259–60, 398n4; Maecenas to Horace, 155–56, 398n4; Pliny the Younger to his childhood nurse, 238, 367n77, 398n4

V

Valentinian II (emperor), 184
Valerian (emperor), 316, 423nn231–32
Vandals, 200, 377n263
Varro, 232, 252; *Antiquities of Human and Divine Things in 41 Books*, 392n85; brother of, 404n38; Cicero and, 206, 366n70, 386n31, 399n31, 405n50; *Imagines*, 376n233; *On the Latin Language*, 54, 56n6; Pompey, biography of, 366n70; proscription of, 366n70; Reate, born in, 353n89, 354–55n109, 355n116, 366n68; rustic language, 420n192; villas, 362n2, 366n68, 398n8. See also *Three Books on Agriculture*
Varro, villa at Casinum, 105, 153–54, 165, 366n68, 371n145, 399n31; aviary-*triclinium*, 23, *23*, 105, 153, 355n116; Cicero's invective against, 366n70
Vedius Pollio, 284; house in Rome, 284, 409n16; Pausilypon villa, 284–85, 305, 409n17
Veii, 294, 388n83, 413n81
Velitrae, 283, 289, 409n11
Venus/Aphrodite, 94, 104, 165, 371n142, 371n146; Corinthian order, 359n12; statues of, 17, 296, 418n161; temples of, 345n59, 417n145, 418n161
Vergil, 242, 266, 342n6, 348n6, 387n57, 390n34, 423n239; *Eclogue*, 379n291; *Georgics*, 115, 160, 162, 347n70, 353n88, 379n288, 393n95; Hadrian's preferring Ennius over, 305, 421n202; honoring of, 357n147; pastoral themes, 422n226; tomb of, 210, 386n50. See also *Aeneid*
Verginius Rufus, Lucius, 228, 386n44, 419n167
Verres, Gaius. See *Verrine Orations*
Verrine Orations (Cicero), 70–73, 345n59; Gaius Heius, 70–72, 346n63, 346n65, , 346–47n66, 347n67; Sthenius, 71, 345nn58–59, 346n60
Vespasian (emperor), 296–99, 302, 315, 414n98, 415n103, 415n113; cypress tree, 297, 302, 415n104; Domitian, son of, 299, 415n107; Gardens of Sallust and, 297, 302; *horti* and, 276; Nero, distancing from, 297, 315, 413n75; Domus Aurea, changes to, 297, 414nn91–92, 414n95; oak tree, 297; reputation, 282, 296, 414n107; Tiberi-

INDEX 479

us, son of, 43; villas, 296, 298, 299
Vesta and Vestal Virgins, 89, 271, 340, 352n70, 406n58, 416nn125–26; College of Vestals, 271, 273, 406n58; Cornelia, trial of, 301, 416n125; House of the Vestals, 420n182
Vesuvius, 181, 229–30, 288, 298
Via Appia, 36, 279, 299, 308, 329, 364n43, 367n87, 369n114; villas and *horti* on, 225, 276, 316, 422n215
Via Aurelia, 40, 307, 309, 403n13, 414n99
Via Cassia, 313
Via Flaminia, 164, 285, 370n131, 424n246
Via Gabina (Via Praenestina): Site 11, 29, 41, 51; phase 1A, 37; phase 1C, 30, *30*, *31*; phase 2A, 32, *32*, *33*; phase 2B/C, 34, *34*, *35*; villa of the Gordiani, 318
Via Latina, 90, 164, 308, 364n43, 366n70, 369n114, 416n129
Via Sacra, 96, 109, 294, 353n92, 406n69, 413n78
Via Salaria, 108, 164, 370n131, 410n32
Via Vitularia, 251, 399nn27–28
Villa Hadriana (Hadrian's villa at Tibur), 43, 281, 302, 305–8, 316, 417–18n151; Canopus, 418n159; literature on, 418n152; "Lyceum and the Academy," 418n157; *opus reticulatum*, 418n154; Prytaneum, 418n158
Villa Iovis (Tiberius's villa at Capreae), 43, *43*, 44, 286–88, 313, 410nn30–31, 421n12; atrocity stories, 288, 411n37, 415n116; debauchery at, 287, 376n230, 410n37; Tiberius's retirement to, 286
Villa Magna, 306, 315, 387n73, 417n140; during Antoninus Pius's reign, 308–10; Hadrian, builder of, 305, 420n186; *triclinium*, 420n192
Villa of Livia. *See under* Livia
Villa of the Quintilii. *See under* Quintilii
Villa Publica, 105–7, 110, 248, 355n115, 366n73
villas: atrocity stories and cruelty at, 282, 284–85, 313, 314, 404n33, 408n103, 409n17, 410n37; debauchery and sexual misconduct at, 53, 274–76, 282, 286, 287, 366n70, 376n230, 407n76, 410nn34–35, 410n37; enslaved personnel at, 79–85; imperial, 34, 281–82; luxury, 82, 138, 202, 205, 245, 265, 266, 283, 310, 354n96, 354n98, 405n53; numinous events at, 283, 296, 315, 409n9, 411n47, 413n78; proscription, and confiscation of, 254, 255, 264, 268–69, 271, 366n70, 404n30, 404nn32–33, 408n100; as refuge, 53, 254, 278–79; terminology, 52–53, 329–41; ubiquity of, 53, 398n12. *See also* hospitality; maritime villas; *otium*

villas, retirement to, 44, 53, 213–14, 228, 319, 387n62, 421n212, 422n225; Ausonias, 183–84; Cicero, 56n5, 73, 205, 260; Diocletian, 282, 316, 320; Domitian, 298, 415n107; Scipio the Africanus, 238, 275–76, 369n111, 369n114; Tiberius, 286–87, 410n28
villas, revenue from, 236, 247, 257, 393–94n1, 395n12, 395n22, 396n28, 397n42; donated to charity, 198, 200, 381n320, 383n326, 384n335; fishponds, 14, 338, 395n8; *fructus* (produce), 53, 93, 311, 333, 337; rental, 367n77, 398n2, 398n4
Visigoths, 377n263, 378n267, 379n292, 383n323; Alans, rupture with, 378n269; Burdigala, occupation of, 377n263, 378n266, 378n274; Sack of Rome, 188, 383n332
Vitruvius. *See On Architecture*
Vopiscus, Manilius: villa at Tibur, 165–67, 358n176, 371n146, 377n155

W
wall painting, 17, *17*, 18, *18*, 22, *22*, 248, 269; Faventinus on, 361n48; imagery, 19, 22, 84, 158–59, 264, 319, 380n305, 380n307, 381n312; Pliny the Elder on, 158–59, 368n100; Third Style, 25, *25*, 361n44; Vitruvius on, 128, 138, 158, 361n44
wine: *cella vinaria*, 40, 87, 98, 128, 140, 331–32, 361n48; Falernian, 167, 224, 372n161, 390n37, 407n77, 416n122; Formian, 224, 390n37; Pliny the Elder on, 416n122; presses, 56n2, 92, 107, 338, 420n192; price of, 397n42; production, 37, 49, 90, 242, 397n42. *See also* Bacchus
Work of Farming, The (Palladius), 124–29, 263, 358–59n180, 361n47; Faventinus as source, 139–40, 358n177; floors, 358n177, 361n48; garden, 129; grafting, 124, 347n74, 375n221; monthly units, 342n2, 358n169, 358n175; *praetorium*, 127, 358n176; specialized workers, 354n99, 358n172; water supply and storage, 125, 126, 128, 129, 132, 358n179
Works and Days (Hesiod), 59–63, 351n66; enslaved persons, 62; Greek tradition, 348n1, 402n4; Palladius and, 125, 358n169; Pandora, 61, 342n12; Perses, Hesiod's brother, 59–62, 343n16, 343n21; as reference, 125, 352n85, 357n151; Strife, 60–61, 342n8; town and country, 352n83

X
xenia, 142, 226, 229, 234, 341, 382n320; depictions, 16–18, *16*, *17*, *18*, 25, *25*, 51, 137, 138, 341; Martial on, 226, 360n34. See hospitality

Xenocrates, 145, 363n21, 408n88
Xenophon, 59, 63–64, 73, 343nn26–27; *Anabasis*, 348n77; dialogues, 386n34; *Memorabilia of Socrates*, 384n7. *See also Oeconomicus*
Xerxes, 269, 405n43

Z
Zeus/Jupiter, 60–61, 63, 66, 69, 94, 260, 299, 312, 352n71, 379n299, 380n309; children of, 195, 363n28, 392n79; Dapalis, 88–89, 335; nanny, 362n5, 365n55; oak tree, 365n61; Stoa of Zeus Eleutherius, 64; temples of, 44, 239, 301, 372n169, 396n38, 415n113; Capitolinus, 301, 415n113; thunder, 158, 415n112